DICTIONARY
of VIRGINIA
BIOGRAPHY

VOLUME 2
Bland–Cannon

DICTIONARY
of VIRGINIA
BIOGRAPHY

VOLUME 2
Bland–Cannon

EDITORS
Sara B. Bearss, John T. Kneebone, J. Jefferson Looney,
Brent Tarter, and Sandra Gioia Treadway

ASSISTANT EDITORS
John G. Deal, Daphne Gentry, Donald W. Gunter,
Mary Carroll Johansen, and Marianne E. Julienne

THE LIBRARY OF VIRGINIA
RICHMOND • 2001

Library of Congress Cataloging-in-Publication Data will be found on the last printed page of this book.

Standard Book Number: ISBN 0-88490-199-8

Library of Virginia, Richmond, Virginia.
© 2001 by the Library of Virginia.
All rights reserved.
Printed in the United States of America.

This book is printed on acid-free paper meeting the requirements of the American Standard for Permanence of Paper for Printed Library Materials.

Jacket illustrations, from back left: Annabel Morris Buchanan (Library of Virginia); Israel LaFayette Butt (Library of Virginia); Mary Virginia Ellet Cabell (Library of Virginia); David Campbell (Library of Virginia); Rosa L. Dixon Bowser (courtesy of McEva Bowser); Anthony Burns (Library of Congress); Mary Willing Byrd (Library of Virginia); Edward Nathan Calisch (courtesy of the Beth Ahabah Museum and Archives, Richmond, Virginia); and Frederic William Boatwright (Foster Collection, Virginia Historical Society).

Jacket design: Sara Daniels Bowersox, *Graphic Designer*, Library of Virginia.

INTRODUCTION

The *Dictionary of Virginia Biography* is a multivolume historical reference work intended for teachers, students, librarians, historians, journalists, genealogists, museum professionals, and other researchers who have a need for biographical information about those Virginians who, regardless of place of birth or death, made significant contributions to the history or culture of their locality, state, or nation. From the late sixteenth through the eighteenth centuries, the term *Virginia* has been applied to territory extending much farther north, south, and west on the North American continent than the state's modern-day borders. For the purposes of the *DVB*, Virginia is defined by the state's current geographic boundaries, plus Kentucky before statehood in 1792 and West Virginia before statehood in 1863. With few exceptions, no person is included who did not live a significant portion of his or her life in Virginia.

A biographical reference work such as the *DVB* cannot possibly include every interesting or successful person who lived in the past, but it should encompass all those who had an important influence on their communities or who achieved extraordinary recognition from their contemporaries or from posterity. The definition of significance necessarily varies from century to century, from one geographic region to another, and from one field of endeavor to another.

Certain categories of people, most of whom were involved in public life, are included automatically because their participation in events of great consequence has made them frequent subjects of requests for biographical information. The categories of automatic inclusion are Virginia-born presidents of the United States; governors and lieutenant governors of Virginia (including absentee royal governors); members of the governor's Council during the colonial period and of the Council of State between 1776 and its abolition in 1851; Speakers of the House of Burgesses, the House of Delegates, and the Senate of Virginia; African American and female members of the General Assembly; Virginia members of the Continental Congress, the Confederation Congress, the United States Congress, and the Confederate States Congress; cabinet officers of the United States and the Confederate States governments resident in Virginia when appointed; justices of the United States Supreme Court and judges of the

United States appellate and district courts resident in Virginia when appointed; judges of the highest appellate court in Virginia; attorneys general of Virginia; members of all Virginia constitutional conventions from 1776 through 1902; Virginia's delegates to the federal constitutional convention of 1787; members of the Virginia ratification convention of 1788 and of the secession convention of 1861; members of the Virginia State Corporation Commission; general officers from Virginia in the American Revolution, the War of 1812, and the Civil War; winners of major national or international awards, such as Pulitzer and Nobel Prizes; presidents of important national or international organizations; and presidents of the major institutions of higher education in Virginia.

Most of the people who are included in the *Dictionary of Virginia Biography* do not fall into one of these automatic categories. Rather, they are Virginians whose lives and careers made them exceptional in their communities or professions. Some are associated with unusually important or notorious events; others are included because they became legendary figures and require a reliable biographical entry that separates fact from fiction. As a historical reference work, the *Dictionary of Virginia Biography* does not include persons living at the time of publication. No one who died after 31 December 1998 is included in volume 2.

Family history research has played an important part in the production of the *DVB*, although the biographies do not contain a full genealogical record of Virginia's most influential families. Authors have noted family relationships, as needed, to find, verify, and correct dates of birth, death, and marriage; to identify or enumerate parents, children, and spouses; to evaluate the role of important family members in a subject's life; and to take notice of other family members whose lives a subject strongly influenced.

The second volume of the *DVB* contains 452 biographies researched and written by 247 contributors in three countries. Classified indexes to the first two volumes are posted on the Library of Virginia's Web site. At the conclusion of the project a comprehensive index to the *DVB* will be published as the final volume.

EDITORIAL STAFF

Since the appearance of the first volume of the *Dictionary of Virginia Biography* the project has said farewell to several staff members and welcomed some new colleagues. Senior editor J. Jefferson Looney stepped down in September 1999 to assume direction of the new Retirement Series of the *Papers of Thomas Jefferson.* This volume of the *DVB* continued to benefit from his enthusiasm, dedication, and critical eye as he honed prose and raised insightful questions on a volunteer basis from Charlottesville. Research associate Mary Carroll Johansen left the *DVB* in July 1999 to accept a full-time teaching position in New Jersey, and assistant editor Daphne Gentry retired in September 1999 after thirty-five years of service to the Library of Virginia and the state. Their detective skills and editorial vigilance will be much missed.

Sara B. Bearss took the helm of the project as senior editor in April 2000. Marianne E. Julienne joined the staff in September 1999 as research associate, and John G. Deal came on board as assistant editor in June 2000. Editors John T. Kneebone, Brent Tarter, and Sandra Gioia Treadway and assistant editor Donald W. Gunter continue to bring to the *DVB* their expertise in Virginia history and keen editorial eyes.

ACKNOWLEDGMENTS

Any project of this scope would have been impossible without contributions from numerous sources. The editors of the *Dictionary of Virginia Biography* are deeply grateful to all those associated with the Library of Virginia who have brought the second volume of this project to a successful completion. They are especially grateful to the Librarian of Virginia, Nolan T. Yelich, and to the members of the Library Board for their continuing support and encouragement.

The talented and dedicated historians, editors, archivists, librarians, and other specialists on the Library of Virginia's staff have provided valuable assistance to the project at every stage. Many colleagues deserve special mention. The contributions of former research associate Antoinette G. van Zelm were invaluable, as were the eagle eyes and rigorous standards of copy editor Emily J. Salmon and the production expertise of Stacy G. Moore. Other Library staff members and former members who have offered indispensable advice, conducted specialized research, checked facts, entered data, read proof, and done whatever else has been necessary to move the project forward are Barbara C. Batson, Sara Daniels Bowersox, Julie A. Campbell, Gregg D. Kimball, Patricia A. Kloke, and Melissa Q. Rosen. The editors are also grateful to the research assistants, interns, and volunteers who have given their time to the *DVB*, particularly Anna Alexander, Lucy Southall Colebaugh, Arnold P. Fleshood, Louise Fleshood, James A. Jacobs, Kristin Jones, Kevin T. Lett, C. Stinson Lindenzweig, Susan Y. Miller, G. W. Poindexter, Emily Walls Ray, Daniel H. Weiskotten, and Ann Drury Wellford.

The editors, research assistants, and contributors have visited the major research libraries containing materials relating to Virginia history as well as many specialized repositories, historical societies, and research centers across Virginia and the nation. Without exception, the staffs of these institutions have offered gracious assistance to the *Dictionary of Virginia Biography* project, for which the Library of Virginia is deeply grateful. Interlibrary loan departments, local reference librarians, college and university registrars and alumni offices, and the keepers of vital statistics on both sides of the Atlantic have proved unfailingly prompt and helpful in answering queries and tracking down elusive details. It is impossible to thank them all individually or to express gratitude to each of the hundreds of researchers who have advised the editors along the way and generously shared their knowledge, enthusiasm, and insights. The editors particularly thank the following people who provided assistance above and beyond the call of duty for this volume: Chris Bell-Puckett, Cincinnati Historical Society Library; Evan M. Duncan, Office of the Historian, Department of State; Jan Ellison, Historic Christ Church, Alexandria; Jane Hutton, State Library of Pennsylvania; Diane Jacob, Virginia Military Institute; Mary Kearns, Lynchburg, Virginia; Marisa Keller, Corcoran Gallery of Art; Jodi L. Koste, Tompkins-McCaw Library for the Health Sciences, Medical College of Virginia Campus, Virginia Commonwealth University; Greta Lowe, Hampton University Library; R. Lloyd Mathews, Pulaski, Virginia; Connie Park Rice, Morgantown, West Virginia; Bruce Saunders, Franklin, Virginia; Linda Whitaker, Richmond, Virginia; and Patrick Williams, *Arkansas Historical Quarterly*.

Sadly, the editors will not have the pleasure of working again with several contributors who died after completing their entries for volume 2. The editors wish to pay tribute to the memories of these departed colleagues and friends: Mary E. Cookingham, Alonzo Thomas Dill, Carolyn H. Leatherman, Constance K. Ring, Alan Simpson, and George J. Stevenson.

ABBREVIATIONS AND SHORT TITLES

Acts of Assembly	*Acts of the General Assembly of Virginia, Passed at the Session of* . . . (1730–). Title varies over time.
Adm	Admiralty Papers, PRO.
Adventurers of Purse and Person	Virginia M. Meyer and John Frederick Dorman, eds., *Adventurers of Purse and Person, Virginia, 1607–1624/5*, 3d ed. (1987).
AHR	*American Historical Review*.
Annals of Congress	*Debates and Proceedings in the Congress of the United States* (1st–18th Congresses, 1789–1824, published 1834–1856), also known as *Annals of Congress of the United States*.
AO	Exchequer and Audit Department Papers, PRO.
Atkinson and Gibbens, *Prominent Men*	George W. Atkinson and Alvaro F. Gibbens, *Prominent Men of West Virginia* (1890).
bap.	Baptized.
Billings, *Effingham Papers*	Warren M. Billings, ed., *The Papers of Francis Howard, Baron Howard of Effingham, 1643–1695* (1989).
Bland, *Bland Family*	Charles L. Bland, *A Vision of Unity: The Bland Family in England and America, 1555–1900* (1982; rev. ed., 1990).
Branch Papers	*The John P. Branch Historical Papers of Randolph-Macon College* (1901–1918); new ser. (1951–1956).
Brent, *Descendants of Giles Brent*	Chester Horton Brent, *The Descendants of Collo. Giles Brent, Capt. George Brent, and Robert Brent, Gent., Immigrants to Maryland and Virginia* (1946).
Brown, *Cabells*	Alexander Brown, *The Cabells and Their Kin: A Memorial Volume of History, Biography, and Genealogy*, 2d ed., rev. (1939).
Bruce, *Rhetoric of Conservatism*	Dickson D. Bruce Jr., *The Rhetoric of Conservatism: The Virginia Convention of 1829–30 and the Conservative Tradition in the South* (1982).

Bruce, *University of Virginia*	Philip Alexander Bruce, *History of the University of Virginia, 1819–1919: The Lengthened Shadow of One Man* (1920–1922).
Bruce, Tyler, and Morton, *History of Virginia*	Philip Alexander Bruce, Lyon Gardiner Tyler, and Richard L. Morton, *History of Virginia* (1924).
BT	Board of Trade Papers, PRO.
BVS	Bureau of Vital Statistics, Commonwealth of Virginia.
BW	Bounty Warrants, 1779–1860, Office of the Governor, RG 3, LVA.
Byrd Correspondence	Marion Tinling, ed., *The Correspondence of the Three William Byrds of Westover, Virginia, 1684–1776* (1977).
C	Chancery Papers, PRO.
Cabell, *Branchiana*	James Branch Cabell, *Branchiana: Being a Partial Account of the Branch Family in Virginia* (1907).
Caldwell, *History of the American Negro*	Arthur B. Caldwell, ed., *History of the American Negro*, vol. 5: *Virginia Edition* (1921).
Calendar of Virginia State Papers	William P. Palmer et al., eds., *Calendar of Virginia State Papers and Other Manuscripts, 1652–1869* (1875–1893).
Catlin, *Convention of 1829–30*	George Catlin, *The Convention of 1829–30*, VHS; painting reproduced with key in Hall, *Portraits*, 271–274.
Cavaliers and Pioneers	Nell Marion Nugent, *Cavaliers and Pioneers: Abstracts of Virginia Land Patents and Grants, 1623–1732* (1934–1979).
Census	United States Census Schedules, Records of the Bureau of the Census, RG 29, NARA. References are to Lists of Inhabitants unless otherwise indicated.
Clay Papers	James F. Hopkins et al., eds., *The Papers of Henry Clay* (1959–1991).
CO	Colonial Office Papers, PRO.

Compiled Service Records	Compiled Service Records of Confederate Soldiers, 1861–1865, War Department Collection of Confederate Records, RG 109, NARA. Records of soldiers who served in units raised by Virginia, records of general and staff officers and nonregimental enlisted men, and records of soldiers in units raised directly by the Confederate government are the groupings cited most frequently, roughly in that order. The exact subsection used is given only when it is not easily conjectured from the subject's service history.
Convention of 1901–1902 Photographs	Virginia Convention of 1901–1902, [*Photographs of Members*], unpublished bound photograph album of convention members [1902], copies at LVA, UVA, and VHS.
Cunningham, *Circular Letters of Congressmen*	Noble E. Cunningham Jr., ed., *Circular Letters of Congressmen to Their Constituents, 1789–1829* (1978).
CW	John D. Rockefeller Jr. Library, Colonial Williamsburg Foundation, Williamsburg.
Debates and Proceedings of 1850–1851 Convention	*Register of the Debates and Proceedings of the Va. Reform Convention* (1851).
Debates and Proceedings of 1867–1868 Convention	*Debates and Proceedings of the Constitutional Convention of the State of Virginia* (1868).
Documents of 1867–1868 Convention	*Documents of the Constitutional Convention of the State of Virginia* [1868].
Draper MSS	Lyman C. Draper Papers, State Historical Society of Wisconsin, Madison, Wis.
Duke	Duke University, Durham, N.C.
DVB Files	*Dictionary of Virginia Biography* Editorial Files, LVA.
E	Exchequer Papers, PRO.
Evans, *Confederate Military History*	Clement A. Evans, ed., *Confederate Military History Extended Edition* (1899; repr. 1987–1989).
Executive Journals of Council	H. R. McIlwaine, Wilmer L. Hall, and Benjamin J. Hillman, eds., *Executive Journals of the Council of Colonial Virginia* (1925–1966).

Foote, *Sketches of Virginia*	William Henry Foote, *Sketches of Virginia, Historical and Biographical* (1850–1856).
Freedmen's Bank Records	Registers of Signatures of Depositors, Freedmen's Savings and Trust Company, 1865–1874, Records of the Office of the Comptroller of the Currency, RG 101, NARA.
Freedmen's Bureau Records	Records of the Assistant Commissioner for the State of Virginia, 1865–1869, Bureau of Refugees, Freedmen, and Abandoned Lands, RG 105, NARA.
French Biographies	S. Bassett French MS Biographical Sketches, Personal Papers Collection, LVA.
Glass and Glass, *Virginia Democracy*	Robert C. Glass and Carter Glass Jr., *Virginia Democracy* (1937).
Hall, *Portraits*	Virginius Cornick Hall Jr., *Portraits in the Collection of the Virginia Historical Society: A Catalogue* (1981).
Hampton	Hampton University, Hampton.
HCA	High Court of Admiralty Papers, PRO.
Hening, *Statutes*	William Waller Hening, ed., *The Statutes at Large: Being a Collection of All the Laws of Virginia, from the First Session of the Legislature, in the Year 1619 . . .* (1809–1823).
Henry and Spofford, *Eminent Men*	William Wirt Henry and Ainsworth R. Spofford, *Eminent and Representative Men of Virginia and the District of Columbia of the Nineteenth Century* (1893).
Hubard, *Brockenbrough Descendants*	William Stebbins Hubard, *Descendants of William Brockenbrough (1650–1700)* (1998).
Hume, "Membership of Convention of 1867–1868"	Richard L. Hume, "The Membership of the Virginia Constitutional Convention of 1867–1868: A Study of the Beginnings of Congressional Reconstruction in the Upper South," *VMHB* 86 (1978): 461–484.
Hummel and Smith, *Portraits and Statuary*	Ray O. Hummel Jr. and Katherine M. Smith, *Portraits and Statuary of Virginians Owned by The Virginia State Library, The Medical College of Virginia, The Virginia Museum of Fine Arts, and Other State Agencies: An Illustrated Catalog* (1977).

Huntington	Huntington Library, Art Collections, and Botanical Gardens, San Marino, Calif.
Jackson, *Free Negro Labor*	Luther Porter Jackson, *Free Negro Labor and Property Holding in Virginia, 1830–1860* (1942).
Jackson, *Negro Office-Holders*	Luther Porter Jackson, *Negro Office-Holders in Virginia, 1865–1895* (1945).
JAH	*Journal of American History.*
Jamerson, *Speakers and Clerks, 1776–1996*	Bruce F. Jamerson, ed., *Speakers and Clerks of the Virginia House of Delegates, 1776–1996* (1996).
Jefferson Papers	Julian P. Boyd et al., eds., *The Papers of Thomas Jefferson* (1950–).
JHD	Virginia General Assembly, House of Delegates, *Journal of the House of Delegates of the Commonwealth of Virginia* (1776–).
JNH	*Journal of Negro History.*
Journal of 1829–1830 Convention	*Journal, Acts, and Proceedings of a General Convention of the Commonwealth of Virginia* [1830].
Journal of 1850–1851 Convention	*Journal, Acts, and Proceedings of a General Convention of the State of Virginia* [1851].
Journal of 1867–1868 Convention	*Journal of the Constitutional Convention of the State of Virginia* [1868].
Journal of 1901–1902 Convention	*Journal of the Constitutional Convention of Virginia* [1902].
Journals of Council of State	H. R. McIlwaine et al., eds., *Journals of the Council of State of the State of Virginia, 1776–1791* (1931–1982).
Journals of House of Burgesses	H. R. McIlwaine and John Pendleton Kennedy, eds., *Journals of the House of Burgesses of Virginia, 1619–1776* (1905–1915).
JSH	*Journal of Southern History.*
JSV	Virginia General Assembly, Senate, *Journal of the Senate of Virginia* (1776–).

Kaminski, *Ratification*	John P. Kaminski et al., eds., *The Documentary History of the Ratification of the Constitution: Ratification of the Constitution by the States*, vols. 8–10: *Virginia* (1988–1993).
Kingsbury, *Virginia Company*	Susan Myra Kingsbury, ed., *The Records of the Virginia Company of London* (1906–1935).
Kukla, *Speakers and Clerks, 1643–1776*	Jon Kukla, *Speakers and Clerks of the Virginia House of Burgesses, 1643–1776* (1981).
LC	Library of Congress, Washington, D.C.
Legislative Journals of Council	H. R. McIlwaine, ed., *Legislative Journals of the Council of Colonial Virginia* (1918–1919; 2d ed., 1979).
LOMC	Land Office Military Certificates, 1782–1876, Virginia Land Office, RG 4, LVA.
Lowe, "Virginia's Reconstruction Convention"	Richard G. Lowe, "Virginia's Reconstruction Convention: General Schofield Rates the Delegates," *VMHB* 80 (1972): 341–360.
LVA	The Library of Virginia, Richmond.
Madison: Congressional Series	William T. Hutchinson et al., eds., *The Papers of James Madison* (1962–1991).
Madison: Presidential Series	Robert A. Rutland et al., eds., *The Papers of James Madison: Presidential Series* (1984–).
Madison: Secretary of State Series	Robert J. Brugger et al., eds., *The Papers of James Madison: Secretary of State Series* (1986–).
Manarin, *Senate Officers*	Louis H. Manarin, *Officers of the Senate of Virginia, 1776–1996* (1997).
Marshall Papers	Herbert A. Johnson et al., eds., *The Papers of John Marshall* (1974–).
MCV	Medical College of Virginia Campus, Virginia Commonwealth University, Richmond.
Meade, *Old Churches*	William Meade, *Old Churches, Ministers, and Families of Virginia* (1857).
Military Service Records	Military Service Records, World War I History Commission Records, RG 66, LVA.

Minutes of Council and General Court	H. R. McIlwaine, ed., *Minutes of the Council and General Court of Colonial Virginia*, 2d ed. (1979).
MOC	Museum of the Confederacy, Richmond.
MVHR	*Mississippi Valley Historical Review*.
NARA	National Archives and Records Administration, Washington, D.C.
Naval OR	United States Department of the Navy, *Official Records of the Union and Confederate Navies in the War of the Rebellion* (1894–1927).
NCAB	*National Cyclopædia of American Biography* (1891–1984).
n.p.	No page number.
OR	United States War Department, *The War of the Rebellion: A Compilation of the Official Records of the Union and Confederate Armies* (1880–1901).
Pecquet du Bellet, *Virginia Families*	Louise Pecquet du Bellet, *Some Prominent Virginia Families* (1907; repr. 1976).
Pollard Questionnaires	John Garland Pollard, comp., data for biographical sketches of members of the Virginia Convention of 1901–1902, compiled 1901, VHS.
por.	Portrait, identifying location of an original or a source reproducing a photograph, painting, engraving, drawing, or sculpture of the subject.
Prerogative Court of Canterbury	Prerogative Court of Canterbury Registered Wills, Principal Probate Registry, London, Eng.
Presidential Pardons	Virginia Case Files for United States Pardons, 1865–1867, United States Office of the Adjutant General, RG 94, NARA.
PRO	Public Record Office, London, Eng.
Proceedings and Debates of 1829–1830 Convention	*Proceedings and Debates of the Virginia State Convention of 1829–1830* (1830).
Proceedings and Debates of 1901–1902 Convention	*Report of the Proceedings and Debates of the Constitutional Convention, State of Virginia* (1906).

Quarles, *Worthy Lives*	Garland R. Quarles, *Some Worthy Lives: Mini-Biographies, Winchester and Frederick County* (1988).
Reese, *Journals and Papers of 1861 Convention*	George H. Reese, ed., *Journals and Papers of the Virginia State Convention of 1861* (1966).
Reese and Gaines, *Proceedings of 1861 Convention*	George H. Reese and William H. Gaines Jr., eds., *Proceedings of the Virginia State Convention of 1861* (1965).
Resolutions of 1901–1902 Convention	[*Resolutions of the Constitutional Convention of 1901–1902*] [1901–1902].
Revolutionary Virginia	William J. Van Schreeven, Robert L. Scribner, and Brent Tarter, eds., *Revolutionary Virginia, the Road to Independence: A Documentary Record* (1973–1983).
RG	Record Group.
SCC Charter Book	State Corporation Commission Charter Book, RG 112, LVA.
SHSP	*Southern Historical Society Papers* (1876–1959).
Slemp and Preston, *Addresses*	C. Bascom Slemp and Thomas W. Preston, eds., *Addresses of Famous Southwest Virginians* [1939].
Smith, *Complete Works*	Philip L. Barbour, ed., *The Complete Works of Captain John Smith (1580–1631)* (1986).
Smith, *Letters of Delegates*	Paul H. Smith et al., eds., *Letters of Delegates to Congress, 1774–1789* (1976–2000).
Southern Claims Commission	Records of the Commissioners of Claims (Southern Claims Commission), 1871–1880, Department of the Treasury, RG 56, NARA.
SP	State Paper Office, PRO.
Sprague, *American Pulpit*	William B. Sprague, *Annals of the American Pulpit; or Commemorative Notices of Distinguished American Clergymen of Various Denominations* (1866–1877).

Stephenson and McKee, *Virginia in Maps*	Richard W. Stephenson and Marianne M. McKee, eds., *Virginia in Maps: Four Centuries of Settlement, Growth, and Development* (2000).
Stoner, *Seed-Bed*	Robert Douthat Stoner, *A Seed-Bed of the Republic: A Study of the Pioneers in the Upper (Southern) Valley of Virginia* (1962).
Supplement, 1850–1851 Convention Debates	Numbered and dated supplements issued with *Richmond Enquirer, Richmond Examiner, Richmond Times, Richmond Republican, Richmond Republican Advocate,* and *Richmond Whig,* 1850–1851.
T	Treasury Office Papers, PRO.
Tyler, *Encyclopedia*	Lyon Gardiner Tyler, ed., *Encyclopedia of Virginia Biography* (1915).
Tyler, *Men of Mark*	Lyon Gardiner Tyler, ed., *Men of Mark in Virginia* (1906–1909); 2d ser. (1936; anonymously edited). References are to original series unless otherwise indicated.
Tyler's Quarterly	*Tyler's Quarterly Historical and Genealogical Magazine.*
UNC	University of North Carolina at Chapel Hill, N.C.
United States Reports	*Cases Argued and Decided in the Supreme Court of the United States* (title varies; first ninety volumes originally issued in seven distinct editions of separately numbered volumes with *United States Reports* volume numbers retroactively assigned; original volume numbers here given parenthetically; citations are to original pagination).
UTS	Union Theological Seminary and Presbyterian School of Christian Education, Richmond.
UVA	University of Virginia, Charlottesville.
VBHS	Virginia Baptist Historical Society, University of Richmond, Richmond.
VCU	Virginia Commonwealth University, Richmond.
VHS	Virginia Historical Society, Richmond.

Virginia Reports	*Cases Decided in the Supreme Court of Appeals of Virginia* (title varies; issued consecutively for the highest appellate court of Virginia under its variant names of Court of Appeals of Virginia [to 1830], Supreme Court of Appeals of Virginia [1830–1971], and the Supreme Court of Virginia [since 1971]; first seventy-four volumes originally issued in ten distinct editions of separately numbered volumes with *Virginia Reports* volume numbers retroactively assigned; original volume numbers here given parenthetically; citations are to original pagination).
Virginia State Bar Association Proceedings	*Proceedings of the Annual Meeting of the Virginia State Bar Association*; variant titles include *Report of the Annual Meeting*.
VM/RHC	Valentine Museum/Richmond History Center, Richmond.
VMHB	*Virginia Magazine of History and Biography*.
VMI	Virginia Military Institute, Lexington.
VPI	Virginia Polytechnic Institute and State University, Blacksburg.
W&L	Washington and Lee University, Lexington.
W&M	College of William and Mary, Williamsburg.
Washington: Colonial Series	William W. Abbot et al., eds., *The Papers of George Washington: Colonial Series* (1983–1995).
Washington: Confederation Series	William W. Abbot, Dorothy Twohig, et al., eds., *The Papers of George Washington: Confederation Series* (1992–1997).
Washington: Presidential Series	Dorothy Twohig, William W. Abbot, et al., eds., *The Papers of George Washington: Presidential Series* (1987–).
Washington: Retirement Series	William W. Abbot, Dorothy Twohig, et al., eds., *The Papers of George Washington: Retirement Series* (1998–1999).
Washington: Revolutionary War Series	Philander D. Chase, William W. Abbot, et al., eds., *The Papers of George Washington: Revolutionary War Series* (1985–).
Wells and Dalton, *Virginia Architects*	John E. Wells and Robert E. Dalton, *The Virginia Architects, 1835–1955: A Biographical Dictionary* (1997).

Willard and Livermore, *Woman of the Century*	Frances E. Willard and Mary A. Livermore, eds., *A Woman of the Century: Fourteen Hundred-Seventy Biographical Sketches Accompanied by Portraits of Leading American Women in All Walks of Life* (1893).
Winfree, *Laws of Virginia*	Waverly K. Winfree, comp., *The Laws of Virginia: Being a Supplement to Hening's The Statutes at Large, 1700–1750* (1971).
WMQ	*William and Mary Quarterly.*
WPA Biographies	Biographical Files, Virginia Writers' Project, Work Projects Administration Papers, LVA.
WVSA	West Virginia State Archives, Charleston, W.Va.
WVU	West Virginia University, Morgantown, W.Va.

DICTIONARY
of VIRGINIA
BIOGRAPHY

VOLUME 2
Bland–Cannon

BLAND, Anna Bennett (d. ca. November 1687), principal in a court case, was born in Virginia, the daughter of Richard Bennett and Maryann Utie Bennett. Occasionally her first name appears as Ann or Anne. Her birth date is unknown, but the death of John Utie, her mother's first husband, occurred probably in the summer of 1637, and later in the decade Maryann Utie married Bennett, a wealthy Puritan who served on the governor's Council for an indefinite period starting in 1642, was governor of Virginia from 1652 to 1655, and sat on the Council again from 1658 until his death in 1675. Sometime in 1660 Anna Bennett married Theodorick Bland (1630–1672), the Speaker of the House of Burgesses, who was about ten years her senior. Her father deeded the couple his house in James City County in 1662, and in 1665 her husband purchased the Charles City County property known as Westover and moved the family there. Theodorick Bland and Anna Bland had three sons, so far as is known, before his death on 23 April 1672. About three years later she married St. Leger Codd, a widower with three children from his first marriage. They had one son and one daughter.

Anna Bennett Bland undertook a prolonged legal defense of the estate of her first husband, and as one consequence the General Assembly of Virginia lost its status as the court of last appeal in the colony. The case pitted against each other two remarkable, powerful women skilled in the use of political patronage. Anna Bland faced a complicated task in managing property that Theodorick Bland had owned outright or controlled as agent or estate administrator. He had settled in Virginia to manage the large landed estate of his brother John Bland, who remained in England. After Theodorick Bland's death, John Bland sent his own son Giles Bland to the colony to take control of the property, but in this capacity Giles Bland laid claim to land that Theodorick Bland had clearly owned, including Westover. Anna Bland fought back, enlisting powerful allies in Virginia, among them her father and Thomas Ludwell, who, like her second husband, was a political ally of Governor Sir William Berkeley.

Her principal adversary was John Bland's wife, Sarah Greene Bland, who had influence at court and with members of the Privy Council. Sarah Bland became her husband's legal representative and launched a counteroffensive in England in 1676. Giles Bland had meanwhile become a leader in Bacon's Rebellion, in the aftermath of which he was executed and his property confiscated. Sarah Bland traveled to Virginia in 1678 as her husband's representative. The claims and legal actions of Giles Bland and Sarah Bland subjected Anna Bland Codd and her second husband to lawsuits, petitions, and counterpetitions for nine years, during part of which they retired to his property in Maryland to avoid legal harassment.

Anna Bland Codd prevailed in the Virginia courts, where Sarah Bland lost both an appeal to the General Court and a further appeal to the General Assembly. Her allies in England were more powerful than those of Anna Bland Codd and St. Leger Codd, however, and in 1682 the Lords of Trade ordered the parties to appear at a hearing in London. Virginia's new governor, Francis Howard, baron Howard of Effingham, implemented the order by proclamation and also announced the Privy Council's decision that all future appeals from rulings of the General Court be made to the Privy Council in England rather than to the General Assembly. The assembly was unable to challenge the proclamation, which thus terminated the last vestige of that body's judicial powers and thenceforth gave Virginia litigants with powerful English connections a big advantage over those lacking such ties. St. Leger Codd went to England to support his wife's case and the Privy Council ordered the matter to arbitration, but the arbitrators finally settled the suit in 1686 in a manner generally satisfactory to Sarah Bland and unsatisfactory to Anna Bland Codd.

Although the legal battles exhausted much of the Codds' estate, Anna Bland Codd succeeded in preserving Westover and other of Theodorick Bland's properties for her sons, who became wealthy planters and prominent public men. Anna Bennett Bland Codd died in Maryland probably about November 1687.

Bland, *Bland Family*, 91–93, 105–108, 120–126; name given as Anna on first husband's gravestone at Westover (*WMQ*, 1st ser., 4 [1896]: 143); numerous references to Anna Bennett Bland Codd and Sarah Greene Bland in Billings, *Effingham Papers*; leading documents in legal dispute in Colonial Papers, folder 2, no. 18, RG 1, LVA, in PRO CO 1/56, and in PRO PC 2/69–70; denial of appeals to General Assembly in *Executive Journals of Council*, 1:1, 57–58, 501–503, and *Journals of House of Burgesses, 1659/60– 1693*, 167, 195–197.

JOAN R. GUNDERSEN

BLAND, Charles Thomas (3 October 1857–28 December 1915), civic leader, was born in Portsmouth, the son of George Washington Bland, a laborer, and Louisa Frances Stewart Bland. He attended the parish school of Saint John's Episcopal Church and the Portsmouth public schools. At age sixteen Bland was apprenticed to a Norfolk carriage manufacturer, and about five years later he moved to Baltimore to work for another carriage manufacturer and there attended the Houck Night School. On 6 August 1878 Bland married Josephine Hyslop, of Portsmouth. They had three sons and three daughters.

Bland worked in North Carolina and Richmond before he became a salesman of carriage varnish, working out of Newark, New Jersey, and New York City. He worked as a carriage painter in Portsmouth in 1882, returned to Baltimore, spent several years first as a carriage painter and then as a salesman in Richmond, and was back in Portsmouth by 1889 as a painter. Within a decade Bland remade himself as a journalist and a lawyer. He wrote for the *Portsmouth Enterprise-Times,* the *Portsmouth Progress*, and the *Portsmouth Star*, became editor and owner of a half interest in the *Portsmouth Evening Times* late in the 1890s, served as night and sports editor of the *Norfolk Virginian*, and in 1900 was a manager of the Portsmouth bureau of its successor, the *Norfolk Virginian-Pilot.* Bland worked as Portsmouth city editor for the *Norfolk Landmark* from about 1902 to 1905, and he also served as southern correspondent of *Carriage Monthly*, a trade journal.

Bland studied law under local attorneys and attended the summer law school of the University of Virginia. He was admitted to the bar

about 1899 and practiced in Portsmouth with a series of partners. Early in the twentieth century Bland helped found the short-lived Portsmouth Dime Savings Bank, and he was also an officer of the 1st Regiment Virginia Artillery and a member for some three decades of the Independent Steam Fire Engine Company Number 1. About 1900 he became owner of Portsmouth's baseball team in the Virginia League, which played at Bland Field, and he reportedly once declined the presidency of the league. Bland's civic service also included membership in a number of fraternal organizations, especially the Ancient Order of Knights of the Mystic Chain, the Benevolent and Protective Order of Elks, the Fraternal Order of Eagles, the Improved Order of Heptasophs, the Junior Order United American Mechanics, the Order of Owls, and the Woodmen of the World. He held office in the Benevolent Order of Buffaloes, the Improved Order of Red Men, the Independent Order of Odd Fellows, and the Knights of Pythias.

Bland was well known not only by virtue of the many organizations to which he belonged and the services he performed but also as a popular speaker at fraternal functions. An active Democrat, he translated his numerous local contacts into political success. Voters of the Portsmouth district sent Bland to the House of Delegates in 1895 and reelected him by wide margins in 1897, 1899, and 1901. He did not run in 1903 but won a fifth and final term in 1905. In his first session he was appointed to the Committee on Manufactures and the Mechanic Arts, and he chaired it during his ensuing three terms. His other important assignments included one or more stints on the Committees on Banks, Currency, and Commerce, on the Chesapeake and its Tributaries, on General Laws, on Privileges and Elections, on Propositions and Grievances, and on Roads and Internal Navigation. In 1909 Bland was elected commonwealth's attorney for the city of Portsmouth, a post he held until his death. At least twice he declined to run when his supporters considered him a potential candidate for the United States House of Representatives.

Charles Thomas Bland died of pneumonia at his Portsmouth home on 28 December

1915. He was buried in Oak Grove Cemetery in Portsmouth.

Birth date in BVS Death Certificate, in William H. Stewart, ed., *History of Norfolk County, Virginia, and Representative Citizens* (1902), 819–823, and in Tyler, *Encyclopedia*, 5:1022–1023; variant date of 27 Nov. 1857 in BVS Birth Register, Portsmouth; Census, Portsmouth, 1860, 1870, 1900, 1910; Portsmouth city directories, 1889–1915; obituaries in *Norfolk Virginian-Pilot* (por.), *Portsmouth Star* (por.), and *Richmond Times-Dispatch*, all 29 Dec. 1915.

W. A. Brown

BLAND, Edward (bap. 5 February 1614–by 9 May 1652), explorer, the fifth of seventeen children of John Bland and Susanna de Deblere Bland, was born probably in London, where he was christened in the parish of Saint Stephen Coleman Street on 5 February 1614. Bland's father, who died in 1632, was a prominent London merchant and shipowner, an investor in the Virginia Company of London that founded the colony of Virginia, a member of its London council, and one of the proprietors of Martin's Hundred.

When Edward Bland was about twenty years old, he married his cousin Jane Bland. They had one known son. Bland spent much of the decade before 1646 in Spain and the Canary Islands managing parts of the family's far-flung commercial interests. His elder brother John Bland traveled to Virginia in the mid-1630s to look after and enlarge the family's landholdings, and his brother Adam Bland probably also visited the colony. By 7 July 1646 Edward Bland had moved to Virginia to take charge of the family's property there. He acquired several large tracts in the vicinity of Lawnes Creek in what is now Surry County and by 1652 owned about 14,700 acres, either outright or with other family members.

Even with the growth in Bland's Virginia landholdings, his family was in serious financial difficulty at the end of the 1640s. John Bland had lost property worth almost £14,000 at the outset of the English Civil Wars and was unable to collect on a large loan he had made to Parliament, while other pressures were also undermining the family finances. In the summer of 1650 Edward Bland joined Abraham Wood, a noted Indian trader and a close friend of Governor Sir William Berkeley, in planning an expedition to the southwest of the settled parts of Virginia. Wood hoped to open up new trading opportunities, and Bland probably hoped to establish a family claim to a large part of the Piedmont of what is now North Carolina.

Bland and Wood, together with Sackford Brewster, Elias Pennant, two servants, and an Appamattuck guide named Pyancha, left Fort Henry (approximately the present site of Petersburg) on 27 August 1650. The seven men returned nine days later, having traveled more than 175 miles. Their route has been the subject of historical conjecture, but they probably reached the Roanoke River below the site of what is now Roanoke Rapids, North Carolina. Bland named the place New Britain and described it as lush and fertile. After his return to Jamestown the General Assembly endorsed his plan to colonize the region. He wrote a detailed history of the expedition that contained much new information about the native inhabitants of the area. John Bland had *The Discovery of New Brittaine* (1651), the resulting sixteen-page pamphlet, published in London.

The Bland family did not gain title to any Carolina land or otherwise profit from the expedition. Edward Bland died shortly thereafter, most likely early in 1652 at his residence near Lawnes Creek. On 9 May 1652 his widow received a patent confirming a previous grant of 4,300 acres of land near the head of Chippokes Creek. To take charge of the family's large Virginia interests after Edward Bland's death, his youngest brother, Theodorick Bland (1630–1672), moved to the colony and became the progenitor of the distinguished Bland family there.

Adventurers of Purse and Person, 124–128; Bland, *Bland Family,* 61–62, 86–91; Neville Williams, "The Tribulations of John Bland, Merchant: London, Seville, Jamestown, Tangier, 1643–1680," *VMHB* 72 (1964): 19–41; move to Virginia by 7 July 1646 documented in Patent Book, 2:50, RG 4, LVA; Alan Vance Briceland, *Westward from Virginia: The Exploration of the Virginia-Carolina Frontier, 1650–1710* (1987), 13–91; grant to widow of 9 May 1652 in Patent Book, 3:200.

Alan Vance Briceland

BLAND, Edward David (October 1848–13 February 1927), member of the House of Delegates, was the son of Frederick Bland and Nancy Yates Bland. He was born a slave, probably in Dinwiddie County. After the Civil War the family resided in Petersburg, where his father was a shoemaker and a preacher, although apparently never the pastor of his own church. Bland learned the shoemaker's trade working with his father and probably also attended one of the local night schools organized by northerners for blacks. On 18 December 1872 he married Nancy Jones, of Petersburg. Their nine children included two sons and four daughters who survived him.

About 1874 Bland and his wife moved to City Point in Prince George County, where he worked as a shoemaker. Using oratorical skills, Bland became involved in local politics. During the 1870s the issue of how to deal with Virginia's huge public debt divided the Democratic Party into Funders, who insisted that the debt be paid in full, and Readjusters, led by William Mahone. Bland was one of those African American Republicans who advocated an alliance with the white Readjusters. On 3 October 1879 a mass meeting of black Republicans in Petersburg divided on that question, and those favoring the Readjusters withdrew to hold their own meeting, at which Bland delivered one of the speeches.

The Readjusters in Prince George organized on 9 October without naming their own candidate to represent Prince George and Surry Counties in the House of Delegates. Instead, they threw their support to Bland, the Republican candidate. Meanwhile the Funders unsuccessfully tried to nominate several men before Robert E. Bland, the white incumbent, finally agreed to run less than a week before the election.

On 17 October 1879 E. D. Bland joined Mahone and others on the speaker's platform at a Readjuster barbecue in Prince George County. Three days later county Republicans, disgruntled by Bland's Readjuster apostasy, called for his removal as the party's nominee. Bland marshaled his supporters for the meeting that ensued at the courthouse on 29 October. Amid so much confusion and crowding that a voice vote could not be taken, everyone went outside to line up for or against Bland. So many men went to his side that his opponents did not bother to form ranks.

Bland and the other ten African American Republicans elected to the House of Delegates in 1879 held the balance of power between the Funders and Readjusters. Their votes gave the Readjusters control of the legislature and sent Mahone to the United States Senate, but the coalition remained shaky. White Readjusters failed to back measures that the blacks introduced, and they, in turn, remained loyal to the national Republican Party. Bland served on the Committees on Executive Expenditures and on Schools and Colleges.

In 1880 Bland was a delegate to the Virginia Republican Party convention and supported the party's national candidates rather than Mahone's slate of uncommitted electors. Needing votes from blacks to carry the next year's legislative elections, Mahone promised federal patronage positions and support for legislation in return for a coalition. Bland was one of the leaders who met on 14 March 1881 in Petersburg to endorse the Readjusters, and he easily won reelection in November. He served on the Committees on Agriculture and Mining, on Claims, and on Retrenchment and Economy. During the session of 1881–1882 blacks obtained legislation creating a state-supported college and an insane asylum for African Americans as well as improved funding for their public schools. Conservatives responded in 1883 with a blatant white supremacy campaign through which they regained control of the General Assembly, although Bland won reelection for a third term. He was appointed to the influential Committee on Propositions and Grievances and the less consequential Committees on Enrolled Bills and on Officers and Offices at the Capitol. Bland also benefited from Mahone's control of federal patronage in Virginia and worked for a time as a gauger, assessing the tax on whiskey and other goods, for the Internal Revenue Service at City Point.

Bland stepped down after the legislative session of 1883–1884. Surry County Republicans made known their desire to have one of their own as the party's next nominee, and he accordingly gave way to William Faulcon. Bland did not retire from politics, however. On 30 September 1885 he complained to William Mahone about the inaction of Republicans in a neighboring district, contrasting it with his own well-organized district, in which he spoke somewhere every night. Bland contemplated another run for the legislature in 1887. On 6 September of that year he requested Mahone's support but promised to step aside if Mahone preferred another man. Goodman Brown, of Surry County, became the party's successful candidate that year. Possibly disenchanted by this snub, Bland supported John Mercer Langston against Mahone's candidate in the 1888 congressional election. By then white Democrats were intent on eliminating blacks from Virginia politics, a process that culminated in the disfranchisement measures of the Constitution of 1902.

Edward David Bland continued to live in Prince George County and moved from City Point to a farm about the turn of the century. He suffered from chronic nephritis during his last years and died on 13 February 1927. Because the local church had recently burned, his large funeral took place at Gillfield Baptist Church in Petersburg, and he was buried at Providence Cemetery, since renamed People's Memorial Cemetery, in that city. A housing project in Hopewell, opened in December 1954, was named the Edward D. Bland Courts in his memory.

Jackson, *Negro Office-Holders*, vi (por.), 3; Census, Dinwiddie Co., 1870, Prince George Co., 1880, 1900 (which gives month and year of birth), 1910; BVS Marriage Register, Petersburg, lists Dinwiddie Co. as birthplace, but BVS Death Register, Prince George Co., lists Nottoway Co.; Personal Property Tax Returns, Prince George Co., RG 48, LVA; political career reported in *Richmond Whig*; James T. Moore, "Black Militancy in Readjuster Virginia," *JSH* 41 (1975): 167–186; Bland letters in William Mahone Papers, Duke; obituary and report of funeral in *Petersburg Progress-Index*, 14, 17 Feb. 1927.

JOHN T. KNEEBONE

BLAND, Giles (bap. 26 October 1647–27 March 1677), participant in Bacon's Rebellion, was born in England and christened in the parish of Saint Olave, Hart Street, in London,

the son of John Bland and Sarah Greene Bland. His family was consequential in London mercantile circles and had interests in Virginia as old as the colony. His paternal grandfather for whom he was named was a shareholder in the Virginia Company of London, and John Bland and the elder Giles Bland both had substantial holdings in the colony.

Bland married Frances Povey, the daughter of Thomas Povey, an influential royal functionary. They had at least one son. The relationship to Povey probably explains Bland's appointment in the mid-1670s as a royal customs collector for Virginia. Coincidentally, the death of Bland's uncle Theodorick Bland (1630–1672), who had managed the family's Virginia property, left a jumble of unresolved debts and claims against the family for settlement by his widow, Anna Bennett Bland. Bearing his father's power of attorney for use in clearing up the family's finances, Giles Bland traveled to Virginia about 1673 and soon assumed his duties as customs collector.

Something of a tart-tongued free spirit, Bland disagreed with his aunt over control of the estate. No pushover, she acted quickly to defend her rights, and their quarrels led to litigation in the General Court. Giles Bland either ignored or failed to recognize a salient quality about his aunt: she had friends in high places. Her supporters included Governor Sir William Berkeley; the deputy governor; the secretary of the colony; numerous other prominent politicians, including St. Leger Codd, whom she later married; and her own father, Richard Bennett, who was a former governor and then a member of the governor's Council, which in its judicial capacity constituted the General Court. With such men Anna Bland understandably found more support than did her pushy nephew, and the highly political litigation that began after Giles Bland arrived in Virginia persisted for a decade.

In September 1674 Bland ran afoul of Thomas Ludwell, the secretary of the colony and a councillor. Accounts differ about the origin of the dispute, though this much is certain: Bland took exception to Ludwell's opinion in the case against his aunt. After the General Court had risen for the day, Bland stopped at

Ludwell's house to argue his point. The secretary offered him a drink. Emboldened by too much alcohol, the men traded insults and threats. Determined to have the last word, Bland took one of Ludwell's gloves and pinned it to the statehouse door with a note declaring its owner "a Sonn of a Whore mechannick Fellow puppy and a Coward." The burgesses complained of Bland's gesture as a "Publique Affront" to the assembly as well as to the secretary and asked the governor to have Bland arrested and made to answer for his insult. Berkeley readily complied, and Bland was forced to apologize publicly, which he did in a "Slight and Scornefull" manner. The General Court also levied a £500 fine, suspended for two years so that Bland could appeal the judgment to England.

Bland did appeal, but he also sought to square accounts with Berkeley. He complained to his superiors in the customs service about the governor's failure to enforce the navigation laws. He probably asserted correctly that the Virginians enforced the trade laws laxly, but Bland had been an irritant to Berkeley almost from the day of his arrival, and the two men had clashed over the extent of Bland's power as customs collector. Differences in personality contributed to their disputes, but so did their overlapping authority. The Crown had charged both men with the same task without delineating their individual responsibilities, and Berkeley had already named his own collectors before Bland's appointment.

The relationship between Bland and Berkeley soured beyond repair within a year of the Ludwell affair. On 16 September 1675 Bland wrote the governor a sharp, accusatory letter alleging that Berkeley had willfully condoned repeated violations of the trade laws and threatening again to complain to London. Infuriated, Berkeley hauled Bland before the Council to demand sworn evidence of his allegations. Bland offered no proof, "would not or could not otherwaies Justifie himselfe," and admitted that he had sent a copy of his letter to the customs board. The Council unanimously suspended him as collector and jailed him until he posted a bond to keep the peace.

Bland's brief association with Virginia is a nearly perfect example of how a mixture of private affairs with personalities and politics can produce unforeseen consequences, the effects of which linger for generations. His troubles with Berkeley, Ludwell, and others probably account for his siding with Nathaniel Bacon (1647–1676) in the rebellion led by Bacon in 1676. Less certain is what the rebel leadership saw in Bland. He had no recorded friendships with Bacon or any other leader of the rebellion before he became one of them. He brought no military skill to the cause, and he had no apparent following among Bacon's malcontented supporters. They intended to send Bland to England to plead their cause in person, as he had already done in letters to his parents, Povey, and other royal officials, but he never got the chance because he proved to be an inept insurrectionary. In September Bacon put Bland in charge of an expedition to seize the governor, but the governor captured Bland instead. Thereafter Bland remained in close confinement aboard a ship as the revolt ran its course. Despite the exertions of family and friends, Bland was too deeply implicated to win the king's pardon. On 8 March 1677 Berkeley presided over a court-martial that condemned him to death. Though originally scheduled to hang on 15 March 1677, Giles Bland was executed in Jamestown on 27 March 1677, when "he made a good penitent end." His place of burial is unknown.

Adventurers of Purse and Person, 124–132; Neville Williams, "The Tribulations of John Bland, Merchant: London, Seville, Jamestown, Tangier, 1643–1680," *VMHB* 72 (1964): 19–41; Thomas Jefferson Wertenbaker, *Virginia Under the Stuarts, 1607–1688* (1914), 139, 174–176, 183, 202–203; Stephen Saunders Webb, *1676: The End of American Independence* (1984), 50–57, 151–154, 203–204; Warren M. Billings, *Virginia's Viceroy, Their Majesties' Governor General: Francis Howard, Baron Howard of Effingham* (1991), 37–38, 43–44, 47; *Minutes of Council and General Court*, 399 (first, second, and third quotations), 423 (fourth quotation), 448–449; Bland to Berkeley, 16 Sept. 1675, and related docs. in Egerton MS 2395, British Library, London; PRO CO 1/31, 1/36, 1/39 (death described on fols. 182–183; fifth quotation), 5/1355.

WARREN M. BILLINGS

BLAND, James William D. (27 February 1844–27 April 1870), member of the Convention of 1867–1868 and member of the Senate of Virginia, was born in Prince Edward County, the son of Hercules Bland and Mary Bland. Bland's father was a free man and a cooper who purchased his wife to ensure their children's freedom. Bland was taught to read and write by a slave in the household of his mother's former owner. He worked with his father as a cooper and carpenter until 1864, when he entered an American Missionary Association school in Norfolk. For two years he studied there and also taught reading, geography, and arithmetic. Although the school refused to license Bland to teach because of alleged smoking and profanity, he was permitted to continue as a substitute.

Bland returned to Prince Edward County and on 21 November 1867 married Mary E. Clarke. A few weeks earlier, on 22 October 1867, Bland and a white former United States Army officer, Edgar Allan, had been elected to represent Appomattox and Prince Edward Counties at a state constitutional convention that met from 3 December 1867 to 17 April 1868. Both men won overwhelming support from African Americans, who were voting for the first time, and they each received the support of only one white voter. Considered one of the convention's most intelligent black members, Bland served on three of the major standing committees: the Elective Franchise and Qualifications for Office, Revision and Adjustment, and Rules and Regulations. He recommended amending the preamble to the constitution by replacing "men" with "mankind, irrespective of race or color." Other black delegates opposed the suggestion because they preferred to keep any references to color or race out of the constitution. Bland voted with the Radical reformers on most major issues that came before the convention. In an attempt at racial conciliation, however, while defending the new constitutional provisions granting full political rights to blacks, he denounced other sections requiring test oaths of former Confederates and denying some of them the right to vote and hold public office. Both white and African American Republicans objected to Bland's comments. Even so, he was vindicated to some extent in 1869 when state voters rejected the provisions of the constitution that disfranchised former Confederates and when Virginia's senators and representatives won admission to Congress a

year later despite this defeat of the disfranchisement provision.

Bland attended every state Republican convention held in 1867, 1868, and 1869. He was appointed assistant assessor of internal revenue for Charlotte and Appomattox Counties in May 1869, and later that year he won election to the Senate of Virginia from the district consisting of Charlotte and Prince Edward Counties. Taking his seat in October 1869, Bland served on the Committee for Courts of Justice. He supported public education as the state's highest priority and sponsored one major bill that passed a month after his death. The measure incorporated Hampton Normal and Agricultural Institute, enabling it to receive federal land-grant funding. Tall, graceful, and modest in demeanor, Bland was popular among his constituents and with the press. Respected by both races as a conscientious legislator, he was a voice of compromise and impartiality in an age of turmoil and partisanship. Political supporters and allies characterized him as an orator of extraordinary ability, and he made a strong impression when he met with members of Congress on the readmission of Virginia to the Union. Detractors accused him of emulating the speech, attire, and mannerisms of the Senate president. In the spring of 1870 Bland may have switched, or contemplated switching, from the Republican to the Democratic Party.

On 27 April 1870 Bland was in a large crowd attending a morning session of the Supreme Court of Appeals in the State Capitol during the appeal of a case concerning Richmond's contested mayoral election. Shortly after eleven o'clock the floor collapsed, killing James William D. Bland and about sixty other people. The Senate passed resolutions in his memory, and the General Assembly appropriated $52 for funeral expenses. Bland was buried in Farmville, where two hundred mourners attended his interment.

Jackson, *Negro Office-Holders*, 3–4, 60 (por.); birth date in Bland to George Whipple, 16 May 1865, American Missionary Association Papers, Amistad Research Center, Tulane University, New Orleans; Prince Edward Co. Marriage Register; Bland letter, 15 Mar. 1868, in Elihu Washburne Papers, LC; Robert C. Morris, *Reading, 'Riting, and Reconstruction* (1981), 99; Richard Lowe, *Republicans and*

Reconstruction in Virginia, 1856–70 (1991), 78, 133, 135, 137, 215, 224; Election Records, no. 427, RG 13, LVA; Hume, "Membership of Convention of 1867–1868," esp. 481; *Debates and Proceedings of 1867–1868 Convention*, 1:250 (quotation); extended references to Bland's politics in *Richmond Whig*, 20 Oct. 1869, 7 Jan., 29 Apr. 1870, *Washington New Era*, 3 Mar., 21 Apr. 1870, and *New Orleans Louisianian*, 24 Sept. 1871; *A Full Account of the Great Calamity, Which Occurred in the Capitol at Richmond, Virginia, April 27, 1870* (1870), 47; obituaries in *Washington New Era*, 12 May, 2 June 1870; funeral reported in *Richmond Daily Dispatch*, 2 May 1870; Senate memorial resolution and eulogies in *Petersburg Daily Index*, 3, 4 May 1870.

ERVIN L. JORDAN JR.

BLAND, Richard (6 May 1710–26 October 1776), member of the Continental Congress and member of the Convention of 1776, was the son of Richard Bland and his second wife, Elizabeth Randolph Bland. His probable birthplace was Jordan's Point in Prince George County, his father's plantation. Orphaned in 1720, he grew up under the guidance and tutelage of his guardians and relatives, the Randolphs of Turkey Island, and he attended the College of William and Mary.

Bland married Anne Poythress on 21 March 1730, and they had six sons and six daughters before her death on 9 April 1758. On 1 January 1759 Bland married Martha Macon Massie, a widow who died eight months after their marriage. He subsequently married Elizabeth Blair Bolling, the widowed half sister of Councillor John Blair (ca. 1687–1771). She died late in April 1775.

Bland managed his inherited plantations, joined many of his friends and family members in speculating in land, studied law and qualified to practice before the colony's General Court, and exhibited a litigious streak. At his death his estate included thirty slaves. An erudite and highly intelligent man and a dedicated student of history and law, Bland assembled a large, excellent library as well as many valuable original documents for a history of the colony that he never wrote. Thomas Jefferson, who acquired some of the most useful books and records after Bland's death, later described him as "the most learned and logical" of all the leading men of that generation. Bland's eyes were failing him by October 1774, when his acquaintance Roger Atkinson described him as having "something of the look of musty old Parch[men]ts w'ch he handleth & studieth much."

Bland served on the Prince George County Court and sat on the local parish vestry, where he sometimes officiated as a lay reader. Like his father before him he sat on the board of visitors of the College of William and Mary. Elected to the House of Burgesses from Prince George County in the spring of 1742, Bland remained in the Virginia legislature without a break until his death more than thirty-four years later. He quickly became a leading burgess with high positions on the most important committees and frequently chaired one or more standing committees or the committee of the whole. His able pen and extensive knowledge of law and history almost always got him onto critical drafting committees for important bills and resolutions concerning Virginia and its place in the British empire. Bland ranked with Speaker John Robinson (1705–1766) and Peyton Randolph (ca. 1721–1775) as one of the most influential and productive burgesses during the last quarter century of the colonial period. Following Robinson's death, Bland lost a bid for becoming Speaker to Randolph.

During the 1750s and 1760s Bland took a leading role in defending the colony's use of paper money to finance its part in Great Britain's war against France. Late in November 1764 he helped to frame the colony's first protests against the Stamp Act, but it is unclear whether, as was later reported, he opposed or was even present when Patrick Henry introduced a second, more inflammatory set of resolutions the following year. Later in the 1760s Bland was a key draftsman of the assembly's stern objections to the Townshend Acts. In addition he opposed creation of an American bishopric to govern the colonial Church of England and maintained that local vestries, rather than the General Court or the bishop of London through the colonial commissary, had full authority over the parishes and the right to select and provide for the support of their ministers. At every turn Bland argued for colonial control of colonial affairs and against any extension of British control over Virginia's internal political and economic life.

Between 1753 and 1774 his newspaper articles, public letters, and pamphlets made him one of the best-known Virginians of his day. Bland's cultivated mind and spirited pen helped lay the groundwork for revolution, although revolution was never his goal nor independence his purpose. Rather, as each new political crisis strained the relationships between the General Assembly and the royal governor, between colony and Parliament, and between colony and Crown, he gradually developed and asserted Virginia's constitutional and legal claim—and ultimately its moral under natural law—to a large measure of self-government.

Bland first emerged as a defender of Virginia's rights during the pistole fee controversy. He helped draft the burgesses' resolutions of November 1753 charging that Lieutenant Governor Robert Dinwiddie's imposition without legislative approval of a fee of one pistole for signing and affixing the colonial seal to land patents was "of dangerous Consequence to the Liberties of his Majesty's faithful Subjects, and to the Constitution of this Government." In response to Dinwiddie's assertion that he had a right to impose the fee as a part of the royal prerogative, Bland likened the controversy to the struggles of Parliament with Charles I in the 1630s and asserted that just as levying a tax in England was illegal without parliamentary action, so too no fee could legally be imposed in Virginia without approval by the people's representatives in the General Assembly. He almost went so far as to maintain that even the royal prerogative could not operate contrary to the laws and legal customs of the colony. Bland spelled out his reasoning in a short essay entitled "A Modest and True State of the Case," now better known as *A Fragment on the Pistole Fee*, the title under which it was first published in 1891.

Bland acquired a much wider fame during the protracted debates following the adoption in 1758 of the second of the so-called Two Penny Acts, both of which he had helped to write. Passed in the wake of tobacco crop failures, the laws, which applied to all transactions and contractual obligations payable in tobacco, permitted parish vestries to substitute for one year a cash payment of approximately two pence per pound of tobacco in lieu of 16,000 pounds of tobacco and cask, which was the legal annual salary of ministers. The laws raised important and complex issues, including whether the General Assembly could amend or repeal the statute establishing ministers' salaries without first obtaining royal consent, whether the assembly's acts diminished ministerial salaries unfairly, and whether these questions could be properly adjudicated in the colony's courts. Bland fired early salvos in a pamphlet war on these subjects. In *A Letter to the Clergy of Virginia, in Which The Conduct of the General-Assembly is vindicated, Against The Reflexions contained in a Letter to the Lords of Trade and Plantations, from the Lord-Bishop of London*, published in Williamsburg in 1760, Bland attacked the leaders of the Virginia clergy and the bishop of London while adducing legal precedents and constitutional and practical justifications for the assembly's actions. He stated that in emergencies the General Assembly of Virginia had the right to do whatever was necessary for the good of the colony, royal instructions to colonial governors notwithstanding. Four years later, after Landon Carter and Commissary John Camm had entered the bitter and highly personal debates, Bland published an extended satiric dialogue, *Colonel Dismounted: or the Rector Vindicated, in a Letter addressed to His Reverence: Containing A Dissertation upon the Constitution of the Colony*, which blasted Camm by name and asserted more boldly than anyone had before that for all strictly provincial purposes the General Assembly of Virginia was the only representative body that could tax or legislate for the colony. In developing his argument Bland distinguished between acts of Parliament made to regulate imperial affairs and those of a purely local nature, a distinction used later in 1764 and in 1765 to help justify the actions of the House of Burgesses and most other colonial assemblies in North America that were busy contesting the power of Parliament to lay a stamp tax on the colonists.

After the Stamp Act crisis, Bland undertook to refute the theory of virtual representation used by defenders of that law against the colonial objection to taxation without representation. In *An Inquiry into the Rights of the British*

Colonies (1766), he took his previous arguments several steps further by denying that Parliament had the authority to lay a tax on a colony or pass legislation respecting its internal affairs. Bland's pamphlet directly challenged Parliament's dominance in the British empire. It emphasized instead the importance of representative assemblies in the governance of the colonies and brought to the forefront the power of natural rights as a counterbalance to parliamentary or even royal power and authority.

Late in the 1760s and early in the 1770s Bland attended all of the recorded Virginia protest meetings and conventions, served on the Virginia Committee of Correspondence, and signed all of the Virginia associations and pacts directed at British policies. A group of bold and energetic younger men soon began to take the lead, but they built on foundations that he had laid, and he supported their efforts. In September 1774 Bland was a Virginia delegate to the First Continental Congress in Philadelphia, where he told John Adams that the meeting was so important to the defense of colonial rights that despite his age he would have gone all the way to Jericho if necessary. Bland returned to the Second Continental Congress in the spring of 1775 but retired at about the end of May because of ill health. On 7 July of that year, after being publicly accused of disloyalty to the colonial cause, he vindicated himself and attacked his accuser, a clergyman named Samuel Sheild, in a public letter to the newspaper. Bland also demanded and received a public endorsement of his patriotism from the Convention of July–August 1775.

Bland served on the eleven-man Committee of Safety that in effect governed Virginia between September 1775 and July 1776, and he represented Prince George County in the Virginia conventions that met in December 1775 and May 1776. He had never aimed at independence, and some of his comments in the spring of 1776 have been interpreted, possibly incorrectly, as indicating a reluctance to take that last big step. Hugh Blair Grigsby, a Virginia historian able to base his assessment on the firsthand knowledge of many of Bland's contemporaries, later remarked that unlike many other men whose utterances were unclear because they knew too little, Bland often expressed himself poorly because he knew too much. In the spring of 1776, when Thomas Paine's *Common Sense* had many Americans exclaiming over its irresistible rhetorical power and conceding the inevitable necessity of declaring independence, Bland, ever the pedant and close student of history, chose to fault Paine's reading of history and reportedly declared "that the Author of common sense is a blockhead and ignoramus for that He has grossly mistaken the nature of the Jewish Theocracy." Bland may merely have been irritated by one of Paine's historical analogies, and there is no reliable evidence that he hesitated when the question of independence became unavoidable. On 15 May 1776 Bland joined the other members of the Virginia convention in instructing the colony's congressional delegation to move a resolution of independence. His infirmities confined him to a relatively inconspicuous role in the Convention of 1776, but he served on the committee that wrote the Virginia Declaration of Rights and the first constitution of the commonwealth, which lodged most governmental power where Bland had always thought it belonged, with the people's directly elected representatives in the House of Delegates, the lower and more numerous branch of the General Assembly.

After returning to Williamsburg early in October 1776 as a member of the House of Delegates, Richard Bland collapsed in the street on 26 October 1776 and died that evening in the house of John Tazewell. He was buried on 7 November in the family cemetery at Jordan's Point.

Clinton Rossiter, "Richard Bland: The Whig in America," *WMQ*, 3d ser., 10 (1953): 33–79; Robert Detweiler, *Richard Bland and the Origins of the Revolution in Virginia* [ca. 1981], based on his "Richard Bland: Conservator of Self-Government in Eighteenth-Century Virginia" (Ph.D. diss., University of Washington, 1968), which includes an annotated bibliography of Bland's publications and surviving manuscripts; effusive but useful character sketch in Hugh Blair Grigsby, *The Virginia Convention of 1776* (1855), 57–61; Bland, *Bland Family*, 151–169 (por. on 160A); MS of Bland's pistole fee essay in Thomas Jefferson Papers, LC; essential documents of his public life during the 1770s in *Revolutionary Virginia*; Thomas Jefferson to William Wirt, 5 Aug. 1815, in Andrew A. Lipscomb and Albert Ellery

Bergh, eds., *The Writings of Thomas Jefferson* (1903), 14:338 (first quotation); *VMHB* 15 (1908): 356 (second quotation); *Journals of House of Burgesses, 1752–1755* and *1756–1758* (third quotation on 143); obituaries in *Williamsburg Virginia Gazette* (Dixon and Hunter) and *Williamsburg Virginia Gazette* (Purdie), both 1 Nov. 1776; estate sale advertised in *Williamsburg Virginia Gazette* (Dixon and Hunter), 31 Jan. 1777.

BRENT TARTER

BLAND, Schuyler Otis (4 May 1872–16 February 1950), member of the House of Representatives, was born in Gloucester County, the son of Schuyler Bland, a merchant, and Olivia James Anderson Bland. His father died when Bland was young, and he was educated by private tutors and at the Gloucester Academy in Summerville. From 1888 to 1890 he attended the College of William and Mary on a state scholarship and then, under the terms of the scholarship, taught school in Northampton County for three years. Following another interval of study at William and Mary from 1894 to 1896, Bland served as principal of a two-room school at Bloxom in Accomack County from 1896 to 1900, concurrently studying law under Richardson Leonard Henley in Williamsburg and Raleigh Minor at the University of Virginia.

S. Otis Bland passed the bar examination in 1899 and settled in Newport News the next year to practice law. He was serving as president of the Newport News Chamber of Commerce at the time of his marriage to Mary Crawford Putzell on 19 January 1911. They had no children. Bland soon became active in local Democratic Party politics, but his election to Congress came about suddenly. On 29 May 1918 the First District Democratic convention deadlocked when attempting to name a candidate to complete the unexpired term of the recently deceased congressman William Atkinson Jones. Bland was campaign manager for one of the contestants, but on the eighty-second ballot he was chosen himself as a compromise candidate. Bland was elected to Congress in June and narrowly defeated G. Walter Mapp on 6 August 1918 in the Democratic Party primary for the full term that began in 1919. Thereafter Bland was reelected without significant opposition for the rest of his life.

In March 1933 Bland became chairman of the Committee on Merchant Marine, Radio, and Fisheries, and he retained this chairmanship in every succeeding Democratic Congress. His most important achievement was sponsorship in 1936 with Senator Royal Copeland, of New York, of the Merchant Marine Act, or Bland-Copeland Act. This measure boosted the slumping shipbuilding industry, a vital concern on the Peninsula, and paved the way for the nation's astounding success in naval construction and marine transport during World War II. Bland's interest in maritime affairs earned him high marks from business and civic leaders in Hampton and Newport News, and almost two decades after his death the library at the United States Merchant Marine Academy at King's Point, Long Island, was named for him.

Along with most other conservative Virginia congressmen during the 1930s, Bland paid lip service to President Franklin Delano Roosevelt but often opposed his administration and frequently voted against New Deal legislation. Bland prided himself on constituent service and interested himself in what many people of the time probably considered minor, local matters. He supported preserving as public historic parks some of the most significant Civil War battlefields in Virginia, and he served on the Yorktown Sesquicentennial Commission in 1931.

Bland suffered from heart disease during the 1940s, and in the spring of 1949 he announced that he would not seek reelection in November 1950. By then he ranked fifth in seniority in the House of Representatives and was the dean of the Virginia delegation. After becoming ill early in February 1950 and checking into Bethesda Naval Hospital in Maryland, Schuyler Otis Bland died there of a cerebral hemorrhage on 16 February 1950. He was buried in Greenlawn Cemetery in Hampton–Newport News.

Bruce, Tyler, and Morton, *History of Virginia*, 6:437; Schuyler Otis Bland Papers, W&M; BVS Birth Register, Gloucester Co.; *Newport News Daily Press*, 20 Jan. 1911; *Commonwealth* 11 (Nov. 1944): 21; por. in possession of U.S. House of Representatives; *New York Times*, 18 Nov. 1968; obituaries, some with long biographical sidebars, in *Newport News Times-Herald*, *Norfolk Ledger-Dispatch*, and *Richmond News Leader*, all 16 Feb. 1950, and *New York Times*, *Newport News Daily Press*, *Norfolk Virginian-Pilot*, and *Richmond Times-Dispatch*, all 17 Feb. 1950; memorial with some errors about early law career in *Virginia State Bar Association Proceedings* (1950): 124–130 (por.); *Memorial Services Held in the House of Representatives . . . with Remarks Presented in Eulogy of Schuyler Otis Bland* (1950).

BRENT TARTER

BLAND, Theodorick (bap. 6 January 1630–23 April 1672), Speaker of the House of Burgesses and member of the Council, was the son of John Bland and Susanna de Deblere Bland. He was born probably in London, where he was christened on 6 January 1630 in the parish of Saint Antholin, Budge Row. His father died in April 1632, after which his elder brother John Bland assumed direction of the family's extensive commercial interests. As a young man Theodorick Bland resided for several years in Sanlúcar de Barrameda, Spain, where the family engaged in the wine trade. In the mid-1640s he succeeded his brother Edward Bland as the family's agent in the Canary Islands, and following Edward Bland's death by May 1652, Bland moved to Virginia to take control of the large landed property that the family owned there. His name first appears in Virginia records as foreman of a Surry County jury on 3 November 1653.

Bland soon moved to Berkeley Hundred in Charles City County, and in September 1656 he was one of three men recommended for appointment to the county court. Bland also became a vestryman of Westover Parish and served as churchwarden in 1663. Sometime in 1660 he married Anna Bennett, daughter of Richard Bennett, who had been governor of the colony between 1652 and 1655. They had three sons. In April 1665 Bland purchased Westover plantation for £170 from its English owner, Sir John Pawlett.

Bland was elected in 1660 to represent Charles City County in the House of Burgesses. He was elected Speaker of the House on 13 March 1660 and presided over the two sessions of the assembly that met that year. During the first session, the assembly arranged for the peaceful transfer of the colony's allegiance from the Protectorate to the Crown. The political situation in England was unclear. Oliver Cromwell had died, and Richard Cromwell had abdicated, but so far as the Virginians knew the exiled son of King Charles I had not yet reclaimed the throne. The House of Burgesses therefore declared itself to be "the supreame power of the government of this country . . . until such a comand and comission come out of England as shall be by the

Assembly adjudged lawfull." Following careful preliminary negotiations, in which Bland took no part, Sir William Berkeley accepted an offer to serve as interim governor until the situation in England was settled. The assembly met again on 11 October, by which time Charles II had been restored to the throne and had recommissioned Berkeley as governor of the colony.

Bland represented Henrico County in the House of Burgesses during the March 1661 and March 1662 sessions, but he was not reelected Speaker. Probably between 2 June and 12 September 1662 Berkeley appointed Bland to the governor's Council. The loss of the Council records for the first eight years of Bland's tenure makes assessment of his service impossible, but he regularly attended its sessions during 1670 and 1671, and considering his family connections and his status as a major landowner and merchant, Bland's opinions undoubtedly carried weight.

Theodorick Bland died probably on 23 April 1672. He was buried on the grounds of the Westover estate, and his widow later had a stone placed over his grave. The date of death on the stone is 23 April 1671, but Bland went to his last recorded Council meeting on 24 November 1671, and on 16 May 1672 the General Court described him as deceased. Because his three sons were all under ten years of age, his elder brother John Bland, still the head of the family, sent his own young son, Giles Bland, to the colony to manage the family's Virginia properties.

Kukla, *Speakers and Clerks, 1643–1776,* 59–61; *Adventurers of Purse and Person,* 128–129; Bland, *Bland Family,* 68–69, 91–93; Joseph Lemuel Chester and George J. Armytage, *The Parish Registers of Saint Antholin, Budge Row, London . . .* (1883), 64; presence in Virginia first documented in Surry Co. Deed Book, 1:31; property transactions and public service documented in numerous Charles City Co. and Surry Co. court records; *Minutes of Council and General Court,* 286, 306; Hening, *Statutes,* 1:530 (quotation); appointment to Council dated from Charles City Co. Deeds, Wills, Orders, Etc. (1655–1665), 359, and *Minutes of Council and General Court,* 507.

DAPHNE GENTRY

BLAND, Theodorick (21 March 1742–1 June 1790), Continental army officer, member of the Confederation Congress, and member of the

Convention of 1788, was born at Cawsons, his father's plantation in Prince George County near the confluence of the James and Appomattox Rivers. He was the son of Theodorick Bland (1719–1784) and Frances Bolling Bland. About 1753 his father, an affluent tobacco planter, sent him to England for a classical education at Wakefield School in Yorkshire. In 1759 Bland began studying medicine at a Liverpool infirmary, and two years later he entered the University of Edinburgh as a medical student. He graduated in 1763 after writing a thesis on digestion, and in 1764 he sailed to Virginia.

Soon after returning to Prince George County, Bland opened a medical practice at Blandford, a village adjacent to Petersburg, and a few years later he became a partner in a Blandford "medicinal shop." He eventually found that the long hours and almost constant travel required of a practicing Virginia physician were undermining his health, and much against his parents' wishes he gave up his medical career. To mollify his family and patients, Bland announced in William Rind's *Williamsburg Virginia Gazette* for 28 March 1771 that, although he would no longer make house calls or keep medical accounts, he would give "advice, and prescribe for any case that shall be properly stated and sent me for that purpose, accompanied with my fee, which is a pistole for prescribing, and a guinea for a consultation."

Between 1771 and 1774 Bland acquired Kippax, a Bolling plantation near Cawsons that his mother apparently had inherited from her father. Renaming the place Farmingdell, Bland settled there with his wife, Martha Dangerfield Bland, whom he had married about 1768. Their one child died young. Bland raised tobacco, wheat, corn, cotton, and cattle there and at another plantation in Amelia County.

A vestryman by 1765 and a justice of the peace as early as 1771, Bland assumed a more prominent public role as an advocate of American rights in 1775. On 8 May 1775 he became a member of the Prince George County Committee, and on 24 June he was one of twenty-four men who removed a large quantity of arms from the governor's palace in Williamsburg. In December, using the pseudonym Cassius, Bland wrote two open letters to the royal governor, the earl of Dunmore, upbraiding him for his unrelenting opposition to the American cause. By the end of 1775 Bland was seeking an army commission, and although he lacked military experience, on 13 June 1776 the Virginia convention appointed him captain of the first of six troops of light-horse to be raised for defense of the colony. During the ensuing weeks Bland recruited men and purchased horses, and on 5 September he arrived in Williamsburg with his troop. On 4 December 1776 the General Assembly named him major commandant of all six troops of Virginia cavalry. About that same time he received orders to join George Washington's army with his new regiment.

Bland's regiment reached Washington's headquarters at Morristown, New Jersey, early in January 1777, and it was immediately dispersed in small detachments to forage, gather intelligence, and provide security for the army. On 14 January Congress took the regiment into Continental service, and on 31 March Washington promoted Bland to colonel. By June 1777 the Virginia contingent of light-horse was so fatigued that Washington let Bland reassemble his regiment to rest and equip it properly. During the Philadelphia campaign later that year, Bland's cavalry performed reconnaissance and acted as a screening force. At the Battle of Brandywine on 11 September 1777, Bland was posted on the army's right flank and belatedly sent Washington irrefutable reports of an impending British attack from that direction. Dissatisfied with his rank relative to other cavalry officers and needing to attend to his neglected private affairs, on 8 November 1777 Bland requested permission to resign his commission. Washington refused, but in March 1778 he sent Bland to Virginia to purchase horses. Bland did not rejoin the army until the following September.

On 5 November 1778 Washington ordered Bland to supervise the march from Massachusetts to Virginia of the so-called convention army, which consisted of the British and German soldiers who had surrendered after the Battle of Saratoga. Bland delivered the prisoners to their new camp near Charlottesville in January 1779 and proceeded to Farmingdell. Reports of disorder at the Charlottesville barracks prompted Washington on 28 February to direct Bland to return to the camp as its commandant. Arriving on 15 April, Bland quickly restored order by appointing a new quartermaster and hospital director and reinforcing the ill-disciplined guards with troops from his own regiment. Bland also established cordial relations with the British and German officers. In October 1779 Washington allowed Bland to go home, and on 10 December Congress accepted his resignation from the army.

On 21 June 1780 the General Assembly elected Bland a member of the state's delegation to Congress. He took his seat on 30 August and served until October 1783. Bland was a member of the medical committee and sat on various committees dealing with financial and military matters, including the one that in January 1781 helped to quell the mutiny of the Pennsylvania State Line. A strong nationalist, he supported increased taxing powers for Congress and urged that Virginia's demand for free navigation of the Mississippi River be moderated to encourage full Spanish participation in the war against England.

The plundering of Farmingdell by British troops in April 1781 did not prevent Bland from resuming his life as a planter there in 1783. In 1785 he became county lieutenant, and from 1786 to 1788 he represented Prince George in the House of Delegates. During his first year he served on the Committees on Commerce, Propositions and Grievances, and Religion, and during his second year he served on the Committees on Commerce, Privileges and Elections, and Propositions and Grievances. As a member of the Virginia Convention of 1788 Bland voted against ratification of the Constitution despite his nationalist views. The new federal government, he later wrote to Richard Henry Lee on 28 October 1788, would threaten "Tyranny and oppression" unless checked by amendments protecting individual rights.

In February 1789 Bland was elected to the House of Representatives as an antifederalist. He was the only announced candidate in his large south-central Virginia district. Bland took his seat at New York on 30 March 1789 and served

on the Committee on Joint Rules. In 1790 he supported Alexander Hamilton's plan for the United States government to assume states' wartime public debts. Theodorick Bland died in New York on 1 June 1790 and was buried in the churchyard of Trinity Episcopal Church. In 1828 his remains were moved to Congressional Cemetery in Washington, D.C. Having no surviving children, Bland bequeathed to his wife all of his property except for mementos to three nephews and a two-acre lot in Blandford set aside for a college that never was built.

Charles Campbell, ed., *The Bland Papers: Being a Selection from the Manuscripts of Colonel Theodorick Bland, Jr., of Prince George County, Virginia* (1840); birth recorded in Bristol Parish Register, 66, Acc. 20335, LVA; "Selections from the Campbell Papers," *VMHB* 9 (1901–1902): 59–77, 162–170, 298–306; Churchill Gibson Chamberlayne, *The Vestry Book and Register of Bristol Parish, Virginia, 1720–1789* (1898), 288, 291; Bland letters in George Washington Papers, LC, Lee Family Papers, UVA, Tucker-Coleman Papers, W&M, and several collections in LVA and VHS; Smith, *Letters of Delegates*, vols. 16–21, 25; Kaminski, *Ratification*, 10:1541, 1557, 1565, 1617–1618; Merrill Jensen et al., eds., *The Documentary History of the First Federal Elections, 1788–90* (1976–), 2:267–268 (quotation); Linda G. De Pauw et al., eds., *Documentary History of the First Federal Congress* (1972–), 1:335, 3:443; Fillmore Norfleet, *Saint-Mémin in Virginia: Portraits and Biographies* (1942), 93 (por.); will in Prince George Co. Deed Book (1787–1792), 404, printed in *VMHB* 3 (1896): 315–316; obituary in *Richmond Virginia Independent Chronicle and General Advertiser*, 16 June 1790.

PHILANDER D. CHASE

BLAND, Thomas (19 January 1793–11 July 1867), member of the Convention of 1850–1851, was born probably in Dumfries, the son of Thomas Bland and Sarah Byrne Bland. His father died a few weeks before Thomas Bland's birth, and about 1794 or 1795 his mother married Jacob Zinn, of Monongalia County. Bland grew up in northwestern Virginia, but little else is known about his youth or education. He was a private in the Monongalia County militia during the War of 1812, helped to defend Fort Meigs when the British besieged it in the spring of 1813, and served at Norfolk when the British invaded the Chesapeake Bay in 1814.

Bland returned to western Virginia after his military service ended and may have lived for a short time in Williamsport (later Pruntytown) in

Harrison County before settling in Weston. He married Mary Newlon on 10 December 1815. They had six sons and three daughters. Bland began as a tanner but became a prominent local businessman and mill owner, operated Bland's Hotel in Weston for many years, and was one of the original directors in 1852 of the Weston branch of the Exchange Bank of Virginia. He served as a founder and vestryman of Saint Paul's Episcopal Church in Weston, as a justice of the peace for Lewis County from 15 March 1825 to 6 July 1831, and as one of the county's school commissioners. With a dozen other Lewis County citizens he joined more than a hundred other delegates from sixteen counties at an education convention in Clarksburg in September 1841 that petitioned the General Assembly and addressed the people of Virginia in behalf of the establishment of a system of free public schools for the state.

From 1823 to 1830 Bland represented Lewis County in the House of Delegates. He served on the Committee on Propositions and Grievances but did not become a leader in the assembly. During the session of 1836–1837 he returned to the House of Delegates to represent the district consisting of the counties of Braxton and Lewis. He was elected to the Senate of Virginia from the district comprising Braxton, Harrison, Lewis, and Wood Counties in 1837 and served three years. On 22 August 1850 Bland was one of four successful candidates in a field of fifteen for seats in a state constitutional convention from the district composed of Barbour, Braxton, Gilmer, Jackson, Lewis, Randolph, and Wirt Counties. Bland served on the Committee on the Right of Suffrage and Qualifications of Persons to Be Elected, which recommended that the convention adopt universal suffrage for adult white males, one of the few democratic reforms to pass the convention with little difficulty. He supported other western proposals for democratizing the political practices and institutions of Virginia and for reducing the weighted advantage the eastern counties had enjoyed in the General Assembly, but he missed the vote on 31 July 1851 that approved the new constitution.

Bland sold Bland's Hotel in Weston and retired from public affairs before the Civil War

began. Several of his close relatives served in the Confederate army, and his son William J. Bland served in the General Assembly during the war. Thomas Bland died at Jane Lew, Lewis County, West Virginia, on 11 July 1867 and was buried in the Arnold Cemetery in Weston.

Bland, *Bland Family*, 373–379 (por. in 1982 ed., 378A; original in possession of George Linn Bland Jr., 1998); Urilla Moore Bland, "Additional Collections for the Ancient Family of Bland," unpublished 1974 paper at UVA; variant marriage date of 8 Dec. 1815 in Earle H. Morris, *Marriage Records: Harrison County, Virginia (West Virginia), 1784–1850* (1966), 92; Virgil A. Lewis, "The Soldiery of West Virginia," West Virginia Department of Archives and History, *Biennial Report* 3 (1911): 175–176; *Education Convention of Northwestern Virginia*, Doc. 7, appended to *JHD*, 1841–1842 sess., 4, 6; Edward Conrad Smith, *A History of Lewis County, West Virginia* (1920), 183, 186–187, 255, 257, 273–274, 417; convention election in *Richmond Enquirer*, 13 Sept. 1850; *Journal of 1850–1851 Convention*, 58, Appendix, 22; Lewis Co. Death Register lists variant birthplace of Fairfax Co. and confirms death date on gravestone; variant death date of 12 July 1867 in obituary in *Morgantown Weekly Post*, 27 July 1867.

STEPHEN W. BROWN

BLANTON, Natalie Friend McFaden (1 January 1895–25 August 1987), writer and civic leader, was born in Marion, the daughter of Frank Talbot McFaden, a Presbyterian minister, and Mary Minge Friend McFaden. The family moved in 1896 to Lynchburg and in December 1903 to Richmond, where her father became pastor of the First Presbyterian Church. She was especially devoted to her father, recalled that her family was "particularly close and harmonious," and remembered many instructive family discussions of woman suffrage and other topics. In 1910 McFaden enrolled in Virginia Randolph Ellett's school (later Saint Catherine's School). There she came under the influence of the school's founder, who groomed her best students for Bryn Mawr College and encouraged McFaden to concentrate on college preparation courses instead of the arts. After graduating from Ellett's school in 1913 McFaden attended Bryn Mawr and received an A.B. in 1917.

On 1 January 1918 she married Wyndham Bolling Blanton, a captain in the Army Medical Corps whom she had known since childhood. After completing an internship in New York City in 1919, he joined a private medical practice in Richmond. They had three sons and one daughter. After her children had all begun school Blanton became active in civic affairs, concentrating first on education. She was appointed to Richmond's school board on 11 August 1931 and served on it for two years. Between 1936 and 1941 Blanton worked part-time as publicity director at Saint Catherine's School, and from 1938 to 1951 she served on the Richmond Public Library Board. She was a member of the Richmond Board of Health from 1948 until September 1955, a charter director of the Richmond Citizens Association, a director of the Friends Association for Colored Children, and a board member of Richmond Forward, a civic association.

Blanton became interested in politics in childhood when her father explained to her the satirical humor of political cartoons. In 1947 and 1948 she was a member of the Governor's Commission on Reorganization of State Government, and from 1950 until June 1956 she served on the Governor's Commission to Provide Suitable Text on Virginia's History, Government, and Geography (later the Virginia History and Government Textbook Commission). In 1957 she sat on the Virginia Advisory Legislative Commission to Study the Milk Commission. Blanton became active in electoral politics in 1949 when she served as Third Congressional District vice chairman of John Stewart Battle's gubernatorial campaign. In 1952 she supported the Democrats for Eisenhower movement, and a year later she chaired the party's Richmond women's division during Thomas Bahnson Stanley's bid for governor. Blanton was vice chairman of the February 1955 Virginia Democratic Party's Jefferson-Jackson Day dinner, and she was elected to the Richmond City Democratic Committee the same year.

On 9 April 1955 Blanton announced her candidacy for the Democratic Party nomination for the House of Delegates from Richmond. She called for improvement in the quality of Richmond's schools and hospitals and in medical treatment for the young, the elderly, and the mentally ill. Blanton received 8,383 votes in the party primary, which placed her ninth in the twelve-candidate field for Richmond's seven seats. The following day the *Richmond Times-Dispatch* expressed regret at her defeat, remarking that "some day this city is going to get over its senseless prejudice against electing women to public office."

Blanton also devoted herself to writing. In 1950 she published *In That Day: Poems of the Second World War,* her first volume of poetry. In sensitive verse she described her concern for the safety of her son serving overseas, her reaction to the bombing of Japan, and her sadness over the losses that her friends and neighbors suffered. A member of the Poetry Society of Virginia, Blanton published *The Door Opened* (1959), *Let's Not Be Grave* (1965), *Songs of Sorrow and Love* (1979), and *Poems for Christmas* (1979). She produced three works based on the papers of Virginia Randolph Ellett, *Miss Jennie and Her Letters: An Effort at Documentation* (1955), *Love Remains* (1960), and *Ninety-Nine Notes to Love Remains* (1962). Blanton published two books on her family, *West Hill, Cumberland County, Virginia: The Story of Those Who Have Loved It* (1964) and *In Gratitude to Frank Talbot McFaden, 1864–1933, and Mary Minge Friend McFaden, 1868–1942* (1966). She also assisted in her husband's research on medical history until his death on 6 January 1960. Blanton later served on the board of the Historic Richmond Foundation, of which her spouse had been president.

In June 1960, at a convocation celebrating the seventy-fifth anniversary of Bryn Mawr's founding, Blanton won recognition for her "able and vigorous" participation in local and state affairs, her career as a writer, and her former service as a president of the Richmond branch of the American Association of University Women. She was one of seventy-five graduates honored for distinguished service. On Alumna Day at Saint Catherine's School in April 1969 Blanton was one of four women to receive a Distinguished Alumna Award.

About 1962 Blanton moved from her home on Seminary Avenue to a restored house on East Grace Street in Church Hill. Long a member of the Woman's Club of Richmond, she served as the organization's president from 1963 to 1964.

By 1966 Blanton had moved to the Berkshire Apartments, where she lived until about 1984. She resided for the last three years of her life at the Westminster-Canterbury retirement center. Natalie Friend McFaden Blanton died there of heart failure on 25 August 1987. Her body was cremated, and her ashes were buried in Hollywood Cemetery in Richmond.

Blanton gave autobiographical data and family history in *West Hill, Cumberland County, Virginia: The Story of Those Who Have Loved It* (1964), first quotation on 45, and *In Gratitude to Frank Talbot McFaden, 1864–1933, and Mary Minge Friend McFaden, 1868–1942* (1966); in *West Hill* she gave her birth place as Marion, but birth was recorded in BVS Birth Register, Lynchburg; letters and family genealogical records in Wyndham Bolling Blanton Papers, VHS; 1918 marriage recorded in BVS Marriage Register, Richmond City, 1917; feature articles in *Richmond Times-Dispatch,* 11 Aug. 1931, 18 Feb. 1955 (por.), and *Richmond News Leader,* 12 Feb. 1963; election campaign covered in *Richmond Times-Dispatch,* 10 Apr., 10, 13 (second quotation) July 1955; Sandra Gioia Treadway, *Women of Mark: A History of the Woman's Club of Richmond, Virginia, 1894–1994* (1995), 82, 114, 140; *Bryn Mawr College: The Seventy-Fifth Anniversary Convocation in Honor of Bryn Mawr Alumnae* (1960), third quotation; *St. Catherine's Bulletin* 32 (summer 1969): 10–11 (por.); obituaries with some errors in *Richmond News Leader* and *Richmond Times-Dispatch*, both 26 Aug. 1987.

FRANCES S. POLLARD

BLANTON, Thomas Hunter (19 October 1895–18 October 1965), member of the Senate of Virginia, was born in Caroline County, the son of James Rawlings Blanton and Cora Lee Blanton Blanton. He was educated in the schools of Caroline County and at the University of Virginia, from which he received his law degree in 1921. Blanton worked his way through law school with such success that when he graduated he had more money than when he entered. On 14 September 1921 he married Blanche Dulany Broaddus. They had two daughters.

Blanton practiced law and participated in public affairs in Bowling Green from 1921 until his death. He served on Bowling Green's town council from 1926 until 1943, sat on the Caroline County school board in 1922 and 1923, and was elected commonwealth's attorney for Caroline County in 1923. On 15 January 1925 Blanton resigned as commonwealth's attorney to become president of the Union Bank and Trust

Company of Bowling Green, a post he held until his death. A cautious and successful bank manager, he took an active role in the Virginia Bankers Association, chairing its 1938 constitutional revision committee and serving as president of the association for the 1940–1941 term. Blanton also invested in a number of local and regional businesses and owned a large farm in the county. At his death he left an estate valued at more than half a million dollars.

Blanton was elected to the Democratic Party's state central committee in 1936, and in 1943 he won election to the Senate of Virginia from the district composed initially of the counties of Caroline, Goochland, Hanover, and King William. He won four additional terms and served until he retired after the legislative session of 1963, citing failing eyesight as his reason for leaving public service. Blanton served on the influential Committees on Privileges and Elections and on General Laws during most of his career. He chaired the Committee on Nominations and Confirmations during his second term, joined the Committee on Finance during his third term, and became chairman of the Committee on Insurance and Banking in 1952, holding that chairmanship until he retired. In recognition of his service as chair of the commission to erect a new state office building adjacent to Capitol Square in Richmond in the 1950s, the building was named the Blanton State Office Building.

Blanton was a presidential elector for Harry S. Truman in 1948. Following the presidential election of 1952, in which many prominent Virginia Democrats supported the presidential candidacy of Dwight David Eisenhower and the Republicans won the state, Blanton took over as chairman of the party's state central committee hoping to reunite the warring factions. During his twelve years as chairman, the party remained deeply divided over issues of national politics as well as between supporters and opponents of party leader Harry Flood Byrd (1887–1966) and the proper response by Virginia to the Supreme Court's 1954 decision against racial segregation in the public schools. During the critical assembly session in the spring of 1959, Blanton voted consistently with the supporters of Massive

Resistance, but after Governor James Lindsay Almond abandoned the party leaders' intractable opposition to school desegregation, Blanton supported Almond's freedom of choice program. Behind the scenes Blanton strove to hold the party together, and he helped direct the Democratic Party's unsuccessful presidential campaigns in Virginia in 1956 and 1960.

Blanton sat on the board of visitors of the University of Virginia from 1960 to 1965 and also served as chairman of the trustees of the alumni association. Thomas Hunter Blanton died in the building of the Union Bank and Trust Company on 18 October 1965 and was buried in Lakewood Cemetery in Bowling Green.

Daphne Dailey, *The First Seventy Years, 1902–1972: A History of Union Bank & Trust Company* (1972), 34–36, 60; banking information supplied by William Beale and Marchant D. Warnom; presidential address in Virginia Bankers Association, *Yearbook* (1941): 61– 67; por. in Union Bank and Trust Company, Bowling Green; obituaries in *Richmond News Leader* and *Richmond Times-Dispatch*, both 19 Oct. 1965, and *Bowling Green Caroline Progress*, 21 Oct. 1965; editorial tribute in *Richmond Times-Dispatch*, 20 Oct. 1965; memorial in *Virginia State Bar Association Proceedings* (1966): 116 –118 (por.).

GEORGE B. OLIVER

BLANTON, Wyndham Bolling (3 June 1890 – 6 January 1960), physician and historian, was born in Richmond, the son of Charles Armistead Blanton and Elizabeth Brown Wallace Blanton. During his youth Blanton was exposed to both medicine and history, for his father and grandfather were physicians and both his parents' families included Virginians who had been famous during the eighteenth and nineteenth centuries. He received his early education at the Glebe School in Richmond, earned a B.A. at Hampden-Sydney College in 1910, and received an M.A. at the University of Virginia two years later.

Blanton studied medicine at the College of Physicians and Surgeons of Columbia University in New York, but he also studied in Europe and was in Berlin when World War I began. In 1915 he volunteered to serve in the American Ambulance Corps at the hospital in Neuilly-sur-Seine, France. He then returned to New York, received an M.D. in 1916, and began his medical

internship at Bellevue Hospital in New York City. After the United States entered World War I, Blanton was commissioned a captain in the Army Medical Corps and served until 1919 without being sent abroad. He then completed his internship at Bellevue Hospital in the same year. On 1 January 1918 Blanton married Natalie Friend McFaden, who became a civic and political activist and a poet. They had three sons and one daughter.

After completing his internship, Blanton returned to Richmond and joined the private medical practice of his brother, Howson Wallace Blanton, and their father. He also began a long association with the Medical College of Virginia as chief of laboratory service at the college's hospital. Blanton became an associate in medicine in 1920, assistant professor in 1925, associate professor by the end of the decade, and professor of clinical medicine in 1939. In 1936 he founded the outpatient department's immunology clinic, which had become one of the largest units of the medical school by the time he retired in 1954. Blanton was active in more than a dozen professional and learned organizations. He served as president of the Richmond Academy of Medicine and the Richmond Society of Internal Medicine and as vice president of the Southern Medical Association and the American Academy of Allergy.

Blanton entered medicine during one of its most exciting periods, as scientific thinking was newly emphasized, hospitals and laboratories were established or reorganized, and X rays and aseptic surgery were employed. During and immediately following World War I he published five articles on bacteria and on such epidemic diseases as polio, acute respiratory infections, streptococcal diseases, and diphtheria in such nationally known medical journals as the *Journal of the American Medical Association* and the *Journal of Medical Research*. During the ensuing decades Blanton's research led to articles in the medical literature on chemical therapeutic drugs; on other infectious diseases including tuberculosis, anthrax, herpes zoster, and infectious jaundice; on such physiological disorders as cardiac standstill, hemochromatosis, and orthostatic albuminuria; on changes in blood-cell counts and types; on fevers, sudden death, and hypertension; and on ways of learning what was occurring within the body without exploratory surgery. Altogether, Blanton published thirty-six articles in fourteen medical journals between 1917 and 1957 as well as two textbooks, *A Manual of Normal Physical Signs* (1926; 2d ed., 1930) and *A Handbook of Allergy for Students and Practitioners* (1942).

Blanton was also a pioneer in the field of medical history. In 1927 he published a historical article in the *Virginia Medical Monthly* and became the first chairman of the historical committee of the Medical Society of Virginia, which hoped to sponsor the publication of a history of medicine in Virginia. The other committee members achieved this goal by deferring to Blanton, who conducted his own research, employed research assistants, and wrote three large volumes entitled *Medicine in Virginia in the Seventeenth Century* (1930), *Medicine in Virginia in the Eighteenth Century* (1931), and *Medicine in Virginia in the Nineteenth Century* (1933). Organized in a coherent and useful fashion and written in a readable and interesting style, the three volumes of *Medicine in Virginia* stood out among other state medical histories published during the same decade. They were milestones in the evolution of American medical scholarship and have stood the test of time. Blanton supplemented his books with about two dozen articles on various aspects of medical history and the history of medical education that appeared in at least ten journals, newspapers, magazines, and reference works between 1927 and 1957.

In 1933 the board of the Medical Society of Virginia elected Blanton editor of its *Virginia Medical Monthly*, a position he filled with distinction until 1942. Following his retirement from that post he remained on the monthly's editorial board as editor emeritus for eighteen more years. From 1939 to 1942 Blanton served on the editorial board of the *Annals of Medical History*. He was a consulting editor of the *Journal of the History of Medicine and Allied Sciences* from its founding in 1946 until his death, and he sat on the editorial board of the *Bulletin of the History of Medicine* from 1953 to 1960. In 1958 the

Medical College of Virginia named him professor emeritus of clinical medicine and the history of medicine.

Blanton did not confine his interests to medicine and medical history. He was one of a group of Richmond men who in the 1930s began to compile a volume of biographies of some of Virginia's leading citizens. The one volume to appear was published in Richmond in 1936 as the start of a projected second series of *Men of Mark in Virginia*, continuing a five-volume work of that name edited by Lyon Gardiner Tyler between 1906 and 1909. The new volume featured a large number of physicians and Richmond residents, suggesting that Blanton exercised a strong influence over its production. He also wrote a centennial history of his church, *The Making of a Downtown Church: The History of the Second Presbyterian Church, Richmond, Virginia, 1845–1945* (1945), prepared a number of short articles and papers on various aspects of Virginia's history, belonged to several historical and patriotic societies, and was a founder of the Historic Richmond Foundation. During service on the board of the Virginia Historical Society from 1945 until his death, he chaired the board's publications committee, supported the publication of additional primary source materials and scholarly articles of a higher quality in the *Virginia Magazine of History and Biography*, and helped make the society's collections more useful and accessible to scholarly researchers. Blanton was serving his second year as president of the Virginia Historical Society at the time of his death.

Blanton sat on the board of trustees of Mary Baldwin College from 1932 to 1940. He was a member of the board of Richmond's Union Theological Seminary from 1941 to 1958 and chairman from 1958 until his death. Wyndham Bolling Blanton died of a heart attack at his home in Richmond on 6 January 1960 and was buried in Hollywood Cemetery in that city.

Tyler, *Men of Mark*, 2d ser., 1:36–39 (por.); feature articles in *Virginia Medical Monthly* 69 (1942): 701–702, and *Bulletin of the History of Medicine* 38 (1964): 80–81; Blanton Family Papers and Wyndham Bolling Blanton Papers, VHS; Blanton's medical history research papers, UVA; bibliography of publications compiled from *Index Medicus*,

1916–1964, in DVB Files; Hall, *Portraits*, 28–29 (por.); obituaries in *Richmond News Leader*, 6 Jan. 1960, and *Richmond Times-Dispatch*, 7 Jan. 1960; memorials in *VMHB* 68 (1960): 226–227, in *Virginia Medical Monthly* 87 (1960): 115, 226, in *Journal of Allergy* 31 (1960): 286–287, and in *Transactions of the American Clinical and Climatological Association* 72 (1960): xli–xlii.

TODD L. SAVITT

BLATTNER, Mildred Ferguson Goodnow (18 November 1892–30 January 1968), librarian, was born in Chicago, the daughter of Charles Newell Goodnow, a lawyer, and Serena DeCamp Ferguson Goodnow. She graduated from Saint Mary-of-the-Woods in Indiana in 1912 and from 1913 to 1916 worked as an assistant in the Chicago Public Library. In March 1916 Goodnow entered the Wisconsin Library School in Madison, by which she was certified as a school librarian in June 1917. She worked as an extension librarian in Springfield, Illinois, from 1917 to 1919; as a librarian in Plymouth, Indiana, in 1919 and 1920; in the library of the National Bank of Commerce in New York City during the years 1921–1923; and in the public library system of Passaic, New Jersey, from 1923 to 1928.

By March 1923 Goodnow had married George Wayman Blattner, whom she may have met while studying in Wisconsin. She temporarily retired from library work in 1929 when she moved to Arlington County with her husband, who became an economist with the Federal Reserve Board in Washington, D.C. Only a few of Virginia's counties had public libraries when Blattner moved to the state, and most were like Arlington's system of small lending libraries run by volunteers. Blattner was an organizer of the Arlington County Library Association, founded on 21 July 1936 to serve as a liaison between the county government and the five small county libraries. The association obtained an appropriation of $3,000 from the county, and Blattner prepared a report on the county's library needs that served as the blueprint for the subsequent development of the library system. She assisted in hiring the first county librarian and worked as cataloger of the library's collections.

On 15 February 1941 Blattner was appointed director of the county's library system. During her sixteen years as director of the Arlington County Public Library, the county's population doubled, and state and county appropriations for library services grew from less than $10,000 in 1941 to almost $275,000 in 1957. Blattner oversaw the expansion of the branch system, increased the professionalism of the staff, enlarged the staff and the size of the collections, and built Arlington's public libraries into the largest county system in Virginia. In 1957, with seven branches, a staff of sixty-seven, and a collection of almost 120,000 volumes, the Arlington County library system served as a model for public library development elsewhere in Virginia.

Blattner chaired a committee of the Virginia Library Association that in 1950 prepared a comprehensive report on professional standards and pay scales for the public libraries of Virginia, and she served as president of the Virginia Library Association for the 1950–1951 term. She also served from 1950 to 1958 on the board of Fairfax County's library system and in June 1957 was elected president of the board. Shortly before Blattner retired on 31 August 1957 she commissioned a new professional study of the future library needs of Arlington County.

Mildred Ferguson Goodnow Blattner died on 30 January 1968 at Commonwealth Doctors Hospital in Alexandria and was buried beside the body of her husband in Arlington National Cemetery.

Oral history interview with Jane B. Nida, and vertical files, Virginiana Room, Arlington Co. Public Library; family history verified by Ted Banvard; *Arlington Northern Virginia Sun*, 14 Feb. 1941, 2 Sept. 1957; Eleanor C. Leonard, "Pioneer Library Work in Arlington County," *Library Journal* 64 (1939): 741–743; Jeanne Rose, "A Brief History of the Arlington County Libraries," *Arlington Historical Magazine* 1 (Oct. 1960): 28–38; Arlington Co. Department of Libraries, *Annual Reports,* 1949/1950–1964/1965; career information verified by Jack H. Foster and Mary Katherine McCulloch; feature articles in *Arlington Personnel News* 2 (Apr. 1953), photocopy in DVB Files (por.), and *Arlington Virginia Citizen*, 22 Mar. 1957; obituaries in *Fairfax Northern Virginia Sun, Washington Post*, and *Washington Star*, all 1 Feb. 1968, and *Virginia Librarian* 15 (spring 1968): 24–25.

SARA J. COLLINS

BLAYNEY, Edward (ca. 1595–by 6 February 1626), member of the Council, was born probably in England. Because other people spelled the surname in a variety of ways, the names of his parents and the place and date of his birth cannot be determined. He may have engaged in trade with the Netherlands before becoming associated with the Virginia Company of London. In April 1620 the Society of Particular Adventurers for Traffic with the People of Virginia in Joint Stock appointed Blayney to succeed Abraham Peirsey as cape merchant for the Virginia colony. Blayney arrived in the colony aboard the *Francis Bonaventure* with the autumn 1620 fleet. As cape merchant, or supercargo, he supervised the sale of supplies from the company's magazine, or warehouse. Blayney was expected to turn a profit by taking the settlers' tobacco in exchange for English goods and thereby relieve the company of the task of supplying the colony. The arrangement was never an economic success.

After less than a year in Virginia, Blayney returned to London in May 1621. Shortly thereafter the Company of Fur Adventurers chose him to be its factor, or agent, in trading with the Indians in Virginia in emulation of the profitable practice of the French. Blayney returned to Virginia on the *Warwick* on 20 December 1621 with supplies valued at £2,000. The other passengers included a number of women sent over as prospective wives for the colonists. On the marriage of each, Blayney was to receive 150 pounds of good leaf tobacco. The scheme, like the magazine, was not profitable, and two years later the sponsors who underwrote the transportation of the women were still seeking payment from Blayney.

Like Peirsey before him, Blayney complained of the debts that the colonists owed to the magazine and of the operation's constant losses. Part of the difficulty resulted from the selling of goods to individual colonists on credit in anticipation of the next tobacco harvest. All too often the tobacco was spent elsewhere. Much of the crop found its way to the floating taverns that shrewd entrepreneurs operated on ships anchored in the James River, where the tobacco was exchanged for substantial quantities of what the governor and Council dismissed as "rotten Wynes." Blayney also lamented that what tobacco he did receive in payment of debt was often so poorly packed in its casks as to be virtually worthless. In June 1625, almost two years after John Hart replaced him as cape merchant, Blayney testified before the General Court that the tobacco the magazine had received from Sir George Yeardley was "soe wett and ill Condicioned" that he returned it. Perhaps because Yeardley had become governor by then, Blayney did not take advantage of the law providing that inferior tobacco be burned in the presence of its owner.

Although Blayney began his association with the colony in relatively modest circumstances, he soon gained the respect of the colony's leaders. George Sandys predicted in 1623 that Blayney "wilbee a Planter amongst us" and suggested that he be appointed to the Council. Sometime before 11 April 1623 Blayney married Margaret Powell, a recent widow with several children whose first husband, William Powell, had served in the 1619 General Assembly. She is not known to have had any children with Blayney. A series of depositions taken in May 1625 indicates that she had had a miscarriage, but it may have taken place before Powell's death. The marriage improved Blayney's economic standing, and he added lands on both sides of the James River to his property in Jamestown. According to a colonial muster, or census, taken in January 1625, he had seventeen servants, fifteen of whom were at his plantation in present-day Surry County.

As one of two representatives of the merchants, Blayney served in the assembly that met from 16 February to 5 March 1624. Representing "the Plantations over the water," he also sat in the session that met for a few days beginning on 10 May 1625. As an assemblyman he signed several documents, including the body's long point-by-point rebuttal of charges in February 1624 that the Virginia Company had mismanaged the colony. The king's commission of 4 March 1626 appointing Sir George Yeardley governor named Blayney one of thirteen members of the governor's Council. Blayney's name also appeared as a councillor on 22 March 1628 in John Harvey's commission as governor. Although these appointments testified to Blayney's reputation in England as a merchant and colonist, he never served on the Council because he had died before he was so named.

The exact date of Edward Blayney's death has not been determined. He testified about Yeardley's tobacco in the General Court on 7 June 1625, but he did not sign a letter that the governor and councillors wrote eighteen days later. His widow remarried before 6 February 1626, when the General Court recorded an agreement concerning the magazine that had been concluded between the governor and Francis West, "in behalfe of Mrs *Margrett West* Administratrix to her late husbande *Edwarde Blayney* Marchant, deceased." Margaret Powell Blayney West had two more children. She died before 31 March 1628, when West, by then the governor of the colony, married the widow of George Yeardley.

Blayney gave age as twenty-eight in a deposition on 7 Jan. 1624 (*Minutes of Council and General Court*, 9–10); autograph with spelling of surname in letter to Sir Edwin Sandys, 17 Sept. 1621, Ferrar Papers, Magdalene College, Cambridge University, Eng.; 1625 muster in *Adventurers of Purse and Person*, 31, 40; numerous references in Kingsbury, *Virginia Company*, vols. 3–4 (first and third quotations on 4:453 and 4:111, respectively), in *Minutes of Council and General Court* (second and final quotations on 64 and 93, respectively), and in Ferrar Papers; 4 Mar. 1626 Yeardley commission in PRO CO 5/1354, fols. 253–261.

JENNIFER DAVIS McDAID

BLAYTON, Thomas (fl. 1669–1695), participant in Bacon's Rebellion, was born in England, probably about the mid-1630s. The names of his parents are not known, and some contemporary spellings of the surname as "Bleighton" may have confused the records as well as given a clue as to the name's pronunciation. With his wife Joan (maiden name unknown), two sons, and two daughters, Blayton settled in Virginia sometime before 23 June 1669. He lived at Martin's Brandon in the southern part of Charles City County that became Prince George County in 1702. Blayton served as a factor and legal agent for some of London's leading mercantile houses, including those under the management of Micajah Perry and Phillip Perry, of John Sadler, and of Thomas Quiney.

Blayton was probably a member of the Charles City County Court by the mid-1670s. He was elected to the House of Burgesses in May 1676 and attended the occasionally tumultuous session of 5–25 June. Fragmentary and contradictory evidence exists on Blayton's actions during that assembly and the remainder of 1676. While the assembly was in session Nathaniel Bacon (1647–1676) demanded from Governor Sir William Berkeley a commission as a general to lead an army against the Indians, but Berkeley refused, and Bacon turned to the assembly for the commission. According to Thomas Mathew's reminiscences, written thirty years later and confused in some details, Blayton opposed the assembly's decision to grant Bacon's request on the ground that issuing commissions was the governor's responsibility. Blayton apparently approved of Bacon's intention to make war on the Indians, however, and Berkeley and his followers later charged that Blayton served as "Bacon's great engin" in attempting to persuade other leading men to support what came to be called Bacon's Rebellion.

Blayton attended Bacon's conference at Middle Plantation at the beginning of August and probably drafted parts of one or both of the declarations addressed to the public by those assembled there. The two declarations charged that by opposing Bacon's plans for a campaign against the Indians, Berkeley had endangered the safety of the colony and brought about a civil war. Bacon's supporters called on the colonists to support Bacon's intended campaign and requested Bacon to summon a new General Assembly, if necessary, to supplant Berkeley's authority until the king could be fully apprised of Bacon's plans and the complaints against Berkeley. Blayton was one of seventy men who signed the declaration of 3 August and one of thirty who signed the declaration of 4 August.

Whether Blayton accompanied Bacon during the ensuing fighting is unclear. He advised Joseph Ingram, who commanded Bacon's followers after Bacon's death in October 1676, until the surrender of 2 January 1677. After the capitulation, Berkeley ordered Edward Hill, colonel of the Charles City County militia, to arrest Blayton and other leaders who had not surrendered with Ingram and to seize their estates. Blayton took sanctuary on a ship, from which Hill was unable to remove him. Hill then seized Blayton's property under circumstances that permitted passing soldiers to carry off some of Blayton's clothing, powder, and shot, as well as his business papers and the papers and property of several other merchants that he had stored in his buildings. On 10 February 1677, when Berkeley pardoned most of Bacon's followers, he excluded Blayton and twenty-five other surviving "active prosecutors, ayders, and abettors of the said Rebellion." Berkeley's exceptions contradicted the king's proclamation of October 1676, and later in 1677 the General Assembly passed an "Act of indemnitie and free pardon" that did include Blayton.

Hard feelings and public recriminations did not end there. On 10 May 1677 Blayton and six other Charles City County men who had supported Bacon signed a long statement that became known as the Charles City County Grievances. Blayton probably helped compile the document, which charged Berkeley with misrule and sharply criticized Hill for his treatment of the men he had been ordered to arrest earlier in the year. Hill replied with a long statement that contains many of the surviving assertions about Blayton's participation in Bacon's Rebellion. Both documents are after-the-fact exculpations, and they contradict each other, leaving details of Blayton's role shrouded in uncertainty.

When Blayton was able to resume his private business affairs, he acted more often as an attorney than a merchant. In November 1678 he was appointed or reappointed a justice of the peace, and in 1682 and 1683 he represented Sarah Greene Bland in her efforts to recover the estate of Giles Bland, her son and Bacon's lieutenant, whom Berkeley had hanged. Blayton's contemporary William Fitzhugh once expressed a low opinion of his legal ability, but in November 1682 Blayton was appointed clerk of the House of Burgesses' Committee on Propositions and Grievances, a post he also held during the April 1684 assembly. In June 1689 he finally petitioned the court of Charles City County to be admitted to the practice of law there. Thomas Blayton continued to practice as late as 3 October 1695, the last documented reference to him. The place and date of his death are not known.

Patent Book, 9:725, RG 4, LVA, records immigration of Blayton and family; presence in Virginia first documented in Surry Co. Deed Book, 1:341–342, 379; scattered references in deed and order books of Surry and Charles City Cos.; June 1676 assembly service recorded in Charles City Co. Order Book (1677–1679), 250, 349; Thomas Mathew, "Beginning, Progress, and Conclusion of Bacon's Rebellion, 1675–1676," in *Narratives of the Insurrections, 1675–1690,* ed. Charles McLean Andrews (1915), 9–41; Middle Plantation declarations of 3, 4 Aug. 1676, PRO CO 1/37, fols. 130–131; Charles City Co. Grievances and Edward Hill's reply in PRO CO 1/40, fols. 140–147, 148–161, printed in *VMHB* 3 (1895–1896): 132–147, 239–252 (first quotation on 249), 341–349, and 4 (1896): 1–15; Berkeley's and assembly's pardons in PRO CO 1/39, fols. 64–65 (second quotation), and Hening, *Statutes,* 2:366–373; Blayton's signatures on Sarah Greene Bland petition, 25 Feb. 1683, and application to practice law in Charles City Co., 3 June 1689, Colonial Papers, RG 1, LVA; last reference to Blayton in Charles City Co. Order Book (1687–1695), 592–593.

DAPHNE GENTRY

BLENNERHASSETT, Harman (8 October 1764–2 February 1831), businessman, was the youngest of three sons and six daughters of Conway Blennerhassett and Elizabeth Lacey Blennerhassett. He was born while his mother was on a visit to Hambledon, Hampshire, England, and grew up at his father's 7,000-acre estate, Castle Conway, at Killorglin, County Kerry, Ireland. At age nineteen Blennerhassett was admitted to the Middle Temple in London to study law. He also studied law at Trinity College in Dublin and traveled on the Continent. In November 1790 he was admitted to the Irish bar as a member of the Honorable Society of the King's Inns, Dublin. His elder brothers having died young, Blennerhassett inherited a large fortune from his father in March 1792.

Blennerhassett was a man of romantic sensibilities and an enthusiastic supporter of the ideals of the French Revolution. In 1793 he joined and became a secretary of the Society of United Irishmen, which secretly plotted to free Ireland from British rule. In 1794 Blennerhassett married his niece Margaret Agnew in violation of the laws of the Church of Ireland. To avoid charges of both treason and incest, he sold Castle Conway for £28,000 and in the summer of 1796 moved to the United States.

Blennerhassett resided briefly in New York City and Philadelphia before moving to Pittsburgh in November 1796. From autumn 1797 until spring 1798 he lived in Marietta in the Northwest Territory. In March 1798 he made a verbal agreement to purchase the upper portion of an island, now known as Blennerhassett Island, situated in the Ohio River near the mouth of the Little Kanawha River. Slavery was legal on the Virginia island but not on the north shore of the Ohio River, and Blennerhassett set himself up as a planter and for a short time became one of western Virginia's most active entrepreneurs. He stimulated the region's cash-starved economy with investments in shipbuilding, fur trading, cattle raising, and opening a chain of stores. On his island Blennerhassett erected a Palladian-style mansion and filled it with fine furniture and objets d'art purchased from Baltimore, Philadelphia, and London. The mansion, set amid landscaped gardens, soon gained a reputation as the finest residence west of the Alleghenies. It also became the region's acknowledged social and cultural center. Margaret Blennerhassett, learned, athletic, and physically attractive, entranced neighbors and travelers alike with her charm, elegance, and command of languages. Her husband composed music for the flute and violin. The Blennerhassetts raised their three sons, two daughters (who both died young), and adopted son according to the principles of Jean-Jacques Rousseau's *Emile: ou de l'Education* (1762).

Blennerhassett's nearly idyllic existence soon ended, however, as a result of his extravagant living, poorly performing investments, and decision to sink the remainder of his fortune into Aaron Burr's controversial 1805–1806 military expedition to the Southwest. Blennerhassett played host to Burr and to Burr's unreliable ally, James Wilkinson, and allowed his island to serve as one of Burr's bases of operation. At the same time Blennerhassett addressed a series of public letters, signed "Querist," to the editor of the *Marietta Ohio Gazette, and Virginia Herald*, suggesting that the economic interests of the Ohio Valley would eventually lead to a separation of the western states from those on the Atlantic Coast. After Burr's arrest was ordered on charges of treason, Virginia militiamen descended on Blennerhassett Island in December 1806 in search of Blennerhassett, but he had

fled, and they ransacked his mansion instead. Blennerhassett was arrested in Lexington, Kentucky, on 14 July 1807, jailed in Richmond, and indicted as an accomplice of Burr. After the latter was acquitted of treason, the prosecutors dropped the charges against Blennerhassett, who was more a victim of Burr's schemes than a knowing participant. Blennerhassett's fortune and reputation, however, were both in ruins.

Blennerhassett unsuccessfully attempted to recoup his finances, first by growing cotton in Mississippi from 1810 to 1814 and then by practicing law in Canada. Attempts to recover a small inheritance in Ireland and to secure a position with the British government proved unsuccessful. About 1822 he directed an essay on the political and commercial connections of the United States and Great Britain to the British colonial department. Margaret Blennerhassett was an accomplished writer and poet in her own right who published *The Widow of the Rock, and Other Poems* in Montreal in 1824. Blennerhassett returned to England the next year and moved to the Channel Islands in 1826. Harman Blennerhassett died of apoplexy on 2 February 1831 on the island of Guernsey. He was buried there in Le Cimetière des Etrangers in a grave that is not marked.

Ronald Ray Swick, "Harman Blennerhassett: An Irish Aristocrat on the American Frontier" (Ph.D. diss., Miami University, 1978) and *An Island Called Eden: The Story of Harman and Margaret Blennerhassett* (2000); collections of Blennerhassett papers in LC, Ohio Historical Society, Columbus, and Missouri Historical Society, Saint Louis; Raymond E. Fitch, ed., *Breaking with Burr: Harman Blennerhassett's Journal, 1807* (1988), frontispiece por., with Blennerhassett giving birth date as 8 Oct. 1764 or 1765, p. 125; 10 Oct. 1764 christening recorded in Hambledon Parish baptismal register, Hampshire Record Office, Winchester, Eng.; approximate year of marriage mentioned in Harman Blennerhassett to Margaret Blennerhassett, 29 June–2 July 1807, Blennerhassett Papers, LC; death date in Therese Blennerhassett-Adams, "The True Story of Harman Blennerhassett," *Century Magazine* 62 (1901): 351–356.

RAY SWICK

BLES, Marcus John (11 March 1904–9 January 1986), real estate developer, was born on a farm near Kelso, Scott County, Missouri, the son of Joseph John Bles and Florence McClanehan Bles. He lost his right eye playing cowboys and Indians when he was a boy and part of a finger in another accident. Because he was needed on the family farm, Bles received only intermittent formal schooling and never completed the sixth grade. About 1925 he moved to Saint Louis, where he trained as a carpenter, sold life insurance, and learned about the construction business as a "boomer" who worked on construction jobs in different parts of the country. On 15 January 1936 he married Alba Julet Trainor. They had one son and one daughter.

In 1939 Bles moved his family to Northern Virginia, where he found construction work. He arrived in the state with very little money but at the start of a remarkable building boom that lasted for half a century, during which he amassed a fortune of approximately $50 million. The Pentagon was among the first projects on which he worked. In 1944 Bles started his own utilities contracting firm, M. J. Bles Construction, which became one of the largest in Northern Virginia and took part in the construction of numerous federal installations and private projects. He received $500,000 when he sold the firm in 1957, in part because of his dissatisfaction over the high taxes he was paying.

Bles continued to work as a general contractor through the 1960s on projects that included the construction of both the Baltimore and Dulles airports, but as the 1940s ended he turned increasingly to real estate development. About 1949 he purchased a farm at Tyson's Corner. Initially he sold gravel dug from the property, but by 1965 he had spent $1.5 million acquiring additional land in the vicinity. The land ultimately became the business and commercial center of Fairfax County, and in the 1960s Bles sold it for a profit of $19 million. He used a portion of the proceeds to buy more than 3,500 acres in Loudoun County, of which he sold about 2,400 in the 1980s for approximately $40 million. At one point during the 1960s he owned almost 6,500 acres, making him one of the largest landowners in Northern Virginia.

Bles retained the marks of his rural upbringing. He wore a string tie and a Stetson hat and avoided the trappings of great wealth. He kept a large herd of cattle in Loudoun County and was awarded four patents for inventions, including a tree-stump remover and a wood splitter. In partnership with his son, James M. Bles, he sold both devices as well as red clover seed. Like many other self-made men, Bles was politically conservative. He complained about high taxes, zoning laws, easy credit, urban renewal, reformers, and lax enforcement of criminal laws. Despite his opposition to big government and to government intervention in the economy, Bles benefited greatly from the enormous expansion of the federal government during and after World War II. That growth, which he helped direct and from which he profited, transformed Northern Virginia from a rural backwater into a densely packed urban and suburban area.

Bles contributed 641 acres of land to Georgetown University in 1969. His epileptic and mentally retarded daughter, Marcey Ann Bles, had been treated in the university hospital, and the university awarded him an honorary Sc.D. in 1971 and named the Marcus J. Bles University Affiliated Center for Child Development for him. Marcus John Bles died of pneumonia in Georgetown University Hospital in Washington, D.C., on 9 January 1986 and was buried in the cemetery of Saint John's Catholic Church in Leesburg.

Nan Netherton, "Three 'Northern Virginians': At Home in a Land of Contrasts," *Northern Virginia Country* (1976), 26–27; oral history interview, 1975, George Mason University; additional information supplied by son James M. Bles; feature articles in *Washington Post*, 7 Sept. 1969, 5 Mar. 1984; obituaries in *Washington Post*, 10 Jan. 1986 (por.), and *Loudoun Times-Mirror*, 16 Jan. 1986.

ROY A. ROSENZWEIG

BLEWETT, William Edward (8 November 1894–6 October 1965), industrialist, was born in Newark, New Jersey, the son of William Edward Blewett and Florence A. Vreeland Blewett. He was educated in the public schools of Newark and at Montclair Academy before graduating from Cornell University in 1918 with a degree in mechanical engineering. Blewett joined the United States Army Air Corps shortly before the end of World War I and worked for a bank in New York for a few months in 1919. In June 1920 he married Eleanor W. Johnson, of Montclair, New Jersey. They had three daughters.

William E. Blewett Jr., as he identified himself throughout his professional life, joined the

Newport News Shipbuilding and Dry Dock Company as a draftsman in August 1919. He worked as a draftsman, an engineer, and an assistant superintendent until 1928, when he was appointed assistant to the president of the company, Homer L. Ferguson. In 1930 Blewett became production manager for the entire shipyard. An independent thinker with outstanding executive skills, he was a keen businessman who earned a national reputation during the 1930s as an astute shipbuilder. Blewett was aggressive, sometimes impatient, and often emphasized his opinions with profanity, but he knew every aspect of his business. After he was appointed a vice president of the shipyard in 1941, he personally directed many of the programs that enabled the shipyard to perform miracles of construction during World War II, for which he received a presidential certificate of merit in 1947. Blewett also served on the wartime board of directors of the shipyard's subsidiary, the North Carolina Shipbuilding Company, of Wilmington, North Carolina.

Some 189 vessels constructed at Newport News, a total of more than two million tons of shipping, took part in World War II. During the four years of the war the shipyard constructed nine aircraft carriers, one battleship, eight cruisers, and some of the largest types of landing craft. The yard also converted passenger liners and freighters into wartime transports and overhauled and repaired damaged ships. The North Carolina Shipbuilding Company turned out almost 250 Liberty ships and other transport vessels. At one time during the war the shipyard in Newport News employed more than 31,000 people, while more than 20,000 worked at the shipyard in Wilmington. Newport News Shipbuilding became the largest industrial establishment and the largest single nongovernmental employer in Virginia.

Blewett was elected to the board of directors and appointed executive vice president in 1947. On 16 December 1953 he became the seventh president of the Newport News Shipbuilding and Dry Dock Company, and he succeeded to the chairmanship of the board in 1961. During the 1950s American construction of merchant vessels declined. The firm built its last

ocean liner, the *United States*, the largest and one of the last of the great passenger liners to be laid down in the United States and also the fastest passenger liner ever. Blewett led Newport News Shipbuilding into new fields and prosperity as an innovative constructor of naval vessels. After he organized his company's Atomic Power Design Department in 1955, the yard built the *Enterprise*, the first nuclear-powered aircraft carrier, which was the largest ship in the world at the time that it was launched. The yard also became a principal builder of atomic-propelled submarines and by 1960 had constructed more nuclear-powered ships than any other yard in the world.

Blewett constantly improved on technical and safety programs in the nuclear-engineering field and eventually developed a separate submarine reactor-plant department within the Atomic Power Division. He enlarged the yard's research facilities and created engineering and electrolysis laboratories. After a shortage of young engineers developed during the 1950s when many young men entered the seemingly more glamorous aerospace industry, Blewett created a program to pay for graduate engineering training for members of the apprentice classes at the shipyard. In addition to building some of the largest and most technologically sophisticated warships in the world, the company also built huge hydraulic turbines and other heavy equipment, including wind tunnels for experimentation at Langley Field, the Virginia research facility of the National Advisory Committee for Aeronautics.

Throughout his career Blewett took an active part in professional organizations. In 1952 he was elected to a two-year term as president of the Society of Naval Architects and Marine Engineers, and in 1958 the society awarded him the Vice Admiral Jerry Land Medal for outstanding accomplishments in marine architecture. He also served as a national vice president of the Propeller Club and belonged to the American Society of Naval Engineers, the Shipbuilders Council of America, the Defense Industry Advisory Council, and the Newcomen Society. For a publication series of the Newcomen Society, Blewett prepared a short history, *"Always*

Good Ships": A History of the Newport News Shipbuilding and Dry Dock Company (1960).

Like his immediate predecessors as shipyard president, Homer Ferguson and John Brockenbrough Woodward, Blewett served on many regional economic and educational committees. He chaired the Lower Peninsula Planning Commission from 1944 to 1948 and participated in the planning for the construction of Patrick Henry Airport near Williamsburg and the Hampton Roads Bridge-Tunnel linking Hampton with Norfolk. In addition, Blewett established and became president of the Newport News Shipbuilding Company Foundation, the philanthropic arm of the firm, sat on the board of visitors of Virginia Polytechnic Institute in 1963 and 1964, and was serving as president of the Mariners' Museum in Newport News at the time of his death. He was also an avid golfer and was president of the Virginia State Golf Association and of the Virginia Senior Golf Association, and he owned a cattle farm near Bevans, Sussex County, New Jersey.

Blewett continued as president of the shipyard until January 1964, when he was appointed chief executive officer. Suffering from cancer, he resigned that post in December of the same year but remained as chairman of the board. William Edward Blewett died in Riverside Hospital in Newport News on 6 October 1965 and was buried in Peninsula Memorial Park.

Franklyn Gale and Harry M. Suplee, comps., *Essex County Heroes of To-day: Bloomfield and Glen Ridge Section* (1919), 106 (por.); William L. Tazewell, *Newport News Shipbuilding: The First Century* (1986), esp. 203–210; por. in offices of Newport News Shipbuilding and Dry Dock Co.; obituaries with pors. and editorial tributes in *Newport News Daily Press*, *Newport News Times-Herald*, and *Richmond Times-Dispatch*, all 7, 8 Oct. 1965.

F. ROBERT TENCH

BLOSSER, Emanuel (28 October 1877–23 August 1953), poultryman, was born several miles west of Harrisonburg, the son of Henry Blosser and Sophia Showalter Blosser. He attended a two-room school near Weaver's Church but never received additional formal schooling. He furthered his education thereafter by reading.

Blosser learned the poultry business as a boy while working on the farm of his father, whose cousin Samuel H. Blosser had pioneered in the artificial incubation of chicken eggs. During the 1890s the family's small-scale operation raised chickens and turkeys and dressed them for sale to markets in Virginia and the North. Believing that demand justified investment in a poultry-dressing business, on 13 April 1908 Blosser, his brother Gabriel Blosser, and Hershey H. Weaver founded the City Produce Exchange in Harrisonburg, with Emanuel Blosser as president. The wholesale operation, which handled eggs and prepared chickens for market, completed construction of a plant in November 1911 and enlarged it the next year.

Rockingham County's poultry industry was then in its infancy. Blosser and his crews scouted the countryside for farmers with chickens to sell. After weighing the poultry at the farm, they moved the birds to the plant, fattened them on corn, killed the chickens, and "New York dressed" them, plucking the feathers by hand and washing the carcasses, but leaving the head and feet attached. To prevent the spread of bacteria and to allow the chicken to stay fresh longer, they took care not to break the skin. Blosser's firm packed the chickens in ice and shipped them in refrigerated boxcars to Baltimore, New York, and Philadelphia. The plant also processed turkeys, for which demand was seasonal. In the autumn Blosser and his crews drove flocks of turkeys from surrounding farms to his plant to be fattened and dressed for the holidays.

A forerunner of modern poultry-processing plants, the City Produce Exchange offered Shenandoah Valley farmers a convenient market for their eggs, chickens, and turkeys. By 1916 the company had expanded operations with large branch facilities in Elkton and Staunton and had also constructed a cold storage plant. It switched to a semiscald method of removing feathers and pins, building what was perhaps the first machine in the industry capable of such an operation. By 1922 the firm had constructed yet another addition to its plant, enabling it to feed up to 60,000 chickens under one roof. The work remained labor-intensive even with improvements and modifications to the processing operation. After the chickens were slaughtered, they were scalded, cooled, run through a mechanical picker, and then sent through a wax dip for easier removal of the remaining feathers.

In 1926 the Harrisonburg Chamber of Commerce boasted that Rockingham County was the leading poultry producer in the state and the second-largest producer nationally. It singled out City Produce Exchange as the largest fattening and packing plant in the world. Even allowing for exaggeration common in such local boosterism, the company clearly operated on a scale seldom duplicated elsewhere. A 1922 study conducted by the University of Virginia School of Economics that described Rockingham County as the egg and poultry center of the state cited census and revenue figures on the "immense" economic returns from poultry livestock. Blosser later stated that after its 1922 expansion the plant was "the largest poultry and egg house in the United States."

In 1924 the partnership incorporated, and four years later the company became the first egg-grading station in Virginia. In 1935 the plant was one of the first to use high-speed mechanical devices for picking and waxing poultry. The City Produce Exchange was shipping about eleven tons of dressed chickens daily by 1939. Two years later it was dressing eight times as many chickens as it had in 1931. Annual shipment totals reached several thousand tons. During World War II the plant shipped dressed poultry overseas.

Blosser and his partners shut down their processing plant in 1948. Since the mid-1930s the company, which advertised itself as "The Oldest in the Valley," had shipped dressed chickens to northern markets using its own fleet of trailer and flatbed trucks. Union stevedores, however, sometimes refused to unload Blosser's cargoes because his drivers were not unionized. After Blosser's drivers joined the union, it demanded that all City Produce Exchange employees become union members. In response, Blosser and his partners hired outside trucking firms to transport their poultry. In 1947 about one hundred company employees staged a walkout, demanding higher wages. To complicate matters, City Produce Exchange's competitors were by then eviscerating chickens and turkeys,

producing a more appealing product that needed only to be washed and cooked. Faced with labor disputes and the need to revamp the production process in order to compete with other processing facilities, Blosser and his partners closed operations at the City Produce Exchange.

Regarded as one of the most knowledgeable poultrymen of his time, Blosser was a pioneering businessman who helped establish Rockingham County as one of the leading poultry-producing areas in the United States. He was also involved in other business and civic activities in Harrisonburg. In 1924 he helped organize the Harrisonburg Loan and Thrift Corporation (later the Spotswood National Bank), serving at various times as president, chairman of the board, director, and treasurer. Blosser also helped organize and served as a director of the National Bank of Harrisonburg and was a vice president of the Harrisonburg Grocery Company. He was a charter member and president of the Harrisonburg Kiwanis Club and belonged to the Harrisonburg Chamber of Commerce and the Rockingham County Historical Society. A lifelong member of the Mennonite Church, Blosser was nominated as a candidate for the ministry in 1910 but did not answer the call.

On 29 May 1901 Blosser married Mary Garber. They had no children. After the death of his wife in 1922, he married Leona Branum on 31 January 1924. They had one son and one daughter. Emanuel Blosser died at Rockingham Memorial Hospital in Harrisonburg on 23 August 1953. He was buried at the Community Mausoleum in Harrisonburg's Woodbine Cemetery.

NCAB, 42:501; John W. Wayland, ed., *Men of Mark and Representative Citizens of Harrisonburg and Rockingham County, Virginia* (1943), 38–39 (por.); Harrisonburg Chamber of Commerce, *Harrisonburg, Virginia: A General Industrial Survey* (1926), 8; Census, Rockingham Co., 1880, 1900; BVS Marriage Register, Rockingham Co.; J. S. Peters and W. F. Stinespring, *An Economic and Social Survey of Rockingham County*, University of Virginia Record Extension Series (1924), 93 (first quotation); *Harrisonburg Daily News-Record*, 15 July 1916, 15 June 1949 (second quotation); family and business history verified by son, Henry Blosser, and daughter, Julia Blosser Grandle; obituaries in *Harrisonburg Daily News-Record*, 24 Aug. 1953 (por.), and *Virginia Poultryman* (Oct. 1953): 104, 106.

DALE F. HARTER

BLOSSER, Samuel H. (3 October 1855– 2 October 1945), poultryman, was born in Rockingham County, the son of Peter Blosser and Magdaline Rhodes Blosser. He worked on the family farm until he was twenty-one years old. On 30 May 1876 he married Emma C. Shiflette. They had six sons and seven daughters. A lifelong member of the Mennonite Church, Blosser never allowed his photograph to be taken. He wore a beard throughout his adult life and described himself as being five feet, eleven inches tall, "of a slender form," with dark hair and gray eyes.

In 1877 Blosser built a house on a ten-acre tract of land his father had given him and began working as a stonemason. He quit that trade as a result of ill health and engaged primarily in farming and carpentry from 1877 until 1885. He began raising bees in 1879.

Blosser also raised chickens and may have been the first Virginian to hatch chickens by artificial incubation. In 1885 he devoted long hours to observing the laying habits of chickens and even spent nights under his chicken house to hear how often hens turned their eggs. Blosser constructed a homemade incubator consisting of a wooden box lined with sawdust and topped with a metal tank. He filled the box with eggs and kept them warm with water heated in a teakettle on his kitchen stove and poured into the tank. The water filtered through the sawdust and had to be changed every three hours. Three weeks later Blosser's first brood of chicks hatched. A model of the incubator, which he never patented, was displayed at the World's Poultry Congress in 1939.

After moving to the nearby town of Dayton in 1910, Blosser established the first commercial chicken hatchery in Virginia in 1911. About ten years later he began experimenting with turkey eggs and became one of the first people in the United States to hatch turkey poults. Blosser continued to run the hatchery until the 1930s, when he turned it over to one of his sons. The hatchery remained in operation until 1975.

Blosser's homemade incubator served as a prototype for later commercial ones. Other Virginia poultrymen and representatives from national incubator manufacturers often sought his advice. The hatchery he established in 1911 paved the way for commercial poultry production in Rockingham County, the state, and perhaps the nation. His cousin's son Emanuel Blosser opened the county's first commercial poultry-processing plant in that same year. According to Charles W. Wampler, another Rockingham County poultry innovator, Blosser always discussed his ideas freely and said that if he had learned anything of value for mankind he wanted everyone to have the benefit of it. Wampler regarded Blosser's successful experimentation with artificial incubation in 1885 as the "most important event for poultry in Virginia, and probably in the whole world."

Although his formal education was probably limited, Blosser was regarded as a well-read man and an interesting conversationalist. He prepared a short autobiographical memorandum in the 1880s and published a *Genealogical History of the Blosser Family* in 1903. Not a robust man, he nevertheless lived until one day before his ninetieth birthday. Samuel H. Blosser died at his home in Dayton on 2 October 1945, survived by ten children, seventy-one grandchildren, eighty-one great-grandchildren, and three great-great-grandchildren. He was buried at Pleasant View Mennonite Church, several miles west of town.

S. H. Blosser, "Sketch of a part of my life" (typescript in possession of son Fred Blosser, 1993), first quotation; family and business history information verified by Fred Blosser; BVS Marriage Register, Rockingham Co.; Charles W. Wampler, *My Grandfather, My Grandchildren and Me* (1968), 77–78 (second quotation), 86; obituary in *Harrisonburg Daily News-Record*, 3 Oct 1945.

DALE F. HARTER

BLOW, George (5 May 1813–2 May 1894), member of the Convention of 1861, was born in Sussex County, the son of George Blow and Elizabeth Waller Blow. He grew up in the household of his maternal grandmother in Norfolk, was educated at the College of William and Mary, and studied law at the University of Virginia. Blow became a lawyer in Portsmouth before moving about 1839 to Texas, where he practiced law in San Antonio and became a prosecuting attorney. He was elected to the Texas House of Representatives and represented Bexar County in the 5th Congress of the Republic of Texas from November 1840 to February 1841. Blow returned to Norfolk after his mother died in 1841 and practiced law in Virginia for the next twenty years. On 27 August 1846 he married Elizabeth Taylor Allmand, of Norfolk. They had six daughters and four sons. Active in the local militia, Blow rose by 28 April 1860 to the rank of brigadier general of the 9th Brigade, 4th Division. Blow served on the board of the Virginia Military Institute from 1851 to 1852, 1857 to 1860, and 1861 to 1862. He was reportedly a friend of Illinois senator Stephen A. Douglas and ran unsuccessfully for presidential elector on Douglas's ticket in November 1860.

On 26 January 1861 Blow was the overwhelming choice of a mass meeting of Norfolk Unionists to represent the city in that year's state convention on the secession question, and on 4 February he defeated James R. Hubard, a secessionist, by a margin of more than two to one. In the convention Blow served on the Committee on Federal Relations and joined in efforts to encourage peaceful federal acceptance of the departure of those states that had already seceded. On 4 April he voted against secession, but the night before the second vote on secession he abandoned all hopes of preserving the Union. On 17 April 1861 he voted for secession, and the next day he was appointed to the seven-man Committee on Military Affairs.

Elements of his old militia brigade were formed into the new 41st Regiment Virginia Infantry later in the spring of 1861, and on 8 July Blow received a commission as lieutenant colonel of the regiment. He served until 3 May 1862, when, for unrecorded reasons, he was not reelected in a reorganization of the regiment. Blow returned to Norfolk, where he was arrested and paroled during the Union occupation of the city.

After the Civil War, Blow resumed the practice of law. On 25 March 1870 the General Assembly elected sixteen circuit court judges to preside over the state's principal trial courts established under the Constitution of 1869. Blow became judge of the First Judicial Circuit, composed of the city of Norfolk and the counties of Isle of Wight, Nansemond, Norfolk, Princess Anne, Southampton, and Surry. He served as circuit court judge until he retired at the end of 1886. George Blow died of a heart attack at his home in Norfolk on 2 May 1894 and was buried in Elmwood Cemetery there.

Blow Family Papers and family Bible, giving 5 May 1813 birth date, W&M; marriage in *American Beacon, and Norfolk and Portsmouth Daily Advertiser*, 28 Aug. 1846; *Biographical Directory of the Texan Conventions and Congresses, 1832–1845* [1941], 53; Harrison W. Burton, *The History of Norfolk, Virginia* (1877), 42–44; Reese and Gaines, *Proceedings of 1861 Convention*, 3:163, 603–605, 4:85–88, 144; Compiled Service Records; William D. Henderson, *41st Virginia Infantry* (1986), 5, 90; por. in possession of great-grandson George Blow, 1999; obituaries with some inaccuracies in *Norfolk Public Ledger*, 2 May 1894, and *Norfolk Landmark* and *Norfolk Virginian* (variant birth date of 15 May 1813), both 3 May 1894.

GUY R. SWANSON

BLOW, Katharine Rowland Cooke (21 April 1897–25 March 1965), local politician, was born in Chicago, the daughter of George Joseph Cooke and Mary Elizabeth Kerwin Cooke. She was educated in the convents of the Sacred Heart in Chicago and in Torresdale, Pennsylvania. On 2 December 1922 she married George Waller Blow, an industrial designer then living in La Salle, Illinois. They moved to New York in 1926 and lived there until early in 1942. Blow was active in society and reviewed restaurants for *The New Yorker*, using the nom de plume Soubise. She had four sons.

In 1942 the Blows moved into the historic Nelson house in Yorktown. Blow lived there for the remainder of her life. Almost thirty years earlier her husband's father, George Preston Blow, had purchased the Nelson house, refurbished it, and landscaped the grounds, creating a town estate that he called York Hall. Blow entered into the polite society of York County and the Peninsula and participated actively in a wide variety of civic and service organizations for more than twenty years. During World War II she worked for the Virginia War Finance Committee, and she helped make the arrangements for the international conference in San Francisco in the spring of 1945 at which the United Nations was founded.

Blow took part in Democratic Party politics as an alternate delegate to the state conventions in 1944 and 1948, an alternate delegate to the national convention in 1948, and a delegate in 1952 and 1956. She joined the critics of the Democratic Party organization, of which Harry Flood Byrd (1887–1966) was the leader, and in the summer of 1949 she endorsed Byrd's principal antagonist, Francis Pickens Miller, for governor. Blow first ran for public office that year. She challenged incumbent Paul W. Crockett for the Democratic nomination in the House of Delegates district composed of the city of Williamsburg and the counties of Charles City, James City, New Kent, and York. Blow was one of three Democratic women who ran for the House that year. One Republican woman and four African American Democratic men also ran for the assembly in 1949, and one of the latter, Charles S. Franklin from Charles City County, challenged Crockett. During her low-key campaign Blow called for increased appointments to office of "men and women of talent and vision," improved programs for public education, and better allocation of road-building funds. She lost the primary by a large margin but outpolled Franklin, and she did much better than the other two Democratic women, Florrye C. Fuller in Madison and Orange Counties and Elizabeth Newton Dew in the city of Richmond. None of the black candidates won nomination, either. The lone Republican woman, Elizabeth Oldfield Duffee, of Norfolk, was nominated in a large, multimember district but lost badly in the general election. Had Blow been nominated and elected, she would have been only the seventh woman to serve in the General Assembly and the first since 1933.

Early in May 1950 Blow sought to become the first woman to represent Virginia in Congress by announcing her candidacy for the House of Representatives in the First Congressional District. In a campaign that the newspapers described as unusually dull, she failed to articulate a program or to distinguish her views from those of the incumbent, Edward J. Robeson, who defeated her by a margin of almost nine to one in the 1 August primary. In July 1955 Blow returned again to electoral politics, and after knocking on virtually every door in her district, she won the Democratic Party nomination for a term on the York County board of supervisors by defeating an incumbent,

R. Nelson Smith, by a vote of 119 to 117. Smith mounted a last-minute write-in campaign against her in the November general election, but she defeated him 132 to 101. Blow was the first woman ever elected to the York County board and served one four-year term beginning on 1 January 1956. In July 1959 Blow sought renomination but lost by a vote of 207 to 99 to Bernard G. White, a pharmacist who promised to bring "a businessman's approach to county government." That setback concluded her career in elective politics.

Katharine Rowland Cooke Blow died of cancer at her home in Yorktown on 25 March 1965 and was buried next to her husband in Arlington National Cemetery.

Feature articles in *Richmond News Leader*, 30 June 1949, and *Richmond Times-Dispatch*, 14 July 1955 (por.); family history information supplied by sons George Blow and John M. Blow; Blow Family Papers, W&M; elections covered in *Newport News Daily Press*, esp. 27 July 1949 (first quotation), *Newport News Times-Herald*, and *Williamsburg Virginia Gazette*; *Newport News Daily Press*, 11 July 1959 (second quotation); obituaries in *Newport News Times-Herald*, 25 Mar. 1965 (por.), and *New York Times*, *Norfolk Virginian-Pilot*, and *Richmond Times-Dispatch*, all 26 Mar. 1965; editorial tribute in *Williamsburg Virginia Gazette*, 2 Apr. 1965.

BRENT TARTER

BLOXOM, Elizabeth James Morris Downes. See **DOWNES, Elizabeth James Morris**.

BLUE, Charles James (28 December 1804– 21 March 1863), member of the Convention of 1850–1851, was born probably in Jefferson County, the son of Mary Blue. The identity of his father is not recorded. In 1826 Blue purchased a small tract of land along Back Creek in Frederick County, but by 1830 he had moved across the mountains into Hampshire County and was a deputy sheriff there. By 1835 he had settled along the North River, about fourteen miles east of Romney near the community of Hanging Rock. During the next twenty years he accumulated more than 1,800 acres of land in the vicinity. A slave owner, Blue was among the ten wealthiest men in his section of the county by the mid-1840s. He married Mary Catharine Vance about 1832 and had two sons and five daughters.

Blue was postmaster at Hanging Rock from March 1835 until July 1837 and from February 1841 until June 1842, when his wife succeeded him and served until her death in 1870. In 1840 and 1860 he was a census enumerator in Hampshire County. During 1842 Blue qualified as a justice of the peace, and in the same year he was elected to the first of three consecutive one-year terms in the House of Delegates. He served on the Committee of Privileges and Elections during the 1842–1843 session and on the Committee on the Militia Laws during the 1843–1844 and 1844–1845 sessions. In 1850 he was elected to represent the district of Frederick, Hampshire, and Morgan Counties in a state constitutional convention that met in Richmond from 14 October 1850 to 1 August 1851. He served on the Committee on the Right of Suffrage and Qualifications of Persons to be Elected, which successfully introduced a constitutional provision for universal white adult male suffrage. Blue supported a change in the basis of representation that gave more assembly seats to western counties, and he voted for the constitution, which the convention approved on 31 July 1851.

On 26 January 1853 an acquaintance unsuccessfully recommended Blue for a presidential appointment as United States marshal of the Western District of Virginia. In a letter lauding Blue's character, enterprise, industriousness, and bookkeeping skills, he described him as "a firm, true and undeviating democrat . . . one of the most prominent and influential men of that party in his section of the state." In 1859 Blue was elected to the House of Delegates again. He was appointed to the Committee of Privileges and Elections and chaired the Committee to Examine the Armory, but he resigned before the session that began in January 1861 to accept the position of deputy marshal and to be near his ailing wife. He was also elected to the assembly that first met in December 1861. He became a ranking member of the Committee on Privileges and Elections and chaired the Committee to Examine the Armory. Blue returned home and as colonel of the county militia participated in a skirmish on 7 January 1862 at nearby Hanging Rock Pass, or Blue's Gap. Immediately thereafter, in retaliation for his having quartered

Southern soldiers, Union forces burned his house, outbuildings, and mill. By 17 January 1862 Blue had resumed his seat in the House of Delegates.

On 20 March 1862 the General Assembly elected Blue superintendent of the state penitentiary by a margin of six votes over the incumbent, James F. Pendleton. He resigned his House seat on 20 November 1862 and assumed his new post on 2 January 1863 but served only briefly. Charles James Blue died on 21 March 1863 following a short illness. His funeral was held from Richmond's Second Presbyterian Church, and he was later buried beside his wife in Indian Mound Cemetery in Romney, West Virginia.

Middle name and birth date from gravestone; mother identified in Frederick Co. Deed Book, 49:267–268; wife and children identified in Romney Church membership roll (microfilm), UTS; *Journal of 1850–1851 Convention*, 58, 419, Appendix, 22; George H. Lee to Franklin Pierce, 26 Jan. 1853, VHS (quotation); *OR*, 1st ser., 5:392, 396, 403–405; Frank Moore, ed., *The Rebellion Record* (1861–1868), vol. 4, Documents, pp. 21–23; several Blue letters to John Letcher in Governor's Office, Letters Received, RG 3, LVA; obituary in *Richmond Enquirer*, 23 Mar. 1863; eulogy by Letcher in *JHD*, Jan.–Mar. 1863 sess., 242–243.

DAPHNE GENTRY

BLUETT, Benjamin (bap. 10 April 1580–by 12 May 1621), member of the Council, was the son of Nicholas Bluett, or Blewett. His mother's name and the date and place of his birth are unknown, but he was christened in Horley Parish, Surrey County, England, on 10 April 1580. Bluett married Johanne Blaker at Cuckfield, Sussex County, England, on 27 July 1601 and had at least one son, John Bluett, born in Sussex in 1603, and one daughter, Elizabeth Bluett, born in London in 1605. She was one of the "maydes" who arrived in Virginia on the *Buona Nova* late in the summer of 1621.

Bluett lived in Sussex and late in the 1610s teamed with David Middleton in supplying provisions to people who were sailing for the colony of Virginia. Bluett became well acquainted with members of the Virginia Company of London, such as the Ferrars and Henry Hastings, fifth earl of Huntingdon. On 5 April 1620 Huntingdon empowered Bluett and Nicolas Martiau to manage the Virginia land to which Huntingdon was entitled as a company shareholder. The company also put Bluett in charge of eighty men who had been sent to Virginia the previous year to establish and operate an iron-mining and smelting operation. On 28 June 1620 the company appointed Bluett a member of the Council in Virginia.

Bluett and Martiau arrived in Virginia together late in the summer of 1620 aboard the *Francis Bonaventure*. Bluett probably went directly to the new ironworks on Falling Creek, in what is now Chesterfield County, where he died within a few months of his arrival, possibly from wounds received in an Indian attack. Whether he ever attended a Council meeting in Jamestown is unknown. News of Benjamin Bluett's death reached London before 12 May 1621, when the company appointed John Berkeley to take over the ironworks in the place of "mr. Blewett lately deceased."

Surname spelled "Bluett" in his few surviving autographs; christening and marriage recorded in registers of Horley Parish, Surrey Co., and Cuckfield Parish, Sussex Co., Eng.; 1620 power of attorney in Hastings Papers, Huntington, and printed in John Baer Stoudt, *Nicolas Martiau: The Adventurous Huguenot* (1932), 8–9; undated "Note of Monies disbursed by me Benjamin Bluett Captain" and other papers relating to ironworks in Ferrar Papers, Magdalene College, Cambridge University, Eng., and in Kingsbury, *Virginia Company*, vols. 1, 3 (quotation on 1:475).

DAPHNE GENTRY

BLUNT, Benjamin (21 June 1746–ca. November 1803), member of the Convention of 1788, was born in Surry County, the son of Richard Blunt and Ann Blunt, whose maiden name may have been Irby. He was christened in Albemarle Parish on 27 July 1746. His father died on 17 April 1747, and in 1758 his mother married Abraham Green in Sussex County. Blunt's guardian and first cousin, Howell Edmunds, returned accounts that were recorded in Southampton County, but unfortunately they are not itemized and reveal nothing about Blunt's education.

From his father Blunt inherited a substantial amount of land in the portion of Isle of Wight County that became Southampton County in 1749. On 29 November 1766 he married Frances Briggs in Sussex County. They had three sons and two daughters. Blunt purchased additional Southampton County land to supplement his inheritance and gifts from his father-in-law. Blunt's family had a pattern of local public service. His brother Richard Blunt was a burgess from Surry County, his brother-in-law Micajah Edwards was a justice of the peace in Isle of Wight County, and Edmunds was a member of the first Southampton County Court.

In the summer of 1775 Blunt marched to Williamsburg with other volunteers to support Patrick Henry after Henry seized a large sum of money from the receiver general of the royal revenue in Virginia and armed conflict between partisans of Henry and of the governor appeared likely. That September the Southampton County Committee nominated Blunt as a major of the local militia, and in November he was elected to the committee. Blunt served through its last recorded meeting in September 1776. He became a justice of the peace in June 1777 and served until 1802 or 1803. In September 1781 Blunt was the commanding officer charged with mobilizing the county militia before the siege of Yorktown. He is first recorded acting as county lieutenant in 1782 and continued in that office until 1792. Blunt also served as sheriff of Southampton County, qualifying in October 1783 and October 1784, and he qualified as county treasurer in November 1789.

Blunt supported the Episcopal Church and signed a December 1785 petition to the General Assembly favoring a religious assessment bill that would have granted public money to churches of all denominations, a failed attempt to prevent passage of the Statute for Religious Freedom that disestablished the Episcopal Church and denied public support for any church. He was also a lay delegate to the Virginia diocesan convention in 1786. Blunt was a trustee for a lottery to fund Millfield Academy in December 1790, and in December 1791 he was named a trustee for the new town of Jerusalem, which became the county seat of Southampton and was later renamed Courtland.

In 1788 Blunt was one of two men elected to represent Southampton County in the convention called to consider ratification of the Constitution of the United States. He was paid for nineteen days of attendance, indicating that he was present throughout the debates, but he evidently did not speak. Blunt voted against requiring prior amendments to the Constitution, against an amendment to weaken the taxing power of Congress, and on 25 June for ratification.

Blunt may have represented Southampton County in the House of Delegates in the session of October–December 1790, but a younger man of the same name, who married Blunt's niece, also lived in the county at that time. Through comparison of signatures most, but not all, references to the two men can be distinguished.

Benjamin Blunt wrote and amended his will early in 1803 and died in Southampton County, probably in November 1803. On an unspecified date in that month his executor began administering the estate by paying the local minister for preaching the funeral sermon. Blunt's will was recorded at the 19 December 1803 meeting of the county court. His children eventually moved to other areas, many of them to Alabama.

Birth and christening dates in Gertrude R. B. Richards, ed., *Register of Albemarle Parish, Surry and Sussex Counties, 1739–1778* (1958), 13; Lyndon H. Hart III and Henry Wilkins Lewis, *A Genealogy of the Southern Virginia Blunts, Including the Descendants of Howell Edmunds of Surry* (1987), 6, 14–17; father's will in Surry Co. Deeds, Wills, Etc., 9:559–560; Sussex Co. Marriage Register; *Revolutionary Virginia*, esp. 3:322, 325, 349, 4:87, 177–178, 229, 357; public service documented in Southampton Co. order books, county committee records, and militia commission records; property holding recorded in Southampton Co. Land and Personal Property Tax Returns, RG 48, LVA; Kaminski, *Ratification*, 10:1539, 1540, 1557, 1565; will, estate inventory, and estate accounts in Southampton Co. Will Book, 5:457–458, 518–519, 542–543.

LYNDON H. HART III

BOATWRIGHT, Cynthia Ellen Elizabeth Virginia Addington (12 December 1898– 5 March 1973), civic leader, was born in the Wise County town of Coeburn, the daughter of James L. Addington and Sarah Frances Blair Addington. Her father established the Addington Mercantile Company and became a prominent and influential businessman as well as a Baptist minister. Addington attended the Coeburn public schools but finished her last two years of high school at Virginia Intermont College in Bristol.

She stayed for two more years and graduated in 1918 with a teacher's degree in voice, harmony, and the history of music. On 12 December 1919 she married Roy Gilley Boatwright, of Scott County. They lived in Coeburn, where he started as a cashier at the First National Bank and later worked in her father's store. From 1944 to 1965 Roy Boatwright was postmaster of Coeburn. They had one daughter.

Boatwright was known for her love of music as well as her pride in Wise County, and she worked hard to promote the mountain region of Virginia. Like many women of her time and economic position, she committed herself to volunteer activities and civic work in place of a paying job working outside the home. On 12 June 1934 Boatwright was elected to the Coeburn town council, becoming the first woman in Wise County to win political office. She served for two two-year terms and was the only incumbent reelected in 1936. Boatwright joined the Coeburn Woman's Club in the 1930s and served as the district vice president of the Virginia Federation of Women's Clubs in 1934 and as president from 1935 to 1938. She was elected vice president of the state federation in 1938 and in 1941 became the first member from southwestern Virginia to serve as president. During Boatwright's years as president, from 1941 to 1944, the VFWC turned its attention to the war effort, donating two ambulances to the American Red Cross, encouraging women to volunteer for civil defense, conservation, and nursing services, and supporting the United Service Organizations. She also served on the Virginia Defense Council. From 1944 to 1947 Boatwright chaired the General Federation of Women's Clubs Aviation Defense Board. She was president of the Coeburn Woman's Club from 1945 to 1946 and president of the Wise County Federation of Women's Clubs from 1944 to 1947.

In 1944 Virginia Agricultural and Mechanical College and Polytechnic Institute merged with the Radford State Teachers College to become Virginia Polytechnic Institute. The fourteen-member board of visitors of the expanded institution included four seats reserved for women. In December 1944 Boatwright was one of the first women appointed to this VPI–Radford College board of visitors. She served until 1953. Boatwright worked strenuously for the Democratic Party in the latter part of the 1940s and the 1950s. She was a member of the Democratic State Central Committee, chair of the Virginia Ninth District Democratic Party Women's Division, and a delegate to the 1952 and 1956 Democratic National Conventions. From 1954 to 1958 Boatwright represented Virginia on the National Democratic Advisory Committee on Political Organization.

Boatwright became a Methodist after she married and actively applied her energies to her church. She played the piano for funeral and Sunday church services throughout her life. From 1947 to 1951 Boatwright served as president of the Big Stone Gap district of the Women's Society of Christian Service. In 1960 she headed a fund drive for additions to buildings at the district Methodist camp. Boatwright also worked for the Virginia Heart Fund, the Virginia Cancer Foundation, Breaks of the Cumberland Park, and the Eastern Wise Chapter of the American Red Cross, and she wrote about Coeburn social and community events for the *Norton Coalfield Progress*.

Cynthia Ellen Elizabeth Virginia Addington Boatwright died in Grundy on 5 March 1973 and was buried in the Laurel Grove Cemetery in Norton.

Biography in Etta Belle Walker Northington, *A History of the Virginia Federation of Women's Clubs, 1907–1957* [1958], 79–82; Cynthia Addington Boatwright Papers, VPI; information supplied by daughter Ida Virginia Boatwright Spraker and by Herbert D. Jones and Ray Richardson; BVS Marriage Register, Wise Co.; Coeburn town council minutes; *Bristol Herald-Courier*, 4 Sept. 1961; *Virginia Club Woman* 13 (Oct. 1940): 12 (por.), 25; obituaries in *Bristol Herald-Courier*, 6 Mar. 1973, and *Norton Coalfield Progress*, 8 Mar. 1973.

LAURA KATZ SMITH

BOATWRIGHT, Frederic William (28 January 1868–31 October 1951), president of the University of Richmond, was born in White Sulphur Springs, West Virginia, the son of Reuben Baker Boatwright and Marie Elizabeth Woodruff Boatwright. He was christened Frederick William, but as an adult he dropped the *k* from his first name and never again used it. Boatwright grew up in Bristol and Marion, where his father was minister at the Baptist churches, and he was educated at Marion Academy and in the local public school.

In 1883 Boatwright entered Richmond College and excelled in languages there. After his 1887 graduation he stayed on to teach introductory Greek and take graduate courses. He received an M.A. in 1888 and also won the Guinn Medal as the most proficient graduate in the school of philosophy. During the 1888–1889 academic year Boatwright served as an instructor of Greek and director of Richmond College's small but expanding athletics program. He spent the following academic year in Europe taking classes in modern languages in Halle, Leipzig, and Paris and spending much time associating with the Baptists in and around Halle.

Boatwright returned to Richmond College in 1890 as professor of modern languages, and on 23 December of that year he married Ellen Moore Thomas. They had one son and one daughter. In frequent contributions to the Baptist journal, the *Religious Herald*, and other venues Boatwright advocated educational reforms, improved education in the sciences, and an expanded social responsibility for Richmond College and its faculty and students. On 11 December 1894 the board of trustees took day-to-day administrative responsibility away from the faculty and elected the twenty-six-year-old Boatwright president of Richmond College. He accepted and was formally inducted on 22 June 1895.

Boatwright served as president of Richmond College, which became the University of Richmond in 1920, until he retired in June 1946. His fifty-one-year tenure was interrupted only once, when he spent the spring semester of 1922 in Europe. Boatwright oversaw the transformation of the institution from a denominational college with 9 faculty members and fewer than 200 students into a small but substantial university with more than 100 faculty members and almost 2,300 students. He was instrumental in the formation of Westhampton College for women as a counterpart to the traditionally all-male Richmond College, with himself as president of the parent university. Boatwright emphasized the natural sciences and welcomed support for a stronger law school and a new school of business, developments that significantly broadened the original classical- and religion-based curriculum. An energetic fund-raiser who increasingly sought donations from alumni and other supporters instead of depending on the educational funds of the Baptist Church, he helped the school erect a new campus west of downtown Richmond during the 1910s, enlarge the faculty, and provide financial assistance for the students. By the time Boatwright retired, the University of Richmond had assets in excess of $7 million. His relations with leading Baptists were occasionally strained. Boatwright tried to keep the university from being dominated by any faction of the divided denomination, and he took a broad view of the university's role in opposition to some influential Baptist leaders who wanted it to remain a traditional church school.

Boatwright's involvement as a Baptist layman included service as president of the American Baptist Education Association in 1897–1898, the Southern Baptist Education Association in 1904–1905, and the Baptist General Association of Virginia in 1937–1939. He served as president of the Association of Virginia Colleges in 1915–1916, helped found the Association of American Colleges, and sat on the board of trustees of Averett College in Danville for twenty-six years. Boatwright received honorary degrees from Baylor University, Georgetown College, the Medical College of Virginia, and Mercer University. He received an honorary doctorate from the University of Richmond when he retired, at which time the board of trustees placed him in the new position of chancellor, which he held until his death. Most fittingly, given his emphasis on teaching and learning, the main library of the University of Richmond was dedicated in 1955 as the Boatwright Memorial Library.

Frederic William Boatwright died at his home in Richmond on 31 October 1951 and was buried in Hollywood Cemetery in that city.

Reuben E. Alley, *Frederic W. Boatwright* (1973), frontispiece por.; Alley, *History of the University of Richmond, 1830–1971* (1977); University of Richmond Archives; por.

by David Silvette in Sarah Brunet Memorial Hall, University of Richmond; obituaries in *Richmond News Leader* and *Richmond Times-Dispatch*, both 1 Nov. 1951, and *Religious Herald*, 8 Nov. 1951, 10–11; editorial tribute by the university's rector, Douglas Southall Freeman, in *Richmond News Leader*, 1 Nov. 1951.

BRENT TARTER

BOATWRIGHT, Herbert Lee (12 September 1862–23 January 1935), tobacco broker, was born in Buckingham County, the son of John Guerrant Boatwright and Pattie Pendleton Phillips Boatwright. He grew up in Danville, where his father practiced medicine after the Civil War, but the latter's death in 1873 disrupted the lives of Boatwright and his siblings. By the age of twelve he was forced to abandon his education and go to work in the local tobacco factory of George S. Hughes. During five years there Boatwright began to acquire an extensive knowledge of the tobacco trade and to become an excellent judge of leaf tobacco.

Careers could be built on such discriminating knowledge in late-nineteenth-century Danville. The discovery of bright tobacco before the Civil War and the proliferation of the innovative, loose-leaf sales system after the war combined to make Danville the leading tobacco market in the United States between the 1870s and World War I. Boatwright made good use of his discerning eye. By 1879, at the age of seventeen, he had become the manager of Ferrell and Flinn, leaf tobacco brokers. During the next quarter century he alternated between his own ventures in the leaf tobacco business and partnerships with other Danville businessmen, most notably John H. Schoolfield.

In 1904 H. Lee Boatwright, as he was known as an adult, joined the firm of Dibrell Brothers and became its secretary-treasurer after it reorganized in 1905. Boatwright was in charge of all leaf tobacco purchases. Along with the president, Richard L. Dibrell, and vice president, Alexander Berkeley Carrington, he was part of the "famous triumvirate," as a company history puts it, that helped lay the foundations of the modern company. Dibrell Brothers became internationally known as a dealer in raw tobacco leaf. During his early years with the firm Boatwright often traveled overseas to help the company expand its foreign operations. He was promoted to vice president when Dibrell died in 1920.

Boatwright's tobacco and business acumen translated into positions of increasing civic responsibility. He served as president of the Danville Tobacco Association from 1903 to 1904, was a founder of the local Young Men's Christian Association, and led in the formation of the Commercial Association, the predecessor of the Danville Chamber of Commerce. Boatwright served as a trustee of the Roanoke College for Young Women (later Averett College) and the University of Richmond. He was also an active Mason and became Worshipful Master of Danville's Roman Eagle Lodge in 1907. A lifelong Democrat, Boatwright guided the local party through the political crisis of 1928, when party members divided over the presidential candidacy of Alfred E. Smith, whose opposition to Prohibition and membership in the Catholic Church alienated many Virginia Democrats. Boatwright chaired the city Democratic committee and supported Smith.

On 18 December 1889 Boatwright married Mary E. Vaughan, of Halifax County. They had three sons and three daughters. Herbert Lee Boatwright died in Danville on 23 January 1935 of heart complications following an influenza attack and was buried in Green Hill Cemetery in that city.

Glass and Glass, *Virginia Democracy*, 3:587–588; George Washington Dame, *Historical Sketch of Roman Eagle Lodge* (1939), 233–234; Buckingham Co. Birth Register; BVS Marriage Register, Halifax Co.; Mary Cahill and Gary Grant, *Victorian Danville* (1977), 27–28; Danville Tobacco Association, Inc., *100 Years of Progress, 1869–1969* (1969), 41–42; *Dibrell Brothers, Incorporated, 1873–1973* (1973), quotation; obituaries in *Danville Bee*, 23 Jan. 1935 (por.), and *Danville Register*, 24 Jan. 1935 (por.); editorial tribute in *Danville Register*, 24 Jan. 1935.

W. Thomas Mainwaring
Gary Grant

BOAZ, William Henry (21 July 1852–9 March 1907), member of the Convention of 1901–1902, was born on his father's farm in southern Albemarle County, the son of William D. Boaz and Cornelia Harris Boaz. He received an M.A. from the University of Virginia in 1873 and a law degree from the same school two years later. After practicing law briefly in neighboring Nelson County, Boaz returned to Albemarle County and lived there the remainder of his life. In an orchard near the family farm he raised apples, specializing in Albemarle pippins, which he marketed directly in England, where that variety was especially popular. Boaz did not have one of the largest orchards in the county, but it was well managed and successful, and in 1897 he sold the yield of his 1,100 trees for $20,000. On 3 March 1897 he was elected one of the founding vice presidents of the Virginia State Horticultural Society, an early organization of commercial fruit producers in Virginia. A quiet and retiring man who preferred the solitude of the country, Boaz evidently never married. In his later years he became quite portly.

Although he was apparently not a close ally of his fellow Albemarle County Democrat, party leader Thomas Staples Martin, Boaz was a typical party member who represented the county in the House of Delegates for the 1889–1890 session and again from 1895 to 1904. During the sessions from 1899 to 1904 he was chairman of the important Committee on Finance, which determined Virginia's tax policy. Boaz opposed almost any large expenditure of public money and always advocated ways to economize.

On 23 May 1901 Boaz and another Democrat, Charlottesville journalist James H. Lindsay, were elected without Republican opposition to a state constitutional convention from the district consisting of Albemarle County and Charlottesville. Boaz was the only candidate in the state endorsed by the *Southern Planter*, an influential agricultural journal. He served on the Committees on Taxation and Finance and on Final Revision. Boaz introduced three resolutions that he hoped would produce a more honest and efficient assessment and collection of local taxes, and he advocated reducing the number of local government officers in order to save money. He filled his contributions to the debates on taxation and legislative appropriations with facts and figures that demonstrated a detailed knowledge of the financial condition of the state government and the operations of local governments. Boaz apparently approved of the suffrage article that the convention adopted, which was intended to reduce the number of African American voters, but he missed the final vote. He voted with the majority on 29 May 1902 in favor of putting the constitution into effect without a ratification referendum.

Boaz contracted Bright's disease about 1906 and withdrew from politics and the management of his orchards as his health deteriorated. He wrote his will on 2 March 1907. William Henry Boaz died at his home seven days later.

Birth date in Boaz's handwriting in Pollard Questionnaires; *Southern Planter* 58 (1897): 168, 547; ibid. 62 (1901): 233; S. W. Fletcher, *A History of Fruit Growing in Virginia* (1932), 33, 34; *Journal of 1901–1902 Convention*, 50, 60, 119, 486–487, 504; *Proceedings and Debates of 1901–1902 Convention*, 1:491–493, 561–562, 925–927, 1003, 2:1713; *Resolutions of 1901–1902 Convention*, nos. 20, 21, 229; *Convention of 1901–1902 Photographs* (por.); obituary and editorial tribute in *Charlottesville Daily Progress*, 11 Mar. 1907.

BRENT TARTER

BOCOCK, Elisabeth Strother Scott (8 February 1901–9 December 1985), civic leader, was born in Richmond, the daughter of Frederic William Scott, a banker, and Elisabeth Mayo Strother Scott. She attended Virginia Randolph Ellett's school in Richmond and in 1919 graduated from Saint Timothy's School in Stevenson, Maryland. On 3 May 1928 Scott married a Richmond attorney, John Holmes Bocock (1890–1958), a grandson of the prominent Presbyterian minister of that name. A year earlier her lifelong involvement in civic affairs had begun when she became a founding member of the Richmond Junior League.

Bocock raised one son and two daughters. Realizing the economic importance of preserving Richmond's historic fabric, she developed a growing interest in historic preservation. Along with her cousin, the Richmond preservationist Mary Wingfield Scott, she fought for the city's architectural heritage and in 1935 helped found the William Byrd Branch of the Association for the Preservation of Virginia Antiquities to salvage properties of architectural or historical value. She was an early advocate of the adaptive reuse of old buildings and urged the city council to save structures that were not only important but that also could be put to good use. On a number of occasions Bocock used her own money to purchase a building imminently threatened by bulldozers, only stopping to raise funds for its preservation after it had been saved from destruction. She frequently served on the board of the William Byrd Branch, and through her efforts as chair of the finance committee she secured the gift of the Ellen Glasgow house to the association in 1947. She chaired the branch's annual tour committee in 1952 and served as vice director in 1940 and 1957.

Bocock helped found the Historic Richmond Foundation in 1956 and was part of its effort to persuade the city council to enact a historic zoning ordinance, which was first employed in the area of Church Hill near Saint John's Episcopal Church. She provided funding for studies of historic areas to show how they could be developed to preserve their integrity and remain economically viable. Throughout her long career, Bocock bought and rented numerous properties in order to save them and on several occasions moved buildings from the path of destruction so they could be reconstructed elsewhere in the city and not lost to modern development. Although her fellow preservationists did not always agree with her methods, Bocock's tireless efforts to preserve the historic structures of Richmond were deeply appreciated, and after her death the General Assembly passed a resolution honoring her work to save the city's heritage.

Bocock involved herself in highway beautification and served as the corresponding secretary for the Associated Clubs of Virginia for Roadside Development (ACVRD) from 1954 to 1956. Constituting an alliance among the Garden Club of Virginia, the Virginia Federation of Garden Clubs, the Virginia Federation of Home Demonstration Clubs, and the Virginia Federation of Women's Clubs, the ACVRD proposed adding roadside plantings to Virginia's new interstate highways to make them attractive and safe for drivers. Rosebushes planted in the medians, Bocock argued, would reduce the glare from oncoming headlights, lessen driver fatigue, and "cushion collisions where cars go out of control." Bocock chaired the ACVRD's turnpike landscape committee from 1955 to 1960, taking women on driving tours of the Richmond-Petersburg Turnpike (which she called an "unbeautiful speedway"), questioning its general manager, and lobbying Senator Harry Flood Byrd (1887–1966). From 1956 to 1958 she also chaired the alliance's finance committee.

A month after her husband died on 14 August 1958, Bocock embarked on the pursuit of a college degree at the age of fifty-seven. Her father had not approved of higher education for women, but this nontraditional student traveled to Ambler Junior College near Philadelphia (a branch of Temple University) in September 1958 to take classes in horticulture. Bocock found her chemistry course especially difficult, describing her professor in her diary as "an embryo Ethan Frome . . . come into our once happy lives to worry and darken our days." Bocock subsequently took courses at Mary Washington College, Westhampton College of the University of Richmond, the University of Virginia, the College of William and Mary, and Mary Baldwin College before bringing her accumulated credits to Richmond Professional Institute (later Virginia Commonwealth University). On 8 June 1969 she finally received a B.A. in English from Virginia Commonwealth University along with a special service award.

Bocock was a woman of action whose life was a flurry of meetings and letters. Her boundless energy and steely determination earned her the family nickname "Mrs. Bulldozer." In 1942 she was Richmond's Christmas Mother, heading the effort to provide holiday relief for the city's needy families. Bocock helped found several cultural organizations in Richmond, among them the Hand Workshop (opened in Church Hill in 1963) and the Richmond Symphony. She also served from 1942 to 1965 as a trustee of the Virginia Museum of Fine Arts. With her own collection of antique carriages Bocock sought "to offer glimpses of [a] 19th Century way of life away from 20th Century speed and pressure." She first displayed them in her Early Virginia Vehicular Museum and later donated them to Maymont Park in Richmond. Always ready to defend Richmond's past, she

opposed expressway construction as a member of the Committee for the Alternative and promoted the historic and architectural value of iron-front buildings on East Main Street through involvement in the Committee to Save a Vanishing Environment.

When buildings were threatened Bocock picketed (and once passed out knitted hats to her fellow protesters), telling her family, "If you don't like my doing it, I'm very sad, and I apologize to you, but I can't go back on my word. I won't be a turncoat." When she disagreed with the direction that the Hand Workshop was taking, she led a group resignation from the board of directors. Bocock reacted to the trimming and eventual felling of a majestic elm near her house on West Franklin Street with a telegram to the city council protesting its "tree butchering." Her love of the outdoors also evidenced itself in October 1960 when a state chapter of the Nature Conservancy was organized at a meeting in her home and she was named a director. Bocock unsuccessfully championed the return of electric trolleys to Richmond streets and wrote letters of protest with a fountain pen nearly always supplied with bright green ink, her favorite color.

Bocock had a lifelong connection to Virginia Commonwealth University. Her house was on the campus. After her husband died and her children were grown she put the spacious residence to good use by housing twenty-two female students in the front of the building while living in the back herself. A traditionalist, Bocock was appalled when male and female students lived together in dormitories and did her part to keep the sexes separate. Her house later became office space for the university. From the winter of 1958 until 1967 the Junior League operated a senior center on the first floor of the Bocock house, offering both classes and recreation.

Late in life Bocock published a short remembrance of Richmond during her childhood. She received the Barbara Ransome Andrews Award from the Richmond Junior League in 1979 and the Individual Service Award from the Federated Arts Council in 1982. When asked what motivated her unrelenting community service work, Bocock replied simply: "How can I expect others to do something for my community if I am not willing to do it myself?"

Elisabeth Strother Scott Bocock died of an apparent heart attack on 9 December 1985 at her Richmond home and was buried in Hollywood Cemetery.

Mary Buford Hitz, *Never Ask Permission: Elisabeth Scott Bocock of Richmond* (2000), pors.; Elisabeth Scott Bocock Papers, VCU (first quotation in Bocock to John J. Pershing, 16 July 1956, second quotation in Bocock to "cousins Sara and Charles," 17 July 1957, third quotation in diary entry, 30 Sept. 1958, fourth quotation in "Purposes of E.V.V.M.," sixth quotation in telegram to city council, 20 Oct. 1964, seventh quotation in "Volunteer for All Seasons," *Leaguer*, 1 Nov. 1982); Bocock, "Now and Then: A Way of Life in Richmond in the Early 1900's," *Richmond Quarterly* 4 (spring 1982): 24–31; BVS Marriage Register, Richmond City; *Richmond News Leader*, 3 May 1928, 6 Feb. 1974 (fifth quotation), 16 Dec. 1985; *Richmond Times-Dispatch*, 10 Dec. 1965, 2 June 1978, 2 May 1982; *Virginia Garden Gossip* 31 (Feb. 1956): 4, (Nov. 1956): 10, (Dec. 1956): 13, 27; obituaries in *Richmond News Leader* and *Richmond Times-Dispatch*, both 10 Dec. 1985.

JENNIFER DAVIS MCDAID

BOCOCK, John Holmes (31 January 1813– 17 July 1872), Presbyterian minister, was born in the portion of Buckingham County that became Appomattox County in 1845. He was the son of Mary Flood Bocock and John Thomas Bocock, a prosperous farmer and sometime member of the General Assembly. His brothers included Thomas Salem Bocock and Willis Perry Bocock, who both became important politicians. Bocock was schooled at home until the beginning of 1832, when he moved in with his minister, Jesse S. Armistead, and there began his theological studies. Bocock enrolled in Amherst College, in Amherst, Massachusetts, as a sophomore in the autumn of 1832. His classmates included a number of men who later became prominent clergymen, among them Henry Ward Beecher.

Following graduation in 1835, Bocock returned to Virginia and taught school before entering Union Theological Seminary in 1836. Studying under George Addison Baxter and other defenders of strict Calvinism and so-called Old School Presbyterianism, Bocock adhered throughout his life to the creed in which he was raised and educated. In 1839 he graduated, was ordained, and became an evangelist, serving the Amherst Presbyterian Church and the Union Presbyterian Church in Appomattox. After a brief interval in Louisiana, where a planter employed him as teacher and pastor to his family and slaves, Bocock returned to Virginia to serve a succession of Presbyterian churches at Parkersburg (1845–1847), Louisa County (1847–1853), and Harrisonburg (1853–1856). He considered himself "a saddle-bags preacher" because he spent much of his career in the rural areas of Virginia. Bocock received an honorary M.A. from Hampden-Sydney College in 1847 and an honorary D.D. from Washington College (later Washington and Lee University) in Lexington in 1856.

On 25 August 1853 Bocock married Sarah Margaret Kemper, of Madison County. They had four sons and one daughter. In 1857 Bocock became pastor of the Bridge Street Presbyterian Church at Georgetown in the District of Columbia. In what was probably the most personally and professionally rewarding time of his life, a great revival swept through the congregation in 1858, and he preached for ninety consecutive nights. With the outbreak of the Civil War Bocock returned to Virginia and was appointed chaplain to the 7th Regiment Virginia Infantry. His health, which had begun to deteriorate during his stay at the Bridge Street Church, soon failed, and he was forced to retire in December 1861. Bocock acted as stated supply at Union Presbyterian Church in Appomattox in 1863, at Halifax Presbyterian Church from 1864 to 1866, and at Fincastle Presbyterian Church from 1867 to 1870.

Well-read in theology and history, Bocock was known best as a frequent contributor to various religious and literary periodicals. Although he was a forceful speaker and debater with a combative disposition, he was also a sensitive man who composed poetry. Bocock wrote occasionally for the *Southern Religious Telegraph* and the *Watchman of the South*. After 1847 his articles regularly appeared in the *Presbyterian Magazine, Princeton Repertory, Princeton Review, Southern Literary Messenger,* and *Southern Presbyterian Review*. In addition to theological essays and discussions of topics under debate within the church, Bocock wrote about southern literature and intellectual history and reviewed religious and secular books. Long after his death his widow published *Selections from the Religious and Literary Writings of John H. Bocock, D.D.* (1891), a 644-page collection of his articles, reviews, sermons, verse, and other writings.

John Holmes Bocock suffered a stroke in 1870 and retired to a house in Lexington, where he died on 17 July 1872. He was buried in that town's Lexington Presbyterian Church Cemetery (later the Stonewall Jackson Memorial Cemetery).

Biographies in *Central Presbyterian,* 10 Nov. 1886, and *Selections from the Religious and Literary Writings of John H. Bocock, D.D.* (1891), ix–xxvii (frontispiece por.; quotation on xii); Alfred Nevin, ed., *Encyclopedia of the Presbyterian Church in the United States of America* (1884), 84–85; Madison Co. Marriage Register; E. C. Scott, ed., *Ministerial Directory of the Presbyterian Church, U.S., 1861–1941* (1942), 65; David F. Riggs, *7th Virginia Infantry,* 2d ed. (1982), 63; copy of tombstone inscription in UTS; obituary in *Lexington Gazette,* 19 July 1872; memorial in *Central Presbyterian,* 7 Aug. 1872.

ROBERT BENEDETTO

BOCOCK, Thomas Salem (18 May 1815–5 August 1891), member of the United States House of Representatives and Speaker of the Confederate House of Representatives, was born in Buckingham County, the son of John Thomas Bocock, a prosperous farmer and sometime member of the General Assembly, and Mary Flood Bocock. His brothers included John Holmes Bocock, a prominent Presbyterian minister, and Willis Perry Bocock, an attorney general of Virginia. Bocock studied with private tutors before spending two years at Hampden-Sydney College, from which he graduated with honors in 1838. He then studied law under Willis P. Bocock and was admitted to the bar in 1840.

Entering politics as a Democrat, Bocock represented Buckingham County in the House of Delegates from 1842 to 1844. During the first session he served on the Committee of Roads and Internal Navigation and during the second on the Committees for Courts of Justice and on Finance. In January 1844 Bocock supported a bill to create Appomattox County from parts of Buckingham, Campbell, Charlotte, and Prince Edward Counties. The bill failed, but a similar statute passed in the next legislative session established the new county. The Bocock family was prominent in its first government, organized on 12 May 1845, with Willis P. Bocock representing Appomattox County in the General Assembly, John T. Bocock becoming clerk of the county court, and Thomas S. Bocock chosen as commonwealth's attorney.

On 2 September 1846 Bocock married Sarah Patrick Flood, with whom he had one daughter before his wife's death on 19 September 1850. Meanwhile, in April 1847 Bocock won election to the House of Representatives, carrying every county except Buckingham in the seven-county Fourth District. He served continuously until early in 1861. He was appointed ranking member of the Committee on Naval Affairs during his second term and served as its chairman from 1853 to 1855 and from 1857 to 1859. Bocock assisted his constituents in a variety of matters, handling inquiries about post office appointments, military pensions, appointments to West Point (among them James Ewell Brown Stuart), and development of the Virginia and Tennessee Railroad. On 4 October 1853 Bocock married Annie Holmes Faulkner, the daughter of his fellow Virginia congressman Charles James Faulkner (1806–1884). They had one son and at least four daughters.

Bocock earned a reputation as an effective orator and a skilled parliamentarian. As early as 1853 he expressed an interest in becoming Speaker of the House of Representatives. By then the issue of slavery's expansion into new territories had divided Congress along sectional lines and helped to destroy the Whig Party. Bocock missed the votes on the Compromise of 1850, probably because of his first wife's death, but he was a vigorous advocate of southern rights who favored the divisive Kansas-Nebraska Act of 1854. He was the Democratic candidate for Speaker when Congress convened in December 1855, but the victory after 133 ballots of Nathaniel Prentice Banks, of Massachusetts, was regarded as the first triumph of the new, anti-slavery Republican Party. Four years later the southern Democratic caucus again nominated

Bocock for Speaker. The Republicans chose John Sherman, of Ohio, and in balloting that lasted for several weeks neither candidate captured a majority. After Bocock withdrew from the contest on 19 December and Sherman withdrew in January, House members compromised on William Pennington, of New Jersey. Some members allegedly became so accustomed to answering "Bocock" or "Sherman" during the balloting that they continued to do so by habit on voice votes for years afterward.

Bocock, who owned more than twenty slaves in 1860, argued during the presidential campaign of that year that Virginia should remain in the Union even if Republican Abraham Lincoln became president and some of the Southern states seceded. He hoped that Virginia could mediate the conflict and gain assurances of Southern rights. Events early in 1861 changed Bocock's mind, and he strongly opposed legislation enabling Lincoln to use force to restore the Union. By April 1861 Bocock favored Virginia's immediate secession.

After the Civil War began and the Confederate capital moved to Richmond, Bocock was elected to the Provisional Congress, taking his seat on 23 July 1861. His previous parliamentary experience made him a valuable member of the body, and he was elected president pro tempore on 10 December 1861. The First Confederate Congress met on 18 February 1862, and its House of Representatives unanimously elected Bocock Speaker. He introduced no bills and seldom participated in debates, but he presided with ability and impartiality, ensuring efficient parliamentary procedures and ably directing much legislation through the House. When the Congress reconvened on 2 May 1864, Bocock was again elected Speaker and presided until its last adjournment on 18 March 1865.

Bocock was concerned about the burdens the war placed on his constituents, but he defended the administration of Jefferson Davis against critics in Congress. He opposed Davis's plan late in the war to arm slaves to fight for the Confederacy, and on 20 January 1865 he was the spokesman when the Virginia congressional delegation met with Davis to express its dissatisfaction with his conduct of the war and to offer recommendations for reorganizing the cabinet. Davis strongly rebuffed the delegation's requests as an affront to his executive authority, although Secretary of War James Alexander Seddon, hurt by criticism from his fellow Virginians, resigned.

Bocock was involved in a peculiar episode in April 1865 that sharply illuminated the changes that the Civil War produced. After the surrender of the Confederate army at Appomattox Court House but before the local army commander had officially proclaimed the Emancipation Proclamation in effect, Bocock purchased several slaves. When the proclamation became effective Bocock informed his former slaves that he would not provide them more than the same support and clothing they had received under slavery. He learned that the man from whom he had recently purchased the additional slaves may not have had legal title to them, and therefore, believing that he had acquired no legal responsibility for those people, he probably refused them any support at all. The freedpeople appealed to the local provost marshal, who told them that they were all entitled to a "liberal compensation" from Bocock, but the marshal also informed Bocock that providing them food and clothing fulfilled that obligation. Bocock later promised his workers that if the crops of the year were good, he would give them a suitable amount of corn. Like many other Virginians, Bocock found himself in an unfamiliar and uncomfortable position with respect to his former slaves and his agricultural laborers, and he did not know how to react. He was unwilling or unable to pay them, but he could not farm his property without them.

A friend later stated that after the war Bocock turned down an offer from an admirer in New York City to guarantee his income if he moved there and opened a law practice. His home in Appomattox County, Wildway, had burned, and Bocock and his family resided in Lynchburg while the house was rebuilt. To recover his finances Bocock worked as a lawyer, including service at different times as counsel for the Atlantic, Mississippi, and Ohio Railroad and for the Richmond and Alleghany Railroad. He also had numerous individual clients in Lynchburg and surrounding counties. Bocock's large library on legal and other topics was reputedly one of the finest in the state.

Bocock also involved himself in postwar politics. On 11 December 1867 he attended a meeting in Richmond to organize what became the Conservative Party, and he made speeches in behalf of Gilbert Carlton Walker, whose successful gubernatorial campaign marked the end of Reconstruction in Virginia. Bocock was at the State Capitol on 27 April 1870 when a section of floor collapsed and killed about sixty people, but he escaped with a badly broken leg. He served on the board of visitors for the new Virginia Agricultural and Mechanical College (later Virginia Polytechnic Institute and State University) from 1873 to 1 January 1876, and he also worked behind the scenes to restore the finances of Hampden-Sydney College. In 1874 friends in the Senate of Virginia schemed unsuccessfully to elect Bocock to the United States Senate, but his only public office after 1865 was a single term representing Appomattox County in the House of Delegates in the session of 1877–1879. He was appointed to the third-ranking positions on the Committee for Courts of Justice and the Committee on Finance, and he was second-ranking member of the Committee on Roads and Internal Navigation.

The issue of handling the state's crushing public debt dominated that session. A moderate Funder, Bocock hoped to stave off the more extreme measures to reduce the debt proposed by the Readjusters. He joined Isaac C. Fowler, of Washington County, to sponsor what became known as the Bocock-Fowler Act. This unsuccessful attempt at compromise asked the state's creditors to exchange their old bonds for new ones at a lower interest rate. Not surprisingly, few creditors took advantage of the offer, and the political divisions over the issue continued and deepened.

Poor health plagued Bocock during the last decade of his life. He rarely traveled far from his estate in Appomattox County, and he suffered a serious stroke in 1883. Thomas Salem Bocock died on 5 August 1891 at Wildway of kidney failure diagnosed as Bright's disease and was buried at the nearby family cemetery. Eulogists recalled his genial disposition and fondness for anecdotes about his experiences in public life, his talent as a partisan orator, and his ability as a legislator to preserve order and extract fair compromises.

Middle name appears as Salem in son's obituary in *Lynchburg Daily Virginian*, 17 Aug. 1859; middle name often given as Stanhope or Stanley in posthumous sources; Thomas Cary Johnson, *The Hon. Thomas S. Bocock* (n.d.); *Confederate Veteran* 10 (1902): 132–133 (por.); Thomas S. Bocock Papers, UVA; Stuart McDearmon Farrar, *Historical Notes of Appomattox County, Virginia* (1989); *Richmond Enquirer*, 29 Sept. 1846, 27 Sept. 1850; Guy L. Keesecker, *Marriage Records of Berkeley County, Virginia* (1969), 18; slave purchase recorded in Thomas S. Bocock Memorandum Book, Papers of Thornhill Family and Thomas S. Bocock, UVA (quotation); *Richmond Dispatch*, 21 Aug. 1883; obituaries in *Lynchburg Daily Virginian*, *Lynchburg News*, and *Richmond Dispatch* (por.), all 7 Aug. 1891, and *New York Times*, 8 Aug. 1891; account of funeral in *Lynchburg News*, 11 Aug. 1891.

Guy R. Swanson

BOCOCK, Willis Perry (22 February 1807–14 March 1887), member of the Convention of 1850–1851 and attorney general of Virginia, was born in the southern part of Buckingham County that in 1845 became Appomattox County. He was the son of John Thomas Bocock and Mary Flood Bocock. His brothers included John Holmes Bocock, an eminent Presbyterian minister, and Thomas Salem Bocock, Speaker of the Confederate House of Representatives. Bocock received a law degree from the University of Virginia in 1833. He practiced at Buckingham Court House for several years while also teaching in a school his father had established. In 1845 Bocock won the first of two consecutive one-year terms in the House of Delegates, serving as a Democrat representing Buckingham and the new county of Appomattox. He chaired the Committee for Courts of Justice during both sessions.

In August 1850 Bocock was elected one of three delegates from the district composed of Appomattox, Charlotte, and Prince Edward Counties to a constitutional convention that met from 14 October 1850 to 1 August 1851. As a member of the Committee on the Basis and Apportionment of Representation he assisted in arranging a mixed apportionment plan based on property and population. This plan awarded a larger proportion of seats in the assembly to the more populous western counties than the old constitution had, but it continued to permit the eastern counties where slaves were numerous to take the slaves' value into consideration in legislative apportionment. Bocock's absence during the floor debate limited his participation in this sectional dispute. An active delegate otherwise and a successful farmer who owned thirty-four slaves, he was a vocal opponent of proposed new taxes on slave property, which he referred to as an important eastern crop. In addition, reacting to constituent concerns over the growing free black population, Bocock proposed a clause requiring that all free blacks remaining in the state longer than twelve months after manumission forfeit their freedom and authorizing the assembly to restrict emancipation and promote removal of free blacks. With the adoption of this language as part of Article IV, the Constitution of 1851 became the first in Virginia to include measures specifically regulating the free black population.

Bocock was unwavering in his support for the interests of eastern Virginia's slave-owning planters, but some of his positions were extreme even for a staunch defender of slavery. He unsuccessfully proposed giving the governor emergency war powers to defend the state against federal encroachments, which carried with it the implication that the governor had the authority to remove Virginia from the Union without consulting the legislature. Despite such strong positions western members respected him for his good humor and integrity as a legal scholar.

Bocock's ability to transcend Virginia's sectional differences may explain his popularity within the Democratic Party, which nominated him for attorney general in 1851. During this first statewide election for that office, the Whigs branded the Democrats as disunionists and characterized Bocock as "even more South Carolinian" than Shelton F. Leake, the candidate for lieutenant governor who had referred to the Compromise of 1850 as a bitter pill forced on the South by federal doctors. Bocock defined the campaign as a battle between theories of limited and unlimited government, asserting that the Whigs intended to "widen and break down the barriers of the constitution." He defeated the Whig incumbent attorney general, Sidney Smith Baxter, and was reelected in 1855. As attorney general, Bocock advised state officials on the new constitution, including the definition of powers of new state agencies, and he also interpreted new statutes regulating manumissions and the transportation out of Virginia of slaves convicted of crimes. On 20 March 1857 he resigned effective 15 May, citing personal circumstances.

On 10 December 1856 Bocock married Mourning S. Gracy, a widow who owned a plantation in Marengo County, Alabama. Having also sustained a crippling fall, Bocock lived the remainder of his life as a private gentleman, dividing his time between his Virginia and Alabama farms, which had a combined value of $572,281 in 1860. After his wife died in 1886 he moved back to Virginia. Willis Perry Bocock died in Appomattox County on 14 March 1887, leaving his large landholdings in both states to the families of his brothers and sisters. He was buried in the family cemetery in Appomattox County.

Birth date in obituary in *Lynchburg Daily News*, 15 Mar. 1887; scattered letters in collections at UNC, UVA, and VHS; *Debates and Proceedings of 1850–1851 Convention*, esp. 226–227, 267–271, 472; *Supplement, 1850–1851 Convention Debates*, nos. 74, 75; *Lynchburg Virginian*, 3 Nov. 1851 (first quotation); *Richmond Semi-Weekly Examiner*, 2 Dec. 1851 (second quotation); opinions as attorney general in Auditor of Public Accounts Papers, RG 48, LVA; several letters, including 20 Mar. 1857 letter of resignation, in Governor's Office, Letters Received, RG 3, LVA; marriage reported in *Richmond Daily Dispatch*, 19 Jan. 1857; Nathaniel Ragland Featherston, *The History of Appomattox, Virginia* (1948), 69 (por.); obituaries in *Lynchburg Daily News*, *Lynchburg Virginian*, and *Richmond Dispatch* (with variant death date of 13 Mar. 1887), all 15 Mar. 1887.

JOHN ALLEY

BODEKER, Anna Whitehead (ca. 26 July 1826–26 October 1904), woman suffrage activist, was born in Midland Park, Bergen County, New Jersey, the daughter of Jesse Whitehead and Sophia Candy Whitehead, both of whom were English immigrants. When she was ten years old the family moved to Virginia. Her father oversaw construction of the Manchester Cotton Mill in the city of Manchester and served for many years as its superintendent. The family lived in a house adjacent to the mill, and Whitehead's parents evidently provided her with a good education. On 15 January 1846 she married Augustus Bodeker, a German immigrant who had settled in Richmond ten years earlier. Then a clerk for a local druggist, he soon opened his own pharmaceutical business. She assumed responsibility for the care of two teenage members of her husband's family, and she had three daughters, the first of whom died in infancy. In 1862 the family purchased a two-and-a-half-story brick house in Church Hill in Richmond. Bodeker spent part of the Civil War in Albemarle County but lived in Church Hill for the remainder of her life.

By late in the 1860s Bodeker was well versed on women's issues and had begun to follow the activities of the National Woman Suffrage Association (NWSA), the larger and more radical of the two major suffrage organizations founded in the United States in 1869. When she learned that NWSA activists, including Paulina Wright Davis, were visiting Richmond late in January 1870, Bodeker invited them to her house to discuss the suffrage movement with friends and neighbors. The visitors left the meeting impressed. Reporting on her trip in the *Revolution*, a prosuffrage weekly, Davis described Bodeker as a "most bril[l]iant woman" and predicted that if she could "be induced to take the lecturing field, she might reach the whole south and do incalculable good."

With this encouragement Bodeker made plans to organize a woman suffrage association in Virginia. She and several other Richmond women drafted and submitted a "Defence of Woman Suffrage" to the *Richmond Daily Enquirer*, which opposed extending the franchise but published the essay in two installments on 18 and 23 March 1870. The article promised benefits to society if women were granted the vote and focused on the connection between the franchise and women's economic opportunity and independence. Bodeker also arranged for the prominent New York suffragist Matilda Joslyn Gage to visit Richmond. On 5 May 1870 Gage addressed a small group of suffrage supporters. The following evening she joined Bodeker and others in founding the Virginia State Woman Suffrage Association, with Bodeker as president.

The founding officers also included United States District Court judge John C. Underwood and his wife; Alexandria attorneys Lysander Hill and Westel Willoughby and their wives; Freedmen's Bureau school superintendent Ralza M. Manly; the novelist Martha Haines Butt, a native of Norfolk, then resident in New York; Elisa Washburne, wife of Richmond's superintendent of schools; Georgianna Smith, a physician's wife; and Sue L. F. Smith, daughter of a former president of Randolph-Macon College.

Bodeker was elated and invited several well-known suffrage leaders to speak in Richmond during the meeting of the General Assembly that began on 7 December 1870. Susan B. Anthony, hoping that Bodeker would be able to ignite a viable suffrage movement in the South, accepted and gave evening talks at the federal courthouse on 9 and 10 December. Anthony advocated a constitutional amendment granting women the vote, but despite advance publicity and personal invitations to the members of the House of Delegates, on both nights the audience consisted of only a few legislators and women. Because many white Richmonders avoided the federal courthouse as a result of its association with Reconstruction, Bodeker attempted unsuccessfully to move the second night's talks to the House chamber in the Capitol. Nevertheless, she used Anthony's second appearance to test her own oratorical skills. In introducing Anthony, Bodeker delivered a fierce denunciation of the subordinate status of women and concluded with a stirring call for immediate legislative action.

Far from being discouraged by the low turnout, Bodeker was energized by Anthony's visit and pushed forward with her own schedule of lectures and appearances. In January 1871 she hosted a presentation by the southern-born suffragist Lillie Devereux Blake, and two months later Paulina Wright Davis, Josephine S. Griffing, and Isabella Beecher Hooker spent several days in Richmond with Bodeker. These speakers attracted larger audiences than Anthony had, but few Richmond women attended their lectures, and their presence failed to create a groundswell of support for the suffrage movement.

At a suffrage convention held in New York in May 1871, Bodeker was one of thirty-four women whom Anthony selected to serve on the National Woman Suffrage Educational Committee, a group charged with coordinating future NWSA activities. The committee urged association members to cite the Fourteenth and Fifteenth Amendments and attempt to vote in local elections in the autumn of 1871. Bodeker accordingly appeared at the designated polling place for the second precinct of Marshall Ward in Richmond to cast her vote. When the election judges refused to accept it, she insisted on placing a paper in the ballot box stating that "by the Constitution of the United States, I, Mrs. A. Whitehead Bodeker, have a right to give my vote at this election, and in vindication of it drop this note in the ballot-box, November 7th, 1871."

During the 1872 assembly session the Virginia Woman Suffrage Association sponsored another suffrage program featuring Matilda Joslyn Gage and Laura de Force Gordon, who had recently campaigned unsuccessfully for a seat in the California state senate. At Bodeker's request, Henry County delegate George William Booker presented her petition for legislation granting women the right to vote. The petition was referred to the Committee for Courts of Justice, which ignored it, and the assembly once again rose without seriously considering woman suffrage.

Whether prompted by frustration at her inability to effect suffrage reform in Virginia or by some other reason, Bodeker late in 1871 began to take a deep interest in spiritualism. By 1872 she believed that she had developed exceptional powers as a medium. Convinced that she could commune directly with Heaven and that she had a responsibility to interpret God's plan to all who would listen, Bodeker began to express her unorthodox spiritual views forcefully at home and in public. Her behavior became so erratic that on 19 September 1873 her family had her confined against her will in the Western Lunatic Asylum in Staunton. Following her release on 20 October 1874 Bodeker returned to her home in Richmond, but she never resumed her suffrage activity and by 1876 had been replaced as Virginia's representative to the National Woman Suffrage Association by Caroline Putnam, a Northumberland County teacher. By 1909, when the suffrage movement revived with the founding of the Equal Suffrage League of Virginia, Bodeker's legacy as the founder of the state's first suffrage organization had faded into obscurity.

In 1882 Bodeker published *Medium We*, a collection of her spiritualist writings. After the death of her husband on 26 July 1884, she continued to live in the family's home with her surviving daughters, neither of whom had married and the elder of whom became the head of the household. Anna Whitehead Bodeker died in Richmond on 26 October 1904 and was buried in Hollywood Cemetery in that city.

Sandra Gioia Treadway, "A Most Brilliant Woman: Anna Whitehead Bodeker and the First Woman Suffrage Association in Virginia," *Virginia Cavalcade* 43 (1994): 166–177; Richmond City Death Certificate gives incomplete birth date of 26 July 182_ but notes age at death as seventy-eight years, three months, and zero days; Hollywood Cemetery interment record (LVA microfilm) gives same age at death, implying birth in 1826; Census, Richmond City, 1900, gives birth date as Sept. 1827, with incorrect first name and birthplace; Benjamin B. Weisiger III, ed., *Marriage Bonds and Ministers' Returns of Chesterfield County, Virginia, 1816–1853* (1981), 18; *Richmond Daily Enquirer*, 3 Feb., 18, 23 Mar., 9 May, 10, 12, 13 Dec. 1870, 7, 9 Mar. 1871, 31 Jan., 1 Feb. 1872; *Revolution*, 17 Feb. (first quotation), 19 May 1870, 26 Jan., 16, 23 Mar., 18 May 1871; *Richmond Dispatch*, 8 Nov. 1871 (second quotation); *JHD*, 1870–1871 sess., 29–30, and 1871–1872 sess., 244; Elizabeth Cady Stanton, Susan B. Anthony, et al., *History of Woman Suffrage* (1887–[1922]), 3:19, 823–824; dates of hospitalization confirmed by Western State Hospital, Staunton; obituary in *Richmond Times-Dispatch*, 30 Oct. 1904 (gives variant birth date of 27 July 1827).

Sandra Gioia Treadway

BOGGESS, Caleb (19 April 1822–14 April 1889), member of the Convention of 1861, was born in Lumberport, Harrison County, the son of Caleb Boggess and Mary Robinson Boggess. He was educated in the common schools of Harrison County and perhaps at Randolph Academy in Clarksburg before attending the Virginia Military Institute for three years and graduating eighth in a class of twenty in 1845. Boggess returned to Harrison County and read law in the Clarksburg office of Edwin Steele Duncan. He was admitted to the bar in 1847.

On 2 November 1848 Boggess married Elizabeth Ann Camden. Of their one son and three daughters, only a daughter survived into adulthood. Their eldest child, Sallie, may have had birth defects or been mentally retarded. Boggess placed her in a Catholic institution, Mount de Chantel, in Wheeling, where she died at age fourteen but received care that so impressed Boggess that the erstwhile Baptist converted to Catholicism.

After his marriage Boggess practiced law in Weston with his wife's cousin Johnson Newlon Camden. In 1858 Boggess helped found the Bank of Weston. He was probably a Whig early in the 1850s but took no recorded part in partisan politics until December 1860, when he presided over a large meeting in Weston that adopted resolutions recommending that Virginia remain in the Union even if other Southern states seceded. On 4 February 1861 Boggess defeated William J. Bland to represent Lewis County in the state convention on the issue of secession. Boggess made no recorded speeches during the convention and voted against leaving the Union when a motion to secede was defeated on 4 April 1861 and again when it passed thirteen days later.

Boggess returned home to Weston before the convention adjourned. His house had been burned during his absence, probably by accident but possibly by local secessionists. Boggess then moved to Clarksburg and lived there for the remainder of his life. He continued to practice law and made a name for himself handling railroad cases. About 1873 he became a counsel for the Baltimore and Ohio Railroad. He argued cases before the United States Supreme Court and often appeared before the West Virginia Supreme Court but declined a nomination for a seat on the latter in 1866 because he disapproved of popular elections of judges. Caleb Boggess died on 14 April 1889 at his home in Clarksburg, West Virginia, and was buried in the Independent Order of Odd Fellows Cemetery in that city.

Atkinson and Gibbens, *Prominent Men*, 2:751–752; George W. Atkinson, ed., *Bench and Bar of West Virginia* (1919), 87–88; Harrison Co. Marriage Register; family history confirmed by great-grandson Robert S. Wilson; some Boggess letters in Jonathan McCally Bennett Papers, WVU; Roy Bird Cook, *Lewis County in the Civil War, 1861–1865* (1924), 11–12 (frontispiece por.); Reese and Gaines, *Proceedings of 1861 Convention,* 3:163, 4:145; obituaries in *Wheeling Intelligencer* and *Wheeling Register*, both 16 Apr. 1889.

DOROTHY UPTON DAVIS

BOGGS, Edmond Mac (23 February 1909–5 February 1989), commissioner of the Department of Labor and Industry, was born in Gilmer County, West Virginia, the son of Edgar M. Boggs and Olive Norman Boggs. When he was three years old the family moved to Goochland County, where he attended the local public schools and worked on his father's farm. Boggs left home at age nineteen, learned the boilermaker's trade the following year, and traveled widely in search of work during the early years of the Great Depression. He joined the Standard Oil Company of New Jersey in 1934 as a salesman in Richmond and later took a similar position with the Richmond Coca-Cola Bottling Works, Inc., before becoming Coca-Cola's plant manager at Urbanna in May 1944.

In January 1945 Boggs resigned to become Virginia district representative for the International Brotherhood of Boilermakers, Iron Shipbuilders, and Helpers of America, a labor union affiliated with the American Federation of Labor. Except in the Hampton Roads area and the mining districts in the southwestern part of the state, organized labor in Virginia had little influence, but even so the state's political leadership harshly criticized unions, especially the Congress of Industrial Organizations, then engaged in an ambitious southern organizing campaign. On 21 January 1947 the General Assembly enacted a stringent right-to-work law, forbidding the requirement of union membership for employment. In this hostile environment Boggs organized locals, negotiated with management, and lobbied for his union.

The administration of Governor William Munford Tuck, who had dramatically prevented several threatened strikes, also reorganized state government for economy and efficiency. On 9 February 1949 the governor's office released a scathing "Report on the Department of Labor and Industry" that pointed out numerous inefficiencies and failings. Shortly before it appeared, Tuck requested the immediate retirement of John Hopkins Hall, the department's head.

Under the 1898 law creating the Bureau of Labor and Industrial Statistics, the institutional ancestor of the Department of Labor and Industry, the commissioner was to be a person "identified with the labor interests of the state." Charles R. Fenwick, state senator from Arlington County, proposed that the governor appoint Boggs, apparently without Boggs's knowledge. Others—union members, friends, and politicians—also endorsed him for the post. On 15 February 1949 Tuck named Boggs acting commissioner and charged him with implementing the report's recommendations. The governor also made him responsible for mediating labor-management conflicts involving public utilities, a duty that Tuck had previously handled himself. Citing Boggs's successful mediation of labor disputes involving the state's two largest electric power companies, Tuck removed "acting" from Boggs's title just three months later. Boggs remained commissioner for twenty-eight years, serving in eight gubernatorial administrations.

The Department of Labor and Industry compiled economic statistics, inspected mines and other workplaces for safety, and monitored compliance with laws governing the employment of women and children. Boggs eliminated overlapping responsibilities and improved methods of statistical reporting. He also informally mediated disputes in industries other than public utilities and won the respect of both union leaders and employers. Boggs believed that unions contributed to stability in labor relations but gradually came to accept and even defend the state's right-to-work laws.

Virginia's economy became overwhelmingly nonagricultural during Boggs's quarter century in office. The department's Division of Research and Statistics charted the change, reporting in ever-greater detail the condition of the state's economy. Responsibilities for monitoring compliance with state and federal labor laws expanded, too, and by 1968 the department had field offices in eleven locations across the state.

Boggs took a special interest in the department's safety program and on 28 April 1949 created the Advisory Council on Industrial Safety consisting of representatives from both labor and management. Rather than compelling employers to eliminate hazards, the department emphasized the costs of injuries and illnesses and, in cooperation with the Virginia Manufacturers Association, designed educational programs to make workplaces safer. Even as industrial employment skyrocketed, accident rates remained below the national average.

Boggs opposed federal legislation setting national safety standards that the United States Department of Labor would enforce. He testified against the legislation in 1962, used his presidency of the International Association of Government Labor Officials in 1963 to campaign against it, and testified against similar legislation in 1968, upholding Virginia's cooperative program as more workable. The Occupational Safety and Health Act became law in 1970, but not until six years later, after protracted negotiation, did his department gain responsibility for safety inspections under the federal program. Virginia conservatives saluted Boggs's position, but throughout the controversy he emphasized safety, not ideology.

Boggs retired as commissioner in 1977, citing "personal and family obligations." He had married Lucyle Mosby, of Fluvanna County, on 22 November 1929, and they had one daughter. Boggs cared for his wife during her final illness. On 20 August 1983 he married Nellie Trice Pierce. Edmond Mac Boggs died at Henrico Doctors Hospital on 5 February 1989 and was buried in Westhampton Memorial Park in Henrico County.

Governor William Munford Tuck Executive Papers, boxes 57–58 (including Boggs's undated autobiographical memorandum of ca. 1949), RG 3, LVA; feature article in *Richmond News Leader*, 21 Feb. 1951 (por.); *Acts of Assembly*, 1897–1898 sess., 894 (first quotation); James Euchner, "Department of Labor and Industry," *Virginia Record* 77 (Aug. 1955): 10–13, 43–48; William Bryan Crawley Jr., *Bill Tuck: A Political Life in Harry Byrd's Virginia* (1978), 80–134; Commissioner's Correspondence/Subject Files, 1950–1987, Department of Labor and Industry, boxes 3–4, RG 19, LVA; *Annual Report of the Department of Labor and Industry* (1949–1978); *Richmond News Leader*, 15 Feb. 1949, 15 Feb. 1952, 21 Feb. 1955, 22 Aug. 1963, 30 Apr.

1977 (second quotation); additional information provided by Janice M. Hathcock; obituaries in *Richmond News Leader* and *Richmond Times-Dispatch* (por.), both 6 Feb. 1989.

JOHN T. KNEEBONE

BOGGS, Moran Lee "Dock" (7 February 1898–7 February 1971), musician, was born in the small Wise County community of Dooley, the son of Jonathan Bishop Boggs, a blacksmith and small farmer, and Elizabeth Emily Phillips Boggs. He was named for a physician in the nearby town of Norton, and his father called him "Dock." Boggs attended school only until about age twelve, when he began working in the local coal mines.

During his childhood Boggs became interested in music. Several members of his immediate family sang or played stringed instruments, and he learned the clawhammer, or knockdown, style of playing the banjo with the thumb and forefinger. About 1908 he met an African American banjo player whose highly syncopated technique of playing with two fingers and thumb Boggs adopted as his own. Although his musical style developed straight out of that of many white Appalachians, African American music influenced him and others among his contemporaries. Despite his lifelong interest in music, which began as a family and neighborhood activity rather than an occupation, Boggs labored in the coal mines from 1910 to 1954. When hard times in the mines of southwestern Virginia and southeastern Kentucky made work hard to find, he supplemented his income by bootlegging. On 26 April 1918 Boggs married Sara A. Stidham, of Letcher County, Kentucky. They had no children. She strongly disapproved of secular music, and consequently he seldom played in public.

Early in 1927 Boggs met a talent scout for the Brunswick Record Company and attended an audition in the ballroom of a Norton hotel. Impressed by Boggs's playing and singing, the agent arranged for him to travel to New York City in March 1927. Boggs recorded eight numbers that the Brunswick Record Company released on four records. Unfortunately the recordings were of poor quality and did not sell well, although "Country Blues," "Down South Blues," "Pretty Polly," and "Sugar Baby" are exceptional performances. Boggs then bought the best banjo he could afford, a Gibson, and formed a band, Dock Boggs and His Cumberland Mountain Entertainers. The group performed on a circuit of tent shows, theaters, and programs at coal camps. In 1929 William E. Myer, an entrepreneur from the Tazewell County town of Richlands, asked Boggs to record for his new Lonesome Ace label. That autumn Boggs traveled to Chicago and recorded four more songs, including "False Hearted Lover's Blues" and "Old Rub Alcohol Blues." The two records suffered from exceptionally limited distribution and low-quality pressings. The paltry record sales and increasing objections from his wife to quit performing caused Boggs to lay down his banjo.

For the next twenty-five years Boggs played only rarely. He joined the Baptist Church during the 1930s, stopped bootlegging, and tried to give up drinking. Not until 1954, when Boggs quit mining and had to rely in part on his wife's garden to make ends meet, did he begin to play again locally. His retirement from the coalfields coincided with a renewal of interest in folk music and sparked a revival of his truncated musical career. Early in the 1960s Boggs met Mike Seeger, a member of the New Lost City Ramblers and a folk music researcher, who encouraged him to resume playing the banjo. Boggs performed throughout the country at folk festivals and appeared several times at the Newport Folk Festival, entertaining audiences that numbered in the tens of thousands. On 4 December 1969 Boggs and Seeger performed at an inaugural music festival at Clinch Valley College of the University of Virginia (later the University of Virginia at Wise). The folk festival became an annual event sponsored by the college and Appalachian Traditions and later took the name Dock Boggs Memorial Music Festival. Seeger recorded Boggs's music and taped interviews with him, and Folkways issued three albums of his music and another of his music and verbal recollections. Gradually, however, his health failed, and he had to lay his banjo aside once more. Moran Lee "Dock" Boggs died in Norton on his seventy-third birthday, 7 February 1971, and was buried there in Laurel Groves Cemetery.

Interest in Boggs and his music surged late in the 1990s, initially as a result of the unexpected commercial and critical success of and publicity for the Smithsonian Folkways reissue in 1997 of Harry Smith's *Anthology of American Folk Music*, originally released in 1952 and containing two of Boggs's songs. In 1998 all of his early work for Brunswick and Lonesome Ace and many of his 1960s recordings were reissued, and he was the subject of a thoughtful review article by William Hogeland in the *Atlantic Monthly*. Boggs's status accordingly shifted from that of a pioneering (albeit unorthodox) country music artist to an icon who influenced Bob Dylan and others in the folk revival.

Barry O'Connell, "Dock Boggs, Musician and Coal Miner," *Appalachian Journal* 11 (1984): 44–57; Kip Lornell, *Virginia's Blues, Country, and Gospel Records, 1902–1943: An Annotated Discography* (1989), 32–34 (por.); Irwin Stambler and Grelun Landon, eds., *The Encyclopedia of Folk, Country and Western Music*, 2d ed. (1983), 54–55; Dock Boggs, "I Always Loved the Lonesome Songs," *Sing Out!* 14 (July 1964): 23, 33, 35, 37; BVS Marriage Register, Wise Co.; Mike Seeger produced several albums on Folkways Records of his field recordings of Boggs, including *Dock Boggs, Legendary Banjo Player and Singer,* FA 2351 (1964), *Dock Boggs: Volume 2,* FA 2392 (1965), *Dock Boggs: Volume 3,* FA 3903 (1970), and *Dock Boggs: Excerpts from Interviews with Dock Boggs, Legendary Banjo Player and Singer*, FA 5458 (1965); *Country Blues: Complete Early Recordings (1927–29),* recording with brochure notes by Greil Marcus and Jon Pankake, Revenant Records 205 (1998); *Dock Boggs: His Folkways Years, 1963–1968,* Smithsonian Folkways recording with brochure notes by Barry O'Connell and Mike Seeger, SFW 40108 (1998); William Hogeland, "Corn Bread When I'm Hungry: Dock Boggs and Rock Criticism," *Atlantic Monthly* 282 (Nov. 1998): 116–124; obituaries in *Norton Coalfield Progress,* 11, 18 Feb. 1971 (por.).

Kɪᴘ Lᴏʀɴᴇʟʟ

BOHANNAN, James Gordon (22 October 1880–19 November 1947), attorney and civic leader, was born at Claremont in Surry County, the son of Aurelius Powhatan Bohannan and Anna Victoria Deal Bohannan. He grew up in Surry, where his father served as county treasurer, and then attended the College of William and Mary from 1895 to 1898. Bohannan taught school in Surry County but returned to William and Mary, from which he earned a B.A. in 1901.

During the 1902–1903 school year he taught at Smithfield Male and Female Institute in Smithfield. Bohannan entered the law school of the University of Virginia in 1903 and graduated in 1905.

J. Gordon Bohannan returned to Surry to practice law and served the county from 1905 to 1911 as commonwealth's attorney. In 1912 he moved to Petersburg and became a partner in a law firm with Charles Evans Plummer until Plummer's death in 1942, after which he practiced with his nephew Willis Wilson Bohannan. Bohannan also invested in local businesses and sat on numerous boards of directors. He was president of the Petersburg Chamber of Commerce during the mid-1920s, sat on the board of Petersburg's Central State Hospital from 1905 until 1923, was a member of the Virginia State Port Authority from 1926 until 1933, the last three years as chairman, and served from 1934 to 1938 on the State Board of Education.

Early in 1929 Bohannan was elected president of the five-year-old Virginia State Chamber of Commerce. In June of the following year he led a twelve-member delegation of Virginia business leaders to Great Britain. Bohannan also served as president of the Virginia State Bar Association in 1929–1930. His presidential address on 6 August 1930 on "The Demand for Certainty and Stability in the Law—The Necessity for Change" called for the freeing of lawyers and judges from legislated restraints so that they could adapt rules of law and procedure to the new economic conditions and institutions of the twentieth century. Bohannan presented a businessman's and corporate lawyer's perspective, and as a businessman, lawyer, and conservative member of the Democratic Party, he opposed programs to intervene in the economy during the Great Depression of the 1930s.

Although he was a man of strong opinions who often involved himself in public affairs, Bohannan held only local elective office. Early in 1926 he was named to fill a vacancy on the Petersburg city council, and on 1 September 1926 the other council members elected him mayor of the city for a two-year term. Under Petersburg's city manager form of government, the office of mayor was largely ceremonial, and the mayor's most important responsibility was presiding over the five-member council.

Bohannan was appointed city attorney for Petersburg in 1936 and held the post for the remainder of his life. From 1938 until 1946 he sat on the board of visitors of the College of William and Mary, serving from 1941 until 1946 as the college's rector and becoming intimately involved in efforts to restore the college's accreditation after a committee of the Association of American Universities issued a report criticizing the administrative structure and management of the college and its Norfolk and Richmond branches.

On 2 June 1909 Bohannan married Elizabeth Edloe Lamb, who died on 2 October 1924, and on 29 October 1937 he married Elizabeth Randolph Macon Tilley, who died two years later. He had no children from either marriage. James Gordon Bohannan died of heart disease at the Medical College of Virginia Hospital in Richmond on 19 November 1947 and was buried in Blandford Cemetery in Petersburg.

Feature article in *Petersburg Progress-Index*, 1 Sept. 1926; BVS Marriage Register, Williamsburg, 1909, and Alexandria City, 1937; Bohannan set out his economic, political, and legal philosophies in annual reports as president of the Virginia State Chamber of Commerce, published as its *Miscellaneous Documents* 26 (1930) and 29 (1931), and in his presidential address to the Virginia State Bar Association, printed in its *Proceedings* (1930): 341–374; Bohannan's correspondence and will in presidential papers of John Stewart Bryan and John E. Pomfret, College Archives, W&M; obituaries in *Petersburg Progress-Index*, 19 Nov. 1947, and *Richmond Times-Dispatch*, 20 Nov. 1947; memorial in *Virginia State Bar Association Proceedings* (1948): 144–146 (por.).

BRENT TARTER

BOHANNAN, Richard Lafon (d. 15 July 1855), physician and medical educator, was born at Shelba in Essex County, the son of Joseph Bohannan, a planter, and Elizabeth Lafon Bohannan. In 1811 Bohannan graduated from the University of Pennsylvania Medical School after studying there under Thomas Chalkley James, a noted author on obstetrics who had recently been appointed to the school's first chair in that field. Bohannan decided to specialize in obstetrics at a time when medical science was just beginning to apply its methods to tasks that had traditionally been the province of midwives.

Following his graduation Bohannan moved to Richmond and on 7 December 1811 announced that at his new practice of medicine, surgery, and midwifery he would "attend and furnish Medicine for the Poor, gratis." He became a leading member of Richmond's medical community and eventually developed an extensive practice in which he delivered up to 150 babies a year. Bohannan was a member of the first Medical Society of Virginia, chartered in 1824. He married Sarah Cabell Whitlocke in Petersburg on 22 February 1838, and they had five sons and two daughters.

In 1837 Bohannan joined physicians Lewis Webb Chamberlayne, John Cullen, and Augustus Warner in successfully petitioning the board of trustees of Hampden-Sydney College to create a medical school in Richmond to be operated under the college's charter. Bohannan continued his private practice, but for the remainder of his life he also taught at the medical school, which in 1854 was separated from Hampden-Sydney and chartered as the Medical College of Virginia. The school's first professor of obstetrics and the diseases of women and children, and the founder who taught there the longest, Richard Lafon Bohannan died at his home in Richmond on 15 July 1855 and was buried in Hollywood Cemetery in that city.

Wyndham B. Blanton, *Medicine in Virginia in the Nineteenth Century* (1933), 45 (gives 1790 year of birth); reminiscence by student J. C. Egan in *Old Dominion Journal of Medicine and Surgery* 1 (1902): 36; French Biographies (gives 1784 year of birth); *Richmond Enquirer*, 31 Dec. 1811 (quotation); marriage and children documented in Chesterfield Co. Marriage Register, *Richmond Enquirer*, 1 Mar. 1838, and Census, Richmond City, 1850 (gives age as sixty), 1860, 1900; William T. Sanger, *Medical College of Virginia before 1925 and University College of Medicine, 1893–1913* (1973), 3–7; Sanger Historical File, MCV, including Bohannan's own lecture notes and student notes from his lectures; Hummel and Smith, *Portraits and Statuary*, 9 (por.); Hollywood Cemetery interment record (LVA microfilm), gives age as seventy-four; obituary in *Richmond Enquirer*, 18 July 1855; memorial with age at death of sixty-eight in *Virginia Medical and Surgical Journal* 5 (1855): 164–165.

JOHN ALLEY
JODI L. KOSTE

BOHUN, Lawrence (d. 19 March 1621), physician and member of the Council, was born probably in England between 1575 and 1585. An acquaintance later wrote that Bohun had been "a long time brought up amongst the most learned Surgeons, and Physitions in Netherlands." Most likely he received his medical education at Leiden, but nothing of his youth or education is definitely known.

Bohun, whose surname contemporaries often spelled "Bohune" or "Boone," sailed for Virginia on 1 April 1610 as personal physician to the new governor, Thomas West, baron De La Warr. Within a month after they arrived in Jamestown on 10 June 1610, Bohun had treated the governor's fever with bloodletting, which De La Warr believed had saved his life. Bohun soon depleted his medical chest treating colonists' frequent illnesses, and during the nine and one-half months he was in the colony he experimented with indigenous native plants and minerals to ascertain their medicinal properties. He used sassafras to purge phlegm, employed a white clay to fight fevers, used the saps of gum trees and white poplar to make a balm for healing wounds, and compounded a medicine for dysentery from myrtle fruit.

Bohun left Virginia with De La Warr on 28 March 1611 bound for Nevis in the West Indies, where the governor hoped to recover from scurvy. The wind drove their ship instead to the Azores, where De La Warr decided to sail to England and recuperate fully before returning to the colony. Bohun found himself back in England a year after he had first arrived in Virginia.

On 12 March 1612 Bohun was one of 325 shareholders named in the third charter of the Virginia Company of London. During the next several years he probably practiced medicine among the court favorites and commercial leaders of London, and his marriage to Alice Barnes, widow of merchant William Barnes, of Lambeth, Surrey County, likely also occurred about this time. She had at least one son and two daughters before her marriage to Bohun, with whom she had one daughter.

Bohun continued his involvement in the affairs of the Virginia Company. In February 1620 he and James Swift were granted a tract of Virginia land for having transported 300 colonists and some cattle to Virginia. In November of that year the company approved Bohun's request that the grant be renewed in his name only, and about the same time he subscribed to a petition that a suitable gentleman of quality be sent to Virginia as governor. The surviving records of the Virginia Company include two veiled references to a "project" of Bohun, which "promised much benefitt but in the end came to nothinge." The scheme probably involved the cultivation of silkworms in Virginia. Bohun enjoyed a long friendship with members of the Ferrar family, who attempted to introduce silk culture in Virginia, and when Bohun sailed for Virginia the second time, he was on a ship transporting silkworm larvae, or "seed," to the colony.

On 13 December 1620 the Virginia Company appointed Bohun physician general of the colony, a position that carried with it an allotment of 500 acres and twenty tenants to work it. The company also appointed him to the Council. Bohun and his stepson, Edward Barnes, embarked on the *Margaret and John*, of which Bohun was part owner, near the end of January 1621. When the ship arrived in the West Indies to take on fresh water, two Spanish warships attacked it. During the two-day battle the English drove off the larger Spanish ships, but the silkworm larvae were destroyed, and ten Englishmen were killed or mortally wounded, including Lawrence Bohun, who fell with his pistol in his hand on 19 March 1621.

Wyndham B. Blanton, *Medicine in Virginia in the Seventeenth Century* (1930), 11–16; Smith, *Complete Works*, 2:238, 273 (first quotation); Kingsbury, *Virginia Company*, vols. 1, 3 (second quotation on 1:576); Harlean MSS, 7009, British Library; Ferrar Papers (with autograph on June 1619 share transfer), Magdalene College, Cambridge University, Eng.; Manchester Papers, nos. 247, 291, PRO 30/15/2; will in Prerogative Court of Canterbury, Savile 30; death reported in PRO SP 14/120, no. 29; Avery E. Kolb, "The Feisty Voyagers of the *Margaret and John*," *Virginia Cavalcade* 28 (1979): 130–137.

DAPHNE GENTRY

BOISSEAU, James (10 June 1822–29 November 1872), member of the Convention of 1861, was born in Petersburg, the son of James Boisseau, a Petersburg merchant of Huguenot extraction, and Jane Inglish Turner Boisseau. When

Boisseau was two years old his father died, and after the death of his mother three years later he lived at Flat Rock, the Dinwiddie County home of his aunt Sally Boisseau, whose estate he managed after he reached adulthood. Boisseau entered the College of William and Mary in 1839 and graduated in 1842. He taught school at Winfield Academy in Dinwiddie County and bought Cedar Lane, a farm south of Five Forks.

Boisseau served as commissioner of revenue for Dinwiddie County from 1848 to 1850 and then studied law briefly at the University of Virginia. From 1852 to 1856 he served as commonwealth's attorney for the county. In 1857 he was elected to the House of Delegates and represented Dinwiddie County in the legislative session that met from December 1857 to April 1858. He sat on the Committees on the Militia Laws and of Propositions and Grievances. He also served as a justice of the peace and by 1860 was the Dinwiddie County Court's presiding justice. On 29 February 1860 Boisseau married Martha Elizabeth Cousins. They had two sons and two daughters.

On 4 February 1861 Boisseau was chosen to represent Dinwiddie County in a state convention on the question of secession. With a small majority of the county's voters he favored leaving the Union, and on 1 March 1861 he moved in the convention that the connection between Virginia and the United States be dissolved. Boisseau made no major convention speeches, but he voted for secession both when the resolution was defeated on 4 April 1861 and again when it passed on 17 April 1861. He also attended the other two sessions of the convention held in the summer and autumn of 1861. Even though he was more than forty years old, Boisseau joined the ranks of Johnston's Artillery, a heavy artillery unit that was organized on 2 September 1861 and reorganized the following spring. Boisseau served in the defenses around Richmond, and from June 1864 until April 1865 he served in the defense of Petersburg. On 1 September 1864 he was promoted to corporal. Boisseau was captured on 13 April 1865 during the retreat of the Confederate army after the fall of Petersburg and briefly held as a prisoner of war.

After the war Boisseau returned home to a looted farmhouse, from which he resumed farming and practicing law. On 14 April 1870 the General Assembly elected him to a six-year term as judge of Dinwiddie County. James Boisseau died on 29 November 1872 in a hotel in Petersburg, where he was attending a convention of North Carolina and Virginia farmers. He was buried at Cedar Lane in Dinwiddie County.

French Biographies; Sterling Boisseau, "James Boisseau," *WMQ*, 2d ser., 2 (1922): 71–72; Virginia Writers' Project, *Dinwiddie County: "The Countrey of the Apamatica"* (1942), 222; BVS Marriage Register, Dinwiddie Co.; Reese and Gaines, *Proceedings of 1861 Convention*, 1:276–277, 3:163–164, 4:144; Sterling Boisseau, *The Union Monument and Other Poems* (1913), 16; Compiled Service Records; obituary in *Petersburg Daily Appeal*, 30 Nov. 1872.

DONALD W. GUNTER

BOLAND, Robert J. (23 October 1850–16 November 1918), physician, was born in or near La Grange, Georgia, the son of an enslaved woman whose name is not recorded. His father, whose name may have been John Boland, was the son of his mother's owner. Early in 1865 Boland escaped from slavery and went to Atlanta, where he worked as a janitor at the Storrs School for Colored Children. He moved to Detroit in 1868 and supported himself as a waiter while completing elementary school and three years of high school. In 1879 Boland began a two-year apprenticeship in the office of Dr. Charles Pratt, training that helped prepare him for admission to the Michigan College of Medicine in 1881. The first African American to attend the Detroit-based medical school, Boland graduated in 1883, at which time he was also a member of Detroit's Young Men's Christian Association and superintendent of the Sunday school of Bethel African Methodist Episcopal Church.

Boland practiced medicine in Detroit for three years. In 1886 he married a seamstress, Perdita E. Golden, and moved to Virginia, where he received a license to practice from the Board of Medical Examiners on 9 April 1886. He may have been the first African American to take and pass the examination that the new Virginia Board of Medical Examiners administered to new physicians. Boland opened his office in

Hampton and had at least one son before 1891, when he moved to Roanoke. He paid $400 for a corner lot at Rutherford Avenue and Second Street in the black neighborhood of Gainsboro. Boland practiced medicine, built a large two-story house, and amassed a substantial amount of property. In 1912 he opened a new two-story office on Commonwealth Avenue two blocks from his previous address. By the time of his death Boland owned eight rental properties in Roanoke and a farm nearby. His personal property included the belongings of a man of education and prosperous social status: a piano, a valuable library, his medical equipment, and an automobile. Indeed, Boland was said to be the first African American in Roanoke to own a car. He married twice after the death of his first wife, but the name of his second spouse has not been discovered. His third wife was Kate Taliaferro. Boland's two additional sons included Jesse L. Boland, a well-known aviator and later, as Master X, a soothsayer and local celebrity in Richmond.

A man of medium size who wore his hair long, Boland was a leading figure in Roanoke's African American community during a time when the population grew rapidly as the shops and headquarters of the Norfolk and Western Railway attracted people to Roanoke in search of work. He was editor of the *Roanoke Weekly Press* in 1891, but the length of his association with the newspaper is uncertain. Boland was a member of Mount Zion African Methodist Episcopal Church, where his third wife played the organ. She also taught piano in their large house. Robert J. Boland died of chronic nephritis, or Bright's disease, in Roanoke on 16 November 1918 and was buried in that city in Old Lick Cemetery.

Leslie L. Hanawalt, "From Slave to Physician: Robert J. Boland (1850–1918)," *Detroit in Perspective: A Journal of Regional History* 2 (1976): 189–203; Board of Medical Examiners, Minutes and Results of Examinations (1884–1902), 34, RG 37, LVA; Roanoke City directories, 1891–1892, 1895, 1912; information provided by Gladys L. Cox; estate inventory and appraisal in records of Commissioner of Accounts, 13:445, Roanoke City Circuit Court; death date in BVS Death Certificate, Roanoke City; obituary giving erroneous death date of 17 Nov. 1918 in *Richmond Planet*, 22 Nov. 1918.

JOHN R. KERN

BOLDEN, Carrie J. Clarke (ca. 1869–11 April 1973), nurse and civic leader, was born in Wytheville, the daughter of Stephen Clarke, a teacher, and Sibbie Jones Redmond Clarke. She later gave her birth date as 21 March 1884, but she was listed as aged eleven in the 1880 census. Little is known about her parents, one or both of whom may have been born into slavery. After her father died in 1880, her mother worked for a time as a laundress and servant and by 1909 had moved to Philadelphia, where she became a caterer. She encouraged her children to achieve. Clarke's siblings included Stephen H. Clarke, a school principal in Portsmouth for fifty years, and Douchette Redmond Clarke, an Episcopal minister.

On 30 September 1886, giving her age as nineteen, Clarke married thirty-year-old Elias Horace Bolden, the presiding elder for the Wytheville District of the African Methodist Episcopal Church. A clergyman since 1878, he had served in 1884 as supervisor of public schools for African Americans in his hometown of Portsmouth. Bolden must have learned from him, but she also brought talents of her own to their childless marriage. When the AME's Virginia annual conference met at Wytheville in April 1897, the delegates organized the Women's Mite Missionary Society of Virginia and elected Carrie Bolden the first state president.

On 11 July 1902, while serving a church in Newport News, Bolden's husband died. She never remarried. Instead, Bolden entered the Hampton Training School for Nurses, commonly called Dixie Hospital, and graduated in 1904. A year earlier Virginia's professional nurses had obtained legislation requiring that all new nurses pass a written examination in order to be registered in the state. Bolden passed the examination at Norfolk in December 1905. Although not the first black nurse to register (the legislation permitted trained nurses already practicing to register without taking the examination), she was, as best as can be determined, the first to take and pass the examination.

Bolden worked for several years as a private duty nurse in association with local physicians. Nurses were regarded as caregivers to their communities, and she brought talents as a leader and organizer to that role. When members of a social club in Hampton lamented to Bolden just before Christmas 1905 that they were unprepared for the holiday's expenses, she organized a Christmas Savings Club with a dozen members. The plan proved so successful that she organized a similar club the following year in Newport News, her place of residence.

In 1908 several African American physicians of Newport News rented four rooms for a hospital, but it soon closed for lack of funds. Black citizens requiring hospitalization faced a choice between the city jail's infirmary or traveling fifteen miles to Dixie Hospital in Hampton. Bolden's appeal to a women's social club, of which she was a founder and president, to help establish a new hospital resulted in an intensive drive to raise money. Their hard work paid off, and in 1914 a foundation was laid for the facility. Whittaker Memorial Hospital, named for deceased African American physician Robert L. Whittaker, was chartered on 27 May 1914. Impressed by such progress, in March 1915 George Benjamin West, white president of the Citizens and Marine Bank, donated two lots on Twenty-ninth Street between Roanoke and Orcutt Streets in Newport News as the site for the hospital. Despite the failure of efforts to obtain an appropriation from the city council to build and equip the hospital, the organizers carried on, and two years later, on 14 March 1917, Whittaker Memorial Hospital opened to the public. In addition to the hospital, Whittaker Memorial eventually included a tuberculosis sanatorium and a training school for nurses.

In 1916 the Newport News board of education hired Bolden as a school nurse, a post she held until 1949. She served in the elementary schools, the only public schools for blacks in Newport News until 1922, giving physical examinations and testing the students' vision. Alumni remembered her as a small woman with a dignified and serious demeanor, an impression that her white uniform and starched cap reinforced. During the deadly influenza epidemic of 1918 Bolden served without pay as a volunteer nurse at the white Walter Reed High School, which the city designated as an emergency hospital.

Whittaker Memorial Hospital operated at a deficit, and community fund-raising helped keep it open. Bolden was at the forefront of every campaign for money. "Without such a person as Mrs. Bolden," an officer of the hospital later declared, "Whittaker would not be in existence." Her diverse activities in behalf of the hospital ranged from weekly bake sales to organizing a women's auxiliary. For more than forty years Bolden served on the hospital's board of trustees. She was vice president when a new fifty-three-bed hospital was constructed during the 1940s. To honor her long service, a new residence for nurses was named the Carrie J. Bolden Nurses' Home on 29 October 1950.

Remembered as a very private person, Bolden knew her community well and quietly exerted her considerable influence. On 5 February 1913 she was confirmed as a member of the Episcopal Church and became active in Saint Augustine's Church. At some point, possibly to avoid age discrimination within the school system, Bolden began giving her birth date as 21 March 1884. She was actually about eighty years old when she finally retired as a school nurse. Residing during the final years of her long life at the hospital she had steadfastly supported, Carrie J. Clarke Bolden died of heart disease at Whittaker Memorial Hospital on 11 April 1973 and was buried at the Pleasant Shade Cemetery in Hampton.

Census, Wythe Co., 1880; BVS Marriage Register, Wythe Co.; Israel L. Butt, *History of African Methodism in Virginia* (1908), 78, 83, 99, 103, 107, 237; Record of Averages of the Nurse Candidates for Registration in Virginia, State Board of Nursing, RG 37, LVA; Peabody Newspaper Clipping File (microfiche ed.), item 268, nos. 78–83, Hampton; Hampton Training School for Nurses and Dixie Hospital, *Annual Report* (1904/1905): 48; Alexander Crosby Brown, ed., *Newport News' 325 Years* (1946), 229; feature articles in *Newport News Daily Press*, 29 Oct. 1950 (por.), *Newport News Times-Herald*, 30 Oct. 1950, 16 May 1969 (quotation), and *Norfolk Journal and Guide*, Peninsula ed., 4 (por.), 11 Nov. 1950; interviews with Olivia Birchette, Carrie Brown, Florence Crittenden, Inetta Edwards, Ralph Haines, Lillian Lovett, Ruth Thornton, and Julia Tucker; obituaries in *Newport News Daily Press*, 13 Apr. 1973, and *Norfolk Journal and Guide*, 21 Apr. 1973.

PATRICIA E. SLOAN

BOLEN, David Winton (17 August 1850–11 December 1932), member of the Convention of 1901–1902, was born in Carroll County, the son of William B. Bolen and Rebecca Morris Bolen. He grew up on the family farm at Fancy Gap, a mountain community twelve miles south of Hillsville. A devout Methodist faith pervaded the Bolen household, but the strict discipline of that creed did not prevent the boy from enjoying such rural pleasures as swimming and horseback riding. His father died of a fever in June 1862 while serving in the Confederate army, leaving the family nearly destitute. For the next seven years Bolen performed agricultural labor to support his mother, two brothers, and two sisters. Brief stints at public schools and the Hillsville Academy constituted the limits of his formal education, but he compensated for this deficiency through extensive reading at home after chores were completed. Emotional nurture came from his mother, to whom he was devoted, and from his grandfather, John Morris, who lived nearby.

Striving for advancement amid the hardships of the post–Civil War era, Bolen began to teach in neighborhood schools in 1869 and also briefly in Nebraska and West Virginia. He earned additional income during the 1870s as a land surveyor. Meanwhile, he started to read law under the direction of Judge Randall M. Brown, of Hillsville. Bolen was admitted to the bar in February 1875, combining work as an attorney with teaching school for the first two years of his practice. On 21 February 1877 he married Nancy Gage Early, the daughter of a local saddler and harness maker. Both of their children died in infancy.

Although Bolen was still new to the practice of law, in January 1879 the General Assembly elected him to fill the vacant office of judge of Carroll County. He served until the end of the year. Casting his lot with the Democratic Party in its struggles with the coalition of Republicans and Readjusters, Bolen won election to the House of Delegates in 1883 and was reelected two years later. He served on the Committees on Counties, Cities, and Towns and on Propositions and Grievances and chaired the Committee on Enrolled Bills. A Republican rival defeated him in 1887, but Bolen remained active in party politics. From 1887 to 1888 he edited a Demo-cratic weekly, the *Hillsville Virginian,* rallying support that enabled him to return to the House of Delegates in 1889. Bolen served on the Committee on Roads and Internal Navigation and chaired the Committee on Counties, Cities, and Towns. In March 1890 the assembly's Democratic majority rewarded his efforts by electing him judge of the Fifteenth Judicial Circuit, which encompassed Bland, Carroll, Giles, Pulaski, Tazewell, and Wythe Counties.

To this point the political star of Judge Bolen, as he was usually called, had been in the ascendant. On 3 March 1892, however, he resigned his judicial post in order to seek the Democratic nomination in the Fifth Congressional District, only to suffer a resounding defeat at the hands of Claude Augustus Swanson. Bolen also lost an 1895 bid for a state senate seat. In 1901 he won the election to represent Carroll County in the convention that drafted the Virginia Constitution of 1902. Bolen served on the Committee on Organization, the Committee on the Organization and Government of Cities and Towns, and the critically important Committee on the Elective Franchise, which fashioned a set of restrictive voter registration requirements intended to reduce African American voting in Virginia. He missed the final vote on the suffrage provision but voted for adoption of the new constitution. Bolen joined an unsuccessful convention effort to allow the voters to accept or reject the constitution by referendum.

Bolen last figured in Virginia politics in 1904, when he was a presidential elector on the Democratic ticket. Carroll County shifted decisively into the Republican column early in the 1900s, further diminishing the erstwhile jurist's political prospects. Thereafter he devoted most of his energies to private law practice. On 14 March 1912 Bolen gained renewed prominence when one of his clients, the notorious Floyd Allen, joined several kinsmen in a gunfight with lawmen inside the Hillsville courthouse. This well-publicized melee left five people dead and several wounded. Present but unharmed during the shootout, Bolen testified at the ensuing trials, and his evidence played a major role in sending Floyd Allen and his son Claude Swanson Allen to the electric chair.

Bolen was also involved in other, less spectacular activities. From 1895 to 1903 he served as a member—and from 1898 to 1901 as president—of the board of directors of Southwestern State Hospital in Marion. He was a member and sometime chairman of the Hillsville district school board from 1910 to 1922. During World War I Bolen headed the county draft board, provided legal counsel for mobilization efforts, and delivered many patriotic speeches.

Bolen's successful law practice enabled him to purchase a large house and other real estate in Hillsville, but he maintained his permanent residence at the 185-acre farm near Fancy Gap. There he wrote sentimental verse and indulged an interest in local history. The Methodist beliefs of Bolen's childhood soon gave way to a Quaker-tinged Unitarianism. A freethinker in religion and an independent-minded Democrat in politics, he enjoyed the respect of Carroll County and the status of a mountain sage during his final years. David Winton Bolen died on 11 December 1932 and was buried in John Morris Cemetery near Fancy Gap.

Brief biographies in Tyler, *Men of Mark*, 5:39–40, and Bruce, Tyler, and Morton, *History of Virginia*, 6:461; BVS Marriage Register, Carroll Co.; Henry C. Ferrell Jr., *Claude A. Swanson of Virginia: A Political Biography* (1985), 14–15, 61; *Journal of 1901–1902 Convention,* 535; *Convention of 1901–1902 Photographs* (por.); Elmer J. Cooley, *The Inside Story of the World Famous Courtroom Tragedy* [ca. 1962], 44–48, 54–67; Edwin Chancellor Payne, *The Hillsville Tragedy* (1913), 97–99; J. J. Reynolds, *The Allen Gang* (1912), 136–147; samples of Bolen's poetry in W. R. Morris, ed., *"Folk Lore" of Early Settlers of America and Their Ancestral Lineage* (1958), 2:71–87 (por.), 3:241–256; gravestone inscription with birth and death dates in Suzanne Burow, ed., *Cemetery Records of Carroll County, Virginia* (1990), 513; BVS death records give variant birth date of 26 Aug. 1850.

JAMES TICE MOORE

BOLLING, Anna Peyton (30 September 1836–8 February 1919), educator, was born on her father's farm in Amelia County, the daughter of John Peyton Bolling and Anne Field Gilliam Bolling. The family moved to Petersburg in 1842. On 12 May 1855 Bolling joined the Tabb Street Presbyterian Church, to which her parents belonged, and she remained a member until her death almost sixty-four years later.

A very private woman who never married or took part in society, she lived with her mother for most of the time between her father's death in 1861 and her mother's death in 1882.

Bolling may have attended one of the schools for women founded in Petersburg and Richmond late in the antebellum period, but nothing is definitely known about her education. She may have taught in one of the many small private schools in Petersburg until 1868. When the city established its first system of public schools in the autumn of 1868, more than two years before the commonwealth of Virginia created a public school system, the local school board appointed Bolling one of two faculty members of the new Petersburg Public High School. The high school offered a three-year course of study patterned on the curriculum of a Boston preparatory school, and each teacher, including the principal, taught all of the subjects in a given grade. During Bolling's first eight years at the school, the two or three teachers were always under the direction of a male principal, except for a brief interval at the beginning of the 1869–1870 school year when Bolling served as acting principal. During the academic year 1876–1877 she and one other woman constituted the entire full-time faculty of the high school. In July 1877 the school board appointed Bolling principal of Petersburg High School, a post she held for thirty years. A dearth of records from some other jurisdictions makes it not quite certain that she was the first woman to serve as principal of a public high school in Virginia, but she was certainly one of the earliest.

Women teachers were common in Virginia during Bolling's years as principal, especially in the lower grades, but women were not regularly entrusted with administrative responsibilities except in grammar schools. The Educational Association of Virginia, initially composed chiefly of college professors, private school principals, and school superintendents, did not even admit "Lady Teachers" into its ranks until 1875, and then only as associate members not allowed to vote or speak at meetings. Virginia's teachers did not form their own organization until 1890, and published accounts of its annual meetings do not indicate that

Bolling was a member. Indeed, Petersburg's public school teachers seldom participated in teachers' associations during the nineteenth century. Bolling evidently took no part in the summer normal institutes that attracted many public school educators as faculty and students between the 1870s and the 1910s. As a result, she was probably not so well known in Virginia as many women educators of lesser stature in their home communities. In Petersburg, however, Bolling and William Gordon McCabe, principal of the prestigious University School, were regarded as the city's best and most influential teachers.

During Bolling's thirty-nine years at Petersburg High School, the enrollment grew from scarcely 50 to 175, and in 1895 the school moved into a new building. Her retirement in June 1907 marked what was recognized at the time as the end of an era in Petersburg's educational history. The double standard for men and women in the teaching profession persisted, however. Bolling's male successor was offered a starting salary substantially higher than hers had been at the end of thirty years as principal of the high school. A formidable woman with an infectious laugh, Bolling demanded much of, and gave much to, her pupils. Because many former students became teachers and administrators in the Petersburg public school system, she left a long and well-remembered legacy. Twenty years after Bolling's retirement and almost a decade after her death, a large new brick school building in Petersburg was named Anna P. Bolling Junior High School. During her retirement she indulged her fondness for travel, as she may have done during summer vacations while she was still teaching. Anna Peyton Bolling died in Westbrook Sanatorium in Richmond, where she spent her last two years, on 8 February 1919 and was buried in Blandford Cemetery in Petersburg.

Birth date from gravestone; Alexander R. Bolling Jr., *The Bolling Family: Eight Centuries of Growth* (1990), 124; *Manual for the Members of the Tabb Street Presbyterian Church, in Petersburg, Virginia* (1887), 34, 43; *Petersburg Index-Appeal*, 12 July 1877; Petersburg Board of Education, *Annual Report* 2 (1870): 15; transcript of E. Reinhold Rogers's memorial address at the dedication of Anna P. Bolling Junior High School, 15 Feb. 1927, and other information in Henry Buckius Brockwell, "History of Secondary Education in Petersburg, Virginia" (master's thesis, UVA, 1939), esp. 112, 130, 303–306; naming and opening of school reported in *Petersburg Progress-Index*, 1, 15 Feb. 1927, and *Virginia Journal of Education* 20 (1927): 301; obituaries in *Petersburg Evening Progress* and *Richmond News Leader*, both 8 Feb. 1919; funeral described in *Petersburg Progress-Index*, 10 Feb. 1919.

BRENT TARTER

BOLLING, Charles Edward (4 May 1852–22 June 1929), civil engineer, was born at his parents' Bolling Island estate in Goochland County, the youngest of ten children of Thomas Bolling and Mary Louisa Morris Bolling. His mother died giving birth to him, and his eldest sister, Julia Calvert Bolling, took primary responsibility for his care. The deaths of four children and a wife undoubtedly contributed to the occasionally erratic behavior of his father, who after the 1845 death of his own father, William Bolling, had lived apart from his own family at his mother's nearby estate of Bolling Hall. In 1850 Thomas Bolling sold some of his land to pay personal debts.

Charles Bolling obtained some schooling in Hanover County at an academy operated by his uncle Charles Morris. He probably passed the years of the Civil War in relative safety at his home in Goochland County. By 1870 Bolling was living with his eldest sister's family in Nelson County. With the aid of some training as a surveyor and engineer, acquired perhaps from his brother Richard Morris Bolling, a civil engineer, he worked for a short time in Lynchburg before moving to Richmond at the end of 1870 to work as a surveyor for the Chesapeake and Ohio Railroad Company. By 1873 Bolling was an assistant engineer engaged in the construction of the railroad tunnel under Richmond's Church Hill.

On 15 February 1873 Bolling became an assistant to the city engineer. Shortly thereafter, Wilfred Emory Cutshaw put him in charge of building a new, enlarged reservoir at what later became Byrd Park to improve the city's undependable water supply. Work began on 18 March 1874, and water was first distributed from the reservoir on 1 January 1876. Bolling was then instructed to divert water from the old James River and Kanawha Canal to provide power for additional pumps. The pumping system was completed in July 1882, and the handsome new pump house, with its pavilion for dances, became a popular destination for pleasure seekers.

In July 1885 Bolling was promoted to superintendent of the city waterworks. During the next two decades he directed renovations and extensions of the system to meet the city's growing demand for water, and in 1900–1901 he served as president of the American Water Works Association. James River water quality was of particular concern. In addition to problems with pollution as population expanded westward along the river, the water was often turbid and muddy. Bolling developed large settling basins to hold river water until mud and other foreign matter dropped out of it. Work began in 1903, and the basins produced their first clear water on 22 December 1909.

In January 1908 Bolling was promoted to city engineer, a post that was renamed director of public works in 1918. He oversaw the paving of miles of streets, extension of sewer improvements to new subdivisions, and construction of a reinforced concrete bridge across the James River. Bolling learned from experience. In 1912 he published a magazine article in the *American City* advising other city engineers to install underground pipes carefully before paving new roads. He had learned that electrolysis from electric streetcar lines in Richmond had damaged older water pipes buried at shallow depth. Richmond's population more than doubled between 1870 and 1920, and Bolling had a hand in almost all the public works projects that provided services to the growing city during that half century. He retired in 1920 but continued to serve the department as a consulting engineer.

On 12 December 1877 Bolling married Imogen Warwick, of Richmond, but she died on 18 July 1879 at the age of twenty-five. On 17 April 1894 he married Parke Chamberlayne Bagby, the twenty-year-old daughter of George William Bagby, a popular writer, and Lucy Parke Chamberlayne Bagby, a civic leader. They had no children. Bolling lived comfortably and without ostentation. He continued to drive his horse-drawn buggy to and from work late into

the 1920s. Admirers maintained that no man in Richmond had more friends. Bolling and his wife shared a devotion to Confederate memorial associations and to the Confederate Museum (after 1970 the Museum of the Confederacy).

Charles Edward Bolling suffered from arteriosclerosis and died in Richmond on 22 June 1929 following the amputation of an infected leg. He was buried in Hollywood Cemetery in that city. To honor his long service to Richmond, the city council voted to set aside each year an amount equal to his $4,000 per annum salary as a memorial fund to maintain the city's trees. The Great Depression soon made such expenditures impossible, and the fund was discontinued in 1932.

Biographies in Robert A. Brock, *Virginia and Virginians* (1888), 2:769, George H. Whitfield, *Story of the Water Works and Annual Report, 1930* (1930), 66–72, and James R. Barker, comp., *Directors of Public Works for the City of Richmond, Virginia: 1828–1956* (1957), 23–24 (por.); Charles Edward Bolling Papers, VHS; Richard T. Couture and Kay Ackerman, eds., "Bolling-Cabell Letters—1861: The Early Letters of Julia (Juliet) Calvert Bolling to Philip Barraud Cabell," *Goochland County Historical Society Magazine* 12 (1980): 23–35, ibid. 13 (1981): 16–32, and ibid. 14 (1982): 20–33; BVS Marriage Register, Richmond City; Charles E. Bolling, "Installing Underground Pipe Connections Before Paving Roads," *American City* 6 (1912): 498–499; obituaries in *Richmond News Leader,* 22 June 1929, and *New York Times* and *Richmond Times-Dispatch,* both 23 June 1929; editorial tributes in *Richmond News Leader,* 22 June 1929, and *Richmond Times-Dispatch*, 24 June 1929.

CAROLYN H. LEATHERMAN

BOLLING, John (27 January 1677–20 April 1729), merchant, was the only child of Robert Bolling (1646–1709) and his first wife, Jane Rolfe Bolling. His mother died when he was very young, and after his father married Anne Stith in 1681 he acquired five half brothers and two half sisters. He was born and grew up at his father's Kippax plantation in a portion of Charles City County south of the James River that in 1702 became Prince George County. On 29 December 1697 Bolling executed a marriage bond and on that date or shortly thereafter married Mary Kennon, the daughter of Richard Kennon and Elizabeth Worsham Kennon. Their one son and five daughters all married into prominent Virginia families, as had Bolling, his siblings, and their father. John Bolling was the great-grandson of John Rolfe and Pocahontas and the first of the so-called Red Bollings.

In November 1704 Bolling purchased Cobbs plantation, located near the mouth of the Appomattox River in the southern part of Henrico County that is now Chesterfield County. He lived at Cobbs for the remainder of his life. A grandson wrote in a brief family history that Bolling "had a gay, lively and penetrating spirit" and that having "devoted himself to commerce" he "received all the profits of an immense trade with his countrymen, and of one still greater with the Indians." Bolling's mercantile affairs are poorly documented and his principal English business contacts have not been identified, but he often sued creditors for large sums in the Virginia county courts and had frequent dealings and conferences about the Indian trade with William Byrd (1674–1744), whose knowledge of the business was extensive. Byrd employed Bolling as a supply agent for the famous surveying expedition to mark the colony's southern boundary that Byrd led the year before Bolling's death.

Bolling inherited about 5,000 acres of land from his father and subsequently acquired much more. He bequeathed Cobbs plantation and 600 acres to his wife, 1,200 acres each to two daughters, and more than 15,000 acres to his only son. He also left cash gifts of more than £700 and at his death owned many slaves.

Many relevant records have been lost, but Bolling served on the Henrico County Court between at least 1699 and 1714. He was probably also a vestryman of Dale Parish, and he became a captain and later a major of dragoons in the county militia. Bolling served in the House of Burgesses from 1710 to 1718 and again from 1723 until his death. John Bolling died at Cobbs plantation on 20 April 1729 and was buried in the family cemetery there.

Birth record in father's copy of John Purvis, *A Complete Collection of All the Laws of Virginia* (1684), LVA, printed in *WMQ*, 1st ser., 5 (1897): 275–276; death date in Robert Bolling (1738–1775), *Memoirs of the Bolling Family*, trans. and ed. John Robertson Jr. (1868), 3–4 (quotation; por. following 4); marriage date in Henrico Co. Records (1697–1699), transcript, 96; numerous references in records of several counties, in Louis B. Wright and Marion Tinling, eds., *The Secret Diary of William Byrd of Westover, 1709–1712* (1941), and in Wright and Tinling's ed. of Byrd, *London Diary, 1717–1721, and Other Writings* (1958); will in Henrico Co. Deeds, Wills, 1:242–243.

PETER V. BERGSTROM

BOLLING, Leslie Garland (16 September 1898–27 September 1955), sculptor, was born in Surry County, the son of Clinton C. Bolling, a blacksmith, and his first wife, Mary Brown Bolling. He was educated in the county schools and took preparatory classes at Hampton Normal and Agricultural Institute from 1916 until 1918. More study followed at the preparatory Academy Department of Virginia Union University in Richmond between the autumn of 1919 and June 1924, when Bolling graduated. He resided in Richmond for the remainder of his life. On 27 May 1928 he married Julia V. Lightner, a widow and seamstress. She died on 14 June 1943, and on 16 October 1948 Bolling married Ethelyn M. Bailey, a divorced woman then working as a maid in Richmond. Neither marriage produced children.

Bolling began carving wood in 1926 without having had any formal art instruction. He always carved in poplar because of its softness. His basic tool kit consisted of several pocketknives, a scroll saw, and a vise. He roughed out the shape of the figure with his scroll saw and used a pocketknife to concentrate on details. Most of his carvings were between twelve and twenty-four inches high, and they usually depicted a single figure engaged in work or play.

Richmond artist Berkeley Williams Jr. noticed Bolling's carvings at a group exhibition at the Young Women's Christian Association and helped bring Bolling to the attention of the writer and photographer Carl Van Vechten, of New York, who purchased two works, *The Boxer* and *Head of a Woman*, both now owned by Yale University. In November 1932 Bolling displayed several pieces in the second annual exhibition of the work of local artists at the Richmond Academy of Arts, where a patron purchased his *Market Woman*. In 1933 Bolling displayed two sculptures, *Washerwoman* and *Figure Reclining*, and won an award at an exhibition sponsored by the Harmon Foundation, of Washington, D.C., which promoted African

American art and artists. Later that year he submitted four figures—*Salome, Shopper, Portrait Bust,* and *George's Delight*—to an exhibition of works by African American artists sponsored by Howard University and the Association for the Study of Negro Life and History in cooperation with the Harmon Foundation. He exhibited *The Workman* and a second version of *Salome* at the Harmon Foundation in 1935.

In 1934 Bolling showed his work again at the Richmond Academy and at the Valentine Museum in Richmond as part of a series of exhibitions highlighting contributions by minority and ethnic groups to Richmond's history. In January 1935 his one-man show at the Richmond Academy was the first there by a black Virginia artist. Thomas Hart Benton, who was in Richmond to lecture on mural painting, visited the exhibition and announced that he would support Bolling for a Guggenheim Fellowship. That same month the Harmon Foundation filmed and photographed Bolling and other black Richmond artists in preparation for a documentary on African American artists. Bolling's *Workman* was exhibited at the New Jersey State Museum in Trenton in April 1935, and two other works, *Fish Man* and *Mama on Wednesday*, were shown at the fourth annual exhibition of the Richmond Academy of Arts.

In 1936 seven of Bolling's figures, including five depicting activities of the days of the week, appeared in an exhibition of African American art assembled for the Texas centennial celebration. The William D. Cox Gallery in New York City hosted a one-man show of seventeen of Bolling's works in June 1937, including the completed days of the week series. He presented a portrait bust of contralto Marian Anderson to her when she performed in Richmond in 1940 and also carved figures of Eleanor Roosevelt and Franklin Delano Roosevelt, hoping that the first lady would accept them for her art collection. In 1941 Bolling carved an overtly political figure, *Save America*, which depicted an American soldier defending two children against a coiled snake. The piece was the last he exhibited, at the ninth exhibition of the work of Virginia artists at the Virginia Museum of Fine Arts in 1943. Bolling's last identified work, a small figure of the radio personalities Lum and Abner, won third place in a 1942 competition sponsored by *Science and Mechanic* magazine.

Bolling is best remembered for his series of seven figures illustrating daily activities typical of blacks. Each carving was named for a day of the week—*Aunt Monday, Sister Tuesday, Mama on Wednesday, Gossip on Thursday, Cousin on Friday, Cooking on Saturday*—and depicted chores, successively laundry, ironing, sewing, gossiping, scrubbing floors, and cooking. A writer for *Opportunity*, the monthly journal of the National Urban League, speculated in June 1940 that the series showed the workweek of a housewife, but a reviewer in 1934 understood it to depict blacks working as domestic servants in Richmond's white households. Completing the cycle was *Parson on Sunday*, which captured a preacher leaning over his pulpit at the height of his sermon.

Bolling usually applied a light wax to his carvings but used paint infrequently. Critics appreciated his technical mastery as well as the absence of symbolism and sentimentality. Elmer John Tangerman praised Bolling in 1940 for the artistic quality of his work and especially for not sanding the surfaces to remove the tool marks. Julia Sully, art critic for the *Richmond News Leader*, wrote that Bolling's "gift lies in motion, rather than in emotion; in rhythm rather than pattern."

Despite Bolling's success in national exhibitions, wood carving remained a hobby for him. He earned his living in Richmond as a porter, as a letter carrier, and as a utility worker. Nevertheless, national recognition in art circles enabled Bolling to work with community leaders to establish the Craig House Art Center in Richmond. Founded under the auspices of the Works Progress Administration, the center offered instruction in art and art appreciation to African Americans and other minorities. Bolling taught wood-carving techniques at Craig House from its opening in 1938 until it closed three years later. He exhibited there in 1939 and 1940.

Although private collectors in Canada, New York, Washington, and London purchased many of the approximately fifty carvings Bolling exhibited during the decade when his work attracted wide attention, the locations of fewer than ten are now known. The Virginia Museum of Fine Arts owns *Cousin on Friday* from the days of the week series. Leslie Garland Bolling died in New York City on 27 September 1955 and was buried in Woodland Cemetery in Richmond.

BVS Delayed Birth Certificate, Surry Co., 1944; BVS Marriage Register, Richmond City, 1928; Richmond City Marriage Register, 1948; Theresa Dickason Cederholm, ed., *Afro-American Artists: A Bio-Bibliographical Directory* (1973), 28–29; Gary A. Reynolds and Beryl J. Wright, eds., *Against the Odds: African-American Artists and the Harmon Foundation* (1989), 159–162 (por.); Thomas Riggs, ed., *St. James Guide to Black Artists* (1997), 62–63; feature articles in *Richmond Times-Dispatch*, 29 May 1932 (por.), 6 Jan. 1935, 16 May 1940, *Richmond News Leader*, 12 Nov. 1932, 5 Jan. 1935 (quotation), 12 June 1937, and *New York Times*, 20 June 1937; Harmon Foundation Collection, NARA; Harmon Foundation Records, LC; vertical files, VM/RHC; Bolling's works illustrated in *Richmond Times-Dispatch*, 12 Jan. 1933, 22 Apr. 1934, 6 Jan. 1935, 5 Sept., 18 Nov. 1940, 30 Nov. 1941, *American Magazine of Art* 26 (1933): 45–46, and 27 (1934): 38, *Art Digest* (15 Feb. 1935): 23, *Opportunity: The Journal of Negro Life* 15 (1937): 240, *Whittling Works of Leslie Garland Bolling at the Gallery of William D. Cox, Inc.* (1937), Elmer John Tangerman, *Design and Figure Carving* (1940), 241–245, Cedric Dover, *American Negro Art* (1960), 71, James A. Porter, *Modern Negro Art* (1969), 263, Harmon Foundation, Inc., *Negro Artists: An Illustrated Review of Their Achievements* (1971), 35, and Ilene Susan Fort, *The Figure in American Sculpture: A Question of Modernity* (1996), 181–182; obituaries in *Richmond News Leader* and *Richmond Times-Dispatch*, both 30 Sept. 1955.

BARBARA C. BATSON

BOLLING, Mary Marshall Tabb (ca. 1737– by 28 October 1814), merchant, was born probably on the Amelia County estate of her parents, Thomas Tabb and Rebecca Booker Tabb. Her father was one of Virginia's wealthiest merchants, and her standing was further secured on 11 April 1758 when she married Robert Bolling, of Dinwiddie County, scion of another wealthy merchant family. They had two sons and four daughters.

Bolling inherited £10,000 from her father in 1769. Following her husband's death on 24 February 1775, she assumed the management of an enormous estate. The property, much of it in Amelia County, included plantations and scores of slaves. Bolling also managed tobacco warehouses, a gristmill, and much of the land on which the rapidly growing town of Petersburg was built. By 1790 she owned thirty-three of the town's most valuable lots, four of its eight tobacco warehouses, and at least thirty-eight slaves who lived in the town. Bolling paid taxes on more than 10 percent of Petersburg's total taxable wealth.

During the American Revolution Bolling earned a reputation for exceptional mettle. Many residents fled when the British army occupied Petersburg briefly in the spring of 1781. Bolling stood her ground, hoping to save her property from destruction. British officers placed her under house arrest and established their headquarters at Bollingbrook, her residence and the largest house in town. Before they left, the British confiscated her horses and burned her tobacco. Bolling persuaded them to return her slaves, however, and the British spared her warehouses and mill. After a visit to Bollingbrook the following year the marquis de Chastellux pronounced its mistress "lively, active, and intelligent; [she] knows perfectly well how to manage her immense fortune, and what is yet more rare, knows how to make good use of it." This combination of character and wealth would likely have won a man high public office, military honors, or distinction in one of the learned professions—perhaps all three. But however great their talents, women were excluded from all such positions of public authority.

Because she never remarried, Bolling could take advantage of a legal system that authorized single women and widows to exercise control over property. In the thirty-nine years of her widowhood she engaged in almost every kind of transaction. Bolling served as an executrix and a guardian. She bought and sold land, rented out houses and shops, and took debtors to court. Like other cautious mothers Bolling settled a separate estate on one daughter to prevent any risk of the property's being seized by the creditors of her son-in-law. Other transactions reflected the institutional development of Virginia towns in the early republic. Bolling invested heavily in two new banks, petitioned the assembly to empower Petersburg to pave its streets, and in 1787 gave land to the town for its municipal offices. She contributed to a fire company, a theater company, the Episcopal Church, and the Female Orphan Asylum.

A tough-minded proprietor, Bolling, unlike some of her female contemporaries in Petersburg, evidently freed none of her slaves. When she wrote her will not long before her death she distributed her wealth, including the slaves, according to her notions of the varying deserts of her heirs, rewarding some and slighting others. This personalized style of bequest became commonplace among Petersburg women later in the century, but Bolling was unusual in stipulating that heirs who contested her will would be cut off. On or shortly before 28 October 1814 Mary Marshall Tabb Bolling died, probably at Bollingbrook. She was buried in the family graveyard.

Bolling Family Notes, Acc. 29121, LVA, give marriage date, variant birth dates of 23 Jan. 1737 and 23 June 1737, and death date of 28 Oct. 1814; Tabb genealogy in *WMQ*, 1st ser., 13 (1904): 126; father's will in Amelia Co. Will Book, 2X:309–310; husband's will in Bolling Family Records, 1653–1843, LVA; C[harles] C[ampbell], "Reminiscences of the British at Bollingbrook," *Southern Literary Messenger* 6 (1840): 85–88; François Jean, marquis de Chastellux, *Travels in North America in the Years 1780, 1781 and 1782*, trans. Howard C. Rice Jr. (1963), 2:422 (quotation); Suzanne Lebsock, *The Free Women of Petersburg: Status and Culture in a Southern Town, 1784–1860* (1984), 6–7, 81–82, 112–116, 176; will, dated 28 Sept. 1814 and proved 7 Nov. 1814, and estate inventory in Petersburg Will Book, 2:102–104, 122–128; Philip Slaughter, *History of Bristol Parish* (1846), 141–142, gives death date of 14 Oct. 1814; printed funeral invitation, 28 Oct. 1814, giving age at death of seventy-seven, in Harrison Henry Cocke Papers, Southern Historical Collection, UNC.

SUZANNE LEBSOCK

BOLLING, Parke Chamberlayne Bagby (27 February 1874–17 January 1947), leader of the United Daughters of the Confederacy, was born in Richmond, the daughter of George William Bagby and Lucy Parke Chamberlayne Bagby. Her mother and her younger sister Ellen Matthews Bagby both became prominent preservationists. Bagby's father, a noted humorous essayist, died when she was nine, and her mother supported the large family as a clerk in the office of the auditor of public accounts. Lucy Parke Bagby instilled in her children the importance of charitable work and a strong sense of civic responsibility. Educated at the Richmond Seminary, Bagby began a lifetime of work to

help Richmond's less fortunate, working first as a visitor for the City Mission. On 17 April 1894 she married Charles Edward Bolling, a widower twenty-one years her senior who became Richmond's city engineer in 1918. They had no children.

In 1896 Bolling became a charter member of the Richmond chapter of the Virginia Division of the United Daughters of the Confederacy. Her father had served briefly as a private in the 11th Regiment Virginia Infantry before being honorably discharged because of ill health. In this organization devoted to objects "historical, educational, memorial, benevolent, and social," Bolling served on a variety of committees and in a number of offices. During her half century with the UDC she was director of the Lee Memorial Chapel in Lexington and vice president and then president of the Richmond chapter. Bolling also served as president of the Virginia Division of the UDC during 1929–1931 and on the national level as first vice president general and from 1940 to 1942 as president general. She traveled widely as president general and represented the organization in many ways. In 1940 she presented a distinguished service citation to Margaret Mitchell, the author of *Gone With the Wind*.

After her term ended in 1942, Bolling agreed to chair the UDC's Patriotic Activities and Civilian Defense Committee (PACD). Her work as vice chairman of the Richmond Red Cross Home Service Committee during the previous world war and as UDC Relief Committee chairman helped prepare her for this post coordinating the patriotic work of UDC members during World War II. In addition to organizing the efforts of five regional divisions nationwide, Bolling also worked in Richmond's Aircraft Filter Center, staffed the War Savings Bond and Stamp Window at the Miller and Rhoads department store, volunteered at the British War Relief Society, and served in the army's Aircraft Warning Service Reserve. Under her leadership the PACD raised funds to train nurses. Women in the military were a particular concern of Bolling, who supported the opening of a dayroom in Richmond offering hospitality, recreation, and "sympathetic aid" to women serving in all branches of the military.

Bolling's public-speaking skills and organizational abilities earned her positions on the boards of several other associations, including the Friends of Stratford Hall, the Confederate Memorial Literary Society, and the Robert E. Lee Memorial Foundation. She was also active in benevolent organizations, including the Red Cross, the Society for the Prevention of Cruelty to Animals, the Associated Charities of Richmond, the Service League of Grace and Holy Trinity Church, and the Instructive Visiting Nurse Association. Bolling served for years on the board of the IVNA, founded in 1902 to provide nurses to Richmond residents who were unable to pay for medical care. The association made thousands of home visits to those who were ailing, taught classes in hygiene, and organized a clinic for expectant mothers, all without regard to the recipients' race. Through the IVNA's progressive program Bolling hoped that health reform and education could help to end poverty.

Parke Chamberlayne Bagby Bolling died in Richmond at the home of a sister on 17 January 1947, ending a six-month struggle with the painful degeneration of her spinal column. A long editorial tribute in the *Richmond News Leader* lamented the passing of a woman who "personified . . . the Daughters of the Confederacy" and worked to alleviate human distress. Bolling was buried next to her husband, who had died on 22 June 1929, in Hollywood Cemetery.

Letters and diaries in Bagby Family Papers, VHS; BVS Marriage Register, Richmond City; United Daughters of the Confederacy, Virginia Division, *Minutes of the Annual Convention*, 1903 (first quotation on 81), 1925–1931; *Bulletin of the United Daughters of the Confederacy*, 1939–1940, 1942 (por. with Margaret Mitchell, Dec. 1940); *Commonwealth* 7 (Jan. 1940): 21–22; *United Daughters of the Confederacy Magazine* 7 (Apr. 1944): 6 (second quotation); obituaries in *Richmond News Leader* and *Richmond Times-Dispatch* (por.), both 18 Jan. 1947; editorial tribute in *Richmond News Leader*, 18 Jan. 1947 (third quotation).

JENNIFER DAVIS MCDAID

BOLLING, Phillip S. (ca. 1849–18 April 1892), member of the House of Delegates, was born into slavery in Buckingham County, the son of Samuel P. Bolling and Ellen Munford Bolling. About 1857 Samuel P. Bolling purchased the freedom of his mother and possibly himself and other family members from the prominent Eppes family of Buckingham and Cumberland Counties.

By 1870 the family had moved to Cumberland County, where Phillip Bolling worked as a farmer. During the 1860s his father had purchased lots in Farmville and Lynchburg, and in 1872 Bolling acquired the Lynchburg property from him. He also worked at his father's brickyard in Farmville. By 1880 both men had moved to Farmville, where that summer's census identified them as brick masons.

Encouraged by his father's success in local politics, Bolling ran for the House of Delegates in the autumn of 1883 in the district comprising Buckingham and Cumberland Counties. He campaigned as a Readjuster against John O. Reynolds, a Democrat and Funder. On election day the Democrats posted notices at voting precincts asserting that Bolling was a resident of Prince Edward County and therefore ineligible to represent Buckingham and Cumberland Counties. Voters ignored the warning and elected Bolling by 538 votes. Two days later the local electoral board affirmed Bolling's election and refused to consider the Democratic challenge to his eligibility.

The General Assembly convened on 5 December 1883. Bolling was appointed to the Committees on Banks, Currency, and Commerce, on Officers and Offices at the Capitol, and on Rules. The Democrats again challenged his election, however, and on 22 January 1884 the Democratic majority of the Committee of Privileges and Elections rejected evidence that Bolling had been registered to vote in Cumberland County, had voted there from 1881 to 1883, and had served as a juror there as recently as June 1883. Because he had been working at a brick kiln in Prince Edward County before the election, the committee ruled that he was "not an actual resident" of the district from which he had been elected and therefore found him ineligible. Noting that voters had cast ballots for Bolling even after being warned of his ineligibility, the committee declined to award his vacated seat to Reynolds, choosing instead to hold a special election on 13 February 1884. On that date Reynolds lost to Edmund W. Hubard, a Readjuster who had just lost his seat in the Senate of Virginia to another Democratic challenge. A sympathetic newspaper account of the Readjuster victory described Bolling's defeat and Hubard's comeback under the headline "Retribution." Bolling no doubt felt somewhat mollified by this outcome and by his father's election in 1885 to represent Buckingham and Cumberland Counties in the House of Delegates. Because their names were similar and some documents confused P. S. Bolling with his father S. P. Bolling, the election of Phillip S. Bolling to the House of Delegates and his brief service there have not been included in standard references on the participation of African Americans in Virginia politics late in the nineteenth century.

Bolling may have married and had one or more children before his entry into politics, but he was listed as single on the license for his marriage on 31 March 1887 to twenty-four-year-old Harriet T. Jackson, of Prince Edward County. Two months later, on 26 May, he was elected to a two-year term on the Prince Edward County board of supervisors. At that time he was working as a mechanic. Bolling later developed a debilitating mental illness, and on 18 March 1892 he was admitted to the Central Lunatic Asylum in Petersburg suffering from what was diagnosed as acute mania. He was also suffering from lung disease, and on 18 April 1892 Phillip S. Bolling died at the asylum of consumption, or tuberculosis.

Census, Cumberland Co., 1870 (gives age as twenty), Prince Edward Co., 1880 (gives age as thirty-one); BVS Marriage Register, Prince Edward Co. (gives age in 1887 as thirty-five); Election Records, no. 416, RG 13, LVA; *Richmond Dispatch*, 9 Nov. 1883; *Richmond Whig*, 19 Feb. 1884; *JHD*, 1883–1884 sess., 226–230 (quotation on 229); Prince Edward Co. Order Book, 32:449; BVS Death Register, Dinwiddie Co. (gives age in 1892 as forty-three).

DONALD W. GUNTER

BOLLING, Robert (26 December 1646– 17 July 1709), merchant, was the son of John Bolling and Mary Bolling, of Tower Street in the parish of All Hallows, Barking, in London. He arrived in Virginia on 2 October 1660, possibly under the sponsorship of Thomas Batte, who lived near the mouth of the Appomattox River.

By the 1670s Bolling was an established merchant in his own right and the part owner of at least one ship. He acquired his first land in January 1675 and eventually purchased and patented in excess of 5,000 acres on the south side of the Appomattox River. Bolling did well enough in Virginia that he was identified as a gentleman when he joined with William Randolph in patenting more than 600 acres at Warwick Swamp on 20 November 1682. He built his house, called Kippax, near the Appomattox River in the southern part of Charles City County that became Prince George County in 1702.

Bolling became a justice of the peace for Charles City County in June 1688 and ran for the House of Burgesses the same year. Edward Hill defeated him at the poll, but Bolling successfully challenged this outcome and was seated. He represented Charles City County in the assembly again from 1691 to 1692 and in 1699, and he represented Prince George County from 1703 until 1706. Bolling also served as sheriff of Charles City County from 1692 to 1694 and from 1699 to 1700, and by 1704 he was a lieutenant colonel in the militia.

In 1675 Bolling married Jane Rolfe, the only child of Thomas Rolfe, who was the only child of John Rolfe and Pocahontas. Robert Bolling and Jane Rolfe Bolling had one child, the wealthy merchant John Bolling. Jane Rolfe Bolling died not long thereafter, and in 1681 Bolling married Anne Stith and had five more sons and two daughters. Robert Bolling recorded his own birth, immigration, and marital history on a blank leaf in his personal copy of John Purvis's *Complete Collection of All the Laws of Virginia* (1684), sometime after the birth of his last child on 30 November 1700. This memorandum is the only certain surviving proof of his marriage to the granddaughter of John Rolfe and Pocahontas and thus of the status of Robert Bolling's first child, John Bolling, as the first of what later came to be known as the Red Bollings, family members descended from Pocahontas.

During the final months of his life Robert Bolling suffered from what William Byrd

(1674–1744) described as dropsy. Bolling continued to manage his business affairs until he died at Kippax on 17 July 1709. He was buried in the family graveyard at Kippax.

Bolling's copy of Purvis's *Complete Collection*, LVA, with his annotations printed in *WMQ*, 1st ser., 5 (1897): 275–276; *Cavaliers and Pioneers,* vols. 2–3; Louis des Cognets Jr., comp., *English Duplicates of Lost Virginia Records* (1958), 222, 323; officeholding documented in Charles City Co. Order Book (1687–1695), 125, 174, 396, and *Journals of House of Burgesses, 1659/60–1693* and *1702/3–1712*; Robert Bolling (1738–1775), *Memoirs of the Bolling Family*, trans. and ed. John Robertson Jr. (1868), por. opp. 3; illness and death documented in Louis B. Wright and Marion Tinling, eds., *The Secret Diary of William Byrd of Westover, 1709–1712* (1941), 8, 60; inscription from gravestone, which was moved to Blandford Cemetery, Petersburg, in 1858, transcribed on 13 May 1837 in diary of William Bolling, VHS, and printed in Edward Duffield Neill, *Virginia Carolorum: The Colony under the Rule of Charles the First and Second* (1886), 416.

JOHN FREDERICK DORMAN

BOLLING, Robert (17 August 1738–21 July 1775), writer, was born at Varina in Henrico County, the son of John Bolling (1700–1757) and Elizabeth Blair Bolling and a great-great-grandson of Pocahontas and John Rolfe. In 1751 his father sent him to the Free Grammar School of Queen Elizabeth in Wakefield, England, which a number of other Virginia boys attended. Bolling excelled in languages. On his way back to Virginia he stopped off in London and on 31 December 1755 was admitted to the Middle Temple for legal studies. Bolling returned to Virginia the next year, arriving at Yorktown on 16 April 1756. For a year and a half he studied law under Benjamin Waller in Williamsburg.

After his father died in 1757, Bolling lived at his father's Chesterfield County plantation, Cobbs, until the middle of 1760, when he built a house called Chellow, or Chellowe, at his plantation in the portion of southern Albemarle County that became Buckingham County in 1761. From 12 January until 16 September 1760 Bolling courted Anne Miller, a distant cousin. His courtship journal, "A Circumstantial Account," and the poems he wrote provide a unique view of courtship among the eighteenth-century Virginia gentry. The romance ended when Miller sailed to Scotland with her father; she later married Sir Peyton Skipwith.

On 5 June 1763 Bolling married Mary Burton, of Northampton County. She died on 2 May 1764, two days after the birth of their daughter. Almost fourteen months later, on 31 May 1765, Bolling posted a marriage bond in Amherst County and married Susanna Watson on that day or early in June. They had two sons and two daughters.

At the first election after Buckingham County was formed, the voters chose Bolling for the House of Burgesses. He attended the assembly of 1761–1765 regularly and was appointed to the prestigious Committee on Propositions and Grievances in 1762. Assuming that the important assembly business was concluded, he left to be married before the last session adjourned, thereby missing the famous meeting of the House of Burgesses on 29 May 1765 when Patrick Henry presented the Virginia Resolves against the Stamp Act. Bolling either did not stand for reelection in the summer of 1765 or was defeated.

Bolling became embroiled in several controversies. He heard George Whitefield preach at Bristol Parish in Blandford in April 1765 and satirized his revivalistic preaching. Later, in Alexander Purdie and John Dixon's *Williamsburg Virginia Gazette* for 20 June 1766, Bolling precipitated a major crisis by questioning whether three members of the General Court had shown partiality in bailing their friend John Chiswell, who had been arrested and charged with murder. Writers hotly debated the question in the newspapers. William Byrd (1728–1777), one of the judges who allowed Chiswell bail, sued Bolling for libel. On 16 October 1766 Lieutenant Governor Francis Fauquier, presiding at a session of the General Court, instructed a grand jury to "punish the Licentiousness of the Press," but the jury refused to indict. Byrd subsequently challenged Bolling to a duel, but a few hours before the duel was to take place both men were arrested and jailed. After being bound over to keep the peace they were released. Bolling was again involved in legal troubles in 1771. His youngest brother, Archibald Bolling, sued him, believing that he should have received the property that their brother Edward Bolling, who died in 1770, had left instead to Robert

Bolling. Archibald Bolling's attorney, George Wythe, and Robert Bolling's attorney, Thomas Jefferson, prepared exhaustive statements of the case, both of which survive. Jefferson's argument remains one of the best examples of his abilities as a lawyer.

Bolling cultivated grapes, made wine on his estate in Buckingham County, and wrote a dissertation on wine making, a portion of which appeared in Purdie and Dixon's *Williamsburg Virginia Gazette* for 25 February 1773. The House of Burgesses awarded him £50 sterling a year for five years beginning in 1773 "in Order to enable him to prosecute his scheme of cultivating Grapes, for the making of Wine."

Bolling is best known as a writer. He published more poetry than any other colonial American between 1759 and his death. His poems appeared in the Williamsburg newspapers on many occasions, such as on the arrival of Governor Botetourt in 1768, and were of several types, including a long elegy in John Dixon and William Hunter's *Williamsburg Virginia Gazette* of 20 May 1775 on the deaths of Virginia militiamen at the Battle of Point Pleasant the previous October. Bolling was probably the greatest student of Italian literature in colonial America, and he wrote poetry in Italian, French, and Latin as well as in English. His verse ranged through the usual genres of eighteenth-century popular poetry but also included some extraordinary pieces, such as the amazingly grotesque poem "Neanthe" (ca. 1763), which reflected elements of Italian anti-Petrarchan traditions, colonial Virginia folklore, and English Hudibrastic poetry. In the earliest appreciation of Bolling's poetry, Pierre Étienne Du Ponceau extravagantly judged him "one of the greatest poetical geniuses that ever existed." Bolling also wrote a brief family history, which was translated from the original French and published in Richmond in 1868 as *Memoir of a Portion of the Bolling Family in England and Virginia*. It recorded his descent from the immigrant Robert Bolling and the granddaughter of Pocahontas.

In many other ways typical of the late colonial Virginia gentry, Bolling served on the Buckingham County Court from its creation in 1761 until his death and by 1774 was the second-ranking member. Against his wishes he was appointed sheriff of Buckingham County in 1765, and he was a colonel of the Buckingham County militia by 1773. Bolling was elected to represent his county in the Virginia Convention of July–August 1775. He was present in Richmond on 17 July 1775 for the convention's opening. Four days later, on 21 July 1775, Robert Bolling died suddenly at Richmond, perhaps of a heart attack. "Poor Bob. Bolling has run his race," one of the delegates wrote, "adieu to Burgundy."

Biography in J. A. Leo Lemay, ed., *Robert Bolling Woos Anne Miller: Love and Courtship in Colonial Virginia, 1760* (1990), 1–43, which also contains courtship journal (MS at W&M) and poems; Bolling gave 17 Aug. 1738 birth date in his commonplace book (MS copy at UVA, p. 21), but date of 28 Aug. 1738 in Bolling, *Memoir*, 5, indicates that at some point he corrected for the calendar change of 1751; Amherst Co. Marriage Bonds; Bolling's MS volume on vineyards and two volumes of belletristic materials and letters, Huntington; several MS songs, Hubard Papers, Southern Historical Collection, UNC; Lemay, "Robert Bolling and the Bailment of Colonel Chiswell," *Early American Literature* 6 (1971): 99–142 (first quotation on 115); Edward Dumbauld, *Thomas Jefferson and the Law* (1978), 94–120; Bernard Schwartz, Barbara Wilcie Kern, and R. B. Bernstein, *Th: Jefferson and Bolling v. Bolling: Law and the Legal Profession in Pre-Revolutionary America* (1997); *Williamsburg Virginia Gazette* (Purdie and Dixon), 11 Mar. 1773 (second quotation); Lemay, "A Calendar of American Poetry in the Colonial Newspapers and Magazines and in the Major English Magazines Through 1765," *Proceedings of the American Antiquarian Society* 80 (1970): 71–222, 353–469; Philip Slaughter, *History of Bristol Parish, Va.,* 2d ed. (1879), 23–26, prints satire of Whitefield; Lemay, "Southern Colonial Grotesque: Robert Bolling's 'Neanthe,'" *Mississippi Quarterly* 35 (1982): 97–126; Robert D. Arner, ed., "The Muse of History: Robert Bolling's Verses on the Norfolk Inoculation Riots of 1768–1769," in *Early American Literature and Culture: Essays Honoring Harrison T. Meserole*, ed. Kathryn Zabelle Derounian-Stodola (1992), 165–183; Du Ponceau quotation in *Columbian Magazine, or Monthly Miscellany* 2 (1788): 211–212; quotation on death in George Gilmer to Thomas Jefferson, 25 July 1775, in *Jefferson Papers*, 1:238; death notices in *Williamsburg Virginia Gazette* (Pinkney), 27 July 1775, ibid. (Purdie), 28 July 1775, and ibid. (Dixon and Hunter), 29 July 1775.

J. A. Leo Lemay

BOLLING, Samuel P. (10 January 1819–8 February 1900), member of the House of Delegates, was born into slavery in Cumberland County, the son of Olive Bolling. The identity of his father, an African American, is not known.

The Bollings were owned by the prominent Eppes family. He may have been a body servant of the Buckingham County physician Willie J. Eppes. Bolling also became an able mechanic and frequently supervised the work of other slaves. Such was his skill at building and farm management that Eppes frequently permitted him to hire out to other slaveholders. By 1857 Bolling had reportedly saved enough money that he and his brother were able to purchase their mother's freedom. Bolling is also said to have purchased his own freedom before the Civil War, but his name does not appear in Cumberland County's free population census of 1860.

At an undetermined date Bolling married Ellen Munford, of Halifax County, North Carolina. The eldest of their two sons and four daughters, Phillip S. Bolling, was born about 1849, and the last was born about 1864. Hardworking and thrifty, Bolling began to acquire property after the Civil War. In 1866 he obtained two lots on Madison Street in Farmville from John W. Eppes. Bolling eventually added five other pieces of property in Farmville, and in 1867 he bought a lot in Lynchburg. In 1874 he purchased an interest in 602 acres of farmland in Cumberland County, and by 1878 he had clear rights to the property, where he later raised tobacco. Bolling eventually amassed more than 1,000 acres in Cumberland County.

The 1870 census shows Bolling and his family living in Cumberland County. He was working as a carpenter. He had established a brickyard in nearby Farmville by 1874 and soon was manufacturing three widely marketed varieties of brick. Bolling's business eventually employed about fifteen workers and operated six months of the year, making from 200,000 to 300,000 bricks annually. He constructed many of the buildings in Farmville and the surrounding countryside, and by 1880 he and his family, including his mother, had moved to a house on Madison Street in Farmville. Bolling's wife was not enumerated in that year's census and may have died by that time.

Bolling's fame as a farmer, builder, and brick maker spread. His name appeared on the front page of the *Cleveland Gazette* in a 23 October 1886 article describing the advances of African Americans in business. The article estimated that the value of his brick-making operation and fine country house was $40,000. When Bolling composed his will in 1889 his estate included a house and three lots in Farmville and the 600-acre farm and house in Cumberland County, plus another 100 acres and a dwelling in the county at which one of his sons then resided. Such industry was characteristic of the family. Bolling's brother was reportedly a successful builder in the Lynchburg area during the 1870s and 1880s.

About 1880 Bolling joined the Readjusters, who proposed to scale down the principal and interest to be paid on the antebellum state debt in order to pay for the new public school system and other public projects. Comprising a fragile alliance of poor whites, Republicans, African Americans, and a few disgruntled Conservatives, the Readjuster Party attempted to expand its appeal by promising blacks a greater role in the state's affairs. Bolling became active at the county level, working at the polls as an election judge from 1880 to 1882 and in 1884 and as election commissioner in 1885.

In May 1883 Bolling ran as a Readjuster and won a one-year term on the Cumberland County board of supervisors. His election provoked criticism from the Democratic *Farmville Journal,* which complained that he lacked adequate education to manage the financial affairs of the county competently. Nevertheless, the voters reelected Bolling supervisor in May 1884. He also encouraged his sons' political activities. Phillip S. Bolling was elected to the House of Delegates from Buckingham and Cumberland Counties in 1883, although he soon lost his seat on a technicality, and in 1883 and 1884 Lewis R. Bolling served as an election judge.

In October 1885 Bolling campaigned for his son's former seat in the House of Delegates from Buckingham and Cumberland Counties. Although the Democrats had surged back into power, Bolling narrowly defeated his Democratic opponent by 176 votes. He served on three standing committees: Claims, Manufactures and Mechanic Arts, and Retrenchment and Economy. Although Readjuster power was ebbing, Bolling still enjoyed the support of the party's leader, William Mahone. In 1887 Bolling ran for the state senate seat representing Amelia, Cumberland, and Prince Edward Counties. In July he wrote to Mahone that he did not think his opponent, Nathaniel M. Griggs, another African American, stood any chance. By August, however, Bolling was complaining that "they are bleeding me on every turn" but that given enough money he could prevail. Mahone unexpectedly threw his support to Griggs, but Bolling stuck it out, campaigning as an Independent Republican. Griggs beat him by a vote of 2,740 to 1,513. Bolling worked in behalf of John Mercer Langston's successful 1888 congressional campaign, but he never again sought public office.

In his later years Bolling sold part of his property in Cumberland County to the area's poorer African Americans. He and his daughters also contributed land and money for a normal and industrial school. Later named in Bolling's memory, the school was situated on land near where he had once worked as a slave. Bolling was also active in the Mount Nebo Baptist Church, serving as deacon, trustee, and treasurer. His daughter Eliza Bolling was well known in Cumberland and Prince Edward Counties for her efforts to promote Booker T. Washington's philosophy of self-help and self-sufficiency. An 1881 graduate of Hampton Normal and Agricultural Institute who taught at Tuskegee Institute in Alabama from 1890 to 1891, she operated small rural schools around the Bolling farm for little or no pay while helping to manage her father's tobacco farm and assisting with the brickyard business.

In December 1899 Bolling became ill, and although he experienced little pain he soon became too weak to stand or feed himself. On 8 February 1900 Samuel P. Bolling died at his Cumberland County farm. The funeral service was conducted at the farm, and he was buried there.

Brief biographies in Jackson, *Negro Office-Holders*, 4 (por. on 68), and *Norfolk Journal and Guide*, 8 Feb. 1947; birth and death dates in Eliza Bolling to H. B. Frissell, 9 Feb. 1900, Eliza Wayles Bolling correspondence in Student Records, Hampton; Bolling was mentioned but not named in W. E. B. Du Bois, "The Negroes of Farmville, Virginia: A Social Study," *U.S. Bureau of Labor Statistics Bulletin* 14 (1898): 23; Bolling letters in William Mahone Papers, Duke (quotation in Bolling to Mahone, 6 Aug. 1887); activities as election judge documented in Warrant Receipt Stub Books, 1879–1882 and 1884–1887, Cumberland Co. Board of Supervisors Records; political activities documented in *Richmond Daily Whig*, 29 May 1883, 6, 9 Nov. 1885, *Richmond Daily Dispatch*, 31 Aug. 1883, 21 Oct., 9 Nov. 1887, and *Petersburg Daily Index-Appeal*, 29 Oct. 1887; Election Records, nos. 19, 23, RG 13, LVA; property transactions recorded in Cumberland Co., Lynchburg City, and Prince Edward Co. Deed Books; Eliza W. Bolling autobiographical statement, *Twenty-Two Years' Work of the Hampton Normal and Agricultural Institute* (1893), 158; *Southern Workman* 57 (1928): 384; Prince Edward Co. Will Book, 16:468; obituaries in *Farmville Herald*, 16 Feb. 1900, and *Richmond Planet*, 24 Feb. 1900.

LYNDA J. MORGAN

BOLLING, Stith (28 February 1835–1 November 1916), Republican Party leader, was born in Lunenburg County, the son of John Stith Bolling and Mary Thomas Irby Bolling. He grew up on his father's farm and was educated at Mount Lebanon Academy before moving to Richmond at age nineteen to become a clerk in a store. The following year he and two brothers founded a wholesale grocery and commission business, which they operated until the summer of 1861. On 9 May 1860 Bolling married Cornelia Scott Forrest, of Lunenburg County. They had three daughters and one son.

On 7 June 1861 Bolling enlisted as a sergeant in the Lunenburg Light Dragoons, which became Company G of the 9th Regiment Virginia Cavalry. He was commissioned a lieutenant on 28 April 1862 and promoted to captain on 17 January 1863. Later that year he was detailed to Brigadier General William Henry Fitzhugh Lee's staff as acting assistant adjutant general, and in 1864 he was detached to brigade headquarters. At one time Bolling led the largest cavalry company in Major General James Ewell Brown Stuart's command, and at another he commanded the 9th Cavalry's fourth squadron of sharpshooters. During the war Bolling sustained six wounds, the most serious being a head injury received at Morton's Ford on 11 October 1863, after which he required three months of convalescence before returning to duty. He refused to surrender with the remainder of the Army of Northern Virginia at Appomattox Court House and led his troops through the lines in a futile attempt to join General Joseph E. Johnston in North Carolina. Soon realizing that further warfare was impossible, however, Bolling surrendered and was paroled on 15 April 1865.

Bolling returned to the family farm in Lunenburg County. On 6 July 1869 he was elected to the House of Delegates. He joined a coalition of Conservatives and moderate Republicans in opposition to the Radical Republicans and chaired the Committee on Public Property. Bolling ran for reelection as a Conservative in 1871. He lost by a margin of eighty-two votes to George M. Jennings, an African American and Radical Republican, but the polling was conducted with such flagrant disregard for the law that the House of Delegates refused to seat either candidate and ordered a new election, which Bolling won on 20 February 1872. He served for the remainder of the session in the spring of 1872 and in the regular session in the winter of 1872–1873 but did not receive any standing committee assignments.

In 1870 the governor appointed Bolling a brigadier general of the militia, and in 1875 Bolling became an inspector general of tobacco in Petersburg. He moved to Petersburg and lived there for the remainder of his life. He followed his fellow townsman William Mahone into the Readjuster movement later in the decade and attended the February 1879 convention in Richmond that founded the Readjuster Party. Bolling campaigned for the Readjusters during the 1880s, and in 1882 Governor William Evelyn Cameron, another Petersburg Readjuster, named him to the board of directors of the Central Lunatic Asylum. Bolling served as the board's first president. After the Readjuster Party collapsed, Bolling became a Republican. He ran unsuccessfully for mayor of Petersburg in 1888 and as a Republican candidate for presidential elector that same year. For the next two decades he regularly played a prominent role in the party's state conventions and on the campaign trail. In recognition of his leadership in the party, Republican presidents twice made Bolling postmaster of Petersburg, from 1882 to 1885 and from 1889 to 1913.

Bolling was a proprietor of the Oaks Tobacco Company in Petersburg. He belonged to the Tobacco Exchange, and he served for eight years as president of the Petersburg Tobacco Association and for several years as vice president of the Petersburg Chamber of Commerce. He also presided over Petersburg's school board and was active in several fraternal organizations. Bolling's special interest in Confederate veterans' groups extended to command in Petersburg of the A. P. Hill Camp of the United Confederate Veterans, service for several years as commander of the 1st Brigade, Virginia Division, of the UCV's Army of Northern Virginia Department, election as grand commander of the Virginia Division on 12 October 1899, and a stint as major general of the Virginia Division from 1907 to 1913. His sustained popularity among Confederate veterans was all the more remarkable considering his active role in the Republican Party. Stith Bolling died of bronchitis and nephritis at his home in Petersburg on the evening of 1 November 1916 and was buried two days later in a local cemetery.

French Biographies; Henry and Spofford, *Eminent Men*, 401–402; Robert A. Brock, *Virginia and Virginians* (1888), 2:637–638; Bolling letters in William Mahone Papers, Duke; Lunenburg Co. Marriage Register; Compiled Service Records; Robert K. Krick, *9th Virginia Cavalry* (1982), esp. 58; *Richmond Daily Whig*, 10, 11 Nov. 1871, 21 Feb. 1872; *JHD*, 1871–1872 sess., 31, 59–60, 72, 204, 215; James Tice Moore, *Two Paths to the New South: The Virginia Debt Controversy, 1870–1883* (1974); William D. Henderson, *Gilded Age City: Politics, Life and Labor in Petersburg, Virginia, 1874–1889* (1980); *Confederate Veteran* 8 (1900): 4 (por.); BVS Death Certificate, Petersburg; obituaries in *Petersburg Daily Index-Appeal*, 1 Nov. 1916, *Petersburg Daily Progress* and *Richmond Times-Dispatch*, both 2 Nov. 1916, and *Confederate Veteran* 26 (1918): 32.

Donald W. Gunter

BOLLING, William (26 May 1777–16 July 1845), educator of the deaf, was the youngest of at least four sons and six daughters of Thomas Bolling and Elizabeth Gay Bolling. His elder brother William Gay Bolling and three of his sisters died early in their childhood. Bolling was born at his father's Cobbs plantation in Chesterfield County and educated there by private tutors.

Between his marriage and his death forty-seven years later Bolling resided at one of his family's plantations, Bolling Hall in Goochland

County. He owned between seventy-five and a hundred slaves and paid taxes on approximately 3,000 acres of land. He served for most of his adult life on the vestry of Saint James Northam Parish and frequently attended the conventions of the Episcopal Church in Virginia. Bolling was a captain in the Goochland County militia during the War of 1812, took the field briefly during the British invasion in 1814, and subsequently became a colonel. He also served for many years as presiding justice of the Goochland County Court.

Deafness afflicted Bolling's family. His parents had been first cousins, and two of his brothers and one of his sisters were deaf. Beginning in 1771 their father sent them to the Braidwood Academy in Edinburgh, Scotland, where they remained until 1783 and at considerable expense to the family learned to speak, read, and write. As the only hearing male of his generation to reach adulthood, William Bolling became the head of the family. His marriage on 23 February 1798 to his first cousin Mary Randolph allowed a shared recessive gene for deafness to assert itself again, and of their two sons and three daughters, William Albert Bolling and Mary Bolling were deaf.

Rather than send his son abroad, William Bolling arranged in 1812 for John Braidwood, who had immigrated to the United States, to tutor him. Braidwood was the grandson of the founder of the Braidwood Academy and had been its director for two years, but he was an alcoholic and so deeply in debt that Bolling had to discharge the obligations in order to keep him out of prison. In 1815 Bolling and Braidwood opened a small school for the education of the deaf at Cobbs. William Albert Bolling and four or five other deaf students attended this first American school founded with the objective of teaching deaf students to speak, read, and write. It closed only a year later, however, in part because of the high financial cost to Bolling and the small number of paying students, but also because of Braidwood's character flaws and inability to manage his business affairs. Nonetheless, Bolling's patronage of Braidwood marked a turning point in attitudes toward the education of the deaf in American society.

William Bolling died at Old Point Comfort on 16 July 1845 and was buried in the family cemetery at Bolling Hall.

Birth and death dates on gravestone; William Bolling Papers, Duke; William Bolling diaries and plantation records, VHS; family history in Thomas Bolling diary and George Harrison Sanford King Papers, VHS; Henrico Co. Marriage Bonds; Elie Weeks, "Bolling Hall," and Richard T. Couture, "Bolling Island," *Goochland County Historical Society Magazine* 3 (spring 1971): 26–31 and 4 (autumn 1972): 25–31; Betty Miller Unterberger, "The First Attempt to Establish an Oral School for the Deaf and Dumb in the United States," *JSH* 13 (1947): 556–566; John Vickrey Van Cleve and Barry A. Crouch, *A Place of Their Own: Creating the Deaf Community in America* (1989), 21–28; obituary, with incorrect death date of 17 July 1845, in *Richmond Enquirer*, 22 July 1845.

BARRY A. CROUCH

BOLTON, Channing Moore (24 January 1843–6 December 1922), civil engineer, was born in Richmond, the son of James Bolton, a surgeon and ophthalmologist, and Anna Maria Harrison Bolton. He was educated in private schools in Richmond and matriculated at the University of Virginia in 1860, where he took Latin, French, and a mathematics course that included surveying.

Bolton entered Confederate service in 1861 and spent the first year of the war helping lay out the defenses around the city of Richmond. He worked as a surveyor in 1862 and became resident engineer during construction of the forty-eight-mile Piedmont Railroad between Danville and Greensboro, North Carolina. In the retreat from Gettysburg in July 1863 Bolton assisted in the construction and subsequent demolition of a pontoon bridge over the Potomac River that enabled the Confederate army to elude pursuing Northern forces. He was commissioned a second lieutenant in the 1st Regiment Confederate Engineer Troops on 6 April 1864, with the commission to date from 29 March of that year, and he remained with the Army of Northern Virginia until the war ended. Frequent references to him after the war as Major Bolton came after he won the rank of major in the United Confederate Veterans.

Bolton began his career in civil engineering as surveyor and engineer during the construction of the Clover Hill Railroad near Richmond.

During 1866 and 1867 he directed the construction of a 600-foot tunnel under Gamble's Hill in Richmond that connected the Richmond and Danville and the Richmond, Fredericksburg, and Potomac Railroads. Bolton worked from 1867 to 1869 as resident engineer of the Louisville, Cincinnati, and Lexington Railroad, and he held the same post for the Chesapeake and Ohio Railroad from 1869 to 1874, during which he participated in the surveying and construction of a railroad line through the mountains between Covington and White Sulphur Springs, worked on other construction projects in western Virginia and West Virginia, and located the route for the line between Richmond and Newport News. During 1872 and 1873 he supervised the construction of a tunnel 4,000 feet in length under Church Hill in Richmond.

From 1876 to 1879 Bolton was in charge of the construction of a canal around the cascades of the Columbia River in Oregon, and he conducted surveys of the entrances to Coos Bay and the Coquille River. He was president of the Richmond City Street Railway in 1879 and 1880 and at the same time supervised construction of a line from Richmond to Lynchburg for the Richmond and Alleghany Railroad. During the next two years he lived in Greenville, Mississippi, serving as engineer and superintendent of the Greenville, Columbus, and Birmingham Railroad. Bolton rejoined the Richmond and Danville in 1882, first as its chief engineer and subsequently as chief engineer of its successor, the Southern Railway Company. He was elected to the American Society of Civil Engineers in 1888 and lived in Washington, D.C., until 1895.

Bolton retired in 1895 and moved to a farm near Charlottesville, where he invested in several businesses. He became president of the Piedmont Real Estate and Loan Company when it was incorporated in 1904, and he served as president of the Charlottesville Canning Company, a director of the Charlottesville Ice Company, and a member of the board of the Jefferson National Bank. In 1906 Bolton supervised the construction of the Church of Our Savior, a small stone Episcopal church at his farm, and he served as president of the local street railway, the Charlottesville and Albemarle

Railway, from 1902 to 1908 and again from 1912 to 1913. In 1907, probably because of his experience with the two Richmond railroad tunnels, he worked briefly for the Northern Pacific and the Chicago, Milwaukee, and Saint Paul Railroads in Montana on the construction of two tunnels through the Rocky Mountains.

Bolton married Lizzie Calhoun Campbell on 17 February 1874. They had two daughters before she died on 6 October 1889. On 6 June 1894 he married Alma Ann Baldwin. They had one daughter and one son. Channing Moore Bolton died in Charlottesville on 6 December 1922 and was buried in Hollywood Cemetery in Richmond.

Tyler, *Encyclopedia,* 3:290–291 (por.); Henry Carrington Bolton and Reginald Pelham Bolton, *The Family of Bolton in England and America, 1100–1894: A Study in Genealogy* (1895), 403–404 and chart opp. 397; Compiled Service Records; Bolton's description of 1873 Church Hill tunnel project and his technical drawings in Henry S. Drinker, *Tunneling, Explosive Compounds, and Rock Drills,* 2d ed., rev. (1882), 581–588, 664, 704, 737–738; Albert E. Walker, ed., "Charlottesville Virginia: 'The Athens of the South,'" *Charlottesville Daily Progress Historical and Industrial Magazine* (June 1906): 16, 18, 24; Jefferson Randolph Kean, "'Forward is the Motto of the Day': Electric Street Railways in Charlottesville, 1893–1936," *Magazine of Albemarle County History* 37/38 (1979/1980): 114, 119–132, 166, 169; obituaries in *Charlottesville Daily Progress,* 6 Dec. 1922, and *Richmond Times-Dispatch,* 7 Dec. 1922; memorial in *Transactions of the American Society of Civil Engineers* 86 (1923): 1633–1635 (gives variant death date of 11 Dec. 1922).

MARTIN S. LANE

BOLTON, James (5 June 1812–15 May 1869), physician, was born in Savannah, Georgia, the son of John Bolton and his second wife (and cousin) Sarah Bolton Bolton. He lived in Savannah until his father, a successful merchant, moved the family to Jamaica, New York. Bolton earned an A.B. from Columbia College in 1831 and an A.M. from the same institution in 1835. He received an M.D. in 1836 from the College of Physicians and Surgeons, then an independent institution but subsequently merged with Columbia. During his training Bolton served as a clinical assistant to Valentine Mott, an eminent surgeon, and he studied ophthalmology and otolaryngology under John Kearney Rodgers.

Bolton married Anna Maria Harrison, of Fredericksburg, on 3 October 1838 and moved to Richmond. Of their eight sons and two daughters, three sons died in infancy. The eldest surviving son was Channing Moore Bolton, a civil engineer. James Bolton attended the Protestant Episcopal Theological Seminary in Alexandria and was ordained in 1845, but after serving briefly as pastor of Saint Luke's Chapel in Richmond he resumed his medical career.

Bolton's association with Rodgers had led to an interest in eye diseases at a time when ophthalmology was not a separate specialty but part of a general surgeon's practice. His first important professional publication was *A Treatise on Strabismus, with a Description of New Instruments Designed to Improve the Operation for its Cure, in Simplicity, Ease, and Safety, Illustrated by Cases* (1842). Strabismus produced chronic squinting resulting from the inability to focus clearly because of an imbalance in the strengths of the eye muscles. The *Treatise* was one of the earliest American reports of successful surgery for this disorder. Bolton published more than fifteen medical papers during the 1840s and 1850s. His articles describing his employment of ether and chloroform during surgery are credited with encouraging their use by physicians concerned about the safety of anesthetics.

Bolton was an active professional who also assumed civic responsibilities. He was one of the physicians who opened Bellevue, Richmond's first private hospital, in Church Hill in June 1854, and he was a founder of the Medico-Chirurgical Society of Richmond, serving as the first treasurer in 1852. Bolton was also a member of the Medical Society of Virginia, an editor of its official organ, the *Stethoscope*, from 1854, and president of the society in 1857–1858. His presidential address, "Origin of the Negro," dealt with the then-controversial question of whether Africans and Europeans belonged to the same species. The text was destroyed in a fire before it could be published. Bolton also joined the American Medical Association and served on several of its committees. An early advocate of public health measures, he presented papers and spoke on issues such as the elimination of cholera and the need to require the labeling of the ingredients of "secret nostrums."

Although Bolton opposed secession until the middle of April 1861, he was commissioned a surgeon in the Confederate army at the end of May 1862 and served at various posts in Richmond and Fredericksburg. He was in charge of the hospital at Howard's Grove that received wounded soldiers during the Seven Days' Battles near Richmond in 1862. Bolton also served on the board of surgeons that attended wounded officers in private quarters in Richmond. During the war he became one of the first proponents of external fixation for long bone fractures, and he published an important article on his method in the *Confederate States Medical and Surgical Journal* in April 1864.

Following the war James Bolton resumed his private medical practice in Richmond until his death from Bright's disease in Albemarle County on 15 May 1869. He was buried in Hollywood Cemetery in Richmond.

L. Laszlo Schwartz, "James Bolton (1812–1869): Early Proponent of External Skeletal Fixation," *American Journal of Surgery* 66 (1944): 409–413; G. E. Arrington Jr., "James Bolton, Surgeon-Oculist: His Place in the History of Ophthalmology," *Virginia Medical Monthly* 87 (1960): 479–490 (por.); Henry Carrington Bolton and Reginald Pelham Bolton, *The Family of Bolton in England and America, 1100–1894: A Study in Genealogy* (1895), 396–399; Wyndham B. Blanton, *Medicine in Virginia in the Nineteenth Century* (1933), 48, 80 (quotation), 91, 117, 146–147, 155, 160, 222, 243, 304, 348–350, 395; Bolton Family Papers, VHS; Bolton's journal, 1853–1861, Baker Library, Harvard University, and his medical daybook, 1862–1864, LVA; *Richmond Enquirer*, 9 Oct. 1838; Compiled Service Records; Presidential Pardons; obituaries in *Richmond Daily Dispatch*, 17 May 1869, *Richmond Daily Enquirer and Examiner*, 17, 18 May 1869, and *Transactions of the American Medical Association* 31 (1880): 1019–1021; memorial by Richmond Academy of Medicine in *Richmond Daily Enquirer and Examiner*, 22 May 1869.

LYNNE U. TURMAN

BOND, William Langhorne (12 November 1893–16 July 1985), airline executive, was born in Petersburg, the son of Thomas Baker Bond and Mary Potter Langhorne Bond. He attended the Petersburg public schools and graduated from Petersburg High School in 1911. Bond worked in a clerical position for the Seward Trunk and Baggage Company in Petersburg until 1917 and then enlisted in the United States Army. He served briefly in France near the end of World War I, after which he joined Langhorne and Langhorne Construction Company, which built railroads in Ohio and West Virginia.

Bond worked for Langhorne and Langhorne for ten years and became manager of its Miami Gravel Company in Miamitown, Hamilton County, Ohio. In June 1929 he moved to Baltimore to supervise construction of an aircraft factory for the Curtiss-Wright Corporation. Although he completed the project a year later, the factory did not open because of the Great Depression. In March 1931 Curtiss-Wright sent Bond to Shanghai, China, to revive the flagging fortunes of the China National Aviation Corporation, part of which it owned. The airline company was only two years old, and the Chinese government, which had a 55 percent stake in it, permitted Bond to manage the business until April 1933, when Pan American World Airways purchased Curtiss-Wright's stock in the company.

Bond remained in charge of the airline under joint Chinese–Pan American ownership. It prospered and became one of Pan American's most successful foreign investments, with passenger traffic increasing from 3,153 in 1932 to 18,588 in 1936. The outbreak of war between China and Japan in 1937 ended this period of growth and prosperity for the civilian airline. After 1937 CNAC became China's lifeline to the outside world, and Bond struggled to keep it in operation during difficult times that included Japanese attacks on its airfields. In November 1940 he surveyed a new high-altitude route over the Himalayan Mountains between China and Burma. After the United States entered World War II, this air supply route "over the hump" became one of the most famous air routes in the world and was essential in keeping China in the war against Japan. Bond played a critical role in CNAC's affairs during the war and often mediated between the Chinese and American governments. In 1945 he was the only foreigner to be awarded the Chinese victory medal.

Bond became Pan American's vice president for the Orient after World War II and supervised the reestablishment of the company's passenger routes throughout Asia. In 1949 an era ended when he negotiated the sale of Pan American's interest in CNAC to the Chinese

government. Bond retired the next year and returned with his family to his native Virginia, where he bought a farm near Warrenton. From 1959 to 1977 he served as chairman of the board of the Kentucky River Coal Company, an outgrowth of Langhorne and Langhorne, and helped return that company to prosperity.

On 15 May 1935 Bond married Katharine Dunlop. They had two sons, the first of whom, Langhorne McCook Bond, served as administrator of the Federal Aviation Agency from 1977 to 1980. William Langhorne Bond died at his vacation home in Ponte Vedra Beach, Saint John's County, Florida, on 16 July 1985 and was buried in Warrenton.

Bond papers and por. in possession of son Thomas Dunlop Bond, 1992; unpublished memoirs in library of National Air and Space Museum, Washington, D.C.; William M. Leary Jr., *The Dragon's Wings: The China National Aviation Corporation and the Development of Commercial Aviation in China* (1976); obituaries in *New York Times*, 27 July 1985, *Richmond Times-Dispatch*, 28 July 1985, and *Washington Post*, 3 Aug. 1985.

WILLIAM M. LEARY

BONHAM, Hezekiah Love (18 February 1866–30 May 1934), horticulturist, was born near Chilhowie in Smyth County, the son of James Scott Bonham and his second wife, Candace Perkins Bonham. He grew up on his father's farm and was educated probably in the local public schools. On 18 March 1891 he married Docia Virginia Copenhaver. They had three sons, three daughters, and one other child who died in infancy. Following Docia Bonham's death on 14 January 1905, her younger sister Eliza Cordia Copenhaver, who already lived with the Bonhams, raised the children.

H. L. Bonham worked as a laborer in the lumber industry as a young man before starting a successful lumber-milling business. In 1911 he gave up manufacturing in favor of commercial farming. At first Bonham raised apples and peaches on his small Smyth County farm, but he soon enlarged his operation and specialized in apples. Bonham consulted research institutions and extension experts and experimented on his own in order to meet or exceed the standards required of the trade. At his death H. L. Bonham Orchards was the second-largest apple producer in Virginia. In 1933 he sold 65,000 barrels of apples. Bonham erected his own apple storage warehouse in 1916 and purchased a large orchard in Johnson County, Tennessee, in 1933. In 1917 he joined the Virginia State Horticultural Society, the organization of the state's commercial fruit growers. He served as vice president of the society from 1922 to 1924 and again in 1929 and was president in 1927 and 1928. Bonham also owned a herd of Hereford cattle that was recognized as one of the state's best, largely as a result of his progressive plan of pasture management. In 1930 Virginia Agricultural and Mechanical College and Polytechnic Institute awarded him a certificate of merit, and the Standard Farm Paper Association also recognized his achievements by awarding him its Master Farmer Medal. After his death his three sons continued the successful orchard business as Bonham Brothers, Incorporated.

Bonham served on the board of trustees of Marion College from 1900 until his death and on the board of Roanoke College from 1910 to 1912. He was also a trustee of the Konnarock Training School, which educated poor children. After joining Chilhowie's Saint James Lutheran Church in 1883 Bonham became a deacon in 1893 and an elder in 1902. In the latter year he was elected a delegate to the church's state conference for the first time. Bonham spent thirty years on the state delegation to the triennial meetings of the United Lutheran Synod of the South and had a long stint on the church's Board of Foreign Missions. He also served on the board of George Ben Johnson Hospital in Abingdon and as a director of the National Bank of Chilhowie.

Although Bonham never displayed any political ambitions, his fellow Republicans nominated him for Smyth County's seat in the House of Delegates in 1915. He won and served on the Committees on Asylums and Prisons, Public Property, and Retrenchment and Economy but did not seek reelection in 1917. Bonham was the county food administrator during World War I.

Hezekiah Love Bonham suffered from tuberculosis during his last years, and following a month's serious illness he died on 30 May 1934 at his home in Chilhowie. He was buried in the Saint James Lutheran Church cemetery.

Elmer B. Hazie, *Bonham, 1631–1973*, rev. ed. (1973), 94; Mildred Manton Copenhaver and Robert Madison Copenhaver Jr., *The Copenhaver Family of Smyth County, Virginia* (1981), 483–490; orchards described in *Virginia Fruit* 21 (Sept. 1933): 5–6; BVS Death Certificate, Smyth Co.; obituary in *Marion Smyth County News*, 31 May 1934; memorial in *Virginia Fruit* 22 (June 1934): 22–25 (por. on cover).

DAPHNE GENTRY

BONNYCASTLE, Charles (22 November 1796–31 October 1840), mathematician, was born in Woolwich, England, the son of John Bonnycastle and his second wife, Bridget Newell Bonnycastle. His father was a professor of mathematics at the Royal Military Academy at Woolwich. Following in his father's footsteps, Bonnycastle was educated at Woolwich and soon distinguished himself through his contributions to the thirteenth edition of his father's noted mathematics textbook, *An Introduction to Algebra,* which was published in 1824, three years after John Bonnycastle's death.

In September 1824 Bonnycastle met with Francis Walker Gilmer, the agent for the new University of Virginia, who was in England to hire faculty members. Negotiations proceeded rapidly, and Bonnycastle formally accepted the university's first professorship of natural philosophy. The fact that he had been educated at the Royal Military Academy obligated him to obtain permission from the British government before accepting any foreign post or risk a fine of £500. Gilmer's imminent departure left Bonnycastle without time to secure the needful permission, and so he incurred the penalty in the belief that matters could be straightened out later. Ultimately Thomas Jefferson himself had to intervene in Bonnycastle's behalf, and the university advanced Bonnycastle the money to settle with his government.

After this inauspicious beginning Bonnycastle enjoyed a fruitful association with the University of Virginia. He served as professor of natural philosophy from the time of his arrival in 1825 until he succeeded Thomas Key in 1827 as professor of mathematics. Bonnycastle continued in the latter post until his death in 1840 and served as chair of the faculty senate from 1833 to 1835. As one of the first professors at the university, Bonnycastle helped shape the curricula of the schools with which he was associated. In his natural philosophy course he taught standard Newtonian physics sprinkled with discussions of some of the more recent but elementary advances in the subject. Bonnycastle also emphasized laboratory work and introduced raised benches in his classroom so that his students might better observe the demonstrations.

As mathematics professor, "Old Bonny," as he was fondly called, replaced the antiquated British approach to mathematical pedagogy typified by his own father's texts with a new approach borrowed from French mathematicians. British writers had imitated Euclid by clinging to the deductive manner of presenting material. They opened their texts with axioms and definitions and proceeded to the derivation of facts and theorems. Although logically satisfying to mathematicians, the method did little to motivate beginning students. French textbook writers, on the other hand, approached mathematics analytically, leading from concrete examples to abstractions. Bonnycastle introduced this method at the University of Virginia and published his own college textbook, *Inductive Geometry, or, An Analysis of the Relations of Form and Magnitude: Commencing with the Elementary Ideas Derived Through the Senses, and Proceeding by a Train of Inductive Reasoning to Develop the Present State of the Science* (1834). Painfully prolix even by nineteenth-century standards, the innovative book was not a financial success.

Bonnycastle also published several articles on mathematical and physical topics in the *Transactions of the American Philosophical Society*. In 1836 he acted to supplement the university's course offerings in the pure sciences with applied subjects by instituting the Department of Civil Engineering. Bonnycastle's interests outside of these scholarly fields included philosophy, metaphysics, ancient languages, and modern literature.

On 10 January 1826 Bonnycastle married Ann Mason Tutt, of Loudoun County. They had one son and two daughters. Charles Bonnycastle died in Charlottesville on 31 October 1840 and was buried in the University of Virginia Cemetery. His estate was valued at more than $23,000, including a library of more than a thousand volumes.

Birth and death dates from gravestone; Harry Clemons, *Notes on the Professors for Whom the University of Virginia Halls and Residence Houses Are Named* (1961), 7–10; Clara Bell Davis, "Charles Bonnycastle," *Alumni Bulletin of the University of Virginia* 6 (1900): 106–107; William B. O'Neal, *Pictorial History of the University of Virginia* (1968), 44 (por.); Bruce, *University of Virginia*, 1:371–372, 2:9–12, 95–98, 126, 145–146; Florian Cajori, *The Teaching and History of Mathematics in the United States* (1890), 191–195; most of Bonnycastle's papers were evidently destroyed by fire in 1895; several letters are in Charles Bonnycastle Papers, Cocke Family Papers, and John Knowles Papers, UVA; Board of Visitors Minutes and Faculty Minutes, UVA; Richard Beale Davis, ed., *Correspondence of Thomas Jefferson and Francis Walker Gilmer, 1814–1826* (1946), 23, 113, 136, 138–141, 144, 146; Bonnycastle's most important publications include "On a New Principle in Regard to the Power of Fluids in Motion to Produce Rupture of the Vessels Which Contain Them; and on the Distinction between Accumulative and Instantaneous Pressure" and "On the Insufficiency of Taylor's Theorem as Commonly Investigated, with Objections to the Demonstrations of Poisson and Cauchy, and the Assumed Generalization of Mr. Peacock, to Which are Added a New Investigation and Remarks on the Development and Continuity of Functions," *Transactions of the American Philosophical Society*, new ser., 7 (1841): 113–123 and 217–250; marriage reported in *Richmond Enquirer*, 21 Jan. 1826; will and estate inventory in Albemarle Co. Will Book, 14:106, 109–113, 15:202–210; obituaries in *Southern Literary Messenger* 8 (1842): 50–51, and *American Almanac and Repository of Useful Knowledge* (1842), 296.

KAREN HUNGER PARSHALL

BONSACK, James Albert (4 October 1859–2 June 1924), businessman and inventor of the cigarette-rolling machine, was born at Bonsack in Roanoke County, the son of Jacob Bonsack and Sarah Whitmore Bonsack. His father operated the Bonsack Woolen Mill on the road between Salem and Lynchburg. James Bonsack gained his early knowledge of machinery there.

In 1876 Bonsack saw an announcement that the tobacco firm of Allen and Ginter in Richmond had offered a prize for the first machine able to roll and cut a complete cigarette. Bonsack and his friends decided to work on the project, but only he had sufficient mechanical ingenuity. The challenge soon became an obsession. Having completed his early education under a Roanoke schoolmaster, Bonsack entered Roanoke College in 1878, only to leave after one year to set up a workshop in his father's mill. The decision proved fortuitous when the carding machine in the mill inspired the solution to one of his most difficult problems, how to measure the tobacco consistently and accurately. Bonsack initially planned to use a tapered tube to form the cigarette paper into a cylinder but then learned that a New Yorker had patented a similar but ineffective device in 1876. Bonsack's father then paid a reported $18,000 for the rights to the earlier patent. James A. Bonsack completed his design with a complicated blade that cut the cylinder into cigarettes of uniform length. He filed for a patent for his cigarette-rolling machine on 4 September 1880 and received patent number 238,640 on 8 March 1881.

Bonsack soon had a completed machine ready to ship to the Allen and Ginter factory in Richmond, but fire destroyed it while it was on a freight car at Lynchburg. Insurance money enabled him to build a second, improved device, which was tested at Allen and Ginter in June 1881. In March 1882 he chartered the Bonsack Machine Company to manufacture the Bonsack Cigarette Machine. The family attorney, Demetrius B. Strouse, was president, with Jacob Bonsack and James A. Bonsack among the trustees. They applied for foreign patents in order to license overseas manufacturers, and in 1882 Bonsack went to Rome to direct the installation of the first European machine. Two years later, seven were operating in the United States, and an equal number, manufactured under license in France, had been built in Europe.

The Bonsack Machine Company prospered from the first. One machine could produce as many cigarettes as forty-eight people could make manually. The early machines were very complicated devices and not without problems. A mechanic employed by the manufacturer directed the operations of the machines. An exceptionally able mechanic, William Thomas O'Brien, made improvements to the two machines installed at the W. Duke, Sons, and Company factory in Durham, North Carolina, enabling that factory to produce up to four million cigarettes a day.

The modern cigarette-manufacturing industry traces its development directly to Bonsack's machine, which produced inexpensive cigarettes at a time when cigarette smoking was growing in popularity. Ironically, through the mid-1880s Allen and Ginter declined to employ the device

throughout their factory and continued to market more expensive hand-rolled cigarettes, losing much of the mass market in the United States to North Carolina manufacturers, especially W. Duke, Sons, and Company, and the European market to tobacco companies operating Bonsack machines there under license from the manufacturer.

The invention brought Bonsack wealth. He moved to Marietta, Pennsylvania, where on 1 February 1883 he married Anna Musser. They had two sons and one daughter and had moved to Philadelphia by the end of the decade. Until 1901 Bonsack continued to improve his cigarette machine, replacing the solid cylinder-forming tube with an ingenious series of inclined belts and obtaining more than a dozen patents for tobacco feeds, tube pasters, and cigarette cutters. The royalties from his inventions appear to have been the major source of family income, enabling him to join the Philadelphia Country Club and other socially prominent organizations. James Albert Bonsack died of apoplexy in the vault of a Philadelphia bank on 2 June 1924.

James Evans Bonsack, "A Sketch of the Early Life of James Albert Bonsack Including a Brief Account of the Invention of the Bonsack Cigarette Machine," typescript dated 30 Nov. 1938, Nannie May Tilley Papers, Duke; Nannie May Tilley, *The Bright-Tobacco Industry, 1860–1929* (1948), 570–577 (por. following 402); other accounts of varying accuracy in *Lynchburg News,* sesquicentennial ed., 11 Oct. 1936, *Roanoke Times and World News*, 14 June 1947, and Deedie Dent Kagey, *Community at the Crossroads: A Study of the Village of Bonsack of the Roanoke Valley* (1983), 114–119; obituaries in *Philadelphia Record*, 3 June 1924, and *Lynchburg News,* 5 June 1924.

JAMES MULHOLLAND

BONTECOU, Eleanor (14 February 1891–19 March 1976), attorney, was born in Short Hills, Essex County, New Jersey, the daughter of Frederic Thayer Bontecou and Amy Vail Bontecou. A descendant of early Dutch settlers in the Hudson Valley, her father was a broker who saw lean as well as affluent years but always insisted on the best education for his daughters. Bontecou attended Miss Beard's School in Orange, New Jersey, noted for its exceptionally high standards, and she entered Bryn Mawr College in 1909 on a scholarship awarded for the highest grades received on entrance examinations from New Jersey and New York. She graduated with highest honors in 1913.

Bontecou entered the New York University law school and graduated in 1917. She was admitted to the New York bar in 1919 and worked as a law clerk in a New York City firm from 1918 to 1921. In 1922 Bontecou returned to Bryn Mawr as dean of the college. She began graduate work at Harvard University law school three years later and studied there under Felix Frankfurter. From 1927 to 1930 Bontecou was a research fellow for the Commonwealth Fund, studying the rule-making activities of administrative agencies of the federal government. She received an M.A. in administrative law from Radcliffe in 1927 and a Ph.D. a year later from the Robert Brookings Graduate School of Economics and Government (later the Brookings Institution) in Washington, D.C.

With this brilliant academic record, Bontecou looked forward in 1929 to her new appointment as a full professor of legal relations at the University of Chicago. She had served just one year when she was stricken with encephalitis lethargica (sleeping sickness). Returning to the Washington area, Bontecou spent most of the 1930s bedridden and disabled in mind and body from the effects of the disease. She derived her bravery and determination to recover from a conviction that bodies could heal themselves and, with the help of her recently widowed mother, worked diligently throughout the decade to regain her strength and coordination. Bontecou never fully recovered, but undaunted by an impaired sense of balance and a slight tremor in her hands, she designed a house overlooking the Potomac River in 1936 and lived in Arlington from 1932 until 1974.

Bontecou joined the Southern Conference for Human Welfare, providing legal advice to its campaign to abolish the poll tax. In 1939 she began working with Ralph Johnson Bunche on a survey of southern suffrage for the New School for Social Research and the Carnegie Foundation Study of the Negro in America. The survey became part of Bunche's monograph, later published separately as *The Political Status of the Negro in the Age of FDR* (1973), which he wrote in 1940 for Gunnar Myrdal's larger work,

An American Dilemma: The Negro Problem and Modern Democracy (1944). Still homebound, Bontecou used her earnings to pay a research assistant and a field-worker to complete the research for her own study, *The Poll Tax*, which the American Association of University Women published in 1942.

In 1943 Bontecou was ready to return to what she called "regular work" and sought a temporary position in the new Civil Rights Section of the Criminal Division at the United States Department of Justice. She named as references two close friends who were associate justices of the United States Supreme Court, Felix Frankfurter and Hugo Black. Tom C. Clark, the director of the Civil Rights Section, recognized her keen legal mind and research skills and soon offered her a permanent position. In matters involving race and cases of discrimination against Japanese Americans, Bontecou was considered the most able attorney in the section. During her first year she completed a study of the treatment of conscientious objectors by the United States and the allied nations in World War I and recommended solutions to conscientious objector problems in World War II. Bontecou was one of the first seven attorneys in the Civil Rights Section, and she believed that this small group paved the way for action by the federal government in later civil rights cases. Especially skillful in the appraisal of witnesses, she was transferred to the War Department in 1946 to help prepare for the prosecution of major war criminals in the Pacific area. In 1947 the War Department sent Bontecou to Nürnberg to inspect and report on all war crimes activities in Germany. The rigors of travel and the nature of the work in Germany proved too great a strain. When Bontecou returned to the United States, she suffered a heart attack and was forced to retire.

Despite her health problems Bontecou soon resumed her research. In 1948 she undertook a study of the federal loyalty-security program for Cornell University. Funded by the Rockefeller Foundation, Bontecou's research covered the work of the Dies Committee, the attorney general's list of subversives, and the work of federal and regional un-American activities committees. *The Federal Loyalty-Security Program*

(1953) was one in a series of volumes that emphasized the effects of the security programs on civil liberties. Bontecou conducted and included interviews with government employees who had faced charges that they were disloyal or were security risks, and the book also had a chapter based on her 1950 study of British loyalty-security programs. Her research affected her deeply, and she put her abhorrence of the miscarriage of justice in the McCarthy era to practical use by counseling, and in some cases raising money for, persons charged with subversive activities. Bontecou also recounted in two impassioned unpublished manuscripts the experiences of other government employees whose careers were destroyed by the "self-appointed guardians of political purity." The most notable among the eight case histories was that of J. Robert Oppenheimer, whom she interviewed shortly after he was denied a clearance by the Atomic Energy Commission in April 1954.

In 1955 the Senate Subcommittee on Constitutional Rights made Bontecou a consultant on loyalty and security problems. She later edited *Freedom in the Balance: Opinions of Judge Henry W. Edgerton Relating to Civil Liberties* (1960), part of the Cornell Studies in Civil Liberty. Bontecou never rose to national prominence. She was confident in her own intellectual endeavors and did not seek recognition beyond a few close associates. Acutely aware that through illness she had missed one important period in law and government in the 1930s, Bontecou seized the opportunity to devote her keen legal mind and her energy to victims of McCarthy-era hysteria in the 1950s.

Eleanor Bontecou never married. She moved to the Goodwin House in Alexandria in 1974 and died of a heart attack on 19 March 1976 at George Washington University Hospital in Washington, D.C. She was buried in Alstead, Cheshire County, New Hampshire.

Birth date and professional data in Office of Personnel Management Records, RG 478, NARA; Eleanor Bontecou Papers, including oral history and unpublished manuscripts (quotation), in Harry S. Truman Presidential Library, Independence, Mo.; Bontecou correspondence and files in Bryn Mawr College Archives and Schomburg Center for Research in Black Culture, New York Public Library; information provided by Doris Bryant, Virginia Foster Durr, Jolande Goldberg, Jean Atherton Flexner Lewinson, Zola Shoup, Edward Squibb, Margaret Squibb Stevens, and George C. Stoney; *Washington Post and Times Herald*, 12 Sept. 1955; obituaries in *Washington Star*, 24 Mar. 1976, *Fairfax Northern Virginia Sun* and *Washington Post* (por.), both 25 Mar. 1976, and *Bryn Mawr Alumnae Bulletin* (summer 1976): 28–29.

MARY KATE BLACK

BOOKER, Edmund (d. by 24 January 1793), member of the Convention of 1788, was born probably in Essex County about 1721, the son of Edmund Booker and Jane Booker. His father moved the family to Amelia County in 1736. On 17 May 1746 Booker married Edith Marot Cobbs, of Amelia County. They had four sons and three daughters.

Booker was a small planter who occasionally speculated in land by buying and selling small tracts of Amelia County farmland. He never achieved great wealth, but at the time of his death he owned 568 acres and eleven slaves. In 1749 he was elected to the vestry of Raleigh Parish. Booker began to emerge as a minor local political leader after his father's death in June 1758. He won election to the House of Burgesses that year but was not reelected in 1761. On 26 June 1760 he took an oath as a justice of the peace for Amelia County, by 1761 he was a captain in the militia, and in October 1772 he became sheriff of Amelia County.

In March 1788 Booker and John Pride were elected to represent Amelia County in the convention called to consider ratification of the proposed United States Constitution. Booker attended the convention from opening day through the vote on ratification on 25 June 1788, but he made no recorded speeches. He voted for prior amendments to the new constitution and then voted against ratification. Booker left the convention on 26 June and so was not present for consideration of the proposed constitutional amendments that the convention recommended on 27 June.

Booker's wife died after 1765, and sometime before September 1776 he wed a woman named Prudence, maiden name unknown. Following her death he married Mary Pride on 28 June 1781. He had no children with his second or third wives, and his third wife predeceased him. Edmund Booker died sometime between

27 December 1792, when he was a security for his namesake son when the latter became sheriff of Amelia County, and the admittance of his will to probate in the Amelia County Court on 24 January 1793.

Family relationships established in wills of Booker, father, and namesake son recorded respectively in Amelia Co. Will Book, 4:342–343, 1:136–137, 5:208–209; Amelia Co. Tithable Lists, 1736–1782, LVA, distinguish several Edmund Bookers; first and third marriages in Kathleen Booth Williams, *Marriages of Amelia County, Virginia, 1735–1815* (1961), 12; Raleigh Parish Vestry Book, 176, LVA photocopy; landholdings and public offices recorded in Amelia Co. Deed and Order Books, with approximate year of birth conjectured from first appearance on tithables lists in 1737, first conveyance of land to Booker by father on 15 Sept. 1742 (Deed Book, 1:416 [originally numbered 287]), and appointment as undersheriff on 19 Aug. 1743 (Order Book, 1:243); Kaminski, *Ratification*, 10:1538–1540, 1565.

DAPHNE GENTRY

BOOKER, George Edward (22 March 1872– 1 April 1951), Methodist minister, was born probably in Petersburg, the son of Fanny Eubank Booker and George Edward Booker, a widely respected clergyman who served in the Virginia Conference of the Methodist Episcopal Church South from 1859 to 1898. Booker received his early education primarily from his father. Initially interested in the law, he attended the College of William and Mary during the academic year 1889–1890, was elected to Phi Beta Kappa, and helped found a chapter of the Kappa Sigma social fraternity.

In 1892 Booker chose the ministry instead of the law and assisted his father on the Sussex Circuit, and in 1893 he entered the Virginia Conference on trial. While assigned to the Ashland Circuit from 1894 to 1896, he took courses in religion at Randolph-Macon College. During the 1905–1906 academic year Booker studied English literature at the University of Virginia. Recipient of an honorary D.D. from Randolph-Macon College in 1908, he served on that institution's board of trustees from 1919 to 1950. On 29 April 1896 Booker married Annie Parham Howle, of Sussex County. She participated actively in church work and was a strong support to her husband. They had one son and two daughters.

Booker rose rapidly through the ministerial ranks after his ordination in 1895 and served some of the major Methodist churches in Virginia, among them First Church in Charlottesville (1904–1906 and 1933–1936), Epworth Church in Norfolk (1906–1910), Washington Street Church in Petersburg (1910–1913), Court Street Church in Lynchburg (1915–1919), and Monument Church (1921–1925) and Centenary Church (1929–1933) in Richmond. From 1925 to 1929 he was superintendent of the Richmond District. A highly esteemed member of the Virginia Conference, Booker was elected to seven successive quadrennial general conferences and served in 1927 as a delegate to the church's international Conference on Faith and Order in Lausanne, Switzerland.

Booker was known for his eloquence while speaking from the pulpit and to civic and college audiences throughout Virginia. A fellow minister recalled his ornate elocutionary style and his impressive silver-haired appearance. An able administrator who showed a strong concern for his churches and parishioners, Booker requested in 1932 that his salary at Centenary Church in Richmond be cut by 20 percent to help meet the church's financial commitments.

Booker contributed articles to the *Virginia Methodist Advocate* and other journals. In 1949 he published *Dreams and Visions and Other Essays*, a collection that reflected his literary interests as well as his personal moral and religious philosophy. The inspirational essays present Booker's personal philosophy on such topics as friendship, unselfish giving, ideal manhood, motherhood, and the essentials for success in life. Moralistic in tone and interspersed with literary allusions and themes, all the essays reflect Booker's love of literature, his faith in people, and his strong belief in Christian principles.

In 1936, three years after his wife's death on 2 August 1933, Booker retired from the ministry and returned to Richmond to live with his daughters. George Edward Booker died in Richmond on 1 April 1951 and was buried in Blandford Cemetery in Petersburg.

Biographies in John James Lafferty, *Sketches and Portraits of the Virginia Conference: Twentieth Century Edition* (1901), 405–409 (por.), Bruce, Tyler, and Morton, *History of Virginia*, 5:160, and W. D. Keene Jr., ed., *Memoirs— 200 Years* (1988), 761–763; all biographies give Petersburg as place of birth, but it is given as Cumberland Co. in BVS Marriage Register, Sussex Co.; Floyd S. Bennett, *Methodist Church on Shockoe Hill: A History of Centenary Methodist Church, Richmond, Virginia, 1810–1960* (1962), 138–144; Joseph D. Eggleston and George E. Booker III, "Some Booker Genealogy," undated typescript at Randolph-Macon College, 9–11; *Minutes of the Virginia Annual Conference of the Methodist Episcopal Church, South*, 1893–1936; *Richmond Times-Dispatch*, 18 Oct. 1933; *Richmond News Leader*, 21 July 1952; information provided by granddaughter Anne Booker Keyser (including material from family scrapbook), Alpheus W. Potts, and Mrs. Meriwether V. Smith; obituary and editorial tribute in *Richmond Times-Dispatch*, 2 (por.), 4 Apr. 1951.

NANCY NEWINS

BOOKER, George William (5 December 1821–4 June 1884), member of the House of Representatives, was born in Patrick County, the son of Edward Booker and Elizabeth Anglin Booker. Educated locally, he farmed and taught school before reading law. Booker was admitted to the bar in Henry County on 8 March 1847 and practiced there the remainder of his life. Elected to the county court in 1856, he served as its presiding justice from 1858 until 1864. Booker was a strong Unionist at the time of the secession crisis, but according to his later testimony he voted for the Ordinance of Secession because he feared reprisals from his neighbors. He avoided being conscripted in 1864 because he was a justice of the peace, and the only part he took in the Civil War was the performance of his duties as a magistrate.

Booker was elected to represent Henry County in the House of Delegates on 12 October 1865 and served until 1867. During the first session he sat on the Committee on Military Affairs and the Committee to Examine the Clerk's Office; during the second he sat on the Committees on Propositions and Grievances and on Militia and Police. He allied himself with other former Unionists and John Minor Botts, the Virginia politician whom he most admired. Although Booker had begun his political career as a Democrat, he took an active role in the emerging Republican Party. The military government of Virginia entrusted him with a series of temporary appointments in 1869 as commonwealth's attorney for the counties of Franklin, Patrick, and Prince Edward. On 7 May 1868 the Republican state convention nominated Booker for attorney general, but no election was held that year, and when the party's radical wing reassembled to nominate candidates for statewide office in March 1869, he did not attend and was dropped from the ticket.

In June 1869 Booker announced his candidacy for the House of Representatives from the Fourth Congressional District comprising Brunswick, Charlotte, Franklin, Halifax, Henry, Lunenburg, Mecklenburg, Patrick, and Pittsylvania Counties. Identifying himself as a "True," or Liberal, Republican, he moderated his earlier contemptuous statements about secessionists and sought to promote reconciliation by advocating removal of all remaining political disabilities from former Confederates. For statewide office he endorsed the Conservative Party ticket headed by gubernatorial candidate Gilbert Carlton Walker. On 6 July 1869 Booker defeated two Radical Republicans by a margin of 3,533 votes out of 27,308 cast, after which one of the defeated candidates unsuccessfully challenged Booker's eligibility because of his service on the Henry County Court during the Civil War. Acquaintances of Booker testified that he had been consistently and conspicuously loyal to the Union during the war and that even though he was too poor to leave Virginia he had vowed to do so if the Confederacy had won. Booker took his seat in Congress on 1 February 1870, partway into the second session, and during his abbreviated term he served on the Committee on Freedmen's Affairs. Although active in introducing bills to remove civil and political disabilities from individual constituents, he submitted no major legislation and seldom spoke. In December 1870 he submitted for printing in the *Congressional Globe* set remarks supporting a bill providing a general amnesty for all Confederates and Southern sympathizers during the Civil War.

Booker did not seek reelection in 1871 but instead ran for and regained his former seat in the House of Delegates, in which he served two more years. He became one of several floor leaders of the Conservative Party, chaired the Committee on Banks, Currency, and Commerce, and on at least one occasion acted as Speaker pro tempore. Booker also served as acting chairman of a special committee appointed in 1872 to investigate allegations that agents for northern bondholders had bribed members of the previous assembly to pass the Funding Act of 1871. He supported free public schools for all of the state's children, and, although his personal views on the issue are unknown, he agreed to submit a petition from a Richmond woman, Anna Whitehead Bodeker, asking that women be permitted to vote.

In June 1872 Booker attended the Conservative Party state convention and was elected a delegate to the Democratic National Convention that nominated Horace Greeley, the candidate of the Liberal Republican Party, for president of the United States. Booker then retired to Henry County, where he continued to practice law. Sometime between 1850 and 1855 he had married Maria Philpott, and they had two or three daughters, one set of twin boys, and a son, born about 1868, whom they named for John Minor Botts. George William Booker died of a stroke at his home near Martinsville on 4 June 1884.

Birth date in French Biographies; imperfect family history, including an account of a namesake son that could be misinterpreted as describing Booker himself, in Virginia G. Pedigo and Lewis G. Pedigo, *History of Patrick and Henry Counties, Virginia* (1933), 93–94; letters from Booker to Christopher Y. Thomas in Gravely Family Papers, LVA; political career documented in Lynchburg and Richmond newspapers, in *JHD*, 1865–1867 and 1871–1872, in *Congressional Globe*, 41st Cong., 2d and 3d sess., and in *Testimony in the Case of George Tucker vs. Geo. W. Booker, Fourth Congressional District of Virginia*, 41st Cong., 2d sess., House Misc. Doc. 44, serial 1433; BVS Death Register, Henry Co.; obituaries in *Lynchburg Daily News* and *Richmond Daily Whig*, both 6 June 1884.

BRENT TARTER

BOOKER, James Edward (9 February 1850–19 March 1940), Presbyterian minister, was born at Charlotte Court House, the son of John Booker and Lucilla Stanley Elliott Booker. His mother died when he was three years old, and his eldest sister, Anne Carrington Booker, raised him until his father, a merchant, enrolled him in private schools in Prince Edward and Charlotte Counties. Booker entered Hampden-Sydney College in 1867. Following his graduation in 1870, his health deteriorated, but he soon recovered and attended universities in Göttingen and

Leipzig, where he studied for a year and a half. After traveling in Europe he returned to Virginia in 1874. A year later Booker entered Union Theological Seminary, then located adjacent to Hampden-Sydney, and graduated in 1878. On 13 September 1877 he married Sarah Bannister Peck, the daughter of a professor at the seminary. They had one son and three daughters.

Booker served as pastor of Second Presbyterian Church in Staunton from 1878 to 1886, as co-pastor of First Presbyterian Church in Charleston, West Virginia, from 1886 to 1888, and as pastor of Hebron Presbyterian Church at Swoope in Augusta County from 1888 to 1900. In 1895 he chaired the state committee on home missions for the Synod of Virginia. Booker served as synod evangelist in the Allegheny Mountains in West Virginia from 1900 to 1902, but his health failed, and he moved to Lexington to recuperate. He served as stated supply for the Timber Ridge and Mount Carmel Presbyterian Churches near Lexington in 1902.

In 1903, his health restored, Booker was appointed superintendent of home missions for the synod. Initially responsible for mission work in both Virginia and West Virginia, he coordinated the effort in nearly a dozen presbyteries. Under Booker's guidance the synod's home mission program grew from a single department of "Evangelism and Sustenation" in 1903 to ten departments by 1926. The home mission effort included working with various minority and ethnic groups, with state institutions such as penitentiaries and hospitals, and with urban as well as rural congregations. It also operated Sunday schools for young people. In addition to its social influences, Booker's mission program greatly contributed to the large increase in Presbyterian church membership in Virginia during this period. He served as superintendent until he retired in 1929 at age seventy-nine. Booker was named superintendent emeritus and served as treasurer of home missions in 1930.

In 1915 Booker moved to Hampden-Sydney College. From there he directed the work of home missions, keeping Presbyterians informed by means of *Multum in Parvo*, a small publication distributed throughout the synod. Booker served as moderator of the Virginia Synod in 1908 and received high praise for his creative work in behalf of the church in Virginia. Widely respected within the Presbyterian Church in the United States, he received honorary D.D. degrees in 1915 from both Hampden-Sydney College and Washington and Lee University. Booker served on Hampden-Sydney's board of trustees from 1918 to 1938 and was a constant presence on its campus throughout his retirement.

James Edward Booker died at his residence at Hampden-Sydney on 19 March 1940 and was buried in the Union Theological Seminary Cemetery at Hampden-Sydney.

Birth date in memorial in *Minutes of the Synod of Virginia* (1940): 586–589, and other church references; E. C. Scott, ed., *Ministerial Directory of the Presbyterian Church, U.S., 1861–1941* (1942), 65; Session Minutes and Register, 1872–1894, Hebron Presbyterian Church, Swoope, 56, and Session Minutes and Register, 1876–1898, Second Presbyterian Church, Staunton, 137 (microfilms at UTS); annual reports of superintendent of home missions in *Minutes of the Synod of Virginia* (1903–1930); obituaries in *Richmond Times-Dispatch*, 20 Mar. 1940 (por.), *Farmville Herald and Farmer-Leader*, 22 Mar. 1940, and *Christian Observer*, 3 Apr. 1940, all giving variant birth date of 12 Feb. 1850.

ROBERT BENEDETTO

BOOKER, Matilda V. Mosley (18 September 1887–27 June 1957), educator, was born probably in Halifax County, the daughter of Killis Mosley and Tamara Smith Mosley. She grew up on her father's farm near Clover in Halifax County. With the encouragement of a grandfather who had been a slave, she entered the Thyne Institute, a normal school at Chase City in Mecklenburg County, at about age thirteen. Living with a cousin, Mosley spent four years there, received a teacher's certificate, and then taught near her parents' home for two years. In 1907 she entered the Virginia Normal and Industrial Institute (later Virginia State University) at Ettrick, near Petersburg.

After graduating in 1911, Mosley was hired as principal of the two-teacher Little Bethel School in Henrico County. The county's rural schools for African Americans followed programs first developed by Virginia Estelle Randolph, a local teacher. Randolph's work inspired a northern foundation, the Negro Rural School Fund, Inc., known as the Jeanes Fund, to subsidize salaries across the rural South for African American teachers and supervisors who used a curriculum based on industrial arts such as sewing and agriculture. Recognizing that local people would have to provide most of the money and labor to improve their schools, the Jeanes Fund also expected teachers to follow Randolph's example and act as civic organizers. With her school's other teacher, Mosley organized two School Improvement Leagues that raised money and used it to lay walks, plant flowers, fence the school, and buy pictures for its classroom walls.

With Randolph's encouragement, Mosley in 1913 became the Jeanes Supervisor for Cumberland County's twenty-three schools for blacks. On arriving there in April, she discovered that the schools had already closed after terms of only five months or less. All but two of the school buildings were in a state of disrepair. Mosley spoke at churches and other meeting places throughout the county, exhorting the citizens to support the schools. By 1920 they had responded by building eight new schools and renovating another thirteen. Mosley also encouraged teachers to attend summer institutes to improve their skills, and she raised the money for the higher salaries to which their new skills entitled them.

On 24 May 1916 Mosley married Samuel Glover Booker, a native of Cumberland County. They bought a small farm and cultivated it in their spare time. In 1919 Samuel Booker opened a store and gasoline station, which he operated for fifty-four years. They had no children of their own, but relatives and foster children regularly filled their home. Matilda Mosley Booker also paid for a new house for her parents in Halifax County.

In 1920 Cumberland County abolished the post of Jeanes Supervisor. The reason is undocumented, but Booker's constant campaign for better schools may finally have made white local officials uncomfortable. She quickly secured employment as the Jeanes Supervisor for Mecklenburg County, more than fifty miles south of her Cumberland home, and for the next thirty-five years she commuted weekly between the two counties. The historian of education of African

Americans in Mecklenburg declared that Booker had a "remarkable ability to inspire the people to make personal sacrifices for their schools." By 1936 her efforts had resulted in the construction of new buildings for more than half of the county's fifty-six schools for blacks. As in Cumberland County, Booker strove to improve the teaching staff and also raised money for school buses and school dental clinics. She asked for and received an assistant in 1925, and grateful supporters later gave her an automobile to use in her travels.

When Booker arrived, Mecklenburg County had no high school for African Americans. A large committee petitioned the school board in 1923 for a county training school at South Hill, but the board declared that it lacked funds for such an undertaking. Under Booker's leadership, citizens raised money to enlarge an existing school building and, beginning in 1926, provided funds each year to add coursework for another grade. The Mecklenburg County Training School graduated its first class in 1930. Residents of the western part of the county subsequently organized to establish a second high school at Clarksville in 1935. By 1940 a standard nine-month term was the norm for all the county's schools.

Building on successful litigation elsewhere in the state, in 1940 Mecklenburg's black teachers and their lawyer, Oliver W. Hill, of Richmond, requested that the board equalize salaries of white and black teachers. By the beginning of the 1943 school term the board had done so. Continued legal pressures for equalization caused the school board to take on new responsibilities, including the building of new schools and the transporting of students. These changes diminished the Jeanes Supervisor's role. From the late 1940s until her retirement in 1955, Booker distributed educational materials, collected funds for charity, and served the county superintendent as, in effect, his assistant for the education of African Americans.

In 1940 Booker's alma mater, then the Virginia State College for Negroes, presented her with a certificate of merit for her achievements in education. The Virginia Teachers Association honored her retirement by reproducing her por-trait on the cover of the March–April 1956 issue of its journal. Matilda V. Mosley Booker had suffered from heart disease for several years when she died in Cumberland County on 27 June 1957. She was buried in the nearby family cemetery.

Biographies and feature articles in Mary Jenness, *Twelve Negro Americans* (1936), 20–34, *Virginia Education Bulletin* 37 (1956): 96–97 (cover por.), *Cumberland County, Virginia, and Its People* (1983), 79–80 (por.), and Jessie Carney Smith, ed., *Notable Black American Women* (1991), 96–98; birth date on death certificate, which gives birthplace as New Brunswick, N.J.; BVS Marriage Register, Cumberland Co.; information provided by sisters-in-law Annie Harris Booker and Aliase B. Crosby; George B. Lancaster, "The Development of Education for Negroes in Mecklenburg County, Virginia, 1865–1946" (master's thesis, Virginia State College, 1947), 54–82 (quotation on 64).

JOHN T. KNEEBONE

BOOKER, Sallie Cook (28 August 1857–20 December 1944), member of the House of Delegates, was born on her father's farm in Franklin County, the daughter of Samuel Shrewsberry Cook and Mildred Dawson Cook. She began teaching school when she was sixteen years old and later attended Piedmont Institute for Young Ladies in Franklin County to complete her preparation for teaching in public schools. On 22 May 1877 she married Jesse Wootten Booker, of Henry County. Shortly after her marriage she resumed teaching in one-room country schools in Henry County. Later she moved to Martinsville, where her husband worked first as a businessman and then as a postal employee and where she continued to teach. Booker attended summer normal institutes several times and taught school for more than twenty-five years. She also brought up four sons and three daughters.

Booker was active in the Women's Christian Temperance Union, the Methodist Church, and the United Daughters of the Confederacy. After she retired from teaching she became active in local Democratic Party politics as well. Early in the 1920s Booker became a member of the state central committee and also of the executive committee, which formulated party policies. On 12 September 1925 she was the surprise, unanimous nominee of the Democratic Party for Henry County's seat in the House of Delegates. According to a story then current, the leading Democratic men of Henry County caucused in a drugstore to settle on a successor to the retiring delegate, and someone suggested that the best person they could send to Richmond was their former schoolteacher. Booker was nominated without debate and elected without Republican opposition.

Sallie C. Booker was the third woman elected to the General Assembly of Virginia, and she served two consecutive two-year terms. In 1927, during her first term, the assembly met in a special session to prepare the constitutional amendments needed to implement Governor Harry Flood Byrd's governmental reorganization plans, which she supported. The Speaker appointed Booker to the Committee on Schools and Colleges, and she also served on the Committees on Counties, Cities, and Towns, on Retrenchment and Economy, and on the Library. During her second term she was the ranking member of the Committee on the Library, and she was fourth in seniority on the thirteen-member Committee on Schools and Colleges. The chair of the education committee during her second term was Sarah Lee Fain, who had been elected to the General Assembly two years before Booker, and another member was Helen Ruth Henderson, also a teacher, who was elected two years after Booker, becoming the fourth woman to serve in the General Assembly.

Booker ran for reelection in 1927 and faced stiff opposition from Reed L. Stone, a Henry County Republican who ran as an independent. He opposed her on the grounds that service in the General Assembly was properly a man's job. Stone declined Booker's challenge to a public debate. Despite the fact that the local Republican Party had a weak political organization, she only narrowly defeated him on 8 November 1927, by a vote of 1,379 to 1,323. During her second term Booker won approval of one of her pet projects, a bill to increase pensions for Confederate veterans and their widows. She did not seek a third term in 1929. Sallie Cook Booker died in Shackelford Hospital in Martinsville on 20 December 1944 and was buried in Oakwood Cemetery in that city.

Biography by Hilda G. Marshall in Virginia Iota State Organization of Delta Kappa Gamma Society, *Adventures in Teaching: Pioneer Women Educators and Influential Teach-*ers (1963), 144–148; BVS Birth Register, Franklin Co. (gives first name as Sally); BVS Marriage Register, Franklin Co.; notes from Essie Smith's undated oral history interview with Booker, WPA Biographies; 1927 campaign covered in *Martinsville Henry Bulletin*, Aug.–Nov. 1927; Election Records, no. 230, RG 13, LVA; por., Special Collections, LVA; obituaries in *Martinsville Daily Bulletin*, 20 Dec. 1944 (por.), and *Richmond Times-Dispatch*, 21 Dec. 1944; editorial tribute in *Martinsville Daily Bulletin*, 21 Dec. 1944.

BRENT TARTER

BOOKER, William (d. by 15 September 1783), member of the Convention of 1776, was born between 1733 and 1736, the son of William Booker and Mary Booker, residents of the part of Amelia County that became Prince Edward County in 1753. He inherited land in Prince Edward County when his father died in 1755, and in 1757 he bought a farm of about 300 acres in the same county, where he lived the remainder of his life. Booker became relatively prosperous, and by the 1780s he owned almost 2,000 acres of land, twenty slaves, and a large, well-furnished house. On 1 April 1755 he married Mary Flournoy in Amelia County. They had at least one son and one daughter who lived to maturity. On 14 May 1768 Booker married his cousin Edith Booker, and they had two or three sons and several daughters. When he composed his will in August 1780, four of his sons and six of his daughters were alive.

Booker was named a justice of the peace for Prince Edward County on 6 November 1766 and in 1775 was elected to the county committee. On 15 April 1776 Booker won election to the last of the Revolutionary Conventions. He attended the convention from opening day on 6 May through adjournment on 5 July. Booker voted for independence, but probably because he was inexperienced in legislative politics he evidently took no active role in the preparation of the Declaration of Rights, the Constitution of 1776, or any of the convention's other work. While in Williamsburg he procured a substantial quantity of arms and supplies for the minutemen of Prince Edward County.

Booker returned to Williamsburg in the autumn of 1776 and again in the spring of 1777 for service in the House of Delegates but then retired to his farm and his county court duties.

Early in 1783 he was named a trustee of Hampden-Sydney College, which probably indicates more that he was a responsible local leader than that he was famed for his learning. At the time of his death his library consisted only of "a parcel of old Books." On 16 June 1783 the Prince Edward County Court recommended that William Booker be appointed county sheriff, but he died between 18 August and 15 September of that year and never served.

Herbert Clarence Bradshaw, *History of Prince Edward County* (1955); father's will of 29 Sept. 1754, listing William Booker as a minor, in Amelia Co. Will Book, 1:115–116; Kathleen Booth Williams, *Marriages of Amelia County, Virginia, 1735–1815* (1961), 14; landholdings and public service documented in Prince Edward Co. Deed Book, vol. 1 (with first land purchase, 10 May 1757, on 92–93), in Land Tax Returns, Prince Edward Co., 1782, 1784, RG 48, LVA, in Prince Edward Co. Order Book, 3:119, 7:77, in *Revolutionary Virginia*, vols. 3–4, 6–7, and in Hening, *Statutes*, 11:272–274; will and estate inventory in Prince Edward Co. Will Book, 1:327–329 (quotation), 340–342; death date range inferred from Prince Edward Co. Order Book, 7, 114, 119.

BRENT TARTER

BOONE, Daniel (22 October 1734–26 September 1820), frontiersman, was born near Reading, Pennsylvania, the son of Squire Boone and Sarah Morgan Boone. Boone's parents were Quakers, but following a dispute between Squire Boone and the Society of Friends, the family left Pennsylvania about the beginning of May 1750 and in October of that year settled near the Yadkin River in what is now Davie County, North Carolina. En route Daniel Boone made his first long trek as a professional hunter. With one companion he left the family's camp in the Shenandoah Valley and spent several months hunting in the Blue Ridge Mountains and along the Roanoke River.

Boone served as a teamster on General Edward Braddock's ill-fated expedition to Fort Duquesne in 1755, after which he returned to the Yadkin Valley and on 14 August 1756 married Rebecca Bryan, a member of a prominent local family. They settled near present-day Farmington, Davie County, North Carolina, and had six sons and four daughters. Early in 1760 Boone temporarily moved his family to Culpeper County to escape the fighting of the Cherokee War and then resumed his life as a professional hunter in the backcountry. He ranged as far as the Holston and Clinch Rivers and won renown for his skills with his gun and traps.

In May 1769 Boone and five companions followed a path through the Cumberland Gap into Virginia's Kentucky wilderness. They spent two years there exploring, hunting, and trapping and returned to the Yadkin Valley in the spring of 1771. In September 1773 Boone set out for Kentucky again, guiding a small party of farmers who intended to establish a settlement there, but during the journey Indians attacked the party and killed one of Boone's sons. Boone retreated to the Clinch River valley with his family and stayed there for two years. In 1774, during Dunmore's War, Boone served as a captain in the Fincastle County militia, overseeing the region's defenses under the command of Colonel William Preston.

In 1775 the North Carolina land speculator Richard Henderson hired Boone to cut a road from the westernmost settlements into Kentucky. The route, later celebrated as the Wilderness Road, ran from present-day Kingsport, Tennessee, through the Cumberland Gap to the Kentucky River, where the first contingent of Henderson's colonists, including Boone's family, built Boonesborough, one of the first settlements in Kentucky. The next summer Indians carried away one of Boone's daughters and two of her companions. Boone tracked the party through the wilderness for three days and rescued the girls on the banks of the Licking River. Boone's fame as a woodsman rested on skills he demonstrated on this and similar occasions, but some of the exploits later attributed to him were embellishments of more modest accomplishments or outright fiction.

In January 1778 Boone led an expedition of about thirty men to the salt springs on the Licking River. While hunting in February he was captured and taken to the Shawnee chief Blackfish, from whom he learned of an Indian plan to drive the settlers out of Kentucky. Hoping to delay the attack, Boone offered to obtain the surrender of his men at the salt springs, accompany the Indians to Boonesborough the following spring, and help them to negotiate the fort's capitulation. He duly persuaded the salt makers to lay down their arms. Some of the captives were sold to the British. Blackfish adopted the remainder, including Boone, who was given the name Sheltowee, or Big Turtle. Boone subsequently escaped in time to return to Boonesborough and lead a successful defense of the settlement. Yet his motives came under suspicion, in part because of the Loyalism of his wife's family, and Boone was later summoned before a court-martial. He was acquitted and soon afterward promoted to major in the militia. Stung by the legal action, Boone and several of his friends formed a new settlement called Boone's Station, and Boone built his own cabin on Marble Creek, several miles away from Boone's Station.

After the creation of Fayette County in 1780, Boone was successively appointed a lieutenant colonel in the militia, elected to the House of Delegates, and commissioned sheriff. While attending the assembly that convened in Richmond in May 1781 but adjourned first to Charlottesville and then to Staunton when the British army marched up the James River, he was taken prisoner but quickly paroled. Boone returned to Kentucky early in 1782, and in August of that year he helped lead an attack on a band of Indians at Blue Lick, where sixty-six Kentuckians died, including another of his sons. About this same time Boone met John Filson, a schoolmaster from Pennsylvania who included a romanticized version of Boone's life in his *Discovery, Settlement and Present State of Kentucke* (1784). The book brought Boone international fame when a French version was published in Paris in 1785.

Boone became deputy surveyor of Fayette County in December 1782 and began speculating in land, but his ventures failed and involved him in expensive and unsuccessful lawsuits. He moved to Limestone in 1783 and opened a trading store and tavern in the small Ohio River port town. When the town was incorporated as Maysville in 1787, Boone was named a trustee, and he won election the same year to the House of Delegates from Bourbon County. In 1789 he moved to Point Pleasant and made another unsuccessful attempt to run a store. In 1791 Boone was elected to the General Assembly a

third time, representing Kanawha County. During all three of his House terms he sat on the Committee for Propositions and Grievances, and in his final term he was also appointed to the Committee for Religion. While attending the legislature Boone contracted to furnish supplies to the county militia. His debts from his store, however, made it impossible for him to obtain credit, and he lost the contract, closed his store, and moved into a cabin in the woods about sixty miles up the Kanawha River from Point Pleasant. Boone was plagued with debts for the remainder of the decade, and a warrant for his arrest was issued in 1798 but never served.

In October 1799 the Spanish governor of Louisiana granted Boone a tract of land at Femme Osage, near the Missouri River. Boone lived the last twenty years of his life in what is now the state of Missouri, but in 1809 a court ruled that he had not satisfied the conditions under which the grant was issued, and he appealed to Congress for a tract of the public domain in recognition of his services to the country. Five years later Congress confirmed his title to the Missouri land. Daniel Boone died at the home of his son Nathan Boone on 26 September 1820 and was buried in the family graveyard. In 1845 bones that were presumed to be those of Boone and his wife were removed from the Missouri graveyard at the behest of the Kentucky legislature and reinterred with much ceremony in a cemetery near the state capitol in Frankfort, Kentucky.

Birth date in family Bible, reproduced in Hazel Atterbury Spraker, *A Genealogical History of the Descendants of George and Mary Boone* (1922), facing 36, is sometimes modernized to 2 Nov. 1734, an innovation Boone resisted; John Mack Faragher, *Daniel Boone: The Life and Legend of an American Pioneer* (1992), por. facing 174; John Bakeless, *Daniel Boone: Master of the Wilderness* (1939), contains evidence for birth date and full bibliography of primary sources; extensive collection of Boone records, including interviews with descendants, in Draper MSS, many of which are compiled as Lyman C. Draper, *The Life of Daniel Boone*, ed. Ted Franklin Belue (1998); obituaries in *Saint Louis Missouri Gazette and Public Advertiser*, 3 Oct. 1820, and *Niles' Weekly Register*, 4 Nov. 1820.

DONALD W. GUNTER

BOONE, Gladys (31 January 1895–23 April 1982), economist, was born in Stoke-upon-Trent,

Staffordshire, England, the daughter of Frederick T. Boone and Florence Adams Boone. Both parents died when she was young, and she was raised in the industrial Midlands of England by an aunt and uncle. Boone was one of the few women who graduated from British universities in the midst of World War I. She received a B.A. in 1916 and an M.A. in history in 1917 from the University of Birmingham. For the next two years Boone worked as a tutor for the Workers' Educational Association in Birmingham in Britain's industrial heartland and thus began a long exposure and commitment to adult education and the workers' education movement, which in Britain had become a firmly established resource for the labor movement and for individual working men and women.

In 1919 Boone obtained a scholarship and traveled to New York to attend graduate school in economics at Columbia University. She thereby entered an intellectual milieu that had inherited from the Progressive era a sense of unlimited possibilities for social and economic change, and she found people who shared her desire to improve the living and working conditions of laboring men and women. Boone joined other strong-minded women activists determined to mitigate what they viewed as the inequitable consequences of industrialization and urbanization.

Boone devoted the next twenty years to undertakings related to labor reform and the burgeoning workers' education movement. She traveled widely and investigated and wrote about the plight of industrial workers in Europe and the United States. In 1920 Boone became an instructor in the Graduate Department of Social Economy and Social Research at Bryn Mawr College, a post she probably used to support her graduate study. At that time M. Carey Thomas, Bryn Mawr's president, was concerned with the education of working women and planning for the influential Bryn Mawr Summer School for Women Workers in Industry. Bryn Mawr's atmosphere of experimentation and commitment to improving women's educational opportunities shaped Boone's career in workers' education and in higher education for women.

In 1922 Boone became an assistant professor of personnel research at the Carnegie Insti-

tute of Technology in Pittsburgh. A year later she moved to Philadelphia to become the executive secretary of the local branch of the Women's Trade Union League. Boone also taught at the Philadelphia Labor College, one of the few organizations in either the United States or Great Britain seeking to break down class barriers and promote the interests of working women by bringing middle- and working-class women together in a difficult and sometimes strained relationship. She stayed in Philadelphia for three years. In 1927 and 1928 Boone was a university fellow at Columbia University. During 1928 and 1929 she worked as assistant editor for the *Encyclopedia of the Social Sciences,* but her own research remained her primary interest, and during summers she worked on her dissertation at her aunt's house in England. Boone's transatlantic focus remained clear, as evidenced by her frequent trips to Europe and attendance at international labor education congresses. This period of her life culminated in the publication of her 1941 Columbia dissertation, the work for which Boone is best known. *The Women's Trade Union Leagues in Great Britain and the United States of America* (1942) broke new ground in the history of the women's reform movement by documenting the efforts of women on both sides of the Atlantic to shape their own public as well as private worlds.

In 1931 Boone joined the faculty of Sweet Briar College. One of a growing number of highly educated activist women recruited by President Meta Glass, Boone taught economics at Sweet Briar until she retired in 1960. A proponent of integrated learning, she helped organize and was the first chair of a new social studies division. She helped shape a coherent liberal arts curriculum and compiled a record of strong participation in faculty and student work at the college. At Boone's death the *Alumnae Bulletin* recalled her as demanding but well liked. An energetic, outgoing faculty member who must have been anything but austere, she continued to tutor students long after her retirement.

Boone's lifelong commitment to reform causes did not wane with her move from the industrial and urban world of the Northeast. In 1934 she produced *Labor Laws in Twelve South-*

ern States, a research report for the National Consumers' League. Three years later Boone completed a study on household employment in Lynchburg for the Young Women's Christian Association and the Interracial Commission. This kind of research formed the backbone of the YWCA's efforts to promote protective labor legislation and ameliorate the condition of black workers in the South. At this time Boone was chair of the economic section of the Lynchburg Interracial Commission, and she probably served on the commission until the end of the 1930s. On the eve of World War II she was conducting research for the state Bureau of Public Administration that led to a joint work entitled *Labor Laws of Virginia* (1940). During the war Boone chaired a regional committee of the National War Labor Board adjudicating labor disputes. She also served as president of the Amherst County Health and Welfare Council for many years.

A committed community activist for causes ranging from public health reform to the amelioration of working conditions, Boone was part of a cadre of tough and dedicated women who provided new professional models and a tradition of reform that white women growing up in the post–World War II South built on in the 1960s. Her life demonstrates that a commitment to labor and racial reform existed in the mid-twentieth-century South, especially among college-educated women, despite the high barriers to change in either the racial mores or the labor laws of the New South. Like many other women of her generation, educational achievement, and career path, Boone never married.

On 23 April 1982 Gladys Boone died in a Lynchburg nursing home. Her body was cremated.

Rowland Andrews Egger, Raymond Uhl, and Vincent Shea, eds., *Who's Who in Public Administration Research in Virginia* (1938), 6; Durward Howes, ed., *American Women: The Standard Biographical Dictionary of Notable Women* (1939–1940), 3:93; *Amherst New Era-Progress*, 27 Apr. 1944; obituaries in *Lynchburg News*, 27 Apr. 1982, *Amherst New Era-Progress*, 29 Apr. 1982, and *Sweet Briar College Alumnae Magazine* (summer 1982): 18 (por.); Richard Rowland, "Memorial Tribute to Gladys Boone," 1982 typescript, DVB Files.

MARION W. ROYDHOUSE

BOOTH, Edwin Gilliam (11 January 1810– 13 February 1886), attorney, was born at Shen-

stone in Nottoway County, the son of Gilliam Booth and Rebecca Hicks Booth. He entered Winfield Academy in Dinwiddie County in 1820, later attended school in Oxford, North Carolina, and matriculated at the University of North Carolina in 1824. After four years there he studied law in Fredericksburg under Judge John Tayloe Lomax and then returned home to learn that much of his personal estate had been lost through the failed speculations of his brother. Booth married Sally Tanner Jones in 1833, and they had three sons and two daughters before her death on 29 August 1860.

Booth opened a law office in Nottoway County and became one of the best-known attorneys in central Virginia. He was elected to the House of Delegates in 1848 and served only one term, but his reputation was so great that he was appointed, along with some of the state's most distinguished lawyers, to the committee to revise the legal code of Virginia. Booth was a Whig and an advocate of education and internal improvements. In January 1849 he sponsored a bill enabling the South Side Railroad Company, of which he was a director, to refinance its debt and resume construction of its line westward from Petersburg into Prince Edward County. Booth also helped found the Virginia Agricultural Society and sat on its board of directors.

In 1860 Booth supported the presidential candidacy of John Bell. He then spent much of the winter of 1860–1861 in Washington, D.C., cooperating with other Unionists in a futile effort to prevent the Civil War. Booth was well-enough known that a Richmond newspaper briefly promoted him in 1863 as a candidate for governor. During the first part of the war, while Booth was living in Virginia, he tried to improve the condition of Union prisoners by providing clothing and medical supplies. Early in 1863 Booth breakfasted with Jefferson Davis. Not long thereafter, having traveled to the North by way of Bermuda and Nova Scotia, Booth ate at the White House with Abraham Lincoln, reputedly becoming the only private citizen to dine with both presidents during the height of the war. Booth then went to Philadelphia, where he married Henrietta Chauncey, the daughter of a wealthy Philadelphia businessman. During the remainder of the war, while he lived in Philadelphia, Booth supplied provisions to Confederate prisoners of war in Northern prisons. In 1864 one of his sons was killed fighting for the Confederacy.

Booth remained in Philadelphia after the war but was at home in both the North and the South and often attended Presbyterian church meetings in Virginia. His second marriage brought him property in nine northern states to go with what he had acquired in Virginia during his successful law practice. He became widely known as an investor in real estate and railroad stock. After the General Assembly of Virginia declined to provide a state building at the centennial exposition in Philadelphia in 1876, Booth built the Old Virginia Building at his own expense and hosted receptions there. In 1879 he bought Carter's Grove, an estate near Williamsburg, and stayed there occasionally on his trips to Virginia. He reputedly had the mansion painted red, white, and blue in observance of the centennial of the siege of Yorktown. Booth's namesake son inherited the property and owned it until 1905. Booth also owned property in Richmond, including Clifton House, which he provided free of rent to the Richmond City Mission for the care of impoverished women.

In 1884 Booth wrote a series of reminiscences and essays for *Progress*, a Philadelphia magazine. A collected edition appeared a year later as *In War Time: Two Years in the Confederacy and Two Years North, With Many Reminiscences of the Days Long Before the War*. Edwin Gilliam Booth died in Philadelphia on 13 February 1886 and was buried in the Chauncey family cemetery in Burlington, New Jersey.

Henry E. Dwight, *The Life and Character of Edwin Gilliam Booth, A Prominent Lawyer, Legislator, and Philanthropist* (1886), frontispiece por.; Booth family genealogical notes, 2:384–388, Kathleen Booth Williams Papers, LVA; Booth letters at UVA and VHS; Mary A. Stephenson, *Carter's Grove Plantation: A History* (1964), 125–132; obituary in *Philadelphia Inquirer*, 15 Feb. 1886.

DONALD W. GUNTER

BOOTHE, Armistead Lloyd (23 September 1907–14 February 1990), member of the House of Delegates and of the Senate of Virginia, was born in Alexandria, the son of Gardner Lloyd Boothe, a Democratic Party leader, and Eleanor Harrison Carr Boothe. After receiving his primary education in the Alexandria public schools he graduated with honors from that city's Episcopal High School in 1924. Boothe enrolled in the University of Virginia in a program that combined a three-year undergraduate course with two years of legal instruction. Graduating as a Phi Beta Kappa in 1928, he was selected as a Rhodes Scholar and spent two years studying law at Oxford University. On 30 June 1934 in Washington, D.C., Boothe married Elizabeth Revenel Peele. They had three daughters.

In 1931 Boothe entered his father's law firm. He became a member of the Alexandria Democratic Committee in 1935 and in 1936 worked as an attorney in the United States Department of Justice. Boothe served from 1939 to 1942 as Alexandria city attorney but left that post for service as a naval air combat intelligence officer in the Pacific theater. While aboard the USS *Hornet*, Boothe had a conversation with a visiting naval officer, Harry Flood Byrd Jr. (b. 1914), that in view of the rest of his political career was ironic and fateful. Byrd's father, a governor and longtime United States senator, headed the dominant faction of the state's Democratic Party. Byrd suggested that Boothe seek state office after the war.

Boothe followed the suggestion and in 1947 won election to represent Alexandria in the House of Delegates. He began his legislative career in the 1948 General Assembly session. For four terms he served on the Committees on Counties, Cities, and Towns, on Currency and Commerce, on Executive Expenditures, and on General Laws. Although affiliated with the Byrd organization, Boothe showed his independence. Persuaded to cosponsor a bill that would have kept President Harry S. Truman's name off the 1948 presidential ballot in Virginia, he thought he had been tricked and helped weaken the bill so much that even though it passed it did not have the intended effect. Leaders of the party, including Boothe's father, had endorsed the bill. Boothe soon took positions favoring a more generous provision of state services and a more liberal policy on race relations than the conservative General Assembly leadership found acceptable. By early in the 1950s Boothe and

Stuart B. Carter, of Fincastle, were leading a group of legislators called the Young Turks. Many of them were World War II veterans elected by the state's growing urban and suburban areas. They formed, in effect, an embryonic progressive wing in the Byrd organization. Most of the measures that they advocated did not pass, but their occasional successes included forcing a legislative reapportionment, securing greater funds for education, and, in a symbolic gesture, gaining Virginia's assent to the Nineteenth Amendment in 1952. In one of their most significant victories, the Young Turks in 1954 deadlocked the General Assembly for hours past its scheduled adjournment and won a compromise by which a portion of the state's surplus revenue was devoted to increased funding of services rather than being returned in its entirety as a tax refund.

Boothe made his definitive break with the Democratic Party organization over the issue of racial segregation. In a 1949 article in the *Virginia Law Review,* he argued that enforcing Virginia's racial segregation statutes was expensive and demeaning. In a prescient passage citing a trend in recent United States Supreme Court cases, he predicted that the Court would soon declare public school segregation unconstitutional. Boothe recommended that Virginia gradually dismantle the state's legal code of segregation. In the 1950 and 1952 assembly sessions he introduced bills to abolish segregation on common carriers and to establish an interracial study group on race relations, but conservatives blocked both proposals.

Early in 1954 Boothe advised the state even more forcefully that school segregation would soon be declared illegal and urged it to prepare for the inevitable transition rather than let change be imposed by the federal government. Legislative leaders again ignored his warnings and sidetracked his bill to establish a race relations study group. After the Supreme Court did declare racially segregated public schools unconstitutional, Boothe acted swiftly. Within a month he sent out a questionnaire surveying the opinions of his legislative colleagues, and by October he had offered his own desegregation plan. Boothe centered his approach on a pupil assignment system designed to limit desegregation to a few students in regions where breaking the color line might be acceptable to the white majority. After his election in 1955 to represent Alexandria in the Senate of Virginia, Boothe joined with Republican Theodore Roosevelt Dalton in proposing a pupil assignment plan permitting limited desegregation. By then Senator Harry Flood Byrd (1887–1966) had issued his call for Massive Resistance to block all desegregation. A strong supporter of public education, Boothe rejected state tuition grants to parents who enrolled their children in segregated private schools, and he led the opposition to these grants in a referendum on 9 January 1956 on the subject.

In January 1959 both state and federal courts declared unconstitutional a central tactic of the Massive Resistance strategy, closing schools that were under court orders to desegregate. Boothe again advanced his assignment plan as an alternative. In the April 1959 legislative special session he voted for the package of measures that Governor James Lindsay Almond proposed. This retreat from Massive Resistance cleared the legislature by only one vote. A professed supporter of segregation even as he opposed Massive Resistance as a threat to the public schools, Boothe became a target for organized segregationists, who strongly backed his conservative opponent in the July 1959 Democratic primary. Despite their efforts, Boothe easily won reelection to the Senate of Virginia. During his two four-year Senate terms he served on the Committees to Examine the Bonds of Public Officers, on Federal Relations, on Insurance and Banking, and on Welfare.

Boothe also sat on the Virginia Code Commission during his service in both houses of the assembly. In 1961 he ran for lieutenant governor. School desegregation and many of the earlier concerns of the Young Turks were major issues. Attacking his Democratic primary opponent, Mills Edwin Godwin Jr., as a Massive Resister and a threat to public education, Boothe advocated increased spending for the schools. Although he received a larger vote than either of his running mates, Boothe lost to Godwin (who had Byrd's support) by a margin of 46 percent to 54 percent.

In 1963 Boothe decided against seeking a third term in the state senate, but in 1966 he ran in the Democratic primary against Harry F. Byrd Jr. for the nomination to fill the United States Senate seat from which Byrd's father had retired. Campaigning on such issues as "one man, one vote" and diplomatic recognition for China and against Byrd's ultraconservative state record, Boothe received the support of more than 49 percent of the electorate, losing by a mere 8,225 votes. That was his last campaign for elective office, but he remained active politically.

After he survived major heart surgery in 1969, Boothe decided to devote the remainder of his career to church work, and he accordingly gave up his law practice at the firm of Boothe, Dudley, Koontz, Blankenship, and Stump. An active Episcopal layman throughout his life, he served six years as director of development at the Protestant Episcopal Theological Seminary (or Virginia Theological Seminary) in Alexandria and four years more as assistant to the seminary's dean. In 1976 Boothe's work for the seminary led him to endorse Byrd, his former opponent, who was successfully seeking reelection to the United States Senate. Although they still disagreed on social matters, Byrd had supported Boothe's position that contributions to colleges should remain tax deductible.

Without bitterness at the frustrations in his political career, Boothe retained a lively interest in public affairs until his final illness, a long struggle with Alzheimer's disease. Armistead Lloyd Boothe died in an Episcopal retirement center in Falls Church on 14 February 1990 and was buried in the cemetery at Virginia Theological Seminary in Alexandria.

Biographies in *Richmond Times-Dispatch*, 5 Jan. 1970, 4 Mar. 1990, *Washington Post*, 30 July 1978, *Richmond News Leader*, 15 Feb. 1990, and Douglas Smith, "'When Reason Collides with Prejudice': Armistead Lloyd Boothe and the Politics of Desegregation in Virginia, 1948–1963," *VMHB* 102 (1994): 5–46 (pors.); Armistead L. Boothe Papers, UVA; information provided by Stuart B. Carter and daughter Eleanor Boothe Smith; J. Harvie Wilkinson III, *Harry Byrd and the Changing Face of Virginia Politics, 1945–1966* (1968); James H. Hershman Jr., "A Rumbling in the Museum: The Opponents of Virginia's Massive Resistance" (Ph.D. diss., UVA, 1978); Armistead L. Boothe, "Civil Rights in Virginia," *Virginia Law Review* 35 (1949): 928–974, "Supreme Court Decision Poses Problem for All," *Virginia Journal of Education* 48 (Sept. 1954): 15–16, "A Virginia Plan for the Public Schools," ibid. 48 (Dec. 1954): 29–31, and campaign statement, ibid. 54 (May 1961): 14, 44; obituaries in *Richmond News Leader*, 14 Feb. 1990, and *Alexandria Gazette Packet*, *Alexandria Journal*, *Richmond Times-Dispatch*, and *Washington Post*, all 15 Feb. 1990.

JAMES H. HERSHMAN JR.

BOOTHE, Gardner Lloyd (1 June 1872–3 May 1964), Democratic Party leader, was born in Alexandria, the son of William Jeremiah Boothe, a businessman, and Mary Leadbeater Boothe. After receiving an education in private schools and reading law under a local attorney, he entered the University of Virginia in 1892. Boothe graduated with a law degree the next year and opened a legal practice in Alexandria. On 7 February 1906 he married Eleanor Harrison Carr, of Petersburg. The elder of their two sons, Armistead Lloyd Boothe, became a prominent state legislator.

Boothe took an active role in Alexandria's political, business, civic, and religious affairs. He became president of the First National Bank in 1909 and retained that position for forty-six years. Boothe served on the boards of directors of the Washington Gas Light Company, the Virginia Electric and Power Company, and the Potomac Electric and Power Company. In 1895 he was elected to the vestry of Christ Church, the city's oldest Episcopal church, and served fifty-eight years. From 1916 to 1956 he was a trustee of Alexandria's Protestant Episcopal Theological Seminary (or Virginia Theological Seminary) and of the Protestant Episcopal Education Society in Virginia. A member of the standing committee of the Diocese of Virginia, Boothe was also a trustee of the Episcopal High School in Alexandria and of Woodberry Forest School in Orange. He promoted various civic and charity endeavors in Alexandria, including service on the advisory board of the Mount Vernon Ladies' Association of the Union from 1935 until 1963.

By the first decade of the twentieth century Boothe was at the center of a group of local leaders who virtually ran Alexandria's political life. He was also a principal figure in his congressional district's politics and from that base became one of the strongest party leaders in northern Virginia, with prominence at the state level. In 1897 Boothe became city attorney, and in 1902 he was elected a member of the State Central Committee of the Democratic Party and chairman of the Eighth District Committee. For the next fifty years he chaired the Eighth District Committee, resigning in 1952 after reapportionment placed Alexandria in the new Tenth District. During that time Boothe was aligned with the dominant faction of the state party, headed after the mid-1920s by Harry Flood Byrd (1887–1966). Boothe was campaign chairman in 1930 for the first of Howard W. Smith's seventeen successful congressional campaigns. On 6 March 1948 Boothe introduced resolutions at a meeting of the state central committee that both roundly condemned Harry S. Truman's civil rights policies and supported Governor William Munford Tuck's unsuccessful attempt to keep the president's name off the ballot in Virginia. The resolutions passed unanimously and urged Virginia's congressmen to oppose proposals for new civil rights legislation.

Boothe's law practice thrived, and in 1952 he became the senior partner in the firm of Boothe, Dudley, Koontz, and Boothe. More than a decade after Boothe's death he was remembered for his characterization of the Virginia gentleman as someone who walked his horse the last mile home, never crushed the mint in his julep, and always sliced his ham very thin. Gardner Lloyd Boothe died at his home in Alexandria on 3 May 1964 after a long illness and was buried in Ivy Hill Cemetery in Alexandria.

Biographies in Tyler, *Encyclopedia*, 5:590–591, and Philip Alexander Bruce, *Virginia: Rebirth of the Old Dominion* (1929), 4:6–8; some Boothe letters in Armistead L. Boothe Papers, UVA; Bruce J. Dierenfield, *Keeper of the Rules: Congressman Howard W. Smith of Virginia* (1987), 22, 32, 35; Douglas Smith, "'When Reason Collides with Prejudice': Armistead Lloyd Boothe and the Politics of Desegregation in Virginia, 1948–1963," *VMHB* 102 (1994): 7–8; *Richmond Times-Dispatch*, 7 Mar. 1948; definition of gentleman in *Washington Post*, 30 July 1978; obituaries in *Alexandria Gazette,* 4 May 1964, and *Washington Post* (por.), 5 May 1964.

JAMES H. HERSHMAN JR.

BORDEN, Benjamin (6 April 1675–by 9 December 1743), land speculator, was born in Monmouth County, New Jersey, the son of Benjamin Borden and Abigail Grover Borden. Little is known about his early life, but in April 1726 his name appeared on a deed as an inhabitant of Freehold, New Jersey, where he was probably acting as a land agent and speculator. Borden married a cousin, Zeruiah Winter, and they had at least three sons and seven daughters.

By April 1734 Borden had taken up residence in Virginia in the northern, or lower, portion of the Shenandoah Valley. On 3 October 1734 Borden received a patent for 3,143 acres in an area of what is now Clarke County that came to be called Borden's Great Spring Tract. He raised tobacco and lived there until his death. In addition to acquiring other tracts in the lower Valley near Apple Pie Ridge, Bullskin Run, and Smith's Creek, Borden received 100,000 acres along the branches of the James River in the upper part of the Shenandoah Valley in May 1735 from the governor's Council. According to an apocryphal story, he obtained this large grant by winning the favor of Lieutenant Governor William Gooch through the gift of a buffalo calf. For the next four years Borden gave much of his attention to fulfilling the settlement requirement for the grant of one family for every 1,000 acres. On 6 November 1739 he solidified his claim to this land by receiving a patent for 92,100 acres of what by then was called the Borden Tract.

Borden was among the most important of those land promoters, also including William Beverley, Jost Hite, and Alexander Ross, whose activities helped populate Virginia's first frontier settlements west of the Blue Ridge. By actively recruiting among recent emigrants from the north of Ireland, Borden furthered the emergence of an ethnically and religiously pluralistic society in the region. After his death the duty of settling the Borden Tract fell to his namesake son, who also served as a militia captain and justice of the peace in Augusta County. Legal disputes over surveys and deeds on the Borden lands were not fully resolved until 1885. Other complaints about large land grants also arose. In 1786 residents of Rockbridge County in the upper part of the Shenandoah Valley protested to the General Assembly that the large colonial grants represented "hard and oppressive" monopolies characteristic of monarchies, "where the natural rights of men are so much abused." They complained that the speculators had avoided paying taxes on their land and had sold the actual settlers small tracts at excessive prices. The petitioners requested the legislators to resurvey the tract and dispose of ungranted land at reasonable prices. Borden's reputation had become that of a beneficiary of privilege rather than an entrepreneur opening to ordinary immigrants the possibility of landownership.

Borden was appointed a justice of the peace for the area northwest of the Blue Ridge in April 1734 and was a member of the Orange County Court in January 1735. His name appeared second in seniority in the list of the first justices of the peace for Frederick County in October 1743, but he did not serve in this capacity. Benjamin Borden wrote his will on 3 April 1742 and died probably about the time that the new county's court began to function in November 1743. His will was proved before the justices of the Frederick County Court on 9 December 1743.

John Alexander Kelly, "Benjamin Borden, Shenandoah Valley Pioneer: Notes on His Ancestry and Descendants," *WMQ*, 2d ser., 11 (1931): 325–329; Hattie Borden Weld, *Historical and Genealogical Record of the Descendants . . . of Richard and Joan Borden* [ca. 1899], 74–82; Richard E. Griffith, "Early Estates of Clarke County," *Proceedings of the Clarke County Historical Association* 11/12 (1951/1953): 116–131; *Executive Journals of Council*, 4:319 (first record of presence in Virginia), 351, 408–409; Patent Book, 15:326–327, 18:360–362, RG 4, LVA; Oren F. Morton, *A History of Rockbridge County, Virginia* (1920), 21–32; William Couper, *History of the Shenandoah Valley* (1952), 1:223–224, 261–263, 274–283, 293–306; Robert D. Mitchell, *Commercialism and Frontier: Perspectives on the Early Shenandoah Valley* (1977), 31–36, 61–78, 80–81; Legislative Petitions, Rockbridge Co., 6 Dec. 1786, RG 78, LVA (quotations); will and estate inventory in Frederick Co. Will Book, 1:4–5, 39–40.

WARREN R. HOFSTRA

BOREMAN, Arthur Ingraham (24 July 1823–19 April 1896), president of the Wheeling Convention of 1861, was born in Waynesburg, Pennsylvania, the son of Kenner Seaton Boreman and Sara Ingraham Boreman. His father moved the family to northwestern Virginia, and Boreman grew up in Tyler County. He was educated in local schools and then read law in the office of his elder brother William Boreman in Middlebourne.

Boreman began his law practice in Parkersburg immediately after his admission to the bar in May 1843. Originally a Whig, he was sympathetic to the nativist American (Know Nothing) Party during the 1850s, and in 1855 he won election to the House of Delegates from Wood County. Boreman was reelected twice and served in all the sessions from December 1855 through April 1861. He sat on the Committee on Banks during his first term and on the Committee on Finance during his final two terms. In addition, during his second term he served on the Committee on Lunatic Asylums and during his first and third terms on the Joint Committee to Examine the Bonds of Public Officers, which he chaired in 1859. An active promoter of internal improvements in his region, Boreman found his assembly service frustrating because the leading politicians of eastern Virginia made it difficult for western representatives to obtain charters for banks and railroads.

Boreman was a committed Unionist during the secession crisis. After the General Assembly adjourned in April 1861 he returned home and took a leading part in the formation of a loyal Virginia government. Boreman served as president of the Second Wheeling Convention that met from 11 to 25 June and 6 to 21 August 1861, during which it declared the state offices of Virginia vacant, elected Francis Harrison Pierpont governor, and sent John Snyder Carlile and Waitman Thomas Willey to the United States Senate. From October 1861 to 1863 Boreman served as a circuit court judge under the authority of the so-called Restored government of Virginia.

After Abraham Lincoln's proclamation that West Virginia would be admitted to the Union effective 20 June 1863, Boreman was elected the new state's first governor on 28 May of that year. He was reelected without opposition in October 1864 and again overwhelmingly elected in October 1866, serving until 26 February 1869. Early in 1869 he successfully ran for the United States Senate. Boreman was an uncompromising Unionist during the war and a Radical Republican immediately afterward. He advocated the disfranchisement of former Confederates, but he gradually moved away from the radical wing of the Republican Party during his one term in the Senate. He sat on the Committees on Claims and on Manufactures, and in the 43d Congress, from March 1873 to March 1875, he chaired the Committee on Territories. During the 42d Congress he made a lengthy speech supporting stronger enforcement of the Fourteenth Amendment in response to Ku Klux Klan activities. Boreman did not seek reelection in 1875, by which time the Democratic Party had won control of the West Virginia General Assembly.

Boreman practiced law in Parkersburg until 1888, when he was elected judge of the West Virginia Fifth Circuit Court. He was also a lay leader in the Methodist Church. On 30 November 1864 he had married Laurane Tanner Bullock, a widow with three young children, and they had two daughters. Arthur Ingraham Boreman died at his home in Parkersburg, West Virginia, on 19 April 1896 and was buried in Odd Fellows Cemetery (later Parkersburg Memorial Gardens) in that city.

Atkinson and Gibbens, *Prominent Men*, 153–156; George W. Atkinson, ed., *Bench and Bar of West Virginia* (1919), 22–23; Isaiah Alfonso Woodward, "Arthur Ingraham Boreman: A Biography," *West Virginia History* 31 (1970): 206–269, and 32 (1970): 10–48; John G. Morgan, *West Virginia Governors, 1863–1980*, 2d ed. (1981), 9–15 (por. on 8); Arthur I. Boreman Papers in WVSA and in West Virginia Collection, WVU; obituary in *Wheeling Intelligencer*, 20 Apr. 1896 (por.).

PAUL D. CASDORPH

BORJES, Charles Simpson (25 November 1891–23 May 1959), photographer, was born in Norfolk, the son of Charles E. Borjes and Gertrude Russell Borjes. His father, a music teacher and conductor, had been born in New York of German-immigrant parents, and his mother was related to the Richmond sculptor Edward Virginius Valentine. He attended public schools in Norfolk and began a career as a professional baseball player with a minor league team in Bristol, but he broke his ankle and later had a foot crushed in an elevator accident, a mishap that ended his baseball career and left him with a permanent limp.

Borjes (pronounced Bŏr′-jēz) became interested in photography as a teenager after his parents gave him a camera as a Christmas present.

He admired the work of the Norfolk photographer Harry C. Mann and spent many hours on the seacoast photographing the dunes. In 1913 Borjes became the first full-time photographer for the *Norfolk Virginian-Pilot*. With the exception of service on the Mexican border with the Norfolk Light Infantry Blues just before the United States entered World War I, Borjes remained the newspaper's principal staff photographer for forty-three years. The credit line "Staff Photo by Borjes" became synonymous with high quality, and young photographers benefited from his tutelage. His energy, resourcefulness, and ability to produce excellent images with unsophisticated equipment eventually won him renown as the dean of Virginia press photographers.

Borjes photographed every president of the United States from Woodrow Wilson through Dwight Eisenhower, and he documented Norfolk's involvement in two world wars, the Great Depression, and the great hurricane of 1933, as well as Ku Klux Klan demonstrations, shipwrecks, sporting events, fires, elections, and the natural beauty of the Cape Henry dunes. He was known in the newsroom for his reckless driving en route to assignments as much as for his patience in setting up and getting the right shot. Locally he was recognized for his action photographs of sporting events, taken before the advent of high-speed film. Borjes gained his first fame outside the Norfolk area when he took photographs of the smoking ruins of the United States Army Air Service's airship *Roma* after it struck a power line and crashed in flames at the Hampton Roads Army Air Base near Hampton on 21 February 1922. Thirty-four people died in the worst air accident in the country to that date.

Borjes retired at the end of 1956 and was presented in January 1957 with a life membership in the Virginia Press Photographers Association. The Norfolk Chamber of Commerce also gave him its citizenship award. A lifelong bachelor, he cared for his invalid mother for many years until her death early in 1959. Charles Simpson Borjes died of lung cancer in Portsmouth General Hospital on 23 May 1959 and was buried in the family plot in Elmwood Cemetery in Norfolk.

Feature article in *Norfolk Virginian-Pilot*, 30 Dec. 1956 (por.); Norfolk City Birth Register; career documented in files of *Norfolk Virginian-Pilot* library, Norfolk; collection of 30,000 prints and negatives in Norfolk Public Library; smaller collection at Mariners' Museum, Newport News; other information supplied by nephews George Borjes and Russell Borjes and by William N. Abourjilie, Alonzo T. Dill, and Louisa Venable Kyle; obituary in *Norfolk Virginian-Pilot*, 24 May 1959; obituary and editorial tribute in *Norfolk Ledger-Dispatch and Portsmouth Star*, 25 May 1959.
STEPHEN S. MANSFIELD

BORLAND, Charles Barney (8 January 1886–3 March 1972), city manager of Norfolk, was born in Norfolk, the son of Thomas Roscius Borland, a Norfolk attorney, and his second wife, Caroline Barney Borland. He was educated in private schools in Norfolk, including the Norfolk Academy, and at Horner Military School in Oxford, North Carolina, from which he graduated in 1903.

From 1903 to 1917 Borland worked in Norfolk in a series of clerkships, for a law office, a cotton broker, and a railroad, and as local agent of the United States Casualty Company. Borland joined the Virginia National Guard in 1903 and went on active duty when the United States entered World War I in April 1917. On 4 August 1917, while in New York, he married Grace Odend'hal, of Norfolk. They had no children. Borland embarked for Europe on 28 June 1918, served in the 112th Field Artillery, 29th Division, in France during the final months of the war, and was discharged with the rank of major on 25 August 1919. He remained affiliated with the Virginia National Guard and on 20 January 1923 was commissioned a lieutenant colonel. Thereafter he was often referred to as Colonel Borland.

On 18 October 1919 Borland was appointed the first inspector of the Norfolk Police Division, and on 29 September 1920 he became chief of police. He was promoted to director of public safety on 17 July 1922, with authority to lead the police and fire departments and supervise the city's public buildings. In April 1934 Borland resumed the title of chief of police but retained the office of director of public safety. He was active in local Democratic Party politics and ran unsuccessfully for city treasurer in 1933. Five years later he supported a slate of reform candidates for city council. They defeated the incumbent councilmen and on 1 September 1938 appointed Borland city manager of Norfolk.

Borland again relinquished his job as police chief but remained director of public safety. When he took office the city devoted more than 40 percent of its revenue to debt service. Borland took on the job of director of finance and with the aid of the council and the General Assembly refinanced the city's bonds and ended deficit financing. He restored the salaries of municipal employees to pre-Depression levels and created a pension system. He also instituted policy changes that enabled the city to hire its first African American police officer in 1941. Borland had served as president of the League of Virginia Municipalities from 1928 to 1929, and he was elected president a second time in 1944.

A population explosion that occurred during World War II brought with it Borland's greatest challenges. Norfolk spent millions of dollars to improve its municipal water system, construct a new municipal airport, and provide housing and schools. Borland helped establish the Norfolk Redevelopment and Housing Authority, and he cooperated closely with the military authorities during the war years. From December 1943 until June 1946 he served on and often chaired the Hampton Roads Sanitation District Commission. Borland was director of civilian defense for Norfolk from 1942 to 1945 and acted as temporary chairman of the Norfolk War Price and Rationing Board from February to June 1943. His military style of management and scandals within the police department drew criticism, but he cited a meddlesome city council as his reason for resigning from all of his city jobs effective 31 December 1945.

Borland became executive vice president of the Jamestown Corporation in June 1946 and supervised the construction of the open-air theater used to stage a drama called *The Common Glory*. He was executive director of the Norfolk chapter of the American Red Cross from September 1947 to May 1949, when he returned to public service as general manager of the Hampton Roads Sanitation District Commission. Borland retired on 30 June 1958 but remained active in the Episcopal Church of the Good Shepherd in Norfolk and in several fraternal, service, and veterans' organizations. His first wife died on 10 May 1959, and on 15 November 1960 Borland married Cornelia McBlair Stribling. They moved to Virginia Beach the following summer. Charles Barney Borland died of congestive heart failure in the Virginia Beach General Hospital on 3 March 1972 and was buried in Elmwood Cemetery in Norfolk.

Biography in Rogers Dey Whichard, ed., *The History of Lower Tidewater Virginia* (1959), 3:59–61; *Virginian-Pilot and the Norfolk Landmark*, 5 Aug. 1917; Military Service Records (contain por. and several transcription errors); Borland city manager scrapbooks, Norfolk Public Library; "With Steady and Capable Hands at the Helm Norfolk Looks to the Future with Confidence" and "Resume of Norfolk Municipal Accomplishments—1939–1944," *Know*, publication of Norfolk Advertising Board (July 1945): 90–92, 93–95, 167–169; *Norfolk Virginian-Pilot*, 16 Nov. 1960; Phyllis A. Hall, "Crisis at Hampton Roads: The Problems of Wartime Congestion, 1942–1944," *VMHB* 101 (1993): 416, 421, 426; obituaries in *Norfolk Ledger-Star* and *Norfolk Virginian-Pilot* (por.), both 4 Mar. 1972; memorial in *Virginia Municipal Review* 50 (1972): 47–48.

R. BRECKENRIDGE DAUGHTREY

BORNSTEIN, Yetta Libby Frieden (15 February 1913–8 December 1968), painter, was born in Waynesboro, Pennsylvania, the daughter of Samuel Frieden and Anna Hoffman Frieden, both of whom had emigrated from Lithuania when young. About 1923 the family moved to Norfolk, where her father joined his elder brother in a mercantile firm. Frieden attended school in Norfolk and worked as a bookkeeper in Norfolk and in Richmond, where she studied art privately and began painting commissioned portraits. On 25 January 1941 in Fredericksburg she married Harry Bornstein, a native of Richmond and a certified public accountant. They moved to Norfolk, where they had two daughters.

In 1959 Bornstein resumed her study of painting at the Norfolk Division of the College of William and Mary (later Old Dominion University), working with Charles K. Sibley, a noted artist and chairman of the Art Department. Under his tutelage she moved away from the traditional methods of her early training to embrace a nonobjective interpretation and learned to improvise. Bornstein joined a garden club when she decided that she needed to study flowers in order to paint them. Her favorite media included collage, and she experimented with combinations of casein, ink, oil, watercolor, and such textural elements as rice paper and foil to develop her abstract style. In the program for Bornstein's first one-woman show at the Norfolk Museum of Arts and Sciences in December 1960, Sibley wrote an introduction lauding as "outstanding" his student's "ability to improvise and to explore with the various media" and declaring that her "technical innovations . . . demonstrate her willingness to do what the more conventional painter often hesitates to do." Norfolk Museum director Henry B. Caldwell described her as "a colorist of the first order."

Within the year Bornstein's work appeared in galleries and museums in Norfolk, Richmond, Virginia Beach, and Williamsburg. After 1961 she began to take her work outside the state, to the annual American Watercolor Society and Audubon Artists exhibitions in New York, to the Lowe Art Gallery in Miami, Florida, and to the Denver Art Museum. Bornstein had a one-woman show at the New York World's Fair in 1965 and others at colleges and museums across the United States between 1963 and 1965. The National Association of Women Artists, to which she belonged, sponsored exhibitions in South America and Europe in 1965 and 1966 featuring her work.

Bornstein received the Tidewater Artists Association's watercolor prize in 1962 and its Dudley Cooper Best in Show Award a year later, took first place in the Biannual of Virginia Artists in Williamsburg in 1962, and won the 1963 Purchase Prize in the Joe and Emily Lowe First National Painting Exhibition in Miami. She served as vice president of the Tidewater Artists Association and in 1966 was the fourth Norfolk artist selected for membership in the Audubon Artists organization of New York City. In March 1967 she was elected to the American Watercolor Society. Bornstein also taught art to children at the Hebrew Academy and the Jewish Community Center, both in Norfolk. In 1967 she opened the Bornstein Gallery, an art supply business near Old Dominion University, which provided a place for local artists to show their work.

Yetta Libby Frieden Bornstein died in Norfolk on 8 December 1968 and was buried in Forest Lawn Cemetery in that city. At the time of her death her works were booked through 1969 in two exhibitions traveling to colleges and museums nationwide. The Tidewater Artists Association posthumously established the Yetta F. Bornstein Scholarship fund, which provides prizes for outstanding Tidewater high school student-artists who compete in the annual Student Gallery in Norfolk.

Bornstein biographical files in Norfolk Public Library, including printed Norfolk Museum exhibition catalog, 30 Nov.–28 Dec. [1960] (quotations), and in Virginia Museum of Fine Arts, Richmond, including her MS and typed biographical reference forms (which give place and date of birth) and printed Jewish Community Center exhibition catalog, 20 Jan.–17 Feb. 1963; Richmond City Marriage Register recording date of marriage in Fredericksburg; feature articles in *Norfolk Virginian-Pilot*, 29 Nov. 1959, 25 June 1964, in *Norfolk Ledger-Dispatch and Star*, 12 Apr. 1962, and in *Norfolk Ledger-Star*, 19 Jan. 1963, 9 June, 28 July 1965, 30 Apr. 1966, 4 Jan. 1967; obituaries with pors. in *Norfolk Ledger-Star* and *Norfolk Virginian-Pilot*, both 9 Dec. 1968.

ANNE B. HARRIS

BORST, Peter Bock (23 June 1826–25 April 1882), member of the Convention of 1861, was born in Schoharie County, New York, the son of Peter I. Borst, a one-term congressman, and Catherine Becker Borst. Little is known of Borst's youth or education. He had studied law and moved to Luray sometime before 27 September 1847, when he qualified to practice law and began a long and successful career at the bar and in business.

In April 1851 Borst married Isabella C. Almond. They had two daughters and two sons. In 1852 he was elected commonwealth's attorney for Page County, a position he held without interruption from 1852 until 1869. By 1860 Borst was one of Luray's most successful businessmen, with $40,000 worth of real estate and a personal estate estimated at more than $10,000. He owned at least four slaves in that year.

On 4 February 1861 Borst was elected to represent Page County in a state convention called to consider the secession question. Unlike many other residents of the lower Shenandoah Valley, he was not a strong Unionist, and early in the convention's proceedings he expressed alarm at shipments of men and arms to United States government military installations in Virginia. Borst voted for secession on 4 April 1861, when the question came up for the first time and failed to pass, and he supported secession again when it passed on 17 April. Borst attended the brief second and third sessions of the Convention of 1861 but took no other official part in the Civil War. He remained in Luray, where he operated a tanyard and sold harnesses to the Confederate army. Because of his wealth, not because he had fought for or held office under the Confederacy, he applied for a presidential pardon on 24 June 1865 and was granted it on 6 July.

The United States Army dismissed Borst from his position as commonwealth's attorney early in 1869, but after a new state constitution went into effect in 1870 he won election to another term. Borst retained an interest in politics and served on the Conservative Party's state committee in 1873. By then his real estate holdings, including a large property in Culpeper County, exceeded $220,000 in assessed value. Borst served as the first president of the Shenandoah Valley Railroad Company, which was incorporated in 1867 and which connected the Pennsylvania Railroad at Hagerstown, Maryland, to the emerging rail hub at Big Lick (later the city of Roanoke). The road was established by Pennsylvania promoters eager to tap the natural resources and markets of the Shenandoah Valley. Borst served as its president for four years, during which construction was begun but not completed. He also promoted and raised money for the Washington, Cincinnati, and Saint Louis Railroad, chartered in March 1871.

In 1852, the year after his marriage, Borst employed his knowledge of Greek Revival architecture, then much in vogue, to design a large new house in Luray. One of his daughters named it Aventine, for one of the Seven Hills of Rome. The mansion is composed of an interesting combination of designs that distinguish it from the Georgian and Federal structures more commonly found in Virginia. Aventine was the main building of the short-lived Luray College and still stands, although it was moved in 1937 from its original site.

Peter Bock Borst continued to practice law in Page County and had just concluded an argument before the bench when he collapsed and died in the courthouse at Luray on 25 April 1882. He was buried in Green Hill Cemetery in that town.

James A. Cross, *A History of Borst Families in America, 1710–1865* (1993), 36; Page Co. Marriage Register (bond dated 1 Apr. 1851); Judith A. Campbell, *Page County, Virginia, Marriages, 1831–1864* (1995), 13, gives marriage date as 3 Apr. 1851; Harry M. Strickler, *A Short History of Page County, Virginia* (1952), 164, 169, 377; Reese and Gaines, *Proceedings of 1861 Convention,* 1:150–151, 3:163, 4:144; Presidential Pardons; Jennie Ann Kerkhoff, *Old Homes of Page County, Virginia* (1962), 161–163; Mason Y. Cooper, *Norfolk and Western's Shenandoah Valley Line* (1998), 11–12, 22, 34, 173; obituaries in *Lynchburg Virginian*, 28 Apr. 1882, and *Berryville Clarke Courier*, 4 May 1882 (gives variant death date of 24 Apr. 1882).

DONALD W. GUNTER

BORUM, John Thomas (13 July 1896–23 January 1969), journalist, was born in Accomac, the son of George B. Borum and Blanche Fogle Borum. Shortly after his birth the family moved to Onancock, where his father was employed by the *Accomack News*. Borum's formal education in the public school system ended at age fourteen when he joined his father on the staff of the newspaper and learned from him the printer's trade. Borum enlisted in the Marine Corps on 21 June 1918 and served in Germany after the end of World War I. He returned to Onancock after his discharge in April 1919. In 1918 Borum had become part owner of the *Accomack News*. He became the publisher in 1919, and a year later he acquired the remaining interest in the paper and became both editor and publisher. On 9 February 1929 Borum married Thelma Virginia Bradley, a bookkeeper in the Northampton County town of Exmore, who was originally from Riverton, Wicomico County, Maryland. She became vice president and secretary-treasurer of the paper. They had no children.

When Borum became its publisher the *Accomack News* was a small eight-page weekly paper, with the four interior pages printed in Baltimore and local advertisements and neighbor-hood news appearing on the front page. He immediately changed the paper's format, put only news on the front page, and moved all printing operations to Onancock. In 1925 Borum changed the paper's name to the *News* after consolidating it with the *Eastern Shore News* of Cape Charles, which he had purchased in 1924. In 1933 he changed the name again, to the *Eastern Shore News*. The weekly paper regularly averaged thirty-six to forty pages, and by the time of Borum's retirement in 1957, it had a paid circulation of more than 7,000 in Virginia's two Eastern Shore counties and a weekly press run of 8,500. The *Eastern Shore News* was one of the largest weekly papers in the South and won several awards from the Virginia Press Association and other trade organizations. Journalism schools regularly requested copies of the paper for classroom study, and the University of Oklahoma listed it among the eleven best weeklies in the nation.

Borum knew all aspects of newspaper work. He had set and distributed type by hand when he was young, and he served as the paper's photographer, sold and composed advertisements, and wrote both news articles and editorials. As the paper's chief reporter Borum cultivated a dedicated corps of volunteer correspondents in the towns and villages of the Eastern Shore. Renowned for his intense energy and tireless devotion to the newspaper, he regularly worked seven days a week and rarely took vacations. In March 1949 Borum began the Eastern Shore's first daily newspaper, the *Eastern Shore Daily News*, but it was not financially successful, and he discontinued it the next month. The printing office was badly damaged in a fire in 1950, but the publishers of the *Peninsula Enterprise* in Accomac printed two editions of the *Eastern Shore News* during repairs, and the paper did not miss a deadline. Borum's plant also printed the *Chincoteague Beacon* and did job work.

In September 1957 Borum and his wife sold the *Eastern Shore News* to two of its employees and retired. They remained in Onancock until 1968, and Borum served as local correspondent for the *Norfolk Ledger-Dispatch* and the *Daily Press* of Salisbury. In 1968 they moved to Naples, Florida. John Thomas Borum died in

Naples on 23 January 1969 and was buried at Mount Holly Cemetery in Onancock.

Philip Alexander Bruce, *Virginia: Rebirth of the Old Dominion* (1929), 4:360–361 (gives incorrect birth year of 1897); Nora Miller Turman, *The Eastern Shore of Virginia, 1603–1964* (1964), 257; BVS Birth Register, Accomack Co.; BVS Marriage Register, Northampton Co.; Military Service Records; information provided by Ben D. Byrd; *Onancock Eastern Shore News*, 27 Jan. 1950, 26 Sept., 3 Oct. 1957, 17 Dec. 1984; Accomack Co. Wills, 33:201; obituaries in *Onancock Eastern Shore News*, 30 Jan. 1969 (por.), and *Virginia Publisher and Printer* 53 (1969): 7.

KIRK MARINER

BOSCHEN, Albert Orlando (25 June 1873–15 August 1957), member of the House of Delegates, was born in Richmond, the son of Margaret Frishkorn Boschen and Henry C. Boschen, a shoe manufacturer and a leading figure in Richmond professional baseball in the 1880s. Boschen was educated in the Richmond public schools, at Saint Mary's Benedictine Institute, and at the Old Dominion Business College. He enrolled in the law department at Richmond College in February 1896 and paid his way through law school by working in his father's factory. In September 1898 he was admitted to the bar, after which he opened a law office in Richmond. On 7 June 1899 Boschen married Mamie Jane Toomey. They had three daughters.

Boschen practiced law in Richmond for more than fifty-five years. For much of that time he was also active in local amateur theatrical groups, performing with local stock companies, taking part in historical pageants, and for twelve years beginning in 1912 directing the dramatic productions of the Samis Grotto Masonic lodge in Richmond. Boschen began participating in Democratic Party politics almost as soon as he started practicing law. He was secretary of the Richmond City Democratic Central Committee from 1900 to 1902, and in 1917 he won election as one of five Richmond members of the House of Delegates. At the very outset of his first term Boschen established himself as an opponent of Prohibition. He was one of only thirteen delegates who voted against ratification of the Eighteenth Amendment on 11 January 1918. He sponsored two measures that passed during his first term, an antitrust act and a law that outlawed the storage of foodstuffs in warehouses with the intention of inflating prices. During the 1920 session of the assembly Boschen sponsored several additional consumer protection bills, including measures to prevent price gouging, ensure sanitary conditions in bakeries, and require manufacturers to place informative labels on processed foods. He remained a vocal critic of Prohibition and introduced a bill during the 1926 assembly session seeking to require public disclosure of private contributions made to the Anti-Saloon League of Virginia.

Boschen unsuccessfully sought the Democratic Party's nomination for commonwealth's attorney of Richmond in 1921. He was reelected to the House of Delegates in 1923 and 1925 but lost the Democratic Party primary on 2 August 1927. Following his defeat Boschen continued his personal crusade against Prohibition by writing *Andrew Trayton: A Novel of Modern Life* (1928). The book attacked moonshiners, bootleggers, and corrupt county officials, whose misdeeds Boschen attributed to the legal prohibition on alcohol. Identifying himself as an "original wet," he did not give up the fight until the Eighteenth Amendment was repealed in 1933.

Boschen failed in a bid to return to the House of Delegates in 1931, but in 1933 he was reelected and served for another twenty years until he was defeated in the primary election in 1953. He sat on the Committee on Appropriations from 1936 through 1952 and chaired the Committee on Asylums and Prisons (renamed Public Institutions in 1950) from 1938 through 1952. Described as "peppery, [and] quick-tempered," Boschen was a vocal and opinionated delegate who criticized high taxes, centralized government, and monopolies of all kinds. He was never one of the party's leaders in the House of Delegates, even though he became one of the senior members in length of service.

Albert Orlando Boschen retired from the practice of law in the mid-1950s and died at his home on 15 August 1957. He was buried in Hollywood Cemetery in Richmond.

Bruce, Tyler, and Morton, *History of Virginia*, 4:176–177; political career in *Richmond Times-Dispatch*, 10 Dec. 1925, 10 Jan. 1926, 3 July, 3 Aug. 1927, 5 Aug. 1931, 11 Jan. 1934, 20 Nov. 1935, 18 Mar. 1936, 13 Jan. 1937 (por.), 17

Jan. 1952, and *Richmond News Leader*, 2, 20 Jan. 1926, 15 July 1953; obituaries in *Richmond News Leader* and *Richmond Times-Dispatch* (por. and quotation), both 16 Aug. 1957.

CATHERINE T. MISHLER

BOSHER, Kate Lee Langley (1 February 1865–27 July 1932), writer and woman suffrage activist, was born in Norfolk, the daughter of Charles Henry Langley and Portia Virginia Deming Langley. She spent her childhood in Norfolk and graduated from the Norfolk College for Young Ladies in 1882. On 12 October 1887 she married Charles Gideon Bosher, of Richmond, a brother of the medical educator Lewis Crenshaw Bosher and part owner of a carriage manufacturing business. They lived in downtown Richmond until their move after World War I to a large house on fashionable Monument Avenue. They had no children.

Bosher was perhaps best known for her success as a writer of popular fiction. Her first book, *"Bobbie"* (1899), published in Richmond under the pseudonym Kate Cairns, is a short novel set in Civil War Virginia. Her remaining works appeared under her own name, starting with *When Love Is Love* (1904). The New York publisher Harper issued eight Bosher novels: *Mary Cary "Frequently Martha"* (1910), *Miss Gibbie Gault* (1911), *The Man in Lonely Land* (1912), *The House of Happiness* (1913), *How It Happened* (1914), *People Like That* (1916), *Kitty Canary* (1918), and *His Friend Miss McFarlane* (1919). *Mary Cary* enjoyed instant success, selling more than 100,000 copies in its first year and doing well for years thereafter. Other successful books were *Miss Gibbie Gault*, *Kitty Canary*, and *His Friend Miss McFarlane*.

These works were often set in Virginia or elsewhere in the South. Focused on the experiences of southerners in the aftermath of the Civil War, most feature as a central character an orphan or a child in need of assistance. Bosher wrote popular novels in the romantic style featuring well-drawn subsidiary characters and treating the differences between the private and public lives of the main characters, most notably in *Mary Cary* and *His Friend Miss McFarlane*. She also contributed shorter works to a variety of national newspapers and magazines and enjoyed her position as a celebrated author.

A different circle of acquaintances and admirers knew Bosher for her advocacy of woman suffrage. A contemporary and friend of Richmond's most famous suffragist, Lila Meade Valentine, she was a planner, promoter, and officer of the Equal Suffrage League of Virginia, founded on 27 November 1909. Bosher used her pen to promote the cause in *The Equal Suffrage League of Virginia*, a small pamphlet published in 1909, to explain the organization's purposes and outline its strategy. She emphasized family themes that resonated in the early twentieth-century South. In Bosher's view, because women paid taxes and were citizens and rational human beings, they should be able to vote. Men, who often had distinct interests, could not represent those matters special to women. The home and the world were no longer separate spheres, and wives and mothers who were responsible for the education, health, and welfare of their families and children needed the vote, without which they lacked effective political influence on issues that directly affected their responsibilities. To be a good mother, according to Bosher's beliefs, a woman had to be an active and voting citizen.

Bosher joined the novelist Mary Johnston and others on 20 January 1912 in the chamber of the House of Delegates to testify before a state legislative committee in favor of woman suffrage. As vice president of the league she addressed the convention of the Virginia Press Association in Staunton on 25 July 1916. The governor, lieutenant governor, attorney general, and secretary of the navy were all on the podium when Bosher presented the case for woman suffrage. She worked and spoke for this cause until it was achieved in 1920 and then helped organize, and remained active in, the new League of Women Voters. Bosher chaired the league's Child Welfare Committee early in the 1920s.

As evidenced in her fiction, Bosher concerned herself with the welfare of orphans and with other issues relating to children even before her involvement with the League of Women Voters. In 1916 the governor appointed her to the board of the Virginia Home and Industrial School for Girls, a boarding school for underprivileged and abandoned young women, and she was reappointed in 1922. Bosher also joined other civic and social groups, including the Richmond Education Association. She helped found the Woman's Club of Richmond, argued eloquently that the organization and its members should take active roles in public affairs, and served as its president in 1922 and 1923. Bosher was also a member of the Country Club of Virginia, the Richmond Writers' Club, the Artists' Club, the Cosmopolitan Club of New York, and several patriotic societies.

Less than a year after the death of her husband on 10 October 1931, Kate Lee Langley Bosher died in Norfolk on 27 July 1932. She was buried in Hollywood Cemetery in Richmond.

Welford Dunaway Taylor, "Recalling Kate Langley Bosher," *Richmond Quarterly* 3 (fall 1980): 33–38; BVS Marriage Register, Norfolk City; a few Bosher letters in VHS; Arthur W. Page, "The Novels That Sell 100,000," *World's Work* 26 (1913): 220–227; Bosher's undated essay, "Legislature's Chance," Adèle Goodman Clark Papers, VCU; *Staunton Daily News*, 26 July 1916; Sandra Gioia Treadway, *Women of Mark: A History of the Woman's Club of Richmond, Virginia, 1894–1994* (1995), 6, 37, 43, 61, 66 (por.), 69, 139; obituary in *New York Times*, 29 July 1932; obituaries and editorial tributes in *Richmond News Leader*, 28 July 1932, and *Richmond Times-Dispatch*, 29 July 1932.

ELIZABETH M. GUSHEE

BOSHER, Lewis Crenshaw (17 February 1860–12 September 1920), physician and medical educator, was born in Richmond, the son of Robert H. Bosher, a prosperous carriage manufacturer, and Elizabeth Eubank Bosher. He attended private academies in Richmond, completed coursework in chemistry at Richmond College in 1881, and received a medical degree from the Medical College of Virginia in 1883. After a year at Richmond City Hospital, Bosher took postgraduate training in surgery at Mount Sinai and Bellevue Hospitals in New York.

Bosher returned to the Medical College of Virginia in 1884 as demonstrator of anatomy and also practiced medicine, first with Francis Cunningham and then on his own after Cunningham's death. In 1893 Bosher served as deputy coroner of Richmond. He became professor of anatomy and clinical lecturer on genito-urinary surgery in 1888, professor of the practice of surgery and of clinical surgery in 1896, and professor of surgery in 1897. Bosher was a popular teacher working during an exciting era, when many of the causes of diseases were discovered and entirely new diagnostic and therapeutic techniques developed. His extant lecture notes reflect his thorough fund of knowledge, attention to detail, and familiarity with current innovations. Yet Bosher could enliven his class with ribald humor, instructing his students (who were all males) on how best to acquire a venereal disease, discussing techniques for relieving chordee, a painful curvature of the "unruly" penis caused by gonorrhea, and referring to the acquisition of subjects for dissection as "body snatching."

Bosher's colleagues elected him secretary of the faculty in 1889. As chairman of the hospital committee he drafted the rules regarding admission of charity patients. Bosher helped expand the medical school program from a two- to a four-year course of study. In 1910 he chaired a joint faculty committee that successfully negotiated the merger of the neighboring and competing University College of Medicine with the Medical College of Virginia. A modest and diligent man who preferred to keep out of the limelight, Bosher hammered out compromises that were crucial to the union of the two medical schools in 1913 and served as the arbitrating member of the committee on curriculum and teaching. When the merger took effect he gave up his chair of surgery in favor of a new professorship of genito-urinary surgery, one of only a few American positions then devoted to urology.

Bosher was not a prolific author but did publish articles on surgery, urology, and pathology that sometimes broke new ground and were always written lucidly and with attention to detail. He reportedly contributed to several textbooks, and he was credited with designing a bladder tenaculum and popularizing the cystoscope. As adviser to the college's *Medical Register* Bosher oversaw editorials on such sensitive subjects as vivisection, eugenics, and the public image of physicians. He also served as president of the Richmond Academy of Medicine and Surgery, 1901–1902, first vice president of the Medical Society of Virginia, 1904–1905, and president of the Southern Surgical and Gynecological Association in 1905.

Bosher chaired the hospital committee of the antiquated Old Dominion Hospital as the 1890s ended and helped plan a new hospital incorporating recent concepts in sanitation. The 150-bed Memorial Hospital opened in 1903. A decade later he joined his colleagues from the Medical College in founding a larger and more modern private facility, Stuart Circle Hospital. As the president of its board of directors, Bosher corresponded widely and traveled to other cities to study design innovations such as electric signaling systems, improvements in boilers, and the best types of flooring. He wrote the regulations for house staff physicians and founded a school of nursing. Even though he had to deal with cost overruns during construction, negotiate labor disputes, and later cope with leaking roofs and malfunctioning elevators, Bosher took pride in the hospital, one of the most modern in the state when it opened in 1913.

Bosher was a lifelong bachelor and a brother-in-law of Kate Lee Langley Bosher, a noted novelist and woman suffrage activist. Cardiac disease forced him to resign his faculty position at the Medical College of Virginia on 28 March 1916. Lewis Crenshaw Bosher died suddenly at his Richmond home on 12 September 1920 and was buried in Hollywood Cemetery in that city.

Biographies in Henry and Spofford, *Eminent Men*, 405, *Old Dominion Journal of Medicine and Surgery* 3 (1905): 359–361, and Tyler, *Men of Mark*, 1:19–22 (por.); "The Legend of Chris Baker," *Scarab* 2 (Mar. 1954): 3–5 (quotations); Bosher notebooks, MCV Board of Visitors Minutes, 1907–1919, MCV Faculty Minutes, 1882–1897, Minute Book of Joint MCV and University College of Medicine Faculty Committee on Amalgamation, 10 Jan.–25 Feb. 1910, Memorial Hospital Board of Trustees Minutes, 1899–1913, all MCV; Minutes and Bylaws of Stuart Circle Hospital Corporation, Stuart Circle Hospital, Richmond (1991); obituary and editorial tribute in *Richmond Times-Dispatch*, 13 Sept. 1920; obituary in *Virginia Medical Monthly* 47 (1920): 282; memorials in *Virginia Medical Monthly* 47 (1920): 333–334, and *Transactions of the American Association of Obstetricians, Gynecologists, and Abdominal Surgeons* 34 (1921): 343–348.

JOHN R. PARTRIDGE

BOSTON, Reuben Beverley (21 April 1834–6 April 1865), Confederate cavalry officer, was born at Red Hill in Fluvanna County, the son of Reuben H. Boston and Margaret Ragland Boston. He was educated by private tutors and at Ridgeway school in Albemarle County, where at age nineteen he became a tutor. In 1855 Boston entered the University of Virginia, where he studied law for two years. He also read law in the office of William J. Robertson in Charlottesville until 1858, when Boston moved to Memphis, Tennessee. There he operated a law office in partnership with Joseph Urquhart until the autumn of 1859, when Boston returned to Fluvanna County to take care of his ailing parents and practice law on his own.

After the Civil War broke out Boston joined the Albemarle Rangers, but he left to help raise an artillery company in Fluvanna County and was elected a lieutenant in Company F of the 3d Regiment Virginia Artillery, Local Defense Troops. In the spring of 1862 he was promoted to captain when his unit was reorganized as Company I of the 5th Regiment Virginia Cavalry. Boston fought in James Ewell Brown Stuart's brigade at Seven Pines and during the Seven Days' Battles when the 5th Virginia served as an advance guard at Gaines's Mill. His regiment also fought at the Second Battle of Manassas (Bull Run) and at Sharpsburg (Antietam). Boston was in the thick of the fighting during Thomas J. "Stonewall" Jackson's famous march around the flank of the Union army at Chancellorsville.

During Robert Edward Lee's northward march into Pennsylvania in June 1863, Colonel Thomas Lafayette Rosser and the 5th Virginia attempted to occupy a gap in the mountains near Aldie in Loudoun County in order to shield Lee's advance. On 17 June Boston led fifty sharpshooters against attacking Union forces in what Stuart described as one of the Civil War's bloodiest cavalry battles. Rosser instructed Boston to hold his forward position at all hazards, but when Rosser was unable to support or recall his skirmishers, the sharpshooters repulsed repeated Union assaults until they ran out of ammunition and Boston was forced to surrender.

Boston was imprisoned at Johnson's Island near Sandusky, Ohio, until he was exchanged on 10 March 1864. On his return he faced a court-martial. Rosser had described Boston as "heroic," but Stuart was furious at the only surrender in the history of his cavalry. No court-martial records survive, but Boston was not convicted, and in May 1864 he rejoined his regiment, which was assigned to Brigadier General Lunsford Lindsay Lomax's brigade. Boston fought at Todd's Tavern in the Battle of the Wilderness and later helped repel Union attempts to seize Spotsylvania Court House. After Colonel Henry C. Pate of the 5th Virginia Cavalry was killed near Yellow Tavern on 11 May, Lomax, citing Boston's "extraordinary skill and valor," elevated him over two senior officers and appointed him colonel of the regiment.

Boston led his unit at Cold Harbor and at Trevilian's Station, where he was again captured but managed to escape. At Ream's Station on 25 August, his soldiers helped defeat a larger Union cavalry force. Boston's regiment joined Jubal Anderson Early in the Shenandoah Valley and fought at Winchester on 19 September and at Cedar Creek on 19 October. In November 1864 remnants of the 15th Regiment Virginia Cavalry were merged into the 5th, and Boston led the regiment through the winter of 1865. He was ill during the fighting that spring but rejoined his command at Amelia Court House following the army's evacuation of Petersburg. On 6 April 1865 Reuben Beverley Boston led the 5th Virginia against superior Union forces at the high railroad bridge near Farmville, where a bullet struck him in the head and killed him. His family later had his body removed from a battlefield grave to the family cemetery at Red Hill.

French Biographies; John Lipscomb Johnson, ed., *The University Memorial: Biographical Sketches of Alumni of the University of Virginia Who Fell in the Confederate War* (1871), 740–743; Peter J. White, "A Memoir of Colonel R. B. Boston," 1911 typescript, VHS; family history information supplied by Joffre H. Boston; Compiled Service Records (quotation in Lomax to S. Cooper, 19 May 1864); *OR*, 1st ser., 27: pt. 2, 747–748; *Confederate Veteran* 17 (1909): 72–75; Robert F. O'Neill Jr., *The Cavalry Battles of Aldie, Middleburg, and Upperville: Small but Important Riots, June 10–27, 1863*, 2d ed. (1993), 40–44; Robert J. Driver Jr., *5th Virginia Cavalry* (1997), esp. 186 (por. on 120); death date in *OR*, 1st ser., 46: pt. 1, 1302; inaccurate 7 Apr. 1865 death date on tombstone.

SANDRA V. PARKER

BOTELER, Alexander Robinson (16 May 1815–8 May 1892), member of the United States House of Representatives and member of the Confederate States House of Representatives, was born into comfortable circumstances in Shepherdstown, the son of Henry Boteler, a physician, and Priscilla Robinson Boteler, the daughter of a wealthy Baltimore merchant and shipowner and a granddaughter of the artist Charles Willson Peale. Boteler's mother died in February 1820, and he lived with his grandparents in Baltimore until his father remarried in 1825.

Boteler studied at the College of New Jersey (later Princeton University) from 1833 to 1835 and received an A.B. in 1835 and the college's essentially honorific A.M. in 1838. He roomed with the promising poet and novelist Philip Pendleton Cooke. Boteler's artistic talent attracted attention at Princeton. On the wall of his room he made a life-size charcoal drawing of the scene from *Macbeth* in which Banquo's ghost appears. The school preserved the artwork until an accidental fire destroyed it. On 26 April 1836 Boteler married Helen Macomb Stockton, of Princeton, New Jersey. They had one son and four daughters.

A few months after Boteler's marriage his father died. He inherited and moved into Fountain Rock, a large mansion near Shepherdstown. Boteler became a successful commercial farmer, producing large amounts of wheat and operating a flour mill. He later converted the mill into a cement-manufacturing plant. Liability for the 1852 bankruptcy of a prominent Shepherdstown merchant fell heavily on Boteler, obliging him to sell half his farm's acreage and other family assets.

Boteler spoke frequently at agricultural fairs and meetings. With interests in progressive agriculture, internal improvements, manufacturing, and education, he became active in the Whig Party. In 1852 Boteler stumped his district as a presidential elector for Winfield Scott. In 1856 he did the same for the American (Know Nothing) Party candidate Millard Fillmore, whose campaigns attracted many former southern Whigs. Boteler won Whig Party nominations for the Senate of Virginia in 1850 and for Congress in 1853 and the American Party nomination for Congress in 1855, but he lost all three races. In his first two races for Congress he lost narrowly to the prominent incumbent, Charles James Faulkner (1806–1884), a former Whig turned Democrat. The district, created by a Democratic legislature, combined emphatically Whiggish Loudoun County, east of the Blue Ridge Mountains, with eight counties in the lower Valley, which together had a Democratic majority sufficient to offset Loudoun. In May 1859 Boteler defeated Faulkner in their third contest by fewer than 300 votes to win a term in the House of Representatives from the district consisting of the counties of Berkeley, Clarke, Frederick, Hampshire, Jefferson, Loudoun, Morgan, Page, and Warren.

Five months later John Brown launched his ill-fated attack on Harpers Ferry. Boteler lived less than ten miles away and observed Brown's bloody repulse of the local militia and his capture the following day. Brown turned out to be the same person whose striking appearance had inspired Boteler to draw a furtive pencil sketch when the two had sat near each other on a train several months earlier. Boteler interviewed Brown at length and sketched him again during the trial.

When Congress convened in December 1859 Boteler and his twenty-two colleagues from what was called the Southern Opposition held the balance of power. Neither Democrats nor Republicans had a majority. Balloting for Speaker of the House dragged on for weeks. After Boteler denounced antislavery Republican Party leaders as equally guilty with Brown of the "abominable outrage" at Harpers Ferry, some of his Southern colleagues promoted Boteler as a compromise candidate for Speaker. On that occasion he made one of his most impressive speeches, but he was not elected. After the House was finally organized, Boteler served on the Committee on Military Affairs.

During the summer of 1860 Boteler became chairman of the national executive committee of the Constitutional Union Party, which included many former Whigs and nominated former Tennessee senator John Bell for president. Bell ran on a simple platform of preserving the Union but carried only Kentucky, Tennessee, and Virginia in the November 1860 election.

Boteler was prominent among Bell's allies in Congress who tried to mediate the subsequent secession crisis. He worked behind the scenes to promote a Union-saving compromise, and he proposed the appointment of a House Committee of Thirty-Three, with one member from each state. Boteler also warned President-elect Abraham Lincoln to do nothing that would undermine the Unionists then in control of the Virginia convention considering the secession question. Early in April 1861 Boteler announced his candidacy for reelection to Congress as a Union man, and he received support from members of all parties.

Lincoln's call on 15 April 1861 for 75,000 troops transformed Boteler and most other Virginia Unionists into firm secessionists and led him to abandon his campaign for reelection to Congress. Elected instead in May 1861 to represent Jefferson County in the House of Delegates, Boteler did not serve because he was subsequently elected to represent Virginia in the Provisional Confederate Congress and the first regular Confederate Congress. He generally supported the war effort and the administration of Jefferson Davis. Boteler served as chairman of the Committee on Ordnance and Ordnance Stores in 1862 and also chaired the Committee of the Flag and Seal, for which he sketched the design subsequently adopted for the great seal of the Confederacy, featuring the equestrian statue of George Washington in Richmond's Capitol Square.

Boteler's wartime role was not, however, primarily legislative. He served on the personal staffs of Generals Thomas J. "Stonewall" Jackson and James Ewell Brown Stuart and as an aide to Governors John Letcher and William "Extra Billy" Smith. Boteler functioned as a go-between for Jackson, conferring with both Jefferson Davis and Robert Edward Lee. He ultimately surrendered with Lee at Appomattox. Continuing to make use of his artistic talent, Boteler also painted oil portraits of Davis, Lee, and several other Confederate generals.

The war blighted Boteler's once-ample estate, valued at $41,000 in 1860. Both his cement mill and his house were burned, and his investment in fifteen slaves was also, of course, lost. Boteler received a presidential pardon in August 1866 but did not have his full civil rights restored until Congress passed a special act in his behalf in 1872. In 1881 an old friend and former classmate, Benjamin Harris Brewster, then United States attorney general, helped Boteler obtain an appointment to the Tariff Commission and jobs as assistant attorney and pardon clerk in the Department of Justice. About 1887 he sold his oil paintings to the Military Historical Society of Massachusetts. Boteler also published significant accounts of his encounters with John Brown and Abraham Lincoln and wrote a long article on Stonewall Jackson that appeared posthumously. An anonymously published pamphlet describing a political rally in Jefferson County, *My Ride to the Barbecue: or, Revolutionary Reminiscences, By an ex-member of Congress* (1860), contains several illustrations in Boteler's style, and the text has also been attributed to him.

A dignified man with persuasive oratorical powers, Boteler supported education, serving for many years on the board of Shepherd College. He also promoted local enterprises and for more than a decade was a director of the Shenandoah Valley Railroad before the Norfolk and Western bought the line in 1890. Perhaps as a matter of local pride, Boteler attempted to win recognition of priority for James Rumsey's 1786 steamboat, which had been demonstrated on the Potomac River near Shepherdstown. Alexander Robinson Boteler died in Shepherdstown, West Virginia, on 8 May 1892 and was buried in Elmwood Cemetery in that city.

Biographies in J. E. Norris, ed., *History of the Lower Shenandoah Valley* (1890), 557–559, "Alexander Robinson Boteler," *Magazine of the Jefferson County Historical Society* 20 (Dec. 1954): 19–27 (por.), and Boyd B. Stutler, "Alexander R. Boteler's Sketches of John Brown," ibid. 25 (Dec. 1959): 32–38; Boteler Papers and scrapbooks, Duke; typescript of diary in William E. Brooks Collection, LC; granddaughter's descriptions of Fountain Rock in *Shepherdstown Register*, 14 Aug., 4, 25 Sept. 1924; *Congressional Globe*, 36th Cong., 1st sess., 582 (quotation); Daniel W. Crofts, *Reluctant Confederates: Upper South Unionists in the Secession Crisis* (1989), 139, 256, 264–265; Compiled Service Records; Presidential Pardons; Boteler's historical writings include "Mr. Lincoln and the Force Bill," in *The Annals of the War Written by Leading Participants North and South* (1879), 220–227, "Recollections of the John Brown Raid," *Century Magazine* 26 (1883): 399–411, and "Stonewall Jackson in Campaign of 1862," *SHSP* 40 (1915): 162–182, and 42 (1917): 174–180; obituary in *Shepherdstown Register*, 13 May 1892.

DANIEL W. CROFTS

BOTETOURT, Norborne Berkeley, baron de (December 1717–15 October 1770), governor of Virginia, was born Norborne Berkeley in the Parish of Saint George's Hanover Square, London, England, where his parents, John Symes Berkeley and his second wife, Elizabeth Norborne Berkeley, resided while Berkeley attended the House of Commons as a Tory member for Gloucestershire. Their only other child, Elizabeth, married Lord Charles Noel Somerset, who became the fourth duke of Beaufort. From 1756 until 1765 Norborne Berkeley served as guardian of his sister's son, who in the latter year became the fifth duke. Berkeley never married but provided handsomely and obtained a commission in the Royal Navy for a son who became Vice Admiral Sir Charles Thompson, baronet (ca. 1740–1799).

Little is known about Berkeley's youth and nothing about his education. When he came of age in 1738, two years after his father's death, he became lord of the manors of Stoke Gifford and Stapleton in Gloucestershire and owner of the Berkeley Liberties in the northern part of the rich and extensive Kingswood coalfields. Berkeley was a very wealthy landowner and a prominent investor in Bristol businesses. Through the influence of the fourth duke of Beaufort he received an honorary doctorate of civil law from Oxford University in 1749. Berkeley served as colonel of militia in both districts of Gloucestershire and was lord lieutenant of the county from 1762 until 1766.

Berkeley was elected to the House of Commons in 1741 and represented Gloucestershire until 1764, when he procured the revival of the barony of Botetourt that had lapsed early in the fifteenth century. The new baron was a friend of George III and of the earl of Bute. He had become a groom of the bedchamber in 1760 and was made constable of the Tower of London in 1767. As a member of the House of Lords, Botetourt supported the ministry's policy of taxing the colonists and voted for the Stamp Act of

1765. Meanwhile he made expensive renovations and additions to the manor of Stoke Gifford and invested about £10,000 in the Warmley Copper Works, a smelting enterprise near Bristol that was one of the largest industrial establishments in England. Its failure early in 1768 plunged him into serious financial difficulty.

During the summer of 1768, following the death of Lieutenant Governor Francis Fauquier, Botetourt and his friends arranged for his appointment as royal governor of Virginia. The office had a salary of £2,000 per annum plus fees that may have been worth almost that much more. Money may have been Botetourt's principal reason for wanting the appointment, but the earl of Hillsborough, the secretary of state responsible for the colonies, had his own reasons for agreeing to name him. Botetourt supported ministerial policies but also recommended himself as an engaging gentleman well versed in commercial and political affairs, accustomed to dealing with large issues in a businesslike manner and with excellent personal and political connections in London. Hillsborough arranged for the dismissal of Governor Sir Jeffery Amherst, who had refused to reside in Virginia, and designated Botetourt in his stead. George III signed Botetourt's commission on 12 August 1768 and ordered a full-rigged ship of the line to take him to Virginia.

Botetourt arrived in Williamsburg on 26 October 1768, ending a succession of administrations by lieutenant governors begun in 1708. Charming, generous, and diligent in attending to business, he lived in the capital for almost two years and became immensely popular. Botetourt restored friendly relations between the government and the church that had been disrupted during Fauquier's administration, and he made himself a patron of education. He attended morning prayers with the students at the College of William and Mary almost every day, instituted the Botetourt Medal to reward scholastic excellence, and became rector of the college in 1769. Botetourt also improved the quality of the county courts by refusing to reappoint justices of the peace with poor attendance records.

The climactic event of Botetourt's administration occurred on 17 May 1769, when he abruptly dissolved the General Assembly after the House of Burgesses adopted an address to the king criticizing parliamentary policies and asserting that only the General Assembly could tax the people of Virginia. The good will that Botetourt had created during his first winter in Virginia kept events from getting out of hand or destroying his influence. Most Virginians believed that Botetourt disapproved of British policies, but in a secret letter of 23 May 1769 the governor advised Hillsborough to take a firm stand against colonial protests.

Norborne Berkeley, baron de Botetourt, died of erysipelas in the governor's palace in Williamsburg on 15 October 1770 and was buried in the chapel at the College of William and Mary. He was honored more than any other royal governor. The assembly named the new counties of Berkeley and Botetourt for him, as well as the town of Botetourt in Gloucester County and the parishes of Berkeley in Spotsylvania County, Botetourt in Botetourt County, and Norborne in Frederick County. The House of Burgesses also commissioned a marble statue of Governor Botetourt that is now at the College of William and Mary.

Bryan Little, "Norborne Berkeley: Gloucestershire Magnate," *VMHB* 63 (1955): 379–409 (por. on 378), citing Harley Miscellany, vol. 5, British Library, for month of birth; Botetourt's letters to secretary of state in PRO CO 5/1347–1348 and to Board of Trade in PRO CO 5/1333; Dianne J. McGaan, ed., "The Official Letters of Norborne Berkeley, Baron de Botetourt, Governor of Virginia, 1768–1770" (master's thesis, W&M, 1971); Beaufort Papers, Badminton, Gloucestershire (selected photocopies at CW), including will; correspondence of the administrators of Botetourt's Virginia estate in Olive A. Hawkins Collection of Virginiana, LVA; estate inventories, the principal source for the interpretation of Colonial Williamsburg's restored governor's palace, printed in *An Inventory of the Contents of the Governor's Palace Taken after the Death of Lord Botetourt: An Inventory of the Personal Estate of His Excellency, Lord Botetourt, Royal Governor of Virginia, 1768–1770* (1981); obituary in *Williamsburg Virginia Gazette* (Purdie and Dixon), 18 Oct. 1770, and supplement of same date not printed until 19 Oct. 1770 or later.

BRENT TARTER

BOTT, Susan Catharine Spotswood (17 January 1774–4 March 1853), Presbyterian lay leader, was born at Orange Grove in Orange County, the daughter of John Spotswood and

Sarah Rowsie Spotswood. She received no formal education, but her parents, especially her mother, instructed her in "drawing, painting, and fine fancy work." In 1798 she requested instruction in painting from Benjamin Henry Latrobe, who responded with a two-volume manuscript "Essay on Landscape," one of his most thorough artistic statements.

Spotswood married John Boswell Bott, a physician, at Orange Grove on 1 April 1802. Their son and daughter both died in infancy. The Botts raised seven orphaned nieces and nephews. After spending the first few years of their married life in Manchester, they moved to a house in Petersburg. After her marriage Bott became a Presbyterian and joined the Tabb Street Presbyterian Church soon after it was founded in 1814. She was one of forty-six Petersburg women who in 1812 petitioned the General Assembly to establish an asylum there to improve "the forlorn and helpless Situation of poor Orphan female Children." Bott also served as secretary of the church's Female Missionary Association, formed in 1819 to collect donations for the Missionary Society of Hanover Presbytery.

Following her husband's sudden death in August 1824, Bott found herself nearly impoverished as she struggled with a debt-ridden estate. She owned little more than a small library of religious literature and one female slave but nevertheless increased her benevolent activities in the church and in the community. Bott assumed leadership of the Female Education Society, which had been established in 1822 to raise money for the training of needy ministerial candidates. She organized fairs to market needlework and other items handcrafted by the women of her church. Bott contributed a prodigious number of items for sale, including wax flowers, morocco needle books, and pincushions. She often inserted inspirational notes or religious tracts inside the pillows that she made, hoping that they would eventually be discovered and read. Tireless in her own work, Bott also encouraged others to undertake similar projects to benefit the church. In response to one acquaintance who offered to work for the Education Society, she requested help in preparing

for the annual fund-raising fair, sent materials for caps and other items, and wrote that "it will afford me pleasure if I can give you patterns to aid you in Yr labour of Love." Under Bott's direction, the Education Society raised nearly $7,000.

Admired and respected by her contemporaries, Bott worked diligently and with considerable success for more than thirty years to advance the goals of the Education Society. In addition to orchestrating moneymaking fairs in Petersburg, she sought other markets for the society's crafts. She shipped them, for example, to the mountain resorts in western Virginia for sale. After her death Bott's personal piety and lifelong devotion to religious benevolence prompted her pastor at Tabb Street Presbyterian Church, Abraham Brooks Van Zandt, to write a biography issued by the Presbyterian Board of Publication in 1857. Van Zandt's memoir, intended to publicize Bott's work and provide other women with a "bright and beautiful example of female piety and usefulness," probably made her even more widely known after her death than she had been in her lifetime.

Susan Catharine Spotswood Bott died of old age, according to the death register, on 4 March 1853. She was then living with a Petersburg friend with whom she had resided since selling her house (acquired after her husband's death) in 1845. The women of Tabb Street Presbyterian Church erected a headstone over her grave in Blandford Cemetery as "a tribute of affection and a memorial of her eminent piety."

Abraham B. Van Zandt, *"The Elect Lady": A Memoir of Mrs. Susan Catharine Bott of Petersburg, Va.* (1857), first quotation on 26, fourth quotation on 15; Edward C. Carter et al., eds., *The Virginia Journals of Benjamin Henry Latrobe, 1795–1798* (1977), 2:457–458 (por.); Orange Co. Marriage Bonds; Legislative Petitions, Petersburg, 9 Dec. 1812, RG 78, LVA (second quotation); Robert P. Davis et al., *Virginia Presbyterians in American Life: Hanover Presbytery, 1755–1980* (1982), 71; Tabb Street Presbyterian Church Records and two of Bott's floral arrangements, UTS; Bott to "Frances," n.d., copy in Dandridge Spotswood Collection, LVA (third quotation); Suzanne Lebsock, *The Free Women of Petersburg: Status and Culture in a Southern Town, 1784–1860* (1984), 203–205, 217–218, 220–222; estate inventories in Petersburg City Hustings Court Will Book, 4:175–176, 192; Petersburg City Death Register; gravestone inscription printed in Works Progress Administration, Virginia Historical Inventory Project, *Blandford*

Cemetery (1980), 189 (fifth quotation); memorial in *Petersburg Daily Express*, 14 Aug. 1857.

JENNIFER DAVIS MCDAID

BOTTOM, Dorothy Eva Rouse (17 July 1896–15 December 1990), civic leader and newspaper publisher, was born in Newport News, the only child of William Elmer Rouse and Edna Sue Hudgins Rouse. She was educated in the local schools and attended Mary Baldwin Seminary (later Mary Baldwin College) for the academic year 1914–1915. On 2 July 1925 she married Raymond Blanton Bottom, an army officer then stationed at Fort Monroe. She lived with her husband at various posts in the United States and in the Philippines until he resigned from the army in December 1930.

They settled in Hampton, and from 1931 to 1953 she led a life typical of the wife of a prominent businessman, civic leader, and newspaper publisher. She was active in various women's clubs and groups and raised one son and two daughters. Raymond Bottom died of a heart attack on 29 October 1953, and Dorothy R. Bottom, with no previous experience in journalism or business, became vice president of the Daily Press, Inc., which owned and published the two daily newspapers in Newport News, the morning *Daily Press* and the evening *Times-Herald*. She succeeded Raymond Bottom as editor of the *Daily Press* and announced that she would make both newspapers more readable and interesting, especially to women. Bottom expanded coverage of women's organizations and society news and at the same time moved into a more prominent role in community affairs, taking her husband's place as a regional booster. She tirelessly promoted tourism at the area's historic sites and also cultivated good relations with the leaders of Hampton Roads' large military installations. The civic project in which Bottom took greatest pride was the erection of a limestone and granite victory arch in 1962 to replace the temporary wooden arch that had been put up in Newport News in 1919 to honor servicemen returning from World War I.

According to some critics the lack of competition from other newspapers combined with Bottom's limited associations with working-class people and minority groups to make the *Daily Press* and the *Times-Herald* bland and complacent during the 1960s and 1970s. Members of the Peninsula's African American community once threatened to boycott the papers because they ignored news of importance to black Virginians. Bottom nevertheless attained a prominent role in Virginia journalism comparable to her husband's. In January 1961 she was elected president of the United Press International Virginia Association of Newspapers, and in 1981 she was made a life member of the Virginia Press Association. During Bottom's career as editor she was involved in several unpleasant disputes, one of which went to court, with members of the Van Buren family, the other principal local owners of stock in the Daily Press, Inc.

Bottom retired in February 1981, and her son, Raymond Blanton Bottom Jr., succeeded her as editor of the *Daily Press*. Both of Bottom's daughters were by then also taking active roles in the company, and the newspapers became more lively and broadened their coverages of the local African American population. In 1986 the Bottoms and the Van Burens sold the Daily Press, Inc., whose newspapers had a combined daily circulation of more than 100,000, to Tribune Co., Inc., a national syndicate. The sale included broadcasting and other associated investments and totaled more than $200 million.

In 1989 Bottom established the Rouse-Bottom Foundation to support cultural, historical, environmental, and educational activities in Virginia, particularly in the Hampton Roads area. Dorothy Eva Rouse Bottom suffered a stroke in 1989 and died in a Hampton nursing home on 15 December 1990. She was buried in the local Greenlawn Cemetery.

BVS Birth Register, Newport News; middle name from Mary Baldwin Seminary *Catalogue* (1914/1915), 87; BVS Marriage Register, Newport News; *Newport News Times-Herald*, 2 July 1925; extensive clipping files on Bottom, her family, the Van Buren family, and the history of the two newspapers in library of Daily Press, Inc., Newport News; feature articles in *Commonwealth* 25 (Aug. 1958): 23–24, 31 (por.), in *Newport News Daily Press*, 1 Feb. 1981, 9 Mar., 15 July, 30 Sept. 1986, in *Newport News Times-Herald*, 2 Feb. 1981, and in *Richmond Times-Dispatch*, 9 Feb. 1986; obituaries in *Newport News Daily Press*, 16 Dec. 1990 (pors.), and *Richmond Times-Dispatch*, 17 Dec. 1990 (which gives variant birth date of 17 May 1896).

BRENT TARTER

BOTTOM, Raymond Blanton (8 September 1893–29 October 1953), newspaper publisher and civic leader, was born in Richmond, the son of Davis Bottom and Ella Virginia Alley Bottom. After completing public school, he worked for the Chesapeake and Ohio Railroad. Bottom was a member of the Richmond Light Infantry Blues until 1916 and entered the United States Army the next year. He joined the air corps and served in France during World War I and in Germany afterward. Thereafter he was stationed at various posts in the United States and the Philippines as a captain in the 61st Coast Artillery. On 2 July 1925, while stationed at Fort Monroe, Bottom married Dorothy Eva Rouse, daughter of William Elmer Rouse, a Newport News businessman. They had one son and two daughters.

Bottom resigned from the army at the end of December 1930 and moved to Hampton to take over management of the Daily Press, Inc., in which his father-in-law had recently purchased a controlling interest. The Newport News company published the city's two daily newspapers, the morning *Daily Press* and the evening *Times-Herald*. Bottom quickly became a respected and influential figure in Virginia journalism. He served as president of the Virginia Press Association from 1935 to 1939. Already involved as publisher in the daily operations of both newspapers, Bottom in 1944 assumed the editorship of the *Daily Press*. He also served as president of the Virginia State Chamber of Commerce from 1938 to 1940.

Bottom was a tireless booster for the Hampton Roads area. Among the civic improvements he advocated were the bridge to link the Peninsula with Gloucester County that opened shortly before his death and a highway link with Norfolk that was constructed after he died. Late in 1945 Bottom traveled to London to invite the United Nations to make its permanent headquarters on a tract of land near Williamsburg. He served in 1951 and 1952 as cochairman of the Virginia Ports Development Committee, a private body that lobbied for the creation of the Virginia State Ports Authority. Bottom also promoted the consolidation of local governments in the Peninsula and helped bring about a referendum in March 1950 on the question of whether to abolish the counties of Elizabeth City and Warwick, the town of Phoebus, and the cities of Hampton and Newport News and replace all the jurisdictions with a new city of Hampton Roads. This ambitious referendum failed, but the idea later led to the consolidation of Hampton and Elizabeth City County and to the consolidation of Newport News and Warwick County.

Bottom held a commission as a major in the army reserves during the 1930s and served in Norfolk with the rank of lieutenant commander in the navy during World War II. In addition to his newspapers he invested in other businesses in the Hampton Roads area. At the time of his death he was president of Hampton Roads Broadcasting Corporation, which owned and operated a radio station. Bottom sat on the boards of directors of several corporations and was one of the organizers of the Virginia Travel Council, founded to stimulate the lucrative tourist industry. He supported improvements at Hampton Institute (later Hampton University) and served on the local committee of the United Negro College Fund, which won him more respect from African Americans than many other editors and publishers of daily newspapers in Virginia enjoyed during the 1940s.

Raymond Blanton Bottom died of a heart attack at his home in Hampton on 29 October 1953 and was buried in the local Greenlawn Cemetery. His widow took over his journalistic enterprises and achieved prominence in her own right.

Feature article in *Commonwealth* 2 (Aug. 1935): 19 (por.); BVS Birth Register, Richmond City; Military Service Records; BVS Marriage Register, Newport News; *Newport News Times-Herald*, 2 July 1925; obituaries in *Newport News Times-Herald*, 29 Oct. 1953, and *Newport News Daily Press*, 30 Oct. 1953 (por.), and shorter notices in most other Virginia newspapers and in *New York Times*, 30 Oct. 1953.

BRENT TARTER

BOTTS, Alexander Lithgow (May 1799–15 May 1860), member of the Council, was born in Dumfries, the son of Benjamin Gaines Botts, a prominent Richmond attorney, and Jane

Tyler Botts. His parents both died in the Richmond Theatre fire on 26 December 1811, and he and his siblings grew up in Fredericksburg with relatives. His brothers included John Minor Botts, who became a member of Congress, and Charles Tyler Botts, the founder of the *Southern Planter*. Botts studied law in Richmond and on 20 September 1818, when he was only nineteen years old, qualified as an attorney and opened his own law office. He married Susan Frances Randolph, of Chesterfield County, on 20 August 1818. They had six sons and four daughters.

On 17 February 1821, even though Botts was a very young man with little legal experience and no prior political office, the General Assembly elected him to the Council of State. By the 1820s the Council had become a comparatively unimportant organ of the executive department, and Botts's routine service as a councillor involved him in few serious political or policy questions. During his ten-year stint he became a senior member, but his colleagues Peter V. Daniel and Wyndham Robertson had been elected shortly before he was, and he never had the opportunity to serve as president of the Council, a post that would have made him acting governor in the event of the incumbent's death or resignation. Botts's salary as a councillor provided him with a much-needed regular income, but while he lived in Virginia, he was in almost constant financial straits.

The new constitution of Virginia that went into effect on 1 April 1831 reduced the number of Council members from eight to three, and on 8 March 1831 Botts resigned. He and his youngest brother, Charles Tyler Botts, opened a law office in Richmond and sought to represent persons pressing claims on the state government for Revolutionary War service. Within a week of his resignation Botts tried to obtain an appointment as a commissioner to settle such claims, but his sponsorship by Daniel, a political adversary of Governor John Buchanan Floyd, probably doomed his bid.

In 1834 Botts moved his family to New York, where he practiced law and made several successful investments. In 1848 his eldest child, Jane Botts, married Henry Chadwick, who became one of the most influential writers on the

rules and strategies of the emerging sport of baseball. Botts participated in New York City's Democratic Party politics as a supporter of Martin Van Buren, and during the war with Mexico Botts aided his Virginia friend John Young Mason, the secretary of the navy, in procuring supplies ranging from ponchos and bedsteads to steamboats. After Botts's wife died in the 1850s, he gradually retired from practicing law and may have withdrawn from politics. Alexander Lithgow Botts died of pneumonia in Washington, D.C., on 15 May 1860. He was buried in a private site in the Congressional Cemetery.

Birth date variously given as 6 May, 20 May, and 29 May 1799 in French Biographies, in *New York Genealogical and Biographical Record* 46 (1915): 163, and in Howard J. Rhodes, comp., *The Rhodes Family in America* (1959), 396, 412; marriage in *Richmond Enquirer*, 28 Aug. 1818; letter of resignation from Council in Governor's Office, Letters Received, 8 Mar. 1831, RG 3, LVA; Richmond City and Chesterfield Co. court records document precarious finances; Botts letters in Mason Family Papers, VHS; death notices in *New York Times*, 17 May 1860, *Richmond Dispatch*, 18 May 1860, and *Washington National Intelligencer*, 19 May 1860.
DAPHNE GENTRY

BOTTS, Charles Tyler (6 March 1809–4 October 1884), journalist, was born in Dumfries, the son of Benjamin Gaines Botts and Jane Tyler Botts. His parents were killed in the Richmond Theatre fire on 26 December 1811, and he grew up in the Fredericksburg household of his guardian, Philip Harrison. Botts's brothers included Alexander Lithgow Botts, who served on the Council of State, and John Minor Botts, who became a congressman.

From 1826 to 1828 Botts attended the University of Virginia, where he studied political economy and jurisprudence. About 1830 he married Margaret Marshall, of Fredericksburg. They had four sons and one daughter. By the winter of 1830–1831 Botts had joined Alexander Lithgow Botts in the practice of law in Richmond. He was also interested in agricultural reforms and was active in the Henrico Agricultural Society. Sometime late in the 1830s or early in the 1840s Botts developed a highly regarded straw-cutting machine. In January 1841 he began publication of a new, monthly agricultural journal, the *Southern Planter:*

Devoted to Agriculture, Horticulture and the Household Arts, which speedily became one of the most influential southern agricultural publications and remained influential in Virginia for a century.

Botts initially supplemented his income from the *Southern Planter* by operating an agricultural supply business and manufacturing and selling his straw-cutter, but his magazine soon prospered. Circulation increased during the first year from 1,200 to 3,000. Botts concentrated on providing useful and practical information. He regularly printed articles reporting on scientific agricultural advances, newly developed implements, and expanded markets, or highlighting rural domestic arts ranging from keeping bees, making butter, mixing whitewash, and growing wheat to cultivating corn, feeding cows, sowing peas, and managing rabbits. He also published news of agricultural societies and urged farmers to form local societies for the exchange of information. The crop reports and wholesale prices Botts printed from Richmond and other principal markets made the magazine a valuable source of information on the southern economy. The *Southern Planter* tended to focus on Virginia agriculture, but Botts sought articles about other regions of the South and regularly reprinted relevant articles from northern agricultural papers. Although he often displayed a southern chauvinism in his editorials, he believed that southern planters could learn from northern farmers.

In December 1846 Botts sold the *Southern Planter*. After serving as editor and one of the publishers of the *Southern Standard*, a new Richmond newspaper that failed within a few months, he obtained an appointment in September 1847 as storekeeper for the United States Navy at Monterey, California. Botts arrived in California in May 1848. The next year he served as a delegate to the first California state constitutional convention and lost a bid to be elected the state's first attorney general by only one vote. In 1850 Botts resigned his navy post and opened a law office in San Francisco. Late in that decade he became publisher of the *Sacramento Standard*, and early in the 1860s he held the state printing contract. Botts also served as state judge

for the Sacramento district during the Civil War. In the 1870s he resumed practicing law in Oakland, where he was a member of Saint Paul's Episcopal Church. Charles Tyler Botts died in San Francisco on 4 October 1884 and was buried in Mountain View Cemetery in Oakland, California.

Family history in Howard J. Rhodes, comp., *The Rhodes Family in America* (1959), 396, 419–420; Botts letters in Charles Campbell Papers, W&M, and Mason Family Papers, VHS; Theodore H. Hittell, *History of California* (1885–1897), 2:756–790, 808–813, 3:588–590, 660–665, 4:48–55; obituaries in *Oakland Daily Evening Tribune* and *San Francisco Chronicle*, both 6 Oct. 1884.

KENNETH E. KOONS

BOTTS, John Minor (16 September 1802–8 January 1869), member of the House of Representatives and member of the Convention of 1850–1851, was born at Dumfries, the son of Benjamin Gaines Botts and Jane Tyler Botts. After his parents died in the Richmond Theatre fire on 26 December 1811, he and his siblings were raised by relatives in Fredericksburg. His brothers included Alexander Lithgow Botts, who served on the Council of State, and Charles Tyler Botts, founder of the *Southern Planter*, an agricultural journal. Botts read law for six weeks and in 1820 was admitted to the bar. On 13 or 14 May 1822 he married Mary Whiting Blair. They had four sons and three daughters. Botts practiced law in Richmond until 1826, when he moved to Half Sink, his Henrico County plantation, where he raised racehorses and farmed using progressive agricultural techniques of the kind advocated in the *Southern Planter*.

In 1831 Botts ran unsuccessfully to represent Henrico County in the House of Delegates, but he was elected in 1833 and again in 1834. He lost to William B. Randolph in 1835 but challenged the result and was seated on 24 December. Botts was reelected in 1836 but defeated by William N. Whiting the next year. Botts again successfully challenged the result and was seated on 20 January 1838. He won his last term later in 1838. During his first four assembly terms Botts served on the Committee of Schools and Colleges, and during his final term he sat on the Committee of Propositions and Grievances. Botts emerged as a spirited and partisan legislator. Although his positions on national issues were often more consistent with those of the Democratic Party, he aligned himself instead with the Whig Party and remained a member until its demise. Unlike most other Whigs, Botts opposed the Second Bank of the United States on constitutional grounds, but he also opposed President Andrew Jackson's veto of the bill to recharter the bank, arguing that Jackson had usurped the power of Congress. During the panic of 1837, Botts favored legislation to relieve state banks of the need to make specie payments and blamed the financial distress of the state and the country on the Democrats. Botts so hated the Democratic Party that the rest of his political career might be defined simply as anti-Democrat in spirit. His frequent publication of his speeches as pamphlets or in the newspapers made his hostility to the Democratic Party widely known.

Botts represented the counties of Charles City, Hanover, Henrico, and New Kent and the city of Richmond in the House of Representatives from 1839 to 1843. During his first term he sat on the Committees on Commerce and on Elections, and during his second he served on the Committee on the Currency and was the second-ranking member to Millard Fillmore on the Committee on Ways and Means. Botts continued to be highly partisan but often acted in unexpected ways. He was one of the few southern representatives to oppose the Democrats' so-called gag rule prohibiting receipt of antislavery petitions. Although himself a slaveholder, Botts argued that the rule violated the right of petition and maintained that hearing petitions against slavery would act as a safety valve releasing abolitionist pressures and preventing sectional agitation. Botts changed his mind on fundamental issues several times. In 1841 he reversed his earlier opposition and declared himself in favor of a national bank. When John Tyler (1790–1862) vetoed a bank bill that year Botts was so angry at what he considered a betrayal of the Whig Party's interests that in 1842 he attempted to impeach the president. A portrait of Botts painted probably in that year depicts him carrying a scroll reading, "I impeach John Tyler."

Defeated for reelection in 1843, Botts remained in the public eye with speeches against the annexation of Texas. He later wrote of his conviction that the Democrats, controlled by John C. Calhoun, had used the Texas issue to divide the Union. Botts was reelected to Congress in 1847 and chaired the Committee on Military Affairs, using this position during the war with Mexico to support the army rather than to oppose the war. He later declared that he would gladly pay Mexico to take back the territory that the United States acquired at the war's end. Botts lost his reelection bid in 1849.

In 1850 Botts was one of six men elected to represent the city of Richmond and the counties of Charles City, Henrico, and New Kent in a state constitutional convention that met from 14 October 1850 to 1 August 1851. He served as chairman of the Committee on the Bill of Rights and proposed or supported such reforms as abolition of the governor's Council and ending capital punishment and also imprisonment for debt. Botts suggested requiring that before slaves could be emancipated, their owners first either arrange for their emigration from the United States or provide for their support if the General Assembly permitted them to remain in Virginia. He also proposed restricting the ability of the assembly to incur a public debt or tax property at different rates in different regions of the state. Unlike many other members from eastern and central Virginia, Botts supported extending the suffrage to all adult white men and the popular election of more public officers, including the governor. He voted for the constitution that the convention successfully submitted to a public referendum.

In 1852 Botts attended the last national convention of the Whig Party and was the only southern delegate who voted for Winfield Scott, a Virginia native who became the party's presidential nominee. The breakup of the Whig Party left Botts with what he called a choice between the "Know-Nothings on the one hand and the Good-for-Nothings on the other." Still a passionate opponent of the Democratic Party, Botts ran for Congress in 1854 on the American (Know Nothing) Party ticket but was defeated. His opposition later in the decade to the proslavery constitution proposed for the new state of Kansas made him increasingly unpopular in

Virginia. Nevertheless, in 1858 a group of southern Unionists began a movement to nominate Botts for president in 1860 as a national rather than a sectional candidate, a man they hoped could unite the old Whigs, the Know Nothings, and the new Republicans. Anna Ella Carroll, a leading Know Nothing pamphleteer from Maryland, actively promoted Botts as a unifying candidate, but the Republicans instead selected Abraham Lincoln, of Illinois, and most southern Unionists and former Know Nothings supported John Bell, of Tennessee, the Constitutional Union Party candidate. Carroll came to believe that Botts was too outspoken and brusque to attract wide support. After his death an appreciative obituary reflected that sentiment, stating that "his nature was too despotic for success" and that voters often "rebelled against his egotism and self-will."

With the election of Lincoln, Botts predicted the immediate secession of the South and called for Virginia to resist the siren song of South Carolina fire-eaters. Defeated as a Unionist candidate for his state's convention on the question of secession, Botts railed against disunion in letters to the newspapers and once again blamed the Democratic Party for the failure of all compromise proposals. Lincoln briefly considered but decided against including him in his cabinet. In April 1861 Botts met privately with the president, who described to him an interview he had had on 4 April with Botts's fellow Unionist John Brown Baldwin, a member of the Virginia secession convention. Because Botts and Baldwin subsequently recalled the events in dramatically different ways, the meeting between Lincoln and Baldwin has long been controversial. As related by Botts in his memoirs, Lincoln told Baldwin that he would evacuate Fort Sumter if the Virginia convention would adjourn without taking the state out of the Union. Botts also maintained that Baldwin kept this offer secret, with the implication that as a result the Virginia convention voted to secede. Botts may have misrepresented Lincoln's suggestion, but Lincoln may also have left Botts and Baldwin with different impressions of his options.

After Virginia seceded, Botts proposed a constitutional amendment to allow the Southern states to withdraw from the Union peacefully. He retired to his farm in Henrico County but continued to speak his mind against both the war and the Confederacy in writings that made him a highly visible target for Confederate officials. On 2 March 1862, the day after Jefferson Davis declared martial law in and around Richmond, Botts was arrested by order of the secretary of war and jailed in a prison formerly reserved for slaves. He was not released until 29 April, and he remained under house arrest in Richmond for four months more. Botts then retired to a farm he had recently acquired in Culpeper County, where he witnessed nine engagements between Union and Confederate armies. He entertained generals from both sides and fed troops from his farm's produce, but he excluded from his hospitality Confederate general James Ewell Brown Stuart, whose troops had trampled Botts's grounds and who briefly had him placed under arrest.

In 1864 the General Assembly of the Restored government, meeting in Alexandria, named Botts to the United States Senate, but he declined. He reentered politics after the war with a plan for reconstruction that included the gradual emancipation of slaves and the enfranchisement of some African Americans. Botts presided over a Unionist conference in May 1866 on those issues and later led the Virginia delegation to a convention of Southern Loyalists in Philadelphia, where he argued against universal manhood suffrage. A leader of the so-called cooperationists, he lost his bid to direct the Southern Union Republican Party to more radical elements of the National Republican Party that promoted both black suffrage and the disfranchisement of all former Confederates. Recognizing the success of the Radicals, Botts at last embraced their positions and joined them, running unsuccessfully on their platform in the October 1867 election of delegates to a Virginia state constitutional convention. He also spoke in favor of their policies at a state Republican meeting in February 1868.

After the Civil War Botts completed and in 1866 published his memoirs to vindicate his political career and to castigate the political leaders with whom he had come into conflict. The title, typical of his style, was *The Great Rebellion: Its Secret History, Rise, Progress, and Disastrous Failure*. John Minor Botts died on 8 January 1869 at his farm in Culpeper County. His body lay in state at the Capitol and was buried in Shockoe Cemetery in Richmond.

John Minor Botts, *The Great Rebellion: Its Secret History, Rise, Progress, and Disastrous Failure* (1866), is largely autobiographical and contains texts of many speeches; Botts family genealogical notes, George Harrison Sanford King Papers, VHS; Henrico Co. Marriage Bonds, 11 May 1822; marriage date given as 13 and 14 May, respectively, in *Richmond Compiler*, 21 May 1822, and *Richmond Examiner*, 21 May 1822; Clyde C. Webster, "John Minor Botts, Anti-Secessionist," *Richmond College Historical Papers* 1 (June 1915): 9–37; Alexander Mackay-Smith, *The Race Horses of America, 1832–1872: Portraits and Other Paintings by Edward Troye* (1981), 29–31; *Richmond Whig*, 20 Aug 1850, 15, 25 Apr., 29 July 1851; *Journal of 1850–1851 Convention*, 66; *Debates and Proceedings of 1850–1851 Convention*, 57, 74, 236; *New York Times*, 21 Nov. 1854 (first quotation); Daniel W. Crofts, *Reluctant Confederates: Upper South Unionists in the Secession Crisis* (1989), esp. 301–306; Janet L. Coryell, *Neither Heroine nor Fool: Anna Ella Carroll of Maryland* (1990), 38–42, 44–45, 51–52; Anna Ella Carroll Papers, Maryland Historical Society, contain Botts letters and unpublished MS biography; some Botts letters in McCue, Martin, and Perry Family Correspondence, UVA, and Pegram Family Papers, VHS; Botts's views on Reconstruction reported in R. J. M. Blackett, ed., *Thomas Morris Chester, Black Civil War Correspondent: His Dispatches from the Virginia Front* (1989), 361–363; *Richmond Portraits in an Exhibition of Makers of Richmond, 1737–1860* (1949), 20–21 (por.); obituaries and accounts of funeral in *Richmond Whig*, 9 (second and third quotations), 11 Jan. 1869, and *Richmond Daily Dispatch*, 9, 11, 12 Jan. 1869.

JANET L. CORYELL

BOTTS, Lawson (25 July 1825–16 September 1862), Confederate army officer, was born in Fredericksburg, the son of Thomas Hutchinson Botts, an attorney, and Ann Carter Willis Botts. His uncles included Alexander Lithgow Botts and John Minor Botts, both prominent politicians, and Charles Tyler Botts, an agricultural journalist. Botts entered the Virginia Military Institute in 1841 but returned home before graduating because of the poor health of his father, in whose office he later studied law. After obtaining a license to practice law, he took up residence in Clarksburg. About 1846 Botts moved to Charles Town, where he became a locally prominent attorney and on 29 January 1851 married Sarah Elizabeth Bibb Ranson. They had a daughter who died in infancy and four sons.

Botts was briefly involved in the trial of John Brown after the October 1859 raid on Harpers Ferry. On 25 October the judge of the circuit court appointed Botts and another local attorney to represent Brown, whose own counsel did not arrive in Charles Town until 28 October. Ignoring the controversy swirling around the case, Botts attempted to save Brown from the gallows by stressing his indulgent behavior toward the civilians in Harpers Ferry and introducing the legal question of his sanity, a defense tactic that Brown rejected. Brown nevertheless reportedly thanked Botts for his hard work on his behalf. In the aftermath of Brown's raid, militia units sprang up in many Virginia communities, and on 4 November 1859 Botts was elected captain of a volunteer company that styled itself the Botts Greys.

Botts presided in August 1860 at the Jefferson County meeting of the Constitutional Union Party that endorsed the presidential nomination of John Bell, of Tennessee. Botts remained committed to the Union until Virginia seceded, but he warned of the danger from Unionists that faced the Virginia militia when the latter received orders from the state convention to seize the United States arsenal at Harpers Ferry. When the Botts Greys were mustered into Confederate service on 3 May, Botts became captain of Company G, 2d Regiment Virginia Infantry, and was assigned to what became known as the Stonewall Brigade. On 12 June he received a commission as major of the regiment. Botts fought at the First Battle of Manassas (Bull Run) on 21 July and on 11 September was promoted to lieutenant colonel. He served as provost marshal at Winchester in November and December 1861. At the Battle of Kernstown on 23 March 1862 his regiment suffered heavy losses, but during the Shenandoah Valley campaign it led in the rout of Union forces at the Battle of Winchester on 25 May. Botts's men, under the command of Colonel James Allen, led the assault on the Union left flank at Port

Republic on 9 June 1862 before marching to the defense of Richmond.

Botts distinguished himself during the Seven Days' Battles that began with the fighting at Mechanicsville on 26 June. During the Battle of Gaines's Mill the next day his 2d Regiment faced intense fire from the Union troops on McGehee's Hill but successfully took the summit. Botts was the only field officer in his regiment to survive. His courage and leadership during the fierce fighting earned him a promotion to colonel as of 27 June. The 2d Virginia also participated in the Confederate assaults during the climactic fight at Malvern Hill on 1 July. Botts commanded the regiment at Cedar Mountain on 9 August and at Groveton on 28 August, when a bullet struck him in the head and knocked him from his horse. The wound proved fatal, although he survived for more than two weeks. Lawson Botts died from a secondary hemorrhage while at the house of a Middleburg minister on 16 September 1862. He was buried at Zion Episcopal Cemetery in Charles Town.

Frederica H. Trapnell, "Colonel Lawson Botts, C.S.A.," *Magazine of the Jefferson County Historical Society* 49 (Dec. 1983): 27–34 (por.); Charles D. Walker, *Biographical Sketches of the Graduates and Elèves of the Virginia Military Institute Who Fell During the War Between the States* (1875), 53–58; Lawson Botts Papers, VMI; Botts family genealogical notes, George Harrison Sanford King Papers, VHS; Stephen B. Oates, *To Purge This Land With Blood: A Biography of John Brown* (1970), 324–325; *Charles Town Virginia Free Press and Farmers' Repository*, 27 Oct., 17 Nov. 1859, 16 Feb., 23 Aug., 27 Sept. 1860; *New York Herald*, 28 Oct. 1859; Compiled Service Records; Dennis E. Frye, *2nd Virginia Infantry* (1984), 1, 16, 32, 34, 39, 85.

DONALD W. GUNTER

BOUEY, Elizabeth A. Coles (14 November 1890–5 February 1957), founder of the National Association of Ministers' Wives, was born at the Bendoo Industrial Mission Station, Cape Mount, Liberia, where her parents, John J. Coles and Lucy Ann Henry Coles, were serving as missionaries for the Baptist Foreign Mission Commission of the United States of America (one of three groups that in 1895 merged to form the National Baptist Convention). Ethnic violence in the region and her father's ill health caused the family to return to her parents' native Virginia in July 1893. In September of that year John J. Coles was elected corresponding secretary of the mission board, but he could not overcome malaria contracted in Africa and died in Richmond on 7 November 1893. Lucy Coles, a graduate of Hartshorn Memorial College (which became part of Virginia Union University in 1932), served out her husband's term as secretary. In the ensuing years, even with several small children to raise, she remained involved in missionary affairs, served for a time as editor of the National Baptist Convention's Sunday school journal, and taught in the night school at Richmond's Armstrong High School. Lucy Coles's discipline set an example for her daughters, and her situation as a woman and a devout and outspoken Christian worker left in an ambiguous relation to the church by the death of her husband must also have made an impression.

Elizabeth Coles announced on 15 June 1911, the night that she graduated as valedictorian of Armstrong High School, that she intended to become a missionary to Africa. The National Baptist Convention did not support unmarried female missionaries, and so she attended the Armstrong Normal School and prepared for a career as a teacher. One day she received a letter from Edward H. Bouey, who like her was the child of missionaries. His father, Harrison Napoleon Bouey, was a former slave and local political leader in Edgefield County, South Carolina, who had led his Baptist congregation to Liberia after whites took control of local government through violence and fraud. Bouey returned to the United States in 1882, married, and served as superintendent of missions in Missouri, where Edward H. Bouey was born. The elder Bouey went to Africa again with his three sons after his wife's death in 1902, and he died there in 1909. Aid from the mission board enabled Edward H. Bouey to graduate from Morehouse College, and he sought a wife who would join him in missionary service. He proposed to Coles on their first meeting, and during his third visit to Richmond they married on 28 April 1920. They had one son and two daughters.

The young couple set out soon afterward for Liberia as independent missionaries, with Lucy Coles organizing support for them at home. They reestablished the Bendoo Station, where her parents had once worked, and during the five years that they successfully operated a school there two of their three children were born. After a short furlough in the United States the Boueys returned to Liberia as supervisors of education for the National Baptist Convention's Foreign Mission Board. They also supervised construction of the Carrie V. Dyer Hospital in Monrovia, which for several years was the only hospital in the Liberian capital.

In 1929 the family returned to the United States, bringing with them an adopted African youth, Johnson Moore, who later became a government official in Liberia. Bouey's husband became pastor of Mount Calvary Baptist Church in Richmond, and she became a teacher in the public schools. In addition to coursework in education, which earned her a master's degree from Columbia University in 1945, she also studied theology at Virginia Union University.

Bouey knew from experience that no specific training was available for the wives of ministers, despite their many responsibilities. In June 1939 at the annual interdenominational Christian Conference for Women at Petersburg she proposed the formation of a national association of ministers' wives. She repeated her proposal to the Richmond Baptist Ministers' Wives Union in October. Others endorsed Bouey's idea, and in November 1939 the first chapter of the National Association of Ministers' Wives was founded at the Second Baptist Church in Richmond.

Bouey devoted the following year to organizing other chapters in Virginia and to corresponding with other ministers' wives throughout the United States. On 8 April 1941 more than one hundred people attended the first national conference in Richmond. Bouey was elected president of the association and held the post until her death nearly sixteen years later. During those years ministers' wives from more than thirty states and from West Africa joined the NAMW. The organization established a quarterly journal, the *Ministers' Wives Herald*, and purchased a headquarters building in Richmond.

Since 1957 the NAMW has grown to become the International Association of Ministers' Wives and Ministers' Widows with more than 40,000 members from more than 100 religious denominations.

In 1950 the *Afro-American* newspaper chain named Bouey that year's "Ideal Mother," noting that in addition to her busy schedule as a teacher, wife, mother, and president of the NAMW she made her home a haven for Africans studying in the United States and even for inmates recently released from prison. Bouey developed cancer in 1955 and had to be returned by ambulance to Richmond from the NAMW's 1956 conference in Washington. Despite her physical pain and the sorrow of her husband's death on 4 August 1956 she maintained her courage and insisted that there be no mourning at her own funeral. Elizabeth A. Coles Bouey died in Richmond on 5 February 1957 and was buried in Woodland Cemetery in that city.

From a Dream to Reality, 1941–1980: The Story of the International Association of Ministers' Wives and Ministers' Widows, International (Interdenominational) (1982), with several pors.; feature article on father and his obituary in *Indianapolis Freeman*, 27 Apr. 1889, and *Richmond Planet*, 11 Nov. 1893; letter to the editor by mother containing biographical information and her obituary in *Richmond Planet*, 22 Oct. 1898, and *Richmond Afro-American*, 13 Aug. 1955; obituary of husband in *Richmond Afro-American*, 11 Aug. 1956; other information provided by daughter Melicent V. Bouey and Shirley Alexander Hart; BVS Marriage Register, Richmond City; Lewis G. Jordan, *Negro Baptist History, U.S.A., 1750–1930* (1930), 227–229, 236–238; C. C. Adams and Marshall A. Talley, *Negro Baptists and Foreign Missions* [1944], 35–36, 43–48; Mrs. S. D. [Mary O.] Ross, *The Minister's Wife* (1946), 12; *Richmond Afro-American*, 13, 20 May 1950; *Norfolk Journal and Guide*, 1 June 1951; obituaries in *Richmond Times-Dispatch*, 6 Feb. 1957, *Richmond Afro-American*, 9, 16 Feb. 1957, and *Norfolk Journal and Guide*, 16 Feb. 1957.

JOHN T. KNEEBONE

BOULDIN, James Wood (ca. 1792–30 March 1854), member of the House of Representatives, was born in Charlotte County, the son of Wood Bouldin (1742–1800), a prominent attorney, and Joanna Tyler Bouldin. Little is known of his youth or education before he was admitted to the bar in Charlotte County on 12 April 1813. Bouldin married Alice Lewis Jouett on 9 December 1813, and they had three sons and two daughters. On 17 February 1825 he married

Martha Goode, and they had one son before her death on 24 July 1827. On 22 July 1829 Bouldin married Almeria Read Kennon, a widow with two children. Their two daughters and two sons included Powhatan Bouldin, who became a prominent newspaper editor in Danville.

Bouldin practiced law and managed a farm in Charlotte County. In 1825 he was elected to one term in the House of Delegates. Otherwise he took no part in politics until the sudden death on 11 February 1834 of his brother Thomas Tyler Bouldin, a member of the House of Representatives for the district composed of Buckingham, Charlotte, Cumberland, and Prince Edward Counties. A meeting of Democrats in Charlotte County nominated Bouldin for his brother's seat. Two of the other three candidates withdrew from the race, and in the special election held in March 1834 Bouldin defeated Nathaniel Beverley Tucker by a margin of about 300 votes out of more than 1,770 cast. During the brief campaign Bouldin came out against the rechartering of the Second Bank of the United States and in favor of President Andrew Jackson's withdrawal of federal deposits from the bank. Bouldin opposed protective tariffs and congressional appropriations for internal improvements, and he indicated that he had disapproved of Jackson's proclamation bolstering federal authority during the South Carolina Nullification Crisis of 1832, the only objection he made to any of Jackson's policies.

Bouldin was sworn in as a member of the House of Representatives on 28 March 1834. In April 1835 he defeated a Whig candidate, Philip A. Bolling, to capture a full term, and in 1837 he won a second time without opposition. Bouldin did not seek a third full term in 1839. He was appointed to the Committee on Elections for the duration of the Twenty-Third Congress and sat on the Committee on the District of Columbia from 1835 to 1839, chairing the latter committee during his final term in Congress. In January 1836 Bouldin spoke forcefully against the proposed abolition of slavery in the District, warning that if such an unconstitutional seizure of property were extended farther south civil war could ensue and suggesting that American slaves were "freer, happier, and more intelligent, and

more pious" than they had been before entering bondage in Africa. He subsequently addressed Congress in support of Texas independence and the state's eventual admission to the Union and favored the policy of Indian removal even as he conceded that Native Americans were "a noble, gallant, injured race."

Family manuscripts hint that Bouldin may have suffered from alcoholism during the 1830s, but the evidence does not indicate whether the condition contributed to his decision not to run for reelection in 1839, nor does it indicate whether it remained a continuing problem for him thereafter. James Wood Bouldin died at his home in Charlotte County on 30 March 1854 and was buried there.

Some family history in Timothy S. Ailsworth et al., eds., *Charlotte County, Rich Indeed* (1979), 275–278, and Alice Riddle Read Rouse, *The Reads and Their Relatives* (1930), 364–365; some Bouldin letters in collections of family papers at UVA and VHS; first marriage recorded in Jouett Family Genealogical Chart, LVA; second marriage reported in *Richmond Enquirer*, 15 Mar. 1825; third marriage documented in Charlotte Co. Marriage Records; elections reported in *Richmond Enquirer*, 18, 21, 28 Mar., 1 Apr. 1834, 17, 24 Apr., 5 May 1835, 27 Apr. 1837; *Register of Debates in Congress*, 24th Cong., 1st sess., 1976, 2003–2004, 2169–2171, 2224–2236, 3728, 4550–4553 (quotations on 2234, 4551); *Remarks of Mr. Bouldin, of Virginia, In the House of Representatives, Tuesday and Wednesday, Jan. 19th and 20th, 1836, . . . on the Subject of Abolition of Slavery in the District of Columbia* (1836); *Speech of Mr. Bouldin on the Bill to Authorize the Issue of Treasury Notes, . . . September 26, 1837* (1837); por. in Special Collections, VHS; wills of Bouldin and widow in Charlotte Co. Will Book, 11:317–318, 12:139.

ALAN L. GOLDEN

BOULDIN, Powhatan (24 May 1830–8 March 1907), journalist, was born in Charlotte County, the son of James Wood Bouldin, a member of the House of Representatives, and his third wife, Almeria Read Kennon Bouldin. He was educated at private schools and entered the Virginia Military Institute in 1848 but withdrew after nineteen months. Bouldin returned to Charlotte Court House to practice law. He served as deputy sheriff and in 1852 as commonwealth's attorney. On 9 March 1855 Bouldin married Ella Fuqua. They had four sons and two daughters.

Bouldin left his law practice to enlist in the Confederate cavalry on 15 May 1861, but poor eyesight led to his discharge that December. He moved to Danville shortly after the war. In the autumn of 1865 Bouldin bought the *Danville Appeal*. He changed its name to the *Danville Times* and edited the paper as a Democratic weekly until about 1894, when severe illness forced him to discontinue it. In 1877 the paper had a weekly circulation of more than 900, and in 1885 Bouldin boasted of its extensive circulation in both Virginia and North Carolina. Too few copies of the *Danville Times* are extant to document or thoroughly describe his editorial career.

At the time of his death the *Danville Register* praised Bouldin for a service he had rendered to the city and the Democratic Party, "which ever afterwards caused him to be held in grateful remembrance." The obituary was almost certainly recalling the period of local Readjuster rule from 1882 to 1883 that terminated with the so-called Danville Riot of 3 November 1883, during which four blacks were killed. The episode put an end to Readjuster political power in Danville and served as a campaign rallying point that restored white Democrats to power in Virginia and led to the downfall of the Readjusters throughout the state. By the turn of the century many white writers regarded the Readjusters' biracial coalition as anathema, erroneously portrayed the period of Readjuster rule as part of Reconstruction (which had ended in Virginia in January 1870), and characterized the brief period when four African Americans sat on Danville's twelve-member city council as a period of "Negro domination." An account of the riot incorporating this interpretation filled seventeen pages of Edward Pollock's 1885 *Sketch Book of Danville*, a book promoting the city as a business center.

The precise nature of Bouldin's service to the white Democratic Party is unclear, but he served as one of three secretaries of the so-called Committee of Forty, put together after the riot to justify the viewpoint of local Democrats. As editor of the *Danville Times* Bouldin presumably both spread the word that the riot had been nothing more than a deplorable street fight that got out of hand and successfully worked for the downfall of the local Readjusters and the rise to power of white supremacist Democrats.

Bouldin also wrote two books. *Home Reminiscences of John Randolph of Roanoke* (1878) depicts Charlotte County's most famous son, as recalled by Randolph's neighbors and acquaintances, including Bouldin's father. *Old Trunk or Sketches of Colonial Days* (1888) uses the contents of a trunk discovered by the author's aged aunt to illuminate his ancestors and the colonial customs of Charlotte County. Both volumes belong to a popular genre of local history that celebrated the customs and local notables of a better and bygone era.

Powhatan Bouldin died at the residence of his son-in-law in Danville on 8 March 1907 and was buried in Green Hill Cemetery in that city.

Timothy S. Ailsworth et al., eds., *Charlotte County, Rich Indeed* (1979), 278, 449, 455, 476; Charlotte Co. Marriage Register; Compiled Service Records; Robert J. Driver Jr., *14th Virginia Cavalry* (1988), 103; W. Thomas Mainwaring, "Community in Danville, Virginia, 1880–1963" (Ph.D. diss., UNC, 1988), 62–78; *Danville Riot, November 3, 1883: Report of Committee of Forty* (1883); Walter T. Calhoun, "The Danville Riot and Its Repercussions on the Virginia Election of 1883," in *Studies in the History of the South, 1875–1922*, ed. Joseph F. Steelman et al. (1966), 3:25–47; Jane Dailey, "Deference and Violence in the Postbellum Urban South: Manners and Massacres in Danville, Virginia," *JSH* 63 (1997): 553–590; obituaries in *Danville Register* (quotation) and *Richmond News Leader*, both 9 Mar. 1907.

W. Thomas Mainwaring
Gary Grant

BOULDIN, Thomas Tyler (d. 11 February 1834), member of the House of Representatives, was born probably in Charlotte County, the son of Wood Bouldin (1742–1800) and Joanna Tyler Bouldin. His father was a prominent local attorney, and his mother was a sister of Governor John Tyler (1747–1813), making him a cousin of President John Tyler (1790–1862). Bouldin read law, possibly in his father's office, and was admitted to the bar on 6 December 1802, by which time he was presumably about twenty-one years old. He married Ann Bickerton Lewis in Richmond on 19 December 1804. They had six sons and five daughters before she died on 25 December 1823. On 7 March 1825 Bouldin married Eliza Watkins Spencer, of Charlotte County. They had four sons.

With the patronage of such local leaders as the inimitable John Randolph of Roanoke, Bouldin won an enviable reputation among the state's legal and political leaders, and on 27 March 1821 he received an interim appointment to the General Court to fill a vacancy caused by the resignation of Peter Randolph. On 8 December 1821 the General Assembly elected him to that seat on the court. He served through 1829, riding circuit to preside over criminal cases, hearing appeals from the county courts, and occasionally meeting at the semiannual sessions in Richmond with other members of the General Court to hear criminal appeals. The few opinions Bouldin wrote are generally characterized by a spare, concise style.

Bouldin's law practice and plantation provided comfortably for his large family. At the time of his death he owned nearly 2,300 acres in three tracts in Charlotte County. His Golden Hills mansion was filled with fine furniture, a law library of more than 300 volumes, and nearly 100 volumes of literature. Thirty slaves worked the property, and he owned an elegant carriage and thirty horses.

Bouldin was a states' rights advocate who ran in April 1829 for the House of Representatives at John Randolph's suggestion and was elected to represent Buckingham, Charlotte, Cumberland, and Prince Edward Counties. He was reelected two years later and served from 7 December 1829 to 3 March 1833. During his second term Bouldin sat on the Committee on Revolutionary Claims. He allied himself with other southern states' rights Democrats. Bouldin's one major congressional speech, delivered on 31 May 1832, was a stirring denunciation of protective tariffs as not only unconstitutional but also economically foolish and wicked. In preparation for the speech, he drafted a memorandum and detailed his stance in a letter to one of his sisters. After Bouldin delivered the address, he had it printed as a twenty-nine-page pamphlet.

In April 1833 Bouldin lost his bid for reelection to none other than his mentor Randolph, but on 26 August 1833 he was again elected to Congress to replace Randolph, who had died. Bouldin took his seat on 2 December. On 11 February 1834 he rose to oppose President Andrew Jackson's removal of federal deposits from the Second Bank of the United States. Before beginning, however, as he started to reply to a comment from a colleague, Thomas Tyler Bouldin suddenly collapsed and died. His wife rushed down from the gallery and had to be carried weeping from the chamber. Bouldin's funeral service was held two days later in the House of Representatives, with the president, the cabinet, and the members of the Supreme Court in attendance. John Quincy Adams recorded the death and funeral in his diary and added that "Bouldin was a man of good disposition and sterling integrity, warped sometimes into great curvature by the political prejudices of the Virginia school." His body was interred temporarily in the Congressional Cemetery in Washington, D.C., and then moved to the family cemetery at his Golden Hills estate near Drake's Branch in Charlotte County.

Timothy S. Ailsworth et al., eds., *Charlotte County, Rich Indeed* (1979), 275–277; Lela Bouldin Shewmake Cowardin, *Golden Hills Plantation in Charlotte County, Virginia* [1970]; birth date of 1781 in standard reference sources evidently conjectured from date of admission to bar; Bouldin Family Papers, VHS; Richmond City Marriage Bonds; Charlotte Co. Marriage Bonds; congressional elections reported in *Richmond Enquirer*, 14, 21, 24 Apr., 1 May 1829, 26, 29 Apr., 10 May, 9, 19 Aug., 6 Sept. 1831, 7 May, 30 Aug. 1833; *Speech of Mr. Thomas T. Bouldin, of Virginia, on the Bill Proposing a Reduction of the Duties of Imports, Delivered in the House of Representatives, June, 1832* (1832); Land Tax Returns, Charlotte Co., 1833–1834, RG 48, LVA; will and estate inventory in Charlotte Co. Will Book, 7:136, 166–169; Charles Francis Adams, ed., *Memoirs of John Quincy Adams* (1874–1877), 9:90–93 (quotation on 92); obituary and report of memorial service in *Washington National Intelligencer*, 12–14 Feb. 1834; obituary in *Richmond Enquirer*, 15 Feb. 1834.

MARK F. FERNANDEZ

BOULDIN, Wood (20 January 1811–10 October 1876), member of the Convention of 1861 and member of the Supreme Court of Appeals, was born at Golden Hills plantation in Charlotte County, the son of Thomas Tyler Bouldin and

Ann Bickerton Lewis Bouldin. Educated in private schools in Richmond and at New London Academy in Bedford County, Bouldin then studied law in the office of William Leigh in Halifax County. After his admission to the bar about 1833, Bouldin practiced law in Charlotte County for about six years. On 22 December 1837 he married Maria Louisa Barksdale. Their one child, Wood Bouldin, served in the Convention of 1901–1902.

After the death of his wife in 1839, Bouldin moved to Richmond, where he practiced law. In Philadelphia on 14 April 1847 he married Martha Daniel, of Lynchburg. They had four sons and six daughters. In 1853 Bouldin purchased a Charlotte County plantation that had belonged to John Randolph of Roanoke and returned to that county to manage the property and practice law. He prospered as both planter and attorney, with real estate valued at about $50,000 in 1860 and personal property, including slaves, worth about $65,000 the same year.

On 4 February 1861 Bouldin was elected by a unanimous vote to represent Charlotte County in a state convention on the question of secession. One week into the convention's deliberations he introduced a declaratory resolution stating that any attempt by the United States government to collect revenue or reclaim installations in any of the states that had left the Union would amount to starting a war in which Virginia would "sustain the seceded States." Bouldin took an active part in the debates, and even though he had no previous legislative experience, his courtroom expertise enabled him to engage in spirited and learned exchanges with some of the most practiced speakers in the convention. Although he stated that he wanted Virginia to remain in the Union, his belief that slavery was endangered with Abraham Lincoln as president led him to vote for secession on 4 April 1861, when it was defeated, and again on 17 April 1861, when it passed.

Bouldin represented Charlotte County in the House of Delegates for the duration of the Civil War. He served on the Committees for Courts of Justice and on Finance and was chairman of the latter in 1863. Early in 1865, in part because he opposed efforts to enlist slaves for the defense of the Confederacy, he decided not to seek reelection. After swearing allegiance to the United States in May and July 1865, Bouldin resumed the practice of law. In 1869 he moved back to Richmond, where he practiced with Hunter H. Marshall and for a time with his own namesake son. Bouldin was in the Capitol on 27 April 1870 when the courtroom floor collapsed and killed about sixty people, but he escaped serious injury.

On 18 March 1872 the General Assembly elected Bouldin to the Supreme Court of Appeals. The most difficult issues faced by the court during his tenure arose from the controversial Funding Act of 1871, which had provided for refinancing what Virginia acknowledged as its share of the antebellum state debt. In *Antoni v. Wright* (1872) Bouldin declared unconstitutional an act of that year repealing the section of the act of 1871 that had made the coupons on 1871 bonds redeemable for payment of state taxes. In *Higginbotham's ex'x v. Commonwealth* (1874) Bouldin rejected the contention that the division of Virginia into two states during the Civil War had extinguished the original state and its debts with it. In both cases he asserted that the law, the state's honor, and good policy required it to fulfill all of its antebellum obligations, earning him the plaudits of the supporters of full funding of the debt.

Bouldin suffered a paralyzing stroke in 1875 and missed the September term of the court. He was able to return for part of the November 1875 term. Wood Bouldin died at his home in Charlotte County on 10 October 1876 and was buried in the family cemetery there.

Biographies in *Green Bag* 5 (1893): 370–373, and George L. Christian, *Reminiscences of Some of the Dead of the Bench and Bar of Richmond* (1909), 39; French Biographies; some letters in Bouldin Family Papers and Baskervill Family Papers, VHS, and in Lyons Family Papers, Huntington; Charlotte Co. Marriage Bonds, 20 Dec. 1837; second marriage in *Richmond Daily Whig,* 13 May 1847; explanatory speeches of 20 Feb. and 6 Apr. 1861 in Reese and Gaines, *Proceedings of 1861 Convention*, 1:118 (quotation), 3:222–226; votes in ibid., 3:163, 4:144; Presidential Pardons; *Antoni* v. *Wright* (1872) (22 Grattan), *Virginia Reports*, 63:833–887; *Higginbotham's ex'x* v. *Commonwealth* (1874) (25 Grattan), *Virginia Reports*, 66:627–641; Hummel and Smith, *Portraits and Statuary*, 10 (por.); obituary in *Richmond Dispatch*, 12 Oct. 1876.

JOHN O. PETERS

BOULDIN, Wood (28 September 1838–11 April 1911), member of the Convention of 1901–1902, was born in Charlotte Court House, the son of Wood Bouldin (1811–1876) and his first wife, Maria Louisa Barksdale Bouldin. His father was a prominent attorney, member of the Convention of 1861, and a judge of the Virginia Supreme Court of Appeals from 1872 until his death.

Bouldin's education began at Rough Creek Church in Charlotte County. He attended the University of Virginia from 1855 to 1857 and returned for one year in 1859 to study law with James P. Holcombe and John B. Minor. Bouldin began the practice of law with his father in Boydton, but on 23 September 1861 he joined the Staunton Hill Artillery and served as a second lieutenant during the Civil War. Afterward he practiced law in Charlotte, Halifax, and Mecklenburg Counties until 1871, when he moved to Richmond. There he practiced in partnership with his father and Hunter H. Marshall and later with James Alfred Jones until 1879. On 9 December of that year he married Florence H. Easley, daughter of James S. Easley, of Halifax County. Bouldin resided for the rest of his life in that county's seat of Houston, later called Halifax. He and his wife had three sons and three daughters.

Bouldin was active in Democratic Party politics in Halifax County for many years and was a longtime member of the State Democratic Central Committee. He campaigned unsuccessfully to represent Charlotte and Halifax Counties in the Convention of 1867–1868. Bouldin attended the 1884 Democratic National Convention in Chicago. In May 1901 he and Joseph Stebbins were elected without opposition to represent Halifax County in a state constitutional convention. Bouldin served on the Committees on Rules and on the Organization and Government of Cities and Towns. He also sat on the important Committee on the Elective Franchise and introduced a resolution to restrict the suffrage to literate property owners and to limit jury service to registered voters. Bouldin's proposal was one of many intended to reduce the number of black Virginians permitted to vote and to keep African Americans out of important public offices and off juries. The restrictive suffrage article that the convention adopted on 4 April 1902 included some of his language. On the important question of whether to call a referendum to ratify the proposed constitution, Bouldin made one of the longest speeches (and the one based on the most legal research) defending the right of the convention to put the constitution into effect without approval by the voters. Bouldin missed the final vote against a referendum on 29 May 1902.

After the convention, Bouldin returned to the quiet practice of law in Houston, but in 1905 he succeeded William Leigh as commonwealth's attorney after Leigh moved from Halifax County. Wood Bouldin subsequently won election to a full term and was a candidate for reelection when he died suddenly at his home on 11 April 1911. He was buried the following day in the graveyard at nearby Saint John's Episcopal Church.

Pollard Questionnaires; several Bouldin letters at VHS; Compiled Service Records (incomplete); BVS Marriage Register, Halifax Co.; *Journal of 1901–1902 Convention*, 49, 50, 113, 486–487, 504; *Resolutions of 1901–1902 Convention*, no. 207; *Proceedings and Debates of 1901–1902 Convention*, esp. 2:3163–3177; *Convention of 1901–1902 Photographs* (por.); obituaries in *Danville Register* and *Richmond News Leader*, both 12 Apr. 1911.

BRENT TARTER

BOUSH, Clifford Joseph (13 August 1854–24 July 1936), naval officer, was born in Portsmouth, the son of George Richard Boush and Adele Virginia Bilisoli Boush. His father was a naval contractor and descendant of Samuel Boush, the first mayor of Norfolk. Boush was educated at the Phillips Academy in Portsmouth and at the United States Naval Academy, from which he graduated in 1876. He was one of eight officers in his class of forty-two who attained the rank of admiral.

Boush devoted his entire professional career to the United States Navy, spending twenty-three years at sea. He rose slowly and unspectacularly through the naval hierarchy, as did most officers of his generation. Still a lieutenant at the time of the Spanish-American War, Boush did not become a captain until 1908 and achieved the rank of rear admiral only three years before his retirement on 13 August 1916. He commanded a division of the Atlantic fleet from 1913 to 1915. Recalled to active duty when the United States entered World War I, he served from September 1917 to September 1919 as commandant of the navy yard at Portsmouth, New Hampshire. Boush won the Navy Cross for his war work.

Boush attained flag rank, but he never achieved prominence as one of the movers and shakers of the new navy that emerged late in the nineteenth century. He served on none of the major policy or operational boards that reshaped American naval power between the 1890s and World War I. Boush had varied but largely routine duty assignments—teaching at the Naval Academy (1885–1887) and at the Naval War College (1904), deep-sea exploration on a fisheries commission steamer, storage development for the Bureau of Ordnance, assignment as lighthouse inspector of the Boston district, hydrographic work with the Bureau of Equipment, and service on the naval examining and retirement board. When he was relieved of his Atlantic fleet assignment in 1915, a lengthy article in the *New York Times* devoted most of its space to the qualifications and accomplishments of the officers most likely to succeed him.

Still, Boush's career is a metaphor for the rise of American naval power late in the nineteenth century and for the expanding reach of United States foreign policy after the Spanish-American War. In 1898 he was a middle-aged junior officer who had served most recently as navigator for the 1897 summer cruise of the Naval Academy midshipmen and as an officer on a training ship for apprentice seamen. Boush suddenly found himself in the midst of the naval blockade of Havana, participating in the bombardment of Spanish batteries, convoying American troops to Cuba and Puerto Rico, and personally piloting his ship through a Spanish minefield in the capture of Nipa Bay. Two years later, when the United States first flexed its military muscle in Asia, he was executive officer of the vessel that landed Marines in Tianjin (or Tientsin) as part of the international expedition to suppress the Boxer Rebellion in China. There-

after Boush commanded the American gunboats that patrolled the Yangtze River as the American symbol of the preservation of the Open Door Policy. When President Woodrow Wilson sought to extend American influence into revolutionary Mexico in 1915, Boush commanded a naval convoy that landed troops at Vera Cruz. Even his last two assignments put him close to America's naval future. Boush was commandant of the naval station at Pearl Harbor in 1915 and 1916, and the Portsmouth Navy Yard played a significant role in America's greatest contribution to the naval war, the development of the convoy system that thwarted German submarine attacks. His career thus was not spectacular, but it involved him in most of the major events that led his country and his navy into the ranks of the great powers of the modern world.

On 30 November 1882 in Lynchburg Boush married Anna Booker Camm, the daughter of a Williamsburg physician. They had one son and one daughter. Clifford Joseph Boush died in Gloucester County on 24 July 1936 and was buried in Arlington National Cemetery.

NCAB, 44:111–112 (por.); BVS Marriage Register, Lynchburg; United States Naval Academy Alumni Association, *Register of Alumni, Graduates, and Former Naval Cadets and Midshipmen* (1956), 144; *Register of Commissioned and Warrant Officers of the U.S. Navy and Marine Corps* (1900–1919); *Navy and Marine Corps List and Directory* (1908–1919); *New York Times*, 21 June 1915; obituaries in *New York Times* (por.) and *Portsmouth (Va.) Star*, both 26 July 1936, and *Army and Navy Journal* 73 (1936): 1109.

RICHARD D. CHALLENER

BOUSH, Samuel (d. by 18 November 1736), merchant and first mayor of Norfolk, was born probably late in the 1650s or very early in the 1660s in or near London, England, where several members of a Boush family of French descent lived. He and his nephew Maximilian Boush had moved to Virginia by early in the 1690s. Maximilian Boush, who died in 1728, became a prominent attorney and landowner in Princess Anne County, was a burgess from 1710 to 1726, and served as the prosecutor in the famous Grace Sherwood witchcraft trials of 1706–1708. His son, also called Maximilian, had sons named Maximilian and Samuel, which has resulted in much confusion in published histories.

Samuel Boush settled in Norfolk, where he was a ship chandler and one of the first merchants of importance in the new town. He evidently made a considerable amount of money supplying the English navy and purchased some of the most valuable land in Norfolk. Boush rapidly rose into the ranks of the local elite and about 1693 or 1694 married Alice Mason Hodge Porten, the twice-widowed daughter of Lemuel Mason, of Norfolk County. They had a son, Samuel Boush, and at least two daughters.

Boush became a justice of the peace for Norfolk County during the 1690s and remained on the court until he died. He was sheriff of the county in 1702, 1708, and 1715, and he became county lieutenant about 1714. The best measure of his local eminence came when Lieutenant Governor William Gooch named Boush the first mayor in the charter he issued on 15 September 1736 incorporating the borough of Norfolk.

Boush died shortly thereafter, but his family carried on his leadership in the community. He and his son were devoted churchmen. Boush presented Elizabeth River Parish an elegant silver chalice engraved with his coat of arms in 1701, and his son reputedly provided the bricks used to erect Saint Paul's Church in 1739. The second Samuel Boush (1694–1759) became a colonel of militia and county lieutenant and was a burgess representing Norfolk County from 1728 to 1747. He served as clerk of the borough and as a councilman and alderman and was also a justice of the peace for many years before mid-June 1742, when he became county clerk. He held that position until 1753, when he was succeeded by his deputy and son, the third Samuel Boush (1720–1784), who was clerk of the county into the 1770s. The third Samuel Boush was also clerk of the borough from 1749 to 1773 and a burgess for Norfolk County from 1752 to 1754. John Boush, son of the third Samuel Boush, was in turn deputy to his father as county clerk for many years, clerk of the borough from 1773 to 1778, and mayor of Norfolk in 1791.

The children and grandchildren of Samuel Boush and Maximilian Boush married into prominent families in Norfolk and Princess Anne Counties. For the remainder of the eighteenth century Boush descendants were among the most important of Norfolk's merchants, shipowners, and civic leaders, and at least one Boush was almost always in office, as mayor, alderman, councilman, or town clerk in Norfolk. Colonel Samuel Boush, as he was usually referred to during the last decades of his life, died between 23 September 1736, when the borough charter appointed him mayor, and the first recorded meeting of the common hall of Norfolk on 18 November 1736, so that he never served in the office of mayor of the borough of Norfolk.

Kenneth C. Boush, "Samuel Boush Family, Norfolk, Genealogy," undated typescript, LVA, contains much information, some conjecture, and some misinformation about the immigrants; family relationships established in Princess Anne Co. Deeds and Wills, 4:158; Brent Tarter, ed., *The Order Book and Related Papers of the Common Hall of the Borough of Norfolk, Virginia, 1736–1798* (1979); most accounts state that Boush was burgess for Norfolk Co. from 1728 to 1736, but there is no record of election of a successor following his death, and so it was probably his son who sat continuously for Norfolk Co. from 1728 to 1747; *St. Paul's Church, 1832: Originally The Borough Church, 1739, Elizabeth River Parish, Norfolk, Virginia* (1934), frontispiece of reputed por.; will and estate inventory in Norfolk Co. Wills and Deeds, H:67–72, I:32.

BRENT TARTER

BOUSHALL, Thomas Callendine (28 March 1894–10 May 1992), banker and civic leader, was born in Raleigh, North Carolina, the son of Joseph Dozier Boushall, an attorney, and Mattie Callendine Heck Boushall. He majored in economics at the University of North Carolina and graduated in January 1915. After serving for a year as secretary of that university's Young Men's Christian Association, Boushall completed the executive training course of the National City Bank in New York City. He enlisted in the Army Medical Corps in November 1917 and was assigned to Base Hospital 45 in France, which was largely staffed by Richmonders. There he met Marie Mikell Lebby, a nurse from Charleston, South Carolina, whom he married on 23 February 1922. They had one daughter.

After the war Boushall helped establish a branch of the National City Bank at Brussels, Belgium. He remained there until January 1921, when he returned to New York and resigned from the bank. During the bank's training course William C. Redfield, the United States secretary of commerce, had addressed the students, and Boushall took Redfield's slogan, "banking organized down to the needs of the people," as his own guide as a banker. On his way to a job interview in Philadelphia he purchased the March 1921 issue of the *American Magazine*, which contained an enthusiastic article about Arthur Joseph Morris. As a young lawyer in Norfolk in 1910, Morris had opened a bank specializing in small loans to tradesmen and consumers whom the commercial banks did not serve. By 1921 there were 104 Morris Plan banks conducting business in thirty-eight states, and Morris had moved his headquarters to New York. Boushall obtained an interview with Morris and proposed combining the eleven Morris Plan banks in North Carolina into a statewide banking system. Morris agreed, but local managers preferred their independence and blocked the move. Undaunted, Boushall then proposed that Morris underwrite a new bank in Richmond. Morris agreed again, and the Morris Plan Bank of Richmond opened its doors on 17 July 1922.

Boushall planned to make the new bank a consumer-oriented competitor of the established commercial banks. From the beginning it advertised heavily and offered higher interest on savings accounts. Boushall soon opened branch offices in Newport News and Petersburg. By the end of 1926 his bank was the seventh-largest Morris Plan bank in the nation.

During this period Boushall battled tuberculosis. At the beginning of 1923 his doctors sent him to a sanatorium at Asheville, North Carolina, and nearly two years passed before he returned to full-time work in Richmond. Boushall suffered recurrent attacks of the disease until a series of operations in 1932 finally restored his health.

At the end of 1927 Boushall learned that the Virginia Bankers Association was seeking a revision of the state's banking code that would block branch banking. He managed to arrange a compromise, accepting limits on the interest paid on savings accounts in return for permission to operate branch banks in cities with populations exceeding 50,000. After establishing additional branches in Norfolk and Roanoke the bank changed its name to the Morris Plan Bank of Virginia.

Even during the Great Depression, Boushall remained convinced that his bank's future depended on expanding services, even at the expense of immediate profits. A new air-conditioned headquarters building opened in Richmond on 28 June 1932. The bank had begun offering automobile and home mortgage loans by 1936, the year that it introduced low-cost checking accounts. Preparation for impending war improved the economy after 1940, and the bank entered the commercial loan business early in 1943. The next year it opened a branch in Portsmouth, the sixth city in which it operated. Finally, effective 31 December 1945, it dropped the words "Morris Plan" from its name and became the Bank of Virginia.

Boushall believed that businesses and businessmen served themselves by serving their communities. In 1935 he and several other veterans of Base Hospital 45 organized the Richmond Hospital Service Association, a group-insurance plan that became Blue Cross of Virginia. Boushall was its first president. He also served as president of the Richmond Community Council into the 1940s. In 1937 he was elected a director of the Chamber of Commerce of the United States and was assigned to its education committee. Boushall arranged for a study to bolster his own belief that high-quality education ensures economic prosperity. Throughout his ten years on the committee and thereafter he propounded in speeches and articles the view that business served its own interest by investing in education. Boushall even proposed unsuccessfully in 1946 that businesses be taxed according to their numbers of employees to support the public schools. He served on the Richmond city school board from 1946 until 1954.

The Bank of Virginia continued to expand its business. In 1947 Boushall began negotiations to open a branch in Alexandria and proposed to open a second branch in Norfolk. These continuing expansion efforts provoked the Virginia Bankers Association to renew its attempt to revise the banking code to prohibit additional branch banking. Despite popular opposition to the change, Boushall could not prevent the ban from becoming law in 1948. With its existing branches in six cities the Bank of Virginia remained the only statewide bank in Virginia until the law was changed in 1962.

A political conservative, Boushall never voted for a Democratic presidential candidate after 1932. He believed in state and local direction of education and other public affairs, and he strongly supported Republican Dwight David Eisenhower's presidential candidacy in 1952 and was a leader of the Democrats for Eisenhower organization in Virginia. Democratic governor John Stewart Battle nonetheless appointed him to the State Board of Education in 1953. Boushall disagreed with the United States Supreme Court's decision in 1954 that declared public school segregation unconstitutional. Virginia's leaders initially responded to the decision with a plan enabling localities to limit desegregation. To implement the plan a referendum was needed to change the state constitution, and Boushall became the primary fundraiser in support of the referendum. Voters approved the plan early in 1956, but the General Assembly moved instead toward Massive Resistance and the closing of schools. In September 1956 Boushall spoke out against Massive Resistance, to which the ardent segregationists responded by forcing him from the Board of Education at the end of his term in 1958.

Boushall retired as president of the Bank of Virginia and became chairman of its board on 1 April 1959, a few days after he turned sixty-five. In addition to daily work at the bank Boushall served on the board of overseers for Sweet Briar College and on the Richmond Library Board. In 1963 he was a founder and first president of Richmond Forward, a successful local political organization. Boushall led the campaign to establish an educational television system in central Virginia and helped to raise money for Longwood College. His speech at the Governor's Conference on Education on 5 October 1966 advocating changing the constitution to permit issuance of general obligation bonds helped turn the state away from its traditional pay-as-you-go approach to financing public education.

Boushall stepped down as chairman of the board of directors of the Bank of Virginia on 20 January 1967 but did not slow his civic activities. In 1969 Governor Mills Edwin Godwin Jr. honored him with reappointment to the State Board of Education. Boushall resigned from that board on 2 August 1972 but remained a vocal advocate of public education late into his eighties. He received numerous awards from banking, education, and civic organizations during his life, and a public middle school in Richmond was named for him. Thomas Callendine Boushall died in a Richmond nursing home on 10 May 1992 and was buried in Hollywood Cemetery in that city.

"The Story of the Bank of Virginia, 1922–1959 from the point of view of Thomas C. Boushall," autobiographical typescript dated Apr. 1963, VHS; Signet Banking Corporation Records, VHS; feature articles in *Richmond News Leader*, 8 Feb. 1954, 20 Mar. 1961, and *Richmond Times-Dispatch*, 21 July 1957, 21 Jan. 1967; Herbert C. Moseley, *In Appreciation to Thomas C. Boushall* (1966), quotation on 2; Thomas C. Boushall biographical file, Literature and History Division, Richmond Public Library; Robbins L. Gates, *The Making of Massive Resistance: Virginia's Politics of Public School Desegregation, 1954–1956* (1964), 77, 84, 169–171; Paul L. Foster, *Bank Expansion in Virginia, 1962–1966: The Holding Company and the Direct Merger* (1971), 3–15; John H. Wessells Jr., *The Bank of Virginia: A History* (1973), frontispiece por.; for Boushall's views on public education, see esp. "Business and Education: An Imperative Partnership," *Commonwealth* 10 (Sept. 1943): 11–13, "Problems, Opportunities, Promises of Education in Virginia," *Virginia Journal of Education* 48 (Dec. 1954): 26–28, "The Challenge and Promise of Better Public Education in Virginia," ibid. 60 (Nov. 1966): 14–20, and *Richmond Times-Dispatch*, 15 Feb. 1981; obituaries in *Richmond News Leader* and *Richmond Times-Dispatch* (por.), both 11 May 1992, and *Washington Post*, 13 May 1992.

JOHN T. KNEEBONE

BOWDEN, George Edwin (6 July 1852– 22 January 1908), member of the House of Representatives, was born in Williamsburg, the son of Henry Moseley Bowden and his third wife, Henrietta Susan Stevens Stubblefield Bowden. He grew up in Williamsburg and in Norfolk, where his father moved the family in 1862. Bowden was educated in private schools. He worked for his father during the latter's service as clerk of the Norfolk circuit and corporation courts, and he subsequently studied law and won admission to the bar. Bowden preferred banking to the law, however, and from 1874 to 1887 he served as president of the Home Savings Bank of Norfolk. On 22 February 1875 he married Ellen Evangeline Jones. They had three sons, one daughter, and another child who died in infancy.

Bowden's father, his uncle Lemuel Jackson Bowden, and his cousin Thomas Russell Bowden all became prominent Unionists and Republicans during and after the Civil War. Bowden himself was a Republican for all of his adult life. President Rutherford B. Hayes rewarded him for his participation in local Republican Party campaigns by appointing him customs collector for the port of Norfolk, a post he held from September 1879 until May 1885. In 1886 Bowden ran for Congress and with strong support from African American voters defeated Marshall Parks, the Democratic Party nominee, with more than 60 percent of the vote. Two years later he won reelection by more than 6,000 votes over Democrat Richard C. Marshall. During his first term in Congress, Bowden served on the Committees on Claims and on Expenditures in the Treasury Department, and during his second term he belonged to the Committee on Rivers and Harbors. He cooperated with Republican congressional leaders and befriended Speaker Thomas B. Reed and Representative William McKinley. In July 1890 Bowden voted with many northern Republicans and against southern Democrats in favor of the so-called Force Bill that would have provided for federal supervision of elections in southern states where many African Americans were being deprived of the right to vote. In November 1890 the Democratic Party regained control of Congress, and Bowden narrowly lost his seat to Democrat John W. Lawson.

Bowden resumed his career in business. From 1895 to 1897 he served as the special master appointed by the federal court to manage the Norfolk and Western Railroad, which had gone into receivership following the financial panic of 1893. Bowden was a Republican Party leader in Virginia for almost twenty years. He presided over the state party convention in Norfolk that nominated William Mahone for governor

on 22 August 1889, and he served on the state executive committee during the campaign that fall. After McKinley became president, in January 1898 he reappointed Bowden to the customs collector's office in Norfolk. Bowden served until March 1899, when he resigned to become clerk of the United States District Court. He sat on the Republican National Committee for many years, attended national party conventions, and during McKinley's administration cooperated closely with Ohio senator Marcus A. Hanna in the distribution of federal patronage in Virginia. After Theodore Roosevelt became president in 1901, Representative Campbell Slemp, of Virginia's Ninth Congressional District, challenged Bowden for control of federal patronage in the state. The Slemp and Roosevelt faction ultimately prevailed, but the contest created serious divisions within the Republican Party in Virginia.

George Edwin Bowden remained clerk of the United States District Court until he died at his home in Norfolk on 22 January 1908. He was buried in Elmwood Cemetery in Norfolk.

Biography in *Norfolk Virginian-Pilot,* Twentieth-Century Edition, June 1900 (por.); Bowden letters in William Mahone Papers, Duke; Norfolk City Marriage Register; William C. Pendleton, *Political History of Appalachian Virginia, 1776–1927* (1927), 502–503, 513; obituaries in *Norfolk Landmark, Norfolk Virginian-Pilot,* and *Richmond Times-Dispatch,* all 23 Jan. 1908.

DONALD W. GUNTER

BOWDEN, Henry Moseley (10 April 1819–11 April 1871), member of the Convention of 1867–1868, was born in James City County, the son of William Bowden and Mildred Davis Bowden, and he grew up on his father's farm near Williamsburg. As a young man he engaged in farming and built houses. On 24 December 1839 he married Elizabeth A. M. White. After her death he married Esprella Eugenia Ann Ware on 23 December 1841, and they had one daughter. Sometime after his second wife's death on 17 April 1850, Bowden was married a third time, to a widow, Henrietta Susan Stevens Stubblefield. Their one child, George Edwin Bowden, served in the House of Representatives.

By the 1850s Bowden and his elder brother Lemuel Jackson Bowden had become prosperous and influential in Williamsburg, an ascendancy symbolized by Henry Bowden's construction for Lemuel Bowden of a large, expensive new house near Bruton Parish Church. Intensely partisan Democrats, the brothers were often at odds with Williamsburg's politically powerful Whigs. Henry Bowden served as sergeant at arms of the Senate of Virginia during the 1850–1851 and 1852–1853 sessions and helped persuade the General Assembly to limit the terms of members of the board of the Eastern Asylum, which sheltered mental patients in Williamsburg. The decision enabled the governor to appoint the first Democrats to the board, with Lemuel J. Bowden becoming its president in 1851 and Henry Bowden joining the board in January 1852. Under the new regime Henrietta Bowden became hospital matron, in charge of female patients, and Henry Bowden joined with other local Democrats in obtaining profitable contracts to sell food and other supplies and lease their slaves to the asylum.

Bowden voted for Democrat Stephen A. Douglas, of Illinois, in the 1860 presidential election and opposed secession in the May 1861 referendum on that issue. His outspoken contempt for secession provoked some of his neighbors to violence. Bowden's house was stoned, he was shot at on several occasions, and to protect himself he sometimes hid in the woods for days at a time. After the Union army took control of Williamsburg, Bowden became clerk of the Eastern Lunatic Asylum in May 1862 and steward a month later. As steward he ran the institution and restored his wife to the position of matron. Bowden freed his slaves during the summer, but after the Union army withdrew from the Peninsula he abandoned his home and property in York County and on 20 August 1862 fled with his family to the safety of Norfolk, taking with him most of the hospital's food and supplies. In January 1866 an investigative committee of the General Assembly concluded that during his wartime management of the asylum Bowden had used or disposed of the hospital's money and foodstuffs without an adequate

accounting and improperly kept possession of the institution's mutilated records. The legislature took no action against him.

Bowden worked initially as a corder of wood and financial agent under the appointment of Union general Benjamin F. Butler after moving to Norfolk. In June 1863 Bowden became clerk of the city's hustings and corporation court. He attended a convention of more than 300 Republicans at Richmond's First African Baptist Church on 17 April 1867 to plan campaign strategy for the election of delegates to the upcoming state constitutional convention. On 22 October 1867 he was elected to represent the city of Norfolk along with Thomas Bayne, who became the most powerful black delegate to the convention. Bowden received 1,815 votes from African Americans but only 62 from whites, many of whom refused to vote. He served on the Committee on Internal Improvements and chaired the Committee on County and Corporation Courts and County Organizations. The latter committee introduced proposals embodied in Articles VI and VII of the Constitution of 1869, which replaced the antebellum local government structure with a popularly elected democratic system modeled on New England town government. Bowden also helped end the sometimes abusive debates on whether oysters could be taxed while tobacco was not by introducing a compromise resolution that became Section 2 of Article X, which exempted from taxation the harvesting of oysters from natural beds but permitted the taxation of oysters sold commercially. He sided with the Radicals on most roll calls before the final vote on the constitution, which he missed.

Bowden served by military appointment in 1869 as a commissioner in chancery for the Norfolk City Hustings Court, and in December 1870 President Ulysses S. Grant appointed him assessor of internal revenue for the Norfolk district. On 6 July 1869 Bowden headed the poll in a six-way race for Norfolk's two seats in the House of Delegates. He served on the Committees on Finance and on Resolutions in the assembly sessions that convened in October 1869 and December 1870 and on the Committee on Immigration in December 1870. Henry Moseley Bowden died aboard a train in Isle of Wight County on 11 April 1871, a few days after the assembly adjourned, and was buried in Norfolk.

Family history information supplied by Lemuel Bowden and Monroe Couper; [Charles H. Porter], "Sketch of a Virginian Family," *Fishkill (N.Y.) Standard*, 27 Nov. 1880; some Bowden letters in VHS; marriage announcements and death notice of second wife in *Richmond Whig and Public Advertiser*, 21 Jan. 1840, 18 Jan. 1842, 26 Apr. 1850; Norman Dain, *Disordered Minds: The First Century of Eastern State Hospital in Williamsburg, Virginia, 1766–1866* (1971), 142–161, 170–174, 192–193; *Calendar of Virginia State Papers*, 11:474–497; documents including testimony of Bowden, 30 Aug. 1865, and wife, 3 June 1872, Claim 36,986, Southern Claims Commission; elections documented in *Norfolk Journal*, 25 Oct. 1867, 9 July 1869; Hume, "Membership of Convention of 1867–1868," 481; obituaries in *Norfolk Journal*, 12, 13 Apr. 1871.

DONALD W. GUNTER

BOWDEN, Lemuel Jackson (16 January 1815–2 January 1864), member of the Convention of 1850–1851 and member of the United States Senate, was the son of William Bowden and Mildred Davis Bowden. He was born in Williamsburg, grew up on his father's farm in James City County, and received an L.B. from the College of William and Mary in 1832. After studying law under James Semple, Bowden was admitted to the bar in 1838. Two years later he married Martha Ellen Shackelford. Their one daughter and two sons included Thomas Russell Bowden, who became attorney general of Virginia. His son-in-law, Charles Howell Porter, represented Chesterfield and Powhatan Counties at the Convention of 1867–1868 and served in the United States House of Representatives from 1870 to 1873. Bowden's law practice was lucrative, and he owned several profitable farms in York County. During the 1850s his younger brother Henry Moseley Bowden built him a large and expensive house near Bruton Parish Church in Williamsburg.

In 1841 Bowden won election to the House of Delegates as a Democrat representing the city of Williamsburg and the counties of James City and York. He was reelected to one-year terms in successive years, and after he lost the election in 1845 he successfully challenged the result and reclaimed his seat, serving a total of five terms. He served on the Committee on Schools and Colleges from 1841 through 1845 and on the Committee on Claims in 1842. As chairman of the Committee on Lunatic Asylums in 1841, 1843, and 1844, Bowden led a legislative fight for uniform admission policies for the state's two mental hospitals, the Eastern and Western Asylums, respectively situated in Williamsburg and Staunton. The selective admission policy in effect at the Staunton institution enabled it to refuse admission to African Americans, paupers, and others who could not pay or might require extensive treatment, forcing the Eastern Asylum, which had no such restrictive policy, to treat most of the state's indigent patients and those requiring the longest and costliest stays.

In 1850 Bowden successfully ran for election to a state constitutional convention from the district composed of the city of Williamsburg and the counties of Elizabeth City, James City, Gloucester, Warwick, and York. In a campaign address on 15 July 1850 he advocated public education of white children, universal white manhood suffrage, popular election of most public officials, including some judges, and retention of the practice of taking the value of slaves and other personal property into account in the distribution of seats in the General Assembly. Bowden served on the convention's Committee on the Judiciary, and he unsuccessfully proposed to reduce the minimum age for service on the Supreme Court of Appeals from thirty-five to twenty-one. He also moved without success to limit the power of the General Assembly to create a public debt. He usually sided with conservative eastern delegates seeking to retain the apportionment scheme that benefited the eastern counties, but he tended to vote with western delegates in favor of other democratic reforms. Bowden was one of only eight eastern Democrats who voted for a crucial compromise on apportionment, and on 31 July 1851 he voted for the constitution as finally approved.

Bowden's intense partisanship often placed him at odds with Williamsburg's socially and economically influential Whigs. In 1850 he and his brother took the lead in persuading the General Assembly to limit the terms of the members of the board of the Eastern Asylum. The

131

move enabled the governor to appoint the board's first Democratic members, including Bowden, who served as president from 1851 until 1854. In 1855 Bowden parted political company with some of his Democratic friends to campaign for the American (Know Nothing) Party in opposition to the successful gubernatorial candidacy of Democrat Henry Alexander Wise.

In 1860 Bowden won election as a presidential elector on the Constitutional Union Party ticket of John Bell and Edward Everett. He opposed secession so strongly in 1861 that he refused to pay his state taxes until the government threatened to auction off his property. In the spring of 1862 Wise, then a Confederate general, issued an order for Bowden's arrest. Bowden made his Williamsburg home available to Union officers in May of that year, and Major General George B. McClellan appointed him mayor of the borough. After McClellan's army withdrew from the Middle Peninsula, Bowden and his family escaped to Yorktown before moving to Norfolk, where he continued to practice law. By then his wife had died, he had lost property valued at almost $8,500, and he was being called a traitor in his hometown.

Later in 1862 Bowden reportedly turned down President Abraham Lincoln's offer of an appointment as a federal judge in Virginia. During the winter of 1862–1863 the General Assembly of the so-called Restored government of Virginia met in Wheeling. Waitman T. Willey declined reelection to the United States Senate, preferring instead to become one of the first senators for the new state of West Virginia. Bowden may have been present, and on 23 January 1863 the assembly elected him senator in Willey's place. He was sworn in on 4 March 1863 and appointed to the Committees on Military Affairs and the Militia, on Pensions, and on Post Offices and Post Roads. Congress adjourned on 14 March and did not reconvene until 7 December 1863, when Bowden was added to the Committee on Commerce. Lemuel Jackson Bowden contracted smallpox three weeks later, died in Washington, D.C., on 2 January 1864, and was buried in the Congressional Cemetery in that city.

Parke Rouse Jr., *Cows on the Campus: Williamsburg in Bygone Days* (1973), 57–61 (por. on 59); family history information supplied by Lemuel Bowden and Monroe Couper; [Charles H. Porter], "Sketch of a Virginian Family," *Fishkill (N.Y.) Standard*, 27 Nov. 1880; some Bowden letters in VHS; Norman Dain, *Disordered Minds: The First Century of Eastern State Hospital in Williamsburg, Virginia, 1766–1866* (1971), 117, 120–121, 137, 142–156, 171; *Address of L. J. Bowden, to the Voters of Gloucester, Elizabeth City, Warwick, York, James City, and the City of Williamsburg* (1850); *Journal of 1850–1851 Convention*, 32–33, 60–61; *Debates and Proceedings of 1850–1851 Convention*, 149–153; Claim 20,775, Southern Claims Commission; *New York Times*, 23 May 1862; *Wheeling Daily Intelligencer*, 26 Jan. 1863; obituaries in *Alexandria Gazette*, *Washington Daily National Intelligencer,* and *Washington Evening* Star, all 4 Jan. 1864.

Donald W. Gunter

BOWDEN, Thomas Russell (20 May 1841–6 July 1893), attorney general of Virginia, was born near Williamsburg, the son of Lemuel Jackson Bowden and Martha Ellen Shackelford Bowden, and grew up on one of his father's farms. In 1859 he entered the College of William and Mary, where he studied Latin, Greek, French, history, and economics for two years. As a member of the college's Phoenix Literary Society, Bowden won a gold medal for his debating skills. He probably also studied law in his father's Williamsburg office.

Bowden's father and his uncle Henry Moseley Bowden were uncompromising Unionists during the winter of 1860–1861. In the spring of 1862, after the Union army occupied Williamsburg and acquired responsibility for the patients in the Eastern Lunatic Asylum, Northern officers appointed Henry Bowden clerk and steward of the institution and made Thomas Bowden collector of its pay-patient fund. With the withdrawal of the Union army later in the summer the Bowden family left Williamsburg, and the events of the Civil War made its members Republicans. Bowden's father represented Virginia in the United States Senate before his death on 2 January 1864, and Bowden's sister later married Charles Howell Porter, a Union army officer from New York who was a member of the Virginia Convention of 1867–1868 and served two terms in Congress from Virginia.

Bowden also entered politics. In May 1863 a convention of Virginia Unionists had nominated a ticket headed by Governor Francis Harrison Pierpont for the so-called Restored government of Virginia, but the candidates for lieutenant governor and attorney general withdrew from the race. Bowden then became the Unionist candidate for attorney general and was easily elected with the rest of the slate on 28 May 1863 by a small turnout of voters in Alexandria and other Virginia jurisdictions occupied by Northern forces. With 2,743 votes Bowden became the youngest attorney general of Virginia at the age of twenty-two.

With the collapse of the Confederacy in the spring of 1865, officials of the Restored government moved to Richmond and began to administer the entire state. Bowden divided his time between Richmond and the family home in Williamsburg. In the autumn of 1865 his younger brother Lemuel Gardner Bowden was serving as president of the board of the Eastern Lunatic Asylum and running unsuccessfully for the House of Delegates. In January and February 1866 the attorney general found himself in the peculiar position of being both a witness and a central figure in a two-pronged legislative investigation, of his uncle's and his own administration of the hospital's funds and the disappearance of its supplies in 1862, and of his brother's and his own alleged improper attempts three years later to influence the votes of hospital employees in the legislative election. The investigating committee ultimately recommended taking no action against Bowden.

On 10 March 1869 a Republican Party convention nominated Henry Horatio Wells, the provisional incumbent, for governor, J. D. Harris, an African American, for lieutenant governor, and Bowden for another term as attorney general. The Republican candidates all lost in the general election held on 6 July. James Craig Taylor defeated Bowden by a vote of 119,446 to 101,129, and on 26 July Bowden resigned as attorney general effective 1 August 1869. During his years in office the military authorities in effect controlled the government, limiting his responsibilities. Bowden's few arguments before the Supreme Court of Appeals were usually confined to technical matters of criminal procedure, and so far as is known he did not seriously influence any consequential public policies.

On 27 April 1869 Bowden married Rosa Marion Sands, of Williamsburg. They had one daughter. Not long after leaving office as attorney general, Bowden moved to Washington, D.C., where he practiced law for more than twenty years. In August 1870 he was arrested in connection with a Richmond forgery case arising out of the administration of an estate in which he had been briefly involved. The count against him was dropped on 13 September, and thanks in part to evidence Bowden produced, former Richmond mayor George Chahoon was subsequently convicted of forgery.

In addition to practicing law, Bowden published *Blunders in Educated Circles Corrected* (1889), a short book dedicated to the correction of common errors in grammar and English usage. Thomas Russell Bowden died in Washington, D.C., on 6 July 1893 and was buried in Cedar Grove Cemetery in Williamsburg.

Family history information supplied by Lemuel Bowden and Monroe Couper; election of 1863 reported in *Alexandria Gazette*, 14 Dec. 1863; official letters and 1866 investigation in *Calendar of Virginia State Papers*, 11:422, 429–431, 474–497; two official opinions in *Lynchburg Daily Virginian*, 12, 20 July 1865; *Richmond Whig*, 11 Mar. 1869; election defeat and resignation documented in memorandum of 18 Aug. 1869, in Military District Number One, *General Orders and Circulars, Headquarters, First Military District, 1869* (1870), and *Index of Special Orders, Headquarters, First Military District, 1869* (1870), no. 155; marriage and forgery case reported in *Richmond Daily Dispatch*, 30 Apr. 1869, 19–22, 25 Aug., 12–14 Sept., 28 Oct. 1870; suicide alleged in John S. Wise, *The Lion's Skin: A Historical Novel and a Novel History* (1905), 192; obituaries in *Washington Post*, 8 July 1893, and *Norfolk Landmark*, 9 July 1893.

DONALD W. GUNTER

BOWEN, Henry (26 December 1841–29 April 1915), member of the House of Representatives, was the son of Rees Tate Bowen, later a congressman, and his first wife, Maria Louisa Peery Bowen. Born at Maiden Spring, his father's Tazewell County farm, he received his early education locally and studied at Emory and Henry College from 1856 to 1858 before returning to the farm. On 29 May 1861 Bowen became first lieutenant in the Tazewell Troop, which was mustered into the Confederate army as Company H, 8th Regiment Virginia Cavalry. He was promoted to captain by 30 July 1863 and served in western Virginia until the summer of 1864, when the regiment was placed under the command of Jubal Anderson Early. After participating in the defense of Lynchburg and Early's raid on Washington, D.C., Bowen was captured at Lacy Spring on 21 December 1864 and spent the remainder of the war imprisoned at Fort Delaware in Delaware.

Bowen returned to the family farm in Tazewell County after his release in the summer of 1865. In the summer of 1869 he won election to represent the county in the House of Delegates. A member of a coalition of conservative Republicans, former Democrats, and others opposed to the Radical Republicans, Bowen served on the Committees on Agriculture and Mining and on Retrenchment and Economy. He won reelection in 1871 and was appointed to the important Committee on Privileges and Elections as well as the less consequential Committees on Militia and Police and on Public Property.

Late in his first assembly term Bowen voted against the controversial Funding Act of 1871, which pledged Virginia to pay the full principal and interest on the outstanding prewar public debt. For more than a decade thereafter state politics hinged on whether to reduce, or readjust, the amount of the principal to be paid back and how to finance, or fund, the principal and interest. Bowen joined the Readjuster Party when it was formed at the end of the 1870s. When Readjuster influence peaked in southwestern Virginia he ran for the House of Representatives in 1882 from the sixteen-county Ninth District and by 4,470 votes defeated one-term incumbent Abram Fulkerson, who had shifted his allegiance from the Readjusters to the Funders. In Congress Bowen sat on the Committees on War Claims and on Expenditures in the Department of Justice. He failed to win renomination in 1884. Two years later, however, after the Readjuster Party had served its purpose and fallen apart, he won the Republican Party nomination for Congress and regained his seat, defeating Robert Randolph Henry by 3,631 votes. During this term Bowen was not assigned to a standing committee, and throughout his congressional service he made no speeches and introduced no important

bills. He ran again in 1888 but lost to Democrat John Alexander Buchanan by only 478 votes. Bowen unsuccessfully challenged the result, alleging corruption and illegal voting.

In 1892 Bowen attended the Republican National Convention but then retired from politics to manage his farm and to raise cattle. He was named commander of the Brown-Harman Camp of the United Confederate Veterans in 1896. On 4 December 1871 Bowen had married Mariah E. Louisa Gillespie, of Tazewell County. Their four sons and two daughters included Margaret Ellen Bowen, who became the first osteopath to pass the Virginia medical examination and who served as president of the Virginia Osteopathic Association from 1922 to 1924. Henry Bowen died at his home on 29 April 1915 following a long illness and was buried in Jeffersonville Cemetery in Tazewell County.

French Biographies; John Newton Harman, *Annals of Tazewell County, Virginia, from 1800 to 1922* (1922–1925), 2:346–348; William C. Pendleton, *History of Tazewell County and Southwest Virginia, 1748–1920* (1920), 636 (por.), which gives incorrect birth date; Jamie Ault Grady, *Bowens of Virginia and Tennessee: Descendants of John Bowen and Lily McIlhaney* (1969–1975), 1:9–9A; Compiled Service Records; Jack L. Dickinson, *8th Virginia Cavalry* (1986), 12, 75; Tazewell Co. Marriage Register; Bowen letters, 1882–1887, in William Mahone Papers, Duke; *Henry Bowen* v. *John A. Buchanan*, 51st Cong., 1st sess., 1890, House Rept. 1214, serial 2811; obituaries in *Roanoke Times* and *Tazewell Clinch Valley News* (por.), both 30 Apr. 1915, *Richmond Times-Dispatch*, 1 May 1915, and *Marion News*, 7 May 1915.

Donald W. Gunter

BOWEN, Rees Tate (10 January 1809–29 August 1879), member of the House of Representatives, was born at Maiden Spring in Tazewell County, the son of Henry Bowen and Ellen Stuart Tate Bowen. His father served in the General Assembly and farmed a large and prosperous tract in the Cove section of Tazewell County. Educated at Abingdon Academy in Washington County, Bowen eventually succeeded his father in charge of the Maiden Spring plantation. The farm was renowned for the quality of its livestock and prospered under his guidance. By 1850 Bowen's real estate was valued at $40,000. During the ensuing decade his wealth increased dramatically. He was a founding director of the Jeffersonville Savings Bank chartered in 1851, and in 1860 his real estate was worth more than $73,000 and his personal assets totaled almost $34,000. In a region sparsely populated with slaves, Bowen then owned fourteen. On 13 January 1835 he married Maria Louisa Peery. They had five sons and four daughters before her death on 1 April 1853 from complications resulting from childbirth. His son Henry Bowen served in Congress in the 1880s.

Bowen was a Democrat who served as postmaster at Maiden Spring from 26 June 1840 to 13 December 1845. In 1849 he became a school commissioner, and in the spring of 1858 he was elected to a vacancy on the Tazewell County Court and often acted as presiding justice in 1860 and 1861. Active in the militia, Bowen in March 1859 was appointed brigadier general of a new brigade of the state militia. Twice during the Civil War he received orders to summon his 28th Brigade to duty, but on neither occasion did it participate in any action. Both Union and Confederate troops camped on his Maiden Spring property, which a Union general found to be of strategic importance during the Battle of Saltville in October 1864.

In 1863 Bowen was elected to represent Buchanan, McDowell, and Tazewell Counties in the House of Delegates. He served on the Committee on Finance during attendance at all three assembly sessions between September 1863 and the spring of 1865. The value of his real estate obliged Bowden to obtain a presidential pardon in the summer of 1865. After the Civil War he joined the Conservative Party, a coalition of Democrats, former Whigs, and some Republicans opposed to what they perceived as the excesses of the Radical Republicans. In November 1872 Bowen won election to the House of Representatives from the new fifteen-county Ninth Congressional District, defeating Republican Robert W. Hughes by a large margin. Bowen served on the Committee on Manufactures and evidently never spoke on the House floor. On 19 February 1875, less than two weeks before his term expired, he denounced the Grant administration's interference in the politics of Louisiana, where Reconstruction had not yet come to an end. Bowen did not deliver his speech in the House but asked that it be published in the appendix to the *Congressional Record*. He also had it printed as a small pamphlet, *Condition of Affairs in the South*.

Bowen did not seek a second term and permanently retired from politics in 1875, returning to his farm to pursue his interests in agriculture, geology, and history. On 1 September 1875 he married Lucy J. Gravatt, of Port Royal. They had one daughter, and a son who died in infancy. Rees Tate Bowen died on 29 August 1879 and was buried in the family cemetery at Maiden Spring in Tazewell County.

John Newton Harman, *Annals of Tazewell County, Virginia, from 1800 to 1922* (1922–1925), 2:345–346; family Bible records with birth and death dates printed in Jamie Ault Grady, *Bowens of Virginia and Tennessee: Descendants of John Bowen and Lily McIlhaney* (1969–1975), 1:9–9A, 2:10A–11, 19–22; Tazewell Co. Marriage Register, 1835; BVS Marriage Register, Caroline Co., 1875; Tazewell Co. Historical Society, *Another Album of Tazewell County, Virginia, Part 1* (1991), 7 (por.); vertical files, Virginia Room, Tazewell Co. Public Library; Presidential Pardons; Election Records, no. 5, RG 13, LVA; Louisiana remarks in *Congressional Record*, 43d Cong., 2d sess., 1519, Appendix, 55–56, also reprinted with biography in Slemp and Preston, *Addresses*, 283–289; obituary in *Richmond Dispatch*, 2 Sept. 1879.

CATHY CARLSON REYNOLDS

BOWERING, Andrew Benjamin (6 August 1842–20 October 1923), musician, was born in Paterson, New Jersey, the son of Benjamin Bowering and Lucinda Voorhees Bowering. About 1849 the family moved to Fredericksburg, where Bowering grew up. His parents took active roles in the cultural life of the city and gave him musical training. On 22 April 1861 he joined the Fredericksburg Grays, which on 1 July was mustered into the Confederate army as Company B, 30th Regiment Virginia Infantry. By 1 July 1861 Bowering was assigned to the regimental band, and the following summer he was appointed principal musician. Serving as both band leader and bugler, Bowering participated in ceremonial and other regimental military functions. He was present at the Battle of Sharpsburg (Antietam) on 17 September 1862 when the 30th Virginia suffered exceptionally severe losses. On such occasions noncombatant personnel, including musicians, performed support duties varying from rear area guard duty to service as stretcher bearers on the front lines.

In the predawn hours of 12 May 1863 Bowering was ordered to report to Richmond for duty at the funeral service for Confederate lieutenant general Thomas J. "Stonewall" Jackson. Unable to locate his sheet music for the "Dead March" from George Frideric Handel's *Saul*, the piece Bowering deemed most fitting for the occasion, by torchlight he arranged it from memory for military band. Later in the day his band played the dirge while leading the procession from the State Capitol down to the James River landing, where Jackson's body was placed aboard a boat to be taken to Lexington for burial. Bowering remained in the army until the war's end. His regiment narrowly escaped destruction at Five Forks on 1 April 1865, and he sounded the call for Sunday services at Appomattox eight days later, likely the final summons to assembly for the Army of Northern Virginia.

Bowering returned to Fredericksburg after the war and on 6 September 1866 married Susan C. Huffman. Of their three sons and one daughter, one son died in infancy. Bowering's wife died on 12 April 1892, and he married Margaret A. Jones on 18 October 1893. They had one son and a second child whose gender is unknown, and after his second wife's death on 5 February 1896 he married her sister Annie Laurie Jones on 25 October 1899. They had no children.

Bowering earned his living teaching music. For several years he was also his father's partner in a foundry, Bowering and Son. In 1875 Bowering became Fredericksburg's commissioner of revenue, a position he held until his death. He served for many years as clerk of the city school board, was active in several fraternal and service organizations, and taught a Bible class at the Fredericksburg Baptist Church, where his parents were longtime members of the choir.

Professor Bowering, as he became known locally, remained active in Fredericksburg's musical life, and two of his children became musicians. He organized and led community bands and supervised the music in ceremonies occasioned by the Spanish-American War, the United States Army's operations in Mexico, and World War I. Bowering served as commander of the Maury Camp of the United Confederate Veterans in Fredericksburg and was one of the most popular figures at a 1921 reunion of Confederate veterans held in Richmond. Late in life he admitted to an interviewer that he disliked "Dixie" and avoided playing it whenever possible. Andrew Benjamin Bowering died at his Fredericksburg home on 20 October 1923. The Fredericksburg band led the procession to his gravesite in the city cemetery, where in November 1925 the band members erected a monument to him.

Chester Goolrick, "He Didn't Like 'Dixie'!" *Virginia Cavalcade* 9 (spring 1960): 5–10 (pors.); Compiled Service Records; Robert K. Krick, *30th Virginia Infantry* (1983), 83 (por. on 71); Fredericksburg Marriage Register, 1866; Spotsylvania Co. Marriage Register, 1893, 1899; family history in parents' obituaries, *Fredericksburg Free Lance*, 7 Feb. 1901, 14 July 1903; Andrew Benjamin Bowering Papers, Fredericksburg Area Museum and Cultural Center; obituary and detailed description of funeral in *Fredericksburg Free Lance*, 23 Oct. 1923; obituary in *Confederate Veteran* 31 (1923): 468.

DONALD W. GUNTER

BOWERS, Fredson Thayer (25 April 1905–11 April 1991), literary scholar, was born in New Haven, Connecticut, the son of Fredson Eugene Bowers, a manufacturing company executive, and Hattie May Quigley Brownell Bowers. His father died in 1911, and three years later his mother married Charles K. Groesbeck. Bowers graduated from New Haven General High School in 1921 and enrolled in Brown University, where he studied English, participated in literary and musical societies, was elected to Phi Beta Kappa in 1924, and graduated with a Ph.B. in 1925.

In the autumn of 1925 Bowers enrolled in graduate school at Harvard, where he studied under John Tucker Murray and George Lyman Kittredge and received his Ph.D. in 1934 with an 1,100-page doctoral dissertation on Renaissance drama. Shortened and revised, it became his first scholarly book, *Elizabethan Revenge Tragedy, 1587–1642* (1940), still considered the standard treatment of the subject. Bowers served as an instructor in English at Harvard while completing his graduate study, stayed on in that position from 1934 to 1936, taught at Princeton from 1936 to 1938, and in 1938 joined the faculty of the University of Virginia. From 1942 to 1945 he worked in Washington, D.C., with the rank of lieutenant commander leading a team of naval intelligence analysts charged with deciphering Japanese naval communications. Bowers was promoted to associate professor at the University of Virginia in 1946 and full professor in 1948. From 1949 through 1964 he also taught summer courses in bibliography at the University of Chicago.

Bowers had one of the most distinguished and influential careers in the history of American bibliographical and textual studies. Besides an astonishing output of critical editions of works by authors from five centuries, he published eight books and more than 200 papers, speeches, and reviews. His theoretical writings became classic statements of the ways in which the processes of book production affect the texts that appear in books, thereby making clear how the physical evidence in books is related to their intellectual content. Bowers raised the study of books and texts to a new level and made it more visible in the scholarly community. He explained, more thoroughly and effectively than his predecessors, the importance of, and the techniques for, describing books as physical objects; and he developed procedures for analyzing the production history of books and applying that knowledge to the editing of texts.

Bowers developed his interest in the physical evidence in books before the war in several pioneering articles and brought it to fruition in *Principles of Bibliographical Description* (1949), an epochal book that amply exhibited his rigorously logical and powerfully synthesizing mind. It instantly became, and remains, the central work in its field. Following this publication with the first volumes of his four-volume edition of *The Dramatic Works of Thomas Dekker* (1953–1961), which was important for its editorial principles, he achieved an unquestioned eminence. In consequence, Bowers was asked to deliver three major series of bibliographical lectures, each of which became a major book. His 1954 Rosenbach Lectures at the University of Pennsylvania were published as *On Editing Shakespeare and the Elizabethan Dramatists* (1955), the 1958 Sandars Lectures at Cambridge University led to *Textual and Literary Criticism* (1959), and the 1959 Lyell Lectures at Oxford University resulted in *Bibliography and Textual Criticism* (1964). These books have been widely read and cited as magisterial basic statements of the role of textual criticism in literary criticism and of analytical bibliography in editing.

During the next thirty years Bowers augmented this impressive record of scholarship with landmark theoretical essays and celebrated works of literary criticism. The most important of them were collected as *Essays in Bibliography, Text, and Editing* (1975) and *Hamlet as Minister and Scourge and Other Studies in Shakespeare and Milton* (1989). In addition, Bowers completed a series of scholarly editions remarkable in its range and amazing in its extent, a total of some sixty volumes of writings by Christopher Marlowe, Thomas Dekker, William Shakespeare, Francis Beaumont and John Fletcher, John Dryden, Henry Fielding, Nathaniel Hawthorne, Walt Whitman, Stephen Crane, William James, and Vladimir Nabokov. In 1948 Bowers published the first annual volume of *Studies in Bibliography* (originally *Papers of the Bibliographical Society of the University of Virginia*), which he edited until his death and which, through his eye for innovative work and the perspicacity of his suggestions to contributors, became a key factor in shaping the course of bibliographical scholarship in the English language.

Bowers was generous with his time in advising editors who wished to set up editorial projects, in delivering lectures that proselytized for the causes of bibliographical and textual studies, and in serving on a number of professional boards. From 1961 to 1968 he chaired the University of Virginia's English Department, and he was dean of the faculty of Arts and Sciences in 1968 and 1969. Bowers helped make his department one of the country's most prestigious and received numerous awards. From

1957 to 1968 he was Alumni Professor and from 1968 until his retirement in 1975 he was Linden Kent Memorial Professor of English Literature. He held Fulbright and Guggenheim Fellowships and received honorary degrees from Brown and Clark Universities in 1970 and from the University of Chicago in 1973. Bowers also received the gold medal of the London Bibliographical Society in 1969 and the Thomas Jefferson Award from the University of Virginia in 1971. He was elected to the American Academy of Arts and Sciences in 1972. In person he was invariably gracious, and in public he had a commanding presence. Bowers never hesitated to expose muddled thinking in print, and he did not shrink from controversy. Throughout much of his career he was at the center of intense scholarly debates about the editorial principles he advocated and the way he applied them in his critical editions.

On 11 November 1924 in New York City Bowers married Hyacinth Adeline Sutphen. They had three sons and one daughter before they divorced early in 1936. His marriage to the celebrated writer Nancy Hale on 16 March 1942 ended only with her death on 24 September 1988. After Bowers ceased teaching at the University of Chicago in 1964, he spent part of each summer at his wife's family's summer place near Rockport, Massachusetts. In addition to his scholarly interests, Bowers collected stamps, enjoyed sports cars, followed the stock market, and wrote nearly 1,200 reviews of some 5,000 musical recordings for the *Richmond Times-Dispatch* between 1939 and 1966. He was also, during his Harvard years, a breeder of Irish wolfhounds. His first book was *The Dog Owner's Handbook* (1936), and he wrote authoritatively on dogs and judged shows for many years.

A conference held in Charlottesville in April 1985 honored Bowers on the occasion of his eightieth birthday, and the Bibliographical Society of America devoted much of the second quarterly issue of volume 79 of its *Papers* to the tributes from that conference. Fredson Thayer Bowers died at his home near Charlottesville on 11 April 1991. His ashes were buried in Forest Hills Cemetery in Boston.

G. Thomas Tanselle, *The Life and Work of Fredson Bowers* (1993), including frontispiece por., citations to numerous critical evaluations of Bowers's scholarship, and a checklist and chronology by Martin C. Battestin; *Dictionary of Literary Biography Yearbook* (1991), 224–253; *Bibliographical Society of Australia and New Zealand Bulletin* 15 (1991): 45–102; *Text* 8 (1995): 25–100; Fredson Bowers Papers, UVA; *A Keepsake to Honor Fredson Bowers* (1974), pors.; information provided by Fredson Thayer Bowers Jr.; memorial by E. D. Hirsch, 23 Apr. 1991, Minutes of Faculty of Arts and Sciences, UVA Archives; obituaries in *Charlottesville Daily Progress, New York Times, Richmond News Leader,* and *Richmond Times-Dispatch*, all 13 Apr. 1991, and *London Independent*, 15 Apr. 1991.

G. Thomas Tanselle

BOWERS, Nancy Hale Hardin Wertenbaker. See **HALE, Nancy.**

BOWIE, Walter Russell (8 October 1882–23 April 1969), Episcopal minister, was born in Richmond, the son of Walter Russell Bowie, an attorney, and Elisabeth Halsted Branch Bowie. His parents were related to several prominent central Virginia families, and he was a cousin of the novelist James Branch Cabell. After his father died of tuberculosis in 1894, his mother opened a boarding house to support her two children. He and his sister often stayed with their aunt and uncle, Mary-Cooke Branch Munford and Beverley Bland Munford, a leading Richmond attorney. Mary-Cooke Munford was a crusader for better conditions for working women, public education for all children, and women's higher education. Her public work in behalf of reforms that were unconventional in the Lost Cause culture of late-nineteenth-century Richmond undoubtedly influenced Bowie. The Munfords may have paid for his education in private schools.

Bowie attended McGuire's University School in Richmond and the Hill School in Pottstown, Pennsylvania. The headmasters of both schools strongly influenced the course of his life. John Peyton McGuire's reinforced Bowie's devotion to the Episcopal Church, and at the Hill School John Meigs introduced him to a less parochial, more biblical, more personal, and at all times more academically rigorous education. After graduating from the Hill School in 1900, Bowie entered the still wider world of Harvard College. He threw himself into his studies, sports, and other activities with zest. Bowie joined at least six organizations and clubs, including the Signet, which chose students who showed intellectual and literary promise. In 1902 and 1903 he won three prestigious scholarships. Bowie and Franklin Delano Roosevelt coedited the *Harvard Crimson,* Bowie joined Phi Beta Kappa, and when he graduated in 1904 he was both the Class Day Officer and Ivy Orator. He received an A.M. from Harvard in 1905.

Bowie taught for one year at the Hill School before entering the Protestant Episcopal Theological Seminary in Virginia (or Virginia Theological Seminary) in Alexandria, from which he received a B.D. in 1908. He spent part of his final year at Union Theological Seminary in New York City and found it immensely stimulating. In the autumn of 1908 Bowie moved to the Blue Ridge Mountains and became rector of Greenwood Parish and pastor of Emmanuel Episcopal Church in Greenwood, a small community in western Albemarle County. There he became close to a remarkable rural social gospel reformer and missionary-minded English archdeacon, Frederick William Neve. At that time Bowie was also deeply impressed by Lewis Carter "Monk" Harrison, a young minister who used his meager salary to support a ministry among the alcoholics and derelicts who worked in a Northumberland County fish factory. Both men represented an ideal of service and a love of people that drew Bowie to his ministry in the church, although he was simultaneously drawn to the intellectual world of his education in the North.

On 29 September 1909 Bowie married a young teacher, Jean Laverack, the daughter of a prominent businessman from Buffalo, New York. They had two sons and two daughters. Early in 1911, at the age of twenty-eight, Bowie became rector of Saint Paul's Episcopal Church in Richmond, the parish in which he had been baptized and grown up. From there his renown as a preacher and pastor quickly spread. During the next twelve years Bowie became critical of the Old South, speaking out from the pulpit and elsewhere against the Ku Klux Klan and for better treatment of African Americans. He also supported the vote and higher education for women. Bowie's unequivocal opinions often clashed with those of his parishioners and of other influential Episcopal leaders in Virginia. Beginning in 1919 he wrote often for the leading Episcopal evangelical journal, the *Southern Churchman,* and served as its editor from 1920 through the end of May 1924. During World War I Bowie served as a Red Cross chaplain at Base Hospital 45, a field hospital that Virginians operated in France. The suffering he witnessed there led him to become a pacifist.

In March 1923 Bowie was called to Grace Episcopal Church in New York, where he remained until April 1939, when he ended his ministerial career because of strain to his voice. In addition to eloquent and often controversial preaching, he wrote many of his popular books in New York: *Some Open Ways to God* (1924), *The Master: A Life of Jesus Christ* (1929), *When Christ Passes By* (1932), the very popular *Story of the Bible* (1934), *Great Men of the Bible* (1937), and *The Story of Jesus for Young People* (1937). Bowie published more than thirty titles, and although several were written specifically for children or young readers, others contained serious scholarship or derived from his thoughtful sermons. His publications earned him a coveted place on the committee of translators who under the auspices of the International Council of Religious Education produced the renowned Revised Standard Version of the Bible. The subcommittee on the translation of the New Testament consisted of six famous biblical scholars and two popular interpreters who possessed an ear for current idiom, with Bowie as one of the latter.

Following his resignation from Grace Episcopal Church in 1939, Bowie remained in New York as professor of pastoral theology at Union Seminary. He served on the five-member editorial board of the Interpreter's Bible. Bowie wrote the exposition for the first six chapters of Luke as well as a preliminary essay on the parables of Jesus. He was serving as dean of students when he reached mandatory retirement age in 1950.

Bowie moved in the highest circles of the Protestant establishment in both parochial and intellectual endeavors. He was a member of the

Commission on the World Conference on Faith and Order that resulted in the great Lausanne Conference of 1927. Bowie gave the Lyman Beecher Lectures at Yale in 1935 and was Hale Lecturer at Seabury-Western Theological Seminary in 1939. He received honorary degrees from Richmond College in 1914, Syracuse University in 1933, and the Virginia Theological Seminary in 1938.

Bowie was a transitional figure in American Protestantism. Trained in the era of great preachers, he distinguished himself in that respect, but he concluded his career in what increasingly came to be the new elite who taught in the theological schools. A liberal evangelical Episcopalian, he emphasized the humanity of Jesus. Despite the almost somber, atonement-centered Christology of his fine hymn, "Lord Christ, when first thou cam'st to men," Bowie strongly criticized neo-orthodoxy in America for what he perceived as its excessive emphasis on sin. On the other hand, he never absorbed Karl Barth's different theology. For a time in the 1950s students branded Bowie derisively as the liberal that he was. A decade later a newer breed of evangelical and charismatic students, dissatisfied with the remoteness of Jesus in the hands of the biblical critics, sought him out.

Bowie was not immune to personal challenges. He worked hard to lay aside his southern accent. A majority of the Episcopal clergy in Richmond questioned his orthodoxy and demanded his removal as editor of the *Southern Churchman*. In New York he publicly clashed with his bishop, and no doubt his membership in the pacifist Fellowship of Reconciliation caused many of his colleagues to regard him with suspicion. At one point Bowie was even called a subversive. His intense desire to be a great preacher added to the strain under which he worked and perhaps contributed to the damage to his voice. Bowie certainly believed that service was the most important work of a minister. At least once he turned down an opportunity to become a bishop; he declined an appointment late in 1928 as bishop-coadjutor of Pennsylvania.

In 1950 Bowie returned to his alma mater as professor of homiletics at the Virginia Theological Seminary in Alexandria. He finally retired from teaching in June 1955. During the 1950s and 1960s Bowie published several more books, among them *Men of Fire: Torchbearers of the Gospel* (1961) and *Women of Light* (1963), both of which consist of short biographies of biblical characters and modern people whose lives reflected their religious beliefs and who put the social gospel into action. *Women of Light* includes a chapter on Mary-Cooke Branch Munford. Earlier Bowie had written full-length biographies of his aunt and the teacher who most seriously influenced his life, *Sunrise in the South: The Life of Mary-Cooke Branch Munford* (1942) and *The Master of The Hill: A Biography of John Meigs* (1917). Shortly before his death he completed and published his memoirs, *Learning to Live* (1969). Walter Russell Bowie died in an Alexandria hospital on 23 April 1969 following a stroke and was buried in the Virginia Theological Seminary Cemetery.

Walter Russell Bowie, *Learning to Live* (1969); Walter Russell Bowie Collection, Virginia Theological Seminary; information supplied by daughter Jean Laverack Bowie Evans and Jack Goodwin; *Richmond News Leader*, 28 May 1937, 18 Oct. 1939, 23 Jan. 1950; *Virginia Seminary Journal* 1 (July 1955): 2–3 (por.), 7–8; obituaries in *New York Times*, *Richmond Times-Dispatch*, and *Washington Post*, all 24 Apr. 1969, and *Virginia Churchman* 78 (June 1969): 3; memorial in *Virginia Seminary Journal* 21 (June 1969): 3.

JOHN F. WOOLVERTON

BOWLER, Jack. See **DITCHER, Jack**.

BOWLER, John Andrew (1 March 1862– 7 October 1935), educator, was born in Richmond, the son of Emily C. Bowler, a slave. His father's identity is not known. He grew up in the household of Mortimer Bowler, his maternal grandfather, who was a shoemaker. At the age of five Bowler entered a school sponsored by the New England Freedmen's Aid Society. Bright and enthusiastic, he became a favorite of Bessie L. Canedy and the other teachers there, who taught him a speech on Abraham Lincoln that he regularly declaimed when visitors came to the school. When the public schools opened in 1869, Bowler attended the Navy Hill School and the Richmond Colored Normal School, from which he graduated in 1877. Determined to continue his education, he shined shoes, sold news-papers, and shoveled snow (for which, he admitted later, he had prayed) to pay his way at the Richmond Theological Institute (later Virginia Union University) until 1881. With but a penny in his pocket Bowler went to New York City to work as a bellman, but the big city did not appeal to him, and he returned to Richmond.

During the autumn of 1881 J. Andrew Bowler helped to organize the East End School, the first school for blacks in the Church Hill neighborhood of Richmond. On 1 January 1882 he began his life's work as a teacher. With an enrollment of 250 pupils, the four-room structure was Richmond's fourth public elementary school for African American students. Overcrowding soon made additional space imperative, but not until 1889 was a six-room brick building completed. The original building continued in use for classes for the older children. Renovation of nearby frame houses added necessary space for classrooms in 1911, the year that the school was renamed the George Mason School. After construction of additional classrooms in the 1930s the school occupied an entire block.

Bowler began teaching the third grade but soon moved to more advanced classes. Eventually he taught the seventh grade, preparing the students who planned to go on to high school. The school always had white principals, but Bowler's long tenure made him the most prominent member of its all-black faculty. During the 1970s alumni still remembered him with affection and admiration. One recalled that Bowler stood outside the school every morning, his pocket watch in his hand, warning the students to hurry to class. He served the students of the George Mason School for fifty-two years.

On 22 December 1887 Bowler married Eva Flournoy Keene, of Richmond. Of their six children, one son and three daughters reached adulthood. His son J. Andrew Bowler Jr. became a journalist at the *Norfolk Journal and Guide*. Bowler's salary as a teacher was insufficient for his growing family, and every summer until 1900 he worked as a bellman in northern resort hotels to earn additional income.

Bowler began preaching regularly at a hotel in Rhode Island at Sunday evening services for the staff. A devout man, he experienced conversion at the age of nine, was baptized, and joined the First African Baptist Church. Bowler was active in the church. He sang in the choir, served as superintendent of the Sunday school, and became a deacon on 14 July 1889. First African licensed him to preach in 1894, and he received formal ordination as a minister there on 14 February 1901. By that date Bowler had already served as the first pastor of the new Mount Olivet Baptist Church in Church Hill for almost a year. The congregation had increased enough by 1913 to purchase land and construct a brick church building, which was enlarged in 1922. Mount Olivet also acquired the old organ from the white Monumental Episcopal Church, an instrument that Bowler had pumped to earn money in his youth. In 1928 Virginia Union University acknowledged his service to his church with an honorary D.D.

In 1933 Bowler's health began to fail, and his congregation hired an assistant to take over some of his duties. A paralytic stroke forced him to retire from the George Mason School the following year. John Andrew Bowler died in Richmond on 7 October 1935 and was buried in Evergreen Cemetery in that city. The superintendent closed Richmond's black schools on the afternoon of Bowler's funeral.

In April 1948, as lawyers from the National Association for the Advancement of Colored People pushed for equalization of school facilities, the Richmond school board decided to convert the white Springfield Elementary School to a school for blacks in order to reduce serious overcrowding at the George Mason School and two other African American elementary schools in Church Hill. On 26 July 1948 the school board announced that the facility would be renamed the J. Andrew Bowler School. On 7 September 1948 Bowler's children and grandchildren unveiled his portrait at the school's formal opening.

Biography in Caldwell, *History of the American Negro*, 464–467 (por.); feature articles in *Richmond Planet*, 7 July 1928, and *Richmond Afro-American*, 14 Feb. 1981; *Freedmen's Record* 4 (June 1868): 97–98; First African Baptist

Church Minutes, 2:430, 3:68 (LVA microfilm); BVS Marriage Register, Richmond City; History of Church Hill Project, Richmond Oral History Association and Oral History Series, Acc. No. 83-JAN-03, Box 16, VCU; *Richmond News Leader*, 11 Jan. 1932; *Richmond Afro-American*, 10, 17 Dec. 1938, 4, 18 Sept. 1948; *Richmond Times-Dispatch*, 27 July 1948; *Inventory of the Church Archives of Virginia: Negro Baptist Churches in Richmond* (1940), 42; obituary in *Richmond News Leader*, 9 Oct. 1935; obituary and editorial tribute in *Richmond Planet*, 12 Oct. 1935 (por.).

JOHN T. KNEEBONE

BOWLER, Thomas (d. by 2 July 1679), member of the Council, was born probably in England during the 1620s, but nothing is definitely known about his background or early life. He had become a prominent and well-connected London merchant by the 1650s, and he made several trips to Virginia before settling about 1662 on a large tract of land on the south side of the Rappahannock River at what became Bowlers Wharf in Essex County. Bowler dealt in tobacco, indentured servants, and slaves, and his Virginia customers and associates included many of the leading men of the colony. With his first wife, whose name is not known, he had a daughter. Between 4 April 1671 and 5 October 1672 he married Tabitha Underwood, and they had one son and one daughter.

On 29 September 1664 Bowler became a justice of the peace for Rappahannock County and was placed on the quorum, indicating that he was one of the more respectable or wealthy members. Because of the loss of county court order books his length of service is unknown. Bowler continued to deal in tobacco. The scant information about his life in Virginia does not reveal what caused Hubert Farrell in November 1673 to insult Bowler and his wife in "Soe High and Soe unjust" a manner that the General Court in 1674 fined Farrell 20,000 pounds of tobacco and required him to ask Bowler's forgiveness "publiquely in Court." The size of the fine attests to Bowler's high standing.

On 9 October 1675 Governor Sir William Berkeley appointed Thomas Bowler, Ralph Wormeley, and Rowland Place to the governor's Council, and Bowler and Place took the oath of office that afternoon. Bowler incurred Berkeley's wrath during Bacon's Rebellion, but no surviving evidence gives the details. Bowler's name is not on either of the August 1676 declarations issued by Bacon's supporters, but on 10 February 1677 Berkeley excluded Bowler and two other councillors from his pardon proclamation. Later that year royal commissioners reporting on the activities of Council members during the rebellion did not mention Bowler at all. His last recorded attendance at a Council meeting was on 21 March 1676, but he is not known to have resigned or been removed.

Thomas Bowler wrote his will on 17 March 1679 and died between then and the probation of his will in the Rappahannock County Court on 2 July 1679.

Minnie G. Cook, "Edloe-Underwood-Bowler," *WMQ*, 2d ser., 16 (1936): 469–473; land acquisitions, headrights, county court service, and numerous business transactions documented in Patent Book, vols. 4–6, RG 4, LVA, and records of Lancaster, old Rappahannock, and York Cos.; *Minutes of Council and General Court*, 368 (quotations), 426, 450; Berkeley's pardon in PRO CO 1/39, fols. 64–65; old Rappahannock Co. Will Book, 2:133–137.

DAPHNE GENTRY

BOWLES, Drury Wood Knight (29 January 1802–11 August 1885), member of the Convention of 1850–1851, was born in Fluvanna County, the son of Knight Bowles and Patty Wood Bowles. On 14 February 1821 he married Mary Ann Richardson. They had at least four sons and at least four daughters. Bowles managed his farm, which consisted of about a thousand acres at Bowlesville near the Goochland County line, and invested in local enterprises including a gold mine, part of which he owned from 1834 until 1838. The mine's owners erected one of America's first powered stamping-mills for refining gold-bearing ore.

Bowles became a lieutenant in the Fluvanna County militia on 26 February 1821 and a colonel by the end of September 1829. He took his oath as a member of the Fluvanna County Court on 25 December 1826 and served for more than forty years. After the office of justice of the peace became elective in 1852 Bowles won four consecutive four-year terms and served as presiding justice of Fluvanna County during the Civil War, by which time he was usually referred to as Judge Bowles.

In August 1850 Bowles, a Democrat, was elected one of three delegates to represent the counties of Fluvanna, Goochland, and Louisa in a state constitutional convention that met from 14 October 1850 to 1 August 1851. He served on the Committee on Education and Public Instruction but seldom if ever spoke on the convention floor. Although reportedly in favor of substantial revisions to Virginia's constitution, Bowles often sided with eastern delegates who opposed many of the alterations advocated by delegates from the western portions of Virginia. On 16 May 1851 he voted against a key compromise on the question of apportionment that ultimately shifted the balance of power in the General Assembly away from the eastern counties, and on 31 July 1851 he cast his vote against the final version of the constitution that was submitted to the voters and ratified later that year.

Bowles represented Fluvanna County in the House of Delegates for the 1857–1858 session, serving on the Committees on Agriculture and Manufactures and on Trade and the Mechanic Arts. He was also a delegate representing Fluvanna and Goochland Counties in the first General Assembly after the Civil War, which sat in three sessions between December 1865 and April 1867. During the first session he was chairman of the Committee on Agriculture and Manufactures, and during the second and third he chaired the Committee on Agriculture and Mining. Probably as a result of financial reverses occasioned by the Civil War, Bowles placed all of his property in trust on 9 December 1868 to satisfy the demands of his creditors and avoid bankruptcy. He served on the Fluvanna County Court from April 1875 until the January 1882 term. Drury Wood Knight Bowles died at the home of his son John S. Bowles on 11 August 1885 and was buried in the family cemetery at Bowlesville. His body and gravestone were later moved to the graveyard of Lyles Baptist Church in Fluvanna County, which he had joined late in life.

French Biographies; birth and death dates on gravestone, transcribed in Point of Fork Chapter, Daughters of the American Revolution, *Tombstone Inscriptions from Church Cemeteries of Fluvanna County, Virginia* (1959), 104; family history in Tyler, *Encyclopedia*, 4:537–538, and in father's will, Fluvanna Co. Will Book, 2:317–320; Fluvanna Co. Marriage Certificates; *Journal of 1850–1851 Convention*, 59, 419, and Appendix, 22; business affairs documented in Fluvanna Co. Deed Book and John D. Horn, "The Golden Paradox of Fluvanna," *Bulletin of the Fluvanna County Historical Society* 20 (1975): 17–25; 1868 deed of trust in Fluvanna Co. Deed Book, 20:200–203; church membership in *Richmond Dispatch*, 22 Feb. 1881; por. in Fluvanna Co. courthouse, Palmyra; death of "Old Age" recorded in Fluvanna Co. Death Register; obituary in *Richmond Dispatch*, 12 Aug. 1885.

JANICE L. ABERCROMBIE

BOWLES, George Ashby (11 May 1883–1 June 1956), commissioner of insurance, was born near Tabscott in western Goochland County, the son of Richard Curd Bowles, a physician, and Sallie Catherine Payne Bowles. He grew up at and eventually acquired the Oaks, the family home on the border between Goochland and Fluvanna Counties. Bowles graduated from high school in Louisa County in 1899 and went to work in 1902 as a telegraph operator with the Richmond, Fredericksburg, and Potomac Railroad. In 1910 he enrolled in the Medical College of Virginia, but a year later he contracted tuberculosis and left school. Bowles recovered fully and from 1911 to 1930 ran a lumber business in Goochland County. On 4 April 1914 in Washington, D.C., he married Georgia Pollard Kennon. Their two sons included George Ashby Bowles (1925–1986), who had a long career in Virginia broadcast journalism.

In 1915 Bowles was elected to the House of Delegates from Goochland and Fluvanna Counties. He was reelected seven times and became influential in the General Assembly's Democratic Party majority. From 1920 through 1923 he chaired the Committee on Labor and the Poor, and from 1924 through 1928 he was chairman of the influential Committee on Roads and Internal Navigation and ranking member of the powerful Committee on Appropriations. Bowles was reelected in November 1929 but gave up the lumber business and politics a month later to become deputy to the state commissioner of banking and insurance.

Bowles may have been influenced in this change of career by his friend William Meade Fletcher, one of the three members of the State

Corporation Commission, for whom the commissioner of banking and insurance worked. Myon Edison Bristow, the incumbent commissioner, headed the commission's banking division, while Bowles was in charge of its insurance division until 1938, when the units were separated. Thereafter Bowles was the sole commissioner of insurance until his death. During his twenty-five-year tenure the staff of the commissioner of insurance grew from about twenty to fifty. Many insurance examiners and fire inspectors were added, and the budget rose from about $56,000 in 1932 to more than $367,500 in 1956.

On 23 June 1937 Bowles was elected president of the National Association of Insurance Commissioners at its annual convention in Philadelphia. He soon proposed that the national mortality schedules life insurance companies used to calculate premium and benefit rates be revised and brought up to date. From 1949 until his death he served as secretary-treasurer of the association. George Ashby Bowles died of heart disease in a Richmond hospital on 1 June 1956 and was buried in the family cemetery at the Oaks.

William Bien, "Virginia's Own George A. Bowles: Nationally Recognized Insurance Commissioner," *Virginia and the Virginia Record* 76 (Apr. 1954): 12 (por.), 77; birth date in *Who's Who in Government* 2 (1932/1933): 239; variant birth date of 30 May 1883 in Fluvanna Co. Birth Register; marriage in *Washington Post*, 5 Apr. 1914; family history information furnished by Richard C. Bowles; *Richmond Times-Dispatch*, 5 Dec. 1929; speech of 2 Dec. 1937 to annual convention of Association of Life Insurance Presidents published as *Insurance Supervision—Its Responsibilities and Its Responses* (1937); obituaries in *Richmond News Leader* (por.) and *Richmond Times-Dispatch*, both 2 June 1956.

RICHARD T. COUTURE

BOWLES, George Ashby (9 March 1925–9 March 1986), journalist, was born at the Oaks, the Bowles family home near Tabscott on the Fluvanna-Goochland County border, the son of George Ashby Bowles (1883–1956) and Georgia Pollard Kennon Bowles. He grew up in Goochland County and in Richmond, where his father served as Virginia's commissioner of insurance from 1930 to 1956. Bowles was educated in the

Fluvanna County public schools and at Saint Christopher's School in Richmond.

On 1 July 1943 Bowles was inducted into the United States Army and served as a supply clerk and military policeman until 14 February 1946. He returned to Richmond, where he attended the Richmond Professional Institute (later Virginia Commonwealth University) and Smithdeal-Massey College of Law. Bowles also served as a master sergeant in the Virginia National Guard, received a commission in the United States Air Force in January 1951, and was on active duty for twenty years, retiring in March 1971 with the rank of lieutenant colonel. He saw combat in Korea, served on the staff of the Office of Special Investigations, and from 1961 to 1964 commanded one of the first guided-missile units stationed in Germany. During World War II Bowles married Evelyn Ogelvie. They had one daughter before divorcing early in 1951. Later that year he married Nancy Thumma, with whom he had four sons.

Bowles retired to his birthplace in the spring of 1971 and almost immediately announced his candidacy for the House of Delegates. After losing a three-way race in the Democratic Party primary, he developed an interest in journalism and began writing political commentary for the *Goochland Gazette* and then for the *Charlottesville Daily Progress*. The column was soon syndicated to about two dozen other Virginia newspapers. From May 1973 through December 1976 Bowles edited the editorial page for the *Daily Progress*, and at the same time he began covering Virginia politics for Charlottesville radio station WINA. By 1979 his radio broadcasts, called *Commonwealth Conversations*, were heard on more than fifty Virginia stations. His distinctive voice became familiar to radio listeners, and his ruddy face was easily recognized around the State Capitol in Richmond. Bowles became the best known and one of the most respected and insightful political commentators in Virginia. He was a founder and president of the Virginia Capitol Correspondents Association in Richmond.

Bowles also wrote and broadcast short features on Virginia personalities and historical subjects, some of which appeared in a short book, *Pages from the Virginia Story* (1979). In 1987 the Virginia News Network established a scholarship in his name, and in 1989 the Virginia Association of Broadcasters created the George A. Bowles Jr. Award for Distinguished Performance in Broadcast News. He suffered from high blood pressure during his later years and was frequently hospitalized with heart problems. George Ashby Bowles died of heart failure at the Oaks on 9 March 1986, his birthday, and was buried on the estate in the family cemetery.

Family history information furnished by widow Nancy T. Bowles; feature articles in *Goochland Gazette*, 3, 24 Mar. 1971; obituaries in *Charlottesville Daily Progress*, 10 Mar. 1986 (por.), *Richmond News Leader*, 10 Mar. 1986, and *Washington Post*, 12 Mar. 1986.

RICHARD T. COUTURE

BOWLES, William Anderson (26 February 1850–10 March 1919), educator of the deaf and blind, was born in Louisa County, the son of Augustus Knight Bowles, a farmer, and Elizabeth Blaydes Anderson Bowles. He was educated in local private schools and then began a career as a teacher. Bowles attended the University of Virginia for one term in 1873, but contrary to later published accounts, he did not graduate. On 13 May 1884 he married Martha A. Hope Jones, a widowed Louisa County teacher. They had one son and two daughters.

For five years beginning about 1879, Bowles conducted a Peabody school in New Hope, Augusta County. He then became principal of the public high school in Staunton and served as superintendent of the city's schools in 1886. At the end of 1886 Bowles moved to Richmond as principal of the Leigh School, and two years later he was appointed principal of Richmond High School. Bowles left the education profession in 1890 and managed the Jefferson Park Hotel in Charlottesville and the Brandon Hotel in Basic City (later part of Waynesboro) until 1896.

On 6 June 1896 the new board of visitors of the recently reorganized Virginia Institution for the Education of the Deaf and Dumb and of the Blind in Staunton elected Bowles superintendent. He took office on 1 July and held the post for the remainder of his life, almost twenty-three years. Bowles's experience as an educator and manager appealed to the board members, who were charged with transforming the institution into a free public school for children whose hearing or eyesight was too poor for them to attend the city or county schools. The objective was to prepare the students for life outside the institution. Bowles reintroduced classes to teach the deaf to speak, which had been neglected under the preceding administration, and in his first annual report he began a brief and successful campaign to have the General Assembly change the name to the Virginia School for the Deaf and the Blind, because he saw its mission as one of education, not institutionalization.

Bowles was not an innovator in education for the deaf or the blind, but he was a competent and sympathetic administrator and by all accounts a kindly superintendent. He developed the school's educational program in its training schools in crafts and trades, and he placed a high value on his pupils' moral education. In 1908 Bowles prepared *Memory Gems: A Compilation of Five Hundred Short and Easy Quotations from Three Hundred Authors* for the deaf students to publish in the school's print shop. He also had this small book of hortatory maxims printed for the blind in New York Point, a variant of Braille. During Bowles's tenure the school slowly grew from an annual enrollment of about 170 to more than 250. At the end of his term the school had seventy-five employees and an annual budget of more than $80,000. In June 1914 Bowles and the Virginia School hosted the annual conference of the American Instructors of the Deaf. He also served on the State Board of Education from 1902 to 1905. William Anderson Bowles became ill and relinquished the day-to-day running of the school at the end of 1918, and he died in Staunton on 10 March 1919. He was buried in Thornrose Cemetery in Staunton.

Biographies in *Virginia School Journal* 11 (1902): 121, Tyler, *Men of Mark*, 1:172–173, and R. Aumon Bass, *History of the Education of the Deaf in Virginia* (1949), 94–98; Louisa Co. Marriage Register; election as superintendent reported in the institution's *Goodson Gazette*, 13 June, 15 July 1896; Bowles outlined his philosophy for the school in his first annual report, 30 Sept. 1897, printed in pamphlet form; por. at Virginia School for the Deaf and Blind,

Staunton; BVS Death Certificate, Staunton; obituaries in *Staunton Daily News*, 11 Mar. 1919, and *Virginia Guide* (formerly *Goodson Gazette*), 15 Mar. 1919 (por.).

BRENT TARTER

BOWLING, Richard Hausber (4 September 1864–26 July 1913), Baptist minister, was the son of Richard Bowling and Venus Anne Russell Bowling. He was born in a rough cabin that his parents owned near Hampton in Elizabeth City County. Bowling's father was a farmer and the owner of a small store. Following a childhood spent helping his father on the farm, in the store, and fishing, he entered Hampton Normal and Agricultural Institute in 1876 and came under the influence of its founder, Samuel Chapman Armstrong. In December 1879 Bowling ran away from Hampton and worked his way on a boat to Boston, where he briefly served in the army. After a year in Boston he went West for a year and a half. Bowling then spent a year in New York working as a butler and attending a private theological school. During the next three years he worked as a farmhand in Connecticut in the winter and as a waiter at a resort in the summer. Whether he was working or on the move Bowling kept his books with him and studied when he had an opportunity.

Feeling a call to the ministry, Bowling joined Mount Olivet Baptist Church in New York and began to establish a reputation as a promising young preacher. In 1885 he returned to Virginia when he was called to the pulpit of a small Baptist church in Waynesboro. He held brief pastorates there, in Harrisonburg, and in Steelton, Pennsylvania, where he erected a new church building. In December 1889, while Bowling was visiting his family in Hampton, he preached a trial sermon at Norfolk's historic First Baptist Church, which was seeking a new pastor. The sermon was so well received that on 1 January 1890 the congregation unanimously offered him the position. On 8 October 1890 Bowling married Eliza Howard Haynes, a Staunton native and graduate of Fisk University. They had three sons and four daughters, three of whom died in infancy. Eliza Bowling died in February 1905. On 31 January 1907 Bowling married Grace P. Melton, of Winton, North Carolina. They had two sons and one daughter.

During his Norfolk pastorate Bowling conducted a number of remarkable revivals and added many members to his church, which became one of the largest African American congregations in Virginia. He encouraged his parishioners to become educated, to invest in property, and to live soberly. On at least two occasions the *Richmond Planet* printed Bowling's sermons, considerably enlarging the reach of his ministry and contributing to his growing reputation as one of the most influential and successful African American clergymen in Virginia. From 1899 until his death he was president of the Virginia Baptist State Convention, which under his leadership paid for and successfully operated the Virginia Theological Seminary and College in Lynchburg. Bowling was also active in many civic and philanthropic efforts. He sat on the boards of the seminary and of other educational, philanthropic, and missionary organizations; he served as president of Norfolk's African American branch of the Young Men's Christian Association; and he helped organize a black insurance company. Bowling was chaplain to the 2d Regiment Virginia Infantry, an African American militia regiment. He cultivated his mind by reading and by writing poetry, which probably contributed to the widely remarked musical quality of his sermons.

In 1904 Bowling's congregation, which then numbered approximately 2,000, began a large new stone church on Bute Street. It cost more than $72,000, and building it during the next two years and paying for it over the next nine years was perhaps the largest achievement of his life. A visitor described the church as "charmingly built," with a sanctuary "contrived in graceful horseshoe style, with graduated, sloping gallery, richly-stained windows, and a vast array of red-cushioned seats." Richard Hausber Bowling died in Norfolk on 26 July 1913 following an illness of several months and was buried in Calvary Cemetery in that city. The following year his eldest son, Richard Hausber Bowling (1891–1961), succeeded him as pastor of First Baptist Church.

Richmond Planet, 2 July 1898; Clement Richardson, ed., *National Cyclopedia of the Colored Race* (1919), 429 (por.); Margaret L. Gordon, ed., *A Documented History of the First*

Baptist Church, Bute Street, Norfolk, Virginia, 1800–1988
(1988), 19–21, 24–25, 195 (por.); Annie Bowling Givens,
"Norfolk's Favorite Son: A Biography of the Reverend
Richard H. Bowling, Jr." (master's thesis, Hampton Insti-
tute, 1963), 8–20; first marriage documented in BVS Mar-
riage Register, Staunton; U.S. Bureau of the Census, *Census
of Religious Bodies, 1916* (1916), 1:458–459; Stephen
Graham, *The Soul of John Brown* (1920), 35–48 (quotations
on 37); Ernest N. Hall, "A Negro Institutional Church,"
Southern Workman 50 (1921): 113–118; Earl Lewis, *In Their
Own Interests: Race, Class, and Power in Twentieth-Century
Norfolk, Virginia* (1991), 70–71; Ralph E. Luker, *The Social
Gospel in Black and White: American Racial Reform,
1885–1912* (1991), 164, 177; sermons printed in *Richmond
Planet*, 26 Dec. 1896, 21 Aug. 1897; obituary in *Norfolk
Virginian-Pilot*, 27 July 1913; obituary and account of
funeral in *Richmond Planet*, 9 Aug. 1913.

RALPH E. LUKER

BOWLING, Richard Hausber (24 October
1891–28 December 1961), Baptist minister, was
born in Norfolk, the son of Richard Hausber
Bowling (1864–1913) and his first wife, Eliza
Howard Haynes Bowling. He attended Norfolk's
public schools and completed high school at Virginia Theological Seminary and College in
Lynchburg. In 1910 Bowling entered Bucknell
University as the only African American in his
class. After winning a junior oratorical contest
and a prize for Greek studies, he graduated
summa cum laude in 1913 and received a gold
watch for the best commencement oration. On
30 June 1915 Bowling married Rebecca Lucinda
Pride in Lynchburg. They had three daughters.

Bowling succeeded his father as pastor of
Norfolk's First Baptist Church on 1 July 1914,
even though some members believed that he
was too young and inexperienced for so large a
church. During summers he studied at New
York's Union Theological Seminary, and he
received an honorary D.D. from Howard University in 1936. Bowling became widely known
for his ministry at First Baptist. Building on the
work that the church had done during his
father's pastorate, he established an institutional program of social services to Norfolk's
African American community in 1919. The
church soon had a paid staff of seven, a drum
and bugle corps, an employment agency, a home
for elderly people and unwed mothers, an information service, a library, a milk dispensary, a
mothers' clinic, a nursery, a kindergarten, a playground, a retirement program for the church's

full-time employees, a thrift club, and gospel
teams for evangelism at the city jail and in
neglected parts of the city. Even during the financially difficult years of the Great Depression, the
church maintained its services to the community.

Bowling was very active in civic affairs and
education. A founder of Norfolk's Community
Hospital, he served on its board of trustees from
1932 to 1950, part of that time as chairman. In
honor of his several years on the advisory committee of Norfolk's Redevelopment and Housing
Authority, the Bowling Park Housing Development was named for him. Bowling also worked
with the Boy and the Girl Scouts of America,
Child and Family Services, City Social Service
Bureau, Colored United Charities, Community
Chest, March of Dimes, Municipal Auditorium
Commission, Municipal Beach for Colored People, Norfolk Committee on Negro Affairs, Red
Cross, United Service Organizations, Welfare
Board, Young Men's Christian Association, and
other community agencies. Deeply devoted to
the Virginia Theological Seminary and College,
he served on its board of trustees for many
years, and in recognition of his support for public and collegiate education in Norfolk the
Bowling Park Elementary School was named
for him. Bowling also joined a number of fraternal and service organizations.

Widely known as a speaker and leader
among Baptists and in ecumenical affairs, Bowling was a member of Norfolk's Baptist and Interdenominational Ministers Alliances and vice
president of the Virginia Council of Churches.
In November 1925, long before the birth of the
modern civil rights movement, he protested that
Norfolk's residential segregation ordinance
"hems the black brother in and keeps his death
and sick rate high, his economic status low, his
living conditions crowded and a disgrace to any
modern city." Bowling continued to speak out
with a regular column, "The Guide Post," that
appeared more than 550 times in the *Norfolk
Journal and Guide* between January 1926 and
December 1937. In October 1950 he broke a
longstanding precedent by becoming the first
African American minister to lead the opening
prayer at a session of Norfolk's city council.

For reasons of health Bowling retired from the active ministry and became pastor emeritus in 1953. After several years of illness, Richard Hausber Bowling died in Norfolk on 28 December 1961 and was buried in Calvary Cemetery in that city.

Annie Bowling Givens, "Norfolk's Favorite Son: A Biography of the Reverend Richard H. Bowling, Jr." (master's thesis, Hampton Institute, 1963), cites family Bible records for date of birth; Norfolk City Birth Register gives variant birth date of 10 Oct. 1891; BVS Marriage Register, Lynchburg; Margaret L. Gordon, ed., *A Documented History of the First Baptist Church, Bute Street, Norfolk, Virginia, 1800–1988* (1988), 20–26, 131–136, 145–149, 197 (por.); Stephen Graham, *The Soul of John Brown* (1920), 35–48; Ernest N. Hall, "A Negro Institutional Church," *Southern Workman* 50 (1921): 113–118; Richard H. Bowling, "Keeping an Old Church Alive," *Southern Workman* 61 (1932): 200–208; *Norfolk Journal and Guide*, 3 July 1915, 21 Nov. 1925 (quotation), home ed. 1 July 1950, home ed. 26 Feb. 1955; *Richmond Afro-American*, 14 Oct. 1950; obituaries in *Norfolk Ledger-Dispatch* and *Norfolk Virginian-Pilot*, both 29 Dec. 1961; obituary and account of funeral in *Norfolk Journal and Guide*, 6 Jan. 1962.

RALPH E. LUKER

BOWMAN, Abraham (16 October 1749– 9 November 1837), Continental army officer, was born near Cedar Creek in Frederick County, the son of George Bowman and Mary Hite Bowman. His brother John Bowman was a frontier militia officer, and another brother Joseph Bowman was an officer in George Rogers Clark's Illinois Regiment. Nothing is definitely known of Abraham Bowman's education, but he probably worked for a local surveyor and may have intended to follow that profession. When Bowman was about seventeen he assisted his neighbors in repelling a band of violent Indians, and when Dunmore County was formed out of Frederick in the spring of 1772, he was appointed one of the new county's first justices of the peace.

On 10 January 1775 Bowman was a founder of the Dunmore County Committee, organized to enforce the nonimportation association that the First Continental Congress had adopted. Shortly thereafter he traveled to Kentucky, where on 5 June 1775 agents of the Transylvania Company appointed him a conservator of the peace at the Boiling Springs community. Bowman returned to Dunmore County in the autumn,

and when John Peter Gabriel Muhlenberg issued his call for volunteers from the lower Shenandoah Valley to form a regiment to fight for Virginia, Bowman was one of the first to respond. On 12 January 1776 the Convention of 1775–1776 appointed Muhlenberg colonel and Bowman lieutenant colonel of the 8th Regiment Virginia Infantry, also called the German Regiment because many of its first soldiers were of German birth or ancestry. Muhlenberg and Bowman took their qualifying oaths on 3 April 1776 and received commissions dated 1 March.

The German Regiment was one of the most famous Virginia regiments in the Revolutionary War. General Charles Lee and other commanders complained of its soldiers' unmilitary deportment during service in Tidewater Virginia in the spring of 1776 and en route to South Carolina early in the summer, but the regiment so distinguished itself during the defense of Charleston on 28 June that Lee singled it out for high praise. Congress voted in principle to take the regiment into the Continental army on 25 March 1776, subsequently ruled that the unit would not be accepted until it was fully manned, and on 13 August 1776 reversed itself and admitted it into the Continental establishment dating from 25 May.

After Muhlenberg's appointment as brigadier general, Bowman was promoted to colonel on 22 March 1777 with his commission to date from 30 January. He led the German Regiment in the Battles of Brandywine and Germantown in the autumn of 1777 and continued to serve until after the Battle of Monmouth in June 1778. Bowman returned to Virginia to recruit more soldiers, but, perhaps because recruitment funds had been exhausted, he did not return to the army.

Bowman moved to Kentucky in 1779 and settled near Lexington in what became Fayette County a year later. During the summer of 1782 he married Sarah Henry Bryan, the widow of John Bowman's stepson. She had one son by her first husband, and the Bowmans had four sons and three daughters. Bowman had begun investing in land during the 1770s, on his own and in partnership with his brothers John Bowman and Joseph Bowman, and he amassed several thousand acres and prospered as a planter. Bowman became a Fayette County justice of the peace on 19 July 1786 and in 1792 served as an elector for the new Senate of Kentucky. He lived to be old and respected, and as one of the most prominent Revolutionary War veterans in central Kentucky he hosted the marquis de Lafayette when the French general visited Lexington in May 1825. Abraham Bowman died at his home in Fayette County, Kentucky, on 9 November 1837.

John W. Wayland, *The Bowmans: A Pioneering Family in Virginia, Kentucky, and the Northwest Territory* (1943), esp. 137 (Bowman's 15 May 1825 address welcoming Lafayette), 162–164 (will), and abstracts of military, land, and family Bible records; service data and marriage date in Revolutionary War Pension and Bounty-Land Warrant Application Files, RG 15, NARA; *Revolutionary Virginia*, 1:122–123, 2:228–229, 5:391, 6:318, 7:757–758; numerous references in Muhlenberg's orderly book, printed in *Pennsylvania Magazine of History and Biography* 33–35 (1909–1911); obituary in *Lexington Kentucky Gazette*, 23 Nov. 1837.

PAUL DAVID NELSON

BOWMAN, Abram Smith (3 March 1868–27 June 1952), entrepreneur, was born at Bellevue in Mercer County, Kentucky, the son of Dudley Mitchum Bowman and Virginia Smith Bowman. His mother was a native of Luray, and his father also descended from Virginians. After graduating from Transylvania University in 1888, Bowman became a salesman for a Kansas City wholesale dry goods company that he helped establish as a major supplier for residents of the Indian Territory (Oklahoma) after it was opened for settlement in 1889. An avid horseman, he returned to Kentucky in 1895 to join his aunt Nannie Smith in the breeding and training of trotting horses and raised the record-setting Red Wilkes.

A. Smith Bowman entered the real estate business in Lexington, Kentucky, in 1900, and he married Katherine Lyttleton DeLong of that city on 20 June 1901. They had two sons, one daughter, and stillborn twins. In 1905 Bowman acquired more than 27,000 acres of land in Alberta, Canada, where he raised cattle and other crops and organized a champion polo team. Following the death of his daughter from pneumonia Bowman moved his family in 1913 to Afton Villa, a plantation in Louisiana. Using his business and real estate experience he formed a transportation company, the New Orleans–Kenner Interurban Line, and he built and operated a distillery that manufactured alcohol for the French government during World War I. In 1917, ever restless after each successful business venture, Bowman sold his Louisiana holdings and moved to Indianapolis, where in 1920 he founded a bus company and established the locality's first citywide coordinated bus system. In 1927 he sold the venture for approximately $500,000.

In response to a newspaper advertisement, Bowman purchased the 3,800-acre Sunset Hills Farm in Fairfax County in 1927 and resided there for the remainder of his life. He raised beef and dairy cattle, cultivated grain, and made the farm virtually self-sustaining. Evidently delighted to reside where members of the Fairfax and Washington families had held sway, Bowman quickly made his mark in local society by hosting balls, entertainments, and receptions at Sunset Hills. He brought six Walker-type hounds from Kentucky and in 1928 established the Fairfax Hunt, of which he served as master of foxhounds twice during the 1920s and 1930s. A thirty-five-room hotel built on the Sunset Hills property in the 1890s was its headquarters.

In 1935, after the repeal of Prohibition, Bowman established the A. Smith Bowman Distillery to produce bourbon, which he began selling at the end of the decade under the brand names Virginia Gentleman and Fairfax County. The operation was housed entirely on Sunset Hills Farm, with a soapstone mill converted into a distillery, an old icehouse as the office, and a brick building that formerly housed a German Reformed church as the warehouse. Bowman initially grew all of the needful barley, corn, and rye, fed the mash to his cattle, and manufactured his barrels from white oak cut from his own land. Eventually he had to purchase additional grain. During World War II the distillery produced alcohol that the United States government used in the manufacture of synthetic rubber and explosives.

In 1947, in partnership with both of his sons, Bowman purchased more than 3,000 additional acres, making Sunset Hills one of the largest farms in Northern Virginia. His distillery, which produced about 2,500 gallons of bourbon whiskey per day, was then and remained for years the only legal distillery in Virginia. After the formation of the partnership his eyesight began to fail. Abram Smith Bowman died at Sunset Hills Farm on 27 June 1952. He was buried in Lexington, Kentucky. A. Smith Bowman Distillery continued to operate in Fairfax County until it moved to Fredericksburg in 1988.

Biographies in *NCAB*, 42:348–349 (por.), and John W. Wayland, *The Bowmans: A Pioneering Family in Virginia, Kentucky, and the Northwest Territory* (1943), 147–155; information provided by Helen Bowman, Katherine Bowman Burton, and Frances Keightley; A. Smith Bowman Jr., "A History of Sunset Hills Farm," in Historical Society of Fairfax County *Yearbook* 6 (1958/1959): 36–43; Fairfax Co. Master Inventory of Historic Sites, no. 172, and vertical files on Bowman's house, both Fairfax Co. Public Library; Nan Netherton et al., eds., *Fairfax County, Virginia: A History* (1978), 554, 600, 614; Netherton, *Reston, a New Town in the Old Dominion: A Pictorial History* (1989), 39–45; J. S. Wamsley, "The Gentlemen of Sunset Hills," *Commonwealth* 30 (Dec. 1963): 38–43; *The History of the Fairfax Hunt, 1929–1972* [ca. 1972]; obituaries in *Washington Post*, 29 June 1952, *McLean Providence Journal*, 3 July 1952, and *Fairfax Herald*, 4 July 1952.

CONSTANCE K. RING

BOWMAN, Alpheus Michael (11 January 1847–2 August 1913), agricultural businessman and member of the House of Delegates, was born on his father's farm in Rockingham County, the son of George M. Bowman and Sarah Zeigler Bowman. He attended local schools until 1863, when he joined the Confederate army. During his service as a private in Company H of the 12th Regiment Virginia Cavalry, Bowman's unit saw action at the Battles of Spotsylvania Court House and Yellow Tavern and participated in cavalry engagements around Brandy Station, Petersburg, and Richmond. He was captured on 1 March 1865 at Mount Crawford and imprisoned at Fort Delaware until 28 May.

After his release Bowman attended New Market Academy for two years and worked on the family farm. On 11 February 1869 he married Marietta "Mollie" V. Killian. They had five sons and three daughters. Bowman managed a farm in Augusta County until 1880. He then moved to Washington County and became a prosperous and well-known cattleman during ten years of residence there. Bowman was also active in Democratic Party politics and attended almost every state convention between 1873 and his death. He chaired the Ninth District committee for six years, belonged to the state central committee for twelve, and attended the party's national convention in 1888. Also Bowman served on the boards of the Southwestern Lunatic Asylum in Marion and the Central State Hospital in Petersburg.

Bowman moved to Salem in 1890. At Bowmont Farm he raised blooded cattle, swine, and several breeds of horses. With one of the largest herds in Virginia, he became one of the state's most successful cattlemen and exported breeding stock to Europe and South America. Bowman served for eleven years as vice president of the American Berkshire Association, was a founding officer of the state chapter of the American Saddlebred Horse Association, belonged to the Percheron Horse Association of America and the American Jersey Cattle Club, and helped found and sat on the board of the American Shorthorn Breeders' Association. As founding president of the Diamond Orchard Company, the largest orchard in the Roanoke Valley, he also raised apples and peaches. Bowman benefited from and helped direct the economic development of the Roanoke region. He was the founding president in 1890 of the Salem Development Company, a founder and later president of the Bank of Salem, founding president of the Salem Dairy Company, and an investor and officer in several other corporations.

In 1901 Bowman was elected to the House of Delegates as one of two representatives from the district composed of Roanoke City and Craig and Roanoke Counties. He campaigned unsuccessfully for the Democratic Party nomination for Congress following the death in 1902 of Peter J. Otey. Bowman won reelection to the House of Delegates from his original district in 1903 and 1905, and after Roanoke County was made a separate one-member district in 1907 he was returned that year and in 1909 and 1911. As a well-known party leader and a prominent and successful cattleman and businessman, he received two choice committee assignments during his first term, to the Committees on Finance and on Agriculture (later Agriculture and Mining). From his second term until his death Bowman was ranking member of the latter, and in 1906 he became chairman of the finance committee. He was credited with arranging the financing for the state's participation in the 1904 Louisiana Purchase Exposition in Saint Louis, he helped pass the appropriations for the 1907 Jamestown Ter-Centennial Exposition, and he served on the Virginia commissions for both fairs.

Bowman was an active Lutheran layman and sat on the board of the Lutheran Orphan Home of the South in Salem. He became a member of the board of Roanoke College in 1886 and was board president from 1907 to 1913. During the last two years of his life, Bowman also served as president of the board of Roanoke Woman's College at Salem and a member of the board of Virginia Agricultural and Mechanical College and Polytechnic Institute. Because of declining health he planned to retire from the House of Delegates at the end of his sixth term. Before the term ended Alpheus Michael Bowman died from complications of Bright's disease and heart disease at his home in Salem on 2 August 1913 and was buried in East Hill Cemetery in that town.

Tyler, *Men of Mark,* 1:152–155 (por.); George S. Jack and Edward B. Jacobs, *History of Roanoke County . . .* (1912), 53–54; Compiled Service Records; Dennis E. Frye, *12th Virginia Cavalry* (1988), 110; Augusta Co. Marriage Register; family history information verified by Geline Bowman Williams and Charles K. Woltz; civic and business activity in Norwood C. Middleton, *Salem: A Virginia Chronicle* (1986); BVS Death Certificate, Roanoke Co.; obituary and editorial tribute in *Roanoke Times,* 3, 5 Aug. 1913.

NORWOOD C. MIDDLETON

BOWMAN, Jean Eleanor (27 September 1917–16 August 1994), painter, was born in Mount Vernon, New York, the daughter of Lewis Bowman, a noted architect, and Eleanor Holwick Bowman. Her parents encouraged her childhood abilities in both art and horseback riding. At age nine Bowman learned about equine art from an English artist whom her family had engaged to paint their horses and dogs, and she decided to make it her life's work. She attended the private Spence School, but after the Great Depression depleted her family's finances she graduated from the public Bronxville High School. Bowman prepared for a career in art by studying at the Grand Central School of Art and at the National Academy of Design in New York and with instructor Scott Clifton Carbee in Boston, while supplementing her formal training with a self-directed study of equine conformation and of George Stubbs's anatomical drawings of horses. She won her first acclaim about 1936 with a first prize from Grand Central for a portrait—not of a horse, but of her younger brother.

Jean Bowman, as she was professionally known throughout her life, moved to Boston following her marriage in 1939 to Richard W. Pentecost. In 1940 she had her first solo show at the Vose Gallery in Boston. Individual and group exhibitions followed at many other venues, including Scott and Fowles, the Grand Central Art Galleries, and M. Knoedler and Company, all in New York City, and in London at the Tryon Gallery and as the first American to exhibit at the Ackermann Gallery. Bowman's name and reputation traveled through the horse world, and she received commissions from numerous wealthy patrons. She painted her first commissioned horse portrait in 1948, for Richard Mellon, the first of several for the Mellon family. Ten years later Bowman began executing commissions for patrons in Great Britain and Europe, including a portrait of Queen Elizabeth II's horse Hopeful Venture. Walter Chrysler, Robert J. Kleberg, of the King Ranch in Texas, Paul Mellon and his wife, and John Hay "Jock" Whitney also commissioned paintings. Bowman's equine subjects ranged from family pets to such famous thoroughbreds as Affirmed, Arkle, Seattle Slew, and Secretariat.

In 1944, following the birth of her one son and her divorce, Bowman moved to Maryland, but not long thereafter she settled near Middleburg in Northern Virginia. She traveled throughout the United States and Europe to paint her subjects, but she lived the rest of her life in Virginia. After 1972 Bowman's home and studio were in an antebellum house called Bonnycastle in the village of Unison, near Middleburg. On 27 February 1949 she married Alexander Mackay-Smith, one of Virginia's best-known horsemen. They divorced on 5 May 1965 but remained friendly and often worked together. In 1971 Bowman married John Holmes Magruder III, a retired Marine colonel and artist who drowned in 1972, just six months after the wedding. On 16 March 1974 she married Charles W. Morgan, who died in 1983.

In 1980, at the suggestion of Mackay-Smith and Joseph Rogers, Bowman and nine other artists founded the American Academy of Equine Art (AAEA) to support and instruct fellow equine artists. The organizers modeled the AAEA, based initially in Middleburg and later in Lexington, Kentucky, after the British Royal Academy. Bowman served as AAEA president for its first ten years and later chaired the board of directors.

Bowman became one of the country's best-known equine artists. Between 1946 and 1998 sixty-eight of her paintings graced the cover of *Chronicle of the Horse*, a weekly magazine published in Middleburg. Bowman also illustrated such periodicals as *Blood Horse, British Race-horse,* the *Maryland Horse,* and *Spur*, and her work appeared in *The Poster Book of Horses: Paintings of American Equestrian Sport by American Artists and Designers* (1978), which Mackay-Smith edited. The National Museum of Racing and Hall of Fame, in Saratoga Springs, New York, and the AAEA, as well as many private collectors, own her canvases.

Jean Bowman signed her oil paintings with a flourish, a hunting crop shaped into a "J" and a "B." In addition to careful use of lighting and accurately depicted anatomy, her portraits of horses might also contain a groom, owner, or rider, or perhaps a four-legged companion of the subject, such as a cat or a mule. Bowman complemented her love of art and animals with a warm personality, ever ready to help fellow horse enthusiasts and artists, often at AAEA workshops.

On 16 August 1994 Jean Eleanor Bowman and the equestrian Gary L. Gardner were killed on a flight to Winchester from Rochester, New York, when their twin-engine aircraft, piloted by Gardner, experienced engine trouble and crashed into a house in Waynesboro, Pennsylvania. Two people in the house were also killed. Bowman was buried in Middleburg. In her memory her family and the AAEA established the Jean Bowman Trust for Equine Artists, from which the AAEA bestows the Jean Bowman

Memorial Award for Painting. Her heirs donated her library to the AAEA and to the National Sporting Library in Middleburg.

Lucretia W. Grindle, "Portrait of the Artist," *Spur* 30 (July/Aug. 1995): 42–45 (por.); *Who's Who in American Art* (1973, 1976, and 1978 eds.); Jim Collins and Glenn B. Opitz, eds., *Women Artists in America: 18th Century to the Present (1790–1980)* (1980), s.v.; *National Sporting Library Newsletter* (winter 1996), por. on back cover; death reported in *Winchester Star,* 18 Aug. 1994; obituaries in *Washington Post,* 19 Aug. 1994, *American Academy of Equine Art Newsletter* (autumn 1994), and *Chronicle of the Horse* (9 Sept. 1994): 51.

JULIE A. CAMPBELL

BOWMAN, John (10 December 1738–4 May 1784), frontier militia officer, was born near Cedar Creek in Frederick County, the son of George Bowman and Mary Hite Bowman. His brother Abraham Bowman served as an officer in the Continental army, and his brother Joseph Bowman was an officer in George Rogers Clark's Illinois Regiment. Toward the end of the French and Indian War, John Bowman became a captain of the Frederick County militia on 6 May 1760, and later in the decade he served on the vestry of Frederick Parish. About 1766 Bowman moved to the southern part of Augusta County, and when the new county of Botetourt was formed in 1770, he was one of its first justices of the peace. He lived there for about a decade and married Elizabeth Bryan, a widow with several children. They had one son, born about 1771.

Bowman first traveled to Kentucky early in 1776 to inspect with his younger brother Joseph land that their brother Abraham had visited the previous year. Together with their cousin Isaac Hite, the Bowmans formed Hite, Bowman and Company, a land and stock venture, to settle the property. At Harrodsburg on 20 June 1776 Bowman signed a petition for the creation of a new county in the West. He then returned home and served as a quartermaster for William Christian's expedition against the Cherokee Indians in the autumn. In 1777 Bowman set out for his new western residence, carrying with him a commission as colonel of the militia of the new Kentucky County. He was also a member of the Kentucky County Court and attended when the court met for the first time at Harrodsburg on 2 September 1777.

Bowman was preoccupied with the security of the western settlements. In August 1777 he marched two companies of militia to Boonesborough, and in May 1779 he led a force of nearly 300 militiamen across the Ohio River and attacked the Shawnee town of Chillicothe. The Kentucky militia plundered and burned the Indian town but withdrew to Kentucky in the face of Shawnee resistance. Bowman was criticized by some for attacking a strong force with too few men and by others for retreating without completing his intended course of destruction. One probable consequence of Bowman's brief campaign was his inability the following month to provide men and supplies for George Rogers Clark's planned expedition to Detroit, which was initially postponed and finally canceled.

After Kentucky County was divided into three parts, Bowman became the county lieutenant, sheriff, and presiding justice of the new Lincoln County in January 1781. In July of that year he was succeeded as county lieutenant. Bowman became one of the founding trustees of Transylvania Seminary, the first college to be founded west of the Allegheny Mountains, and attended the first meeting of the board on 11 November 1783. He was in poor health by then, resigned as county sheriff the same month, and wrote his will on 5 February 1784. John Bowman died at his home, called Bowman's Station, on 4 May 1784 and was buried there.

John W. Wayland, *The Bowmans: A Pioneering Family in Virginia, Kentucky, and the Northwest Territory* (1943), esp. 108 (physical description), 161–162 (will), and 175–176 (abstracts of land documents); Draper MSS; William Dodd Brown, "Dangerous Situation, Delayed Response: Col. John Bowman and the Kentucky Expedition of 1777," *Register of the Kentucky Historical Society* 97 (1999): 137–157; James Alton James, ed., *George Rogers Clark Papers*, published in *Collections of the Illinois State Historical Library,* vol. 8 (1912); Hening, *Statutes,* 11:283.

WILLIAM DODD BROWN

BOWMAN, John-Geline MacDonald (30 March 1890–14 April 1946), business executive and president of the National Federation of Business and Professional Women's Clubs, was born in Atlanta, Georgia, the daughter of John Angus MacDonald and his second wife, Rowena Winter Thompson MacDonald. Her father, a native of Canada and a member of the publishing firm of N. D. MacDonald and Company, died when she was little more than a month old. She and her mother moved to Richmond to live with her mother's elder half sister John-Geline Woolfolk Binford. Binford's husband, Thomas Mayo Binford, was a businessman who died in 1902.

Geline MacDonald grew up in the Richmond household of her aunt and mother, attended local schools, and then entered the Academy of the Holy Cross in Washington, D.C. She graduated in 1909 with special training in voice, piano, and the harp, returned to Richmond, and became a professional singer, performing in churches. A charter member of the Musicians' Club of Richmond, she sang at the annual members' recital in 1918. On 29 October 1913 she married Jacob Killian Bowman, a Richmond businessman and son of Alpheus Michael Bowman, a prominent state legislator from Salem. Their twin son and daughter were born in 1924.

Before World War I Bowman joined a network of Richmond women with a special interest in economic and educational opportunities. In 1914 she helped to establish the Virginia Bureau of Vocations for Women (later the Alliance for Guidance of Rural Youth) and served as its treasurer for many years. In the spring of 1917 the local chapter of the Young Women's Christian Association created a Business Women's Club, and Bowman became a leader in its campaigns to sell Liberty Bonds and War Savings Stamps. She became a talented public speaker and reportedly sold more thrift stamps than any other woman in the state.

Bowman's efforts brought her to the attention of Thomas McAdams, a banker who hired her after the war to head the new women's department of Merchants National Bank. She used direct-mail advertising to attract female customers to the bank. In 1922 the owner of the Expert Letter Writing Company, a local producer of such advertising, invited Bowman to manage the firm. She agreed to a trial but continued to give the bank half of her time. After six months Bowman resigned from the bank and in 1923 purchased the company. She had continued her singing career at Sunday church services until early in the 1920s, but operating the Expert Letter Writing Company and her growing organizational responsibilities ultimately left her no time for professional singing.

Bowman's most important work involved the National Federation of Business and Professional Women's Clubs. Following World War I the YWCA organized the various clubs for businesswomen into a national body. Representatives from several such Virginia organizations met in Richmond on 27 June 1919 to create the Virginia Federation of Business and Professional Women's Clubs and to select delegates to attend the founding meeting of the national body in Saint Louis in July. Bowman was a charter member of the Virginia organization and attended the Saint Louis meeting. She served as president of the Virginia federation from 1920 to 1923 and as president of the Richmond club from 1926 to 1928. In 1928 she became first vice president of the national federation. Bowman then organized the federation's first biennial meeting, which took place in Richmond from 6 to 11 July 1931. At that meeting she was elected president of the National Federation of Business and Professional Women's Clubs. Delegates reelected her to that post two years later.

An active president, Bowman estimated that she devoted 90 percent of her working time to the federation. She traveled widely, spoke often, made radio broadcasts, and wrote magazine articles, all in the interest of opening business and professional opportunities for women. The Great Depression threatened the position of working women as states and localities attempted to curtail government employment of married women, supposedly to reserve jobs for family men. Bowman forcefully protested this practice at the federation's 1935 meeting and helped to thwart proposed restrictions on federal employment of married women. At that meeting, despite her reluctance to serve a third term as president of the National Federation of Business and Professional Women's Clubs, she accepted renomination but was defeated by fourteen votes.

Bowman's work for the federation had involved her with political issues, but she had long shared with her husband an active interest in the Democratic Party. In 1936 she was a Virginia delegate to the party's national convention and made campaign speeches in behalf of Franklin Delano Roosevelt, including one to an unfriendly audience on Wall Street in New York City. In 1938 Bowman unsuccessfully sought appointment as postmaster of Richmond.

Bowman continued to operate the Expert Letter Writing Corporation, which had become one of the largest such enterprises in the South. She also served a number of civic organizations in Richmond and helped to found the Richmond Symphony Orchestra. For many years Bowman sat on the board of the Southern Woman's Educational Alliance, which became the Alliance for Guidance of Rural Youth. She supported improved educational opportunities for women, including their admission to the College of William and Mary. Bowman campaigned for Roosevelt again in 1940, and during World War II she served on the speakers' bureau of the war fund drives. Her son, Jay Killian Bowman, was shot down over Germany while flying in the Army Air Corps on 14 January 1945 and killed in action.

By then Bowman was undergoing treatment for breast cancer. She displayed great courage as the family waited for confirmation of the young man's fate. John-Geline MacDonald Bowman died in Richmond on 14 April 1946 and was buried in Hollywood Cemetery in that city. In 1961 her formal portrait was unveiled at the headquarters of the National Federation of Business and Professional Women's Clubs in Washington, D.C. Her daughter, Geline Bowman Williams, served as mayor of Richmond from 1988 to 1990.

Biographies in Glass and Glass, *Virginia Democracy*, 3:558–563, and Charlotte Allen, comp., *A Record of Twenty-Five Years, an Interpretation: Virginia Federation of Business and Professional Women, 1919–1944* (1946), 24–26; BVS Marriage Register, Richmond City; *Richmond Times-Dispatch*, 4 Sept. 1932; *Richmond News Leader*, 30 Dec. 1936, 28 Mar. 1941; *Catholic Virginian* 6 (Sept. 1931): 8, 17–18; letter to editor in *Richmond Times-Dispatch*, 3 July 1932; National Federation of Business and Professional Women's Clubs, *Proceedings of the Biennial Convention* 2 (1933): 11–21; *Richmond Times-Dispatch*, 9 Jan. 1961 (por.); obituaries in *Richmond News Leader* and *Richmond Times-Dispatch*, both 15 Apr. 1946; editorial tributes in *Richmond News Leader,* 15 Apr. 1946, and

Richmond Times-Dispatch, 16 Apr. 1946; memorial in *Virginia Business and Professional Woman* 10 (Apr. 1948): 3.
SUZANNE H. FREEMAN
JOHN T. KNEEBONE

BOWMAN, Joseph (8 March 1752–14 August 1779), officer of George Rogers Clark's Illinois Regiment, Virginia State Forces, was born near Cedar Creek in Frederick County, the son of George Bowman and Mary Hite Bowman. His brother Abraham Bowman served as a Continental army officer, and another brother John Bowman was an officer in the frontier militia. Joseph Bowman was a young captain in the Dunmore County militia in 1774 when his company was called into the field during Dunmore's War. Many of his men deserted, and it took Bowman two years to recover the value of the equipment and supplies that they took with them.

In 1775 Bowman went to Kentucky, perhaps in company with his elder brother Abraham Bowman. At Harrodsburg on 20 June 1776 he was among those who petitioned to have a new western county established. Evidently Bowman favorably impressed George Rogers Clark, who was also at the Harrodsburg meeting. In January 1778 Clark offered Bowman a captain's commission if he would raise a company of men in the lower Shenandoah Valley and join the army Clark was recruiting for western service. Bowman again lost men to desertion, but he and his company joined Clark, and on 12 May 1778 the expedition started down the Monongahela and Ohio Rivers bound for the Illinois country. They marched overland to the Mississippi River and captured Kaskaskia on 4 July 1778 without firing a shot. Clark sent Bowman and thirty men up the Mississippi River, and by 7 July Bowman had taken Prairie du Rocher, Saint Philippe, and Cahokia. Within a few weeks Vincennes surrendered without a fight, and Clark's Virginia army controlled most of the land between the Ohio River and the Great Lakes.

Bowman served as military commander at Cahokia, which Clark called Fort Bowman, and as judge of a civil court that the Americans established there. He also attempted to win the support of neighboring Indian tribes. In February 1779, after the British commander Henry Hamilton recaptured Vincennes, Bowman took part in Clark's winter march east to the Wabash River, where he commanded the second division during the fighting that led to Hamilton's surrender. On 25 February the Virginians took possession of the fort, but during the attendant military festivities an explosion badly burned Bowman and five other men. Two days later he received news from Williamsburg that he had been promoted to major effective 14 December 1778.

Bowman spent the spring and summer recovering from his burns, and by 5 August 1779 he seemed well enough to be put in charge of recruiting new men. Joseph Bowman, however, died at Vincennes, possibly from the effects of his burns, on 14 August 1779.

John W. Wayland, *The Bowmans: A Pioneering Family in Virginia, Kentucky, and the Northwest Territory* (1943), esp. 114–115 (will) and abstracts of family and land records; Bowman documents in Draper MSS and Bowman Family Papers, 1774–1836, Filson Historical Society, Louisville, Ky.; James Alton James, ed., *George Rogers Clark Papers*, including Bowman's journal and letters, published in *Collections of the Illinois State Historical Library*, vols. 8, 19 (1912–1926), with variant death date of 19 Aug. 1779 in Thomas Quirk to George Rogers Clark, 22 Aug. 1779, 8:360; John D. Barnhart, ed., *Henry Hamilton and George Rogers Clark in the American Revolution* (1951), 187; death certificate, given by George Rogers Clark in Lincoln Co. on 5 Feb 1782, in Draper MSS, 17J16, 118.
WILLIAM DODD BROWN

BOWMAN, Paul Haynes (5 July 1887–4 April 1964), president of Bridgewater College, was born near Flourville in Washington County, Tennessee, the son of Samuel Joseph Bowman, a dentist and minister, and his first wife, Susan Virginia Bowman Bowman. After joining the nearby Knob Creek Church of the Brethren in 1900, he attended the Boones Creek Seminary from 1902 to 1906. Bowman was called to the ministry in 1907 but continued his education. He graduated from Bridgewater College in 1910 and received an M.A. from the University of Pennsylvania in 1913 and a B.D. from Crozer Theological Seminary the same year.

From 1910 to 1915 Bowman was pastor of the Bethany Church of the Brethren in Philadelphia. On 12 August 1913 he married Flora Etta Hoover, a fellow Bridgewater graduate. They had two sons and two daughters. In 1915 Bowman became president of Blue Ridge College in

New Windsor, Maryland, one of several small colleges that the Church of the Brethren operated in the southern states. He returned to Virginia in 1918 as professor of biblical literature and theology at Bridgewater College. Later that year, at age thirty-one, Bowman was elected acting president of Bridgewater College and became professor of philosophy. The board elected him president in 1921, and he served until he retired in 1946.

During his presidency Bowman brought about the consolidation of Bridgewater College with Blue Ridge College, with Daleville College in Botetourt County, and with Hebron Seminary in Prince William County, measures that helped the institution grow into one of the strongest independent colleges in Virginia. After the mergers, the institution was officially known as Bridgewater-Daleville College from July 1924 until 1951. Bowman's other accomplishments included raising educational standards, gaining accreditation from the Association of Colleges and Secondary Schools of the Southern States in 1925, building Cole and Rebecca Halls, and guiding the college through the difficult years of World War II. A consummate mediator and diplomat, Bowman was instrumental in freeing Bridgewater from strong religious controls while at the same time maintaining high measures of respect for and confidence in the college and himself. His work for the college continued even after his retirement. Bowman chaired the college's Crusade for Excellence campaign that, among other things, funded the building of the Alexander Mack Memorial Library, dedicated the day before Bowman's death.

Bowman received honorary degrees from Blue Ridge College in 1918, Juniata College in 1925, Roanoke College in 1940, and Bridgewater-Daleville College in 1944. He was named the Bridgewater College alumnus of the year in 1955. Bowman was also one of the most respected leaders in the Church of the Brethren and held key national posts during his presidency of the college. Elected to the denominational Council of Boards (later the General Brotherhood Board) in 1925, he was often either president or vice president during his almost continuous service from then until 1958. Bowman also sat for many years on the church's General Education Board. He chaired the Brethren's 250th anniversary celebration and the committee that erected the new church headquarters building in Elgin, Illinois. Bowman was moderator at the church's national conferences in 1937, 1942, and 1949, and he frequently served on the annual conference committee. In 1940 religious conviction led Bowman, along with leaders of the Mennonite Church and Society of Friends, to organize the Civilian Public Service, a program that enabled men who conscientiously opposed combat to serve their country during World War II in nonmilitary and conservation efforts. Bowman acted as its first national director.

Bowman also remained active at the district level of the church, and he was involved in business and civic matters. A founder of the Rockingham County Public Library, he was one of its directors for many years. Bowman was vice chairman of the Farmers and Merchants Bank at Timberville, a member of the board of directors of the Rockingham Memorial Hospital, and a founder of the Bridgewater Rotary Club. He also served as a special consultant to the United States Office of Education. Bowman was president of the Association of Virginia Colleges in 1942 and belonged to the Virginia Academy of Science and Tau Kappa Alpha.

After retiring from Bridgewater-Daleville College in 1946, Bowman and his wife lived on her family's farm in Timberville. He acted as interim pastor of Brethren churches in Waynesboro, Pennsylvania, and Mill Creek and Bridgewater in Virginia. Bowman wrote *Brethren Education in the Southeast* (1955) and *The Adventurous Future* (1959) and left uncompleted a history of the Church of the Brethren in Tennessee. In 1960 the Bowmans built a house near the Bridgewater campus. Paul Haynes Bowman lived there for four years and died in a Harrisonburg hospital on 4 April 1964. He was buried in Oak Lawn Cemetery in Bridgewater.

Biographies in Bruce, Tyler, and Morton, *History of Virginia*, 4:250, Donald F. Durnbaugh et al., eds., *Brethren Encyclopedia* (1983–1984), 1:168, and Joseph B. Yount III, ed., *Tunker House Proceedings, 1972* (1973), 89–91; BVS Marriage Register, Rockingham Co.; Paul Haynes Bowman Papers and vertical files, Bridgewater College Library;

information provided by daughter Rebecca Gene Johnson; Bowman, *Brethren Education in the Southeast* (1955), 145–172, 245–264; Bridgewater College *Bulletin*, n.s., 8 (Dec. 1918): 3–4; ibid. 21 (Aug. 1945): 1–2; John Walter Wayland, ed., *Fifty Years of Educational Endeavor: Bridgewater College, 1880–1930, Daleville College, 1890–1930* (1930), 126–157 (por. facing 132); Francis Fry Wayland, *Bridgewater College: The First Hundred Years, 1880–1980* (1993), 261–431 (por. on 263); obituaries in *Harrisonburg Daily News-Record*, 6 Apr. 1964 (with editorial tribute), Bridgewater College News Release, 8 Apr. 1964 (DVB Files), and *Gospel Messenger* (30 May 1964): 8–9.

EMMERT F. BITTINGER

BOWMAN, Warren Daniel (9 April 1894–23 April 1987), president of Bridgewater College, was born in the Rockingham County town of Dayton, the son of Benjamin Franklin Bowman, a farmer, and Mary Elizabeth Miller Bowman. He attended the Bridgewater public schools, graduated from Bridgewater High School, and entered Bridgewater College, which one of his grandfathers had helped found. Bowman left school and entered the army on 16 November 1917. Initially assigned to a machine gun unit, he was transferred to the medical department and served at Camp A. A. Humphreys in Virginia until discharged with the rank of sergeant on 22 January 1919. Bowman returned to college and graduated in 1920. In June 1921 in Bridgewater he was ordained a minister of the Church of the Brethren.

Bowman was principal of the high school in McGaheysville during the 1921–1922 academic year. From 1923 to 1930 he taught in the education department at the State Teachers College at Farmville (later Longwood College). Bowman concurrently pursued his higher education at the University of Chicago, receiving an M.A. in 1922 and a Ph.D. in education and psychology in 1930. He was also interim pastor of the Roanoke Central Church of the Brethren in 1925 and 1926. On 11 June 1925 Bowman married Olive Murrann Smith, of Columbus, Georgia. They had one son and three daughters.

From 1930 to 1937 Bowman headed the Department of Education and Psychology at Juniata College in Huntingdon, Pennsylvania. Until 1935 he was also dean of men. During several summers Bowman taught at George Peabody College for Teachers in Nashville, Emory University, the Lake Junaluska branch

of Duke University, the University of Virginia, and the Virginia Agricultural and Mechanical College and Polytechnic Institute. In 1937 he moved to the District of Columbia, where he served as pastor of the Washington Church of the Brethren for twelve years.

In Washington Bowman focused his creative energies on family problems in the urban parish in the context of Brethren doctrine and practice. In 1938 the Elgin Press, forerunner of the Brethren Publishing House, published his book, *Home Builders of Tomorrow*. Bowman's interest in pastoral counseling, especially problems of marriage and the family, and his premarital counseling program became well-known and led to his *Counseling with Couples before Marriage* (1945). He often lectured on marital and family problems and served on several church commissions and committees relating to family life, including the Commissions on Marriage and the Home of both the National Council of Churches and the Washington Federation of Churches. Bowman also helped refine Church of the Brethren doctrine on anointing and healing by adapting and applying its use within the modern medical and therapeutic setting, and in 1942 he published *Anointing for Healing*. As a member of the church's National Christian Mission in 1940 and 1941, he visited Brethren churches in several cities, and he served as moderator of the denomination's national conference in 1945.

In February 1949 the board of visitors of Bridgewater-Daleville College (after 1951 again designated Bridgewater College) unanimously elected Bowman president of the college, a position he held with energy and distinction until his retirement on 30 June 1964. During his administration Bridgewater increased its capital assets by more than 400 percent, boosted enrollment by one-third, and raised the proportion of faculty holding advanced degrees to a level above the national average. The college added a bachelor of science program in business administration and created new departments of health and physical education, physics, and Spanish. In 1953, with neither fanfare nor difficulty, it admitted its first African American as a private student. In keeping with Church of the Brethren doctrine, the college had never had any formal restrictions on admission of students by reason of race or religion. Bridgewater also constructed several new buildings, including a new library. A science building erected in 1953 was later named Bowman Hall in joint recognition of service to the college of Bowman and his distant relations Samuel H. Bowman, a founder, and Paul Haynes Bowman, a previous president.

Bowman remained active in his church while he was president of the college. He served as moderator of various district conferences, sat on the General Brotherhood Board from 1952 to 1956, and belonged to the Brotherhood Committee on Higher Education. Following his retirement Bowman served part-time or as an interim minister at Brethren churches in Lebanon (1964–1968), Barren Ridge (1968–1969), Cedar Grove in alliance with the Valley Central United Church of Christ (1970), Middle River (1971–1972), Harrisonburg (1972–1973), Linville Creek (1973), and Bridgewater (1974).

In 1951 Bowman was an organizer of the Virginia Foundation for Independent Colleges. He received honorary degrees from Bethany Theological Seminary in 1960 and Bridgewater College in 1966, and he received the latter's Distinguished Alumnus Award and was named president emeritus of the college in 1964. He suffered a stroke in 1975. Two years later he and his wife moved into a retirement center, the Bridgewater Home. Warren Daniel Bowman died there on 23 April 1987 and was buried at Oak Lawn Cemetery in Bridgewater.

Harry Anthony Brunk, *David Heatwole and His Descendants* (1987), 757–759; Donald F. Durnbaugh et al., eds., *Brethren Encyclopedia* (1983–1984), 1:169; feature article in *Richmond Times-Dispatch*, 27 Sept. 1959; Military Service Records; Warren Daniel Bowman Papers, Bridgewater College Library; information provided by daughter Helen Elizabeth Bowman Moore; Roger E. Sappington, *The Brethren in Virginia: The History of the Church of the Brethren in Virginia* (1973), 415–419; Francis Fry Wayland, *Bridgewater College: The First Hundred Years, 1880–1980* (1993), 467–566 (por. on 468); obituary in *Harrisonburg Daily News-Record*, 25 Apr. 1987.

EMMERT F. BITTINGER

BOWSER, James (b. ca. 1730), Continental army soldier, was born probably in Nansemond County. The names of his parents are not known, but his ancestors included persons of both African and European or Native American descent. Local parish records in 1760 and 1762 document medical treatment for "Bowsers Wife" and "Mary Bowzer" but fail to disclose whether one or two women were involved or their relationship to James Bowser. According to family tradition he was a farmer who was born free.

James Bowser's name first appears in a 1780 army size roll that records data on certain Virginians enlisting or reenlisting in the Continental army. He was described as a man of mixed race background with black hair and eyes, about fifty years old and five feet, six and three-quarters inches tall. Bowser enlisted for eighteen months on 26 September 1780. General John Peter Gabriel Muhlenberg and Colonel Thomas Meriwether certified in May 1783 that by then Bowser had served in the Continental army for four years.

Bowser probably first joined the army late in 1778 or early in 1779 as part of the 1st Regiment, Virginia State Line, becoming one of approximately 5,000 men of African descent who served in the Continental army or navy during the American Revolution. During his first enlistment he may have served under Muhlenberg in Pennsylvania or New Jersey. After reenlisting in 1780 Bowser joined a rendezvous of about 500 other Continental soldiers in Chesterfield County and went on active duty in Virginia. He was very likely present at the siege of Yorktown in October 1781. Bowser differed greatly from most of his fellow soldiers, being twenty-five or thirty years older than most privates, serving longer in the Continental army, and as an African American. The southern state governments had not encouraged the enlistment of African Americans early in the war, but as enlistment quotas became progressively harder to meet, Virginia began enlisting black men. Bowser may have been among the first. Some of the African American soldiers acted as guides or spies, but most probably served in support or logistical roles rather than on the front lines. Having served to the war's end, he was issued a warrant in May 1783 for 200 acres in Ohio.

Another James Bowser from Nansemond County, who was nineteen years old in 1782, also served in the Continental army. The two men were probably related, and later traditions may have conflated episodes in their lives.

In 1828 Bowser's name appeared on an official list of Revolutionary War officers and soldiers who were entitled to but had not applied for or who had not received their land bounties. In mid-October 1833 eight free African Americans of Nansemond County established to the satisfaction of a local justice of the peace that they were Bowser's heirs at law, and with his service as a private in the Continental army proved, on 26 February and 20 March 1834 Governor John Floyd certified that the heirs were entitled to receive the warrant, "if not heretofore drawn."

The date and place of James Bowser's death are not known. He was fifty-three years old when his enlistment expired, and he may have died not long after the war ended. His name does not appear on any extant late-eighteenth-century Nansemond County tax list, but he may have owned no taxable property. Bowser family members remained in Nansemond and the lower Tidewater for generations. The heirs who filed in the 1830s may not all have been literate, but they were all free. After the end of slavery one family member, Florence Brickhouse Bowser, founded a school, which was later named for her, in nearby Driver. In August 1981 a state historical highway marker was erected near the site of the Bowser farm to commemorate the service of one of the few identified African American Continental army soldiers from Nansemond County.

Wilmer L. Hall, ed., *The Vestry Book of the Upper Parish, Nansemond County, Virginia, 1743–1793* (1949), 152; William Lindsay Hopkins, ed., *Suffolk Parish Vestry Book, 1749–1784, Nansemond County, Virginia, and Newport Parish Vestry Book, 1724–1772, Isle of Wight County, Virginia* (1988), 24; Chesterfield Supplement, "Size Roll of Troops Join'd at Chesterfield Courthouse Since Sept. 1st 1780," RG 2, LVA; LOMC, no. 606; Revolutionary War Pension and Bounty-Land Warrant Application Files, RG 15, NARA (quotation); *List of the Names of Such Officers and Soldiers of the Revolutionary Army as Have Acquired a Right to Lands from the United States and Who Have Not Yet Applied Therefor*, 20th Cong., 1st sess., 1828, Senate Doc. 42, serial 164, 65; Thomas E. Barden, ed., *Virginia Folk Legends* (1991), 69–70; *Norfolk Virginian-Pilot*, 15 Aug. 1981.

SYLVIA R. FREY

BOWSER, Mary Elizabeth (fl. 1860s), Union spy, was probably born a slave in or somewhere near Richmond. Her mother's first name may have been Caroline, but the full identities of her parents, the dates of her birth and death, and the course of her life after 1865 are not known. Documentary evidence about her life is virtually nonexistent now, and almost nothing about her life before 1861 is known for certain. According to an account compiled early in the twentieth century, Elizabeth Van Lew, of Richmond, either purchased her in order to free her or freed her after acquiring her in some other way and then sent her to Philadelphia to be educated. At about the time the Civil War began, Van Lew persuaded her to return to Richmond to act as a spy for the Union. Bowser kept or later prepared a record of her Civil War espionage, but members of the Bowser family of Richmond discarded it early in the 1950s before historians had an opportunity to examine it.

This much is known. On 16 April 1861 in Richmond, an African American woman named Mary married an African American man named Wilson Bowser. The record of the marriage establishes the free status of both, because slaves could not be legally married, and it identifies them as servants in the Van Lew household. At some stage during the Civil War, Mary Elizabeth Bowser acted as a waitress, and probably had other duties as well, in the official residence of President Jefferson Davis. She gathered information by listening to conversations and by surreptitiously reading documents, and then she passed on what she had learned to a Union spy named Thomas McNiven, who posed as a baker and made daily delivery rounds in his wagon to private homes and government offices. His couriers spirited information out of Richmond, but he often passed Bowser's intelligence to the Union army through the agency of Elizabeth Van Lew, who ran the most important ring of Northern espionage agents in the capital of the Confederacy. McNiven stated before his death in 1904 that Van Lew's "girl Mary" was one of the Union's best agents and that she could repeat word for word everything that she read on Davis's desk. It is not known when or for how long Bowser was in the Davis household, whether she posed as free or slave, as married or unmarried, what name she was known by, how

Van Lew had arranged to place her in the Davis home, or whether any Confederate authorities were aware of an earlier connection between Bowser and Van Lew.

The official records of Van Lew's espionage and such information about her agents as she may have supplied to the army were removed from the files of the Department of War before the end of the 1860s and could not be found by the end of the century. Portions of Van Lew's personal records and some of her later correspondence did survive. After her death in 1900 her executor, John P. Reynolds Jr., of Boston, Massachusetts, drew on information in the papers and his personal knowledge to prepare two biographical memoranda on Van Lew that briefly mentioned her spy in the Davis household. From that source and from Richmond and Boston newspaper obituaries of Van Lew, William Gilmore Beymer wrote and published an article in 1911 that served as the basis for a chapter in his widely read book on Civil War intelligence operations, *On Hazardous Service: Scouts and Spies of the North and South* (1912). In both publications Beymer included a short paragraph about the spy in the Davis household, and for the first time he publicly identified that spy as Elizabeth Van Lew's former slave, Mary Elizabeth Bowser, of whose subsequent fate he stated that he knew nothing.

The remainder of what has appeared about Bowser in histories of Richmond and on the Civil War, in books of reference and on women, and in fiction and on film consists of unsubstantiated embellishment on that original paragraph or embellishment of the embellishments. Despite the paucity of information about her life, Bowser's accomplishments were recognized in 1995, when the United States Army Military Intelligence Corps inducted her into its Hall of Fame in Fort Huachuca, Arizona.

Although Bowser's name does not appear in any records yet uncovered, she may have remained in the vicinity of Richmond, where a large and notable family of Bowsers resided for generations and where her own record of her espionage rested until it disappeared. She could also have gone elsewhere, perhaps to the North. Either way she could have been lost to view by

acquiring a new surname through remarriage. It is also possible that Mary Elizabeth Bowser, after aiding materially in the victory of the Union over the Confederacy and in the consequent destruction of slavery, died too young to enjoy her freedom fully.

The basic sources are two undated memoranda (ca. 1901–1909) of John P. Reynolds Jr. in Elizabeth Van Lew Papers, New York Public Library (LVA microfilm), William Gilmore Beymer, "Miss Van Lew," *Harper's Monthly* 123 (June 1911): 90, and Beymer, *On Hazardous Service: Scouts and Spies of the North and South* (1912), 75; presence of an unnamed servant of Van Lew in the Davis household reported in *Richmond Evening Leader*, 27 July 1900; Anna I. Whitlock to John Albree, 25 Apr. 1913, Elizabeth Van Lew Papers, W&M, contains a cryptic comment that "Caroline was the mother of Mary Bowers"; marriage recorded in J. Staunton Moore, ed., *Annals of Henrico Parish, Diocese of Virginia* (1904), 248; modern, edited transcript of the recollections of Thomas McNiven, LVA; Ruth Ann Coski, "White House Spy Legend Lives On," *Museum of the Confederacy Newsletter* (spring/summer 1999): 6–7, includes Varina Davis's denial that spying took place in the Confederate White House.

BRENT TARTER

BOWSER, Rosa L. Dixon (7 January 1855–7 February 1931), educator and civic leader, was probably born into slavery in Amelia County, the daughter of Henry Dixon, a carpenter, and Augusta A. Hawkins Dixon, a domestic servant. After freedom came in 1865, the family moved to Richmond and started a new life. Religion and education were the foundations of the family, and they joined Richmond's largest congregation, First African Baptist Church. Dixon first taught in the Sunday school there. Her father recognized her aptitude and enrolled her in the Richmond public schools, where she initially received instruction from northern teachers of the Freedmen's Bureau.

The superintendent of the Freedmen's Bureau schools in Richmond, Ralza M. Manly, identified exemplary students and selected them for teacher training at the Richmond Normal and High School (after 1870 the Richmond Colored Normal School). Dixon became one of Manly's protégés and excelled in English, mathematics, music, and reading. She graduated with the second-highest marks in the class of 1872–1873 and remained in school for an additional year to study Greek, Latin, music, and teaching strategies.

In 1872 Dixon passed the examination for teacher certification and began her teaching career. On 4 September 1879 she married James Herndon Bowser, a fellow teacher who had been the valedictorian in her class at the Richmond Colored Normal School. Soon after their marriage he left teaching and worked instead as a clerk in the Richmond post office until his death from consumption, or tuberculosis, on 25 April 1881. Their only child, Oswald Barrington Herndon Bowser, became a successful Richmond physician.

For a time after her marriage and the birth of her son, Bowser taught music in her home and continued to teach in the Sunday school. Regarding the community as her extended family, she formed literary circles and taught childrearing and housekeeping techniques. In 1883 the city school board appointed Bowser to teach in the primary grades at Navy Hill School. The next year Bowser became supervisor of teachers at the Baker School in Richmond and in 1896 principal teacher as well in the night school for men. In addition, she taught classes in social skills at the Young Men's Christian Association in Jackson Ward, the heart of Richmond's African American community.

Bowser organized reading circles in order to give experienced teachers a forum for sharing information with new colleagues about their reading, their students, and their classroom strategies. The success of these groups led directly to the formation in 1887 of the Virginia Teachers' Reading Circle, the first professional African American educational association in the state. Bowser was president of the organization, in 1889 renamed the Virginia State Teachers Association, from 1890 to 1892. Over a period of more than thirty years she often taught at Peabody institutes, sessions of summer teaching courses at various black normal schools in Virginia.

The presidency of the association opened the door for Bowser to play major roles in other African American organizations, including the Hampton Negro Conferences and their successor, the Negro Organization Society. She chaired the conferences' Committee on Domestic Science from 1899 to 1902. At the July 1897 conference Bowser made one of her most notable speeches, "Some of Our Needs," and appealed to the conference to form girls' meetings to teach ladylike qualities and to sponsor mothers' clubs to advise young mothers on childrearing. In response to her appeal, additional girls' and mothers' meetings were organized in scores of Virginia communities. Bowser also called for reforms in education, increased teacher salaries, and improved housing and education for wayward children. She joined with such influential black Virginians as Janie Porter Barrett and Maggie Lena Mitchell Walker to form the Woman's Department of the Negro Reformatory Association of Virginia, which raised money for the development of the Industrial Home School for Colored Girls and the Virginia Manual Labor School for Colored Boys, both in Hanover County.

Although Bowser did not seek an active role in public affairs, in August 1895 she founded and became first president of the Richmond Woman's League. By July 1896 she had led the league in raising $690 to pay the legal bills of three black Lunenburg County women who were appealing murder convictions, two of them death sentences. Bowser became involved in other social causes and supported the founding and funding of organizations for treatment of tuberculosis, improved medical facilities, and medical insurance. As a result of an alliance she forged, the Federated Insurance League joined with the Woman's League to support a Richmond branch of the Virginia Colored Anti-Tuberculosis League.

Bowser became active in the woman's club movement that swept the nation late in the nineteenth century. She joined the Woman's Era Club, of Boston, Massachusetts, an organization that raised money to create kindergartens for African American children, and for several years served as field editor, or reporter, from Virginia for its journal, the *Woman's Era*. In July 1896 she participated as a member of its successor organization, the National Federation of Afro-American Women, and as president of the Richmond Woman's League, in founding the

National Association of Colored Women. Bowser was nominated for president of the new association but was not elected. She was also a founder of the Virginia State Federation of Colored Women's Clubs in 1908.

In 1912, working with Mary Church Terrell and Maggie Walker, Bowser attempted to aid a young girl sentenced to be electrocuted for murder. Their combined efforts included a direct appeal to the governor of Virginia to reopen the case and commute the sentence. Despite the backing of the National Association of Colored Women, the girl was executed. Bowser and the association also publicly opposed lynching and racial segregation and supported universal woman suffrage.

Bowser continued her community work, teaching in the public schools until she retired in 1923. She taught Sunday school classes at First African Baptist Church for more than fifty years, until diabetes forced her to relinquish the work. In recognition of her many contributions to education, the first branch of the Richmond public library to be opened to African Americans was named for Bowser in 1925. A Richmond vocational training school for boys later bore her name. Rosa L. Dixon Bowser died of complications from diabetes on 7 February 1931 at her home in Richmond and was buried in Evergreen Cemetery in that city.

Birth date on gravestone; names Augusta, Henry, and Rosa appear in roster of William J. Barksdale's Clay Hill plantation in Amelia Co., 1856 (Gibson Jefferson McConnaughey, ed., *Amelia County, Virginia, Miscellaneous Records, 1735–1865* [1995], 117); biographies in M. A. Majors, *Noted Negro Women, Their Triumphs and Activities* (1893), 149–151, L. A. Scruggs, ed., *Women of Distinction: Remarkable in Works and Invincible in Character* (1893), 283–287, *Richmond Planet*, 12 Jan. 1895 (por.), D. W. Culp, ed., *Twentieth Century Negro Literature* (1902), insert between 176 and 177 (including por.), "Rosa D. Bowser: Talent to Spare, Talent to Share," *Richmond Literature and History Quarterly* 1 (fall 1978): 45–46 (giving middle name as Lewis), and *Richmond Afro-American*, 21 Feb., 14 Mar. (por.) 1981; information provided by granddaughter-in-law McEva Bowser; BVS Marriage Register, Richmond City; Bowser, "Some of Our Needs," Hampton Negro Conferences, 1897, State and National Organizations, RG 5, Hampton, abstracted in *Southern Workman and Hampton School Record* 26 (1897): 177–178; Bowser, "What Role Is the Educated Negro Woman to Play in the Uplifting of Her Race?" in Culp, *Twentieth Century Negro Literature*, 177–182; *A History of the Club Movement among the Colored Women of the United States of America* (1902), 39, 42, 53, 62, 85–87, 122; Lauranett Lee, "More than an Image: Black Women Reformers in Richmond, Virginia, 1910–1928" (master's thesis, Virginia State University, 1993), 16–31; BVS Death Certificate, Richmond City; death notice in *Richmond Times-Dispatch*, 9 Feb. 1931; obituaries in *Norfolk Journal and Guide* and *Richmond Planet*, both 14 Feb. 1931.

VERONICA ALEASE DAVIS

BOWYER, Claude Bernard (25 December 1880–29 July 1947), physician, was born in the Elk Creek section of Grayson County, the son of Henry L. Bowyer and Kate M. Bowyer. His father named him for a noted French physician and physiologist and determined at once that his eldest son would follow in his footsteps and continue a century-old family tradition by becoming a doctor. He also decided to educate his son at Emory and Henry College and by 1890 had moved to Emory as the college physician.

At age fourteen Bowyer began two years of study in Emory and Henry's preparatory department. His academic performance at the college was by no means brilliant. He spent five more years there before earning the bachelor's degree in 1902, but he was captain of the football team and took part in such college pranks as releasing a billy goat in a lecture room. Bowyer always believed that his seven years as a student set a record at the college. He entered the Medical College of Virginia in 1902 and received an M.D. on time in 1906.

Soon after receiving his medical degree Bowyer took a job as a physician for the Stonega Coke and Coal Company in Stonega in Wise County, where he spent the rest of his life except for a one-year internship at Memorial Hospital in Richmond in 1908–1909. In 1910 he became director of the Stonega Hospital, which the company owned and operated for its employees. A pioneer in industrial medicine, Bowyer took special courses in that field at New York Postgraduate Medical School (1912) and Harvard University (1921). In 1918 he was both a charter member of the American Medical Association's College of Industrial Physicians and Surgeons and an industry adviser to the commission that drafted the first Virginia Workmen's Compensation Act.

Bowyer organized the Clinch Valley Medical Society and helped found the Wise County

Medical Society. From 1918 to 1942 he sat on the council of the Medical Society of Virginia, and in 1943 he was elected president of the society. He delivered his presidential address entitled "Physicians, Wake Up!" the following year and called on doctors to cooperate with industrial and labor organizations and the insurance industry to provide affordable medical care in rural areas and to the urban poor before the state or federal government intervened. Bowyer also served on the governing boards of both of his alma maters. In 1936 he was named both a trustee of Emory and Henry College and a member of the board of the Medical College of Virginia, positions he held until his death. On the latter board Bowyer proposed that medical scholarships be given to "country boys" to ease the shortage of physicians in rural Virginia. He also proposed that the efficacy of rehabilitating injured workers be demonstrated at state expense. Neither proposal made much headway during years of depression and war.

Bowyer was active in the business and civic affairs of Wise County. He was a successful farmer and cattleman, a director of the First National Bank of Appalachia, and a founder and president for fifteen years of the Lonesome Pine Country Club. He never married but had many friends and was a storyteller and wit. Claude Bernard Bowyer died at his home in Big Stone Gap on 29 July 1947, probably from a heart attack. He was buried in Emory.

Feature articles in *Virginia Medical Monthly* 70 (1943): 584–585 (por.), and *Commonwealth* 11 (Feb. 1944): 15; *Emory and Henry Bulletin* 28 (July 1936): 33; Bowyer files at Emory and Henry College and MCV; presidential address in *Virginia Medical Monthly* 71 (1944): 557–561; obituaries in *Tazewell Clinch Valley News*, 1 Aug. 1947, and *Virginia Medical Monthly* 74 (1947): 442; memorial resolutions in Bowyer file at MCV and *Virginia Medical Monthly* 74 (1947): 434, 542.

ELIZABETH W. ETHERIDGE

BOWYER, John (d. 24 April 1806), member of the Convention of 1776, was the son of Michael Bowyer, a Shenandoah Valley pioneer. The date and place of his birth and the identity of his mother are not known. Bowyer was a young man with little property in the autumn of 1753 when he started teaching school in Augusta County. On 4 February 1754 he married very well to a twice-widowed older woman, Magdalene Woods McDowell Borden, and he became the guardian of her underage children. Financially independent after his marriage, Bowyer became a captain in the militia and by 1757 was a justice of the peace, although his gambling (sometimes on the bench even while court was in session) and his violent temper brought him into occasional conflict with his fellow justices.

Bowyer eventually acquired a substantial amount of land near the James River in the southern part of Augusta County. He was sheriff of the county when the area in which he lived was carved off to form the new county of Botetourt at the end of 1769, and he was immediately appointed a justice of the peace for the new county. Bowyer represented Botetourt in the House of Burgesses from 1770 until 1776 and sat in all five of the Revolutionary Conventions. As a member of the Convention of 1776, which unanimously voted for independence and adopted the Virginia Declaration of Rights, he served on the large and distinguished committee that reported the draft declaration and the first constitution of the commonwealth. Bowyer also served in the House of Delegates in 1776 and 1777, and following the formation of the new county of Rockbridge in 1778 he represented it in that year and again in 1782, 1784–1786, 1789–1796, and 1799–1802. He served at different times on the Committees of Courts of Justice, Privileges and Elections, Propositions and Grievances, and Public Claims. Because of alterations in county lines, Bowyer held important positions in three counties without moving.

Bowyer was the first presiding justice of the Rockbridge County Court, served as county lieutenant throughout the 1780s, and in 1780 became Rockbridge's second sheriff. In January 1781 when the British invaded Virginia, he marched more than 200 men down to the Tidewater, but he returned home in April and was not, as has been asserted, the Colonel Bowyer reportedly wounded and captured at Jamestown early in July 1781. Bowyer was a member of the board of trustees of Liberty Hall Academy, which later became Washington and Lee University, when it received its first charter in 1782.

On 12 August 1784, after the death on an unknown date of his first wife, he married Mary Baker in a Presbyterian ceremony in Botetourt County. Bowyer is not known to have had any children with either wife.

When the state militia was reorganized in 1792, Bowyer was appointed brigadier general of the 13th Brigade. References to him thereafter as General Bowyer usually distinguish him from his namesake nephew and principal heir, who was a well-known attorney in Augusta and Rockbridge Counties. The following year Bowyer began construction of Thorn Hill, a large brick residence of Georgian design with fine interior detailing, on his property near Lexington. He served as a presidential elector in 1792, sat on the Republican committee in Rockbridge County early in 1800, and was chosen in December of that year as a presidential elector for Thomas Jefferson. Bowyer was too feeble to attend court by 1804. When he wrote his will on 7 May 1804 he owned three tracts of land totaling about 1,325 acres in Rockbridge County. After his second wife died he added a codicil to his will on 9 November 1805. John Bowyer died at his home on 24 April 1806 and was buried in Lexington.

Brief and incomplete biographies in *Washington and Lee University Historical Papers* 2 (1890): 68–70, Joseph A. Waddell, *Annals of Augusta County, Virginia, From 1726 to 1871,* 2d ed. (1902), 180, and Maryetta Frances Bowyer, *The Bowyers of Old Virginia, 1607–1979* (1979), 48–54; published genealogies contain errors and differ irreconcilably; family connections and land acquisitions detailed in Augusta Co. records, some of which are abstracted in Lyman Chalkley, ed., *Chronicles of the Scotch-Irish Settlement in Virginia* (1912–1913); John T. Vogt and T. William Kethley Jr., eds., *Augusta County Marriages, 1748–1850* (1986), 46; Botetourt Co. Marriage Register; variant date of second marriage as 14 Aug. 1784 in John T. Vogt and T. William Kethley Jr., eds., *Botetourt County Marriages, 1770–1853* [1987], 1:53; Royster Lyle Jr. and Pamela H. Simpson, *Architecture of Historic Lexington* (1977), 122–125; Rockbridge County Will Book, 3:3–5; death notice in *Richmond Virginia Argus,* 29 Apr. 1806.

ROYSTER LYLE JR.

BOXLEY, George (ca. 1780–5 October 1865), antislavery leader, was born in Spotsylvania County, the son of a farmer, Thomas Boxley. Very little is known about his family and early life. He farmed for a time, operated a general store, and owned a tannery in Fredericksburg. On 27 March 1805 he married Hannah Jenkins. They had at least seven children, perhaps as many as eleven. He paid taxes on from three to eight slaves between 1801 and 1816, but in the latter year he was described as being in "desperate circumstances."

Boxley served as an ensign in the militia during the War of 1812. By some accounts he was passed over for promotion, and he reportedly also had political ambitions thwarted when he was forced to defer to a member of a more prominent family. During the second half of 1815 Boxley began to conspire against slavery. Few observers agreed about his motivations or even his deeds. Some people assumed that Boxley acted out of resentment for past slights, some that he had become an abolitionist, some that he had become demented, and some that religious delusions motivated him. He allegedly told people that God had spoken to him through a white bird and convinced him of the evils of slavery. Boxley spoke out against slavery and attempted to organize African Americans in Spotsylvania and the neighboring parts of Louisa and Orange Counties. He may have been trying either to help slaves flee Virginia or to mount an armed campaign to free them, but before anything took place his activities were exposed by a female slave. Boxley turned himself in on 27 February 1816 and was charged with fomenting an insurrection.

At least twenty-seven slaves were arrested and charged with complicity in Boxley's alleged uprising. In the largest prosecution for insurrection in Virginia between the discovery of Gabriel's conspiracy in 1800 and Nat Turner's rebellion in 1831, five slaves were executed, and six others were sentenced to be transported out of Virginia. Boxley was ordered tried for capital felony and stealing two slaves, but while he was awaiting trial his wife smuggled him a file with which he sawed his way out of the Spotsylvania County jail and escaped.

On 13 November 1816 Boxley executed a power of attorney in Washington County, Pennsylvania, that enabled him to sell his two tracts of Spotsylvania County land totaling 460 acres. During the next several years he moved from place to place in Ohio, Illinois, and Indiana. In

1818 the superior court in Spotsylvania County outlawed Boxley after he again failed to appear for trial, and on several occasions bounty hunters attempted to capture him and return him to Virginia. One took him prisoner, but Boxley's friends rescued and released him.

In 1828 Boxley built a cabin north of Indianapolis, Indiana. A nearby town was called Boxleytown and later Boxley. He continued to speak out against slavery and also denounced banks, taxes, courts, and government generally. He may have assisted people escaping from slavery, and his zeal made him appear to fit the stereotype of the wild-eyed radical abolitionist, but he also taught at one of the first schools in Hamilton County, Indiana. George Boxley died at his home on 5 October 1865, two months before the ratification of the Thirteenth Amendment made slavery illegal anywhere in the United States. He was buried in Boxley.

Census, Spotsylvania Co., 1810, and Hamilton Co., Ind., 1850 (gives age as seventy); Jeremiah Chandler Marriage Register, Baptist Church Records, LVA; William H. B. Thomas, "'Poor Deluded Wretches!' The Slave Insurrection of 1816," *Louisa County Historical Magazine* 6 (1974): 57–63; Philip J. Schwarz, *Twice Condemned: Slaves and the Criminal Laws of Virginia, 1705–1865* (1988), 271–272, 329–330; Schwarz, *Migrants against Slavery: Virginians and the Nation* (2001), 85–101; Louisa Co. Minute Book (1815–1818), 38–39; Spotsylvania Co. Minute Book (1815–1819), 52–53, 70–71; Spotsylvania Co. Superior Court Law Orders, G:235; *Richmond Enquirer*, 13 Mar. 1816; Edward Herndon to James Frazer, 5 Apr. 1816, Felix G. Hansford Papers, WVU; trial records and correspondence, 1816, and letters from bounty hunters, 4, 29 Mar., 2 Aug. 1819, 10 Aug. 1826, 30 Mar. 1827, 4 Sept. 1831, Governor's Office, Letters Received, RG 3, LVA (quotation in Waller Holladay and James M. Bell to Wilson Cary Nicholas, 25 Feb. 1816); Spotsylvania Co. Deed Book, V:14–16; Thomas B. Helm, *History of Hamilton County, Indiana* (1880), 103–104; Augustus Finch Shirts, *A History of the Formation, Settlement, and Development of Hamilton County, Indiana* (1901), 164–167; John F. Haines, *History of Hamilton County, Indiana* (1915), 146–151, 257–258, 973–974; Frank S. Campbell, *The Story of Hamilton County, Indiana* (1962), 130–135; death date on gravestone.

PHILIP J. SCHWARZ

BOXLEY, William Wise (17 July 1861– 12 January 1940), contractor and mayor of Roanoke, was born in Louisa County, the son of James Boxley, a planter, and Sallie Ann Lipscomb Boxley. He attended the county schools and worked on his father's plantation, which was badly damaged in the Civil War. As a young man Boxley began working with a mule-drawn cart and a shovel for his distant relative James C. Carpenter, a railroad contractor and fellow Louisa County native. Boxley soon rose to foreman and later to superintendent, and in 1890 he became Carpenter's partner in constructing the Neuse River Railroad, later part of the Southern Railway System, in North Carolina.

On 18 December 1884 Boxley married Fannie Fife Haley, of Louisa County. They had two sons and moved several times when the firm began new construction projects. Boxley and Carpenter built sections of rail lines for the Norfolk and Western, the New York Central, the Baltimore and Ohio, the Richmond, Fredericksburg and Potomac, the Virginian, and the Chesapeake and Ohio railroads. The firm's notable achievements included constructing the Little Bend Tunnel for the C&O near Hinton, West Virginia, and a headquarters building with the first elevator in Clifton Forge.

In 1893 Boxley's wife and younger son drowned in an accident, probably near one of Boxley's construction sites on the New River near Hinton. On 10 February 1903 he married another Louisa County native, Willie Maria Saunders, in Richmond. They had one son and two daughters. In 1906 Boxley moved to Roanoke and built a large house there. His partnership with Carpenter grew and won contracts for more than 100 miles of railroad construction valued in 1906 at more than $3.6 million. They concentrated on straightening and double-tracking main-line railroads. After Carpenter's death in 1910, Boxley bought his share of the firm. W. W. Boxley and Company participated in construction of a section of the New York City subway system in Brooklyn and sections of the Croton and Catskill aqueducts that carried water forty miles from the Catskill Mountains to New York City. In 1912 Boxley won a contract to provide 2,500 tons of rock ballast for railroad construction daily for six months. To meet the demand the firm opened four rock quarries in Botetourt, Giles, and Tazewell Counties between 1908 and 1917.

Known to his acquaintances as Captain Boxley, he was elected in 1918 on a nonpartisan ticket to a four-year term as the first Roanoke mayor under its new city manager form of government. During his service the council approved the annexation of five suburban neighborhoods and began appropriating funds for the city's first library. Reflecting his own business interests, Boxley also promoted street construction. His term was notable for the acumen and executive ability he brought to the position. Even though a professional city manager was in charge of the city workers, Boxley was more than a titular mayor and spent many hours a day in the mayor's office.

One of Roanoke's wealthier citizens, Boxley earned more than $65,000 in 1915. Reflecting the success of his construction business and his prominence in the city, W. W. Boxley and Company erected the first skyscraper in Roanoke in 1921 and 1922. The eight-story Boxley Building is a granite and brick structure with an imposing facade and an unusually fine top-story ornamented cornice. It dominated the city's skyline and signaled Roanoke's coming of age as a major business center. In the 1930s Boxley began turning over the rock-quarrying operations to his sons. In addition to furnishing the stone for the Boxley Building, the quarries supplied material for the Patrick Henry Hotel, the Memorial Bridge, and other Roanoke structures.

Boxley had a broad range of business and civic interests. He was president of the Roanoke Chamber of Commerce, a founder and vice president of Colonial-American National Bank, an officer and director of Liberty Trust Company, a member of the boards of Roanoke College and the Baptist orphanage in Salem, and a member of the board of Virginia Military Institute from 1924 to 1937 and chairman of its building committee.

William Wise Boxley died on 12 January 1940 at his home in Roanoke after a heart attack and was buried in Evergreen Burial Park in that city.

NCAB, 30:244 (por.); Gertrude Blair, "William Wise Boxley," WPA Biographies; William Couper, *History of the Shenandoah Valley* (1952), 3:472–473; information provided by grandson Frank A. Boxley; nomination form for Boxley Building, May 1983, National Register of Historic Places Inventory, 128-47, Virginia Department of Historic Resources, Richmond; BVS Marriage Register, Louisa Co. and Richmond City; *Richmond News Leader*, 10 Feb. 1903; *W. W. Boxley Company, The First 100 Years* (1985); obituary and editorial tribute in *Roanoke Times*, 13, 14 Jan. 1940.

GEORGE A. KEGLEY

BOYCE, Upton Lawrence (19 October 1830–24 December 1907), railroad executive, was born in Greenup County, Kentucky, the son of William Boyce and Catherine Lawrence Shreve Boyce. About 1856 he moved to Saint Louis, Missouri, where he practiced law and about 1860 married Belinda Frances Wright, the daughter of fellow Saint Louis lawyer Uriel Sebree Wright, a Virginia native. Boyce's sympathies during the Civil War are not certain. Conflicting sources credit him with service in the Confederate forces and in the Union cavalry. In later life he was called Colonel Boyce, but whether this designation was honorific or for military service is not clear. In the summer of 1865 Wright and Boyce moved to Virginia and opened law offices in Berryville and Winchester.

The Boyces had one son before they moved to Virginia and two sons and two daughters afterward. In 1866 Belinda Boyce inherited an interest in the Tuleyries, a fine house and estate in Clarke County. Boyce later bought out the other heirs and made the Tuleyries one of the most elegant and fashionable estates in the county. He hosted English-style house parties when he could afford to do so. After Wright's death in 1869, Boyce shifted his interest from law to investments, and as a result his financial fortunes waxed and waned with the business cycles of the nineteenth century. In addition to spending a large sum on the Tuleyries, he invested in a number of local enterprises, only some of which made money. The failures included a scheme to manufacture and market a smokeless coal-burning stove.

Boyce made his principal contribution to the region as a financier for the Shenandoah Valley Railroad. Pennsylvania promoters proposed it at the end of the 1860s as a line from Hagerstown, Maryland, into the ore- and timber-rich eastern portion of the Shenandoah Valley. The depression that followed the panic of 1873 slowed the sale of stock, and construction was halted before much track was laid. Boyce bought stock in the railroad, persuaded the citizens of Clarke County to invest heavily in it, and according to later accounts ingeniously promoted the railroad at the end of the 1870s. He may have gone to England one or more times to sell securities. Construction resumed in 1879, and by the end of June 1882 the road was in operation from its connection with the Pennsylvania Railroad at Hagerstown to a junction with the Norfolk and Western at Big Lick (later Roanoke), a distance of almost 250 miles. Boyce was the vice president of the Shenandoah Valley Railroad from April 1876 until 1890. With pardonable exaggeration local writers later compared him to James J. Hill, the financial wizard who created the Great Northern Railroad.

Early in 1881 Boyce joined his Philadelphia bankers and other investors in purchasing the assets of the Atlantic, Mississippi, and Ohio Railroad, which had gone into receivership. When they reorganized it into the new Norfolk and Western on 3 May 1881, Boyce was a member of the board of directors, on which he served until 1896. In 1882 the Norfolk and Western purchased a controlling interest in the Shenandoah Valley Railroad, which had not become a financial success. The older company had incurred large debts building its line and purchasing locomotives and rolling stock. It also faced competition from the Baltimore and Ohio and from the Chesapeake and Ohio, and the mineral deposits that the original promoters had hoped to tap were not rapidly developed. The Shenandoah Valley Railroad went into receivership at the end of March 1885, and after its creditors foreclosed the Norfolk and Western purchased the road on 1 October 1890 and incorporated it into its rapidly expanding network of freight and passenger service.

The town of Boyce in Clarke County began as a country station on the Shenandoah Valley Railroad line and is named for him. Late in the 1890s Boyce suffered a stroke that partially paralyzed him and impaired his eyesight. Following his wife's death on 31 October 1902, he sold the Tuleyries and went to live with his sons on their farm near Stanton, New Castle County, Delaware. Upton Lawrence Boyce died there on 24 December 1907 and was buried in Old Chapel Cemetery in Clarke County.

Birth date in notes on the Tuleyries in Richard E. Griffith Papers, Clarke Co. Historical Association Collection (LVA microfilm); marriage date surmised from Census, Clarke Co., 1900; Richard E. Griffith, "Early Estates of Clarke County," *Proceedings of the Clarke County Historical Association* 11/12 (1951/1953): 60–62; Stuart E. Brown Jr., *Annals of Clarke County, Virginia* (1983–1987), 1:151–154, 2:115–116; *Corporate History, Shenandoah Valley Railway Company* [ca. 1891]; Norfolk and Western annual reports, 1881–1896; Richard E. Prince, *Norfolk and Western Railway* (1980), 55–59; Mason Y. Cooper, *Norfolk and Western's Shenandoah Valley Line* (1998), 15–17, 27 (por.), 31–32, 55; obituaries of wife, with some inaccuracies, in *Winchester Evening Star*, 31 Oct. 1902, and *Berryville Clarke Courier*, 5 Nov. 1902; obituaries in *Winchester Evening Star*, 26 Dec. 1907, and *Berryville Clarke Courier*, 1 Jan. 1908.

BRENT TARTER

BOYD, Andrew Hunter Holmes (4 June 1814–16 December 1865), Presbyterian minister, was born in Berkeley County, the son of Elisha Boyd, a prominent attorney and member of the Convention of 1829–1830, and his second wife, Ann "Nancy" Holmes Boyd. He was named for his great-uncle Andrew Hunter Holmes, a Presbyterian minister. Boyd was educated at Martinsburg Academy and received an A.B. in 1830 from Jefferson College (later Washington and Jefferson College) in Canonsburg, Pennsylvania. He studied under Nathaniel William Taylor at Yale Divinity School from 1830 to 1832, at Princeton Theological Seminary from 1833 to 1836, and in Scotland at the University of Edinburgh in 1837. Boyd returned to Virginia and married Eleanor Frances Williams on 11 January 1838. They had three sons.

On 30 September 1837 the Winchester Presbytery licensed Boyd to preach and ordained him on 20 April 1839. He served short terms as the stated supply of Presbyterian congregations in Leesburg, at Middleburg in Loudoun County, at Cook's Creek in Rockingham County, and in Harrisonburg until March 1842, when he moved to Winchester as pastor of the Loudoun Street Presbyterian Church. Doubling as minister at nearby Opequon Church until 1850, Boyd regularly preached three times every Sunday during much of his time in Winchester. From 1850 until his death he also served as stated supply at

Opequon. In 1853 Delaware College (later the University of Delaware) in Newark awarded him a D.D.

As a former pupil of Taylor, Boyd was one of the minority of Virginia Presbyterian clergymen to align themselves with the so-called New School Presbyterians, who differed from their Old School brethren on some questions of church governance, more readily embraced the evangelical movement, and endorsed a milder form of Calvinism. Loudoun Street was a newly formed New School congregation when Boyd became its pastor, and during the remainder of the antebellum period he was widely recognized as one of the leading New School ministers in Virginia. During the 1850s many northern New School Presbyterians became so critical of slavery that in 1857 Boyd joined other regional New School ministers in forming the United Synod of the Presbyterian Church in the U.S.A., a separate southern church.

Boyd defended the institution of slavery without apology. His *Thanksgiving Sermon, Delivered in Winchester, Va., on Thursday, 29th November, 1860* (1860) accorded full responsibility for divisive sectionalism to Northern opponents of slavery. At that time Boyd earnestly espoused the cause of the Union, but after Virginia seceded he was equally vocal in his opposition to the Union army, which occupied Winchester several times. Between 1862 and 1864 he was arrested several times for refusing to take the oath of allegiance to the United States, for defiance of Union authority, or to serve as hostage to guarantee the good behavior of Winchester's citizens and was imprisoned for months in Wheeling and at Fort McHenry in Maryland. His health irretrievably damaged by the experience, Andrew Hunter Holmes Boyd died at his home in Winchester on 16 December 1865 and was buried in Mount Hebron Cemetery in that town.

Joseph Clay Stiles, *Address on the Life and Death of Rev. A. H. H. Boyd, D.D., of Winchester, Va.* (1866); Quarles, *Worthy Lives,* 42–43 (por.); family records in possession of Robert L. Boyd, 1992; Shenandoah Co. Marriage Register; Robert Bell Woodworth, Clifford Duval Grim, and Ronald S. Wilson, *A History of the Presbyterian Church in Winchester, Virginia, 1780–1949* (1950), 113–115; death date from gravestone; death notice in *Winchester Journal,* 22 Dec. 1865 (variant death date of 15 Dec. 1865).

R. STANLEY HARSH

BOYD, Charles Rufus (30 or 31 October 1841– 16 April 1903), geologist, was born in Wytheville, the son of Thomas Jefferson Boyd and Minerva Ann French Boyd. He studied at home and at a military academy in Wytheville. Boyd may have developed his early interest in surveying and geography through the influence of his father, who speculated in land and promoted mining and railroads in southwestern Virginia in addition to serving in the House of Delegates from 1848 to 1853 and on the Virginia Board of Public Works from 1853 to 1859, as president after 1857. In his youth Boyd worked as an assistant engineer on the Covington and Ohio Railroad and then served on the Virginia and Kentucky Railroad under Claudius Crozet, the noted state engineer who was a leader in Virginia's internal improvement programs.

Boyd enlisted as a private in the 4th Regiment Virginia Infantry on 24 April 1861 and took part in the First Battle of Manassas (Bull Run). On 30 July 1861 he was detached to engineer duty as a second lieutenant in the Volunteer Forces of Virginia, in which capacity he helped build defensive works around Richmond. On 1 May 1862 Boyd enlisted in the 30th Battalion Virginia Sharp Shooters and was elected second lieutenant on 16 July. He resigned on 5 May 1864 to accept his appointment of 30 April as second lieutenant of engineers, assigned to the 3d Regiment of Engineers, Confederate States Army. Boyd served to the end of the war and won promotion to first lieutenant of engineers on 5 January 1865, with his commission to date from 19 October 1864.

A dearth of business opportunities in Wytheville in 1865 caused Boyd to follow his elder brother David French Boyd to Louisiana after the war. On 22 April 1868 Boyd married Sallie Stafford. They had two sons and two daughters. His brother remained in Louisiana and became a noted educator considered the founder of Louisiana State University, but Boyd could not get settled in business in Baton Rouge and returned to Virginia in 1871. In 1873 he matriculated at the University of Virginia, where he took classes in Latin, Greek, mathematics, chemistry, and mineralogy and geology. Boyd's instructors included Francis Henry Smith, a student of the director of the first geological survey of Virginia, William Barton Rogers. In 1874 the university certified Boyd as proficient in mineralogy and geology.

From 1874 until his death Boyd resided in Wytheville and worked as a consultant throughout southwestern Virginia and western North Carolina, surveying and evaluating mineral claims and consulting for state agencies and railroad officials. He was a stockholder and director of the Boyd Land Company of Wytheville. With a deep interest in the economic aspects of geology, Boyd encouraged the development of Virginia's economic resources, especially those located in his part of the state. In 1881 he published his most important treatise, *Resources of South-West Virginia*, a lengthy work that included data on the mineral resources of western North Carolina. Boyd also sought to attract development to his region by publishing several maps, the most important being *South West Virginia and Contiguous Territory: Mineral Resources and Railway Facilities* (1886, revised 1891, 1903). He emphasized the importance of railroads in marketing and contended that the resources of southwestern Virginia had helped the state pay its debts after the Civil War.

Boyd represented Virginia's interests at home and abroad by serving as commissioner from Virginia to expositions at Philadelphia in 1876, Paris in 1878, and New Orleans in 1884. He attended meetings of the British Association for the Advancement of Science in 1888 and the International Congress of Geologists in 1891 and served on the general committee for the reception and entertainment of the British Iron and Steel Institute when its members visited the United States in the autumn of 1890. Boyd belonged to the American Institute of Mining Engineers, the American Society of Civil Engineers, the Franklin Institute of Pennsylvania, and the Association of Engineers of Virginia, of which he was second vice president in 1891.

Boyd often spoke and wrote in behalf of southwestern Virginia, and he called unsuccessfully for improving dissemination of information on Virginia's geological resources by reestablishing the state's geological survey. His writings drew on his highly regarded library on geology and southwestern Virginia resources and evinced a thorough knowledge and understanding of his state's political and economic history as well as its geological and mineral resources. Boyd reportedly left behind many incomplete maps and unpublished reports, but if they have survived their location is unknown. Active in both civic and educational activities in Wytheville, he was esteemed as a scholar and a man of strong professional ethics who placed local interests above his own.

Charles Rufus Boyd died in Rockfish in Nelson County on 16 April 1903, after suffering what was probably a stroke, incurred while gathering geological specimens intended for exhibition at the Louisiana Purchase Exposition in Saint Louis. He was buried in East End Cemetery in Wytheville.

Birth date of 31 Oct. 1841 and material probably supplied by Boyd in *South-West Virginia and the Valley, Historical and Biographical* (1892), 283–285; birth date of 30 Oct. 1841 in French Biographies and in Boyd Family Genealogical Scrapbook, Leroy Stafford Boyd Papers, Louisiana State University, Baton Rouge; some Boyd letters at LSU and VHS; Compiled Service Records; Joseph K. Roberts, "Contributions of Virginians to the Geology of the State," *Virginia Journal of Science* 1 (1940): 75; Roberts, *Annotated Geological Bibliography of Virginia* (1942), 50–52, 117–121; obituary in *Roanoke Evening News*, 17 Apr. 1903.

MARIANNE M. McKEE

BOYD, Elisha (6 October 1769–21 October 1841), member of the Convention of 1829–1830, was born in Frederick County, the son of John Boyd and Sarah Griffith (or Gryfith) Boyd. He attended Liberty Hall Academy (later Washington and Lee University) and studied law under Philip Pendleton before beginning a legal practice in Berkeley County in the 1790s. In 1795 he married Mary Waggoner, and they had one daughter. Boyd wed Ann "Nancy" Holmes in 1806. Their two sons and two daughters included Andrew Hunter Holmes Boyd, who became a prominent Presbyterian clergyman in Winchester, and Mary Boyd Faulkner, whose husband, Charles James Faulkner, served in the House of Representatives. Ann Boyd died on

20 July 1819, and Boyd then married Elizabeth Byrd, who died childless on 16 November 1839.

Boyd became one of the most successful attorneys and prominent men in Berkeley County. He acquired thousands of acres in western Virginia, and after he moved into Martinsburg early in the nineteenth century he built Boydville, then the finest residence in the town. Boyd also had a long career in public office. He became commonwealth's attorney of Berkeley County in 1798, and during the British invasion in the summer of 1814 he served in Tidewater Virginia as a lieutenant colonel of militia. On 8 January 1825 the General Assembly elected him brigadier general of the 16th Brigade Virginia Militia, after which he was referred to as General Boyd.

Boyd represented Berkeley County for five terms in the House of Delegates during assemblies that met from 1795 to 1798, 1804 to 1805, and 1813 to 1814, sat for the district comprising Berkeley, Hampshire, Hardy, and Morgan Counties in the Senate of Virginia from 1823 through 1827, and returned to the House for two more terms from 1828 to 1830. He served another term in the Senate from 1830 to 1833, representing Berkeley, Hampshire, and Morgan Counties, and he sat for Berkeley County in the House of Delegates for a final term from 1836 to 1837. During his legislative service Boyd tended to be assigned to important committees, including those on Claims, Courts of Justice, Finance, Internal Improvements, and Propositions and Grievances. He was chair of the Senate Committees on Claims and on General Laws in the 1826–1827 session, during his final three Senate sessions he chaired the former committee and was ranking member of the latter, and in his last year as a senator he was also chairman of the Committee on Privileges and Elections.

Politically Boyd began as a Federalist and ended as a Whig. As early as 1798 he supported calls for a state constitutional convention, and on 15 March 1827 he persuaded the grand jury of Berkeley County to issue a long presentment against the General Assembly for failing to call one. Boyd was one of four men elected in May 1829 to represent the counties of Berkeley, Hampshire, Hardy, and Morgan in a constitu-

tional convention that met from October 1829 to January 1830. He served on the Committee on the Judicial Department and favored most of the reforms that the delegates debated, which included extending the franchise to all adult white men, democratizing the county court system, abolishing the Council of State, choosing the governor by popular election, and reapportioning seats in the General Assembly to give the western counties more representation. Because the convention agreed to only a few modest reforms, on 14 January 1830 Boyd voted against the constitution as it was submitted to the electorate and approved later that year.

Elisha Boyd died at his home in Martinsburg on 21 October 1841 and was buried in the family graveyard adjoining Norborne Cemetery in that town.

F. Vernon Aler, *Aler's History of Martinsburg and Berkeley County, West Virginia* (1888), 185–188; French Biographies; Boyd letters in Faulkner Family Papers, VHS; Land Tax Lists, Berkeley Co. and Morgan Co., 1841, West Virginia State Auditor's Office, LVA; *Richmond Constitutional Whig*, 27 Mar. 1827; *Richmond Enquirer*, 29 May 1829; Bruce, *Rhetoric of Conservatism*, 37; Catlin, *Convention of 1829–30* (por.); death date on gravestone and in Aler and French Biographies; obituary with variant death date of 24 Oct. 1841 in *Charlestown Virginia Free Press*, 28 Oct. 1841.

Don C. Wood

BOYD, Maria Isabella "Belle" (9 May 1844– 11 June 1900), Confederate spy, was born in Martinsburg, the daughter of Benjamin Reed Boyd and Mary Rebecca Glenn Boyd. Her father owned and operated a store. Both of her parents were from prosperous and socially prominent Virginia families, and the Boyds possessed several slaves. Belle Boyd developed a reputation early for energy and assertiveness. At age twelve she entered Mount Washington Female College near Baltimore, where she pursued an academic curriculum that placed special emphasis on languages and literature. Following her education Boyd spent the winter of 1860–1861 as a Washington debutante in a season that was, she later reported, "pre-eminently brilliant" despite, or perhaps because of, the atmosphere of intense political crisis in the capital. She undoubtedly met some of the most eminent political and military figures of the day, acquaintanceships that she later turned to her advantage.

After Virginia seceded and Boyd's father joined the Confederate army, she returned to Martinsburg and witnessed its occupation by the United States Army early in July 1861. She was active in the Confederate cause from the outset and soon volunteered to nurse sick and wounded Southern soldiers. On 4 July 1861 Union soldiers confronted Boyd and her mother after being told that the younger woman had decorated her room with rebel flags. When the men moved to raise a Union banner over the house, Boyd's mother objected. One of the soldiers responded with a curse, and Belle Boyd drew a hidden pistol and wounded him mortally. An investigation exonerated her, but the incident seems to have emboldened her to work systematically against the Union. Northern soldiers soon intercepted a message containing information about troop positions that she had obtained conversing with soldiers sent to monitor her movements. Boyd was excused with a severe reprimand, but her parents removed her to the care of an aunt and uncle in Front Royal.

While continuing her nursing efforts, Boyd remained eager to undertake further intelligence work. In October 1861 she became a courier for Confederate generals Thomas J. "Stonewall" Jackson and Pierre G. T. Beauregard, often transmitting to them information from their subordinate, Colonel Turner Ashby. After 23 March 1862 Northern officials detained Boyd for a week, but she was freed in time to make what she regarded as her most significant contribution to the Southern cause. After the Union army took Front Royal in May 1862, she was in excellent position to gain significant information from the occupying troops. Boyd subsequently recalled spying on a gathering of Northern officers through a hole in a closet floor and then riding fifteen miles by night to report her findings to Ashby. Later in the same month she urged Jackson's advancing troops to hurry their attack on Front Royal so as to seize the town before Union forces destroyed its supply depots and transportation lines. By then Boyd was becoming a celebrity, and newspapers both North and South described the young woman waving her sunbonnet to cheer on Confederate troops amid a hail of bullets.

Union officials had learned to regret their earlier leniency, and when opportunity presented itself late in July 1862 they seized Boyd and sent her to the Old Capitol Prison in Washington. She was treated well during a month of incarceration and evidently enthralled the superintendent, who, believing that she was engaged to be married, was said later to have sent her a wedding trousseau across the Confederate lines. Released in a prisoner exchange late in August, Boyd was sent to Richmond. By then a thoroughly public figure, she enjoyed fame and admiration during travel throughout the South in the autumn and winter of 1862–1863. Jackson reportedly affirmed her status by appointing her an honorary aide-de-camp with the rank of captain.

When Boyd returned home to Martinsburg late in the summer of 1863, the town had become part of the state of West Virginia, and she was again arrested. This time her imprisonment in Washington lasted longer, but in December 1863 she was banished to the South. Boyd left for England carrying Confederate dispatches in May 1864, but her ship was stopped on the 10th of that month. Once again she captivated her captors, escaped punishment, and made her way first to Canada and then to England, where on 25 August 1864 she married Samuel Hardinge Jr., the Union naval officer who had seized her ship. Almost immediately after the marriage Hardinge returned to the United States, perhaps hoping to clear his name of the suspicions of treason attendant on the escape from his custody of and his subsequent marriage to a Confederate agent. He was imprisoned and apparently died sometime after his release in February 1865. The end of the Hardinge marriage and, indeed, the end of Hardinge himself are shrouded in mystery, and some have doubted Boyd's assertion that he never rejoined her abroad.

Pregnant with Hardinge's daughter, Boyd remained in England and turned to writing to support herself. In May 1865, with the assistance of George Augustus Sala, an English journalist who had reported the American Civil War for a London newspaper, she published *Belle Boyd in Camp and Prison*. The veracity of this highly dramatic two-volume account of her wartime experiences, and of Boyd's exploits more generally, have often been challenged, but following a careful examination of Boyd's text Louis A. Sigaud was able in 1944 to confirm its fundamental accuracy using notes taken from Boyd's papers and corroborating statements from respected contemporaries, chiefly Union and Confederate military figures. *Belle Boyd in Camp and Prison* appeared in a one-volume edition in New York later in 1865 and was reprinted in 1867, 1968, and 1998.

In 1866 Boyd took up acting, first in England and then in the United States after her return to her native country a year later. On 17 March 1869 she married John Swainston Hammond, an English-born businessman who had served in the Union army. They had two sons and two daughters before divorcing in Texas on 1 November 1884. On 9 January 1885 she married Nathaniel Rue High, a young actor from Toledo, Ohio. Boyd's all-but-unbelievable adventures became the basis for her postwar livelihood, and she began touring the country speaking on her wartime experiences. Her popular lectures promoted sectional reconciliation but also inspired imitation, and she occasionally had to identify herself as the real Belle Boyd. Her veracity often challenged and her character at times assailed, she nevertheless supported herself with her lectures about her Civil War exploits. Maria Isabella Boyd Hardinge Hammond High—Belle Boyd to everyone who knew her story—died of a heart attack on 11 June 1900 in Kilbourn City (later Wisconsin Dells), Columbia County, Wisconsin, where she had gone to perform before an audience of members of the Grand Army of the Republic. She was buried in Kilbourn (later Spring Grove) Cemetery.

Louis A. Sigaud, *Belle Boyd, Confederate Spy* (1944), pors. opp. vii; *Belle Boyd in Camp and Prison*, ed. with extensive introduction by Curtis Carroll Davis (1968), quotation on 120; Ruth Scarborough, *Belle Boyd, Siren of the South* (1983); Mary Elizabeth Massey, *Bonnet Brigades* (1966), 96–98, 184; Louis A. Sigaud Papers, Blennerhassett Island Historical State Park, Parkersburg, W.Va.; *OR*, ser. 2, 4:309–310, 349, 461; *Naval OR*, ser. 1, 27:687 (giving Harding as spelling of first husband's name); obituaries in *Milwaukee Journal*, 12 June 1900, and *New York Times*, 13 June 1900.

DREW GILPIN FAUST

BOYD, Thomas Munford (25 September 1899–2 September 1985), attorney and legal educator, was born in Roanoke, the son of James Boyd, an Episcopal minister, and Emma Munford Boyd. At age three he became permanently blind after contracting scarlet fever. His mother encouraged him to surmount his handicap, and Boyd persevered and became the first blind student to complete elementary education in the Roanoke public schools. After his family moved to Richmond, he attended and graduated from John Marshall High School, where he excelled academically and participated in wrestling. In 1920 Boyd took his undergraduate degree from the University of Virginia and entered its law school, where he became associate editor of the *Virginia Law Review*. He received an LL.B. and passed the Virginia bar examination in 1923.

T. Munford Boyd found it difficult to break into the legal profession. He practiced in Charlottesville until 1940 and for a time supplemented his income by writing for the local newspapers. From 1925 to 1930 Boyd served part-time as judge of the Juvenile and Domestic Relations Court. On 10 September 1929 he married Dorothy Leigh Pilkington. They had one son. Boyd worked in Washington, D.C., from 1940 to 1943 on the legal staffs of the Office of Production Management, the National Defense Advisory Commission, and the War Production Board. In 1943 he moved back to Richmond and joined the firm that became Christian, Barton, Parker, and Boyd.

In 1947 Boyd accepted an offer to teach law at the University of Virginia. He taught Virginia procedure, bankruptcy, and professional ethics, among other subjects. Boyd's phenomenal memory, comprehensive knowledge of Virginia law, and sense of humor endeared him to his colleagues and students. In 1957 he received the university's highest faculty honor, the Thomas Jefferson Award. Colleagues joked that Boyd's greatest handicap as a lawyer had been that he knew more about Virginia procedure than the judges before whom he appeared. He served as special counsel to the Virginia Code Commission from 1953 to 1958 and was a consultant on the revision of the procedural statutes in the 1970s. Boyd's principal publications included *Virginia Bar Examinations, Annotated* (1925), (with William W. Koontz) the fourth edition of

Martin Parks Burks's *Common Law and Statutory Pleading and Practice* (1952), and (with Edward S. Graves and Leigh B. Middleditch Jr.) *Virginia Civil Procedure* (1982).

Taking a leave of absence from teaching in 1961, Boyd ran for the Democratic Party nomination for attorney general on a ticket with gubernatorial candidate Allie Edward Stokes Stephens and Boyd's good friend Armistead Lloyd Boothe, running for lieutenant governor. They were not members of the party's inner circle and opposed the hard line against court-ordered desegregation of the public schools that the Democratic leaders had imposed on Virginia. All three candidates lost, and Robert Young Button was instead nominated for attorney general. When Harry Flood Byrd Jr. (b. 1914) ran for reelection to the United States Senate as an independent in 1970, Boyd was his campaign manager in Charlottesville and Albemarle County.

After taking mandatory retirement from teaching at age seventy in 1970, Boyd went back into law practice immediately by joining a Charlottesville firm and serving as counsel for a firm in Norton. A vigorous man to the end of his life, he was respected for his analytical mind and loved for his modesty, dignity, and sharp wit. Boyd's friend and colleague Emerson G. Spies wrote that "his other senses were so acute that his blindness seemed almost an asset." Boyd served on the board of directors of the National Federation of the Blind from 1954 to 1962.

Thomas Munford Boyd died of throat cancer in Charlottesville on 2 September 1985 and was buried in the University of Virginia Cemetery.

Feature articles in *New York Herald Tribune Magazine,* 8 Sept. 1929, *Virginia Law Review* 56 (1970): 731–738, and *Richmond Times-Dispatch,* 30 Oct. 1983; BVS Marriage Register, Charlottesville; information provided by son Thomas Munford Boyd Jr.; *Richmond News Leader,* 8, 21 Apr. 1961; obituaries in *Charlottesville Daily Progress, Richmond News Leader,* and *Richmond Times-Dispatch* (por.), all 4 Sept. 1985; memorial in *Virginia Law School Report* 10 (winter 1985): 31 (quotation).

MARSHA TRIMBLE

BOYD, William Watson (ca. 22 December 1815–8 April 1866), member of the Convention of 1861, was born in Botetourt County, the son of James Boyd and Mary Bryan Boyd. His father

died in 1816, and his mother married Thomas Martin on 19 February 1819. Boyd grew up in Botetourt County and married Jane Caperton Erskine in Greenbrier County on 18 September 1849. They had four sons and four daughters.

On 12 August 1839 Boyd qualified to practice law in Botetourt County and opened an office in Pattonsburg, but he soon moved his office across the James River to the town of Buchanan, which had been established on the property of his father. As an attorney Boyd concentrated on land sales in the western counties and the trusteeship of estates. He was also active in the economic development of the Blue Ridge region of Virginia. In September 1839 he began publishing the *Buchanan Commercial Journal,* a weekly in which he supported the Whig Party and advocated commercial ventures in western Virginia, such as railroad construction and completion of the James River and Kanawha Canal. The newspaper survived for only a year or two, but Boyd became a board member of the James River and Kanawha Company and invested in other businesses and banks. He acquired almost 26,000 acres in and around Botetourt County and several town lots in Buchanan. In 1859 Boyd paid taxes on nine slaves, and he also owned a library of almost 650 volumes, including 310 law books. With his brother he provided land in the 1840s for a Presbyterian church on High Street in Buchanan.

Boyd explained his views on the sectional crisis in a lengthy public letter of 22 December 1860 that appeared in the *Fincastle Valley Sentinel* on 4 January 1861, and he was one of two Unionists elected to represent Botetourt and Craig Counties in the state convention on the secession question that convened in Richmond on 13 February. Three days later he was appointed to the key twenty-one-member Committee on Federal Relations. Boyd did not take an active part in convention deliberations until 21 March, when he introduced a resolution calling for use of the Missouri Compromise line to govern the expansion of slavery into the western territories. He sought support for the resolution up to the moment of its rejection on 13 April. Boyd had voted against secession on 4 April but, like many others, reversed his position on 17 April 1861. During the war he operated an iron furnace in Botetourt County, but he took no other part in the war, perhaps because of ill health. When the Union army occupied Buchanan in the summer of 1864, Boyd's wife convinced him to leave home rather than risk arrest and imprisonment.

Boyd took the amnesty oath on 28 July 1865 and received a presidential pardon two weeks later, actions required of him not as a former Confederate official but rather as a man of some wealth. In October 1865 he was elected to the Senate of Virginia from the district comprising the counties of Alleghany, Bath, Botetourt, and Highland. He served on the Committees on Banks and on Roads and Internal Navigation during the first postwar assembly session, which met from 4 December 1865 to 3 March 1866. William Watson Boyd died at Oak Hill, his home overlooking the town of Buchanan, on 8 April 1866 and was buried in the family cemetery there.

Gravestone gives correct death date but incorrect birth date of 1817; mentioned by name in father's will, Botetourt Co. Will Book, C:60; Norma P. Evans, ed., *Register of the Marriages Celebrated in Greenbrier County, 1781–1849* (1983), 58; recollections of widow in record for Oak Hill, Botetourt Co., in Works Progress Administration, Virginia Historical Inventory, LVA; wealth documented in Land and Personal Property Tax Returns, Botetourt Co., RG 48, LVA; Reese and Gaines, *Proceedings of 1861 Convention*, 1:38, 2:129–130, 3:163–164, 673–674, 680–686, 4:144; Presidential Pardons; estate inventory and sales in Botetourt Co. Will Book, L:183–198, 482–485; death notice and death date in *Lynchburg Daily News*, 16 Apr. 1866.

DAPHNE GENTRY

BŎŸE, Herman (16 November 1792–20 March 1830), cartographer and engineer, was born in Rudkøbing, on the Danish island of Langeland, the son of Christen Nielson Bŏÿe, a merchant and shipowner. Details of his education are not known, but he probably intended to join his father's trading firm. On 14 September 1811 Bŏÿe received a certificate of proficiency in navigation from the Board of Longitude in Copenhagen. He served as a corporal in the Danish military from 1813 to 1814 but was identified as a merchant a year later.

Planning to settle in Philadelphia, Bŏÿe departed from Norway in 1816 and landed early in May at Plymouth, Massachusetts. Within two years he had moved to Virginia, where he worked for about four years as an engrossing clerk in the office of the clerk of the House of Delegates. Having become known to many of the most important men in the state government, Bŏÿe was well placed to take maximum advantage when opportunity came his way. In order to facilitate Virginia's internal improvement program of road and canal construction, the assembly on 27 February 1816 passed "An Act to provide an accurate chart of each county and a general map of the territory of this Commonwealth." Bŏÿe worked as principal assistant to John Wood, who was overseeing the drafting of county maps preparatory to producing a map of the whole state. Following Wood's death Bŏÿe applied to the governor for the vacant position on 15 May 1822, observing that he had actually executed "the graphical part of all the work, done by Mr. Wood for the public on this occasion" and asserting his "perfect competency for the geometrical and astronomical part still unfinished." Isaac Briggs, who was completing the term of the recently deceased principal engineer of the Board of Public Works, endorsed Bŏÿe's application, praised his mathematical skill, and described him as "intelligent and ardent in pursuit of science, yet modest and amiable in his manners." On 22 November 1822 Bŏÿe was awarded the contract to complete Wood's work by finishing maps of two counties and directing the preparation and printing of the state map, which he did using drafting instruments he borrowed from Thomas Jefferson.

The *Map of the State of Virginia Constructed in conformity to Law, from the late Surveys authorized by the Legislature and other original and authentic Documents* was printed in Philadelphia from nine copperplates that engraver Henry S. Tanner executed under Bŏÿe's supervision in 1825 and 1826. It was copyrighted on 14 April 1826, and the first prints were made about that time, but most copies were printed and distributed in 1827. Typical of the state maps of the period, it was very large, approximately 62 by 93 inches, and elaborately and beautifully decorated. On 1 May 1827 the state contracted with Bŏÿe to publish 400 copies of the map and to prepare a smaller version and have it engraved and printed in an edition of 800 copies, all to be completed by 1 December of that year. For this work he was to receive $6,000. The legislation authorizing the publication of the reduced map allocated the proceeds from the sale of 650 of the copies to support the state library (later the Library of Virginia). Bőÿe was also made responsible for transporting the maps and printing plates from Philadelphia to Richmond. Eight of the nine plates for the large map and all four plates for the reduced map are in the Library of Virginia.

The two maps served as the most accurate representations of Virginia until they were updated in 1859 by Ludwig von Buchholtz, who added new roads, new county boundaries, and other details to the original copper printing plates. The revised nine-sheet map was printed by Selmar Seibert, of Washington, D.C.

While in Philadelphia on 18 June 1825, Bőÿe declared his intention to become a naturalized American citizen. After the completion of the Virginia maps, beginning on 28 August 1828 Bőÿe worked on construction of the Chesapeake and Ohio Canal as resident engineer at the site where an aqueduct was being built at the confluence of the Monocacy and Potomac Rivers. Working conditions were conducive to fevers and disease, and during the latter part of 1829 Bőÿe was often ill. He wrote his will on 1 March 1830, naming two Richmond friends as executors and carefully identifying which of his friends were to receive his drafting implements, prints, musical instruments, jewelry, clothing, and papers. Herman Bőÿe died on 20 March 1830, probably in Georgetown, D.C. The next day an undertaker billed his estate $57.75 for supplying a lined mahogany coffin, making funeral arrangements, and digging a grave at an undisclosed location.

Herman Bőÿe Papers, Huntington, including naturalization application giving birth date; a few letters in Coolidge Collection of Thomas Jefferson Manuscripts, Massachusetts Historical Society, Boston, and VM/RHC; letters and contracts printed in *Calendar of Virginia State Papers*, vol. 10; Bőÿe to governor, 15 May 1822 (first quotation), Isaac Briggs to governor, 24 May 1822 (second quotation), and other letters, Governor's Office, Letters Received, RG 3, LVA; Stephenson and McKee, *Virginia in Maps*, 121–123; Chesapeake and Ohio Canal Company, *Annual Report of the President and Directors* (1830); will and estate inventory in Richmond City Hustings Court Will Book, 5:225–226, 310–312, 508–509; death date in Benjamin Wright to Charles Mercer, 20 Mar. 1830, Records of the Chesapeake and Ohio Canal Company, National Park Service, RG 79, NARA.

MARIANNE M. McKEE

BOYKIN, Maury Wood (25 November 1893–11 April 1984), civil engineer, was born at Pocahontas in Tazewell County, the son of Christopher C. Boykin, a druggist, and Florence Gatewood Jeffries Boykin. He grew up and was educated in Norfolk and attended the Virginia Military Institute, from which he received a B.A. in 1917. During World War I he joined the United States Navy in August 1917 and rose from ensign to lieutenant junior grade during service that took him to France and by 1 March 1919 to direction of the naval training unit at the Virginia Agricultural and Mechanical College and Polytechnic Institute.

Boykin returned to Norfolk and worked as a real estate developer. He was teaching history and civics at the city's Maury High School on 1 May 1923, when he published *Plan for Projecting An Atlantic Coastal Trunk Line Railroad Through Norfolk*, a pamphlet containing a detailed plan for a direct railroad link between Norfolk and Hampton. He modeled his plan on the railroad tunnel that had been constructed under the Detroit River in 1910 to link Detroit, Michigan, and Windsor, Ontario. Boykin suggested building causeways north from the end of Willoughby Spit to the Rip Raps and south from Hampton to a spot near Old Point Comfort and connecting the two with a tunnel under the main channel of the James River. He proposed that the tunnel be built from prefabricated steel sections to be buried in a trench dredged in the bed of the river. Boykin calculated that constructing causeways and using the trench tunnel design would cost much less than a tunnel dug underneath the entire width of the river. He estimated that the project could be completed for about $16 million.

Boykin argued that a direct rail link would stimulate the growth of the whole Hampton Roads region by integrating the economies of all the cities, giving Hampton and Newport News a link with southern and western railroads converging on Norfolk, and connecting the city directly to the railroads that already came to Hampton and Newport News from the north and northwest. He believed that the plan would attract Northern Neck commerce away from Baltimore, forge closer ties between Norfolk and the Northeast, and benefit the military during wartime. Calculating costs and benefits in an analysis similar to later urban-planning studies, Boykin sought endorsements for his plan from engineers in the War Department and from the chief engineer of the Detroit railroad tunnel. He also had copies sent to James Aylor Anderson, professor of engineering at VMI, and other notable engineers. Boykin was unable to persuade the state, the localities, and the railways to construct the bridge-tunnel, but in 1928 VMI awarded him an honorary M.A. in recognition of his pioneering design.

After World War II Boykin's scheme was revived as an automobile bridge-tunnel proposed for the same route with much the same design as he had originally suggested. He was recognized as the originator of the concept for the Hampton Roads Bridge-Tunnel, which was constructed between 1954 and 1957, while Anderson was the state commissioner of highways. Boykin also recommended using the same principles to erect a longer bridge-tunnel linking Norfolk to Cape Charles on the Eastern Shore via a route that closely paralleled the one selected by the engineers for the Chesapeake Bay Bridge-Tunnel in the 1960s.

Boykin never married. He worked as a civil engineer for the city of Norfolk from 1929 to 1941. During World War II he served as a major in the chemical warfare department of the United States Army and late in the 1940s was a representative for the Veterans Administration. By 1951 he had returned to engineering and spent about fifteen years with Norfolk's Department of Public Works until he retired in 1966. Maury Wood Boykin died at his home in Norfolk on 11 April 1984 and was buried in Elmwood Cemetery in that city.

Military Service Records; feature articles with pors. in *Norfolk Virginian-Pilot*, 1 May, 21 June, 2 Nov. 1957, *VMI Alumni Review* 51 (fall 1974): 11–13, and *Norfolk Ledger-Star*, 6 Mar. 1976; extensive alumnus file in VMI Archives;

obituaries in *Norfolk Virginian-Pilot*, 14 Apr. 1984, and *VMI Alumni Review* 61 (summer 1984): 66.

MARTIN S. LANE

BOYLE, Sarah Lindsay Patton (9 May 1906– 20 February 1994), writer and civil rights leader, was born in Albemarle County, the daughter of Robert Williams Patton, an Episcopal minister, and Jane Stuart Stringfellow Patton. She was tutored at home but suffered from undiagnosed dyslexia and did not learn to read until she was a teenager. She enrolled in 1926 at the Corcoran School of Art in Washington, D.C., and studied painting there for six years.

On 26 December 1932 Patton married Eldridge Roger Boyle, a speech and drama instructor at the University of Virginia, and moved to Charlottesville. After the birth of the first of her two sons in 1939, she gave up painting to care for her child and concentrate on the freelance writing with which she supplemented the family's income. Boyle was a successful nonfiction writer who published an average of one article a week in popular women's magazines. In spite of a long line of Episcopal clergymen in her family background, she rebelled against Christianity as a young adult and experimented with a variety of religious forms. Late in the 1940s, as her marriage became more difficult, Boyle turned back to Christianity and became a practicing Episcopalian, which she continued for the remainder of her life.

This resurgence of faith in the 1940s anticipated the spiritual awakening Boyle experienced in the summer of 1950 when she learned that the first African American was to be admitted to the University of Virginia's law school. She realized for the first time that segregation was an "enormous injustice," but her draft article welcoming the student, Gregory H. Swanson, to the university community offended him. Seeking to understand how she had given offense, Boyle submitted the draft to Thomas Jerome Sellers, the associate editor in charge of the Charlottesville branch office of the *Tribune*, a weekly African American newspaper headquartered in Roanoke. He criticized her article frankly and constructively, showing Boyle that her condescending tone and endorsement of gradualism in the ending of segregation implied that although the law student might be welcome at the university, other blacks were not. Though Sellers had barely known Boyle, they began a personal dialogue that forced her to change her mind on many matters, and early in the 1950s she began writing and speaking in behalf of immediate integration. Under the nom de plume of "A White Southerner," from about the beginning of 1952 until 31 January 1953 Boyle wrote a weekly feature column for the Charlottesville and Roanoke versions of the *Tribune* in which she sought to explain that, despite objectionable attitudes, typical white southerners were neither hostile to nor contemptuous of African Americans and would renounce segregation when the system's injustices were exposed. She also involved herself directly in the civil rights movement by becoming president in 1954 of the Council for Social Action, a new interracial organization in Charlottesville that worked to secure adequate housing, education, and jobs for all of the city's residents. Boyle began by directing a drive to marshal votes for a fair housing referendum.

Boyle's opinions did not attract much attention in Charlottesville until late in 1954, when she was one of the few white witnesses who appeared before a committee of the General Assembly to denounce efforts to block the desegregation of the state's public schools. She wrote an article entitled "We Are Readier Than We Think" for the *Saturday Evening Post*, intending it to reassure other white southerners that segregation could be ended without animosity. The magazine published it in February 1955 as "Southerners Will *Like* Integration," and with the inflammatory new title it brought Boyle severe criticism. Local segregationists burned a cross in her yard, and few white liberals were willing to join her public stand against discrimination. Very much an idealist, she was prepared neither for her critics' attacks nor for the lack of support from her friends, and she became so depressed that she contemplated suicide.

Despite her depression Boyle continued to campaign tirelessly for civil rights. In 1955 she joined the interracial Virginia Council on Human Relations and stumped across the state for three years as the organization's only field-worker, promoting interracial dialogue, establishing local discussion groups, and evaluating community needs. Boyle organized a local Council on Human Relations in Charlottesville in July 1956 but had withdrawn from active membership in the state council by 1960, criticizing it as a refuge for moderates. She preferred to work with the National Association for the Advancement of Colored People.

Boyle's first book, a spiritual autobiography entitled *The Desegregated Heart: A Virginian's Stand in Time of Transition* (1962), described her change of heart in 1950 and her slow recovery from the disillusionments that came later that decade. The best-selling book earned her a national reputation as a civil rights expert. Boyle was appointed to the Virginia Advisory Committee of the United States Commission on Civil Rights in 1963 and the following year published a second book, *For Human Beings Only: A Primer of Human Understanding* (1964). She took part in a number of marches and nonviolent demonstrations during the 1960s and worked with several interracial organizations, including the Southern Regional Council, the Congress of Racial Equality, and the NAACP. Martin Luther King Jr. commended her writings in behalf of civil rights in *Why We Can't Wait* (1964). Numerous awards for her work included a woman-of-the-year award from the National Council of Negro Women in 1956, the Russwurm Award of the National Newspaper Publishers Association in 1958, citations from the Southern Christian Leadership Conference and the NAACP, and the first Bishop Ireton Award from the Catholic Interracial Council of Richmond in 1963. The emergence of separatist ideologies within the civil rights movement convinced Boyle that her call for Christian brotherhood was no longer relevant, and she retired from the movement in 1967, deeply saddened by, yet with an empathy for, frustrated young African Americans' demands for black power.

The Boyles divorced in 1965, and she moved to Arlington. Her final book, *The Desert Blooms: A Personal Adventure in Growing Old Creatively* (1983), confronted the issue of age discrimination. Having nursed her mother-in-law through terminal cancer in the 1950s and cared for her own aged mother, who died in the 1960s, Boyle in her retirement battled stereotypes associated with age. In her final book, as in all of her writings, she tried to cultivate people's ability to love and understand one another as the best means of eradicating perceived social barriers. She remained active in behalf of equal rights for the elderly and the handicapped for another decade. Sarah Lindsay Patton Boyle died in Arlington on 20 February 1994 and was buried near her birthplace in Albemarle County.

Jennifer Ritterhouse, "A Crisis of Convictions: Sarah Patton Boyle's Desegregated Heart" (master's thesis, UNC, 1994); Ritterhouse, "Speaking of Race: Sarah Patton Boyle and the 'T. J. Sellers Course for Backward Southern Whites,'" in *Sex, Love, Race: Crossing Boundaries in North American History,* ed. Martha Hodes (1999), 491–513; Kathleen Murphy Dierenfield, "One 'Desegregated Heart': Sarah Patton Boyle and the Crusade for Civil Rights in Virginia," *VMHB* 104 (1996): 251–284 (pors.); Joanna Bowen Gillespie, "Sarah Patton Boyle's Desegregated Heart," in *Beyond Image and Convention: Explorations in Southern Women's History*, ed. Janet L. Coryell et al. (1998), 158–183; BVS Marriage Register, Albemarle Co.; Sarah-Patton Boyle Papers, UVA; other letters in Benjamin Muse Papers, UVA, James McBride Dabbs Papers, Southern Historical Collection, UNC, and P. D. East Papers, Boston University Library; oral history interview, 7 Jan. 1994, copy in author's possession; Boyle, *The Desegregated Heart: A Virginian's Stand in Time of Transition* (1962; repr. 2001), quotation on 50; John Egerton, *A Mind to Stay Here: Profiles from the South* (1970), 128–145; feature article in *Richmond News Leader*, 17 Dec. 1980 (por.); obituary in *Charlottesville Daily Progress*, 5 Mar. 1994.

JENNIFER RITTERHOUSE

BOYS, John (fl. 1619–1627), member of the first General Assembly, was a literate gentleman of unknown parentage who may have come from one of several prominent Kentish families. A number of men of that name were born there late in the sixteenth century, and some may have been connected with men of the same name resident in the Netherlands at the same time, but no certain identification has been made. Boys may also have been related to one or more of at least three other contemporaneous Virginia colonists whose surnames, like his, were variously spelled Boys, Boyse, Boise, Boyce, or Boice.

John Boys probably arrived in Virginia aboard the *Guift of God* early in 1619 in company with the original group of settlers sent to Martin's Hundred, located on the north bank of the James River about ten miles downriver from Jamestown and near the later site of Carter's Grove plantation. Martin's Hundred was one of the particular plantations, large settlements owned by and operated for the benefit of specific groups of investors rather than the Virginia Company of London. Boys was one of two men who represented the hundred in the first General Assembly, which met in Jamestown from 30 July to 4 August 1619. He served on the assembly's first committee, appointed to consider reforms in the granting of land. The following November the governor named Boys one of the colony's four official tobacco tasters, charged with assessing quality and recommending prices for the different grades of that product.

His new post may have encouraged Boys to remain in Jamestown, for on 3 April 1620 some of the proprietors of Martin's Hundred complained to the Virginia Company that "one Boyse" had "forsaken their plantation and settled himselfe elsewhere." If he had been absent then, Boys returned to Martin's Hundred and was serving as its warden by the first months of 1621. His responsibilities included accepting and assigning laborers on behalf of influential investors. He may also have erected the first and most substantial palisaded dwelling at the Martin's Hundred site.

Boys survived the devastating Powhatan uprising of 2 March 1622, but Martin's Hundred suffered the most fatalities of any Virginia settlement. Five of his servants were killed, as were Thomas Boys and his child. The wives of John Boys and Thomas Boys, whom the records do not identify by name, were initially identified as killed, but one or both may have been among the approximately twenty women who were captured. The following year one of the captives, identified only as Mistress Boys, was allowed to return to the settlements and plead for the captives' ransom. Whether she was John Boys's wife is unknown.

What happened to John Boys thereafter is not clear. The few survivors at Martin's Hundred were dispersed to other sites, and when William Harwood arrived in the autumn of 1622 as the new commander of a rejuvenated plantation there, Boys may have been reassigned to transatlantic transport duties on behalf of the investors. Perhaps he sailed to England with the fall 1623 tobacco fleet, as his name does not appear on lists of Virginia inhabitants compiled in February 1624 and in 1625.

In April 1624 Boys's name was first on a petition of "poore Planters in Virginia" who had recently arrived in England and wanted the king to reduce the tax on tobacco. An unidentified grouping of them also complained to the Virginia Company's officers about the conduct of the governor and other officials in Jamestown. On 7 April 1625 colonist William Perry informed the governor that Boys and other Virginia planters had recently been in England and there encountered difficulties in getting their tobacco through customs because "the pryse of Tobacco was very lowe."

Boys disappears from extant Virginia records after 1625 except for a brief mention in the 1628 General Court minutes concerning an earlier, undated incident. English documents appear to show that in the summer of 1627 he imported some tobacco from Virginia. The surname survived in Virginia through descendants of Cheyney Boys, whose relationship to John Boys is unknown. Cheyney Boys, along with Luke Boys, also served briefly in the General Assembly.

John Boys was one of many relatively insignificant figures in Virginia's early history who played specific roles in important events for short periods of time and then faded into obscurity, leaving few documents and no descendants to recount their contributions. The date and place of his death are not known.

Kingsbury, *Virginia Company*, 1:331–332 (first quotation), 2:518–522 (second quotation on 519), 3:228–229, 450–451, 4:98, 229; *Minutes of Council and General Court*, 52 (third quotation), 166; Edward Waterhouse, *A Declaration of the State of the Colony and Affaires in Virginia* (1622), 41–42; William J. Van Schreeven and George H. Reese, eds., *Proceedings of the General Assembly of Virginia, July 30–August 4, 1619* (1969), 14–15, 24–25; Smith, *Complete Works*, 2:301–302, 309, 315; Ivor Noël Hume, *Martin's Hundred*, rev. ed. (1991), 340–345; J. Frederick Fausz, "The Missing Women of Martin's Hundred," *American History* 33 (Mar. 1998): 56–60, 62; tobacco importation recorded in PRO E 190/31/1 and E 190/32/8; a will of a John Boyse, dated 7 Aug. 1649 and proved 31 May 1650, was written

preparatory to a voyage from England to Virginia but cannot be linked to the colonist (Prerogative Court of Canterbury, Pembroke 59).

J. FREDERICK FAUSZ
DAPHNE GENTRY

BRACKEN, John (bap. 2 May 1747–15 or 16 July 1818), president of the College of William and Mary, was born probably in Westmorland County, England. On 2 May 1747 he was christened in the town of Winton, parish of Kirkby Stephen, the son of Joseph Bracken and a woman whose name is not recorded in the parish registers. Bracken's youth and education are not well documented. He arrived in Virginia not later than the summer of 1769, probably to tutor the children of one of the merchant families residing in or near Petersburg. In the summer of 1772 Bracken went back to England to be ordained a minister of the Church of England and with an expectation that he would become curate of Raleigh Parish in Amelia County.

On 12 June 1773, soon after Bracken returned to Virginia, the vestry of Bruton Parish in Williamsburg elected him rector. He filled the post until his death forty-five years later. Bracken's first months were filled with controversy because Samuel Henley, one of the professors at the College of William and Mary, had sought the position and complained in the newspapers about Bracken's selection, drawing him into a protracted public debate between factions within the colonial church. In November 1775 Bracken succeeded Thomas Gwatkin as master of the college's grammar school, and on 1 April 1777 he was formally appointed to the post with the rank of professor of humanity. He also took charge of the college's library. Early in September 1776 Bracken married Sarah Burwell, of Carter's Grove. They had one son and two daughters.

Bracken preached the opening sermon at the first convention of the Protestant Episcopal Church in Virginia in 1785. He served as secretary of the second and third conventions and president of the 1789 convention and attended regularly during the 1790s as the clerical delegate from Bruton Parish. Two months after Bracken preached the funeral sermon for Bishop James Madison (1749–1812), he presided over a special Episcopal convention that on 14 May 1812 named him bishop-elect of Virginia to succeed Madison. Several younger delegates objected that Bracken lacked the youth and vigor to revive the languishing church. He declined to be consecrated and resigned on 26 May 1813.

Bracken lost his post at the College of William and Mary when the grammar school was abolished during an institutional reorganization in December 1779. He opposed the concurrent reform of the college and thereby incurred the enmity of Governor Thomas Jefferson and others. Bracken twice sued the college to reclaim his position and salary, but he lost both cases on appeal. In 1780 he opened a school in his house in Williamsburg, and in January 1787 he took charge of a school conducted in the old Capitol. William and Mary's board of visitors revived the grammar school in 1792 and appointed Bracken to the faculty, and in 1793 it granted him a D.D. On 9 March 1812 the board elected Bracken to succeed Madison as the ninth president of the College of William and Mary. The institution was at one of its historic nadirs, and Bracken was no more able to revive the college than the church. He was in poor health, may have had a drinking problem, and was widely regarded as ineffectual. The board requested his resignation, and he complied in June 1814. The college had only thirty-two students when Bracken became president and probably no more than that when he resigned. During his short term the board abolished the grammar school and appointed professors of chemistry, law, mathematics, and natural philosophy, but Bracken may not have contributed anything to these changes.

The prominence and prosperity of his wife's family enabled Bracken to live in some style in Williamsburg, where he acquired several lots. He also purchased plantations in Gloucester and York Counties and the property known as the Secretary's Land in James City County. He held stock in and sat on the board of directors of the Dismal Swamp Land Company, served several years during the 1790s and in 1800 as mayor of Williamsburg, and was president of the board of the Public Hospital in Williamsburg. John Bracken died in Williamsburg on 15 or 16 July 1818 and was buried in the Burwell family cemetery at Carter's Grove in York County.

Rutherfoord Goodwin, "The Reverend John Bracken (1745–1818), Rector of Bruton Parish and President of William and Mary College in Virginia," *Historical Magazine of the Protestant Episcopal Church* 10 (1941): 354–389; christening date, estimated time of immigration, other personal information, and ordination papers in Fulham Palace Papers, 26:91–95, Lambeth Palace Library, Eng.; undated marriage notice in *Williamsburg Virginia Gazette* (Purdie), 13 Sept. 1776; journals of church conventions in Francis L. Hawks, *Contributions to the Ecclesiastical History of the United States of America* (1836–1839), 1: appendix, 4, 12, 18, 26, 89; Susan H. Godson et al., *The College of William and Mary: A History* (1993), 1:169–173, 199–202; obituaries in *Norfolk American Beacon and Commercial Diary*, 22 July 1818 (with 16 July 1818 death date), and *Richmond Enquirer*, 24 July 1818 (with 15 July 1818 death date).

DAPHNE GENTRY

BRADFORD, John (17 April 1747–ca. 21 March 1830), printer and publisher, was born in the portion of Prince William County that in 1759 became Fauquier County, the son of Daniel Bradford and Alice Morgan Bradford. Little is known of his education, but his intelligence and ingenuity later earned him the sobriquets Old Wisdom and the Kentucky Franklin. On 26 February 1770 he married Elizabeth James, of Fauquier County. They had five sons and three daughters.

Bradford traveled to Kentucky about 1779 as deputy surveyor to George May. In 1780 he participated in a campaign against the Indians at Chillicothe and Piqua. Bradford returned to Fauquier County and was commissioned an ensign in the militia in 1781. He had moved to Kentucky permanently by the spring of 1785 and lived on 6,000 acres he had claimed in Fayette County near Lexington.

In 1786 a convention meeting in Kentucky sought to attract a printer to the district to found a newspaper that would promote statehood. After several attempts to secure a printer from the East proved unsuccessful, Bradford volunteered his services, although he had no experience as a printer or publisher. His brother acquired a printing press in Pennsylvania and shipped it and a set of type to Lexington. On 11 August 1787 Bradford produced the first issue of the *Kentucke Gazette*. He changed the paper's name to the *Kentucky Gazette* in March 1789. In addition to articles on both sides of the statehood question, Bradford published international and national news, government documents, and advertisements. Until 1795 his was the only newspaper in central Kentucky.

After statehood was won in 1792, the paper advocated Jeffersonian political philosophy against the Federalists during the remainder of the decade. Although Bradford allowed both sides to speak through the paper, the *Gazette*'s position was obvious. Articles, editorials, and even poetry denounced aristocracy and encouraged unpretentious agrarian values. The *Gazette* praised the French Revolution, played down its excesses, and held Federalist leaders accountable for anti-French, antiwestern, and antidemocratic policies. Bradford was instrumental in forming several Democratic societies and played a significant role in bringing western dissatisfaction to the attention of the government.

Bradford was Kentucky's first official state printer and published the acts of the General Assembly from 1792 to 1798, except in 1796. Three of Bradford's sons became prominent newspaper printers in Kentucky, Louisiana, and Tennessee, and the Bradfords were perhaps the premier family of early nineteenth-century western printers. In 1798 he and his son James Bradford founded a newspaper in Frankfort, the *Guardian of Freedom*. Bradford published the *Kentucky Gazette* until he relinquished it to his son Daniel Bradford in 1805. In addition to newspapers and the other routine work of printers, Bradford published *The Kentucky Almanac* in 1788 and 1794. So that western journalists could share their knowledge, in 1805 he established the Printers and Booksellers Association, of which he was elected president.

For many years Bradford was a trustee of Lexington. He encouraged local improvements and supported an immigration society to entice a better class of people to Lexington with the hope of making it the "Athens of the West." Bradford encouraged a horticultural society, a Kentucky branch of the Society for the Promotion of Useful Knowledge, and the Kentucky Vineyard Association and also helped found a public library and an Episcopal church in Lexington.

Beginning in 1792 he served on the board of Transylvania Seminary and in 1798 was instrumental in creating Transylvania University through a union of the seminary with the Kentucky Academy. Bradford remained on the university's governing board until 1827, for part of the time as chairman. He served in the Kentucky House of Representatives in 1797 and again in 1802.

From 1826 to 1829 Bradford wrote and published sixty-six historical articles in the *Kentucky Gazette* under the title "Notes on Kentucky." The articles were based on his personal knowledge of many of the early settlers and events of Kentucky and earned him a reputation as one of the first historians of the state. John Bradford died at his home in Lexington on or about 21 March 1830. The discovery of a marker bearing his name near the site of Lexington's First Baptist Church suggests that he was buried in the vicinity of that church.

J. Winston Coleman Jr., *John Bradford, Esq., Pioneer Kentucky Printer and Historian* (1950); John E. Kleber et al., eds., *The Kentucky Encyclopedia* (1992), 111–112; Mrs. Philip Wallace [Martha W.] Hiden, "The Bradford Family of Fauquier County, Virginia," *Tyler's Quarterly* 27 (1945): esp. 116–120, gives 17 Apr. 1747 birth date from family Bible records, which agrees with age of eighty-three reported at death, but gives variant 22 Mar. 1830 death date; other accounts, including James Melvin Lee in *Dictionary of American Biography,* 1:557–558, give 6 June 1749 birth date without documentation and variant 20 Mar. 1830 death date; John Bradford Papers and Samuel Mackay Wilson Papers, University of Kentucky, Lexington; Fauquier Co. Marriage Bonds and Ministers Returns; Samuel M. Wilson, "The 'Kentucky Gazette' and John Bradford Its Founder," *Papers of the Bibliographical Society of America* 31 (1937): 102–132; J. Merton England, "Some Early Historians of Western Virginia," *West Virginia History* 14 (1953): 91–107; Richard Miller Hadsell, "John Bradford and His Contributions to the Culture and the Life of Early Lexington and Kentucky," *Register of the Kentucky Historical Society* 62 (1964): 265–277; Daniel A. Yanchisin, "John Bradford, Public Servant," ibid. 68 (1970): 60–69; Herndon J. Evans, *The Newspaper Press in Kentucky* (1976); Leland A. Brown, "The Family of John Bradford," *Kentucky Press* 9 (Sept. 1937): 2, 3, 5; E. Merton Coulter, "The Efforts of the Democratic Societies of the West to Open the Navigation of the Mississippi," *MVHR* 11 (1924): 376–389; "Notes on Kentucky," reprinted in George W. Stipp, ed., *John Bradford's Historical &c Notes on Kentucky from the Western Miscellany* (1932), and Thomas D. Clark, ed., *The Voice of the Frontier: John Bradford's Notes on Kentucky* (1993), frontispiece por.; notice reporting death on 21 Mar. 1830 at age eighty-three in *Lexington Kentucky Reporter*, 24 Mar. 1830;

obituary giving 19 Mar. 1830 death date in *Olive Branch and Danville (Ky.) Advertiser,* 27 Mar. 1830, reprinted in *Lexington Kentucky Gazette,* 2 Apr. 1830.

LINDSEY APPLE

BRADFORD, John Howard (6 October 1881–6 May 1965), director of the budget, was born in Centre, Cherokee County, Alabama, the son of Thomas Bradford, a local probate court judge, and Louisa Wills Bradford, a native of Mecklenburg County. He studied law in his father's office and was admitted to the bar in 1903. From 1904 to 1908 Bradford served as deputy solicitor for Cherokee County. He then moved to Washington, D.C., where from 1908 until 1919 he worked briefly for Alabama congressman John L. Burnett and then as a special agent or officer for a succession of federal agencies, including the Immigration Service, the Tariff Commission, the Department of Commerce and Labor, and the Federal Trade Commission. Having attracted the attention of LeRoy Hodges, who in 1919 helped Governor Westmoreland Davis prepare Virginia's first state budget, Bradford moved to Richmond in April 1919 to work for Hodges as a statistician in the budget office. When Hodges resigned as state budget director in 1924, Governor Elbert Lee Trinkle appointed Bradford acting director of the budget.

Late in February 1926 Governor Harry Flood Byrd (1887–1966) made John H. Bradford's appointment permanent. Thereafter the frugal, hard-working bachelor devoted his life to saving Virginia money. He lived at the Commonwealth Club, took his meals at moderately priced restaurants, worked sixty to eighty hours a week, never missed a day of work, and had no hobbies. Along with such men as Everett Randolph Combs, the state comptroller, and Carlisle Havelock Morrissett, the tax commissioner, Bradford helped institutionalize and protect the lean-budget, low-tax state government that the Virginia Democratic Party promised under Byrd's leadership. Taciturn and usually inflexible, Bradford routinely reduced even the modest funding requests of agency heads.

In February 1939 Governor James Hubert Price enlarged the office of the budget, added to its responsibilities, and placed Rowland A. Egger in charge, relegating Bradford to a minor job.

The effective demotion was one of the last in a series of actions by which Price removed several key Byrd appointees from influential posts, but in 1940 the General Assembly, over Price's objections, created for Bradford the position of legislative director of the budget. At the end of January 1942, shortly after becoming governor, Colgate Whitehead Darden Jr. reappointed Bradford director of the budget and also made him head of the state personnel system, so that he could keep a close watch on salaries. Bradford administered the personnel system until 1948, when a separate office was established. On compensating public employees he reportedly said, "Get 'em as low as you can and keep 'em as long as you can."

Bradford was often addressed as Judge or Colonel, even though he never held any judicial or military office. His decisions did not always make him popular with legislators or state employees. Although he was once dubbed the "most cussed" man in Virginia, every governor from Harry Byrd to James Lindsay Almond (including even Price) praised Bradford's work. By 1950 his penny-pinching had produced a fund of unexpended state money that was estimated at more than $59 million. An admirer once observed that "compared to Mr. Bradford, Harry Byrd is a spendthrift."

John Howard Bradford retired at the end of July 1958 and moved back to Centre. He died there, after suffering a fall on a visit to Richmond, on 6 May 1965 and was buried in his hometown at Centre Cemetery.

Feature articles in *Richmond Times-Dispatch,* 29 Jan. 1950, 3 July, 3 Aug. 1958 (third quotation), *Commonwealth* 21 (Feb. 1954): 25–27 (por.), and *Richmond News Leader,* 27 June 1958 (second quotation); other information, including an Associated Press biographical sheet (1939), furnished by James H. Latimer; obituaries in *Richmond News Leader* (first quotation) and *Richmond Times-Dispatch,* both 7 May 1965; editorial tribute in *Richmond News Leader,* 7 May 1965.

BRENT TARTER

BRADSHAW, Booker Talmadge (26 February 1904–29 December 1984), businessman and civic leader, was born in Saint Louis, Missouri, the son of Marion H. Bradshaw, a Pullman car porter, and Priscilla Brannon Bradshaw, a teacher. He completed his grammar and high school education in Saint Louis and began his college education at the University of Illinois, where he supported himself with such odd jobs as pressing clothes, waiting tables, clerking in a store, and working in a packinghouse. In 1925 he moved to Richmond to work with his brother William Tecumseh Bradshaw, who was an agent for the Atlanta-based Standard Life Insurance Company, but he returned to Illinois to complete his education and received a B.S. in the commerce department in 1928.

After graduation Bradshaw resumed working in Richmond as an agent for Standard Life and later for the National Benefit Life Insurance Company. He compiled an impressive record of salesmanship until the Great Depression forced National Benefit Life into receivership. In January 1933 Bradshaw and two associates pooled their resources to found the Virginia Mutual Benefit Life Insurance Company, initially a small company with assets of less than $2,500. It grew steadily, began issuing hospitalization insurance in 1949, and by 1965 employed 169 people and had assets worth nearly $3.5 million, including a $450,000 headquarters building constructed the previous year in Richmond. Bradshaw worked for the company for more than forty years, serving as its first president and treasurer. After he retired in 1973 he was chairman of the board until his death. On 5 April 1931 he married Emma Adele Forrester, of Richmond. They had one son.

Despite the demands of his business, Bradshaw found time to serve his community in many ways. Although he was reserved, his numerous organizational affiliations attest to his willingness to contribute to Richmond's social and economic development. Bradshaw was appointed to Selective Service Draft Board 55 during World War II and headed it for twenty-five years. He served as president of the Virginia Trade Association and vice president of the National Negro Business League. In 1951 he joined the board of directors of Consolidated Bank and Trust Company in Richmond. Bradshaw also sat on the boards of the Richmond Urban League, the United Givers Fund, and the Jefferson Townhouse Corporation. He served as state cochair-

man of the United Negro College Fund campaign and as a trustee and treasurer of the finance committee of the board of Virginia Union University. In 1968 he became the first African American rector of Virginia State College (later Virginia State University), which in 1956 had conferred on him an honorary LL.D. Bradshaw also belonged to the National Association for the Advancement of Colored People, the National Conference of Christians and Jews, and Kappa Alpha Psi fraternity. He received numerous honors and awards for his public service, sat on the board of the Central Virginia Educational Television Corporation, became a vice president of the Robert R. Moton Memorial Foundation, and from 1965 to 1970 served one term as the first African American member of the State Library Board.

Bradshaw's most important public service came as a member of the Richmond city school board. In August 1953 the city council appointed him to a vacancy on the board, making him the first black member in nearly seventy years. Subsequently appointed to two full five-year terms, he was the board's vice chairman when he retired as his eligibility to serve expired in 1965. Bradshaw earned respect for his leadership as he and such white members as Thomas Callendine Boushall and Lewis Franklin Powell charted a cautious course during the state's Massive Resistance to court-ordered desegregation of the public schools. Bradshaw believed that African Americans could make more progress with a gradualist approach than by confrontation, and he acquiesced in policies that fell far short of full desegregation but could at least command the support of the city's white political leaders. Although sometimes criticized for not being militant enough in his approach, Bradshaw took pride in his service on the school board at a time that he once characterized as "a second emancipation—an emancipation of the intellect."

Booker Talmadge Bradshaw died in a Richmond hospital on 29 December 1984 and was buried in Riverview Cemetery in Richmond.

Undated biographical memorandum, with incorrect marriage date, Library Board Files, RG 35, LVA; Merah Steven Stuart, *An Economic Detour: A History of Insurance in the Lives of American Negroes* (1940), 239–240; BVS Marriage Register, Richmond City; SCC Charter Book, 170:86;

Richmond Planet, 13 Feb. 1937; *Virginia Education Bulletin* 33 (1953): 6–7; *Richmond Times-Dispatch*, 19 Aug. 1953, 1 July 1965, 26 Sept. 1968; *Richmond Afro-American*, 22 Aug. 1953, 5 Oct. 1968; *Richmond News Leader*, 25 Aug. 1953, 11 May 1964, 6 (quotation), 12 Aug. 1965; Robert A. Pratt, *The Color of Their Skin: Education and Race in Richmond, Virginia, 1954–89* (1992), 18, 33–39; obituaries in *Richmond Times-Dispatch*, 1 Jan. 1985 (por.), and *Richmond Afro-American*, 5 Jan. 1985.

ROBERT A. PRATT

BRADSHAW, Mildred Roberts Lawrence Glenn (9 February 1902–13 June 1989), nurse and educator, was born in Suffolk, the daughter of Joseph Robert Lawrence and his second wife, Angelina Christian Jones Lawrence. She received her early education in parochial schools and graduated in 1920 from Saint Joseph's Academy in Portsmouth. After teaching in Oak Grove, in Wake County, North Carolina, Lawrence enrolled in 1924 in the school of nursing at Norfolk's Saint Vincent's Hospital and graduated in 1927.

Lawrence taught at Saint Vincent's for nine months after graduation and then became director of nurses at Martha Jefferson Hospital in Charlottesville. She remained there until 1932, when she began fourteen years as the director of nurses at King's Daughters' Hospital in Portsmouth. On 30 May 1936 she married Arthur Glenn in that city. After he was badly burned in an accident at the naval shipyard where he worked, he committed suicide on 20 September 1941. On 11 November 1944 she married Herbert Oscar Bradshaw, of Portsmouth. They separated in 1948, and she obtained a divorce on the grounds of desertion on 16 June 1950.

Mildred L. Bradshaw, as she was professionally known for much of her career, became a national leader in the education of licensed practical nurses. In January 1946, in cooperation with the Norfolk city school system's vocational education program, she started a course in practical nursing at Leigh Memorial Hospital. At the time only about thirty-five practical nurse education programs existed in the United States, and the only other school of practical nursing previously established in Virginia had been short-lived. Bradshaw's program at Leigh was the first in the country to receive national accreditation for practical nurse education. She was president of the Graduate Nurses' Association of Virginia from October 1942 to May 1946. In 1951 Bradshaw was elected to the first of two consecutive two-year terms as president of the National Association for Practical Nurse Education. By the time she retired from nursing in 1964, practical nurse education programs in the United States numbered approximately 700.

In 1954 Bradshaw and her sister Martha G. Lawrence formed the Practical Nurse Digest Publishing Company and began issuing *Practical Nurse Digest*, a monthly journal that served for fifteen years as the official organ of the Federation of Licensed Practical Nurses. Bradshaw wrote a regular column entitled "Let's Talk About It" and contributed to other nursing publications. She was also a delegate to the 1960 White House Conference on Children and Youth and to the 1961 White House Conference on Aging. In 1954 the board of the National Association for Practical Nurse Education created a national service award and named it for her. Bradshaw was herself the recipient of the Bradshaw Award in 1959, and three years later she won the Virginia State Nurses Association's biennial Nancy Vance Award for distinguished service. The Virginia Licensed Practical Nurses Association created a similar biennial award and named it the Mildred L. Bradshaw Award.

Bradshaw retired from Leigh Memorial Hospital in 1964 but continued to publish the *Practical Nurse Digest* and remained active in Saint Paul's Catholic Church. She was also a leader in the Norfolk chapter of the Pilot Club, a women's service organization, and in 1958 she became the first Virginian to serve as president of the Pilot Club International. The Norfolk Pilot Club created and named in her honor the Mildred L. Bradshaw scholarship award. Mildred Roberts Lawrence Glenn Bradshaw suffered a stroke in January 1989 and died in Norfolk on 13 June 1989. She was buried in Portsmouth Catholic Cemetery.

Virginia's Voc Ed Voice 8 (Apr. 1986): 2; *New York Times*, 17 May 1951, 6 May 1953; *Norfolk Virginian-Pilot*, 25 Jan. 1953, 11 Oct. 1962; *Norfolk Ledger-Dispatch*, 18 July 1957; *Richmond Times-Dispatch*, 28 July 1957; *Norfolk Ledger-Dispatch and Star,* 12 July 1958; *Virginia Nurse Quarterly* 30 (winter 1962): 44–47 (por.); dates of marriages and divorce verified by BVS; obituaries in *Norfolk Virginian-Pilot*, 14 June 1989, and *Virginia Nurse* 57, no. 3 (1989): 50.

DAPHNE GENTRY

BRADY, James Dennis (3 April 1843–30 November 1900), member of the House of Representatives, was born in Portsmouth, the son of Bartholomew Brady, a carpenter, and Elizabeth Brady. His parents emigrated from Ireland to New York before moving to Virginia. About three years after they died in an 1855 yellow fever epidemic, Brady secured employment as a clerk in New York City. He also attended an evening school and joined the Demilt Literary Association, participating in its debates and other activities.

Brady's service in the Civil War reflected his identity as a Catholic Irish-American. In December 1861 he became a first lieutenant in the 63d Regiment New York Infantry, part of the famous Irish Brigade commanded by Thomas Francis Meagher, an exiled Irish revolutionary leader. Brady almost certainly belonged to the Fenians, a secret society devoted to the liberation of Ireland, but hard experience probably tempered his revolutionary zeal. In 1862 he was wounded at Sharpsburg (Antietam) and again in the hard fighting at Fredericksburg late that year, and he nearly died on 3 June 1864 at Cold Harbor when a musket ball passed entirely through his body. Brady won promotions throughout the war and served as an adjutant and then in the inspector general's department of the Second Corps. He became a lieutenant colonel on 26 January 1865 and at the age of twenty-two was in command of his regiment with the rank of colonel when it mustered out of service at Alexandria on 30 June 1865.

Brady remained in Virginia and opened a grocery business in Petersburg. On 28 March 1866 he addressed a Fenian meeting in Richmond. On 3 October 1866 Brady was appointed the naval storekeeper at the Gosport Navy Yard in Portsmouth and moved to that city. There he also became president of the Soldiers' and Sailors' Association of Portsmouth and superintendent of the Saint Paul's Catholic Church Sunday School. On 3 January 1867 Brady married Margaret A. Campbell, a fellow Portsmouth native. They had two sons and four daughters.

As a Union army veteran residing in Virginia and a recipient of a federal patronage position, Brady naturally took an interest in the success of the Republican Party. He played an inconspicuous role in the campaigns of 1867 and 1869, but following his election in 1870 as clerk of the Portsmouth Hustings Court he resigned from the navy yard. Brady ran for state senator in 1875 and carried Norfolk County, but the results in Portsmouth gave victory to his opponent, John H. Gayle. Brady immediately contested the election. Testimony before a Senate committee revealed fraud so palpable that even John Warwick Daniel, a leading Democrat, voted with a majority of the Committee of Privileges and Elections recommending that Brady be seated. By a close and partisan margin, however, the whole Senate gave Gayle the seat.

Brady sought appointment as United States pension agent in Norfolk but fell victim to factional conflicts within the national Republican Party. Nonetheless, as secretary of the party's state committee he played a large role in the 1876 presidential campaign, and on 11 December of that year he received his reward, appointment as an inspector of customs in Richmond. In 1877 Brady was appointed collector of internal revenue for the district headquartered at Petersburg. The customhouse remained politicized under his direction, but it handled large sums of money efficiently and honestly.

Also resident in Petersburg was William Mahone, leader of the faction of the Democratic Party that favored readjustment of the state's huge prewar public debt. Brady became one of the first prominent Republicans to endorse a coalition with the Readjusters, and by 1881 he was identified as Mahone's chief advocate within the party. The following year Brady chaired the board of commissioners charged with choosing a site for the new Virginia Normal and Collegiate Institute and at Mahone's urging ensured that the new school (later Virginia State University) would be constructed near Petersburg. On 5 January 1883 Brady accepted an appointment as clerk of the Virginia Supreme Court of

Appeals, a more secure patronage position than the one he then held, but at Mahone's behest he subsequently declined the post.

Early in 1884 Republicans in Petersburg who resented Mahone's domination nominated Joseph P. Evans, an African American and former state senator, for the House of Representatives from an eleven-county district centered on Dinwiddie and Nottoway Counties. Mahone controlled the district convention, however, and secured the official nomination for Brady, his loyal supporter. Evans stayed in the race, and the Democrats, seeing opportunity in Republican division, nominated George S. Rives, but Brady won the election in a very close race. Brady's term in Congress was the quiet one typical of new members. He served on the Committees on Banking and Currency and on Pensions. Brady looked forward to reelection in 1886, but Mahone instead asked him to step aside so that he could take his place, and the ever-loyal Brady complied. Mahone then endorsed another Republican for Congress and ultimately permitted William Embre Gaines, whom Brady considered a political enemy, to secure the nomination and win the election. Embittered, Brady published a letter in September 1886 detailing Mahone's machinations, and he joined the throng of former allies who wound up as Mahone's enemies.

With a Democratic president controlling patronage, Brady's chances of obtaining an appointment disappeared. Instead, he won admission to the bar and supported his family by practicing law in Petersburg, but he remained active in politics. He backed John Mercer Langston for Congress in 1888 against Mahone's candidate and then served as one of Langston's attorneys when that pioneering African American successfully challenged the election of his Democratic opponent. The Republican National Committee, of which Brady was the member from Virginia, arranged a truce between Mahone and his enemies for the 1889 gubernatorial campaign. On 22 July 1889, two days after Brady agreed to the compromise, President Benjamin Harrison reappointed him collector of internal revenue at Petersburg. Brady and

Mahone quickly fell out over how many of Brady's subordinates Mahone could select, however, and Mahone blocked Brady's confirmation in the post until mid-March 1890.

When the Democrats returned to the White House in 1893, Brady again resumed his law practice. He remained active in state politics and served as counsel in contested congressional elections in 1894 and 1898. As secretary of the state party committee, he directed William McKinley's 1896 presidential campaign in Virginia. McKinley reappointed Brady collector of internal revenue.

About 1898 Brady developed a kidney ailment diagnosed as Bright's disease. A short hospital stay in Washington, D.C., seemed to help, but he suffered a relapse after returning to Petersburg. James Dennis Brady died suddenly at his home in Petersburg on 30 November 1900. In his memory the officials and clerks of the internal revenue and of the post office in Petersburg placed a reproduction in oils of Bartolomé Esteban Murillo's *Immaculate Conception* at Saint Joseph's Catholic Church in that city. Brady is buried in the church's cemetery.

James H. Bailey, "Colonel James Brady of Virginia," *Catholic Virginian*, 9, 16, 23 July 1948; French Biographies; James Dennis Brady Papers, LC; James Dennis Brady Scrapbooks, UVA; William Mahone Papers, Duke; BVS Marriage Register, Portsmouth; Frederick Phisterer, *New York in the War of the Rebellion, 1861 to 1865*, 3d ed. (1912), 2587, 2594; *JSV,* 1875–1876 sess., 54, 333–334; *Report of the Committee of Privileges and Elections in the Contested Election from the Eleventh Senatorial District*, Doc. 21 appended to *JSV*, 1875–1876 sess.; *Minority Report of the Committee of Privileges and Elections in the Case of Brady vs. Gayle, in the Senate of Virginia*, Doc. 24 appended to *JSV*, 1875–1876 sess.; William D. Henderson, *Gilded Age City: Politics, Life and Labor in Petersburg, Virginia, 1874–1889* (1980); *Petersburg Daily Index-Appeal*, 16 Aug. 1881, 1 Sept. 1884, 23 Sept. 1886, 17 Mar. 1890; obituaries in *New York Times*, *Petersburg Daily Index-Appeal* (with editorial tribute), and *Richmond Dispatch* (por.), all 1 Dec. 1900.

JOHN T. KNEEBONE

BRADY, Samuel (25 May 1756–1 January 1796), frontiersman, was born at Shippensburg, Pennsylvania, the son of John Brady and Mary Quigley Brady, and after 1768 lived on a farm in the Susquehanna River valley. During the summer of 1775 he joined one of the companies of volunteer riflemen that marched to the defense of Boston and thereby became one of the first soldiers in the Continental army. On 17 July 1776 Brady became a first lieutenant, and when the company was attached to the 8th Regiment Pennsylvania Infantry in November he was appointed captain lieutenant.

Brady fought with distinction at the Battle of Brandywine on 11 September 1777, and ten days later when a British force surprised General Anthony Wayne's division in a night attack at Paoli, Pennsylvania, Brady eluded capture and led his men to safety. He fought again at Germantown on 4 October 1777 and spent the difficult winter with Washington's army at Valley Forge. In June 1778 Brady's regiment was transferred to western Pennsylvania. That summer a party of Delaware Indians killed one of his brothers, and in April 1779 other Native Americans killed his father. Tradition relates that Brady swore vengeance on each occasion. While pursuing a Delaware party in June 1779 Brady led a dawn attack on the Indians' camp and killed one of the men whom he believed was responsible for the death of his brother.

On 2 August 1779 Brady was appointed captain of the army scouts who patrolled the areas between the American forts on both sides of the Ohio River in western Virginia. Later that month he took part in Daniel Brodhead's expedition to attack the villages and crops of the Seneca and Delaware. In the only resistance encountered, Brady's scouts drove off a Seneca party that had fired on the advancing columns. Brodhead employed Brady as a scout and spy until 17 January 1781, when Brady was transferred to the 3d Regiment Pennsylvania Infantry, in which he served until the Revolutionary War ended.

In 1784 Brady married Druscilla Van Swearingen in Washington County, Pennsylvania, and settled in that county at Chartiers Creek. The first of their two sons was born there in 1786. About 1788 Brady moved to Van Swearingen Fort on the Ohio River above Wellsburg in what became Brooke County. Later, the Bradys lived at nearby Short Creek.

Brady's prowess made him the premier scout and frontiersman in the upper reaches of the Ohio River valley. He was compared to Francis Marion and Daniel Boone and, as with them, his achievements passed into legend. Nineteenth-century literature on the Ohio frontier abounds with stories of his skillful tracking ability, stealthy and deadly approaches to Indian camps, daring rescues of captives, narrow escapes, long-distance runs to elude capture, and miraculous leaps over dangerous rivers. Family tradition held that James Fenimore Cooper drew on Brady's exploits in composing the *Leatherstocking Tales*. Some of the exaggerated stories later told about Brady undoubtedly had some basis in fact, and his involvement in some controversial episodes is well documented. In March 1791 Brady and a troop of rangers trailed and attacked a band of Delaware Indians. Governor Beverley Randolph refused a request from the governor of Pennsylvania that Brady be arrested and extradited to stand trial for the murder of the Indians, and he was ultimately tried and acquitted for the killings in Pittsburgh on 21 May 1793. Samuel Brady concluded his army service as a scout in Anthony Wayne's 1793–1794 expedition against the Indians and died at his home on 1 January 1796. He was buried in West Liberty, Ohio County.

Birth and death dates documented in Brady Papers, ser. E, Draper MSS; published accounts mixing facts and legends include Cecil B. Hartley, *Life and Adventures of Lewis Wetzel, the Virginia Ranger* (1860), 191–241, J. H. Newton, G. G. Nichols, and A. G. Sprankle, *History of the Pan-Handle, Being Historical Collections of the Counties of Ohio, Brooke, Marshall, and Hancock, West Virginia* (1879), 145–147, Cyrus Townsend Brady, "Captain Samuel Brady, Chief of the Rangers," in *Brady Family Reunion and Fragments of Brady History and Biography*, ed. William G. Murdock (1909), 25–37, C. Hale Sipe, *The Indian Wars of Pennsylvania* (1929), 573–582 (giving death date from gravestone), and Ralph Emmett Fall, "Captain Samuel Brady (1756–1795), Chief of the Rangers, and His Kin," *West Virginia History* 29 (1968): 203–223.

DONALD W. GUNTER

BRAGG, George Freeman (25 January 1863–12 March 1940), journalist and Episcopal minister, was born into slavery in Warren County, North Carolina, the son of George Freeman Bragg, a carpenter, and Mary Bragg, a seamstress. At the age of two Bragg moved with his family to Petersburg, where his grandmother Caroline Wiley Cain Bragg lived. A devout

Episcopalian, she was instrumental in the founding of Saint Stephen's Episcopal Church in 1867, and her extended family composed a majority of the congregation.

Bragg attended his family's church and Saint Stephen's Normal and Theological School as well, where he studied under Giles Buckner Cooke, a former Confederate staff officer and dedicated educator of freedpeople. Bragg also became involved in the field of journalism. From an early age he delivered newspapers and accordingly established relationships with prominent white residents of Petersburg, among them an editor of the *Petersburg Index*, John Hampden Chamberlayne, who in time gave him practical experience in every aspect of newspaper publishing. Chamberlayne also introduced Bragg to the world of Virginia politics, for the editor was a close ally of William Mahone, of Petersburg, who created the Readjuster Party and actively courted black voters.

Bragg moved quickly through the normal school at Saint Stephen's and entered its theological department in the autumn of 1878. Six months later the church's white rector expelled him for insufficient humility, just in time for Bragg to become caught up in the campaigns of the Readjusters. He worked at Mahone's headquarters in Petersburg throughout the successful legislative campaign of 1881, assisting with distribution of literature and other political tasks. For his efforts Bragg was appointed a page in the 1881–1882 session of the House of Delegates.

On 1 July 1882 Bragg put his knowledge of journalism to work by founding a weekly newspaper, the *Petersburg Lancet*. Its first motto was "Sworn to no Party; of no Sect am I; I can be silent, but will not be." The second issue's motto altered the second portion to "I can't be silent, but will not lie." Bragg was concerned above all with civil rights, and he encouraged African Americans to become politically active in order to demonstrate and protect their citizenship. At that time black political activity in Virginia was closely tied to the Readjuster Party. In 1884, following the previous year's electoral defeat for the Readjusters, a split developed between Mahone and black political leaders over the local congressional nomination. Mahone's

candidate, James Dennis Brady, defeated Joseph P. Evans, a black man, for the seat from the Fourth Congressional District, which included Petersburg. Bragg supported Evans and accused Mahone of dictatorial behavior concerned less with black rights than black votes. The nasty split and Evans's subsequent loss disillusioned Bragg about politics. He blamed Evans's defeat on Mahone's corruption and on black voters' willingness to be corrupted.

On 12 September 1885 Bragg announced that the *Lancet* would eschew partisan politics and instead urge blacks to concentrate on moral, educational, and commercial pursuits. Two months later it declared that it would henceforth focus on the activities of black Episcopalians. In January 1886 the paper adopted a new motto reflecting the change in Bragg's outlook: "For what is a man profited, if he shall gain the whole world, and lose his own soul." Beginning on 6 February of that year the paper appeared as the *Afro-American Churchman*, which was published for a time by Bragg's younger sister Carrie Bragg.

Bragg's journalistic shift coincided with his return to the seminary. A change in the rectorship at Saint Stephen's Church allowed him to reenter what had become Bishop Payne Divinity and Industrial School in the autumn of 1885, and in July 1886 he gave up publication of the *Afro-American Churchman*. Ordained a deacon on 12 January 1887, Bragg took over the ailing Holy Innocents Episcopal Church in Norfolk, which depended on missionary support for survival. On 19 December 1888 he was ordained a priest at Saint Luke's Episcopal Church in Norfolk, thus becoming only the twelfth black Episcopal priest in the United States. During his five years in Norfolk Bragg invigorated and expanded his congregation, making it into the fully self-supporting Grace Episcopal Church. He also established the Industrial School for Colored Girls and served from 1887 through 1890 on the board of Hampton Normal and Agricultural Institute. On 20 September 1887 Bragg married Nellie Hill, a member of another prominent family in Petersburg's black community. They had two sons and two daughters.

On 17 November 1891 Bragg was called to resurrect another church, the Saint James African Episcopal Church in Baltimore. Starting with sixty-nine members and dependent on financial aid from the bishop, he made the church self-sufficient, tripled the size of its congregation within a few years, and erected a new church building in 1901. Bragg helped establish the Maryland Home for Friendless Colored Children in 1899 and devoted much time to preparing twenty black men for the ministry. During his forty-eight years in Baltimore he returned to his roots in publishing by editing a monthly newspaper, the *Church Advocate*, and writing and printing more than a score of books and pamphlets, several of which dealt with the history of blacks in Virginia. His most important works included *The Colored Harvest in the Old Virginia Diocese* (1901), *Afro-American Church Work and Workers* (1904), *The Story of Old St. Stephen's, Petersburg, Va.* (1906), *A Bond-Slave of Christ: Entering the Ministry Under Great Difficulties* (1912), *History of the Afro-American Group of the Episcopal Church* (1922), and *The Hero of Jerusalem* (1926), which commemorated the centennial of the birth of William Mahone.

In recognition of Bragg's contributions to the church and to black historiography, Wilberforce University awarded him an honorary D.D. in 1902. He was a central figure in the Conference of Church Workers Among the Colored People, the national black Episcopal organization, which argued that the appointment of black bishops would increase the number of African Americans in the church. Twice Bragg was proposed for elevation to bishop. He was suggested as bishop of Haiti in 1911 and as suffragan bishop of Arkansas in 1917 but was not selected either time.

George Freeman Bragg continued his ministry at Saint James Church until his death at Provident Hospital in Baltimore on 12 March 1940 following a brief respiratory illness.

Memoirs and birth date in Bragg, *Colored Harvest* (1901), 15–19; Mildred Louise McGlotten, "Rev. George Freeman Bragg: A Negro Pioneer in Social Welfare" (master's thesis, Howard University, 1948); J. Carleton Hayden, "'For Zion's Sake I Will Not Hold My Peace': George Freeman Bragg, Jr., Priest, Pastor, and Prophet," *Linkage* (Oct. 1986): 10–11, 23; George Freeman Bragg Papers, Mooreland-Spingarn Research Center, Howard University, Washington, D.C., and Virginia State University; George Freeman Bragg Papers and George Freeman Bragg Photograph Collection, Schomburg Center for Research in Black Culture, New York Public Library; BVS Marriage Register, Petersburg; Lawrence L. Hartzell, "The Exploration of Freedom in Black Petersburg, Virginia, 1865–1902," in *The Edge of the South: Life in Nineteenth-Century Virginia,* ed. Edward L. Ayers and John C. Willis (1991), 139–145; William D. Henderson, *Gilded Age City: Politics, Life and Labor in Petersburg, Virginia, 1874–1889* (1980); Bragg, *Story of Old St. Stephen's* (1906), title page por; obituaries in *Baltimore News-Post* and *Petersburg Progress-Index,* both 12 Mar. 1940, *Richmond Afro-American,* 16 Mar. 1940 (por.), and *Journal of Negro History* 25 (1940): 399–400.

LAWRENCE L. HARTZELL

BRANCH, Blythe Walker (16 March 1864– 22 May 1942), civic leader, was born in Petersburg, the son of John Patteson Branch, a banker, and Mary Louise Merritt Kerr Branch. He grew up in Richmond and attended Episcopal High School in Alexandria. From 1888 to 1889 he worked in Richmond as a clerk for his family's banking and brokerage firm, Thomas Branch and Company, and became a partner in the company in 1891.

Branch traveled extensively in Europe after completing his education, and in 1899 he married Marie Thérèse Tarrant in Paris. Branch resigned from the family firm and as director of the Paris office of the Galena Oil Company became one of the foremost American businessmen in that city. By March 1923 he had been elected president of the American Chamber of Commerce in France. Branch also served as a vice president of the American Hospital in Paris and as a warden of the Church of the Holy Trinity. An admirer of French arts and culture, he entered into Parisian society during thirty-two years of residence there or in the suburb of Neuilly-sur-Seine. Branch also maintained a house in the south of France.

Following the death of his wife on 14 July 1931, Branch visited Virginia for the first time in eighteen years and decided to move back to Richmond, where he quickly became a leader in cultural and artistic life. He was a founding member of the first Richmond Symphony Orchestra, and following his election as its president on 26 January 1933 he led fund-raising efforts in order to expand the orchestra's scope by sending the symphony to other Virginia cities to perform and by attracting guest solo artists to Richmond. Branch was also one of the first Virginians to express public alarm over the rise of the Nazis in Germany. In letters to the editor in the *Richmond News Leader* in 1933 and 1940 he warned that Adolf Hitler's rise to power could prove dangerous to the United States.

Branch made his most important civic contribution as a founder and president of the Virginia Museum of Fine Arts. In 1934 he contributed $10,000 toward its creation, one of the dozen largest initial contributions, and later that year the General Assembly appointed him to the museum's first board of directors. The other board members elected him vice president on 11 February 1935, and for two years he chaired the Committee on Education in Art. On 19 June 1937 Branch succeeded John Garland Pollard as president of the board and chairman of the executive committee. Branch was reelected in 1938, 1939, and 1940, despite his expressed desire to relinquish the presidency to a younger and more vigorous person. In 1940 the board also awarded him the first Webster S. Rhoads Medal honoring contributions to art in Virginia. During Branch's seven years as a board officer and president, the museum's membership more than doubled, and the institution took its place among the best of such state museums in the Southeast.

The board reelected Branch president of the Museum of Fine Arts yet again on 21 May 1941. His health deteriorated during the following winter, which he spent in Palm Beach, Florida. Soon after his return to Richmond he entered the hospital and on 21 April 1942 submitted his resignation to the museum's board of directors. Blythe Walker Branch died of urinary intravasation at Stuart Circle Hospital in Richmond on 22 May 1942 and was buried in Hollywood Cemetery in that city.

Branch letters and Branch and Company Records, VHS; Virginia Museum of Fine Arts, Minute Book, vol. 1; Hollywood Cemetery interment record (LVA microfilm); obitu-

aries with pors. in *Richmond News Leader* and *Richmond Times-Dispatch*, both 23 May 1942; memorial in Virginia Museum of Fine Arts *Museum Bulletin* 3 (Sept. 1942): [1–2].

DONALD W. GUNTER

BRANCH, James Read (28 July 1828–2 July 1869), banker and Confederate artillery officer, was born at New Market, near Petersburg in Prince George County, the son of Thomas Branch and his first wife, Sarah Pride Read Branch. After an early education in the Petersburg schools he attended Randolph-Macon College, then at Boydton, and received an A.B. in 1848. An excellent student, Branch was elected principal of the preparatory school at Ridgeway, Warren County, North Carolina, one of four schools in that state then associated with the college. After a year there, he joined his father's business in Petersburg. With his younger brother John Patteson Branch, they formed a partnership called Thomas Branch and Sons, which became one of the largest commission-merchant houses in that city. On 3 December 1856 Branch married his second cousin Martha Louise Patteson, of Richmond. They had one son and four daughters.

Branch shared his father's Unionist convictions and his eventual support of secession. He organized an artillery company and entered active Confederate service on 11 May 1861. A family tradition has it that with only two cannons Captain Branch's company checked two dozen Union guns during the bloody Confederate defeat at Malvern Hill on 1 July 1862. His battery also fought effectively in the Battles of Antietam (Sharpsburg) and Fredericksburg, earning him promotion to major to rank from 2 May 1863 and to lieutenant colonel on 25 August 1863. As chief of artillery for Robert Ransom's brigade, Branch took part in the successful siege of occupied Plymouth, North Carolina, on 17–20 April 1864. During the fighting his horse was shot and fell on him, breaking Branch's leg in three places. He returned to Richmond, where his wife and children had moved in 1863, but recovery came slowly, and he resigned from the army on 28 March 1865.

After the war Branch helped to reorganize Thomas Branch and Sons as a banking house in

Richmond. He became a leader among those businessmen struggling to rebuild the city's economy and helped to found the Merchants' Exchange, the Corn and Flour Exchange Association, and the Tobacco Exchange. Branch was also the Richmond banker for William Mahone and advised him in his effort to consolidate his railroad properties.

Branch soon became involved in politics, too. After racially polarized voting in October 1867 resulted in a Radical Republican majority at a state constitutional convention, white leaders organized as the Conservative Party. Branch was elected secretary of the party's executive committee. Unlike most other committee members he had not been politically prominent before the Civil War, but his future seemed bright, and Conservatives in Richmond nominated him for the Senate of Virginia in 1869. Deeming defeat of the hated Radicals to be all important, the Conservatives entered into an alliance with moderate Republicans to back Gilbert Carlton Walker for governor, and they even sought support from black voters. Branch endorsed that tactic and urged Conservative speakers to appeal to the reason of black voters rather than abuse them.

Branch attended a barbecue sponsored by the Colored Walker Club of Richmond on 2 July 1869, four days before the election. A temporary bridge provided access to an island in the James River where the event took place, but a policeman refused to permit those without tickets to cross. Already on the island, Branch stepped onto the bridge and shouted to the policeman to open the gate to all. The crowd streamed onto the bridge, which suddenly collapsed. James Read Branch fell under the broken timbers and chains of the bridge and drowned. After funeral services at Saint Paul's Episcopal Church two days later, thousands of people followed Branch's casket to Hollywood Cemetery. Members of the Colored Walker Club joined the procession, and along the way other African Americans taunted them as traitors.

Martha Patteson Branch never remarried and taught her children to revere their father's memory. Others remembered him, too. John Sergeant Wise's racist novel about Reconstruction, *The Lion's Skin*, published in 1905 shortly after a new state constitution disfranchised African Americans, recounted the drowning death of "a leading banker" who had sought to win blacks to the cause of the Conservatives as "an ill omen" of the futility of that tactic. Branch's youngest daughter, Mary-Cooke Branch Munford, later explained her activism as inspired by the example of her father.

Cabell, *Branchiana*, 61–69; BVS Marriage Register, Richmond City; Branch and Company Records, VHS; Richard Irby, *History of Randolph-Macon College, Virginia* (1898), 109–110 (por.), 117; Compiled Service Records; Presidential Pardons; Jack P. Maddex Jr., *The Virginia Conservatives, 1867–1879: A Study in Reconstruction Politics* (1970), 48, 55, 279, 284; John S. Wise, *The Lion's Skin: A Historical Novel and A Novel History* (1905), 242–245 (quotations); Walter Russell Bowie, *Sunrise in the South: The Life of Mary-Cooke Branch Munford* (1942), xiii, 11–17, 152; extended reports of death and funeral in *Richmond Daily Enquirer and Examiner*, *Richmond Dispatch*, and *Richmond Whig*, all 3, 5, 6 July 1869.

JOHN T. KNEEBONE

BRANCH, John Kerr (1 May 1865–1 July 1930), banker, was the son of John Patteson Branch, a Petersburg broker and merchant, and Mary Louise Merritt Kerr Branch. He was born in Danville, where his mother had gone for refuge from the fighting at Petersburg. The extended Branch family transferred its enterprises to Richmond after the Civil War and into banking. Branch attended McGuire's University School in Richmond and then studied under private tutors in France and Germany until he turned twenty-one. At nineteen, in the Black Forest of Germany, he met Beulah Frances Gould, of Pawling, Dutchess County, New York. They married on 27 October 1886 and had one son and two daughters.

Branch began his business career as a clerk for the family-owned Thomas Branch and Company, a Richmond banking house with expanding ties to New York City's financial markets. As his father had done for him, John Patteson Branch prepared his son for increased responsibilities in the firm. Thus, John Kerr Branch conducted business in New York for the company and became a member of the New York Stock Exchange on 8 October 1896. He also purchased Elmwood Farm, an estate at Pawling, where his family spent part of each year.

In 1892 Branch became a director of the Merchants National Bank in Richmond, of which his father was president, and in 1898 he became the bank's vice president. In 1895 Thomas Branch and Company faced a crisis when Frederic Robert Scott, a longtime partner, withdrew. John Patteson Branch responded by making his sons, Blythe Walker Branch and John Kerr Branch, full partners in the reconstituted company. The elder son's move to Paris and departure from the firm in 1899 made John Kerr Branch the heir apparent to the family's enterprises. His father also put him in charge of his Kingsland Land Corporation and in 1903 gave him a block of land on Monument Avenue.

Branch continued his father's practice of diversified investment in manufacturing concerns and financial institutions, which helped to maintain the family firm as one of the South's most prominent banking houses. He used that power and prestige effectively in 1913 and 1914 as chairman of a committee of bankers and businessmen who successfully lobbied to have Richmond chosen as the site of the headquarters bank of District Five of the new Federal Reserve System. Branch's proud father stood with him at the formal announcement of the city's selection on 2 April 1914. Following his father's death the next year, Branch became president of Merchants National Bank and successfully guided it through the economic strains associated with World War I. He chaired all four of the Liberty Loan campaigns in Richmond during the war.

For decades Branch and his wife spent part of each year in Europe, where they developed an appreciation for Italian Renaissance art and culture. With expert advice they purchased furniture, paintings, sculpture, and many other works of art. Until his father's death Branch and his wife lived with him when they were in Richmond. Branch's responsibilities as president of the bank encouraged the couple to construct a winter residence on their Monument Avenue property in Richmond. Designed by John Russell Pope, the architect of Richmond's Broad Street Station and Washington's Jefferson Memorial, the magnificent Tudor Revival residence was completed in 1919. Its 28,000 square feet of interior space provided a setting for their art collection and a place for entertaining friends, in addition to broadcasting Branch's wealth and status.

Branch served as president of the Richmond Chamber of Commerce in 1920 and 1921 and took an active part in Democratic Party fundraising later in the decade. On 9 January 1923 he stepped down as president of Merchants National Bank to become chairman of the board and turned the reins over to a cousin. The bank consolidated with another in 1926 to become the First and Merchants National Bank. By then Branch and his wife had purchased a villa in Florence in their beloved Italy, and he spent much of his time there during his retirement years. John Kerr Branch died of pneumonia at the villa on 1 July 1930. He was buried in Hollywood Cemetery in Richmond. Branch's estate was reportedly worth more than $4.5 million. His widow returned to Richmond and lived in the Branch house until her death in 1952. The mansion became a Virginia Historic Landmark. Following the death of Beulah Gould Branch, her will and the generosity of a daughter brought many pieces from the Branch art collection to the Virginia Museum of Fine Arts.

Cabell, *Branchiana*, 81–82; Tyler, *Encyclopedia*, 5:1055–1057 (gives marriage date); *NCAB*, 44:99; Branch and Company Records, VHS; New York Stock Exchange, *Yearbook* (1930), 36; Frances Leigh Williams, *A Century of Service, Prologue to the Future: A History of the First and Merchants National Bank* (1965), 97–98; Edmond H. Brill, *History of the Richmond Chamber of Commerce* [1967], 12; *Richmond Times-Dispatch*, 3 Apr. 1914, 8 Nov. 1953, 19 Jan. 1992; *Richmond News Leader*, 9 Jan. 1923, 1 Nov. 1952; *New York Times*, 30 July 1930; Kathy Edwards, Esme Howard, and Toni Prawl, *Monument Avenue: History and Architecture* (1992), 39–40, 61, 64, 178–179; obituaries and editorial tributes in *Richmond News Leader*, 2 July 1930 (por.), and *Richmond Times-Dispatch*, 3 July 1930 (gives variant death date of 30 June 1930); obituary in *New York Times*, 3 July 1930.

JOHN T. KNEEBONE

BRANCH, John Patteson (9 October 1830–2 February 1915), banker, was born in Petersburg, the son of a prosperous commission merchant, Thomas Branch, and his first wife, Sarah Pride Read Branch. He attended Petersburg's best schools, but poor health prevented him from entering college. In 1848 he became a clerk in his father's office. His elder brother, James Read

Branch, soon joined him and with their father formed a partnership, Thomas Branch and Sons, which was one of Petersburg's most prominent commission houses.

Branch remained with the family business after the Civil War began. On 12 May 1863 he married Mary Louise Merritt Kerr, of Petersburg, daughter of a Methodist minister. They had two sons, Blythe Walker Branch and John Kerr Branch, both of whom became prominent in Richmond during the twentieth century, and two daughters. On 29 February 1864 Branch mustered into Confederate service in Company E of the 44th Virginia Battalion, a volunteer unit organized the preceding year for the defense of Petersburg, and he was elected a lieutenant. His business experience best suited him for work under the unit's quartermaster, but he served in the field with the Army of Northern Virginia until the surrender at Appomattox.

The Branch family reunited in Petersburg after the war. He applied for and received a presidential pardon and briefly resumed the mercantile business. With the end of slavery the partners' antebellum role as brokers and middlemen in the plantation economy offered diminished prospects for prosperity, so Branch and one of his brothers, James Read Branch, opened a Richmond operation, called Thomas Branch and Company, specializing in banking, securities, and other financial enterprises. Thomas Branch joined them there to found the Merchants National Bank in November 1870. James Read Branch had died in an accident the previous year, and John P. Branch ascended to the primary position among Thomas Branch's several sons and sons-in-law associated with the firm.

With a brother-in-law, Frederic Robert Scott, Branch purchased the elder Branch's share of Thomas Branch and Company in 1872. He directed the firm further into banking and invested in railroads, especially the Richmond and Danville Railroad, which united his interests with those of several other leading Richmond capitalists. Branch and Company also purchased coupon bonds and other forms of the Virginia debt, and Branch served on the finance committee of the state Democratic Party during the 1880s, helping to protect the investments

against the Readjusters. By then the firm operated exclusively in finance, and Branch held a seat on the New York Stock Exchange.

On 11 January 1881 Branch succeeded his father as president of the Merchants National Bank, only a few years after he blocked a nervous stockholder attempt to sell off the bank as unprofitable. General economic conditions improved in the 1880s, and Branch led the bank to prosperity. Deposits doubled by 1890 and again by 1900; in 1910 the total resources of the bank stood at nearly $7 million. By then he had earned a reputation as one of the ablest bankers in Richmond, and his forceful insistence on conducting business as usual during the financial panic of 1907 became part of the city's banking lore. He served on the executive committee of the American Bankers Association from 1893 to 1896.

Branch also invested widely in real estate, especially in suburban land to the west of Richmond, forming corporations under family direction to develop the properties. During the 1880s he purchased land along what became Monument Avenue, subdivided and sold numerous lots in the area, and provided the next generation of his family with the space for the erection of magnificent houses that dominate the avenue's architecture.

A devout member of the Methodist Church since adolescence, Branch followed his father as a member of the board of trustees of Randolph-Macon College and served from 1883 until his death. He supported the college generously, with his two most conspicuous gifts being dormitories erected in 1906 and 1913 to honor, respectively, his wife and his father. He also provided funding for publication of the John P. Branch Historical Papers, a series of scholarly essays published by the college's historians between 1901 and 1918. The college awarded him an honorary LL.D. in 1913. Branch also served on the board of Centenary Methodist Church in Richmond and in 1908–1909 paid for installation of electrical lighting and magnificent stained-glass windows. He presented $25,000 to the city of Richmond for construction of the Branch Public Baths, which opened on 30 January 1908.

For many years Branch spent the summer at the White Sulphur Springs resort and also traveled regularly in Europe, where his wife sought medical treatment as a result of her ill health. Mary Kerr Branch died on 20 December 1896 in Munich, Bavaria, where she had gone several months earlier for treatment. John Patteson Branch died in Richmond of a severe respiratory ailment on 2 February 1915 and was buried in Hollywood Cemetery. His estate was worth $2,795,000 and was divided among his children.

Cabell, *Branchiana*, 77–82; Tyler, *Men of Mark*, 2:46–50 (por.); Tyler, *Encyclopedia*, 4:412–415, 5:1056–1057; BVS Marriage Register, Petersburg; Branch and Company Records, VHS; Compiled Service Records; Presidential Pardons; W. Asbury Christian, *Richmond: Her Past and Present* (1912), 383, 455, 464, 515, 536; *Richmond* 1 (Oct. 1914): 11; Floyd S. Bennett, *Methodist Church on Shockoe Hill: A History of Centenary Methodist Church, Richmond, Virginia, 1810–1960* (1962), 108–110, 114–119; Frances Leigh Williams, *A Century of Service, Prologue to the Future: A History of the First and Merchants National Bank* (1965), 94–97; C. S. Alling, "'A Felt Presence and Power in Society': The Business Records of Thomas Branch and Family," Virginia Historical Society *An Occasional Bulletin* 49 (Dec. 1984): 1–5; Kathy Edwards, Esme Howard, and Toni Prawl, *Monument Avenue: History and Architecture* (1992), 34–40, 61–67; James Edward Scanlon, *Randolph-Macon College: A Southern History, 1825–1967* (1983), 195, 287, 289; "Will of Jno. P. Branch," *Southern Banker* 23 (Mar. 1915): 47; obituary in *New York Times*, 3 Feb. 1915; obituaries and editorial tributes in *Richmond News Leader* and *Richmond Times-Dispatch*, both 3 Feb. 1915; memorials in *Journal of the American Bankers Association* 7 (1915): 549, and *VMHB* 24 (1916): xxxiii–xxxvii.

JOHN T. KNEEBONE

BRANCH, Samuel (d. 1 September 1847), member of the Convention of 1829–1830, was born probably in Chesterfield County late in the 1780s, the son of Samuel Branch and Jane Martin Branch. His father died before December 1789, and his mother married Thomas Whitworth and moved with her son to Charlotte County. About 1807 Branch enrolled at Hampden-Sydney College and joined the Philanthropic Society, a literary club, but he did not graduate from the school. On 27 November 1807 he married Winifred Jones Guerrant, daughter of John Guerrant, a former member of the Council of State from Goochland County. They had six sons and four daughters.

On 1 October 1807 Branch purchased 500 acres of land on Little Cub Creek in Charlotte County from his mother and stepfather. He raised tobacco there until 1817, when he purchased an 822-acre tract from Claiborne West and moved to Buckingham County. Branch's wife died on 29 October 1828, and on 4 April 1831 he married Ann N. Haskins Watkins, a widow. By marriage he obtained a life estate only in her 972-acre farm in Prince Edward County, but Branch bought out his wife's remaining interest in the land, presumably intending to use it to provide for his children by his first marriage. The couple lived there until 1835 or 1836 and then moved to Campbell County, where Branch had purchased 1,032 acres in 1833. He eventually acquired other property in Campbell County, including a mill. By 1842 Branch owned almost 3,000 acres in Campbell County, and by the late 1830s he owned more than fifty slaves.

In addition to cultivating tobacco, Branch practiced law. He served as commonwealth's attorney for Prince Edward County from April 1813 until June 1845 and for Charlotte County from June 1816 until June 1825. During the War of 1812 Branch was an ensign with the 4th Regiment Virginia Militia, and he subsequently rose to the rank of captain. He was elected to the board of trustees of Hampden-Sydney College on 22 July 1820 and remained a member until his death. Branch became a Whig and ran unsuccessfully for presidential elector on Henry Clay's ticket in 1832.

In May 1829 Branch lost a bid to represent Bedford, Buckingham, and Campbell Counties at a state constitutional convention. On 26 November 1829 one of the district's four delegates, Callohill Mennis, resigned because of ill health, and under the statute providing for the election of delegates the remaining three members from the district chose Branch to succeed him. He took his seat on 2 December 1829. Extant records do not credit Branch with participation in the debates, but he attended the convention until it adjourned on 15 January 1830, a day after he voted in favor of the conservative constitution that the convention approved and the voters ratified.

By January 1842 Branch was heavily in debt, probably as a result of obligations acquired in his law practice and his numerous land purchases. Through a series of deeds of trust he sought to satisfy his creditors and provide for his wife. His son William Daniel Branch acted as trustee and sold his Campbell County properties at public auction on 10 March 1842. Samuel Branch continued to practice law but owned little personal property when he died at Prince Edward Court House on 1 September 1847.

Death date in *Palmer, Branch, Christian and Guerrant Families, and Their Intermarriages, by a Descendant* (n.d.), 6–9; Alfred J. Morrison, *College of Hampden Sidney Dictionary of Biography, 1776–1825* (1921), 142–143; Land and Personal Property Tax Returns, RG 48, LVA, document changes in county residence; *Richmond Enquirer*, 5 June 1829; *Journal of 1829–1830 Convention*, 60, 66, 296; Catlin, *Convention of 1829–30* (por.); indebtedness documented in Campbell Co. Deed Book, 24:100–104, 148–150, 157–160, and *Lynchburg Virginian*, 3 Feb., 10 Mar. 1842.

DAPHNE GENTRY

BRANCH, Tazewell (13 May 1828–30 April 1925), member of the House of Delegates, was born in Prince Edward County, the son of Richard Branch and Mary Hays. Until emancipation he was owned by the Thackston family, for whom he worked as a house servant and shoemaker. Branch learned to read and write, and many of his contemporaries characterized him as unusually intelligent. About 1859 he married Harriet Lacy, also a slave. They had four sons and six daughters.

With both literacy and a trade, Branch quickly took advantage of his freedom. He was one of the trustees who purchased land in 1868 and 1869 for what became Beulah African Methodist Episcopal Church. By 1873 he owned property of his own in Farmville and served on the town council. Like other Piedmont counties with large African American populations, Prince Edward maintained an active Radical Republican Party organization, and Branch received the party's nomination for the House of Delegates in 1873. As a county native respected by whites as well as blacks, Branch differed from Edgar Allan, the British-born Union army veteran and Republican candidate for both the state senate and commonwealth's attorney. Thus, more than

a play on words may have been behind Allan's description of him as one of the party's "olive branches." The Republicans carried the county, and Branch easily defeated his opponent, Joseph T. Lyon.

Two years later Branch and many other county Republicans cooperated with moderate Conservatives to form a ticket for local offices. The fusion ticket won, but the Republicans split over Branch's candidacy for reelection. Allan repeated a Conservative charge that Branch had a poor attendance record in the legislature, and Branch damned Allan as a party wrecker. As a result largely of defections from Allan's allies, Branch won reelection. During both of his terms in the assembly he served on the Committee on Claims and voted with the small Republican minority.

Branch was said to have become too disgusted with politics to seek reelection in 1877, but he accepted a federal patronage position as an assistant assessor of internal revenue. Because he refused to follow other Republicans into a coalition with the Readjusters, he was dismissed from this position in October 1881. Branch remained out of politics thereafter, although in 1888 he supported the successful bid of John Mercer Langston to become Virginia's first African American congressman.

Making a living in Farmville proved difficult, as factory-produced shoes took customers away from Branch's shop. Although he unsuccessfully operated a grocery store for a time, Harriet Branch's income as a laundress became the family's most important source of income. Perhaps the couple's greatest achievement was to pass their ambition and love of learning to their children. All of them attended college or normal school, and four became teachers. Their son Clement Tazewell Branch received an M.D. from Howard University in 1900, settled in Camden, New Jersey, and in 1920 became the first African American to serve on that city's school board. Their daughter Mary Elizabeth Branch attended Virginia Normal and Collegiate Institute (later Virginia State University) and then taught there for about twenty years; its Branch Hall was subsequently named in her honor. In 1930 she became president of Tillotson College in Austin, Texas, a faltering institution that she transformed into a well-respected and fully accredited African American college.

Branch was a typical postwar African American politician in several respects: he had a close-knit nuclear family and possessed occupational skills, literacy, and property. Branch's independence and willingness to cooperate with moderate white Conservatives limited his political influence but earned him a lasting local reputation for integrity. He lived in Farmville until after 1911, when he sold the last of his property and moved to New Jersey to live with his son. Tazewell Branch died in Camden on 30 April 1925 and was buried in Odd Fellows Cemetery in Farmville.

Jackson, *Negro Office-Holders*, 5, 67 (por.); birth and death dates from New Jersey death certificate; family history in Mary Jenness, *Twelve Negro Americans* (1936), 85–100; Herbert Clarence Bradshaw, *History of Prince Edward County, Virginia* (1955), 426–435, 438, 451–452, 688, 695; Election Records, no. 2, RG 13, LVA; political career reported in *Farmville Mercury*, 1873–1875 (quotation in 6 Nov. 1873); *Richmond Whig*, 28 Oct. 1879; *Washington People's Advocate*, 8 Oct. 1881; information provided by Toni Gutwein of Camden County Historical Society and Patricia Whitney of public library at Moorestown, N.J.; eulogy in *Farmville Herald*, 15 May 1925.

LYNDA J. MORGAN

BRANCH, Thomas (23 December 1802– 15 November 1888), merchant, banker, and member of the Convention of 1861, was born at the Chesterfield County plantation of his parents, Thomas Branch and Mary Patteson Branch. Little is known about his early life. His father died in 1818, and his mother died in 1825, leaving the bulk of her estate to Branch's four younger siblings.

On 19 October 1825 Branch married Sarah Pride Read, of Amelia County. They resided in Petersburg and had eight sons and five daughters. Branch owned a small stable of thoroughbred racehorses and operated the nearby Newmarket track in 1829 and 1830, but after the spring season of 1831 his name no longer appeared in the reports of the races. He experienced a religious conversion at a Methodist camp meeting that year. The sudden death of his eldest child in July may have contributed to his joining the church, and he remained a devout Methodist for the rest of his life.

By 1831 Branch was the town sergeant, a post he held until 1836. His duties included auctioning the properties of debtors, a responsibility he exercised in his own interest. In 1836 he and an elder brother, David Henry Branch, formed a business partnership known as Thomas Branch and Brother to operate as commission merchants—middlemen selling goods to planters and in turn marketing their crops to purchasers elsewhere—and as auctioneers of estates, slaves, and other properties. The business flourished, and Branch became one of Petersburg's leading citizens. He won election as an alderman and served a term as mayor in 1842–1843. In 1846 Branch became a member of the board of trustees of Randolph-Macon College, the small Methodist school then located in Boydton.

In May 1848 Thomas Branch and Brother suddenly went under. Most likely the effect of uncertain political conditions in Europe on market prices for commodities combined with the recent collapse of another Petersburg mercantile house to provoke demands from creditors that the firm could not meet. David H. Branch had also acquired a large personal indebtedness, and Thomas Branch dissolved the partnership on 1 June. He retained the trust of both planters and merchants, quickly rebuilt his business, and eventually paid the old firm's debts. More important, he brought his eldest sons, James Read Branch and John Patteson Branch, into the firm, which by 1853 had become Thomas Branch and Sons. The new firm was one of Petersburg's largest, importing fertilizer and other commodities for sale to planters and marketing local wheat and tobacco to the world. In 1854 he also organized Branch and Company, a Richmond-based commission-merchant house, but it failed in the economic recession of 1857.

On 3 May 1855 Branch's wife died. On 22 April 1857 Branch married Anne Adams Wheelwright, of Westmoreland County. They had one son and two daughters.

Branch was a Unionist and supported the moderate candidate of the Democratic Party, Stephen A. Douglas, for the presidency in 1860. A majority of voters in Petersburg shared his views and elected him the city's delegate to the state convention called to consider the secession crisis. He served on none of the convention's select committees, but Branch was a bluff, plain-spoken man, and he took part often in the convention's debates. At first he counseled caution, but after his constituents delivered a petition early in March endorsing secession and President Abraham Lincoln called for troops to put down the rebellion, he spoke, worked, and voted for secession.

Five of Branch's sons and three of his sons-in-law entered the Confederate service. He continued to operate the business through much of the war and even entered a partnership in Richmond to handle money and stocks. That company fell with the Confederacy. Branch spent the last year of the war in Raleigh, North Carolina, with his wife and youngest children. Because of his wealth he had to apply for and duly received a presidential pardon.

Branch's sons all returned safely from the war, and he set about expanding Thomas Branch and Sons. Another son, Thomas Plummer Branch, and a son-in-law, Frederic Robert Scott, joined the partnership, and Scott organized an office of Branch Sons and Company in Augusta, Georgia, where yet another son, Melville Irby Branch, joined him. James Read Branch and John Patteson Branch meanwhile moved to Richmond and established Thomas Branch and Company, a private banking house. Branch continued to operate the commission-merchant business in Petersburg until about 1872, but the family businesses were firmly headquartered in Richmond by then.

On 12 November 1870 Branch organized the Merchants National Bank. He subscribed for half of the capital stock, and Scott took a third. Not surprisingly, the stockholders elected Branch president and Scott vice president. The sometimes irascible Branch guided the bank through the economic doldrums of the 1870s, but he had long been accustomed to conducting his businesses as he pleased and found banking regulations an irritant. Scott eventually took over many of the executive duties. In 1872 Branch sold his interest in the bank to Scott and to Branch's eldest surviving son, John Patteson Branch, who on 11 January 1881 succeeded him as president.

Branch's distinguished portly figure became as familiar a sight in Richmond as it had been in Petersburg. He joined Centenary Methodist Church in Richmond and remained one of the leading Methodist laymen in the state. Branch helped to engineer Randolph-Macon College's move to Ashland in 1868. Through a quirk in the school's new charter, which prohibited its president from serving as a trustee, Branch became the president of the board in 1874. He was the first layman to hold that post. The next legislature amended the charter, but he remained on the board until 1883. Thomas Branch died in Richmond on 15 November 1888 and was buried in Blandford Cemetery in Petersburg.

Cabell, *Branchiana,* frontispiece por., 51–57; Tyler, *Encyclopedia,* 5:1056; *American Turf Register and Sporting Magazine* (Sept. 1829–July 1831); Branch and Company Records, VHS; Presidential Pardons; John Herbert Claiborne, *Seventy-Five Years in Old Virginia* (1904), 50–51, 305–309; Reese and Gaines, *Proceedings of 1861 Convention,* 1:113–117, 306–307, 404–407, 2:16–19, 37–40, 541–544, 589–590, 3:163, 752–753, 4:144, 164–165; Frances Leigh Williams, *A Century of Service, Prologue to the Future: A History of the First and Merchants National Bank* (1965), 92–96 (por.); C. S. Alling, "'A Felt Presence and Power in Society': The Business Records of Thomas Branch and Family," Virginia Historical Society *An Occasional Bulletin* 49 (Dec. 1984): 1–5; Edward Leigh Pell, ed., *A Hundred Years of Richmond Methodism* (1899), 132–138; James Edward Scanlon, *Randolph-Macon College: A Southern History, 1825–1967* (1983), 125–139; obituaries and accounts of funeral in *Richmond State,* 15 Nov. 1888, *Petersburg Daily Index-Appeal,* 16, 17 Nov. 1888, *Richmond Daily Times* and *Richmond Dispatch,* both 16, 18 Nov. 1888, and *Richmond Christian Advocate,* 22 Nov. 1888; editorial tribute in *Richmond Daily Times,* 16 Nov. 1888; will described in *Richmond State,* 21 Nov. 1888, and *Richmond Daily Times* and *Richmond Dispatch,* both 22 Nov. 1888.

JOHN T. KNEEBONE

BRANDER, Thomas Alexander (12 December 1839–28 January 1900), leader of the Virginia division of the United Confederate Veterans, was born in Richmond, the son of Alexander Carter Brander and Louisiana Harris Adkins Brander. He grew up in Richmond, worked in a local mercantile house, and joined a prestigious militia unit, Company F of the 1st Virginia Regiment. When the Civil War began he became a second lieutenant in Company A of the 20th Regiment Virginia Infantry. For his bravery in July 1861 in the Rich Mountain campaign he was commissioned a first lieutenant on 15 February 1862 and assigned to the newly organized Letcher Artillery for service in the Confederate army. Brander was seriously wounded at Fredericksburg on 13 December 1862. On 3 May 1863 Captain Greenlee Davidson was killed at Chancellorsville, and Brander was promoted to captain on 23 May to succeed him in command of the unit. During the remainder of the war Brander served in nearly every campaign of the Army of Northern Virginia and rose to major on 1 March 1865. About this time he was assigned to William T. Poague's artillery battalion and was with that command when the army surrendered at Appomattox Court House in April 1865.

On 10 January 1865 Brander married Elizabeth Louisa Walke. They had six sons, two daughters, and a stillborn child of unrecorded gender. After the war Brander's various jobs included work as a grocer, supply agent for the Richmond and Danville Railroad Company, fish inspector, and director of a general insurance company that he established. He was active in local Democratic politics and was customs inspector during the first presidential administration of Grover Cleveland, from 1886 to 1887, and again from 1889 to 1890.

Brander was best known for his participation in Confederate veterans' activities. He began as a vice president of the F Company Military Memorial Association in Richmond. In 1888 he became first lieutenant commander and in 1889 commander of the R. E. Lee Camp, No. 1, Confederate Veterans, and when the Virginians joined the United Confederate Veterans in 1892, Brander was appointed major general and commander of the Virginia division and served until 1899. He became one of the best-known veterans' organization leaders in the United States, attended every reunion of Confederate veterans that he could, and often marched or rode at the head of parades. Brander led the veterans' wing of the Jefferson Davis reinterment procession in Richmond in 1893 and chaired the Virginia committee that assisted in raising funds for the Davis memorial that was erected in the city. In addition, Brander served from 1891 until his death as a vice president of the board and chairman of the executive committee of the R. E. Lee Camp

Confederate Soldiers' Home in Richmond. He supported the establishment of the Confederate Memorial Literary Society in Richmond and successfully urged that it receive most of the Confederate memorabilia belonging to the Soldiers' Home.

Thomas Alexander Brander died at his home in Richmond on 28 January 1900. His funeral service was held at Grace Episcopal Church, where he was a vestryman for many years. He was buried in Hollywood Cemetery in Richmond, wearing his Confederate army uniform as he had requested.

Return Jonathan Meigs, *A Record of the Descendants of James Brander Who Settled in Virginia about 1780* (1937), 6–8; Compiled Service Records; Evans, *Confederate Military History*, 4:749–750; G. L. Sherwood and Jeffrey C. Weaver, *20th and 39th Virginia Infantry* (1994), 5, 41; Peter S. Carmichael, *The Purcell, Crenshaw, and Letcher Artillery* (1990), 123, 149–150, 155 (por.), 160; BVS Marriage Register, Powhatan Co.; Robert E. Lee Camp Confederate Soldiers' Home, Minutes, 4 Dec. 1884–13 June 1901, RG 52, LVA; Hall, *Portraits*, 31; obituaries in *New York Times*, *Richmond and Manchester Evening Leader*, and *Richmond News* (por.), all 29 Jan. 1900, and *Richmond Dispatch* and *Richmond Times*, both 30 Jan. 1900.

RUTH ANN COSKI

BRAUN, Johannes. See **BROWN, John** (1771–1850).

BRAXTON, Allen Caperton (6 February 1862–22 March 1914), member of the Convention of 1901–1902, was born at the home of his grandfather Allen Taylor Caperton in Union in Monroe County, the son of Tomlin Braxton and Mary Caperton Braxton. He grew up at Chericoke, the Braxton family plantation in King William County. Braxton attended nearby Pampatike Academy until he was sixteen, when he left school and went to work, serving as a tutor and holding several jobs on railroads in West Virginia. He also read law, attended one summer course under John B. Minor at the University of Virginia, and eventually used funds supplied by friends to begin a practice in Staunton in the autumn of 1883.

A. Caperton Braxton, as he was professionally known, became a leader of the Staunton bar, helped send his younger brothers to law school, and after his father's death at the end of

1892 welcomed his mother and siblings into his bachelor household. From 1886 to 1890 he served as commonwealth's attorney of Augusta County and city attorney of Staunton. Braxton shared with many of his contemporaries both a strong belief in the inherent inferiority of African Americans and support for the growing movement in Virginia during the 1890s to devise a means of eliminating black citizens from the political process. He also favored reducing the participation of poor and uneducated white voters. On 23 May 1901 Braxton easily won election as one of two delegates to represent Augusta County and Staunton in a state constitutional convention that met from 12 June 1901 through 26 June 1902. He was chair of the temporary Committee of Privilege and Election, and on 21 June he was appointed chair of the Committee on Corporations and a member of the Committee on Judiciary. In preparation for the convention Braxton read widely on the legal ramifications of the different methods proposed for eliminating African Americans from public life in Virginia, and in support of the suffrage provisions that the convention adopted Braxton denounced the Fifteenth Amendment and advocated the measures that effectively disfranchised most African Americans and about half the previously qualified white voters in Virginia. He voted for the constitution as approved and for the decision to promulgate it without approval by the electorate.

Braxton opposed the state's Democratic Party leader, Thomas Staples Martin, a United States senator and former railroad lawyer whom he believed to be a corrupting influence in state government and politics. Large corporations in general, and railroads in particular, used their power to keep corporate taxes low, water their stock, and profit from discriminatory freight rates. Before the convention met, Braxton thoroughly researched the legal methods for regulating corporate abuses, and as chair of the corporations committee he drafted what became Article XII of the Constitution of 1902, which created the Virginia State Corporation Commission. With a few like-minded delegates he worked to reassure other members of the convention that their essentially conservative intent was to reduce the political power of big business and regulate corporations in the public interest. Braxton's objectives actually included cutting the ground out from under radical reformers. Nevertheless, corporate pressures made his task difficult, and he worked and spoke tirelessly and skillfully to obtain adoption of the commission article. The State Corporation Commission, of which he was regarded as the founder, consisted of three members appointed by the governor and confirmed by the General Assembly. The commission possessed legislative, executive, and judicial powers to charter corporations and regulate their activities in Virginia.

Between 1901 and 1904 Braxton published scholarly legal articles defending and explaining the most important work of the convention. His swift rise to prominence in Virginia and the innovative character of the State Corporation Commission brought him a brief national reputation, and his name was mentioned at the 1904 Democratic National Convention as a possible candidate for vice president. The following year Braxton contemplated challenging Martin for the senatorial nomination, but because he shared Martin's conservatism on most issues he could not rally a following among members of his party's small progressive faction.

Braxton moved to Richmond in 1904 and there expanded his law practice and became general counsel to the Richmond, Fredericksburg, and Potomac Railroad. In 1906 he was elected president of the Virginia State Bar Association. In December 1912 Braxton contracted Bright's disease. He spent most of 1913 in Atlantic City, New Jersey, under the care of Mary Patterson Miller, a longtime friend from Staunton whom he married on 23 November 1913. Allen Caperton Braxton died at his home in Staunton on 22 March 1914 and was buried in the family plot at Hollywood Cemetery in Richmond.

Tyler, *Men of Mark*, 1:220–223; Bernard M. Caperton, *The Caperton Family* (1973), 77–79, gives incorrect death date; Braxton family Bible records, 1781–1961, LVA; Pollard Questionnaires; Allen Caperton Braxton Papers, UVA; Braxton's publications include "Powers of Conventions" and "The Powers of the Approaching Constitutional Convention in Virginia," *Virginia Law Register* 7 (1901): 79–99 and 100–106 (jointly reprinted as *The Legitimate Functions and Powers of Constitutional Conventions . . .* [1901]), *Brief Digest of the New Constitution of Virginia* (1902), "The Fifteenth Amendment—An Account of Its Enactment," *Virginia State Bar Association Proceedings* (1903): 243–308, "The Civil Jury," *American Law Review* 38 (1904): 220–228, "The Virginia State Corporation Commission," *Virginia Law Register* 10 (1904): 1–18, and "The Eleventh Amendment," presidential address in *Virginia State Bar Association Proceedings* (1907): 172–193; Victor Duvall Weathers, "The Political Career of Allen Caperton Braxton" (M.A. thesis, UVA, 1956); Wythe W. Holt Jr., *Virginia's Constitutional Convention of 1901–1902* (1990); Thomas Edward Gay Jr., "Creating the Virginia State Corporation Commission," *VMHB* 78 (1970): 464–480; George Harrison Gilliam, "Making Virginia Progressive: Courts and Parties, Railroads and Regulators, 1890–1910," *VMHB* 107 (1999): 189–222; *Richmond Times*, 12 June 1901; *Proceedings and Debates of 1901–1902 Convention; Convention of 1901–1902 Photographs* (por.); marriage reported in *Staunton Daily News*, 25 Nov. 1913; obituaries in *Richmond Times-Dispatch*, 23 Mar. 1914 (por.), and *Staunton Daily News*, 24 Mar. 1914; editorial tribute in *Staunton Daily News*, 25 Mar. 1914; memorials in *Virginia State Bar Association Proceedings* (1914): 54–57, and *Virginia Law Register* 20 (1914): 81–90.

WYTHE W. HOLT JR.

BRAXTON, Carter (10 September 1736– 10 October 1797), member of the Continental Congress and member of the Council, was the younger of two sons of George Braxton (d. 1749) and Mary Carter Braxton and was born at Newington, the King and Queen County estate of his grandfather George Braxton (ca. 1677– 1748), a prosperous immigrant merchant and planter. His mother, who died as a consequence of his birth, was the youngest daughter of the fabulously wealthy Robert "King" Carter.

In his youth Braxton enjoyed riches and privilege. On 16 July 1755, while attending the College of William and Mary, he married Judith Robinson, a niece of John Robinson (1705–1766), the powerful Speaker of the House of Burgesses. Braxton purchased Elsing Green in King William County. Judith Robinson Braxton died giving birth to the second of her two daughters in December 1757, after which Braxton traveled in Europe for two years. On 15 May 1760 he married Elizabeth Corbin, daughter of Richard Corbin, a member of the governor's Council and deputy collector of the royal revenue in Virginia. They had ten sons and six daughters. Braxton purchased Chericoke plantation in King William County, not far from Elsing Green, and lived there until the end of 1776.

When his elder brother died in October 1761 Braxton inherited the remainder of the family estate, but both brothers had lived extravagantly, and he was burdened with large debts. Even after selling land to satisfy some of his many creditors, he owned more than 12,000 acres and about 165 slaves during the 1770s and engaged in large-scale tobacco planting and the transatlantic tobacco trade. As a well-connected member of the landed elite, Braxton served on the vestry and as a justice of the peace and sheriff. He was elected to represent King William County in the House of Burgesses in 1761 and attended sixteen of the nineteen meetings of the General Assembly between then and 1775. He served on the Committee of Propositions and Grievances from 1764 to 1775, joined the Committee for Religion in 1768, and was appointed to the Committee for Trade in 1769.

During the imperial crises that led to the American Revolution, Braxton sided with moderate critics of British policies and usually opposed such bold leaders as Patrick Henry. On 3 May 1775 Braxton alone confronted Henry and a large company of volunteer militiamen who were marching on Williamsburg to demand restoration of or reimbursement for Virginia gunpowder that the royal governor had removed from the colony's powder magazine. Braxton's pledge to have the powder paid for out of his father-in-law's royal accounts probably averted a violent clash.

Braxton represented King William County in the first four Revolutionary Conventions. The convention of July–August 1775 elected him to the Virginia Committee of Safety, which oversaw the arming of the colony, and on 15 December the Convention of 1775–1776 elected him to the Continental Congress. Braxton served in Congress from 23 February 1776 until the first week in August. He was not a leading member, nor did he advocate independence until late in the spring, but he voted for independence on 2 July 1776 and supported and signed the Declaration of Independence.

In the spring of 1776 Braxton wrote and published a pamphlet, *An Address to the Convention of the Colony and Ancient Dominion of Virginia, on the Subject of Government in General, and Recommending a Particular Form to Their Consideration*. Intended as a corrective to what he perceived as excessively democratic ideas in John Adams's *Thoughts on Government* of the same year, the pamphlet, together with rumors that Braxton's wife and father-in-law were Loyalists, brought him severe criticism from many of the Revolutionary leaders in Virginia. The Convention of 1776 reduced the number of Virginia delegates to Congress late in June 1776 in order to remove Braxton and his friend Benjamin Harrison (1726–1791) from the delegation.

Braxton returned to Virginia and sat in the House of Delegates from King William County in nearly every assembly between the autumn of 1776 and January 1786. When present, he held influential committee appointments. In 1776 and 1777 he served on the Committees of Privileges and Elections and of Propositions and Grievances and was chair of the Committee for Religion, and in 1777 he became ranking member of the Committee of Trade. He chaired the Committee of Privileges and Elections in 1779 and 1780 and in 1783 was ranking member of the Committees of Propositions and Grievances and of Trade.

After a fire destroyed the dwelling at Chericoke on 19 December 1776, Braxton moved to a smaller but elegant house in the town of West Point, where he lived and conducted his business until 1786. During the Revolutionary War Braxton and Robert Morris, of Philadelphia, financed the *Phoenix*, a privateer that seized a Portuguese vessel illegally. The resulting lawsuits cost both investors dearly. In a separate disaster in 1779, Braxton lost a £40,000 tobacco ship to the British. Though still owning large tracts of land, he was virtually insolvent by the end of the war.

In the autumn of 1785 Braxton sought appointment to the Council of State, the governor's executive advisory board and a salaried office. The General Assembly duly elected him, and he served from 23 January 1786 through 30 March 1791 and again from 31 May 1794 until his death. By the time he joined the Council Braxton had made his political peace with Patrick Henry, and they worked together harmoniously while Henry was governor in 1786. Braxton served as a commissioner of the Pamunkey Indian lands and a lay delegate to the founding convention of the Episcopal Church in Virginia. Although not a delegate to the Convention of 1788, he supported ratification of the United States Constitution. Carter Braxton died in Richmond on 10 October 1797 and was buried either in that city or at Chericoke.

Alonzo Thomas Dill, *Carter Braxton, Virginia Signer: A Conservative in Revolt* (1983), frontispiece por.; L. Tomlin Stevens, "Carter Braxton, Signer of the Declaration of Independence" (Ph.D. diss., Ohio State University, 1969); birth, death, and second marriage dates in John Sanderson, *Biography of the Signers to the Declaration of Independence* (1828), 5:87–107; first marriage in Middlesex Co. Marriage Bonds, printed in *WMQ*, 1st ser., 4 (1895): 119; other biographical and family information in *Richard Brooke* v. *William H. Macon et al.* suit papers, U.S. Circuit Court Record Book, vol. 17, LVA; personal and business letters at Historical Society of Pennsylvania, Philadelphia, in Papers of the Continental Congress, NARA, and in several collections at UVA and VHS; death notice without date in *Virginia Gazette, and Petersburg Intelligencer*, 17 Oct. 1797.

ALONZO THOMAS DILL

BRAXTON, Carter Moore (5 September 1836–27 May 1898), Confederate artillery officer and civil engineer, was born in Norfolk, the son of Carter Moore Braxton and his third wife, Elizabeth Teagle Mayo Braxton. Elliott Muse Braxton, who served in the House of Representatives after the Civil War, was his elder half brother. Carter Moore Braxton lived in Norfolk and in King and Queen County until his father died in 1847, after which he lived in Fredericksburg. He was educated at Hanover Academy and prepared for a career in civil engineering. By the time the Civil War broke out in 1861, Braxton was chief engineer in charge of construction for the Fredericksburg and Gordonsville Railroad.

Braxton had a distinguished career in the Confederate army. He became a captain in the Fredericksburg Artillery on 8 May 1861. His company, known as Braxton's Battery, saw action in the Seven Days' Battles and at Cedar

Mountain, the Second Battle of Manassas (Bull Run), Chantilly, Sharpsburg (Antietam), and Fredericksburg. When the Army of Northern Virginia reorganized its artillery, Braxton was promoted to major on 4 April 1863, with the commission to date from 2 March. After fighting at Chancellorsville and distinguishing himself at Gettysburg and Mine Run, he was promoted on 14 March 1864 to lieutenant colonel to rank from 27 February 1864. He served at the Battles of the Wilderness and of Cold Harbor and saw action in the Shenandoah Valley in 1864 and at Chaffin's Farm near Richmond early in 1865. Braxton fought at Hatcher's Run and Five Forks in the last days of the war and surrendered with the Army of Northern Virginia at Appomattox Court House on 9 April 1865. Although often in the thick of the fighting and described by one later account as having had seven horses killed under him, he was never wounded. After the war Braxton prepared and published a *Map of the Battle Field of Fredericksburg, Explained by Extracts from Official Reports* (1866).

Braxton married Fanny Page Hume in Orange County on 16 February 1865, but she died in Richmond on 16 June of that year. He returned to Fredericksburg and to his career as a civil engineer, first in overseeing the repair of the Aquia Creek bridge of the Richmond, Fredericksburg, and Potomac Railroad, and briefly in 1869 as Fredericksburg city surveyor. In June 1866 Braxton became president of the Fredericksburg and Gordonsville Railroad, which he extended during the following decade to Orange as the Potomac, Fredericksburg, and Piedmont Railroad. He also supervised the surveying and construction of the Fredericksburg and Alexandria Railroad, which later became part of the Richmond, Fredericksburg, and Potomac Railroad. Braxton married Nannie Clementina Alsop, of Fredericksburg, on 26 March 1868, and they had nine daughters.

In 1881 Braxton directed the completion of the Chesapeake and Ohio Railway line for the few miles from Lee Hall into Newport News. He moved to the latter town, where from 1881 to 1889 he was in charge of maintenance for the C&O. In July 1889 Braxton began supervision of the massive excavations for the Chesapeake

Dry Dock and Construction Company, which changed its name within the year to the Newport News Shipbuilding and Dry Dock Company. He formed his own engineering construction firm, Braxton, Chandler, and Marye, and also developed real estate as president of the Central Land Company and of the Newport News Land and Development Company. Braxton was founding president of the Newport News Street Railway Company, which began with horse-drawn carriages but soon converted to electricity. In 1891 he became vice president of the First National Bank of Newport News, and he was also vice president of the Newport News Gas Company.

Braxton was active in the First Baptist Church of Newport News and from 1887 until his death was commander of the McGruder Camp of the United Confederate Veterans. Carter Moore Braxton died of Bright's disease at his home in Newport News on 27 May 1898 and was buried in the local Greenlawn Cemetery.

Biographies in Evans, *Confederate Military History*, 4:750–752, and Henry and Spofford, *Eminent Men*, 405–406; some letters at UVA and VHS; Robert K. Krick, *The Fredericksburg Artillery* (1986), esp. 91 (por.), 98; Compiled Service Records; BVS Marriage Register, Orange Co., 1865, Fredericksburg, 1868; obituary (giving 1839 birth year) and report of funeral in *Newport News Daily Press*, 28, 29, 31 May 1898.

MARTIN S. LANE

BRAXTON, Corbin (3 May 1792–12 February 1852), member of the Convention of 1850–1851, was born at Hybla in King William County, the son of George Braxton and Mary Walker Carter Braxton. His grandfather Carter Braxton signed the Declaration of Independence, and his mother was the aunt of Robert Edward Lee. Braxton attended Washington College (later Washington and Lee University) for at least three semesters beginning no later than May 1807. He entered the medical school of the University of Pennsylvania in October 1811 and graduated in April 1814.

Braxton returned home to Chericoke in King William County and began the practice of medicine. He served briefly in the field as a second lieutenant of militia in an artillery company during the British invasion in the autumn of 1814 and subsequently won promotions to major in July 1815, lieutenant colonel in September 1817, and colonel in May 1818. On 11 January 1843 the General Assembly elected Braxton general of the 14th Brigade Virginia Militia.

On 12 February 1824 Braxton married Mary Williamson Tomlin. One each of their three sons and four daughters died young. By the 1830s Braxton had ceased practicing medicine full time and devoted most of his attention to his two plantations and marshland property, which together contained almost 1,400 acres. At the time of his death he owned sixty-five slaves. Braxton was one of the most successful planters in the county and among the first in Tidewater Virginia to purchase and experiment with Cyrus McCormick's reaper.

Braxton was elected in 1816 to a single term representing King William County in the House of Delegates. In 1837 he won a special election to fill a vacancy in the Senate of Virginia from the district comprising Gloucester, King and Queen, King William, Mathews, and Middlesex Counties. He served on the Committee of Privileges and Elections and the Joint Committee to Examine the Penitentiary. His term expired after the session held in the spring of 1838, and he did not seek reelection. From May 1845 through 1851 Braxton sat on the board of visitors of the Virginia Military Institute and served as president of the board from 1846 to 1850.

Despite ill health and without seeking the nomination, Braxton was elected one of five delegates to represent the district of Caroline, Hanover, King William, and Spotsylvania Counties in a state constitutional convention that met from 14 October 1850 to 1 August 1851. He served on the standing Committee on the Executive Department and Ministerial Officers and also chaired a committee that set the compensation for the convention's employees. Braxton opposed many of the reforms that delegates from the western counties successfully proposed. The changes included white manhood suffrage, popular election of local officials and the governor, and, most productive of controversy, a reapportionment of seats in the General Assembly based on the white population that gave the western counties majorities in both houses of the legislature. Like many other eastern Democrats in the

convention, Braxton opposed the key compromise on reapportionment, and he voted against the constitution that the convention approved on 31 July 1851.

On 12 February 1852 Corbin Braxton suffered a hemorrhage of the lungs and died at Williams Ferry in King William County, where he had gone to offer medical care to a sick woman. He was buried probably in the family graveyard at Chericoke.

Frederick Horner, *The History of the Blair, Banister, and Braxton Families* (1898), 157–167; birth date in Braxton family Bible records, 1781–1953, LVA; Braxton family Bible records, 1781–1961, LVA; Tomlin family Bible records, 1778–1915, LVA; marriage date in Coalter family Bible records, 1802–1930, VHS; Braxton letters in various collections at UVA, VHS, VMI, and W&M; William Couper, *One Hundred Years at V.M.I.* (1939), 1:197, 227, 235, 250–253, 260–262; *Journal of 1850–1851 Convention,* 27, 31, 59, 419, Appendix, 22; por. at VMI; undated obituary in *Richmond Enquirer,* 2 Mar. 1852; death date in Braxton Family Genealogical Notes, LVA, and *Catalogue of the Officers and Alumni of Washington and Lee University, Lexington, Virginia, 1749–1888* (1888), 61.

DAPHNE GENTRY

BRAXTON, Elliott Muse (8 October 1823–2 October 1891), member of the House of Representatives, was born in Mathews County, the son of Carter Moore Braxton and his second wife, Anna Muse Braxton. A younger half brother, Carter Moore Braxton (1836–1898), became an eminent civil engineer in Newport News. During his childhood Braxton lived in the city of Norfolk and in King and Queen County, and as a young man he studied law in the office of his father, who died in 1847.

Braxton was admitted to the bar in 1849 and shortly thereafter moved to Richmond County to practice law. In October 1851 he defeated the veteran Whig legislator Robert W. Carter for a seat in the Senate of Virginia representing the counties of Lancaster, Northumberland, Richmond, and Westmoreland. In May 1853 Braxton was narrowly reelected to a four-year term by defeating another Whig, John T. Rice. Braxton's contemporaries attributed his success as a Democrat in an essentially Whig district to his personal popularity. Throughout his Senate service he sat on the Committee for Courts of Justice and the Joint Committee to Examine the

First Auditor's Office. Braxton chose not to seek reelection in 1857.

On 23 November 1854 Braxton married Anna Maria Marshall, a granddaughter of jurist John Marshall. They had four daughters and four sons. In 1859 or 1860 he moved his family and his law practice to Fredericksburg. Braxton entered Confederate service on 1 July 1861 with a company of volunteers he raised from Stafford County and was elected its captain on 18 July. The company became part of the 30th Regiment Virginia Infantry in September 1861, and he was reelected captain on 16 April 1862. In August 1862 Braxton was promoted to major and assigned the office of brigade quartermaster. He retained this rank and assignment until the end of the war despite an attempt to obtain an army judicial post in the autumn of 1864.

In the spring of 1865 Braxton returned to Fredericksburg and opened a law office with C. Wistar Wallace, with whom he had served in the 30th Virginia. Braxton was elected to the Fredericksburg city council in 1866 and served until it was reorganized by the state's military government in April 1868. In 1870 he ran for the House of Representatives as a Conservative and defeated Republican incumbent Lewis McKenzie in the district comprising Culpeper, Fairfax, Fauquier, Loudoun, Louisa, Madison, Orange, Prince William, Rappahannock, Spotsylvania, and Stafford Counties. McKenzie challenged the outcome, charging that Conservative Party workers had intimidated and threatened voters. Despite its Republican majority the Committee on Elections decided unanimously on 9 January 1872 that Braxton had been duly elected, and he served in Congress from 4 March 1871 to 4 March 1873. He ran for reelection in November 1872 but lost to James B. Sener, a lawyer and owner of a Republican newspaper who had testified against him in the contested election case. During his one unremarkable congressional term Braxton served on no committees but spoke several times in defense of Virginia, states' rights, and the Conservative Party and moved unsuccessfully to compensate the Lee family for Arlington, the estate that the federal government had seized during the Civil War.

Elliott Muse Braxton practiced law in Fredericksburg until he developed heart disease during the 1880s. He died at his home on 2 October 1891 and was buried in that town's Confederate Cemetery.

Biography with some errors in Evans, *Confederate Military History*, 4:752; Braxton Family Genealogical Notes, LVA; *Richmond Enquirer*, 3 June 1853; Compiled Service Records, including one Braxton letter; Robert K. Krick, *30th Virginia Infantry* (1983), esp. 83; *Congressional Globe*, 42d Cong., 1st sess., 75, 2d sess., 1197–1199, 1741–1743; *McKenzie* v. *Braxton: Papers in the Case of Lewis McKenzie* v. *Elliott M. Braxton*, 42d Cong., 1st sess., 1872, House Misc. Doc. 35, serial 1472; *McKenzie* v. *Braxton*, 42d Cong., 2d sess., 1872, House Rept. 4, serial 1528; Robert A. Hodge, *A Roster of the Citizen Burials in the Fredericksburg Confederate Cemetery* (1981), 11–12; obituary in *Fredericksburg Free Lance*, 6 Oct. 1891.

DONALD W. GUNTER

BRAXTON, George (ca. 1677–1 July 1748), merchant, was born in England and immigrated to Virginia sometime during the 1690s. Documentary evidence about his early years in Virginia is very scarce, but he prospered rapidly and by 1702 was a member of the King and Queen County Court, a captain in the county militia, and a merchant of considerable prominence. By then Braxton had married a daughter of Thomas Paullin and Elizabeth Davis Paullin, also of King and Queen County, and by 1704 he had acquired Newington, a 2,800-acre estate on the Mattaponi River. The couple had one son and two daughters.

Braxton acted as a factor, or agent, on behalf of and in partnership with some of the most important English mercantile houses, including the Perrys, of London, and Noblett Ruddock and Isaac Hobhouse, both of Bristol. Braxton exported tobacco to England and imported manufactured goods from England and slaves from Africa and the West Indies. Following the death of the prominent merchant John Baylor (ca. 1660–1720), Braxton became the wealthiest and most important merchant operating anywhere along the Mattaponi. By the mid-1720s Braxton's namesake son had joined him in his mercantile ventures and also in land speculation. On their own and in conjunction with other partners and relatives they acquired large grants, including one 10,000-acre tract in

Spotsylvania County and one 25,000-acre holding in Goochland County. The two George Braxtons were partners in business and served together on the county court and in the militia. As a consequence of the loss of many local records their careers are presented confusingly in some old county and family histories.

Braxton continued his service on the county court and rose to colonel in the militia. In 1718 he was elected to the House of Burgesses from King and Queen County. Reelected three times, he served through October 1734 and sat on the Committee of Propositions and Grievances at every session he attended. Eight years after Braxton retired from the House, his son succeeded him as a burgess. His son married a daughter of Robert "King" Carter and acquired such standing that in 1736 Lieutenant Governor William Gooch unsuccessfully recommended him for a seat on the governor's Council. The second George Braxton (d. 1749) had two sons, a third George Braxton (1734–1761) and Carter Braxton (1736–1797), who signed the Declaration of Independence.

George Braxton, founder of the Braxton family of Virginia, died on 1 July 1748 and was buried at the Lower Church of Saint Stephen's Parish in King and Queen County.

Malcolm H. Harris, *Old New Kent County: Some Account of the Planters, Plantations, and Places in New Kent County* (1977), 1:404, 411; earliest reference in Virginia in undated enclosure from Francis Nicholson to Board of Trade, 21 Mar. 1702, CO 5/1312, pt. 2, fol. 217; numerous references to business affairs, land speculation, and officeholding in *Journals of House of Burgesses, Executive Journals of Council*, Patent Book, vols. 10–26, RG 4, LVA, and *Williamsburg Virginia Gazette*; gravestone inscription (photograph in George Harrison Sanford King Papers, VHS) gives age as seventy-one and death date.

DAPHNE GENTRY

BRAY, James (d. 24 October 1691), member of the Council, was born probably in England early in the 1630s. He may have been a member of or an attorney for a London mercantile house before arriving in Virginia sometime before 26 October 1657. Bray eventually acquired land at Middle Plantation, on the boundary between York and James City Counties, engaged in agriculture and commerce, and practiced law in the courts of James City, New Kent, and York Counties, as well as in the General Court. In 1658 he was undersheriff in York County, and by 1672 he was a member of the quorum for the James City County Court. By 24 August 1658 Bray was married to Angelica Fisher, a widow with whom he had at least three sons and one or two daughters.

On 3 March 1675 Bray and three other men were appointed to the governor's Council, and Bray was sworn in the next day. During Bacon's Rebellion the following year, Bray remained an ally of Governor Sir William Berkeley, although he may have tried to adopt a conciliatory pose at the tumultuous June 1676 session of the General Assembly. A contemporary allegation that Bray signed one of Nathaniel Bacon's two declarations of August 1676 is not substantiated on extant copies of either document. In mid-September, when Bacon began fortifying Jamestown, he forced the wives of several Berkeley supporters, including Angelica Bray, to stand on the ramparts to shield his workmen. After the rebellion Berkeley prosecuted one of its leaders, William Drummond, at Bray's Middle Plantation residence.

Bray and others of Berkeley's followers soon clashed with Berkeley's successor, Herbert Jeffreys, who recommended that they be removed from the Council. On 14 March 1679 the king duly excluded James Bray, Philip Ludwell, and Thomas Ballard (d. 1690) from the Council "for their unworthy behaviour and demerits." Bray then resumed his law practice in the area courts. During the 1670s and 1680s his friends and clients included such prominent men as Daniel Parke and William Byrd (ca. 1652–1704). A hot-tempered and opinionated man, Bray had once been arrested in 1662 for "uncivil wrangling and rude deportment" in the York County Court. In 1683 a litigant in the same county complained that "there was noe Justice done at Yorke Courtt this day but what was done for Esq. Bray."

In 1688 Bray was elected to the House of Burgesses from James City County and was immediately appointed chairman of the important Committee for Public Claims. He was also elected to the first session of the assembly that met in April 1691, but with one other burgess-elect, Arthur Allen (ca. 1652–1710), he refused to take the oaths of allegiance and supremacy to William and Mary, probably because he would not renounce his prior loyalty oaths to James II. The House repeatedly pressed Bray to take the oaths, but feigning sickness and angering the burgesses in the process, he stayed away from the House until 18 May, when he finally refused to take the oaths and was declared ineligible, only three days before the assembly adjourned.

James Bray died on 24 October 1691 and was buried probably in the churchyard of Bruton Parish, which he had served as a vestryman from at least the 1674 date of the earliest extant record. Early in the eighteenth century his son David Bray sold part of the Middle Plantation estate to the colony for the establishment of the new capital at Williamsburg. David Bray's only son, also named David, was appointed to the governor's Council on 12 June 1731 but died sixteen days before the Council reconvened on 21 October and consequently never served.

Mary A. Stephenson, "A Record of the Bray Family, 1658–ca. 1800" (1963 typescript, CW), 1–2; other family history in Hening, *Statutes*, 4:370–376, and Winfree, *Laws of Virginia*, 381–384; residence in Virginia first documented in York Co. Deeds, Orders, Wills, 3:4; numerous business and legal references in York Co. court records (second and third quotations from York Co. Deeds, Orders, Wills, 3:168–169, 6:497); *Minutes of Council and General Court*; *Richmond Enquirer*, 12 Sept. 1804; exclusion from Council in PRO CO 5/1355, fols. 266–273 (first quotation on 271); oath controversy in *Journals of House of Burgesses, 1659/60–1693*, 340, 345, 356, 357, 363; death date in Bruton Parish Register, W&M.

DAPHNE GENTRY

BREAZEALE, William McSwain (9 May 1908–11 December 1970), nuclear engineer, was born in New Brunswick, New Jersey, the son of William E. Breazeale, a professor of mathematics and astronomy at Rutgers University, and Josephine McSwain Breazeale, a professor of French at Agnes Scott College before her marriage. He received a B.S. from Rutgers in 1929, an M.S. from Vanderbilt University in 1932, and a Ph.D. in physics from the University of Virginia in 1935, with a dissertation entitled "The Electro-Optical Kerr Effect in Ammonia, Nitrogen, and Oxygen." While pursuing his education Breazeale worked as a test engineer for the Western Electric Company and from 1932

to 1935 as an instructor in physics at the University of Virginia.

From 1935 to 1941 Breazeale taught electrical engineering at Vanderbilt University. On 22 June 1938 he married Mary Rutledge, a librarian at Vanderbilt. They had one son and one daughter. During World War II Breazeale served on the staff of the radiation laboratory at the Massachusetts Institute of Technology, but he also spent several months in London in 1943 and 1944 working on scientific research and development, probably on problems associated with radar and microwave receivers. He taught electrical engineering at the University of Virginia, from 1945 to 1946 as an associate professor and from 1947 to the summer of 1949 as a professor. From 1949 to 1953 he was the principal physicist at the Oak Ridge National Laboratory in Tennessee. Breazeale taught nuclear engineering at Pennsylvania State University from 1953 to 1956 and directed the university's reactor facility.

From 1956 until his death Breazeale held various research and administrative positions in Lynchburg with the Babcock and Wilcox Company. Babcock and Wilcox, a major industrial supplier of boilers for power plants and ships, became one of the nation's most important engineering firms in the field of nuclear power and nuclear propulsion. In 1962 Breazeale advanced from assistant manager of the company's Atomic Energy Division to director of the Nuclear Development Center of the company's Research and Development Division. He had overall responsibility for engineering design work on the nuclear power plant for the NS *Savannah,* the world's first nuclear-powered merchant ship. In its futuristic vision the *Savannah* project appropriately symbolized the grand expectations for nuclear power in the 1950s and early in the 1960s, but the financial failure of the *Savannah* project, in part because some ports refused admittance to the nuclear-powered ship, symbolized the guarded apprehension about nuclear power that began to emerge later in the 1960s. The *Savannah* proved to be the United States' only effort at building a nuclear-powered merchant vessel, although both Germany and Japan launched their own prototypes, and the Soviet Union developed a nuclear-powered icebreaker.

Breazeale published about twenty research papers and with Lawrence R. Quarles wrote *Lines, Networks, and Filters* (1951), a textbook on transmission lines. He worked as a consultant on various "swimming pool" reactors, in which the nuclear fuel rods were suspended vertically in a pool of water in the reactor's core. Such reactors operated at relatively low temperatures and pressures and were used for research. Breazeale received the first reactor operations license issued by the Atomic Energy Commission and served on its committee on reactor safeguards. In 1960 he was a representative at the Intergovernmental Maritime Consultative Organization's international conference on the safety of life at sea, which considered the safety implications of nuclear-powered ships.

William McSwain Breazeale died suddenly of a cerebral hemorrhage at his home in Lynchburg on 11 December 1970. His body was cremated.

American Men of Science: A Biographical Directory, 11th ed. (1965), 563; *Commonwealth* 29 (Oct. 1962): 41–42; information provided by widow Mary R. Breazeale; obituaries in *Lynchburg Daily Advance*, 12 Dec. 1970 (por.), and *Lynchburg News* and *New York Times*, both 13 Dec. 1970.

PAUL R. WAIBEL

BRECKINRIDGE, Cary (5 October 1839– 11 May 1918), Confederate cavalry officer and educator, was born at Catawba near Fincastle in Botetourt County, the son of Cary Breckinridge and Emma Walker Gilmer Breckinridge. His grandfather James Breckinridge represented Virginia in Congress, and his cousin John Cabell Breckinridge was vice president of the United States and a major general and secretary of war of the Confederate States.

Breckinridge grew up at his grandfather's Federal-style mansion, Grove Hill. From it his father managed his plantations and became a wealthy planter, owning nearly 150 slaves in 1860, more than any other person in Botetourt County. After study at home, Breckinridge entered the Virginia Military Institute in 1856. He was an unexceptional student and graduated eighteenth in a class of forty-one on 4 July 1860,

but during his final year at VMI he served as cadet second lieutenant and ranked first in his class in infantry tactics.

Breckinridge and all four of his brothers fought for the Confederacy, and three of them died. A diary kept by their sister Lucy Gilmer Breckinridge between 1862 and 1864 recorded the constant worry and grief experienced by the family on the home front. Cary Breckinridge enrolled as second lieutenant of the Botetourt Dragoons on 17 May 1861. On 30 January 1862 he was elected captain of Company C, 2d Regiment Virginia Cavalry, and less than three months later, on 24 April 1862, he received a major's commission. Breckinridge was an aggressive combatant and during the course of the war reportedly had five horses shot from under him. At the Second Battle of Manassas (Bull Run), on 30 August 1862, he suffered a saber cut to his face, the first of his five war wounds. Breckinridge was captured at Kelly's Ford on 17 March 1863 and briefly imprisoned in the Old Capitol Prison in Washington, D.C. After he was exchanged and enjoyed a week of recuperation at home he returned to his regiment. In January 1865 Breckinridge was promoted to lieutenant colonel retroactive to 7 December 1864. During the waning days of the war he was promoted to brigadier general, but having never held that rank in battle he refused to claim it later in life.

Breckinridge returned to Fincastle after the war and on 27 June 1866 married Mary Virginia Calwell, a young woman he had first met and reportedly become infatuated with on a short furlough home in January 1864. She was a native of Greenbrier County, West Virginia, and the granddaughter of James Calwell, the manager of the White Sulphur Springs resort. Four of their five sons and both of their daughters survived to maturity. Breckinridge's father died in 1867, but he and his wife chose to reside in Fincastle rather than at Grove Hill, where his mother and then his younger brother George William Breckinridge maintained the family estate. Breckinridge and his contemporaries identified him as a farmer, but some accounts state that he also engaged in banking. His standing as a former Confederate officer and his family background undoubtedly helped make him the choice of local Conservatives to run for the House of Delegates in 1869. Indeed, those qualities, combined with his imposing physical stature (contemporaries described him as a "giant"), might have won him greater political prominence had he sought it. Breckinridge carried Botetourt County with nearly twice as many votes as his opponent in 1869. He voted with the Conservative majority in the House of Delegates and served on the Committees of Claims and on Militia and Police. He did not seek reelection.

Breckinridge remained a stalwart of the local Conservative Party and its successor, the Democratic Party, sitting on the county executive committee, attending nominating conventions, and serving between 1887 and 1902 on the county electoral board. He also served on the board of visitors of the Virginia Military Institute from 1888 to 1890. Breckinridge's most important public service was as superintendent of public schools of Botetourt County from 1886 to 1917. At the close of his three decades in this post, nearly half of the county's schools remained one-room structures, but the county also boasted a dozen graded schools and seven high schools, two of which were accredited four-year institutions. During Breckinridge's last year as superintendent, although past the age of seventy-five, he made 114 official visits to different public schools.

Cary Breckinridge died of heart failure on 11 May 1918 at Aspen Hill, his home in Fincastle, and was buried nearby at Godwin Cemetery. His youngest son, William Norwood Breckinridge, a physician, shared his father's devotion to the Democratic Party, served for many years as mayor of Fincastle, and had the Breckinridge Elementary School there named in his honor.

Birth and marriage dates in Cary Breckinridge alumnus file, VMI; variant marriage date of 27 June 1866 in Larry G. Shuck, ed., *Greenbrier County Marriages, 1782–1900* (1988–), 1:59; Mary Selden Kennedy, *Seldens of Virginia and Allied Families* (1911), 1:456–458, citing family Bible records and giving marriage date of 2 June 1866; John Frederick Dorman, *Prestons of Smithfield and Greenfield in Virginia* (1982), 128–132; Krick, *Lee's Colonels*, 58; Compiled Service Records; Robert J. Driver Jr., *2nd Virginia Cavalry* (1995), esp. 169 (por.), 199; Mary D. Robertson, ed., *Lucy Breckinridge of Grove Hill: The Journal of a Virginia Girl,* *1862–1864* (1979); *Fincastle Herald*, 20 July 1893; *Virginia School Report, 1916–1917* (1918), 64; obituaries in *Lynchburg News* and *Roanoke Times*, both 12 May 1918, and *Confederate Veteran* 26 (1918): 452 (quotation).

LINDSAY ROBERTSON

BRECKINRIDGE, James (7 March 1763– 13 May 1833), member of the House of Representatives, was born near what is now Fincastle, in the southern part of Augusta County that in 1770 became Botetourt County. He was the son of Robert Breckinridge, or Breckenridge, and his second wife, Lettice Preston Breckinridge. His elder half brother Robert Breckinridge served in the Convention of 1788, and his brother John Breckinridge represented Kentucky in the United States Senate and served briefly as attorney general of the United States. Breckinridge received his early education from private tutors. After his father's death about 1773, his uncle William Preston became his guardian. During the Revolutionary War Breckinridge enlisted as a private in a company of Botetourt riflemen that Preston commanded, and in 1781 he served as an ensign under General Nathanael Greene in North Carolina. Breckinridge then returned home and attended Liberty Hall Academy (later Washington and Lee University). On 13 June 1782 he was appointed deputy clerk of Botetourt County.

Breckinridge studied law under George Wythe at the College of William and Mary in 1788. A visit to that year's state convention in Richmond impressed him with the eloquence of the debates over the ratification of the new federal Constitution. Breckinridge returned to Botetourt County early in 1789 and on 10 February presented his license to practice law to the county court. He opened a law office in Fincastle and supplemented his income with work as an inspector of federal tax collection for an eight-county district. In November 1789 Breckinridge was appointed trustee for the town of Fincastle, and on 14 April 1790 he was sworn in as a captain in the county militia. He also served as commonwealth's attorney for Botetourt County until 13 June 1797. In Richmond on 1 January 1791 he married Ann Selden, of Elizabeth City County. At Grove Hill, their residence just northwest of Fincastle, Breckinridge built an elegant twenty-six-room house in the fashionable Federal style. They had five sons and five daughters.

In the spring of 1789 Breckinridge won election to the first of two consecutive one-year terms representing Botetourt County in the House of Delegates. He sat on the Committee for Courts of Justice during both terms and on the Committee on Privileges and Elections during the second. From 1796 to 1802 Breckinridge again represented the county in the House of Delegates. In addition to service on the same committees he was a member of the Committee on Claims in 1796 and of the Committee on Propositions and Grievances thereafter. Breckinridge speedily became a leader among the General Assembly's Federalists, who unsuccessfully nominated him for United States senator in 1796 and for governor in 1799. Breckinridge also lost when he ran as the Federalist candidate for presidential elector in 1800. He returned to the House of Delegates from 1806 to 1808, when he served again on the influential Committees on Claims and on Propositions and Grievances. The assembly elected him a brigadier general of militia, with a commission dated 1 February 1809.

In 1807 Breckinridge lost a poorly organized campaign for Congress to the incumbent Republican, Alexander Wilson, of Rockbridge County. He defeated Wilson in 1809 and was reelected three times, serving from December 1809 to March 1817 as the representative of a district that initially included the counties of Botetourt, Greenbrier, Kanawha, Monroe, and Rockbridge. Breckinridge sat on the Committee for the District of Columbia during his first term, on the Committee on Public Lands during his next two terms, and on the Committee on the Post Office and Post Roads during his fourth term. He seldom spoke in Congress but kept his constituents informed of his Federalist foreign policy views, including fear of Napoleon's expansionistic schemes. Breckinridge believed that France was a greater threat to the United States than Great Britain was. Breckinridge opposed the declaration of war on Britain in 1812, but following the burning of Washington, D.C., he received orders on 6 October

1814 to lead his brigade of Virginia militiamen north from Richmond to reinforce the defenses around Washington and Baltimore. His regiment crossed the Potomac River into Maryland and encamped until the danger of further damage from the British fleet was over and his troops were sent home that December.

Breckinridge did not seek reelection to Congress in 1817. The previous year he had been president of a convention in Staunton at which representatives from the Piedmont and western counties unsuccessfully called for a state constitutional convention to reduce the disproportionate political power of Tidewater counties in the General Assembly. Breckinridge was also one of the commissioners who met with Thomas Jefferson on 1 August 1818 to determine the site of the University of Virginia and served on the committee that reported the commission's recommendations to the assembly. In 1819 the governor appointed him to the new university's board of visitors, a position he held until his death. Reelected to the House of Delegates in 1819, Breckinridge served on the Committees on Finance and on Schools and Colleges and used his influence to push through the assembly a loan bill for the university, thus enabling the construction of buildings to proceed. After two terms he declined to run for reelection in 1821, but he served again during the session of 1823–1824 and was appointed to the Committees on Militia Laws and on Roads and Internal Navigation. In 1829 Breckinridge lost his last campaign, as a candidate for a state constitutional convention, and received the fifth-largest number of votes for the four seats from a seven-county district.

A successful land speculator, Breckinridge owned about 4,000 acres by 1804. He was a planter, but his diverse business interests also included a brickyard, a tannery, a forge, and the Catawba Mill, mostly built and operated by slaves, which for many years ground cornmeal and graham flour. Not surprisingly, Breckinridge supported internal improvement proposals in the legislature, particularly construction of the James River and Kanawha Canal, and he attended a meeting in Charlottesville on 14 July 1828 to recommend that the General Assembly supplement the state's internal improvement fund and improve Virginia's roads and canals.

James Breckinridge died at Grove Hill on 13 May 1833 and was buried with military honors in the family cemetery there.

Katherine Kennedy McNulty, "General James Breckinridge, Frontier Man for All Seasons," *Journal of the Roanoke Historical Society* 7 (winter 1971): 1–21 (por.); Roy Albert Lamb Jr., "James Breckinridge: Federalist Politician in Jeffersonian Virginia" (master's thesis, UVA, 1986); Stoner, *Seed-Bed*, 278–280; Breckinridge Family Papers in LC, UVA, and VHS, and in Joint Collection University of Missouri–Columbia Western Historical Manuscript Collection and State Historical Society of Missouri Manuscripts, Columbia, Mo.; Breckinridge letters in Kaminski, *Ratification*, 8:136–137, 171–172, 320–321, 329–330, 10:1620–1621, 1661–1663; Henrico Co. Marriage Bonds; Cunningham, *Circular Letters of Congressmen*, 2:679–683, 767–769; Daniel P. Jordan, *Political Leadership in Jefferson's Virginia* (1983); *Richmond Virginia Gazette and General Advertiser*, 10 Dec. 1799; *Richmond Enquirer*, 17 Apr. 1807, 18, 28 Apr. 1809, 19, 30 Apr. 1811, 20 Apr. 1813, 19 Apr., 3 May 1815, 8 Apr. 1817, 11 Aug. 1818, 29 May 1829; Stuart Lee Butler, *A Guide to Virginia Militia Units in the War of 1812* (1988), 32, 252, mistakenly identifies him as John Breckinridge; obituaries in *Lynchburg Virginian*, 20 May 1833, and *Richmond Enquirer*, 24 May 1833.

Donald W. Gunter

BRECKINRIDGE, Robert (1754–10 September 1833), member of the Convention of 1788, was born in Augusta County, the son of Robert Breckinridge, or Breckenridge, and his first wife, Sarah Poage Breckinridge. His younger half brothers included James Breckinridge, who represented Virginia in the House of Representatives, and John Breckinridge, who was briefly attorney general of the United States, represented Kentucky in the United States Senate, and founded the distinguished Breckinridge family of that state. His mother died when he was about four years old and his father soon remarried, but he and his brothers did not get along well with their stepmother, Lettice Preston Breckinridge. The family moved to the portion of the county that in 1770 became Botetourt County, and about 1772 he and his brothers were apprenticed to a carpenter and builder in Hanover County.

Breckinridge enlisted in the army on 2 March 1776, reportedly as a sergeant in the 8th Virginia Regiment. A year later he was commissioned an officer (probably an ensign), and on 14 September 1778 he became a first lieutenant. Breckinridge was serving with the 4th Virginia Regiment on 12 May 1780 when he was taken prisoner at the surrender of Charleston, South Carolina. After his exchange in July 1781, he remained in the army until the end of the summer of 1783 and soon thereafter moved west to Jefferson County, near Louisville.

Robert Breckinridge learned surveying, which became his profession in Kentucky, where he gained a reputation as one particularly knowledgeable about the earliest Jefferson County surveys and the many conflicting claims that arose from some of them. He also speculated in land, patenting 20,545 acres in Kentucky and acting as agent for many Virginians in the management of their western landholdings. As a result he accumulated a considerable fortune. Described as shy, compassionate, and quiet, Breckinridge nevertheless quickly became a figure of importance in his new home. He was named a justice of the peace in Jefferson County and a deputy surveyor in 1785. Appointed a commissioner in 1787 to sell the town lots in Louisville not disposed of by the original trustees, he also served from 1786 until at least 1792 on the commission to assign bounty lands on the north side of the Ohio River to soldiers who had served with George Rogers Clark in the Illinois Regiment.

In 1788 Breckinridge was elected one of Jefferson County's two delegates to the convention that met in Richmond to consider ratification of the Constitution of the United States. He made no significant speeches during the June convention, but he broke ranks with the majority of his fellow Kentuckians by voting for the new constitution on 25 June 1788. Breckinridge missed or abstained from the vote two days later to impose certain limits on Congress's power to tax. In 1788 he was also elected to a seat in the House of Delegates, which began its sessions while the convention was still in progress. Breckinridge served only one year and sat on the Committees of Claims and of Propositions and Grievances.

By then Kentucky was debating the question of separation from Virginia, and Breckinridge was elected a delegate in 1787 and 1789 to conventions considering that question. He was a member of the Kentucky constitutional convention of 1792 and was subsequently elected to three one-year terms in the Kentucky House of Representatives, where he served as the first Speaker of the House. In subsequent years Breckinridge filled other important posts in Kentucky, including service as a brigadier and major general in the state militia. He never married but in 1801 became guardian of the children of his brother Alexander Breckinridge. He spent the years after 1815 in Louisville and became reclusive toward the end of his life. Robert Breckinridge died in Louisville, Kentucky, on 10 September 1833 and was buried in the Floyd-Breckinridge Cemetery on his own property.

Birth year and death date on gravestone; Joseph A. Waddell, *Annals of Augusta County, Virginia, From 1726 to 1871*, 2d ed. (1902), 119–120; John Mason Brown, *Memoranda of the Preston Family* (1870), 6–20; James C. Klotter, *Breckinridges of Kentucky, 1760–1981* (1986), xvi, 5, 8, 12; Breckinridge Family Papers, LC, UVA, and University of Kentucky, Lexington; suit papers in *Hite and Fishback* v. *Breckinridge*, in Robert Emmett McDowell Papers and Preston Family Papers, both Filson Historical Society, Louisville, Ky.; certificate of Sam Finley, 23 Aug. 1783, BW; Draper MSS, 6J89, 8ZZ50; Kaminski, *Ratification,* 10:1539, 1540, 1565, 1651; Willard Rouse Jillson, *Kentucky Land Grants* (1925), 23, 148; G. Glenn Clift, *"Corn Stalk" Militia of Kentucky, 1792–1811* (1957), 1, 15; description of later years and funeral in Derek Colville, "A Transcendentalist in Old Kentucky," *Register of the Kentucky Historical Society* 55 (1957): 326–327; will, written 7 Sept. 1833, in Jefferson Co. Archives, Louisville, Ky., and in Jefferson Co., Ky., Will Book, 2:527.

GEORGE H. YATER

BREEDEN, Edward Lebbaeus (28 January 1905–1 June 1990), member of the House of Delegates and member of the Senate of Virginia, was born in Norfolk, the son of Edward Lebbaeus Breeden, a general contractor, and Cora Lee McCloud Breeden. He attended public schools in Norfolk, spent the academic year 1922–1923 at Hampden-Sydney College, and studied law at George Washington University from 1924 to 1925 but did not receive a degree. Breeden returned to Norfolk and served as deputy clerk of the Norfolk City Circuit Court from 1926 to 1930. He passed the bar in 1927 and entered private practice in 1930. On 8 September 1928 he married Billye Holland. They had one son and one daughter.

In 1935 Breeden won election to the first of four two-year terms in the House of Delegates.

During his eight years representing the city of Norfolk in the House he served on the Committees on Asylums and Prisons, on Counties, Cities, and Towns, and on Enrolled Bills. During his first term he belonged to the Committee on the Chesapeake and Its Tributaries, and after his first term he sat on the powerful Committee on Appropriations. Breeden became a member of the Virginia Advisory Legislative Council in 1942 and served until 1945, at which time he was the chair. He was chief patron in 1942 of the bill creating the Elizabeth River Tunnel Commission to direct construction of a bridge and tunnel that opened in 1952, linking Norfolk and Portsmouth by road. Breeden later supported a bond issue that financed a second tunnel between the two cities. It opened in 1962.

In 1943 Breeden was elected to the first of seven four-year terms representing Norfolk in the Senate of Virginia. He served on the Committee on Courts of Justice for twenty-eight years and was its ranking member from 1956 through 1970. Breeden's other major committee assignments were on the Committee on Finance, Insurance, and Banking, which he chaired after 1964, and the Committee on Rules, the extremely powerful five-member committee of the Senate's most influential members, which he joined in 1954. He also served twice on the Governor's Advisory Board on the Budget. Breeden was copatron in 1950 with Senator Harry Flood Byrd Jr. (b. 1914) of the Byrd Tax Credit Act, which provided that when state tax revenue exceeded expenditures the surplus would be refunded to the taxpayers. Four years later Breeden successfully urged that the legislation be repealed so that revenue could be made available for capital outlay needs. When he retired from the Senate at the end of 1971 he was the senior member of the General Assembly and had himself written or chaired the committees that wrote and published more than two dozen major reports on issues ranging from taxation to commerce and public health.

Breeden ran initially under the auspices of the dominant faction of the Democratic Party, which was loyal to Harry Flood Byrd (1887–1966), but during his long legislative tenure he exhibited a political independence that led to his estrangement from the Byrd organization. Breeden responded more to the desires of his urban constituency than to the conservative party orthodoxy. He opposed the poll tax as a prerequisite to voting, was friendly with leaders of organized labor in his district, and in 1947 voted against Virginia's right-to-work law. Breeden maintained ties with leaders of Norfolk's African American community from the beginning of his political career. In 1959 he served on a legislative commission that recommended adoption of a local option approach as an alternative to the Byrd organization's policy of closing schools as part of its Massive Resistance to court-ordered desegregation of the public schools. In April 1959 Breeden presided over the Senate when it debated as a committee of the whole and by a one-vote margin adopted the commission's recommendations, thereby dealing Massive Resistance a fatal legislative blow.

Toward the end of his legislative career, Breeden moved away from the pay-as-you-go philosophy of the Byrd organization and helped pass the first sales tax bill in Virginia and in 1968 campaigned for passage of an $81 million bond referendum for the construction of higher education and mental health facilities. A vigorous advocate of port development, Breeden chaired the Virginia State Ports Study Commission in 1969 and three years later became a member of the board of commissioners of the Virginia Port Authority.

Breeden's opposition to Massive Resistance as well as a dispute over a judicial appointment in Norfolk produced the most serious electoral challenge of his political career in the 1959 Democratic Party primary. By a margin of only 1,200 votes out of some 22,260 cast Breeden defeated Reid M. Spencer, who was supported by the segregationist Defenders of State Sovereignty and Individual Liberties and during the bitter campaign branded Breeden as an advocate of racial integration. Breeden easily defeated a Republican candidate in the general election. He chaired the Second District Democratic Committee from 1952 to 1960 and supported the party in presidential elections until 1972. Although he considered running for lieutenant governor on several occasions, Breeden never sought statewide office.

A man of prodigious energy, Breeden maintained an active law practice during his years of public service and after his retirement. He received an honorary LL.D. from Hampden-Sydney College in 1973. Following the death of his first wife on 13 November 1964, he married Virginia Hurt Sneed on 16 April 1966. Edward Lebbaeus Breeden died of a stroke in a Norfolk hospital on 1 June 1990 and was buried in Forest Lawn Cemetery in that city.

E. Randolph Trice, comp., *The Elks Parade: A Centennial History and Catalogue of Members of Upsilon Chapter of Kappa Sigma* [ca. 1983], 52; *Record of the Hampden-Sydney Alumni Association* (July 1944): 8–9; Edward Lebbaeus Breeden Papers, UVA; author's interview with Breeden, 23 Apr. 1973; other information supplied by son Edward L. Breeden III; *Norfolk Ledger-Dispatch*, 10 Sept. 1928, 3 Jan. 1955; *Norfolk Virginian-Pilot*, 17 Apr. 1966, 9 Mar. 1971; *Richmond Times-Dispatch*, 9 Mar., 4 July 1971; political career thoroughly documented in Norfolk newspapers, 1935–1971; obituaries in *Norfolk Virginian-Pilot* (por.) and *Richmond News Leader,* both 2 June 1990, and *Richmond Times-Dispatch*, 3 June 1990; editorial tribute in *Norfolk Virginian-Pilot*, 5 June 1990.

JAMES R. SWEENEY

BREEDLOVE, William (ca. 1820–15 June 1871), member of the Convention of 1867–1868, was born in Essex County, the son of James Davis, a white man, and Polly Breedlove, a free African American. Little is known of Breedlove's early life. The 1850 census identifies him as a blacksmith and literate. With his wife, Susan Breedlove, the daughter of Cordelia Drake, he resided in the Tappahannock household of Henry Adams, next to the blacksmith shop of the elderly James Lewis, from whom Breedlove may have learned his trade. When Susan Breedlove died of typhoid fever in December 1857, they had at least two sons and one daughter, of whom only George W. Breedlove survived to adulthood. On 9 December 1858 Breedlove married Eliza Ann Davis, the daughter of a black man and a white woman and therefore also free. They had at least two sons and two daughters.

By 1860 Breedlove had accumulated real estate worth $1,500 and personal property worth $250. He may also have begun operating a ferry service across the Rappahannock River by then. Free people of color usually lived inconspicuously, but during the Civil War that became difficult. They faced the threat of being impressed to labor on Confederate fortifications and might also receive nearly irresistible appeals for help from slaves attempting to escape behind the lines of the United States Army. On 2 November 1863 Breedlove and another free black named William Chandler, his employee at the ferry, transported an African American man across the river under the impression that he had a pass authorizing him to travel, when in fact the man was attempting to escape from slavery. Breedlove and Chambers were arrested and on 16 November 1863 convicted in Essex County of assisting in a slave's escape. The penalty prescribed by law was that both convicted men be "sold into absolute slavery."

The prosecuting attorney and some of the justices of the peace who convicted them recommended gubernatorial clemency, believing that Breedlove and Chandler had not known that the man was a slave. Other local dignitaries, including Lieutenant Governor Robert Latané Montague, also wrote in Breedlove's behalf and described him as an honest and industrious blacksmith, a man of good character, and a valuable member of the community. Governor John Letcher pardoned Breedlove on 19 December 1863, and Governor William "Extra Billy" Smith pardoned Chandler on 29 January 1864.

These legal travails may have sparked Breedlove's postwar political activism. On 1 October 1867 the local agent of the Freedmen's Bureau reported that blacks in Tappahannock were holding meetings to select a candidate for the state constitutional convention. They settled on William Breedlove, and their counterparts in neighboring Middlesex County, the other county in the electoral district, agreed. In the balloting on 22 October, Breedlove received votes from only three white men, but black voters outnumbered white voters in both counties, and he easily defeated the white candidate, William G. Jeffries. Brigadier General John McAllister Schofield, then the military commander of Virginia under Congressional Reconstruction, observed that Breedlove lacked formal education but was "honest and intelligent." During the constitutional convention Breedlove sat on the Committee on Taxation and Finance. He served inconspicuously and voted consistently with the Radical majority.

On 19 July 1869 the military commander in Essex County appointed Breedlove one of six new justices of the peace for the county. Breedlove also served on the town council of Tappahannock, and his appointment on 3 March 1870 as postmaster there outraged many local whites. He stepped down as postmaster on 13 March 1871, possibly because of failing health. William Breedlove died of "Brain Fever" near Tappahannock three months later, on 15 June 1871, survived by his wife and four children, the youngest less than a year old. Several of his children acquired property in Tappahannock, and George W. Breedlove served as a constable for a time, carrying on for another generation the respectable and constructive reputation that William Breedlove had fashioned before the war.

Jackson, *Negro Office-Holders,* 5, 62; age given as about twenty-three on 24 July 1843 in "Register of Free Blacks, 1810–1843, Essex County," *Tidewater Virginia Families* 9 (Nov./Dec. 2000): 191; age given respectively as thirty, forty, and fifty in Census, Essex Co., 1850, 1860, 1870; BVS Marriage Register, Essex Co., records second marriage in 1858 at age thirty-eight with clerk's marginal note identifying Breedlove's parents and the races of his and his wife's parents; *Commonwealth* v. *Breedlove and Chandler* and accompanying documents, Pardon Papers, Dec. 1863, Executive Papers of Governor John Letcher, RG 3, LVA (first quotation); Watson R. Wentworth to O. Brown, 1 Oct. 1867, Freedmen's Bureau Records; Election Records, no. 427, RG 13, LVA; Lowe, "Virginia's Reconstruction Convention," 358 (second quotation); Hume, "Membership of Convention of 1867–1868," 481; James B. Slaughter, *Settlers, Southerners, Americans: The History of Essex County, Virginia, 1608–1984* (1985), 210–211; Essex Co. Circuit Court Order Book, 3:231; Records of Appointment of Postmasters, Virginia, Essex Co., Post Office Department, RG 28, NARA; *Richmond Dispatch,* 15 Mar. 1870; death dates of Breedlove and first wife in BVS Death Register, Essex Co. (third quotation).

JOHN T. KNEEBONE

BRENNAN, Andrew James (14 December 1877–23 May 1956), bishop of the Catholic Diocese of Richmond, was born in Towanda, Bradford County, Pennsylvania, the son of James Brennan, a railroad worker, and Ellen Flood Brennan. The close and devout Irish-Catholic family lived in Towanda, where Brennan attended Saint Agnes Parochial School and the local high school and worked evenings and summers in a toy factory and in his elder brother's confectionery store. Brennan attended Holy Cross College in Worcester, Massachusetts, and won honors as a student and as the catcher for the college's baseball team. After graduation in 1900, he began preparing for the priesthood at Saint Bernard's Seminary in Rochester, New York. The following year Brennan moved on to the Pontifical North American College in Rome, where in competition with students from around the world he won a gold medal for his knowledge of canon law. Ordained at the Cathedral of Saint John Lateran in Rome on 17 December 1904, he received his doctorate in sacred theology in June 1905.

Assigned in September 1905 to Saint Peter's Cathedral in Scranton, Pennsylvania, his home diocese, Brennan also taught Latin and Greek at Saint Thomas's College (later the University of Scranton). Bishop Michael John Hoban soon recognized Brennan's talents and on 1 January 1908 appointed him chancellor of the diocese and secretary to the bishop. On 24 February 1923, at Hoban's suggestion, Pope Pius XI appointed Brennan auxiliary bishop. Three years later, on 28 May 1926, Brennan received promotion to the See of Richmond following the resignation of Bishop Denis Joseph O'Connell. Brennan's formal installation took place on 16 December 1926 at the Cathedral of the Sacred Heart in Richmond.

Brennan found himself in charge of a diocese that, despite its name, encompassed all of the Catholic parishes in Virginia except those on the Eastern Shore. He created new institutions and offices to organize the diocese's activities. He founded a Society for the Propagation of the Faith in 1927 to collect alms for missionary work, appointed a superintendent of parochial schools in 1929, arranged for graduate training in social work for the director of the Bureau of Catholic Charities, and in 1931 purchased the *Virginia Knight*, a monthly published in the interests of the Knights of Columbus, to become the diocesan newspaper, the *Catholic Virginian*. In October 1930 Brennan announced an ambitious five-year building program that included the

completion of Saint Joseph's Villa, an orphanage in Richmond, and the erection of a Catholic hospital there. He supported construction of two other orphanages in the diocese, Saint Vincent's Home for Boys in Roanoke and the Barry-Robinson Home in Norfolk. Brennan carried on in spite of the Great Depression, arguing that deflation had lowered building costs and that the projects would help to relieve unemployment. Between 1927 and 1933 he established five new parishes in the diocese.

Constituting only a small proportion of the state's population, the diocese's 36,000 communicants watched with anger and dismay as state treasurer John M. Purcell, a Catholic, ran far behind the rest of the Democratic ticket in 1925 and as Virginia voters rejected Alfred E. Smith, the first Catholic presidential candidate, three years later. Convinced that Protestant ill will grew out of a misunderstanding of Catholicism, Brennan joined several hundred other Catholics, as well as Protestants and Jews, in a "good will" dinner in Richmond on 16 February 1928. He also encouraged the organization of a Catholic Laymen's League to combat bigotry and educate non-Catholics. When the Tidewater branch of the Laymen's League arranged in 1930 for a series of statewide radio talks on Catholicism, Brennan gave the first address, on "Catholic Belief and Practice."

Brennan relaxed from his work by collecting and tending a flock of tropical and other foreign birds at his Richmond residence at the cathedral. On 26 February 1934, during a visit to Norfolk, he suffered a series of cerebral hemorrhages that paralyzed his right side and left him unable to speak. A gradual recovery gave hope, but another stroke in May 1935 ended Brennan's active ministry. That autumn Peter Leo Ireton was appointed bishop coadjutor, and after Brennan resigned on 1 May 1945 Ireton succeeded him as bishop of the Diocese of Richmond. Inarticulate and barely able to walk even with the aid of a cane, Brennan spent his winters at DePaul Hospital in Norfolk and his summers at Mercy Hospital in Scranton, but he attended mass every day and prayed. Although he remained entitled to wear a bishop's ring and episcopal robes, he did so only on the celebration of the fiftieth anniversary of his ordination in 1954. Andrew James Brennan died of a cerebral hemorrhage in DePaul Hospital in Norfolk on 23 May 1956. In accordance with his wishes he was buried under the sanctuary of the Saint Joseph's Villa chapel in Richmond.

NCAB, 42:217; John J. Delaney and James Edward Tobin, eds., *Dictionary of Catholic Biography* (1961), 173; *Scranton Times*, 12 Jan. 1969; John P. Gallagher, *A Century of History: The Diocese of Scranton, 1868–1968* (1968), 313–317; *Richmond News Leader*, 1 June, 16 Dec. 1926; *Richmond Times-Dispatch*, 16 June 1935; F. Joseph Magri, "Three Constructive Years: An Appraisal of the Rule Over the See of Richmond of Right Reverend Andrew J. Brennan, D.D., Eighth Bishop," *Virginia Knight* 5 (Jan. 1930): 1–2, 29; *Catholic Virginian* 20 (June 1945): 3, 44–45; ibid. 31 (1 June 1956): 1–5, 8; Brennan, "Five-Year Program" and "Catholic Belief and Practice," *Virginia Knight* 5 (Oct. 1930): 1, 34–35, and 6 (Nov. 1930): 3–4, 29–32; obituaries in *Richmond News Leader* (por.) and *Scranton Times*, both 23 May 1956, *New York Times* and *Richmond Times-Dispatch*, both 24 May 1956, and *Catholic Virginian* 31 (25 May 1956): 1, 16.

JOHN T. KNEEBONE

BRENT, George (ca. 1640–by 1 September 1700), attorney, acting attorney general of Virginia, and member of the House of Burgesses, was born in Worchestershire, England, the son of George Brent and Marianna Peyton Brent. His grandfather Richard Brent was lord of Admington and Lark Stoke but lost much of his property during the English Civil Wars because of his Catholicism. With family fortunes declining in Great Britain, George Brent migrated to Maryland between 1660 and 1663. By 1670 he had moved to the Aquia Creek area of Stafford County where his relatives, including his uncle Giles Brent (1600–1672) and aunt Margaret Brent, once major political leaders in Maryland, had created a refuge for other Catholics and acquired substantial amounts of property.

Brent initially practiced law. In December 1670 he was identified as "George Brent of Oquia Creeke, Gent.," in a record authorizing him to act as an attorney for a London haberdasher who had an interest in land in Westmoreland County. Brent became a successful tobacco planter and raised livestock, owned a sawmill, ran a ferry, and accumulated land and laborers. He became surveyor of Stafford County in 1679 and by 1687 had also become surveyor of Westmoreland County. By 1683 he had become the law partner of William Fitzhugh, a powerful local Protestant. Brent speculated in land on a large scale and joined three London investors in acquiring a 30,000-acre tract known as Brenton, or Brentown, from the Northern Neck proprietors in 1687. The investors hoped to attract French Huguenot settlers and obtained a grant of toleration from James II in 1687, but the venture failed.

In 1677 Brent married Elizabeth Greene, of Bermuda. They had three sons and two daughters before she died in childbirth on 26 March 1686. Brent's subsequent marriage on 27 March 1687 to Mary Sewall Chandler, a widow with two sons and three daughters, renewed his ties to Maryland's most prominent Catholic families. They had at least one son and three daughters before she died during childbirth on 12 March 1694. One of his stepsons, Richard Chandler, became a Benedictine priest.

Despite his faith Brent participated in public life in Virginia, where laws against Catholics' holding office were largely ignored. As Major Brent he was commanding Stafford County's troop of horse in 1675 when he and George Mason (1629–1686) pursued and killed some Doeg Indians who were accused of murdering settlers, leading indirectly to the outbreak of Bacon's Rebellion the next year. Vague references in some of the surviving records of the conflict have resulted in confusion concerning the roles of Brent and his cousin Giles Brent (ca.1652–1679), but George Brent probably took little or no other part in the rebellion.

In 1681 Brent and Fitzhugh provisioned the Potomac garrison, and three years later Brent led an expedition to defend the inhabitants of Rappahannock River settlements from attacks by the Seneca. He also served as receiver general for the area north of the Rappahannock River in 1683 and was acting attorney general of Virginia from the autumn of 1686 until the spring of 1688. In the latter year Brent won election to the House of Burgesses from Stafford County and was allowed to take his seat even though he declined to take the anti-Catholic oath of supremacy. During the session he was an active and responsible member.

Unfortunately for Brent, events in England in 1688 ended his promising public career. The Glorious Revolution unleashed anti-Catholic feelings in the colonies, and as the most prominent Catholic in Virginia he suffered the consequences. When rumors spread in March 1689 that Brent was conspiring with Maryland Catholics and Indians to kill Protestants, some of Virginia's leaders ordered him to take refuge at William Fitzhugh's house for his own safety. In February 1690 a Franciscan priest fleeing persecution in Maryland found shelter with Brent at Woodstock, his residence.

Brent tried to make the best of the situation, proposing to turn the Brenton tract into a refuge for English Catholics, but anti-Catholicism took its toll on him. He never again held public office, and despite efforts by Stafford County leaders to shield him he also apparently lost the right to practice law. Brent did continue serving the Northern Neck proprietors, who appointed him ranger general in charge of defense in 1690. Three years later he and Fitzhugh became joint agents for the proprietors. In that capacity they favored each other and their friends with large tracts of land, enriching themselves but retarding settlement. In this way Brent acquired a great deal of land and owned more than 15,000 acres in Virginia plus land in Maryland and England at the time of his death.

Brent acted as an agent for the Northern Neck proprietors at least through the autumn of 1696. George Brent died before 1 September 1700, when his eldest surviving son wrote his own will. He was buried near the bodies of his wives at Aquia Cemetery in Stafford County.

W. B. Chilton, ed., "Pedigree of the Brents, of Cossington, in the County of Somerset," *VMHB* 12 (1905): 440–441; estimated birth date in Brent, *Descendants of Giles Brent*, 42–43, 64–80; earliest record of Virginia residence in Westmoreland Co. Deeds, Patents, Wills, Etc. (1665–1677), 113 (quotation); numerous references in Stafford Co. records; royal commissioners' 1677 "True Narrative of the Rise, Progress, and Cessation of the late Rebellion in Virginia," PRO CO 5/1371, fol. 188; *Minutes of Council and General Court*, 403, 523; *Executive Journals of Council*, 1:14, 334; *Journals of House of Burgesses, 1659/60–1693*, lvi, 218, 288, 291, and documentation as acting attorney general, liii, 282, 300, 303; Richard Beale Davis, ed., *William Fitzhugh and His Chesapeake World, 1676–1701: The Fitzhugh Letters and Other Documents* (1963), 26, 28, 41–44, 46, 70–71,

92–93, 120–121, 210–211, 250, 361; Bruce E. Steiner, "The Catholic Brents of Colonial Virginia: An Instance of Practical Toleration," *VMHB* 70 (1962): 387–409; will fragment, said to have been dated 6 Apr. 1694, in *VMHB* 18 (1910): 96–100.

Beatriz Betancourt Hardy

BRENT, George William (August 1821–2 January 1872), member of the Convention of 1861, was born in Alexandria, a part of the District of Columbia until 1846, the son of George Brent, collector of the port of Alexandria, and Elizabeth Parsons Brent. After completing the study of law at the University of Virginia in 1842, he opened an office in Warrenton. On 16 December 1844 Brent married Cornelia D. Wood in Albemarle County. She died on 15 November 1848, and on 30 January 1851 he married Lucy Goode, daughter of Thomas Goode, proprietor of the Hot Springs in Bath County. They had at least three sons and five daughters.

Late in 1851 Brent was elected to a one-year term in the Senate of Virginia representing the counties of Fauquier and Rappahannock. He sat on the Committee for Courts of Justice and on the Joint Committee to Examine the Second Auditor's Office. Brent also served on the board of visitors of the Virginia Military Institute in 1852 and 1853. By the latter year he had moved to Alexandria and was practicing law there. During the 1860 presidential campaign Brent was an unsuccessful candidate for presidential elector for Stephen A. Douglas, the nominee of the Northern Democratic Party. On 4 February 1861 the citizens of Alexandria County elected Brent to the state convention called to consider the question of secession. He won by a three-to-one margin over David Funsten, leader of the local Southern faction of the Democratic Party that had supported John C. Breckinridge for president in 1860. On 8 March 1861 Brent delivered a long pro-Union, proslavery convention speech in which he defended the union of states as "preeminently a Virginian conception," first envisioned under "the hallowed roof of Mount Vernon." He called for a conference of border states to propose constitutional amendments designed to protect the South and serve as a basis for the settlement of the questions dividing the nation. He went on to prophesy that "if this

Union is to be involved in war, the institution of slavery will vanish from our midst. The perpetuity of that institution depends upon peace and upon repose. Let civil war once sound its horrid tocsin in this land, and slavery is at once ended." Brent voted against secession on both 4 April, when it failed, and 17 April, when it passed, but he later signed the Ordinance of Secession.

True to his promise in his March speech that "my lot is cast with that of Virginia; come weal, come woe," Brent obtained a commission as a major in the 17th Regiment Virginia Infantry on 2 May 1861. He was promoted to lieutenant colonel to date from 1 May 1862 and fought with the Army of Tennessee at the Battle of Shiloh, and he served as assistant adjutant general on the staffs of Generals Braxton Bragg and Pierre G. T. Beauregard in the Department of the West. In March 1864 Brent was back in Richmond, where he presented a report on the hospitals used for prisoners of war in the city. He surrendered with General Joseph Eggleston Johnston on 26 April 1865 in Greensboro, North Carolina.

After the war Brent resumed his law practice in Alexandria. On 27 April 1870 he was one of more than 300 persons in the Supreme Court of Appeals in the Virginia State Capitol in Richmond when the floor collapsed. Sitting just in front of the railing surrounding the judges' bench when the floor beneath him gave way, Brent sprang forward, clutched that railing, and clung to it until a piece of timber from the ceiling above knocked him into the gallery of the House of Delegates. Rescued in such a disfigured condition that his friends did not recognize him, he incurred a broken right leg, a severe cut in his throat, and serious bruises. Brent remained in Richmond for several weeks before returning to Alexandria to recuperate.

George William Brent died at his home in Alexandria on 2 January 1872, four days after contracting typhoid and pneumonia. He was buried in the cemetery of Saint Mary's Catholic Church in that city.

George William Brent Papers, Duke; Albemarle Co. Marriage Bonds; Constance Corley Metheny and Eliza Warwick Wise, comps., *Bath County Marriage Bonds and Ministers' Returns, 1791–1853, With an Addendum of Newly Found Ministers' Returns* (1998), 108; *Alexandria Gazette and Virginia Advertiser*, 24 Nov. 1848, 14 Sept. 1860, 5 Feb. 1861, 28 Apr. 1870; Reese and Gaines, *Proceedings of 1861 Convention*, 1:493–518 (quotations on 505, 516, 518), 3:163, 4:144; *OR*, ser. 1, vols. 2, 8, 10, 16–17, 20, 23, 28, 30–32, 39–40, 42, 44–45, 47, 49, 51–52, ser. 2, vols. 3–6, 8, ser. 4, vols. 2–3; Compiled Service Records; *Richmond Daily Whig*, 2 May 1870; obituaries in *Alexandria Gazette and Virginia Advertiser*, 3 Jan. 1872 (with partial birth date), and *Richmond Enquirer*, 4 Jan. 1872.

DAPHNE GENTRY

BRENT, Giles (ca. 5 April 1652–2 September 1679), participant in Bacon's Rebellion, was born probably near Aquia Creek in the portion of Northumberland County that became Westmoreland County in 1653 and Stafford County in 1664. His parents were Giles Brent (1600–1672) and Mary Brent, the daughter of a tayac, or emperor, of the Piscataway. A Catholic of both Indian and English heritage, Brent was an anomaly in seventeenth-century Virginia, and like others in his strong-minded family he frequently provoked controversy.

Brent's father had a remarkable career before arriving in Virginia. The younger son of a prominent Gloucestershire family, he had migrated to Maryland in 1638 with three siblings. His Catholicism, affluence, and education led to his quick attainment of positions of authority, such as member of the assembly, councillor, and chief militia officer on Kent Island. More often than not the Brents opposed proprietary prerogatives, both in protection of their own interests and in rallying dissident groups against the Calverts. Despite earlier conflicts Lord Baltimore appointed him acting governor in April 1643. An ardent Royalist, the elder Giles Brent antagonized Protestant supporters of Parliament and helped set off an uprising in the colony before being dismissed from office and transported to England in 1645. After obtaining his freedom he returned to Maryland and was briefly reinstated as a councillor. A final break with the Calverts prompted Brent and his equally influential sister Margaret Brent to move to Virginia about 1649 and settle near Aquia Creek. Giles Brent married the orphaned daughter of a Piscataway leader who had been raised by Margaret Brent and Jesuit missionaries who had converted her and her father to Christianity. If he had hoped that the marriage would secure him a claim to Indian lands and that he could promote her right of succession to her father's title, he was disappointed on both counts. Despite legislation restricting the rights of Catholics and occasional complaints about Catholic influence, the Brent family prospered in Virginia. The senior Brent became a militia officer, and his nephew George Brent (b. ca. 1640) held several responsible public offices in the Northern Neck.

Giles Brent dwelt in two worlds. He learned the Indian language from his mother, but after his father's death early in 1672, he inherited all of his father's extensive landed estate and became a prosperous young planter and a captain in the militia. In 1674 Brent became a local collector of the tobacco export tax. His primary importance in Virginia history arises from his involvement in Bacon's Rebellion. In July 1675, as Captain Brent, he served in a party commanded by George Mason (1629–1686) and George Brent that pursued a contingent of Doeg Indians into Maryland and killed several of them in retaliation for the Indians' having killed some Virginians. Bacon's Rebellion grew from that episode and other clashes on Virginia's frontier. Vague references in some of the surviving records of the struggle have resulted in confusion concerning the roles of Giles Brent and his cousin, George Brent. Giles Brent definitely joined forces loyal to Nathaniel Bacon (1647–1676) in order to battle the Pamunkey and other tribes. Referred to during those weeks as Colonel Brent, he collaborated with Bacon until the rebel leader turned his forces against the governor, Sir William Berkeley, in the autumn of 1676 and laid siege to Jamestown. Brent then turned against Bacon and gathered approximately 1,000 men to confront Bacon's forces. When the men learned that Bacon had burned Jamestown, however, they quickly lost heart and deserted Brent, whose role in the conflict then ended.

Brent's last conflicts were domestic in nature. Just as his fiery temperament had led him to confront the neighboring Indians, it began to threaten members of his own household, which consisted of a wife, whose name is unknown, and at least two sons and two daughters. In May 1679 Brent's wife petitioned the governor and Council for protection and a separate mainte-

nance, an action that the prominent Northern Neck attorney William Fitzhugh described as unprecedented in Virginia. The court records are lost, but according to Fitzhugh the petition graphically described Brent's "inhumane usage" of his wife. The Council ordered Brent to live apart from her and "to allow her a Maintenance, according to his Quali[ty] & Estate." A later attorney who examined the court papers before they were destroyed concluded that Brent was "a terrible fellow." Before any further proceedings in the case could take place, Giles Brent died in Middlesex County on 2 September 1679. He may have converted from Catholicism to the Church of England, because his death was recorded in the register of Christ Church Parish and he was buried in the cemetery of that Anglican church in Middlesex County.

Brent, *Descendants of Giles Brent*, 82–89; deed of 5 Apr. 1673 appears to establish birth date (*VMHB* 16 [1908]: 100–101); Bruce E. Steiner, "The Catholic Brents of Colonial Virginia: An Instance of Practical Toleration," *VMHB* 70 (1962): 387–409; Charles M. Andrews, ed., *Narratives of the Insurrections, 1675–1690* (1915), 17–18, 71–73, 123–124, 126; *VMHB* 12 (1905): 292–293; *Journals of House of Burgesses, 1659/60–1693*, 68–69; Richard Beale Davis, ed., *William Fitzhugh and His Chesapeake World, 1676–1701: The Fitzhugh Letters and Other Documents* (1963), 97–99 (first and second quotations); *VMHB* 9 (1901): 187 (third quotation); *Parish Register of Christ Church, Middlesex County, Va., from 1653 to 1812* (1897), 22.

DAVID W. JORDAN

BRENT, Richard (d. 30 December 1814), member of the House of Representatives and member of the United States Senate, was born in the 1760s at Richland, the Stafford County plantation of his parents, William Brent, a member of the Convention of 1776, and Eleanor Carroll Brent. His parents descended from wealthy Catholic families, but his father converted to the Church of England. Richard Brent's adult religious affiliation, if any, is unrecorded. He never married.

Little is known about Brent's education, but he studied law and read widely. Contemporaries regarded him as a polished orator with a cultivated mind. He inherited one-third of his father's land in 1782, including all of his property in King George County. Brent obtained land in other counties as well, altogether more than 1,750 acres, which qualified him to represent Stafford County in the House of Delegates in 1788 and Prince William County, where he resided, in 1793 and 1794. While a delegate for Stafford he sat on the Committees for Courts of Justice and of Privileges and Elections. During the 1793 and 1794 sessions he served on the Committees on Claims, for Courts of Justice, and of Propositions and Grievances.

In 1795 Brent defeated Federalist incumbent Richard Bland Lee for the seat in the United States House of Representatives from the district comprising the counties of Fairfax, Loudoun, and Prince William. He was a Jeffersonian Republican, and although he rarely spoke during his first term he joined fellow Republicans in voting against an appropriation to carry out the Jay Treaty. During the diplomatic crisis with France that arose during his second term he addressed the House three times in opposition to a Federalist bill to raise a provisional army, contending that the measure gave unconstitutional powers to the president. Brent voted against the Alien and Sedition Acts in 1798, though he did not participate in the debate. He either did not run for a third term or was defeated in 1799. Brent was a presidential elector for Thomas Jefferson in 1800. He returned to the House of Delegates for the session of 1800–1801, when he represented Prince William County and sat on the Committees of Privileges and Elections and of Propositions and Grievances. A third term in Congress followed in 1801. Although silent during most debates, Brent regularly sided with Jefferson on such issues as taxes, appropriations, and reform of the federal judiciary.

Brent gave up the practice of law, and between 1803 and 1808 he probably spent his time running his plantations, making use of the labor of the sixty-five slaves he owned in 1810. He was elected to the Senate of Virginia in 1808 from the district composed of the counties of Fairfax and Prince William. In 1809 the General Assembly elected him to the United States Senate. Republicans had reason to be pleased with the selection because President James Madison was confronting factionalism in the Senate,

and among the mavericks giving the president trouble was Brent's fellow senator from Virginia, William Branch Giles. Brent's voting record in the Senate through the War of 1812 solidly favored the administration. He supported increases in the army and navy and even voted in December 1814 to renew the charter of the Bank of the United States despite instructions from the Virginia assembly to oppose the bill.

In 1811 Madison asked Brent to help persuade Governor James Monroe to accept the office of secretary of state. The addition of Monroe to the administration reduced factional infighting in the Republican Party. The Senate, however, remained evenly divided on the question of peace or war with Great Britain, and some independent Republicans occasionally sided with the Federalists. Knowing that Brent would support the administration, the British ambassador instructed an aide to get Brent drunk so that he could not participate in the vote on declaring war. The aide reported that he had succeeded in getting Brent drunk, but the trick failed. Drunk or sober, Brent seldom missed a roll call, and on 17 June 1812 he voted for the declaration of war, which was adopted 19 to 13.

Brent's health was "always delicate," according to newspaper reports, and he became ill during the session of Congress that began in November 1814. One of his last acts was to vote on 8 December for the bank charter bill. Richard Brent died on 30 December 1814 in Washington, D.C. He was buried in the family vault at Richland.

Brent, *Descendants of Giles Brent,* 126–132; 1757 birth date in older reference works not supported by known documentation; age is listed as between twenty-six and forty-five in Census, Prince William Co., 1810, suggesting 1767 birth as plausible; Richard Brent Papers, Duke; Land and Personal Property Tax Returns, Prince William Co., RG 48, LVA; Daniel P. Jordan, *Political Leadership in Jefferson's Virginia* (1983), 131, 175, 187, 195; Norman K. Risjord, *The Old Republicans: Southern Conservatism in the Age of Jefferson* (1965), 118–119; 1812 episode in Irving Brant, *James Madison* (1941–1961), 5:477; Ellen G. Miles, *Saint-Mémin and the Neoclassical Profile Portrait in America* (1994), 253 (por.); Prince William Co. Will Book, K:411–413; obituary in *Washington Daily National Intelligencer,* 31 Dec. 1814 (quotation), reprinted in *Alexandria Gazette,* 3 Jan. 1815; tribute in *Washington Daily National Intelligencer,* 14 Jan. 1815, reprinted in *Richmond Virginia Argus,* 21 Jan. 1815.

NORMAN K. RISJORD

BRENT, William (26 July 1733–by ca. 8 April 1782), member of the Convention of 1776, was born in Stafford County, the son of William Brent and Jane Brent. About 1754 he married Eleanor Carroll, of Maryland, whose brother John Carroll became the first Catholic bishop in the United States. Brent and his wife descended from noted Catholic families, but he converted to the Church of England, and they both attended services at Overwharton Parish. Two of their three sons and their four daughters found spouses among the prominent Virginia and Maryland families of Ambler, Carroll, Hill, Lee, and Sewall. Richard Brent, their middle son, served in the House of Representatives and the United States Senate.

Brent inherited several thousand acres in King George, Prince William, Stafford, and Westmoreland Counties as well as in Maryland and points west. He raced and bred a noted stable of thoroughbred horses. An astute businessman, Brent earned large stud fees for his stallions Figure and Republican and owned Ebony, a famous brood mare. When advertising the stud services of Don Carlos in 1777, he offered to accept either money or young slaves in payment.

In May 1757 Brent became a justice of the peace in Stafford County. He joined the other justices in resigning to protest the Stamp Act in October 1765, but the resignation was ignored, and he continued as a justice until his death. Brent signed the Westmoreland Association in February 1766, also in protest of the Stamp Act, and in 1774 he was elected to the Stafford County Committee to enforce the nonimportation associations enacted by the Virginia Revolutionary Conventions and the Continental Congress. On 8 April 1776 he was elected one of two delegates from Stafford County to the last Revolutionary Convention. Brent served on the Committee on Privileges and Elections and voted for independence, for the Virginia Declaration of Rights, and for the first constitution of the commonwealth.

On 23 July 1776 a raiding party from HMS *Roebuck* landed in Stafford County and destroyed a number of buildings, including Brent's elegant brick mansion called Richland at the mouth of Aquia Creek. Brent rebuilt his house and remained in public life. He represented Stafford County in the House of Delegates in the autumn of 1776, when he served on the Committee on Privileges and Elections, and again in 1778, when he sat on the Committee on Propositions and Grievances. Brent was elected to the Senate of Virginia in the spring of 1780 to represent the district consisting of King George, Stafford, and Westmoreland Counties. He wrote his will on 7 January 1782 and added a codicil on the next day and a second codicil on 9 January. William Brent died between that date and the April 1782 meeting of the Stafford County Court at which his will was proved. The court should have met on 8 April, but its sessions could have been prolonged for several days. Brent was buried in the family vault at his estate.

Brent, *Descendants of Giles Brent,* 123–131; birth recorded in George Harrison Sanford King, ed., *Register of Saint Paul's Parish, 1715–1798* (1960), 15; Brent family research notes, George Harrison Sanford King Papers, VHS; Francis Barnum Culver, *Blooded Horses of Colonial Days* (1922), 52, 79, 82, 106, 121; numerous references in the various *Williamsburg Virginia Gazette*s; *Revolutionary Virginia,* 1:25, 160–161, 2:204, 3:159, 5:162, 6:349, 356, 7:25, 61, 329, 723; HMS *Roebuck* logbook and journal, PRO Adm 52/1965, pt. 3, fols. 1–10; John Wollaston's pors. of Brent and wife in Georgetown University Art Collection, Washington, D.C.; family records and copy of will in Fredericksburg District Court Papers, files 49, 263.

Daphne Gentry

BREWBAKER, John Joseph (6 June 1895–10 March 1976), educator, was born near Springwood in Botetourt County, the son of Abram Joseph Brewbaker and Claudia V. Styne Brewbaker. His father was a tenant farmer who was able to purchase land for the first time three years after Brewbaker's birth. Brewbaker received his early education in rural schools and at Springwood and graduated from Buchanan High School in 1915. He received an A.B. from Roanoke College in 1918 and then entered the army's officer training school at Camp Lee. World War I ended shortly before Brewbaker completed training, and he was then discharged from the army and worked as assistant cashier of a bank in Buchanan from 1918 to 1922. On 19 February 1921 he married Carolyn Louise Fitch, of Clifton Forge. They had two sons.

Brewbaker began his career as an educator by serving as principal of Buchanan High School from 1922 to 1926 and of Saint Paul High School in Wise County for the 1926–1927 academic year. In 1927 he moved to Norfolk to become principal of Robert E. Lee Elementary School and served there for twelve years. Brewbaker attended summer sessions at the University of Virginia and received a master's degree in education in 1939 with a thesis entitled "Salaries of Norfolk Teachers," completed at the very time that the city's school district was involved in a lawsuit to equalize the pay scales of African American and white teachers. He was principal of James Madison Elementary School and Maury Night School in Norfolk from 1939 until 1942, business manager of the Norfolk public school system in 1942, and assistant superintendent from 1943 to 1949.

In 1949 the Norfolk school board elected Brewbaker superintendent of schools. His administration coincided with the postwar baby boom and annexations of portions of Norfolk and Princess Anne Counties. The school system expanded rapidly. By the time Brewbaker retired in 1960, Norfolk had built eighteen new schools at an expense of some $20 million and had an enrollment of about 50,000 students. The school district also began a program to use educational television. But these were also years in which every southern school administrator had to face challenges resulting from the United States Supreme Court's opinion in *Brown* v. *Board of Education* that mandatory racial segregation in public schools was unconstitutional.

The crisis of Brewbaker's career and of Virginia public education generally came in 1957 and 1958, when federal courts considered cases from several Virginia cities, including Norfolk, growing out of the General Assembly's adoption of laws to implement a policy of Massive Resistance to court-ordered desegregation. The laws authorized the governor to take over and even close any school that was ordered to desegregate. Brewbaker was no advocate of racial integration, but he believed that some degree of desegregation was inevitable and that it must be very gradual in areas with substantial black populations. His worst fear was that a collision between state policy and federal court orders would endanger

or destroy the public school system, which he considered the most important and significant institution in American life.

On 11 February 1957 the United States District Court enjoined the Norfolk school board from denying enrollment in any of its schools because of race, and by August 1958 more than 150 black pupils had applied for admission to formerly all-white schools. Caught between the court injunction and the state's school-closing laws, the board and the administration attempted to reject all of the black applications under an elaborate pupil-testing program. After the courts disallowed that ploy, Brewbaker's administration drew up a plan to admit seventeen black students to three high schools and three junior high schools. The governor immediately closed those schools, an order that locked more than 10,000 white students out of classes.

A group of white parents in Norfolk then sued the governor. They asserted that their children were denied equal protection of the laws, because schools were provided in other parts of Virginia while theirs were closed. On 19 January 1959 the federal court agreed, and on the same day the Virginia Supreme Court of Appeals ruled that the Massive Resistance laws violated the state constitution. Norfolk schools reopened on 2 February 1959 and admitted the black students without serious incident. Brewbaker received much credit for the calm desegregation, which he later cited as the high point of his career. Determined opponents of desegregation criticized him, and conflicts with them and with the mayor contributed to his decision in June 1960 to retire at age sixty-five, one year before his term expired. Brewbaker chronicled the school crisis and its resolution in a fifteen-page pamphlet, *Desegregation in the Norfolk Public Schools* (1960).

From July 1960 through May 1963 Brewbaker served as a consultant for the Southern Regional Council, advising school administrators who were facing desegregation. His views on desegregation do not seem to have moved much beyond gradualism and tokenism during the 1960s, thus making his position appear increasingly conservative as time passed. In a 1971 autobiography Brewbaker quoted with approval a 1955 court opinion that the United States Constitution did not require integration, only an end to enforced segregation. Doubting the constitutionality of other court interpretations, he endorsed neighborhood schools and could not reconcile himself to busing as a means of desegregation.

In 1973 and 1974 Brewbaker served as headmaster of Eastern Academy, a private Norfolk school, which was renamed Brewbaker Academy after his death. He was active in numerous civic and professional organizations and was an elder in the First Christian Church (Disciples of Christ) of Norfolk. Brewbaker received a distinguished service award from Phi Delta Kappa of the University of Virginia in 1960 and the Liberty Bell Award from the Norfolk-Portsmouth Bar Association in 1964 for outstanding public service in the spirit of the Constitution. In 1967 he was named one of Roanoke College's twelve outstanding alumni. John Joseph Brewbaker died in Norfolk on 10 March 1976 and was buried in Forest Lawn Cemetery in that city.

John Joseph Brewbaker, *Autobiography, Including Brief Family Sketches of Close Relatives* (1971), pors.; Henry Smith Rorer, *History of Norfolk Public Schools, 1681–1968* (1968), 70; Forrest R. White, *Pride and Prejudice: School Desegregation and Urban Renewal in Norfolk, 1950–1959* (1992); Thomas C. Parramore, Peter C. Stewart, and Tommy L. Bogger, *Norfolk: The First Four Centuries* (1995), 362–376; *Richmond News Leader,* 15 Feb. 1957; *Norfolk Virginian-Pilot,* 29, 30 June 1960; *Virginia Journal of Education* 54 (Nov. 1960): 30–31; *Southern School News,* esp. Mar. 1957, June 1958–Feb. 1959; July 1960–May 1963 reports, Southern Regional Council Papers, Atlanta University Center; obituaries in *Norfolk Ledger-Star* and *Norfolk Virginian-Pilot,* both 11 Mar. 1976.

PAUL E. MERTZ

BREWER, John (d. by 11 July 1635), member of the Council, was born in England, perhaps at Chard in Somersetshire, where his grandfather William Brewer was a physician, or in London, where his grandfather Richard Drake was a cloth maker. He was the son of Thomas Brewer and Ann Drake Brewer, but nothing else is known of him before his marriage on 12 February 1616 in the Parish of Saint Vedast, Foster Lane, London, to his first cousin Mary Drake, with whom he had three sons and three daughters.

Brewer was a grocer in London and was probably associated with his uncle, who was also named John Brewer and with whom he has been confused. The uncle was a London citizen (a freeman with voting privileges) who worked as a wholesale grocer at Bartholomew Lane dealing in spices, dried fruits, and sugar and belonged to the powerful Grocers Guild, an organization highly interested in foreign trade. John Brewer arrived in Virginia between about 1624 and 1628, most likely as a factor for his uncle. On 20 January 1629 he purchased 1,000 acres at Stanley Hundred, also called Bruers Borough, near the Warwick River in what is now part of the city of Newport News. Brewer's early activities in Virginia are unknown, but most likely he continued as a factor or merchant while settling his family on his property and becoming a planter. With Thomas Flint, from whom he had purchased his estate, he represented Warwick River in the General Assembly in 1630.

Brewer returned to England at least once. When he was in London late in 1630 or early in 1631 he joined Francis West, William Claiborne, William Capps, and Robert Sweet in a petition calling on the king to support the faltering tobacco market. Acts passed at the February and September 1632 assembly sessions, probably after his return to Virginia, made Brewer a commissioner, or justice, of the Warwick River County Court. He had been appointed to the governor's Council and was serving on it by the time the assembly met on 1 February 1633, but his name does not appear on any of the few other extant Council documents from the period of the controversial tenure of Governor Sir John Harvey. Brewer's allegiance when some of the major planters clashed with the governor is thus impossible to determine, and he was almost certainly dead before the May 1635 confrontation in which a Council faction drove the governor from the colony.

John Brewer died in Virginia before 11 July 1635, on which date Thomas Butler, minister of Denbigh Parish in Warwick County, who had married Brewer's widow, patented 1,000 acres at Brewer's Neck near the Nansemond River, using headrights to which Brewer had become entitled for the transportation of himself, his wife, and eighteen other people to Virginia. Brewer's will, dated 4 September 1631, was proved in London on 13 May 1636. His eldest son, also named John Brewer, inherited the property at Stanley Hundred, laid claim to the Brewer's Neck property after the death of Thomas Butler, and represented Isle of Wight County in the 1658 session of the House of Burgesses.

Marvin Talmadge Broyhill III, "The Brewer Families of Colonial Virginia, 1626–1776" (1992 typescript, LVA), 27–32; Ben R. Brewer, *The Long Brewer Line* (1993), 15–26; marriage in *Publications of the Harleian Society* 30 (1903): 10; *Minutes of Council and General Court*, 180 (first documented presence in Virginia), 200; Hening, *Statutes*, 1:147–148, 168–169, 186–187, 202; undated petition in Kingsbury, *Virginia Company*, 3:580–581; *Cavaliers and Pioneers*, 1:26 (earliest record of death), 91, 507; will in 66 Pile, Will-Register Books, Greater London Principal Probate Registry, printed in *New-England Historical and Genealogical Register* 47 (1893): 273–274.

NANCY D. EGLOFF

BREWER, John Bruce (26 August 1846–20 June 1929), president of Roanoke College (later Averett College), was born in Wake Forest, North Carolina, the son of John Marchant Brewer, a merchant and planter, and Ann Eliza Wait Brewer. After receiving private instruction from his grandfather Samuel Wait, a founder of the North Carolina Baptist Convention and a founder and first president of Wake Forest College, he enrolled in the Bethel Hill Academy in Person County, North Carolina. In 1864 Brewer joined the 2d Regiment North Carolina Junior Reserves and took part in the Battles of Kinston and Bentonville. He farmed for a year after the war before entering Wake Forest College. Brewer received a bachelor's degree in 1868 and a master's degree three years later. On 2 July 1873 he married Anne Elizabeth Joyner, of Franklin County, North Carolina. They had two sons and seven daughters.

From 1868 to 1870 Brewer taught at Maple Springs Academy in Franklin County, North Carolina. From 1870 to 1875 he was a principal of the coeducational Wilson Collegiate Institute in Wilson, North Carolina. Thereafter Brewer became a leader in higher education for Baptists and women. From 1875 to 1881 he presided over the Wilson Collegiate Seminary for Young Ladies, and from 1881 to 1896 he served as principal of the Chowan Baptist Female Institute in Murfreesboro, North Carolina. During Brewer's tenure Chowan became one of the most highly regarded colleges for women in the state. He then moved to Virginia and from 1901 to 1907 directed the Franklin Female Seminary in Franklin.

Much sought after as an experienced and successful woman's college administrator, Brewer rejected other offers of employment and in June 1907 became president of Roanoke College (later Averett College) in Danville. The college's ambitions had outrun its resources, but Brewer immediately had a positive effect. Inheriting an institution suffering from declining enrollment, financial difficulties, dilapidated facilities, and academic overextension, he quickly moved to cut costs by abolishing such expensive departments as the kindergarten and teacher education. Brewer then brought honesty to the degree structure by cutting a year from the four-year collegiate program. He put in place rigid entrance requirements and improved the curriculum by adding an elective system. In 1910 Brewer changed the name of the institution from Roanoke College to the Roanoke Institute in order to reflect the changes in curriculum. He also affiliated the school with the state Baptist educational system, a move that guaranteed additional students, attracted hefty contributions, and thus promised permanence. Most important, in April 1911 Brewer relocated the campus to a new site on West Main Street. Unquestionably one of the most successful and important leaders in history of the college, he placed the institution on a sound financial basis and nearly doubled its enrollment to almost 200 students.

Brewer retired in 1914 after forty-six years of teaching and academic administration. Nevertheless, four years after leaving Roanoke he returned to North Carolina to serve for two years as president of what had become Chowan College since his departure. During his career he also served on the governing boards of Wake Forest College, Meredith College, and Thomasville Baptist Orphanage. John Bruce Brewer died of a heart attack on 20 June 1929 in Blowing Rock, North Carolina, where he was staying with a daughter. He was buried the next day in the Brewer plot in the town cemetery in Wake Forest.

Tyler, *Encyclopedia*, 4:457–458; William S. Powell, ed., *Dictionary of North Carolina Biography* (1979–1996), 1:220–221 (variant birth date of 26 Oct. 1846); Jack Irby Hayes Jr., *A History of Averett College* (1984), 61–71 (por. on 62); statement of purpose and por. in Roanoke College for Young Women, *Annual Catalogue* 47 (1907); North Carolina Bureau of Vital Statistics, Death Certificate; obituaries in *Danville Register*, 21 June 1929, and *Religious Herald*, 27 June 1929.

JACK IRBY HAYES JR.

BREWER, Richard Lewis (27 May 1864–5 April 1947), Speaker of the House of Delegates, was born in Prince George County, the son of Richard Lewis Brewer and Judith Anne Robinson Brewer. His father had been the first mayor of Suffolk in 1852, taught school, served as superintendent of the county school system, and owned and operated a jewelry store in Suffolk. Richard L. Brewer Jr., as he referred to himself for most of his life, attended Suffolk Military Academy. He went to work in his father's jewelry store and following his father's death in 1902 was the sole proprietor of R. L. Brewer and Son until he sold the concern in 1923. Brewer developed other business interests as well. By the 1920s he was involved in investments, insurance, and banking. At various times he was chairman of the National Screen Company in Suffolk, vice president of American Bank and Trust Company, and president of the Gloucester-Yorktown Ferry, Inc. He belonged to many of the fraternal organizations of Suffolk, including the Masons, and for all of his adulthood was an active Methodist lay leader. On 28 January 1892 Brewer married Lelia Jackson Vellines, of Isle of Wight County. They had one daughter. Following his first wife's death on 30 April 1930, he married Belle Ashburn, principal of a primary school in Nansemond County, on 23 July 1931.

Brewer was elected mayor of Suffolk in 1892 and served for twelve years. He acquired the honorary title of colonel during the administration of Governor William Hodges Mann. In 1911 Colonel Brewer, as he was usually known thereafter, was elected to represent Nansemond County and Suffolk in the House of Delegates for the first of eleven consecutive two-year terms. At the beginning of his second term, in January 1914, the House created the new Committee on Appropriations. Brewer became its first chairman and held the position for six years. He played an important legislative role in introducing Virginia's first executive budget system, which went into effect in 1920. In January 1920, with support from advocates of Prohibition, Brewer defeated Kenneth N. Gilpin in the Democratic Party caucus and was elected to the first of three consecutive terms as Speaker of the House of Delegates. Brewer later cited the erection of a new state office building in Capitol Square as one of his most important legislative achievements. Another significant development came during his second term as Speaker when the House decided to install the nation's first mechanical vote-recording device.

On 30 June 1921 Brewer attended a ceremony in London at which his daughter unveiled a bronze reproduction of Jean-Antoine Houdon's statue of George Washington, a gift from Virginia to the United Kingdom. In January 1924 Brewer easily survived a half-hearted behind-the-scenes attempt by the state Democratic Party chairman, state senator Harry Flood Byrd (1887–1966), to replace him with Thomas W. Ozlin because Brewer supported the issuance of public bonds to finance road construction. Shortly thereafter Brewer announced that he would not seek a fourth term as Speaker in 1926. He subsequently subsided into the background, although he did not retire from the House of Delegates until 1933. In the meantime, in April 1922 the General Assembly appointed Brewer to the State Board of Charities and Corrections, and he served on that board and its successor, the State Board of Public Welfare, for twenty-five years. Richard Lewis Brewer died in Lakeview Hospital in Suffolk on 5 April 1947 and was buried in Cedar Hill Cemetery in that city.

Bruce, Tyler, and Morton, *History of Virginia*, 5:491 (por.); Rogers Dey Whichard, ed., *The History of Lower Tidewater Virginia* (1959), 3:342–344 (por.); BVS Marriage Register, Isle of Wight Co., 1892, and Suffolk City, 1931; obituaries in *New York Times*, *Norfolk Virginian-Pilot*, and *Richmond Times-Dispatch*, all 6 Apr. 1947, and *Suffolk News-Herald*, 7 Apr. 1947, including description of funeral services.

BRENT TARTER

BRIDGER, Joseph (bap. 28 February 1632–15 April 1686), member of the Council, was born probably at Woodmancote, the seat of his parents, Samuel Bridger and Mary Bridger, in the parish of Dursley, Gloucestershire, England. Old transcriptions of lost parish records note his baptism on 28 February 1632. At least one brother and other near relatives settled in Virginia, and members of the Driver, Holladay, and Pitt families who had lived nearby also immigrated to the colony. Some of them settled in Isle of Wight County, intermarried there, and came to control the county's land and politics. Sometime before 1670 Bridger married Hester Pitt, daughter of an immigrant. They had at least three sons and four daughters.

Little is known of Bridger's childhood and education. He may have matriculated at the College of Gloucester, of which his father was auditor. Certainly he was literate and well-read. The first record of Bridger's presence in Virginia is his election to the House of Burgesses from Isle of Wight County for the 1658 assembly session. He amassed considerable property in that county and left his children at least 9,500 acres at his death. Bridger evidently imported ample quantities of goods from England, and he may have been exporting wine and other products to Virginia before moving there himself. He continued to ship merchandise until shortly before his death.

Bridger took an active and constructive role during service in the House of Burgesses in 1658 and again from 1662 until 1670. He participated in adjusting boundary disputes with Maryland and served on a commission that sought to raise leaf tobacco prices by negotiating with Maryland and North Carolina a cessation of tobacco planting during the 1667–1668 seasons.

Bridger was appointed to the governor's Council on an unrecorded date and took his seat on 10 November 1673. He remained on the Council until his death. During at least part of that time Bridger also commanded the colony's militia in the southern counties, and he was a frequent companion and informal adviser to Governor Sir William Berkeley and his successors. Bridger supported Berkeley during Bacon's Rebellion of 1676 and received so many threats from the rebels that he temporarily took refuge in Maryland. Before the rebellion subsided he returned and "was very active & Instrumentall," according to one official report, "in Reducinge to their obedience the south part of James River," even though his own property was plundered "to a good vallue." In 1682 Bridger was again the object of some public criticism after helping suppress the plant cutters who illegally and violently sought an increase of tobacco prices, the same end that Bridger had attempted to achieve by negotiation fifteen years earlier. Bridger was customs collector for the lower district of the James River at least as early as the summer of 1675, and by the time of his death he was the adjutant general of the colony with the title of colonel.

Bridger was well respected in Virginia and Maryland, and substantial public funds passed through his hands as customs collector. He lived at White Marsh plantation in a fifteen-room house that may have been the largest in Isle of Wight County, and he enjoyed many comforts and luxuries that only a wealthy man could have acquired. Although no other evidence impugns his honesty, in October 1738 a slave working on Bridger's former plantation found a cache of money consisting chiefly of many gold and silver coins dating from the reigns of Elizabeth I, James I, and Charles I. The man who found the money spent some of it. Suspicious white neighbors seized most of the remainder and spent it, also. When this incident was reported in the *Williamsburg Virginia Gazette,* the printer speculated that the money either had been hidden during Bacon's Rebellion or that Bridger had collected it and kept it for himself or his family.

One year before he died Bridger disinherited his eldest son for leading an unprofitable and dissolute life, thereby depriving his namesake of an extremely valuable inheritance. Joseph Bridger died on 15 April 1686 and was buried on his property in Isle of Wight County.

Baptismal record in John A. Brayton, "Joseph Bridger of Dursley, Gloucestershire," *Virginia Genealogist* 41 (1997): 183–184; John Bennett Boddie, *History of Seventeenth-Century Isle of Wight County, Virginia* (1938), 409–433, quoting gravestone, which gives death date and inconsistent age at death of fifty-eight; gravestone now at Saint Luke's Church (Old Brick Church), Isle of Wight Co.; *Minutes of Council and General Court*, 361, 434, 522; *Executive Journals of Council*, 1:7, 9, 13; PRO AO 3/305, fols. 7–8; PRO CO 1/20, pt. 1, fols. 193–194, 295; "A list of the Names of those worthy persons," Samuel Wiseman's Book of Record, Pepysian Library 2582, Magdalene College, Cambridge University (quotation); *Williamsburg Virginia Gazette*, 30 Mar. 1739; Hening, *Statutes*, 6:448–450; disinheritance, will, and estate inventory in Isle of Wight Co. Wills, Deeds, Etc., 2:242, 250–251, 255–262.

TIMOTHY E. MORGAN

BRIDGES, Charles (bap. 2 April 1670–by 18 December 1747), painter, was christened in the parish of Barton Seagrave in Northamptonshire, England, on 2 April 1670, the son of John Bridges and Elizabeth Trumbull Bridges. He came from a well-educated gentry family, and his brother John Bridges was a barrister and one of the first and most laborious historians of Northamptonshire. Charles Bridges married Alice Flower on 4 August 1687 at Saint Marylebone, near London. They had at least one son and two daughters. He was an agent of the Society for Promoting Christian Knowledge by 1699 and served as a liaison with local charity schools at least until 1713, when his name disappears from the society's records. Bridges may have been trained as a painter and begun a career as a portraitist, though the only English portrait firmly attributable to him is one of Thomas Baker, a fellow of Saint John's College, Cambridge University, painted after 1717.

In 1733 Bridges, probably by then a widower, contemplated moving to Georgia. Men approaching their mid-sixties seldom relocated to the colonies, but two years later he arrived in Williamsburg with his children. Armed with recommendations from Thomas Gooch, master of Gonville and Caius College, Cambridge, and Edmund Gibson, the bishop of London, Bridges presented himself to Lieutenant Governor William Gooch and Commissary James Blair. Their influence and his own talent enabled him to receive commissions for portraits from William Byrd (1674–1744) and others, and in December 1735 he witnessed the will of Sir John Randolph. That same month Byrd introduced Bridges to Alexander Spotswood as "a man of a good family," who was forced "either by the frowns of fortune, or his own mismanagement," to earn a living as a painter. Byrd stated that, although Bridges was not a portraitist of the first rank, had he lived back "when places were given to the most deserving, he might have pretended to be serjeant-painter of Virginia." Bridges was the first documented painter to live and work in Virginia and to produce work of good quality. The more than two dozen portraits of Virginians attributable to him include members of the Blair, Bolling, Carter, Custis, Grymes, Lee, Ludwell, Moore, Page, and Randolph families. The work includes appealing double portraits of children, forthright images of great planters and their wives, and coats of arms for county governments. Portraits by Bridges can be seen at the College of William and Mary, the Colonial Williamsburg Foundation, the Virginia Historical Society, and Washington and Lee University.

Bridges also explored with Blair and Gibson the possibility of establishing a charity to teach Christianity to the colony's African Americans. Because baptism was linked in many minds with notions of freedom, which the planters certainly opposed, and because Blair and Bridges lacked funds and youthful energy, nothing came of this humanitarian ambition. One of Bridges's daughters died in Williamsburg on 24 August 1736, and that December he rented a house in the borough for twelve months. Thereafter he moved to Hanover County, where he evidently stayed until he returned to England about 1744. Charles Bridges died in his native Northamptonshire and was buried in the church of Warkton Parish near Barton Seagrave on 18 December 1747.

Henry Wilder Foote, "Charles Bridges: 'Sergeant-Painter of Virginia,' 1735–1740," *VMHB* 60 (1952): 3–55; Susanne Neale, "Charles Bridges: Painter and Humanitarian" (master's thesis, W&M, 1969), giving variant christening date of 2 Apr. 1672; Thomas Thorne, "Charles Bridges, Limner," *Arts in Virginia* 9 (winter 1969): 22–31; Graham Hood, *Charles Bridges and William Dering, Two Virginia Painters, 1735–1750* (1978), 1–98 (derivation of christening date on 1); William Gooch to Thomas Gooch, 26 May 1735, transcription at CW, records first presence in Virginia; William Byrd (1674–1744) to Alexander Spotswood, 22 Dec. 1735, in *Byrd Correspondence*, 2:468 (quotations); burial record from Warkton Parish register giving age at death as seventy-seven printed in *Northamptonshire Notes and Queries* 6 (1896): 79.

GRAHAM HOOD

BRIDGMAN, Ralph Parkhurst (22 November 1896–31 December 1991), president of Hampton

Institute (later Hampton University), was born in Boston, the son of Frank Easter Bridgman and Mary Louise Parkhurst Bridgman. Educated at Roxbury Latin School in Boston, Bridgman attended Harvard University from 1914 to 1916 but left before graduating to serve until 1919 as Young Men's Christian Association secretary and English teacher in government schools in Osaka, Japan. After returning to the United States, Bridgman received a B.A. from Harvard in 1921 and in 1924 both a B.D. from Union Theological Seminary in New York and a master's degree from Teachers College, Columbia University. He completed a Ph.D. at Teachers College in 1948. On 25 May 1925 Bridgman married Charlotte Frances Bradley, of New York City. They had three daughters.

After two years of teaching religious education at Union Theological Seminary, Bridgman entered the field of parent and family life education in 1926 as director of the Parents' Council in Philadelphia. In 1931 he returned to New York to join the faculty of the Child Development Institute at Teachers College. The following year Bridgman became executive director of the National Council of Parent Education in New York City and remained there until 1938, when he became an instructor of mental hygiene at New York University. He frequently published articles on parent and family education and from 1934 to 1938 edited the journal *Parent Education*. Bridgman was dean of students at Brooklyn College in New York from 1939 to 1943.

In 1943 the board of trustees of Hampton Institute elected Bridgman president. He took office in February 1944 as the last in a line of white presidents who had led the institute since its founding in 1868. Other historically black colleges had begun hiring black presidents, and before Bridgman's election some Hampton faculty members had called for the selection of an African American. Bridgman announced that successful administration of Hampton depended on democratic interracial cooperation and a sound relationship among the trustees, faculty, student body, and alumni, but his administration quickly foundered on these issues during a time of change and conflict.

Disappointed by the lack of racial progress during World War II, many African Americans demanded government protection of their civil rights, particularly equal access to education. In the field of higher education black leaders were promoting liberal arts programs and questioning the usefulness of the industrial education that Hampton still offered. In his 1944 annual report Bridgman recognized the need for Hampton to decide whether to become a liberal arts college or remain a college of applied arts and sciences offering vocational training. He appeared to favor a shift toward the liberal arts when he supported more stringent faculty standards in a bid to gain accreditation from the American Association of Colleges and Universities. On 29 February 1944 a faculty committee recommended that instructors hold master's degrees and professors hold doctorates. The proposal also required professional study as well as work experience for the faculty in the trade school. Bridgman endorsed the proposal, and the faculty and board of trustees approved it in 1945. Although he succeeded in raising faculty salaries and reducing course loads, his decision in October 1946 to "correct" the statute on faculty rank by mandating additional years of graduate study for Hampton's teaching staff aroused faculty ire. Longtime staff members, particularly in the trade school where few members of the faculty held degrees, feared dismissal. Bridgman countered by blaming unrest on those seeking to remain at Hampton despite incompetence or weak academic credentials.

Postwar enrollment in Hampton's trade school, boosted by returning veterans, increased more than 50 percent above its previous high. Bridgman raised the possibility of further changes in the student body by arguing in 1945 that a segregated black college was not a proper institution for a democracy. The institute operated a biracial summer farm camp for women in 1944, and in a 1947 experiment three Hampton students exchanged with five white students at Antioch and Grinnell Colleges.

By the autumn of 1947 Bridgman had lost the confidence of both faculty and students. Black leaders in Virginia, including the editors of the *Richmond Afro-American*, called for his replacement by a black president. Bridgman submitted his resignation to a divided board of trustees, effective 31 August 1948, and went on administrative leave on 20 February 1948.

After he left Hampton, Bridgman became chairman of the Department of Family Life at Merrill-Palmer School in Detroit in September 1948. In 1950 he developed a family court center in Toledo that received international recognition. Ten years later, at the request of the Japanese government, he received a Fulbright scholarship to teach and lecture for a year at the Institute of Research and Training in Tokyo. Bridgman and his wife retired to Black Mountain, North Carolina, after their return from Japan, and he became director and chief counselor of the counseling and continuing education program of the Diocese of Western North Carolina of the Episcopal Church. Charlotte Bridgman died in 1989. Ralph Parkhurst Bridgman died in Black Mountain on 31 December 1991 and was cremated.

Commonwealth 11 (June 1944): 18–19 (por.); Ralph Parkhurst Bridgman Papers, Hampton; William Hannibal Robinson, "The History of Hampton Institute 1868–1949" (Ph.D. diss., New York University, 1953); *Norfolk Journal and Guide*, 18 Sept., 6 Nov. 1943, 1 Mar., 11, 18, 25 Oct., 1 Nov. 1947, 7, 14 Feb. 1948; *Washington Post*, 28 Jan., 4 Mar. 1947; *Richmond Afro-American*, 25 Oct. 1947, 7, 14 Feb. 1948; *New York Times*, 2 Sept. 1948; North Carolina Bureau of Vital Statistics, Death Certificate; obituary in *Asheville Citizen-Times*, 3 Jan. 1992.

MARY CARROLL JOHANSEN

BRIGGS, David (6 January 1780–5 November 1836), member of the Council, was born probably on his father's farm near Falmouth in Stafford County. His father, David Briggs (originally Bridges), was a native of Fifeshire, Scotland, who had studied for the Presbyterian ministry before immigrating to Virginia, where he became a prosperous merchant and landowner. His mother, Jean McDonald Briggs, was the daughter of the rector of Brunswick Parish in King George County.

Little is known about his early life, although he may have attended the College of William and Mary about 1803. On 28 June 1808 Briggs married Mary Frazer Vowles, of Falmouth. They had five sons and seven daughters. Before his

marriage Briggs had begun the practice of law in Falmouth and the neighboring county courts, and in 1816 he moved across the Rappahannock River to Fredericksburg. His practice eventually extended to the state appellate courts and the federal district court in Richmond. Briggs helped found the Fredericksburg Colonization Society in 1819. On 21 March 1820 he was elected mayor of Fredericksburg for a one-year term, and he served on the city council in 1821 and 1822. In the latter year Briggs was appointed a director of the Fredericksburg branch of the Bank of Virginia.

Briggs won election to the House of Delegates from Spotsylvania County in 1824 and was reelected in 1825 and 1826. He served on the Committees on Courts of Justice, on Finance, and on Schools and Colleges. Late in the night of 15 December 1826 the General Assembly elected Briggs to the Council of State. Twelve men had been nominated for two vacant positions, and it took the assembly all day and six hotly contested ballots to fill them. Briggs completed his own assembly term before taking his seat on the Council on 29 May 1827.

In order to attend to the routine duties of his new office while supporting his many children, Briggs moved his family and his law practice to rented rooms in Richmond. On 6 January 1830, in accordance with a constitutional provision requiring the assembly to remove two councillors every third year, Briggs and another member lost their Council seats. Partisan politics evidently played little part in the assembly's decision, but the legislators still needed several ballots to decide whom to displace. Briggs stayed at his post until his successor appeared to take the oath of office on 29 May 1830.

On 8 December 1829 the members of the Virginia Convention of 1829–1830 elected Briggs to replace George Wythe Munford, who had resigned as secretary of the constitutional convention. He served until the body adjourned on 15 January 1830. David Briggs remained in Richmond practicing law and died there on 5 November 1836. In spite of many years of successful practice he never accumulated any significant amount of property, and even though he was an attorney he evidently left no will.

Birth date in Briggs family Bible record (VHS typescript); Dolorus Briggs Mansfield, "History of the Briggs-Bridge Family" (unpublished MS, 1960, VHS), 10–14; Briggs letters in several collections, VHS; Fredericksburg City Council Minutes (1801–1829), 287; *Fredericksburg Virginia Herald*, 1 July 1808, 29 May 1819; *Richmond Enquirer*, 16 Dec. 1826, 7 Jan. 1830; *Richmond Daily Whig*, 7 Jan. 1830; *Proceedings and Debates of 1829–1830 Convention*, 567; Catlin, *Convention of 1829–30* (por.); obituaries in *Richmond Courier and Daily Compiler*, *Richmond Enquirer*, and *Richmond Whig and Public Advertiser*, all 8 Nov. 1836, and *Fredericksburg Virginia Herald*, 9 Nov. 1836.

DAPHNE GENTRY

BRIGGS, John Howell (d. 2 March 1808), member of the Convention of 1788 and member of the Council, was born probably in Sussex County sometime late in the 1750s, the son of Gray Briggs and Dorothy Pleasants Briggs. His father, a merchant and landowner, represented Sussex County in the House of Burgesses from 1754 to 1758 and later moved to Dinwiddie County.

Briggs may have studied briefly at the College of William and Mary. He served as an ensign in a cavalry troop of Sussex County militia during the last two years of the Revolutionary War. In April 1785 he received a commission as a lieutenant colonel of militia, and in August 1786 he became a justice of the peace. Briggs was elected to the House of Delegates in 1784 and served through the end of 1789. His committee assignments included Commerce, Courts of Justice, Privileges and Elections, and Propositions and Grievances, but he never obtained a major chairmanship. In March 1788 Briggs was elected one of the two county delegates to a state convention called to consider ratification of the proposed constitution of the United States. He made no recorded speech during the debates. On 25 June Briggs voted with the minority in favor of requiring constitutional amendments before ratification and then voted against the successful motion to ratify.

On 28 November 1789 the General Assembly elected Briggs to fill a vacancy on the Council of State. He took his seat on 21 December, following the end of the legislative session. Briggs served almost four years, during which the business of the Council was largely routine. He was evidently regular in attendance. In March 1793 Briggs ran for the House of Representa-

tives from the district composed of the counties of Prince George, Southampton, Surry, and Sussex, but he lost to Carter Bassett Harrison. On 28 October 1793 he resigned from the Council, citing "my own inclination, but more my domestic Concerns." Briggs remained interested in politics, though. He supported Thomas Jefferson for president in 1800 and in November of that year was one of three commissioners to supervise the voting for presidential electors in Sussex County.

The earliest extant land tax return for Sussex County, taken in 1782, shows that Briggs then owned 3,412 acres, most of which he had inherited from his grandfather Howell Briggs. During the 1780s and 1790s Briggs sold a number of tracts in Sussex County and acquired one, leaving him with more than 1,900 acres in Sussex at the time of his death. In 1802 he purchased Mattoax, a 425-acre Chesterfield County plantation of the Randolph family, to which he moved about 1805. In the summer of 1804 Briggs made a ten-week tour of the western springs and visited several prominent state politicians whom he had known while still active in public affairs. His journal of the trip attests to his curiosity about his surroundings, his ability to play the flute and violin, and his wide acquaintance among the influential families of Virginia.

John Howell Briggs died at Mattoax on 2 March 1808. He had never married and left no will. His complicated estate was not settled until 1820.

Biography in *Journals of Council of State*, 5:380; Land and Personal Property Tax Returns, Sussex Co., 1782–1809, RG 48, LVA; Kaminski, *Ratification*, 8:194–195, 10:1539, 1541, 1565; Briggs to Henry Lee, 28 Oct. 1793, House of Delegates, Executive Communications, RG 79, LVA (quotation); Briggs, "Journal of a Trip to the Sweet Springs commencing July 23d and ending September 29th 1804," in *First Resorts: A Visit to Virginia's Springs*, [ed. E. Lee Shepard] (1987), 5–32; family relationships and estate settlement papers in *Atkinson* v. *Watkins et al.* (1820), Sussex Co. Court Loose Papers, box 226; death notice in *Norfolk Gazette and Publick Ledger*, 7 Mar. 1808.

DAPHNE GENTRY

BRIGHT, John (25 September 1908 –26 March 1995), biblical scholar, was born in Chattanooga, Tennessee, the son of John Bright, a Railway Express cashier, and Elizabeth Nall Bright. After graduating from the McCallie School in Chattanooga in June 1924, he entered the Presbyterian College of South Carolina in Clinton, from which he graduated with a B.A. in May 1928. Bright then matriculated at Union Theological Seminary in Richmond, and during his attendance there he did fieldwork at Presbyterian churches in Moorefield, West Virginia, and Greensboro, North Carolina. He received a B.D. in 1931.

Bright remained at the seminary as the Walter W. Moore Fellow, working toward a degree in theology and teaching in the Department of the Old Testament as an assistant professor of Greek and Hebrew. He received a master's degree on 9 May 1933 with a thesis entitled "A Psychological Study of the Major Prophets." During the summers of 1932 and 1934 Bright worked on excavation teams at two biblical sites. He was not an archaeologist, only a student earning his keep by driving a truck and doing odd jobs, but this experience and the influence of the archaeologists William Foxwell Albright and James Leon Kelso caused Bright to devote his life to biblical study.

Licensed and ordained on 17 May 1935 by the Atlanta Presbytery of the Presbyterian Church in the United States, Bright entered the doctoral program in oriental studies at the Johns Hopkins University. He soon found himself struggling with the role of human reason in understanding and interpreting Scripture. Bright wondered whether the literary and archaeological tools employed in secular scholarship could be used to unlock the meaning and to enrich understanding of sacred writings. He specifically asked how higher criticism could contribute to biblical scholarship. With these unanswered questions in mind, Bright withdrew from the degree program to become associate pastor at the First Presbyterian Church in Durham, North Carolina. In October 1936 he applied to enter the doctor of theology program at Union Theological Seminary, for which he embarked on a study of the poetic books of the Old Testament with a minor in the Pauline epistles. Bright still struggled with the questions he had raised, and in September 1937, after accepting charge of the Catonsville Presbyterian Church in Maryland, he was allowed to withdraw from his graduate

work with the privilege of rematriculating at his discretion. Bright served at Catonsville until 1 January 1940, when he resigned to complete his doctoral residence work at the Johns Hopkins. His dissertation, completed in June 1940, was entitled "The Age of King David: A Study in the Institutional History of Israel."

On 1 July 1940 Bright became associate professor in the biblical department of Union Theological Seminary and on 13 May of the following year was elected Cyrus H. McCormick Professor of Hebrew and the Interpretation of the Old Testament. He retained the latter post until he retired on 31 May 1975. Bright was granted a leave of absence on 12 July 1943 to serve as a United States Army chaplain. Assigned to several artillery units, from the final months of 1944 until the end of the war he participated in campaigns in Europe, part of the time in central Germany, where his only brother had died in a prisoner of war camp. Bright returned to the United States with the rank of captain in February 1946 and resumed teaching at the seminary that spring.

Bright published *The Kingdom of God: The Biblical Concept and Its Meaning for the Church* (1953) and *Early Israel in Recent History Writing* (1956). Using his archaeological experience and a writing style readable equally by specialists and the laity, he provided evidence in support of biblical narrative and won acclaim as one of the world's foremost biblical scholars. Bright's third book, *A History of Israel* (1959), expanded on his doctoral dissertation and quickly won acceptance as a standard textbook. This brilliant work answered the questions that he had struggled with early in his career. Bright's approach employed the tools of modern secular scholarship without denying a role for revelation. He used both science and faith to enhance scriptural exegesis and deepen understanding of God's revealed will. *A History of Israel* was reprinted six times during Bright's life including translation into several other languages. He published a definitive study of the book of Jeremiah for an Anchor Bible series on books of the Bible in 1965 and concluded his scholarly publications with *The Authority of the Old Testament*

(1967) and *Covenant and Promise: The Prophetic Understanding of the Future in Pre-Exilic Israel* (1976).

Bright received an honorary D.D. from Presbyterian College of South Carolina in 1947 and was named its Man of the Year and recipient of its principal alumni award in 1953. From June 1963 to January 1964 he lectured at Presbyterian theological seminaries in Brazil, and during the summer of 1966 he preached and taught in South Africa as part of an exchange program. Later in 1966 Bright lectured at Cambridge, Edinburgh, London, Oxford, and elsewhere in Great Britain, and in 1968 he was one of four United States delegates to the assembly of the World Council of Churches in Sweden. In November 1975 Bright was the fifth man to be named honorary president of the ninety-five-year-old Society of Biblical Literature, the world's largest organization of biblical scholars.

On 28 July 1938 in Atlanta, Bright married Carrie Lena McMullen, director of religious education at First Presbyterian Church in that city and a daughter of missionary parents in China. They had two sons. John Bright died in Richmond on 26 March 1995 and was buried at the Union Theological Seminary in Virginia Cemetery at Hampden-Sydney College. He left his large library to the seminary.

Birth date and personal and professional information from archives, alumni records, files on deceased faculty members, and oral history videotapes, UTS; "How to Win Funds and Influence People—Dr. John Bright Knows," *Star and Lamp of Pi Kappa Phi* (May 1954): 4–5 (por.), 13; *Richmond Times-Dispatch*, 21 Nov. 1952, 1 Feb. 1965, 15 June, 5 July 1968, 8 Nov. 1975; *Richmond News Leader*, 4 Jan. 1956, 19 Feb. 1966, 17 May 1975; obituaries in *Richmond Times-Dispatch*, 28 Mar. 1995 (por.), and *New York Times*, 1 Apr. 1995.

DAPHNE GENTRY
G. SCOTT HENRY

BRIGHT, John Fulmer (17 November 1877–29 December 1953), Richmond city mayor, was the son of Mary Samuel Davies Bright and George Hilliard Bright, a physician and native of South Carolina who settled in Richmond after the Civil War. He was born in the family home on West Grace Street and lived there all his life. Bright attended public schools and the Medical College of Virginia, where he received

an M.D. in 1898. After graduation he established a successful private practice and also accepted a professorship in anatomy at his alma mater. Bright remained on the faculty through 1910, after which he became professor emeritus. He joined the Virginia National Guard in 1907 as a medical officer and rose to command the 1st Regiment Virginia Infantry, attaining the rank of colonel in 1920. During World War I he was a major in the 3d Battalion of the 116th United States Infantry at Camp McClellan, in Anniston, Alabama. From 1918 to 1923 Bright served as coroner for Henrico County. He never married.

J. Fulmer Bright first entered politics in 1922 with a successful bid to be one of the five men representing Richmond in the House of Delegates. He sat on the Committees on Asylums and Prisons, on Militia and Police, on Printing, and on Roads and Internal Navigation. In 1924 he defeated three-term incumbent mayor George Ainslie and thus began a sixteen-year tenure that gained him the reputation as probably the most colorful figure ever to preside over Richmond's affairs. The 1924 mayoral contest offered a striking contrast between Ainslie's attention to economic development, exemplified by road construction and maintenance, new schools, and enlarged police and fire services, and Bright's call for retrenchment and economy.

Bright captured the April primary by nearly 1,300 votes, largely as a result of strong support in the heavily working-class Jefferson and Madison Wards. The *Richmond Labor Journal* had for several years chided the Ainslie administration for neglecting public improvements in such neighborhoods. Labor and its press failed to recognize that as mayor Bright intended to reduce the overall role of local government in public improvements, rather than expand services to those previously neglected. Throughout his four terms as mayor, Bright consistently resisted appeals for government action either to encourage urban development or to resolve social and economic problems. Planning also took a back seat in his restricted conception of government's proper role.

Bright could point to an array of accomplishments during his four terms in office, including the establishment of Byrd Flying Field as a municipal airport, construction of bridges and a system of traffic lights, erection of the Virginia War Memorial Carillon in Byrd Park, and expansion of sewers, paving, curbs, and gutters, but he opposed many of these projects at least initially. The tone and substance of the Bright administration was better captured by the mayor's ample use of his veto power to halt projects and to assert preeminence in local policy-making. His relations with the common council and board of aldermen were stormy. On 7 June 1936 the latter body set a record by overriding five of Bright's vetoes in a single meeting.

A feud Bright began with the Richmond newspapers as early as 1925 raged for the next two decades. In 1932 he responded to a journalistic investigation of questionable purchasing practices by cutting off all official city advertising. Relations with the press broke down again at the end of that year after Bright arrested two communists who came to Richmond to organize the unemployed. When editorials questioned the arrests, the mayor ordered the police department to sever all relations with the newspapers. The papers, in turn, complained that the irritable mayor's fearful reaction to the radicals actually publicized their agitation.

Communists and labor organizers were not alone in angering the mayor. Bright fiercely opposed the New Deal, and his stubborn refusal to seek relief from the federal government during the darkest days of the Great Depression set Richmond apart from other southern cities. By the mid-1930s he acknowledged the need to tackle such problems as slum conditions but remained adamantly opposed to public housing. Instead, he insisted that solutions were the responsibility of local businessmen rather than government.

Bright's unwavering opposition to the federal housing program became a central issue in the election of 1940. His opponent, Gordon Barbour Ambler, hammered away at him for refusing to improve housing, back annexation, finance necessary public improvements, or reorganize city government. Bright responded by attempting to establish his record as a racial moderate and show that Richmond had not stood still dur-

ing his tenure, but he could not overcome his reputation as an opponent of change and lost the election.

The Virginia National Guard was called into federal service in February 1941, but a disappointed Colonel Bright was relieved from active duty because of defective vision and arterial hypertension. In April he retired with the formal rank of brigadier general. Bright then ran for a seat in the House of Delegates but lost the primary. In December 1941 he was appointed assistant coordinator of the Virginia Defense Council in charge of tire rationing and, in May 1942, became state director of the Federal Office of Price Administration. In 1944 Bright considered another run for the mayor's office but, declaring that his duty must prevail over his desire, decided to retain his state position.

Throughout the 1940s Bright vociferously opposed various changes in Richmond's governmental structure and services. He waged a strident one-man crusade against a new city charter designed to replace Richmond's thirty-two-member bicameral city council with a single nine-member body. On 4 November 1947 the voters overwhelmingly approved the new charter, an action that, combined with reforms to reduce the mayor's power, ended the style of city government that Bright had practiced during his years in office. Thereafter he wore a piece of black crepe in his lapel as a sign of mourning. Bright was more successful in his opposition to an expressway plan for central Richmond in 1950 and 1951. Twice he forced city leaders to subject the plan to a referendum, and both times Richmond voters rejected it.

Bright belonged to a variety of fraternal organizations. He remained active in the Freemasons and Acca Temple until the end of his life. In 1950 John Fulmer Bright became medical adviser to the Industrial Commission of Virginia, a post he held until his death from a heart ailment on 29 December 1953. His will left funds to the city's poor children, made bequests to ten local churches, and specified that money from a trust fund he established for the three sisters who survived him be used after their deaths to improve public parks in East End neighborhoods. The newspapers with whom he had often feuded marked Bright's passing with editorials praising his courage and devotion to Richmond. He was buried in Hollywood Cemetery in that city.

Glass and Glass, *Virginia Democracy*, 3:108–109; BVS Birth Register, Richmond City; Military Service Records; Harry M. Ward, *Richmond: An Illustrated History* (1985), 246–247 (por.); *New York Times*, 15 Jan. 1933; *Richmond News Leader*, 1 Sept. 1934, 3 Aug. 1940; *Richmond Times-Dispatch*, 8 Sept. 1937 (por.), 29 May 1990; Virginius Dabney, *Richmond: The Story of a City* (1976), 313–314, 320; Christopher Silver, *Twentieth-Century Richmond: Planning, Politics, and Race* (1984), 90–93, 130–131, 146–150, 176–181, 188–189; obituaries in *Richmond News Leader* and *Richmond Times-Dispatch*, both 30 Dec. 1953, and *New York Times,* 31 Dec. 1953; memorials in *Richmond News Leader*, 30 Dec. 1953, 1, 18 Jan. 1954, *Richmond Times-Dispatch*, 31 Dec. 1953, *Report of the Adjutant General of the Commonwealth of Virginia* (1954): 51, and *Virginia Medical Monthly* 81 (1954): 142.

CHRISTOPHER SILVER

BRIMM, Henry Muller (3 February 1898– 1 August 1984), librarian, was born in Columbia, South Carolina, the son of Daniel Johnson Brimm and Elizabeth Muller Brimm. His father was a Presbyterian minister and professor of New Testament literature and exegesis at Columbia Theological Seminary. A doctrinal dispute caused him to resign in 1900, but after several years as a teacher in secondary schools, he became in 1910 professor of the Bible at the Presbyterian College of South Carolina at Clinton. Henry Muller Brimm received a solid educational background at home and in local schools. He received a B.A. from Presbyterian College in 1917. Brimm served in the United States Navy during World War I and received his discharge in 1919.

Brimm discovered his vocation when he worked as librarian for his alma mater from 1923 to 1925. In 1927 he attended Columbia University's School of Library Service and received his B.S. the following year. He returned to Columbia University in 1935–1936 for further graduate study. During his first stint in New York he began what became a close lifelong friendship with Robert Beach, the librarian of Union Theological Seminary there. Armed with his professional degree, Brimm in 1928 became assistant librarian at the University of South Carolina in Columbia.

In 1930 Brimm moved to Richmond as the first full-time librarian of Union Theological Seminary in Virginia. Although the school's president, Benjamin Rice Lacy, had emphasized the library's importance, in 1929 it owned only 47,000 inadequately cataloged books and pamphlets. More important, only about one hundred borrowers, limited almost entirely to the seminary's faculty and students, used the collections. During his forty years at the seminary Brimm enlarged the collections and developed a distinguished library staff. By his retirement in 1970 the library boasted not only a substantially expanded facility but also holdings of more than 135,000 volumes and nearly 800 periodical subscriptions.

Brimm gave as much attention to opening the library's resources to more users as he did to developing it into one of the nation's finest theological collections. He helped to establish Union Theological Seminary's continuing education program for working clergymen, which included circulation of library materials by mail. Brimm also spread the word throughout the local community that the library was open to anyone, including African Americans, a policy that made it one of the first library facilities in Virginia to extend full and equal services to black patrons. By 1970 the library had nearly 3,000 registered borrowers.

Brimm's efforts to place the library at the center of the seminary's instruction also resulted in his appointment in 1940 as professor of bibliography. He was the first nonordained faculty member to hold that rank. In 1947 he helped found *Interpretation: A Journal of Bible and Theology* and established a bibliographical lecture series at the seminary. Brimm conceived and in 1960 began publication of *Scholar's Choice*, a bibliographical journal serving theological libraries. The seminary recognized his achievements in 1965 by creating the Henry Muller Brimm Chair of Bibliography.

Brimm was a charter member of the American Theological Library Association in 1947 and served as its president in 1953–1954. He also sat on the Committee on Library Standards of the American Association of Theological Schools and chaired the Library Section of the Presbyterian Educational Association. Honorary doctorates were awarded him in 1943 by Davis and Elkins College in Elkins, West Virginia, and in 1965 by his alma mater, Presbyterian College. Following World War II Brimm helped to organize relief assistance to the Faculté Libre de L'Eglise Réformée in Montpellier, France, and the school expressed its appreciation with an honorary degree in 1965.

An active churchman, Brimm was an elder in the Ginter Park Presbyterian Church and served on numerous committees of Hanover Presbytery. He also represented his denomination on the Commission on Civil and Religious Liberty of the North American Area of the Alliance of Reformed Churches throughout the World holding the Presbyterian System. With William Munford Ellis Rachal he edited and published *Yesterday and Tomorrow in the Synod of Virginia* (1962), a collection of essays.

In 1938 Brimm married Josephine Craven Robinson, a widowed music teacher from Raleigh, North Carolina, who had one daughter from her previous marriage. After retiring from the seminary in 1970 he moved briefly to Kentucky, where he served as visiting librarian at Louisville Presbyterian Seminary until 1972. Henry Muller Brimm died in Richmond on 1 August 1984 and was buried at the Union Theological Seminary in Virginia Cemetery at Hampden-Sydney College.

Connolly Gamble Jr., "Henry M. Brimm, Librarian," *Virginia Librarian* 2 (1956): 43 (por.); Henry Muller Brimm Papers and oral history interview, UTS; Martha B. Aycock, "Oral History at Union Theological Seminary," *Journal of the Richmond Oral History Association* 1 (winter 1977): 9–13; obituaries in *Richmond News Leader*, 2 Aug. 1984, *Richmond Times-Dispatch*, 3 Aug. 1984, *Presbyterian Outlook*, 3 Sept. 1984, and *Virginia Librarian Newsletter* 30 (1984): 96.

JOHN BOONE TROTTI

BRISBY, William Henry (August 1836–16 November 1916), member of the House of Delegates, was born in New Kent County to Roger Lewis, a free African American, and Marinda Brisby, who was of Pamunkey Indian origins. Lewis was much older than Marinda Brisby and died before March 1838. She returned to her family, who had not approved of Lewis, and the boy took his mother's name. Little else is known of his early life. He had a brother and probably sisters; a nephew and a niece lived with him at one time.

Brisby may have inherited land from his father in New Kent County. Ambitious and industrious, Brisby soon established himself in that free black community. He worked on the construction of the Richmond and York River Railroad and used his wages to purchase a set of blacksmith's tools. With a partner, Brisby set up a blacksmith shop at Talleysville in 1859. The following year he bought his partner's tools and on 29 January 1860 purchased the lot where his shop was located. One year later he acquired thirty-two acres of land nearby.

The advance toward Richmond of the Union army during the Peninsula campaign of spring 1862 brought war to New Kent County. Free people of color were being forced to work on Confederate fortifications near Yorktown. To avoid impressment Brisby served for several months as a blacksmith for a troop of Confederate cavalry stationed in the county. He traveled with the cavalry but at least could still oversee his farm and smithy.

On his own again in 1863, Brisby expanded his enterprises in April by purchasing for $900 in inflated state currency a large net for catching fish, which he salted and packed in barrels. He often traveled to Richmond to sell fish and crops and to buy iron and other goods. His cargo on the return trips sometimes included fugitive slaves and escaped Union prisoners. Confederate authorities twice imprisoned him for short periods at Castle Thunder on suspicion of aiding the enemy. When Union troops under Major General Philip H. Sheridan commandeered his property in May 1864, Brisby showed Sheridan a testimonial by three Union officers whom he had helped escape, and Sheridan ordered Brisby's three cows returned to him.

Brisby later testified that the slave regime's withholding of education made him a Unionist, and as late as 1860 he signed with his mark. Somehow, though, Brisby learned to read and write. The 1863 note for the fishing net bears his own signature. Thereafter he continued to study and obtained books, and he took a special interest in the law.

In April 1867 Brisby was one of three delegates from New Kent County who attended the Union Republican State Convention in Richmond. After a constitutional convention organized a new state government, Republicans in New Kent County nominated him for the House of Delegates in 1869. Brisby won the election by just nineteen votes and was assigned to the Committee on Officers and Offices at the Capitol. In the General Assembly he voted with the Republican minority and was a leader among the African American delegates who condemned the erratic behavior of William H. Andrews, a black Republican delegate from Surry County.

On 11 September 1871 county Republicans nominated Brisby for a second term. Newton M. Brooks, a former agent of the Freedmen's Bureau in New Kent, had sought the nomination for himself and afterward asked Brisby to withdraw. When he refused, Brooks threatened to run against him. Fearing that the presence of a third candidate would give the election to the Conservatives, Brisby called for a second convention at which his African American friend and neighbor William H. Patterson received the nomination and went on to win the election.

When Brisby petitioned the Southern Claims Commission in 1873 for payment for property that Sheridan's soldiers had taken in 1864, Brooks exacted his revenge. At his instigation, several men testified about Brisby's Confederate service as a blacksmith. Their testimony forced Brisby to submit additional evidence and delayed payment of his claim until 1878.

On 4 November 1869 Brisby married nineteen-year-old Ann Rebecca Cumber, daughter of a long-resident free family. Of as many as twelve children, six sons and two daughters survived. Brisby remained active in local politics. During the 1876 election campaign the Republican Congressional Executive Committee named him a district canvasser for the Second Congressional District. Brisby served from 1871 until at least 1881 on the county board of supervisors, attended the county organizing meeting of what became the Readjuster Party in 1879, and served as a justice of the peace until at least

1896 and possibly into the first decade of the twentieth century.

In 1885 Brisby and his brother, Matthew Brisby, went into debt to buy a steam sawmill, which they moved to his 129-acre property. The sawmill proved unprofitable, and his brother died before 1891, leaving Brisby responsible for all that they owed. He fell further into debt, assisted, according to family tradition, by a combination of alcohol and unscrupulous white men. Brisby began selling his property to stave off his creditors. Finally, in 1907 the county sold the last of his land at auction. A year later he sold the sawmill for $150 and, past the age of seventy, contracted to work there for the new owner.

For all of Brisby's local prominence, his life ended sadly. A strict, sometimes violent disciplinarian, he drove his sons out of the household as soon as possible. Ann R. Brisby died suddenly on 1 August 1894, and his beloved younger daughter, Nannie J. Brisby, became convinced that he had caused her death. Her alienation grew when he married Victoria Pearman Holmes, a widow, on 20 February 1901.

Sometime after 1908 Brisby began to suffer from dementia. He and his second wife moved into the Henrico County home of his unforgiving younger daughter. In July 1916 his physical condition worsened, and he was committed to Central State Hospital in Petersburg. William Henry Brisby died there of kidney failure on 16 November 1916. The place of his burial is unknown.

Claim 19204, Southern Claims Commission; birth date from Census, New Kent Co., 1900; BVS Marriage Register, New Kent Co.; Jackson, *Negro Office-Holders*, 6, 82 (por.); Helen Jackson Lee (a granddaughter), *Nigger in the Window* (1978), 40–43; Personal Property Tax Returns, New Kent Co., 1863, RG 48, LVA; New Kent Co. Deed Book, 1:112, 4:83, 125, 137–138, 272, 5:29, 337–338, 340, 6:560–561, 7:283, 8:131, 10:241–242, 11:52, 356–357; *Organization, Resolutions and Address of the Union Republican State Convention of Virginia, held at Richmond, April 17, 1867* (1867), 2; *JHD*, 1869–1870 sess., 54, 106, 211, 395; *Richmond Whig*, 27 Feb. 1879; additional information provided by Sue Harwell, Renata Jackson, Helen Jackson Lee, and Helen C. Rountree; BVS Death Certificate, Dinwiddie Co.

JOHN T. KNEEBONE

BRISTOW, Joseph Allen (17 September 1838–30 April 1903), member of the Convention of

1901–1902, was born at Stormont in Middlesex County, the son of Larkin Stubblefield Bristow and Catherine Seward Bristow. He attended local private schools and began the study of medicine, but on 18 July 1861, before he completed his studies, he joined the Confederate army. Bristow was a sergeant in the 24th Regiment Virginia Cavalry when he was captured near Petersburg on 28 July 1864. He spent six months in the prison camp at Elmira, New York, before being exchanged on parole on 25 February 1865.

His father had died during the war, and Joseph A. Bristow returned to manage Pleasant View, the family farm. On 24 January 1866 he married Mary Mildred Roane, also of Middlesex County, and they had two sons and one daughter before she died at the end of 1871. On 3 October 1875 Bristow married Lucy Elizabeth Chambers, of Person County, North Carolina. They had five sons and five daughters. A nephew, Myon Edison Bristow, served as Virginia's commissioner of insurance and banking during the Great Depression.

Bristow broadened his interests beyond farming into several other businesses and made himself an expert on oysters. He helped develop a special oyster tong that enabled watermen to extend their catch into the deep waters of the Rappahannock River and the lower Chesapeake Bay. On 29 April 1890, three years after the first patent for a deepwater tong had been issued to a man in Maryland, Bristow and William M. Dixon received patent number 426,909 for their design.

Bristow and several members of his family joined the Republican Party in 1872, and most of them supported the Readjusters, who wished to reduce the antebellum state debt rather than pay it off in full. Bristow was one of William Mahone's loyal local leaders and remained the most important Republican in Middlesex County for more than thirty years. In 1892 he was an unsuccessful candidate for presidential elector. In 1898 the Republicans of the First Congressional District nominated Bristow for Congress. He did not campaign and lost the dull election to the incumbent, Democrat William Atkinson Jones, by a margin of more than two to one. That same year Bristow was rewarded for his party loyalty with appointment as postmaster at Saluda, an office he held until his death in 1903, when his son Burke Bristow succeeded him.

In the spring of 1901 the Democratic Party nominated a former Populist leader, John Hill Carter Beverley, for the seat in a state constitutional convention from the district of Essex and Middlesex Counties. In protest, many conservative Democrats either did not vote or sided with the Republicans. As a result Bristow won the election by a vote of 1,533 to 1,005. With no legislative experience and as one of only a dozen Republicans in the 100-member convention and the only one from east of the mountains, he could not have expected to wield much influence. Bristow held the lowest-ranking seat on the Committee on the Organization and Government of Counties, and he took little part in the debates. He introduced resolutions intended to protect private oyster beds and to enable watermen and farmers to sell their catches and produce free from local licensing ordinances and discriminatory freight rates. Bristow's resolution that naturally occurring oyster beds should be held as a public trust for the use of the people of Virginia evolved into section 175 of the Constitution of 1902. He voted against the restrictive voter-registration provisions that the convention adopted, against putting the constitution into effect without a referendum on ratification, and, on 6 June 1902, against the adoption of the constitution.

Joseph Allen Bristow died at Pleasant View on 30 April 1903 after an illness of four months and was buried in the family cemetery on the estate.

Brief biography in *Richmond Times*, 12 June 1901; birth date recorded in Pollard Questionnaires; Gordon Byron Woolley, *John Bristow of Middlesex County, Virginia, and Descendants through Ten Generations* (1969), 110; Compiled Service Records; Middlesex Co. Marriage Register, 1866; Person Co., N.C., Marriage Register, 1875; Bristow letters in William Mahone Papers, Duke; Election Records, nos. 43, 45, RG 13, LVA; *Journal of 1901–1902 Convention*, 49–50, 486–487, 504, 535; *Resolutions of 1901–1902 Convention*, nos. 203, 241, 246; *Convention of 1901–1902 Photographs* (por.); obituary in *Richmond Times-Dispatch*, 1 May 1903.

BRENT TARTER

BRISTOW, Myon Edison (2 November 1879–11 November 1955), commissioner of insurance and banking, was born in Saluda, Middlesex County, the son of physician Lewis Shuck Bristow and his second wife, Nellie Blanche Games Bristow. He was a nephew of Joseph Allen Bristow, a member of the Convention of 1901–1902. Myon Bristow attended public schools in Saluda until age eighteen, when he enlisted in the United States Navy. He saw service in the Spanish-American War. On 8 June 1905 Bristow married Emerald Alvin Christian in Baltimore. They had one son and four daughters.

Bristow was discharged from the navy in 1899 and entered Richmond College as a law student. After graduation in 1901, he was admitted to the bar and practiced law in Cape Charles, Hampton, and Gloucester Court House. He served as commonwealth's attorney of Gloucester County from 1904 to 1906. In 1915 Bristow was elected to the House of Delegates representing Gloucester County for one term. During the 1916 legislative session he served on the Committees on the Chesapeake and its Tributaries and on Insurance and Banking and on the minor Committees on Enrolled Bills and on House Expenses.

Bristow's association with banking paralleled his law career. He helped organize the Bank of Gloucester in 1906 and served as its cashier for five years. Bristow returned to the Naval Reserve during World War I, but by the time he completed officer training school and was assigned to duty as a storekeeper the war was over, and so he did not serve overseas. After leaving the navy in 1919, he became an assistant bank examiner for the State Corporation Commission. The following year he joined the Farmers and Merchants Trust Bank in Cape Charles, but in March 1923 he again became an assistant bank examiner and was promoted to chief examiner of banks on 1 August 1923. A reorganization of state government eliminated that position effective 1 March 1928, and beginning the next day Bristow carried out his former duties with an increased salary under the new title of deputy commissioner of insurance and banking. On 15 January 1930 he became commissioner of insurance and banking. After the Bureau of Insurance and Banking was divided on 20 June 1938, Bristow served as commissioner of banking until 31 January 1939.

Bristow became a certified public accountant in 1930 and in 1938 earned a degree from the graduate school of banking at Rutgers University. Between 1924 and 1934 he compiled and published five volumes in a series of Virginia statutes relating to banks. During his career Bristow served as president of the National Association of Supervisors of State Banks (1929–1930) and of the National Association of Supervisors of Building and Loan Associations (1937–1938). He occasionally taught evening classes at the University of Richmond's School of Business Administration and at the Virginia Mechanics' Institute.

Bristow led the state's banking division during its most difficult time, the Great Depression. Between 1928 and 1935 the number of state banks in Virginia fell from 323 to 195. As a result of mergers, 90 state banks disappeared, and an additional 72 went bankrupt or were liquidated. Twenty-nine Virginia state banks failed to reopen after the federal bank holiday of 6 March 1933. The most visible of them was the American Bank and Trust Company of Richmond, which Bristow ordered placed in receivership. He worked in concert with federal authorities during the banking crisis of the 1930s and urged banks chartered under Virginia laws to join the new Federal Deposit Insurance Corporation. Bristow's bureau recommended legislation to discourage the formation of too many new banks and to encourage mergers in order to strengthen the banking system. His published annual reports as commissioner chart the health of Virginia's banking system during the depression.

Bristow resigned as commissioner on 31 January 1939. From then until his retirement in 1954, he worked as an insurance examiner for the Bureau of Insurance. Active in veterans' affairs, Bristow served as department commander of the United Spanish War Veterans (1929–1930) and the American Legion (1932–1933). He was divorced in 1939 and on 20 June 1942 married Rebecca Anne Thornton in Las Vegas. They had no children. Myon Edison Bristow died in McGuire Veterans Hospital in Richmond on 11 November 1955 and was buried in Arlington National Cemetery.

NCAB, 46:393–394 (por.); Gordon Byron Woolley, *John Bristow of Middlesex County, Virginia, and Descendants through Ten Generations* (1969), 111, 159–160; Glass and Glass, *Virginia Democracy*, 3:42–43; Military Service Records; David C. Parcell, *State Banks and the State Corporation Commission: A Historical Review* (1974), 52–63; Bristow, "Money and Banking," in *Richmond, Capital of Virginia: Approaches to Its History*, ed. Hamilton J. Eckenrode (1938), 252–262; obituaries in *Richmond News Leader*, 11 Nov. 1955, and *Richmond Times-Dispatch*, 12 Nov. 1955; memorial in *Virginia State Bar Association Proceedings* (1956): 107–108 (por.).

DAVID C. PARCELL

BRITT, Lula Emily Vanderslice Ivey (24 August 1863–17 May 1945), Methodist lay leader, was born in Amherst County, the daughter of George Curtis Vanderslice and Susan A. Pettit Vanderslice. As the daughter of a prominent minister of the Methodist Episcopal Church South, Virginia Conference, she became active in the church at an early age by participating in the children's missionary society. Vanderslice was educated in Virginia public schools and at Farmville Female Seminary (later Longwood College). She taught several years at Finney College in Suffolk and in South Carolina. On 31 July 1883 she married Robert James Ivey, a Lynchburg tobacconist who died on 24 October 1888. They had one son. On 26 September 1894 she married Lee Britt, an attorney and lay leader of Suffolk's Main Street Methodist Church, where her father was then minister. Her second husband died on 26 January 1936. The death of her only child in a Lackawanna Railroad accident on 4 July 1912 left her emotionally scarred.

Britt taught the adult women's Sunday school class at Main Street Methodist for forty years and was a member of the congregation's board of stewards. Her service expanded beyond her local church when she became secretary of the Woman's Missionary Society in the Portsmouth district in 1897. From 1908 until 1912 she served as recording secretary of the Woman's Foreign Missionary Society of the Virginia Conference. After the 1910 General Conference united the Woman's Board of Home Missions and the Woman's Board of Foreign Missions to create the Woman's Missionary Council, Britt became a member of the missionary council's executive committee and held that position for twenty years. In 1913 she became president of the Woman's Missionary Society of the Virginia Conference and served in that office continuously for twenty-seven years, until failing health forced her resignation in 1940. Through the power of her personality and the length of her tenure Britt dominated Virginia's Methodist missionary efforts through the first half of the twentieth century.

After 1918 the Methodist Episcopal Church South granted women lay rights and began to allow them more opportunities to serve in positions of authority. Britt was often the first woman in these new leadership roles. In 1919 she was one of the first four women delegates elected to the Virginia Annual Conference. Eleven years later Britt was the first woman elected from the Virginia Conference to attend the General Conference. She went then and again in 1934 as an alternate. She was a member of a special conference called in 1924 to consider unification of the northern and southern divisions of the church, a delegate to the Uniting Conference in 1939, and a delegate to the first General Conference after unification in 1940.

Britt sat on the executive committee of the board of trustees at Scarritt College for Christian Workers in Nashville and chaired the board of trustees of Brown Hall, a Methodist dormitory at the College of William and Mary. She served as a charter member of the board of trustees at Ferrum Training School (later Ferrum College). As part of a committee of five, Britt launched a campaign in 1940 to raise funds for a larger library at Ferrum. The building was completed in 1942 and named Lee Britt Library (later redesignated Britt Hall when its function changed).

Britt's leadership also extended into civic areas. She was one of the organizers and the first president of the Suffolk Woman's Club. Lula Emily Vanderslice Ivey Britt died in Suffolk on 17 May 1945 as a result of injuries sustained in a fall several weeks earlier. She was buried in Cedar Hill Cemetery in Suffolk.

Catherine Davis Morgan, *United Methodist Women in Virginia, 1784–1984* (1984), 27, 33, 50, 54; *Who's Who in*

Methodism (1952), 85; BVS Marriage Register, Lynchburg, 1883, and Nansemond Co., 1894; Frank Benjamin Hurt, *A History of Ferrum College: An Uncommon Challenge, 1914–1974* (1977), 13, 18, 25, 83, 95–96; Clinton T. Howell, ed., *Prominent Personalities in American Methodism* (1945), 1:41; information provided by niece Anne Vanderslice; obituaries in *Suffolk News-Herald*, 18 May 1945, *Richmond Times-Dispatch*, 19 May 1945, and *Virginia Methodist Advocate*, 24 May 1945; memorials in Virginia Conference of the Methodist Church, *Proceedings of the Annual Session* 163 (1945): 166–167, and Woman's Society of Christian Service, *Annual Report* 6 (1946): [3–5] (por.).

JOANNE SNAPP

BROADDUS, Andrew (4 November 1770– 1 December 1848), Baptist minister, was born in Caroline County, the son of John Broaddus, a farmer and teacher, and Frances Pryor Broaddus. He received only a few months of formal schooling, but his studious inclinations convinced John Broaddus that his son should seek ordination in the Episcopal Church. The father's ambitions had been thwarted earlier when an older son, educated for the Anglican ministry, died just before he was to be ordained. Andrew Broaddus caused his father a second disappointment. Ignoring strict parental admonitions, he began attending services conducted by the Baptist revivalist Theodoric Noel, who baptized him on 28 May 1789 as a member of the Upper King and Queen Baptist Church. By December of that year Broaddus was a lay exhorter, and on 16 October 1791 he was ordained a Baptist minister, thereby casting his lot with a community that his father considered both socially inferior and religiously wrongheaded.

Broaddus began his ministry as pastor of Burrus's Church in Caroline County, where he served from 1793 to about 1810. He also preached at the County Line Church in Caroline County for part of that time. During a long career Broaddus eventually served the Bethel, Salem (1820–1848), Upper King and Queen (1827–1848), Beulah (1839–1845), Union at Mangohic (1839), Upper Zion (1841–1842), and Mount Calvary (1847) congregations. He helped revive and reorganize the Fredericksburg Baptist Church in 1804 and served as pastor until 1815. During Broaddus's ministry, urban Baptists in the South sought and attained higher levels of social respectability, but he was uncomfortable with the expectations of genteel congregations and unwilling to live in a city. Apart from a six-month stay in Richmond as assistant pastor of the First Baptist Church early in the 1820s, he remained in Caroline and King and Queen Counties throughout his ministry and declined opportunities for pulpits in Boston in 1811 and 1812, Philadelphia in 1811, 1819, 1824, and 1825, Baltimore in 1819, Norfolk in 1826, New York City in 1832, and Richmond in 1833. His intense nervousness before large audiences probably kept Broaddus in rural Virginia. He once declined the offer of an honorary D.D. from Columbian College (later George Washington University) in Washington, D.C., because he considered such honors inappropriate for a minister.

Once in the ministry Broaddus pursued an informal education and attained some mastery of both Greek and Latin. He also conducted a private school. Despite occasional bouts of stage fright, Broaddus gained recognition as a preacher able to offer luminous and moving interpretations of Scripture. In 1832 he was elected moderator of the Dover Association, then the largest association of Baptist churches in the United States, and he held that position for eight of the subsequent nine years before he declined reelection in 1841 because of his advanced age.

Broaddus greatly extended his influence using his abilities as a writer. In his *Age of Reason and Revelation* (1795) he argued against the deism of Thomas Paine and for the reasonableness of Christianity. Broaddus contended that Paine had exaggerated the capacities of human beings to reason and ignored their susceptibility to passion and prejudice. Broaddus maintained that reason could discern the power and majesty of God in the works of creation, that the biblical miracles and prophecies validated the revelatory character of the Scriptures, and that the intrinsic worth of biblical teaching and the historical progress of Christianity in the face of adversity demonstrated Christianity's truthfulness.

Broaddus wrote frequently for a popular readership in the *Religious Herald*, the newspaper of the Baptist General Association of Virginia. Eventually he completed a biblical commentary for family use, a catechism for children, and a manual of Baptist polity, in addition to a polemic against Alexander Campbell, *The Extra Examined: A Reply to Mr. A. Campbell's M. Harbinger, Extra, on Remission of Sins, Etc.* (1831). Broaddus defended a common Baptist interpretation of rebirth as an inward change resulting from the immediate influence of the Spirit. By insisting that regeneration was an inward change, an act of the heart, rather than an outward act of baptism, as Campbell taught, Broaddus aligned himself with the tradition of seventeenth-century Calvinist pietism. His thought therefore embodied both the orthodox rationalism and the evangelical piety that became normative in popular southern Protestantism.

Believing that music had been instrumental in his conversion, Broaddus gave expression to his own piety with *A Collection of Sacred Ballads* (1790), *The Dover Selection of Spiritual Songs* (1828), and *The Virginia Selection of Psalms, Hymns, and Spiritual Songs* (1836). He intended the books for popular use in public worship services and in social meetings. The hymnals typified the democratizing of religious music that accompanied the popular revivals of the early national period.

Broaddus married four times. About 1793 he married Fanny Temple. Before her death about 1804 or 1805, they had two sons and three daughters. His second wife, Lucy Honyman (Honeyman), died childless. On 29 December 1815 Broaddus married Jane C. Honyman Broaddus, a sister of his second wife and the widow of one of his nephews. On both of these grounds the marriage violated Virginia's law against incest. They married again on 8 March 1816 in the District of Columbia, where the near relationships were not defined as incestuous. Later in the year the attorney general of Virginia, ignoring the second wedding, moved in the court of chancery to have the marriage nullified and the husband and wife forced to live separately. Broaddus successfully appealed citing technicalities in the method of the prosecution. He and his third wife had two sons and one daughter, but following the conclusion of the legal proceedings they became estranged and lived apart until her death more than twenty years later. For a time during that period public sympathy turned against Broaddus, and he lost his pulpit

for several months. In 1817 he traveled to Kentucky when contemplating moving his ministry and family out of Virginia, but he soon returned. Broaddus married Caroline W. Boulware in 1843. They had one son. Broaddus's namesake son by his third wife eventually succeeded him as minister at Salem and Upper King and Queen Baptist Churches, and a namesake grandson followed, so that for 106 consecutive years an Andrew Broaddus officiated at Salem Baptist Church.

Among antebellum Baptist ministers who remained pastors of small country churches, Broaddus was one of the best known and most respected in Virginia. In 1852 a son extended that reputation by publishing a posthumous edition of his sermons with a lengthy biographical introduction by Jeremiah Bell Jeter. Enfeebled by poor health late in life, Andrew Broaddus died at his home at Newton in King and Queen County on 1 December 1848 and was buried in the graveyard of Salem Baptist Church in Caroline County.

Andrew Broaddus, ed., *The Sermons and Other Writings of the Rev. Andrew Broaddus, With a Memoir of His Life* (1852), frontispiece por.; James B. Taylor, *Virginia Baptist Ministers*, 2d ser. (1859), 238–277; Sprague, *American Pulpit*, 6:290–296; Andrew Broaddus Papers, VBHS; Andrew Broaddus, *A History of the Broaddus Family, From the Time of the Settlement of the Progenitor of the Family in the United States down to the year 1888* (1888), 64–92; *Fredericksburg Virginia Herald*, 13 Mar. 1816; *Richmond Enquirer*, 18 Apr. 1817, 19 Feb. 1818; *Attorney General* v. *Broaddus and Wife* (1818) (6 Munford), *Virginia Reports*, 20:iii–vi, 116–117; John L. Blair, ed., "A Baptist Minister Visits Kentucky: The Journal of Andrew Broaddus I," *Register of the Kentucky Historical Society* 71 (1973): 393–425; Paul A. Richardson, "Andrew Broaddus and Hymnody," *Virginia Baptist Register* 24 (1985): 1198–1209; obituaries in *Richmond Enquirer*, 14 Dec. 1848, and *Richmond Whig and Public Advertiser*, 19 Dec. 1848; obituary and account of funeral in *Religious Herald*, 21 Dec. 1848; Jeremiah B. Jeter, "Funeral Sermon of Rev. Andrew Broaddus," *Baptist Preacher* 8 (1849): 37–52; memorials in *Minutes of the Dover Baptist Association* (1849): 20, and *Minutes of the Rappahannock Baptist Association* (1849): 16–17.

E. BROOKS HOLIFIELD

BROADDUS, John W. (ca. 1804–4 May 1874), member of the Convention of 1867–1868, was born in Caroline County, the son of Thomas Broaddus and Martha Jones Broaddus. His middle name is not recorded, and the early part of his life is poorly documented. By the age of twenty Broaddus had moved to Amherst County, where on 11 January 1825 he married Elizabeth E. Taliaferro. They had one daughter and may also have had a son.

Shortly after his marriage Broaddus purchased a small farm. He served as a justice of the peace for about ten years beginning on 20 February 1832. For several years Broaddus operated a mercantile firm in partnership with Edmund W. Hill and John C. Whitehead until they dissolved the firm of Broaddus, Hill, and Company in the spring of 1842. Broaddus was probably in financial difficulty at the time. During the summer of 1842 he sold part of his farm to satisfy his debts and transferred his personal estate to his wife. Two years later his father-in-law specified that Elizabeth Taliaferro Broaddus's inheritance was to be placed in trust for her children, an action suggesting a need to shield her inheritance from her husband's creditors.

During the 1840s Broaddus ran freight on the canal between Lynchburg and Richmond, and by 1860 he was an inspector, probably at a freight depot. From the 1830s through the 1850s he owned between five and a dozen slaves, according to census and tax returns. His obituary writer later stated that Broaddus had been an active member of the Baptist Church, but otherwise his name seldom appeared in public records until he was elected county surveyor on 25 January 1866. On 12 October 1867 a committee of two men from each magisterial district in the county unanimously nominated Broaddus as the Conservative Party candidate to represent Amherst County in the convention called to write a new constitution for Virginia. Ten days later he defeated the Radical candidate, John C. Deane, by a margin of just 6 votes. Broaddus received 1,161 votes from white voters and only 28 from black voters, while Deane won a scant 2 white votes and 1,181 black votes. In the convention that met in Richmond from 3 December 1867 through 17 April 1868, Broaddus served on the Committee on Internal Improvements, but he did not participate in the recorded debates. He missed several significant roll call votes but sided regularly with opponents of reform, and on 17 April 1868 he voted against the constitu-

tion. Three days later Broaddus signed an "Address of the Conservative Members of the late State Convention to the People of Virginia," which denounced the constitution that the convention had approved.

Elizabeth Taliaferro Broaddus died sometime during the 1860s. On 4 January 1872 Broaddus married a widow, Elizabeth Cox Heiskell. She died on an unrecorded date between 24 February and 16 April of that year. John W. Broaddus died at the residence of a grandson in Amherst County on 4 May 1874. He left a personal estate valued at only $85.10.

Andrew Broaddus, *A History of the Broaddus Family, From the Time of the Settlement of the Progenitor of the Family in the United States down to the year 1888* (1888), 39, 180; Alfred Percy, *Amherst County Story: A Virginia Saga* (1961), 87, indicates without citing any authority that Broaddus's middle name was Woodford; Census, Amherst Co., 1850, 1860, 1870, gives age as forty-six, fifty-six, and sixty-five, respectively; Amherst Co. Marriage Bonds, 1825; Amherst Co. Marriage Register, 1872; partnership dissolution and transfers of property in Amherst Co. Deed Book, Y:154, 249; father-in-law's will in Amherst Co. Will Book, 11:416–418; *Lynchburg News*, 15 Oct. 1867; Election Records, no. 427, RG 13, LVA; Hume, "Membership of Convention of 1867–1868," 481; Lowe, "Virginia's Reconstruction Convention," 350; *Journal of 1867–1868 Convention*, 389; *Richmond Daily Dispatch*, 20 Apr. 1868; estate inventory in Amherst Co. Will Book, 18:473–474; obituary giving seventy as age at death in *Lynchburg Daily News*, 11 May 1874.

DAPHNE GENTRY

BROADDUS, Willey Richard (30 December 1895–14 September 1982), attorney, was born in West Point, the son of Willey Richard Broaddus, a newspaper publisher and educator, and Hauzie Temple Tuck Broaddus, founder and principal of the West Point Female Seminary. He graduated from West Point High School in 1913. Broaddus's studies at the University of Richmond were interrupted by military service as a second lieutenant with the field artillery in France during World War I. After the Armistice, Broaddus attended the University of Leeds in England until June 1919. Returning to the University of Richmond, he received a B.A. in 1920 and a law degree the following year. In June 1921 Broaddus opened a law office in Martinsville and became a leading citizen there. Building a successful practice, he represented local banks and manufacturing companies. On 16 November 1921 he married Honlu Evans, of Clio, Marlboro County, South Carolina. They had one son and one daughter.

W. Richard Broaddus, as he was generally known, was a Democrat who served as commonwealth's attorney for Martinsville from 1929 to 1942 and for Henry County from 1942 to 1946. He represented Henry County and Martinsville in the House of Delegates from 1946 until 1954 and served on the Committees on Courts of Justice, Game and Inland Fisheries, Privileges and Elections, and Welfare. During this period Broaddus also sat on the Virginia Advisory Legislative Council and the Judicial Council of Virginia, a select committee of judges and lawyers that streamlined rules of procedure in the state courts.

Following the United States Supreme Court's school desegregation decree of 1954, the leaders of the Democratic Party in Virginia adopted a program of Massive Resistance, asserting a state's right to interpose its sovereignty between the federal government and the residents of the state. Broaddus was one of two delegates who represented Henry, Patrick, and Pittsylvania Counties and the cities of Danville and Martinsville at a convention that met from 5 to 7 March 1956 to consider amending the state constitution to bolster Virginia's segregation policy. Broaddus chaired the key Committee on Privileges and Elections, which proposed an amendment permitting the appropriation of state funds for private schools. The convention unanimously adopted the measure, which was designed to allow localities ordered to integrate their public schools to shut them down while still providing schools for white pupils. As committee chair, Broaddus also moved a resolution that commended the Virginia legislature for invoking the doctrine of interposition. After a spirited debate, in which he took no part, the convention adopted this motion by a vote of 35 to 3.

Following the collapse of Massive Resistance, Broaddus became chief counsel to the governor's Commission on Public Education (called for its chair the Perrow Commission) in 1959. This commission, dominated by moderates although including a few Massive Resisters,

reluctantly accepted the inevitability of some desegregation and recommended tuition grants to private schools. In its report the commission sought to marshal support for compromise measures and vowed that "no child will be forced to attend a racially mixed school."

Active in both professional and civic organizations, Broaddus was elected president of the Virginia State Bar Association in 1950. His presidential address, "Modernization and the Virginia Lawyer," was a plea for improved efficiency in the administration of justice in the state's trial and appellate courts. He was also a fellow of the American College of Trial Lawyers. Broaddus was a trustee of the University of Richmond from 1936 to 1969 and became vice rector of the university in 1951. In addition, he was a trustee of Fork Union Military Academy and served on the school board of both Henry County and Martinsville. Broaddus was a life deacon and trustee of the First Baptist Church in Martinsville, where he taught the men's Bible class for more than fifty years. He was a member of the Commonwealth Club and participated in Kiwanis, the American Legion, and the Knights of Pythias.

After the death of Broaddus's first wife on 12 March 1967, he married Margaret May Terpstra Copenhaver on 12 November 1968. She died on 23 May 1980. Willey Richard Broaddus died in Martinsville on 14 September 1982 after a long illness. He was buried at Oakwood Cemetery in that city.

Glass and Glass, *Virginia Democracy*, 2:430–432; *Commonwealth* 17 (Sept. 1950): 20 (por.); Military Service Records; marriage dates confirmed by BVS; *Richmond News Leader*, 6, 7 Mar. 1956; *Richmond Times-Dispatch*, 7 Mar. 1956 (por.); *Journal of the Constitutional Convention of the Commonwealth of Virginia* (1956); Report of the Commission on Education, Senate Doc. 2, 1959 extra sess., quotation on 6; *Virginia State Bar Association Proceedings* (1951): 246–257; obituaries in *Martinsville Bulletin*, *Richmond News Leader*, *Richmond Times-Dispatch*, and *Roanoke Times and World-News*, all 15 Sept. 1982.

JAMES W. ELY JR.

BROADDUS, William Francis Ferguson (30 April 1801–8 September 1876), Baptist minister, was born near Woodville in the portion of Culpeper County that in 1833 became Rappahannock County, the son of Susannah Ferguson

White Broaddus and her second husband, Thomas Broaddus. Dissatisfied with the awkwardness of his name, he asked his mother for permission to drop one of his middle names. She agreed, and he was always known thereafter as William F. Broaddus, but he never disclosed which name he had dropped. His father died when Broaddus was about ten years old. He attended local schools and by the age of sixteen was sufficiently educated to become a schoolmaster. On 28 October 1819 he married Mary Ann Farrow. They had four sons and two daughters.

In 1823 Broaddus joined the F. T. Baptist Church in Culpeper County, and the following year he was ordained as its pastor. He was a natural and easy speaker, described as laborious rather than studious in his preparation. In 1826 Broaddus moved to Bethel Baptist Church in Frederick County. He became a supporter of those Baptists who advocated missionary work and evangelism and opposed the views of those who feared that innovations such as traveling ministers, Sunday school associations, and other evangelical work would corrupt the principle that individual salvation was possible only through God's intervention. In 1827 the Ketocton Baptist Association defeated Broaddus's proposal that money be raised to spread the gospel among the poor, and some members threatened to abstain from fellowship with any Baptist who advocated missionary efforts. Four years later he was criticized for organizing a four-day revival meeting. In 1833 the association denied Broaddus a seat at its annual meeting, and shortly thereafter the Columbia Baptist Association also refused to admit him to its conference. Angered, delegates from Bethel and from the Long Branch Baptist Church, of which he was also pastor, withdrew from the Ketocton and Columbia Baptist Associations and formed the evangelical Salem Union Baptist Association. In 1835 the Columbia Association relented and allowed Broaddus to participate, but five antimissionary congregations left the association. The rift was not healed for many years, but later church historians gave Broaddus much of the credit for the eventual evangelical triumph over antimission Baptists in the region.

Between 1834 and 1839 Broaddus was pastor of Bethel, Long Branch, Middleburg, and Upperville Baptist Churches in Frederick and Loudoun Counties. He also conducted a boarding school for girls at Middleburg in Loudoun County. In 1836 Broaddus engaged in a public exchange with another minister, Henry Slicer, over the nature of baptism. He argued that only repentant believers should be baptized in *Letters to Rev. Mr. Slicer, in Reply to his "Appeal" on "Christian Baptism."*

From 1840 to 1845 Broaddus was minister of the First Baptist Church in Lexington, Kentucky. From 1845 to 1851 he was president of the Shelbyville Female Institute in Shelbyville, Kentucky, and during part of the time he served the Baptist church in Versailles as well. A fire at the institute destroyed the diary that Broaddus had kept since his youth. His wife died on 8 September 1850, and on 29 July 1851 he married a widow, Susan Burbridge, of Kentucky, before moving to Washington, D.C., as an agent raising funds for Columbian College (later George Washington University). Broaddus had been a trustee from 1838 to 1841 and served again from 1859 to 1872. As Columbian's agent he raised an endowment of more than $40,000. In 1854 the college awarded Broaddus an honorary D.D. His second wife died on 21 April 1852 and exactly one year later he married another widow, Lucy Ann Semple Fleet. They had one daughter.

Broaddus moved back to Virginia in 1853 as pastor of Fredericksburg Baptist Church, and on 1 October of that year he opened the Fredericksburg Female Academy. Principally a minister and educator rather than a scholar, he nonetheless engaged in another debate on baptism, this time with Archibald Alexander Hodge. In *Strictures on Rev. A. A. Hodge's Four Sermons on Infant Baptism* (1858), Broaddus maintained that infant baptism was contrary to Scripture because only repentant believers could be baptized. In 1859 his church granted him a year's sabbatical to study at the Southern Baptist Theological Seminary in Greenville, South Carolina.

The Civil War disrupted Broaddus's ministry. On 29 July 1862 the United States Army arrested him and eighteen other Fredericksburg residents and held them in Washington's Old Capitol Prison until they could be exchanged for prisoners of war being held in Confederate prisons. He and one of the other captives, Maria Isabella "Belle" Boyd, were paroled on 29 August and traveled together to Richmond, where Broaddus worked out a prisoner exchange with the Confederate government. Broaddus obtained his own release on 24 September 1862 and returned to Fredericksburg. Wartime damage to his house destroyed a draft autobiography and all the diaries he had kept since the Shelbyville fire.

Broaddus served as pastor of the Charlottesville Baptist Church from January 1863 until 1868, when he resigned and returned to Fredericksburg to raise money under the auspices of the Baptist General Association of Virginia for the education of children of deceased or disabled Confederate soldiers. In three years he helped more than 2,000 children receive school tuition.

In 1867 Broaddus delivered and published a *Centennial Sermon of the Potomac Baptist Association, of Virginia*. This history of the early churches of the northeastern Piedmont in part described his own role in the split over evangelism and missionary work. From 1868 to 1876 Broaddus served as a trustee of the Southern Baptist Theological Seminary, and he was an overseer of Columbian College from 1872 until he resigned in 1874. His eyesight began failing during the last years of his life, and he suffered the effects of dementia near the end. William F. Broaddus died in Fredericksburg on 8 September 1876 and was buried with Masonic rites in the city cemetery. A tablet commemorating his service was later placed in the Fredericksburg Baptist Church.

Andrew Broaddus, *A History of the Broaddus Family, From the Time of the Settlement of the Progenitor of the Family in the United States down to the year 1888* (1888), 112, 118–119, 133–135, 157–169 (por. on 158); George Braxton Taylor, *Virginia Baptist Ministers*, 3d ser. (1912), 237–247; Oscar H. Darter, *History of Fredericksburg Baptist Church, Fredericksburg, Virginia* (1959), 74–78, 115, 150–152, 153, 169–170; Garnett Ryland, *The Baptists of Virginia, 1699–1926* (1955), 243–250, 311; Reuben Edward Alley, *A History of Baptists in Virginia* (1974), 203–205; a Broaddus letter (VBHS) and diary (LVA photocopy) printed respectively in John S. Moore, ed., "A 19th Century Minister's Problems," and W. Harrison Daniel, ed., "The Prison Diary of William F. Broaddus," *Virginia Baptist Register* 21 (1982): 993–997 (por.), and 998–1019; obituaries in *Fredericksburg News* and *Fredericksburg Virginia Herald*, both 11 Sept. 1876, and *Religious Herald*, 21 Sept. 1876.

DONALD W. GUNTER

BROADWATER, Charles (1722 or 1723–20 March 1806), planter, was the only child of Charles Broadwater and Elizabeth Semmes Turley West Broadwater. Born in that part of Stafford County that became Fairfax County in 1742, he grew up in an extended family that included children born of his mother's two previous marriages. His father was a former sea captain who made several trips to Virginia between 1710 and 1717, settled in Stafford County, and died in 1733 or 1734, leaving his son 1,700 acres. By the 1760s Broadwater ranked with Fairfax County's largest land- and slaveholders.

Broadwater became a justice of the peace in the 1740s and served until 1803. He had an eye for good terrain and a talent for negotiation with landholders, gained perhaps when he served as a chain carrier for his uncle Guy Broadwater on surveying expeditions to the frontier areas as early as 1741. The county court accordingly directed him almost every year from 1749 to 1790 to plan and supervise the route and construction of new roads in the county's northern quadrant. He also worked to improve old routes and maintain existing roadbeds and inspected, repaired, and maintained the Broad Run and Difficult Run bridges that linked Fairfax to points west.

When Broadwater accepted public offices he served with loyalty and diligence. As a justice he sat with remarkable regularity and attended more than 500 times out of 1,200 sessions. Broadwater held the post of county coroner from 1747 until 1803. He also served two terms as sheriff, from 1751 to 1753 and 1755 to 1757. After accepting a militia commission in 1749, Broadwater served in the field in 1756 during the French and Indian War, became a major in 1758, and had risen to colonel by 1789. He also sat continuously from 1744 to 1797 on the Truro and Fairfax Parish vestries.

As befitted a leading planter and office-holder, Broadwater supervised repair and maintenance of official tobacco warehouses, first at the Falls of the Potomac and later at Alexandria's Hunting Creek. When he and other tobacco planters turned more to grain cultivation, he set up a gristmill.

Broadwater signed the 1770 nonimportation association that George Washington publicly posted to pressure British merchants to persuade Parliament to repeal obnoxious taxes. In 1774 Broadwater and Washington represented Fairfax County in the first Virginia Convention, and the next year voters elected Broadwater to the second, third, and fourth of the Revolutionary Conventions.

In the summer of 1774 Broadwater and George Washington were elected to represent Fairfax County in the House of Burgesses. When the assembly met in June 1775 Washington was attending the Continental Congress and Broadwater was the only member from Fairfax County in Williamsburg. He served on the Committees of Propositions and Grievances and on Religion, and he was a member of special committees appointed to revise a draft bill for improving the navigation of the Potomac River and to prepare a bill to regulate smallpox inoculation in Virginia. Following the American Revolution, Broadwater represented the county in the House of Delegates in 1782 and 1783.

Between 1745 and 1750 Broadwater married Ann Amelia Markham Pearson, a widow with two sons and two daughters. They had a son and four daughters. Following his wife's death on 29 June 1796, Broadwater married Sarah Ann Harris, the widow of Benjamin Harris. They had no children. Charles Broadwater died on 20 March 1806 at Springfield, his Fairfax County home in what became Vienna, and was buried there.

Deposition by Broadwater giving age as "48 or 49" on 19 Sept. 1771 in Fairfax Co. Land Records of Long Standing (1742–1770), 347–349; estate records of father in Prince William Co. Will Book, C:8–11, 33–34, 86–88, 189, 228–230; Donald A. Wise, "Some Eighteenth Century Family Profiles," *Arlington Historical Magazine* 6 (Oct. 1977): 18–20; Beth Mitchell and Donald M. Sweig, *An Interpretive Historical Map of Fairfax County in 1760* (1987), 24, 67;

service in county offices documented in Fairfax Co. Court Order Books, 1749–1803; *Revolutionary Virginia*, vols. 1–6; will and estate inventory and accounts in Fairfax Co. Will Book, I-1:471–475, L-1:84–92, 112–118; age given as eighty-six in obituary in *Alexandria Daily Advertiser*, 21 Mar. 1806.

JAMES D. MUNSON

BROCAS, William (d. by 7 May 1655), member of the Council, was born in England probably about 1600, but almost nothing is known of his background or early years. He may have traveled widely and learned several languages, for at his death he owned a number of volumes in Italian, Latin, and Spanish, most of them by then old and worn.

Brocas settled in Virginia before 1635, probably in Charles River County, which became York County in 1643. By 1650 he had moved to land that he had acquired on the south side of the Rappahannock River in the portion of Lancaster County that later became Middlesex County. Like other planters Brocas raised tobacco, but he also cultivated a vineyard and made what was described as excellent wine. Unlike some of his contemporary planters, he did not rely entirely on English laborers. By the time of his death Brocas had eleven men, women, and children of African descent at his plantation.

Brocas married at least three times. His first wife, possibly named Tabitha, may have accompanied him to Virginia from England. In May 1635 they gave refuge to Sir John Harvey after a majority of the Council ousted him from the office of governor. An unfriendly contemporary stated that Harvey felt secure enough at Brocas's house to dismiss his guard and charged that Brocas's wife "was generally suspected to have more familiarity wth him then befitted a modest woman." By March 1646 Brocas had married again, to Mary Adams Wormeley, widow of Christopher Wormeley, a former councillor. By June 1648 Brocas had married Eleanor Eltonhead, member of a well-connected English family from Lancashire. Through his marriages Brocas acquired an extended family with such notable English and Virginia surnames as Burnham, Chicheley, Conway, Corbin, and Wormeley.

When Harvey returned to Virginia as governor for a second time in January 1637, his royal commission named new Council members known to have supported him during his first administration or thought likely to support him during his second. Brocas was among them and took the oaths of office soon after Harvey's return. Brocas was present at the Council meeting on 20 February 1637, the first documented meeting. The loss of the journals from his tenure on the Council makes it possible to say of his service only that he was reasonably reliable in attendance. Brocas remained on the Council until 30 April 1652. On that date, following the surrender of the colony to supporters of Parliament, the General Assembly reelected some councillors and displaced others. Brocas was not reelected.

William Brocas died after the tithable list for Lancaster County was compiled on 6 February 1655 and before 7 May 1655, when the county court granted administration of his estate to his widow, who married John Carter (1620–1669) within a year. Brocas had written a will, but for some unexplained reason it was not acknowledged in court. His principal heir at law was his sister's son, indicating that he had no living children. The long and detailed estate inventory of Captain William Brocas, Esquire, as he was then identified, itemized the personal property of an important gentleman who had once owned several hundred acres and lived in considerable comfort and elegance, but whose household furnishings and farming implements, like his books, were by then all old, worn, and dilapidated.

Landholdings documented in *Cavaliers and Pioneers*, vol. 1, and in York Co. and Lancaster Co. records; *Perfect Description of Virginia* (1649), 14, in *Tracts and Other Papers, Relating Principally to the Origin, Settlement, and Progress of the Colonies in North America,* ed. Peter Force (1836–1846), vol. 2; Samuel Mathews to Sir John Wolstenholme, 25 May 1635, PRO CO 1/8, fol. 178 (first record of residence in Virginia and quotation); appointment to Council in PRO CO 1/9, fol. 103; attendance documented in scattered accounts in York Co. records and in PRO CO 1/10; Hening, *Statutes*, 1:371–372; last two marriages and family relationships mentioned in York Co. and Lancaster Co. records; Lancaster Co. Deeds, Etc., 1:174, 189–192, 202–204 (estate inventories), 283, 2:40 (estate inventory), 161; Lancaster Co. Orders, Etc. (1655–1666), 37.

DAPHNE GENTRY

BROCK, Robert Alonzo (9 March 1839–12 July 1914), antiquarian, was born in Richmond, the son of Robert King Brock, a lumber dealer, and Elizabeth Mildred Ragland Brock. He received little formal education outside the home and went to work clerking for the family business a few years after his father's death in May 1850. Under the guidance of his mother he became a voracious reader and collector of books. On 21 April 1861 Brock enrolled in Company F, 1st Virginia Volunteers (later the 21st Regiment Virginia Infantry), served in the field, and was promoted to corporal in April 1862. After 11 September 1862 he worked as a steward at Camp Winder, a military hospital in Richmond. On 29 April 1869 Brock married Sallie Kidd Haw, of Hanover County, and they had two daughters before her death on 6 February 1887. He married Lucy Ann Peters, of Cumberland County, on 16 October 1889, and they had one son.

Brock made himself a widely recognized authority on Virginia history and genealogy. From 1879 to 1882 he was editor of literary, historical, and genealogical subjects for the *Richmond Standard*, and he wrote regularly on history and genealogy for the newspaper. Over the decades Brock contributed dozens of articles to newspapers, learned society publications, and encyclopedias, such as *Hardesty's Historical and Geographical Encyclopedia, Illustrated* (1884), for which he prepared brief biographies of Confederate veterans from nearly a dozen Virginia counties. He also compiled and published *Virginia and Virginians* (1888), the state's first large biographical reference work. Brock seldom refrained from public comment during any discussion involving any aspect of Virginia history, and historians, writers, genealogists, and collectors from all over the United States and western Europe appealed to him frequently for assistance and advice on Virginiana. One of his obituaries asserted that he belonged to about sixty-five learned, patriotic, and genealogical societies in North America and Europe.

Brock was elected corresponding secretary of the Virginia Historical Society in 1875 and took charge of its collections of books, paintings, maps, and manuscripts. In 1881 he retired from the family lumber business to devote all of his time to history and genealogy, and the following year he revived the society's publications program. Brock began the new series of the Virginia Historical Society's *Collections* with a volume of *The Official Letters of Alexander Spotswood*. During the next decade he edited and published two volumes of the papers of Robert Dinwiddie, a one-volume *Abstract of the Proceedings of the Virginia Company of London, 1619–1624*, Hugh Blair Grigsby's *History of the Virginia Federal Convention of 1788*, and several smaller works and compilations, the whole filling eleven volumes by 1892. The series made valuable contributions to Virginia's colonial and revolutionary history and was respectably done judging by the editorial standards of the time. In part because of the financial burden that the publications placed on the society's meager financial resources, but also because some board members resented the fact that Brock was doubling as secretary of the Southern Historical Society, he was eased out as corresponding secretary and librarian of the Virginia Historical Society at its December 1892 annual meeting.

In 1887 Brock had become secretary of the Southern Historical Society and editor of its *Papers*. He held the positions until shortly before his death. Unlike the valuable documentary editing he did for the Virginia Historical Society, Brock's work in producing volumes fifteen through thirty-eight of the *Southern Historical Society Papers*, published annually from 1887 through 1910, largely consisted of reminiscences, commemorative speeches, and excerpts from books, articles, and retrospective newspaper accounts of the Civil War. The exception is volume fifteen, which contained the roster of the more than 26,000 Confederate soldiers who surrendered at Appomattox.

An indefatigable collector, Brock accumulated one of the largest and most valuable private collections of Virginiana ever assembled. After his death the Virginia State Library declined to purchase it from his heirs, ostensibly because of lack of funds, and evidently neither the Virginia Historical Society nor any other Virginia library made any attempt to acquire it. In October 1922 Henry Edwards Huntington pur-

chased the entire collection, which included a substantial quantity of official Virginia government documents that should never have been in private hands, as well as books and other materials that had clearly belonged to the Virginia Historical Society. A few items that were Brock's personal property remained at the historical society, evidence that in his collecting and filing of books and manuscripts he had not distinguished between what was his and what was the society's. His collection contained some 50,000 manuscripts, 17,000 books, and 65,000 pamphlets and other small printed items. All of the manuscripts and many of the printed items are still in the Huntington Library, Art Collections, and Botanical Gardens, of San Marino, California.

Robert Alonzo Brock died at his home in Richmond on 12 July 1914 and was buried in Hollywood Cemetery in that city.

Brock included his biography in *Virginia and Virginians*, 2:549–550, and probably submitted the information for his entries in Tyler, *Men of Mark*, 1:175–178 (por.), and Tyler, *Encyclopedia*, 4:3–4; small collection of Brock's personal papers at VHS, including two diaries, 1858–1861 and 1871–1872, and a microfilm copy of his commonplace book, 1874–1892; Compiled Service Records; BVS Marriage Register, Richmond City; first wife's death reported in *Richmond Daily Dispatch*, 8 Feb. 1887; BVS Marriage Register, Cumberland Co.; Virginius Cornick Hall Jr., "The Virginia Historical Society: An Anniversary Narrative of Its First Century and a Half," *VMHB* 90 (1982): 56–64; Randall M. Miller, "The Birth (and Life) of a Journal: A 100-Year Retrospective of the *Virginia Magazine of History and Biography*," *VMHB* 100 (1992): 146–150 (por.); James I. Robertson Jr., ed., *An Index-Guide to the Southern Historical Society Papers, 1876–1959* (1980), 1:xvi–xvii; descriptions of Brock collection in *Huntington Library Bulletin* 1 (1931): 66–67, in Louis B. Wright, "For the Study of the American Cultural Heritage," *WMQ*, 3d ser., 1 (1944): 207–209, and in Beverley Fleet, ed., *Virginia Colonial Abstracts*, repr. ed. (1988), 3:558–559; the sale away from the state of the Brock collection provoked an angry editorial from Douglas Southall Freeman's *Richmond News Leader*, 1 Nov. 1922; obituaries in *Richmond News Leader* and *Richmond Times-Dispatch*, both 13 July 1914, and *SHSP* 39 (1914): 215–217 (which gives variant death date of 11 July 1914).

BRENT TARTER

BROCK, Sarah Ann (18 March 1831– 22 March 1911), writer who often published under the pseudonym Virginia Madison, was born at Madison Court House, the daughter of

Ansalem Brock and Elizabeth Beverley Buckner Brock. She and her siblings studied with their father, who was a tavern keeper and teacher, and with a graduate of Harvard University, whose name is not recorded but who lived with the family for four years. About 1850 the family moved to Charlottesville, where Brock's father ran a residence hotel for students at the University of Virginia while her brothers attended medical school. Eight years later the family relocated to Richmond, where Ansalem Brock kept a hotel at Richmond College.

In 1860 Sallie A. Brock, as she was usually known, was a tutor in a household in King and Queen County. At the outbreak of the Civil War she returned to her parents in Richmond. Brock's two brothers served as doctors for the Confederate army, and she contributed to the cause herself by nursing, knitting, and rolling bandages. She was acutely aware of the war's effect on the residents of the city. Brock experienced the anxiety of the average citizen forced to learn about political and military situations through a combination of unreliable rumors and newspaper reports. After her mother died in 1864, she took charge of her father's household.

At the end of the war Brock tapped her literary skills in an attempt to earn money. Later, in her only published novel, she described a governess who supplemented her income by writing magazine fiction under an assumed name. Perhaps Brock had also been writing in this way, but the first evidence of her career dates from a visit to New York City during the summer of 1865, when she began a manuscript recounting her experiences in wartime Richmond. The volume appeared in 1867 as *Richmond During the War: Four Years of Personal Observation*. Released under the pseudonym A Richmond Lady, it is an intelligent interpretation of the Civil War as experienced by a woman in the Confederate capital. Brock's grasp of the events that led to war and her analysis of its progress are accurate, well considered, and surprisingly conciliatory. Her presentation is alternately comprehensive and anecdotal and provides both an overall view and detailed stories of how food shortages, the booming population, crime, stress, and chaos affected the city and its citizens. Brock's biases and convictions are typical of a woman of her

time and social position and only sporadically distract the modern reader from the story. The book remains in print, a tribute to its enduring value as a frequently cited source for events and everyday life in the capital of the Confederacy.

The success of *Richmond During the War* spurred Brock to other work. In 1869 she gathered the most significant poetry that southerners had written about the Civil War into an anthology entitled *The Southern Amaranth: A Carefully Selected Collection of Poems Growing out of and in Reference to the Late War*, published for the benefit of a women's memorial association to aid in the reinterment of Confederate soldiers in the South. Brock included four of her own poems, one under the name Virginia Madison, a pseudonym she sometimes used that referred to her birthplace. Her best-known work in the collection was "Stonewall Jackson's Pall." Early critics considered *The Southern Amaranth* one of the best southern collections inspired by the Civil War. In 1869 Brock began organizing another poetry anthology to be entitled *American Poets in Their Poetry* that juxtaposed brief biographies of major American poets with their favorite example of their own verse. Although this work is listed under variant titles in several reference works as having been published, no examples have been located, and the volume may never have appeared.

Brock traveled through Europe in 1869–1870 and wrote letters about her experiences that appeared in several magazines. After her return she wrote for Frank Leslie's *Lady's Magazine*. Brock also contributed to the *New York Home Journal,* predecessor of *Town and Country*. Later in life she described her work as consisting of editorials, historical articles, reviews, essays, letters, travel sketches, short stories, biographies, and translations. Brock was respected by her peers but not widely known, perhaps because few articles in ladies' magazines of the period were signed. One measure of her talent is the inclusion of her description of Weyers Cave in Augusta County in William Cullen Bryant's *Picturesque America: or, The Land We Live In* (1872–1874), a notable travelogue of sixty-five articles, only two of which were by women.

In 1873 Brock published *Kenneth, My King*, a romance set in the South and a transparent imitation of *Jane Eyre* that is very readable but shows no talent for plotting. A savage review in the *New York Times* of 8 March 1873 dismissed it as "really a hopeless book." On 19 March 1873 the *Richmond Daily Enquirer* predicted that the novel would "find many readers and admirers in her native State, as well as elsewhere." Its strong female protagonist probably reflects Brock's estimation of her own life to that point—unmarried, intelligent, and left to fend for herself, she chose to work rather than rely on her relatives for assistance.

In Richmond on 11 January 1882 Brock married Richard Fletcher Putnam, an Episcopal minister and member of the Boston publishing family. Although she continued to contribute to magazines after she married, she wrote more for enjoyment than for a livelihood, and her output diminished considerably. The couple lived in New York and Connecticut and traveled frequently. Brock retained her literary contacts and participated in a display of books by Virginia authors at the World's Columbian Exposition in 1893. She wrote two more novels and started a third but published none of them, although her draft novel "Myra" is sometimes listed as published.

Sarah Ann Brock Putnam died in New York on 22 March 1911, five years after her husband's death on 16 January 1906, and was buried next to him in Hollywood Cemetery in Richmond.

Birth and death dates from gravestone; age given as twenty-five in Census, King and Queen Co., 1860, and as forty-six in BVS Marriage Register, Richmond City, 1882, implying a later birth year; [Mary T. Tardy], ed., *Living Female Writers of the South* (1872), 404–406; Willard and Livermore, *Woman of the Century*, 591–592 (por.); family history in William Armstrong Crozier, *Buckners of Virginia and the Allied Families of Strother and Ashby* (1907), 160–161; Armistead Churchill Gordon Jr., *Virginian Writers of Fugitive Verse* (1923), 95, 108, 252–254; a few letters in VHS; *Richmond Daily Dispatch*, 12 Jan. 1882; obituaries and accounts of funeral in *Richmond Times-Dispatch*, 23 Mar. 1911, *Richmond Virginian*, 25 Mar. 1911, and *Madison Exponent*, 31 Mar. 1911.

SARAH SHIELDS DRIGGS

BROCKENBROUGH, Eleanor Sampson (22 February 1910–13 August 1985), librarian, was born in Richmond, the daughter of John Mercer Brockenbrough, a civil engineer, and Clara Doyle Kenny Brockenbrough. She was educated at the school operated by Virginia Randolph Ellett (later Saint Catherine's School) in Richmond, and in 1927 she graduated from the Academy of the Sacred Heart, a Catholic school in Noroton, Connecticut. After returning to Richmond, Brockenbrough lived with her parents and sisters and was tutored in business courses. Her father frowned on women's working outside the home, and she held no job until after he died in 1930.

Brockenbrough began working as assistant house regent at the Confederate Museum in 1939. At that time the museum housed its entire collection of artifacts and archives in the White House of the Confederacy, which had been built in 1818 by her great-great-uncle John Brockenbrough. The historic house became her second home. She aided India Thomas, the house regent, and the visiting public with a proprietary zeal. Brockenbrough started work the same year as the release of the film *Gone With the Wind,* and when foreign visitors asked if the movie correctly portrayed conditions in the South she generally responded that "every family in the South has stories worse than that."

In 1946 Brockenbrough resigned because of her low pay. The museum had been hard-pressed financially, especially during the Great Depression and World War II, but she was quickly reinstated at an increased salary of $100 per month. With Thomas, who retired in 1963, Brockenbrough identified and cataloged thousands of unique items and documents in the collections, continuing the work Douglas Southall Freeman began in 1907. Serving at times as assistant director (1963–1968 and 1969–1977), interim director (1968–1969 and 1977–1978), bookkeeper, and librarian, Brockenbrough remained on the job for forty years and saw in a new age. The institution changed its name in 1970 to the Museum of the Confederacy and six years later completed construction of a new exhibition and library building adjacent to the old house. As assistant director, Brockenbrough was an active proponent of the venerable organization's new identity.

A respected archivist and librarian, Brockenbrough nevertheless had to make her mark in a world of predominantly male Civil War historians. With her deep knowledge of the museum's collections and their historical nuances, she succeeded. Brockenbrough influenced and guided the research of several generations of scholars, including Clifford Dowdey and Douglas Southall Freeman in the 1930s and 1940s; Richard B. Harwell, Frank E. Vandiver, and Bell I. Wiley in the era of the Civil War centennial; and James I. Robertson Jr., Emory M. Thomas, and many others after 1965. Over many years Brockenbrough thus assisted in the development of a broad reinterpretation of the social, political, and military history of the Confederacy. Robert K. Krick wrote in 1979 that "those who think [Varina Howell] Davis is the First Lady of the Confederacy have never worked with Eleanor Brockenbrough."

Beginning in the 1970s Brockenbrough suffered a series of debilitating falls and illnesses that confined her to a wheelchair. She retired from the museum in 1979 but returned on 10 April 1981 for the dedication of the Eleanor S. Brockenbrough Library. She was then named librarian emeritus in recognition of her many years of service as scholarly ambassador.

Always an active gardener, Brockenbrough belonged to the Garden Club of Virginia and the James River Garden Club, which under her persuasion designed the gardens at the Museum of the Confederacy. As long as possible she lived with her sisters at Doolough, the family home, but she eventually moved to the University Park Nursing Home in Henrico County. Eleanor Sampson Brockenbrough died in Richmond on 13 August 1985 and was buried beside her sisters in Hollywood Cemetery in that city.

Feature article in *Richmond Times-Dispatch,* 18 Apr. 1981 (por. and first quotation); Hubard, *Brockenbrough Descendants*, 56; information provided by sister Mary Austin Brockenbrough Morrison and by Peter Rippe and Margaret Rucker; Confederate Memorial Literary Society Archives Minute Books, MOC; *The Dedication of the Eleanor S. Brockenbrough Library* (1981 program, DVB Files); Krick, *Lee's Colonels*, viii (second quotation); obituaries in *Richmond News Leader* and *Richmond Times-Dispatch,* both 14 Aug. 1985.

RUTH ANN COSKI

BROCKENBROUGH, John (8 May 1773– 3 July 1852), banker and political leader, was born in Essex County, the eldest son of John Brockenbrough, a physician, and Sarah Roane Brockenbrough. After receiving his early education in Tappahannock he entered the medical school of the University of Edinburgh, from which he graduated in 1795 after completing a thesis on rabies in dogs. Brockenbrough returned to Virginia and married Gabriella Harvie Randolph, a widow with one son, in Goochland County on 18 April 1797. Their one son died in childhood, but his wife's son and other relatives often lived with them in Richmond, and he later served as guardian of his wife's grandchildren.

Brockenbrough occupied a secure social position as a member of an established and prestigious family. He gave up the practice of medicine to manage the large property holdings that his wife brought to their marriage. On Clay Street near the Virginia State Capitol, Brockenbrough built two impressive residences, one of which later served as the White House of the Confederacy. He became a member of the board and cashier of the new Bank of Virginia in 1804. In January 1812 the board appointed him the institution's second president. Brockenbrough served in that capacity until he retired from business in 1843. During most of that time only three chartered banks were operating in the eastern portion of the state, giving Brockenbrough and his bank a major role in the economic development of Virginia.

Brockenbrough had extensive business interests outside the bank. He managed his and his wife's considerable holdings in the city of Richmond and in Henrico County. The governor appointed Brockenbrough in 1808 to a committee charged with devising a plan to promote domestic manufacturing, and he was a delegate to the 1828 state convention to encourage internal improvements. He owned Belle Isle in the James River and rented part of it to the Belle-Isle Rolling and Slitting Mill and Nail Manufactory, of which he, one of his brothers, and a brother-in-law eventually became proprietors. The mill was incorporated as Belle Isle Manufacturing Company in March 1832 and operated at a loss throughout much of the 1840s but remained a family business until 1852, when it was sold at public auction and became the profitable Old Dominion Ironworks. Brockenbrough also had a longstanding interest in the Warm Springs Company and Hotel in Bath County. He joined it as a partner in 1828, used the annuities of his wards to purchase the outstanding shares in the 1840s, and was its sole proprietor by 1852. At the time of his death Brockenbrough's real estate holdings alone were worth $77,000, and he and his wife owned fifty-seven slaves.

Throughout his life Brockenbrough involved himself in public affairs. At various times beginning in 1803 he was a trustee and president of the Richmond Academy. Brockenbrough also served as a commissioner to establish wards and boundaries in the city of Richmond in 1805, a member of the 1807 grand jury that indicted Aaron Burr for treason, and a member and occasional president of Richmond's common council in 1812–1813, 1817–1818, 1819–1821, 1824–1825, and 1827. He played an important role on two council committees in the design selection and construction of two architecturally sophisticated Richmond landmarks designed by Robert Mills, Monumental Church, completed in 1814, and a new city hall erected between 1816 and 1818.

Perhaps the most important but elusive aspect of Brockenbrough's career was his involvement in state and national politics. He probably wrote the article on the building of towns for the 22 September 1804 issue of the *Richmond Enquirer* that was part of the so-called Rainbow Series published in Richmond newspapers. Staunch Republicans, the authors were known as the Richmond Junto, a small circle of politically astute leaders whom many opponents believed wielded almost dictatorial power over Virginia politics. Brockenbrough's role in the informal working of the group cannot be precisely documented, but he was a close family, political, and often business ally of many of its most prominent members, including his younger brother William Brockenbrough, a jurist and vocal critic of their near neighbor John Marshall, United States chief justice. John Brockenbrough was in regular communication with prominent party

members in Virginia and in Washington, D.C., and he almost certainly advised both Thomas Ritchie, influential editor of the *Richmond Enquirer*, and Martin Van Buren. He corresponded with and greatly admired John Randolph of Roanoke. Like most other surviving members of the Junto, Brockenbrough moved into the Jacksonian faction during the transitional years of the second party system.

Shortly after retiring from politics and from the management of his Richmond business interests, John Brockenbrough moved to Bath County in 1844 and died there on 3 July 1852. He was buried in Warm Springs Cemetery in Bath County.

Birth recorded in Roane-Ritchie-Brockenbrough family Bible records, LVA; birth and death dates on gravestone; Hubard, *Brockenbrough Descendants*, 7–8, 11–12 (contains some errors); Kenneth Shorey, ed., *The Collected Letters of John Randolph of Roanoke to Dr. John Brockenbrough, 1812–1833* (1988); marriage date in Goochland Co. Ministers' Returns; letters in Harrison Family Papers and Carter Braxton Page Papers, VHS, and in collections of Thomas Jefferson Papers at Huntington, LC, and UVA; James K. Sanford, ed., *Richmond: Her Triumphs, Tragedies, and Growth* (1975), 50–51, 56–57; Harry Ammon, "The Richmond Junto, 1800–1824," *VMHB* 61 (1953): 395–418; Joseph H. Harrison Jr., "Oligarchs and Democrats: The Richmond Junto," *VMHB* 78 (1970): 184–198; F. Thornton Miller, "The Richmond Junto: The Secret All-Powerful Club—or Myth," *VMHB* 99 (1991): 63–80; wills and estate inventories of Brockenbrough and wife in Bath Co. Will Book, 5:469–470, 525–526, 534–537, 556–558, 575–584; obituary in *Richmond Daily Dispatch*, 8 July 1852.

NANCY BOWMAN
TUCKER H. HILL

BROCKENBROUGH, John Mercer (1 August 1830–25 August 1892), Confederate army officer, was born in Richmond County, the son of Moore Fauntleroy Brockenbrough, who represented Richmond County for ten terms in the House of Delegates, and his second wife, Sarah Waller Smith Brockenbrough. In 1850 he graduated from the Virginia Military Institute, standing eleventh in a class of seventeen.

Brockenbrough decided against becoming a soldier after his graduation. Instead, he returned to his native region and settled into the life of a gentleman farmer on 281 acres of land. In 1860 he owned eight slaves. On 10 December 1856 Brockenbrough married his distant cousin

Austina Brockenbrough, of Essex County. They had five sons and four daughters.

With the call to arms in 1861, Brockenbrough sprang to the forefront of military preparations on the Northern Neck. He assembled men from all over the region and in June 1861 formed them into the 40th Regiment Virginia Infantry. His commission as colonel of the regiment dated from 1 July 1861. For the remainder of that year and into 1862 Brockenbrough participated in the defense of his home counties. He first experienced combat on 26 June 1862 in the opening moments of the Seven Days' Battles. From June until late in August, Brockenbrough led his regiment through some of the fiercest fighting of the Civil War, eliciting occasional praise from his superiors.

On 30 August 1862 Brockenbrough became brigade commander when Brigadier General Charles W. Field was wounded during the fighting at the Second Battle of Manassas (Bull Run). His brigade saw little action at Sharpsburg (Antietam). At Fredericksburg two of Brockenbrough's regiments were heavily engaged while the rest remained in reserve, but at Chancellorsville on 2 May 1863 Brockenbrough led his brigade in Thomas J. "Stonewall" Jackson's famous flank march around the Union army. When the offensive resumed the next day, Brockenbrough's veterans were conspicuous on the front lines and suffered a 50 percent casualty rate as they helped drive the Army of the Potomac back to the Rapidan River.

On the first day of fighting at Gettysburg, Brockenbrough and his brigade participated in the assaults on McPherson's Ridge and Seminary Ridge, operations that dislodged the defenders and contributed to the rout of two Union corps. On 3 July, in preparation for the attack up Cemetery Ridge, Brockenbrough's force, down to just 500 men, was placed on the left of the Confederate lines in an unprotected position exposed to a destructive enfilade fire from Union gunners. Demoralized, some of the Virginians remained in a swale when the brigade resumed its advance after pausing to regroup. When the 8th Ohio launched an attack against Brockenbrough's wavering lines, the brigade faltered and then disintegrated as the stunned veterans headed to the rear.

This dismal performance reflected poorly on Brockenbrough, whose problems were compounded on 14 July 1863 while the army was retreating across the Potomac at Falling Waters. His brigade repelled an attack while in a defensive position. Ordered to withdraw across the river, Brockenbrough instead sent his troops forward under the command of his aide Wayland Dunaway, while he departed with the main force. During the close fighting, the Union troops received reinforcements, and when the brigade attempted to disengage nearly 700 men were captured, including Dunaway. The 40th, 47th, and 55th Regiments lost their battle flags.

After the campaign, and amid much protest, Lieutenant Colonel Henry Harrison Walker was promoted over Brockenbrough to brigade commander. Considering Walker unfit for command and stung by what he later termed the "puerile exertions" of his successor, Brockenbrough resigned on 19 July 1863. On this occasion Major General Henry Heth, the division commander, wrote to Jefferson Davis that Brockenbrough had commanded his brigade with conspicuous gallantry, although he did not cite any specific recognition or recommend promotion. Brockenbrough's greatest support came from his brigade, men who had twice criticized their superiors in writing. Fifty commissioned officers signed a note to Robert Edward Lee, commander of the Army of Northern Virginia, protesting the change of command and citing Brockenbrough's gallantry in every engagement since Second Manassas. The colonel solicited but did not receive another assignment. His resignation was accepted on 21 January 1864.

Returning home to the Northern Neck, Brockenbrough became colonel of the 2d Regiment Virginia Reserves. After the war ended, he resumed farming in Richmond County. In 1872 Brockenbrough was the founding president of the Agricultural and Immigrant Society for the Counties of Richmond, Westmoreland, Lancaster, and Northumberland. He had moved to Essex County by January 1876. After his first wife's death in 1874, Brockenbrough married

Kate C. Mallory, a native of Elizabeth City County, on 8 November 1877 in Norfolk. They had one son and one daughter.

During the controversy over the payment of Virginia's prewar state debt, Brockenbrough became a prominent Readjuster. When the party triumphed in the General Assembly, he was elected register of the Land Office and superintendent of public buildings. Brockenbrough held the posts from 11 December 1879 through 17 December 1883 and moved accordingly to the state capital. He remained in Richmond until 1886, lived for a time in Chicago, and then returned to Richmond. John Mercer Brockenbrough died there of lung congestion after a brief illness on 25 August 1892 and was buried in Hollywood Cemetery in that city.

Hubard, *Brockenbrough Descendants*, 15–16, 31–32, 34; Robert E. L. Krick, *40th Virginia Infantry* (1985); Brockenbrough alumnus file, VMI; Compiled Service Records (quotation in Brockenbrough to James A. Seddon, 22 Jan. 1864); BVS Marriage Register, Essex Co., 1856, and Norfolk City, 1877; *Richmond Daily Whig*, 9, 12 Dec. 1879; James Tice Moore, *Two Paths to the New South: The Virginia Debt Controversy, 1870–1883* (1974), 141; Agricultural and Immigrant Society for the Counties of Richmond, Westmoreland, Lancaster, and Northumberland, *The Northern Neck of Virginia as a Home for Immigrants* (1872); BVS Death Register, Richmond City; obituaries in *Richmond State*, 25 Aug. 1892, and *Richmond Daily Dispatch* and *Richmond Times*, both 26 Aug. 1892; variant death date of 24 Aug. 1892 on grave marker.

ROBERT E. L. KRICK

BROCKENBROUGH, John White (23 December 1806–20 February 1877), legal educator, United States District Court judge, and member of the Provisional Confederate Congress, was born at Westwood in Hanover County, the son of William Brockenbrough, a prominent jurist, and Judith Robinson White Brockenbrough. He attended the College of William and Mary (1824–1825), the University of Virginia (1825), and the private law school of Henry St. George Tucker in Winchester (1827–1828), where he learned Tucker's perceptive blending of practice and theory through a balanced mix of readings, classroom lectures, and appearances before a moot court.

After Brockenbrough obtained his law license he returned to Hanover County to begin his practice. Like many other young lawyers he served briefly as commonwealth's attorney. About 1834 Brockenbrough moved to Rockbridge County, where he married Mary Colwell Bowyer on 15 April 1835. They had six sons and one daughter. Brockenbrough developed a successful practice in the local courts of the Lexington area and before the federal and state courts in Richmond. Following in his father's scholarly footsteps, he collected and published *Reports of Cases Decided by the Honourable John Marshall . . . in the Circuit Court of the United States for the District of Virginia and North Carolina from 1802 to 1833 Inclusive* (1837), which he dedicated to the American bench and bar.

In 1840 Brockenbrough and fellow Lexington Democrat John Letcher lost bids for Rockbridge County's two seats in the House of Delegates as a result of a statewide Whig victory. Brockenbrough and Letcher had a long and at times stormy personal and political relationship. Briefly in 1841 Brockenbrough followed Letcher's lead and served as an editor and publisher of the *Valley Star*, a party organ published in Lexington. Shortly thereafter he acted as counsel for the Virginia Military Institute and was elected to its board in 1843.

When the judge of the United States District Court for the Western District of Virginia resigned in 1845, Brockenbrough actively sought the vacated seat. The influence of his uncle John Brockenbrough, second president of the Bank of Virginia, and of Thomas Ritchie, editor of the *Richmond Enquirer*, prevailed over the quiet opposition of Letcher. The president nominated Brockenbrough on 23 December 1845, his thirty-ninth birthday, and the Senate confirmed the nomination the next month. The district was huge, and Brockenbrough held court semiannually in Charleston, Clarksburg, Staunton, Wheeling, and Wytheville. Reportedly, not a single one of his opinions was overturned on appeal during his sixteen-year tenure.

Brockenbrough supplemented his judicial salary by educating aspiring attorneys in western Virginia. In October 1849 he opened a private law school that met in annual six-month sessions. With a curriculum similar to Tucker's,

Brockenbrough commenced his school in a room in the Franklin Society Hall in Lexington. By 1852 he had more than a dozen students, and by the opening of the Civil War he had graduated more than 200. Brockenbrough's lectures were known for their clarity of organization and argument. He published two of them, *Introductory Address to the Law Class of Lexington, . . . October 31, 1849* (1849), and *Introductory Lecture, Delivered in the Franklin Hall, Lexington, Va., to the Law Class, 1858–9* (1858). Brockenbrough timed his classes so that his students could also attend nearby Washington College (later Washington and Lee University). In July 1852 the college board elected him a trustee. Brockenbrough was certainly well loved by his students and held in high esteem by the local community, but he had a notoriously hot temper. His emotions led him into an altercation at least once with the president of the college.

Despite being a federal judge, Brockenbrough remained active in Virginia politics. Mentioned as a possible gubernatorial candidate of the American (Know Nothing) Party in 1855, he completely disavowed the party. Three years later, however, he stood ready to accept the draft of the Democratic convention as candidate for governor. Supported by Henry Alexander Wise and a coalition of eastern and northwestern Democrats who wished to block John Letcher's nomination, Brockenbrough came close to defeating his longtime rival. Brockenbrough was correctly perceived as hostile toward abolition and a strong proponent of southern rights.

Brockenbrough lost again to Unionists in February 1861 when he ran for a state convention called to consider secession. That same month the Virginia assembly appointed him a representative to the so-called Peace Conference held in Washington, D.C. Arriving at the conference with some optimism, Brockenbrough quickly became thoroughly disillusioned and declared to the Northern antislavery delegates that if they persisted in characterizing slavery as "a sin, the sum of all villa[i]nies, then we may as well separate. We cannot live together longer."

On 4 May 1861 Brockenbrough resigned as United States district judge. Three days later he took the oath as the first of Virginia's delegation to be seated in the Provisional Confederate Congress in Montgomery, Alabama. Later that month that Congress elected him Confederate States judge of the Western District of Virginia, but he continued to serve simultaneously in Congress until mid-February 1862. He sat on the Committee on the Judiciary. After the ratification in 1862 of the permanent Constitution of the Confederate States, which forbade dual officeholding, in April 1862 the Confederate Congress confirmed his appointment as district judge. On the bench he consistently decided cases in favor of the Jefferson Davis administration.

Following the end of the war Brockenbrough announced in May 1865 the reopening of his private law school and obtained a presidential pardon. In the spring of 1866 he attended a convention in Staunton that formally organized the Valley Railroad. Late in 1867 Brockenbrough helped form a local unit of the Conservative Party. In perhaps his most memorable postwar contribution, he helped persuade Robert Edward Lee to serve as president of Washington College. Appointed rector of the college in the summer of 1865, Brockenbrough reportedly donned a suit of borrowed clothes and spent his last remaining funds traveling to Lee's temporary residence in Powhatan County to argue that the former general should devote his remaining years to the college education of young southern men.

Brockenbrough's relationship with Washington College deteriorated during his last years. At the urging of the board of trustees he agreed in 1867 to merge his private law school with the college. The merger was completed in June 1870, but the appointment of John Randolph Tucker as a second law professor led to increasing friction between the judge and the college. After a series of angry confrontations and misunderstandings, Brockenbrough terminated his long relationship with the law school he had founded and returned to the practice of law. In 1873 he unsuccessfully tried to revive his private law school. John White Brockenbrough died of heart disease in Lexington on 20 February 1877 and was buried in the Lexington Presbyterian Church Cemetery, later known as Stonewall Jackson Memorial Cemetery.

W. Hamilton Bryson, ed., *Legal Education in Virginia, 1779–1979: A Biographical Approach* (1982), 98–104 (por.); Matthew W. Paxton Jr., "A Judge's School: A Brief Biography of John White Brockenbrough," *Proceedings of the Rockbridge Historical Society* 8 (1970/1974): 85–104; "Brockenbrough Family Bible," in Hanover Co. Historical Society *Bulletin* 30 (June 1984): 7–8; Rockbridge Co. Marriage Register; a few Brockenbrough letters and letters referring to him in Rockbridge Historical Society, VHS, and W&L; L. E. Chittenden, *A Report of the Debates and Proceedings in the Secret Sessions of the Conference Convention for Proposing Amendments to the Constitution of the United States* (1864), quotation on 281; election to Provisional Confederate Congress on 29 Apr. 1861 in Reese and Gaines, *Proceedings of 1861 Convention,* 4:612–615; Presidential Pardons; Ollinger Crenshaw, *General Lee's College: The Rise and Growth of Washington and Lee University* (1969); obituary in *Lexington Gazette and Citizen,* 23 Feb. 1877.

E. LEE SHEPARD

BROCKENBROUGH, William (10 July 1778–10 December 1838), member of the Council, General Court judge, and judge of the Virginia Court of Appeals, was born in Tappahannock, the son of John Brockenbrough, a physician, and Sarah Roane Brockenbrough. He attended the College of William and Mary in 1798 and studied law. Brockenbrough represented Essex County in the House of Delegates from 1801 to 1803 and served on the Committee on Propositions and Grievances during his first term and on the Committee for Courts of Justice during both terms. He was then elected to the Council of State and served from 3 June 1803 until mid-May 1806, having been voted off that body on 17 December 1805 under a constitutional provision that required the assembly to remove two councillors every third year. Brockenbrough represented Hanover County in the House of Delegates from 1807 to 1809 and again sat on the Committee for Courts of Justice.

In the assembly Brockenbrough wrote his first newspaper essays, using the pseudonym Aristogitan. His most noted political writing consisted of attacks on the jurisprudence of the United States Supreme Court and Chief Justice John Marshall. Republican Party leaders in Virginia regarded the Court's 1819 decision in *McCulloch* v. *Maryland* as a declaration that the national government held supreme sway over the states and would exercise a power that, through the implied powers clause, had no fixed limits.

Virginia's political leaders met the challenge with a strong defense of the states' rights interpretation of the Constitution and federal system. Brockenbrough wrote essays under the pseudonym Amphictyon in the 30 March and 2 April 1819 issues of the state's leading newspaper, the *Richmond Enquirer*. He condemned the Court for construing the Constitution too broadly and allowing the national government to expand its power at the expense of the states. The states' rights countermovement succeeded in putting Marshall and the nationalists on the defensive, and the chief justice entered the fray with a public response to Brockenbrough's attack.

Throughout his adult life Brockenbrough was identified as a member of the Richmond Junto. This leadership clique included his brother John Brockenbrough, the president of the Bank of Virginia; Thomas Ritchie, the editor of the *Richmond Enquirer*; and his kinsman Spencer Roane, a member of the Court of Appeals who like Brockenbrough wrote essays sharply critical of the Marshall Court. Political rivals described the Junto as a secret, omnipotent organization that controlled the state's politics by dominating the Republican Party caucus, but if the Junto formally existed at all, its power was greatly exaggerated. That Brockenbrough was identified as one of its leaders attests to his contemporary stature. He was a respected member of the state judiciary and an architect, along with Roane and John Taylor of Caroline, of the southern states' rights constitutional doctrines. Brockenbrough was a presidential elector for James Monroe in 1820, William Harris Crawford in 1824, and Andrew Jackson in 1828.

On 7 February 1809 the General Assembly elected Brockenbrough to a seat on the General Court. During twenty-five years of service he heard appeals from lower courts in criminal cases and met twice a year with other General Court judges as the state's final appellate court for criminal cases. From 1809 to 1812 Brockenbrough was judge for the circuit of seven western counties reaching from Montgomery on the northeast to Lee on the southwest. Thereafter he presided over the circuit for the city of Richmond. By seniority Brockenbrough became president of the General Court in November 1820.

During his tenure he wrote his most influential newspaper articles, and with Hugh Holmes he edited and published a *Collection of Cases Decided by the General Court of Virginia* (1815). Brockenbrough subsequently edited and issued a second volume, *Virginia Cases, or Decisions of the General Court of Virginia* (1826), which included his own "Brief Sketch of the Courts of this Commonwealth." As a member of the committee that the assembly appointed in 1816 to revise the laws of the state, Brockenbrough also published *Draughts of Such Bills as Have Been Prepared by the Revisors of the Laws* (1817). In 1818 he served on the Rockfish Gap Commission, which recommended Charlottesville as the site of the new University of Virginia.

On 20 February 1834 the assembly elected Brockenbrough to the Court of Appeals, on which he served until his death four years later. None of those weighty and controversial constitutional issues about which he wrote in the newspapers came before the Court of Appeals. Brockenbrough's work there consisted of interpreting Virginia statutes and ruling on appeals from lower Virginia courts on the construction of deeds and wills and on procedural matters of civil law and in equity.

Brockenbrough married Judith Robinson White at White Plains in King William County on 22 December 1803. Their six daughters and two sons included John White Brockenbrough, who became a federal judge and prominent legal educator. William Brockenbrough died in a Richmond boardinghouse on 10 December 1838 and was buried at White Plains.

NCAB, 19:316–317; Hubard, *Brockenbrough Descendants*, 7–8, 12; Benjamin Blake Minor, "Judge William Brockenbrough," *SHSP* 27 (1899): 350–358, reprinted in *Virginia Law Register* 5 (1900): 731–739 (por.); W. Hamilton Bryson, ed., *The Virginia Law Reporters Before 1880* (1977), 7–10; Roane-Ritchie-Brockenbrough family Bible records, LVA; "Brockenbrough Family Bible," in Hanover Co. Historical Society *Bulletin* 30 (June 1984): 7–8; letters in Harrison Family Papers, VHS; Eric Tscheschlok, "Mistaken Identity: Spencer Roane and the 'Amphictyon' Letters of 1819," *VMHB* 106 (1998): 201–211; Harry Ammon, "The Richmond Junto, 1800–1824," *VMHB* 61 (1953): 395–418; Joseph H. Harrison Jr., "Oligarchs and Democrats: The Richmond Junto," *VMHB* 78 (1970): 184–198; F. Thornton Miller, "The Richmond Junto: The Secret All-Powerful Club—or Myth," *VMHB* 99 (1991): 63–80; Hummel and Smith, *Portraits and Statuary*, 12 (por.); obituary in *Richmond Enquirer*, 11 Dec. 1838.

F. THORNTON MILLER

BRODNAX, John (bap. 16 October 1664–by 17 August 1719), gold- and silversmith, was born probably in London, England, where he was christened on 16 October 1664 in the Parish of Saint Gregory by Saint Paul's. He was the son of Robert Brodnax, a goldsmith, and Ann Brodnax. After Robert Brodnax died about 1688, Ann Brodnax operated his goldsmith's shop in Tucke Court in the Holborn district of London. John Brodnax's grandfather John Brodnax (ca. 1608–by November 1657) migrated to Virginia in the 1650s, and a younger brother William Brodnax also settled in the colony, acquired substantial property on Jamestown Island, and represented James City County or Jamestown in nearly every assembly between 1715 and 1726.

Brodnax probably learned to work gold and silver in his father's shop. An elder brother, also trained as a goldsmith, was favored to inherit the business. John Brodnax's residence in Virginia is first documented in a Henrico County lawsuit alleging that he reneged on a large gambling debt after a horserace held in April 1686. In March 1687 Brodnax bought his first 100 acres of land, and during the next seven years he acquired more than 1,550 acres, some of it located south of the James River. He returned to England at least twice and acquired some of his land by virtue of headrights for immigrants whose passage he paid for when he returned to Virginia. During his first years in Virginia Brodnax combined goldsmithing with keeping a store in Henrico County. In August 1691 he executed a metal seal engraved with the device of Henrico County for use in marking inspected tanned and cured leathers.

By February 1695 Brodnax had moved to James City County. He often appraised or audited estates, and committees of the House of Burgesses met in his house in 1695 and 1696. After the seat of government moved to Williamsburg, Brodnax served as keeper of the Capitol and public jail from 12 September 1709 until his death. He acquired three lots in Williamsburg, including the one where he resided and engaged in gold- and silversmithing. Brodnax is the earliest documented silversmith in Virginia for whom identified metalwork survives. Archaeological excavations at Williamsburg and Yorktown sites have uncovered two silver spoons with the maker's mark "IB." A small gold ring bearing the same maker's mark and the inscription "Fear God Mary Brodnax" is believed to have been his daughter's christening ring and is among the oldest pieces of attributed southernmade gold. The estate inventory of Brodnax taken in 1719 lists the tools and raw materials of his trade, including filings, broken silver and gold, and more than 902 ounces of silver and finished items such as silver casters, porringers, buckles, and soupspoons. Imported extravagances including diamond rings, a snuffbox topped with a gold device, and a silver-handled scimitar may have been personal or business stock. Artisans were often regarded as distinct from the elite social ranks, but Brodnax bridged the gap in Virginia. Some legal documents call him a gentleman, and he died relatively wealthy, with a personal estate valued at more than £1,000, excluding slaves and real estate.

A letter from William Byrd (ca.1652–1704) to his London factors suggests that Brodnax may have had a wife, name unknown, who died of smallpox by 10 November 1686. Brodnax married Mary Skerme, of Henrico County, by 1698. They had at least three sons and at least three daughters. Mary Brodnax is not named in her husband's will and probably predeceased him. Their son Winfield Brodnax served an apprenticeship to a master silversmith in England and later returned to Williamsburg to practice his craft. John Brodnax dated his will on 2 July 1719 and died between then and 17 August 1719, when the will was proved in the York County Court. His silversmithing tools were sold to Richard Packe, another practicing Williamsburg silversmith.

Mildred Seab Ezell, *Brodnax: The Beginning* (1995), 101–113, 135–153; parish register of Saint Gregory by Saint Paul's, London, Eng.; family relationships documented in *Robert Gibbon v. William Brodnax et al.,* PRO C 5/486/46; Henrico Co. Order Book (1678–1693), 235 (first record in Virginia), 374; Henrico Co. Deeds, Wills, Etc. (1677–1692), 431, and (1688–1697), 219 (gives age as twenty-six on 1 Aug. 1691), 228, 247; Patent Book, 8:61, 394, RG 4, LVA; *Journal of House of Burgesses, 1695–1702,* 8, 49, 62; *Executive Journals of Council,* 3:222; George Barton Cutten, *The Silversmiths of Virginia (Together with Watchmakers and Jewelers) from 1694 to 1850* (1952), 187; death of "poor Mrs. Brodnax" reported in William Byrd to Perry and Lane, 10 Nov. 1686, in *Byrd Correspondence,* 1:65–66; will and estate records in York Co. Orders, Wills, Etc., 15:475–477, 510–512, 16:307, 316, 319.

CATHERINE B. HOLLAN

BRODNAX, William Henry (ca. 1786–23 October 1834), member of the Convention of 1829–1830, was born in Brunswick County, the son of William Brodnax, a lawyer, and Frances Belfield Walker Brodnax. About 1804 or 1805 he attended Hampden-Sydney College, which awarded him an honorary M.A. in 1830. After studying law in Petersburg, Broadnax established a lucrative practice in that city and in neighboring Brunswick, Dinwiddie, and Greensville Counties. Eventually he became very prosperous, married Anne Eliza Withers, and lived on the 1,600-acre Kingston plantation in Dinwiddie County. They had four sons and two daughters.

Brodnax represented Greensville County in the House of Delegates for the session of 1818–1819 and served on the Committees for Courts of Justice and on Propositions and Grievances. The assembly elected him a brigadier general of the state militia on 24 January 1824 and later that year detailed him to lead the welcoming escort when the marquis de Lafayette entered Virginia on his triumphal return to the United States. Brodnax was also a presidential elector for William Harris Crawford in 1824.

In May 1829 Brodnax received the most votes of the eleven candidates for the four seats from the district comprising Brunswick, Dinwiddie, Lunenburg, and Mecklenburg Counties in a convention called to revise the Virginia constitution. He sat on the Committee on the Legislative Department. Brodnax seldom took part in the debates but generally voted with opponents of democratic reforms. He supported a conservative compromise that extended the suffrage to most adult white men but apportioned seats in the General Assembly on the basis of the number of white people reported in the 1820 census, a minor reform that effectively continued the eastern counties' domination of the legislature. The denial of true white-basis democracy escalated tensions between slave-holding and nonslaveholding Virginians for decades to come.

In 1830 the voters of Dinwiddie County elected Brodnax to the first of three consecutive one-year terms in the House of Delegates. During his first term he served again on the Committee for Courts of Justice and also on the Committees of Privileges and Elections and of Schools and Colleges. During his second and third terms he chaired the Committee for Courts of Justice. In August 1831 Brodnax commanded the militia-men who marched from Brunswick and Greens-ville Counties to help suppress Nat Turner's Rebellion in Southampton County. At the ensuing assembly session Brodnax chaired a special committee to consider petitions relating to the place of free blacks, slaves, and slavery in Virginia society. Unlike some members from eastern Virginia he favored a full debate on the subjects of slavery and emancipation, but on 16 January 1832 his committee concluded that it was "inexpedient for the present to make any legislative enactments for the abolition of slavery."

Brodnax owned or had a life interest in more than 100 slaves, according to his estate inventory. He condemned abolitionists for seeking to violate the property rights of slave owners but expressed equal disdain for apologists for slavery. In a long speech begun in the House of Delegates on 19 January 1832 Brodnax characterized slavery's influence on Virginia as "a mildew" and called it "the *incubus* which paralyzes her energies and retards her every effort at advancement." A member of the American Colonization Society, he proposed that the state pay for the annual removal from Virginia of 6,000 free blacks and manumitted slaves. Hoping for a decline in the market value of slaves and a resulting increase in manumissions, Brodnax calculated that in eighty years Virginia could be entirely free of African Americans and of the institution of slavery at a cost of about $200,000 per annum. The delegates rejected his plan in 1832 and again when he proposed it at the next session of the House of Delegates.

Brodnax emphatically supported the southern states' rights political philosophy all of his public life. Like many other Virginia political leaders he condemned Andrew Jackson's han-

dling of the Nullification Crisis early in the 1830s and thereafter allied himself with the evolving Whig Party. In his last political act Brodnax sent to a meeting of Petersburg Whigs a public letter dated 14 October 1834 and printed ten days later in the *Richmond Whig and Public Advertiser*. Perhaps fearful of an outbreak of cholera in the area, he excused his absence on the basis of his poor health but used the opportunity to denounce Jackson for betraying the principles of 1776 and the promises he made when elected. Despite his precautions, William Henry Brodnax contracted cholera and died at his Kingston plantation on 23 October 1834. He was buried in the cemetery at Dinwiddie Court House.

NCAB, 19:228–229; H. F. Turner, "General William Henery Brodnax," *Branch Papers* 3 (1909): 14–26; "Brodnax Family," *WMQ*, 1st ser., 14 (1905): 52–58 (por.), based on family Bible records; William Henry Brodnax Papers, LVA and W&M; Brodnax Family Papers, VHS; American Colonization Society Papers, LC; *Richmond Enquirer*, 2 June 1829; Catlin, *Convention of 1829–30* (por.); Bruce, *Rhetoric of Conservatism*, 36; Alison Goodyear Freehling, *Drift Toward Dissolution: The Virginia Slavery Debate of 1831–1832* (1982); *JHD*, 1831–1832 sess., 15, 99 (first quotation); *Speech of William H. Brodnax, (of Dinwiddie) in the House of Delegates of Virginia, on the Policy of the State With Respect to its Colored Population* (1832), 10–11 (second and third quotations); will and estate inventory in Dinwiddie Co. Will Book, 1:384–386, 435–438; obituary giving cause of death and age at death as about forty-eight reprinted in Henry Howe, *Historical Collections of Virginia* (1845), 148; death notice and tributes in *Richmond Enquirer*, 31 Oct., 4 Nov. 1834.

ALISON GOODYEAR FREEHLING

BROOKE, David Tucker (28 April 1852–28 March 1915), member of the Convention of 1901–1902, was born in Richmond, the son of Henry Laurens Brooke and Virginia Sarah Tucker Brooke. He attended private schools in Virginia after the death of his mother and his father's relocation to Baltimore. Brooke matriculated at the University of Virginia in 1870 and then taught in schools in Stafford County and in Jefferson County, West Virginia, before moving to Norfolk in 1873. He continued to teach until 1880 or 1881, but in the meantime he read law with local attorney Tazewell Taylor, was admitted to the bar in 1874, and began practicing law in the first of two partnerships. After Brooke stopped teaching he undertook the full-time practice of law. On 7 April 1880 he married Lucy Borland Higgins, the daughter of a Norfolk bank clerk. They had one son and five daughters.

On 24 January 1884 the General Assembly elected D. Tucker Brooke to fill an unexpired term as judge of the corporation court of the city of Norfolk. He was reelected in his own right in 1888 but declined further service on the court when his six-year term expired at the end of 1894. Brooke then resumed his law practice and his participation in local Democratic Party politics. In 1901 he won election to a state constitutional convention as a result of factional infighting among Norfolk Democrats. Alfred P. Thom, a prominent attorney, was opposed by several powerful leaders of the local party because of his role in local patronage disputes and because they feared he was too much indebted to local corporate interests. To prevent a serious split in the party, political brokers arranged to pair Thom with Brooke, who was acceptable to business leaders but also on good terms with Thom's critics, as a team for the city's two seats in the convention. On 24 April 1901 Thom and Brooke easily won the party's primary, and on 23 May they were elected without Republican opposition.

Brooke chaired the convention's Committee on the Organization and Government of Cities and Towns, served as ranking member of the Committee on Corporations, and also sat on the Committee on Final Revision. As chairman of the committee on municipal government, he prepared the first draft of what became the considerably revised Article VIII of the new constitution and led the floor debates on this section. A conservative man who several times denounced the convention's innovations, Brooke refused to sign the report of the Committee on Corporations that successfully recommended creation of a strong State Corporation Commission, and during floor debate he usually sided with Thom in favor of weakening amendments. Brooke voted against the restrictive suffrage provisions adopted on 4 April 1902, and on 29 May he disapproved when a majority decided to implement the constitution without a popular referendum on ratification. He voted for the final text of the constitution on 6 June 1902.

Brooke was a good public speaker but seldom a willing one. On 6 February 1902 he opened his principal speech in the convention against the corporation commission by remarking on "how largely I am possessed of that quality of modesty which adorns a woman and destroys a lawyer." He practiced law with a succession of partners, the final one being his son. David Tucker Brooke died of heart disease at his home in Norfolk on 28 March 1915. He was buried in Forest Lawn Cemetery in that city.

Henry and Spofford, *Eminent Men,* 409–410; Pollard Questionnaires; BVS Marriage Register, Norfolk City; *Norfolk Virginian-Pilot,* 27 Mar., 18, 24, 25 Apr. 1901; Election Records, no. 43, RG 13, LVA; *Journal of 1901–1902 Convention,* 486–487, 504, 535; *Proceedings and Debates of 1901–1902 Convention,* 1:884–886, 1165–1168, 1415–1419, 2:1888–1899, 2038–2040, 2209–2219 (quotation on 2:2209); *Richmond Times,* 12 June 1901; *Convention of 1901–1902 Photographs* (por.); obituaries in *Norfolk Ledger-Dispatch* and *Norfolk Virginian-Pilot and the Norfolk Landmark* (por.), both 29 Mar. 1915; editorial tribute in *Norfolk Virginian-Pilot and the Norfolk Landmark,* 30 Mar. 1915.

BRENT TARTER

BROOKE, Francis Taliaferro (27 August 1763–3 March 1851), Speaker of the Senate of Virginia and judge of the Virginia Court of Appeals, was born at Smithfield in Spotsylvania County, the son of Richard Brooke and his first wife, Ann Hay Taliaferro Brooke. He had a twin brother, John Brooke, who was born a few minutes before he was. Brooke received a classical education in local schools and from a private tutor. At age sixteen he joined the Continental army as a lieutenant. He served in Virginia and the southern theater during the remainder of the Revolutionary War. Brooke then spent about two years hunting foxes, racing horses, and reading history. He studied medicine for a year with one of his brothers and then read law with another, Robert Brooke, who subsequently served as governor and attorney general of Virginia.

Francis T. Brooke obtained his law license early in 1788, moved to Morgantown, and practiced there for a little more than two years, part of the time as commonwealth's attorney. In 1790 he moved to Tappahannock, where he lived for about six years before returning to

Fredericksburg. Brooke married Mary Randolph Spotswood in October 1791. They had two sons and two daughters before her death on 5 January 1803. On 14 February 1804 Brooke married Mary Champe Carter, who died on 25 October 1846. They had two sons and one daughter. Soon after his second marriage Brooke built a beautiful two-story brick house of Federal design on his plantation near Fredericksburg and named it Saint Julien.

In 1794 Brooke was elected to the House of Delegates from Essex County and served for two years, during which time he sat on the Committees on Claims, Courts of Justice, and Propositions and Grievances. In December 1800 he was elected to the Senate of Virginia as a Jeffersonian Republican from the district comprising Culpeper, Madison, Orange, and Spotsylvania Counties to complete the term of the recently deceased French Strother. In 1802 Brooke was elected a brigadier general of militia, and on 7 December of that year he was unanimously chosen Speaker of the Senate. He presided over that body for thirteen months.

On 12 January 1804 the General Assembly elected Brooke a judge of the General Court. He rode a large circuit for the next seven years, holding trial courts and hearing appeals. In January 1811 the assembly elected Brooke to the Virginia Court of Appeals, on which he served for the remainder of his long life. As senior judge during the latter part of 1822 and 1823 he usually presided in the absence of President William Fleming, and after Fleming's death on 15 February 1824 Brooke succeeded him as president. In 1831, when the court was reorganized under the new constitution and renamed the Supreme Court of Appeals, partisans of Andrew Jackson in the General Assembly replaced Brooke in the presidency with Henry St. George Tucker. Early in 1842 Brooke was again elected president of the court. He declined because of his age, even though his health appears to have remained remarkably strong until late in the 1840s, and he continued to attend the court's western sessions in Lewisburg and to visit the fashionable western spas. Along with Fleming and William H. Cabell, who was president when Brooke died, he had one of the longest tenures on the court of any

judge. Because of Fleming's long absences late in life, Brooke and Cabell shared the honor of longest actual service.

Brooke was a respected judge but not a learned legal scholar or influential jurist like some of his colleagues, most notably John W. Green, Spencer Roane, and Henry St. George Tucker. Brooke's opinions tended to be comparatively brief and simple, with less show of legal learning than the opinions of his more renowned colleagues. During Brooke's presidency the judges began producing long and scholarly opinions that reflected well on the erudition of the court but may also have complicated and protracted its work and certainly lengthened the reports of its decisions. Although not so insistent a critic of the federal courts as Roane, Brooke praised the states' rights philosophy of the Virginia Resolutions of 1798 that Roane often relied on. In an 1814 opinion Brooke ruled that a section of the federal Judiciary Act of 1789 was unconstitutional and on that basis rejected the appellate authority of the United States Supreme Court as a violation of dual sovereignty.

Although he was a judge, Brooke was keenly interested in politics and was for more than forty years perhaps the closest friend Henry Clay had in Virginia. Brooke kept Clay informed of changing events in Virginia and advised him on campaign strategy, and Clay looked after Brooke's western land investments, acquired in part as a result of his Revolutionary War service. Brooke completed a brief autobiography early in 1849. Much of it deals with his Revolutionary War experiences and recalls some of the most famous Virginians of that period. Curiously, it does not mention his long friendship with Clay or treat his forty-seven-year career as a judge. Francis Taliaferro Brooke died at Saint Julien on 3 March 1851 and was buried there.

Francis T. Brooke, *A Narrative of My Life; for My Family* (1849); *Virginia State Bar Association Proceedings* (1928): 407–422; 1847 prose portrait by John S. Skinner in *VMHB* 80 (1972): 172–174; Manarin, *Senate Officers*, 36–39 (por.); Brooke family papers, VHS; Brooke correspondence with Henry Clay in *Clay Papers*; *Hunter* v. *Martin* (1814) (4 Munford), *Virginia Reports*, 18:16–25; Hall, *Portraits*, 32–33 (por.); will and estate inventory in Spotsylvania Co. Will Book, T:212–213, 283–287; obituaries in *Richmond Daily Times*, 8 Mar. 1851, *Richmond Enquirer* and *Rich-*

mond Whig and Public Advertiser, both 11 Mar. 1851, and *Virginia Historical Register* 4 (1851): 116–117.

BRENT TARTER

BROOKE, George (d. 7 April 1782), member of the Convention of 1776 and treasurer of Virginia, was born probably sometime during the 1720s at the King William County residence of his parents, Humphrey Brooke, a prominent local merchant who died in 1738, and Elizabeth Braxton Brooke, the daughter of another notable merchant, George Braxton (ca. 1677–1748). His younger brother Humphrey Brooke represented Fauquier County in the Convention of 1788. About 1749 Brooke married Anne (or Hannah) Tunstall. They had at least two sons and four daughters. She died on 25 March 1779.

About the time of his marriage Brooke moved to King and Queen County and formed a mercantile partnership with one of his Tunstall kinsmen. He operated the business alone after October 1769. For many years Brooke was deeply involved in the effort to clear up the complicated affairs of his Braxton relations following the death in 1749 of his uncle, the second George Braxton. Brooke's growing reputation as a reliable man of business resulted in his being engaged in 1767 as agent by the administrators of the tangled and politically sensitive estate of Speaker John Robinson (1705–1766).

Brooke owned approximately 777 acres of land in King William County. In 1764 he acquired and thereafter lived at Mantapike, a plantation of more than 1,500 acres in King and Queen County. Brooke was probably appointed to the King and Queen County Court for the first time early in the 1750s and was a member of the quorum by 1765. He was elected to the House of Burgesses in 1765, 1771, and 1774. Brooke sat on the Committee for Courts of Justice during his first term, on the Committee of Propositions and Grievances in his second, and the Committees of Propositions and Grievances and for Trade during his last.

During the 1770s Brooke took part in all of the local committees formed to enforce the associations that the Virginia Revolutionary Conventions and the Continental Congress adopted to try to force Parliament to repeal the obnoxious taxes and other laws that eventually brought on the American Revolution. As a burgess he was eligible to attend the first Virginia Convention in August 1774. Brooke was elected to the other four conventions, although bad weather delayed the election for the fifth and final convention in King and Queen County. He consequently took his seat a month late and missed the 15 May 1776 vote on independence, but he served on the Committee of Propositions and Grievances and was present when the convention unanimously adopted the Virginia Declaration of Rights on 12 June and the first constitution of Virginia on 29 June 1776. Brooke served as paymaster to the 1st and 2d Virginia Regiments in 1775 and 1776 and to the 7th and 8th Virginia Regiments during the spring of 1776.

In August 1776 Brooke was elected to the Senate of Virginia to represent the district comprising Essex, King and Queen, and King William Counties. He served until the spring of 1779, when for some undisclosed reason he was declared ineligible. On 23 December 1779 the General Assembly elected him treasurer of Virginia. Brooke began his work four days later and held office through the tumultuous final years of the Revolutionary War. He supervised the transfer of the state's treasury and its records to the new capital of Richmond in the spring of 1780, and he attempted to hold the fiscal affairs of the state together in 1781 after British raids dispersed the government's officers and scattered its records. George Brooke died of apoplexy in Richmond on 7 April 1782. He may have been buried at Mantapike.

St. George Tucker Brooke, "The Brooke Family of Virginia," *VMHB* 11 (1903): 202–203, and 14 (1907): 436–437; numerous references in the *Williamsburg Virginia Gazette*s and in *Revolutionary Virginia*, esp. 6:348, 7:23, 29, 212, 349; *JHD*, 1779 sess., 128; Braxton and Robinson estate records and copy of will in *Richard Brooke* v. *William H. Macon et al.* suit papers, U.S. Circuit Court Record Book, vol. 17, LVA; will printed in *VMHB* 11 (1903): 95, 200–202; death notices in *Richmond Virginia Gazette, or the American Advertiser* and *Richmond Virginia Gazette, and Weekly Advertiser*, both 13 Apr. 1782.

DAPHNE GENTRY

BROOKE, George Doswell (15 September 1878–23 August 1982), railroad executive and president of the Chesapeake and Ohio Railway

Company, was born at Sutherlin in Pittsylvania County, the son of Thomas Vaden Brooke, a physician, and Fanny Baylor Doswell Brooke. Like his father, George D. Brooke attended the Virginia Military Institute. He graduated first in the class of 1900 and won the Jackson-Hope Medal, First Honor, for academic achievement.

Brooke taught mathematics and military tactics for two years at Culver Military Academy in Indiana and then went to work in 1902 for the Baltimore and Ohio Railroad. He quickly rose in the organization as a civil engineer and transportation manager and from 1919 to 1924 served as superintendent of transportation in Cincinnati. In 1924 Brooke moved to Richmond as an assistant to the vice president of the Chesapeake and Ohio Railway Company. In 1926 he was appointed general manager and was promoted to a vice presidency in 1930. In December 1936 Brooke was named executive vice president of the C&O. Brooke succeeded William Johnson Harahan as president of the C&O in December 1937 and relocated to Shaker Heights, Ohio, near the corporation's administrative headquarters in Cleveland. Brooke soon thereafter assumed the presidencies of the Pere Marquette Railroad and the New York, Chicago, and Saint Louis Railroad, usually called the Nickel Plate, two railroads in which the C&O owned controlling interests. In April 1938 he was elected to the board of directors of the Erie Railroad. By then Brooke's annual salary was $60,000, in addition to income from his other investments. He sat on the boards of directors of the First and Merchants National Bank in Richmond, the Belt Railway Company of Chicago, the Norfolk and Portsmouth Belt Line Railroad, and the Cincinnati Union Depot and Terminals Company.

It was not a propitious time for someone with a civil engineering background rather than experience in high finance to be placed in charge of a major national network of railroads. All of the lines for which Brooke was responsible were in financial difficulty during the Great Depression of the 1930s, and the C&O was a valuable asset that at least two major groups of investors were trying to take over and control. One of them was under the direction of Robert Ralph Young. In May 1939 Brooke managed to oust Young

from the chairmanship of the board of the Nickel Plate, but Young gained control of the C&O and its subsidiary lines and in December 1942 forced Brooke's retirement from the presidencies of all three railroads. By then Brooke's salary was $75,000 per annum, and his severance agreement gave him a retirement salary of $20,000 a year plus a $25,000 retainer to serve as a consultant. Both payments were cut off in February 1943, however, when Brooke became chairman of the board of the Virginian Railway Company.

Brooke moved to Norfolk and lived in Tidewater Virginia for the remainder of his life. The Virginian was a major freight-hauling line that operated almost six hundred miles of track from Norfolk through southern Virginia into the coalfields of Virginia and West Virginia. For a few months in 1944 Brooke served as acting president, as well as chairman, until he brought in Frank Dunnington Beale, a former associate from the C&O, to replace Carl Bucholtz as the president of the Virginian. They remained in office until late in 1959, when the Norfolk and Western Railway Company absorbed the Virginian Railway in a major merger that substantially increased the Norfolk and Western's trackage in the coalfields and strengthened its competitive position with respect to the Chesapeake and Ohio. Following the merger, Brooke retired.

Brooke had married Sue Scott Herbert, of Alexandria, on 14 June 1906, when he was living in Cumberland, Maryland. They had two sons and three daughters. After his retirement Brooke lived in Virginia Beach, where he tended his vegetable garden, helped found the Virginia Beach General Hospital, and played golf as often as possible. Until he had to give up the game at age ninety-seven, he frequently shot his age or better, and at age eighty-six he made a hole in one at the Princess Anne Country Club. Brooke served for twenty-three years on the board of the VMI Foundation and was its president from 1946 to 1949. For his hundredth-birthday party, the VMI color guard traveled to Norfolk to salute him as the institute's oldest living alumnus. George Doswell Brooke died at his home in Virginia Beach on 23 August 1982 and was buried in the Eastern Shore Chapel Cemetery in that city.

James M. Morgan Jr., *The Jackson-Hope and the Society of the Cincinnati Medals of the Virginia Military Institute: Biographical Sketches of All Recipients, 1877–1977* (1979), 77–79 (por.); feature articles in *Richmond Times-Dispatch*, 30 Dec. 1937, *Commonwealth* 5 (Feb. 1938): 25, and *VMI Alumni Review* 55 (fall 1978): 13; BVS Birth Register, Pittsylvania Co.; BVS Marriage Register, Alexandria City; Charles W. Turner, *Chessie's Road* (1956), 199–227; *New York Times*, 11 May 1939; *Richmond Times-Dispatch*, 16 Dec. 1942, 28 July 1944; obituaries in *Norfolk Ledger-Star*, 24 Aug. 1982 (por.), and *Norfolk Virginian-Pilot* and *Richmond Times-Dispatch*, both 25 Aug. 1982; memorial in *VMI Alumni Review* 59 (fall 1982): 45.

BRENT TARTER

BROOKE, Humphrey (d. by 24 May 1802), clerk of the Senate of Virginia and member of the Convention of 1788, was born probably in King William County sometime between September 1728 and 1738. His parents were Humphrey Brooke, a locally prominent merchant who died in 1738, and Elizabeth Braxton Brooke, daughter of another influential merchant, George Braxton (ca. 1677–1748). His elder brother George Brooke was a member of the Convention of 1776. Nothing is known about Brooke's education, but he probably served an apprenticeship in the office of the secretary of the colony in Williamsburg before being appointed first clerk of the new county of Fauquier in the spring of 1759.

Late in 1760 Brooke purchased a 568-acre farm in Fauquier County. He sold part of it two years later and for most of his life paid taxes on holdings ranging from 150 to 400 acres. By the 1780s Brooke owned about twenty slaves, and the number once reached twenty-seven, probably more than were necessary to work his land. He may have leased some of his bondsmen to his neighbors. Before June 1763 Brooke married Ann Whiting, and they had three sons and five daughters. After her death and sometime before March 1793 he married Mildred Tomkies, a widow from Gloucester County. They had no children.

When Leeds Parish was created in 1770 Brooke was one of its first vestrymen. He was also a militia officer and served as county lieutenant during the Revolutionary War. Even though he never served in the General Assembly, Brooke became known well enough in Rich-mond, where his brother had been treasurer of the state from 1779 to 1782, that on 12 November 1785 he was elected clerk of the Senate of Virginia. He served until his death nearly seventeen years later. On 24 March 1788 Brooke and Martin Pickett easily defeated two other candidates in the election to represent Fauquier County in a state convention called to consider the proposed constitution of the United States. Brooke did not speak in the debates, but he opposed requiring amendments before ratification and voted to ratify the Constitution on 25 June 1788.

Brooke also served as clerk of the district court that met in Dumfries between March and December 1789, when one of his sons succeeded him. On 25 March 1793 he resigned after thirty-four years as clerk of Fauquier County in favor of another son. He also retired from the management of his farm about that time. Humphrey Brooke dated his will on 17 April 1802 and died before 24 May 1802, when the will was proved in court.

Manarin, *Senate Officers*, 295–296, and St. George Tucker Brooke, "The Brooke Family of Virginia," *VMHB* 15 (1907): 201–202, both contain some inaccuracies; Fauquier Co. Minute Book (1759–1762), 1–2, and (1791–1793), 323; Land and Personal Property Tax Returns, Fauquier Co., 1782–1802, RG 48, LVA; T. Triplett Russell and John K. Gott, *Fauquier County in the Revolution* (1976), 16, 26, 33, 50, 179, 255–256, 393; *JSV*, 1785–1786 sess., 6; Kaminski, *Ratification*, 9:587–588, 10:1539, 1540, 1556, 1565; Fauquier Co. Will Book, 3:380, 388–390.

DAPHNE GENTRY

BROOKE, James Vass (10 October 1824–9 October 1898), member of the second and third sessions of the Convention of 1861, was born in Falmouth in Stafford County, the son of William Brooke, a merchant, and Jane Morrison Brooke, a native of Scotland. He was named for his mother's half brother James Vass, a Fredericksburg merchant. Following study at a private school Brooke began to read law in 1841 with Richard Cassius Lee Moncure and supported himself by keeping accounts for various Fredericksburg merchants. In 1842 Brooke moved to Warrenton and continued to read law in the office of Samuel Chilton, his brother-in-law and soon to be a Whig congressman.

Brooke qualified as an attorney on 26 September 1843 and began a fifty-five-year practice in Warrenton that earned him a widespread reputation for ability and integrity. For more than four decades he also served variously as alderman, recorder, or mayor of Warrenton. During Brooke's many years on the town council Warrenton installed modern streetlights and waterworks. He served as superintendent of the Sunday school of the Warrenton Presbyterian Church for twenty-five years, frequently attended the district general assembly, and filled the pulpit more than once when the church was without a pastor.

Brooke was an admirer of Henry Clay. Following the demise of the Whig Party he took an active part in the American (Know Nothing) Party and was its state secretary in 1855. In January 1861 Brooke announced his candidacy for the state convention that had been called to consider the secession crisis. He spoke against secession for more than thirty minutes at a public meeting at the Fauquier County courthouse on 28 January 1861, but he withdrew his name before the election. On 19 June 1861, following the death of John Quincy Marr, one of the Fauquier delegates, Brooke defeated former governor William "Extra Billy" Smith by a vote of 598 to 506 to succeed Marr in the convention. Brooke attended the final seven days of the twenty-day second session, which adjourned on 1 July, and the entire third session that met from 13 November through 6 December 1861. While in Richmond he signed the Ordinance of Secession that had been adopted on 17 April, an act that led some later writers to misconstrue his role during the secession crisis.

In March 1862 Brooke organized and became captain of Company A of the 12th Battalion, Virginia Light Artillery. While his company was on duty in the lower part of the Shenandoah Valley late in 1862, he broke his ankle. Brooke nevertheless participated in the Battle of Chancellorsville in May 1863. Surgeons ruled that his disability prevented further military service, and on 24 July 1863, after his battery's participation in the Battle of Gettysburg, he resigned his commission. Almost as soon as he returned home Brooke was elected to represent Fauquier County in the House of Delegates. He served in the three assembly sessions held between September 1863 and the end of the war. Brooke was assigned the ranking position on the Committee for Courts of Justice and also sat on the Committee to Examine the Bonds of Public Officers.

Brooke resumed his law practice at the end of the war and in 1866 formed a partnership with Robert Taylor Scott, later elected attorney general of Virginia. Their extensive practice carried them into the courts of the counties surrounding Fauquier as well as the Virginia Supreme Court of Appeals and the United States Supreme Court. Brooke remained active in politics and in 1871 was elected to a two-year term in the House of Delegates on a platform critical of the Funding Act of 1871. He chaired the Committee for Courts of Justice, which in 1873 recommended publication of George Wythe Munford's revision of the state code. Brooke emerged as one of the Conservative Party's leading assemblymen and in August 1873 became a member of the party's state committee.

In 1877 Brooke was elected to the Senate of Virginia for a two-year term from the district composed of Fauquier and Rappahannock Counties. He served on the important Committees for Courts of Justice and on Finance and on the minor Committee to Examine the Bonds of Public Officers. Settlement of the huge prewar state debt remained the most controversial and important issue in state politics. Brooke took a middle position between those called Funders, who advocated paying the full principal and interest, and those called Readjusters, who wished to reduce the principal and refinance the debt at a lower rate. On 17 January 1878 he introduced a bill that provided for a small readjustment of the public debt but retained some features of the Funding Act of 1871, such as making the interest coupons on the debt redeemable for state taxes. Brooke's bill passed the Senate on 7 February but died in the House of Delegates. On 20 February 1878 he voted for the so-called Barbour Bill that provided for a more extensive readjustment of the debt, but the governor vetoed it. Brooke did not seek reelection in 1879 and left the Senate before the end of the protracted political controversy over the debt question. For the remainder of his life he was a Democrat.

On 22 May 1844 Brooke married Mary Elizabeth Norris, of Warrenton. Their two daughters and four sons included Richard Norris Brooke, a noted artist. Mary Elizabeth Norris Brooke died at their Warrenton home in April 1879, and James Vass Brooke died there of pleurisy on 9 October 1898. He was buried in the Warrenton Cemetery.

French Biographies; Annie G. Day, *Warrenton and Fauquier County, Virginia* (1908), 28 (por.); James V. Brooke, "Ancestry and Biography of Hon. James Vass Brooke, of Warrenton, Va.," in Fauquier Historical Society *Bulletin* 4 (1924): 460–467 (por.); Fauquier Co. Marriage Bonds and Returns, 5:299; *Warrenton Flag of '98,* 24 Jan., 27 June 1861; Compiled Service Records; Michael J. Andrus, *The Brooke, Fauquier, Loudoun and Alexandria Artillery* (1990), 21–30, 100; *Richmond Dispatch*, 22 Jan.–8 Feb. 1878; Partnership Matters of Brooke and Scott (ledger), LVA; Brooke law practice documents in various collections, VHS; obituary in *Richmond Dispatch*, 11 Oct. 1898; memorial in *Virginia State Bar Association Proceedings* (1899): 106–108.

DAPHNE GENTRY

BROOKE, John Mercer (18 December 1826– 14 December 1906), naval officer, was born at Fort Brooke on the shores of Tampa Bay, Florida, the son of George Mercer Brooke, a career army officer, and Lucy Thomas Brooke, of Duxbury, Massachusetts. His great-grandfather George Brooke served in the Convention of 1776. Brooke grew up at a series of frontier army posts. His mother died in 1839 and on 3 March 1841 he entered the navy as an acting midshipman at the age of fourteen. After spending several years sailing on routine cruises, Brooke graduated in 1847 from the United States Naval Academy as a member of its first class.

Brooke was assigned to the Coast Survey in 1849. On 6 November of that year he married Mary Elizabeth Selden Garnett, of Norfolk, whose brother Richard Brooke Garnett later became a Confederate general and died at Gettysburg. Of their four children, only one daughter survived infancy. Brooke's next assignment was to the African Squadron, and he found the separation from his wife difficult. Returning to the United States in 1851, he worked at the Naval Observatory in Washington, D.C., under the command and keen eye of Matthew Fontaine Maury. At the observatory Brooke invented a deep-sea sounding lead that first made it possible to determine depth accurately and to map and bring up sediment from the deep ocean floor. His sounding work won him the Prussian Gold Medal of Science in 1861, although his resignation from the navy delayed his receipt of the medal until 1867.

In 1853 Brooke was assigned to a surveying and exploring expedition in the North Pacific Ocean. He made soundings with his deep-sea lead and determined the precise position of many places in the vast area traversed. Lieutenant John Rodgers, whom Brooke admired, took command of the expedition at Hong Kong shortly after Matthew C. Perry opened Japan for limited trade with the United States. Rodgers directed Brooke to survey the east coast of Japan from Shimoda to Hakodate. Brooke later landed on the Chukchi Peninsula of Siberia to make observations. He was promoted to lieutenant on 22 October 1855 and returned the next year to Washington, where he helped prepare the expedition's charts and improved the design of his deep-sea lead.

In 1858 Brooke undertook to survey the best steamship route between San Francisco and Hong Kong. He erased hundreds of reported or imaginary dangers from the old charts. Brooke also hoped to survey the recently opened Japanese ports, but shortly after arriving at Yokohama a terrific storm drove his ship ashore, and an investigation revealed that it was not worth salvaging. Brooke returned home in 1860 aboard the Japanese naval vessel that escorted that nation's first diplomatic mission to the United States.

Brooke resumed work on his charts, but following Virginia's secession he resigned his naval commission on 20 April 1861. Not himself a defender of slavery, his wife strongly influenced his decision to side with Virginia. Brooke was commissioned a lieutenant first in the Virginia State Navy on 23 April 1861 and subsequently in the Confederate States Navy on 2 May 1861. He began as a naval aide to the Virginia commander, Robert Edward Lee. Brooke immediately recognized the need for ironclad ships to break the Union blockade of Confederate ports.

After writing to the Confederate secretary of the navy, he received orders to draw up plans for an ironclad. Brooke designed a casemated vessel with extended submerged ends. The latter unique feature earned him a Confederate patent. To save time, the navy decided to make use of the former USS *Merrimack*, a steamship that had been scuttled near Norfolk. Brooke secured iron plates from the Tredegar ironworks in Richmond and devised heavy rifled ordnance for the ship, which was renamed the CSS *Virginia*. A prolonged dispute later erupted between Brooke and John Luke Porter, the naval constructor, over credit for the design. Stephen R. Mallory, the secretary of the navy, sided with Brooke.

In November 1861 Brooke received responsibility for examining all improvements proposed for the ordnance and equipment of naval vessels. He was promoted to commander on 13 September 1862, and in March 1863 he became chief of the Bureau of Ordnance and Hydrography. Meanwhile Brooke had begun designing rifled cannons and smoothbores. He reinforced cast-iron muzzleloaders with wrought-iron bands shrunk onto the barrel. The Brooke guns, as they were known, became the most powerful in the Confederacy. From a personal point of view the war years were sad for Brooke. Two of his young daughters died, and on 14 June 1864 his wife died of consumption.

After the war Brooke quickly renewed contacts with former colleagues in the United States Navy, and he applied for and in August 1866 received a presidential pardon. He joined the faculty of the Virginia Military Institute in October 1865 as professor of practical astronomy, geodesy, meteorology, and physical geography. Brooke firmly believed that the South had to educate its young men in order to recover economically. He taught at the institute until he retired in June 1899.

Soon after the war Brooke, Robert Minor, and Catesby Jones formed a company to supply foreign governments with naval ordnance and materièl, but they accomplished little. Brooke also tried unsuccessfully to augment his meager income through inventions. He wrote articles on naval ordnance late in the 1870s, and in 1879 he received a one-year appointment to the board of visitors of the United States Naval Academy.

On 14 March 1871 Brooke married Kate Corbin Pendleton, the widow of Alexander "Sandie" Swift Pendleton. They had two sons and one daughter. John Mercer Brooke died of a stroke in Lexington on 14 December 1906 and was buried in the Lexington Presbyterian Church Cemetery (later the Stonewall Jackson Memorial Cemetery).

George M. Brooke Jr., *John M. Brooke, Naval Scientist and Educator* (1980), includes pors., cites official reports, and lists principal publications; Tyler, *Men of Mark*, 1:43–45; *NCAB*, 22:29; George M. Brooke Jr., *John M. Brooke's Pacific Cruise and Japanese Adventure, 1858–1860* (1986); Norfolk City Hustings and Corporation Court Marriage Bonds, 5 Nov. 1849 (first marriage); Fredericksburg Marriage Register (second marriage); John Mercer Brooke papers in author's possession (2001); Presidential Pardons; obituary in *Lexington Rockbridge County News*, 20 Dec. 1906.

GEORGE MERCER BROOKE JR.

BROOKE, Richard Norris (20 October 1847–25 April 1920), painter, was the son of James Vass Brooke and Mary Elizabeth Norris Brooke. He was born in Warrenton, where his father was a prominent lawyer and politician. Brooke attended the Warrenton Academy and then went to Philadelphia in October 1865 to study painting at the Pennsylvania Academy of Fine Arts. He also taught art at different academies in that city between 1866 and 1870. In September 1871 Virginia Military Institute's board of visitors selected Brooke as head of the Department of Fine Arts. Brooke assisted the regular teacher of the drawing classes, but a lack of funds put an end to more ambitious plans for art instruction at the institute, and he left after a year.

In May 1873 Brooke received a recess appointment as United States consul in La Rochelle, France, thanks to his fellow Warrentonian John Singleton Mosby, whose support for President Ulysses S. Grant in 1872 had given him a say in some federal patronage decisions. Brooke was not a Republican and, at Mosby's suggestion, hastily wrote to his mother explaining the opportunity and assuring her that his political views had not changed. After being recommissioned in February 1874, Brooke remained in that post until the consulate was closed in mid-August 1876. He then entered the

Paris studio of Léon Bonnat, a Realist painter and teacher whose American pupils had included Thomas Eakins. Brooke returned to Virginia in 1879 and in December 1880 moved to Washington, D.C.

Brooke concentrated at first on painting genre scenes of African American life, using people and places in Warrenton as his models. He later stated that he had been inspired by Jules Breton, a French painter of peasant life. The best known of these works is *The Pastoral Visit* (1881). The Corcoran Gallery of Art in Washington later purchased the painting, which is generally dismissed today as nostalgic and patronizing. Brooke's *Incoming Tide* is also in that collection. Other works from this period include *The Dog Swap*, first exhibited in 1881 and now at the National Museum of American Art, and a copy of William D. Washington's portrait of John Marshall, originally painted for the Fauquier County courthouse and now in the collection of the United States Capitol. Brooke's full-length portrait of Pocahontas, based on the Booton Hall likeness and painted about 1905, belongs to the Virginia Museum of Fine Arts in Richmond, and a *Virginia Scene* (ca. 1910) is owned by the Virginia Historical Society.

Brooke's genre paintings did not sell well. Although he also painted portraits and landscapes, his main contribution came as a teacher and artistic leader in the capital. In 1885 he helped to found the Art Students' League of Washington and taught there for several years. For fifteen years he was president of the Society of Washington Artists, founded in 1890, which sponsored highly regarded annual exhibitions. Brooke became vice principal of the Corcoran School of Art in 1901 and remained on its faculty until ill health forced his retirement in 1918.

Brooke traveled regularly to Europe, several times in the employ of a wealthy collector for whom he purchased Dutch masterworks. During a particularly lengthy European stay from 1887 through 1889, he spent a year studying in Paris under the painter Benjamin Constant. Brooke's paintings won prizes at the Atlanta Exposition in 1895 and at the annual exhibitions of the Society of Washington Artists in 1901 and 1904.

Brooke regularly visited family members in Warrenton and was present on 15 November 1889 to help rescue the town's portrait of John Marshall from a fire at the courthouse. A deeply religious member of the Presbyterian Church, he returned to Warrenton weekly from May 1896 to January 1897 to lead mission services at the Baptist church. In 1899 Brooke established a studio in Warrenton for painting during the summers.

Brooke never married. When his health failed in his last year, he unsuccessfully sought relief in the mountains at Asheville, North Carolina. Richard Norris Brooke returned to the home of a niece in Warrenton and died there on 25 April 1920. His funeral was held at the Presbyterian church, and he was buried in the Warrenton Cemetery.

Birth date in French Biographies and on gravestone; Annie G. Day, *Warrenton and Fauquier County, Virginia* (1908), 28 (por.); William Couper, *One Hundred Years at V.M.I.* (1939), 3:202–203, 232; John Singleton Mosby to Joseph Bryan, 30 Jan. 1904, in *The Letters of John S. Mosby*, ed. Adele H. Mitchell (1986), 128; Jessie J. Poesch, "Growth and Development of the Old South, 1830 to 1900," in *Painting in the South, 1564–1980* (1983), 91–93; Guy C. McElroy, *Facing History: The Black Image in American Art, 1710–1940* (1990), 93; Marie Louise Evans, *An Old Timer in Warrenton and Fauquier County, Virginia* (1955), 34–36; Leila Mechlin, "Art Life in Washington," *Records of the Columbia Historical Society* 24 (1922): 174–181; James C. Kelly and William M. S. Rasmussen, *The Virginia Landscape: A Cultural History* (2000), 37; Rasmussen and Robert S. Tilton, *Pocahontas: Her Life and Legend* (1994), 33–34; Peter Hastings Falk, ed., *Who Was Who in American Art* (1985), 79; *Warrenton True Index*, 21 May 1887, 13 Mar. 1892, 9 May 1896–30 Jan. 1897; Lee Moffett, *The Diary of Court House Square, Warrenton, Virginia, U.S.A.* (1988), 59, 63, 68; Nancy Chappelear Baird and Carol Jordan, *Fauquier County, Virginia, Tombstone Inscriptions* (1994), 1:155; obituaries in *Richmond Times-Dispatch*, 26 Apr. 1920, *Warrenton Fauquier Democrat*, 1 May 1920 (birth date given as 10 Oct. 1847), and *American Art Annual* 17 (1920): 265.

BETTY A. STACY

BROOKE, Robert (d. 27 February 1800), governor and attorney general of Virginia, was born probably in Spotsylvania County about 1760, the son of Richard Brooke and his first wife, Ann Hay Taliaferro Brooke. About 1774 he and an elder brother traveled to Edinburgh, Scotland, to attend the university. When the American

Revolution began they were temporarily stranded and unable to get back to Virginia. Brooke may have studied law before he returned via France in the autumn of 1780. He immediately joined a volunteer cavalry troop and was captured at Westham during the British invasion of Virginia in January 1781.

In the autumn of 1781 Brooke opened a law office in Spotsylvania County. By 1785 he had moved his office to Fredericksburg and taken one of his younger brothers as a partner. Brooke purchased a small farm just west of Fredericksburg in June 1786 and later built a stately mansion on the property that a subsequent owner named Federal Hill. In that same year Brooke married Mary Ritchie Hopper, the daughter of Archibald Ritchie and the widow of William Hopper. They had one son.

In 1791 Brooke won election to the House of Delegates from Spotsylvania County, and he was reelected in 1792, 1793, and 1794. He was quickly recognized as one of the ablest young men in the assembly. During his third year Brooke chaired the Committee of Privileges and Elections, served as ranking member of the Committees of Propositions and Grievances, of Religion, and for Courts of Justice, and was third in seniority on the Committee of Claims. During his fourth year he again chaired the Committee of Privileges and Elections, was ranking member on the Committees for Courts of Justice and of Propositions and Grievances, and was fourth in seniority on the Committees of Claims and of Religion.

Brooke's fourth year in the assembly was dramatic. Governor Henry "Light-Horse Harry" Lee left the state to command the federal army assembled to quell the Whiskey Rebellion, and in his absence his political enemies declared the office of governor vacant. On 20 November 1794 the assembly elected Brooke the new governor by a vote of 90 to 60 over veteran Council president James Wood. Brooke was reelected without opposition for a second one-year term on 26 November 1795. His two years as governor were relatively quiet ones for the executive, and during his occupancy of a position with few independent powers, he made no significant

attempt to alter the status quo. Brooke's wife died on 5 July 1796.

On 16 November 1796, with many members mistakenly anticipating that Patrick Henry would become the next governor, the assembly elected Brooke attorney general. His close friendship with James Monroe and other Virginians who supported Thomas Jefferson for the presidency in 1796 placed Brooke squarely in the emerging Republican Party, and its members gave him an 89 to 71 vote victory over Bushrod Washington, a Federalist some members regarded as better qualified. When some friends attempted to persuade Robert Brooke and his younger brother Francis Taliaferro Brooke to run for Congress in 1797, they both declined rather than risk losing the income from their private law practices.

As attorney general, Brooke was able to practice law and earn a private income at the same time. He held the relatively undemanding office of attorney general for the remainder of his life. The young men who assisted him and studied law in his office included Henry Clay. In 1796 the assembly formed a new county out of Ohio County in the northwestern part of the state and named it Brooke County. Brooke was an active Freemason. In November 1795 he was elected grand master of the Grand Lodge of Virginia to succeed John Marshall, and he was elected to a second term the next year.

By the summer of 1798 Brooke was heavily in debt, probably from serving as security on loans of his brother-in-law Fontaine Maury. Monroe called on several influential Republican friends to assist Brooke, and with their help he paid off his most insistent creditors. Robert Brooke died in Fredericksburg on 27 February 1800, a few months before his benefactors finished paying the rest of his creditors.

Francis T. Brooke, *A Narrative of My Life; for My Family* (1849), 7–9, 56; *NCAB*, 5:443, and several other references give birth year as 1751, but a date ca. 1760 is more consistent with Brooke's birth order, educational history, and participation in the American Revolution; St. George Tucker Brooke, "The Brooke Family," *VMHB* 19 (1911): 100–101, 320, gives approximate birth date of 1761; Richard R. Beeman, *The Old Dominion and the New Nation, 1788–1791* (1972), 136–137; Norman K. Risjord, *Chesapeake Politics, 1781–1800* (1978), 448, 513–514, 664;

Virginia Gazette, and Richmond Chronicle, 21 Nov. 1794; *Madison: Congressional Series*, 15:407, 16:414, 445, 17:253–254; *Richmond Virginia Gazette, and General Advertiser*, 6 July 1796; Thomas Evans to John Cropper, 6 Dec. 1796, John Cropper Papers, VHS; debts described in Brooke to James Monroe, 29 Aug. 1798, James Monroe Papers, LC; John Dove, *Proceedings of the M. W. Grand Lodge of Ancient York Masons of the State of Virginia, from Its Organization, in 1778, to 1822* (1874), por. of son Richard Brooke, adapted to represent Robert Brooke, facing 1:138; death notices in *Fredericksburg Virginia Herald*, 28 Feb. 1800, and *Richmond Virginia Argus*, 7 Mar. 1800.

DAPHNE GENTRY

BROOKS, Albert Royal (ca. 1817–15 July 1881), businessman, was born in Chesterfield County, the son of Peggy Henderson, a slave. As a young man he was hired out to a tobacco manufacturer in Richmond, a pivotal event that introduced Brooks to a milieu in which slaves could earn money and a few earned enough to purchase their freedom. Hardworking, ambitious, and lucky, Brooks was among those few. He was permitted to hire his own time, a common though illegal practice whereby slaves negotiated paid employment, their owners received a fixed payment, and the slaves kept leftover earnings. Using money from his factory labors and a second job as a driver, A. R. Brooks, as his name usually appears, invested in an eating house and a hack and livery stable.

Brooks married Lucy Goode, another Richmond slave, on 2 February 1839. They set up house in the city, joined fellow Richmond blacks in forming the First African Baptist Church when that congregation split from the First Baptist Church in 1841, and had at least five sons and four daughters, of whom four sons and three daughters survived early childhood. Two sons, Prince Albert Brooks and Robert Peel Brooks, were named for prominent British figures of the day. The death of Lucy Brooks's master in 1858 threatened the dispersal of the family among the decedent's heirs. She persuaded local buyers to purchase four children and allow them to remain in Richmond. One buyer reneged, however, and sold the eldest daughter, Margaret Ann Brooks, to an owner in Tennessee, where she died in 1862. At Albert Brooks's urging, Daniel Von Groning, a tobacco merchant and diplomat, purchased Lucy Brooks and the younger children and kept them in Richmond.

Brooks reported in 1865 that he had purchased his own freedom for $1,100, perhaps during the Civil War because he was not listed as free in censuses taken in 1850 or 1860. The emancipation of the rest of his family can be dated exactly. Von Groning freed Lucy Brooks and her young children on 21 October 1862, following the receipt of $800 from Albert Brooks, and the United States Army freed the remaining children on 3 April 1865. Although Albert Brooks's good fortune depended in part on vital white support and protection, his success in conducting businesses while enslaved and his purchase of freedom for himself and other family members were indisputably heroic feats attesting to remarkable industry, self-discipline, talent, and tact.

Although it brought freedom, the war nearly ruined Brooks economically. Confederate authorities confiscated or destroyed most of his equipment, and by 1865 his working stock had been reduced to three hacks and one horse. His business was further threatened in June 1865 when police of Richmond's freshly restored civilian government arrested him for failing to procure a pass signed by a white person. Caught in a joint police and army campaign to expel African American refugees from the city using the pass laws of the slavery regime, Brooks and a dozen other prominent Richmond blacks swore depositions accusing the authorities of reimposing slavery on the only truly loyal element in Richmond. A large gathering held in the First African Baptist Church chose seven local black men and a reporter from the *New York Tribune* to take those depositions and a protest statement to President Andrew Johnson. The city administration was subsequently deposed, and the oppressive pass and curfew laws were repealed.

The ambivalent civil rights record of Presidential Reconstruction weighed heavily on Richmond freedpeople, and they cheered the northern electorate's massive repudiation of Johnson and his policies late in 1866. A cautious optimism, a sense that the liberating work begun with Emancipation would soon resume, swept over the black community and energized Brooks. With James Hunnicutt, the leading white radical in the city and editor of the *New Nation*, Brooks traveled to Washington, D.C., in January 1867 to present Republican congressmen with a petition signed by 2,400 Richmonders calling for the enactment of universal suffrage. That spring he sat on the racially mixed petit jury considering treason charges against Jefferson Davis. Brooks was simultaneously active in the Republican Party, which was being formed as a mass political organization in Virginia. He served as a delegate to the party's first convention in Richmond in April 1867. At a nominating meeting six months later Jefferson Ward Republicans unsuccessfully proposed Brooks as a candidate for the state constitutional convention. The Republican slate won but managed to attract only a handful of white Richmond voters. Alarmed by their party's weak showing with whites and by the division of white Unionists into warring camps, several black Republicans, including Brooks, called on white Unionists to bury their differences and join them in building a powerful, biracial, and progressive Republican Party in Virginia. Despite its eloquence their appeal failed.

Brooks withdrew from public involvement in Republican affairs in 1868, apparently for financial rather than ideological reasons. His businesses depended on white customers, and Republican activists were frequently threatened with economic reprisals for their political actions. Scores of Richmond tobacco workers lost their jobs for voting Republican late in 1867. Brooks may also have feared that his exposed political position jeopardized friendships with whites that had proved valuable in the past. In any event, he retreated from the political stage after 1867. Brooks and his family remained warm supporters and beneficiaries of such basic Reconstruction principles as universal suffrage, equal justice, public education, black uplift, and civil rights.

Brooks's real estate holdings were valued at $2,000 in 1870 and $1,700 in 1880. A successful businessman and deacon of the First African Baptist Church, Brooks supported his wife's philanthropic endeavors and his children's educational aspirations. Lucy Goode Brooks was a moving force behind the establishment of the Friends' Asylum for Colored Orphans in 1867. Brooks sent his youngest sons, Walter Henderson Brooks and Robert Peel Brooks, to high school,

college, and professional school. The former became an outstanding Baptist minister in Washington, D.C., and the latter was one of the first black lawyers admitted to the bar in Richmond. The youngest daughters, Alberta Maria Brooks and Lucy Gertrude Brooks, were educated in Richmond public schools, a legacy of Reconstruction, and became teachers. Having lived to see his family free and prospering, Albert Royal Brooks died at his home on 15 July 1881 and was buried probably in Union Mechanics Cemetery, one of the Barton Heights cemeteries in Richmond.

Charlotte K. Brooks, Joseph K. Brooks, and Walter H. Brooks III, *A Brooks Chronicle: The Lives and Times of an African-American Family* (1989), pors. on 9, 65; Michael B. Chesson, *Richmond After the War, 1865–1890* (1981), 100; Jackson, *Free Negro Labor*, 77, 179; Brooks's 1865 deposition, Freedmen's Bureau Records; *Richmond Daily Whig*, 24 Jan. 1867; *Organization, Resolutions and Address of the Union Republican State Convention of Virginia, held at Richmond, April 17, 1867* (1867); *Richmond New Nation*, 18 Apr., 10 Oct., 14 Nov. 1867; Freedmen's Bank Records; estate values in Census, Richmond City, 1870, and Land Tax Returns, Richmond City, Madison Ward, 1880, RG 48, LVA; obituaries in *Richmond Dispatch*, 16 July 1881, and *Washington, D.C., People's Advocate*, 30 July 1881.

JOHN T. O'BRIEN

BROOKS, John Mitchell (1 September 1917–8 August 1980), civil rights activist, was born in Braddock, Pennsylvania, the son of William H. Brooks and Jeannette Mitchell Brooks. His parents had moved there from Richmond to obtain work and apparently returned to Richmond by 1922. They died while Brooks was a boy. He grew up in Richmond with his grandparents John M. Mitchell, a laborer, and Sarah Mitchell. Brooks became one of the city's first African American Eagle Scouts. He attended Virginia Union University for one year and West Virginia State College for an additional semester before joining the United States Army as a first lieutenant in November 1943. Brooks served in Italy as a medical assistant, won the Bronze Star, and left the service in June 1946.

After the war Brooks returned to Richmond and opened a restaurant with a friend. About 1947 he married Helen Mae Sampson, a Richmond elementary school teacher. They had one son. While continuing to operate the restaurant,

Brooks began working at a department store owned by Samuel Z. Troy, a Russian Jewish immigrant who quickly recognized his talent and made him assistant manager and then manager of the store. According to his son, Brooks was the first African American in Richmond to manage a white-owned store. Brooks had given up the restaurant by 1951.

During this period Brooks got to know William Lester Banks, executive secretary of the Virginia branch of the National Association for the Advancement of Colored People, and William S. Thornton, a young chiropodist. They became dissatisfied with what they considered the undue caution of local black political organizations in contrast to the activism of the NAACP. The trio's frustration grew as Virginia's white leaders prepared to resist school desegregation. On 9 January 1956 voters approved a referendum that opened the way for state support of private schools and, by implication, the closing of the public schools. Blacks overwhelmingly opposed the referendum, but in Richmond only a minority were registered to vote.

Brooks and Thornton began discussing ways to increase the number of registered voters in the city. William Ferguson Reid, a surgeon, soon joined them. Late in August 1956 they announced a plan to organize the black-majority precincts in the city, with each precinct itself organized by blocks. The plan worked, and, as precincts competed against one another for voters, registrations increased each year. A supporter, Christopher Foster, suggested that the organization be called the Crusade for Voters, and Brooks, the most charismatic public speaker among the founders, became its executive secretary.

To assist the new organization and Brooks, who resigned from the department store, Banks hired him on 1 September 1957 as assistant to the executive secretary, and later as field secretary, for the NAACP and put him in charge of the Virginia conference's own voter registration effort. On 24 March 1958 Brooks was named director of registration and voting for the national NAACP. The South, where whites had devised a variety of methods to restrict the ballot, was the primary focus of his activity. The

NAACP's officers accordingly permitted Brooks to base himself in Richmond, thus enabling his wife to retain her teaching post.

Brooks typically worked with leaders of local branches of the NAACP to organize campaigns for voter registration, but he also spoke regularly at churches and colleges about the value of the ballot. Within a year, grassroots campaigns existed in every southern state except Alabama. These efforts helped lay the groundwork for the expanded voting-rights campaign that began in the spring of 1962 funded by the Voter Education Project, in which Brooks and the NAACP participated.

In his work for the nonpartisan NAACP, Brooks emphasized voter registration, but at home in Richmond he helped guide the Crusade for Voters into political action. If the Crusade's endorsements of candidates were to carry weight, the organization had to deliver votes, and voter education thus became as important as registration. Once the poll tax and other barriers to the ballot were removed, black Richmonders went to the polls in ever-greater numbers during the 1960s. The Crusade for Voters, with its strategic endorsements of candidates and reputation for political integrity, became powerful in local politics. Johnny Brooks, as he was known, was one of the insiders responsible for its success, which climaxed in 1977 with the election of a black majority to the city council.

Because the federal government protected voting rights after 1965, the NAACP's voter registration campaign gradually lost its significance. Brooks remained at his post—retitled director of voter education—until 16 March 1973, when it was abolished. The decision especially dismayed him because the NAACP could not afford pensions for its employees. He and his wife opened a nursing home in Richmond, from which he retired early in 1980. John Mitchell Brooks died on 8 August 1980 at a local hospital after brain surgery and was buried in Riverview Cemetery in Richmond.

John M. Brooks biography file, NAACP Library, Baltimore; information provided by son, Milton E. Brooks, and William S. Thornton; William C. Hocker, *Richmond's Negro Boy Scouts* (1989), 15; marriage date approximated from Richmond City Lists of Teachers, 1946–1947 and 1947–1948;

Brooks NAACP files, VCU; *Richmond Afro-American*, 25 Aug. 1956; *Crisis* 65 (1958): 5–8, 60–61; ibid. 65 (1958): memo insert, [1–2]; *Ebony* 18 (Sept. 1963): 144 (por. with Medgar Evers); *Richmond Times-Dispatch*, 24, 25 Apr. 1966, 16 June 1991; birth and death dates verified by BVS; obituaries in *Richmond News Leader* and *Richmond Times-Dispatch*, both 9 Aug. 1980, and *Richmond Afro-American*, 16 Aug. 1980 (pors.).

JOHN T. KNEEBONE

BROOKS, Lucy Goode (13 September 1818–7 October 1900), civic leader, was born probably in or near Richmond, the daughter of Judith Goode, a slave, and an unidentified white man. Her nephew John Henry Smyth became the United States minister to Liberia. On 11 November 1838 Lucy Goode became a member of the First Baptist Church of Richmond, and she joined other blacks in forming the First African Baptist Church when that congregation split from its parent in 1841.

Late in the 1830s Lucy Goode met Albert Royal Brooks, another Richmond slave. Goode had learned to read, perhaps from listening to the lessons taught to her master's children. As she and Albert Brooks fell in love, she passed her reading skills on to him, and they conspired to write the passes that enabled him to court her. When Goode's master died in 1838, she became the property of a man named Sublett. Her new master not only consented to her marriage on 2 February 1839 but also agreed that she could live with her husband, whose own master allowed him to operate a livery stable and eating house in return for regular payments. Brooks was permitted to keep his leftover earnings and used them eventually to purchase his freedom. The Brookses had at least five sons and four daughters, but one boy and one girl died in childhood. One son, Robert Peel Brooks, became a leader of the postwar Republican Party and was one of the first black lawyers to practice in Richmond.

Lucy Brooks's master died by 1858, when his heirs sold her and her three youngest children to Daniel Von Groning, a local tobacco merchant known to Albert Brooks. Von Groning permitted them to live with their husband and father, and Albert Brooks agreed to pay him in installments for their freedom. Lucy Brooks then set out for Richmond's business district to find

buyers for her eldest daughter and the three eldest boys, walking along Main Street with her younger children in tow. Three local men bought her sons and agreed to allow them to live at the Brooks home so long as the youngsters came to work in the tobacco factories each day. A fourth buyer purchased her daughter and promised not to sell her away but broke his pledge. Aged eighteen, literate, and subject of a photographic portrait that reveals a self-possessed, promising young woman, Margaret Ann Brooks was sold off to slavery in Tennessee, where she died in 1862. The betrayal pained her parents for the rest of their lives, but their brave efforts saved their other children from that fate.

Albert Brooks was one of Richmond's most successful antebellum black entrepreneurs, but to buy his wife and three youngest surviving children from Von Groning took four years. The deed of manumission was dated 21 October 1862. The older boys did not become free until the Union army occupied Richmond on 3 April 1865. Walter Henderson Brooks, later a prominent Baptist minister in Washington, D.C., recalled the care his parents took to keep him and his siblings from realizing that they were slaves subject to being sold away from home.

After Emancipation former slaves flocked to Richmond to seek better opportunities and look for missing family members. Lucy Brooks noted some children were separated from their parents and abandoned by former masters. Having lost one of her own children to the slave trade, she had a special concern for the plight of parentless children. Brooks convinced the Ladies Sewing Circle for Charitable Work, of which she was a leader, that a home for orphans was a worthy project. She then obtained support for an orphanage from the local Cedar Creek Meeting of the Society of Friends. Brooks had probably already won the backing of several black churches, whose representatives were included in the plans that the Quaker leaders devised for governance of the orphanage.

On 12 April 1867 the Richmond city council deeded a lot to the organization, and the orphanage building was completed in 1871. The General Assembly incorporated the Friends' Asylum for Colored Orphans in March 1872.

Seventeen years later the white trustees turned the institution over to representatives of Richmond's black Baptist churches. The orphanage operated until 1932, when the organization became a child-placement agency working primarily with foster families. The building that housed the orphanage was razed in 1969. Today, the renamed Friends' Association for Children operates a family center and a playground. The Lucy Brooks Foundation, created in 1984 to raise funds for the association, was named in honor of its founder.

The number of Richmond children whose lives Brooks touched cannot be known, but the long life of the institution she founded to aid children without families is proof of the great need for such work. Her own children's accomplishments can be traced to her teachings and the example she set, not least her courageous struggle to preserve her family during slavery. Albert Royal Brooks died on 15 July 1881. Lucy Goode Brooks died at her home on 7 October 1900 and was buried in Union Mechanics Cemetery, one of the Barton Heights cemeteries in Richmond.

Charlotte K. Brooks, Joseph K. Brooks, and Walter H. Brooks III, *A Brooks Chronicle: The Lives and Times of an African-American Family* (1989), pors. on 14, 93; manumission in Richmond City Hustings Court Deed Book, 78A:393–394; Lucy Brooks described as unable to write in April 1868 in Freedmen's Bank Records and in Census, Richmond City, 1870; *Charter and By-Laws of the Friends' Asylum for Colored Orphans, in the City of Richmond, Va.* (1883); Friends' Association for Colored Children, *Annual Report* (1946, 1959); obituary in *Richmond Planet*, 13 Oct. 1900.

JOHN T. KNEEBONE

BROOKS, Lyman Beecher (27 May 1910–20 April 1984), president of Norfolk State College (later Norfolk State University), was born at Blakes in Mathews County, the son of John Robert Brooks, a farmer and waterman who supplemented his family's income by giving music lessons, and his second wife, Mary Anna Burrell Brooks, a schoolteacher. His mother named him for Lyman Beecher Tefft, president of Hartshorn Memorial College (later Virginia Union University), her alma mater.

Brooks enjoyed a stimulating home environment in which books and newspapers were readily available, and visiting preachers and other dignitaries often stayed with the family. He began reading at three years of age and received his early education in a one-room school at which his mother taught. Because Mathews County had no high school for African Americans, Brooks lived with an aunt so that he could attend the Middlesex Training School, which did offer three years of secondary education. He spent his fourth year of high school at Virginia Union University's secondary school in Richmond and then went on to major in mathematics there. Brooks graduated second in his class.

Brooks taught at the Middlesex Training School until 1934, when he became founding principal of the new Essex County High School. His duties included teaching, coaching athletic teams, building ties to the local community, and pressing the school board for more funds and equipment. After taking a summer course at the University of Michigan in 1936, Brooks decided to resign his job and pursue graduate studies at that institution. In 1937 and 1942, respectively, he received M.A. and Ph.D. degrees in education.

Meanwhile, on 8 June 1938 Brooks accepted an offer to become the director of the Norfolk Unit of Virginia Union University, a two-year, junior college division of that private Baptist university, which had been entirely dependent on local support since its founding in 1935. By 1938 the school had 115 students, operated on a budget of less than $12,000, and was housed in rooms rented from the Young Men's Christian Association. Brooks immediately located a suitable building and indebted himself to purchase it so that his college could start the new academic year in more appropriate quarters.

Brooks raised money, hired the best faculty that he could attract, added new programs, and increased enrollment. In March 1942, seeking financial support from the city, state, and federal governments, the school severed its ties with Virginia Union and became an independent junior college called Norfolk Polytechnic College. With the change in name, Brooks's title changed from director to president. On 29 February 1944 the school finally won financial support from the state and became the Norfolk Division of Virginia State College.

In April 1951 the city of Norfolk donated fifty-five acres in the middle of the city, previously the site of a golf course, and the college moved there in 1955. Earlier, in 1950, Brooks had created a committee to reorganize the school's curriculum and won approval from the state to become a full degree-granting institution. The first four-year programs began in elementary education and business in 1956. By 1975 twenty-nine departments offered sixty-two baccalaureate degree programs.

Enrollment at the Norfolk Division of Virginia State College exceeded that of its senior institution by the mid-1960s. Brooks began planning for separation in 1965, and on 1 February 1969 Norfolk State College became independent. In 1979, four years after Brooks retired, it became Norfolk State University. The state authorized the college to grant master's degrees in 1972, and two years later the Graduate School of Social Work began operation. Throughout the school's growth, it remained committed to Brooks's conviction that any student, given excellent teaching and motivation, could be educated. Thus, the school offered both honors programs for the most talented students and remedial programs for those less prepared.

Between 1962 and 1964 Brooks chaired a project, funded by the Cooperative Research Branch of the United States Office of Education, to study the effectiveness of vocational education in assisting unskilled workers to secure jobs. Brooks was the senior author of project reports published as *Training the Hard-Core Unemployed: A Demonstration-Research Project at Virginia State College, Norfolk Division* (1964) and *Re-Education of Unemployed and Unskilled Workers (Summary)* (1965).

Brooks married Evelyn Fields, a local schoolteacher, on 27 December 1954, and they had two daughters. His busy schedule included community service on the boards of Norfolk Community Hospital, the Hunton YMCA, and the Bank Street Baptist Church. When Brooks retired in 1975 after more than thirty-seven years

at the helm of Norfolk State, the college had an enrollment of 7,500 students, occupied some 100 acres of land, and was one of the largest historically black colleges in the nation. He spent the first years of his retirement researching and writing the partly autobiographical *Upward: A History of Norfolk State University (1935 to 1975)*, which was published in 1983. Lyman Beecher Brooks died on 20 April 1984 at Norfolk Community Hospital following a heart attack and was buried at Calvary Cemetery in that city. The Lyman Beecher Brooks Library at Norfolk State University honors his long period of leadership there.

Lyman Beecher Brooks, *Upward: A History of Norfolk State University (1935 to 1975)* (1983), pors.; W. Augustus Low and Virgil A. Clift, eds., *Encyclopedia of Black America* (1981), 193; information provided by widow, Evelyn Fields Brooks; *Norfolk Journal and Guide*, 22 Feb., 1 Mar. 1975; obituaries in *Richmond Times-Dispatch*, 22 Apr. 1984, *Norfolk Virginian Pilot*, 23 Apr. 1984, and *Norfolk Journal and Guide*, 25 Apr. 1984.

TOMMY L. BOGGER

BROOKS, Robert Peel (29 October 1853– 10 October 1882), attorney and Republican Party leader, was born into slavery in Richmond, the sixth of at least nine children of Albert Royal Brooks and Lucy Goode Brooks. His parents, owned by different masters, struggled to keep their family together. After Lucy Goode Brooks's master died in 1858, she found local buyers for the four eldest children, and Albert Brooks persuaded a tobacco merchant to buy his wife and their other children. Permitted to hire his time, Albert Brooks managed to save $800, with which he bought his wife and younger children. Robert Peel Brooks was accordingly manumitted on 21 October 1862.

Freedom for the remaining members of his family did not come until 1865 and the defeat of the Confederacy. Even while a slave, Albert Brooks had established a successful livery business, and he invested in the education of his younger sons. In 1865 Robert Peel Brooks and his elder brother, Walter Henderson Brooks, later a well-known Baptist minister in Washington, D.C., entered a school in Richmond sponsored by the New-England Freedmen's Aid Society. Later that year the brothers attended the Wilberforce Institute in Carolina, Washington County, Rhode Island, and they entered Lincoln University in Chester County, Pennsylvania, in 1866. They graduated in 1871, and Robert Peel Brooks went on to study law at Howard University in Washington, D.C.

Peel Brooks, as his friends called him, graduated from Howard's law school in the class of 1875 and qualified in January 1876 to practice law before the Henrico County Court and the Richmond City Hustings Court. He was one of the first African American lawyers to practice in Richmond. The first, Walter G. Wynn, also a Howard graduate, qualified before the court in 1871 but moved from Richmond soon thereafter. Two other Howard-trained lawyers joined Brooks in Richmond. William Cabell Roane was a boyhood friend, and Henry B. Fry was a classmate who became Brooks's partner until his departure for Arkansas in 1880. The trio contributed occasional pieces about Richmond to the *People's Advocate*, an Alexandria newspaper published by blacks. In the issue of 13 May 1876 Roane reported that the white lawyers and judges in Richmond were "gentlema[n]ly and polite, and treat them in all respects like the white members of the bar."

In March 1877 a group of Richmond blacks started the *Richmond Virginia Star,* a newspaper that existed for at least five years. The fact that only eleven issues are known to survive makes it impossible to determine exactly when Brooks became the paper's editor. His name was on the masthead by the end of 1878, and except for a brief hiatus early in 1880, when he reported on Richmond's African American community for the white *Richmond Southern Intelligencer*, Brooks served as editor of the *Virginia Star* for at least two years and probably longer.

Those years saw turmoil in state politics, as Virginians who were determined to ease the burden of the state's huge prewar debt organized as the Readjusters in opposition to the Funders, who were adamant that the debt be paid in full. The dispute divided both the white Democratic Party and the Republican Party. During an 1879 election campaign in which the Readjusters triumphed, Brooks traveled the state advocating full payment of the debt, though he remained a

Republican. At Petersburg, before an audience that included numerous white Funders, he denounced the Democratic Party for its efforts to eliminate blacks from politics. On 1 May 1880 Brooks was elected secretary of the Republican State Central Committee.

By then Brooks had concluded that the hostility of white Democrats required blacks, for their own "self-defense" and "self-respect," to support the Readjusters. In Petersburg on 14 March 1881 a convention of African American leaders endorsed a coalition with the Readjusters. Brooks did not attend, but he was present in Lynchburg in August when the Republican Party convened. After some Republicans rejected a coalition and left the convention, Brooks led the rest of the party into the Readjuster camp and then canvassed the state in that autumn's election campaign. Friends sought his appointment as United States district attorney afterward in appreciation for these efforts but were unsuccessful.

Brooks maintained his law practice and also gave legal instruction to James Highland Hayes, later a member of the Richmond city council. Robert Peel Brooks had engaged to marry a Miss Jennings, but in September 1882, already ill with tuberculosis, he contracted typhoid fever and after a month's struggle died at his mother's home in Richmond on 10 October 1882, not long before his twenty-ninth birthday. He was buried in Union Mechanics Cemetery, one of Richmond's Barton Heights cemeteries. Brooks's reputation as a lawyer and orator outlasted his short career. A year after his death, the Alexandria journalist Magnus L. Robinson credited a young lawyer with "that element of 'push' and 'tact' that characterized the late lamented R. Peel Brooks." As late as 26 May 1934 a correspondent for the *Richmond Planet* listed Brooks as one of the city's ten greatest blacks.

New York Freeman, 14 Feb. 1885 (por.); Charlotte K. Brooks, Joseph K. Brooks, and Walter H. Brooks III, *A Brooks Chronicle: The Lives and Times of an African-American Family* (1989); Brooks letter in William Mahone Papers, Duke; manumission in Richmond City Hustings Court Deed Book, 78A:393–394; James T. Moore, "Black Militancy in Readjuster Virginia, 1879–1883," *JSH* 41 (1975): 167–186; *Alexandria People's Advocate*, 13 May 1876 (Roane quotation), 25 Oct. 1879, 1 May, 26 June 1880,

2, 30 Apr., 19 Nov. 1881, 28 Jan. 1882; *Richmond Whig*, 23 Oct. 1879; *Richmond Southern Intelligencer*, 5 Apr. 1880 (Brooks quotations); *Washington Bee*, 8 Dec. 1883 (Robinson quotation); list of Richmond's great blacks partially reprinted in *Richmond Quarterly* 5 (spring 1983): 52; obituaries and memorials in *Richmond Daily Dispatch* and *Richmond Daily Whig*, both 11, 12 Oct. 1882; memorial service described in *Richmond Virginia Star*, 11 Nov. 1882.

JOHN T. KNEEBONE

BROOKS, Vernon Asbury (31 July 1882– 18 October 1955), mayor of Portsmouth, was born in Mathews County, the son of George Gamaliel Brooks and Evelyn Marshall Brownley Brooks. He grew up in Portsmouth and graduated from Portsmouth High School. Brooks studied medicine and pharmacy at the University College of Medicine in Richmond and received an M.D. in 1904. After completing his internship in Richmond, he returned to Portsmouth in 1907 to practice medicine.

Brooks established a private practice and was also a staff physician at King's Daughters' Hospital of Portsmouth, an examining physician for the Chesapeake and Potomac Telephone Company in Portsmouth, and a surgeon for the Seaboard Air Line Railway. He was Portsmouth's city health officer for more than a decade beginning in 1912, and during World War I he was a medical examiner for the local draft board. Brooks never sent bills to his patients, assuming that if they could pay they would. He helped found the Portsmouth Kiwanis Club, belonged to the Benevolent and Protective Order of Elks, and sat on the boards of the American National Bank and the Citizens Trust Company.

On 31 January 1920 at Monumental Methodist Church Brooks married Lillian Blanche Ablett Griffin, of Portsmouth. They had one son, one daughter, and one stillborn child. Lillian Brooks was active in many local organizations and served from 1954 to 1958 as vice president of the Southern Candy Company in Portsmouth. She was also president of the Woman's Society of Christian Service of Monumental Church in 1956 and president of the Woman's Club of Portsmouth.

In April 1920 Brooks ran with a slate of reform candidates who captured the Democratic Party nomination for seats on the Portsmouth city council, and they defeated all of the Republican candidates in June. Reelected to the city council every four years through 1934, he became council president and mayor of Portsmouth in September 1926. The council reelected him to two-year terms as mayor in 1928 and 1930. Brooks relinquished the office of mayor in 1932 but was again elected council president and mayor two years later. After a charter amendment abolished at-large elections in favor of a ward system, he was defeated for mayor in his final campaign in 1936 and did not seek reelection to the council when his term expired in 1938.

Throughout his service on the council, Brooks advocated construction of a bridge-tunnel for vehicle traffic across the Elizabeth River between Norfolk and Portsmouth, an idea that originated about the time he was first elected. When he chaired the joint Norfolk County– Portsmouth Ferry Commission in 1928 he proposed building the tunnel, but other Portsmouth councillors and the owners of a ferryboat opposed the plan because the city and Norfolk County profited significantly from the ferry. Plans for construction made little progress until the General Assembly created the Elizabeth River Tunnel Commission in 1942 to plan the work. Brooks was one of the initial members of the commission, which issued bonds to pay for construction, which finally began in 1950. The bridge-tunnel, later known as the downtown tunnel, opened on 23 May 1952.

Vernon Asbury Brooks suffered from heart disease later in life and died in King's Daughters' Hospital of Portsmouth on 18 October 1955. He was buried in Oak Grove Cemetery in Portsmouth.

Rogers Dey Whichard, ed., *The History of Lower Tidewater Virginia* (1959), 3:206–208 (por. facing 206); BVS Birth Register, Mathews Co.; information provided by daughter, Lillian Ann Brooks Hall; Vernon Asbury Brooks Papers, Portsmouth Public Library; BVS Marriage Register, Portsmouth; *Portsmouth Star*, 7 Apr., 9 June 1920, 11 June, 1 Sept. 1924, 2 Sept. 1926, 4 Apr., 13 June, 1 Sept. 1928, 3 Sept. 1930, 15 June, 1 Sept. 1932, 1 Sept. 1934, 10 June 1936; *Norfolk Ledger-Dispatch*, 16 Oct. 1920; obituaries in *Norfolk Ledger-Dispatch and Portsmouth Star* and *Norfolk Virginian-Pilot*, both 19 Oct. 1955.

DEAN BURGESS

BROUGHTON, Thomas Greene (27 September 1786–24 August 1861), journalist, was born in Princess Anne County, the son of Charles Broughton and Elizabeth Greene Broughton. He grew up there but as a young man moved to Norfolk, where on 6 May 1808 he married Ann Bell, a native of Carlisle, England. They had six sons and six daughters. In addition, Broughton was serving as guardian of a young woman at the time of her marriage in 1811.

Beginning in 1808 Broughton worked for seven years as an editor for James O'Connor, publisher of the *Norfolk and Portsmouth Herald*. In 1815 Broughton became O'Connor's partner and part owner of the newspaper, and following O'Connor's death in July 1819 he became sole publisher and editor. Originally issued on Wednesdays and Saturdays, the newspaper under Broughton's editorship expanded from a triweekly publication with a separate edition for outlying areas to a daily paper (except Sundays) beginning on 13 August 1840. With name changes to the *Norfolk and Portsmouth Herald and General Advertiser* in 1833, the *Norfolk and Portsmouth Herald and Daily Commercial Advertiser* in 1843, and back to the *Norfolk and Portsmouth Herald* by 1847, the paper was one of the most successful and long-lived of all the lower Tidewater papers and circulated in northeastern North Carolina as well as Virginia. Broughton's son Thomas Gibson Broughton became a partner with him in the ownership and publication of the paper in 1836 as Thomas G. Broughton and Son, and later another son, Richard Gatewood Broughton, joined them. By the mid-1840s T. G. Broughton and Company served also as a general printer. The firm continued publishing the daily newspaper until a shortage of paper forced it to suspend publication sometime in the summer of 1861. Broughton's death shortly thereafter and the turmoil associated with the Civil War in Norfolk kept his sons from resuming publication thereafter.

Broughton and his sons supported the Whig Party from early in the 1830s until its demise in the mid-1850s. They backed John Bell, the Constitutional Union Party candidate who carried Virginia in the 1860 presidential race, and they were Unionists during the secession crisis. Besides becoming the senior journalist in Norfolk, Broughton was also a respected community leader. He sat on the Norfolk common council, was secretary of the board of health during a cholera epidemic in 1832, and served for two decades before his death as a ruling elder in the local Presbyterian church. Thomas Greene Broughton died in Norfolk on 24 August 1861 and was buried in Cedar Grove Cemetery in that city.

Birth date in French Biographies; Norfolk Co. Marriage Bonds; family history provided by Lemuel Bowden and Monroe Couper; one Broughton letter in Norfolk Spanish Consulate Papers and political references in Hugh Blair Grigsby, diary, 1828, both VHS; *Norfolk and Portsmouth Herald and General Advertiser*, 25 Aug. 1819, 1 Jan., 12 Sept. 1836; William S. Forrest, *Historical and Descriptive Sketches of Norfolk and Vicinity* (1853), 100–101; obituaries in *Richmond Daily Whig* and *Richmond Enquirer*, both 27 Aug. 1861.

W. A. BROWN

BROWN, Abram (d. August 1840), Baptist lay leader, was born in the eastern portion of Charles City County sometime between 1767 and 1774, the son of Abram Brown and Sarah Brown. The family had been free for at least two generations before Brown's birth. Brown's paternal grandmother, identified in local records as being of mixed racial background, bound out his father and two uncles as apprentices during the 1740s. By 1769 Brown's father had purchased two farms containing a total of 273 acres. The elder Abram Brown acquired additional land and at least three slaves, and as a respectable property owner he joined a large number of county residents in signing a petition to the General Assembly in 1780.

Following his father's death about 1790, Abram Brown inherited 130 acres, on which he raised wheat and corn and enjoyed a comfortable existence rare for African Americans in Virginia during the early republic. By the time of his death he had acquired books, silver spoons, a brass candleholder and snuffers, a mantle clock, and a considerable quantity of household and kitchen furniture. One of the wealthiest men in Charles City County's black community, Brown was paying taxes on a gig, or pleasure carriage, by 1828.

Brown was instrumental in founding his community's religious and institutional heart. Many local African Americans, including his father and siblings, had been affiliated with the First Baptist Church in Petersburg, but he apparently did not join that church until 1809 or 1810. Soon thereafter Brown helped establish a separate church in Charles City County (known originally simply as the Baptist Church but by 1813 called Elam), and in autumn 1813 the church successfully petitioned for membership in the Dover Baptist Association, the regional church conference. He became a frequent delegate to the association's annual conferences, and in 1819 he served on a biracial committee that visited and reported on conditions at Hanover Baptist Church. On 20 November 1818 Brown deeded to the church the small tract of land on which its meetinghouse stood, thus securing himself the credit as founder of Elam Baptist Church. The original building burned in 1919, but the congregation survived and is one of the oldest black churches in Virginia.

Brown's other legacy to Charles City County was his family, which continued its leadership of the church and the black community of Ruthville. With his wife, Susanna Brown, whose maiden name and marriage date are unknown, he had perhaps as many as ten children, of whom four sons and four daughters reached maturity. Their son Christopher Brown inherited the Browns' house and 20 acres of land, and the other three brothers inherited and divided the remaining 110 acres. The youngest son, Samuel Brown, eventually acquired from the other heirs the entire tract his father had owned and bequeathed it in turn to his sons. Samuel Brown became the county's most prominent black citizen in the first generation after the Civil War. Identified in the 1850 census as a Baptist clergyman, he became the county's first licensed black minister in 1866. Officials of the Freedmen's Bureau described Brown as an educated and respectable man. Immediately after the Civil War he opened a short-lived school at Elam for the county's black children. Brown was

appointed, then elected, county superintendent of the poor in November 1870 and held that post until his death in November 1881.

Members of subsequent generations of the Brown family also achieved positions of social and political prominence. Samuel Brown's son Samuel Allen Brown, grandson of Abram Brown, served as pastor of Petersburg's historic Gillfield Baptist Church for almost forty years. Abram Brown's grandson Crawford Brown served intermittently as a justice of the peace and district overseer of the poor in Charles City County from the 1870s through the 1890s. Two other county justices, Seaton Brown and Fleming Brown, the county's only nineteenth-century black supervisor, William S. Brown, and a twentieth-century supervisor, Howard D. Brown, may also have been related to Abram Brown.

Comparatively little is known about the family and personal life of Abram Brown, but he was the central figure in the history of a family that was for generations before and after Emancipation a pillar of one of the state's largest, most prosperous, and most stable black communities. Abram Brown wrote his will on 12 April 1836 and died sometime in August 1840. He was "decently and plainly intered" as specified in his will, probably at his home or in the graveyard of Elam Baptist Church in Charles City County.

Given names of Brown and father appear in records both as Abram and as Abraham; father's will, dated 11 July 1789 (Charles City Co. Will Book, 1:16–18), suggests that Brown was born probably after July 1767, and his name on the county tithable list for 1790 indicates that he was born probably no later than 1774; Daryl Cumber Dance, *The Lineage of Abraham: The Biography of a Free Black Family in Charles City, VA* (1998), 9–15, 20, 22, 117, 152–153; incomplete and inexact family histories in Caldwell, *History of the American Negro*, 35, [Alexander Q. Franklin], *History of Elam Baptist Church, Charles City Co., Va.* (1910), 5, and Willnette D. Carter et al., eds., *Organization and Development of Elam Baptist Church* (1976), 67; "Charles City's Brown Families: Tangled Roots and Obscure Origins," *Charles City County Historical Society Newsletter* (Mar. 1997): 11–17; published records of Dover Baptist Association contain details and church history; property holdings recorded with variations in Land and Personal Property Tax Returns, Charles City Co., RG 48, LVA, and in Census, Charles City Co., 1830; death in Aug. 1840 recorded in Charles City Co. Free Negro Register; will and estate inventory in Charles City Co. Will Book, 4:375 (quotation), 388–390.

JOHN M. COSKI

BROWN, Alexander (5 September 1843–24 August 1906), historian, was born at Glenmore in Nelson County, the son of Robert Lawrence Brown, a farmer, merchant, and teacher, and his first wife, Sarah Cabell Callaway Brown. Both of his siblings died young and his mother died in 1849. After his father's remarriage to Margaret Baldwin Cabell, Brown was raised by his grandmother Mary Elizabeth Cabell and educated by private tutors at Benvenue in Nelson County from 1851 to 1856 and at the Charlottesville school of Horace W. Jones from 1856 to 1860. Brown entered Lynchburg College in 1860, but the Civil War ended his education. He joined the Staunton Hill Artillery in September 1861 and served until the end of the war. He suffered a severe and permanent loss of hearing in his right ear in December 1864 after an explosion at Fort Fisher, North Carolina.

For about three years Brown worked as a salesman in Washington, D.C. He then returned to Nelson County, where he was a merchant, farmer, and writer for the remainder of his life. On 27 December 1873 Brown married Caroline Augusta Cabell, who died on 31 July 1876, and on 28 April 1886 he married her elder sister, Sarah Randolph Cabell. He had no children by either marriage. Brown purchased and lived at Union Hill, a Cabell family estate near Norwood in Nelson County. By 1876 he was beginning to lose the hearing in his left ear and had begun his career as a writer. Brown lived very simply and employed his own resources and a network of friends and acquaintances in the United States and Europe to acquire a significant collection of books and primary source records relating to the founding of Virginia and to his own family. He wrote and published several important books on the Jamestown colony: *New Views of Early Virginia History, 1606–1619* (1886), the two-volume *Genesis of the United States* (1890), *The First Republic in America* (1898), *The History of Our Earliest History* (1898), and *English Politics in Early Virginia History* (1901). Brown also produced a valuable, detailed genealogy, *The Cabells and Their Kin* (1895).

During America's great age of gentleman scholars at the end of the nineteenth century, Brown was the leading and most prolific amateur historian of early Virginia. In addition to his books, he wrote often for the *Virginia Magazine of History and Biography*, the *Magazine of American History*, the *Atlantic Monthly*, and two Richmond newspapers, the *Dispatch* and the *Standard*. Brown was a fellow of the Royal Historical Society of England and a member of the American Historical Association, the Society of American Authors, and the state historical societies of Maine, Maryland, Massachusetts, Tennessee, and Virginia.

Brown made his most lasting contribution as a tireless, pioneering compiler of important and little-known documents on seventeenth-century Virginia. Generations of later historians have benefited from the full or extracted transcriptions of essential sources that he published, most notably the often-ignored Spanish documents that he included in his massive *Genesis of the United States* and in *The First Republic in America*. Brown was the first Virginian to publish records of the Virginia Company of London, to include translations of Spanish documents, and to print eyewitness accounts by the first English colonists. His extensive biographical entries in *Genesis* inspired an interest in genealogy and prosopography, and his perspectives on Virginia's contributions to civil liberties anticipated the work of such later professional historians as Thomas Jefferson Wertenbaker.

Brown based his books on the premise that a fair and full history of the founding of Virginia had never been published, but that was virtually his only uncontroversial statement. However significant his contributions in searching for data and encouraging popular interest in early Virginia history, he failed as an interpretive historian. Although his keen judgment and indefatigable tenacity in assembling essential documents rivaled the skills of professional archivists, Brown remained a mediocre and amateurish historian whose interpretations of those sources were often unconvincing and blatantly biased. Most of his conclusions are suspect, not only because his undocumented assertions are difficult to verify but also because of his intrusive, shrill, and redundant denunciations of Captain John Smith's writings.

Brown believed that the directors of the Virginia Company constituted a "patriot party" that made early Jamestown a veritable "republic" until Smith's popular narratives discredited and overshadowed them. Brown saw it as his special mission to resurrect the company's reputation, but such serious students as Frederick Jackson Turner and William Wirt Henry severely criticized his lack of objectivity, animosity toward the company's critics, and partisanship in behalf of the company's leaders. "Brown committed a great mistake," Henry wrote in 1898 at the conclusion of a fourteen-page dissection of *The First Republic in America*, "in his bungling effort to depreciate some of the noblest of these men, and to magnify some of the most unworthy. As a collector of historical matter he proved to be a great success, as a historian he is a lamentable failure."

The popularity of Brown's writings as well as his own obsessions with heroes and villains may be explained in part by the longing of his generation to restore Virginia's once-glorious reputation as the first republic in America. Thirty years after Appomattox, he wrote nostalgically about his distinguished ancestors. Scholars found fault with Brown's interpretations, but his fellow citizens appreciated and rewarded his efforts to uncover the forgotten heritage of the first founders. The University of the South at Sewanee, Tennessee, honored him with a doctorate of civil law in 1893, the same year that he received a medal from the Columbian Historical Exposition in Madrid. The College of William and Mary elected him to membership in the Alpha Chapter of Phi Beta Kappa and in 1901 conferred on him an honorary doctorate of laws.

Brown was the elder half brother of William Cabell Brown, a missionary and Episcopal bishop of the Diocese of Virginia from 1919 until 1927. After years of deafness and incapacitating paralysis, Alexander Brown died at Union Hill on 24 August 1906 and was buried in the family cemetery in Nelson County.

NCAB, 19:171 (which gives death date as 25 Aug.); Marvin Ellis Harvey, "Alexander Brown and the Renaissance of Virginia History" (master's thesis, W&M, 1947); Eliza-

beth Jean Inge, "Alexander Brown and the History of Colonial Virginia" (master's thesis, UVA, 1984); Alexander Brown Papers, W&M; Charles Dean Papers, Massachusetts Historical Society, Boston; Compiled Service Records; Nelson Co. Marriage Register, 1873, 1886; Brown, *Cabells*, 466–468; Brown, *The Genesis of the United States* (1890), v–xviii; critical reviews by Henry and Turner, respectively, in *AHR* 4 (1898): 162–165, and 7 (1901): 159–163; Henry's review and Brown's lengthy rejoinder in *VMHB* 6 (1898–1899): 209–222 (quotation on 222), 324–334; por., Special Collections, LVA; obituaries in *Lynchburg News*, 26 Aug. 1906, *Richmond News Leader*, 27 Aug. 1906, and *AHR* 12 (1907): 441–442 (which gives death date as 29 Aug.).

J. FREDERICK FAUSZ

BROWN, Alexander Gustavus (22 February 1833–16 March 1900), Methodist minister and college administrator, was born in Stephensburg in Frederick County, the son of Gustavus Alexander Scott Brown, a physician, and Ann Murphy Brown. His father died before Brown reached the age of two. He was educated at a succession of private academies, including Greenway Court in Clarke County and Hillsboro and New Lisbon in Loudoun County. His parents were Methodists, and during the summer of 1848 Brown underwent a conversion experience at a camp meeting in Rappahannock County. He entered the itinerancy in 1853 and in October of that year became a probationary minister of the Methodist Episcopal Church South. After his ordination in 1857, Brown became the chaplain at Randolph-Macon College in Boydton, where he also took courses. On 6 January 1859 he married Fannie A. Cooksey, of Fairfax County. They had three sons and five daughters.

Like other educated Methodist ministers, Brown served a succession of urban churches. He was at Third Street Methodist Church in Lynchburg (1858–1860), Trinity Methodist Church in Richmond (1860–1862), and High Street Methodist Church in Petersburg (1862–1864). In November 1864, during the Union army's siege of Petersburg, Brown left the city to take charge of the Bedford Circuit. He was presiding elder of the Lynchburg Circuit (1866–1870) and the Norfolk District (1870–1871) and financial secretary at Randolph-Macon College (1871–1875). Brown returned to the High Street and Battersea Churches in Petersburg for two years and then served successively at Trinity and Clay Street Methodist Churches in Richmond,

Main Street Methodist Church in Danville, and Cumberland Street Methodist Church in Norfolk. In 1889 he was again elevated to the supervisory position of presiding elder, this time for the Charlottesville District, and in 1890 he held the same post for the West Richmond District. Brown retired from the ministry in April 1899 after his health began to fail.

Brown's congregations were seldom the largest in the cities he served, leaving him time to undertake other church responsibilities. He edited and published the Virginia Annual Conference's yearly minutes from 1878 through 1887, received an honorary D.D. from Emory and Henry College in 1889, and won recognition as a skillful debater as a delegate to his denomination's quadrennial General Conferences in 1870, 1890, 1894, and 1898. In 1884 Brown represented the Methodist Episcopal Church South at the Centenary Conference of American Methodism. In 1868 he became chairman of the joint board of finance for the Virginia Conference, a post he held until 1898. Brown oversaw the disbursement of collections to the widows and orphans of ministers. These collections rose from $3,400 in 1868 to $12,200 in 1898, very little of which even in the later years came from investments. In 1890 Brown took over the management of the conference colportage, which sold religious books primarily through itinerant ministers working on commission. During his first year the sale of more than 14,300 books, tracts, and hymnals brought in $8,100.

On 27 July 1871 Brown was elected a trustee of Randolph-Macon College, which had moved to Ashland in 1868. Two days later he was also elected financial secretary, a new post combining the work of a number of officers who had attempted to organize the school's finances. The college was near insolvency, and Richmond banks refused to honor its checks. Brown had to manage the school's physical plant, raise money, and lobby the governor and legislators to pay full interest on Virginia bonds during the controversy over completely funding or partially repudiating the state's prewar debt. He succeeded. By 1872 Brown had helped persuade the General Assembly to enact two bills enabling incorporated colleges and seminaries to receive full interest on their state bonds. Between 1873 and 1875 he built a hotel near the railroad tracks in Ashland. It served meals to the students and also satisfied a stipulation that the Richmond, Fredericksburg, and Potomac Railroad made in a grant of land to the college. The book value of the college's net assets rose from $36,000 in 1872 to $71,000 in 1875, but the panic of 1873 left Randolph-Macon $2,862 short of meeting its expenses in 1875, and the real value of its holdings had fallen by a third. Citing bad financial times, Brown resigned on 9 November 1875, and the position of financial secretary was then abolished. He remained an esteemed and active member of the board until his death. Brown's well-written reports suggest both a clarity of vision and an enthusiasm for financial undertakings, highly prized virtues in the age of Andrew Carnegie and John Pierpont Morgan.

Brown suffered a stroke in July 1899. Paralyzed on his left side, he was confined to bed for the rest of his life. Alexander Gustavus Brown died on 16 March 1900 at his Ashland home across the railroad tracks from the college campus. He was buried in Hollywood Cemetery in Richmond.

A Memorial of Alexander Gustavus Brown (1901), frontispiece por.; Alexander Gustavus Brown Papers and a few letters in various other collections at VHS; details of career in Virginia Annual Conference, Methodist Episcopal Church South, *Minutes,* which occasionally printed his reports and essays, including "An Essay on the Grace of Giving as Developed in Both Testaments" (1881), 96–109; Fairfax Co. Marriage Register; Trustees Minutes, Randolph-Macon College; Richard Irby, *History of Randolph-Macon College, Virginia* [1898], 207–208 (por.), 222, 225, 227, 235–237; James E. Scanlon, *Randolph-Macon College: A Southern History, 1825–1967* (1983), 123, 133, 135, 136 (por.), 248, 267; obituary in *Richmond Dispatch,* 17 Mar. 1900; memorial in Virginia Annual Conference, *Minutes* (1900): 33–37, reprinted in W. D. Keene Jr., ed., *Memoirs—200 Years! 1785–1987* (1988), 293–297.

JAMES E. SCANLON

BROWN, Aubrey Neblett (6 May 1908–6 August 1998), Presbyterian minister and editor, was born in Hillsboro, Texas, the son of Aubrey Neblett Brown and Virginia Rose Sims Brown. He grew up in Andrews and Midland in western Texas and in 1925 graduated from high school in Mineral Wells, Texas. Brown received a B.A. in 1929 from Davidson College, where he edited the college newspaper, and a B.D. from Union Theological Seminary in Richmond in 1932.

On 4 October 1932 Aubrey N. Brown Jr., as he was known throughout his life, married Sarah Dumond Hill, of Richmond, the daughter and granddaughter of prominent Presbyterian clergymen. They had three sons and five daughters. Brown began his ministerial career in 1932 in Ronceverte, West Virginia. Six years later he transferred to a congregation in Montgomery, West Virginia. During this time Brown became one of several departmental editors of the *Presbyterian of the South and Presbyterian Standard*, a privately published weekly religious journal founded in 1819 and printed in Richmond. Early in the 1940s the publication experienced financial difficulties and was seized by its printer for debt. A stock company raised some $11,600 to recover the magazine and invited Brown to move to Richmond as full-time editor and manager of the journal, which he did effective 1 November 1943. He changed the name to the *Presbyterian Outlook* in April 1944 and in September 1947 made his brother James S. Brown business manager of Outlook Publishers and its bookselling branch, the Outlook Book Service.

The magazine Brown took over was in financial straits, but it was also becoming the voice of change within the Presbyterian Church in the U.S., as an alternative to the conservative *Presbyterian Journal*. Brown's education had drawn him away from the biblical literalism and strict Calvinism of traditional southern Presbyterian teaching. He was influenced by such American writers and religious thinkers as Harry Emerson Fosdick and by his own long personal acquaintance with Ernest Trice Thompson, his immediate predecessor as editor. Brown opened the pages of the *Presbyterian Outlook* to advocates of biblical criticism, opponents of rigid Calvinism, and writers who believed that the church should engage in more social justice work. In his unambiguous editorials he lobbied for change within the church and supported those who wished to reunite the Presbyterian

Church in the U.S. with its northern counterpart, the Presbyterian Church in the U.S.A., and with other churches within the Reformed tradition. Although Brown always made his positions clear, he permitted a wide variety of opinions to appear in the magazine. To a reader who complained that he did not agree with everything that appeared in the *Presbyterian Outlook*, Brown once replied, "Neither do I."

Unlike many southern Presbyterians, Brown supported the ecumenical movement and participation in the Federal Council of Churches (later the National Council of Churches) and its international counterpart. From 1962 to 1973 he served on the North American council of the Alliance of the Reformed Churches throughout the World holding the Presbyterian System (after 1970 the World Alliance of Reformed Churches [Presbyterian and Congregational]) and attended the alliance's general council in Kenya in 1970. Brown advocated admitting women to positions in church governance and the ministry, and he was one of the few white Virginia clergymen who opposed racial discrimination and segregation from the beginning of the civil rights movement. From 1957 to 1959 he was the first president of the Richmond chapter of the Virginia Council on Human Relations. Brown was president of the state council from 1963 to 1965 and for a time chaired the Virginia Advisory Committee of the United States Commission on Civil Rights.

As a forceful editor, a persistent advocate of change, and a clergyman who publicly participated in biracial organizations, Brown exercised a wide influence within the community of southern Presbyterians. Few of its leaders were as widely known. Awarded an honorary D.D. from Maryville College in 1961, Brown also received the first Torch of Liberty Award from the Virginia Chapter of B'nai B'rith in 1966. In 1979 he delivered the annual Sprunt lecture at Union Theological Seminary. Entitled "Credible Discipleship in a World of Affluence and Poverty," the talk strongly challenged the Presbyterian Church to improve its ministry to the poor.

Brown edited the *Presbyterian Outlook* until he retired at the end of 1978. Beginning in 1946 he began compiling the *Going to College*

Handbook, an annual magazine, issued by Outlook Publishers. Containing feature articles about Presbyterian colleges in the United States and essays useful to students and parents, its circulation grew to several thousand copies, and its last issue in 1980 contained more than seventy pages. Brown served twice as interim pastor of All Souls Presbyterian Church in Richmond. After retirement he continued to write for the *Presbyterian Outlook*, led the Sunday discussions of the Ginter Park Presbyterian Peace Forum, took charge of the Wednesday night programs of the Ginter Park Presbyterian Church, and participated in interdenominational and other church-related conferences. Brown published *The Church Publicity Book: Techniques for Communication* (1986) and delivered a series of talks on aspects of his career that was published in 1997 as *Aubrey Brown Remembers: The Purpose of an Independent Church Press, The Church's Record in Race Relations, The Struggle for Women's Status in the Church, The Movement Toward Christian Unity*.

Sarah Hill Brown died on 3 July 1995. Aubrey Neblett Brown Jr. died at the Hermitage, a Richmond retirement home, on 6 August 1998. He donated his body to science.

E. C. Scott, ed., *Ministerial Directory of the Presbyterian Church, U.S., 1861–1941*, rev. ed. (1950), 79; family records, including autobiographical memoranda, courtesy of daughter Katherine Brown Weisiger; BVS Marriage Register, Richmond City; Aubrey N. Brown Jr. Papers, VHS; Aubrey Brown Papers and several audio- and videotape interviews and recordings, UTS; *Richmond Times-Dispatch*, 5 Oct. 1932, 18 Jan. 1997, 11 Aug. 1998 (quotation); Janet Harbison, "Man of Right Much Courage," *Presbyterian Life* (15 July 1959): 6–7, 31–33; *Presbyterian Outlook* 175 (31 May 1993): 10, 16–20; Ernest Trice Thompson, *Presbyterians in the South* (1963–1973), 3:335, 490, 530–535, 542, 550–551; valedictory in *Presbyterian Outlook* 160 (18 Dec. 1978): 8; obituary in *Richmond Times-Dispatch*, 7 Aug. 1998; tributes in *Presbyterian Outlook* 180 (7 Sept. 1998): 5–10 (pors.), and (14 Sept. 1998): 8–15.

Brent Tarter

BROWN, Bedford (1 January 1825–13 September 1897), physician, was born in Caswell County, North Carolina, the son of Bedford Brown (1795–1870) and Mary Lumpkin Glenn Brown. His father was a planter who from 1829 to 1840 served in the United States Senate, and his mother was a native Virginian from Halifax County. After attending several North Carolina academies Brown began studying medicine in 1846 as a private pupil of Benjamin W. Dudley in Lexington, Kentucky. He also attended two years of lectures at the medical department of Transylvania University and graduated in 1848. Brown then took a course of lectures at Jefferson Medical College in Philadelphia and graduated in 1854. On 1 July 1852 he married Mary Elizabeth Simpson in Washington, D.C. Of their ten children, only two sons and one daughter reached adulthood.

Brown began practicing medicine in Virginia, first in Albemarle and Fauquier Counties, but he soon returned to North Carolina and practiced there until 18 July 1861, when he was commissioned surgeon of the 14th Regiment North Carolina Volunteers (redesignated the 24th Regiment North Carolina Troops). In August 1861 Brown's regiment was assigned to Brigadier General John Buchanan Floyd's Army of the Kanawha in western Virginia. During the battle at Carnifex Ferry on 10 September 1861, Brown was conspicuous for his attention to the injured and dying and personally treated Floyd's wounds. Brown resigned in October 1861 but was recommissioned as surgeon of the 43d Regiment North Carolina Troops on 24 March 1862. In December 1862 he was appointed medical director on the staff of Major General Gustavus W. Smith. Brown's final military appointment was as an inspector of hospitals and camps in North Carolina.

Brown moved back to Virginia after the Civil War and established a private practice in Alexandria. He became known as one of the most highly accomplished and experienced physicians in the state. His courtly manners and a kind and sympathetic disposition won him the confidence and esteem of his patients and a large, lucrative practice. Brown wrote prolifically on many medical subjects both before and after the war. His most important contributions to the medical literature were probably two clinical studies of severe head wounds published in 1860 and 1894, the former described as one of the first cases on record in which the effect of chloroform was clearly demonstrated.

Brown was a member of the American Medical Association and served as a vice president of the Medical Society of Virginia in 1880–1881 and 1883–1884 and as its president in 1886. He helped found the Southern Surgical and Gynecological Association and was its vice president in 1887 and president in 1893. In 1894 Brown was made an honorary member of the Medical Society of the District of Columbia. In November 1896 he served as honorary chairman of the section on general surgery at the Pan-American Medical Congress when it met in Mexico City. At the conference he presented a paper on autumnal fevers, his last major work. In 1884 Brown was one of the original members of the first Virginia State Board of Medical Examiners. He also served as surgeon of the R. E. Lee Camp of the United Confederate Veterans in Alexandria and was active on the Council of Confederate Veterans and in the Episcopal Church.

In his last year Brown contracted what was believed to be Bright's disease, also identified in contemporary accounts as an affliction of the bladder and chronic cystitis. Following unsuccessful surgery Bedford Brown died at his Alexandria home on 13 September 1897. He was buried in Rock Creek Cemetery in Washington, D.C.

NCAB, 5:442; Henry and Spofford, *Eminent Men*, 413–415 (por.); William B. Atkinson, ed., *Physicians and Surgeons of the United States* (1878), 389–390, with partial list of publications; Irving A. Watson, ed., *Physicians and Surgeons of America* (1896), 447–448, with list of other publications; marriage in *Washington Daily National Intelligencer,* 7 July 1852; Wyndham B. Blanton, *Medicine in Virginia in the Nineteenth Century* (1933); Brown's key articles include "Case of Extensive Compound Fracture of the Cranium: Severe Laceration and Destruction of a Portion of the Brain, Followed by Fungus Cerebri, and Terminating in Recovery," *American Journal of the Medical Sciences*, new ser., 40 (1860): 399–403, "Personal Experience in Observing the Results of Good and Bad Sanitation in the Confederate States Army," *Virginia Medical Monthly* 20 (1893): 589–599, "Observations on the Action of Chloroform on the Functions of the Human Brain and Spinal Cord, as Witnessed in Extensive Injuries of the Cranium and Brain," *Therapeutic Gazette*, 3d ser., 10 (1894): 793–802, "Therapeutic Action of Chloroform in Parturition," *Journal of the American Medical Association* 25 (1895): 354–358, and "Autumnal Fevers of the Southern Atlantic States and Their Treatment," printed in both *Journal of the American Medical Association* 27 (1896): 1319–1325 and *Virginia Medical Semi-Monthly* 1 (1896): 493–502; obituaries in *Alexandria Gazette* and *Washington Evening Star*, both 13 Sept. 1897, and *Washington Post*, 14 Sept. 1897; memorials in *Virginia Medical Semi-Monthly* 2 (1897): 372, and *Transactions of the Medical Society of Virginia* (1898): 274–275.

JOAN ECHTENKAMP KLEIN

BROWN, Charles Edward (24 September 1888–30 June 1975), educator and civil rights leader, was born in Charlotte County, the son of Thomas Brown, a farmer, and Henrietta Morton Brown. After Brown's father died in 1902, his mother insisted that he and his siblings continue to attend school and encouraged them to aspire to achievement. He attended Virginia Normal and Industrial Institute (later Virginia State University), paying his way with work in the North during the summers, and graduated in 1909.

Brown returned to Charlotte Court House as principal of the school he had once attended. It had two rooms and offered only elementary instruction during a five-month term. Brown's salary was $20 a month, or $100 for the term. He raised the money to add another room to the building and furnish it with a blackboard and modern desks. Except for a $25 contribution from the Negro Organization Society, funds to cover the improvements all came from local citizens. Brown also enlarged the faculty to three teachers and had the school placed on the state's graded school list, although it lost that status shortly after his departure.

Brown's work in Charlotte County won him the attention of Jackson Davis, state supervisor of rural black elementary schools, and in 1914 Davis invited Brown to transfer to York County. A few years earlier the directors of the John F. Slater Fund had agreed to help support central training schools for blacks in rural southern counties. The Slater schools offered courses above the elementary level with special attention to training teachers and providing vocational education in home economics and agriculture. Even with help from the Slater Fund, school quality depended largely on local contributions. Principals necessarily had to be effective community organizers.

Brown accepted Davis's invitation and arrived in York County in October 1914. He found that an old store was serving as the schoolhouse and immediately set to work. The community raised $1,500, and with help from the county school board the new four-room York County Training School opened in 1916. Two years later the federal government claimed 12,000 acres for a new naval mine depot, and the land included the new school and the residences of most of its patrons. Brown arranged for teaching to continue at Shiloh Baptist Church, using curtains to separate the class areas, and began raising money once again. Contributions paid for a five-acre site, and together with the government's payment for the previous school and a $1,600 gift from the Julius Rosenwald Fund, a new building with six classrooms, an auditorium, an office, and a library opened in 1921.

The York County Training School initially offered coursework only through the eighth grade, but Brown soon raised the money to hire two more teachers and added high-school courses. In the 1917–1918 term nine students were enrolled in the high school, but the number advanced to twenty by 1920–1921 and sixty-eight by 1933–1934. The teaching faculty also grew to nine, including Brown, who taught four periods daily in addition to his duties as principal. In 1934 the York County Training School became an accredited state high school.

After nineteen years as principal, Brown resigned in 1934 to become an educational adviser for the Civilian Conservation Corps, a New Deal program that put unemployed men to work building and repairing roads and bridges and undertaking conservation projects. He taught at night and provided vocational and other training for young men who in many instances had received little previous education.

In 1942 Brown became the first African American to hold a white-collar job at the naval mine depot. As a time and leave clerk he won the respect of his coworkers and supervisors and was able to recommend others, black and white, for jobs at the depot. Brown also became the first black man to hold a supervisory post, when he was named supervisor of inventory. He held the latter position for eight years until he retired in 1959.

As a leader in his community, Brown helped to found in 1936 and for twelve years served as president of the York County Voters' League (later known as the York County Civic Association). In that year the county had only ninety-two registered black voters, nearly all of them men. Brown made a special effort to convince women to register and vote. By 1961 more than 800 African Americans were on the county's voting rolls. Brown had joined the National Association for the Advancement of Colored People early in the 1920s and in 1940 helped organize the York–James City–Williamsburg branch of the NAACP and served for seventeen years as its president. Employment with the federal government helped to shield him from economic retaliation for his activism, but his long struggle to improve conditions for African Americans in York County still required courageous determination. In recognition of his services, Brown was elected president of the Virginia Conference of Branches of the NAACP in 1968 and served through 1970.

In 1970 Brown's neighbors, many of them graduates of the York County Training School, honored him with a surprise birthday party at Shiloh Baptist Church. A list of his civic activities—from campaigning for the NAACP through organizing a troop of Boy Scouts to serving on the church's board of trustees—filled nearly a page of the printed program. Above all, the program declared, Brown gave "courage, inspiration, and hard work" to his community.

On 11 August 1915 Brown married Annie Williams, of Fayetteville, North Carolina. They had one son but later divorced. On 25 December 1928 Brown married Lucy Ann Hobday, a home economics teacher. After her death on 4 October 1954, he married Ethel Oliver Fowlkes, a music teacher, on 7 July 1956. She had one son and three daughters from an earlier marriage and died on 18 October 1965. Charles Edward Brown died at his York County residence on 30 June 1975. He was buried between his second and third wives in the Old Shiloh Baptist Church cemetery.

Birth date in BVS Birth Register, Charlotte Co.; Caldwell, *History of the American Negro*, 351–353 (por.), gives variant birth date of 21 Sept. 1887 and date of first marriage; BVS Marriage Register, Gloucester Co., 1928; third marriage and wives' death dates confirmed by BVS; *Newport News Daily Press*, 8 June 1969 (por.); *Norfolk Journal and Guide*, national ed., 17 Oct. 1970; information provided by Louise Billups, Alexander Lee, John M. Robinson, and Beulah Wallace; *This is Your Life . . . Charles Edward Brown* (1970), with quotation and variant birth date of 24 Sept. 1889, and copy of funeral obsequies, courtesy of Louise Billups, in DVB Files; obituaries in *Williamsburg Virginia Gazette*, 4 July 1975, and *Norfolk Journal and Guide*, 12 July 1975 (por.).

JOHN T. KNEEBONE

BROWN, Duncan McGregor (4 November 1856–27 January 1908), educator, was born in Petersburg, the son of Charles C. Brown, a baker, and Mary McGregor Brown. His parents had recently immigrated to the United States from England and Scotland, respectively. Brown attended the local high school, part of a public school system that Petersburg established in 1868, two years before a statewide public school system began. The high school offered only three years of classes but emphasized Latin and science. After completing his studies in 1873, Brown attended Hampden-Sydney College and graduated in 1877.

Brown returned to Petersburg and in 1878 became the third principal of the Peabody School, established in 1874 as the first public high school for African Americans in Virginia. Whites taught all the classes, but the school offered the same classical course of study as the white high school. Brown moved in 1881 to the Anderson Public School, a white grammar school, as principal, and the school board also named him principal of schools. He reported directly to the school board and had responsibilities similar to those of the superintendent of schools, who reported to the State Board of Education.

Brown soon found himself the victim of political conflict. The local branch of the Readjusters, a coalition of white and black Republicans and disaffected Democrats led by William Mahone, of Petersburg, held a slight majority on the city council. They supported the effort of local blacks to hire African American teachers for their schools, an action the school board refused to take. Turning to the Readjuster-controlled State Board of Education, in August 1882 they obtained a ruling that the school board members had failed to qualify legally. The state board then named a new, more tractable local school board. In addition to hiring black teachers for the first time, Petersburg's new school board replaced Brown as principal of schools with the Readjuster superintendent of schools, Edward B. Branch.

Brown immediately embarked on a new career. He entered the Medical College of Virginia, graduated on 31 March 1884, returned to Petersburg, and began a practice as a physician. At the end of May 1886, after the Democratic Party captured control of the State Board of Education, it removed Branch as superintendent of schools in Petersburg. Brown was named as his replacement and assumed his new duties on 1 July 1886. For the next few years he identified himself in city directories as both superintendent and physician, but he eventually gave up his medical practice for a full-time career as an educator. Brown regularly lectured at summer teachers' institutes across the state and gained a reputation for expertise on educational legislation. He also eventually served as clerk and treasurer of the Petersburg school board, attesting to the board's willingness to defer to his authority as superintendent.

Brown had an effective working relationship with the school board but lacked sufficient resources for the public schools as Petersburg's economy declined. Two attempts to reintroduce a four-year course of study in the high school failed for lack of funds in 1886 and 1888. In annual reports to the state superintendent of public instruction Brown warned regularly that without increased appropriations the city could not improve its schools further. He managed to obtain funding for a new high school building, which opened in October 1895, but until 1910 the curriculum remained the same as in his school days, despite some local sentiment for making the program more practical in nature. Courses in home economics were introduced in 1899, but manual training courses did not begin until a decade after Brown's death.

On 30 April 1896 Brown married Lucy Adelaide McAllister, a native of Surry County and a former student at the Petersburg High School. They had one son and one daughter.

Early in the twentieth century Brown developed tuberculosis of the throat, and in 1907 the school board granted him a four-month leave of absence. Duncan McGregor Brown died at his home in Petersburg on 27 January 1908. The schools closed for his funeral. Black teachers and students attended the service but were seated in the balcony at Saint John's Episcopal Church, which Brown had long served as vestryman and church treasurer. He was buried in Blandford Cemetery in Petersburg. To honor Brown's contributions to the city, a new elementary school (later an administration building) was given his name in 1908.

Biography in Martha Short Dance, *Peabody High School: A History of the First Negro Public High School in Virginia* (1976), 24–25 (por.); Henry Buckius Brockwell, "History of Secondary Education in Petersburg, Virginia" (master's thesis, UVA, 1939), 97–99, 103, 107–110, 133, 300; James G. Scott and Edward A. Wyatt IV, *Petersburg's Story: A History* (1960), 264; William D. Henderson, *Gilded Age City: Politics, Life and Labor in Petersburg, Virginia, 1874–1889* (1980), 132–139; *Petersburg Rural Messenger*, 26 Aug. 1882; *Petersburg Daily Index-Appeal*, 30, 31 Aug. 1882, 1 June 1886, 1 May 1896; BVS Marriage Register, Surry Co.; obituaries and accounts of funeral in *Petersburg Daily Index-Appeal*, 28, 30 Jan. 1908, *Petersburg Daily Progress*, 29 Jan. 1908, *Virginia Journal of Education* 1 (Feb. 1908): 25, and *Virginia Normal and Industrial Institute Gazette* 14 (Apr. 1908): 3.

JOHN T. KNEEBONE

BROWN, Edward C. (ca. July 1877–24 January 1928), entrepreneur, was born in Philadelphia, the son of Robert Brown and Anna M. Cooper Brown. His father was one of the first African American policemen in Philadelphia, and a sister became one of the first professional black librarians in the public library system of Cincinnati. Brown attended local schools and the Spencerian Business College in Philadelphia before working first as a mail clerk and then as a stenographer for a white official of the National Railway Company. He must have held that job only briefly before moving to Newport News, where he was listed as an insurance agent in an 1897–1898 city directory. Brown later stated that when he arrived in Virginia he worked as a waiter in a resort hotel. The 1900 census gave his occupation as a real estate agent, even though he was then still a lodger. Apparently Brown added about seven years to his age when he reported to the census taker, perhaps to lend credibility to his business reputation, and he also added several years to his age on 29 August 1901 when he married Estelle A. Smith, of Hampton. They had no children.

On 1 November 1905 Brown and four other men obtained a charter for E. C. Brown, Incorporated, with the declared intention of dealing in insurance and real estate. Black capitalists faced nearly insuperable obstacles. Real estate and banking markets were restricted to the segregated black community, African Americans had limited access to capital for investment, and young people entering business had few opportunities to gain experience. To bolster his new business, Brown published at least one issue of the *Dollar Mark* (June 1906), a magazine that carried articles encouraging thrift, arguing for investment in African American enterprises, and explaining why stock in E. C. Brown, Incorporated, would be a good investment. On 10 June 1908 he opened the Crown Savings Bank in Newport News, with capital of $5,000. The bank's success spurred Brown's ambitions. He established the Brown Savings Bank in Norfolk on 10 April 1909, followed later by the Beneficial Insurance Company of Norfolk and by the Brown Realty Company, probably a branch of E. C. Brown, Incorporated.

Brown soon looked beyond Tidewater. Retaining his business associations in Virginia, he returned to Philadelphia in 1913 and started a real estate company there. In partnership with Andrew F. Stevens, a respected local political and civic leader in the African American community, Brown established the Home Extension and Insurance Association. In 1915 the partners founded the private banking firm of Brown and Stevens. Business was good. Full employment during World War I and the many blacks who moved from the South to Philadelphia brought Brown customers who borrowed money to buy houses and had wages sufficient enough to open savings accounts. The bank's advertisements emphasized the institution's growth as evidence of its stability and exhorted customers to develop the habit of thrift.

Success seemed to expand Brown's ambitions. He created the Quality Amusement Corporation, which operated the legendary Lafayette Theater in New York City and controlled theaters in several other cities, including Newport News and Norfolk. In 1917 he formed the Payton Apartments Corporation to purchase a New York apartment complex valued at nearly $1 million. To finance these and other ventures, Brown invested his bank's funds and borrowed against his properties, climbing an ever-steeper ladder of mortgages. Compounding the situation, he and his wife acquired expensive tastes. Salesmen from Bonwit Teller reportedly brought gowns to the Brown household so that Estelle Brown could select her finery free from the snubs that black customers often faced in public. His cream-colored Stutz and her Pierce Arrow automobiles helped lend credence to the gossip.

The nation suffered an economic recession after World War I, and Brown's empire cracked. His Quality Amusement Corporation failed, and its expensive theaters had to be sold at a loss. Brown liquidated his Virginia properties and concentrated on his bank and his real estate in New York and Philadelphia. The bank's solvency came into question as a result of its bad investments and expensive loans, leading to a run on the bank by nervous depositors on 7 February 1925. Because the bank's assets were tied up in real estate, Brown could not halt the panic. On 10 February 1925 the Brown and Stevens Bank collapsed, bringing down two branch banks and taking with it the savings of thousands of depositors. A bank examiner regarded it as "the greatest example of irresponsibility" he had ever encountered. Even the bank building itself had several mortgages on it. To maintain his honor, Stevens gave up his own property and wealth to restore what little he could of the lost savings, but in stark contrast only a judge's restraining order prevented Brown from conveying his remaining assets to his wife to protect them from the bank's creditors.

Without a word of contrition, Brown fled to New York City to escape public anger. Remembered in the North only as a cautionary example of spectacular failure, Brown left a more enduring institutional legacy in Virginia. In 1919 the Brown Savings Bank in Norfolk changed its name to the Metropolitan Bank and Trust Company and in 1922 merged with the Tidewater Bank and Trust Company to become the nation's largest black-owned financial institution. Despite its size the bank could not survive the Great Depression and closed forever in June 1933. The much smaller Crown Savings Bank continued to operate in Newport News until 4 September 1964.

The collapse of his enterprises ruined his health, and Edward C. Brown died of kidney failure and heart disease on 24 January 1928 in a tenement in New York City. He was buried in the Eden Cemetery in Philadelphia, but no obituary appeared in that city's black newspaper.

Birth date not recorded in Philadelphia; biographies in W. N. Hartshorn, ed., *An Era of Progress and Promise, 1863–1910* (1910), 472–473 (gives 1876 year of birth), and *National Cyclopedia of the Colored Race* (1919), 452–453 (por.; gives 1877 year of birth); Census, Warwick Co., 1900 (gives July 1870 birth date); BVS Marriage Register, Elizabeth City Co. (gives age as twenty-seven on 29 Aug. 1901); New York City Bureau of Records, Death Certificate, signed 24 Jan. 1928 (gives age as fifty); family information in Wendell P. Dabney, *Cincinnati's Colored Citizens: Historical, Sociological and Biographical* (1926), 321; information provided by Dorothy Warrick Taylor; SCC Charter Book, 58:22–24, 66:65–66; Abram L. Harris, *The Negro as Capitalist: A Study of Banking and Business Among American Negroes* (1936), 84–88, 125–143; Earl Lewis, *In Their Own Interests: Race, Class, and Power in Twentieth-Century Norfolk, Virginia* (1991), 44–45, 122–123; Alexander Crosby Brown, ed., *Newport News' 325 Years: A Record of the Progress of a Virginia Community* (1946), 253–254; *Norfolk Journal and Guide,* 4 Mar. 1922, 14 May 1927, 20 Jan. 1951, 12 Sept. 1964; financial troubles detailed almost weekly in *Philadelphia Tribune,* 14 Feb. 1925 through 1926 (quotation, 21 Mar. 1925); obituaries in *New York Age* and *Norfolk Journal and Guide,* both 28 Jan. 1928, and *New York Amsterdam News,* 1 Feb. 1928.

JOHN T. KNEEBONE

BROWN, Edward Thomas (7 January 1859–9 March 1933), developer of Endless Caverns, was born in Gainesville, Georgia, the son of Warren A. Brown, a prosperous merchant, and Louisa C. Hoyt Brown. Bright and ambitious, he had by the age of nineteen graduated from Davidson College in North Carolina, studied law in an Atlanta judge's office, and been admitted to the bar. Brown practiced law in Athens,

Georgia, and served as solicitor general of that state's Western Judicial Circuit from 1885 to 1889. He was elected to a two-year term as mayor of Athens in 1890. On 12 July 1887 Brown married Mary Celestine Mitchell, of Norwalk, Ohio. The couple had two sons and one daughter.

In 1899 Brown moved to Atlanta, where he continued to practice law and became more deeply involved in politics. He was the state's attorney for the Western and Atlantic Railroad from 1899 until 1903, and he also served as legal counsel for the American Telephone and Telegraph Company and for the Seaboard Air Line Railway. A stalwart Democrat, Brown was chairman of the Democratic State Committee from 1900 to 1904 and supported the conservative Democrat Allen Daniel Candler for governor in two successful campaigns in 1898 and 1900. After his appointment as lieutenant colonel on Candler's staff, he was known as Colonel Brown. His business acumen and political savvy gained him a reputation as one of the most influential political leaders in the state. When Woodrow Wilson, his cousin by marriage, ran for president in 1912, Brown played an important role in the campaign in Georgia. Two years later Wilson appointed him vice chairman and deputy agent of the Federal Reserve Bank of Atlanta.

Brown's life changed following the death of his younger son in February 1919 from injuries suffered in World War I. Later that year Brown and his wife traveled to Washington, D.C., to visit their other son, Edward Mitchell Brown. En route they stopped in New Market, where townspeople informed them of the area's natural caverns. In August 1919 Brown purchased the Rockingham County land that the caverns occupied and formed a partnership with his son to develop the site as a tourist attraction. This sort of enterprise had already proved financially successful; during the 1870s Luray Caverns in Page County, illuminated with thousands of candles, attracted visitors and international publicity.

After moving to Washington, D.C., Brown, his son, and a nephew, Gordon Brown, prepared the cave for tourists. The process involved opening up areas with drills and explosives, erecting stone safety walls along the steep cliffs, wiring the caverns for electricity, building an elaborate entrance, and launching an aggressive, international advertising campaign. Brown also persuaded the Rockingham County board of supervisors to appropriate money for a road to the caverns from the nearby Valley Pike (U.S. Route 11), which provided direct highway links to New York and Atlanta. He called the cave Endless Caverns because no end had yet been discovered. The attraction opened to the public on 14 August 1920 and met with immediate success. Four years later, over the three-day Labor Day weekend in 1924, 3,000 people visited the caverns, and from 800 to 1,000 cars with out-of-state license plates were counted in the parking lot.

By that date New Market was the acknowledged tourist hub of the Shenandoah Valley, able to lodge 700 travelers in its hotels and private homes. Brown had done more than anyone else to unite the Valley for the promotion of tourism. As the region's tourist industry grew he advocated further improvements in transportation. Brown purchased and donated adjacent land to the Valley Pike so that the road could be widened, and he convinced other property owners to grant free rights-of-way. He secured the support of the State Highway Commission, and improvement of the road commenced. In 1928 Brown leased another cave near Melrose in Rockingham County and opened it to the public as the Caverns of Melrose. He also developed the Natural Chimneys in Augusta County as a tourist attraction.

Sometime after the death of his wife on 27 March 1925, Brown gave up his Washington residence and settled near New Market. In the autumn of 1932, his own health failing, he relinquished management of the Endless Caverns to his son, his nephew, and his son-in-law, Ben King. Brown moved to the Mayflower Hotel in Washington, D.C., but in spite of his poor health he was planning to open a law office and to remain politically active. At the presidential inauguration of his friend Franklin Delano Roosevelt on 4 March 1933, Brown caught a cold, which developed into bronchial pneumonia.

Woodrow Wilson's former personal physician attended him, but Edward Thomas Brown died in the Mayflower Hotel on 9 March 1933. During his funeral in Athens, Georgia, on 13 March 1933, residents of New Market honored him by closing the doors of their businesses for half an hour.

Lucian Lamar Knight, *Standard History of Georgia and Georgians* (1917), 6:2971–2973; Clark Howell et al., eds., *The Book of Georgia: A Work for Press Reference* (1920), 206 (por.), 288; Noah Daniel Showalter, *Atlas of Rockingham County, Virginia* (1939), 63; John W. Wayland, ed., *Men of Mark and Representative Citizens of Harrisonburg and Rockingham County, Virginia* (1943), 391; *New York Times*, 3 Oct. 1914; *New Market Shenandoah Valley*, 17 June, 19 Aug. 1920, 4 Sept. 1924; Elizabeth Atwood, " 'Saratoga of the South': Tourism in Luray, Virginia, 1878–1905," in *Edge of the South: Life in Nineteenth-Century Virginia*, ed. Edward L. Ayers and John C. Willis (1991), 157–172; obituaries and accounts of funeral in *Harrisonburg Daily News-Record*, 10–11, 13–15 Mar. 1933, and *Atlanta Constitution*, 11 Mar. 1933.

STACY G. MOORE

BROWN, Edward Wellington (d. 15 September 1929), editor and officer of the Grand Fountain United Order of True Reformers, was born into slavery in Southampton County, the son of Edward Brown and Euseba Clements Brown. Accounts of his early life are vague and inconsistent. Various reference works give dates of birth ranging from 1860 to 1878, with later birth years given as his life progressed. During his second year as commissioner of revenue for Prince George County in 1888, he signed his reports "Edward Willie Brown." He may have adopted the middle name himself.

Brown's father died before the end of the Civil War. His maternal grandparents, who had acquired some education during slavery, encouraged him to attend a local school at Drewrysville. Brown studied under John Wesley Cromwell, a pioneer black teacher, and after joining the local Baptist church he became close to Joseph Gregory, its pastor and a political activist. The church elected Brown its clerk when he was only twelve years old. With his obvious potential he received encouragement to continue his education. Brown studied at Hampton Normal and Agricultural Institute (later Hampton University) from 1878 to 1880 and then accepted a teaching post in Prince George County.

In addition to teaching, Brown at various times engaged in farming and operated a store. He also entered politics and on 26 May 1887 was elected county commissioner of revenue as part of the successful Republican ticket. The next year Brown abandoned party regularity to support the independent Republican candidacy of John Mercer Langston for Congress, but he returned to the fold in time for reelection as commissioner of revenue, thus becoming one of the few African Americans who held public office into the 1890s. Despite the county's black majority, white Democrats finally regained control over the ballot box, and Brown lost his bid for reelection in May 1895. On 27 December 1894 he married Nannie Ruffin Allen, a native of Prince George County. They had one daughter and one son, George William Clement Brown, who became a noted educator.

Brown moved his family to Richmond after the 1895–1896 school term concluded. He planned to study medicine but accepted work as a clerk at the Savings Bank of the Grand Fountain United Order of True Reformers, a fraternal beneficiary organization. Brown had been a charter member of a fountain, as local lodges were called, in Prince George County in 1889. The order sent him to Southampton County, where he organized five fountains. In May 1897 Brown succeeded John Henry Smyth as editor of the order's weekly newspaper, the *Reformer*, which was published in Richmond.

Only two issues of the four-page paper from Brown's tenure are known to survive. They show that the activities of the True Reformers filled the news columns. Brown's editorials boosted the order's various enterprises while condemning the new segregation laws and anti-Negro prejudice, but his was a conservative editorial voice by comparison with the *Richmond Planet*. In 1898 the *Reformer* counted a circulation of 5,800, and even more people probably read it at the order's many lodges throughout the eastern United States. As did many other small newspapers, the *Reformer* also operated a printing shop, at which his brother Benjamin R. Brown worked.

In 1910 the True Reformers' bank went into receivership, and the order's finances collapsed. Unlike several of the other officers, Brown was not charged with criminal offenses, but he shared in the general discredit. Members attempting to save the order ousted all of the officers in August 1911, and he left the newspaper. Brown's wife had died in September 1905, and on 18 October 1906 he married Minnie Odessa White, daughter of the pastor of Mount Carmel Baptist Church, at which Brown was a lay leader. Perhaps his new father-in-law convinced him to become an ordained minister. Brown served a Baptist church at Tappahannock until about 1917, when he became pastor of the First Baptist Church in the Brighton neighborhood of Portsmouth. He guided the congregation through construction of a new brick building in 1918 but left the ministry in the mid-1920s to join his son's real estate and insurance agency in Norfolk. Edward Wellington Brown suffered a stroke and died in Norfolk on 15 September 1929. He was buried in Richmond.

Biographies in *Twenty-Two Years' Work of the Hampton Normal and Agricultural Institute* (1893), 147 (gives 1860 birth date), in W. P. Burrell and D. E. Johnson, *Twenty-Five Years History of the Grand Fountain of the United Order of True Reformers, 1881–1905* (1909), 52 (por.), 159, 200, 212, 268, 418–421 (gives 1864 birth date), in William N. Hartshorn, ed., *An Era of Progress and Promise, 1863–1910* (1910), 454 (por.; gives 1864 birth date), and in Caldwell, *History of the American Negro*, 487–489 (gives 11 Jan. 1873 birth date); Census, Richmond City, 1900 (gives Jan. 1862 birth date), Richmond City, 1910 (gives 1865 birth date), Portsmouth, 1920 (gives 1873 birth date); BVS Marriage Register, Prince George Co. (gives age as thirty-one on 27 Dec. 1894), Richmond City (gives age as forty-three on 18 Oct. 1906); BVS Death Certificate, Norfolk City (gives 1878 birth date); *Petersburg Daily Index-Appeal*, 28 May 1887, 25 May 1895; *Richmond Southern News*, 15 Oct. 1892; *Richmond Reformer,* 27 Jan. 1900, 28 Jan. 1905; *Richmond Planet*, 13 Oct. 1906, 25 Feb., 12, 26 Aug. 1911; Lelia Lawrence Barnes, *The Best of Brighton—As I Remember* (1988), 65–68; obituary in *Norfolk Journal and Guide*, 21 Sept. 1929.

JOHN T. KNEEBONE

BROWN, George O. (August 1852–17 May 1910), photographer, was born in Orange County, the son of Willis Brown and Winnie Brown. According to family tradition the family was enslaved and may have changed its surname after emancipation. Sometime after the Civil War the family moved to Richmond. He was probably the George Brown who was baptized and joined Ebenezer Baptist Church on 7 May 1871. Brown opened an account at the local bank of the Freedmen's Savings and Trust Company on 23 March 1872. The bank records identify him as working in a photographic gallery. Most likely Brown learned photography on the job at one of Richmond's busy studios. By 1879 he was working at the photographic gallery of George W. Davis.

On 21 July 1881 Brown married Bettie G. Mason, a teacher at Navy Hill School in Richmond. They had two sons and two daughters, but two children did not survive infancy. About 1888 they moved into a house near Ebenezer Baptist Church in Jackson Ward, the center of black residential, commercial, and cultural life in Richmond. In 1895 Brown signed a three-year partnership agreement with Rebecca P. Farley to operate the Jefferson Fine Art Gallery. Farley's husband James Conway Farley had also worked as a photographer for G. W. Davis, and he joined forces with Brown in operating the new studio. Brown had been the head photographic printer at Davis's gallery and continued that specialty with his new partner. By 1899 Brown had opened his own studio, the Old Dominion Gallery, on East Broad Street, and in 1905 he moved his enterprise to 603 North Second Street in the heart of Jackson Ward.

Brown's two children who reached adulthood, Bessie Gwendola Brown and George Willis Brown, joined the family business. The Browns, whose slogan was "Makers of Portraits That Please," became the most important visual chroniclers of Richmond's African American population, producing thousands of studio portraits and documenting community life at schools, sporting events, and fraternal meetings. The studio produced pictures for schools and institutions throughout the state, including Virginia Union University, Virginia Normal and Industrial Institute (later Virginia State University), Hampton Normal and Agricultural Institute (later Hampton University), Saint Paul's Industrial School (later Saint Paul's College) in Lawrenceville, and the Virginia Industrial School for Girls. The *Richmond Planet* and its successor, the *Richmond Afro-American*, frequently ran images by the Browns. The quality of Brown's work brought into his studio such notable Virginians as the banker and entrepreneur Maggie Lena Mitchell Walker and the dancer and film star Bill "Bojangles" Robinson, but for the most part his images documented the everyday experience of African Americans, capturing weddings, funerals, country church congregations, and other typical scenes. The photographs are readily identifiable by the studio mark "The Browns." In 1907 Brown won a silver medal for his photographs at the Jamestown Ter-Centennial Exposition, and the studio depicted the award in its advertisements.

George O. Brown died in Richmond on 17 May 1910. He owned a plot in Union Sycamore Cemetery, one of the Barton Heights cemeteries, and was most likely buried there. The family business that Brown founded continued to thrive for almost sixty years after his death. George Willis Brown died on 10 May 1946, but Bessie Gwendola Brown, who lived with her brother's widow, operated the studio until 1969. Bessie Gwendola Brown died on 28 December 1977. George Willis Brown Jr. worked for a short time with his father and aunt but left after disagreements about the operation of the firm. One of his two sons, Albert Wilder Brown, has worked as a photographer since 1982. George O. Brown's legacy and his pioneering role as a photographer are reflected in recent interest in his work. Exhibitions on African American photographers at the Smithsonian Institution and at Chicago's DuSable Museum of African-American History have featured his photographs. Richmond's Valentine Museum has also exhibited photographs and equipment from the Brown studio and owns several collections of photographs that include numerous examples of the studio's work both before and after his death.

Family and business history in *Richmond Planet*, 29 Aug. 1925, and *Richmond News Leader*, 7 Feb. 1985 (por.); month and year of birth in Census, Richmond City, 1900; BVS Marriage Register, Richmond City; information provided by great-grandsons Albert Wilder Brown and Michael Gregory Brown, who recall his middle name as Oscar; family papers in possession of Julia Turner Brown, 2001; Ebenezer Baptist Church Minute Book, 1858–1876 (LVA microfilm), 175; Freedmen's Bank Records; Richmond city directories, 1871–1910; *Richmond Planet*, 31 Aug., 7 Sept. 1895, 28 May 1910; Anacostia Museum and Center for African American History and Culture, Smithsonian Institution, *Reflections in Black: A History of Black Photographers, 1840 to the Present* (2000), 2, 4; Giles B. Jackson and D. Webster Davis, *The Industrial History of the Negro Race of the United States* (1908), 246, 396; obituary in *Richmond Planet*, 21 May 1910.

GREGG D. KIMBALL

BROWN, George William Clement (1 May 1895–3 January 1973), educator, was born in Prince George County, the son of Edward Wellington Brown, a teacher and county commissioner of revenue, and Nannie Ruffin Allen Brown. The family moved to Richmond in 1896. Brown's mother died in 1905, and the following year his father, then editor of the weekly *Reformer*, married Minnie Odessa White, who helped raise Brown and his sister. He completed his secondary education in Richmond and graduated from Virginia Union University in 1917.

Brown served for one year as assistant principal of the Corey Memorial Institute, a private secondary school in Portsmouth, and the following year he worked as a bookkeeper for the Mutual Savings Bank. On 9 June 1919 he became assistant secretary of the new Tidewater Bank and Trust Company of Norfolk. Brown moved to Norfolk and on 29 November 1919 in Richmond married Elaine Hucles, daughter of a longtime treasurer and business manager of Virginia Normal and Industrial Institute (later Virginia State University) near Petersburg. They had one son and two daughters.

In March 1921 Brown left the bank and worked in several local businesses until 1925, when he established Brown and Brown, Inc., a real estate agency, in partnership with his wife and father, who had also moved to Norfolk. The business expanded into loans and insurance, and after the death of his father in 1929 the firm was called G. W. C. Brown Insurance Agency. For a time after 1930 Brown was also district manager for the Victory Life Insurance Company, of Chicago.

Early in 1935 the Norfolk Federation of Parent-Teacher Leagues, which Elaine H. Brown served as secretary, revived an effort to create a local junior college for African Americans. G. W. C. Brown was elected chairman of the publicity committee at an organizational meeting in June and later became cochairman of the campaign itself. Virginia Union University agreed to make the junior college an extension division and established enrollment centers at local high schools and at Brown's insurance agency.

The Norfolk Unit of Virginia Union University opened on 18 September 1935 with eighty-five day students and forty-seven evening students meeting in rooms at the Young Men's Christian Association. Brown agreed to serve as the school's business manager. He and his wife operated their insurance agency until after World War II, but Brown gave most of his attention to the new school. His college classmate John Malcus Ellison served as liaison with Virginia Union, and Brown worked with him to get the junior college accredited. The university's support, however, did not extend to financial aid, and Brown had to conduct continuous fund-raising campaigns. As a lay leader of the Bank Street Baptist Church who was also active in numerous civic organizations, he had the connections and the respect to mobilize community leaders behind the growing school.

Lyman Beecher Brooks became director of the school in 1938, and he and Brown, who was also secretary of the school's advisory board, worked effectively together. They recognized that to obtain government funding the connection to Virginia Union, a private Baptist school, would have to be severed, and in March 1942 Brown helped bring about reorganization as the independent Norfolk Polytechnic College. On 29 February 1944 the school became part of the state's system of higher education as the Norfolk Division of Virginia State College.

Brown helped arrange for Teachers College of Columbia University to offer graduate courses at the school from 1942 to 1945, and he earned a master's degree in education in 1945. Virginia State College assumed responsibility for the graduate program into the 1960s. Brown continually sought additional professional training and on 3 October 1950 became the first African American admitted to a course at what later became Old Dominion University.

In 1952 Brown stepped down as business manager in order to become supervisor of the evening school, and to enable him to carry out his responsibilities he earned a professional certificate from Columbia University. He also supervised the school's audiovisual center from 1952 to 1956. In May 1957 he organized a successful National Conference on Adult Education at the school. One year later, the college graduated its first four-year class.

Brown retired in 1967, and his friends organized a public tribute in his honor. Two years later the school that Brown had helped to create became Norfolk State College (later Norfolk State University), an independent institution of higher learning. To generate private gifts the Norfolk State College Foundation was chartered in 1971, with Brown serving as chairman until his death. His numerous awards include an honorary doctorate from Virginia Union University in 1950, and a scholarship fund and campus building at Norfolk State University bear his name, but as a 1967 editorial tribute observed, Norfolk State itself was "his monument."

George William Clement Brown died in Norfolk on 3 January 1973 and was buried in Roosevelt Memorial Park in Chesapeake.

Caldwell, *History of the American Negro*, 257–260 (por.; gives variant date and place of birth as 23 Sept. 1894 in Richmond); Prince George Co. Birth Register gives 1 May 1895, recorded by his father as commissioner of revenue; Census, Richmond City, 1900, gives birth date as Sept. 1895; BVS Marriage Register, Richmond City (gives age as twenty-five on 29 Nov. 1919); Social Security application, Social Security Administration, Office of Earnings Operations, Baltimore, Md., gives birth date as 23 Sept. 1895; *Norfolk Journal and Guide*, 7 Jan. 1950, 3 (quotation), 10 June 1967; *Richmond Afro-American*, 14 Oct. 1950; *Congressional Record*, 90th Cong., 1st sess., 13737–13738; Lyman Beecher Brooks, *Upward: A History of Norfolk State University (1935 to 1975)* (1983); obituaries in *Norfolk Virginian-Pilot*, 4 Jan. 1973, and *Norfolk Journal and Guide*, home ed., 6 Jan. 1973 (por.).

JOHN T. KNEEBONE

BROWN, Goodman (24 July 1840–4 July 1929), member of the House of Delegates, was born in Surry County, the son of Herbert Brown, a farmer, and Parthena Bell Brown, both of whom were free African Americans. His grandfather Scipio Brown received his freedom in 1804 from James Bell, of Surry County, and in 1809 married Amy Johnson, a free woman. Herbert Brown and his brother Benjamin Brown both owned property in Surry County before the Civil War. Goodman Brown worked on his father's fifty-acre farm until age nineteen and obtained some rudimentary education in a night school.

On 1 November 1862, near Cape Fear, North Carolina, Brown enlisted in the United States Navy as a cabin boy aboard the USS *Maratanza*. He was discharged at Savannah, Georgia, on 20 December 1864. Brown's whereabouts immediately before and after his Civil War naval service are not known. An unsubstantiated later account indicates that he served in the United States Army. Possibly Brown worked for the army in some civilian capacity. After the war he returned to Surry County and quickly emerged as a community leader. When the new county agent of the Freedmen's Bureau sought to identify the most respectable African American men in the county, local black residents provided him with eight names in April 1867, among them Goodman Brown, his brother Bedford Brown, and their father and uncle. Later two other members of the family, James Brown and W. T. Brown, served as overseers of the poor in Surry County. In 1872 Brown married Mary Todd Park (or Parke), of Richmond. A pioneering black teacher in Surry County, she helped him continue his education. Of their nine children, four sons and four daughters survived.

During the 1870s Brown became involved in politics. On 14 March 1881 he attended a meeting in Petersburg at which regional African American leaders resolved to support the Readjuster Party and its leader, William Mahone. Brown corresponded with Mahone and in a letter dated 14 May 1883 identified himself as chairman of the Surry County Readjuster Committee. He used his relationship with Mahone to seek patronage positions for local men and ask that prominent political leaders be scheduled to speak in the county. After the Readjuster Party ceased to exist, Brown followed Mahone into the Republican Party. Several times Brown sought the Republican nomination to the House of Delegates from the district consisting of Prince George and Surry Counties but lost to candidates from Prince George County. In October 1887 he finally secured the nomination and despite opposition within his own party defeated

Democratic candidate John Wilson by a margin of more than two to one. During the campaign newspapers identified Brown as a Mahone supporter. The Democratic Party then fully controlled the assembly, and as a Mahone Republican and an African American, Brown received the lowest-ranking appointments on the Committee on Immigration and the inconsequential Committee on Retrenchment and Economy. He did not seek renomination in 1889.

Brown had been acquiring land since the end of the war. By the time he entered the assembly he owned five tracts totaling almost 226 acres, on which he raised corn and peanuts. Brown resided in the Cobham district near Bacon's Castle. He belonged to the Mount Nebo Baptist Church after 1875 and for four decades was one of his county's leading African American men. Goodman Brown died of uremia in Surry County on 4 July 1929 and was buried near Bacon's Castle.

Jackson, *Negro Office-Holders*, 6 (frontispiece por.); family history provided by great-great-granddaughter Gertie Williams; Index to Rendezvous Reports, Civil War, 1861–1865, and muster roll of USS *Maratanza*, 1 Jan. 1863, Records of Bureau of Naval Personnel, RG 24, NARA; J. F. Wilcox to O. Brown, 4 Apr. 1867, Freedmen's Bureau Records; several Brown letters in William Mahone Papers, Duke; *Richmond Daily Whig*, 18 Mar. 1881; *Petersburg Daily Index-Appeal*, 22, 29 Oct. 1887; Election Records, no. 24, RG 13, LVA; birth and death dates confirmed by BVS and in obituary in *Richmond Planet*, 27 July 1929.

MICHAEL PLUNKETT

BROWN, Henry Box (1815 or 1816–after 9 May 1878), abolitionist lecturer and performer, was born Henry Brown at the Hermitage, a plantation about ten miles from Yanceyville in Louisa County. Brown, his parents (names unknown), three brothers, and four sisters were slaves of John Barret, a former mayor of Richmond. After Barret's death on 9 June 1830, Brown was separated from his family and sent to Richmond to work in the tobacco factory of Barret's son William Barret, whose property he became.

In Richmond about 1836 Brown married Nancy, a slave owned by a different master. They had three children. The family joined the First African Baptist Church, where Henry Brown sang in the church's choir. He had become a skilled tobacco worker and earned enough money through overwork to set up his family in a rented house. Then, in August 1848, Nancy Brown's master suddenly sold her and their children (she was pregnant with their fourth child), and they were taken away to North Carolina.

After mourning his loss for several months, Brown resolved to escape from slavery and conceived an unusual method. Through James Caesar Anthony Smith, a free black and fellow member of the church choir, he contacted Samuel Alexander Smith, a white shoemaker and sometime gambler, who agreed for a price to help Brown escape. The three men rejected several possible means before Brown had the inspiration to be shipped in a box by rail to Philadelphia. Samuel Smith accordingly contacted James Miller McKim, a Philadelphia leader of the Pennsylvania Anti-Slavery Society who was involved in Underground Railroad activities.

On 23 March 1849 the Smiths sealed Brown into a box about three feet long, two and one-half feet deep, and two feet wide, and had it conveyed by train to Philadelphia. On the steamboat transfer up the Potomac River to Washington from the Richmond, Fredericksburg, and Potomac Railroad's terminus at Aquia Creek, Brown was turned head down in the box for several hours and nearly died. At other transfers the box was roughly handled, but he endured silently. After the parcel finally arrived in Philadelphia early on 24 March 1849, McKim took delivery at the office of the Pennsylvania Anti-Slavery Society, where the box was opened with great trepidation. After twenty-six hours' confinement, Brown emerged, alive and free.

At the end of May Brown appeared before the New England Anti-Slavery Convention in Boston, where his daring escape was celebrated as proof that slaves desired liberty, and he was renamed Henry Box Brown. He had a fine voice and performed the hymn of thanksgiving that he had sung on his arrival in Philadelphia. That summer he appeared at antislavery gatherings. Published sheets with the lyrics to "Song, Sung by Mr. Brown on being removed from the box" and "Escape from Slavery of Henry Box Brown" were probably sold by Brown after his perfor-

mances. Early in September 1849 the *Narrative of Henry Box Brown*, written by Charles Stearns, was published in Boston. Brown and Stearns toured New England selling the book and delivering antislavery lectures into the early part of November 1849.

Samuel Smith attempted another shipment of slaves from Richmond to Philadelphia on 8 May 1849 but was discovered and arrested. That November he was sentenced to six and one-half years in the state penitentiary. James C. A. Smith had aided Smith in the attempt but avoided arrest until 25 September 1849. A divided panel of magistrates enabled him to escape conviction. James C. A. Smith had joined Brown in Boston by December.

Late in 1849 Brown engaged the Boston artist Josiah Wolcott and others to begin work on an ambitious moving panorama about slavery. In January 1850 *The Resurrection of Henry Box Brown at Philadelphia,* a lithograph probably reproducing an image created for the panorama, was published in Boston and became one of the earliest of many pictorial representations of that scene. On 11 April 1850 the moving panorama, *Henry Box Brown's Mirror of Slavery,* opened in Boston. Brown and Smith exhibited it in New England through the summer.

On 30 August 1850, with passage of the Fugitive Slave Bill imminent, Brown was assaulted on the street in Providence, Rhode Island. Believing himself at risk of being captured and returned to Virginia under the law, Brown, along with Smith, sailed to England in October 1850. They exhibited the panorama in Liverpool from 12 November to 5 December 1850, showed it in Manchester from 14 December 1850 to 1 January 1851, and toured Lancashire and Yorkshire through the spring. Early in May 1851 the "First English Edition" of the *Narrative of the Life of Henry Box Brown* was published in Manchester.

In June 1851 Brown's and Smith's partnership ended after a bitter dispute involving money and Smith's complaint that Brown had made no effort to purchase his own family. Smith strongly criticized Brown in letters to prominent American abolitionists as well as to those English activists who had helped them get started in that country. Out of both necessity and choice Brown moved from the abolitionist circuit entirely into English show business. He exhibited his panorama throughout England during the 1850s, developing the character of the African Prince as another part of his persona and dressing in fine clothes and jewelry. In July 1852 Brown won a libel case against a newspaper that had published racial slurs about his performances. By 1859 he had remarried and with his wife, name unknown, was also exhibiting a panorama of the Indian Mutiny of 1857. About that time Brown began to perform as a mesmerist, entertaining audiences with the actions of persons under his hypnotic influence. As late as 1864, when billing himself in Wales as the "King of all the Mesmerisers," he still occasionally showed the *Mirror of Slavery*.

In 1875, accompanied by his wife and daughter Annie, Brown returned to the United States. Billing himself as "Prof. H. Box Brown," he performed as a magician. He carried over from his previous shows his portrayal of the African Prince and continued to climb into his original box. The Browns performed at Milbury and Worcester, Massachusetts, at the beginning of 1878, and an extant handbill announces a performance at Brookline on 9 May 1878. No later information on them has been found. The date and location of Henry Box Brown's death are not known.

More than a century later, the man who escaped slavery in a box has become a symbol of the Underground Railroad, and his confinement and triumphant emergence from the box have inspired works by several contemporary artists. Brown has been featured in a short film, at least two plays, an opera, and an exhibit at a wax museum. The writer Anthony Cohen paid homage to Brown's courage by traveling from Philadelphia to New York inside a box. Brown's famous passage to freedom was not a thing apart from the rest of his life, and he displayed the attributes that enabled him to succeed as a fugitive time and again during his long career as a performer.

Charles Stearns, *Narrative of Henry Box Brown, Who Escaped from Slavery Enclosed in a Box 3 Feet Long and 2 Wide, Written from a Statement of Facts Made by Himself with Remarks upon the Remedy for Slavery* (1849), with frontispiece por. and birth year of 1816 on 14; *Narrative of the Life of Henry Box Brown, Written by Himself, First English Edition* (1851), with birth year of 1815 on 1; William Still, *The Underground Rail Road* (1871), 81–86; Jeffrey Ruggles, "Go and Get a Box: Henry Brown's Escape from Slavery, 1849," *Virginia Cavalcade* 48 (1999): 84–95; *Liberator*, 8 June, 14 Sept. 1849, 19 Apr., 31 May 1850; Cynthia Griffin Wolff, "Passing Beyond the Middle Passage: Henry 'Box' Brown's Translations of Slavery," *Massachusetts Review* 37 (spring 1996): 23–44; *Liverpool (Eng.) Mercury*, 5, 12 Nov., 3 Dec. 1850; *Manchester (Eng.) Examiner and Times*, 14, 21 Dec. 1850; *Leeds (Eng.) Mercury*, 24 May 1851; C. Peter Ripley et al., eds., *The Black Abolitionist Papers* (1985), 1:293–301; R. J. M. Blackett, *Building an Antislavery Wall: Black Americans in the Atlantic Abolitionist Movement, 1830–1860* (1983), 158–159, 209–210; Audrey A. Fisch, *American Slaves in Victorian England: Abolitionist Politics in Popular Literature and Culture* (2000), 73–83, 119–121; *West London (Eng.) Observer*, 12 Mar. 1859; *Merthyr (Wales) Star*, 10 Mar. 1864; *Worcester (Mass.) Evening Gazette*, 29 Dec. 1877, 1, 2, 9 Jan. 1878; Kimberly Rae Connor, "To Disembark: The Slave Narrative Tradition," *African American Review* 30 (spring 1996): 35–57; Anthony Michael Cohen, *The Underground Railroad: A Personal Journey Through History* (1998); 1878 handbill reproduced in David Price, *Magic: A Pictorial History of Conjurers in the Theater* (1985), 58.

JEFFREY RUGGLES

BROWN, Henry James (12 October 1811–9 April 1854), painter, was born in Cumberland County, the son of Daniel Brown, a farmer, and Nancy Hobson Walton Brown. He spent his childhood there and at Somerset, a nearby farm that his father had purchased in Powhatan County. Brown learned to farm and gained business experience in his father's store and gristmill. Although he appears to have had little or no formal education, his devoutly Methodist mother encouraged him to follow a religious vocation. In 1828, when he was seventeen, the Methodist Church licensed Brown as an exhorter. That same year he painted his first portrait. Dissatisfied with a local artist's painting of him, Brown declared that he could do a better likeness himself, and shortly thereafter he proved his point.

In October 1833 Brown married Susan Ann Hobson. They had two sons and five daughters. Three of them died young, and another child died in infancy. In 1838 Brown bought a farm in Saline County, Missouri, and moved there to grow corn and hemp. He continued his Methodist evangelism and was licensed to preach in

1840. At the same time Brown pursued his artistic vocation, seeking and fulfilling portrait commissions, and he studied for a time under George Caleb Bingham. From 1840 to 1847 Brown served as postmaster of the nearby village of Cow Creek.

Brown returned to Virginia briefly in 1843 to bury one of his children in the family plot at Somerset. Four years later he relinquished the management of his farm in Missouri, moved back to Virginia, and settled in Ballsville, a small community in Powhatan County. Most of Brown's surviving portraits date after his return to Virginia. Income from the Missouri farm enabled him to spend much of his time painting and even to study in the Philadelphia studio of Thomas Sully, America's foremost portraitist. Sully's influence can be seen in several of Brown's later works, especially a portrait of Emily Lee Bondurant and a group portrait of his own daughters. Brown also studied and copied works by other artists, such as Chester Harding's portrait of John Randolph of Roanoke.

In 1848 Brown became interested in the newly revived Female Collegiate Institute in Buckingham County. Virginia's first college for women, the institute had been founded in 1837 but failed six years later. With Methodist support, it reopened to students for the academic year 1849–1850, and Brown was appointed vice president of its board of directors and put in charge of recruiting. Though not listed among the faculty, he may have taught art there as well. The 1850 census lists Brown as living at the institute, and about 1852 he built an imposing brick house that still stands on the institute grounds. A color lithograph of the institute's principal building, "drawn by Rev. Henry Brown," was published in 1852 on the cover of the "Buckingham Polka," a musical composition dedicated to the institute's students. Approximately fifty of Brown's paintings have been located, most of them still in the hands of family members. A copy portrait of Peter Livingston attributed to Brown belongs to Sweet Briar College. The Woman's Club of Lynchburg mounted an exhibition of his works in 1941, and several were shown at the Lynchburg Fine Arts Center in 1963. Henry James Brown died of pneumonia in Buckingham County on 9 April 1854 and was buried in the family cemetery at the Somerset estate.

Birth and death dates on gravestone, Brown family cemetery, Powhatan Co.; variant death date of 13 Mar. 1854 in BVS Death Register, Buckingham Co.; Charles E. Worsham, "Henry James Brown, American Artist: His Life and Works" (master's thesis, Hunter College, City University of New York, 1969), frontispiece por.; Lucille McWane Watson, "Virginia Planter-Painter Henry James Brown," *Antiques* 100 (1971): 591–595, gives marriage date as 20 Oct. 1833, citing family register, but Powhatan Co. Marriage Register (later transcription) gives date as 14 Oct.; Henry James Brown Papers, UVA; Census, 1850, Buckingham Co.; Sue Roberson West, *Buckingham Female Collegiate Institute: First Chartered College for Women in Virginia* (1990), 84–88, 101–102; *Lynchburg News*, 16 Oct. 1941.

Virginius C. Hall

BROWN, James (17 June 1780–3 January 1859), second auditor of Virginia and superintendent of the Literary Fund, was born probably in Mecklenburg County, the son of John Brown (1750–1810) and Anne Geddy Brown. His father was clerk of Mecklenburg County in 1780 but moved to Richmond in 1781 after being elected clerk of the General Court. Little is known about the early life of James Brown or why until his death he called himself James Brown Jr. He probably grew up in Richmond, where he was also educated and where his father served as clerk of the Virginia Court of Appeals from 1785 until his death. On 9 December 1802 Brown married Frances Gooseley in Yorktown. They had five sons and five daughters.

Brown was licensed in Richmond as a vendue master, or auctioneer, of land and slaves. In that capacity he undoubtedly became interested in proposals to develop regional transportation networks. On 24 February 1823 the General Assembly passed an act to make more effectual improvements of the navigation of the James and Kanawha Rivers. The act also created the position of second auditor of Virginia to manage the Fund for Internal Improvement and to serve as secretary to the Board of Public Works. The board and the fund had been established in 1816 to oversee the state's investments in, and to supervise the construction of, canals, turnpikes, and other transportation improvements in Virginia, eventually including railroads. Brown was elected second auditor on 25 February 1823 and held the post until 31 December 1852, when he resigned. He was thus centrally placed to help direct some of the state's most important and expensive undertakings. In 1829 Brown was also named superintendent of the Literary Fund, which oversaw the disbursement of public revenue for educational purposes, and on 10 March 1835 he became one of the commissioners of the Sinking Fund created to oversee the retirement of the public debt. Under the Constitution of 1851 the second auditor ceased to be secretary of the Board of Public Works, but Brown continued to be responsible for the financial records of the Fund for Internal Improvement.

Brown's numerous responsibilities required him to keep detailed records, submit extensive annual reports to the General Assembly, and maintain a voluminous correspondence with engineers, accountants, company presidents and board members, contractors, and school superintendents. His success in managing his tasks and the genteel and literate manner in which he did so made him one of the best-known and most highly regarded state officials of his time. Brown's regular correspondents included such notables as Claudius Crozet, the brilliant and irascible principal engineer of the Board of Public Works, and William Barton Rogers, the University of Virginia professor and later a founder of the Massachusetts Institute of Technology who directed the Geological Survey of Virginia between 1835 and 1848. Brown became an early advocate of a strong, centralized public school system for Virginia, but the concept met with widespread local resistance until after the Civil War.

James Brown died on 3 January 1859 from injuries he had sustained a few days earlier in an odd accident at the Richmond and Fredericksburg Railroad depot in Richmond. A locomotive ran over his foot and ankle. His obituary stated that although the injury would not have killed a younger or more vigorous man, the "very advanced age of Mr. Brown and his rather feeble physical condition rendered his recovery doubtful from the time of the accident." After his funeral at Saint Paul's Episcopal Church, the

Richmond Light Infantry Blues, of which he had been a member, marched in his honor, and he was buried in Shockoe Cemetery in Richmond.

Albertina Brown Parker, *The History of John Francis Deane Brown and Members of His Family in Virginia, Montana, and California* (1963), 12–13; Brown, *Cabells*, 379; Richmond City Common Council Records, no. 4, 18 Nov. 1814, no. 6, 16 Sept. 1816, no. 7, 30 Nov. 1819, no. 7, 17 Apr. 1820; *Richmond Enquirer*, 15 Jan. 1820; official correspondence in Office of the Second Auditor, RG 50, and Board of Public Works, RG 57, LVA; A. J. Morrison, *The Beginnings of Public Education in Virginia, 1776–1860* (1917), 94; William Arthur Maddox, *The Free School Idea in Virginia Before the Civil War* (1969), 82–83, 101, 115–116, 134–135; obituary in *Richmond Dispatch*, 4 Jan. 1859 (quotation).

JOHN S. SALMON

BROWN, James Andrew (22 December 1815– 4 March 1900), Lutheran minister, was born five miles north of Wytheville, the son of Christopher Brown (originally Braun), a Wythe County farmer, and Anna Marie Rader Brown. At the age of twenty he entered Pennsylvania College (later Gettysburg College) and the nearby Lutheran Theological Seminary. After six years of collegiate and theological study, Brown walked home to Virginia in 1841 with a diploma and a license for the Lutheran ministry. He was the first member of his local church community to receive a college education.

On 9 July 1843 Brown married Eleanor C. Herbst, daughter of a Lutheran clergyman, in Gettysburg. He was ordained by the Evangelical Lutheran Synod of Western Virginia and Adjacent Parts in August of the same year and began his ministry as an assistant pastor of Saint John's Lutheran Church, his home congregation, in Wythe County. Brown later became its pastor and within three years was pastor of three other small churches, Saint Paul, Saint Peter's, and Zion, in southern Wythe County, and of Luther Chapel (formerly South Fork), a congregation that he organized at Lodi in Washington County. In 1854 he became pastor of Lebanon Lutheran Church in what was then Cripple Creek Parish, Wythe County, and in 1875 he organized Rosenbaum Chapel at Crockett, also in Wythe County. Brown was elected secretary of the Synod of Western Virginia (after 1867 the Evangelical

Lutheran Synod of Southwestern Virginia) for twelve nonconsecutive one-year terms between 1845 and 1879 and treasurer for two one-year terms in 1871 and 1872. He served one-year terms as president of the synod in 1848, 1849, 1862, 1867, 1868, 1869, 1873, and 1874. Brown was also a president, director, and secretary of its Education and Missionary Society.

In addition to his work as pastor of three or four congregations at a time, Brown had other church assignments. He preached to congregations in eastern Tennessee that were too poor to afford to pay a regular minister, helped start a Lutheran mission in Richmond, and gave an address at the synod's fiftieth-anniversary service in 1891. In 1880 Brown served on a three-member committee to recommend a plan of care and financial assistance for disabled ministers. During his ministry of more than fifty-six years, he married 500 couples, baptized hundreds of their children, and conducted many funerals. Brown was recognized as one of the most important Lutheran clergymen in southwestern Virginia during the period when the church and its congregations made the transition from the German to the English language.

Brown also took an interest in education and served as a charter trustee of Roanoke College from 1853 to 1867 and as a trustee of Marion College from 1873 to 1878. He was a founder of what became Bald Hill School near his home in Wythe County, and in the mid-1850s he helped found Wytheville Female Seminary. It operated for about twelve years, with a three-year suspension from 1865 to 1868, until heavy debt forced it to close. Brown was the largest subscriber to a sinking fund to rescue the school from its financial problems in 1866 and the only person to pay his pledge in full. By the time the seminary shut its doors in 1870 he had contributed some $11,000 to the unsuccessful attempt to save the school.

On 30 May 1868 Brown was the speaker at a Memorial Day service in the national cemetery in his wife's hometown of Gettysburg. He established a scholarship for ministerial students at the seminary, and in 1892 he received an honorary D.D. from Roanoke College. Brown

reported regularly on weather conditions for the Smithsonian Institution and on farming practices for the United States Department of Agriculture.

Brown had no children. His wife died suddenly on 20 July 1879. On 18 September 1880, at the age of sixty-four, he married twenty-four-year-old Alice Virginia Sharitz, of the Wythe County community of Lebanon. They had one son and two daughters and adopted another daughter. In 1881 Alice Sharitz Brown served as treasurer of the Women's Missionary Society of the Evangelical Lutheran Synod of Southwestern Virginia. James Andrew Brown died in Wythe County on 4 March 1900 and was buried in the Saint John's Lutheran Church Cemetery in that county. The synod adopted a memorial praising him as a "preacher of more than ordinary ability" and "a friend of education."

Frederick B. Kegley and Mary B. Kegley, *St. John's Evangelical Lutheran Church, Wythe County, Virginia: Its Pastors and Their Records, 1800–1924* (1961), 29, 52–68 (quotations on 67), 197, 378 (por.); *Biographical Sketches of Lutheran Pastors in Virginia, 1820–1987* (1992), 29 (por.); Brown family papers in possession of George A. Kegley, 2001; BVS Marriage Register, Wythe Co., 1880; C. W. Cassell, W. J. Finck, and Elon O. Henkel, *History of the Lutheran Church in Virginia and East Tennessee* (1930), 119; William Edward Eisenberg, *The Lutheran Church in Virginia, 1717–1962* (1967), 177, 307, 318, 354–359, 430, 574, 579, 581, 583, 669–670, and *The First Hundred Years: Roanoke College, 1842–1942* (1942), 32, 34, 471; George B. Gose, *Pioneers of the Virginia Bluegrass* [1964], 101–103; Thomas W. West, *Marion College, 1873–1967* (1970), 211; will and estate inventory in Wythe Co. Will Book, 17:172–175, 217–219, 460–461.

MARY B. KEGLEY

BROWN, James Henry (25 December 1818–28 October 1900), member of the West Virginia Convention of 1861–1863, was born in Cabell County, the son of Benjamin Brown, a physician, and a North Carolinian of unknown first name whose maiden name was Scales. He graduated from Augusta College in Bracken County, Kentucky, in 1840, read law under John Laidley, of Cabell County, and was admitted to the bar in 1842. In 1848 Brown moved to Charleston in Kanawha County, where he prospered by successfully litigating land cases. About 1843 he married Louisa Mayer Beuhring. They had at least two sons and four daughters.

Brown was an active Democrat before the Civil War and attended the Democratic state conventions in 1854 and 1856, but he ran for public office only once during that period, when he lost an 1855 bid for a seat in the Senate of Virginia. He opposed the movement for secession during the winter of 1860–1861 and on 23 May 1861 was elected from Kanawha County to the House of Delegates, the Unionist delegates of which were later designated the legislature of the Restored government of Virginia. That autumn Brown represented Kanawha County at the convention that wrote the constitution for the new state of West Virginia. As a ranking member of the Committee on the Judiciary he was instrumental in drafting the section that created the court system for West Virginia. Brown also served on the standing Committees on Fundamental and General Provisions and on the Legislative Department, on the committees on the boundaries of the proposed new state and on the convention's order of business, and on a special committee on forfeited, waste, and unappropriated lands.

Brown's most controversial activity at the convention was his attempt to move the proposed border of the new state eastward to the Blue Ridge Mountains. He joined the successful effort to include within the new state the counties that now form its eastern and southern tier, but he also argued for annexation as far east as the Blue Ridge in order to extend protection to the Unionist minority in those counties and retain their natural resources and transportation facilities. Ultimately the convention rejected Brown's proposal. He took a lesser part in the debates over including the eastern panhandle counties in the new state. Brown's steadfast loyalty to the Republican Party in later years appears to contradict accusations that by trying to extend West Virginia's borders into areas loyal to the Confederacy he was surreptitiously working with opponents of separate statehood. His other losing battle during the convention was his proposal to name the new state Kanawha. Brown did not vote on the boundary proposal on 13 December 1861. On 18 February 1862, after casting his vote to approve the new constitution, he resigned from the convention, although he returned to the recalled session in February 1863, when he was appointed to a special committee on compensation for emancipated slaves and to the Committee on Revision.

On 26 December 1861 Brown won election as judge of the Eighteenth Circuit Court under the authority of the Restored government. He resigned his seat in the General Assembly on 14 January 1862 and assumed his seat on the bench in February. Brown conducted trials in areas where the United States Army was in precarious control. Several times he narrowly escaped capture by Confederate raiders. At the constitutional convention, Brown had resisted antislavery proposals, but after Congress voted to make emancipation a requirement for the admission of West Virginia to the Union, he counseled acquiescence and campaigned for ratification of the constitution, which provided for abolition, in the referendum held on 26 March 1863.

On 28 May 1863 Republicans elected Brown an associate judge of the Supreme Court of Appeals of West Virginia. His political future dimmed, however, after former Confederates regained their voting rights. Brown was defeated for reelection in 1871, lost an attempt to regain his office five years later, and failed in campaigns for the United States Senate in 1875 and the House of Representatives in 1883 and 1886. His one electoral victory in later years was a term in the state legislature in 1882.

After leaving the bench, Brown resumed his law practice in Charleston in partnership with his son. After his wife died in 1872, he married Sallie S. Shrewsburg Lovell, the widow of Fayette A. Lovell, another Kanawha County lawyer. James Henry Brown remained healthy and active until shortly before his death from pneumonia on 28 October 1900 at his home in Charleston, West Virginia. He was buried in Spring Hill Cemetery in that town.

Atkinson and Gibbens, *Prominent Men*, 270–272 (por.); George W. Atkinson, *Bench and Bar of West Virginia* (1919), 9–11; W. S. Laidley, *History of Charleston and Kanawha County, West Virginia, and Representative Citizens* [1911], 97–100; some Brown letters in Waitman T. Willey Papers, West Virginia and Regional History Collection, WVU; Charles H. Ambler, F. H. Atwood, and W. B. Mathews, eds., *Debates and Proceedings of the First Constitutional Convention of West Virginia (1861–1863)* (1939); Kyle

McCormick, "Why Is Mercer County in West Virginia Instead of Virginia?" *West Virginia History* 19 (1957): 60–65; Richard Orr Curry, *A House Divided: A Study of Statehood Politics and the Copperhead Movement in West Virginia* (1964), 89, 126–127; death notice in *Wheeling Daily Intelligencer*, 30 Oct. 1900; Rose W. Peterson, comp., *Spring Hill Cemetery, Charleston, WV* (1995), 1:65.

JOHN R. McKIVIGAN

BROWN, John (ca. 1728–24 March 1803), Presbyterian minister, was born in Ireland, most likely in Londonderry, the son of James Brown and Jennet Stevenson Brown. By 1747 he had followed some of his brothers to America and in that year began studies with Samuel Blair at Fagg's Manor Academy in Pennsylvania. In 1749 he was a member of the second graduating class of the College of New Jersey (later Princeton University).

Brown subscribed to the evangelical, or pro–Great Awakening, theology of the so-called New Side Presbyterians. After his graduation the Presbytery of New Castle licensed him as a supply, or visiting, pastor for vacant congregations in the Valley of Virginia. Brown also preached on occasion in western North Carolina. The effectiveness of his early ministry is evinced in the recollection of the distinguished Presbyterian minister Alexander McWhorter, whom Brown led to conversion in North Carolina early in the 1750s through a sermon entitled "If the Wicked Turn Not." With Samuel Davies presiding, Brown was ordained on 11 October 1753 at Fagg's Manor to serve as pastor for Timber Ridge and New Providence Presbyterian Churches in the region that became Rockbridge County. He officiated at Timber Ridge until 11 October 1767 and at New Providence until mid-September 1795.

As one of the Valley's earliest settled Presbyterian clergymen, Brown continued throughout the colonial period to supply the region's vacant pulpits. During the French and Indian War he also traveled extensively to conduct services for Virginia's troops. Emphasizing saving conversion, Brown's sermons followed the plain style of American Calvinistic rhetoric, in which a few points were drawn from Scripture, elaborated with reasons and examples, and finally made applicable to the audience. Never an admirer of bombastic preaching, he withheld his

support from the emotional Hampden-Sydney Revival late in the 1780s.

Brown served as a founding member of the Hanover Presbytery, the Lexington Presbytery, and the Synod of Virginia. Before the American Revolution he championed the right of the Hanover Presbytery to depose any of its member ministers for misconduct, and he pressed the issue successfully during the protracted 1765–1771 sexual assault case against Alexander Miller. After the Revolution Brown actively advocated increased independence for Virginia Presbyterians through the separation of church and state. In a ministry notable for its support and direction of education, he was a founder of both primary and secondary schools and taught at and served as a trustee of the classical school that evolved into Augusta Academy, Liberty Hall Academy, and eventually Washington and Lee University. Brown's important accomplishments as a preacher, educator, and church government official, combined with the many examples of evangelical eloquence that have survived in his letters and sermon notes, explain the high esteem in which he was held. He may have expressed his Christian point of view best in 1772 following the death of a son: "there is but a narrow passage between Death & Life, and it is attended with such important Consequences that it is the greatest Wisdom to prepare for a happy Eternity."

About 1754 Brown married Margaret Preston, also a native of Ireland, a niece of the wealthy and politically influential James Patton and sister of William Preston, a surveyor, militia leader, and Brown's intimate friend. They had nine sons and two daughters, of whom five sons and both daughters survived to maturity. Their eldest surviving son, John Brown (1757–1837), served in the House of Representatives from Virginia and in the United States Senate from Kentucky, and another, James Brown (1766–1835), served as a United States senator from Louisiana and as American minister to France.

Shortly after retiring from the ministry in 1795, Brown and his wife moved to Woodford County, Kentucky, where they lived with their eldest son. Margaret Preston Brown died in Frankfort, Kentucky, in 1802, and John Brown died there on 24 March 1803. They were buried locally in the churchyard at Pisgah Presbyterian Church, but the family graves were later moved to the Frankfort Cemetery.

Richard Webster, *History of the Presbyterian Church in America* (1857), 656–657; James McLachlan, *Princetonians, 1748–1768: A Biographical Dictionary* (1976), 15–17; John White Stuart III, "The Rev. John Brown, of Virginia (1728–1803): His Life and Selected Sermons" (Ph.D. diss., University of Massachusetts, 1988); gravestone inscription giving age at death as seventy-five quoted in Foote, *Sketches of Virginia,* 99; Brown family Bible records, 1755–1775, VHS; several letters in Preston Family Papers, LC, and Draper MSS, 2QQ49–5QQ119 (quotation in John Brown to William Preston, 18 Mar. 1772, 2QQ133); James R. Bentley, ed., "Letter of Rev. John Brown to John Brown, Jr., 10 June 1786," *Filson Club History Quarterly* 45 (1971): 72–76; John Brown, memorandum book, 1753–1797, and papers, 1755–1796, Presbyterian Historical Society, Philadelphia; obituary in *Frankfort Kentucky Gazette*, 29 Mar. 1803.

JOHN WHITE STUART III

BROWN, John (12 September 1757–29 August 1837), member of the Confederation Congress and member of the United States House of Representatives, was born near Staunton, the son of John Brown (ca.1728–1803), a Presbyterian minister, and Margaret Preston Brown. Brown's twin brother died in infancy. His younger brother James Brown was the first secretary of state of Kentucky, a United States senator from Louisiana, and American minister to France.

Brown probably began his education at Augusta Academy (later Washington and Lee University), where his father taught. He assisted at James Waddel's school on the Northern Neck while continuing his studies and then followed in his father's footsteps by attending the College of New Jersey (later Princeton University). The British army disrupted his studies late in 1776, and Brown returned to Virginia to complete his education at the College of William and Mary, where he read law briefly under George Wythe. Brown's education again became a war casualty when British troops marched through Williamsburg on their way to Yorktown. A tradition that Brown served as an aide to the marquis de Lafayette during the American Revolution may have no basis in fact, but he could have served with the Virginia militia under Lafayette's command during the siege of Yorktown. In Williamsburg Brown formed several lifelong and valuable friendships, including those he made as an early member of Phi Beta Kappa.

Brown began working as a lawyer in 1782 and resided for a time in Albemarle County, where he profited from access to Thomas Jefferson's library. He moved the next year to Kentucky, settling first in Danville and afterward in Frankfort, where he looked after land grants of his uncle William Preston as well as some of his own. Brown was elected to the Senate of Virginia in 1784 and served one four-year term from the huge Kentucky district that included counties as far east as Botetourt and Washington. Two issues then dominated Kentucky politics, statehood and the free navigation of the Mississippi River. As a state senator Brown combined the roles of colonial agent and territorial delegate. He strongly advanced his constituents' beliefs, which were often at odds with those of many eastern Virginians. The great distance between the capital and the western settlements was inconvenient and frequently dangerous to residents of Kentucky. A false alarm of an impending Indian attack late in 1784 led to a convention of concerned westerners who thought it ludicrous to seek permission from Richmond before responding to Indian incursions, a procedure that might take months. The Kentuckians began a protracted movement to achieve statehood.

On 23 October 1787 the assembly elected Brown to the Virginia delegation to the Congress of the United States in order to provide the residents of Kentucky with representation. During his attendance at the almost moribund Confederation Congress from late in January until August 1788, he sought separate statehood for Kentucky, but several other states opposed the admission of new states to the Union. Brown went so far as to speak with the Spanish ambassador about what an independent Kentucky could expect from Spain, an incident that haunted him later in life.

Unlike many other Kentucky residents, Brown favored ratification of the United States Constitution, but in 1789 the voters of the western district nevertheless elected him to the first of two terms in the new House of Representatives. He acted as an important link between Kentucky and the federal government. Brown shared letters from prominent Kentuckians with George Washington and other members of Washington's administration. He also did errands for western residents, such as buying books and other items unavailable in the West. After Kentucky was admitted to the Union in 1792, Brown was elected one of the first United States senators from the new state. Reelected twice, he served until 1805. Brown disagreed frequently with his fellow Kentucky senator, Humphrey Marshall, who supported Jay's Treaty and became a Federalist. Brown's friendship and political agreements with Jefferson and James Madison, with whom he had frequently conferred about Kentucky affairs, placed him firmly in the emerging Jeffersonian Republican camp. During his final two years in office, Brown was president pro tempore of the Senate.

On 19 February 1799 Brown married Margaretta Mason, the daughter of a New York clergyman. They had four sons and also one daughter who died young. Brown constructed a substantial multistory house in Frankfort and called it Liberty Hall. Thomas Jefferson proposed a simpler, single-floor structure, but Brown erected a larger house, of which Jefferson, contrary to some assertions, was not the architect.

The legislature did not reelect Brown to the Senate in 1805. He became a director of the Bank of Kentucky, but his return to private life was not entirely peaceful. Although Aaron Burr visited Brown in Kentucky in 1805, Brown was not seriously implicated later when Burr's western plans led to his indictment for treason. In 1806 the partisan *Frankfort Western World*, with John Wood and Humphrey Marshall slinging most of the dirt, began a series of articles accusing Brown and other early Kentucky Jeffersonians of involvement in a Spanish conspiracy that had allegedly begun with Brown's 1788 interview with the Spanish ambassador and was even then continuing.

During his remaining years Brown was rarely in the spotlight. He focused on family and business concerns but did become county sheriff in 1829. Brown met President James Monroe when he passed through Kentucky during his 1819 western tour and in 1825 greeted the marquis de Lafayette. John Brown died in Frankfort,

Kentucky, on 29 August 1837, one of the last survivors of the Confederation Congress. He was buried in Frankfort Cemetery.

Richard A. Harrison, ed., *Princetonians, 1776–1783: A Biographical Dictionary* (1981), 217–222 (por.); John E. Kleber et al., eds., *The Kentucky Encyclopedia* (1992), 128–129 (gives variant marriage and death dates of 21 Feb. 1799 and 28 Aug. 1837); Elizabeth Warren, "John Brown and His Influence on Kentucky Politics, 1784–1805" (Ph.D. diss., Northwestern University, 1937); Stuart S. Sprague, "Senator John Brown of Kentucky, 1757–1837: A Political Biography" (Ph.D. diss., New York University, 1972); Sprague, "Kentucky Politics and the Heritage of the American Revolution: The Early Years, 1783–1788," *Register of the Kentucky Historical Society* 78 (1980): 98–114; Bayless E. Hardin, "The Brown Family of Liberty Hall," *Filson Club History Quarterly* 16 (1942): 75–87; Rebecca K. Pruett, *The Browns of Liberty Hall* (1966); Brown papers in several collections at Filson Historical Society, Louisville, Ky., in Kentucky Historical Society, Frankfort, in Breckinridge Family Papers, James Brown Papers, and Harry Innes Papers, LC, in John Mason Brown and Preston W. Brown Papers, Yale University, in Smith, *Letters of Delegates*, vols. 24–25, and in *Madison: Congressional Series*, esp. vol. 11; obituary in *Lexington Kentucky Gazette*, 31 Aug. 1837 (gives death date as 29 Aug.).

STUART S. SPRAGUE

BROWN, John (5 October 1762–6 October 1826), judge of the Superior Court of Chancery, was born near Harrisburg, Pennsylvania, of Scots-Irish ancestry. The names of Brown's parents and the date he moved to Virginia have not been discovered. He was a student at Liberty Hall Academy (later Washington and Lee University) from 1782 to 1783 and later served on its board of trustees from 1807 to 1817. As a young man the red-headed, freckled-faced Brown seldom lost a footrace or wrestling match. Even late in life he could reportedly leap up and tap the door lintel with his boot heel. On 21 February 1784 he married Frances Peyton, of Prince William County. They had two sons and two daughters.

Brown studied law and from the mid-1780s to 1802 practiced in the courts of Frederick, Hampshire, and Hardy Counties. He lived at Moorefield in Hardy County. On 24 January 1799 the General Assembly elected Brown brigadier general of militia in the district composed of Hampshire, Hardy, and Pendleton Counties. He held the post until he left the district in December 1802. On 27 January 1802, after the assembly reorganized the courts of chancery into three districts, it elected Brown judge of the Superior Court of Chancery that was to meet in Staunton and hear cases from all Virginia counties west of the Blue Ridge Mountains. He accordingly moved to Staunton and purchased the Spring Farm estate, where he lived until his death. Further divisions in the chancery court districts reduced the number of counties in each district, but Brown was appointed judge of two other districts, and he held yearly sessions after 1812 in Wythe County and after 1814 in Greenbrier County.

Chancellor Brown, as he was sometimes known, necessarily traveled a great deal, but for at least some of the time he may have continued to practice in the common law and county courts. The bar in the Valley of Virginia was then composed of some of the most able and distinguished attorneys in the state, who appeared before his bench or tested their mettle with him in court. Brown acquired a good library with more than 100 works on law, in excess of 150 volumes of history, literature, and poetry, and a few volumes on religious subjects.

Keenly interested in national and state politics, Brown was a presidential elector for Thomas Jefferson in 1800 and supported James Madison in the campaign of 1808. Although he was suspicious of banks as a whole, he favored the expansion of banking into the western parts of Virginia rather than permitting financial institutions to remain concentrated in Richmond. Brown guardedly approved of most of the objectives of the convention of western Virginians that met in Staunton in 1816 and called for amendment of the state constitution to give westerners more equitable representation in the assembly, fairer taxation, and an expansion of the suffrage.

John Brown died of apoplexy on 6 October 1826 while sitting quietly on the porch of his residence in Staunton. He was buried in the churchyard of Trinity Episcopal Church in Staunton, but his remains were later moved to Thornrose Cemetery in the same town after the burial there of his widow.

Birth and death dates from gravestone in Thornrose Cemetery, Staunton; Thomas D. Ranson, "Judge John Brown," *Washington and Lee University Historical Papers* 4 (1893): 176–179; Horace Edwin Hayden, *Virginia Genealogies* (1891), 504–505; *Calendar of Virginia State Papers*, 9:4, 75, 190, 276; Brown letters in Brown Family Papers and Stuart-Baldwin Papers, UVA, and in Grinnan Family Papers, VHS; records and order books, Superior Court of Chancery for the Western District, Augusta Co. Courthouse, Staunton (LVA microfilm); por. at W&L; inventory and estate sale in Augusta Co. Will Book, 16:111–136; obituaries in *Fredericksburg Virginia Herald*, 11 Oct. 1826, and *Lynchburg Virginian*, 19 Oct. 1826; memorials in *Richmond Enquirer*, 20 Oct. 1826.

KENNETH W. KELLER

BROWN, John (21 July 1771–26 January 1850), German Reformed clergyman, was born Johannes Braun, the son of Hermann Daniel Braun and Adelheit Lürssen Braun, a respected middle-class German family of Vegesack, near Bremen. He received a good classical education in preparation for a career in teaching, but like many other young men of the Hanseatic port cities he left Bremen in 1797 in order to escape the turmoil of the wars precipitated by the French Revolution.

John Brown, as he always signed his name in English-language documents, arrived in Baltimore but was unable to find a teaching position. While working as a laborer, he attended services at the local German Reformed church. Its minister, William Otterbein, noticed his educational background and guided him toward a ministerial career. He recommended Brown to Philip Stock, who trained theological students at his parsonage in Chambersburg, Pennsylvania. After several months of intensive instruction, Stock sent Brown to the scattered and leaderless Reformed congregations in the Shenandoah Valley to aid them in organizing their services and assess their need for clergymen. Brown identified seventeen congregations, some of them near dissolution. He returned for several months of additional study under Stock before the German Reformed Synod in Pennsylvania sent him back to Virginia in 1799 as a preacher and missionary. Seven churches extended Brown an official call. He made his home near Bridgewater in Rockingham County.

Brown regularly visited the churches in Rockingham and Augusta Counties and occasionally traveled to Reformed congregations in Page and Shenandoah Counties and adjacent areas in the western mountains. During his fifty years in the ministry, to which he was finally ordained in 1803, he consolidated the Reformed churches and created the basis for a regional, independent organization of the Reformed Classis of Virginia in 1825. Brown's deep attachment to the German language was a positive factor in his ministry as long as German was still in general use, but by the 1820s, when younger church members began to prefer an English ministry, he reluctantly consented to provide services in both languages. In 1830 Brown published a seventy-two-page bilingual textbook, *Eine kurze Unterweisung Christlichen Religion, nach dem Heidelbergischen Catechismus, in den deutschen und englischen-sprachen.*

Brown was the only Reformed clergyman in his part of Virginia for thirty-five years. Despite his heavy pastoral workload, he found time for writing and translating. In close cooperation with the Lutherans and Mennonites, Brown helped bring the singing school movement to German denominations. His most significant publication was a 400-page address to the Reformed congregations in the Valley, *Circular-Schreiben an die deutschen Einwohner von Rockingham und Augusta, und den benachbahrten Caunties* (1818). The work included Brown's "Treatise on Slavery and Serfdom," in which he maintained that any form of serfdom placed the Christian character in jeopardy, although he believed that abolition of slavery was a political rather than a religious matter. By translating excerpts from the writings of Thomas Jefferson and St. George Tucker on this subject, Brown afforded those Germans who could not read English a glimpse into the thinking of leading Virginians on the subject of slavery.

Together with his friend Archibald Rutherford, Brown founded the Rockingham Bible Society in 1814, and he became its first president. His lifelong interest in education ranged from active support of Marshall College in Pennsylvania, a Reformed institution that conferred an honorary D.D. on him in 1841, to service as county school commissioner and treasurer of the pauper schools in Rockingham County in the 1820s and 1830s.

By 1802 Brown had married Elizabeth Falls in Rockingham County. They raised four

sons and five daughters in the small parsonage in Bridgewater. Father Brown, as John Brown had become known in the Valley, died at his home in Rockingham County on 26 January 1850 and was buried in the churchyard of his favorite congregation, Friedens Church near Mount Crawford.

Klaus Wust, "Johannes Braun (1771–1850), Geistiger Führer der Virginia-Deutschen," *Europa und die niederdeutsche Welt* 19 (1955): 120–123; Wust, trans. and ed., *Shenandoah Valley Family Data, 1799–1813, from the Memorandum Book of Pastor Johannes Braun* (1978); Brown Family Collection, James Madison University, Harrisonburg; Brown's MS memorandum book, including personal notes, list of his books, and accounts as Rockingham Co. schoolmaster, 1823–1825, in possession of Joseph H. Meyerhoeffer, 2001; three Brown letters and records of Classis founding meeting in 1825, Historical Society of Pennsylvania, Philadelphia; Record Book of Virginia Classis, Evangelical and Reformed Historical Society, Lancaster Theological Seminary Library, Lancaster, Pa.; J. Silor Garrison, *The History of the Reformed Church in Virginia, 1714–1940* (1948), 58–59, 82–83 (por.); Rockingham Co. Will Book, A:178–180.

KLAUS WUST

BROWN, John (ca. January 1830–after 19 June 1900), member of the Convention of 1867–1868, was born into slavery in Southampton County. The names of his parents are not known. His owner, Robert Ridley, was a large-scale planter who sat in the Convention of 1850–1851. Ridley died in 1852, and, possibly as a result of that event, Brown's wife, two daughters, and perhaps a brother were later sold and taken to Mississippi. He maintained sporadic contact with them until the Civil War.

Brown resided on Ridley family land until at least 1870. About 1861 he remarried, to a woman named Chloe with whom he had six children, including three sons and two daughters. In April 1867 Brown dictated a letter that the local agent of the Freedmen's Bureau wrote for him and addressed to Holly Springs, Mississippi, to his daughters from his first marriage. Evidently it did not reach them.

Although modern scholarship has largely discredited the old stereotype of illiterate former slaves elevated to high public office during Reconstruction, Brown showed by his example that some blacks did overcome all the handicaps of enslavement to gain postwar political prominence and that ambitious Virginia freed-people briefly enjoyed enlarged opportunities. Brown won his convention seat at a remarkable moment in Virginia's political history. During the summer of 1867 newly energized freedmen sought to break free from the subservient position to which they had long been assigned. Armed for the first time with the ballot, blacks dared to assert themselves in ways that would have been unthinkable at any time in the past.

Brown and other politically active blacks in Southampton spurned an alliance with moderate white former Whigs who hoped to win black votes. They boldly took matters into their own hands. In an astonishing display of group cohesion and discipline, almost 98 percent of registered black men appeared at the polls on 22 October 1867. All 1,242 black voters and a lone white supported Brown, who easily defeated two white candidates. Nothing since Nat Turner's Rebellion in 1831 so shocked the local gentry. Available evidence does not indicate how Brown emerged as the spokesman for Southampton's freedpeople, but in the short time after Emancipation he must have exhibited impressive leadership abilities to command a unanimous following.

Brown was appointed to the Committee on the Judiciary, excepting County and Corporation Courts. He did not assume a conspicuous role at the convention. In assessing the delegates John McAllister Schofield, the army general then in control of Virginia, dismissed Brown as a man with "no force of character." Brown regularly voted with the Radicals to reform and democratize the state constitution and protect the rights of freedpeople. Unfortunately for him and his fellow Radicals, their startling 1867 victory galvanized opposition. Both in Southampton County and statewide, former Whigs and Democrats mobilized to counter the black political initiative by building similar political unity among whites. The resulting Conservative Party gained control of the state in 1869. Voters approved the new constitution but struck out a clause that disqualified prominent former Confederates from office.

The 1870, 1880, and 1900 census takers listed Brown as unable to read or write. Described as a carpenter who owned no land in 1870, he paid taxes on one horse and several other animals. In 1880 and 1900 Brown was identified as a farmer. He may have been related to a Brown family of African Americans from New Bern, North Carolina, some of whom moved to Norfolk after the Civil War and became active in the Republican Party. John Brown died on an unknown date after the census enumeration of his district on 19 June 1900. Neither he nor his wife was listed in the 1910 census.

Month and year of birth and year of second marriage in Census, Southampton Co., 1900; Jackson, *Negro Office-Holders*, 7; John Brown to Manerva Ann Brown and Ann Eliza Brown, 24 Apr. 1867, Freedmen's Bureau Records; Daniel W. Crofts, *Old Southampton: Politics and Society in a Virginia County, 1834–1869* (1992), 246–258, 396; *Clarksville Tobacco Plant*, 11 Oct. 1867; *Richmond Daily Whig*, 28, 30 Oct. 1867; Election Records, no. 427, RG 13, LVA; Lowe, "Virginia's Reconstruction Convention," 354 (quotation); Hume, "Membership of Convention of 1867–1868," 481.

DANIEL W. CROFTS

BROWN, John Dudley George (16 June 1868–20 January 1915), the model for Walter C. Kelly's "Virginia Judge," was born in Hanover County, the son of Joseph Booth Brown and Fanny Lavinia Taylor Brown. Brown's grandfather, for whom he was named, was a prominent planter in Hanover County who won some posthumous notoriety for his 1866 will bequeathing his descendants "bitter hatred, and everlasting malignity" toward Yankees.

Brown attended Oakland Academy in Louisa County and enrolled in the University of Virginia for the 1891–1892 term. After being admitted to the bar he moved to Newport News in 1893 and opened a law practice in partnership with Ellyson S. Robinson. Brown soon won a reputation for preparation and probity. On 14 October 1896 he married Nellie Grace Allen, a native of Connecticut. They had two sons.

In January 1896 the General Assembly incorporated Newport News as a city and named interim public officers to oversee the new city until the legislation took effect on 1 July 1896. Brown was named a justice of the peace for the Fourth Ward. At its first meeting on 20 January 1896, the interim city council chose Brown as the first justice of the police court. These courts meted out justice to those arrested for any number of offenses against the civic peace. Charges of disorderly conduct, drunkenness, fighting, and petty theft dominated each day's docket. The justices enjoyed wide discretion in their treatment of people charged with these crimes, and to modern eyes the harsh sentences handed down for small offenses can appear capricious. Nonetheless, the records of the Newport News Police Court show Brown to have been consistent in his sentencing and efficient in operating his court.

Such courts had nothing inherently humorous about them, but newspaper reporters found occasional amusement in the repartee between the justice and well-known repeat offenders. More often, laughter resulted from the desperate attempt of some unfortunate person caught red-handed to explain away the offense. Tales first recounted to fellow journalists became in time a subgenre of humor writing. As early as 1892 Peter J. Burton published *Police Court Pictures at Richmond, Virginia*, a series of anecdotes that depended on racial stereotypes for their humor. He even rendered the speeches of well-educated African American attorneys in dialect. At Newport News, where sailors from around the world regularly faced Brown after a debauch ashore, the ethnic mix was more varied, but blacks still made up the majority of those charged with crimes. One day, probably about 1897, Walter C. Kelly, a native of New York who was then a machinist and man-about-town, wandered into Brown's court in the basement of city hall. After spending the morning listening to the exchanges as a succession of defendants appeared in court, Kelly promised himself "that this heretofore undiscovered 'gold mine' of comedy and pathos should not be lost to mankind."

Several years later in New York City, Kelly developed a vaudeville act, "The Virginia Judge," in which he performed the voices of the plaintiffs and defendants as well as the judge. His monologues proved an immediate hit with audiences everywhere, and he toured as "The Virginia Judge" for some thirty years. Despite their reliance on racial and ethnic stereotypes, Kelly's monologues found the humor in recognizably human situations. In 1935 he cowrote the story for and starred in a moderately successful film entitled *The Virginia Judge*. The movie was actu-

ally based on the dialect stories of Octavus Roy Cohen. Kelly always credited Brown as his inspiration for "The Virginia Judge," and his monologues retained Newport News place-names, but many Richmonders came to believe that John Crutchfield, that city's flamboyant police justice, was the original "Virginia Judge." The impression was strengthened in 1934 with the publication of John H. Gwathmey's *Justice John: Tales from the Courtroom of the Virginia Judge*.

Brown wore his measure of fame lightly. He was diagnosed with tuberculosis late in 1913 but continued to perform his duties until 17 December 1914, when he stepped down from the court. John Dudley George Brown died in Newport News on 20 January 1915. A large gathering of black and white citizens attended his burial at Greenlawn Cemetery. After Walter C. Kelly was struck by an automobile in Hollywood, California, and died of his injuries three weeks later on 6 January 1939, the Newport News Police Court adjourned in his honor on the motion of a black attorney.

Tyler, *Encyclopedia*, 5:981–982; Hanover Co. Will Book, 1:352 (first quotation), reported in *Lynchburg Tri-Weekly News*, 20 Mar. 1872, *Richmond Times-Dispatch*, 6 Dec. 1959, and elsewhere; BVS Marriage Register, Newport News; Walter C. Kelly, *Of Me I Sing: An Informal Autobiography* (1953), 12–16 (second quotation on 15), por. facing 55; Alexander Crosby Brown, ed., *Newport News' 325 Years* (1946), 7, 9; Newport News Police Court Docket Books, LVA; *The Motion Picture Guide* (1985–1987), 8:3695; *New York Times*, 12 Mar. 1933, 7 Jan. 1939; *Norfolk Virginian-Pilot*, 8 Jan. 1939; obituary and account of funeral in *Newport News Daily Press*, 21, 22 Jan. 1915.

JOHN T. KNEEBONE

BROWN, John Robert (14 January 1842–4 August 1927), member of the House of Representatives, was born in Franklin County, the son of Frederick Rives Brown and his first wife, Jane Prunty Brown. He was educated in the schools of Franklin County. Brown entered the Confederate army on 11 June 1861 as a sergeant in Company D of the 24th Regiment Virginia Infantry but received a medical discharge for phthisis, a shrinking of the eye, six weeks later. Despite the brevity of his military service, he was active in a veterans' camp in later years. On 26 October 1862 Brown married Ann Eliza Vial. They had three sons and seven daughters.

After the Civil War ended Brown and his father operated a tobacco factory under the name of J. R. and F. R. Brown at Shady Grove in Franklin County. In 1882 Brown moved to Edgewood (later Stanleytown) in Henry County, and he later moved the business to Martinsville. Log Cabin, the company's most popular brand of plug tobacco, won prizes at world's fairs in Chicago in 1893 and Saint Louis in 1904 and at the 1907 Jamestown Ter-Centennial Exposition. The Browns also operated a warehouse and sold leaf tobacco in Martinsville. An active lay leader of the Broad Street Christian Church in Martinsville, Brown was one of the organizers of the Henry County Bank. He and his father built handsome identical houses when they moved to Martinsville, and the street on which they lived was named in their honor.

A lifelong Republican, Brown was elected mayor of Martinsville in 1884, and in 1886 he ran for the House of Representatives as an independent Republican after the party failed to hold a nominating convention. In a stunning victory over the incumbent Democrat, George Craighead Cabell, he won by a margin of more than 3,000 votes out of 22,387 cast. Brown took his seat representing the Fifth Congressional District, which comprised the counties of Carroll, Floyd, Franklin, Grayson, Henry, Patrick, and Pittsylvania and the cities of Danville and North Danville. The Democratic Party then controlled the House of Representatives, and he consequently received only one insignificant committee assignment and played no important part in the deliberations. In compliance with Republican Party platforms adopted in other Virginia congressional districts, Brown introduced two bills to abolish the internal revenue taxes on tobacco and on spirits distilled from fruit. Neither bill made it out of committee. He also introduced a bill to grade and pave the road to Danville's national cemetery. Other Republicans sometimes criticized him as a poor public speaker, and in 1888 he lost the Republican Party nomination to John D. Blackwell, of Danville, who in turn lost the general election.

Brown remained active in Republican Party politics and in 1896 challenged Democratic representative Claude Augustus Swanson, who had been elected for the first time in 1892. Brown lost a spirited election by only 551 votes, the best showing that any Republican made in the district for more than a century following his own election in 1886. He challenged the vote count, charging that some Democratic election officers had behaved improperly. The Republican Party had gained control of the House, but Swanson kept his seat because the Committee on Elections could not document enough misbehavior to overturn his victory and did not want to expose some reported Republican irregularities.

Brown continued to manage his tobacco business until he retired well after the beginning of the twentieth century. When he celebrated his eighty-second birthday, he was recognized as one of the oldest and most honored citizens in Martinsville. John Robert Brown died at his home in Martinsville on 4 August 1927 and was buried in Oakwood Cemetery there.

Judith Parks America Hill, *A History of Henry County, Virginia* (1925), 64; Virginia G. Pedigo and Lewis G. Pedigo, *History of Henry and Patrick Counties, Virginia* (1933), 96–97; Marshall Wingfield, *Franklin County, Virginia: A History* (1964), 212; Wingfield, *Pioneer Families of Franklin County, Virginia* (1964), 23–24; Martinsville–Henry County Woman's Club, *Martinsville and Henry County: Historic Views* (1976), 46; Franklin Co. Marriage Register; family history information confirmed by granddaughter Ellen Finley Andrews, who owns por.; Compiled Service Records; Ralph White Gunn, *24th Virginia Infantry* (1987), 72; Election Records, nos. 22, 58, RG 13, LVA; *Richmond Dispatch,* 2 Sept. 1888; *John R. Brown vs. Claude A. Swanson*, 55th Cong., 2d sess., 1898, House Rept. 1070, serial 3720, pts. 1 and 2; *Congressional Record*, 55th Cong., 1st sess., 360; 55th Cong., 2d sess., 3800–3804, 4212, 4226; 55th Cong., 3d sess., 804–805, 2236–2237; obituary in *Martinsville Henry Bulletin*, 12 Aug. 1927.

VIRGINIA STONE WINDLE

BROWN, John Sinclair (30 September 1880 – 15 January 1965), Speaker of the House of Delegates, was born in Warm Springs, the son of George Langhorne Brown, a Presbyterian minister, and Margaret Anderson Brown. In 1886 the family moved to Rockingham County, where Brown attended public and private schools before going to Burnsville Academy in Braxton County, West Virginia. He taught school for two years and in 1899 began working as a timekeeper in railroad construction camps in West Virginia and Pennsylvania. By spring 1904 he had been promoted to assistant manager. Intending to open a hardware store in Enid, Oklahoma, Brown traveled to Salem, Virginia, in 1904 to learn the trade from an uncle. He chose to remain in Salem, where he became a partner in his uncle's hardware business. On 9 October 1907 Brown married Jane Lewis Johnston, of Salem. They had one son and one daughter.

J. Sinclair Brown helped found Sears and Brown, a construction firm, about 1909. He invested in other local businesses, including insurance companies. By 1 April 1922 Brown had become president of the Farmers National Bank of Salem, a post he retained until 1954. He was chairman of the board from 1929 until 1962 and became chairman emeritus in 1963. Active in the American Bankers Association, he was president of the Virginia Bankers Association in 1935 and 1936.

In August 1915 Brown defeated one-term delegate Orren Lewis Stearnes for the Democratic nomination to the House of Delegates from Roanoke County. Brown won the general election in November, was repeatedly reelected without serious opposition, and served for almost twenty years. During his first year he and several other new members of the General Assembly, including Harry Flood Byrd (1887–1966) and Absalom Willis Robertson, were named to a joint committee that prepared the first master plan for a statewide system of highways for Virginia. In 1920, when Richard Lewis Brewer became Speaker of the House, Brown succeeded him as chairman of the important Committee on Appropriations. He retained the chairmanship of the committee until 1930, through Byrd's gubernatorial administration. From the 1924 through the 1928 legislative sessions Brown was also the ranking member of the House Committee on Roads. On 8 January 1930 Brown was elected without opposition to succeed Thomas W. Ozlin as Speaker of the House of Delegates. Brown served as Speaker for three terms, or six years. Those were the worst years of the Great Depression in Virginia, during which the assembly had to grapple with budget cuts and at the same time find means to take advantage of the New Deal programs that Congress was enacting.

Brown did not seek reelection to the assembly in 1935. The winter of 1935–1936 saw some discussion of a possible gubernatorial bid by Brown against James Hubert Price in 1937. Byrd distrusted Price and had been encouraging Congressman Thomas Granville Burch to seek the post. After Burch's candidacy fizzled in November 1935, Byrd began quietly asking people to urge Brown to run. Price was so popular that the campaign would have been difficult for a challenger. Despite several newspaper endorsements Brown declined to enter the race, and Byrd's effort to block Price collapsed. This failure ended Brown's political prominence, although he continued to hold public posts. He served on the Commission on Game and Inland Fisheries from 1937 until 1939 and on the State Board of Education from 1939 until the end of 1940. In May 1945 Brown presided over a brief constitutional convention that produced an amendment to permit servicemen to cast absentee ballots, and in 1952–1953 he sat on a commission to evaluate the state Alcoholic Beverage Commission. He was longtime chairman of the Roanoke County School Trustee Electoral Board, the body that selected school board members.

During his political retirement Brown continued to manage his business affairs and operate two cattle farms that he owned in Roanoke County. John Sinclair Brown died on 15 January 1965 in Salem in the Snyder Nursing Home, to which he had added a wing, and was buried in East Hill Cemetery in that town.

Glass and Glass, *Virginia Democracy*, 3:481–482; *NCAB*, 51:617–618; Jamerson, *Speakers and Clerks, 1776–1996*, 128–129 (por.); biographies in *Richmond Times-Dispatch*, *Roanoke Times*, and *Roanoke World-News*, all 8 Jan. 1930; Bath Co. Birth Register (where name appears as Sinclair Brown); Roanoke Co. Marriage Register; *Roanoke Times*, 11 Oct. 1907; Norwood C. Middleton, *Salem: A Virginia Chronicle* (1986), 326, 347; *Report of the State Road Commission*, Doc. 5, supplement to *JSV*, 1918 sess.; Byrd's attempt to get Brown into the 1937 gubernatorial race documented in Jan.–Feb. 1936 correspondence with John M. Miller, Charles Reed, and James P. Woods in Harry Flood Byrd (1887–1966) Papers, UVA; obituaries in *Richmond News Leader* (por.) and *Roanoke World-News* (por.), both 15 Jan. 1965, and *Richmond Times-Dispatch* and *Roanoke Times*, both 16 Jan. 1965.

BRENT TARTER

BROWN, John Thompson (19 February 1861– 15 May 1921), member of the Convention of

1901–1902, was born in Hanover County, the son of Henry Peronneau Brown, a planter, and A. Frances Bland Coalter Brown. He grew up in Petersburg, was educated at McCabe's University School in that city, and attended the University of Virginia during the 1879–1880 and 1880–1881 academic years. In 1882 Brown married Cassie Dallas Tucker, of Richmond, and moved to Ivy Cliff, the Brown family estate in Bedford County. They had four sons and two daughters.

Brown lived the life of a gentleman farmer, enjoying a certain prominence won by his involvement in community and state affairs. He was a Scottish Rite Freemason and an Episcopalian, a trustee of New London Academy, and a member of the board of the agricultural high school of Bedford County. Brown also sat on the board of visitors of Virginia Agricultural and Mechanical College and Polytechnic Institute (later Virginia Polytechnic Institute and State University) from 1889 to 1895, from 1897 to 1908, and from 1912 until his death. He was rector from 1900 to 1908 and from 1912 to 1921, and in the spring of 1906 and summer of 1919 he served briefly as acting president of the college. Brown chaired the state livestock sanitary board, sat on the state board of crop pest commissioners, and from 1891 to 1893 belonged to the executive committee of the Virginia State Agricultural and Mechanical Society. Brown was a leader of the Farmers' Alliance during the 1880s, but when it evolved into the People's, or Populist, Party, he ceased his activity and remained a loyal Democrat.

Brown represented Bedford County in the House of Delegates during the 1891–1892 session, when the press identified him as a Farmers' Alliance member. He sat on the prestigious Committee on Privileges and Elections and on the Committees on the Chesapeake and Its Tributaries and on Roads and Internal Navigation. During consideration of a bill to create a state railroad commission, Brown offered amendments that weakened the rate-making powers of the proposed commission but secured its power to review and reduce excessive rates. His amendment may have saved the bill from defeat. In 1892 Brown was a presidential elector for Grover Cleveland.

In the spring of 1901 Brown was one of two Democrats nominated for the county's two seats

in a state constitutional convention, and they both easily defeated their one Republican opponent. Brown served on the Committees on Education and Public Instruction, on Taxation and Finance, and on the Journal. Speaking ably on a variety of subjects, he supported a proposal that small counties be combined into judicial districts to make the administration of justice less costly. Brown's primary concerns were education and agriculture. He advocated restructuring the State Board of Education to give seats to the presidents of Virginia's major institutions of higher learning and supported a recommendation that members of the State Board of Agriculture and of the board of visitors of the Virginia Agricultural and Mechanical College and Polytechnic Institute serve ex officio on each other's board. Brown also favored a proposal that the commissioner of agriculture be elected by the voters rather than appointed by the governor and believed that the new constitution should establish a railroad regulatory commission. On the convention's major issues, Brown voted with the majority for the restrictive suffrage provisions designed to reduce the number of African American voters and for proclaiming the constitution in effect rather than submitting it to the electorate for approval.

John Thompson Brown died in a Lynchburg hospital on 15 May 1921 and was buried the following day in the graveyard of the Episcopal Church of the Good Shepherd in Campbell County.

Pollard Questionnaires, including autobiographical memorandum and birth date; family history in Daisy I. Read, *New London Today and Yesterday* (1950), 104–106; D. L. Kinnear, *The First 100 Years: A History of Virginia Polytechnic Institute and State University* (1972); *Harrisonburg Rockingham Register*, 22 Jan. 1892; *Richmond Daily Dispatch*, 12 June 1901; *Journal of 1901–1902 Convention*, 487, 504, 535; *Proceedings and Debates of 1901–1902 Convention*, 1:578–580, 658, 669, 676, 827–829, 1074–1075, 1125–1128, 1160, 1273–1275, 1652–1655, 2:2056–2062; *Convention of 1901–1902 Photographs* (por.); Hall, *Portraits*, 34; obituary in *Bedford Bulletin*, 19 May 1921.

Donald W. Gunter

BROWN, Mary Moore. See **MOORE, Mary**.

BROWN, Samuel Allen (27 February 1876– 25 December 1960), Baptist minister, was born at Ruthville in Charles City County, one of a pair of twin boys, sons of Samuel Brown and Martha Bowman Brown. His grandfather Abram Brown was the patriarch of a free family and a founder of the Elam Baptist Church. Brown's father served as pastor of that church after 1860, six years later became the first black clergyman the Charles City County Court authorized to perform marriages, and was county overseer of the poor from 1871 until his death in 1881. Samuel Allen Brown grew up in a respected but hardly wealthy family. He attended local schools before entering the Virginia Normal and Collegiate Institute (later Virginia State University) in 1895 for his secondary education. He earned the funds for his schooling himself. Brown completed the collegiate course in 1902 and also read theology with a private tutor.

Immediately after his graduation Brown went to Fredericksburg as principal of that city's lone public school for blacks. On 2 September 1903 he married Clementine Poole, of Hampton, also a graduate of Virginia Normal and Collegiate Institute and a teacher from 1901 until their marriage. They had three sons and three daughters. Not long after his arrival in Fredericksburg, a nearby Baptist church called Brown to become its pastor. Although he had ambitions for a career in medicine, he consulted his heart and agreed to be ordained. Brown served two churches, Second New Hope Baptist Church in Brooke, Stafford County, and Mount Garland Baptist Church in Louisa County, and later Shiloh Baptist Church in Chesterfield. Meanwhile, in 1905 an unsuccessful proposal to create a regional high school for blacks sparked action by local leaders. At a meeting that September fifteen men pledged funds for a school and elected Brown its president. The Fredericksburg Normal and Industrial Institute opened in a church basement the following month. In 1906 the trustees purchased a tract of land south of the city, including a large farmhouse, for use as the high school's permanent home. Known as Mayfield and subdivided into 300 lots, the tract eventually became the city's largest black residential area.

Brown and his family lived first at the school and then in their own house nearby. On 22 January 1912 a local man, angered by Brown's corporal punishment of the man's niece at the school, assaulted Brown outside his home. The experience contributed to Brown's resignation from the high school at the end of the term. He continued to serve as principal of the public school and as pastor of his churches.

Early in November 1912 Brown received a call to the Gillfield Baptist Church in Petersburg. The responsibilities officiating at a 1,500-member church established more than a century before made him hesitate. Then one night he dreamed that the late Henry Williams, pastor there from 1865 to 1900, endorsed him to the congregation. The next day, 18 November 1912, Brown accepted the call. He was installed as pastor on 1 January 1913 but waited until August, after a parsonage was purchased, to move his family to Petersburg.

Gillfield Baptist Church was financially weak when Brown arrived. Its treasury lacked the money to pay for the coal just delivered for the winter's heating. With support from his deacons, Brown modernized the church's methods of collecting contributions from its members, and soon the church significantly increased its support for missions and other church activities. In 1917 he led the church in an ambitious remodeling of the sanctuary that included installation of a pipe organ, steam heat, electric lights, stained-glass windows, a steel ceiling, and a metal roof. Dedicatory services in December 1918 celebrated both the improvements and the congregation's ability to raise the $30,000 that they cost.

Brown participated in various civic activities in Petersburg, but his ministerial responsibilities always came first. In 1926 he organized a Boy Scout troop at the church, soon followed by a Girl Scout troop. To strengthen the church's large Sabbath school, Brown instituted a teacher training class, and he organized and taught both the men's and women's Bible classes. During his thirty-eight years at Gillfield Baptist Church, he calculated that he conducted 1,597 funerals and baptized about 950 people. Brown strongly supported the Virginia Theological Seminary and College in Lynchburg and its philosophy of self-help, and the school awarded him a D.D. For several years he served as president of the

Mattaponi Baptist Association. Brown retired on 7 May 1951, and his appreciative church named him pastor emeritus and gave him a pension.

On 17 January 1942 Clementine Poole Brown died after a brief illness. On 27 January 1943 Brown married Bessie Lee Garland Lockett, a widow from Summit, New Jersey. After his retirement he remained in Petersburg. Samuel Allen Brown died of pneumonia at his home on 25 December 1960. He was buried in the family plot at People's Memorial Cemetery in Petersburg.

Joseph B. Earnest Jr., *The Religious Development of the Negro in Virginia* (1914), 207; Clement Richardson, ed., *National Cyclopedia of the Colored Race* (1919), 1:340 (por.); Caldwell, *History of the American Negro*, 35–38 (por.); Daryl Cumber Dance, *The Lineage of Abraham: The Biography of a Free Black Family in Charles City, VA* (1998), 7, 52, 58 (por.), 120 (gives variant death date of 12 Dec. 1961); James P. Whittenburg and John M. Coski, eds., *Charles City County, Virginia: An Official History* (1989), 79; William Henry Johnson, *A Glimpse of the Happenings of the Gillfield Baptist Sabbath School, Petersburg, Va.* (1928), 27–28; Luther P. Jackson, *A Short History of the Gillfield Baptist Church of Petersburg, Virginia* (1937), 29–43; *Fredericksburg Daily Star*, 23, 30 Jan. 1912; H. C. P. Burke, "A Tribute to the Reverend Samuel A. Brown and A Brief History of Gillfield Baptist Church" and "Dr. Brown's Self-Help Rest: The Editor's Personal Message," *Expected* 21 (Dec. 1951): 2, 4–5; access to materials in the Heritage Room of the Gillfield Baptist Church provided by Thomasine Mason Lane Burke; Warwick Co. Marriage Register, 1903; Richmond City Marriage License, 1943; obituary in *Petersburg Progress-Index*, 27 Dec. 1960.

JOHN T. KNEEBONE

BROWN, Thomas Henry (4 January 1864–8 February 1952), civic leader, was born in Petersburg, the son of Pleasant Brown and Nancy Brown. At birth he was probably a slave, but little is known of his family. Brown lived with a grandmother. Her illness required him to leave school about 1872 to work in a tobacco factory. Somehow he acquired an informal education, and his intelligence and determination carried him onward.

About 1882 Brown joined the Knights of King Solomon, a fraternal order based in Danville. He became state deputy of the order in 1885 and traveled to organize new lodges. After one year Brown returned to Petersburg as a clerk in the pharmacy of William S. Fields, one of the first African Americans to operate a drugstore in

that city. Brown joined the Petersburg Blues, a local militia company, and used his organizer's skills in behalf of John Mercer Langston's bid for the House of Representatives in 1888. Brown's testimony to a congressional committee investigating charges of election fraud in that campaign helped Langston belatedly win his seat in Congress. Brown remained active in the local Republican Party and also organized the city's black lodge of the Improved, Benevolent and Protective Order of Elks of the World. He was also a founding member of Ebenezer Baptist Church in Petersburg.

On 26 December 1888 Brown married Ellen Booth Cooper, of Petersburg. They had one daughter. Two years later they moved to Charlotte, North Carolina, to operate a drugstore for a physician there. The family soon returned to Petersburg, where Brown worked as a janitor for Thomas Scott, an undertaker, who was also keeper of Providence Cemetery adjacent to the white Blandford Cemetery. Providence was part of the Negro Burying Ground, established on land donated for that purpose after the War of 1812 by white militia officers to honor their slaves who went to war with them. As the cemetery expanded, several associations were formed to manage different sections. In 1893 the city threatened to sell Providence Cemetery to meet delinquent property taxes. To pay the arrears, Brown organized the People's Memorial Cemetery Association and became its first president. Members labored to clean the property and built a road to it, but in 1894 another association charged them with trespassing. The mayor's court ruled that the cemetery belonged to Brown's group.

War with Spain began in 1898, and the Petersburg Blues became part of the 6th Regiment Virginia Infantry. Brown served as the unit's hospital steward at Camp Corbin. The regiment suffered discrimination and never saw combat. Captain Brown, as he was later called, became a leader of the Virginia United Spanish War Veterans.

Brown continued working for Scott until 1897. Having learned the undertaking business, bringing to it knowledge acquired at the drugstores, Brown opened his own establishment in

1897 and was licensed by the Board of Funeral Directors and Embalmers on 10 August 1899.

Brown's name does not appear in the Petersburg city directories between 1909 and 1914, and he may have worked in Alexandria as an undertaker during that time. He had returned to Petersburg by 1914. About 1916 Brown opened a funeral home in nearby Hopewell and again worked to organize community institutions. In addition to the Hopewell Benevolent Beneficial Association, established in April 1916, he helped found the Sweet Home Baptist Church. During World War I Brown was a labor agent for the DuPont Company in Hopewell. In March 1928 he founded the Race Advancement Association. Its short-lived newspaper, the *Virginia Race Advocate*, called on black citizens to pay their poll taxes and vote as a unit. Later that year, on 24 October 1928, the Colored Funeral Directors and Licensed Embalmers Association of Virginia held its organizational meeting at one of Brown's funeral homes, and he served the association for many years as secretary. In 1929 he arranged for Petersburg's new city manager to address a mass meeting of African Americans. A smoker in Brown's honor took place afterward, and, typically, he proposed the creation of a civic association and declared again that only through unity could African Americans exert any influence on the city's affairs.

Brown continued to devote his considerable energies to the cemetery. As its keeper since 1921, he dreamed of making it a proper place for burials, with gravesites identified and avenues named in honor of community leaders buried there, but contributions proved sufficient only to control the growth of weeds and brush. The city government ignored his pleas for assistance, but for years Brown organized cleanup days and implored the community to respect the dead through care of the cemetery. By 1943 some 8,900 people were buried in the cemetery that came to be known as People's Memorial Cemetery.

Brown's wife died on 19 November 1939. He married Daisy Valentine on 1 December 1942, and one month later, on 4 January 1943, the community gathered to celebrate the wedding and Brown's seventy-ninth birthday. He continued to champion the cemetery and ran for city council in 1950, sixty-two years after he had campaigned for John Mercer Langston. One of two African Americans in the race, Brown at age eighty-six was said to be the oldest person ever to seek elective office in Petersburg, but he finished last.

Thomas Henry Brown died of pneumonia in McGuire Veterans Hospital in Richmond on 8 February 1952 and was buried at People's Memorial Cemetery in Petersburg. His grandson James Wilbert Brown Burke accepted responsibility for the cemetery, but after his death in 1966 it fell into decay again. Finally, in 1986, the city took possession and began clearing the brush and vines that covered the cemetery. On 28 May 1990, nearly a century after Thomas Henry Brown took responsibility for it, People's Memorial Cemetery formally opened as a city-owned historic site.

Feature article in *Richmond Planet*, 15 Feb. 1936; birth date in *Petersburg Progress-Index*, 5 Jan. 1943, and *Norfolk Journal and Guide*, 9 Jan. 1943; BVS Death Certificate gives variant birth date of 18 Jan. 1864; BVS Marriage Register, Petersburg, 1888; information, including middle name, provided by granddaughter Thomasine Mason Lane Burke, who shared copies of *Virginia Race Advocate*, May and June 1928, and three works by Thomas Henry Brown, *Autobiography* (1939), "History of Peoples Memorial Cemetery & 51 Years Struggle of the Writer of This History" (MS dated 24 Oct. 1943), and *A Brief History of the City and Colored People of Petersburg* (1948); *Norfolk Journal and Guide*, 3 Nov. 1928; *Petersburg Progress-Index*, 1, 4 Oct. 1929, 26 May 1943, 2, 5 Apr. 1950; Michael Trinkley and Debi Hacker, *The African American Cemeteries of Petersburg, Virginia: Continuity and Change* (1999), 25–28, 57, 60, 63, 67–68; *Richmond News Leader*, 24 May 1990; *Richmond Times-Dispatch*, 30 Dec. 1990; obituaries in *Petersburg Progress-Index*, 9 Feb. 1952 (por.), and *Norfolk Journal and Guide*, 23 Feb. 1952.

JOHN T. KNEEBONE

BROWN, William (ca. 1748–ca. 13 January 1792), physician, was born in Haddingtonshire, Scotland, the son of Richard Brown, who was then studying for the ministry, and Helen Bailey Brown. His father's Maryland family included several physicians, and after receiving his early education in King and Queen Parish in Saint Mary's County, Maryland, Brown also decided to study medicine. He attended the University of Edinburgh, where he took his degree in 1770 with a thesis entitled *Specimen Inaugurale Pathologicum, de Viribus Atmosphaerae*.

Brown began his practice in Alexandria, where he rented a house from George Washington. In March 1773 he married a cousin, Catharine Scott, of Prince William County. Their nine children included Gustavus Alexander Brown, also a noted Alexandria physician. William Brown was one of twenty-five men elected in July 1774 to the Fairfax County Committee that adopted two dozen resolutions specifying colonial grievances against British policy. He offered his services to the new Virginia armed forces and in the autumn of 1775 became surgeon of the 2d Virginia Regiment. On 20 September 1776 Congress appointed Brown an assistant physician to William Shippen, of Philadelphia, who in 1777 became director general of all Continental army hospitals. On 2 July 1777 Brown became surgeon general of the middle department, an area extending from the Potomac to the Hudson River, and on 6 February 1778 he succeeded his superior, Benjamin Rush, as physician general of the middle department.

Despite the demands of supervising the care of battlefield casualties and dealing with the distressing conditions in which the sick were treated, Brown found time to write a thirty-two-page pamphlet, *Pharmacopoeia Simpliciorum et Efficaciorum in Usum Nosocomii Militaris* (1778), the first work of its kind issued in the United States. Written in Latin, it described eighty-three medical and sixteen surgical procedures and was intended to fill a critical need by describing simple and inexpensive drugs and medical procedures for use in army camps and hospitals.

After his two former superiors, Rush and Shippen, became embroiled in a controversy, Brown requested permission to resign on 15 July 1780, and six days later Congress accepted his resignation with a resolution affirming its "high opinion" of his "abilities, integrity and past services." Because he had not served for three years in a Virginia regiment he was ineligible for the benefits typically allowed physicians. During its October 1782 session the General Assembly passed a special act entitling Brown to back pay and a land bounty. Accordingly, on 2 June 1783 he received a military certificate entitling him to 6,000 acres. Three years later Brown received two grants totaling 1,300 acres at the confluence of the Cumberland and Ohio Rivers.

In July 1783 Brown purchased a small but elegant frame house in Alexandria, one well suited to a professional man of standing with a growing family. He also established a partnership with Gustavus B. Campbell. Brown had been a founder of the city's Sun Fire Company in 1777 and was instrumental in founding the Alexandria Academy in 1785. He was also a charter member of the Society of the Cincinnati. William Brown died in Alexandria after a long illness, most likely on 13 January 1792. He was buried in a private graveyard at Preston, the home of a kinsman, in Fairfax County. In 1921 the bodies in that graveyard were moved to the graveyard of Pohick Episcopal Church near Alexandria.

Death date of 11 Jan. 1792 and age at death of forty-three from gravestone transcription in Edna May Stevens, comp., *Tombstone Records of Pohick Church, Fairfax County, Virginia* (1981), 54–55; Joseph M. Toner, *The Medical Men of the Revolution* (1876), 81; Bessie Wilmarth Gahn, "Dr. William Brown, Physician-General to the American Army," *Journal of the American Pharmaceutical Association* 16 (1927): 1090–1091 (por.; gives incorrect death date of 20 Dec. 1792); Gay Montague Moore, *Seaport in Virginia: George Washington's Alexandria* (1949), 119–124 (printing misidentified and unlocated obituary giving death date of 13 Jan. 1792), 152; Wyndham B. Blanton, *Medicine in Virginia in the Eighteenth Century* (1931), 130–132; marriage announced in *Williamsburg Virginia Gazette* (Rind), 11 Mar. 1773; several letters in Papers of the Continental Congress, RG 360, NARA, and in George Washington Papers, LC; *Revolutionary Virginia*, 1:133, 5:90–91, 101–102, 6:230, 7:93, 662; Worthington C. Ford et al., eds., *Journals of the Continental Congress* (1904–1937), 5:808, 8:525, 10:131, 17:649 (quotations); Hening, *Statutes*, 11:106–107; LOMC; *Virginia Medical Monthly* 47 (1920): 458–459; estate settlement and sale of library in *Virginia Gazette and Alexandria Advertiser*, 1 Nov. 1792; obituary giving age as forty and death date of 13 Jan. 1792 in *Georgetown Weekly Register*, 28 Jan. 1792.

DONALD W. GUNTER

BROWN, William (11 September 1811–22 April 1894), Presbyterian minister and editor, was born in Rockbridge County, the son of Samuel Brown, pastor of New Providence Presbyterian Church, and Mary Moore Brown. His mother had been abducted by Indians when she was a child, an experience that her eldest son, James Moore Brown, made famous in *The Captives of Abb's Valley: A Legend of Frontier Life* (1854). Brown's parents died when he was a child, and he was cared for by his elder sister

Frances Brown, who married James Morrison, her father's successor at the New Providence church. Morrison taught Brown at home before his enrollment in Washington College at Lexington.

Following his graduation in 1830, Brown taught school for two years and then entered Princeton Theological Seminary, where he and several of his brothers prepared for the Presbyterian ministry. He returned to Virginia after three years, and on 17 October 1835 the Lexington Presbytery licensed him. Brown then studied for one term at the Union Theological Seminary in Virginia, then in Prince Edward County, before his ordination on 28 October 1836 at the venerable Augusta Stone Church north of Staunton. Immediately installed as the church's pastor, he filled the post successfully for nearly twenty-five years. On 19 May 1836 Brown married Elizabeth Hill Smith, of Harrisonburg, the daughter and sister of Presbyterian ministers. They had no children.

Brown's talent and piety won respect from Presbyterians beyond his congregation. He was elected a trustee of Union Theological Seminary in Virginia in 1853 and served continuously until 1890. Brown served even longer as a trustee of Washington College, from 1853 until his death, during which time the school became Washington and Lee University and, with Brown dissenting, severed its formal ties to the church.

In 1860 Brown accepted an invitation to move to Richmond and become editor of the *Central Presbyterian*. This established independent religious weekly reported on actions of Presbyterian bodies in Virginia and elsewhere and reprinted sermons and stories from other religious papers. Through his editorials Brown helped to shape public opinion in Virginia and other southern states where the Presbyterian Church had a strong presence. He reported on the bitter separation of the northern and southern Presbyterians in 1861 and championed the cause of the Confederacy. By 1865 war-related paper shortages had reduced the *Central Presbyterian* to publication of a single sheet, but Brown continued to seek donations to help send the paper to soldiers in the field.

The *Central Presbyterian* temporarily suspended publication with the issue of 16 March 1865, but Brown resumed publication on 20 July. He remained resentful of criticisms from northern Presbyterians and opposed admitting African Americans to the Presbyterian ministry, but his editorials emphasized religious faith, not political controversy. From their arrival in Richmond, the Browns had resided in the home of Moses Drury Hoge, one of his predecessors as editor of the *Central Presbyterian*, and in 1866 and 1867 the two ministers and friends jointly published the *Richmond Eclectic: A Monthly Magazine of Foreign Literature, Religious and Secular*. During this same period Elizabeth Brown helped to found the Hollywood Memorial Association, served as its secretary, and devoted much effort to the reinterment at Hollywood Cemetery in Richmond of Confederate dead from Gettysburg.

The General Assembly of the Presbyterian Church in the U.S.—the name that the southern Presbyterians adopted after the Civil War—elected Brown its permanent clerk in 1865, and he held the post until 1884. As such, he became an authority on Presbyterian Church government, and other ministers frequently sought his advice in the development of church policies. In 1874 the General Assembly appointed Brown chair of a committee to discuss the restoration of relations with the northern Presbyterians. After several years of sometimes acrimonious debate, in 1882 he guided through the assembly a resolution calling for fraternal relations without reunification. The northerners responded favorably, and in 1883 Brown was one of the first southern delegates to attend a meeting of the northern assembly.

Brown's eyesight failed late in the 1870s, and on 11 June 1879 he retired as editor of the *Central Presbyterian*. He and his wife moved to Fredericksburg to live with her brother James Power Smith, a Presbyterian minister. Elizabeth Brown died there of pneumonia on 2 March 1881. On 15 May 1882 Brown married Lucy Gray Wellford, of Fredericksburg, and they moved to Florida in 1883 and in 1889 settled at Bayview, Hillsborough County (later Pinellas County). He was by then completely blind, but he still ministered to a small congregation. William Brown died in Bayview on 22 April 1894 after several months of failing health. He was buried in Florida, but friends had his remains disinterred for final burial on 5 November 1912 in Richmond's Hollywood Cemetery next to the grave of his first wife.

Alfred Nevin, ed., *Encyclopaedia of the Presbyterian Church in the United States of America* (1884), 109 (por.); J. N. Van Devanter, *History of the Augusta Church from 1737 to 1900* (1900), 40–48 (por.); E. C. Scott, comp., *Ministerial Directory of the Presbyterian Church, U.S., 1861–1941* (1942), 90; Ollinger Crenshaw, *General Lee's College: The Rise and Growth of Washington and Lee University* (1969), 200–201; Ernest Trice Thompson, *Presbyterians in the South* (1963–1973), 2:196, 212–215, 245–256, 435–436; obituary of first wife and report of second marriage in *Central Presbyterian*, 9 Mar. 1881, 17 May 1882; obituaries in *Richmond Dispatch*, 24 Apr. 1894, *Fredericksburg Free Lance*, 27 Apr. 1894, *Central Presbyterian*, 9 May 1894, and *Minutes of the Synod of Virginia* (1894): 333–335; reburial reported in *Presbyterian of the South*, 13 Nov. 1912.

ROBERT BENEDETTO

BROWN, William Ambrose (3 January 1877– 12 July 1965), Episcopal bishop, was born in Albemarle County, the son of Henry William Brown, a gardener, and Sarah Slade Runyard Brown. His parents were natives of England who immigrated to Virginia about 1872. After 1880 the family moved to Danville, where Brown grew up. He attended Epiphany Episcopal Church in Danville and became an ardent admirer of the rector George Washington Dame. Brown earned an A.B. from Roanoke College in 1898 and an A.M. from the same school in 1901. He received a B.D. from the Protestant Episcopal Theological Seminary in Virginia (also known as the Virginia Theological Seminary) in 1902.

Brown was ordained a deacon in June 1901 and a priest in May 1902. He was in charge of Christ Episcopal Church in Blacksburg in 1901 and 1902 and became rector of Magill Memorial Episcopal Church in Pulaski in the latter year. In 1904 Brown moved to Portsmouth to become rector of Saint John's Episcopal Church. He married Mary Ramsay on 29 October 1902. They had one son and a daughter, Mary Ramsay Brown Channel, who was one of the first women in Virginia to become a licensed architect.

Seven times between 1919 and 1937 Brown was a deputy to the national General Convention, and he served as secretary of the Diocese of Southern Virginia from 1909 until 1938. In

Petersburg on 11 January 1938 a special meeting of the diocesan council elected Brown bishop of the diocese. He was consecrated at Saint John's on 3 May 1938 and continued to reside in Portsmouth while administering the diocese from its headquarters in Norfolk. Brown's annual addresses to the councils of his diocese lamented the disruptions and dislocations occasioned by World War II, particularly the disintegration of the family and local problems caused by the war. He also expressed a generalized interest in greater unity with the Presbyterian Church. Brown preferred simplicity and decried high-church elements that he believed were slipping into the American branch of his denomination.

During Brown's twelve years as bishop, he became a familiar and outspoken but beloved participant in the national councils of the Episcopal Church as well as the international Lambeth Conference of Anglican Bishops. Called a "one-man interfaith movement" by a Baptist colleague, he participated in the services of various Christian denominations. Brown was an intensely loyal Virginian, and his frequent references to the state's heritage made many people throughout the United States and Great Britain aware of the Old Dominion's history. As a bishop whose diocese included Jamestown, Williamsburg, and Yorktown, he often participated in commemorative ceremonies during visits by presidents, royalty, prime ministers, and other dignitaries. Even in such distinguished company, Brown was frequently the most impressive figure on the platform. His strong features, silver hair, authoritative baritone voice, eloquence, wit, and warmth made him unforgettable. The author of Brown's obituary began, fifteen years after his retirement, by identifying him as the "jovial bishop."

Brown received a D.D. from the Virginia Theological Seminary in 1917 and an LL.D. from Roanoke College in 1938. During his tenure as bishop he was president of the board of Saint Paul's Polytechnic and Industrial Institute (later Saint Paul's College) in Lawrenceville, a historically black institution, and he served on the board of the Bishop Payne Divinity School in Petersburg, which trained African Americans for the Episcopal ministry. Brown was also a trustee of the Virginia Theological Seminary, the Episcopal High School of Virginia, several other schools, and the Children's Home Society of Virginia. He retired as bishop on his birthday in 1950.

Four years after the death of his first wife on 9 May 1935, Brown married Winifred Washington Watts, of Portsmouth, on 7 September 1939. She died on 3 April 1959. William Ambrose Brown died in Portsmouth on 12 July 1965 and was buried in Cedar Grove Cemetery in that city. In January 1969 the Diocese of Southern Virginia named its new administrative headquarters in Norfolk in his honor.

NCAB, 51:326 (por.); Julius C. Schwarz, ed., *Religious Leaders of America* (1941), 2:153; *Who's Who in America* 25 (1948/1949): 321; information provided by daughter, Mary Ramsay Brown Channel; Alf J. Mapp Jr. and Ramona H. Mapp, *Portsmouth: A Pictorial History* (1989), 153 (por.), 161; Parke Rouse Jr., *Below the James Lies Dixie: Smithfield and Southside Virginia* (1968), 47–52 (first quotation on 47); BVS Birth Register, Albemarle Co.; Alexandria City Marriage Register, 1902; Diocese of Southern Virginia, *Journal of the Annual Council* (1939–1951); *Norfolk Virginian-Pilot*, 4 May 1938, 8 Sept. 1939; *Norfolk Ledger-Star*, 28 Nov. 1963, 18 Jan. 1969; *Newport News Daily Press*, 20 Nov. 1983; obituary and editorial tribute in *Norfolk Virginian-Pilot*, 13 July 1965 (second quotation); memorial in Diocese of Southern Virginia, *Journal of the Annual Council* (1966): 40–41, 70 (gives variant birth year of 1878).

ALF J. MAPP JR.

BROWN, William Cabell (22 November 1861–25 July 1927), Episcopal bishop, was born in Lynchburg, the son of Robert Lawrence Brown and his second wife, Margaret Baldwin Cabell Brown. His elder half brother Alexander Brown was a prominent historian of seventeenth-century Virginia. Brown was educated at the Norwood High School in Nelson County, where his father taught. In 1876, aged just fifteen, he was named principal of Nelson County's public high school. The title carried more prestige than authority, for only in his second year was Brown able to hire his first staff member. It was well for both him and his family that he became a wage earner then, because within four years of his appointment both his parents had died, leaving him to support a younger brother in Virginia and to provide partial financial support for two sisters and another brother who resided with his eldest brother in Kansas.

In 1881 Brown joined the faculty of the Episcopal High School in Alexandria, a post he held for seven years until he enrolled in 1888 in the Protestant Episcopal Theological Seminary in Virginia (known as the Virginia Theological Seminary), also located in Alexandria. A remarkable student of languages, he learned Greek, Hebrew, Latin, and Portuguese and taught himself French and German. During the 1890–1891 academic year Brown again taught at the Episcopal High School while completing his studies at the theological seminary. In 1891, after graduating from the seminary, he was ordained a deacon and priest in the Protestant Episcopal Church and assigned his first parish as a missionary to Brazil. On 4 August 1891 in Georgetown, District of Columbia, Brown married Ida Mason Dorsey, a member of a socially prominent Baltimore family and a granddaughter of James Murray Mason, a United States senator from Virginia and Confederate envoy. They had three sons and two daughters.

Within a month of their wedding, the Browns traveled to Rio Grande do Sul in Brazil, where, except for infrequent furloughs, he served as a missionary for the next twenty-three years. His most notable achievements there included the establishment of a theological seminary and his translation into Portuguese of the Book of Common Prayer, an effort judged so excellent by the British and Foreign Bible Society that it commissioned him to translate the Bible into Portuguese. Brown worked from Greek and Hebrew texts but also consulted sources in nine other languages in order to achieve the best interpretation. In 1900 he received a D.D. from the University of the South.

In 1904 Brown was nominated as bishop of Puerto Rico, but he declined. Ten years later he was recalled from Brazil and consecrated on 28 October 1914 as bishop coadjutor of Virginia, the first of his denomination to be recalled from the missionary field to accept a bishopric in Virginia. After the death of Bishop Robert Atkinson Gibson on 17 February 1919, Brown became bishop of the Diocese of Virginia. He was an authority on parliamentary procedure as well as an expert on questions of theology and church doctrine. Combining an ecumenical spirit with evangelical zeal, Brown quadrupled the scope of the diocese's foreign and domestic missionary work. Tireless in his efforts at both the diocesan and national levels, he served as president of the boards of the Virginia Theological Seminary and the Episcopal High School, chairman of the House of Bishops of the Episcopal Church of America (in 1922 and in 1925), chairman of the Diocesan Missionary Society, and chairman of the Commission on Message and Method and first vice president of the Committee on Cooperation in Latin America at the Panama Congress in 1916. Brown was a member both of the National Council and of the Joint Commission on Revision and Enrichment of the Prayer Book.

Brown lived in Richmond while serving as bishop of the diocese. At the urging of his friends, who feared that his constant exertions had undermined his health, he and his wife departed in 1927 for an extended vacation in England and Scotland. William Cabell Brown suffered a heart attack in London and died there on 25 July 1927. His body was returned to Virginia and interred in the graveyard of Emmanuel Episcopal Church in Henrico County.

NCAB, 25:220–221; Ida Mason Dorsey Brown, "Life and Reminiscences of William Cabell Brown. Written for his children by 'Mother,'" and other documents in Ida Mason Dorsey Brown Papers, VHS; Brown and Dorsey family Bible records and Protestant Episcopal Church, Virginia Diocese, Papers, VHS; a few Brown letters in Brown Family Papers, 1801–1889 and 1861–1964, VHS, and Frederick William Neve Papers, UVA; Brown sermons, ca. 1891–1927, VHS; Brown, *Cabells*, 466–468; *Washington Post*, 5 Aug. 1891; *Richmond Times-Dispatch*, 29 Oct. 1914; obituaries and editorial tributes in *Richmond News Leader*, 25, 26 July 1927, and *Richmond Times-Dispatch*, 26 July 1927 (por.); memorial in *Virginia Churchman* 43 (1927): 123–125 (por.).

ROBERT F. STROHM

BROWN, William G. (25 September 1800–19 April 1884), member of the House of Representatives, member of the Convention of 1850–1851, and member of the Convention of 1861, was born at Kingwood in the part of Monongalia County that became Preston County in 1818. He was the son of James Brown and Rachel Hawthorn Brown, natives of Scotland who lived in Ireland until the 1780s, when they fled to the United States after British authorities sought to arrest James Brown for advocating Irish independence.

Brown attended school in the Kingwood area, studied law in Parkersburg, and in the spring of 1823 joined the bar of Preston County. He was commonwealth's attorney from 1823 to 1832. On 3 July 1828 Brown married Juliet A. R. Byrne. They had no children before her death in 1851. On 8 June 1855 Brown married Margaret Patterson Gay, of Morgantown. Their one child, William Gay Brown, represented West Virginia in the House of Representatives.

Brown was an active and lifelong Democrat. He campaigned for Andrew Jackson in the presidential elections of 1824, 1828, and 1832. In 1829 Brown headed the polls in Preston County but lost overall when ten candidates ran for four seats to represent a five-county district in a state constitutional convention. He was elected to the House of Delegates from Preston County in 1832 and served on the Committee of Privileges and Elections. During debates on South Carolina's attempt to nullify federal tariff laws, Brown defended Jackson's proclamation condemning nullification. He then returned to his law practice in Kingwood until 1840, when he was again elected to the House of Delegates. The Whigs held a majority in the House that session, and Brown was appointed only to the relatively minor Committee to Examine the Executive Expenditures. Reelected in 1841, he served on the same committee and chaired the equally unimportant Committee to Examine the Register's Office. In 1842 Brown won reelection without opposition, and the Democrats regained control of the House. In his final assembly term he served on the Committee on Banks and the Committee for Courts of Justice.

In 1844 Brown was elected to the House of Representatives from the district consisting of the counties of Brooke, Marion, Marshall, Monongalia, Ohio, Preston, Randolph, and Tyler, and he was reelected two years later. He served on the Committee on Manufactures, chaired by John Quincy Adams from 1845 to 1846, and during his first term he also sat on the Committee on Expenditures in the Post Office Department. Brown forcefully supported American expansionism, including President James Knox Polk's policies toward Mexico, the war that resulted, and the ensuing acquisition of territory. Even though he regarded Polk's compromise settlement of the northwestern boundary dispute with Great Britain as a surrender of American rights, as a loyal Democrat he defended the peaceful resolution of the controversy.

Brown was one of four men elected in 1850 to represent Marion, Monongalia, Preston, and Taylor Counties in a convention called to revise the constitution of Virginia. He served on the critically important Committee on the Basis and Apportionment of Representation and like most western delegates supported democratic reforms and equitable treatment of western interests. In his principal recorded speech on 21 February 1851 Brown argued at length for equalizing representation in the assembly and thereby ending the political advantage that small eastern slaveholding counties had enjoyed over the more populous western counties. He voted for virtually unrestricted adult white manhood suffrage and for taxation of slaves on the same basis as other property, and he approved the constitution that the convention prepared.

In 1860 Brown was a delegate to the Democratic National Convention that met in Charleston, South Carolina. He supported Stephen A. Douglas for president, and after the party split between Northern and Southern factions he attended a second Democratic convention in Baltimore that nominated Douglas as the Northern candidate. On 4 February 1861 the voters in Preston County elected Brown as one of two delegates to the state convention called to consider the question of secession. He won all but 27 of approximately 2,500 votes cast. Brown served on the Committee of Privileges and Elections and remained steadfast both in his support for the institution of slavery, although he owned only a few household slaves himself, and in his opposition to secession. Brown reflected the sentiments of the majority of his constituents. Like many other Upper South Unionists, he seems to have been prompted by loyalty to the Union and fear of civil war. Brown voted against disunion on 4 April and again on 17 April 1861. His outspoken opposition to secession led him to call for the western counties to separate from Virginia, and on 29 June 1861 the convention expelled him and eleven other similarly inclined westerners.

Brown had recently been elected to the House of Representatives from the northwestern Virginia district and was one of only two members from Virginia to serve a full term during the first two years of the Civil War. He sat on the Committees on Manufactures and on the Militia, and in June 1862 he presented to Congress petitions requesting statehood for West Virginia. After the new state's admission to the Union Brown was reelected and represented West Virginia in the House of Representatives from 1863 to 1865. He served on the Committee of Claims, and on 31 January 1865 he voted for the Thirteenth Amendment to the Constitution, which ended slavery throughout the United States. In 1868 he sought another term in the House of Representatives but lost to Republican James C. McGrew.

Brown was assistant prosecuting attorney for Preston County in 1868 and 1869 and a delegate to the West Virginia Constitutional Convention of 1872. He also served in the West Virginia House of Delegates in 1872 and 1873. Brown then retired from politics and practiced law in Kingwood for the rest of his life. An active member of the Kingwood Presbyterian Church and president of the National Bank of Kingwood, he was at his death one of the largest landowners in his part of West Virginia. William G. Brown died in Kingwood on 19 April 1884 and was buried in Maplewood Cemetery there.

Samuel T. Wiley, *History of Preston County (West Virginia)* (1882), 236–241 (por. on 237), published during Brown's lifetime and perhaps from information he supplied, gives middle name as Guy; some sources give middle name as Gay based on son's middle name and second wife's maiden name; Atkinson and Gibbens, *Prominent Men*, 235 (middle name as Guy); *A Reminiscent History of Northern West Virginia* (1895), 129–137; Oren F. Morton and J. R. Cole, *History of Preston County, West Virginia* (1914), 571–572; BVS Marriage Register, Monongalia Co., 1855; *Richmond Enquirer*, 12, 29 May, 5 June 1829; *Congressional Globe*, 30th Cong., 1st sess., 720–722; 37th Cong., 2d sess., 2526, 2933; 37th Cong., 3d sess., 283; 38th Cong., 2d sess., 531; *Journal of 1850–1851 Convention*, 226, 419; *Debates and Proceedings of 1850–1851 Convention*, esp. 317–321; Reese and Gaines, *Proceedings of 1861 Convention*, esp. 1: 442–444, 2:6–8, 3:163, 520, 4:80–82, 131–132, 145, 197; Reese, *Journals and Papers of 1861 Convention*, vol. 1, Journal, 306, 310–311; Granville Davisson Hall, *The Rending of West Virginia: A History* (1902; repr. 2000), 474–476, 529–531; obituaries in *Wheeling Sunday Register*, 20 Apr. 1884, *Wheeling Intelligencer*, 21 Apr. 1884, and *Morgantown Weekly Post*, 3 May 1884.

MICHAEL J. GORMAN

BROWN, William Moseley (27 February 1894–8 January 1966), educator and fraternal organization leader, was born in Lynchburg, the son of William Nicholas Brown and Emily Carrington Moseley Brown. The family moved to Atlanta for a few years and then returned to Virginia. Brown's father, who operated a grocery in Danville, served in the House of Delegates from 1906 through 1912 and later as the city's postmaster.

Brown attended public schools and graduated from Danville High School in 1911 and from Washington and Lee University in 1914. He taught German at Washington and Lee from 1914 to 1917 and also biology in the 1915–1916 term, and in 1915 he received a master's degree from the university. In 1914 Brown helped found Omicron Delta Kappa, a service fraternity that soon spread to other colleges. In addition to choosing the organization's Greek-letter name, he served as general secretary from 1916 to 1920. During America's participation in World War I Brown entered the army and rose to the rank of second lieutenant in the production division of the air service.

After the war Brown returned to Danville, where he taught, served as assistant principal of the high school, and was secretary of the city school board until 1920. He then returned to Washington and Lee as associate professor of education and psychology. During the 1922–1923 academic year Brown was on leave. He earned a second master's degree in 1922 from Columbia University and a doctorate from the same school in 1923 with a thesis published as *Character Traits as Factors in Intelligence Test Performance*. On 27 June 1922 he married Gloria Graham, a native of Birmingham, England. They had two sons.

Teaching at Washington and Lee did not fill all of Brown's time. He occasionally taught in summer sessions at George Washington University and at the University of Virginia. He also served as national president of Omicron Delta Kappa from 1922 to 1925 and as executive secretary of the organization from 1925 to 1937. Brown plunged into Freemasonry, too. Between January and June 1922 he became a Master Mason, a Royal Arch Mason, and a Knight Templar, took the Scottish Rite degrees, and joined the Shrine.

In 1928 Brown was first elected to statewide office in the Masonic order. That same year he served as the sixth president of the Virginia Academy of Science and as head of the Association of Virginia Colleges.

In 1928 Brown was drawn into politics. A Presbyterian elder and an ardent prohibitionist, he joined many fellow southern Democrats in supporting Republican presidential candidate Herbert Hoover after the Democratic Party nominated Alfred E. Smith, the Catholic governor of New York and an opponent of Prohibition. Hoover carried Virginia in the November 1928 election. Virginia's gubernatorial election of 1929 won national attention as a test of whether the desertion of the anti-Smith Democrats in 1928 was a temporary phenomenon or the beginning of effective two-party politics in the South. Virginia Democrats nominated John Garland Pollard, a Baptist layman and prohibitionist who had supported Smith in 1928. On 18 June 1929 anti-Smith Democrats chose William Moseley Brown to run against Pollard after Brown stated that he would enter the campaign if the Republicans also backed him. Eight days later the Republican state convention nominated Brown.

Brown promised a nonpartisan administration if elected governor and condemned anti-Catholicism in politics. His speeches, however, lurched between unsuccessful attempts to tie Virginia's Democrats to Smith and ineffective criticism of the popular administration of retiring governor Harry Flood Byrd (1887–1966). The campaign went steadily downhill, and some Democrats circulated a leaflet that appealed for racial solidarity by predicting that a Republican victory would return the franchise to African Americans. In November Pollard and the regular Democratic Party organization defeated Brown by a margin of two to one. Brown carried only three of the state's one hundred counties and lost every congressional district.

Brown had resigned his position at Washington and Lee to run for governor. In February 1930, through the influence of state Republicans, he found work as a research associate for the president's National Commission on Law Observance and Enforcement. Two months later

Brown announced the creation of Atlantic University in Virginia Beach, of which he was the president. The school was the brainchild of the psychic and healer Edgar Cayce. Brown had taught Cayce's son at Washington and Lee and as a psychologist had become interested in Cayce's beliefs. Unfortunately for Brown, Cayce quarreled with his financial supporters, and the school closed in 1931.

In 1932 Brown contemplated running for Congress, and he delivered a speech to the Virginia Young Republicans in 1936, but he did not again campaign for office. He served as Grand Master of Masons in Virginia in 1934, Grand Commander of the Knights Templar of Virginia the next year, and Grand High Priest of the Royal Arch Masons in Virginia in 1936. Brown became editor of the monthly *Virginia Masonic Herald* in August 1936. Earlier that year his *Freemasonry in Virginia (1733–1936)* was published, followed by *Templary in the Old Dominion* (1938), both of which were chronological compendiums of early Masonic documents, records of lodge charterings, and lists of officers.

At the end of 1937 Brown became director of the Vick Chemical Company's new school of applied research in New York. He resigned as executive secretary of Omicron Delta Kappa and in the spring of 1939 resigned as editor of the *Masonic Herald*, but he retained ties to Virginia by preparing several other volumes on Masonry in the state. During World War II Brown served in the air force and retired as lieutenant colonel in February 1954. In 1949 he became a professor of social science at Elon College in North Carolina and executive director of the Elon College Foundation. During his time at Elon, Brown published a biography of another prominent Virginia fraternal leader and independent political figure, *From These Beginnings: The Life Story of Remmie LeRoy Arnold* (1953). In 1960 he retired and moved to Florida. William Moseley Brown died in Saint Petersburg, Florida, on 8 January 1966 and was buried with other family members in the cemetery in Louisville, Jefferson County, Georgia. On 29 June 1966 he was reinterred in Arlington National Cemetery.

Dr. William Moseley Brown, Independent Candidate for Governor of Virginia (1929 campaign biography, including por.); BVS Birth Register, Lynchburg; Estelle Stevenson, *George Cabell Moseley of Ingleside, Bedford County, Virginia* [1953], 32; *Virginia Masonic Herald* 29 (Mar. 1934): 8–9; *Commemorating the Silver Anniversary: Omicron Delta Kappa Fraternity, 1914–1939* (1939); Alvin L. Hall, "Virginia Back in the Fold: The Gubernatorial Campaign and Election of 1929," *VMHB* 73 (1965): 280–302; *Dr. Brown, Republican Candidate for Governor* [1929]; Harmon Hartzell Bro, *A Seer Out of Season: The Life of Edgar Cayce* (1989), 329–336; Brown's publications also include *Freemasonry in Staunton, Virginia: A Saga of Two Centuries* (1949), *Freemasonry in Winchester, Virginia, 1768–1948* (1949), and *Blandford Lodge No. 3 A. F. & A. M. Petersburg, Virginia* (1957); obituaries in *Richmond Times-Dispatch*, 9 Jan. 1966, *Richmond News Leader*, 10 Jan. 1966, and *New York Times*, 12 Jan. 1966; memorials in *Virginia Masonic Herald* 59 (Mar.–Apr. 1966): 10, and *Virginia Journal of Science* 18 (1967): 5.

JOHN T. KNEEBONE

BROWNE, Henry (d. by 1 March 1662), member of the Council, was born in England probably during the first decade of the seventeenth century, but the date and place of his birth, the identities of his parents, and the extent of his education are not known. Most likely he had established connections with prominent English merchants or Virginia colonists by the time he settled in Virginia early in the 1630s. The first certain record of Browne's presence in Virginia is a General Court order dated 12 December 1634 permitting him to take up 2,000 acres of land. On 14 July 1637 he received a patent for 2,250 acres on the south side of the James River in the part of James City County that in 1652 became Surry County. Browne renewed the patent in November 1643 and added another 200 acres to it. Portions of his property were later known as Pipsico Plantation and Four Mile Tree Plantation. Browne resided at Four Mile Tree for the remainder of his life and eventually became a vestryman of Southwark Parish.

Governor Sir John Harvey appointed Browne to the Council sometime between the summer of 1634 and April 1635. The governor and some of the councillors were then engaged in a dispute, the causes of which included Harvey's refusal to forward a petition from the General Assembly to the king objecting to a royal proposal to establish a monopoly on tobacco exports from the colonies to England. Browne's opinion on that question is not known, but his appointment by Harvey suggests that the governor believed that Browne agreed with him on at least some of the divisive issues. The author of a letter written in July 1634 estimated that only two members of the Council then supported Harvey, one of whom was "an honest and plain man, but of small capacity and less power." Some scholars have identified this councillor as Browne. After matters reached a climax on 28 April 1635, an eyewitness to the councillors' dramatic confrontation with and arrest of Harvey reported that Browne had been absent, by reason of "a paine that hee had in his belly," but that "hee opposed him as did the rest." The ambiguous wording seemed to place Browne with the rebellious majority. Harvey, however, did not list Browne with the councillors who had opposed him, and Browne continued to serve on the Council for nearly two decades, including Harvey's second administration, from 1637 to 1639.

The loss of most of the Council records for the period obscures Browne's service. For reasons that extant records do not disclose, the Council suspended Browne from office in October 1641 but reinstated him on 10 March 1642. Following the colony's surrender to Parliament as a consequence of the English Civil Wars, the General Assembly on 30 April 1652 elected a new Council that did not include Browne. Sometime between 13 and 27 March 1660 Browne's friend Governor Sir William Berkeley reappointed him to the Council.

Henry Browne died probably during the winter of 1661–1662 and certainly before 1 March 1662, when a document recorded in Surry County refers to his orphans. He had one son and one daughter then living, and his widow, whom the records identify only as Ann Browne, was also still alive. A bond dated 20 October 1662 indicates that she was engaged to marry the widower Thomas Swann. Browne was buried most likely in the graveyard in his orchard at Four Mile Tree Plantation in Surry County.

Cavaliers and Pioneers, 1:61 (first record in Virginia), 149–150, 154; Surry Co. Deeds, Wills, Etc., 1:27, 115–116, 163, 186, 197, 5:75; James D. Kornwolf, *Guide to the Buildings of Surry and the American Revolution* (1976), 59–60; Council service imperfectly recorded in *Minutes of Council and General Court*, 491–492, 498–499, Hening, *Statutes*, 1:235, and PRO CO 1/9–10 and 5/1354; Edward D. Neill, *Virginia Carolorum: The Colony under the Rule of Charles the First and Second* (1886), 118–119, 133 (first quotation), 156, 184, 186, 193, 198; John Zouch to Sir John Zouch, 5 May 1635, PRO CO 1/32, fols. 7–8 (second and third quotations); indenture, 1 Mar. 1662, in Surry County Deeds, Wills, Etc., 1:178–179.

DAPHNE GENTRY

BROWNE, Orris Applethwaite (8 August 1842–28 September 1898), agricultural reformer, was born at Accomac Court House, the son of Peter Fielding Browne, a physician, and Sally Cropper Bayly Browne. Through his mother he was related to several of the Eastern Shore's leading families. His distinguished relatives included his grandfather Thomas Monteagle Bayly, his uncle Thomas Henry Bayly, and his younger brother Thomas Henry Bayly Browne, all of whom served in the House of Representatives. Browne received his early education from private tutors before entering the Virginia Military Institute in 1858. As a cadet he stood guard at the hanging of John Brown on 2 December 1859. VMI named him, along with many other alumni Confederate veterans, an honorary graduate in 1875. In 1860 Browne transferred to the United States Naval Academy, from which he resigned on 25 April 1861 following Virginia's secession from the Union. He joined the Virginia State Navy and on 8 July 1861 was commissioned an acting midshipman in the Confederate States Navy. Browne saw duty in Richmond, Paris, and London. Promoted to acting passed midshipman during the summer of 1864, he was assigned late in 1864 to the new armed cruiser CSS *Shenandoah*. He remained on that successful commerce raider until her belated surrender to British authorities at Liverpool on 6 November 1865.

Fearing that the United States government might indict him for piracy, Browne fled to Argentina, where he prospected and farmed on the Rio Paraná. After his father secured a presidential pardon for him, which he received in September 1866, Browne returned to Virginia the following year. He assumed the inspectorship of the third district of the oyster police force that oversaw enforcement of Virginia's oyster-harvesting laws, and in this connection he issued a *Report to the Auditor of Public Accounts on the Oyster Beds of Virginia* (1872). After the oyster navy disbanded in the mid-1870s, Browne engaged in farming, horse breeding, and the manufacture of fertilizer near Accomac Court House. In 1888 he moved to Hollywood Place near Cape Charles in Northampton County. Until his death Browne managed this 2,200-acre truck farm, then owned by the Pennsylvania railroad magnate William Lawrence Scott.

Browne had an active mind and a facile pen, and he ceaselessly promoted a host of rural reforms, including crop diversification, improved methods of cultivation, fence laws, use of fertilizers, and selective breeding of livestock. He also championed expanded banking facilities, improved roads, and emigration of laborers from Europe. Convinced that overharvesting would deplete the state's natural oyster bottoms, Browne suggested that Virginia grant barren tracts to entrepreneurs willing to plant seed oysters. He published his views in numerous magazine and newspaper articles, particularly in the *Accomac Court House Peninsula Enterprise*. Browne held office in various oystermen's and truckers' associations, the Grange, the Farmers' Alliance, and the Virginia State Good Roads Association. From 1888 to 1893 he served on the State Board of Agriculture.

Browne was chairman of the Democratic Party in Accomack County before moving to adjacent Northampton County, but his interest in agricultural reform led him in 1892 to renounce his ties to the party in order to run for the House of Representatives from the First District on the ticket of the People's, or Populist, Party. Browne's populism was of that aristocratic kind peculiar to Virginia, and William Atkinson Jones, the one-term Democratic incumbent from Richmond County, scored heavily by characterizing Browne as the lackey of a railroad baron and denouncing him as the advocate of legislation that would place the oyster bottoms under the control of monopolists. Jones won a decisive victory over Browne in the thirteen-county district that included the Eastern Shore, the Northern Neck, and the city of Fredericksburg.

A large, genial man, Browne was much admired as a host and raconteur and as an expert on matters of the turf who raised successful harness racers. On 10 December 1891 he married

Nannie Bruce Howard, of Richmond. They had one daughter. Orris Applethwaite Browne died of stomach cancer in a Baltimore hospital on 28 September 1898 and was buried on the Mount Custis estate near Accomac Court House.

Leonard W. Johnson, *Ebb and Flow: A History of the Virginia Tip of the Delmarva Peninsula, 1561–1892* (1982), 217–222; Orris Applethwaite Browne and Josephine Browne Tidball Scrapbooks, Eastern Shore of Virginia Historical Society, Onancock; *Register of Officers of the Confederate States Navy, 1861–1865*, rev. ed. (1983), 24; *Naval OR*, ser. 1, 3:757, 779–780, 785, 792; ibid., ser. 2, 2:657, 771, 819; Presidential Pardons; BVS Marriage Register, Richmond City; Charlotte Jean Shelton, "William Atkinson Jones, 1849–1918: Independent Democracy in Turn-of-the-Century Virginia" (Ph.D. diss., UVA, 1980), 112–117; *Accomac Court House Peninsula Enterprise*, 13 June 1885; *Staunton Valley Virginian*, 21 Aug. 1890; *Warsaw Northern Neck News*, 9, 23 Sept., 11 Nov. 1892; *Fredericksburg Free Lance*, 28 July 1896; Thomas Whitehead, comp., *Virginia: A Hand-Book* (1893), frontispiece por.; death date on grave marker; death notice in *Baltimore Sun*, 29 Sept. 1898; obituaries in *Richmond Daily Times*, 30 Sept. 1898, and *Accomac Court House Peninsula Enterprise*, 1 Oct. 1898 (with variant death date of 29 Sept.).

BROOKS MILES BARNES

BROWNE, Thomas Henry Bayly (8 February 1844–27 August 1892), member of the House of Representatives, was born at Accomac Court House, the son of Peter Fielding Browne, a physician, and Sally Cropper Bayly Browne, through whom he was related to several of the Eastern Shore's leading families. His grandfather Thomas Monteagle Bayly and his uncle Thomas Henry Bayly both sat in the House of Representatives, and his elder brother Orris Applethwaite Browne was a prominent agricultural reformer.

Browne was studying with a private tutor when the Civil War began, and in the summer of 1861 he enlisted as a sergeant in an Eastern Shore company that was part of the 39th Regiment Virginia Infantry. It disbanded when an overwhelming Union force invaded the Delmarva Peninsula. Escaping across the Chesapeake Bay, Browne joined Chew's Battery, Stuart Horse Artillery, in May 1864 as a private and served for the remainder of the war.

In 1865 Browne entered the law school of the University of Virginia. During his final term he was elected president of the Jefferson Society. After graduating in 1867, Browne returned to the Eastern Shore to establish a law practice at Accomac Court House. On 5 February 1873 he took out a license to marry Anna Drummond Fletcher. They had three sons and one daughter. Active in the Democratic Party, Browne was elected on 4 November 1873 to a three-year term as commonwealth's attorney that began the following January. During that decade a controversy over paying off the state debt split the party. One faction, called Funders, insisted on paying off the entire debt regardless of the expense and the effect on public schools. The other, called Readjusters, proposed to reduce the amount of the principal and refinance the remainder of the debt at lower interest. Browne embraced the cause of readjustment. He served as county committeeman and canvasser for the Readjusters in Accomack County and in 1883 ran unsuccessfully as a Readjuster candidate for the House of Delegates.

Browne was among the Readjusters who moved into the Republican Party, and in 1884 he was a candidate for Republican presidential elector. In 1886 and 1888 he won election to the House of Representatives from the First District, which included the two Eastern Shore counties, the city of Fredericksburg, and eleven counties west of the Chesapeake Bay. By exploiting the popularity of Republican tariff policies with the Tidewater's truck farmers and avoiding embroilment in volatile racial issues he defeated one-term incumbent Democratic representative Thomas Croxton in 1886 and Gilmor S. Kendall, a little-known Northampton County candidate, in 1888. During his first term Browne served on the Committee on Commerce, and during his second term he served on the Committees on Commerce, on Expenditures in the Navy Department, and on Pensions.

In 1890 Democrat William Atkinson Jones defeated Browne in his bid for a third term by almost 2,800 votes out of 26,768 cast. Browne had voted for the higher rates in the McKinley tariff bill, which may have alienated some of his constituents, and during a time of intense backlash in Virginia against African American participation in politics, he was vulnerable because he did not strenuously oppose a federal elections enforcement bill that would have protected African American voters from intimidation. As a Republican Browne also lost support when his party seated John Mercer Langston, an African American Republican who successfully challenged the election of a white Democrat from Virginia's Fourth Congressional District.

Browne was an indefatigable organizer, a formidable stump speaker, and a capable legislator who succeeded in winning generous appropriations for his congressional district. As a politician, he supported the protective tariff, aid to education, sectional reconciliation, and racial cooperation. Like many other Readjusters he admired the Republican Party for its nationalism and thus moved quite easily into its ranks. As a lawyer, Browne enjoyed a reputation for clear thinking and attention to detail. For several years he served as the leading counsel on the Eastern Shore for the New York, Philadelphia, and Norfolk Railroad.

Thomas Henry Bayly Browne died of cancer at Accomac Court House on 27 August 1892 and was buried nearby on the Mount Custis estate.

Leonard W. Johnson, *Ebb and Flow: A History of the Virginia Tip of the Delmarva Peninsula, 1561–1892* (1982), 217–222; Orris Applethwaite Browne and Josephine Browne Tidball Scrapbooks, Eastern Shore of Virginia Historical Society, Onancock; Compiled Service Records; Samuel T. Ross, "Recollections of Bench and Bar of Accomack," address delivered 19 June 1900, in *Onancock Eastern Shore News*, 22 Feb. 1935; Browne letters in William Mahone Papers, Duke; Charlotte Jean Shelton, "William Atkinson Jones, 1849–1918: Independent Democracy in Turn-of-the-Century Virginia" (Ph.D. diss., UVA, 1980), 88–101; obituaries in *Fredericksburg Free Lance*, 2, 9 Sept. 1892, and *Accomac Court House Peninsula Enterprise*, 3 Sept. 1892.

BROOKS MILES BARNES

BROWNE, William Washington (20 October 1849–21 December 1897), leader of the Grand Fountain United Order of True Reformers, was born in Habersham County, Georgia, the son of Joseph Browne and Mariah Browne. His parents were Virginia slaves who met after being sold and transported to Georgia. Browne's original given name was Ben. When he was about eight years old he was moved to a plantation near Memphis, Tennessee, and then sold to a horse trader. After his sale Browne adopted the given names William Washington. He escaped from bondage in 1862 after the United States Army occupied Memphis and subsequently served first on a Union gunboat and then in the infantry. After being discharged in 1866 Browne attended school in Prairie du Chien, Wisconsin, before returning to the South in 1869 to teach school. He met Mary A. Graham while teaching in Alabama, and they were married on 16 August 1873.

Browne's education won him immediate respect in the black community. He further enhanced his standing throughout Georgia and Alabama by speaking out against the Ku Klux Klan during the early part of the 1870s and by becoming a leading temperance advocate. Browne sought the endorsement in Alabama of the Independent Order of Good Templars, a white temperance society. The Good Templars refused to be formally associated with blacks but offered Browne a compromise according to which he would receive a charter and sponsorship under the separate name of the Grand United Order of True Reformers. Browne accepted, quit his teaching position, and began his rise to national prominence.

A superb speaker and organizer, Browne soon founded fifty local chapters, or subfountains, which was the number of chapters Good Templar guidelines required for the establishment of a state organization, called a grand fountain. To enhance his authority and expand his audience, Browne looked to the church. The Colored Methodist Episcopal Church Conference of Alabama licensed him to preach and ordained him in August 1876.

In 1876 the Grand Lodge of Good Templars of Virginia invited Browne to lead its new branch of the True Reformers in Richmond. Although a bastion of black temperance, the city proved quite a challenge. After an auspicious start, interest in the Reformers quickly dwindled. Browne returned to Alabama, where he developed plans to transform his temperance society into an insurance organization with a bank, but he could not obtain the state charter necessary for the enterprise. In 1880 he moved to Richmond to take control of the weak Grand Fountain of Virginia and there continued to work on his plan to create a business empire out of the True Reformers. Shortly after his arrival in Richmond he also

served for a time as pastor of the Leigh Street Methodist Episcopal Church.

Browne's first insurance effort, the Mutual Benefit and Relief Plan of the United Order of True Reformers, was a poorly planned savings and death-benefit system that depended on continual recruitment of new members, which made it little more than a Ponzi scheme. In January 1884 the General Assembly passed a bill incorporating the Supreme Fountain Grand United Order of True Reformers (later the Grand Fountain United Order of True Reformers), and in 1885 after further study the True Reformers instituted the first insurance plan of an African American fraternal society that was based on actuarial calculations of life expectancies. Members and prospective members paid varying fees for their insurance according to their ages.

The insurance system proved quite profitable and soon supported other Reformer enterprises. Browne established the Rosebud department to instill principles of thrift in members' children. He also began to expand the order's business operations by purchasing real estate in Richmond and elsewhere as the order spread across Virginia and the eastern United States. Browne's most daring move came on 2 March 1888, when the order received a state charter for the nation's first black-owned, black-operated bank. The True Reformers' bank prospered for years and was the only bank in Richmond able to continue honoring checks during the financial panic of 1893.

In May 1891 the Reformers dedicated a new hall that housed the various operations of the order. The building contained the bank, several business offices, three stores, four large meeting rooms, and a concert hall. The largest building in the city owned by blacks, it was also constructed entirely by African Americans. By that time the order's membership approached 10,000, and it soon acquired a hotel, published a weekly newspaper, ran a general merchandise store, and operated a home for aged members. From the True Reformers' humble beginnings as a temperance society Browne built the order into the largest black fraternal society and black-owned business in the country. The impressive new True Reformers' Hall in Richmond symbolized the order's premier position.

Success notwithstanding, Browne engendered controversy in Richmond's African American community. His conservatism and enormous ego irritated many of his contemporaries, most notably John Mitchell Jr., the editor of the *Richmond Planet*. Two incidents in 1895 particularly raised hackles. After Mitchell and a black Massachusetts legislator presented themselves in March at the governor's mansion for a reception tendered to the visiting Massachusetts Committee on Mercantile Affairs, Browne wrote to a local newspaper criticizing their behavior and explaining his own less confrontational view of race relations: "Legal equality and cordial relation—to the extent of building up the negro race—are the desires of respectable and sensible negroes; and they are as much opposed to social equality between whites and blacks as are the whites themselves." The following September Browne arranged to sell his copyrighted plans for the True Reformers to the order for $50,000. Many in Richmond, and Mitchell in particular, regarded the transaction as an overwhelming proof of Browne's greed.

Nonetheless, Browne's standing was widely recognized. He was one of only eight men, including Booker T. Washington, selected to represent African Americans at the Cotton States and International Exposition in Atlanta in 1895. The True Reformers' exhibition there enhanced Browne's stature and that of his order in what proved to be his last major achievement. In 1897 physicians discovered a cancerous tumor and urged him to have the affected arm amputated, but he refused. The cancer spread quickly, and William Washington Browne died in Washington, D.C., on 21 December 1897. He was buried in Sycamore Cemetery, and his funeral was one of the largest ever seen in Richmond's black community. Browne bequeathed his estate to his widow, except for small legacies to the boy and girl they had adopted. After his death the True Reformers initially continued to prosper, but the order collapsed in the wake of the scandalous failure of its bank in 1910.

W. P. Burrell and D. E. Johnson, *Twenty-Five Years History of the Grand Fountain of the United Order of True Reformers, 1881–1905* (1909); James D. Watkinson, "William Washington Browne and the True Reformers of Richmond, Virginia," *VMHB* 97 (1989): 375–398 (por. on 377); David M. Fahey, *The Black Lodge in White America: 'True Reformer' Browne and His Economic Strategy* (1994), which includes a reprint of D. Webster Davis's 1910 biography, *The Life and Public Services of Rev. Wm. Washington Browne*; *Acts of Assembly*, 1883–1884 sess., 18–19, 1887–1888 sess., 423–424; *Richmond Dispatch*, 23 Mar. (quotation), 9 Apr. 1895; obituary and account of funeral in *Richmond Dispatch* and *Richmond Planet*, both 25 Dec. 1897.

JAMES D. WATKINSON

BROWNING, George Landon (3 April 1867–26 August 1947), judge of the Virginia Supreme Court of Appeals, was born at Greenfield in Rappahannock County, the son of Mary Lewis Willis Browning and John Armistead Browning, a prominent farmer and orchardist who represented the county in the House of Delegates from 1889 to 1892. He was educated in the Rappahannock County public schools, attended the University of Virginia in the academic years 1886–1887 and 1888–1889, and worked for several years as a messenger in the United States House of Representatives. While in Washington, Browning attended Georgetown University and in 1895 received an LL.B.

Browning began the practice of law in Madison Court House in 1899 in partnership with James Hay, who represented the district in the House of Representatives. In 1909 Browning moved to nearby Orange Court House. There he practiced law with John G. Williams until Williams's death in 1911, when he formed a new partnership with Alexander T. Browning, a distant cousin. Starting in 1922, after Alexander Browning was elected a circuit court judge, George L. Browning practiced with Severn M. Nottingham. While he was in practice in Orange County, Browning was active in the Democratic Party, and he represented the county in the House of Delegates from 1914 to 1916. During the 1914–1915 sessions he sat on the Committees on Confirmations, for Courts of Justice, on Executive Expenditures, and on Special, Private, and Local Legislation. During the 1916 session he served on the Committees for Courts of Justice, on Privileges and Elections, on Rules, and on Special, Private, and Local Legislation. On 27 February 1906 in Washington, D.C., Browning married Evelyn Byrd Hill Ransom, a widow with one son and one daughter. They had three sons.

After many years of successful law practice in Orange County, Browning was considered by the Democratic caucus for a seat on the Supreme Court of Appeals during the 1930 session of the General Assembly. He was not chosen initially, but soon thereafter a vacancy occurred when one of the justices died, and the Democratic caucus selected him on 11 February 1930 by a one-vote margin over Joseph William Chinn, who was placed on the court to fill another vacancy almost two years later. The vote for Browning in the General Assembly was unanimous. He was elected to a full twelve-year term in 1940 and served until his death. Regarded like the other justices during his tenure as conservative, Browning was the author of judicial opinions noted for their clarity, incisiveness, and brevity. He wrote nearly three hundred formal opinions during his seventeen years on the Supreme Court of Appeals and filed more than fifty dissenting opinions.

One of Browning's most significant opinions struck down a 1944 Virginia law creating a special fund and registration procedure by which the poll taxes of the state's servicemen could be paid and they could accordingly be registered to vote in state and local elections. Writing for the court in *Staples* v. *Gilmer*, he stated laconically that it required "no mental ingenuity" to perceive that the law was merely "a scheme to circumvent the intendment and the terms of the Constitution, and to avoid the State's declared policy. The fact that it was conceived in altruistic motives renders it none the less obnoxious and offensive to constitutional restrictions and limitation." As a result, the General Assembly summoned a special limited-purpose convention that in April and May 1945 drafted an amendment to the state constitution exempting members of the armed services from the state's poll tax requirement and permitting them to register to vote while on duty outside Virginia.

In 1940 Georgetown University awarded Browning an honorary LL.D. He served on the board of visitors of the Virginia Military Institute from 1907 to 1920 and was active in the Episcopal Church, as senior warden of Saint Thomas Episcopal Church in Orange from 1911 until 1947 and as a lay delegate to several general conventions of the Diocese of Virginia and to the General Convention of the Episcopal Church. Browning was an enthusiastic and extroverted person. He loved hunting and fishing and spending the evenings singing and dancing with friends. The Browning home was one of the social centers of Orange County. After his wife died on 21 March 1940, he spent most of his time in Richmond. George Landon Browning died on 26 August 1947 at Johnston-Willis Hospital in Richmond after months of illness and the amputation of a leg. He was buried in Graham Cemetery in Orange.

NCAB, 36:406; marriage date in *Washington Evening Star*, 28 Feb. 1906, and wife's obituary, *Orange Register*, 28 Mar. 1940; *Richmond Times-Dispatch*, 12 Feb. 1930, 31 Aug. 1947; elections to court in *JHD*, 1930 sess., 280, and 1940 sess., 265; *Staples* v. *Gilmer* (1944), *Virginia Reports*, 183:338–352 (Browning's opinion, 340–350; quotations on 345, 349); Hummel and Smith, *Portraits and Statuary*, 13 (por.); obituaries and editorial tributes in *Richmond News Leader*, 26 Aug. 1947, and *Richmond Times-Dispatch*, 27 Aug. 1947; memorial in *Virginia State Bar Association Proceedings* (1948): 146–150 (por.).

W. HAMILTON BRYSON

BRUCE, Charles (17 August 1826–6 October 1896), planter, was born in Halifax County, the son of James Bruce, a wealthy planter and merchant, and his second wife, Elvira Cabell Henry Bruce. He graduated with an A.B. from the University of North Carolina in 1845 and from the law school at Harvard University in 1847. In the latter year Bruce came into his fortune on attaining his majority. In rapid succession he hired John Evans Johnson to build a country mansion, left for a grand tour of Europe, and after his return married Sarah Alexander Seddon, a native of Fredericksburg and sister of future Confederate secretary of war James Alexander Seddon, on 19 September 1848.

Johnson, known as an extravagant architect, built for Bruce the Gothic Revival confection in Charlotte County known as Staunton Hill. It cost more than $50,000, but the cost overrun did not faze Bruce, who was once described by his half brother, James Coles Bruce (1806–1865), as "quite a sybarite" in his tastes. One of the wealthiest tobacco growers in Southside Virginia, Bruce owned land valued at a quarter of a million dollars in 1860 and slaves worth twice that. He served two consecutive terms in the Senate of Virginia, representing Charlotte and Mecklenburg Counties from 1857 to 1865. Bruce did not become a Senate leader. From 1859 until the end of his second term he was a member of the Committee on Finance and Claims (the Committee on Finance after 1862), but most of his other appointments were to minor or routine committees, with the exception of seats on the Committee on General Laws in 1859 and the Committee on Confederate Relations during the 1864–1865 session.

After the Civil War began Bruce raised and fitted out an artillery battery called the Staunton Hill Artillery and served as its captain from 23 September 1861 until the unit was reorganized on 23 May 1862. During part of that time it was assigned to duty in Georgia. Bruce returned to Virginia to run his plantations and a year later received from James Coles Bruce a plea that Staunton Hill supply more produce for the Confederate cause, an appeal ending with the appalling injunction to "put your wife and children on the smallest amount of food, kill dogs, and old negroes if necessary to keep our army alive."

Bruce lost heavily in the Civil War. His investment in Confederate bonds and the emancipation of his slaves reduced him to genteel penny-pinching but by no means to poverty. He retained Staunton Hill and several thousand acres of good land, and after the war he managed his land and invested in other ventures. In 1870 Bruce placed a steamboat in operation on the Staunton River in an unprofitable attempt to improve the market for his tobacco and other crops in a region with no railroads. After 1865 he repeatedly resisted appeals from local and state political leaders to run for office.

Bruce adapted to the great changes of the Civil War with a minimum of adjustment in his personal life. A scion of the convivial, horse-racing, Episcopalian gentry, he kept his cheerful outlook on life even after Appomattox swept away much of the world he had known. His stern-willed wife, three years his junior, had a gloomier

disposition. That the Bruces still retained their hauteur, even without all of their fortune, is suggested by Sarah Bruce's comment after the war that the greater portion of happiness in life lay in having good servants. According to local folklore three kinds of people lived in Charlotte County: blacks, whites, and Bruces.

The Bruces should have been happy in their family. They had eight sons and two daughters. Their younger daughter, Anne Seddon Bruce, married Thomas Nelson Page, who wrote nostalgic fiction about life in antebellum Virginia. Their sons included Charles Morrelle Bruce, who served as acting governor of Arizona Territory; James Douglas Bruce, a professor at Bryn Mawr College and the University of Tennessee; Philip Alexander Bruce, a historian and founding editor of the *Virginia Magazine of History and Biography*; and William Cabell Bruce, who represented Maryland in the United States Senate and was the father of the diplomat David Kirkpatrick Este Bruce.

Charles Bruce died at Staunton Hill on 6 October 1896, mourned by apologists for the old order as the last representative of the Southside plantocracy. Eight former slaves bore his coffin to the Staunton Hill family cemetery. After the death of Bruce's widow in 1907, he was reburied at her side in Hollywood Cemetery in Richmond.

William Cabell Bruce, *Recollections* (1936), 15–37, 121 (por. by Thomas Sully facing 24); life dates in Bruce family Bible records, LVA; Richmond City Marriage Bonds, 18 Sept. 1848; genealogy in *VMHB* 12 (1904): 93–94 and 85 (1977): 239, and in Brown, *Cabells*, 365–366 (with variant birth date of 7 Aug. 1826); Bruce Family Papers, including James Coles Bruce to Charles Bruce, 6 Sept. 1844 (first quotation), and 13 Apr. 1863 (second quotation), VHS; Bruce Family Papers, LC; Henry W. Lewis, *More Taste than Prudence: A Study of John Evans Johnson (1815–1870), an Amateur with Patrons* (1983), 74–96; Timothy S. Ailsworth et al., *Charlotte County, Rich Indeed: A History from Prehistoric Times through the Civil War* (1979), 293–296; *Speech of Charles Bruce, Esq., in the Senate of Virginia, on the Internal Improvement Policy of the State, Delivered Feb. 16, 1858* (1858); Census, Charlotte Co., 1860; Compiled Service Records; Presidential Pardons; William Cabell Bruce, "A Plantation Retrospect," *Virginia Quarterly Review* 7 (1931): 546–561; lightly fictionalized account of postwar life at Staunton Hill in William Cabell Bruce, *Below the James: A Plantation Sketch* (1918); Hall, *Portraits*, 34–35; obituary with variant death date of 4 Oct. in *Charlotte Gazette*, 22 Oct. 1896; reburial on 30 Apr. 1908 in Hollywood Cemetery interment record (LVA microfilm, with variant death date of 5 Oct. 1896).

NELSON D. LANKFORD

BRUCE, David Kirkpatrick Este (12 February 1898–5 December 1977), intelligence officer and diplomat, was born in Baltimore, the son of William Cabell Bruce and Louise Este Fisher Bruce. His father, who became a United States senator from Maryland, was a son of the prominent planter Charles Bruce (1826–1896), a brother of the historian Philip Alexander Bruce, and a brother-in-law of the writer Thomas Nelson Page. Bruce considered himself a Virginian because of his family's strong ties to the state, even though he grew up in Baltimore and lived abroad for much of his career. Educated at the Gilman Country School for Boys in Baltimore, he spent two years at Princeton University in the class of 1919 before joining the army when the United States entered World War I in April 1917. Bruce reached France as an artillery sergeant before the armistice but saw no action. As a second lieutenant for the army courier service after the war, he carried messages between the Paris peace conference and American embassies, thus beginning his lifelong love affair with Europe.

Bruce did not finish his Princeton degree after returning home in 1919. Instead, he studied law at the Universities of Virginia and Maryland, passed the Maryland bar at the top of his class, and represented Baltimore in the Maryland House of Delegates from 1924 to 1926. On 29 May 1926 Bruce married Ailsa Mellon, daughter of Andrew Mellon, then the secretary of the treasury and one of the wealthiest men in the United States. They had one daughter. Bruce's first foray into diplomacy, as vice consul in Rome (1926–1927), was cut short when his wife developed a malady that the doctors could not diagnose, the first evidence of neurotic behavior that became increasingly debilitating.

Returning to America, Bruce lived in Washington and New York, dabbled on Wall Street, sat on corporate boards, and helped his father-in-law create the National Gallery of Art, which he later served as president from 1939 until 1945. Bruce wrote a book of biographical essays on American presidents from George Washington through Andrew Jackson, *Seven Pillars of the Republic* (1936), which he enlarged to treat all of the presidents through Abraham Lincoln and published as *Revolution to Reconstruction*

(1939). He later revised the biographies further and issued them as *Sixteen American Presidents* (1962).

Bruce purchased and restored Staunton Hill, the family's former estate in Charlotte County, which his grandfather Charles Bruce had built. His philanthropy made possible the construction of eleven public libraries in Hanover County and Southside Virginia. A supporter of the conservative state Democratic Party leader Harry Flood Byrd (1887–1966), Bruce defeated one of Byrd's critics in the 1939 party primary and represented Charlotte County in the House of Delegates during the session of 1940. He served on the Committees on Courts of Justice, on Finance, on the Library, and on Militia and Police and made a favorable impression on the party's inner circle of leaders. He was reelected in 1942, retained his committee appointments, and also chaired the Committee on the Library.

Chafing at the bonds of a failed marriage and dependence on Mellon influence, Bruce volunteered for an American Red Cross mission to London in 1940. His firsthand experience of the Battle of Britain and the Blitz reinforced his strong pro-British sentiments, and he became an emblematic figure in the Anglo-American special relationship during the war years and after. At home Bruce opposed isolationism and joined the fledgling intelligence agency that became the Office of Strategic Services, a predecessor of the Central Intelligence Agency. With the rank of major, and later lieutenant colonel, in the Army Air Corps, he contributed to the OSS most notably as administrative head of its London base, the largest overseas office. Despite much intramural squabbling with British intelligence and the American military, Bruce's organization of more than 3,000 people trained teams of agents to assist French partisans and provided tactical intelligence for the American army after D-Day. He observed the invasion of Normandy and reached Paris on the day of its liberation in August 1944.

On 20 April 1945 Bruce and his wife were divorced in a Florida court. Three days later in Boston he married Evangeline Bell, a member of an Anglo-American diplomatic family he had met in wartime London. They had two sons and one daughter. As a supporter of an active, interventionist foreign policy, the financially independent Bruce served as assistant secretary of commerce (1947–1948), head of American aid to France under the Marshall Plan (1948–1949), and ambassador to France (1949–1952). He served briefly as undersecretary of state (1952–1953) in the waning days of the Truman administration but disliked the Washington bureaucracy. In 1953 President Dwight David Eisenhower appointed the conservative Democrat envoy to the European Coal and Steel Community and to the European Defense Community, and he served until 1955. Bruce worked hard to promote the EDC, which hoped to rearm Germany so that it could assist in Western defense against the Soviet Union. An advocate, like his friend Jean Monnet, of European integration, Bruce was depressed when the French government defeated the EDC.

After two unsatisfying and inactive years back in the United States, Bruce accepted Eisenhower's appointment as ambassador to West Germany. He served in Bonn from 1957 to 1959 but found the post much less congenial than Paris. Mentioned as a leading candidate for secretary of state in the Kennedy administration, Bruce received instead the plum diplomatic posting to the Court of Saint James's. Bruce's strong ties with the British establishment made him the most effective twentieth-century American ambassador to the United Kingdom as well as the longest serving, from 1961 to 1969. He returned to diplomacy in 1970 and 1971 as American envoy at the frustrating peace talks between the United States and North Vietnam held in Paris. Bruce was also the first United States emissary to the People's Republic of China from 1973 to 1974 and ambassador to the North Atlantic Treaty Organization from 1975 to 1976.

Between appointments Bruce lived at his house in Georgetown in the District of Columbia or at Staunton Hill, his rural retreat. In his later years he and his wife spent a portion of each year at their London flat. With his independent means and her flair for creating a classic salon of politicians, intellectuals, and artists, the Bruces earned a reputation for representing their country with style. A tall, cultured, courtly man, Bruce had few intimate friends but a vast array of acquaintances in London, New York, Paris, Washington, and other cities. Fluent in French, he was a connoisseur of eighteenth-century art, English furniture, and French wine. Both a raconteur and an astute listener, he loved the good life, but his enjoyment did not inhibit his ability to make hardheaded decisions and to craft long, incisive telegrams that became legendary within the foreign service. In 1945 Bruce received the Distinguished Service Medal and the French Legion d'Honneur and was made an honorary Commander of the British Empire (military). He received the Presidential Medal of Freedom in 1976.

Two tragic deaths marred Bruce's final years. His first daughter died in an airplane crash in 1967, and his second daughter died in mysterious circumstances at Staunton Hill in 1975. David Kirkpatrick Este Bruce died of a heart attack in Washington, D.C., on 5 December 1977 and was buried in Oak Hill Cemetery in that city.

Nelson D. Lankford, *The Last American Aristocrat: The Biography of David K. E. Bruce, 1898–1977* (1996), pors.; Lankford, ed., *OSS against the Reich: The World War II Diaries of Colonel David K. E. Bruce* (1991); David Kirkpatrick Este Bruce Papers, including diaries and *David K. E. Bruce* (privately printed memorial booklet, 1977), VHS; interviews with widow, Evangeline Bell Bruce, and son David Surtees Bruce; Hall, *Portraits*, 35–36 (por.); obituaries in *Baltimore Sun*, *New York Times*, *Richmond Times-Dispatch*, and *Washington Post*, all 6 Dec. 1977; editorial tributes in *New York Times*, 7 Dec. 1977, and *Richmond Times-Dispatch*, 10 Dec. 1977.

NELSON D. LANKFORD

BRUCE, Edward Caledon (November 1825–24 November 1900), painter and writer, was born in Winchester, the son of Sidney Smith Bruce and John Bruce, first president of the Winchester and Potomac Railroad Company. At age fourteen he lost his hearing as a result of scarlet fever and remained completely deaf for the rest of his life. A precocious youth with a pronounced artistic bent, Bruce went to Philadelphia to develop his talent and received instruction from Thomas Sully and John Neagle. In 1847 he moved to Richmond to seek work painting portraits, but by mid-1848 he had returned to Winchester and purchased the *Winchester Virginian*, for which he served as managing editor until he sold it in 1857.

On 11 October 1854 Bruce married Eliza Thomson Hubard, of Norfolk. They had one son and two daughters. Bruce probably moved to Charles Town after he sold his newspaper. He published "Loungings in the Footprints of the Pioneers," an illustrated travel narrative depicting the James River and Tidewater Virginia and North Carolina, in the May 1859 and May 1860 issues of *Harper's New Monthly Magazine*. Bruce resumed his artistic career after his marriage, and the engravings in the latter issue included a self-portrait disguised as a painting of a seventeenth-century adventurer. The April 1861 issue of the same periodical carried Bruce's article "A Dish of Capon," and the March 1866 issue featured his "In and Around Richmond."

Although Bruce was described as an ardent secessionist, his deafness presumably disqualified him from active service in the Confederate military. He worked instead as a clerk in the Confederate quartermaster's department in Richmond. Bruce also painted portraits, the most celebrated being a full-length life-size portrait of Robert Edward Lee, "begun at Petersburg from life, in the fall [or] the winter of '64–'65." After the Senate of Virginia defeated a bill to purchase the portrait, the artist exhibited it in eastern cities as far north as Montreal, but it took him more than two decades to sell the portrait, and it has long since dropped from sight. Several of Bruce's preliminary studies of Lee's head survive, one of them at the Virginia Historical Society.

Bruce wrote several poems about the Civil War, including "The Viking." His signed travel articles on "Wanderings with Virgil" and "Up the Thames" appeared in *Lippincott's Magazine* between October 1875 and February 1876. In the latter year the Philadelphia publisher J. B. Lippincott collected Bruce's essays and others by Sarah B. Wister into a volume entitled *The Tiber and The Thames: Their Associations, Past and Present*, and in 1877 the same publisher issued Bruce's only full-length book, *The Century, Its Fruits and Its Festival: Being a History and Description of the Centennial Exhibition, with a Preliminary Outline of Modern Progress*, featuring the author's detailed sketches. He illustrated other books and articles on a variety of topics. A lively illustrator and a competent portrait painter, Bruce rose on occasion to excellence, as seen in his portrait of John Singleton Mosby, owned by the Museum of the Confederacy. Edward Caledon Bruce died at his daughter's house in Moundsville, West Virginia, on 24 November 1900 and was buried in Mount Hebron Cemetery in Winchester.

L. Moody Simms Jr., "Edward Caledon Bruce, Virginia Artist and Writer," *Virginia Cavalcade* 23 (1974): 30–37 (self-por.); Alexander C. Brown, "Painter of Robert E. Lee—Edward C. Bruce Recorded Tidewater Scene," *New Dominion Magazine* supplement to *Newport News Daily Press*, 23 July 1972; BVS Marriage Register, Norfolk City; Alexander Wilbourne Weddell, *Portraiture in the Virginia Historical Society* (1945), 143–144, giving month and year of birth (quotation, citing Bruce to Thomas H. Ellis, 8 Feb. 1896); Laura MacMillan, comp., *North Carolina Portrait Index, 1700–1860* (1963), 37 (por.); Presidential Pardons; obituaries in *Moundsville Daily Echo*, 24 Nov. 1900, *Richmond Times*, 25 Nov. 1900, *Richmond Evening Leader* and *Richmond News*, both 26 Nov. 1900, and *Charles Town Spirit of Jefferson*, 4 Dec. 1900.

Virginius C. Hall

BRUCE, James (20 March 1763–12 May 1837), merchant and planter, was born in Orange County, the son of Charles Bruce and Diana Banks Bruce. Bruce's mother died when he was a child, and his father later married Frances Stubblefield. Bruce grew up in comfortable circumstances at his father's Soldier's Rest plantation, where he studied under a tutor who lived with the family.

According to family tradition, at age sixteen Bruce went to work for a Petersburg merchant who imported goods for planters and took their tobacco in payment. Bruce quickly proved his aptitude for business and as his employer's partner took charge of a new branch store in Amelia County. By about 1785 he had moved to Halifax County in partnership with his kinsman John Pannill, with whom he purchased 350 acres of land in 1788. Not long afterward his younger brother, Charles Bruce, joined him there. Many years later Bruce declared that a young man living among strangers had the advantage of relying on himself for success without family obligations.

Although early records identify Bruce as a merchant, he soon purchased sufficient property—nearly 2,000 acres in Halifax alone by 1798—to be considered an important landowner. He augmented his stature on 1 August 1799 by marrying Sarah Coles, whose father, Walter Coles, was a pioneer political and economic leader in the county. They had three children, two of whom died in childhood. She died on 21 May 1806, four months after giving birth to James Coles Bruce, who later represented the county in the Convention of 1861.

Bruce continued to purchase land and at various times owned properties in Alabama, Kentucky, North Carolina, several Virginia counties, and the city of Richmond. He also expanded his mercantile operations. The historian Kathleen Eveleth Bruce, a great-granddaughter who enjoyed access to more of his papers than now survive, reported that between 1802 and 1837 Bruce owned and operated six plantations producing tobacco and wheat, several flour mills, a fertilizer factory, and a large-scale blacksmith shop. He was also the dominant partner in at least nine stores. Bruce attracted talented young entrepreneurs to operate these stores, collect debts, and otherwise act as his business agents.

On 20 April 1819 Bruce married Elvira Cabell Henry, a widow of one of Patrick Henry's sons and known for her charm, piety, and wit. With her help their Woodburn estate, near Halifax Court House, became famous for its hospitality. When the Bruces traveled in their carriage, however, they reputedly refused to acknowledge their poorer neighbors. Of their two sons and two daughters, one son died as a child. Late in 1825 Bruce inherited the estate of his unmarried brother, Charles Bruce, in whose memory he named his youngest son the next year. Charles Bruce (1826–1896) went on to become one of the wealthiest men in Charlotte County and the father of several distinguished children.

The writer William Cabell Bruce, son of the younger Charles Bruce, reported a tradition that James Bruce made his fortune by purchasing tobacco at depressed prices during the War of 1812 and selling it at a great profit after the war's end. Already wealthy before 1812, Bruce would have been one of the few merchants with the resources to continue purchasing tobacco during the war, but such actions could also have enabled smaller producers to survive those years even if Bruce wound up earning the most. His letter books show that he was a prudent and tough-minded businessman without being a speculator or an extortionist.

Bruce organized production thoroughly on his plantations, but the prices for commodities in the markets still determined his agricultural profits. He therefore had to keep abreast of changing market conditions in Lynchburg and Richmond so that he could ship his tobacco and flour wherever prices seemed best, as balanced against the cost of transportation. Bruce also took a special interest in efforts to improve the navigation of the Roanoke River and its tributaries, the Banister, Dan, and Staunton Rivers, to provide a water route to the coast. A prominent investor in the Roanoke Navigation Company, chartered in Virginia in 1816, he sat on its board of directors and was the company's president in 1827–1828. Bruce also served as a trustee of Hampden-Sydney College from 1805 to 1829 and in 1831 was elected a founding member of the Historical and Philosophical Society of Virginia (later the Virginia Historical Society).

Men of wealth and power could hardly avoid public office. Bruce served early in the nineteenth century as a justice of the peace and was sheriff of Halifax County in 1822–1823, but he did not seek political power. He was one of several candidates in 1829 for seats in a state constitutional convention from the district composed of Charlotte, Halifax, and Prince Edward Counties, but he ran far behind the victors and did not even mention his own candidacy in a letter about the election to an associate in Richmond.

Early in the 1830s Bruce began investing in bank stocks, which he called "convenient property for an old man winding up his business." President Andrew Jackson's opposition to the Second Bank of the United States angered him. Bruce nonetheless supported Jackson for reelection in 1832 and regarded him as a better representative of southern interests than Henry Clay, who favored federal spending on internal improvements and protection of manufacturers. When Jackson vetoed the bill to renew the bank's charter, however, Bruce condemned the action, disposed of his shares in the bank, and lent the proceeds to local planters and merchants at 6 percent annual interest. Earlier, in 1831, he had lent $35,000 to the city of Richmond.

Bruce called himself a capitalist but expressed little interest in the manufacturing enterprises that defined the Industrial Revolution elsewhere. He even predicted that fifty or one hundred years would pass before railroads played a significant role in the agricultural economy of Southside Virginia. Nevertheless, Bruce occupied a dominant place in the early economic history of Virginia. An honest, disciplined man, he preferred to appeal to his debtors' honor rather than the law, although he prudently insisted on two names as security when he made a loan. Bruce's surviving correspondence primarily concerns business matters, but evidence of his love for his wife and children can be found there, too.

Bruce went to Philadelphia in January 1837 to receive medical treatment for what was probably cancer. In March his doctors abandoned hope for recovery. James Bruce died in Philadelphia on 12 May 1837 and was buried there in the cemetery at Saint Andrew's Church. His will left plantations and bank stocks to his widow and each of his children and bequeathed monetary gifts to his grandchildren and business agents. The entire estate was worth an estimated $2 million, and his contemporaries judged him Virginia's wealthiest man, perhaps surpassed in the nation only by the merchants John Jacob Astor and Stephen Girard. Through their inheritances his surviving sons became two of the wealthiest planters in Southside Virginia. His elder son, James Coles Bruce, later erected a monument to his memory in the family cemetery at Berry Hill plantation in Halifax County.

Kathleen Eveleth Bruce, "James Bruce," in *Memorial Volume of Virginia Historical Portraiture, 1585–1830*, ed. Alexander Wilbourne Weddell (1930), 368–370 (por.); William Cabell Bruce, *Recollections* (1936), 15–17; family history in *VMHB* 11 (1904): 328–331; birth, marriage, and death dates in Bruce family Bible records, 1763–1858 and 1763–1896, LVA; Bruce Family Papers, including letter books (quotation from Bruce to Messrs. Joseph Marx and Son, 23 Feb. 1832), UVA; William Cabell Bruce Collection of Papers Relating to John Randolph of Roanoke, LVA; Bruce Family Papers, 1828–1938, VHS; Wirt Johnson Carrington, *A History of Halifax County (Virginia)* (1924), 118–133, 273; Kathleen Bruce, "Materials for Virginia Agricultural History," *Agricultural History* 4 (1930): 10–14; *Richmond Enquirer*, 19 June 1829; Hall, *Portraits*, 36; will and estate inventories in incomplete Halifax Co. Will Book, 18:183–196, 215–221, 233–245, 255ff; obituary in *Richmond Whig and Public Advertiser*, 19 May 1837.

JOHN T. KNEEBONE

BRUCE, James Coles (26 January 1806–28 March 1865), planter and member of the Convention of 1861, was born in Halifax County, the son of James Bruce, a wealthy merchant and planter, and Sarah Coles Bruce, who died four months after his birth. His father remarried in 1819, and Bruce's younger half brother, Charles Bruce (1826–1896), became one of the wealthiest men in Southside Virginia. Bruce received his early schooling at Hampden-Sydney College in 1823, subsequently attended classes at the University of North Carolina, continued his education at Harvard University in 1826, and studied law at the University of Virginia from 1827 to 1828. On 21 July 1829 he married Eliza Wilkins. They had eleven children, of whom eight sons and two daughters survived. During the 1830s they lived at Tarover plantation in Halifax County, traveled occasionally to northern cities, and wintered in New Orleans, Cuba, or the West Indies.

Bruce was elected to the House of Delegates in 1831 and reelected in 1832 and 1833. He served on the Committee of Schools and Colleges during all three sessions and on the Committee of Finance during the first two. In 1833 he chaired the Committee to Examine the First Auditor's Office. During his first assembly term, a few months after Nat Turner's Rebellion in Southampton County, the members engaged in an extended debate about the future of slavery in Virginia. Even then Bruce owned probably more slaves than any other legislator, although not nearly so many as he owned later. His major speech on the subject, delivered on 13 January 1832, began by characterizing slavery as an evil, but he justified the practice as a necessity, denounced all proposals for its abolition, and opposed further discussion of the subject as likely to stimulate more slave revolts. The other major issue discussed while Bruce was in the assembly was South Carolina's attempt to nullify the operation of the tariff and President Andrew Jackson's proclamation condemning nullification. Bruce strongly supported the states' rights position and vindicated the action of South Carolina.

After his father died in 1837, Bruce acted as executor of the estate, estimated to be worth $2 million and probably including several hundred slaves. His share of the inheritance made him rich in land and slaves, and with his growing family he devised a plan for a large and elegant new residence. In 1842 Bruce employed a local architect, John Evans Johnson, and a local builder, Josiah Dabbs, to plan and erect an elegant new mansion modeled after the Parthenon. Completed in 1844, Berry Hill has been called the purest example of Greek Revival architecture in Virginia. A registered state and National Historic Landmark, it is certainly one of the finest residences built in the state during the period.

An able and sometimes witty orator, Bruce addressed the second annual meeting of the alumni of the University of Virginia in 1840 and the graduating class of the University of North Carolina the following year. Speaking on 4 July 1847 before the combined agricultural societies of Granville County, North Carolina, and Mecklenburg County, Virginia, he suggested stimulating the South's agricultural economy through crop rotation, a more diversified commercial agriculture, better use of capital and credit, and the sale of surplus slaves (whom he considered "dead capital") to reduce the region's labor force to a size appropriate to its needs. Bruce recommended that each planter retain no more than ten slaves and supplement their services with wage labor. In 1853 he addressed the Danville Lyceum and elaborated on a subject that he had been pressing ever since his assembly service. Noting that Virginia lagged behind other states in political power and in commercial and industrial prosperity, he urged the formation of a state system of public schools open equally to young men and women.

Even though he feared that the South lacked economic vitality, Bruce prospered. By 1860, according to his half brother's granddaughter, the historian Kathleen Eveleth Bruce, he had doubled his inheritance and was worth as much as $4 million. Bruce was reputedly one of the wealthiest men in the country and one of the largest slaveholders in the South. In February 1861 he was one of two men elected to represent Halifax County in a state convention called to consider the question of secession. Bruce served on the critically important Committee on Federal Relations and made several long speeches during the convention. He reiterated his lifelong devotion to states' rights and condemned abolitionists and unfair tariffs as the sources of sectional discord. Hoping initially that a compromise plan could be devised that would allow Virginia to remain in the Union, Bruce voted against secession on 4 April, but he voted for it on 17 April 1861.

Bruce's last public service was as a member and president of the board of visitors of the Virginia Military Institute in 1861 and 1862. He invested heavily in Confederate war bonds and contributed outright an estimated $50,000 to the war effort, but later family tradition suggests that he was resigned to the inevitable ruin of his class as a consequence of the defeat of the Confederacy that was near at the time of his death. James Coles Bruce died at home on 28 March 1865 and was buried beside the body of his wife, who had died on 28 May 1850, in the cemetery at Berry Hill in Halifax County.

Family history in *VMHB* 11 (1904): 330–332, 441; Bruce family Bible records, 1763–1858, 1763–1896, and 1806–1906, LVA; Bruce Family Papers, UVA and VHS; Wirt Johnson Carrington, *A History of Halifax County (Virginia)* (1924), 121–124; Faye Royster Tuck, "Berry Hill," *Virginia Cavalcade* 34 (1985): 162–173 (por. on 168); Clifton Coxe Ellis, "Building Berry Hill: Plantation Houses and Landscapes in Antebellum Virginia" (Ph.D. diss, UVA, 2000); Kathleen Bruce, "Materials for Virginia Agricultural History," *Agricultural History* 4 (1930): 10–14; Alison Goodyear Freehling, *Drift Toward Dissolution: The Virginia Slavery Debate of 1831–1832* (1982), table 7; *Richmond Enquirer*, 26 Jan. 1832; Bruce's publications include *An Address Delivered before the Society of Alumni of the University of Virginia* (1840), *An Address Delivered before the Alumni and Graduating Class of the University of North Carolina at Chapel Hill* (1841), speech in *Richmond Whig and Public Advertiser*, 17 Aug. 1847 (quotation), and *Popular Knowledge the Necessity of Popular Government: Lecture Delivered before the Danville Lyceum, March 13th, 1853* (1853); Reese and Gaines, *Proceedings of 1861 Convention*, 2:238–246, 254–270, 3:163, 488–490, 529–536, 4:144, 312–315; Halifax Co. Will Book, 28:707–710; obituary in *Richmond Whig*, 31 Mar. 1865.

DONALD W. GUNTER

BRUCE, John (5 March 1793–31 December 1855), president of the Winchester and Potomac Railroad Company, was born near Perth, Scotland, the son of George Bruce and Margaret Balmain Bruce. He received an A.M. from the University of Saint Andrews. At the invitation of his uncle Alexander Balmain, rector of Frederick

Parish, Bruce immigrated to Winchester in 1818 and became principal of the Winchester Academy, a classical school of which Balmain had been a founder. Bruce taught Latin and other subjects at the academy until 1835. On 6 April 1820 he married Sidney Smith, the daughter of Edward Smith, a prominent local landowner. The eldest of their four sons was the artist and writer Edward Caledon Bruce.

In 1828 Bruce took charge of the construction of Christ Episcopal Church, which still stands in Winchester. It was designed by the eminent architect Robert Mills, whose wife was a cousin of Bruce's wife. In the spring of 1831, as construction of the Baltimore and Ohio Railroad and the Chesapeake and Ohio Canal improved commercial transportation links on the Potomac River, Bruce and other citizens sought to exploit a new opportunity. Representatives of large landowners along the Shenandoah River suggested that a canal be built to carry their crops to the Potomac River markets. At a meeting he convened in Winchester on 5 March 1831, Bruce instead proposed construction of a railroad from that town to Harpers Ferry. He argued that a canal would funnel trade away from Winchester but that a railroad would make the town a commercial center. The railroad proposal won local support, and on 8 April 1831 the General Assembly chartered the Winchester and Potomac Railroad Company. Bruce was the first president.

Bruce oversaw construction of the line to Harpers Ferry. Problems delayed the work, and he had to give so much time to the railroad that he resigned from the Winchester Academy in 1835. The fact that the line ran through hilly limestone country made construction slow and expensive. Undercapitalized from the beginning, the railroad had to borrow $40,000 from the state in 1834 and another $150,000 in 1838. Partly because of high prices charged by landowners along the Shenandoah River for right-of-way, construction costs soared to $600,000, nearly twice the original estimate. Such conflicts between local planters and commercial interests in Winchester contributed to the separation of Clarke County from Frederick County in 1836.

On 9 March 1836 the first train departed Winchester at 11:00 A.M. and returned from Harpers Ferry at 2:45 P.M. Bruce described the train as "the greatest novelty exhibited since the first settlement of the country." His journal also documents his busy schedule, including trips between Winchester and Harpers Ferry and several journeys to Baltimore in the interest of the railroad. Despite continual trouble with engines and track, Bruce remained convinced that the railroad, which primarily carried flour to the Baltimore and Ohio Railroad at Harpers Ferry for transshipment to Baltimore merchants, would prove successful.

Stockholders were less sanguine about the railroad's prospects and replaced Bruce as president at the annual meeting in August 1839. The Winchester and Potomac never managed to lower freight rates sufficiently for local merchants to compete with those at Baltimore. Competition from other railroads thwarted Bruce's dream that Winchester would become the commercial hub of western Virginia. The Winchester and Potomac Railroad survived until the United States Army took it over during the Civil War. After the war the line was absorbed into the Baltimore and Ohio system, and Winchester became just one stop on a longer line.

In 1841 Bruce returned to Scotland to visit family and friends. The 1850 census gives his occupation as farmer, but he also served on the city council and maintained his interest in commercial development and new technologies. In 1849 he and several other citizens obtained a charter for the Winchester and Harpers Ferry Telegraph Company, which was eventually acquired by the Western Union system. John Bruce died of stomach cancer on 31 December 1855 and was buried at Mount Hebron Cemetery in Winchester.

Birth and death dates on gravestone; Garland R. Quarles, *The Schools of Winchester, Virginia* (1964), 1, 3, *The Story of One Hundred Old Homes in Winchester, Virginia* (1967), 38–39, and *Worthy Lives,* 21–24, 47; Bruce Family Papers, 1836–1906, VHS, including biographical data and typescript of "Private Journal of John Bruce," 9 Mar. 1836–12 July 1839 (quotation 9 Mar. 1836); Frederick Co. Marriage Register; "John Bruce's Account of Charges for Building the Edifice Corner Water and Washington Streets, He Having Charge of Same and Furnishing Design," Christ Episcopal Church, Winchester; *Winchester Star,* 18 Nov. 1986; Rhodri Windsor Liscombe, *The Church Architecture of Robert Mills* (1985), 18; *Proceedings of Two Meetings Held in the Town of Winchester to Take into Consideration the Expediency of Constructing a Rail-road from Winchester to Some Point on the Potomac River, at or Near Harper's Ferry* (1831); Charles Conrad Wright, "The Development of Railroad Transportation in Virginia" (Ph.D. diss., UVA, 1930), 21, 61, 76; Charles W. Turner, "The Virginia Railroads, 1828–1860" (Ph.D. diss., University of Minnesota, 1946), 22; Warren R. Hofstra, *A Separate Place: The Formation of Clarke County, Virginia* (1986), 69–78, 94–97; annual reports, Winchester and Potomac Railroad Company, 1831–1850; *Charles Town Virginia Free Press*, 8 Aug. 1839; Frederick Co. Will Book, 24:320–323; BVS Death Register, Winchester; obituary in *Washington Daily National Intelligencer*, 4 Jan. 1856.

CONNIE JEAN CASILEAR
JOHN T. KNEEBONE

BRUCE, Kathleen Eveleth (21 October 1885–26 April 1950), historian, was born in Richmond, the daughter of Thomas Seddon Bruce and Mary Bruce Anderson Bruce. She was a granddaughter of Joseph Reid Anderson, manager of the Tredegar ironworks in Richmond, and of Charles Bruce (1826–1896), one of the wealthiest planters in Southside Virginia. The historian Philip Alexander Bruce was her uncle, and she was related to other prominent Virginia families. She began her education in Richmond, but after her mother's poor health caused the family to move to the dry western climate, she attended public schools in Tucson, Arizona, and El Paso, Texas.

Although her mother opposed college education for women, Bruce entered Radcliffe College, from which she received a B.A. in 1918, an M.A. in 1919, and a Ph.D. in history in 1924. Professors at Harvard University, which then refused to admit women to graduate study in history, conducted classes on the Radcliffe campus or allowed women to attend classes at Harvard. Bruce studied with Edward Channing, a historian of colonial America, and with Frederick Jackson Turner, the foremost historian of the frontier and of American regionalism. She was one of a limited number of students to complete a doctoral dissertation under Channing. Published in 1931 as *Virginia Iron Manufacture in the Slave Era*, Bruce's dissertation clearly demonstrated that some industrialization had taken place in the South before the Civil War and that slave labor had been pivotal to Virginia's industrial development. Her pioneering use of the voluminous business records of her grand-father's Tredegar ironworks made *Virginia Iron Manufacture* one of the first and most durable contributions to early southern industrial and labor history.

Having taken advantage of untapped primary sources available to her from one side of her family, Bruce turned to the records of her father's family and published two noteworthy articles in the journal *Agricultural History*. "Materials for Virginia Agricultural History" in the January 1930 issue used the Bruce family papers to outline research opportunities for studying Virginia's plantation economy and related subjects. Bruce's "Virginian Agricultural Decline to 1860: A Fallacy" in the January 1932 issue suggested that to maintain their land's productivity, Virginia farmers beginning about 1810 had implemented modern and innovative agricultural techniques, such as adding marl and lime to the soil to reduce acidity, and subscribed to agricultural journals that disseminated scientific information. She attacked the prevailing thesis that Virginia planters were careless, unconcerned farmers who accelerated the state's agricultural decline by excessive cultivation of tobacco and cotton. Bruce did not hesitate to challenge the conclusions of both Channing and Turner. She posited instead that without the Civil War agricultural profitability would have been much greater in nineteenth-century Virginia than historians had suggested.

Bruce contributed articles and reviews to the *Dictionary of American Biography* and other reference works and to the *Mississippi Valley Historical Review*, two multipart articles on ordnance manufacture during the Revolutionary War and the Civil War to the journal *Army Ordnance* between 1925 and 1927, and a brief biography of her great-grandfather James Bruce to *Virginia Historical Portraiture* (1930). She also wrote a chapter on Massachusetts women in the American Revolution for the multivolume *Commonwealth History of Massachusetts: Colony, Province and State* (1927–1930).

Bruce taught at Wheaton College, in Norton, Massachusetts, from 1924 to 1926, at the College of William and Mary from 1926 to 1932, at Hollins College from 1933 to 1936, and at Sophie Newcomb College of Tulane University in New

Orleans from 1943 to 1946. She taught at Westhampton College of the University of Richmond from 1948 until her death and began research in the collections of the Virginia State Library (later the Library of Virginia) to compare and contrast conditions after the Civil War with conditions following the two world wars. Bruce received a Social Science Research Council Grant-in-Aid in 1928–1929, was a research associate at the Museum of Science and Industry in Chicago from 1930 to 1932, and was joint director of the Nettie Fowler McCormick Biographical Association in Chicago in 1932 and 1933. In September 1936 she became the regional director of the survey of federal archives in Virginia under the Works Progress Administration. Bruce served on the board of editors of the *Mississippi Valley Historical Review* between 1934 and 1937, was an associate editor of *Agricultural History* from 1932 until her death, and sat on the executive council of the Southern Historical Association in 1935–1937.

Bruce's book on iron manufacturing and industrial slavery remains the standard work in the field and was reprinted in 1968. Her articles on agricultural history paved the way for revision of old ideas about southern agricultural and economic history. Working throughout her career in the predominantly male academic world, Bruce earned her successes with in-depth research in original records, clear analysis, and persuasive writing. When she was passed over in favor of a man for a choice appointment to the history faculty at Smith College in 1936, she lamented the irony that women's colleges were preparing women for professional positions that those same colleges often denied to women, especially in the field of history. While teaching at Westhampton College, Bruce constructed a small house in which to work, which she bequeathed to the college for the use of female faculty members actively teaching and doing research.

Bruce did not marry. She loved to travel and during the 1920s and 1930s visited Asia, Europe, and South America. She toured China and the Soviet Union, including Manchuria and Siberia. Kathleen Eveleth Bruce died in Richmond on 26 April 1950 after a long illness and was buried in Hollywood Cemetery in that city.

Durward Howes, ed., *American Women: The Official Who's Who among the Women of the Nation, 1935–36* (1935), 76; *NCAB*, 42:224–225; BVS Birth Register, Richmond City; *Richmond News Leader*, 3 Feb. 1928, 17 Aug. 1933, 3 Oct. 1936, 9 Oct. 1941, 6 Feb. 1943, 3 Nov. 1950; Bruce, "Archives Survey: A Mystery Project," *Commonwealth* 6 (May 1939): 21, 30–31; Jacqueline Goggin, "Challenging Sexual Discrimination in the Historical Profession: Women Historians and the American Historical Association, 1890–1940," *AHR* 97 (1992): 776–777; obituaries in *Richmond News Leader,* 26 Apr. 1950 (por.), *Richmond Times-Dispatch*, 27 Apr. 1950, *New York Times,* 30 Apr. 1950, and *JSH* 16 (1950): 413.

MARY E. COOKINGHAM

BRUCE, Patrick Henry (21 or 25 March 1881–12 November 1936), painter, was the son of James Coles Bruce (1857–1899) and Susan Seddon Brooks Bruce and a member of the wealthy Bruce family that lost much of its land during the Civil War. Family records indicate that he was born on 21 March 1881 at Tarover in Halifax County, but his birth was recorded in Campbell County as taking place there on 25 March 1881. The family moved to Richmond about 1885. Bruce received his early education at McCabe's University School in Richmond and attended evening classes at the Art Club of Richmond.

Although his family had shown little interest in art, Bruce devoted his entire life to searching for a manner of expressing himself through oil paint. While supporting himself working in the real estate business, he studied with the sculptor Edward Virginius Valentine and in the evenings took drafting and mechanical drawing classes at the Virginia Mechanics Institute in Richmond. His fellow students in Richmond included Adèle Clark. Bruce's earliest-known oil painting, a portrait of Littleton Waller Tazewell Wickham, was completed about 1900, although his first extant dated work is a 1901 charcoal drawing.

Bruce moved to New York in 1902, where he studied under Robert Henri, William Merritt Chase, and Kenneth Hayes Miller at the New York School of Art and became a friend of Edward Hopper. Bruce had moved to Paris by early in 1904. From then until 1907 he painted primarily portraits showing the influence of Henri and Chase. One of Bruce's portraits was exhibited at the National Academy of Design in New York in January 1904. On 24 August 1905 he married Helen Frances Kibbey, whom he had met when they were students in New York. They had one son and separated about 1919.

By mid-1907 Bruce was friendly with Gertrude Stein and Leo Stein, the noted expatriate Americans living in Paris. The Steins and their circle of avant-garde artists probably influenced Bruce's style, which took a more modernist approach beginning that year. In 1908 he became a student of Henri Matisse as one of the first students at the new Académie Matisse in Paris. As a result, his paintings became strongly influenced by that great French artist as well as by the works of Paul Cézanne. Bruce produced still lifes and landscapes showing this influence until late in 1912. During these years he and his wife sold antiques to support their family.

In the spring of 1912 Bruce's work underwent another drastic stylistic change under the influence of the French artist Robert Delaunay and his Ukranian-born wife, Sonia Delaunay. A noted cubist, Delaunay experimented with bold colors and geometrical shapes. For the remainder of his life Bruce painted abstract compositions based on conceptual ideas and not on actuality. Four of his works were exhibited in the famous Armory Show in New York in 1913, and thirty-three, mostly landscapes and still lifes, were shown at the Montross Gallery in New York in 1916. The zenith of Bruce's career began in 1917 with large and colorful paint-and-pencil works on canvas that made use of flat geometric masses interspersed with bold diagonal bars. He eventually became most noted and respected for his twenty-five surviving works in this style. Bruce ceased signing his works in 1916 and finally stopped exhibiting them because he believed that his generation could not understand his art.

Always reclusive, Bruce spent his last dozen years in a state of despondency because of his lack of recognition and his separation from his wife and son. Impoverishment forced him to rely on funds supplied by his sister, Mary Bruce Payne, and he suffered from continuing stomach problems. By May 1933 he had moved to Versailles to conserve his resources. Bruce destroyed many of his paintings during this period of depression. On 29 July 1936 he sailed for New York to live with his sister. Patrick Henry Bruce committed suicide in New York on 12 November 1936. His ashes were scattered in Paris.

The major galleries that own Bruce's canvases include the Corcoran Gallery of Art and the Hirshhorn Museum and Sculpture Garden in Washington, D.C., the Metropolitan Museum of Art and the Whitney Museum of American Art in New York, the Museum of Fine Arts in Houston, and the Yale University Art Gallery. Bruce produced at least 150 works, but his paintings did not attract serious and favorable attention until the 1960s. In 1965 an exhibition of synchromist art at M. Knoedler and Company, New York, featured some of Bruce's works, and in 1979 the Houston Museum of Fine Arts organized a major retrospective of his paintings, which were also exhibited on tour at the Museum of Modern Art in New York and the Virginia Museum of Fine Arts in Richmond. The Parsons-Bruce Art Association, the South Boston chapter of the Virginia Museum of Fine Arts, honored sculptor Edith Stevens Parsons and Patrick Henry Bruce with its name.

William C. Agee and Barbara Rose, *Patrick Henry Bruce: American Modernist* (1979), including texts of relevant documents, citation of New York death certificate, and pors., 7–10; Agee and Rose, *Patrick Henry Bruce: American Modernist, A Catalogue Raisonne* (1979); Agee, "Patrick Henry Bruce: A Major American Artist of Early Modernism," *Arts in Virginia* 17 (spring 1977): 12–32; William D. Judson, "Patrick Henry Bruce, 1881–1936" (master's thesis, Oberlin College, 1968); BVS Birth Register, Campbell Co.; some Bruce letters at Yale University and in several private collections; *Chesterfield County's News Journal* 44 (Dec. 1979): 34.

FREDERICK R. BRANDT

BRUCE, Philip Alexander (7 March 1856–16 August 1933), historian, was born at Staunton Hill in Charlotte County, the son of Charles Bruce (1826–1896), a wealthy planter, and Sarah Alexander Seddon Bruce. His brother William Cabell Bruce represented Maryland in the United States Senate, his brother-in-law was the writer Thomas Nelson Page, his nephew David Kirkpatrick Este Bruce served as American ambassador to France, West Germany, and the United Kingdom following World War II, and his niece Kathleen Eveleth Bruce became an eminent historian. After attending the Norwood School in Nelson County from 1871 to 1873, Bruce spent the next two years at the University of Virginia and graduated from the law school of Harvard University in 1878. He continued his law study at the University of Virginia under John B. Minor in the 1878–1879 academic year before establishing his own practice in Baltimore in 1879.

Bruce never enjoyed the practice of law and began to think seriously about the southern economy. A disciple of the New South ideal of a business and industrial revival based on values traditionally associated with the region, he initially regarded African Americans as an obstacle to progress. Bruce wrote a series of articles on the subject for the *New York Evening Post* in 1884 and expanded them the following year for his first book, *The Plantation Negro as a Freeman: Observations on His Character, Condition, and Prospects in Virginia*, for which he did not find a publisher until 1889. The volume reflected the thinking of many white southerners who then regarded African Americans as a socially and intellectually inferior laboring class. In later work Bruce recommended that blacks not needed for agricultural labor be resettled outside the South.

In 1887 Bruce moved to Richmond as secretary and treasurer of the Vulcan Iron Works, of which his brother Thomas Seddon Bruce was president. By 1890 Bruce had joined the editorial staff of the *Richmond Times*. His varied work included articles critical of women in the pulpit and editorials on race relations and economic development. Drawn toward historical scholarship, Bruce left the newspaper in 1892 to become corresponding secretary and librarian of the Virginia Historical Society. The following year he helped start the society's quarterly historical journal, the *Virginia Magazine of History and Biography*. During Bruce's five-year tenure as the founding editor, the magazine published historical documents and genealogical accounts focused on the leading colonial families, an agenda that continued for decades.

In his own research Bruce combined a nostalgia for the traditions of the Old South, the boosterism of the New South, and a new interest in the earliest period of Virginia's history. He conceived of a three-part project intended to demonstrate that the idealized society of his

youth had its basis in the seventeenth century. The first fruit of this research was Bruce's two-volume *Economic History of Virginia in the Seventeenth Century: An Inquiry into the Material Condition of the People, Based upon Original and Contemporaneous Records* (1896), which made significant contributions to understanding Virginia's early economic history and the rise to wealth of its great landed families.

On 19 October 1896 Bruce married Elizabeth Tunstall Taylor Newton, a Norfolk widow. They had one daughter. Resigning from the Virginia Historical Society in 1898, Bruce made the first of several extended research trips to England. While there he publicized the New South gospel and tried to explain to British readers his views on race. Before publishing the results of his further research on seventeenth-century Virginia, Bruce wrote *The Rise of the New South* (1905), a work that established him as a leader in a school of historical scholarship that sought the origins of the New South in the ruins of the Old. Characterized by high optimism, it reads like an industrial gazetteer of the South and became one of the capstones of the New South crusade, one facet of which was restriction of African American suffrage. Modifying his stern views of two decades earlier, Bruce acknowledged a limited but useful place for black laborers in southern industry.

Bruce moved to Norfolk in 1907. He had inherited more than 1,400 acres of land from his parents' estate in Charlotte County, the income from which enabled him to engage in historical scholarship for the remainder of his life. In 1907 Bruce published the second part of his series on seventeenth-century Virginia, the one-volume *Social Life of Virginia in the Seventeenth Century: An Inquiry into the Origin of the Higher Planting Class, together with an Account of the Habits, Customs, and Diversions of the People*. Its focus on the "higher planting class" fit the then-current notions of social history. Bruce sought the origins of the present in the past and attempted to discover how Virginia's great early planters evolved into the celebrated colonial squirearchy and its commercial leaders, the forerunners of the New South. He concluded his three-part Virginia history in 1910 with the two-volume *Institutional History of Virginia in the Seventeenth Century: An Inquiry into the Religious, Moral, Educational, Legal, Military, and Political Condition of the People, Based on Original and Contemporaneous Records.* Once again he focused almost exclusively on the social and political elites. Summing up all five of Bruce's volumes on seventeenth-century Virginia, an unsigned article in the *American Historical Review* praised Bruce for employing new primary source materials "in lavish but discriminating profusion" and accorded him "no small measure of praise as a scholar and a thinker."

The stereotype of the Old South took firm root in Bruce's memory of his own childhood, his views of the past, and his scholarship. This vision is clearly evident in the laudatory popular biography of Robert Edward Lee that Bruce published in 1907 and in *Brave Deeds of Confederate Soldiers* (1916), both reflecting his lifelong allegiance to the Lost Cause and to the mythology and symbolism of the Old South. In 1916 Bruce moved to Charlottesville as centennial historian of the University of Virginia. Working in the library and from the university's archives he wrote the five-volume *History of the University of Virginia, 1819–1919: The Lengthened Shadow of One Man* (1920–1922). Bruce treated the university as both an educational and a cultural institution. The subtitle summed up his belief that Thomas Jefferson's influence had been pervasive throughout the university's history and that in turn the university's influence had been profoundly significant in the history of Virginia.

The lives of great Virginians formed the subject of Bruce's last major publication, *The Virginia Plutarch* (1929). Its two volumes contained biographies of the figures he deemed the most important and influential in Virginia's history, all eminent white men except for Powhatan and Pocahontas. Bruce published numerous articles and reviews throughout his career, several small works, and one textbook, *A School History of the United States* (1903). He wrote the section on Virginia's history through 1763 for a three-volume *History of Virginia* published in 1924 and supplemented with three additional volumes of densely printed biographical data

supplied by the subjects themselves. A revised and extended version of that essay, carrying Virginia's history up to World War I, appeared as *Virginia: Rebirth of the Old Dominion* (1929). Bruce also contributed entries on Sir Samuel Argall, Nathaniel Bacon (1647–1676), Sir William Berkeley, and Norborne Berkeley, baron de Botetourt, to the *Dictionary of American Biography*. He occasionally wrote poems, some of them in imitation of Edgar Allan Poe, and he published a small volume of verse, *Pocahontas and Other Sonnets* (1912). Bruce's works of popular history and on the Civil War have long been forgotten, and most of his scholarly works have been superseded. His writings on race and on elite whites are no longer persuasive, but his five volumes on the economic, institutional, and social history of seventeenth-century Virginia are still cited as important works of scholarship. Bruce did painstaking research in colonial land and court records and grounded his work in the available primary sources. The volumes have all been reprinted and have influenced subsequent textbook authors, giving his most important scholarly work an enduring place in the literature of Virginia's history.

Bruce received honorary doctorates from the College of William and Mary in 1907 and from Washington and Lee University in 1908, and he was a vice president of the Virginia Historical Society from 1918 to 1933. After 1930 he was often ill. Philip Alexander Bruce died at his home in Charlottesville on 16 August 1933 and was buried in the University of Virginia Cemetery in that city.

NCAB, 42:175–176; William S. Powell, "Philip Alexander Bruce, Historian," *Tyler's Quarterly* 30 (1949): 165–184; Darrett B. Rutman, "Philip Alexander Bruce: A Divided Mind of the South," *VMHB* 68 (1960): 387–407 (por. facing 387); Philip Alexander Bruce Papers, UVA and VHS; L. Moody Simms Jr., "Philip Alexander Bruce: His Life and Works" (Ph.D. diss., UVA, 1966); Simms, "A Childhood at Staunton Hill," *Virginia Cavalcade* 16 (autumn 1966): 23–28; Simms, "Philip Alexander Bruce and the New South," *Mississippi Quarterly* 19 (1966): 171–183; Simms, "Philip Alexander Bruce and the Negro Problem, 1884–1930," *VMHB* 75 (1967): 349–362; Simms, "History as Inspiration: Philip Alexander Bruce and the Old South Mystique," *McNeese Review* 18 (1967): 3–10; Simms, "Philip Alexander Bruce: The Charlottesville Years," *Magazine of Albemarle County History* 29 (1971): 69–79;

Norfolk City Marriage Register; Randall M. Miller, "The Birth (and Life) of a Journal: A 100-Year Retrospective of the *Virginia Magazine of History and Biography*," *VMHB* 100 (1992): 149–156; *AHR* 16 (1910): 139–143 (quotations); Hall, *Portraits*, 36–37; obituaries in *Charlottesville Daily Progress*, 17 Aug. 1933, and *New York Times*, 19 Aug. 1933; obituaries and editorial tributes in *Richmond News Leader*, 17, 18 Aug. 1933, *Richmond Times-Dispatch*, 18 Aug. 1933, and *University of Virginia Alumni News* 22 (Jan. 1934): 94, 96.

L. MOODY SIMMS JR.

BRUNK, George Reuben (31 December 1871– 30 April 1938), Mennonite bishop, was born in Geneseo, Illinois, the son of Henry G. Brunk and Susan Heatwole Brunk. In 1873 the family moved to Kansas, where Brunk's father and three of his seven siblings died from typhoid fever shortly after their arrival. His mother later married Matthias Cooprider and had three more children. Hardship and poverty typified his early life.

Brunk's formal education ended in grade school, but he loved reading and educated himself continuously throughout his life. He attended the Sunday schools of several Christian denominations, and at age seventeen, influenced by the preaching of the pioneer Mennonite evangelist John S. Coffman, he experienced a conversion. That same year he took responsibility for his mother's mortgaged farm and proudly returned it to her free of debt four years later. His mother's prayers and the counsel of a respected uncle helped direct Brunk to a religious career, and he studied the Bible at night after farmwork.

On 1 October 1893, at the age of twenty-one, Brunk was ordained a Mennonite minister in McPherson County, Kansas. Five years later, on 23 October 1898, he received ordination as a bishop. Brunk soon showed himself to be an articulate exponent of Mennonite practice and doctrine, and he helped to organize Mennonite congregations in several states. During evangelistic work in Rockingham County, he met Katherine E. Wenger, of Edom, whom he married on 15 July 1900 after a six-week courtship. They had four sons and five daughters. The Brunks spent ten years in Kansas before moving in 1910 to the Mennonite colony at Denbigh, later in the city of Newport News.

Brunk's sons all became ministers. Truman Henry Brunk succeeded him as bishop in 1938 and continued to preach until shortly before his death in 1995, and George Rowland Brunk II and Lawrence Brunk engaged in major tent evangelistic campaigns during the 1950s. Several daughters married ministers, and one eventually became an ordained minister herself. Brunk did not favor ordination of women but encouraged his daughters to speak in public and serve the church. The children remembered growing up in a home of harmony and love, with a father who was gentle, kindly, sometimes even playful, but also a firm disciplinarian. The call of the church usually came first, and on ten occasions he was away from his family at Christmas.

Shortly after moving to Virginia, Brunk became bishop over several eastern Virginia congregations. He was widely known among Mennonites, partly as a progressive for his support of revival meetings and of voting in certain political elections but primarily as a champion of orthodox doctrine, conservative Christian faith, and plain dress. He wrote for the church papers, sat on several committees of the national Mennonite General Conference, and exerted a major influence within the Virginia Mennonite Conference. Brunk impressed many listeners with his commanding pulpit presence (he was six feet, three inches tall), his oratorical skills, his strong convictions, and his self-assurance that his critics viewed as a large ego. His writing was equally colorful and fearless. A self-made theologian, he strongly opposed Calvinism and the doctrine of salvation by faith alone, advocating instead the Arminian belief that man must cooperate with God in his own salvation.

Brunk's sharp pen and straightforward preaching drew criticism from colleagues, and sometimes even from fellow conservatives, to whom he responded that a gentle, lenient policy would not prevent the church from drifting into error. He also became a major warrior in the Modernist-Fundamentalist controversies among Mennonites in the 1920s and opposed what he saw as religious liberalism's overemphasis on man at the expense of God. In 1926 Brunk published *Ready Scriptural Reasons* to defend his theological positions. Three years later he founded a quarterly, the *Sword and Trumpet*, in which he advocated "Defense of a Full Gospel" and fought "The Drift" toward Modernism and Calvinism. Yet those who best knew the seemingly stern and uncompromising Brunk also experienced his kind and friendly side.

Brunk sat on the Mennonite Board of Education for many years. Early in the twentieth century he and others, fearful that Goshen College in Goshen, Indiana, had drifted toward liberalism, founded an alternative. He presided in 1909 at the opening ceremonies of a more conservative school, later Hesston College in Hesston, Kansas. Brunk was a moving spirit in the founding of Eastern Mennonite School (later Eastern Mennonite University) in Harrisonburg in 1917 and served on its board until his death. His son George Rowland Brunk II served as dean of the seminary at Eastern Mennonite and was succeeded in the position by his own son George Rowland Brunk III.

Occasional bouts with a heart ailment interrupted George Reuben Brunk's ministry, but he always returned to his work until 30 April 1938, when he died suddenly from a heart attack at his home. He was buried in the cemetery of the Warwick River Mennonite Church in Newport News.

John C. Wenger, *Faithfully, George R.: The Life and Thought of George R. Brunk I* (1978); Gladys Shank Baer, "The Life and Work of George R. Brunk," *Sword and Trumpet* (second quarter 1954–third quarter 1955); Brunk Papers, Eastern Mennonite University Archives, Harrisonburg; Harry Anthony Brunk, *History of Mennonites in Virginia* (1959–1972), vol. 2 (por. on 285), and *The Progeny of Jacob Brunk I, The Will-Maker* (1978), 252–257; Ivan W. Brunk, *Jacob's Ladder* (1982), 102–103; obituaries in *Newport News Daily Press*, 1 May 1938, and *Harrisonburg Daily News-Record* and *Newport News Times-Herald*, both 2 May 1938; tributes in *Sword and Trumpet* (memorial number, third quarter 1938).

JAMES O. LEHMAN

BRYAN, Albert Vickers (23 July 1899– 13 March 1984), United States District Court judge and Fourth Circuit Court of Appeals judge, was born in Alexandria, the son of Marion Beach Bryan and Albert Bryan, a bank cashier who served on the Alexandria city council and was active in the Democratic Party. He graduated from Alexandria's public high school, attended the University of Virginia, where he was a member of Phi Beta Kappa, and received his law degree in

1921. Returning to Alexandria to practice law, Bryan married Marie Elizabeth Gasson on 1 December 1923. They had two sons.

While he was a young attorney Bryan made important political connections. His law partner was the namesake son of Howard Worth Smith, who in 1930 began a thirty-six-year tenure in the House of Representatives. Like the elder Smith, Bryan became a loyal supporter of Harry Flood Byrd (1887–1966), who was then the new leader of the dominant faction of the Democratic Party in Virginia. Bryan served as the Alexandria city attorney from 1926 to 1928, when he was appointed and subsequently elected commonwealth's attorney. He practiced law and served as commonwealth's attorney until 1947, when President Harry S. Truman appointed him a federal judge of the Eastern District of Virginia. Bryan was sworn into office on 10 June 1947 and served until August 1961, the last two years as chief judge of the district.

Bryan was completely a product of Virginia's traditional society. Courtly and scholarly, he was, in the words of a fellow federal judge, "the epitome of a Southern gentleman." As a jurist, Bryan was equally known and respected for the clarity of his legal writing and his strict adherence to precedent. During his years on the federal bench he had to deal with several major cases involving school desegregation and legislative apportionment—matters that brought into conflict Virginia's traditional society and the United States Supreme Court rulings he was required to enforce.

In 1952 Bryan sat on a three-judge federal panel that heard the case challenging public school segregation in Prince Edward County. Writing for the court and basing his decision on longstanding precedent, he ruled in *Davis* v. *County School Board of Prince Edward County* that racial separation was constitutional. In 1954 the Supreme Court reversed Bryan's ruling and sixty years of precedent in the landmark *Brown* v. *Board of Education of Topeka*. Two years later, while presiding over the desegregation case involving the Arlington public schools, Bryan in *Thompson* v. *County School Board of Arlington County* adopted the narrowest possible interpretation of the ambiguous wording of the Supreme Court's implementation decree. When two fellow federal judges issued desegregation orders in 1958 that triggered a confrontation with the state's Massive Resistance laws, Bryan, again in *Thompson* v. *County School Board of Arlington County*, gave that county until February 1959 to comply. The delay helped the Byrd organization's leadership avoid an embarrassing confrontation with liberals and moderates in a community where opponents of Massive Resistance were fully prepared to keep the public schools open even if the state's school-closing laws were invoked. After state and federal courts invalidated the Massive Resistance statutes in January 1959, Bryan's decree covering the Arlington and Alexandria schools, along with a similar court order in Norfolk, brought about the first public school desegregation in Virginia. In 1969 in *Griffin* v. *State Board of Education,* closely adhering again to Supreme Court precedent, Bryan struck down the last vestige of Massive Resistance, state tuition grants to students attending segregated private schools.

In 1961, in a move intended to conciliate Howard W. Smith, by then the powerful chair of the House Committee on Rules, President John F. Kennedy raised Bryan to a newly created seat on the Fourth Circuit Court of Appeals. Sworn in on 24 August 1961, Bryan faced another important issue in Virginia politics the very next year. In the reapportionment case of *Mann* v. *Davis*, he ruled that in order to reflect demographic changes, the General Assembly would have to be reapportioned to increase the number of seats for Northern Virginia and the Tidewater cities. Once again, by closely following precedent set by the Supreme Court in *Baker* v. *Carr*, he helped undermine a major bulwark against change—control of the legislature by the most tradition-minded regions of Virginia. Bryan took senior status and in effect retired on 16 August 1971, a month after his son Albert Vickers Bryan Jr. was appointed a federal district judge.

Bryan sat on the board of visitors of the University of Virginia from 1956 to 1964 and was rector of the university from 1960 until his term on the board ended. He was also a vestryman of Christ Episcopal Church in Alexandria for many years and senior warden at the time of his death.

Albert Vickers Bryan died on 13 March 1984 in Fairfax Hospital after open-heart surgery and was buried at Ivy Hill Cemetery in Alexandria. In 1995 Congress named the courthouse for the Eastern District of Virginia, in Alexandria, the Albert V. Bryan United States Courthouse.

Biography in *Washington Post*, 15 Mar. 1984 (por.); Fairfax Co. Marriage Register; Bryan correspondence in Ralph Eisenberg Papers, John Paul Judicial Papers, and John Lee Pratt Papers, and oral history interview (transcription and audiotape), all UVA; Bruce J. Dierenfield, *Keeper of the Rules: Congressman Howard W. Smith of Virginia* (1987), 23, 29; Richard Kluger, *Simple Justice: The History of Brown v. Board of Education and Black America's Struggle for Equality* (1975), 2:605, 614–641; Adolph H. Grundman, "Public School Desegregation in Virginia from 1954 to the Present" (Ph.D. diss., Wayne State University, 1972), 136–137, 183–186, 219, 268; James H. Hershman Jr., "A Rumbling in the Museum: The Opponents of Virginia's Massive Resistance" (Ph.D. diss., UVA, 1978), 302; *Richmond News Leader*, 10 June 1947; *Richmond Times-Dispatch*, 24, 25 Aug. 1961, 17 Aug. 1971; obituaries in *Alexandria Journal, Fairfax Northern Virginia Sun, Richmond News Leader*, and *Richmond Times-Dispatch* (quotation), all 15 Mar. 1984.

JAMES H. HERSHMAN JR.

BRYAN, Corbin Braxton (17 April 1852– 17 March 1922), Episcopal minister and educator, was born at Eagle Point in Gloucester County, the son of John Randolph Bryan and Elizabeth Tucker Coalter Bryan. His elder brothers included Joseph Bryan (1845–1908), the noted Richmond industrialist and newspaper publisher. Bryan was educated in various private schools and at Norwood School in Nelson County before entering the University of Virginia's engineering department in 1871. He felt himself called to the ministry after two years and enrolled in 1875 at the Protestant Episcopal Theological Seminary in Virginia. Bryan graduated in 1878 and was ordained in June 1879. In 1882 he married Mary Sidney Caldwell Scott, of Lenoir, North Carolina. They had two sons and four daughters.

C. Braxton Bryan spent the years 1878– 1881 in Lynnhaven Parish, Princess Anne County, the years 1881–1891 at Christ Church, Millwood, in Clarke County, the years 1891– 1893 at Epiphany Episcopal Church in Danville, and the years 1893–1905 at Saint John's Church in Hampton. At Hampton he developed a keen interest in the students at Hampton Normal and

Agricultural Institute (later Hampton University), including the Native Americans from the western states and territories. Bryan traveled to the West several times to visit the Indian schools from which many Hampton students came. He helped found Saint Cyprian's Church, Hampton's first African American Episcopal congregation, and he came to believe that the influence of Christianity would markedly improve the lives of black Virginians, for whom he believed that he and his fellow whites, as a superior race, had a special responsibility.

During the academic year 1903–1904 Bryan received a D.D. from Hampden-Sydney College. Early in 1905 he moved to Petersburg to become the minister of Grace Episcopal Church, and on 10 March of that year he was elected dean and principal of the Bishop Payne Divinity and Industrial School (after 1910 the Bishop Payne Divinity School), which was also in Petersburg. Organized in 1881, it was the oldest theological seminary for the education of African American Episcopal clergymen in the South. Bishop Payne was a small institution boasting only four teachers and sixteen students in 1908, but by 1921 it had educated more than 60 percent of all the African American Episcopal ministers in the United States, and several of its alumni were serving as missionaries or ministers in other countries. Bryan served as dean and principal until his death.

Bryan also served as historiographer of the Diocese of Southern Virginia, from 1907 to 1919 was the diocese's clerical delegate to the denomination's national conventions, and was dean of the Central Convocation of Southern Virginia at the time of his death. He resigned from Grace Church in February 1922 because of poor health, and on 12 March of that year he suffered a heart attack while in Hampton, where he was conducting Sunday Lenten services at Saint John's, his former church. Corbin Braxton Bryan traveled to Richmond, where he died at the home of a nephew on 17 March 1922. He was buried in Hollywood Cemetery in that city.

Paul Brandon Barringer, James Mercer Garnett, and Rosewell Page, eds., *University of Virginia* (1904), 2:38–39; Bryan letters in several collections and microfilm of his

scrapbook containing genealogical data, correspondence, photographs, and other family records, VHS; John Stewart Bryan, *Joseph Bryan: His Times, His Family, His Friends* (1935), por. facing 216; Frederick G. Ribble, "The Bishop Payne Divinity School For Colored Students, Petersburg, Virginia," in *History of the Theological Seminary in Virginia and Its Historical Background*, ed. William A. R. Goodwin (1923), 2:488–520; Bryan's views on race in "The Negro in Virginia," *Southern Workman* 34 (1905): 51–54, 100–108, 170–179; obituaries in *Petersburg Progress and Index-Appeal*, 18, 19 Mar. 1922, *Richmond Times-Dispatch*, 18 Mar. 1922, and *Richmond News Leader*, with a signed editorial tribute by Douglas Southall Freeman, 18 Mar. 1922 (por.); memorials in *Southern Churchman* 87 (25 Mar. 1922): 14, and (13 May 1922): 7, and in *Southern Workman* 51 (1922): 156–157.

BRENT TARTER

BRYAN, Daniel (ca. 1789–22 December 1866), poet, was born in rural Rockingham County, the son of William Bryan, who served as a major in the militia during the Revolutionary War. His mother's name may have been Nancy Kelly Bryan. Bryan attended Washington Academy (later Washington and Lee University) in the academic year 1806–1807 but did not graduate, apparently as a result of financial difficulties. He then studied law at home and became interested in writing poetry. His first book, *The Mountain Muse* (1813), was published in Harrisonburg and consisted primarily of "The Adventures of Daniel Boone," an ambitious epic poem of more than 5,600 lines. Perhaps the poem's subject persuaded some later writers that its author was the nephew of the famed frontiersman. Boone did have a nephew named Daniel Bryan, but he was not the poet.

By 1815 Bryan was practicing law in Harrisonburg, and on 5 October of that year he married Rebecca Davenport, of Jefferson County. She died on 5 July 1816. On 8 April 1818 Bryan married Mary Thomas Barbour, sister of James Barbour (1775–1842) and Philip Pendleton Barbour, who were then representing Virginia in Congress. They had two sons, three daughters, and another child who died in infancy. Later that year Bryan was elected to represent Rockingham and Shenandoah Counties for a four-year term in the Senate of Virginia. During the 1819–1820 session he sat on the Committee of Privileges and Elections. Bryan served without attracting particular notice until 26 January 1820, when he cast the only vote against a Senate resolution advocating Missouri's entry into the Union as a slave state. He also delivered an impassioned speech defending his lonely stand, in which by denouncing slavery and urging gradual emancipation he placed himself in direct opposition to the pro-Missouri positions of his brothers-in-law and the rest of Virginia's Jeffersonian-Republican establishment.

In April 1821 Bryan accepted an appointment as postmaster of Alexandria. He failed to appear in Richmond when the new legislative session began in December, and on 6 December 1821 the Committee of Privileges and Elections declared his Senate seat vacant. Shortly afterward Bryan's poetry began to appear regularly in periodicals, often anonymously or bearing only the initials "D.B.," and in his own short books. Bryan's most notable works during the 1820s, his most productive decade, were *The Lay of Gratitude* (1826), a tribute to the marquis de Lafayette, and *The Appeal for Suffering Genius* (1826), an attempt to encourage support for struggling artists. He also gained a reputation as an orator, having spoken at various academies, at Hampden-Sydney College in 1828, and at the Alexandria Lyceum, for which he gave the inaugural lecture opening its new building on 10 December 1839. Bryan sometimes delivered his speeches in verse form.

Throughout his career Bryan's poetic style remained essentially unchanged. Quite fashionable in 1813, the neoclassical conventions of *The Mountain Muse* had become antiquated by the 1830s. Of his later works, only "Strains of the Grotto," a somewhat gothic poem inspired by Weyers Cave in Augusta County that first appeared anonymously in the *Southern Literary Messenger* in 1837, betrays any influence of the romantic movement then burgeoning in American literature. Thematically Bryan's writings often expressed intense nationalism as well as support for various reform causes, including temperance, women's education, and the antidueling movement. He corresponded with some of the important figures of his day, including Edgar Allan Poe, who had praised Bryan's verse. His last published work appeared in 1841, and Bryan is now remembered chiefly for his epic about Daniel Boone, a minor poem

that nonetheless provides a wealth of information about American ideals and aspirations in that period.

With a change in presidents Bryan resigned his postmastership early in 1853 to accept a new position in the library of the Treasury Department. He staunchly opposed secession and remained a firm Unionist while living in occupied Alexandria during the Civil War. Immediately after hostilities ended, he and his wife moved across the Potomac River to Washington, D.C., where they lived in the residence of a married daughter. Daniel Bryan died there on 22 December 1866 after a prolonged illness and was buried in Washington's Oak Hill Cemetery.

Wayne M. Studer, "The Frustrated Muse: The Life and Works of Daniel Bryan, ca. 1790–1866" (Ph.D. diss., University of Minnesota, 1984), por., painted by George Peter Alexander Healy in 1856, p. 263; Elizabeth Binns, "Daniel Bryan: Poe's Poet of 'the good old Goldsmith school,'" *WMQ*, 2d ser., 23 (1943): 465–473; correspondence in possession of great-granddaughter Mrs. Frederic C. Lawrence, 1984, and in several repositories, including UVA, VHS, Boston Public Library, Chicago Historical Society, Filson Historical Society, and Historical Society of Pennsylvania; Bryan's other works include *Oration on Female Education* (1816), *Thoughts on Education in Its Connexion with Morals* (1830), "Strains of the Grotto" in *Southern Literary Messenger* 3 (1837): 445–447, and *A Tribute to the Memory of the Rev. George C. Cookman . . . and The Lost Ship, A Poem on the Fate of the Steamer President* (1841); year of birth conjectured from Census, Alexandria, 1850 (age given as sixty-two), 1860 (age given as seventy-one); otherwise unreliable tombstone gives 1792 year of birth; *Charles Town Farmer's Repository*, 26 Oct. 1815, 10 July 1816; Orange Co. Marriage Register, 1818; Senate speech in *Richmond Enquirer*, 15, 17 Feb. 1820; *Alexandria Gazette and Virginia Advertiser*, 12 Dec. 1839, 30 Mar., 2 Apr. 1853; obituaries in *Alexandria Gazette and Virginia Advertiser*, 28 Dec. 1866, and *Charles Town Virginia Free Press*, 3 Jan. 1867 (with age at death of seventy-seven); memorial in *Charles Town Virginia Free Press*, 30 Apr. 1868.

WAYNE M. STUDER

BRYAN, David Tennant (3 August 1906– 9 December 1998), newspaper publisher, was born in Richmond into one of the city's most influential families, the son of John Stewart Bryan and Anne Eliza Tennant Bryan. His paternal grandparents were Isobel Lamont Stewart Bryan, a civic leader and preservationist, and Joseph Bryan (1845–1908), a wealthy industrialist and publisher of the *Richmond Times-Dispatch*. In 1908 his grandfather acquired the *Richmond*

News Leader, which Bryan's father published from 1908 until his death in 1944. Bryan attended the forerunner of Saint Christopher's School in Richmond, graduated from Episcopal High School in Alexandria in 1925, and studied at the University of Virginia from 1925 to 1928, but he left college without graduating.

D. Tennant Bryan joined the staff of the *Richmond News Leader* as a reporter in 1928 and became circulation manager in 1932, a vice president and assistant treasurer the next year, and business manager in 1934. In 1940, following the family's reacquisition of the *Richmond Times-Dispatch*, which it had sold in 1914, and the creation of Richmond Newspapers, Inc., Bryan became vice president and general manager of the corporation. After his father's death in 1944 while Bryan was on active duty in the Pacific as a lieutenant commander in the United States Navy, he was named publisher of both newspapers and president of the corporation, although he did not assume these duties until early in 1946.

Bryan could have directed the policies of the news departments as well as the editorial pages, but he avoided virtually all contact with the former and gave great leeway to the latter. He generally communicated with the news staff only to alert them to the deaths of socially prominent people or to criticize poor grammar. Even though Bryan lacked a college degree, he understood the nuances of the English language and insisted on correct usage. He was a conservative man by temperament, tradition, and personal philosophy. Invariably polite and impeccably dressed, Bryan was always the last person to enter an elevator and the last to leave.

Both newspapers supported the conservative Democratic Party in Virginia most of the time, but as long as Bryan was publisher neither paper endorsed a national Democrat for president. After the United States Supreme Court ruled in 1954 that segregated public schools were unconstitutional, both newspapers opposed desegregation. While Virginius Dabney, editor of the *Times-Dispatch*, took a less bold stance, James Jackson Kilpatrick, editor of the *News Leader*, cooperated with the state's Democratic Party leadership to devise and promote the policy of Massive Resistance to court-ordered desegregation and urged the states to interpose their sovereignty against federal encroachment. Bryan personally published a book in 1956 compiling Kilpatrick's editorials on the subject. Thirty years later Bryan acknowledged that Massive Resistance had been a silly and doomed policy, although it had seemed to him a good idea at the time.

After members of Richmond's local of the International Typographical Union walked off the job on 31 March 1971, Bryan and one of his daughters assisted in composing the next day's issue. Although picket lines remained in place for more than a year, his newspapers quickly hired replacements and automated more of their production, thus effectively breaking the viability of the union.

Bryan's influence in journalism extended far beyond Richmond and Virginia. He was president of the American Newspaper Publishers Association (ANPA) from 1958 to 1960, a director of the Associated Press from 1967 to 1976, head of the Virginia Associated Press Newspapers, a director of the Southern Newspaper Publishers Association, and a trustee of the Washington Journalism Center. Bryan's thoughts on the role of newspapers in society could seem contradictory. Both Richmond newspapers had strong editorial voices, but he repeatedly stated that an independent press should publish unbiased news and allow readers to make up their own minds. Bryan was no crusader, but as chairman of an ANPA committee in 1968 he opposed a proposal by the American Bar Association to restrict coverage of crime news. He denounced the plan forcefully before the ABA's House of Delegates and at conferences of lawyers and judges, but the ABA overwhelmingly adopted the new guidelines.

In 1969 Bryan helped form and became chairman of the board of Media General, a newspaper holding company that eventually expanded into broadcasting, cable television, newspaper recycling, and financial information services. He retired as publisher of the two Richmond papers in 1977 and as chairman of Media General in 1990 but remained on the board of directors until 1997. By then the company owned twenty-one daily newspapers and fourteen television stations and provided cable television service for nearly a quarter of a million customers.

Bryan's other interests included higher education, local charities, and Emmanuel Episcopal Church, which his ancestors had started and which he served as senior warden. The Raven Society at the University of Virginia elected him a member in 1976. Bryan received an honorary doctorate of laws from the University of Richmond in 1973 and an honorary doctorate of humane letters from the College of William and Mary in 1990, and he was appointed an honorary trustee of Virginia Union University. He was elected to the Virginia Communications Hall of Fame in 1987 and later to the Virginia Business Hall of Fame. Bryan was a trustee of the Virginia Historical Society from 1965 to 1986, president from 1978 to 1980, and an honorary vice president from 1987 until his death. In 1949 he donated his family's estate, Laburnum, as the site for the new Richmond Memorial Hospital. Bryan served on the hospital's board of directors and was chairman emeritus at the time of his death.

On 11 May 1932 Bryan married Mary Harkness Davidson. They had two daughters and one son, John Stewart Bryan, who succeeded his father as publisher of the Richmond newspapers and chief executive officer of Media General. Mary Bryan died on 15 February 1987. David Tennant Bryan died at his home in Richmond on 9 December 1998 and was buried in the cemetery at Emmanuel Episcopal Church in Henrico County.

Shelah Kane Scott and St. George Bryan Pinckney, comps., *The Brook Hill Calendar VIII 1998* [1999]; David Tennant Bryan Vertical File, VHS; Bryan Family Papers, UVA; Earle Dunford, *Richmond Times-Dispatch: The Story of a Newspaper* (1995), 13–16, 160, 300–328, 401–402, 439–442; feature articles in *Richmond Times-Dispatch*, 1 July 1990, and *Richmond News Leader*, 30 May 1992; *Richmond Times-Dispatch* anniversary edition supplement, 15 Oct. 2000 (pors.); obituaries and description of funeral in *Richmond Times-Dispatch*, 10 (pors.), 13 Dec. 1998, and *New York Times*, 12 Dec. 1998; critical editorial in *Richmond Free Press*, 17 Dec. 1998.

J. EARLE DUNFORD JR.

BRYAN, Isobel Lamont Stewart (20 August 1847–11 September 1910), historic preservationist and civic leader, was born in Richmond, the daughter of John Stewart and Mary Amanda Williamson Stewart. Her father, a native of Scotland, immigrated as a youth to Virginia and became a wealthy tobacco merchant. Brook Hill, their Henrico County home, had been owned by her mother's family since 1714. Known to her family as Belle, Stewart may have attended the Brook Schoolhouse across the road from Brook Hill when it was open, but her education primarily occurred at home through the tutoring of a Scottish governess. Stewart was an avid reader, and a grandson described her as the most intellectual member of her family. She regularly attended Emmanuel Episcopal Church after her father built it across from the family residence. In 1855 Stewart traveled with her family to Europe to visit Scottish kinsmen. She spent the years 1865–1866 in Edinburgh, where she studied French and calisthenics. During another trip in 1870 she traveled to Dresden, Venice, and other European cities.

During the Civil War Confederate soldiers regularly camped on the Brook Hill property, where Stewart's father established a hospital to tend to the ill and wounded. Robert Edward Lee visited the Stewart home, and the girl developed a profound admiration for the Confederate leader. These adolescent experiences greatly influenced her later.

Even as a young woman, Belle Stewart gained an enviable reputation for intelligence and wit. On 1 February 1871 she married Joseph Bryan (1845–1908), a young lawyer and Confederate veteran. After their marriage, Bryan and her husband resided at Brook Hill. Between 1871 and 1882 she gave birth to six sons, five of whom lived to adulthood. Her children included John Stewart Bryan, president of the College of William and Mary from 1934 to 1942. The family moved in 1885 to their newly built home, Laburnum, near Brook Hill.

About this time Bryan began developing a larger public role for herself. In 1887 she helped to found the Richmond Woman's Christian Association. The new organization concerned itself first with providing appropriate housing for women coming to the city to work in factories and shops. Services for the association's residents included medical care, a library, sewing classes, educational entertainments, and prayer groups, all supervised by a matron and board of managers.

For a decade starting in 1889, Bryan served as president of the association, which became part of the national Young Women's Christian Association in 1906. After developing residences for unmarried working women, the association established a day nursery and kindergarten to care for the children of married working women. Voluntary contributions and a small grant from the Richmond city council enabled the association to employ a qualified teacher to administer the kindergarten. Shortly after it opened in 1890, the entire program was renamed the Belle Bryan Day Nursery. Costs often exceeded available funds, and Bryan regularly solicited contributions from churchwomen's groups and others to meet the budget.

Examples of women's activism and other social reform efforts spurred Bryan and other advocates of the YWCA in their concern for wage-earning women. Perhaps even more important were the moral precepts that moved these women organizers to establish social ministries. Bryan herself had long been active in her church and felt called to make the gospel message a social reality through her actions. Her remarkable talents as an organizer and motivator of others contributed to the success of her projects.

In 1890 Bryan became president of the Ladies' Hollywood Memorial Association, which cared for the graves of Confederate soldiers in Richmond's Hollywood Cemetery. She served the organization well. In addition to arranging for the Hollywood Cemetery Company to transfer to the association ownership of the section occupied by the graves of Confederate soldiers, Bryan led the effort to refurbish the mansion in which President Jefferson Davis had lived during the Civil War. The so-called White House of the Confederacy had become a school after the war, but the city decided to close it in 1889 and offered the building to Bryan's group. To accept, the association had to obtain a state charter under the new name of the Confederate Memorial Literary Society, with Bryan as its first president.

In 1893 the society held a memorial bazaar that raised $31,300 to renovate and fireproof the White House of the Confederacy, redesignated the Confederate Museum and after 1970 the Museum of the Confederacy. The museum opened on 22 February 1896. Three years later the society elected Bryan president of the museum for life. She rallied members of the United Daughters of the Confederacy in each southern state to adopt a room in the museum and decorate it as a shrine for that state's Confederate heroes. Joseph Bryan supported his wife's work and served on the Confederate Memorial Literary Society's advisory board. In the years before World War I, the Confederate Museum housed a library and an archival collection for historical research and hosted about 7,000 visitors yearly.

In 1890 Bryan also became president of the new Association for the Preservation of Virginia Antiquities, a position that she held until her death. The APVA's mission was to raise funds for the purchase and restoration of Virginia historical sites and to correct what elite Virginians perceived as misinterpretations of Virginia's glorious colonial past by historians from New England. The APVA's leaders hosted public events to raise funds, but they also used contacts through family and friends to win government support for their various projects. Under Bryan's leadership, the APVA secured Jamestown Island with a protective seawall, preserved the old Jamestown church, erected a statue of Captain John Smith (which Belle Bryan financed as a memorial to Joseph Bryan, who had died on 20 November 1908), and placed a cross at the falls of the James River. Bryan also aided the APVA's successful effort to save Mary Ball Washington's house in Fredericksburg.

Throughout her public career, Bryan suffered from periods of nervous exhaustion, a condition then called neurasthenia, but those who knew her remembered her boundless energy and engaging personality, not her infirmities. In her later years glaucoma diminished her eyesight. Isobel Lamont Stewart Bryan died in Richmond on 11 September 1910 after a short illness and was buried in the cemetery at Emmanuel Episcopal Church in Henrico County.

In 1949 the Bryan family donated their Laburnum estate to Richmond Memorial Hospital. Additional acreage went to the city of Richmond for creation of Joseph Bryan Park. The Belle Bryan Day Nursery formally closed in 1972 with its sale to the Medical College of Virginia. Proceeds went to the Belle Bryan Day Nursery Foundation, which grants funds to charities that assist needy families with young children.

John Stewart Bryan, *Joseph Bryan: His Times, His Family, His Friends* (1935), 165–175; correspondence in Bryan Family Papers, LVA, and in Bryan Family Papers, Stewart Family Papers, Association for the Preservation of Virginia Antiquities Papers, and numerous other collections, VHS; interview with grandson David Tennant Bryan; Mrs. Joseph [Isobel Lamont Stewart] Bryan, "The Woman's Christian Association, Richmond, Virginia," *International Messenger* 2 (1896): 136–137; Mrs. Ralph R. [Naomi C.] Chappell and Mrs. J. W. S. [Ellen V.] Gilchrist, "A History of the Y.W.C.A. of Richmond, Virginia, 1887–1937" (1937 typescript), VHS; Virginia Capital Bicentennial Commission, "A Short History of the Belle Bryan Day Nursery," *Sketches of Societies and Institutions, Together with Descriptions of Phases of Social, Political, and Economic Development in Richmond, Virginia* (1937), pt. 8; Betsy Brinson, " 'Helping Others to Help Themselves': Social Advocacy and Wage-Earning Women in Richmond, Virginia, 1910–1932" (Ph.D. diss., Union for Experimenting Colleges and Universities, 1984), 84–87; James M. Lindgren, *Preserving the Old Dominion: Historic Preservation and Virginia Traditionalism* (1993), 50–51, 63, 72–73, 91, 93, 125, 130, 137 (por.), 175; Malinda W. Collier et al., *White House of the Confederacy: An Illustrated History* (1993), 23–26 (pors.); obituaries in *Richmond News Leader* and *Richmond Times-Dispatch*, both 12 Sept. 1910.

BETSY BRINSON

BRYAN, John Stewart (23 October 1871–16 October 1944), newspaper publisher and president of the College of William and Mary, was born at Brook Hill in Henrico County, the son of Joseph Bryan (1845–1908), a wealthy industrialist and newspaper publisher, and Isobel Lamont Stewart Bryan, a noted preservationist. Aided by the wealth that Joseph Bryan had accumulated, the family was one of the most influential in Richmond during John Stewart Bryan's lifetime. The Bryans were well educated and well read, loved to travel and write letters, and acquired notable collections of art, books on Virginia, and literature in several languages. In 1935 Bryan published *Joseph Bryan: His Times, His Family, His Friends,* a biography of his father that vividly describes the family's elegant lifestyle and expresses a reverence for a romanticized view of Virginia's history that he and other family members labored to preserve.

A childhood accident blinded Bryan in his right eye but did not keep him from leading an active life. Educated at Thomas H. Norwood's private school in Richmond and Episcopal High School in Alexandria, he graduated in 1893 from the University of Virginia with both B.A. and M.A. degrees. In 1894 Bryan began to study law at the University of Virginia, but after the death of his professor John B. Minor, he transferred to Harvard University, from which he graduated in 1897. Bryan practiced briefly in New York before returning to Richmond to practice with Murray Mason McGuire. In 1898, as a member of the Virginia State Bar Association's Committee on Library and Legal Literature, Bryan completed an able essay on early compilations of Virginia statutes based on personal examination of a number of rare volumes and a close reading of the historical scholarship then available.

In 1900 Bryan gave up the law to become a reporter for Joseph Bryan's *Richmond Dispatch,* and the next year he became vice president of his father's publishing company, which owned the morning *Richmond Dispatch* and the evening *Richmond Leader.* In 1903 the Bryans sold the *Leader,* acquired the *Dispatch*'s morning competitor, the *Richmond Times,* and merged it with the *Dispatch* to form the *Richmond Times-Dispatch.* Shortly before Joseph Bryan's death in 1908, the family acquired the afternoon *Richmond News Leader*, of which John Stewart Bryan then became publisher. He remained the owner and publisher of the *Richmond News Leader* for the rest of his life. In 1915 Bryan hired Douglas Southall Freeman as editor of the *News Leader*, and during the following decades he supported Freeman's time-consuming historical research and writing. Bryan sold the *Richmond Times-Dispatch* in 1914, but in 1940 his Richmond Newspapers, Inc., bought it back, so that during most of his adult life, he owned and published one or both of the city's major daily newspapers. They were the two most influential papers in Virginia and, with the exception of the *Norfolk Virginian-Pilot,* probably the best edited.

Bryan was an original member of the reorganized Associated Press in 1900 and an active member of the American Newspaper Publishers Association, of which he was secretary for fifteen years and president from 1926 to 1928. In 1917 he founded and helped supervise *Trench and Camp*, the wartime newspaper of the Young Men's Christian Association. Following a visit to England on YMCA business at the end of World War I, Bryan went to Paris to cover the opening of the peace conference. In 1927 he and Samuel Emory Thomason, a Chicago publisher and his predecessor as president of the American Newspaper Publishers Association, bought the *Tribune* of Tampa, Florida. Later that year they purchased the *Record* of Greensboro, North Carolina, and in 1928 they acquired the *Chicago Daily Journal*. They sold the Chicago paper in August 1929 and the Greensboro paper the following year, but they remained owners and publishers of the *Tampa Tribune* until Thomason's death in March 1944.

Bryan married Anne Eliza Tennant on 4 June 1903. They had one daughter and two sons, including David Tennant Bryan, who succeeded his father as publisher and president of Richmond Newspapers. Following the deaths of his parents, John Stewart Bryan lived at the elegant and showy new Laburnum mansion that Joseph Bryan had constructed in Henrico County after a fire destroyed the original in 1906. The family made Laburnum a center of Richmond society, and Bryan became a popular toastmaster and after-dinner speaker. More than six feet, two inches tall, he cut an impressive figure and carried himself with an easy dignity. Bryan had a wonderful memory and a copious stock of apt anecdotes, literary and historical allusions, and poetic references.

Bryan seldom participated directly in politics. His views reflected the conservative, business-oriented opinions of his industrialist father, but both men disliked the machine politics characteristic of the leaders of Virginia's Democratic Party, successively Thomas Staples Martin, Claude Augustus Swanson, and Harry Flood Byrd (1887–1966). The conservative Bryans were occasionally at odds with the party's even more conservative leaders. Nevertheless, Bryan was a delegate to the Democratic National Conventions of 1920, 1924, and 1932, and in 1924 he accepted the chairmanship of Carter Glass's favorite-son presidential campaign.

Bryan's influence in Richmond and Virginia extended to many fields but focused on the arts and education. He helped found a short-lived symphony orchestra in Richmond during the 1930s, and he was one of the first vice presidents of the Virginia Museum of Fine Arts. Active as a lay leader in the Episcopal Church, Bryan often attended its triennial national councils during the 1910s and 1920s. He chaired the board of the Richmond Public Library, sat on the boards of a number of charitable organizations, and in 1936 and 1937 was president of the Virginia Historical Society. Bryan also served for many years as president of the local regional council of the Boy Scouts of America. He supported the Co-Operative Education Association of Virginia, founded in 1904 to advocate improvement of public education in the state. Bryan sat on the board of visitors of the University of Virginia from 1918 to 1922 and was rector from 1920 until his term expired in 1922. From 1937 to 1943 he served on the board of overseers of Harvard University.

In 1926 Bryan became a member of the board of visitors of the College of William and Mary. Early in the 1930s, as vice rector, he shouldered more than his share of the additional burdens faced by board members as a result of the failing health and sometimes erratic behavior of President Julian Alvin Carroll Chandler. Following Chandler's death, the board named Bryan president of the college on 30 June 1934. Bryan's eight-year administration was remarkable for the long list of famous guests who visited him and the college, beginning with President Franklin Delano Roosevelt, who spoke at Bryan's inauguration.

During Bryan's presidency the college made significant strides in broadening its curriculum and strengthening its reputation as a liberal arts college. The student body improved in quality, as did an enlarged faculty. Bryan bolstered the college's financial standing, reduced its debt, and took responsibility for the beautification of the campus and the planting of boxwood in the sunken garden. The small and underfunded School of Jurisprudence came under criticism, but alumni rallied to the school's support, and reorganized as the School of Law, it survived to grow in size and gain in stature beginning shortly after Bryan's death. He eliminated other schools, including programs in business administration, economics, education, and secretarial science, in order to focus on the liberal arts.

Bryan continued to pursue his other varied business and professional interests and was thus a part-time college president. He used administrative practices similar to those he had followed as a newspaper publisher, when he hired the business managers and editors and gave them the freedom to do their jobs. Bryan's habit of interviewing candidates for appointment to the faculty caused some deans to worry that this interference with their traditional responsibilties might result in a weakening of academic standards. Although too much presidential involvement in some academic affairs rankled, inadequate supervision in others may have exacerbated certain problems. The college's Richmond affiliate, then known as Richmond Professional Institute (later Virginia Commonwealth University), operated virtually without supervision. The Norfolk division (later Old Dominion University) was academically inferior to the main campus. In the spring of 1941 the Norfolk dean was found to have altered student transcripts, thus endangering the academic reputation of the entire institution. Bryan and members of the board reluctantly bowed to public pressure from leading citizens of Norfolk and allowed the dean to remain in the college administration, although Bryan assigned the college bursar, Charles J. Duke, to run the Norfolk campus.

Partly as a result of that episode, the Committee on Classification of Universities and Colleges of the Association of American Universities suspended William and Mary from its approved list on 30 October 1941. The AAU had been reviewing its accreditation of the institution since 1937, largely because of complaints about the Norfolk division. Despite many improvements made during Bryan's presidency, the committee in its suspension cited a high rate of student failures, low faculty salaries, inadequate library and laboratory facilities, misman-

agement of the Norfolk division, and inefficient administrative procedures made worse by the schedule of the president, who had too many other demands on his time to give proper attention to the administration of the college. William and Mary continued making administrative changes to meet some of the committee's objections, and Bryan submitted his resignation on 11 April 1942, citing poor health and the need for new leadership during World War II. He relinquished his position on 15 September 1942, the day his successor, John Edwin Pomfret, took office. Within two months the Association of American Universities restored William and Mary's accreditation. The board of visitors revived the ceremonial office of chancellor of the college for Bryan, and he was formally vested at Pomfret's inauguration on 8 February 1943.

As a result of his careers in journalism and education, Bryan received honorary degrees from Washington and Lee University (1911), the University of Richmond (1920), Ohio University (1928), the College of Charleston (1935), Dartmouth College (1936), the University of Pennsylvania (1940), Syracuse University (1941), and the College of William and Mary (1942). After he retired from William and Mary, he continued to run his newspapers and engage in other business and civic pursuits, but his health rapidly deteriorated. John Stewart Bryan died of a cerebral hemorrhage at the Medical College of Virginia Hospital in Richmond on 16 October 1944 and was buried in Henrico County at Emmanuel Episcopal Church, to which he had belonged all his life.

Douglas Southall Freeman, "John Stewart Bryan, a Biography" (1947 typescript), VHS; *Richmond Times-Dispatch* anniversary edition supplement, 15 Oct. 2000; BVS Birth Register, Henrico Co.; *Richmond Times-Dispatch*, 5 June 1903; Bryan Family Papers, LVA; Bryan Family Papers and John Stewart Bryan Papers (including diary, 1899–1900, and scrapbooks, 1903–1942), VHS; W&M Archives; Bryan, "Report of Committee on Library and Legal Literature," *Virginia State Bar Association Proceedings* (1898): 55–70; Earle Dunford, *Richmond Times-Dispatch: The Story of a Newspaper* (1995), 3–5, 9–12, 40, 310; Susan H. Godson et al., *The College of William and Mary: A History* (1993), 2:637–692; James R. Sweeney, *Old Dominion University: A Half Century of Service* (1980), 23–31; obituaries in *New York Times*, *Richmond News Leader*, and *Richmond Times-Dispatch* (por.), all 17 Oct. 1944, and *Williamsburg*

Virginia Gazette, 20 Oct. 1944; editorial tributes in *Richmond News Leader* and *Richmond Times-Dispatch*, both 17 Oct. 1944, and *VMHB* 53 (1945): 57–63.

BRENT TARTER

BRYAN, Joseph (13 August 1845–20 November 1908), industrialist and newspaper publisher, was born at Eagle Point in Gloucester County, the son of John Randolph Bryan and Elizabeth Tucker Coalter Bryan. His Georgia-born father was the godson, namesake, and foster child of John Randolph of Roanoke, and his mother was Randolph's favorite niece. John Bryan owned Eagle Point as well as another plantation, Carysbrook, in Fluvanna County, and by 1860 he held more than a hundred slaves. As a youth Joseph Bryan viewed the world through a planter's eyes, and his perspective subsequently underwent few changes. In 1897 he wrote to a friend that "the older I get, the more I admire the old civilization that made patriots and heroes out of the white people, and civilized human beings out of the cannibals of Africa."

Bryan attended Episcopal High School in Alexandria from 1856 to 1861, and his budding states' rights sentiments led him to support the Southern Democrats in the 1860 election. The Civil War, more than any other event, shaped his life. With great reluctance, Bryan deferred to his father's wish that he not enter the military until he was eighteen and instead matriculated at the University of Virginia. When he reached eighteen he joined the niter and mining bureau but took leave in May 1864 to serve briefly with the Richmond Howitzers. In October 1864 Bryan joined Mosby's Rangers and that same month was wounded twice in a clash near Upperville. He returned to action in December and served until the end of the war. The defeat of the Confederacy hardened Bryan's loyalties to the Southern cause while impoverishing his family. His father lost Eagle Point and eventually Carysbrook as well.

Bryan reentered the University of Virginia after the war and studied law under John B. Minor during the 1867–1868 session. He practiced in Fluvanna County until 1870, when he moved to Richmond. On 1 February 1871 Bryan married Isobel Lamont Stewart, of Brook Hill, daughter of a Scottish merchant who had become one of the city's foremost capitalists. Bryan blended his planter heritage with the Stewart wealth to establish himself as a rising influence in Virginia's economy and society. They had six sons, five of whom reached adulthood.

Throughout his life Bryan labored to reverse the dramatic changes unleashed by emancipation and Reconstruction. He deplored the democratic provisions of the Virginia Constitution of 1869 and supported the Conservative Party. Bryan opposed the reform program of William Mahone and the Readjusters, but he failed in 1873, 1875, and 1877 to win a seat in the House of Delegates from Henrico County, defeats he attributed to the unscrupulous workings of mass democracy. The active participation of African Americans in the Readjuster and Republican Parties deeply offended Bryan. He openly violated the Readjusters' debt payment laws and challenged them in court, making a name for himself and earning large legal fees.

No sooner had the Readjusters been defeated than Bryan confronted the popular democracy of the People's (or Populist) Party. He feared its program of empowering the masses and challenging the traditions of social hierarchy, political conservatism, and laissez-faire economics that characterized Virginia's culture. Bryan led a drive to create a Gold Democratic Party in Virginia after the national party adopted the Populists' inflationary platform in 1896. Caught in the middle of this unsettling discord, he subsequently lent his weight to those who demanded that Virginia restrict its electorate, pass sweeping segregation laws, and revise its constitution to restore the old order as far as possible.

Committed to local rule and elite leadership, Bryan opposed the increased federal powers associated with the Reconstruction amendments to the United States Constitution, the Populist platform, and the Republican Party. "A Virginian is first and foremost a Virginian," he told *Richmond Times* readers on 17 May 1901. "This sentiment is distinctly Southern and it should be preserved as one of the bulwarks of the rights of the States against the constant aggression of centralized power." Bryan's advocacy of cultural traditionalism buttressed his states' rights philosophy. At every opportunity he aided the commemoration of the Lost Cause and believed that trends following the Civil War proved the righteousness of the Confederacy. Bryan accordingly endorsed the study of Virginia's history and served as president of the Virginia Historical Society from 1892 to 1902 and again from 1906 to 1908. He was also an influential adviser to the Association for the Preservation of Virginia Antiquities, of which his wife was president. Bryan sought and found in Virginia's history inspiring role models, values, and traditions whose preservation could guide the future. His wife was equally committed to the same goals and in her own right exerted a powerful influence in behalf of preserving traditional values.

Bryan feared that Virginia would lose not only its political and social identity but also its economic independence. By the end of the century he was Richmond's preeminent capitalist. A refined and cultured gentleman, Bryan symbolized the transition from planter to industrialist. As Virginia's economy was transformed by New South development, he often battled workers and farmers to implement his industrial agenda. In the 1870s Bryan had established his legal career by representing corporate bondholders, and as an investor he purchased defaulted bonds and joined with the tobacco magnate Lewis Ginter to parlay them into valuable holdings. In 1887 he bought the failing *Richmond Times* and introduced new printing technology to break the printers' union. Bryan transformed the newspaper into an energetic booster of industry, conservative politics, and traditional culture. He hired William L. Royall, a notorious opponent of the Readjusters, of African American participation in civic life, and of labor unions, as editor of the paper. In 1896 Bryan secretly acquired the *Manchester Evening Leader*. Seeking a monopoly to guarantee his newspapers' profitability, Bryan in a complicated maneuver then divested himself of the *Leader* (which merged with the evening *News* to become the *Richmond News Leader*) and purchased instead the rival morning *Richmond Dispatch,* which in 1903 he merged with the *Times* into the *Richmond Times-Dispatch*. His acquisition by 1908 of the *Richmond News Leader* made him the owner of both of the capital's major daily papers.

Bryan's entrepreneurial activity reflected his belief that through economic growth and diversification Virginia could reestablish its traditional hierarchy and regain the independence it had lost at Appomattox. In pursuit of that dream he purchased an insolvent machine company late in the 1880s and turned it into the Richmond Locomotive and Machine Works. At its height, the factory produced 200 locomotives a year and employed 3,000 workers. Through his advocacy of the piece-rate system and the open shop Bryan followed management trends common at other American locomotive works and maintained practices that supported his conservative views on labor. He also invested heavily in the iron industry of Alabama and in the construction of a Nicaraguan canal. Bryan served as director and first vice president of Sloss-Sheffield Iron and Steel Company of Birmingham beginning in 1887. In 1881 he helped organize the Georgia-Pacific Railway and served as its president, and when it was absorbed into the Southern Railway he became a director of that line. Through this wide-ranging economic activity Bryan labored to develop a southern economy that could stand free from northern interference. The Spanish-American War, which he initially regarded as an unwarranted act of American aggression, gave him hope that his Birmingham iron and his Richmond locomotives, together with other southern products, would find new markets far away through an isthmian canal. Bryan therefore abandoned his anti-imperialism and embraced expansionism.

In each case, however, northern capital undermined Bryan's efforts. His promotion of southern-owned railroads faltered during the hard times of the 1890s, and the region's railroads came under northern control. Wall Street's tight credit policy and favoritism toward northern factories forced Bryan to sell the Richmond Locomotive Works to northern investors in 1900. He remained as chief operating officer of the American Locomotive Company's Richmond factory, but it closed shortly after his death. Moreover, Bryan's iron foundry in Alabama fell victim to a combination of competition from better-financed northern concerns and the panic of 1907. The Nicaraguan canal venture fell victim to a rival plan for a canal through Panama.

Bryan's dreams of an economically independent South faded.

Still wealthy and respected, Bryan built Laburnum, a luxurious residence near Richmond. It burned in 1906, and he replaced it with an even more luxurious building with the same name. Bryan also purchased and restored Eagle Point. He and his wife were prominent members of Richmond society, and their five sons who lived to maturity all had successful careers. The eldest, John Stewart Bryan, took over management of the family's newspapers after Bryan's death and served as president of the College of William and Mary.

Bryan's interests extended beyond business. The family perceived no contradiction between its religious beliefs and practices on the one hand and its hard-headed approach to business on the other, and Bryan's youngest brother, Corbin Braxton Bryan, was a prominent Episcopal clergyman. Bryan was a vestryman of Emmanuel Episcopal Church near Richmond for thirty-six years, a vestryman of Abingdon Episcopal Church in Gloucester County, and a lay delegate to the Episcopal General Convention several times between 1886 and 1907. He served on the board of visitors of the University of Virginia and held such diverse positions as president of the Virginia State Good Roads Association, governor of the Society of Colonial Wars, and director of the Jamestown Ter-Centennial Exposition in 1907.

Joseph Bryan died of heart failure at Laburnum on 20 November 1908. His funeral, befitting a man of his sentiments, harkened back to the past. Eight family servants bore his coffin to his grave in the yard of Emmanuel Episcopal Church. Bryan was buried in his old Confederate uniform, and his casket was draped with a Confederate flag. In 1949 the Bryan family gave the Laburnum estate to Richmond Memorial Hospital and donated land to the city of Richmond for creation of Joseph Bryan Park.

W. Gordon McCabe, *Joseph Bryan: A Brief Memoir* (1909); *NCAB*, 31:519; "Joseph Bryan: A Model Character for His Fellow-Men," *Confederate Veteran* 18 (1910): 164–166; John Stewart Bryan, *Joseph Bryan: His Times, His Family, His Friends* (1935), birth date on 19; *Richmond Times-Dispatch* anniversary edition supplement, 15 Oct. 2000; Joseph Bryan Letter Books and Papers, VHS (first quotation in Bryan to Thomas Pinckney, 22 May 1897); Bryan Family Papers, LVA; Bryan's published addresses include "The Physical and Industrial Resources of Virginia," *Addresses Delivered at the Pan-American Exposition, Buffalo, New York, on Virginia Day, August 23, 1901* (1901), 7–27, and *Christian Stewardship: An Address Delivered before the Y.M.C.A. of Richmond College on February 20, 1908* (1909); James M. Lindgren, " 'First and Foremost a Virginian': Joseph Bryan and the New South Economy," *VMHB* 96 (1988): 157–180 (por. on 158); Lindgren, "The Apostasy of a Southern Anti-Imperialist: Joseph Bryan, the Spanish-American War, and Business Expansion," *Southern Studies*, new ser., 2 (1991): 151–178; W. David Lewis, "Joseph Bryan and the Virginia Connection to the Development of Northern Alabama," *VMHB* 98 (1990): 613–640; Lewis, *Sloss Furnaces and the Rise of the Birmingham District: An Industrial Epic* (1994); Hall, *Portraits*, 37; obituaries and accounts of funeral in *Richmond News Leader*, 21 Nov. 1908 (with incorrect birth month), *Richmond Times-Dispatch*, 21 (with incorrect birth month), 22 Nov. 1908, and *Confederate Veteran* 17 (1909): 606–607.

JAMES M. LINDGREN

BRYAN, Joseph (30 April 1904–3 April 1993), writer, was born at Laburnum in Henrico County, the son of Joseph St. George Bryan and Emily Nelson Page Kemp Bryan and a grandson of the preservationist Isobel Lamont Stewart Bryan and of the Richmond industrialist and newspaper publisher Joseph Bryan (1845–1908). He was known as Joseph Bryan III throughout his life. Bryan was educated successively at Chamberlayne School (later Saint Christopher's School) in Richmond, Episcopal High School in Alexandria, and Princeton University, where he earned a B.A. in 1927. He edited Princeton's humor magazine, the *Princeton Tiger*, and was voted the most entertaining and most witty man in his class and runner-up for best-dressed man and best-all-around man outside athletics.

Following graduation Bryan and several friends toured Europe, Africa, the Middle East, and India. From 1928 to 1930 he worked as a reporter and editorial writer for the *Richmond News Leader* and the *Chicago Daily Journal*, both published by his uncle John Stewart Bryan. The Great Depression made earning a living as a freelancer difficult and forced Bryan into frequent job changes. He was associate editor of *Parade* magazine in Cleveland in 1931 and 1932, then worked briefly for *Time*, *Fortune*, and the *New Yorker*, and from 1933 to 1937 was managing editor of *Town and Country*. From 1937 until he resigned in June 1940 Bryan was an associate editor of the *Saturday Evening Post*.

As a result of his Reserve Officers' Training Corps work at Princeton, Bryan held a commission as a second lieutenant and then lieutenant in the field artillery for several years following his graduation. In January 1942 he was commissioned a lieutenant commander in the navy and assigned to naval air combat intelligence in the Pacific. Reassigned to naval public relations in 1944, Bryan spent much of 1945 aboard the carrier *Yorktown*. From the late 1940s until 1953 he worked for the Central Intelligence Agency with a concurrent commission as lieutenant colonel in the air force, giving him the unusual distinction of having been an officer in all three major branches of the armed services. In 1953 Bryan was promoted to colonel in the air force reserve. He lived in Washington from World War II until 1959, when through a complicated family trust he inherited the right to live at Brook Hill, an ancestral home in Henrico County.

As J. Bryan III he wrote about three dozen articles for *Collier's*, *Reader's Digest*, the *Saturday Evening Post*, and the *Saturday Review of Literature* during the 1930s and 1940s. After leaving government service he resumed his career as a freelance writer. From 1953 through 1974 Bryan wrote about fifty articles for *Holiday* magazine and numerous pieces for other journals. His writings included travel, humor, and personality profiles, some of which evolved into books or reappeared as portions of his books. The pieces Bryan published in national magazines included biographical works on the Aga Khan, the duke of Edinburgh, Britain's Princess Margaret, and Katharine Hepburn, and in 1965 he wrote a biography of John Armstrong Chaloner for the *Virginia Magazine of History and Biography*. His only work of fiction, a short story entitled "First Patrol," appeared in *Esquire* in 1956.

Bryan's principal books included *Mission Beyond Darkness* (1945), written with Philip Reed for the navy about the USS *Lexington* in the South Pacific; *Admiral Halsey's Story* (1947), an authorized biography written with William F. Halsey; *Aircraft Carrier* (1954), based on the diary Bryan kept while aboard the USS *Yorktown* during 1945; *The World's Greatest Showman: The Life of P. T. Barnum* (1956), written for

young readers; and *The Windsor Story* (1979), a dual biography of the duke and duchess of Windsor, written with Charles J. V. Murphy. He also published two volumes of short writings. *The Sword over the Mantel: The Civil War and I* (1960) features reminiscences and character sketches derived from his youth in Richmond, and *Merry Gentlemen (And One Lady)* (1985) contains memorable pen portraits of Fred Allen, Robert Benchley, Dorothy Parker, and other personalities of the Algonquin Round Table who flourished during Bryan's years in New York. His last two books, *Hodgepodge: A Commonplace Book* (1987) and *Hodgepodge Two: Another Commonplace Book* (1989), reflect his wide and omnivorous reading, his love of travel, and his singular sense of humor.

Bryan married three times. On 4 October 1930 he married Katharine Lansing Barnes, of New York. They had two sons and one daughter and were divorced in 1954. On 22 February 1960 Bryan married a widow, Jacqueline Vandesmet, viscountess Guy de La Grandière, of Paris. She died on 8 March 1988, and on 28 August 1991 he married Elizabeth Mayo Atkinson McIntosh, of Richmond. Joseph Bryan III died of cancer at his home in Richmond on 3 April 1993 and was buried with other family members in the yard of Emmanuel Episcopal Church in Henrico County.

Feature articles based on interviews with Bryan in *Richmond News Leader*, 1 May 1980 (por.), and *Richmond Times-Dispatch*, 15 Nov. 1987 (por.); Joseph Bryan III Papers, VHS; first marriage reported in *New York Times*, 5 Oct. 1930, and second in *Richmond News Leader*, 23 Feb. 1960; Shelah Kane Scott and St. George Bryan Pinckney, comps., *The Brook Hill Calendar IV 1998* [1999]; obituaries in *Richmond Times-Dispatch*, 4 Apr. 1993, and *New York Times*, 6 Apr. 1993.

BRENT TARTER

BRYANT, James Fenton (22 February 1841– 16 January 1909), educator, was born in Southampton County, the son of James DeBerry Bryant, a prosperous farmer and slave owner, and Elizabeth Sugars Bryant. He attended a nearby private school, went to the Brookland School in Albemarle County from 1856 through 1858, and enrolled at the University of Virginia for the 1858–1859 and 1859–1860 terms. An enthusiast for the South's secession who designed a flag for the embryonic Confederacy in his Latin notebook, Bryant enlisted in the Southampton Cavalry on 7 May 1861. A year later the unit became part of the 13th Regiment Virginia Cavalry. Private Bryant's surviving letters to his family document his transformation from a youth who complained that he had no manservant to fix his meals into an experienced, hardened soldier. Wounds suffered at Brandy Station in June 1863 prevented him from accompanying the Army of Northern Virginia to Gettysburg, and he was wounded again at Five Forks on 1 April 1865. At the war's end, Bryant lay disabled at home.

Recovering sufficiently to return to the university for the 1865–1866 session, Bryant began the study of medicine, reportedly to fulfill his mother's dying request. The next year he enrolled in New York University's medical department, from which he received an M.D. in the spring of 1867. Bryant served as an intern at Bellevue Hospital in New York City before returning to Southampton County, where on 24 June 1867 he began the practice of medicine at Franklin Depot. Railroads that passed through the county employed him as a surgeon, and he was a vice president of the Southside Virginia Medical Association, the health officer for the county, and from 1892 until his death a member of the board of visitors of the Medical College of Virginia.

When the town of Franklin was incorporated, Bryant served as its first mayor from 15 March through 30 June 1876. An ardent Democrat, as was his father, he chaired the county committee for many years, sat on the state central committee, and twice was a delegate to national party conventions. Three times Bryant unsuccessfully sought the Second District's nomination for Congress. In 1883 he lost a campaign as a conservative Democrat against a Readjuster for the Senate of Virginia. Bryant unsuccessfully contested his defeat on the grounds that the victor had been a county judge at the time of the election and was therefore not legally qualified to run. The following year, after the death of his opponent, Bryant lost again to another Readjuster in a special election.

Bryant made his most important public contribution as the first superintendent of public schools for Southampton County. Taking office on 11 October 1870, he appointed trustees in each magisterial district and arranged for a census of the school-age population. That year only 450 of 4,015 eligible children were enrolled in the county's twenty-five schools. Bryant visited the schools, collected statistics, distributed funds, and organized teachers' institutes. Few attended one such institute in May 1874 because of resentment that a civil rights bill pending in Congress would have prohibited racially separate schools. Bryant made clear in his report that year that he would have abandoned the public schools had the bill passed. A greater problem was the state government's diversion of funds intended for the schools to pay instead Virginia's massive prewar debt. In November 1878, with the county's schools closed until the new year for lack of money, the school board adopted resolutions protesting the practice. The state finally restored full funding at the end of 1879, and by the end of the 1880–1881 academic year Southampton County had sixty schools serving almost 2,000 students.

In 1879 the Readjusters had gained control of the General Assembly, and in 1881 the Senate of Virginia rejected the reappointment of Bryant and several other Democratic superintendents. The Democrats returned to power in 1885, and Bryant became superintendent once again and held the post until 30 June 1905. Although the number of schools in the county increased to 114 by 1905 and enrolled 4,752 students, the schools remained inadequate. African American teachers were paid far less than white ones, and African American students received an education inferior to that of whites. Bryant was a racial conservative, but he sought to hire college-trained teachers for the black schools and served from 1893 to 1897 on the board of the Virginia Normal and Collegiate Institute (later Virginia State University). He was also president of the Franklin Academy, a local private secondary school, from its chartering in 1890 until 1907.

On 23 April 1871 Bryant married Lydia Gabrielle Barrett, of Southampton County. They had two sons and three daughters before her death on 22 September 1882. Bryant married

Margaret Gunter, of Halifax County, North Carolina, on 12 December 1888. They had one son and one daughter. James Fenton Bryant died at his home in the city of Franklin on 16 January 1909 and was buried in Poplar Springs Cemetery in Franklin.

Birth date from gravestone; *Virginia School Journal* 2 (1893): 79–80 (gives variant birth year of 1842); Tyler, *Men of Mark*, 4:39–41; French Biographies; James Fenton Bryant Student Note Book, 1859–1860, VHS; James Fenton Bryant Papers, LVA, printed in [Edgar Jackson, ed.], *Three Rebels Write Home* (1955), 37–73; Compiled Service Records; Daniel T. Balfour, *13th Virginia Cavalry* (1986), 67; Balfour, *Southampton County and Franklin: A Pictorial History* (1989), 47 (por.); *JSV,* 1883–1884 sess., 25, 102–103, 115; Superintendent of Public Instruction, *Annual Report* (1870/1871–1904/1905), including John J. Deyer, "History of the Public Schools of Southampton County," in *Annual Report* (1884/1885): 272–277; Southampton Co. Marriage Register, 1871 (gives age as thirty in April 1871); second marriage confirmed by Halifax Co., N.C., registrar of deeds; obituary in *Richmond Times-Dispatch*, 16 Jan. 1909 (gives age as sixty-seven); memorial in Medical Society of Virginia *Transactions* (1909): 177.

JOHN T. KNEEBONE

BRYCE, Clarence Archibald (8 January 1849– 21 September 1928), physician and editor, was born at the Louisa County residence of his maternal grandmother, the son of Benjamin Franklin Bryce and Mildred Chewning Bryce. He was educated at Morris's Academy in Hanover County, attended Richmond College, and studied medicine privately before entering the Medical College of Virginia on 2 October 1869. Bryce graduated on 1 March 1871 and opened a medical office in Richmond the following year.

In October 1878 Bryce began editing and publishing the *Southern Clinic: A Monthly Journal of Medicine, Surgery and New Remedies*. The early numbers of the journal offered standard medical fare for practicing physicians, but Bryce sought (often without success) original articles from nationally prominent doctors. He published the *Southern Clinic* until September 1919, a circumstance that suggests that advertisements and subscriptions covered the costs of production, but it is doubtful, despite assertions by Bryce's business stationery, that it was ever the leading medical journal of the South and Southwest. In addition to publishing the *Southern Clinic*, Bryce printed and sold *The Physi-*

cian's Companion: A Pocket Reference Book for Physicians and Students (1890) and forms and record books for physicians. He sold galvanic batteries to patients at his office in Richmond and distributed Bryce's Urethral Applicator by mail to doctors.

At the October 1881 annual meeting of the Medical Society of Virginia, Bryce found himself embroiled in the first of several controversies with professional organizations. The president of the society, Hunter Holmes McGuire, charged that Bryce had insulted the integrity of the society's publishing committee. Bryce accused the committee of granting an unduly expensive publication contract for the society's annual volume of *Transactions* to Landon B. Edwards, the society's secretary, without competitive bids. Bryce probably wanted the contract himself, but McGuire argued that Bryce's public complaints and charges of fraud in the *Southern Clinic* went too far and threatened the very existence of the society. He moved for expulsion, and after an ad hoc committee investigation and a heated debate, Bryce resigned. Embittered by the affair, Bryce became a vehement critic of orthodox medical organizations, such as the Medical Society of Virginia and the American Medical Association, which presumed to speak for the medical profession at large.

Bryce became open to fresh approaches to medicine and in 1896 taught a six-week course at the National College of Electro-Therapeutics, in Indianapolis, where he was a professor of surgery until at least 1899. Bryce was also chief surgeon of a sanitarium called the Hickories near Richmond, which specialized in the use of electrical treatments for nervous afflictions. His beliefs were often unconventional or untested, and his renegade personality alienated him from some other members of the medical profession. Bryce embraced remedies regardless of their source if he thought them effective. Individual conscience in all of life was his guide, a conviction that made him sympathetic to homeopathic medicine, but he had no use for Christian Science.

On 8 September 1885 Bryce married Virginia Keane, an accomplished portraitist who had conducted an art school in Richmond. Her painting entitled *The Charity Patient* (1888), which depicts Bryce caring for an elderly black woman, is in the collections of the Virginia Historical Society. The Bryces had one son, who was killed in World War I, and four daughters. Beginning in January 1899 Bryce's children produced a small magazine called the *Hoppergrass*, which he edited, printed, and advertised in the pages of the *Southern Clinic* for almost seven years. He also wrote *"Ups and Downs" of a Virginia Doctor By His Lifelong and Personal Friend* (1904), a book that was probably inspired by events of his own early practice and was illustrated by his daughter Mildred Bryce; *Kitty Dixon, Belle of the South Anna: A Wee Bit of Love and War* (1907), a fictional account of post–Civil War reconciliation based on the life of his friend John Cussons, to whom it was dedicated; and *The Gentleman's Dog: His Rearing, Training and Treatment* (1909), a handbook for birddog owners.

In 1905 Bryce ran as an independent candidate for a seat in the House of Delegates from Hanover County but lost by a margin of more than two to one to William Duvall Cardwell, who was elected Speaker of the House the following January. Two newspaper accounts of the campaign described Bryce as "scholarly," as "aggressive, original and ready with ink," and as "an Achilles in matters controversial." In a long article for the *Richmond Times-Dispatch* of 8 May 1921, Bryce reminisced about memorable personalities in Richmond's Jackson Ward and recounted unscrupulous methods local white political leaders had used to obstruct voting by African Americans during the 1870s and 1880s. The tone of his comments suggests that by then, even if not earlier, he had developed a sympathy with black Richmonders, whom he may have regarded as fellow victims of established powers.

In the twilight of his career Bryce was a founding officer of the Medical Society of the United States, organized in 1916 as an alternative to the American Medical Association. The new society opposed the older association's influence over the practice of medicine, represented a reaction against increased medical specialization, and celebrated the old family physician. Members viewed themselves as brothers nobly associated together to serve humankind, unattached to and unsullied by any particular school of medicine. Bryce was the vice president for Virginia in 1916–1917 and was elected president of the society in October 1919. In his partly autobiographical presidential address, "Crossing the Medical Rubicon," he told his brethren that "I am a Virginian by birth; an American in spirit—absolutely independent in religion, politics, medicine and everything else." The self-assessment serves as a fitting epitaph for a feisty man who lived by his own lights.

Clarence Archibald Bryce died of angina pectoris at his home in Richmond on 21 September 1928. After cremation his ashes were buried in Hollywood Cemetery in that city.

Birth date in Bryce Family Papers and genealogical notes, VHS; Wyndham B. Blanton, *Medicine in Virginia in the Nineteenth Century* (1933), 124–125; BVS Marriage Register, Richmond City (gives birthplace as Louisa Co.); *Southern Clinic* 4 (1881): 437–454; *Virginia Medical Monthly* 8 (1882): 431–435; *Hoppergrass* 7 (Sept. 1905): frontispiece por.; *Richmond Evening Journal*, 23 Oct. (first and third quotations), 7 Nov. 1905 (second quotation); *Richmond News Leader*, 8 Nov. 1905; Bryce, "Crossing the Medical Rubicon," *Southern Clinic* 42 (1919): 270–275 (fourth quotation); Hall, *Portraits*, 38; BVS Death Certificate, Richmond City (gives variant birthplace as Hanover Co.); obituaries in *Richmond News Leader*, 21 Sept. 1928 (por.), and *Richmond Times-Dispatch*, 22 Sept. 1928 (both giving 9 Jan. 1849 birth date); brief memorial in *Virginia Medical Monthly* 55 (1928): 518.

J. STUART MOORE

BRYDON, George MacLaren (27 June 1875–26 September 1963), Episcopal clergyman and historian, was born in Danville, the son of Robert Brydon, a pharmacist and native of Scotland, and Ellen Page Dame Brydon, the daughter of George Washington Dame, an Episcopal minister in Danville. His sister Mary Evelyn Brydon became a physician and public health administrator.

Even before Brydon graduated from Danville High School in 1892, he had decided to enter the Episcopal ministry, and he supplemented his coursework in Latin with private lessons in Greek. The Protestant Episcopal Theological Seminary in Virginia, in Alexandria, had closed its preparatory school and recommended instead that young men preparing for the ministry attend Roanoke College, in its judgment the least denominational of the state's small colleges. Brydon graduated from Roanoke in 1896, after serving as president of his senior class, and from the theological seminary in 1899.

Ten of the seventeen members of Brydon's class volunteered for missionary work. He was one of four who applied for service in Japan, but the bishop of the Diocese of Southern Virginia demanded at least one of the new deacons, and Brydon went instead to Randolph Parish in Halifax County for a year. On 31 May 1900 he was ordained and again applied unsuccessfully for service in Japan. After eight months as an assistant at Emmanuel Episcopal Church in Baltimore, Brydon became rector of three churches in Loudoun County. What made that call attractive to him was the parish rectory, where a married man could live comfortably. On 5 September 1901 Brydon married Nathalie Page Coleman, whom he had met in Halifax County. They had three sons and one daughter.

Brydon returned to Baltimore as rector of Emmanuel from 1904 to 1907 and then served for four years as rector of Trinity Episcopal Church in Morgantown, West Virginia. From 1911 to 1914 he was rector of Saint Paul's and Hanover Parishes in King George County, where the church buildings that survived from the colonial era triggered his lasting interest in the church's early history in Virginia. Brydon also became concerned about the state of public education and invited Jesse Hinton Binford, of the Co-Operative Education Association of Virginia, to organize neighborhood leagues to support the public schools in King George County. That work drew the attention of the bishop of the Diocese of Virginia, who in 1914 called Brydon to Richmond as executive secretary of the Diocesan Missionary Society, church missionary for the city of Richmond, and Archdeacon of Colored Work for the diocese.

Brydon held the post of city missionary until 1917, when he became rector of Saint Mark's Church. His effectiveness in administering the Diocesan Missionary Society soon brought him additional responsibilities. The diocese reorganized its finances under a single officer in 1919, and Brydon in effect took charge of the diocese's headquarters by becoming treasurer,

executive secretary, and secretary of the council of the diocese. In 1920 he also became secretary and treasurer to the board of trustees of the diocese's new Corporation of Church Schools, and he became registrar of the diocese in 1922.

Brydon's policy as Archdeacon of Colored Work from 1914 to 1930 and from 1937 to 1941 was to make the small African American congregations self-supporting. Since the 1880s the Diocese of Virginia had administered the black Episcopal churches under its missionary program, which limited the participation of priests and laymen in diocesan councils and probably contributed to the slow growth in the number of African American communicants of the Episcopal Church. When Brydon took office in 1914 the diocese had four black ministers, seven congregations, and about 400 communicants. In 1937 he reported that although the numbers had not increased significantly, the churches were on more solid footing. The diocese also changed its policy and admitted black clergymen to seats on the diocesan council, and Saint Philip's Episcopal Church in Richmond was admitted as a congregation with the right to lay representation.

Brydon's resignation from Saint Mark's Church after his election as treasurer left his Sundays free. He organized a group of lay readers and clergymen to hold services in every vacant parish within an hour's drive of Richmond. In time this program expanded to the entire diocese, but it also resulted in a call to return to active ministry. Brydon served as minister at Saint James the Less, in Ashland, from 1926 to 1949.

In May 1925 Brydon was elected historiographer of the diocese. Because of his many other duties historical research and writing remained an avocation, but he published numerous articles and pamphlets on the early history of the Protestant Episcopal Church in Virginia. Brydon sat on the editorial board of the *Historical Magazine of the Protestant Episcopal Church* from 1932 until his death and served the Virginia Historical Society as a member of the executive committee from 1934 to 1960, as vice president from 1941 to 1960, and as president in 1960. He became active in a number of patriotic and genealogical societies and was chaplain of the Virginia Society, Sons of the American Revolution, the Virginia Society of Colonial Wars, and the Virginia Society of the Cincinnati. Roanoke College awarded him an honorary D.D. in 1928, and the Virginia Theological Seminary honored him with another in 1942. Brydon was then hard at work on a history of the Episcopal Church in Virginia. To obtain more time for the task he resigned as treasurer in 1940 and as Archdeacon of Colored Work the next year.

In 1947 Brydon published the first volume of *Virginia's Mother Church and the Political Conditions Under Which It Grew.* The work treated the years 1607 to 1727. Brydon updated and significantly revised William Meade's *Old Churches, Ministers, and Families of Virginia* (1857). Using documents unavailable to Meade, Brydon argued that the church in colonial Virginia was far more stable and the clergy more effective than Meade had recognized. Reviewers generally greeted the book warmly, but some remarked on Brydon's partisanship—he wrote as a proud Virginia Episcopalian—and suggested that the copious extracts from contemporary documents made the text slow going. The second volume of *Virginia's Mother Church*, carrying the narrative up to 1814, appeared in 1952. Brydon did not lament the rise of other denominations during the eighteenth century or the disestablishment of the Episcopal Church after the American Revolution, but he concluded the volume with the seizure of the property of the parishes of the former established church, which he regarded as an injustice. Without formal training as a historian, Brydon did thorough research and argued fairly from the evidence. Students of Virginia's colonial history still consult his works today. Brydon collected materials for a third volume to carry his church's history into the twentieth century, but he did not complete it.

Brydon held definite opinions, such as strong opposition to desegregation, but at the core of his personality were generosity and irrepressible humor. He and his wife opened their Richmond home to innumerable guests of all types who needed a place to stay, sometimes to the consternation of their children. Even in retire-

ment and poor health, Brydon continued to work. He founded the diocesan library in 1960 and bequeathed it $5,000. For about forty years he sat on the board of Saint Paul's College, a historically black institution in Lawrenceville that enjoyed Episcopal support, and in his will he left $3,500 for aid to its students. George MacLaren Brydon died from the effects of arteriosclerotic heart disease on 26 September 1963 and was buried in Forest Lawn Cemetery in Richmond.

Albert C. Muller, "George MacLaren Brydon: A Memoir," and Lawrence L. Brown, "The Rev. G. MacLaren Brydon, D.D., and the Historiography of the Episcopal Church," *Historical Magazine of the Protestant Episcopal Church* 32 (1963): 285–286 and 287–288 (frontispiece por.); Bruce, Tyler, and Morton, *History of Virginia,* 4:76–78; George MacLaren Brydon Papers (including diary, 1898–1899, and autobiographical "My Obit," typescript dated 7 Sept. 1960), and Protestant Episcopal Church, Virginia Diocese, Papers, sections 1–5, 10, VHS; BVS Marriage Register, Halifax Co.; Anne Page Brydon, "Lame-Duck Lodge," *Richmond Quarterly* 7 (summer 1984): 42–45; *Richmond Times-Dispatch,* 31 Aug. 1956, 16 Sept. 1960; George MacLaren Brydon, *The Episcopal Church Among the Negroes of Virginia* (1937), esp. 21–26, and "The Unity of the Church," *Episcopal Churchnews,* 24 June 1956; obituaries in *Richmond News Leader* and *Richmond Times-Dispatch,* both 27 Sept. 1963; editorial tribute in *Richmond Times-Dispatch,* 29 Sept. 1963; memorials in Diocese of Virginia, *Journal of the Annual Council* 169 (1964): 53–54, 105–107, 111–113.

JOHN T. KNEEBONE

BRYDON, Mary Evelyn (2 June 1878–13 April 1930), physician and public health officer, was born in Danville, the daughter of Robert Brydon, a pharmacist and native of Scotland, and Ellen Page Dame Brydon, daughter of George Washington Dame, minister of the Episcopal Church in Danville from 1840 to 1895. Her brother George MacLaren Brydon was a prominent Episcopal clergyman and historian.

Following graduation from Danville High School, Brydon entered the Joseph Price Hospital in Philadelphia for training as a nurse. She then returned to Virginia and settled in Richmond, where she met and came under the influence of Sarah "Sadie" Heath Cabaniss, who had pushed for the professional training of nurses in Virginia and who became the first president of the Virginia State Association of Nurses (later the Virginia Nurses Association). Brydon was a founder of the association and served as its third president in 1906–1907. Cabaniss and other Richmond nurses established the Instructive Visiting Nurse Association in 1900. Modeled on similar programs elsewhere in the nation, it provided nursing care and health education to the urban poor. The IVNA accomplished a great deal in Richmond by giving guidance to new mothers, assisting the bedridden, and leading public campaigns against tuberculosis.

About 1904 Brydon moved back to Danville, a small industrial city with no organized means to provide medical care to the poor, and she there put the ideals of the IVNA to work. She convinced the local chapter of the King's Daughters, a Christian women's service organization, to provide supplies and a nominal salary for a visiting nurse. To get the work under way Brydon took the job herself. The streetcar company gave her free tickets, but during the next three years she still walked many miles through Danville's streets to reach patients who needed her help. In 1910 Danville finally appointed its first city health officer, and the King's Daughters relinquished to the city responsibility for the visiting nurse program.

In 1907 Brydon enrolled in the Woman's Medical College of Pennsylvania, in Philadelphia. She received an M.D. in 1911, completed her internship at the Woman's Hospital in Philadelphia, and spent short terms working at the Jackson Clinic in Milwaukee and as physician at Agnes Scott College in Decatur, Georgia. In 1915 Brydon became resident physician at the State Normal School for Women at Farmville (later Longwood College). When the United States entered World War I in 1917, she attempted more than once to enlist for foreign medical service, but the military would send no female physicians overseas. Brydon remained in Virginia and volunteered with the Red Cross and other service organizations.

Reports of the poor physical condition of the men drafted into the military inspired public support for government-sponsored health programs in Virginia and elsewhere. In 1918 the General Assembly authorized public schools to hire nurses and required teachers to inspect the health of their students. Administration of the program fell to the ten-year-old State Board of

Health, and in June 1918 Brydon began working there as a field health officer to carry out the provisions of the legislation. Within a year she had acquired the title director of the Bureau of Child Welfare and School Hygiene. Brydon delivered more than 100 lectures annually to normal schools and teachers' institutes, helped develop a manual for teachers who had to inspect their students' physical condition, and instituted Physical Inspection Day on 3 November 1919 in all of the state's schools. The State Board of Education then ruled that persons requesting a teacher's certificate must have completed training in the physical inspection of schoolchildren. Brydon hired physicians and nurses to conduct the training at eleven summer institutes. To publicize the program, she wrote a monthly column for the *Virginia Journal of Education* from September 1919 through December 1921.

By 1925 the Bureau of Child Welfare had a staff of two physicians, one dentist, six nurses, four teachers, a librarian, and six secretaries and clerks. It conducted programs for child welfare and hygiene, public health nursing, dental hygiene, infant and maternal care, and midwife education. In addition to her many administrative duties, Brydon also continued to campaign for better health care for children. She organized activities in Virginia for the national Child Health Day program and in 1926 developed a program to commend schools whose students breathed through their noses, were of a proper weight, had healthy teeth, and enjoyed adequate vision and hearing. Brydon expanded the campaign in 1929 to encourage students' families to equip their houses with sanitary sewerage, clean water, and window screens.

On 5 September 1925 Brydon married George L. MacKay, a Richmond salesman who was a widower with one daughter. She took his name in private life but in public and professional roles remained Dr. Mary E. Brydon. Her marriage and responsibility for a stepdaughter scarcely slowed her pace. From January through March 1930, for example, Brydon attended 114 conferences, delivered 61 speeches, and traveled 3,236 miles. At the end of March she developed a severe cold, which swiftly worsened into pneumonia. Mary Evelyn Brydon MacKay died in Richmond on 13 April 1930. On the day after her death child health care workers from Iowa and Mexico arrived in Richmond to study her work. Ennion G. Williams, the state health commissioner, stated that "her untimely death was the severest blow that the Health Department has ever sustained." Following the funeral in Richmond she was buried in her family's plot in Green Hill Cemetery in Danville with a gravestone inscribed to her as "Doctor, Nurse, Humanitarian."

BVS Birth Register, Danville; BVS Marriage Register, Richmond City; *Highlights of Nursing in Virginia, 1900–1975* (1975), 3, 29; Jane Gray Hagan, *The Story of Danville* (1950), 46–47; *Annual Report of the State Board of Health*, 1918–1930; Brydon, "Public Health Nurses for Rural Schools" and "The New Viewpoint for the Health Program in Virginia Schools," *Virginia Journal of Education* 12 (1919): 42–45 and 20 (1926): 21–23; por. in Virginia Nurses Association Records, Special Collections and Archives, Tompkins-McCaw Library, MCV; obituaries in *Richmond News Leader* and *Richmond Times-Dispatch*, both 14 Apr. 1930, *Danville Bee*, 14, 15 Apr. 1930, *Danville Register* (with editorial tribute), 15 Apr. 1930, and *Virginia Journal of Education* 23 (1930): 435; memorials in *Virginia Medical Monthly* 57 (1930): 136, 210, 563–564, and *Annual Report of the State Department of Health* (1930): 11 (first quotation); *Green Hill Cemetery, Danville, Virginia: Gravestone Records* (1988), 2:304 (second quotation).

JOHN T. KNEEBONE

BUCHANAN, Andrew (d. 3 October 1804), member of the Convention of 1788, was born probably in King George County late in the 1730s or early in the 1740s. Many aspects of his personal and family life are obscure as a result of the loss of many of the county records of the region, the fragmentary survival of family documents, and the existence in Virginia during his lifetime of several Buchanan families, including at least three men named Andrew Buchanan. Most likely he was the son of Gilbert Buchanan, an attorney in King George County during the mid-1730s, but the name of his mother is not known, nor is his relationship to several prominent merchants and other men named Buchanan who lived in the same part of Virginia.

By early in the 1770s Andrew Buchanan enjoyed a lucrative legal practice in King George County, where he also acted as prosecuting attorney. His clients included William Allason, a prominent Falmouth merchant. After the American Revolution ended, Buchanan vigorously pursued the collection of debts that planters and other Virginians had owed to Allason since before the war. Following the death in 1781 of Thomas, sixth baron Fairfax of Cameron, Buchanan also acted as the local legal agent for Fairfax's executors.

In August 1770 Buchanan was a member of the county committee formed to enforce the first of several nonimportation associations created to pressure Parliament to repeal obnoxious taxes. In January 1775 he was elected to the committee for the town of Falmouth and acted as its spokesman because he was the member "most accustomed to speak in Publick." Buchanan was named a captain of the county minutemen that September and was promoted to major before the unit was disbanded in October 1776.

Buchanan served as a trustee for the town of Falmouth, where he owned lot number 59, the site of Clear View, his house overlooking the Rappahannock River. He also owned 364 acres of land adjoining the town. The tax lists after 1782 annually charged Buchanan for from nine to fifteen slaves, and he owned twenty-six at the time of his death. The town of Falmouth was in a portion of King George County that in 1777 was added to Stafford County. In April 1786 Buchanan received the most votes in a close contest of three candidates for Stafford County's two seats in the House of Delegates. He sat on the Committees of Commerce, for Courts of Justice, and of Propositions and Grievances. Reelected in 1788, 1789, and 1790, he served on the Committees for Courts of Justice and of Privileges and Elections and in 1790 also on the Committee of Propositions and Grievances. Buchanan served a final one-year term in the House of Delegates in 1795. He arrived a week after the session began and was added to the Committees on Claims, for Courts of Justice, on Privileges and Elections, and of Propositions and Grievances. Buchanan never held a committee chairmanship or played a leading role in the assembly.

On 10 March 1788 the voters of Stafford County elected Buchanan and Fairfax County's George Mason (who owned land in Stafford

County and was therefore eligible) to the convention called to consider ratification of the proposed constitution of the United States. Buchanan did not take an active role in the convention and made no recorded speech. He and Mason voted in favor of requiring amendment of the Constitution before ratification and then against the motion to ratify.

Buchanan married three times. His first wife, whose given name is unknown, was a daughter of James Hewitt and Susannah Crump Hewitt. They had one son and two daughters. After her death Buchanan married Anne Hooe, the daughter of his first wife's sister. They had one son before her death in 1792. On 10 January 1803 Buchanan wrote a will that divided his real estate and personal property among his children. Six months later, on 16 July 1803, Buchanan married Anne Baxter in Fredericksburg, and seven months after that, on 25 February 1804, he wrote a second will dividing his estate differently. When both wills were presented for probate on 9 October 1804, the court ruled on the basis of evidence presented to it that Buchanan had not been of sound mind when the second will was written and therefore rejected it "upon the ground of insanity." Andrew Buchanan died at his home in Falmouth on 3 October 1804.

Family data in file on Clear View, Stafford Co., George Harrison Sanford King Papers, VHS; earliest appearance in records, dated 4 Apr. 1763, in King George Co. Will Book, A:165; *Executive Journals of Council*, 6:390; *Williamsburg Virginia Gazette* (Rind), 30 Aug. 1770; ibid. (Purdie), 22 Sept. 1775, 1 Mar. 1776; *Journal of Council of State*, 1:156, 174, 183; numerous references in fragmentary surviving records of King George and Stafford Cos., esp. Stafford Co. Deed Book, S:381; William Allason Letter Book, 1770–1789, William Allason Papers, LVA; *Revolutionary Virginia*, 4:99–100, 5:228–229, 6:92, 7:743, 745 (first quotation); Mutual Assurance Society Declarations, nos. 125 (1796), 820 (1805), LVA; Kaminski, *Ratification*, 8:479, 10:1539, 1541; Fredericksburg Marriage Bonds, 16 July 1803; will dated 10 Jan. 1803 and estate inventory in Fredericksburg District and Superior Court Wills, Bonds, and Inventories, A3:220–221, 287–291; will dated 25 Feb. 1804 and record of its rejection in *Hooe* v. *Beckwith* suit papers, file 142, Fredericksburg District Court (second quotation); death notice in *Fredericksburg Virginia Herald*, 5 Oct. 1804.

DAPHNE GENTRY

BUCHANAN, Annabel Morris (22 October 1888–6 January 1983), composer and folklorist, was born in Groesbeck, Limestone County, Texas, the daughter of Anna Virginia Foster Morris, a teacher, and William Caruthers Morris, editor and publisher of a local newspaper. She changed her given name from Annie Bell to Annabel at the age of eighteen. When Morris was ten her father gave up journalism to become a minister in the Cumberland Presbyterian Church and by 1901 had moved the family to Maury County, Tennessee. Showing precocious musical talent, Morris won a scholarship at age fifteen to the Landon Conservatory in Dallas, where she studied piano, violin, voice, and composition and graduated with honors in 1906. Morris taught music during the 1907–1908 academic year at Halsell College in Oklahoma and from 1909 to 1912 at the Stonewall Jackson Institute (later Stonewall Jackson College) at Abingdon.

On 14 August 1912 in Salem she married John Preston Buchanan, a lawyer who served in the Senate of Virginia from 1916 to 1919, during part of which time his father and law partner, Benjamin Franklin Buchanan, was lieutenant governor. The couple settled in Marion, where, into the 1920s, Buchanan was involved primarily with her home and family of two daughters and two sons. She also found time to serve as organist and choir director at a local church, to compose songs, and to write articles about gardening for such magazines as *Better Homes and Gardens* and *Woman's Home Companion*. In 1923 Buchanan organized the Marion Monday Afternoon Music Club and through that group became active in the Virginia Federation of Music Clubs, for which she served two terms as state president in 1927–1930, and the National Federation of Music Clubs, for which she sat on the board of directors from 1933 to 1937 and chaired the Department of American Music from 1933 to 1935.

A turning point in Buchanan's life came about 1927 when she met John Powell, a composer and pianist from Richmond, who not only employed themes from folk music in his works but also believed ardently in preserving Anglo-Saxon cultural forms. Powell inspired Buchanan to study and collect folk music and to use its musical themes in her compositions. She included performances by folk musicians in the first Virginia State Choral Festival, which she and Powell organized in 1928.

In 1931 Buchanan cofounded and directed the White Top Folk Festival, held each year (except 1937) until 1939. The festival, which took place atop a mountain in Grayson County and gained nationwide attention in 1933 when Eleanor Roosevelt was guest of honor, was only part of what Buchanan saw as her larger work of preserving and disseminating the traditional music of the region. From 1933 to 1936 she organized a series of prefestival seminars that brought folklorists, composers, and writers together with traditional musicians for classes and concerts. Through these meetings, and later through correspondence with such folklorists as Phillips Barry, Anne Gilchrist, and Donald Knight Wilgus, Buchanan continued to study and write about folk music. Her *Folk Hymns of America* (1938) explored traditional use of secular tunes for sacred songs. Buchanan also provided musical arrangements for many of the traditional hymns she had collected from family members and other informants. The collection was well received by musicians and scholars alike.

Buchanan called all her folklore activities the "White Top work." Besides the establishment of one of the nation's first large regional folk festivals, her accomplishments in this field include published articles on the White Top festival and on other aspects of folk music, four book-length manuscripts on folk music and folklore, and her collection of more than 800 traditional songs, mainly from southwestern Virginia, western North Carolina, eastern Kentucky, and Tennessee. This collection is particularly valuable because Buchanan, with her musical training, was one of the few collectors to record tunes as well as lyrics on paper in the years before the widespread availability of recording machines.

Buchanan used folk themes in much of her own substantial body of musical compositions, especially the three choral-symphonic works—a choral ballad called "The Legend of Hungry Mother," a work for women's chorus entitled "Rex Christus," and a suite for chorus and symphony orchestra called *When the Moon Goes Down*—that she believed were her most important contributions to the fine arts. She also published more than 100 original art songs and hymns as well as the arrangements for nearly 250 folk songs and folk hymns.

In 1936 Buchanan moved to Richmond to work for the Works Progress Administration's Federal Music Project and withdrew from active involvement in the White Top festival, partly as a result of her new position and partly from escalating disagreements with promoters John Augustus Blakemore and John Powell over the growing commercialization of the festival. Buchanan's husband, who had remained in Marion and from whom she had become alienated, died on 15 September 1937. She sold their Smyth County home and to support herself taught music at the New England Music Camp in Kennebec County, Maine, at the University of Richmond as a professor of musical theory, and at Madison College (later James Madison University) in Harrisonburg. In 1948 Buchanan retired from teaching to devote more time to her manuscripts and compositions. Three years later she moved to Paducah, Kentucky, to be near her family. Buchanan worked with the National Federation of Music Clubs as its national folk music archivist from 1958 to 1963. Through correspondence with members and folklorists all over the country, she collected more than a thousand folk songs that were deposited in the Archive of Folk Song at the Library of Congress. In 1963 Annabel Morris Buchanan took a six-month world tour, after which she returned to Paducah, where she died on 6 January 1983. She was buried in Round Hill Cemetery in Marion. Later that year, when Marion music enthusiasts reactivated the Monday Afternoon Music Club, the organization she had founded was renamed in her honor the Annabel Morris Buchanan Federated Music Club of Smyth County.

Lyn Wolz, "Annabel Morris Buchanan: Folk Song Collector," *Ferrum Review* 5 (fall 1982): 27–34 ("White Top" quotation on 29); Wolz, " 'White Top Folk Trails': Annabel Morris Buchanan's Folk Music Legacy" (master's thesis, UNC, 1983); Grace Caroline Lelear, "Annabel Morris Buchanan: A Profile of Her Contributions to Folklore" (MLS thesis, UNC, 1978); Buchanan Papers and index to folksong collection, Southern Historical Collection, UNC; correspondence in John A. Blakemore Papers, Southern Historical Collection, UNC, and John Powell Papers, UVA; BVS Marriage Register, Roanoke Co.; John A. Blakemore,

Buchanan: The Family History of James Buchanan, Son of Alexander Buchanan of Pennsylvania, 1702–1976 (1978), 276; *Marion Smyth County News*, 15 Aug. 1912, 16, 23 Sept. 1937; Annabel Morris Buchanan, "Adventures in Virginia Folkways," *Richmond Times-Dispatch* Sunday magazines, 24 May–12 July 1936; David E. Whisnant, *All That Is Native and Fine: The Politics of Culture in an American Region* (1983), 181–252 (por. on 217); Ulrich Troubetzkoy, "Music on the Mountain," *Virginia Cavalcade* 11 (summer 1961): 4–10 (por. on 4); obituaries in *Paducah Sun*, 6 Jan. 1983, and *Marion Smyth County News*, 11 Jan. 1983.

LYN WOLZ

BUCHANAN, Archibald Chapman (7 January 1890–3 May 1979), Virginia Supreme Court of Appeals judge, was born in Tazewell County, the son of Augustus Beauregard Buchanan and Nancy Emerine Chapman Buchanan. His father served for five years as deputy clerk of the Tazewell County Court and for eight years as postmaster of Tazewell during the presidency of Woodrow Wilson. Buchanan graduated from Tazewell High School in 1906. He received a B.A. from Hampden-Sydney College in 1910 and an LL.B. from Washington and Lee University in 1914. Both institutions subsequently bestowed honorary doctor of laws degrees on him, and Buchanan recalled that he had been especially influenced by William H. Whiting, a Latin teacher at Hampden-Sydney, and Martin Parks Burks, dean of the Washington and Lee Law School and later a judge of the state Supreme Court of Appeals.

In partnership with his uncle John William Chapman and George Campbell Peery, who later served as governor, Buchanan practiced law in Tazewell from 1915 to 1927 in the firm of Chapman, Peery, and Buchanan. He served from 1917 to 1921 as mayor of Tazewell and from 1919 to 1927 as the county's commissioner of accounts. On 8 April 1927 the state legislature elected Buchanan to fill a vacancy caused by the death of the circuit judge for the 22d Judicial Circuit, which consisted of Bland, Giles, and Tazewell Counties. He was subsequently elected to a full term on 19 January 1928. He sat from 1928 to 1932 on the first Judicial Council of Virginia, which the legislature created to advise it on improving the administration of justice in the courts. Buchanan also helped the Virginia Advisory Legislative Council develop recommendations for revision of the probation and parole system, which the legislature enacted into law on 6 February 1942.

In 1946 Preston White Campbell, of Abingdon, chief justice of the Supreme Court of Appeals, notified Governor William Munford Tuck of his intention to retire and expressed a preference that Buchanan be appointed to Campbell's seat. On 12 September 1946 Tuck duly appointed Buchanan, who had already been mentioned with respect to earlier court vacancies, to replace Campbell.

A modest man, Buchanan was known to his associates as the scholar of the court. "Citizens need to know what they can and cannot do under the law," he declared in an interview following his retirement. "The fundamental principles of the law are generally well established," he continued, "and courts should only with great reluctance depart from them or modify them." In 1955 Buchanan wrote an opinion upholding Virginia's ban of interracial marriage as a proper governmental objective and one that had traditionally been open to state regulation. The court reaffirmed its validation of the state ban in 1966, but the United States Supreme Court declared the state law unconstitutional the following year. Buchanan also wrote the majority opinion that in 1963 absolved the state legislature of any constitutional obligation to operate free public schools in Prince Edward County. The nation's high court reversed this decision, too. In 1959, however, Buchanan voted with the majority on the state court that struck down Virginia's plan of Massive Resistance to desegregation in the public schools on the grounds that it violated the state's constitutional mandate requiring the legislature to "maintain an efficient system of public free schools throughout the State."

Buchanan lived in Tazewell throughout his life and traveled to Richmond and Staunton for the sessions of the state's high court. He married Olivia McCall on 18 December 1915, and they had one son and one daughter. Buchanan was a Presbyterian teacher and elder, a member of the Tazewell Rotary Club, and a director of the Tazewell National Bank and the Lynn Camp Coal Corporation. He also served on the boards of trustees of Hampden-Sydney College from 1928 to 1969 and of Mary Baldwin College from 1948 to 1962. He retired from the bench in 1969 after forty-two consecutive years as a jurist, and that year the Virginia Trial Lawyers Association honored him with the Virginia Distinguished Service Award. Archibald Chapman Buchanan died on 3 May 1979 after a long illness and was buried in Maplewood Cemetery in Tazewell.

Glass and Glass, *Virginia Democracy*, 3:157–158 (birth date of 7 Jan. 1890); *Richmond Times-Dispatch*, 13 Sept. 1946 (variant birth date of 17 Jan. 1890), 14 Sept. 1969; author's interview with Buchanan, 29 Oct. 1970 (first and second quotations); Tazewell Co. Marriage Register; Thomas R. Morris, *The Virginia Supreme Court: An Institutional and Political Analysis* (1975), 47, 54, 57, 100; family information provided by son, A. C. Buchanan Jr.; pors. in Tazewell County Courthouse and Hummel and Smith, *Portraits and Statuary*, 13; obituaries in *Richmond Times-Dispatch*, 5 May 1979 (por.), and *Tazewell Clinch Valley News*, 9 May 1979.

THOMAS R. MORRIS

BUCHANAN, Benjamin Franklin (4 October 1857–21 February 1932), lieutenant governor of Virginia, was born at his family's Plaster Cove Farm in Smyth County, the son of Patrick Campbell Buchanan and his first wife, America Virginia Copenhaver Buchanan. His parents' families had been prosperous and prominent in southwestern Virginia for several generations. He graduated from Marion Academy in 1876, received a B.A. from the University of Virginia in 1880, became a member of Phi Beta Kappa in 1883, and earned an LL.B. from the University of Virginia in 1884 after studying law under John B. Minor. On 2 March 1887 Buchanan married Eleanor Fairman Sheffey. Of their four sons and three daughters, two sons died in infancy.

Buchanan formed a partnership with his cousin John Alexander Buchanan and practiced law in Marion and Abingdon until February 1894, when his partner became a judge of the Virginia Supreme Court of Appeals. From then until 1912 Buchanan practiced in partnership with James L. White in Marion. In the latter year his son John Preston Buchanan joined him in the firm of Buchanan and Buchanan. Specializing in corporate law, the firm served clients including the Norfolk and Western Railway and the Mathieson Alkali Works. Buchanan also served as general counsel to the office of the United States comptroller of the currency from 1915 to 1921. He

invested in the Marion Light and Power Company, the Rich Valley Railroad, and the Smyth County Telephone Company, and he was a director at various times of the Bank of Marion, the Marion National Bank, and the First National Bank of Saltville.

Buchanan had become chairman of the Democratic Party in Smyth County by 1893 and in November of that year was elected to the Senate of Virginia to represent Smyth and Washington Counties. During both sessions of his four-year term he sat on the Committees for Courts of Justice and on Public Institutions and Education, and during the second session he served on the Committee on County, City, and Town Organizations. Buchanan did not seek reelection, but he remained active in politics and was a delegate to the Democratic National Convention in 1900, 1912, and 1920. In 1913 he was returned to the same seat in the state senate to fill a vacancy and this time attracted notice as a talented legislator. During the two sessions of his term he served on the Committees on Finance, on Fish and Game, on General Laws, and on Public Institutions and Education and also on several minor committees. Buchanan did not seek reelection, and his son and law partner won that Senate seat in the assembly of 1916.

In 1917 Buchanan obtained the Democratic Party's nomination and won election as lieutenant governor of Virginia. He served from 1 February 1918 to 1 February 1922. Because Governor Westmoreland Davis was often at odds with the party's leadership, Buchanan gained distinction and influence as the highest-ranking state official in good standing with the party's most powerful leaders. He might have received the party's nomination for governor in 1921 had he sought that honor, but instead he supported Elbert Lee Trinkle, of Wytheville, who won the nomination and the election.

Buchanan continued to practice law during and after his time in office. He was returned to the Senate of Virginia in 1923 and reelected in 1927 and 1931. Buchanan served on the Committees for Courts of Justice, on Finance, and on Insurance and Banking, and in 1932 he became chair of the justice committee and a member of the powerful Committee on Rules. He also chaired the Committee on the Library from 1924 until his death. Because he was one of the most popular and respected Democrats in the state, party leaders often referred to him in private during the 1920s as Governor Buchanan. He was also one of the assembly's foremost authorities on taxation. In 1914 the lieutenant governor had appointed Buchanan to a special committee to study Virginia's tax laws, and in a special assembly session the following year the legislators adopted the committee's proposals, reinforced by a 1924 law, that led in two steps to the separation of taxing authority between the state government and the city and county governments. The localities received exclusive power to tax land and personal property, and the state retained authority to tax other sources of revenue. Buchanan was also a principal legislative architect of the pay-as-you-go policy by which Harry Flood Byrd (1887–1966) financed highway construction from current revenues and avoided a bonded debt.

Buchanan served on the boards of the Marion Female College from 1894 until 1932, the State Female Normal School (later Longwood College) from 1900 to 1904, and the University of Virginia from 1904 to 1908 and again from 1927 until his death. Hampden-Sydney College conferred an honorary LL.D. on him in 1922. Benjamin Franklin Buchanan died of a heart attack on 21 February 1932 at the Westmoreland Club in Richmond, where he was attending a session of the General Assembly. He was buried in Round Hill Cemetery in Marion. In 1934 the assembly designated the road that became state highway 16 in Smyth County the B. F. Buchanan Highway.

Marvin E. Winters, "Benjamin Franklin Buchanan, 1859–1932" (master's thesis, UVA, 1969); biographies in *NCAB*, 48:490–491, Goodridge Wilson, *Smyth County History and Traditions* (1932), 340–349, and Manarin, *Senate Officers*, 136–138 (por., with 1852 birth date); Smyth Co. Birth Register; gravestone gives variant birth date of 4 Oct. 1859; Smyth Co. Marriage Register; family history confirmed by daughters Eleanor Buchanan Starcher and Josephine Buchanan, granddaughter Betty Blair Stewart, and cousin Margaret Buchanan; a few private letters in family possession and some official correspondence in Executive Papers of several governors, RG 3, LVA; Commonwealth of Virginia, *Report of the Joint Committee on Tax Revision* (1914), esp. 211–215; *JSV*, 1932 sess., 71–72; obituaries and editorial tributes in *Richmond News Leader*, *Richmond Times-Dispatch*, and *Roanoke World-News*, all 22 Feb. 1932, and *Roanoke Times*, 22, 23 Feb. 1932; obituaries in *Marion Democrat*, 23 Feb. 1932, and *Marion Smyth County News*, 25 Feb. 1932.

MARVIN E. WINTERS

BUCHANAN, John (d. by 16 August 1769), surveyor, probably moved to Virginia from Pennsylvania as a young man late in the 1730s and settled early the next decade in the portion of the Shenandoah Valley that is now Augusta County. He may have been the son of James Buchanan and Jane Sayers Buchanan. Records of his early life are sparse, and at least two men named John Buchanan lived in the same part of Virginia and engaged in similar pursuits, which has resulted in confusion about their lives and careers.

Buchanan was probably the "John Buchanan, Gent.," who acquired land in Beverley Manor in 1738. He soon became prominent and was appointed a justice of the peace for the Augusta district of Orange County in November 1741. On 24 June 1742 Buchanan qualified as a captain of militia. He was present at Balcony Falls, near modern-day Glasgow, in Rockbridge County, on 19 December 1742 when militiamen clashed with Iroquois warriors. According to contemporary accounts, for forty-five minutes Buchanan led his small contingent against superior numbers and finally forced the Iroquois to retreat. As a result of this action, in September 1743 he was commissioned a lieutenant colonel in the Orange County militia.

Buchanan worked for James Patton, a land speculator who helped sponsor large-scale immigration to western Virginia. Buchanan explored unsettled land southwest of the settled portion of Augusta County. After receiving his report on 1 May 1743, Patton petitioned the governor's Council for a grant of 200,000 acres fifty miles west of the headwaters of the Roanoke River. On 30 March 1745 the Orange County Court instructed Patton and Buchanan to survey a public road from Frederick County south to Wood's River (now the New River), near the present-day city of Radford. What had once been a trail from Pennsylvania to the Virginia frontier became a major route of migration to western Virginia and into the areas that became Kentucky, Tennessee, and Ohio.

On 26 April 1745 Patton was awarded 100,000 acres in the watershed of the New, Holston, and Clinch Rivers, after which he organized the Wood's River Land Company and appointed Buchanan surveyor. Years later litigants disputing some land titles based on Buchanan's surveys argued that he had not been licensed either as a surveyor by the College of William and Mary or as a deputy to the county surveyor, as the law required. In October 1745 Buchanan made an inspection tour of the Patton grant, and his journal records that he helped John Peter Salley prepare an account of the latter's search for a route to the Mississippi River.

Buchanan was a founding member of the Augusta County Court in 1745. On 10 October 1746 he became agent for the Wood's River Land Company. In April 1748 Buchanan accompanied Patton and Thomas Walker on an expedition of exploration that took them west as far as Cumberland Gap. Buchanan married Margaret Patton, daughter of his patron and partner, in June 1749. They had at least three sons and four daughters. The following year Buchanan moved to Anchor and Hope, a plantation of approximately 1,700 acres on Reed Creek near Max Meadows, where he continued to act as an agent for Patton.

In November 1752 Buchanan was appointed a colonel of militia. His importance in the migration to the western borders of settled Virginia became clear in 1754 when reports circulated that some Indians and their French allies had placed a bounty on his and other leading Englishmen's lives. The French and Indian War soon reached Buchanan's neighborhood, and a party of Shawnee killed Patton on 31 July 1755 at Draper's Meadows. Buchanan sent militiamen in pursuit but failed to apprehend any of the perpetrators, and his pleas for help to Lieutenant Governor Robert Dinwiddie produced no assistance. Buchanan succeeded Patton as commander of the Augusta County militia, and the following spring he withdrew from his exposed residence at Max Meadows to Cherry Tree Bottom, Patton's plantation on the James River.

On 27 July 1756 Buchanan presided over a council of war at the Augusta County courthouse to plan construction of a chain of forts in the Allegheny Mountains. George Washington, commander of Virginia's armed forces during that portion of the French and Indian War, visited Cherry Tree Bottom and was briefed by Buchanan on recent conflicts with the Indians. Buchanan accompanied Washington part of the way back to his headquarters in Winchester, inspecting the small defensive forts as they went. In 1757 Buchanan erected Fort Fauquier near the site in Botetourt County of the modern town of Buchanan, which is named for him. He became county lieutenant, the commanding officer of the entire county militia, on 30 September 1758 and commanded the militia at Fort Fauquier in 1758 and 1759.

Buchanan was sheriff of Augusta County in 1761–1762. After the end of the war the British government issued the so-called Proclamation of 1763 barring colonial settlement of Indian lands west of the Allegheny Mountains. Buchanan considered but decided against traveling to London to seek title for his western investments. Reportedly during a journey to his property at Max Meadows, John Buchanan died on an unrecorded date at the residence of William Preston. He was already sick on 25 June 1769 when he wrote his will, which was proved at a meeting of the Augusta County Court on 16 August 1769.

Mary B. Kegley and Frederick B. Kegley, *Early Adventurers on the Western Waters* (1980–1995), esp. 1:87, 200–202; Patricia Givens Johnson, *James Patton and the Appalachian Colonists* (1983) and *The New River Early Settlement* (1983); numerous references and letters in Preston and Virginia Papers, Draper MSS, ser. 1QQ–2QQ, esp. Oct. 1745 journal, 1QQ38–56; David John Mays, ed., *Letters and Papers of Edmund Pendleton, 1734–1803* (1967), 1:374–375; Robert A. Brock, ed., *The Official Records of Robert Dinwiddie, Lieutenant-Governor of the Colony of Virginia, 1751–1758* (1883–1884), 1:267–268, 2:154–155, 199, 488–490, 492–493, 537, 566, 569, 719; *Washington: Colonial Series*, 3:431–434, 4:1, 13, 30; will and estate inventories in Augusta Co. Will Book, 4:389–391, 490–492, 12:375–380.

DONALD W. GUNTER

BUCHANAN, John (1748–19 December 1822), Episcopal clergyman, was born near Dumfries, Scotland. His father's name may have been Archibald Buchanan, but his mother's name is not known. His elder half brother James Buchanan moved to Virginia about 1757 and became one of the most influential and prosperous merchants in Richmond. John Buchanan briefly studied law in London, but the subject did not interest him, and about 1771 he joined his brother in Richmond. Commerce did not satisfy him either, and after fifteen months he returned to Scotland and may have received an A.M. from the University of Edinburgh in April 1774. On 13 August 1775 the bishop of London licensed Buchanan for the ministry of the Church of England in Virginia.

Buchanan lived in or near Richmond for about three years while serving at Deep Run Church in Henrico County as curate to Miles Selden, the rector of Henrico Parish. Buchanan supplemented his income with work as a tutor for Jaquelin Ambler's family. On 1 October 1779 he began preaching in Lexington Parish in Amherst County and became its rector in January 1780. On 10 May 1785 he succeeded Selden as rector of Henrico Parish and minister of Saint John's Church in Richmond. He inherited much of the large and valuable estate of James Buchanan, who was one of the directors of the state's public buildings in Richmond when he died on 10 October 1787, and he was probably the principal heir of his one known full brother, Alexander Buchanan, who died in Richmond about 1802. Buchanan's inheritances enabled him to live an easy life and indulge his social nature. A jovial man with a subtle sense of humor who became one of the most popular people in Richmond, he hosted the Richmond Quoit Club at his farm just outside the city and contributed to many philanthropic causes. Buchanan also served for several years as president of the Amicable Society.

The College of William and Mary awarded Buchanan an honorary D.D. in 1794, and he was the founding president of the Bible Society of Virginia in 1813. For several years when Saint John's Church was in disrepair he preached to his congregation in the Virginia State Capitol, alternating Sundays with the Presbyterian minister John Durburrow Blair. Buchanan and Blair became close friends. A lifelong bachelor, Buchanan spent many hours in Blair's household and with Blair's children. Buchanan and Blair traded puns and doggerel verse in a lighthearted way, and they preached religious tolerance and set an ecumenical example that distinguished them from some of the Methodists and Baptists of the city.

After the loss of seventy-six lives in the Richmond Theatre fire of 26 December 1811, Buchanan and Blair led the campaign to construct Monumental Church on the site of the disaster. The two clergymen may have intended that they and their congregations share the church, but the more numerous Episcopalians appropriated the building for themselves. The division between the congregations did not disrupt the friendship between the ministers. Their legendary friendship and the example of religious tolerance they set was well known to their contemporaries and embellished many years later in George Wythe Munford's *Two Parsons* (1884). The winning personalities of the two principals and Munford's nostalgic prose style made the book a popular interpretation of Richmond's early history.

Buchanan served for thirty-seven years as rector of Henrico Parish and for twenty-nine years as treasurer of the Diocese of Virginia. He turned down the proffered post of bishop after the death of the incumbent James Madison (1749–1812), citing his own advanced age. John Buchanan died in Richmond on 19 December 1822, about three weeks before his friend Blair, and was buried beneath the chancel of Saint John's Church in Richmond.

Sprague, *American Pulpit,* 5:324–327; J. Staunton Moore, ed., *Annals of Henrico Parish* (1904), 25–27, 35, 36; Meade, *Old Churches*, 1:29–30, 141–143, 2:57, 264–267; Ordination Papers, 26:231–234, Fulham Palace Papers, Lambeth Palace Library, Eng.; Buchanan letters in Munford-Ellis Family Papers, Duke; two MS sermons attributed to Buchanan in George Wythe Munford Papers, LVA; Hall, *Portraits*, 38–39 (por. by John Blennerhassett Martin); Richmond City Hustings Court Will Book, 3:268–271; death notices in *Richmond Commercial Compiler* and *Richmond Daily Mercantile Advertiser*, both 20 Dec. 1822; obituaries in *Richmond Commercial Compiler* (with age at death of seventy-three) and *Richmond Enquirer*, both 21 Dec. 1822, and *Evangelical and Literary Magazine* 6 (1823): 52; memorial in *Richmond Enquirer*, 24 Dec. 1822 (with year of birth).

MAURICE DUKE

BUCHANAN, John Alexander (7 October 1843–2 September 1921), member of the House of Representatives and judge of the Virginia

Supreme Court of Appeals, was born in Smyth County, the son of James Augustus Buchanan, a prosperous farmer, and Mary Glenn Thomas Buchanan. In July 1861, when he was not yet eighteen years old, Buchanan enlisted in the Smyth County Blues, which became Company D of the 4th Regiment Virginia Infantry, part of the Stonewall Brigade. Buchanan spent lengthy intervals at home on sick leave in October 1861 and again in September 1862, but he still saw action in various campaigns before being wounded and captured at Gettysburg on 3 July 1863. He spent most of the remainder of the war in a succession of Maryland prison camps (Fort McHenry, Fort Delaware, Point Lookout) but won his release in a February 1865 prisoner exchange.

Buchanan enrolled at Emory and Henry College and graduated as valedictorian in 1870. He studied law at the University of Virginia during the academic year 1870–1871 and in April 1872 gained admission to the bar in Washington County. For the next two decades Buchanan practiced law in southwestern Virginia. In 1885 he was elected to a two-year term representing Washington County in the House of Delegates. Buchanan served on the Committees on Asylums and Prisons, on Banks, Currency, and Commerce, and for Courts of Justice. He declined to seek a second term, but in 1888 the Democratic Party nominated him for Congress from the fourteen-county Ninth District, which lay west of Craig and Pulaski Counties. Buchanan defeated the Republican incumbent, Henry Bowen, and won reelection in 1890 but declined to seek a third term in 1892.

During his first term in Congress the Republicans were in the majority, and Buchanan received a low-ranking appointment to the Committee on Patents. He introduced an income tax bill and made only one major speech. Along with Virginia's other Democratic congressmen Buchanan opposed the Federal Elections Bill, also known as the Force Bill of 1890, which would have provided federal protection of the voting rights of African Americans in the southern states. He spoke against it on 30 June 1890. The bill passed the House of Representatives but failed in the Senate. During Buchanan's

second term the Democrats were in the majority, and he served on the Committee on Merchant Marine and Fisheries and was active on the Committee on the Judiciary. He did not speak often but presided over the House during debate in the committee of the whole on the revenue bill on 27 May 1892 and on the Post Office appropriation bill on 31 May and 1 June 1892.

From 1885 until 1895 Buchanan practiced law in partnership with his cousin Benjamin Franklin Buchanan, later a lieutenant governor of Virginia. On 6 January 1894, a year before the expiration of the twelve-year terms of the five judges of the Virginia Supreme Court of Appeals, all of whom had been chosen by the Readjusters, the General Assembly elected Buchanan and four other Democrats as their successors. He was reelected in 1906 and served from 1 January 1895 until 12 January 1915, when he became the first member of the court to take advantage of a new law permitting judges who had attained the age of seventy and had served at least twelve years to retire at 60 percent pay. Membership on the court remained comparatively stable during Buchanan's twenty years of service. Three of the four men elected with him still sat on the court when he retired.

Despite the wide variety of civil and less-frequent criminal cases that came before the court, the judges seldom disagreed during Buchanan's tenure, and he filed dissenting opinions in only a few cases. Most of his court opinions concerned the interpretation of deeds and wills and cases arising in chancery proceedings. Buchanan's decisions were decidedly empirical and generally eschewed displays of legal erudition. Important rulings from his time on the bench included *Taylor* v. *Commonwealth* (1903), which affirmed the validity of the Constitution of 1902 even though it had been proclaimed in effect rather than submitted to the voters for ratification through referendum, and *Winchester and Strasburg Railroad Company* v. *Commonwealth* (1906), which upheld the constitutionality of the State Corporation Commission.

Buchanan sat on the board of the Stonewall Jackson Institute (later Stonewall Jackson College), a school for young white women in Abingdon, for more than a quarter of a century, served from 1878 to 1920 on the board of Emory and Henry College, and was also a ruling elder in the Presbyterian Church. He never married and in retirement lived alone on his farm near Emory. John Alexander Buchanan died at his home on 2 September 1921 and was buried in Glade Spring Presbyterian Church Cemetery at Old Glade in Washington County.

Biographies in *South-West Virginia and the Valley: Historical and Biographical* (1892), 299, Lewis Preston Summers, *History of Southwest Virginia, 1746–1786, Washington County, 1777–1870* (1903), 763 (por.), Tyler, *Men of Mark*, 3:52–53, David B. Trimble, *Buchanan and Gillespie of Southwest Virginia* (1992), 187, and French Biographies; Compiled Service Records; speech against Force Bill reprinted in Slemp and Preston, *Addresses*, 363–373; Hummel and Smith, *Portraits and Statuary*, 14 (por.); obituaries in *Richmond Times-Dispatch*, 3 Sept. 1921, and *Confederate Veteran* 29 (1921): 391; memorial in *Virginia Reports* 179 (1942): vii–x, reprinted in *Virginia State Bar Association Proceedings* (1942): 111–113.

PETER WALLENSTEIN

BUCHANAN, John Lee (19 June 1831–19 January 1922), president of the Virginia Agricultural and Mechanical College and superintendent of public instruction, was born on a farm in Smyth County, the son of Patrick Campbell Buchanan and Margaret Ann Graham Buchanan. He obtained his early education in a neighborhood school and subsequently clerked in a store where the wit and wisdom he heard around the legendary cracker barrel instilled an interest in the classics and a desire to attend college. In 1851 Buchanan enrolled in nearby Emory and Henry College as a preparatory student, and one year later he entered the freshman class to pursue a traditional liberal arts course.

Buchanan found the rigors of the classical tradition congenial. He captured the available academic honors, served as an assistant instructor of Greek and Latin in the academic years 1852–1853 and 1853–1854, and graduated as valedictorian of the class of 1856. His facility with ancient languages earned him an invitation to remain and teach in the place of his mentor, William E. Peters, who had taken leave to study in Germany. In 1858 Buchanan became a full professor of mathematics at Emory and Henry, and the next year he received its M.A. On 4 August 1859 he married Frances Elizabeth Wiley, daughter of the president of the college. They had five sons and four daughters.

After the Civil War began Buchanan, a proficient blacksmith, carpenter, and furniture maker, moved back to his father's farm to mine saltpeter, used for the manufacture of gunpowder. He remained there until 1865, when he resumed teaching mathematics at Emory and Henry. In 1866 Buchanan began a twelve-year tenure as chairman of ancient languages, and in June 1877 Emory and Henry granted him an honorary LL.D. He accepted a position on the faculty of Vanderbilt University in 1878, but he returned to Emory and Henry the following year as president-elect. Six months later, however, Buchanan resigned to become president of the Virginia Agricultural and Mechanical College (later Virginia Polytechnic Institute and State University), the land-grant college in Blacksburg. The institution, which had been directed to emphasize the military elements of education, was wracked by internal dissension and suffered from declining enrollment. It soon became a victim of state politics. After control of the state government shifted to the Readjusters, the new General Assembly replaced the board of visitors and ordered it in turn to replace the faculty and administrators of the college. Buchanan, a Democrat, was elected president on 10 December 1879, took office on 1 March 1880, but was dismissed in June of that year. During the swift political changes on the board, he was offered the presidency again and declined in August. After one distinguished educator resigned almost immediately and another refused the job twice, Buchanan accepted the presidency a second time in May 1881 and returned to office in August of that year, only to be removed again on 17 January 1882 by a new board appointed by the incoming governor.

With his father-in-law, Ephraim E. Wiley, Buchanan conducted Martha Washington College, a private school for women in Abingdon, from 1882 to 1884. He sat on a committee that selected Farmville as the site for the new State Female Normal School (later Longwood College) and served as vice president of the school's board of trustees. At the end of December 1885 the Democratic General Assembly elected Buchanan superintendent of public instruction.

That appointment placed Buchanan on the State Board of Education ex officio and enabled him to be present when the members of the board of the Agricultural and Mechanical College who had dismissed him the second time were themselves dismissed.

As superintendent of public instruction from 15 March 1886 until he resigned effective 1 January 1890, Buchanan had responsibility for the struggling public school system and for the administration of such funds as a parsimonious General Assembly saw fit to appropriate. Many Virginians dismissed the public schools as unnecessary and irrelevant, but during their brief existence school enrollments had mushroomed. Buchanan served the public trust with distinction and contributed to a more rational organization of the system. He kept a low profile concerning financing, preferring that economic growth bring necessary financial resources rather than asking for an increase in taxes. Buchanan's philosophy of education derived from the mental discipline of his own education. He regarded education as the transmission of culture from one generation to another, perpetuating civilization through emphasis on virtue and intelligence, the hallmarks of good citizenship. Buchanan published four annual reports containing statistical compilations about Virginia's public schools, and as superintendent he coedited four volumes of the semiofficial *Educational Journal of Virginia*.

Declining an offer to become president of the College of William and Mary, Buchanan left office as superintendent of public instruction to teach Latin at Randolph-Macon College. On 8 January 1894 he became president of the Arkansas Industrial University (after 1899 the University of Arkansas). His eight-year reform administration, which included creation of the Departments of Economics and Sociology, earned him the respect and affection of the university and the community. In June 1902 Buchanan suffered a stroke and retired. Named emeritus professor of Latin by the university, he lived in Fayetteville until his wife's death in June 1908 and then returned to the family farm in Virginia, where he devoted his time to gardening and splinting chairs. John Lee Buchanan died of a cerebral hemorrhage at his brother's home in

Smyth County on 19 January 1922 and was buried beside the body of his wife in Evergreen Cemetery in Fayetteville, Arkansas. All University of Arkansas and public school classes in the town were dismissed during the funeral, and Fayetteville stores closed at 3:00 P.M. in Buchanan's honor.

Biographies in *NCAB*, 29:218–219, Bruce, Tyler, and Morton, *History of Virginia*, 4:154–155, and John Hugh Reynolds and David Yancey Thomas, *History of the University of Arkansas* (1910), 431–433; autobiographical material in Reynolds-Thomas Research Papers, Biographies, 1908–1909, University of Arkansas Libraries, Fayetteville; John Benjamin May, "The Life of John Lee Buchanan" (Ph.D. diss., UVA, 1937), contains bibliography of manuscripts; BVS Marriage Register, Washington Co.; George J. Stevenson, *Increase in Excellence: A History of Emory and Henry College* (1963), 88, 92, 102–103 (pors. following 96, 144); D. L. Kinnear, *The First 100 Years: A History of Virginia Polytechnic Institute and State University* (1972), 99–110, 119, 137–139 (por. facing 147); Peter Wallenstein, *Virginia Tech, Land-Grant University, 1872–1997: History of a School, a State, a Nation* (1997), 64–67; *Educational Journal of Virginia* 16 (1885): 557–558, and 21 (1890): 32–33; BVS Death Certificate, Smyth Co.; obituary, editorial tribute, and account of funeral in *Fayetteville Daily Democrat*, 19, 20, 23 Jan. 1922; obituaries in *Richmond Times-Dispatch*, 20 Jan. 1922, and *Marion News*, 26 Jan. 1922.

GEORGE J. STEVENSON

BUCK, Carrie Elizabeth (2 July 1906–28 January 1983), principal in a court case, was born in Charlottesville, the daughter of Frank W. Buck, a tinner, and Emma A. Harlow Buck. Her father died when she was very young. In April 1920 her mother was committed to the Virginia State Colony for Epileptics and Feeble-Minded in Lynchburg with a diagnosis of feeblemindedness, a vague term that was less a medical finding than a reflection of the examiners' distaste for her sexual behavior. Carrie Buck had been removed from her mother's care when she was three and placed with a foster family. She attended local schools, where her records indicate normal progress each year, but before she completed sixth grade her foster family withdrew her to perform housework for them.

In 1923 Carrie Buck became pregnant, by her account as the result of rape committed by a nephew of the foster family with whom she had lived for almost fourteen years. Believing that the pregnancy was evidence of promiscuity and thus of feeblemindedness, the foster family sought to have her committed, like her mother, to the Virginia State Colony for Epileptics and Feeble-Minded. At a hearing on 23 January 1924, Buck was adjudged epileptic and feebleminded. Following the birth on 28 March 1924 of an illegitimate daughter, Vivian Alice Elaine Buck, Buck entered the colony in Lynchburg on 4 June. Her former foster family took her infant daughter into their home and gave her their name.

Shortly after Buck's commitment, Albert Sidney Priddy, superintendent and physician at the colony, selected her to be the subject of the test case for the constitutionality of Virginia's recently enacted involuntary sterilization statute. This law provided that the state could sterilize anyone found to be incompetent because of alcoholism, epilepsy, feeblemindedness, insanity, or other factors. Behind the law was the eugenic assumption that these traits were hereditary and that sexual sterilization could thus prevent their transmission. Uncertain that the new law could withstand a constitutional challenge, the framers and supporters of the law arranged to test it in court. They chose Buck in the belief that she had inherited her feeblemindedness from her mother and that her daughter showed signs of slow mental development as well.

The litigation went to circuit and appeals courts in Virginia, where the judges approved Buck's sterilization. Eventually styled *Buck* v. *Bell* (referring to John Hendren Bell, the superintendent of the Virginia colony following Priddy's death in 1925), the case went on to the United States Supreme Court in April 1927. On 2 May of that year the Court ruled that Virginia's law was constitutional and that Buck should be sterilized. In the majority opinion Justice Oliver Wendell Holmes enthusiastically declared that the "principle that sustains compulsory vaccination is broad enough to cover cutting the Fallopian tubes." In an oft-quoted phrase, he concluded that "three generations of imbeciles are enough." Consequently, Buck and approximately 8,300 other Virginians, including her younger half sister, were sterilized under the state law between 1927 and 1972.

After being surgically sterilized on 19 October 1927 and released from the Virginia colony

to work for a family in Bland County, Buck married William Davis Eagle, a widowed carpenter, on 14 May 1932. A quarter century after his death on 23 July 1941, she married Charles Albert Detamore, of Front Royal, on 25 April 1965. Friends, relatives, and professionals who knew her later in life deny the accuracy of her diagnosis as mentally retarded. She was independent and a helpful person to others for most of her life. Carrie Elizabeth Buck Eagle Detamore died on 28 January 1983 in a nursing home in Waynesboro and was buried in Oakwood Cemetery in Charlottesville. Vivian Dobbs, the daughter from whom she was separated shortly after giving birth, is buried on an adjacent hillside. Belying Justice Holmes's famous opinion, Dobbs was an honor student when she died of enterocolitis on 3 July 1932 at age eight. The practice of involuntary sterilization did not cease in Virginia institutions until 1972, and the enabling act remained on the books until April 1974.

J. David Smith and K. Ray Nelson, *The Sterilization of Carrie Buck* (1989), gives birth date from commitment records (pors.); grave marker gives variant birth date of 15 Mar. 1903; parents' marriage in BVS Marriage Register, Charlottesville, 1896; Bland Co. Marriage Register, 1932; *Buck* v. *Bell* (1927), *United States Reports*, 274:200–208 (quotations on 207); *Charlottesville Daily Progress*, 24, 26 Feb. 1980; *Richmond Times-Dispatch*, 27 Feb. 1980; Paul A. Lombardo, "Eugenic Sterilization in Virginia: Aubrey Strode and the Case of *Buck* v. *Bell*" (Ph.D. diss., UVA, 1982), and "Three Generations, No Imbeciles: New Light on *Buck* v. *Bell*," *New York University Law Review* 60 (1985): 30–62; death notice in *Charlottesville Daily Progress*, 30 Jan. 1983.

J. DAVID SMITH

BUCK, Dorothea Dutcher (31 July 1887–9 May 1983), president of the General Federation of Women's Clubs, was born in Milwaukee, Wisconsin, the daughter of socially prominent parents, Pierpont Edwards Dutcher, a banker, and Fanny Louise Bull Dutcher. She attended Briarcliff College in Briarcliff Manor, New York, and a private school in Florence, Italy. She studied briefly at Milwaukee-Downer College (later Lawrence University) and pursued interests in painting and portraiture at the Art Students' League in New York.

After her marriage to James Lawrence Blair Buck in Magnolia, near Gloucester, Massachusetts, on 19 September 1914, she moved to Hampton, where her husband served on the faculty at Hampton Normal and Agricultural Institute (later Hampton University). They had one son and two daughters. Mrs. J. L. Blair Buck, as she usually gave her name, began her long career in public service and volunteerism by organizing a series of canteens during World War I. In 1926 she became the first president of the Woman's Club of Hampton. Buck later enjoyed recalling that she arrived after the start of the first meeting, took the only available seat, which was in the front row, and because of the prominence of her entrance was elected president.

In 1930 the Bucks moved to Richmond, where she joined the Richmond Woman's Club, the Ginter Park Woman's Club, and the Tuckahoe Woman's Club. Her organizational abilities at the local club level led to her election that year as president of the Virginia Federation of Women's Clubs. Buck served from 1930 to 1932. During these worst years of the Great Depression, the state federation worked for unemployment relief and thrift programs in the local club communities. Buck also served as the Virginia director of the national General Federation of Women's Clubs and in 1933 moved into its leadership after chairing the arrangements committee for the federation's meeting in Richmond. She was defeated in a three-way race for recording secretary in 1935 but was elected chair of the budget (1935–1938), treasurer (1938–1941), second vice president (1941–1944), and first vice president (1944–1947).

Buck's service to the General Federation of Women's Clubs culminated in her term as president from 1947 to 1950. The first Virginian to hold that office, she promoted a program of building world peace and advocated support of the United Nations. To honor her lobbying for the Marshall Plan, Secretary of State George Catlett Marshall attended the 1948 GFWC convention. Buck participated in the Town Hall World Seminar tour in 1949 and spoke in several countries on the need for building world peace. She also emphasized the work that local clubs could do to better their communities. Buck's administration initiated a continuing nationwide project of the federation, the Build a Better Community Program, which she considered her greatest accomplishment. She also strongly supported the federation's America Home and Youth Conservation Programs. President Harry S. Truman appointed Buck to the Citizens' Food Committee. During her term as president of the federation, she represented it on more than thirty national boards and traveled to China, Cuba, Denmark, Egypt, France, Great Britain, Greece, India, Japan, Korea, the Philippines, and Turkey on official federation business.

After her term concluded, Buck resumed her many civic activities in Richmond, which included membership in the Richmond chapter of the American Red Cross, the Richmond Theatre Guild, and the Virginia League for Planned Parenthood. Briefly in 1951 she worked for the Federal Civil Defense Agency as the regional director of women's activities. Buck was a member of the Virginia Democrats for Eisenhower in 1952 and in 1954 was elected president of the Virginia United Nations Association. From 1954 to 1956 she chaired the Virginia Centennial Committee of the Young Women's Christian Association.

Buck possessed many qualities that made her a natural leader. She had sensitivity, balanced judgment, and the ability to designate the appropriate person for each job. Buck's home was always open to visitors, and she was a brilliant conversationalist. She enjoyed many outdoor activities and sports including golf, sailing, swimming, and tennis. A woman of deep convictions, Buck and her husband moved their membership from Richmond's Grace Covenant Presbyterian Church to the new Saint Giles' Presbyterian Church in 1937 when Grace Covenant's congregation split as a result of the participation of its pastor, John Blanton Belk, in what became the Moral Re-Armament movement. The Bucks supported Belk and were charter members of the new church, and she was elected its first woman elder after her husband's death on 16 March 1964.

Buck pursued her many artistic, church, civic, family, and world interests until 1979, when failing health prompted her to move to a nursing facility in Chester, Connecticut, near the home of one of her daughters. Dorothea Dutcher Buck died there on 9 May 1983 and was buried beside the ashes of her husband in Washington Cemetery in Washington, Connecticut.

Current Biography: Who's News and Why, 1947 (1948), 72–74; Etta Belle Walker Northington, *A History of the Virginia Federation of Women's Clubs, 1907–1957* [1958], 64–69; family history verified by son, Pierpont B. Buck; *Gloucester (Mass.) Daily Times,* 29 Sept. 1914; Presidents' Papers and State Federation Records (Virginia Federation of Women's Clubs), General Federation of Women's Clubs Archives, Washington, D.C.; Mary Jean Houde, *Reaching Out: A Story of the General Federation of Women's Clubs* (1989); Mildred White Wells, *Unity in Diversity: The History of the General Federation of Women's Clubs* (1953); Sandra Gioia Treadway, *Women of Mark: A History of the Woman's Club of Richmond, Virginia, 1894–1994* (1995), pors.; *New York Times,* 5 May 1935 (por.), 26, 28 June, 10 July, 11, 12 Nov. 1947, 26 May 1948, 26 Apr., 11 May 1949, 30 May 1950; *Richmond News Leader,* 20 June 1947; Louis A. Skidmore and Chloris B. Fohl, *A History of St. Giles' Presbyterian Church* [ca. 1987], 62, Appendix 2, 15, 30; obituaries in *Richmond News Leader* and *Richmond Times-Dispatch,* both 10 May 1983.

LISA C. MANGIAFICO

BUCK, James Lawrence Blair (13 April 1886–16 March 1964), educator, was born at Fort Benton, Montana, the son of Horace Riverside Buck and Mary Elizabeth Jewett Buck. His father, a justice of the Montana Supreme Court, died in 1897, after which Buck's mother moved the family back to her native New Haven, Connecticut. He was educated at the Hopkins Grammar School in New Haven and the Gunnery School in Washington, Connecticut.

J. L. Blair Buck, as he was known as an adult, graduated from Yale University with a Ph.B. in electrical engineering in 1906. He worked for the General Electric Company in West Lynn, Massachusetts, for one year before becoming an electrical engineer for the Pennsylvania Railroad in Altoona, Pennsylvania. After taking courses in agriculture at Pennsylvania State College, Buck in 1911 purchased a farm in Charles County, Maryland, but his dream of living a simple agricultural life quickly soured. Later that same year he and a Yale classmate visited Hampton Normal and Agricultural Institute (later Hampton University). The classmate's father, the school's president, offered Buck a job as an assistant to the director of agriculture, and Buck accepted.

Having begun his career in education, Buck believed he was settled enough to start a family.

On 19 September 1914 he married Dorothea Dutcher, the sister of another Yale classmate and later a prominent women's organization leader. They had one son and two daughters. Because northern philanthropists had traditionally provided a large proportion of the institute's funding, during Buck's years at Hampton his household hosted a number of prominent businessmen, educators, and politicians visiting the school, including Andrew Carnegie, William Cameron Forbes, George Foster Peabody, and William Howard Taft. In November 1915 Buck joined Battery D of the 1st Virginia Field Artillery, Virginia National Guard, and he was absent from Hampton for more than a year attending officer training schools. He was promoted to captain on 15 August 1917 and to major in the coast artillery on 13 October 1918. World War I ended shortly before Buck was scheduled to go to Europe, and on 13 January 1919 he was discharged at Washington, D.C. He returned to Hampton as director of extension work, a new position in which he worked with black schools. Buck also traveled on fund-raising campaigns in 1924 and 1925. In 1927 he received an Ed.M. from Harvard University.

By the time Buck joined the faculty, Hampton Institute had become primarily a school for training teachers. The trade school and the agricultural and home economics departments preserved the industrial education tradition on which Hampton had been founded. Buck naively believed that the institute was grounded in a progressive philosophy of learning by doing and never made the connection between the school's curriculum of menial labor and the persistent economic and educational deprivation experienced by southern blacks. Buck showed little evidence that racial segregation troubled him, but on 27 November 1925 he represented Hampton Institute at a meeting in the city of Hampton at which spokesmen for the Anglo-Saxon Clubs of America charged the school with advocating equality of the races and intermarriage. He was one of two among the 300 people present who spoke against a proposed resolution condemning Hampton Institute and requesting legislation requiring segregated seating at public assemblages. Buck did not persuade the crowd to withdraw the resolution, but it was watered down to charge only that the institute's teachings tended to encourage racial intermarriage. In the context of the time, he had won a small victory against racial unfairness.

In 1930 Buck moved to Richmond as assistant state supervisor of secondary education under Harris Hart, Virginia's superintendent of public instruction. He was therefore strategically placed in 1931 when the next superintendent, Sidney Bartlett Hall, began a controversial curriculum revision. Hall invited a number of prominent educational innovators to come to Virginia and tried to involve classroom teachers in the development of the new curriculum. As supervisor of secondary education in the Division of Instruction, Buck played a key role in devising the new curriculum, which was based on the belief that schools should lead their communities out of dependence on old ideas of individualism and into a future of collective planning. In January 1938 he was appointed director of the Division of Instruction in the Department of Education, and in 1941, the year Hall resigned under pressure, Buck became director of the Division of Teacher Education. He received an award in 1940 from the professional honor society, Phi Delta Kappa, for his service to education.

With the outbreak of World War II, Buck tried to enlist in the army but was rejected as too old. During the war he served as president of the Richmond Children's Aid Society and sat on the board of the Richmond Public Forum. Buck also turned his attention to completing his doctoral dissertation, begun under a General Education Board grant awarded for graduate work at the University of Michigan in 1933 and 1934. He received his Ph.D. in 1942, and a decade later the Virginia State Board of Education published his dissertation as *The Development of Public Schools in Virginia, 1607–1952,* the first modern comprehensive history of education in the commonwealth.

Buck spent the 1947–1948 academic year in England as a visiting professor of education at the University of London's Institute of Education. He and his wife, who was serving as president of the General Federation of Women's Clubs, also traveled through Europe. During his ten-month leave of absence Buck was named

coordinator of teacher education in the Virginia Department of Education's Division of Teacher Education (after June 1952 the Division of Teacher Education and Certification). In 1951 he served as vice president of the Southern Association of Colleges and Secondary Schools. He also sat on the central committee of the Department of Interracial Cooperation, an affiliate of the Virginia Council of Churches. Buck was deeply disturbed when the state government responded with a program of Massive Resistance to the United States Supreme Court's ruling in 1954 that racial segregation in the public schools was unconstitutional. On 1 July 1956, at age seventy, he retired, but as head of the Virginia Committee for Public Schools he continued to combat the hysteria that opponents of desegregation promoted.

Buck was an admirer of Frank N. D. Buchman, the founder of what came to be known as the Oxford Group movement, or Moral Re-Armament, devoted to nondenominational Christian evangelism. In 1937 Buck and his wife moved their membership from Richmond's Grace Covenant Presbyterian Church to the new Saint Giles' Presbyterian Church after Grace Covenant's congregation split as a result of the participation of the pastor, John Blanton Belk, in Moral Re-Armament. The Bucks supported Belk and were charter members of the new church. After his retirement Buck traveled thousands of miles each year promoting the Moral Re-Armament movement in Latin America and Europe.

James Lawrence Blair Buck began work on a family history and his memoirs but had not completed them when he died in Richmond on 16 March 1964 after exploratory cancer surgery. His ashes were buried in Washington Cemetery in Washington, Connecticut.

MS autobiography in possession of daughter Frances Buck Hamilton, 2000, who verified family history; feature article in *Richmond Times-Dispatch,* 4 Jan. 1962 (por.); some Buck letters in Editorial Correspondence Files of the *Norfolk Virginian-Pilot,* Kathryn H. Stone Papers, and Louise O. Wensel Papers, all UVA; birth date in Military Service Records; *Gloucester (Mass.) Daily Times,* 29 Sept. 1914; *Newport News Daily Press,* 28, 29 Nov. 1925; *Virginia Journal of Education* 41 (Oct. 1947): 104–105; published works include Buck, *The Patrons' League on a Business Basis* (1922); obituaries in *Richmond Times-Dispatch,* 17 Mar. 1964 (por.), and *Virginia Journal of*

Education 57 (Apr. 1964): 39; editorial tribute in *Richmond Times-Dispatch*, 19 Mar. 1964.

MICHAEL E. JAMES

BUCKE, Richard (1581 or 1582–by January 1624), Anglican minister, was the son of Edmund Bucke and a mother whose name is unknown. He was born in the county of Norfolk, England, and attended a local school. On 26 April 1600 he was admitted at age eighteen as a sizar, or student on scholarship, to Gonville and Caius College, Cambridge University. Bucke was married, possibly to Elizabeth Browne, on 7 July 1607 in Tharston Parish, Norfolk, and had at least one daughter before, on the recommendation of the bishop of London, he was appointed chaplain of the expedition headed by Sir Thomas Gates that departed Plymouth Sound for Virginia on 2 June 1609.

The *Sea Venture*, on which Bucke and his family traveled, ran afoul of a hurricane late in July. After about five days of tumultuous weather, the vessel wrecked on one of the Bermuda islands. During the nine and a half months that the 150 colonists were stranded on the island, Bucke delivered sermons twice on Sundays, mostly on the subjects of thanksgiving and unity, and performed a marriage, two baptisms, and five funerals. Finally able to build two smaller vessels, the party left the island on 10 May 1610, arrived at Point Comfort on 21 May, and landed on 23 May at Jamestown. There Bucke made "a zealous and sorrowfull Prayer, finding all things so contrary to our expectations, so full of misery and misgovernment."

The minister in the colony having died, Bucke found himself the only clergyman in Virginia and conducted twice-daily services in an effort to improve the colonists' morale during this unsettling period. Later his fellow minister Alexander Whitaker characterized him in 1613 as "an able and painfull Preacher." In April 1614 Bucke performed the marriage ceremony for John Rolfe, with whom he had traveled on the *Sea Venture*, and Pocahontas, and he later witnessed Rolfe's will. On 30 July 1619 Bucke opened the initial meeting of the first legislative assembly in Virginia with prayer. At least twice in 1621 he requested Sir Edwin Sandys's assistance in getting the Virginia Company of London to fulfill the terms of its agreement with him, both in payments and in supplying indentured servants, because the terms of the latter already assigned to him were soon due to expire. Bucke resided on a 750-acre tract, including glebe land, in Jamestown promised him by the company and patented in 1620.

Bucke may have returned to England at least once. It is possible that his wife died and that he remarried, perhaps to a woman named Bridget. Bucke had three sons and one daughter born in Virginia between 1611 and 1620. Two of these children won some notice in their own right. Mara Bucke, the eldest, was the subject of a case heard in the General Court in 1624. Following testimony regarding rumors that David Sandys, a minister, planned to steal the thirteen-year-old away from her guardians' house and marry her, the court instructed her guardians to give security that they would thwart any marriage attempts. Benoni Bucke, born in 1616, proved incapable of managing his inheritance and, deemed "the first Ideott found in that plantation," became in 1637 the first subject of a commission to determine competency. The names given the four children born in the colony reflect the possible Puritan philosophy of Bucke as well as the hardships he endured in Virginia: Mara (bitter), Gershon (expulsion), Benoni (sorrow), and Peleg (division).

The exact date of Richard Bucke's death is unknown. He is not listed among those killed during the Powhatan uprising in March 1622, but the census of January 1624 omitted him and described his four youngest children as living in three different households, which strongly suggests that he was dead by then. On 21 June 1624 the General Court ordered his daughter's guardians to give £100 security to the executors of the minister's estate.

Adventurers of Purse and Person, 140–143; James T. Buck, *Rev. Richard Buck and Family at Jamestown* (n.d.); William Curry Harllee, *Kinfolks: A Genealogical and Biographical Record* (1935), 2:1209–1222; John Venn and J. A. Venn, comps., *Alumni Cantabrigienses* (1922–1954), pt. 1, 1:245; Tharston Parish Register, Norfolk, Eng.; Bucke letters with signature in Ferrar Papers, Magdalene College, Cambridge University, Eng.; William Strachey, "A True Reportory," in Samuel Purchas, *Purchas His Pilgrimes* (1625; repr. 1905–1907), 19:37–38, 41, 44 (first quotation), 59; Alexander Whitaker, *Good Newes from Virginia* (1613), C1v (second quotation); Kingsbury, *Virginia Company*, 3:155, 443–444, 460–461, 4:555–556; Seth Mallios with Garrett Fesler, *Archaeological Excavations at 44JC568, The Reverend Richard Buck Site* (1999); *Minutes of Council and General Court*, 16, 86, 100, 117; PRO CO 1/9, fols. 128 (third quotation), 129–131, CO 1/10, fols. 65–68.

IRENE W. D. HECHT

BUCKLAND, William (14 August 1734–by 15 December 1774), builder, was born in Oxford, England, the son of Francis Buckland, a farmer, and Mary Dunsdown Buckland. At age thirteen on 5 April 1748, with his fee paid as a charitable act by the University School of Oxford, he was apprenticed to an uncle in London, James Buckland, a member of the Worshipful Company of Joiners. Less than a year later this uncle died, and Buckland continued his training under a new master, John Whiteaves, a carpenter and fellow native of Oxford.

In 1755 Buckland completed his training, which included exposure to the latest English architecture and pattern books. Skilled craftsmen with such a background were much in demand in the American colonies, where potential clients were anxious to import the best English goods and services. On 4 August 1755 Buckland signed an indenture in London with Thomson Mason, brother of George Mason, who was building a new house in Fairfax County. Buckland spent the next four years finishing Gunston Hall, Mason's plantation house, and creating its interior details. Buckland's work at Gunston Hall has long been known, but much of his original work decorating the interior was lost, making the extent of his design influence on the house uncertain. Twentieth-century investigations uncovered many of the details created under his direction and executed by the craftsmen whom he supervised. By the time Buckland's contract ended, Gunston Hall was a tastefully finished residence exhibiting elegant classical details. On 8 November 1759 George Mason marked the conclusion of Buckland's service by praising him as "a complete Master of the Carpenter's & Joiner's Business, both in Theory & in Practice."

In 1758 or 1759 Buckland married Mary Moore, whose father, William Moore, owned a small plantation. They had two sons and two daughters, the latter of whom both married prominently in Annapolis, Maryland. Buckland moved to Richmond County in 1761 and later purchased a farm there. He established a workshop patterned on the guild tradition of his background. Buckland employed two native-born apprentices and several English indentured craftsmen. He executed several public and private commissions during the 1760s, but few examples of his work survive. The papers of Landon Carter, of Sabine Hall, and John Tayloe (1721–1779), of Mount Airy, refer frequently to Buckland, but most of the work he did for them is lost. Serving tables he designed for Tayloe are in the collections of the Colonial Williamsburg Foundation and the Museum of Early Southern Decorative Arts.

In 1771 Buckland moved to Annapolis, probably at the urging of Tayloe's son-in-law Edward Lloyd. Buckland quickly proved his ability as a designer and architect. A wealthy merchant and planter, Lloyd had purchased a half-finished brick house in Maryland's capital. Buckland agreed to complete its construction and designed the striking decorative details that distinguish the interior. In 1774 he began a new house for Mathias Hammond, his only known opportunity to design and build a house from the beginning. The Hammond-Harwood House, as it is now known, attests to Buckland's knowledge of English Palladianism and the current fashion in decoration. It also demonstrates his talent for design. The house is visually pleasing in scale and proportion and also rich in high-style decoration.

Buckland was a skilled joiner and designer noted for bringing the time-honored standards of the English building trades to Virginia and Maryland. In the progression of his career from joiner to architect during his two decades in America, he helped establish a tradition of fine decorative and architectural design in the Chesapeake region. In a portrait begun in 1774 but completed more than a decade later, Charles Willson Peale depicted Buckland as a man of slight build, with brown hair, hazel eyes, and an engaging smile. In the painting he is dressed modestly and seated at a baize-covered table with books, drafting tools, and a sketch of the Hammond-Harwood House, his last commission, beside him.

Buckland evidently designed a courthouse for Maryland's new county of Caroline. He probably attended a meeting convened at Melvills Warehouse in that county on 16 and 17 November 1774 for contractors bidding to erect the new structure. William Buckland died, probably on Maryland's Eastern Shore, sometime before 15 December 1774, when the sale of his estate was advertised. His burial place is unknown.

Rosamond Randall Beirne and John Henry Scarff, *William Buckland, 1734–1774: Architect of Virginia and Maryland* (1958), prints essential documents, frontispiece por., and 19 Dec. 1774 estate inventory (quotation on 143); Saint Peter in the East Parish Register, Oxford, Oxfordshire Record Office, Eng.; Worshipful Company of Joiners, Register of Apprenticeship Bindings, 5 Apr. 1748, and its Court Book, 6 Mar. 1749, both in Guildhall Library, London, Eng.; 4 Aug. 1755 indenture with George Mason's subjoined testimonial, Gunston Hall Archives, Mason Neck, Va. Charles A. Phillips and Paul Buchanan, "Physical Study of Gunston Hall" (unpublished research reports, 1982–1989), Gunston Hall Archives; Luke Beckerdite, "William Buckland and William Bernard Sears: The Designer and the Carver," and "William Buckland Reconsidered: Architectural Carving in Chesapeake Maryland, 1771–1774," *Journal of Early Southern Decorative Arts* 8 (Nov. 1982): 7–41, 43–88; Barbara Allston Brand, "William Buckland: Architect in Annapolis," *Building by the Book* 2 (1986): 65–100; death recorded at Dec. 1774 court session, Anne Arundel Co. Testamentary Papers, 83:141, Maryland State Archives, Annapolis; estate sale advertised in *Annapolis Maryland Gazette*, 15 Dec. 1774.

BARBARA ALLSTON BRAND

BUCKNER, John (d. by 10 February 1696), merchant and sponsor of the first printing press in Virginia, was born probably in London early in the 1630s. The dates of his birth and marriage and the names of his parents and wife are all unknown. He had one son born about 1657 and at least three other sons and at least one daughter, all born after that year. Buckner immigrated to Virginia, probably early in the 1660s, and by February 1665 had acquired property in Gloucester County. During the next twenty-four years he obtained, alone and in conjunction with several other men, patents for more than 26,000 acres in the watersheds of the Rappahannock and York Rivers. His brother Philip Buckner immigrated to Virginia in 1667 and settled in Stafford County.

John Buckner planted tobacco and acted as a merchant on his own account. Most likely he also engaged in the slave trade, although whether as an importer or local retailer is not certain. Buckner became a man of consequence within a few years of his arrival and by November 1677 was named clerk of Gloucester County, a position he held until at least July 1693. His service on the vestry of Petsworth Parish made him the senior member at the time of the parish's earliest extant record, dated 23 January 1677, and in September 1684 he became churchwarden for the middle and lower part of the parish. Buckner was elected to the House of Burgesses from Gloucester County early in 1682 and served in the sessions that met in April and November of that year. On 2 December 1682 he and three other prominent men posted a bond of £2,000 to guarantee the appearance of Robert Beverley (1635–1687) before the General Court to face charges arising from the plant-cutting riots of the previous year.

Sometime in 1681 or 1682 Buckner assisted in the immigration to Virginia of William Nuthead, a printer who brought the first printing press to the colony. Early in 1683 Nuthead printed some of the laws passed at the November 1682 session of the General Assembly and several other documents that are not described in surviving records. English law required prior approval to print public records, and on 21 February 1683 the governor and Council charged Buckner with having the laws printed "without lycense." In the printer's defense Buckner stated that Nuthead had printed only two sheets intended for presentation to the governor for his approbation, but the Council ordered Buckner and Nuthead to post a secured bond of £100 sterling to print nothing else until the king's "pleasure shall be known therein." In December 1683 Charles II accordingly instructed the new governor, Francis Howard, baron Howard of Effingham, "to provide by all necessary orders and directions that noe person bee permitted to use any press for printing upon any occasion whatsoever."

Nuthead probably left Virginia soon after the Council's prohibition, and he became the first printer in Maryland. Following his death early in 1695, his widow, Dinah Nuthead, succeeded him as the second printer in that colony. The prohibition against printing in Virginia was modified in

October 1690 when royal instructions to Lieutenant Governor Francis Nicholson specified that "noe person use any Press for Printing upon any occasion whatsoever without your Especiall Leave first obtained." No one attempted to set up a press again in Virginia until William Parks opened a branch of his Annapolis printing office in Williamsburg in 1730 and printed the laws of Virginia then in force under the express authority of the assembly three years later.

Buckner's prominent status was not diminished by this incident, nor did the episode prevent his sons from playing responsible roles in the colony's government. Buckner may have represented Gloucester County in the House of Burgesses in the autumn of 1693, but it is possible that the burgess that year was his namesake son, who certainly served in the assembly in 1715. Buckner's sons also included Thomas Buckner, who served in the House in 1698, 1715, and 1718; Richard Buckner, clerk of the House of Burgesses from 1712 to 1715; and William Buckner, who represented York County in the House in 1698, 1699, 1710, and 1712–1714 and became deputy surveyor general of the colony in 1709.

John Buckner's attendance at a meeting of the Petsworth Parish vestry on 7 December 1694 is the last reference to him in the public records. He missed the next meeting, on 7 October 1695, and may have been dead by then. If not, he died not long thereafter. An inventory valuing his personal estate (including eight slaves) at more than £168 sterling was returned to the Gloucester County Court on 10 February 1696.

Genealogy in William Armstrong Crozier, ed., *The Buckners of Virginia and the Allied Families of Strother and Ashby* (1907), 20–26, contradicted in some vital particulars by two depositions of William Buckner in 1693 and 1697 (PRO C 22/1003, fol. 1, and C 22/908, fol. 26); George Harrison Sanford King, "The Buckner Family," *Virginia Genealogist* 42 (1998): 243–246; numerous references in *Cavaliers and Pioneers* (earliest record in Virginia, 1 Feb. 1665, on 1:450), and Richard Beale Davis, ed., *William Fitzhugh and His Chesapeake World, 1676–1701: The Fitzhugh Letters and Other Documents* (1963); Polly Cary Mason, *Records of Colonial Gloucester County, Virginia* (1948), 2:86; Churchill G. Chamberlayne, ed., *The Vestry Book of Petsworth Parish, Gloucester County, Virginia, 1677–1793* (1933), esp. 1, 5, 40, 41; Lawrence C. Wroth, *A History of Printing in Colonial Maryland, 1686–1776* (1922), 1–16; Douglas C. McMurtrie, *The First Printing in Virginia* (1935), 3–4, and *The Beginnings of Printing in Virginia* (1935), 5–7; 21 Feb. 1683 action of Council in PRO CO 1/51, fols. 98–99 (first quotation), partially transcribed and abstracted in Hening, *Statutes,* 2:518, and in *Executive Journals of Council,* 1:493; Billings, *Effingham Papers,* 44 (second quotation); instructions to Nicholson in PRO CO 5/1357, fol. 338 (third quotation); estate inventory in Essex Co. Deeds, Wills, Etc., 9:6.

DAPHNE GENTRY

BUCKNER, Richard (d. by 14 March 1734), clerk of the House of Burgesses, was born probably in the mid-1670s in Gloucester County, the youngest son of John Buckner, who by himself and in partnership with several other men patented more than 26,000 acres of land between 1667 and 1691. The name of his mother is not known. His immigrant father made the family an important one in a short time and represented Gloucester County in the House of Burgesses in 1682 and perhaps again in 1693; his brother William Buckner lived in Yorktown and represented York County in 1698, 1699, 1710, and 1712–1714 and became deputy surveyor general of the colony in 1709; his brother Thomas Buckner represented Gloucester County in the House of Burgesses in 1698, 1715, and 1718; and his brother John Buckner may have been a member of the House in 1693 and represented Gloucester County in 1715.

On 22 September 1682 John Buckner assigned the patent to a 500-acre tract of land in Rappahannock County to his underage son, Richard Buckner. That land was in the portion of the county that in 1692 became Essex County, and Richard Buckner lived all of his adult life on that property. By 1704 he owned three tracts totaling about 1,200 acres. On 10 June 1703 Buckner became clerk of Essex County, a position he held until the beginning of 1715. In September 1704 the governor's Council named Buckner and three other men to conduct the trial of several Nanzatico Indians accused of murdering a family in Richmond County, and in 1706 the Council appointed him and three other men to meet on behalf of the colony with deputies of the proprietor of the Northern Neck to determine the location of the main channel of the Rappahannock River. When the commissioners proved unable to agree, that attempt to establish the southern boundary of the proprietary failed.

Like his father, Buckner engaged in land speculation, occasionally in conjunction with other men. He bought and sold town lots in Tappahannock and property in the counties of King and Queen, King George, Prince William, and Spotsylvania. In May 1713 Buckner was a silent partner with Larkin Chew and others in acquiring rights to more than 4,000 acres in the upper part of Essex County that Chew sold four weeks later to Lieutenant Governor Alexander Spotswood. The land contained rich iron ore deposits. Spotswood later settled a party of German miners on the property, which he called Germanna, and made his fortune.

Buckner had evidently allied himself with Spotswood soon after Spotswood's arrival in the colony in 1710, and the lieutenant governor appointed Buckner clerk of the House of Burgesses for the session that began on 22 October 1712. Buckner served as clerk until 1715. In 1714 Spotswood gave Buckner custody of the weights and measures for tobacco at Tappahannock, for the use of which Buckner was allowed to charge fees. Spotswood was then attempting to create a friendly faction in the assembly by giving members lucrative tobacco inspectorships and other valuable offices. When a new assembly convened in 1718, resentful burgesses retaliated against Spotswood. Among other things, they demanded to know why Buckner, Spotswood's appointee, had entered Spotswood's dissolution speech in the journal of the House, an action contrary to previous practice. The burgesses had Buckner arrested and brought before them on 28 May 1718. The former clerk explained that he had entered the speech in the journal because he was informed "that it was the Governours pleasure that his Said Speech should be added." The burgesses denounced Spotswood's action as "without president & unwarrantable" before releasing Buckner from custody. Nevertheless, dissolution speeches routinely appeared in the assembly journals thereafter.

Buckner had retired from public life by then but continued to speculate in land. When the new county of Caroline was formed in 1728, it included his place of residence, and he was appointed to the county court. Buckner was also elected to the House of Burgesses, took his seat on 21 May 1730, and served on the Committee for Courts of Justice. He may have missed the next assembly session because he was not reappointed to the committee when it was revived, and his name does not appear in the journal. Richard Buckner died between 18 October 1733, when he sold some property in Spotsylvania County, and 14 March 1734, when his will was proved in Caroline County. His wife, Elizabeth Cooke Buckner, and at least one son survived him.

William Armstrong Crozier, ed., *The Buckners of Virginia and the Allied Families of Strother and Ashby* (1907), 34–35, contains numerous errors; references in T. Elliot Campbell, *Colonial Caroline* (1954), confuse Richard Buckner with his namesake son and grandson; George Harrison Sanford King, "The Buckner Family," *Virginia Genealogist* 42 (1998): 245–248; land transactions and public offices documented in county court records, in colonial patent books, and in chancery suit *Thornton* v. *Buckner*, probably decided in General Court, Apr. 1730, reported in Robert T. Barton, ed., *Virginia Colonial Decisions* (1909), 1:R30–R34; *Journals of House of Burgesses, 1712–1726*, 191, 195, 211–212 (quotations); service as House clerk verified in two attested manuscript journals in PRO CO 5/1414, fol. 106, and CO 412/28, fol. 195, but a transcription error in a copy text resulted in name appearing as Robert Buckner for 1712–1714 session in *Journals of House of Burgesses, 1712–1726*, 3; last reference in Spotsylvania Co. Deed Book, B:504–515; Caroline Co. Order Book (1732–1740), 126–127; partial estate inventory in Spotsylvania Co. Will Book, A:214–215.

DAPHNE GENTRY

BUCKTROUT, Benjamin (d. by 1 June 1813), cabinetmaker, was a native of England who had arrived in Williamsburg from London by September 1765 and probably began his Virginia residence as a journeyman with the cabinetmaker Anthony Hay. The following year he announced in the *Virginia Gazette* that he had opened a shop "on the main street near the Capitol in Williamsburg," at which he made "all sorts of cabinet work, either plain or ornamental." Bucktrout was talented and well trained, as evidenced by his offer to make the "mathematical Gouty Chair," which apparently afforded relief to sufferers of that affliction. In 1767 he announced that he also could make and repair spinets, harpsichords, and other musical instruments.

In 1767 Bucktrout married Mary Martin, the widow of James Martin. She may have been the daughter of John Earnshaw, the customs collector for the Upper District of James River. Bucktrout's shop "near the Capitol" may have been in the house of James Martin. When settling Martin's estate, Bucktrout described that house in an advertisement as "nigh the Capitol."

After Hay purchased the Raleigh Tavern in 1767, Bucktrout occupied his cabinet shop and took in William Kennedy as a partner. During this period Bucktrout created the only signed piece of Williamsburg furniture yet to come to light. This piece is an elaborate Masonic master's chair with highly refined carving, reputed to have been given to Williamsburg's Lodge Number 6 by Norborne Berkeley, baron de Botetourt, the royal governor from 1768 to 1770. The chair is arguably the finest surviving piece of ceremonial furniture made in colonial America.

After his partnership with Kennedy ended in 1769, Bucktrout remained at the Hay shop until Hay's death the next year. He then moved to the house of John Chiswell on Francis Street. At the Chiswell site he expanded his business by retailing a variety of imported goods, engaging in paper hanging, and, like most cabinetmakers, conducting funerals.

Just after the Revolutionary War began Bucktrout constructed a hand-powered gunpowder mill in Williamsburg, for which he tried and failed to gain support from the state government. On 22 February 1777 he did receive an appointment as purveyor of the public hospitals in and around Williamsburg and as such provided necessary supplies to the Vineyard Military Hospital and the Public Hospital. He remained in that position probably until the autumn of 1779, when he intended to leave the state. Where Bucktrout went and why he left Virginia are unknown, but he was back in Williamsburg by November 1781, when he was accused of having joined the British army. Nothing came of the accusation.

Bucktrout visited England briefly in 1784 and 1788 but continued to work at his trade in Williamsburg until at least 1797, when he married Mary Bruce, of Bruton Parish. They had three sons and one daughter. In 1804 the Williamsburg court appointed Bucktrout surveyor and directed him to report on encroachments on streets and public lands belonging to the corporation. He may have served previously

as city surveyor, because in August 1800 he prepared a map of Williamsburg that proved of essential value for the twentieth-century restoration of the colonial capital. Unfortunately the Williamsburg city records are lost, and with them Bucktrout's report on the streets and public lands. Benjamin Bucktrout continued to reside in Williamsburg until his death between the compilation of tax lists on 29 June 1812 and 1 June 1813.

Williamsburg Virginia Gazette Daybook, 28 Sept. 1765, UVA; *Williamsburg Virginia Gazette* (Purdie and Dixon), 25 July 1766 (first, second, and third quotations), 8 Jan. 1767, 27 Oct. 1774; Wallace B. Gusler, *Furniture of Williamsburg and Eastern Virginia, 1710–1790* (1979), 75–77; *Williamsburg Virginia Gazette* (Rind), 21 Apr. 1768, 2 Feb. (fourth quotation), 9 Mar. 1769; Norfolk City Order Book, 1:239; *JHD*, 1777 sess., 103; *Williamsburg Virginia Gazette* (Dixon and Nicolson), 28 Aug. 1779; *Calendar of Virginia State Papers*, 2:620; *Richmond Virginia Gazette and Weekly Advertiser,* 17 July 1784, 14 Aug. 1788; Mrs. Peachy Wills to Mrs. John Coalter, 30 Apr. 1797, Tucker-Coleman Collection, W&M; Vincent Watkins, comp., *Marriages of York County, Virginia* (1986), 6; order of Williamsburg Court of Common Council, 28 June 1841, Southall Papers, folder 197, W&M; John W. Reps, *Tidewater Towns: City Planning in Colonial Virginia and Maryland* (1972), 158–163; Ronald L. Hurst and Jonathan Prown, *Southern Furniture, 1680–1830: The Colonial Williamsburg Collection* (1997), 192–198; Land Tax Returns, Williamsburg, 1812, 1813, RG 48, LVA.

HAROLD B. GILL JR.

BUFORD, Abraham (31 July 1749–26 June 1833), Continental army officer, was born in Culpeper County, the son of John Buford and Judith Early Buford. His immigrant ancestors had spelled the surname Beauford, but he always used the shorter spelling. Buford was one of the few Virginians to serve as an officer throughout the Revolutionary War. In 1775 he became the captain of a company of the Culpeper Minutemen and spent much of that winter of 1775–1776 and the ensuing year attached to the 2d Virginia Regiment in the field near Norfolk. On 13 November 1776 Buford was commissioned a major in the 14th Virginia Regiment. He was promoted to lieutenant colonel of the 5th Virginia Regiment as of 1 April 1777 and to colonel on 15 May 1778. Buford spent the winter of 1777–1778 at Valley Forge, Pennsylvania, and fought at Monmouth

Court House on 28 June 1778 before being transferred to the 11th Virginia Regiment. The following year he saw action in several skirmishes in northern New Jersey, but in 1780 he returned home to recruit new troops for the defense of the southern states.

Stalemate in the North led the British to try a southern strategy. In 1780 they laid siege to Charleston, South Carolina, and Buford was given command of one of several Virginia units sent to reinforce the city. En route he received word of Charleston's capitulation on 12 May, and he was then ordered to Camden to remove supplies and escort the governor of South Carolina, John Rutledge, to safety in North Carolina. Slowed by heavy wagons and muddy roads, Buford proceeded northward.

The British columns pushed deep into South Carolina and toward North Carolina to reestablish royal control. Their commander, General Charles Cornwallis, second earl Cornwallis, dispatched Lieutenant Colonel Banastre Tarleton and 270 British soldiers and Loyalists of his mixed cavalry-infantry legion in pursuit. Tarleton caught up with Buford, his 380 men, and a detachment of cavalry on 29 May 1780 at Waxhaw, in South Carolina near the North Carolina border. Tarleton called for Buford's surrender, but Buford first delayed responding until Rutledge and the wagons were safe and then refused the demand. Tarleton ordered his heavy dragoons to crash into the center of the American defenses while his infantry and cavalry swept up the flanks. Overwhelmed, Buford offered to surrender and had his men lay down their arms. According to Tarleton's account, his horse was shot from under him, and the British, seeing their commander go down, became inflamed and attacked the unarmed Americans with sabers and bayonets. According to American accounts, Tarleton deliberately ignored Buford's white flag and unleashed his Loyalists to slaughter their fellow Americans at will.

The carnage was horrific. Buford lost 113 killed, 150 wounded, and 53 captured. Warfare in the South was immediately changed by "Bloody Ban" Tarleton's perceived outrages. Whenever loyal and rebel Americans clashed thereafter, the niceties of eighteenth-century warfare were forgotten, but the Waxhaw killings were not. In October 1780 at Kings Mountain, American backwoodsmen shouted, "Give them Buford's play," when Loyalists under British major Patrick Ferguson tried to surrender. The following year men under the command of Lieutenant Colonel Henry "Light-Horse Harry" Lee and Colonel Andrew Pickens cried, "Remember Buford," as they butchered Loyalists at Haw River.

Buford was not among the officers captured at Waxhaw and remained in the army as commander of the 3d Virginia Regiment until the end of the war. Entitled to more than 8,000 acres of land on the basis of his wartime service, he had moved to Lincoln County, Kentucky, by January 1783 and on 4 October 1788 married Martha McDowell, daughter of a fellow Virginia Continental army veteran. They moved to Georgetown in the area that in 1792 became Scott County and had five sons and one daughter. Working as a surveyor while speculating in land, Buford plotted out choice tracts in the bluegrass section and eventually held title to more than 50,000 acres. Evincing a longtime interest in racehorses, he was one of several Kentuckians who began to import prime racing stock from Virginia shortly after the turn of the century. Abraham Buford died at his home in Georgetown on 26 June 1833 during a cholera epidemic.

Marcus Bainbridge Buford et al., *History and Genealogy of the Buford Family in America* (1924), 36–38, 134–141; J. Tracy Power, "'The Virtue of Humanity Was Totally Forgot': Buford's Massacre, May 29, 1780," *South Carolina Historical Magazine* 93 (1992): 5–14; Banastre Tarleton, *A History of the Campaigns of 1780 and 1781, in the Southern Provinces of North America* (1787), 27–31, 77–84; Buford letters in Papers of the Continental Congress, RG 360, NARA, and George Washington Papers, LC; MS report to General Assembly, 2 June 1780, Emmet Collection, New York Public Library; Revolutionary War Pension and Bounty-Land Warrant Application Files, RG 15, NARA (variant death date of 29 June 1833 in A. D. Hiller to Mrs. Byron Wilson, 6 Dec. 1938); Thomas Sumter Papers, Draper MSS, 12VV251–269; John C. Dann, ed., *The Revolution Remembered: Eyewitness Accounts of the War for Independence* (1980), 202; death date in notice in *Lexington Observer and Reporter*, 4 July 1833.

JOHN MORGAN DEDERER

BUFORD, Algernon Sidney (2 January 1826–6 May 1911), president of the Richmond and

Danville Railroad, was born in North Carolina in the part of Rowan County that became Davie County in 1836, the son of William Buford and Sarah Robertson Shelton Buford, both natives of Southside Virginia. He spent most of his childhood in Pittsylvania County, where he attended a school that his father conducted.

After a brief interlude as a teacher, Buford entered the University of Virginia to study law and graduated in 1848 with an LL.B. He then established a law practice in Danville and quickly became prominent in the affairs of the city. In 1852 Buford bought the *Danville Register*, then an organ of the disintegrating Whig Party, and used it to voice his steadfast opposition to the completion of the Richmond and Danville Railroad, ironically the same road of which he later became president. Buford may have had an interest in the rival Roanoke Navigation Company, a system for river transportation that the coming of the railroad doomed. He represented Pittsylvania County in the House of Delegates for the 1853–1854 session and served on the Committee on Banks, but after his term expired he abandoned his campaign against the railroad, sold his newspaper, and returned to the practice of law.

Buford enlisted in the Confederate army on 23 April 1861 and became a sergeant major in the 18th Regiment Virginia Infantry. His formal military service ended early in December 1861, when he was reelected to the House of Delegates, where he served for the duration of the war. He sat on the Committees on Banks and on Roads and Internal Navigation and chaired the former during his second term. From 1863 until 1865 he also served as a state agent to distribute supplies to Virginia soldiers in the Confederate army, in which capacity he received a brevet commission as lieutenant colonel of militia. Although he never held this rank in the field, he was known thereafter as Colonel Buford.

After the war ended Buford applied for a presidential pardon on 19 July 1865 and received it two days later. He returned to Danville, but Governor Francis Harrison Pierpont summoned him back to Richmond in September 1865 to assume the presidency of the Richmond and Danville Railroad. Many of the railroad's stockholders had preferred former Confederate general Joseph Eggleston Johnston for the presidency. Pierpont, however, desiring to send a conciliatory signal to the North, used the state's 40 percent interest in the line to push for Buford, whose legislative experience on the House committee dealing with railroads also enhanced his candidacy. In the September elections Buford received 2,288 votes to Johnston's 1,728.

Pierpont's choice proved wise. When Buford assumed the presidency the Richmond and Danville consisted of a mere 140 miles of war-damaged track connecting the two cities. He moved energetically to repair and refinance the prostrated line. In December 1868 his annual report to stockholders stated that "the period of poverty and extreme peril to your corporate interests is passed, and the dawn of a permanent and increased prosperity arisen."

Two challenges even more formidable than rebuilding awaited Buford: maintaining the railroad's market share against rival lines and guarding its autonomy from the encroachment of northern financial interests. Through skillful maneuvering Buford extended the railroad north from Richmond to West Point on the York River, with connections to the Chesapeake Bay's commerce, and south from Danville all the way to Atlanta, Georgia. This expansion enabled Buford to stave off rival lines, but it also forced him to seek financial assistance, and in 1871 ownership of his burgeoning railroad network passed to a holding company dominated by Thomas A. Scott, of the Pennsylvania Railroad.

A New York syndicate headed by Thomas Clyde and William P. Clyde bought the Richmond and Danville Railroad in 1880. Buford remained the line's president and continued to manage day-to-day operations, but effective control had passed from his hands. Another change in ownership and removal of company headquarters to New York City in 1886 caused Buford finally to resign the presidency of the Richmond and Danville after a tenure of more than two decades. Eight years later the railroad network that he had developed was reorganized into the new, sprawling Southern Railway System. In an industry moving inexorably toward regional and national consolidation, Buford had fought a losing battle to retain local control.

Buford continued to play an active role in local and Virginia affairs. He represented the city of Richmond in the House of Delegates in 1887–1888, when he chaired the Committee on Finance and also sat on the Committees on Roads and Internal Navigation and on Public Property. For four years he served as president of the Virginia State Agricultural and Mechanical Society. In 1893 Buford made a brief run for the governorship but finished a distant third at the Democratic Party Convention that nominated Charles Triplett O'Ferrall.

Buford married three times. He wed Emily Whitmell Townes on 5 December 1854, and they had one daughter. Another daughter resulted from Buford's marriage to Kate A. Wortham on 16 December 1869. Kate Buford died on 29 December 1874, and on 21 May 1879 Buford married Mary Cameron Ross Strother, with whom he had two sons and two daughters. Buford had been in declining health when a severe fall at his Richmond residence in the spring of 1911 confined him to his bed. Failing to recover, Algernon Sidney Buford died on 6 May 1911 and was buried in Hollywood Cemetery in Richmond.

Tyler, *Men of Mark*, 5:54–58 (por.); Marcus Bainbridge Buford, *A Genealogy of the Buford Family in America* (1903), 289–290 (por.); BVS Marriage Register, Pittsylvania Co., 1854, Richmond City, 1869, 1879; Compiled Service Records; Presidential Pardons; Maury Klein, *The Great Richmond Terminal* (1970), 31–32, 56–64, 86–101; Annual Reports and Stockholders' and Directors' Minutes, Richmond and Danville Railroad Company, Southern Railway Archives, VPI (quotation in Annual Report [1868], 284); obituary in *Richmond Times-Dispatch*, 7 May 1911.

BRUCE HAMMOND

BUFORD, Martha "Pattie" Hicks (14 March 1836–17 January 1901), educator, was born near Lawrenceville in Brunswick County, the daughter of Edward Brodnax Hicks, a well-to-do lawyer and landowner, and Elizabeth Stone Hicks, daughter of a former governor of North Carolina. Her mother died when Pattie Hicks, as she was called, was less than a year old, and thereafter her aunt Martha Hicks lived with the family and raised the children. Family tradition remembered Edward Hicks as imperious and severe, but he believed in education and sent Pattie Hicks, his youngest daughter, to Saint

Mary's School, an Episcopal institution in Raleigh, North Carolina. Edward Hicks was an invalid for many years, and she often eased his discomfort by reading to him. On 24 November 1858, just three days before her father died, Hicks married Francis Emmet Buford, a lawyer, at the home of her sister. A strong-willed woman, she may have married on that date in order to escape the clause in her father's will that would have required approval from her uncle and brother for her to marry.

The Bufords built a house called Sherwood on land inherited from her father about a mile south of Lawrenceville. They had two daughters and four sons. In 1862 F. E. Buford entered the Confederate army and became captain of Company G, 3d Regiment Virginia Light Artillery, a local-defense unit called up to help protect the city of Richmond. After the Civil War he served Brunswick County as commonwealth's attorney, judge of the circuit court, and member of the General Assembly.

Brunswick County experienced dire poverty after 1865, as former slaveholders and newly freed slaves struggled to survive in a weak agricultural economy. One striking example of the changed situation for Pattie Buford was the shift of the freedpeople into their own churches. From her girlhood she had conducted a Sunday school for the slave children on her father's plantation. After the war many local freedpeople joined the Zion Union Apostolic Church, an independent church founded by James R. Howell, who served as its bishop. By early in the 1870s Zion Union counted 2,000 adherents from Brunswick and adjoining counties southward into North Carolina.

In the spring of 1875 Buford asked two female members of the church if she might conduct a Sunday school. They agreed, and she discovered an unquenchable thirst for education among the freedpeople and their children, regardless of religious doctrine. Buford appealed for assistance to the Diocese of Virginia and to the Committee for Domestic Missions of the national Protestant Episcopal Church's Domestic and Foreign Missionary Society. Alvi Tabor Twing, minister and secretary of the committee, took up her cause, and her appeals for aid appeared regularly in the society's periodical, *Spirit of Missions*.

Buford was soon receiving regular contributions of money and bundles of clothing and books from a network of supporters throughout the northeastern states. She sent the best of her pupils out to teach the Episcopal catechism at other Zion Union churches and estimated in 1879 that twenty-eight schools and 1,400 children benefited from the donations. With contributions of $165 Buford had also built the Chapel of the Good Shepherd, where a regular school opened in March 1879 with more than 100 pupils in attendance. That month Francis M. Whittle, bishop of the Diocese of Virginia, recognized her work by appointing her a regular teacher, sustained by the General Board of the diocese.

On 30 April 1879 at Buford's new church, fifteen ministers and more than 1,000 members of Zion Union petitioned two representatives of the bishop for affiliation with the Diocese of Virginia. At that year's annual council Buford received credit for accomplishing "an amazing work (unaided and alone, except by her Heavenly Father's help)." The Episcopal Church, however, required an educated ministry. Only Zion Union's young secretary, James Solomon Russell, who had spent two years at Hampton Normal and Agricultural Institute, impressed the bishop's representatives as a candidate for the priesthood. At the diocese's expense, Russell attended what became the Bishop Payne Divinity and Industrial School (later the Bishop Payne Divinity School) in Petersburg, and after graduating he returned to Brunswick County and founded at Lawrenceville what became Saint Paul's College. He always credited Buford with making his ministry possible.

Suddenly, on 25 August 1881, Buford learned that Bishop Whittle and the Diocese of Virginia would no longer recognize and support her school. The motivation behind the decision is unclear— " for some reason, God only knows what, I have never known," Buford wrote years later. Possibly her conviction that the "plantation negro" was unsuited for all but the most rudimentary education conflicted with the diocese's intention to provide full training for black clergymen. The likeliest reason for the break

came less than a week earlier, when the ministers of Zion Union, with whom Buford's schools were still connected, voted not to require use of the Episcopal prayer book in their services, an implicit act of disaffiliation from the diocese.

The decision might have stymied a less determined person, but it inspired Buford to greater effort for what she turned into a private charity. In autumn 1881 she appealed to her northern supporters for funds to establish a hospital for blacks. They responded generously, and in 1882 the General Assembly incorporated the Church Home for Infirm and Disabled Colored People, which opened in October 1883. The continuing expenses of that institution, soon filled with a steady stream of patients, and of her overcrowded school, which offered instruction in sewing and the rudiments of nursing for the women students, required Buford to devote much of her time to raising funds. In addition to articles in church papers, she issued annual appeals and often traveled for weeks at a time soliciting help from Episcopal circles in the North. Nonetheless, she did not neglect her family, including a daughter born in 1884 when Buford was forty-eight years old. Her sons assisted in her work, and her devoted husband stood by her at every step. They reportedly differed only about thunderstorms, which he hated but she found exhilarating. Buford was also known for her lovely flower beds, especially a rose garden in which she spent much of her spare time.

From childhood Buford had suffered from a chronic and sometimes debilitating illness, possibly rheumatoid arthritis. Whenever possible she taught daily in her school, and through the years she recruited several others to assist her, including two friends and neighbors, Indie Davis and Sarah Wilkes. Margaret Weddell, of Petersburg, served as her personal secretary for the last eighteen years of Buford's life.

On 17 March 1891 the hospital burned to the ground. During the previous year it had served 53 patients on the premises and provided outpatient care to another 1,012 persons. Buford set to work and quickly raised the money for an even larger hospital, which opened in January 1892. The new three-story building, which still stands, had a raised basement and eight wards, each containing eight to ten beds. A separate building housed orphaned children, and an adjacent outbuilding provided beds for patients with extremely contagious diseases. In September 1892 Buford reported that the new hospital buildings cost $7,840. Other contributions since January amounted to $3,340, but expenses had totaled $5,538. To cover the difference, Buford used the surplus from the building fund. The high expenses and the continuing need help to explain the insistent tone of her fund-raising letters. Buford often declared that one had only to witness the suffering to feel and act as she did. In 1893 the hospital cared for 81 patients and helped 721 outpatients.

Family tradition records that the death of her youngest son on 14 May 1900 broke Buford's heart. Martha "Pattie" Hicks Buford died at her home less than a year later, on 17 January 1901, following a long bout with her illness. She was buried in the family plot at Sherwood. Buford's will stipulated that the hospital and the twenty acres set apart for its work should revert to her estate if it did not operate as a hospital for five years. The last known report of the work is dated 30 September 1907, and at some point thereafter the property did indeed pass back to her estate. Despite holding racial views common to southern whites of her day, this courageous and unsung white woman for twenty-five years dedicated her life to caring for the black people of Brunswick County.

Birth and marriage dates in Hicks family Bible records, 1822–1935, LVA; Robert P. Buford IV, *A Buford Family Sourcebook* (1982), includes "She and God," a memoir by her granddaughter Florence deLaunay Buford, and excerpts from diaries, published articles, "Mrs. Buford's Annual Report and Appeal," ca. 1897 (second quotation), and will; Buford's writings include "A Wonderful Work among the Plantation Negroes," *Spirit of Missions* 44 (1879): 102–110, 256–262, and 45 (1880): 262–269, and *Aunt Sally* [ca. 1892]; untitled pamphlet [ca. 1882], reprinting three Buford letters from *Spirit of Missions* and an untitled, unidentified magazine article, Boston Public Library; Brunswick Co. Marriage Licenses; BVS Marriage Register, Brunswick Co.; *Southern Churchman*, 8, 29 (first quotation) May 1879, 1 Sept. 1881; James S. Russell, *Adventure in Faith: An Autobiographic Story of St. Paul Normal and Industrial School, Lawrenceville, Virginia* (1936), 15–16; Frances Ashton Thurman, "The History of St. Paul's College, Lawrenceville, Virginia, 1888–1959" (Ph.D. diss., Howard University,

1978), 24–28; death notice in *Richmond Dispatch*, 19 Jan. 1901; obituaries in *Richmond Times*, 19 Jan. 1901, and *Southern Churchman*, 9 Feb. 1901.

GAY W. NEALE

BUFORD, Paul Chalmers (13 March 1893–13 August 1960), president of the Shenandoah Life Insurance Company, was born in College Hill in Lafayette County, Mississippi, the son of Paul Chalmers Buford, a farmer, and Louise Barry Buford. He was educated in public schools in his native county and in Shelby County, Tennessee, and at Mississippi Heights Academy, at Blue Mountain, Mississippi. Buford attended Southwestern Presbyterian University in Clarksville, Tennessee, and graduated from Washington and Lee University in 1913. He earned a law degree there in 1915 and entered the Roanoke law firm of Martin and Chitwood.

In August 1917 Buford joined the army and after going through the officer training program was commissioned a second lieutenant of field artillery. From July 1918 until May 1919 he served in France. Discharged with the rank of first lieutenant on 24 May 1919, Buford returned to the practice of law in Roanoke. His law partners during the next twenty years included such distinguished attorneys as Harvey Black Apperson and Abram Penn Staples, both of whom served as attorney general of Virginia. Buford was president of the Roanoke Bar Association in 1927 and of the Roanoke Chamber of Commerce in 1929, and he became a member of the board of Colonial-American National Bank during the 1920s. He also took part in local Democratic Party politics. On 29 February 1924 Buford married Anne Warren, of Evanston, Illinois. They had two sons and two daughters.

On 28 October 1939 the board of directors of the Shenandoah Life Insurance Company, a Roanoke firm established in 1916, reorganized the business and elected Buford chairman of the board and general counsel. Elbert Lee Trinkle, the president of the company and a former governor of Virginia, died less than a month later. The board then elected Buford president effective 1 January 1940. He was a quiet manager who disliked conflict, delegated authority, and instituted firm management practices. The company, which specialized in offering group life insurance to businesses and governments, had experienced hard times during the 1930s but grew steadily during the following two decades. Under Buford's leadership the company gradually retired its outstanding capital stock and in 1955 completed its conversion to a mutual insurance company.

In 1946 Shenandoah Life sold its seven-story office in downtown Roanoke and began construction of a new headquarters building of modified Georgian design in a thirty-five-acre park in a residential section on the outskirts of the city. An early example of a suburban office building in Virginia, the headquarters became a local landmark. The company innovated in other ways as well. As part of an increase in advertising it entered the communications field and began operating a radio station, WSLS, on 1 October 1940. It also created WSLS-TV, the first Virginia television station west of Richmond, which went on the air on 10 December 1952. Both ventures succeeded and were sold for a profit after Buford's death.

Buford was stricken with leukemia and resigned as president in December 1956. He remained chairman of the board and kept an office at Shenandoah Life's headquarters. His health improved, and when his successor resigned in June 1959 Buford returned as president of the company. During his two terms as chief executive covering a twenty-one-year period, Shenandoah Life increased its assets from approximately $9 million to $57 million. Insurance in force increased threefold to almost $600 million. One of the largest life insurance companies in Virginia, with twenty-four branch offices by 1960, it was an early leader in selling group insurance policies and also one of the first to install modern automation in its Roanoke office.

Buford also held many civic leadership posts. He received the Algernon Sydney Sullivan Award from Hollins College in 1957 and a citation for community service from Roanoke College the next year. Virginia governors twice appointed him to the Commission on State Capital Outlays and Means of Financing, on which he served from 1955 to 1960. As president of the Hospital Development Fund in Roanoke, Buford helped raise $2.5 million for Roanoke

Memorial and Burrell Memorial Hospitals and served as a trustee of the former. He was a member of the school board of Roanoke from 1938 to 1940 and was a trustee of Hollins College from 1940 to 1960. Several regional businesses also placed Buford on their boards, and he was an elder and trustee of the Second Presbyterian Church of Roanoke.

His leukemia recurred during his second term as president of the Shenandoah Life Insurance Company, and Paul Chalmers Buford died at Roanoke Memorial Hospital on 13 August 1960. He was buried in Evergreen Burial Park in Roanoke.

Glass and Glass, *Virginia Democracy*, 2:262–263; biographical data sheet approved by Buford, 18 Jan. 1956, copy in author's possession; information provided by sons Guy Warren Buford and Paul C. Buford Jr.; Ben Dulaney, "Shenandoah Life Insurance Company," *Commonwealth* 23 (Sept. 1956): 13–17, 40; Hiram J. Herbert, *Shenandoah Life: The First Fifty Years, 1916–1966* (1966), 65–90 (por. on 66); obituary in *Roanoke Times*, 14 Aug. 1960; memorial in *Virginia State Bar Association Proceedings* (1960): 106–109.

GEORGE A. KEGLEY

BULLARD, Chester (12 March 1809–27 February 1893), Disciples of Christ minister, was born in or near Framingham, Massachusetts, the son of Mary Walker Nutt Bullard and her second husband, Daniel Bullard. His relatives included tanners, shoemakers, and ministers, and two of his three brothers became clergymen. In 1818 Bullard moved to Virginia with his sister Mary Bullard Snow and her husband, Asiel Snow. They lived in Staunton until 1826, when they moved to Christiansburg. Economic hardship curtailed Bullard's opportunities for formal education, but while in Staunton he attended a school taught by a Methodist. He studied medicine with David J. Chapman in Giles County in 1830 and 1831 and practiced sporadically thereafter. On 26 January 1831 Bullard married Elsey K. Pearce. They had one daughter before his wife died in 1839.

Reared in the Congregational Church, Bullard united with the Methodists at age seventeen, but on 11 December 1830 Landon Duncan, an early Virginia ally of Thomas Campbell and Alexander Campbell, baptized him and in the spring of 1834 helped him become an ordained minister in what was then called the Christian Association. His ability to draw on the income of the farms and foundries of his brother-in-law, the founder of Snowville in Pulaski County, allowed Bullard the financial freedom to become a traveling evangelist. By 1836 he had established six churches in southwestern Virginia, including Cypress Grove Church, his home church at Snowville, and by 1840 he had begun cooperating with Alexander Campbell and the Disciples of Christ in eastern Virginia. Bullard traveled throughout the state on preaching tours and founded scores of churches, many of them in the southwestern counties. In October 1849 cooperating congregations in southwestern Virginia elected him a traveling evangelist, and in 1860 he was appointed one of the state's six general evangelists. During his career Bullard baptized by his estimate three thousand people in southwestern Virginia.

Bullard was instrumental in battling the rural isolation of the Disciples of Christ in southwestern Virginia and worked tirelessly to expand their horizons. He opposed the notion that theological unanimity was a condition of Christian fellowship and, believing that Christian belief and unity could be found in the New Testament, joined the Campbells in eschewing creeds and formal confessions of faith. Bullard regarded his ministry as extending beyond the congregations he served and also beyond preaching. When starvation threatened many people in Scotland and Ireland in 1847, he joined other Disciples of Christ in raising relief money. An early advocate of equal education for women, Bullard called for coeducation at the Disciples' Bethany College, and in 1849 he welcomed the development of the Sunday school. During the 1840s he encouraged the ministry of Harry Chapman, of Giles County, often called the first African American preacher among the Disciples of Christ. Bullard pleaded for preachers and tracts for the freedpeople during Reconstruction and in 1869 printed two appeals for assistance in the *Millennial Harbinger*.

Bullard married three more times. On 2 November 1842 in Lunenburg County he married Sophia Adeline Stone, who died about two years later, and on 14 June 1846 in Albemarle County he married Mary Saunders Dunkum, who died in 1864. Of their two sons, only William Stone Bullard survived childhood, and he also became a minister. On 29 January 1866 Bullard married Elizabeth Craig. At least two of his wives came from slaveholding families, and the other two were daughters of moderately wealthy landed men. Bullard owned real estate worth an estimated $7,500 in 1850 and real and personal property, including twelve slaves, worth about $23,000 in 1860. During the Civil War he leased his slaves to nearby farms whose white workforce had joined the Confederate war effort.

Chester Bullard died on 27 February 1893 at his house, called Humility, near the Snowville church that he served. Benjamin King, a former slave, presented the eulogy at the funeral. Bullard was buried on Chester Hill in the slave cemetery overlooking his home. After the death of his fourth wife he was reinterred with her in the cemetery behind the Snowville Christian Church.

Autobiographical "Dr. Chester Bullard," ed. F. D. Power, *Christian Standard* 29 (1893): 210, 247–248, 307–308; Mary A. Kearns, "A Merging of Two Restoration Movements: Contributions of Dr. Chester Bullard to the Stone-Campbell Movement" (master's thesis, Emmanuel School of Religion, Johnson City, Tenn., 1996); Frederick Arthur Hodge, *The Plea and the Pioneers in Virginia* (1905), 200–205; J. W. West, *Sketches of Our Mountain Pioneers* (1939), 21–28 (por.); biographical file including sermons, copies of contributions to *Christian Standard* (1880–1891), Mary S. Dunkum Bullard's journal (1846–1847, providing third marriage date), and photograph of gravestone inscription, Disciples of Christ Church Historical Society, Nashville, Tenn.; autobiographical writings, scrapbooks, and other materials in Charles C. Ware Carolina Discipliana Collection, Barton College, Wilson, N.C.; major writings include Bullard, "The Great Want of the Colored People" and "Needed—Two Tracts for the Negro," *Millennial Harbinger* (1869): 169–170, 345–346; first, second, and fourth marriages in E. J. Bullard, *Other Bullards: A Genealogy, Supplementary to Bullard and Allied Families* (1928), 23 (citing record in Bullard's Bible); second marriage bond dated 1 Nov. 1842 in Emma R. Matheny and Helen K. Yates, comps., *Marriages of Lunenburg County, Virginia, 1746–1853* (1967), 16; third marriage bond dated 13 June 1846 in Albemarle Co. Marriage Bonds and Consent Papers; *Millennial Harbinger* (1838): 286, 381, (1839): 469, (1840): 382, (1849): 357, 378–382, (1850): 655, (1860): 652; *Pulaski Southwest Times,* centennial edition, 13 Aug. 1939; gravestone inscription giving birth and death dates printed in Malita Warden Murphy and James L. Douthat, *Gates to Glory: Cemeteries of Pulaski County, Virginia* (1983), 1:178.

DAVID A. JONES

BULLITT, Cuthbert (d. 8 August 1791), member of the Convention of 1776 and member of the Convention of 1788, was born in Prince William County, probably by 1732, the son of Benjamin Bullitt, of Huguenot descent, owner of a small plantation and sometime justice of the peace, and his second wife, whose name was most likely Elizabeth Harrison Bullitt. He received a classical education, may have attended the College of William and Mary, and read law. By 1759 Bullitt was a practicing attorney in Prince William and Fauquier Counties. He married Helen Scott, the daughter of an Anglican clergyman, about 1760. They lived in a well-furnished brick house overlooking the Potomac River about three miles east of Dumfries and had at least four daughters and two sons, including Alexander Scott Bullitt, who was elected lieutenant governor of Kentucky in 1800.

In addition to practicing law, Bullitt acquired land in Fauquier and Prince William Counties and produced tobacco and wheat with a workforce that eventually included about forty slaves. In 1765 he was present when one of his brothers-in-law met John Baylis to fight a duel. Bullitt's attempt to reconcile them failed so badly that Baylis attacked Bullitt, who shot and killed him. An examining court exonerated him on grounds of self-defense.

Bullitt was elected to the Dumfries Committee of Correspondence on 31 May 1774 and to the Prince William County Committee on 19 December of that year. After he criticized the Virginia Convention in November 1775 for undermining revolutionary virtue by paying extravagant salaries to its clerk, chaplain, and other officers, the county committee defended him against charges of disloyalty. On 1 April 1776 Bullitt defeated Thomas Blackburn for one of the county's two seats in the fifth and final Virginia Revolutionary Convention. Bullitt probably attended every session between 6 May and 5 July 1776. He sat on the Committees on Privileges and Elections and on Propositions and Grievances and on the committee appointed on 15 May 1776 to draft the Declaration of Rights and the first constitution of Virginia. He voted on 15 May for the resolution instructing the Virginia delegates to the Continental Congress to declare independence, and he voted for adoption of the Declaration of Rights and the state constitution. Despite his earlier complaints, Bullitt offered no recorded proposal to reduce the pay of the convention's officers.

Bullitt's elder brother, Thomas Bullitt, served as adjutant general of Virginia during the early years of the American Revolution. Cuthbert Bullitt represented Prince William County in the House of Delegates for two terms from October 1776 to January 1778 and became influential there. He served on the Committees of Privileges and Elections and of Propositions and Grievances during both terms. In the two sessions of the second term Bullitt also sat on the Committees for Courts of Justice and of Religion. He was elected to the House of Delegates again in 1785 and served four consecutive terms through the session of October–December 1788. Bullitt arrived late at the sessions of October 1785, October 1786, and October 1787 and so did not receive choice committee assignments, but in the first session of 1788 he sat again on the Committee of Privileges and Elections and chaired the Committee for Courts of Justice. Between those legislative terms he was commonwealth's attorney for Fauquier and Prince William Counties and a tax commissioner for the latter. In October 1779 Bullitt borrowed a large sum of tax money from the sheriff of Prince William County. Although such loans were not then illegal, the assembly investigated the affair and passed a law prohibiting private use of public funds thereafter.

In politics Bullitt supported Patrick Henry, whose niece married Bullitt's elder son in 1785. Like Henry, Bullitt opposed ratification of the Constitution of the United States, and he and another opponent, George Grayson, were elected to represent Prince William County in the state ratification convention that met in 1788. Bullitt supported Henry's attempt to call a second convention to amend the proposed constitution. He served on the Committee of Privileges and Elections but took no active part in the debates. Bullitt voted for amendment of the Constitution prior to ratification and when that motion was defeated voted on 25 June 1788 against ratification.

On 27 December 1788, probably through Henry's sponsorship, the General Assembly elected Bullitt a judge of the General Court. A painful illness not identified in surviving records cut short his career on the bench. Cuthbert Bullitt died on 8 August 1791 at Warm Springs in Bath County, a popular spa he had visited hoping to recover his health. He was buried probably at Warm Springs.

Bob Wohlhueter, "Cuthbert Bullitt" (typescript, ca. 1991, copy in DVB Files); family history sources are incomplete and sometimes contradictory; Bullitt had reached his majority by 30 May 1753, when he stood as bondsman for his brother, in Prince William Co. Minute Book (1752–1753), 129; Horace Edwin Hayden, *Virginia Genealogies* (1891), 597–600 (gives birth year as 1740), 604–607; Virginia Writers' Project, *Prince William: The Story of its People and its Places* (1941), 87; *Revolutionary Virginia*, 2:93, 204, 5:162–163, 167–168, 6:51, 293, 299–300, 7:24, 47, 143, 158; *Calendar of Virginia State Papers*, 3:629, 4:537, 5:359; *Madison: Congressional Series*, 10:373–375, 11:387–388, 420–421; Robert A. Rutland, ed., *The Papers of George Mason, 1725–1792* (1970), 2:550–552; Kaminski, *Ratification*, 8:309, 479, 9:577, 909, 10:1539, 1541, 1557, 1565; Prince William Co. Will Book, G:533–535; death date reported in J. Dawes to Beverley Randolph, 12 Aug. 1791, Governor's Office, Letters Received, RG 3, LVA (printed in *Calendar of Virginia State Papers*, 5:358).

PHILANDER D. CHASE

BULLOCK, Hugh (ca. 1577–by 2 November 1650), member of the Council, was born probably in Middlesex County, England. When he married Alice Nashe in London on 19 September 1603 he was identified as a mariner of Stepney, Middlesex, and she as the daughter of a mariner of the same place. He may have been related to the William Bullock whose name appears in the 1625 muster of Virginia residents, but that man was not, as was once assumed, Hugh Bullock's son.

By the time Hugh Bullock settled in Virginia sometime between 1626 and 1628, he probably owned one or more trading vessels. While he was in Virginia, he left his only son, William Bullock, in London to manage that end of the family business. Bullock made several voyages to England during the 1630s and invested a large amount of money, several thousand pounds of which he and his son lost in joint ventures with untrustworthy associates, one of whom they identified as William Brocas, who served on the Council with Bullock.

Sometime between 29 May 1630 and 20 December 1631 Governor Sir John Harvey appointed Bullock to the Council. The most significant political event during Bullock's tenure occurred in the spring of 1635 when the Council arrested Harvey and deprived him of the governorship. Bullock is not known to have taken sides in the dispute and may have been in England on one of his business trips at that time. The king subsequently reinstated Harvey and reappointed councillors who had supported the governor or were believed willing to support him. An undated memorandum written in London in June 1637 names Bullock and three other men as fit to serve on the Council. He was in London that July, and he probably remained on the Council until he left Virginia for the last time about 1639.

Bullock acquired 5,500 acres in Warwick County. He built and operated sawmills and gristmills there and made other valuable improvements to the property. After Bullock received a royal monopoly in 1628 for use of a device that he had invented to square timber, he may have erected one of these machines in Warwick County. Before departing Virginia in 1639 he leased his plantations to men whose mismanagement may have cost the family as much as £5,000. In part because of their large financial losses, the Bullocks became justifiably dissatisfied with the manner in which political and commercial affairs in Virginia were conducted. In the spring of 1649 William Bullock wrote and published a long pamphlet entitled *Virginia Impartially Examined,* in which he offered detailed proposals for reforming the government of the colony and for giving its economy a more varied agricultural and industrial base. Although he had never been in Virginia, William Bullock drew on his father's intimate knowledge of Virginia and interviewed many of the colony's leading merchants and political leaders. *Virginia Impartially Examined* thus contains valuable information about life in Virginia during the period when Hugh Bullock lived there. Despite its calls for change the pamphlet held out enough promise that Englishmen could get rich in Virginia (if they allied themselves with the proper sort of business associates) that it came to be regarded as one of the best of the early colonial promotional pamphlets.

Later in 1649 William Bullock traveled to Virginia for the first time to attempt to recoup the family's losses, but he died a few months after his arrival. In 1670 Hugh Bullock's grandson and principal heir, Robert Bullock, armed with a letter of introduction to the governor from Charles II, traveled to Virginia and filed suit in the General Court to gain control of the estate, "wch. his Grandfather at great Charge did gayne Plant & improve." The court ruled in Robert Bullock's favor in April 1671 and ordered the county sheriff to assist him in wresting possession of the property from adjoining landowners who had encroached on it after Hugh Bullock's death. Robert Bullock then sold part or all of the land and returned to England.

Sometime before 8 July 1637 Hugh Bullock married a second time, to a woman named Mary whose surname is unknown. She died before 22 October 1649, when Bullock wrote his will, stating that he was then of the parish of All Hallows Barking, London, and suffering from failing vision. The will indicates that Bullock had purchased the right to operate the signal lights at Dungeness, which guided ships along the treacherous coast of Kent County, England. He also held an appointment in the royal customs service and hired a deputy to do the work. Hugh Bullock died in London on an unrecorded date before 2 November 1650, when his will was proved there.

Mary Bullock Aker, comp., *Bullocks of Virginia and Kentucky and Their Descendants* (1952), and James Garland Bullock, *Families of Bullock/Roebuck* (1977), contain factual errors; Bullock gave his age as fifty-nine in a deposition on 23 Jan. 1635 in PRO HCA 13/52, fol. 260, and as seventy-two on 22 Oct. 1649 in his will, Prerogative Court of Canterbury, Pembroke 168; first marriage recorded in *Allegations for Marriage Licenses Issued by the Bishop of London, 1520–1610* (1887), 278; second wife mentioned in indenture dated 8 July 1637 and recorded 27 June 1652 in York Co. Deeds, Orders, Wills, 1:135; a few references in *Minutes of Council and General Court*, including first record of presence in Virginia, 29 Mar. 1628, on 169; first documented service as councillor is signature on document dated 20 Dec. 1631, PRO CO 1/6, fol. 93; undated (ca. June 1637) memorandum identifying Council members in PRO CO 1/9, fol. 141; Robert Bullock's petition to Charles II and the king's letter to Governor Sir William Berkeley in PRO CO 1/33, fol. 104 (quotation), and CO 324/2, fol. 24; William Brocas mentioned in PRO PC 2/50, fol. 558; monopoly in PRO Indexes (formerly Signet Office), 6808; appraisal of Bullock's land, 1653, in Charles City Co. Records, 1642–1842, VHS.

DAPHNE GENTRY

BULLOCK, Rice (17 December 1755–9 April 1800), member of the Convention of 1788, was born in Louisa County, the son of John Bullock and Ann Rice Bullock. He must have received a good education, but nothing else is definitely known of his early life. Bullock served at least two years, from 8 November 1779 until December 1781, as an ensign, lieutenant, and assistant quartermaster in Joseph Crockett's regiment, part of the Virginia State Forces under the command of George Rogers Clark. Extant records place him in a militia company in 1776, and he or someone of the same name served in the 15th Virginia Regiment. As a consequence of his Revolutionary War military service Bullock received land grants totaling at least 2,666⅔ acres, and his family later received a posthumous half-pay pension retroactive to 6 February 1781.

Before April 1785 Bullock settled in Jefferson County, probably in Louisville. On 4 March 1788 he was elected one of two Jefferson County delegates to the state convention called to consider ratification of the proposed constitution of the United States. Given his lack of previous political and governmental experience, Bullock was not an obvious choice. He may have been selected simply because he was available. Bullock was at the courthouse in Louisville early in March, serving on juries and tending to his own legal affairs, when the election took place. His service as an army officer, his literacy, and perhaps his political beliefs recommended him to the voters, who may also have concluded that because he was not married he could make the long round trip to Richmond more easily than some other men. Bullock duly attended the convention in June 1788, voted for ratification, and opposed the motion demanding amendments before approving the document. In voting for the Constitution he could have been influenced by his fellow Jefferson County delegate Robert Breckinridge, one of only two other Kentucky representatives who favored ratification.

Bullock apparently lived quietly in or near Louisville until about 1791, when his name disappears from Jefferson County records. He first appears in the records of the Northwest Territory (in what in 1803 became Hamilton County, Ohio), in January 1795. In 1799 and 1800 he served as first auditor of public accounts for the Northwest Territory. Rice Bullock resided in Cincinnati until his death there on 9 April 1800.

Mary Bullock Aker, comp., *Bullocks of Virginia and Kentucky and Their Descendants* (1952), 9, cites family Bible records for birth date; signed quartermaster records in George Rogers Clark Papers, Auditor of Public Accounts, RG 148, LVA; *List of Officers of the Illinois Regiment, and of Crockett's Regiment, Who Have Received Land for Their Services*, Doc. 32, supplement to *JHD*, 1833–1834 sess., 10; Dec. 1785 purchase of three half-acre lots recorded in Louisville Board of Trustees Minute Book, 1781–1825, Filson Historical Society, Louisville, Ky.; Michael L. Cook and Bettie A. Cummings Cook, comps., *Jefferson County, Kentucky Records* (1987), 1:184, 231–232, 242, 248–249, 262–265, 410; Kaminski, *Ratification*, 10:1539, 1540, 1557, 1565, 1651; *Abstract of Book 1 and Book A Probate Record, 1791–1826, Hamilton County, Ohio* (1977), 24, 36, 57, 58 (will entered on unrecorded date after 20 June 1800); death notice and estate settlement in *Cincinnati Western Spy, and Hamilton Gazette,* 9 Apr., 23 July 1800; administrator's account in Louisa Co. Will Book, 9:51, recording half-pay warrant through 17 Mar. 1800.

JAMES J. HOLMBERG

BUNDICK, William Thomas (15 February 1847–9 December 1908), temperance lecturer, was born near Locust Mount in Accomack County, the son of John B. Bundick, a farmer, and Margaret Floyd Bundick. He received his only formal education in a country school near his father's farm. On 8 January 1868 Bundick married Catherine S. Ames, also of Accomack County. They had two sons and three daughters.

Bundick had a natural talent for oratory. He reputedly entertained his playmates on Sundays by preaching to them from a tree stump. Despite his youthful sermonizing, Bundick never felt a call to the ministry, but he read widely and continued to practice oratory. When the temperance movement revived in the latter part of the nineteenth century, he found a use for his talent. Bundick became active in the Friends of Temperance, organized at Petersburg in 1865, and in November 1882 he was elected state lecturer. Speaking engagements for the Friends of Temperance took him across Virginia and northward to Baltimore and other places in Maryland.

In January 1884 Bundick opened a butcher shop and provision store in Accomac Court House and withdrew from the movement. His growing family no doubt required the income and security of storekeeping. Bundick did not even participate in the hard-fought campaign of 1886 to implement the state's new local-option law permitting localities to outlaw the saloon by referendum. In that same year he added a freezer for ice cream and moved his store to Onancock, where he resided for the rest of his life.

A local newspaper reported on 21 April 1894 that Bundick was in Ashland, and the following day he experienced conversion at a Baptist revival. Nearly a year passed before the meaning of those events became public. In March 1895 announcements proclaimed that Bundick was representing the Keely Institute, of Ashland, which treated alcoholism. He announced that at his lectures he would describe his own experiences with alcohol and the manner in which he had been cured. A few months earlier Bundick had become state Deputy Grand Chief Templar of the Independent Order of Good Templars, a national order that superseded the Friends of Temperance in Virginia. He spent 1895 recruiting and organizing for the Good Templars on the Eastern Shore, and the following year he campaigned for the Prohibition Party. In December 1896 Bundick announced that he had sold his store to his son so that he could dedicate his own life to temperance work.

On 24 February 1897 Bundick was unanimously elected chairman of the Virginia Prohibition Party. He also worked as an organizer and lectured across the state. Bundick's efforts did not greatly improve the small party's fortunes, but he won increasing recognition as an effective temperance lecturer. Speaking engagements in 1900 took him to Alabama, New York, North Carolina, Pennsylvania, Tennessee, and other states. On 4 September 1900 Bundick resigned as party chairman in order to devote all of his time to the lecture circuit.

The party nonetheless chose him as its candidate for lieutenant governor in 1901, but the Prohibition ticket received barely 1 percent of the vote. In addition to calling for a ban on alcohol, its platform condemned the practices of the dominant Democratic Party, and, at a time when white supremacy was a central political issue, the convention even included two African American delegates. The dismal results of that political strategy transformed the Prohibition movement. After 1902 the single-issue pressure-group tactics of the Anti-Saloon League rapidly replaced the broader crusade of the Prohibition Party in Virginia.

Bundick took no active part in the Anti-Saloon League beyond speaking at its 1904 convention, but his lectures helped lay the groundwork for the league's eventual success. A genial man with an impressive white goatee, he traveled throughout the eastern states and as far west as Nebraska to speak against the saloon. Bundick's own struggles with alcoholism informed his addresses, and he never condemned the drunkard. Instead, he emphasized the personal responsibility of his audiences. He tried to persuade abstainers to vote their principles rather than follow their party preferences and implored moderate drinkers to recognize that they helped sustain the liquor trade and its attendant social evils. In 1904 Bundick published six of his most popular addresses in a volume entitled *Bundick's Lectures*.

On 8 October 1908 William Thomas Bundick suffered a stroke while lecturing in Maryland. He returned to Onancock and died there on 9 December 1908 following a second stroke. Bundick was buried in the Onancock cemetery.

Biographies in *Bundick's Lectures* (1904), 1–3 (frontispiece por.), and Ernest Hurst Cherrington, ed., *Standard Encyclopedia of the Alcohol Problem* (1924), 2:450–451; BVS Marriage Register, Accomack Co.; Kirk Mariner, *Revival's Children: A Religious History of Virginia's Eastern Shore* (1979), 176–178; Accomack County Women's Christian Temperance Union, *The Temperance Movement on Virginia's Eastern Shore* (1966), 54–57; Charles C. Pearson and J. Edwin Hendricks, *Liquor and Anti-Liquor in Virginia, 1619–1919* (1967), 152–222; Jack S. Blocker Jr., *Retreat from Reform: The Prohibition Movement in the United States, 1890–1913* (1976), 210–221; numerous references to lectures in *Accomac Court House Peninsula Enterprise* and *Onancock Eastern Shore News*; obituaries in *Accomac Court House Peninsula Enterprise* and *Onancock Eastern Shore News*, both 12 Dec. 1908.

JOHN T. KNEEBONE

BUNN, Benjamin Franklin (11 February 1906–1 December 1989), Baptist minister and civil rights activist, was born in Nash County, North Carolina, the son of William H. Bunn and Mary Westray Bunn. When he was a child his family moved to Rocky Mount, North Carolina, where his father worked as a building contractor. Bunn attended elementary school in Rocky Mount and Booker T. Washington High School, where he was senior class president. The family then moved to East Orange, New Jersey, where the pastor of the Calvary Baptist Church became his mentor and persuaded him to enter the ministry. At Calvary Baptist on 9 September 1932 Bunn was licensed to preach.

Bunn earned a B.A. in 1936 and an M.Div. in 1939 from Virginia Union University. He was an active student leader and served as president of the campus chapter of the National Association for the Advancement of Colored People. One of the first black students to be admitted to Union Theological Seminary in Richmond, Bunn received a master of sacred theology degree in 1944 with a thesis entitled "The Way of Salvation." He also pursued advanced studies in philosophy at the University of California at Los Angeles. On 10 June 1939 Bunn married Imogene Morgan, a nurse with a degree from the University of Michigan. They had no children.

Bunn was ordained at Beulah Baptist Church in Woodford, Caroline County, in July 1937 and at Mount Zion Baptist Church in Downings, Richmond County, in July 1941. He served as pastor at First Liberty Baptist Church in Buckingham County, at Lebanon Baptist Church in New Kent County, at Saint John Baptist Church in Essex County, and at Bright Hope Baptist Church in Louisa County before taking charge of the First Colored Baptist Church (later the First Baptist Church, Main) in Charlottesville on 1 October 1944. During Bunn's thirty-six years there the church membership expanded more than fivefold, from about 100 to about 550 congregants.

Bunn became an advocate for civil rights for black people, promoted social concern for all citizens, and worked to unite the community in opposition to racism. Dismayed to find that Charlottesville lacked a chapter of the NAACP, he organized a public meeting at Jefferson High School in February 1954 at which a Charlottesville chapter was founded with Bernard A. Coles as president. Bunn maintained his membership in the chapter until his death and served periodically on its board until 1985.

Bunn was a pioneer in establishing interracial cooperation in the Charlottesville area. In December 1944 he became the first chair of the new Charlottesville Inter-Racial Commission, a group of about thirty concerned citizens, with approximately equal numbers of white and black members. At his church Bunn also established a Young Adult Fellowship program, which was renamed the Church Council on Human Relations. He charged the organization with investigating job opportunities and housing in the Charlottesville–Albemarle County area. The Inter-Racial Commission adopted the designation of the church group and in the 1950s became the Charlottesville Chapter of the Human Relations Council. Bunn also fostered interracial cooperation as a church leader, and his First Baptist Church was the first predominantly black church to join the Albemarle Association, Southern Baptist Convention.

Bunn strongly encouraged black voter registration. In 1940 the estimated number of black voters in Charlottesville was only 255. In 1946, when about 317 African Americans were registered in Charlottesville, Coles ran for the city council and received enough votes from white citizens to bring his total to 448, still far too few to win. Through a registration drive that Bunn promoted, the number of registered blacks in Charlottesville increased to 645 in 1948. Active in the local Democratic Party, he was influential in securing the first appointments of black citizens to Charlottesville's public welfare and public school boards.

Bunn's wife, too, was a leader in the church, in the work of interracial cooperation, and in the community, and the work of each spouse complemented that of the other. She worked in the school nurse program in Charlottesville, was director of the Negro Program at the Charlottesville Recreation Department, and became a staff nurse of the Instructive Visiting Nurse Association of Charlottesville. In 1975 she received an award as the outstanding member of the Virginia State Nurses Association.

Bunn retired as pastor of the First Baptist Church, Main, of Charlottesville on 1 January 1980, when he became pastor emeritus. On 22 March 1987 he received the Roy Wilkins Award for service to the community from the Charlottesville chapter of the NAACP. Benjamin Franklin Bunn died in Charlottesville on 1 December 1989 after a short illness and was buried in Oakwood Cemetery in that city. On 19 January 1990 he posthumously received a humanitarian award for outstanding contributions to the community as longtime pastor of the First Baptist Church, Main.

Richard I. McKinney, *Keeping the Faith: A History of the First Baptist Church, 1863–1980, in Light of Its Times* (1981), 113–114, 121–127 (por. on 122), 188–199, 287–302; information provided by widow, Imogene Morgan Bunn; Benjamin F. Bunn Papers and Charlottesville-Albemarle Chapter of the Virginia Council on Human Relations Papers, both UVA; John Hammond Moore, *Albemarle: Jefferson's County, 1727–1976* (1976), 433; Kathleen Murphy Dierenfield, "One 'Desegregated Heart': Sarah Patton Boyle and the Crusade for Civil Rights in Virginia," *VMHB* 104 (1996): 271–272, 274; *Charlottesville-Albemarle Tribune*, 26 Mar. 1987; obituaries in *Richmond Times-Dispatch*, 3 Dec. 1989, *Charlottesville Daily Progress* and *Richmond News Leader*, both 4 Dec. 1989, and *Charlottesville-Albemarle Tribune*, 14 Dec. 1989 (por.).

MICHAEL PLUNKETT

BURCH, Thomas Granville (3 July 1869– 20 March 1951), member of the House of Representatives and member of the United States Senate, was born in Henry County, the son of John Waller Burch, a farmer and tobacco manufacturer, and Sarah Frances Minter Burch. He attended public schools in the county and then moved about 1886 to Martinsville, where he sold insurance and invested in various local businesses. In 1922 Burch founded the Piedmont Trust Bank of Martinsville and served as its president from then until 1930, when he became chairman of the board.

Burch entered politics working in Democratic Party campaigns and then became a member of the Martinsville town council. He was elected mayor in 1912 and served until 1914, when he resigned to accept appointment as United States marshal for the Western District of Virginia. Burch held the appointment, which resulted from his party work during the presidential election of 1912, until 1921. The United States district attorney during those years was Richard Evelyn Byrd (1860–1925), a former Speaker of the House of Delegates, through whom Burch was probably introduced to many of the Democratic Party's other state leaders. Burch also sat on the State Board of Agriculture and Immigration in 1912, the State Board of Education in 1930–1931, and the advisory committee on the reorganization of the state government that Byrd's son Harry Flood Byrd (1887–1966) appointed as governor in 1926. By late in the 1920s Burch was chairman of the Democratic Party in the Fifth Congressional District.

In the summer of 1930 Burch mounted a successful primary campaign to challenge Joseph Whitehead, the incumbent Democratic congressman, on the grounds that in 1928 Whitehead had refused to support the party's presidential nominee, Alfred E. Smith. Burch won the general election and every succeeding one without serious opposition until he announced his intention early in 1946 to retire. He represented an eight-county district lying along the North Carolina border. Reapportionment added a ninth county beginning with the 74th Congress. During his sixteen years in the House, Burch served on the Committee on Post Offices and Post Roads and chaired it from 1943 to 1946. He was credited with creating affordable air parcel post and with getting some postmasters a regular salary in lieu of a fee system that had paid them according to the number of letters canceled in their offices.

Burch was a conservative politician and on issues of state politics generally agreed with Harry Byrd, who became a United States senator in 1933. The two also shared a growing dislike of the New Deal. Because of Burch's ability and conservatism, Byrd and his few intimate advisers began passing the word in the autumn of 1935 that Burch was to be their candidate for governor in 1937. On 13 November 1935, however, Burch surprised them by proposing an expensive plan under which the state government would pay all teachers' salaries and use a uniform pay scale, thereby eliminating inequalities in salaries and educational opportunities among the various regions of Virginia. Such a plan clearly would have required additional taxes, and although Burch quickly hedged and then repudiated his suggestion, the damage was done. Within weeks Byrd and his closest political friends began

a futile search for an alternative gubernatorial candidate to Lieutenant Governor James Hubert Price, around whom dissident Democrats and supporters of the New Deal were already beginning to coalesce.

After that episode Burch was never again part of the party organization's inner circle, although he was briefly Byrd's colleague in the United States Senate. Following the death of Senator Carter Glass on 28 May 1946, Burch's close friend Governor William Munford Tuck appointed him to fill the vacant seat. Burch declined to run in the special election that autumn and served as a senator only from 31 May to 5 November 1946. He then retired from public life except for service in 1947 as chairman of a commission Tuck appointed to advise him on another reorganization of the state government. Burch remained interested in politics, however. He was the most prominent Virginia Democrat to endorse the presidential candidacy of J. Strom Thurmond on the Dixiecrat ticket in 1948. Burch stated that, unlike Joseph Whitehead twenty years before, he was adhering to the platform of the Virginia Democratic Party, and he charged that President Harry S. Truman had abandoned the party's traditions.

Burch married Mary E. Anson, daughter of an Episcopal clergyman, on 22 April 1903. They had no children. Thomas Granville Burch died of a heart attack in Martinsville General Hospital on 20 March 1951. His estate was worth approximately $1 million, and his will left more than $100,000 to charities. Burch also bequeathed his house on West Church Street to the public library in Martinsville. He was buried in Oakwood Cemetery in that city.

NCAB, 39:313; Henry Co. Birth Register; BVS Marriage Register, Henry Co.; letters concerning Burch in Harry Flood Byrd (1887–1966) Papers and other collections, UVA, and in William Munford Tuck Papers and other collections, W&M; obituaries in *Richmond News Leader*, 20 Mar. 1951 (por.), and in *Martinsville Bulletin*, *New York Times*, and *Richmond Times-Dispatch*, all 21 Mar. 1951; estate described in *Martinsville Bulletin*, 1 Apr. 1951.

BRENT TARTER

BURDETT, John Sinsell (20 December 1818–4 April 1904), member of the Convention of 1861, was born at Pruntytown, in Harrison

County, the son of Frederick Burdett and Susan Sinsell Burdett, both natives of Fauquier County. As a boy he clerked in his father's mercantile business and garnered an adequate education in the local schools, although he was largely self-taught. Burdett took over the family business and eventually became a successful merchant in his own right, but his interests extended beyond the ledger book to the realm of public affairs.

On 1 July 1845 Burdett married Abby Ann Johnson, of Bridgeport, Harrison County, a sister of Waldo P. Johnson, who later served as United States senator from Missouri. The couple had four sons and three daughters. The next year Burdett's own career as a public servant began with his election to the House of Delegates representing Taylor County, which had been formed in 1844 from portions of Barbour, Harrison, and Marion Counties. An able politician, he was returned to the legislature in the next two elections. During the 1846–1847 session Burdett served on the Committee to Examine the Register's Office, and during the 1847–1848 session he added to that assignment a seat on the Committee on Trade and Mechanic Arts. In 1850 he became a census taker for Taylor County, and in 1852 he served another term in the General Assembly, when he again sat on the Committee on Trade and Mechanic Arts and the Joint Committee to Examine the Register's Office.

Like many of his contemporaries in western Virginia, Burdett was a Unionist who feared that the political goals of the slaveholding class would have serious consequences for his own region. When the legislature called for a state convention to assemble in Richmond on 13 February 1861 to deal with the secession crisis, Burdett was elected a delegate from Taylor County. On 4 April he voted with the majority against secession. On 17 April, when the question was reintroduced, Burdett spoke against disunion and asserted that his county would be overwhelmed by one or the other of the antagonists if secession passed and war broke out. Later that day, however, the delegates voted to secede, and that night Burdett left for home to work in behalf of pro-Unionist forces, an activity for which the convention expelled him on 29 June.

On 13 May 1861 Burdett represented Taylor County at a meeting in Wheeling at which it was determined that if Virginia voters ratified the Ordinance of Secession, then western Virginia would hold elections on 4 June to select delegates to its own convention. After secession was approved on 23 May, the rebellious western counties duly held their elections. Burdett was chosen one of two delegates to join Taylor County's state senator and member of the House of Delegates at the convention, which assembled in Wheeling on 11 June. The delegates declared the offices of the Richmond government vacant, elected new state officers, and passed an ordinance for the purpose of seeking statehood.

During the Civil War Burdett was a captain in the commissary service of the United States Army and served with the 3d Brigade, Fifth Corps, Army of the Potomac. Afterward he resumed his political career and served from 1866 to 1867 in the West Virginia Senate from a district comprising Monongalia, Preston, and Taylor Counties. In 1868 Burdett and his family moved to Charleston, and that same year he was a delegate to the Republican National Convention. During the 1870s, however, he nominally attached himself to the Democratic Party to win election as state treasurer. Burdett served two terms, beginning in March 1871, but he was impeached, found guilty of two of the twenty-one articles, and removed from office effective 30 January 1876 for corruption, conspiracy to defraud the state of $40,000, and attempted bribery of a bank official. He resumed his former party affiliation and in 1888 served on the Republican National League's executive committee. After a long life in public service, John Sinsell Burdett died at his home in Charleston on 4 April 1904 following a stroke and was buried at Spring Hill Cemetery in that city.

Atkinson and Gibbens, *Prominent Men*, 676–679 (por.); *Men of West Virginia* (1903), 1:55–57 (por.); *A Reminiscent History of Northern West Virginia* (1895), 256–258; Theodore F. Lang, *Loyal West Virginia, From 1861 to 1865* (1895), 122–124; Reese and Gaines, *Proceedings of 1861 Convention*, 3:163–164, 4:95–96, 144; Granville Davisson Hall, *The Rending of Virginia: A History* (1902; repr. 2000), esp. 541–547; *Journal of West Virginia House of Delegates,* 1875 adjourned sess., 105–121, 191–193; *Proceedings of the Senate Sitting for the Trial of the Impeach-*

ment of John S. Burdett, Treasurer of the State of West Virginia (1875); Wheeling Intelligencer, 14, 15, 24–25, 28–29, 31 Jan., 1 Feb. 1876; Kanawha Co., W.Va., Death Register (variant death date of 7 Apr. 1904); obituary in Charleston Daily Mail, 4 Apr. 1904 (giving death date of 4 Apr. 1904); estate settlement described in Charleston Daily Gazette, 9 Apr. 1904.

RANDALL S. GOODEN

BURGES, Albridgton Samuel Hardy (ca. 1792–by 18 September 1865), member of the Convention of 1850–1851, was born probably in Southampton County, the son of Henry John Burges, an Episcopal clergyman, and Sarah Albridgton Jones Burges. His father's politics during the American Revolution led to his jailing by the British. After independence Parson Burges, as he was known, served as a justice of the peace and conducted an academy.

After the death of his father late in the 1790s, Burges lived with Simmons Baker, a physician, and then studied medicine at the University of North Carolina from 1805 to 1809. He began his practice in Raleigh, where on 18 May 1814 he married Mary Allen Gilmour. They had at least two children, one a son, before she died on 3 December 1822. Burges returned to low-lying Southampton County, where endemic diseases such as typhoid and malaria kept doctors busy. According to family tradition Burges also wrote on medical topics. He prospered and resided in a handsome three-story house at Burges Crossroad about a mile south of Berlin. On 2 April 1833 Burges married nineteen-year-old Louisa Wellons. They had at least three sons and two daughters.

A. S. H. Burges, although plainly a man of local stature, played no significant political role until the 1840s, when he became a local leader of the Whig Party. He served as an election commissioner in his voting district and in the October 1851 primary ran an unsuccessful race for the House of Delegates. Burges and his relatives in the prominent Kello and Urquhart families gave their part of the county a decidedly Whiggish complexion. He had won election in 1850 to a convention called to revise Virginia's constitution. Burges was the beneficiary of political intrigue to which he was no more than an interested bystander. One of the county's best-known Democrats, John Young Mason, lived in Rich-

mond, and party leaders from the other five counties in the district (Greensville, Isle of Wight, Nansemond, Surry, and Sussex) refused to nominate him. Southampton County Democrats accordingly cut a deal with Whigs to create a bipartisan convention ticket that comprised Mason; another local Democrat, Robert Ridley; Burges; and John Randolph Chambliss (1809–1875), a states' rights Whig from Greensville County. Enjoying bipartisan support from the largest county in the district, all four candidates were elected.

Democrats had most likely been willing to divide their ticket because the issues confronting the convention tended to break along regional rather than party lines. Burges voted with the other eastern delegates against basing representation in the General Assembly exclusively on the white population. In so doing he acted to protect the advantage that the eastern counties, with their large population of slaves, enjoyed over the western counties in the apportionment of assembly seats. Instead, Burges proposed on 1 April 1851 combining population and property as the basis of representation. He served on the Committee on Education and Public Instruction but did not play an important role or often speak insofar as surviving records of the debates disclose. Because Burges was absent when the final vote on the new constitution was taken, his opinion of the document is not known.

Ten years later local Democrats, hoping to find a prominent Whig who favored secession, offered to nominate Burges to a state convention called to consider the secession crisis. Torn by conflicting loyalties, he declined. In the February 1861 election Burges supported an antisecession candidate but abstained on the vote to require a popular referendum to approve secession if the convention voted in favor of leaving the Union. The Civil War sharply depleted his estate, which in 1860 included fifteen slaves and was valued at almost $20,000. A postwar inventory valued Burges's assets at less than $4,000. He had probably ceased to practice medicine by then. Identified in the 1860 census as a farmer, Burges may have given his medical books to his son Richard Urquhart Burges. The younger man served as a surgeon in the Confederate army and won

Southampton County's seat in the House of Delegates in the pivotal 1869 election when local Conservatives, joined by many former Whigs, narrowly defeated Joseph Gregory, a black minister who led Southampton's Republicans during Reconstruction.

Albridgton Samuel Hardy Burges added a codicil to his will on 30 May 1863 and died possibly during 1864 and certainly no later than 18 September 1865, when his will was proved in the Southampton County Court.

Census, Southampton Co., 1850, 1860, with age given as fifty-eight on 18 Sept. 1850 and sixty-seven on 7 Aug. 1860; French Biographies, giving 1864 year of death; first marriage in *Raleigh Star*, 20 May 1814; second marriage in Southampton Co. Marriage Register; Emerson Macaulay Babb, *History of Ivor and Its Environs* (1965), 25–29, 37; Daniel W. Crofts, *Old Southampton: Politics and Society in a Virginia County, 1834–1869* (1992), 12, 13, 156, 162–163, 176, 190, 270; *Journal of 1850–1851 Convention,* 226; *Supplement, 1850–1851 Convention Debates*, nos. 24, 33; will and estate inventory in Southampton Co. Will Book, 18:321, 399–401.

DANIEL W. CROFTS

BURGWYN, Collinson Pierrepont Edwards (5 April 1852–23 February 1915), civil engineer, was born in Jackson, North Carolina, the son of Henry King Burgwyn, a successful planter, and Anna Greenough Burgwyn. His mother belonged to a distinguished New England family, and his father had family roots in both New England and North Carolina. Several of Burgwyn's elder brothers were educated in the North, and the Civil War proved particularly difficult for the family because of its many ties to New England. One brother died fighting for the Confederacy at Gettysburg, and another was wounded and captured in 1864 at Cold Harbor.

The family moved from North Carolina to Boston immediately after the Civil War. About a year later the family relocated to Richmond, where Burgwyn attended a private school before returning to Boston to enter the Boston Latin School, from which he graduated in 1869. He then enrolled in Harvard University, where he won prizes for his Latin poetry before graduating in 1874. Burgwyn went on to receive a civil engineering degree in 1876 from Harvard's Lawrence Scientific School.

C. P. E. Burgwyn returned to Richmond and in 1877 entered the competition for the commission to design a westward expansion of Hollywood Cemetery. Although young and inexperienced, he produced a winning design that showed attention to detail, relied on the natural topography, and was compatible with the original 1848 plan of John Notman. In the autumn of 1878 Burgwyn supervised the installation of Richmond's first telephone lines, which stretched across rooftops and through trees from the state penitentiary to the central business district.

For about two years Burgwyn worked for the United States Coast Survey on the development of waterways between Norfolk and eastern North Carolina and into the Dismal Swamp. After he returned to Richmond he was one of the engineers employed by the federal government until 1891 on river and harbor improvements on the James River. Burgwyn published several articles, complete with detailed information on geology, topography, climate, and water power, extolling the potential of the James River for commercial development. He later served as a consultant on several dock construction proposals.

By 1886 Burgwyn was working for the city engineer, Wilfred Emory Cutshaw, with whom he supervised the construction of the new city hall. Bypassing the city's contractors, the Richmond city council gave Cutshaw and Burgwyn the unusual task of constructing a public building with the use of day labor. Through this project Burgwyn evidently gained an interest in the plight of the working man, and by 1888 he had become the principal of the Virginia Mechanics' Institute, a post he held for more than twenty years. The institute had begun as a trade school but expanded to include basic academic courses.

In 1887 Burgwyn laid out the first section of Monument Avenue, working as a consulting engineer for Otway Slaughter Allen, the developer of the property. Burgwyn's knowledge of Boston's Commonwealth Avenue, a broad boulevard of stately homes, and Monument Place in Baltimore, which Allen himself admired, probably influenced Burgwyn's design of axial streets with treed medians crossing at a traffic circle.

He traveled to Paris to inspect Marius-Jean-Antonin Mercié's equestrian statue of Robert Edward Lee before it was packed and shipped to Richmond for placement on Monument Avenue. Burgwyn's glowing reports of the statue's dignity, especially when compared with famous equestrian monuments in European capitals, were published in Richmond's newspapers.

Burgwyn's early interest in literature and poetry emerged again in 1889 when he published *The Huguenot Lovers: A Tale of the Old Dominion*. The novel dealt with a young Boston woman who traveled to the South and was persuaded by the gallantry of its people to alter her preconceived ideas about the Civil War, after which she fell in love with a former Confederate officer. Burgwyn's writing, though sometimes melodramatic, offers articulate descriptions of the Richmond area during Reconstruction. In 1894 he published *The Lost Diamond,* a play on a similar theme.

During the 1890s Burgwyn continued his efforts to develop the Richmond area as an industrial and commercial center. He served as president of the Virginia Dredging and Dock Company, the Petersburg Iron Works Company, and the Bermuda Hundred Construction Company, which built a new line of the Farmville and Powhatan Railroad. Burgwyn became vice president of the Warwick Park Transportation Company, which developed a park on the bank of the James River four miles below Richmond and transported visitors to and from the park by steamboat. He was also a director of the Virginia Navigation Company, the successor to the Virginia Steamboat Company, which ran steamboats between Norfolk and Richmond. By 1902 Burgwyn had designed and supervised the construction of a hydroelectric plant on the Meherrin River in Emporia.

Burgwyn's vision for Richmond's development influenced the location of the Main Street railway station. When a large terminal was being planned on a site north of the city, the Chamber of Commerce hired him to prepare preliminary sketches for a downtown passenger station. Burgwyn's sketches convinced officials of the Richmond, Fredericksburg, and Potomac Railroad and the Atlantic Coast Line Railroad of the advantages of building closer to the city's center, and Main Street Station (1901) was the result.

On 15 October 1884 Burgwyn married Rosa Bayley Higginbotham, of Henrico County. They had no children, and she died on 30 April 1909. In his later years Burgwyn lived at the Westmoreland Club, of which he was a longtime member. Collinson Pierrepont Edwards Burgwyn died at the Richmond home of a nephew on 23 February 1915 after two months' illness and was buried in Hollywood Cemetery.

Biographical information and newspaper clippings, vertical files, VM/RHC; Burgwyn Family Papers, Southern Historical Collection, UNC; Burgwyn letters in VM/RHC and various collections, VHS; family information in Archibald K. Davis, *Boy Colonel of the Confederacy: The Life and Times of Henry King Burgwyn, Jr.* (1985); BVS Marriage Register, Henrico Co.; Mary H. Mitchell, *Hollywood Cemetery: The History of a Southern Shrine* (1999), 98–101, 121 (por., pl. 31); Virginia Capital Bicentennial Commission, untitled typescript on history of the telephone system in Richmond, 1879–1937, in *Sketches of Societies and Institutions, Together with Descriptions of Phases of Social, Political, and Economic Development in Richmond, Virginia* (1937), pt. 36; Carden C. McGehee Jr., "The Planning, Sculpture, and Architecture of Monument Avenue, Richmond, Virginia" (master's thesis, UVA School of Architecture, 1980); Sarah Shields Driggs, Richard Guy Wilson, and Robert P. Winthrop, *Richmond's Monument Avenue* (2001), 31, 33–34, 48, 99–100, 107, 138–139; *The City on the James: Richmond, Virginia* (1893), 59–60, 115–116; principal professional publications include *Report of Colonel C. P. E. Burgwyn, Civil Engineer, on the Natural Advantages and Water-Power Facilities of the City of Manchester and the County of Chesterfield, with Accompanying Maps* (1888), and *Report on Terminal, Dock and Manufacturing Facilities* (1888); obituaries in *Richmond Times-Dispatch* and *Richmond Virginian*, both 24 Feb. 1915; funeral reported in *Richmond Virginian*, 26 Feb. 1915.

SARAH SHIELDS DRIGGS

BURK, John Daly (1771 or 1772–11 April 1808), writer and historian, was born John Burk in County Cork, Ireland. Very little is known of his youth, except that he was the son of James Burk, a schoolmaster, and that he was reared a Protestant. On 5 June 1792 at age twenty Burk was admitted as a sizar, or student on scholarship, to Trinity College, University of Dublin. Like many of his fellow students, he imbibed anti-British attitudes and was inspired by the French Revolution. Burk may have joined the Society of United Irishmen, a revolutionary organization seeking

Catholic emancipation, reform of the oligarchic Irish parliament, and self-government for Ireland. His pamphlet lamenting the failure of the Irish revolution of the 1780s and hoping for Hibernian independence brought him to the attention of the board of Trinity College. Burk was charged with disseminating atheism rather than with sedition. In defending himself against his accusers, he denied, among other things, the biblical creation story and the divinity of Christ and consequently on 11 April 1794 was dismissed from the university. As he did several times later in life, he published an account of his disputes with the authorities as *The Trial of John Burk, Late of Trinity College, for Heresy and Blasphemy* (1794).

Burk joined and organized several secret revolutionary republican societies. Betrayed by an informer, he narrowly eluded arrest on treason charges in February 1796 with the assistance of a woman named Daly. In gratitude Burk took Daly as his middle name. Forced to flee Ireland, he took passage on a brig bound for Boston, where he had arrived by April 1796. Burk reportedly left behind a wife and son whose names and fates are not known.

During the next several years Burk pursued a stormy career as a dramatist and newspaperman. On 6 October 1796, with the support of several prominent men, he began publication of Boston's first daily newspaper, the *Polar Star and Boston Daily Advertiser*. Burk regarded the United States as an example for his native land, a sentiment he affirmed by spending the long ocean voyage to Boston writing a "republican tragedy" entitled *Bunker-Hill: or, The Death of General Warren, An Historic Tragedy* (1797). The piece characterized the American Revolution as the beginning of a new era, but with little plot or character development, it was primarily patriotic propaganda. In February 1797 *Bunker-Hill* began a run of nine performances at the Haymarket Theatre in Boston under the direction of Charles S. Powell, a Republican activist. By May 1797 two Burk pantomime plays, *The Indian War Feast: or The American Heroine* and *Island of Calypso*, a retelling of the tale of Odysseus's son Telemachus, had also been performed in Boston.

After the *Polar Star* failed in February 1797, Burk moved to New York City during the summer. He wrote three plays in New York that year, *Female Patriotism: or, the Death of Joan d'Arc*; *Prince of Susa: A Tragedy*; and *The Exiles: A Tragedy*. Burk also started but never completed an epic poem, *Columbiad*. In April 1798 he began working for the *Time Piece*, a Republican newspaper formerly edited by Philip Freneau, and by June of that year he had become chief editor. The meteoric rise of the *Time Piece* and Burk's relentless onslaught on the Federalists as betrayers of the republican ideal produced stiff counterattacks from prominent Federalists. When Burk insinuated that President John Adams had altered the wording of letters from France so as to incite war, he was arrested and charged on 6 July 1798 with sedition and libel, making him and Benjamin Franklin Bache the only Republican editors to be indicted for seditious libel under common law before the passage of the Sedition Act of 1798.

While awaiting settlement of his case Burk wrote a *History of the Late War in Ireland, With an Account of the United Irish Association* (1799). Less history than autobiography and contemporary account, it was primarily an apology for the United Irishmen and an argument that the French Republic remained true to the principles of the international republican movement. By contrast, a disillusioned Burk described the United States as retreating from the cause of republican liberty.

With Aaron Burr, his friend and Republican patron, negotiating in his behalf, the government agreed to drop the charges on condition that Burk leave the United States. Instead, during the summer of 1799 he fled to Virginia, where he lived under an assumed name briefly before being named president of the short-lived Jefferson College in Amelia County. After the expiration of the Alien and Sedition Acts in June 1800 and March 1801, respectively, and Thomas Jefferson's inauguration as president, Burk resumed his own name and moved to Petersburg. He was admitted to the bar there on 8 September 1801 and became a moderately prosperous attorney. After the repeal of the Naturalization Act of 1798, Burk became an American citizen on 1 November

1802. During this time his wife, Christianna Borne Curtis Burk, a Massachusetts native whom he had most likely married while in Boston, died and left Burk with their own son and responsibility for her two sons by her first husband. Burk was a shareholder in the Battersea Paper Mills and in 1807 was president of the Petersburg Company of Riflemen.

Burk continued to pontificate about politics and culture and indulge his love of belles lettres. He wrote and publicly recited poetry. Theaters staged productions of his *Bunker-Hill* and two new plays, *Oberon, or the Siege of Mexico* (1802) and *Bethlem Gabor, Lord of Transylvania, Or, The Man Hating Palatine* (1807). Burk expressed his Irish cultural nationalism by assembling a collection of Irish music prefaced by a historical essay strongly tinged with Gaelic traditionalism. Published posthumously as *A Selection, From the Ancient Music of Ireland, Arranged for the Flute or Violin* (1824), it included fourteen poems that he had written to be performed to Irish airs.

Burk's gratitude toward and admiration of Jefferson inspired him to write his most enduring work, a *History of Virginia* (1804–1805). As early as 1800 Jefferson had urged him to produce a history of Virginia illustrating the growth of freedom in an agrarian society. Burk wrote not as a newly minted Virginian but as a Virginia patriot, a cosmopolitan republican, an Irish revolutionary, and a defender of the French Revolution. He prepared a brief for Virginia as the historical mother of American republicanism and, more important, as representative of the qualities he considered characteristically American, in contrast to the doctrines of Federalists and New Englanders. In keeping with his theme, Burk was one of the first Virginia historians to interpret Bacon's Rebellion of 1676 as a revolt against English tyranny rather than an episode in the continuing conflicts between settlers and Native Americans or a civil strife between contending political leaders. The three-volume *History of Virginia* carried the story through 1775. As might have been expected, Burk clearly regarded Virginia's role in the American Revolution as an integral part of the age of international republican revolution. As the first attempt at a complete history of Virginia, his volumes strongly influenced succeeding generations of Virginians.

Burk was unable to complete his history, although a fourth volume carrying the narrative to 1781 was begun by Skelton Jones and finally completed and published in 1816 by Louis Hue Girardin. Aroused by French attacks on American shipping, Burk denounced the French government in 1808 and at a dinner called the French people a "pack of rascals." Felix Coquebert, a young Frenchman residing in Virginia, then challenged him to a duel. The confrontation took place near Petersburg on 11 April 1808, and John Daly Burk was shot and killed. He was buried at Cedar Grove plantation near Petersburg, and in 1905 a monument in his memory was erected in Blandford Cemetery.

Joseph I. Shulim, "John Daly Burk: Irish Revolutionist and American Patriot," *Transactions of the American Philosophical Society*, new ser., 54, pt. 6 (1964); Joseph T. Buckingham, *Specimens of Newspaper Literature: With Personal Memoirs, Anecdotes and Reminiscences* (1850), 2:294–300; Charles Campbell, ed., *Some Materials to Serve for a Brief Memoir of John Daly Burk, Author of a History of Virginia* (1868); Edward A. Wyatt IV, *John Daly Burk, Patriot—Playwright—Historian*, in *Southern Sketches*, 1st ser., no. 7 (1936); Arthur H. Shaffer, "John Daly Burk's *History of Virginia* and the Development of American National History," *VMHB* 77 (1969): 336–346; George Dames Burtchaell and Thomas Ulick Sadleir, eds., *Alumni Dublinenses: A Register of the Students, Graduates, Professors and Provosts of Trinity College in the University of Dublin (1593–1860)*, new ed. (1935), 114; Burk letters in Thomas Jefferson Papers, LC; Aaron Burr to James Monroe, 25 Dec. 1798, in Mary-Jo Kline et al., eds., *Political Correspondence and Public Papers of Aaron Burr* (1983), 1:361–362; Petersburg Hustings Court Minute Book (1800–1804), 123; Petersburg Hustings Court Will Book, 2:32; death notice and accounts of funeral in *Richmond Enquirer*, 12, 19 Apr., 6 May 1808 (quotation).

Arthur H. Shaffer

BURKE, Emmett Carroll (5 January 1875– 26 December 1953), banker, was born in Richmond, the son of Charles Burke, a laborer, and Martha Burke. He graduated from the Richmond Colored Normal School in 1893, taught briefly, and then became the valet of a local physician. He joined the Grand Fountain United Order of True Reformers, a fraternal insurance order, and when the founder, William Washington Browne, visited Burke's lodge, Browne was so impressed by Burke that he offered him a job as a teller in the order's bank. Burke began his career in banking there on 30 July 1894.

Nine years later, in October 1903, Burke left the Savings Bank of the Grand Fountain United Order of True Reformers to become the cashier of the new Saint Luke Penny Savings Bank. Maggie Lena Mitchell Walker, the Grand Worthy Secretary of the Independent Order of Saint Luke, another fraternal insurance organization, had decided to expand the order's work by creating a bank. Opened on 2 November 1903, the bank was at first an adjunct to the order's various other enterprises, which included a printing shop, a newspaper, and a dry goods store. In addition to his duties with the bank, Burke served as treasurer of the store until its demise in November 1911. Survival for the small bank may have seemed unlikely. Indeed, shortly after his marriage on 29 June 1904 to Amy Blanche Moseley, a teacher, Burke announced his resignation and intention of entering the railroad service, but he soon reversed his decision.

The much larger True Reformers' Bank failed suddenly in 1910, as did another local black institution, the Nickel Savings Bank. New state regulations adopted in the aftermath of the failures required the separation of the Saint Luke Penny Savings Bank from the Independent Order of Saint Luke. The bank became a private enterprise, owned by stockholders, although its officers remained the same. State banking examiners who visited regularly expressed concern occasionally at Burke's lack of formal training in accounting, but they usually judged the bank well run.

Two new banks owned by African Americans opened in Richmond in 1920, but the Saint Luke Bank and Trust Company (its name starting in 1923) was by far the largest. The vaunted prosperity of the 1920s ended early for black Richmonders, in that the three banks' resources in 1928 were less than they had been two years earlier. Officers of the banks began discussing a merger. On 2 January 1930 the Saint Luke Bank and Trust Company and the Second Street Savings Bank combined to form the Consolidated Bank and Trust Company, and one year later the Commercial Bank and Trust Company merged

with the new institution. With the merger, Burke succeeded Walker as president. A newspaper story at the time commented on his parsimonious approach to lending the bank's money. Burke's fiscal conservatism served the bank well during the Great Depression. In 1935 the Federal Housing Administration authorized the bank to make its mortgage loans. Total assets declined during that decade, but the bank survived the hard times.

Burke's own reputation for probity and intelligence bolstered public confidence in the bank. In 1926 he earned a bachelor of laws degree from Virginia Union University, and he served on the school's board of trustees from 1943 until his death. A writer for the *Richmond Planet* identified Burke in 1934 as one of the ten greatest African Americans in the capital. A white judge named him the following year to a special grand jury investigating two city officials charged with embezzlement, a rare appointment for an African American at that time. More important than personal honors, however, Burke's careful lending policies helped establish the flourishing black business district in the bank's Jackson Ward neighborhood.

On 17 January 1950, shortly after Burke's seventy-fifth birthday, the board of directors elected him to another year's term as president of the bank, but that spring he fell ill at the bank and required assistance to do his work. Some board members became concerned that his health was failing and requested at the end of May that he step down from active leadership. Stung by the board's proposal that he move to an upstairs office and accept a reduced salary, Burke angrily severed all connections with the bank on 5 June 1950.

Burke had one son who survived him. In retirement he remained active in Ebenezer Baptist Church, which he served as treasurer for forty-one years. Emmett Carroll Burke died in Richmond of complications resulting from arteriosclerosis on 26 December 1953 and was buried in Evergreen Cemetery in that city.

Biography in W. P. Burrell and D. E. Johnson, *Twenty-Five Years History of the Grand Fountain of the United Order of True Reformers, 1881–1905* (1909), 496–497 (provides birth date); information provided by grandson Emmett M. Burke Jr.; BVS Birth Register, Richmond City (birth date of 28 Jan. 1875 for Emmel Burke, a female); BVS Marriage Register, Richmond City; *Richmond Planet*, 1 Aug. 1903, 18 June, 2 July 1904, 3, 10 Jan. 1931, 6 July 1935; *Richmond Afro-American*, 10, 17 June 1950; Consolidated Bank and Trust Company, *"Let Us Have A Bank That Will Take The Nickels And Turn Them Into Dollars"* [ca. 1991], 4–14 (pors.); bank's fiscal health documented in annual reports of State Corporation Commission's banking section; "Richmond's Greatest Blacks: A 1934 Nomination," *Richmond Quarterly* 5 (spring 1983): 52; obituaries in *Richmond Times-Dispatch*, 29 Dec. 1953, *Richmond Afro-American*, 2 Jan. 1954, and *Norfolk Journal and Guide*, 9 Jan. 1954.

JOHN T. KNEEBONE

BURKE, John Woolfolk (21 January 1825–8 November 1907), banker, was born at Ivy Mount in Caroline County, the son of John Muse Burke and Sophia Frances Woolfolk Burke. Little is known about his youth and education. At age twenty-three he moved to Alexandria, and in 1852 he and Arthur Herbert opened a private brokerage and banking business, Burke and Herbert's Banking and Exchange Office. Later that same year, on 23 November 1852, Burke married Julia Thompson. She died following the birth of their only child, a son, and in Philadelphia on 13 October 1858 Burke married Martha Jefferson Trist, daughter of the diplomat Nicholas Philip Trist and great-granddaughter of Thomas Jefferson. They had four sons and three daughters.

From the beginning the Burke and Herbert firm was active in the financial development of northern Virginia. It played a role in the completion of the Alexandria Canal, which joined the city to the Chesapeake and Ohio Canal at Georgetown; in establishing the Washington and Alexandria Steamboat Company; and in financing the Orange and Alexandria Railroad. During the Civil War, when Alexandria was occupied by the United States Army, Herbert became colonel of the 17th Regiment Virginia Infantry. Burke remained in Alexandria. He refused to take a loyalty oath to the United States, was placed under house arrest, and had his bank closed. After being accused of participation in treasonable meetings, Burke was arrested and confined in the infamous Old Capitol Prison in Washington, D.C., for about ten weeks in 1862. Even then he managed to safeguard $200,000 in bonds and money that the Mount Vernon Ladies' Association of the Union

had paid to John Augustine Washington, the last private owner of Mount Vernon, to acquire the first president's estate.

In June 1865 Burke reestablished his business as John W. Burke, Broker. Herbert resumed his role as a partner in November, along with a temporary third partner, Jourdon W. Maury, an Alexandria businessman who provided needed capital and remained with the firm until 1869. The renamed Burke, Herbert and Company resumed its promotion of the region's financial development. The bank helped manage the Greenbrier Hotel, the world-famous spa at White Sulphur Springs, West Virginia, and it sold railroad bonds and acted as an agent for the purchase of both United States government bonds and Virginia securities. In 1899 Herbert sold his shares to Burke's three sons, but the bank's name did not change. Burke also took an active part in Alexandria's civic affairs. He represented the city's First Ward on the board of aldermen and the school board.

Burke and Herbert's bank was unusually successful. The reputations that the founders earned, the careful stewardship of Burke's sons, and the role the firm played in the regional economy enabled it to prosper and endure. The bank survived financial crises, depressions, and other national emergencies that doomed many other private as well as publicly chartered banks. As waves of mergers and takeovers reduced the number of small and regional banks in Virginia during the last years of the twentieth century, the Burke and Herbert Bank and Trust Company, as it was known by the 1960s, survived and remained independent.

John Woolfolk Burke died at his Alexandria home on 8 November 1907. He was buried in Ivy Hill Cemetery in that city.

Biography by John Randolph Burke in George Gree Shackelford, ed., *Collected Papers of the Monticello Association of the Descendants of Thomas Jefferson* (1965–1984), 2:151–154, giving second marriage date of 12 Oct. 1858; Dorothy Holcombe Kabler, *A History of Burke and Herbert's Century of Service to Alexandria and Virginia, 1852–1952* (1952), 3–48 (por. on 7); Alexandria Association, *Our Town: 1749–1865, Likenesses of This Place and Its People Taken from Life by Artists Known and Unknown* (1956), 83–84; several Burke letters in Nicholas Philip Trist Papers, Southern Historical Collection, UNC; *Alexandria*

Gazette, 25 Nov. 1852, 16 Oct. 1858 (giving second marriage date of 13 Oct. 1858); "A Century of Banking: The Burke and Herbert Bank and Trust Company of Alexandria," *Commonwealth* 20 (Feb. 1953): 20–21; Dorothy Troth Muir, *Presence of a Lady: Mount Vernon, 1861–1868* (1946), 47–50; obituaries in *Alexandria Gazette* and *Washington Evening Star,* both 8 Nov. 1907, and *Richmond Times-Dispatch,* 9 Nov. 1907; account of funeral in *Alexandria Gazette,* 11 Nov. 1907.

DENNIS J. PFENNIG

BURKE, Richard Floyd (29 December 1851–21 February 1924), banker, was born in Nottoway County, the son of Richard Henry Leigh Burke, a physician, and Sarah Jane Irby Burke. His father died before Burke was five years old, and he grew up on the Nottoway County estate of his maternal grandparents, William Blunt Irby and Sarah Washington Stith Irby. Following his mother's marriage on 23 October 1867 to William Henry Hallowell, agent for the South Side Railroad Company (later part of the Norfolk and Western Railway), Burke learned telegraphy from his stepfather and then joined the railroad as assistant agent while still in his teens. In 1872 he was assigned to Appomattox Junction (later the town of Appomattox), where he worked until he resigned in 1901. On 27 May 1874 Burke married Lucy Alice Sears, of Appomattox County. They had three sons and six daughters.

On 8 April 1901 Burke, John Randolph Atwood, and Henry DeLaWarr Flood opened the Bank of Appomattox. For almost two decades it was the county's only bank. Atwood was president, Flood vice president, and Burke, with a reputation for integrity and good business management established during his twenty-nine years as railroad agent, was cashier and in charge of daily financial operations. His second son, Richard Leigh Burke, who had also worked for the railroad, served as assistant cashier and became a member of the bank's board of directors. Following Atwood's death in 1912, Burke became vice president, and after Flood's death in December 1921, Burke became president. By 1908 the bank's surplus had equaled its capital, and when Burke assumed the presidency in 1922, the Bank of Appomattox had a capital of $20,000 and a surplus of about $16,100, and each of its 400 shares was worth $84.50.

On 29 June 1903 Burke became treasurer of Appomattox County following the elected treasurer's resignation. In the Democratic Party primary in August Burke won the nomination and in November was elected to a full term as treasurer. He was repeatedly reelected and served until his death. Only when local party factionalism caused an opposition slate to be nominated in 1915 did Burke face a serious challenge. That year he defeated D. Mott Robertson, whom he had succeeded as county treasurer twelve years earlier, by a vote of 467 to 409.

Throughout his life Burke played a significant role in community affairs. After the county courthouse burned in 1892, he helped lead the successful movement to build the new courthouse at Appomattox Junction rather than at Appomattox Court House, three miles from the railroad. Later, as a bank officer, Burke assumed a major role in the organization of the Appomattox Tobacco Warehouse Company, which helped the town maintain its position as one of the best exclusively dark tobacco markets in the state. He also guaranteed the financial support necessary to secure an agricultural high school for the town in 1909, and he helped reorganize the local telephone company. During World War I, Burke or a member of his family chaired every local Liberty Loan campaign, and he was active in all government programs in the county. He was a member and deacon of Liberty Baptist Church and twice master of the local Masonic lodge.

Burke's children kept the family name at the center of Appomattox County's public life for many years. Richard Leigh Burke succeeded him as county treasurer and as president of the bank and served two terms in the House of Delegates. Another son, Jerry Allen Burke, was a successful businessman and longtime superintendent of county schools, and Burke's daughter Eula May Burke served as deputy county treasurer and was involved in many local charitable activities.

Richard Floyd Burke died of vascular heart disease at his home in Appomattox on 21 February 1924 and was buried there in the cemetery of Liberty Baptist Church.

Biography in Bruce, Tyler, and Morton, *History of Virginia,* 5:263–264; William R. Turner, *Notes Concerning the Irby*

Family [1930], [18]; Nathaniel Ragland Featherston, *The History of Appomattox, Virginia* (1948), 70 (por.); Vara Smith Stanley, *A History of Appomattox County* [1965], 35; Thomas R. Terry, *Appomattox County: A Pictorial History* [1984], 60 (por.); annual reports, Assessment of Bank, Banking Association, Trust, or Security Company Records, RG 48, LVA; county government and politics covered in county newspaper, variously called *Appomattox and Buckingham Times*, *Appomattox Times*, and *Appomattox Times-Virginian*; *Farmville Herald,* 17 Aug. 1915; *Lynchburg News,* 21 Aug., 3 Nov. 1915; *Appomattox Times-Virginian,* 10 Nov. 1915; obituary in *Appomattox Times-Virginian,* 21 Feb. 1924.

DAPHNE GENTRY

BURKE, Silas (1 November 1796–14 September 1854), farmer and local official, was born probably in Prince William County, the son of James Burk, a farmer, and Chloe Burk. His family had purchased 187 acres of land in Fairfax County by December 1798 and most likely moved to that county soon thereafter. Burke was most likely educated in local private schools. His name first appeared in Fairfax County records in 1813 when he was seventeen and working as a member of a surveying party. When Burke was twenty the county court appointed him an ensign in the 60th Regiment of the Virginia militia. He rose to the rank of lieutenant colonel by 1827 and retained that rank until his death. In 1824 Burke married Hannah Coffer, of Fairfax County. They had one son and one daughter and lived in a large frame house that he erected about the time of his marriage.

From 1823 until his death Burke managed the vast Ravensworth estate, first for its owner, William Henry Fitzhugh, a member of the Convention of 1829–1830, and after Fitzhugh's death in 1830 for his widow, Anna Maria Sarah Goldsborough Fitzhugh. Burke was the founding president in 1850 of the Fairfax Agricultural Society, dedicated to the increased local acceptance of the principles of scientific farming that he had always practiced. Interested in transportation because of its central role in moving merchandise and agricultural commodities, he served as a county road commissioner from 1835 to 1844, and from 1837 to 1852 he sat on the board of directors of the Fairfax Turnpike Company, where he represented the interest that the state government had by virtue of its ownership of company stock. After petitions and letters from prominent citizens urged his appointment, Burke was named a state director of the Orange and Alexandria Railroad in 1850.

Burke served as a local school commissioner from 1830 to 1841 and as a justice of the peace from 1835 until his death. The office of justice of the peace became elective for the first time in 1852, and although several local incumbent justices were defeated, Burke was elected and then chosen presiding justice of the Fairfax County Court. At various times during his life he also served as county sheriff, acting coroner, and commissioner of public buildings. The postal village of Burke's Station grew up around Burke's house. Early in the twentieth century the village's name was shortened to Burke.

Burke speculated in land and by 1850 had accumulated real property valued at $12,000. The inventory of his personal estate in 1855 indicates that he had extensive commercial and agricultural interests. Burke operated a public house, dealt in firewood, and owned a store, a mill, a blacksmith shop, and a brickyard. In addition to livestock and farm equipment, he owned fourteen slaves. Burke's account book listed thousands of dollars in accounts receivable, indicating that he carried on a significant trade and that he may have been lax in collecting bills due to him.

Silas Burke suffered a stroke and died in Alexandria on 14 September 1854. He was buried in a small family cemetery near his residence. His name has been perpetuated to a remarkable extent in the naming of more than a hundred streets and roads, places, businesses, and organizations in the immediate area of the post village that took his name. In 1991 the Virginia Department of Historic Resources approved the placement of a historical highway marker in front of the Silas Burke house to recognize the contributions he made to his county, region, and state.

Birth date from gravestone, which before being broken gave variant death date of 1 Oct. 1854; some letters in files of Fairfax Turnpike Company and of Orange and Alexandria Railroad in Board of Public Works Papers, RG 57, LVA; Nan Netherton et al., *Fairfax County, Virginia: A History* (1978), 305; Ross Netherton and Nan Netherton, *Fairfax County in Virginia: A Pictorial History* (1986), 56; Nan Netherton and Ruth Preston Rose, *Memories of Beautiful*

Burke, Virginia (1988), 9, 12, 13, 50; *Alexandria Gazette*, 15 Apr. 1850; Robert L. Lisbeth, "Fairfax County Post Offices and Postmasters, 1774–1890," Fairfax County Historical Society *Yearbook* 14 (1976/1977): 27; Fairfax Co. Death Register, giving variant birthplace of Fairfax Co.; will and estate inventory in Fairfax Co. Will Book, X1:406–409, Z1:373–375; obituaries and memorials in *Alexandria Gazette and Virginia Advertiser*, 15, 16, 20 Sept. 1854, and *Washington Daily Evening Star*, 15 Sept. 1854.

NAN NETHERTON

BURKHOLDER, Peter (ca. 27 August 1783–27 December 1846), Mennonite bishop, was born in Lancaster County, Pennsylvania, the son of Peter Burkholder and Margaret Huber Burkholder. His father emigrated from the Rhine Palatinate as a child in 1755. About 1790 the Burkholders moved to Rockingham County and settled near Broadway. Burkholder's mother died in 1798, and a year later his father died during a trip to Pennsylvania. The details of Burkholder's education are not recorded, but like most Mennonite children he received religious instruction and learned to read and write in German, and he probably learned English at the same time.

On 11 October 1803 Burkholder married Elizabeth Coffman, of Greenbrier County. They had five sons and four daughters. In 1805, at age twenty-one, Burkholder became the youngest man up to that time to be ordained in the Mennonite ministry in Virginia. Two years later he purchased and moved to a farm west of Harrisonburg. There he became a strong advocate of the Mennonite Church and its doctrine and traveled frequently to preach at other churches in the region. As a Mennonite minister, Burkholder was open to change. He supported the transition from holding worship services in private homes to the use of meetinghouses, and he participated in the building of at least one church. Burkholder's Church (later Weaver's Church) became one of the leading Mennonite congregations in Virginia. Burkholder also accepted the change from the German to the English language that began during his life. When a controversy among Virginia Mennonite leaders over these issues as well as over the preaching of Frederick Rhodes nearly led to a schism in 1825, Burkholder counseled unity rather than division.

Burkholder's earliest published work was *Eine Verhandlung, Von der äusserlichen Wasser-Taufe, und Erklärung einiger Irrthümer, wie auch von der Feuer-Taufe und wie in Christo das gesetzliche Osterlamm aufgehöret* (1816). This pamphlet, printed in Harrisonburg by Laurentz Wartmann, defended Mennonite teachings on baptism and communion and later appeared in two English translations. John F. Funk published it in the 1870s as *Discussion of the Outward Water Baptism and an Explanation of Several Errors, as Also of the Baptism of Fire, and How in Christ the Passover of the Old Dispensation Ceased*; Abraham Blosser's 1881 version was entitled *A Treatise on Outward Water-Baptism*.

Burkholder's status as the most respected and influential Mennonite in Virginia led to his ordination as bishop on an unrecorded date in 1836 or 1837. In the latter year he completed his most important work, for many years called the Burkholder Confession, or Virginia Confession, of Faith. Compiled in German by Burkholder and translated into English by Joseph Funk, it was published in Winchester as *The Confession of Faith, of the Christians Known by the Name of Mennonites, in Thirty-Three Articles; With a Short Extract from Their Catechism. Translated from the German, and Accompanied with Notes. To Which is Added an Introduction. Also, Nine Reflections, from Different Passages of the Scriptures, Illustrative of Their Confession, Faith and Practice* (1837).

The most systematic explication of Mennonite theology by any nineteenth-century American, this 461-page volume combined earlier writings with Burkholder's own contributions. As the title indicates, Burkholder worked from standard authorities, including the thirty-three articles of faith by Pieter Jansz Twisck, but he probably wrote the Nine Reflections, a biblical exposition on such themes as Christian humility, modest attire, peaceful nonresistance, and qualifications for the ministry. He also most likely wrote three short sections arguing that infant baptism is unscriptural as well as an article on the fallacies of the doctrine of predestination. Joseph Funk, Burkholder's translator, taught singing and for decades printed songbooks in both English and German in Singers Glen.

A gifted speaker, Burkholder could move his audience to tears with his powerful messages.

He frequently spoke in churches of other denominations and preached funeral sermons for non-Mennonites. Of medium height and heavyset, Burkholder had a long flowing beard that turned gray and gave him the appearance of a patriarch. He owned about 237 acres of land but no slaves. Peter Burkholder died at his home near Harrisonburg on 27 December 1846 and was buried in the nearby Shank and Burkholder family cemetery. Two of his sons became Mennonite ministers, including the youngest, Martin Burkholder, who succeeded his father and served for nearly fifteen years as bishop in the middle district of Virginia. He presided over the change from the use of German to English in the Mennonite churches in the Shenandoah Valley and advocated uniting the Mennonites with other denominations within the German Reformed tradition.

Birth date derived from gravestone inscription, which gives death date and age at death as sixty-three years and four months; Harry A. Brunk, "Bishop Peter Burkholder of Virginia, 1783–1846," *Mennonite Quarterly Review* 14 (Jan. 1940): 52–56; Brunk, *History of Mennonites in Virginia, 1727–1900* (1959), esp. 1:87–99; *Burkholder Family Reunion* 1–9 (1926–1933), esp. 7:60; Harry M. Hoover, *The Huber-Hoover Family History* (1928), 28–29, 44, 50–51; Nancy Burkholder Hess, *By the Grace of God* (1979), 85–99; Christian Burkholder birth register in family martyrbook in possession of Amos Hoover, 1991; L. J. Heatwole papers on Peter Burkholder and copy of 1839 will in Eastern Mennonite University Library, Harrisonburg.

GERALD R. BRUNK

BURKHOLDER, Robert Calhoun (3 June 1826–11 December 1914), architect, was born probably at Cumberland Gap in Lee County, the son of James Burkholder and Mary Newton Burkholder. Orphaned at an early age, he was reared by his uncle Isaac Burkholder, probably in Botetourt County. Burkholder most likely worked as an apprentice carpenter in New York City, and he may have done some study or apprentice work in architecture there. In 1850 he was working as a carpenter in Lynchburg, and by February 1851 he was in partnership with John H. Walker. They advertised themselves as carpenters but added that Burkholder could provide architectural services. In 1852 he identified himself as a "General Architect" capable of providing "plans for houses, green houses, and gardens." On 23 November of that year Burkholder married Mary Eliza Crumpton, of Lynchburg, a relative of one of the city's leading tobacconists. They had five sons and five daughters.

Burkholder was one of the first professional architects in western Virginia, and he was among the first, along with William Sharswood Ellison and Stephen G. Morgan, to live and work in Lynchburg. Like other nineteenth-century architects in the smaller cities of Virginia, Burkholder restricted his work to the immediate vicinity, within which realm he helped shape the profession. Lacking formal architectural training, he worked his way up from construction, carpentry, and millwork. The earliest project attributed to Burkholder was a set of alterations made between 1852 and 1854 to Margaret Sullivan's residence at Eighth and Commerce Streets in Lynchburg. He drew plans for a new Lynchburg courthouse in 1852, but Ellison received the responsibility for the project. Whether he made use of Burkholder's drawings is unknown.

On 10 May 1861 Burkholder enlisted in Shoemaker's Company of the Virginia Horse Artillery (also known as the Beauregard Rifles). By July he was serving as a hospital steward. Promoted to fourth corporal in January 1862, Burkholder was discharged in August of that year as overage. He resumed his work as a carpenter, contractor, and builder, along with his architectural practice. Burkholder was the general contractor for the Lynchburg Female Orphan Asylum (sometimes designated the Miller Female Orphan Asylum), a building designed by the Baltimore architect John Ellicott and built in 1870–1872. Described as one of the grimmest, gauntest structures ever built in Lynchburg, it was razed in 1959.

Burkholder did most of his work as an architect between 1875 and 1885, a decade of substantial prosperity and growth for Lynchburg. In addition to many residences in Lynchburg and nearby communities, important buildings attributed to him include the Lynch House (1873), the Court Street Baptist Church (1879–1881), alterations to the Masonic Hall (1880), the Guggenheimer and Company building (1880–1881), the G. W. Smith Tobacco Factory (1880–1881), alterations to the Bedford Alum Springs Hotel in Bedford County (1881), the Lynchburg National

Bank building (1881), and an addition to the Lone Jack Tobacco Factory in Lynchburg (1884).

Burkholder's buildings show an acquaintance with contemporary architectural theories of form, fashion, and construction. For his own residence in Lynchburg he designed and built a unique house in the shape of a Y. Burkholder was evidently familiar with the popular interest in polygonal and geometrical plans for residential buildings and may have been influenced by Orson Squire Fowler, who promoted construction of octagonal houses in *A Home for All* (1848); by Harriet Morrison Irwin, of Charlotte, North Carolina, who patented a plan for a hexagonal residence in 1869; and by Thomas Jefferson's octagonal villa, Poplar Forest, in nearby Bedford County. Fowler and Irwin argued the practical advantages of ventilation, light, and view in polygonal buildings, and Burkholder seems to have adopted some of their ideas.

Burkholder's design for the Court Street Baptist Church was typical of the fashionable Second Empire style. He employed a longitudinal plan, an axial tower with a mansard roof, and coupled arched windows. Burkholder incorporated iron structural members into the masonry structure. The Lynch House was also in the Second Empire mode. Other buildings that Burkholder designed were in the popular Italianate style. His experience with mass-produced architectural millwork evidently made him comfortable with the elements of that style. Burkholder's commercial buildings also showed his expertise with mass-produced architectural elements. He used cast-iron storefronts from Asa Snyder's ironworks in Richmond, and he employed plate-glass windows, made possible by new advances in glass technology, to provide light and allow for display of merchandise. Burkholder's design for the Guggenheimer and Company building featured a cast-iron front fabricated in Philadelphia. Cast iron provided the strength necessary to support large panes of glass. Catalogs and pattern books promoting building components, designs, and entire buildings were coming into nationwide use, and the country's expanding railway network could deliver these products almost everywhere. Burkholder's use of these varied styles and new construction materials contributed to the distinguished and distinctive architectural character of late-nineteenth-century Lynchburg.

Burkholder occasionally involved himself in other civic activities. From 1869 to 1873 he was one of three Conservatives who represented the city and Campbell County in the House of Delegates. During the 1869–1871 sessions Burkholder sat on the minor Committees on Manufactures and Mechanic Arts and on Officers and Offices at the Capitol, and during the 1871–1872 sessions he remained on the former committee while chairing the Committee on Public Property. In March 1871 he was an incorporator of the Lynchburg and North Carolina Railroad. Burkholder retired from architecture, moved to Bedford County in 1884, and began farming, although he continued to work on small projects and occasionally assisted his son's building business. His wife died in Lynchburg on 3 December 1906. Robert Calhoun Burkholder died in Bedford County on 11 December 1914 and was buried in Spring Hill Cemetery in Lynchburg.

Richard H. Ryan, "Robert C. Burkholder of Lynchburg, Virginia: A Typical Victorian Architect" (master's thesis, UVA, 1981), por.; Wells and Dalton, *Virginia Architects,* 55–57; family information provided by William H. Burruss III; *Lynchburg Daily Virginian,* 12 Aug. 1852 (quotations); Lynchburg Marriage Register; Compiled Service Records; S. Allen Chambers Jr., *Lynchburg: An Architectural History* (1981); Diuguid Funeral Home Burial Records, 17:106, Jones Memorial Library, Lynchburg; obituary in *Lynchburg News,* 12 Dec. 1914.

JOHN E. WELLS

BURKS, Edward Calohill (20 May 1821– 4 July 1897), attorney and Virginia Supreme Court of Appeals judge, was born in Bedford County, the eldest son of Louisa Claiborne Spinner Gooch Burks and her second husband, Martin Parks Burks, a locally prominent planter who owned fifty-one slaves in 1850 and served as a justice of the peace and county sheriff. A younger brother, Jesse Spinner Burks, achieved fame as a Confederate army officer. Edward C. Burks's mother gave him a love of learning and made certain that he received a good education. He attended the New London Academy, graduated from Washington College (later Washington and Lee University) in 1841, studied law under

Henry St. George Tucker, and received a law degree from the University of Virginia in 1842.

Burks returned to Bedford County to practice law. On 15 October 1845 he married Mildred Elizabeth Buford, and they had at least four sons and three daughters. She died on 4 January 1873. Burks was a Whig before the Civil War and in 1860 was elected to complete an unexpired term representing Bedford County in the House of Delegates, where he was appointed to the Committee on Military Affairs. Initially opposed to secession, Burks supported the Confederate cause after Virginia left the Union. Two of his brothers had died as children, but the other six all served in the Confederate army. A frail man all his life, Burks did not serve in the military, but he was elected to the House of Delegates for the full 1861–1863 term. He served on the Joint Committee on the Library and chaired the Joint Committee to Examine the Bonds of Public Officers, but he did not seek reelection.

After the Civil War Burks became a Democrat and was later a supporter of full funding of the antebellum state debt. On 15 December 1876 the General Assembly elected him to complete the term of Wood Bouldin (1811–1876) on the Virginia Supreme Court of Appeals, and he began serving on 1 January 1877. In 1882, after the Readjusters had secured majorities in both houses of the General Assembly and as Burks's four colleagues were completing their twelve-year terms, the assembly elected five new members of the court. The Readjusters asserted that Burks had been elected to finish Bouldin's term and that his term, too, was thus nearing completion. Believing that he was entitled to serve a full twelve years, Burks filed suit and took the case to the very court on which he claimed continued membership, but on 15 January 1883 the new members, as their first item of business, rejected his claim by a vote of three to one and ruled that Burks's term had expired on 31 December 1882. Drury A. Hinton accordingly took Burks's seat. During his six years on the court Burks seldom prepared decisions in criminal cases, but he wrote opinions in most other areas of the law and especially relished suits in equity. He became the court's foremost authority on equitable separate estates for women and wrote the

leading decisions on that subject. A diligent student of the law, Burks read new law books as other men read the latest novels.

After leaving the court, Burks practiced briefly in Lynchburg before moving to Bedford, where he practiced with two of his sons, including Martin Parks Burks (1851–1928), later himself a judge of the Virginia Supreme Court of Appeals. In March 1884, after the Readjusters lost control of the General Assembly, the legislature chose Edward C. Burks, Waller Redd Staples (another former judge of the Supreme Court of Appeals), and John W. Riely (a future judge of that court) to produce a new edition of Virginia's legal code, which they completed in 1887. During the next decade he carried on a wide correspondence with other Virginia attorneys who often sought his advice. Burks represented many clients before his successors on the Supreme Court of Appeals. He was one of the attorneys who argued the case of Bettie Thomas Lewis, a young Richmond woman who was the daughter of a wealthy white man and one of his former slaves. William A. Thomas had intended to make his daughter his principal heir, but he never executed a valid will. Nonetheless, in 1892 the Supreme Court of Appeals ruled in her favor.

In 1885 Burks received an honorary LL.D. from Washington and Lee University, and five years later he was elected to a one-year term as president of the Virginia State Bar Association. In 1895 he founded and began editing the monthly *Virginia Law Register*, in which he reported and abstracted court decisions of importance for Virginia attorneys and often added his own learned commentaries. Edward Calohill Burks died of Bright's disease at the Bedford County residence of his daughter on 4 July 1897. His funeral was conducted at Saint John's Protestant Episcopal Church in Bedford, to which he had belonged, and he was buried in Longwood Cemetery in that town.

Biography in *Green Bag* 5 (1893): 415–416; French Biographies; Mary Denham Ackerly and Lula Eastman Jeter Parker, *"Our Kin": The Genealogies of Some of the Early Families Who Made History in the Founding and Development of Bedford County, Virginia* (1930), 107–113 (por. facing 112); Burks letters in Holmes Conrad Papers and Robert Taylor Scott Papers, VHS, and Stafford Gorman Whittle Papers, UVA; some letters printed in James Elliott Walmsley, ed., "The Change of Secession Sentiment in Virginia in 1861," *AHR* 31 (1925): 82–101; Bedford Co. General Index to Marriage Bonds, Licenses, Ministers' Returns, Etc.; Presidential Pardons; *Burks* v. *Hinton* (1883), *Virginia Reports,* 77:1–51; *Thomas's Administrator* v. *Bettie Thomas Lewis and als* (1892), *Virginia Reports*, 89:1–86; presidential address in *Virginia State Bar Association Proceedings* (1891): 109–151; Hummel and Smith, *Portraits and Statuary*, 14 (por.); obituaries in *Lynchburg News* and *Richmond Dispatch* (with editorial tribute), both 6 July 1897; memorials in *Virginia State Bar Association Proceedings* (1897): 127–145, and *Virginia Reports* 94 (1898): v–xx.

PETER WALLENSTEIN

BURKS, Jesse Spinner (20 March 1823–16 June 1885), Confederate army officer, was born in Bedford County, the son of Louisa Claiborne Spinner Gooch Burks and her second husband, Martin Parks Burks, a successful farmer and judge. His eldest brother Edward Calohill Burks was a judge of the Virginia Supreme Court of Appeals. Jesse S. Burks studied at the New London Academy before attending Washington College (later Washington and Lee University) in 1840. The next year he entered the Virginia Military Institute, from which he graduated sixth in a class of nine in 1844. In 1845 Burks traveled to Saint Charles County, Missouri, where on 3 December of that year he married Elizabeth Royal Otey, who had grown up in Bedford County. They had three sons during the next five years before her death on an unrecorded date.

Burks was living in Bedford County again by 1851 and the next year was elected a district court judge, in which capacity he served until 1856. Increasingly interested in state politics, he was elected by his Whiggish constituents in Bedford to the 1853–1854 session of the House of Delegates. There Burks served on the Committees on Militia Laws and on Schools and Colleges. On 24 March 1856 he attended a meeting of the American (Know Nothing) Party at the Bedford courthouse and was among those selected to attend the state convention scheduled for 6 and 7 May in Staunton. The delegates to that convention enthusiastically endorsed Millard Fillmore for president while blaming the Democratic Party for Virginia's distressed financial condition.

On 17 February 1855 Burks married Charlotte Frances Thomson. They had one son and six daughters. A successful planter by 1861, Burks

was sufficiently prosperous to own seventeen slaves and to move his family into Wyoming, a Bedford farm with an elegant twelve-room brick house. But the daily rounds of domestic life were interrupted when Virginia seceded from the Union in April and the citizens of Bedford urged Governor John Letcher to appoint Burks to lead a regiment. Their petition was successful, and on 11 June, despite solicitations from officers of the 42d Regiment Virginia Infantry in behalf of another candidate, Letcher named Burks its colonel. He assumed command on 15 July 1861.

Early in September 1861 Brigadier General William Wing Loring installed Burks as one of his brigade commanders. During September and October Loring's army participated in Robert Edward Lee's unsuccessful Cheat Mountain and Sewell Mountain campaigns in the western Virginia highlands. Some of Burks's subordinate officers, though attesting to his toughness and personal courage, criticized him as insensible to the harsh conditions suffered by his troops and unwilling to take advice. Burks reverted to command of the 42d Regiment when the army was reorganized in December, but in January 1862 Major General Thomas J. "Stonewall" Jackson restored him to brigade command. Burks supported Loring in that officer's controversial feud with Jackson, but in the quarrel's aftermath he retained his brigade command while Loring was transferred to another theater of operations.

On 23 March 1862 Burks confirmed Jackson's opinion of him when he helped avert a Confederate disaster at Kernstown. Jackson had attacked what he thought was an inferior force, but as Union strength developed he found himself unable to extract his army from increasing danger. During the fighting Burks helped to stem late Union attacks, coolly riding along his lines, encouraging his soldiers by his own example. Bullets struck his horse and penetrated his clothing, and one may have wounded him slightly in the hip. Though defeated, Jackson's forces avoided catastrophe, and Burks proved his worth.

In April 1862, while Burks was on leave, the men of the 42d Regiment unanimously reelected him their colonel. But he was suffering from a severe hernia that had developed at

Kernstown, and he reluctantly submitted his resignation on 23 May, effective 21 July 1862.

After the war Burks sought and received a presidential pardon, returned to farming, and resumed his political career. He served as one of three representatives from Bedford County in the House of Delegates for a single term from December 1875 to April 1877. He sat on the minor Committees on Agriculture and Mining and on Public Property. On 5 December 1880 Burks's second wife died, and on 20 March 1883 he married Mary J. Tinsley Claggett, a widowed Powhatan County schoolteacher. They had no children. Jesse Spinner Burks died of heart failure at his home on 16 June 1885 and was buried next to his second wife at Saint Thomas Episcopal Church near his home in Bedford County.

Mary Denham Ackerly and Lula Eastman Jeter Parker, *"Our Kin": The Genealogies of Some of the Early Families Who Made History in the Founding and Development of Bedford County, Virginia* (1930; repr. 1976), 107–108, 114–115, and French Biographies (both with variant death date of 15 June 1885); Parker, *History of Bedford County* (1954; repr. 1988), 121–122; Census, Bedford Co., 1850, 1860, 1870; 1844 class file, VMI Archives; Robert W. Wentz, ed., *The 1989 Register of Former Cadets of the Virginia Military Institute* (1989), 53; Richard M. McMurry, *Virginia Military Institute Alumni in the Civil War: In Bello Praesidium* (1999), 101; interviews with Phillip Parks Burks, Pettigrew Wright Burks, Mary Burks Deane, and Louise H. Forsyth; John Buford Papers, UVA; W. Harrison Daniel, *Bedford County, Virginia, 1840–1860* (1985), 23, 59, 60, 103; *Calendar of Virginia State Papers*, 11:132, 149; John D. Chapla, *42nd Virginia Infantry* (1983), 3, 5–8, 72; Chapla, "Quartermaster Operations in the Forty-second Virginia Infantry Regiment," *Civil War History* 30 (1984): 17, 19; *SHSP* 43 (1920): 140, 146, 152, 156, 158–159, 162; Compiled Service Records; *OR*, 1st ser., 5:1046–1047; ibid. 12: pt. 1, 381–382, 385, 400–403, 405–407, 409; ibid. 51: pt. 2, 283; *Daily Richmond Whig*, 3 Apr. 1862; *Richmond Daily Dispatch*, 8 Apr. 1862; Presidential Pardons; death date given as 16 June 1885 in Bedford Co. Death Register and obituary in *Lynchburg Daily News*, 17 June 1885.

JOHN D. CHAPLA

BURKS, Martin Parks (23 January 1851– 30 April 1928), legal educator and Virginia Supreme Court of Appeals judge, was born in Liberty (later Bedford) in Bedford County, the son of Mildred Elizabeth Buford Burks and Edward Calohill Burks, a prominent attorney who served as judge of the Supreme Court of Appeals from 1877 through 1882. Educated at Sunnyside School, a local school for boys, Burks

attended Washington College (later Washington and Lee University) during Robert Edward Lee's presidency and graduated in 1870. He studied law with John B. Minor at the University of Virginia, received a law degree in 1872, and began to practice law with his father in Bedford. On 31 December 1874 Burks married Roberta Gamble Bell. They had one son and one daughter. In politics Burks was a Democrat, and in religion, like his parents, he was Episcopalian.

Burks's law practice led to many roles in addition to being an attorney. A legal scholar like his father, he published *Notes on the Property Rights of Married Women in Virginia* (1893) when professional colleagues urged him to share his expertise in a rapidly changing field of the law. In 1895, when five new judges on the Supreme Court of Appeals took their seats, they discharged the incumbent court reporter and appointed Burks, who served as reporter for the next twenty-two years. He compiled and published volumes 91 through 119 of the court's official *Virginia Reports,* revised the indexes to conform to standard legal terms, and prepared abstracts of the decisions. Early in his tenure Burks published a number of articles and abstracts of court decisions in the journal that his father had founded, the *Virginia Law Register.*

From 1899 to 1917 Burks taught law at Washington and Lee University, where he was affectionately known as Daddy Burks. After the law school experienced a period of instability, he consented to serve as dean beginning in 1903. During his tenure in that position Burks urged the school to require a second year of study for all law students and later pushed for a third. In his teaching he began to supplement the traditional reliance on lectures and textbooks with discussions of case materials. As dean, Burks recommended that the entire program move in that direction, and in 1916 the school hired Edwin Merrick Dodd, a graduate of Harvard University's law school, where the casebook approach had originated. In these ways Burks nudged Washington and Lee into conformity with dominant characteristics of other American law schools in the twentieth century.

Following the practice of many other law professors of the time, Burks published some of his lectures, first as *Notes on Pleading and Practice* (1905) and later in extended form as *Pleading and Practice in Actions at Common Law* (1913). Three subsequent editions attest to that work's enduring value. Like his father, who had helped revise the legal code of Virginia in 1887, Burks was among those who, beginning in 1914, compiled the Virginia code of 1919. He received honorary LL.D.s from Roanoke College in 1903 and from Washington and Lee in 1920.

Burks capped his career with eleven years of service on the Virginia Supreme Court of Appeals. In March 1917 the governor appointed him to a vacancy when a judge retired. Burks assumed office on 22 March 1917 at the age of sixty-six, older than any other new judge in the history of the court. He relinquished his positions as court reporter and as law professor and dean at Washington and Lee. His extensive experience as practicing attorney, code reviser, court reporter, and law professor gave Burks extraordinary preparation for his new post, and the assembly elected him in February 1918 to a full twelve-year term. He wrote fewer decisions than most of his colleagues. Many of his opinions concerned complicated property transfers, procedural matters, and death and injury cases arising under the law of master and servant.

On 16 April 1928 Burks submitted his resignation because of poor health. It was to have taken effect on 1 June, but Martin Parks Burks died on 30 April 1928 at Saint Elizabeth's Hospital in Richmond, where he had contracted pneumonia after an operation. He was buried in Longwood Cemetery in Bedford.

Tyler, *Men of Mark*, 2:51–53; Charles V. Laughlin, "Martin Parks Burks," in *Legal Education in Virginia, 1779–1979: A Biographical Approach*, ed. W. Hamilton Bryson (1982), 117–126 (por. on 118), which contains a bibliography of his publications; French Biographies; Bedford Co. Marriage Register; Ollinger Crenshaw, *General Lee's College: The Rise and Growth of Washington and Lee University* (1969), 344–345; Burks to Harry Flood Byrd, 16 Apr. 1928, Secretary of the Commonwealth, Executive Papers, RG 13, LVA; *Richmond Times-Dispatch*, 20 Apr. 1928; Hummel and Smith, *Portraits and Statuary*, 15 (por.); BVS Death Certificate, Richmond City; obituaries in *Lynchburg News* and *Richmond Times-Dispatch*, both 1 May 1928; account of funeral and editorial tribute in *Lynchburg News*, 2 May 1928; memorial in *Virginia State Bar Association Proceedings* (1928): 143–148.

PETER WALLENSTEIN

BURLEY, James (ca. 1800–4 January 1870), member of the Convention of 1861, was born in Greene County, Pennsylvania, the son of Jacob Burley, a farmer who served as county sheriff there before moving to Virginia and settling in the part of Ohio County that became Marshall County in 1835, when he became one of the first justices of the peace of the new county. Burley's mother's name is not recorded. By 1829 he had married Elizabeth Alexander. They had one son and one daughter before she died of cholera in Wheeling in 1832. Burley subsequently married Margaret Alexander and had one more son and three more daughters before his second wife died on 11 November 1858.

A productive Moundsville farmer who evidently owned no slaves, Burley was worth almost $100,000 according to the 1860 census. He served as the first president of the Marshall County Agricultural Society. Not known to have been politically active until past middle age, Burley was commissioned a justice of the peace on 1 July 1850. On 4 February 1861 he was elected to represent Marshall County in a state convention that assembled in Richmond nine days later to deal with the secession crisis. Burley unconditionally opposed secession, but he did not take an active part in the debates. Instead, on 1 March he presented to the convention several resolutions that his constituents had adopted, which declared that the Union must be preserved. Sixteen days later he introduced six resolutions that he probably drafted himself, declaring nullification and secession to be "fallacies and heresies," stating that the right of revolution was not strictly reserved to the several states, as advocates of secession had argued, and adding that aggrieved citizens could organize and separate from their own state government, an argument that foreshadowed the withdrawal of the western counties from Virginia after secession. Burley voted against secession on 4 April when it failed to pass and again on 17 April when it was approved by a large majority. The next day Old Man Burley, as the younger convention colleagues from his region called him, and several other western delegates decided to return home to work to preserve the Union and await the outcome of the May referendum on the Ordinance of Secession.

On 23 May 1861 the ordinance was approved by a majority of Virginia's voters, although the western counties remained strongly opposed. Elections for the General Assembly were also held that day, and Burley was elected to represent the district comprising Marion, Marshall, Tyler, and Wetzel Counties in the Senate of Virginia. On 29 June 1861 the Virginia convention expelled Burley and several other Unionist delegates from western counties, and on 3 July Burley took his senatorial seat in the rump meeting of the Virginia General Assembly held in Wheeling, where he chaired the Committee on Finance and Claims. He also served in the third of the Wheeling Conventions of 1861 and was appointed to the Special Committee on the Division of the State. When the legislature at Wheeling reconvened on 2 December Burley resumed his seat and served until the session concluded on 13 February 1862. He was present again in May for a brief session and finished out his term in the next session, which ran from 4 December 1862 through 5 February 1863. On 20 June 1863 West Virginia was admitted to the Union, completing a complex political process brought about through the efforts of Burley and other similarly determined western residents.

Undeterred by age Burley continued his work in the Senate of West Virginia, where he served on eleven standing committees and chaired the Committee on Executive Expenditures in 1864, the Committee on Townships in 1865, the Committee on Internal Improvements and Navigation in 1866, and the Committee on Humane and Criminal Institutions in 1867 and 1868. After an accident disabled him, he announced his retirement from politics in 1869. James Burley died at his home in Marshall County on 4 January 1870.

Gibson L. Cranmer et al., *History of the Upper Ohio Valley* (1890), 1:682; Scott Powell, *History of Marshall County* (1925), 107–108, 116; John H. Brantner, comp., *Historical Collections of Moundsville, West Virginia* (1947); Census, Marshall Co., 1850, 1860; Personal Property Tax Returns, Marshall Co., 1860, RG 48, LVA; *Wheeling Daily Intelligencer*, 30 Jan., 1, 4, 6 Feb., 25, 28 May 1861; Reese and Gaines, *Proceedings of 1861 Convention*, 1:281–282, 723–725 (quotation on 723), 3:163, 4:144; Reese, *Journals and Papers of 1861 Convention*, vol. 1, Journal, 306, 311; Granville Davisson Hall, *The Rending of Virginia: A History* (1902; repr. 2000), 203–204; Virgil A. Lewis, *How West Virginia Was Made* (1909), 27–28, 31; obituaries in *Wheeling Daily Register* (giving age at death of sixty-nine) and *Wheeling Intelligencer*, both 5 Jan. 1870.

David T. Javersak

BURNHAM, Horace Blois (10 September 1824–10 April 1894), Virginia Supreme Court of Appeals judge, was the son of Judson Williams Burnham and Mary Blois Burnham. He was born probably in Columbia County, New York. The family moved to eastern Pennsylvania, where Burnham grew up and studied law. He was admitted to the bar at Wilkes-Barre on 12 August 1844. By 1848 he had married Ruth Ann Jackson. They had one son and two daughters. Burnham lived in Mauch Chunk (later Jim Thorpe), Pennsylvania, and practiced law until the outbreak of the Civil War.

On 26 July 1861 Burnham began recruiting a regiment and on 31 October was commissioned lieutenant colonel of the 67th Regiment Pennsylvania Infantry, which was called into federal service on 31 March 1862. The unit was initially assigned guard duty in Maryland but had the majority of its personnel captured at the Second Battle of Winchester on 15 June 1863. Burnham avoided this fate, and except for an interval in New York City during which he briefly commanded a brigade putting down the draft riots in mid-July 1863, he led the two-company rump of the regiment until the captured men were exchanged and returned to duty that October. In December 1863 Burnham was detailed to Washington for service as a judge advocate, and with the expiration of his three-year term of enlistment he resigned on 18 November 1864 as lieutenant colonel of the 67th and accepted a commission as major and judge advocate, to date from 31 October of that year. When his painful sciatica permitted he served on general courts-martial under the orders of the Department of War. Burnham was awarded the brevet ranks of lieutenant colonel and colonel of volunteers on 13 March 1865. From 23 May 1866 until April 1867 he served in the Bureau of Military Justice, and on 25 February 1867 he was transferred to the permanent military establishment.

On 18 April 1867 Burnham was appointed chief judge advocate of Military District Number One, the army unit that administered Virginia during Reconstruction, and he moved to

Richmond. On 11 September 1867 the commanding general appointed him judge of the Richmond City Hustings Court to succeed William H. Lyons, who had died. Burnham presided over the Hustings Court in the trial of civil and criminal cases. A separate bench composed of the city's aldermen (sometimes called the Hustings Court of Magistrates) dealt with misdemeanors, issued licenses to keepers of ordinaries, and attended to similar administrative duties. The Mayor's Court dispensed summary judgments in cases involving petty misbehavior. Burnham first convened his court on 16 September 1867 with a charge to the grand jury promising that "no distinction will be tolerated which discriminates between individuals by reason of caste or color." He was described at the time as small in stature, with bright blue eyes and auburn hair. Burnham attended the court faithfully, often six times a week, until the commanding general appointed him to the Virginia Supreme Court of Appeals on 9 June 1869.

Burnham took office six days later as one of three new members, all appointed by the general after he dismissed the sitting judges from office in compliance with a new federal law that required replacement of all Virginia and Texas officials with any previous record of Confederate activity. Burnham became president of the court by election of its membership. He was not a dominant jurist. Appearing in the minority more often than his two colleagues, he wrote no majority opinions and only one dissenting opinion in the eight cases the court decided while he was a member that were recorded in the official volumes of the *Virginia Reports*. Burnham had a brief and stormy career on the court. He and his fellow justices, Orloff Mather Dorman and Westel Willoughby, met for the first time from 22 to 28 June 1869 and adopted new rules of practice. The court met again on 12 October 1869 but decided only one case before adjourning until January. In announcing the decision Burnham explained that because Virginia had adopted a new constitution and awaited only congressional approval to implement it and replace military appointees with new officials, it would be expedient for the court to defer further business until the next term. Newspaper reports suggested that the sudden adjournment resulted less from such questions of delicacy than from a desire to head off an effort by those who doubted the court's legitimacy to seek a restraining order from the United States Supreme Court against further action by the Virginia tribunal.

The Supreme Court of Appeals reconvened on 11 January 1870, but its validity was brought into dispute with passage on 26 January of an act of Congress ending Reconstruction in Virginia, restoring civilian rule, and thereby implementing a new state constitution under which the General Assembly would select new judges. Critics argued that the court's proceedings were a mere nullity after the end of military rule, but it doggedly remained sitting until it completed its business and adjourned on 25 February 1870. The General Assembly passed a statute on 5 March 1870 authorizing the new judges to hear appeals of any rulings issued during the last session of the so-called military court. Two cases were duly appealed at the November 1870 session, but after protracted discussions the new judges ruled by a vote of 3–2 that the law of March 1870 was an unconstitutional legislative infringement on judicial power. In effect, that ruling sustained the legality of the decisions Burnham and his fellow judges had rendered.

Burnham no doubt welcomed this judicial endorsement of the court's validity, even though he had been unceremoniously ousted from office late in the court's last session. On 10 February 1870 a member of the House of Delegates moved that the Committee for Courts of Justice report whether the judges of the court were exercising their functions lawfully. Six days later the committee reserved judgment on the status of Dorman and Willoughby but reported that Burnham was unquestionably not entitled to his office because under Virginia law he could not serve on a state court while holding a commission in the army. A joint resolution removing Burnham from the Court of Appeals quickly passed both houses of the General Assembly and received the governor's approval on 22 February 1870. Ironically, Burnham's removal was cited as key evidence supporting the legitimacy of the court, because in leaving his fellow military appointees in office the assembly tacitly approved the court's functioning with judges the commanding general of the army had appointed.

Burnham's brief judicial experience during Reconstruction subjected him to some strong criticism and abuse. One highly prejudiced newspaper story published in 1867 declared that when he practiced law in Pennsylvania he had been a "fifth-rate lawyer and first-class libertine" who "'mixed' with black women" and had escaped an adultery conviction only by bribing the wronged husband to absent himself from the trial.

With the end of Reconstruction in Virginia, Burnham continued to serve until 1 June 1870 as judge advocate of the new military Department of Virginia, which encompassed four states. He was then assigned to the Department of the South. Burnham served in the Department of Texas from 24 April to 2 November 1872. From 20 November 1872 to 10 September 1886 he was stationed at Omaha as judge advocate of the Department of the Platte and won promotion on 5 July 1884 to deputy judge advocate general. Burnham concluded his career in San Francisco with service in the Department of California and Military Division of the Pacific.

Burnham retired from the army on 10 September 1888. He returned to Virginia and lived at Aspen Shade, the Henrico County estate he had acquired during the 1860s. The hard feelings of Reconstruction had somewhat subsided, and the author of an obituary in a Richmond newspaper described him as quiet, unostentatious, and highly esteemed. Horace Blois Burnham died at Aspen Shade on 10 April 1894 of what was variously described as pneumonia and as neuralgia of the heart brought on by a severe cold. He left an estate valued at more than $10,000 and was buried with Masonic honors in Arlington National Cemetery.

Burnham probably contributed biographical information to William H. Powell, *Powell's Records of Living Officers of the United States Army* (1890), 98–99 (birthplace given as Columbia Co., N.Y.); Burnham's publications are *Reply of the Judge Advocate to the Argument of the Accused, Colonel L. Schirmer, 15th New York Artillery* [1865], and dissenting opinion in *Wright* v. *Commonwealth* (1870) (19 Grattan), *Virginia Reports*, 60:634–639; Census, Carbon Co., Pa., 1860; Compiled Military Service Records, Records of the Adjutant General's Office, RG 94, NARA; *OR*, 1st ser., 21:963; ibid., 25: pt. 2, 590; ibid., 27: pt. 3, 799; ibid., 29: pt.

2, 122; Richmond City Hustings Court, Chancery Order Book (1860–1868) and Common Law Order Book (1866–1868), LVA; *Richmond Daily Dispatch*, 17 Sept. 1867 (first quotation), 10 June, 13 Oct. 1869, 4 Feb. 1870; *Richmond Whig and Public Advertiser*, semiweekly ed., 17 Sept. 1867, 15 Oct. 1869; Burnham may be the unnamed "aged Colonel of Volunteers" lampooned in John S. Wise, *The Lion's Skin: A Historical Novel and a Novel History* (1905), 197–199; Supreme Court of Appeals Order Book, 22:55, 59, RG 100, LVA; validity of Jan.–Feb. 1870 session of Court of Appeals sustained in *Griffin's Executors* v. *Cunningham* and *Washington, Alexandria and Georgetown Railroad Company* v. *Alexandria and Washington Railroad Company et al.* (1870) (20 Grattan), *Virginia Reports*, 61:31–123; *JHD*, 1869–1870 sess., 63, 88, 115; removal from office in *Acts of Assembly*, 1869–1870 sess., 11; *Richmond Southern Opinion*, 2 Nov. 1867 (second quotation); *New York Times*, 10 Sept. 1888; original will and estate inventory in Henrico Co. Wills, LVA, with copies in Henrico Co. Will Book, 22:301–305, 445–446, 23:49–65, 163–165; BVS Death Register, Henrico Co.; obituaries in *New York Times* and *Richmond Dispatch* (birthplace given as Cooperstown, N.Y.), both 11 Apr. 1894.

J. JEFFERSON LOONEY

BURNLEY, Hardin (19 March 1761–11 March 1809), member of the Council, was born in Orange County, the son of Zachariah Burnley and his second wife, Mary Bell Jones Burnley. His father was a planter and land speculator, a justice of the peace for almost fifty years, and a member of the House of Burgesses from Bedford County for the 1758–1761 term and from Orange County for the years 1766–1768 and 1772–1774. Three of Burnley's paternal uncles were involved in transatlantic trade and had Loyalist sympathies during the American Revolution, but Zachariah Burnley served on the Orange County Committee in 1774, was appointed county lieutenant in May 1778, and served in the House of Delegates during the 1780–1781 session.

Hardin Burnley was a student at the College of William and Mary between 1776 and 1781 and afterward studied law under George Wythe. He began his practice in Orange County on 24 March 1785. Six months later Burnley became a major in the county militia, and in 1787 he was elected to the first of four successive one-year terms in the House of Delegates. He served all four years on the Committee for Courts of Justice, and he sat on the Committee of Propositions and Grievances during his first two years and on the Committee on Privileges and Elections during his last two. Burnley opposed ratification of the United States Constitution in 1788 and worked with friends of James Madison in the General Assembly in behalf of the amendments that Congress submitted to the states in 1789, ten of which became the Bill of Rights when the Virginia legislature ratified them in December 1791.

On 26 November 1790 the assembly elected Burnley to the Council of State to replace Thomas Madison, who had resigned. Burnley assumed his seat on 4 March 1791. He moved to Richmond and attended Council meetings regularly until his health began to deteriorate eight years later. On 31 January 1799 Burnley was elected president of the Council. The day after James Wood's term as governor expired on 6 December 1799, and until James Monroe arrived in Richmond to be sworn in as the new governor, Burnley, as president of the Council, became lieutenant governor of Virginia, in effect acting governor. Rather than take on this responsibility he pleaded his poor health and resigned from the Council on 9 December 1799.

Burnley married Elizabeth Overton, probably the daughter of William Overton, of Hanover County, and their one child was a daughter Hardenia, called "the elder." Elizabeth Overton Burnley died on 30 April 1793. About two years later Burnley married Mary Overton, daughter of Samuel Overton and Elizabeth Harris Overton and a cousin of his first wife. Their two sons and four daughters included a probably posthumous daughter, also named Hardenia and called "the younger." After leaving the Council Burnley retired to Bear Island, his 1,096-acre plantation in Hanover County, which he had acquired from the estate of William Overton. He lived the life of a wealthy planter for nearly ten years. He must have had periods of improved health, for he returned to Richmond on five occasions to sit on the grand jury of the United States District Court, of which he served as the foreman in November 1800, November 1806, and November 1807 and as the ranking member in November 1803 and May 1805. Hardin Burnley died at Bear Island on 11 March 1809 and was buried in the family cemetery there. His grave is not marked.

Birth date in Burnley-Jones family Bible record, LVA; Emma Dicken, *Our Burnley Ancestors and Allied Families* (1946), 52–53; family history documented in Leon M. Bazile Papers, VHS, and in *Duke* v. *Burnley* suit papers, 1782–1855, Hanover Co. Circuit Court (LVA microfilm); Burnley letters in *Madison: Congressional Series*, 10:327–328, 11:398–399, 12:455–457, 460, 14:135–136; *JHD*, 1790 sess., unpaginated entry for 26 Nov. 1790; Journal of the Council of State (1 Nov. 1798–25 Oct. 1799), 73, and (1 Nov. 1799–7 Feb. 1801), 26, 28, RG 75, LVA; obituary in *Richmond Enquirer*, 17 Mar. 1809.

DAPHNE GENTRY

BURNS, Anthony (31 May 1834–27 July 1862), principal in a fugitive slave case, was born a slave in Stafford County. He was the thirteenth and last child of the family cook of John F. Suttle and of her third husband, who supervised other slaves working in a stone quarry. After Suttle and his wife died, Burns became the property of their eldest son, Charles F. Suttle, a merchant who eventually moved to Alexandria. Burns remained with his mother in Stafford County and learned to read and write. He joined the Baptist Church and may have preached, which would have been a violation of Virginia law. As an adult Burns was about six feet tall with a dark complexion and scars on his cheek and right hand.

Suttle hired his slaves out to various men in Stafford County, and Burns worked for a time for William Brent, of Falmouth. In 1852 Suttle directed Brent to hire Burns out in Richmond, where Burns apparently persuaded Brent to let him hire his own time. Burns used some of the money he accumulated in this way to arrange for his escape from slavery with the assistance of friends and mariners from the North whom he met in Richmond. In February or March 1854 he secretly traveled to Boston. Once there, Burns wrote a letter to one of his brothers in Virginia. Although he had the letter mailed from Canada in an attempt to conceal his location, its contents disclosed that he was in Boston, and, as was the custom, the postmaster delivered the letter to the slave's owner. Suttle and Brent immediately went to Boston, where on 24 May 1854 they had Burns arrested and instituted proceedings to recover possession of him under the Fugitive Slave Act of 1850. One of the most famous and dramatic fugitive slave rendition cases of the 1850s resulted.

The United States marshal kept Burns incommunicado after his seizure and early the next morning carried him before a United States commissioner who expected to hear evidence from Suttle and Brent and promptly sign the necessary papers to turn Burns over to them. Richard Henry Dana Jr., a prominent antislavery attorney, passed the courtroom at that time, however, and saw what was happening. He intervened on Burns's behalf, even though Burns initially rejected this offer of legal counsel because he believed that his return to Virginia in accordance with the Fugitive Slave Act was inevitable and that at this juncture it would be better for him if things went smoothly for Suttle. Arguments by abolitionists of both races soon convinced Burns to accept Dana's assistance.

For the next nine days an extended courtroom drama paralyzed Boston, and an antislavery crowd attempted to rescue Burns from jail. During the violence that ensued, a newly deputized marshal was killed. Hundreds of police, militiamen, and federal troops guarded the courthouse while Dana tried to persuade the commissioner that Burns was not Suttle's slave. The commissioner rejected Dana's arguments and ordered Burns returned to Virginia. It required more than 1,500 troops to conduct him safely through the angry crowd from the courthouse to the revenue cutter that transported him back to Virginia. The government had proved that it could enforce the Fugitive Slave Act of 1850, even in Boston, but at a cost estimated at between $40,000 and $50,000 and at the expense of inflaming public opinion in both North and South.

Burns spent four months chained in one of the Richmond slave jails, an ordeal that left him permanently crippled and in ill health. Suttle then sold Burns to a North Carolina slave trader for $910. Burns lived briefly in Rocky Mount, but in the spring of 1855 a group of African Americans in Boston, acting through their Baptist minister, Leonard Grimes (a black man who had been born free in Virginia), bought his freedom for $1,300. Burns subsequently studied theology at Oberlin College and possibly at the Fairmont Theological Seminary in Cincinnati. By August 1858 he was in Maine preparing to present a panorama entitled the *Grand Moving Mirror*

exhibiting the "degradation and horror of American slavery" and using the occasion to sell copies of a narrative of his travails by Charles Emery Stevens in order to support his continuing studies. Burns planned to travel with the exhibition through Massachusetts and New Hampshire in the autumn and winter. In 1860 he took a position at a Baptist church in Indianapolis, but shortly thereafter he moved to the Zion Baptist Church in Saint Catharines, Upper Canada (later Ontario). Anthony Burns died there of consumption two years later, on 27 July 1862, never having regained his health. He was buried in Saint Catharines Cemetery.

Charles Emery Stevens, *Anthony Burns, a History* (1856); Jane H. Pease and William H. Pease, *The Fugitive Slave Law and Anthony Burns: A Problem in Law Enforcement* (1975), 25–54; Albert J. Von Frank, *The Trials of Anthony Burns: Freedom and Slavery in Emerson's Boston* (1998), por. facing 161; legal proceedings collected in *The Boston Slave Riot, and Trial of Anthony Burns* (1854); the trial, associated violence, and controversy were thoroughly covered in most American newspapers including all the major Virginia papers; *Liberator*, 13 Aug. (quotation), 3 Sept. 1858; Fred Landon, "Anthony Burns in Canada," *Ontario Historical Society Papers and Records* 22 (1925): 162–166, which transcribes the now-broken gravestone with birth and death dates and quotes from an unidentified local obituary; obituary in *Liberator*, 22 Aug. 1862.

PAUL FINKELMAN

BURR, David Judson (16 October 1820–3 August 1876), business and civic leader, was born in Richmond, the son of Annabella Shedden Reeve Burr and her second husband, David Judson Burr, one of Richmond's most enterprising antebellum manufacturers and a partner in the foundry of Burr, Pae, and Samson. Burr attended Yale College as a member of the class of 1839 and after brief study at the law school returned to Richmond and read law under Peachy R. Grattan. On 10 April 1844 in New York City he married Julia Ellen Denison, daughter of a South Carolina physician. They had three sons and three daughters.

Despite forming a partnership with A. Judson Crane, Burr did not pursue a legal career, nor did business take all his energy, even though it easily could have. Burr may best be described as a man of affairs, one of Richmond's consummate insiders. Both before and after the Civil

War he engaged in profitable business ventures, working sometimes as a commission merchant in family concerns. Burr also served as president of a steamship company and as secretary and one of the founders of the Virginia Home Insurance Company, chartered in 1866. He joined Edward N. Spiller as a partner in 1861 in establishing a small-arms factory, one of the few in the Confederacy. Spiller and Burr produced a revolver that James Henry Burton fabricated. After the Confederate secretary of war ordered Burton to Georgia, the owners moved the plant to Atlanta in 1862 and sold it to the Confederate government, which shifted it to Macon in 1864.

Except for his election to one term on Richmond's board of aldermen in 1847, Burr did not hold elective office before the worsening of the sectional crisis. When Richmond called, he was ready. In 1859 Burr was elected to the common council, where his financial expertise was invaluable. He served until 1866 and also represented Richmond in the House of Delegates for the sessions from September 1863 to March 1865. Burr served on the Committee on Finance and on the Joint Committee to Examine the Armory. He proposed various measures in response to the bread riot of April 1863 and led in the destruction of liquor supplies when Confederate forces evacuated the capital two years later. With Mayor Joseph Mayo, other members of the common council, and several dignitaries Burr formally surrendered Richmond to the United States Army on the morning of 3 April 1865. He tried unsuccessfully to get Virginia back into the Union quickly by attempting to convene the General Assembly. Burr also represented the city in negotiations with military authorities during the summer of 1865, successfully proposed a reduction in the tax rates, and moved to repeal the slave and black codes when civilian government was restored in October 1865. He tried to protect Richmond's local investors from hostile railroad interests in 1866 and 1867. A careful man, Burr moved from the antebellum Whig Party, which had dominated Richmond, into support of the Confederacy, although his letter requesting a presidential pardon after the Civil War cited the staunch Unionist and political maverick John Minor Botts as a reference. In the

postwar years Burr naturally moved toward the Conservative Party and then the reconstituted Democratic Party. He was one of three Conservatives on the six-member Richmond school board in 1869–1870.

Burr managed to retain a large measure of his substantial wealth during and after the Civil War. In 1867 he reorganized the old Board of Trade, of which he had been first vice president before the war, and founded the Richmond Chamber of Commerce. He was its president until October 1872, when he retired with resolutions of thanks from the chamber, which is his most enduring monument. In March 1874 David Judson Burr suffered the first of a series of paralytic strokes, which eventually left him completely disabled, and died in Richmond on 3 August 1876. He was buried in Hollywood Cemetery in that city. The capital's leading newspaper, the *Daily Dispatch*, eulogized Burr as "'a man out of a thousand' . . . distinguished by public-spirited actions and devotion to the interests of his native city."

Biographies in *Obituary Record of Graduates of Yale College Deceased from June 1870 to June 1880* (1880), 260–261, and Louis H. Manarin, ed., *Richmond at War: The Minutes of the City Council, 1861–1865* (1966), 627, the latter giving incorrect birth year of 1821 (por. on 307); birth date reported by father in David Judson Burr to Elizabeth Sherman Burr Baldwin, 19 Oct. 1820, Baldwin Family Papers, Yale University, New Haven, Conn.; several Burr documents in James Henry Burton Papers, Yale; marriage in *Richmond Whig and Public Advertiser*, 16 Apr. 1844; Richmond City Council Records, vols. 14–15; W. Asbury Christian, *Richmond, Her Past and Present* (1912), 209, 291, 307, 310, 353; Matthew W. Norman, *Colonel Burton's Spiller and Burr Revolver: An Untimely Venture in Confederate Small-Arms Manufacturing* (1996), esp. 13–14, 41, 95, 101–105; Presidential Pardons; Michael B. Chesson, *Richmond After the War, 1865–1890* (1981), 154–155; Edmond H. Brill Jr., "History of the Richmond Chamber of Commerce" (1967 typescript, LVA), 2–4; obituary in *Richmond Daily Dispatch*, 4 Aug. 1876 (quotation).

MICHAEL B. CHESSON

BURRELL, Isaac David (10 March 1865– 21 March 1914), physician and pharmacist, was born in the village of Chula in Amelia County, the son of Robert Burrell, a farmer who was probably a slave before Emancipation. The name of his mother is unknown. During Reconstruction Burrell attended a public school in Amelia

County and then went to Pennsylvania, where in 1888 he graduated from Lincoln University in Chester County. He subsequently attended the Leonard Medical College of Shaw University in Raleigh, North Carolina, and received an M.D. in 1893.

Burrell then moved to Roanoke and began practicing medicine. In the 1890s Roanoke was a young industrial town crowded with laborers working for the Norfolk and Western Railway Company, several of whom had the surname Burrell. Family connections are now difficult to unravel, but the doctor was probably drawn to the city by the presence of one or more relatives. On 28 December 1897 Burrell married Margaret H. Barnette, a native of Lynchburg and a graduate of Hampton Normal and Agricultural Institute. She was a teacher in the public schools described as "a woman of culture and refinement." They had no children.

Burrell's medical practice prospered, and soon after arriving in Roanoke he opened a drugstore where his younger brother later worked. For many years his was the only black-owned drugstore in southwestern Virginia. About the time of his marriage Burrell purchased an old hotel building and moved his pharmacy and residence into it. By 1905 he had prospered enough to build a large house atop a hill on Patton Avenue in the Gainsboro area of Roanoke. With its commanding view of the city and with its electricity, gaslights, and central heating, the Burrell house became a well-known landmark. Many African American visitors to the city took advantage of the family's hospitality, and Lucy Addison, an accomplished educator who taught in the city's public schools, lived with the family.

The Burrells and several of the city's teachers were members of Fifth Avenue Presbyterian Church. Its minister, Lylburn Liggins Downing, had been one of Burrell's classmates at Lincoln University, and Burrell became an elder in the church. He was involved in fraternal affairs and belonged to the Masons, the Knights of Pythias, and the Odd Fellows. He also served as president of the Magic City Medical Society, the local organization of African American physicians. Because black patients were denied admission to the city's white hospitals, the African American

doctors of Roanoke had long hoped to build their own hospital. The need for such an institution came into grim focus in 1914 when Burrell himself became ill. In great pain and knowing his condition to be critical, he made the 220-mile journey by train to Freedman's Hospital in Washington, D.C., accompanied by his wife and a fellow black physician. Isaac David Burrell died there on 21 March 1914 shortly after undergoing surgery for gallstones. His body was brought back to Roanoke for burial in Midway Cemetery (later Williams Memorial Park Cemetery).

Burrell's widow took over operation of the drugstore for a time, and in 1915 the black physicians of Roanoke opened a hospital for their patients. The ten-bed facility on Henry Street was named Burrell Memorial Hospital. Its first director was Lylburn Clinton Downing, a son of Burrell's minister. In 1919 the city purchased the abandoned buildings of the Allegheny Institute and leased it to the doctors, who operated it as the city's black hospital from 1921 until 1955, when a modern brick hospital was constructed with the help of a woman's auxiliary. In the wake of the civil rights movement, white hospitals in Roanoke began to accept black patients, and in 1978 Burrell Memorial Hospital closed. During more than six decades of operation, however, the hospital was a fitting memorial to the city's pioneering black physician.

Birth and death dates from gravestone, transcribed in Roanoke Valley Historical Society, *Roanoke County Graveyards through 1920* (1986), 245; biography in Caldwell, *History of the American Negro*, 303–305 (por. and quotation); transcription of interview with widow, 8 Jan. 1940, in WPA Biographies; *Richmond Planet*, 25 Dec. 1897, 1 Jan. 1898, 15 July 1905 (por.); information provided by Walter S. Claytor and Dorothy Stuart; *Roanoke Tribune*, 6 Aug. 1955; "Street by Street, Block by Block: How Urban Renewal Uprooted Black Roanoke," special section of *Roanoke Times and World-News*, 29 Jan. 1995; files and scrapbooks on Burrell Memorial Hospital at Roanoke Public Library and Gainsboro Branch Library; J. Daniel Pezzoni, "The Burrell Pharmacy Site" (ca. 1993 report for Preservation Technologies, Inc.; photocopy in DVB Files); obituary in *Richmond Planet*, 28 Mar. 1914.

Ann Field Alexander

BURRELL, William Patrick (25 November 1865–18 March 1952), business leader, was the first of the children of William Patrick Burrell and Mildred Burrell to be born free. His father worked as a butler and waiter in Richmond, and his mother took in washing. His uncle James Burrell obtained an education during slavery and became a leader in the city's black community immediately after the Civil War. Burrell attended the Baker School and the Richmond Colored Normal School, from which he graduated in 1884. At age twelve he joined the Moore Street Baptist Church and eventually became its treasurer and a deacon.

Early in 1881 the church's sexton introduced Burrell to William Washington Browne, who had recently arrived in Richmond from Alabama to reinvigorate the Grand United Order of True Reformers, a temperance organization. Browne proposed to make the True Reformers a mutual benefit society, requiring members to purchase a death-benefit certificate that obligated the order to pay a sum of money to the member's heirs. After Richmond members agreed to his plan, Browne hired Burrell as his secretary.

Although steadfastly in favor of temperance and self-discipline, the Grand Fountain United Order of True Reformers made its insurance features the focus of the order's work. It grew from twelve chapters in 1883 to fifty-one in 1885. In May 1884 Burrell became the order's Grand Worthy Secretary and made the insurance system more actuarially sound by adopting a fee structure based on members' ages. He also taught school in Richmond from 1885 to 1889, by which time the order boasted 254 chapters and 6,500 members. With D. E. Johnson Sr., Burrell wrote the *Twenty-Five Years History of the Grand Fountain of the United Order of True Reformers, 1881–1905* (1909).

On 24 December 1885 Burrell married Mary E. Cary, a native of Richmond and a teacher. They had two sons. She joined the True Reformers, assisted in the secretary's office, and proved to be a fine speaker and organizer. The True Reformers continued to expand, and on 3 April 1889 the Savings Bank of the Grand Fountain United Order of True Reformers opened in Richmond, the first chartered bank in the United States owned by African Americans. Mary Burrell served as the bank's first clerk. Although the majority of the order's members were Virginians, chapters existed in more than a dozen other states by the mid-1890s.

The Burrells became important community and state leaders. He served for many years as president of the Richmond Baptist Sunday School Union, and she helped found the Women's Baptist Missionary and Educational Association of Virginia, chaired its executive committee, and served as secretary of the Virginia State Federation of Colored Women's Clubs. Both helped to establish the Richmond Hospital in 1902. Burrell became chair of the hospital's finance committee, and his wife was secretary of the women's auxiliary in charge of the hospital's charity work.

In January 1901 the governor named Burrell one of the state curators for Hampton Normal and Agricultural Institute (later Hampton University), and he served three consecutive terms in that post through 1912. He attended the annual Hampton Negro Conference and several times addressed it on business-related subjects. Burrell's call at the 1904 conference for insurance companies operated by blacks to cooperate in compiling statistics for actuarial tables inspired the formation of the Federated Insurance League, a business association of which he became the first president. In 1909 a natural interest in improving health conditions for blacks led him to organize Richmond's branch of the Virginia Colored Anti-Tuberculosis League.

By 1903 the True Reformers had about 60,000 members with chapters in almost every state east of the Mississippi River. The order owned real estate valued in that year at more than $385,000, and in December 1899 it chartered the Reformers' Mercantile and Industrial Association, which operated retail stores in several cities. The order borrowed heavily from its funds in the Reformers' Savings Bank to finance those businesses, but the stores proved unprofitable. In the spring of 1910 the board of directors closed them, hoping that the action would strengthen the order's finances. Early in October, however, prompted by some $50,000 in unpaid death benefits, the state sent a bank examiner to study the savings bank's accounts. On 21 October he informed Burrell that the bank was insolvent. Stunned, Burrell called a meeting of the board of directors. They studied the bank's books for themselves and came to the same conclusion. On 26 October 1910 they closed the bank and put the True Reformers into receivership. That evening, the bank's cashier disappeared with more than $50,000 that he had embezzled.

The bank's depositors and the order's members grew ever angrier as investigation revealed that the True Reformers' real estate assets were overvalued and heavily mortgaged. Burrell denied that he was guilty of wrongdoing and maintained that he had unsuccessfully protested the board's speculations, but the audience at one public meeting walked out when he attempted to speak. Early in August 1911 he and the five other directors were indicted on twenty counts, including permitting a bank that they knew to be insolvent to continue receiving deposits. Two weeks later Burrell tendered his resignation as Grand Worthy Secretary. He was the first officer to be tried, in a proceeding that began on 22 April 1912 and went to the jury on 26 April. The jury deadlocked, and the judge dismissed the case. Indicted again, Burrell went on trial on 28 May 1912. That jury acquitted him, and the prosecutor then dropped the charges against the others. The *Richmond Planet* reported on 8 June 1912 that the outcome had produced widespread dissatisfaction.

The Burrells and their two sons moved first to Brooklyn, New York, and by 1915 to Newark, New Jersey. There they constructed new careers of civic activism. In 1915 Burrell helped to organize the Federation of Colored Organizations of New Jersey, which he and his wife both served as officers. Mary Burrell also became a leader of the Federation of Colored Women's Clubs of New Jersey, and husband and wife were both active in the Republican Party. Burrell served as a doorkeeper (1928–1929) and a file clerk (1930–1931) for the state legislature. During the 1930s he became a social worker, and in 1942, at the age of seventy-seven, he was ordained a Baptist minister. His younger son, John Mercer Burrell, an attorney, represented Essex County in the New Jersey legislature from 1933 to 1936. William Patrick Burrell died in a Newark hospital on 18 March 1952 and was buried in Heavenly Rest Cemetery in that city.

Biography in Burrell and D. E. Johnson, *Twenty-Five Years History of the Grand Fountain of the United Order of True Reformers, 1881–1905* (1909), 498–506 (several pors.); BVS Marriage Register, Richmond City; James D. Watkinson, "William Washington Browne and the True Reformers of Richmond, Virginia," *VMHB* 97 (1989): 375–398; Abram L. Harris, *The Negro as Capitalist: A Study of Banking and Business among American Negroes* (1936), 62–74; Burrell, "Labor and Business in Virginia," in Hampton Negro Conference *Proceedings* (1903): 47–56, and "Negro Life Insurance" and "Colored Anti-Tuberculosis League, Richmond Branch," in Hampton Negro Conference *Annual Report* 14 (1910): 44–45, 51–57; bank failure and its consequences reported in *Richmond Planet*, 5 Nov. 1910–8 June 1912, and *Richmond Times-Dispatch*, 23, 25 Apr., 31 May 1912; information provided by New Jersey Historical Society and Newark Public Library; obituaries in *Newark Evening News*, 21 Mar. 1952, and *Newark New Jersey Afro-American* (por.) and *Richmond Afro-American*, both 29 Mar. 1952.

JOHN T. KNEEBONE

BURRESS, Withers Alexander (24 November 1894–13 June 1977), army officer, was born in Richmond, the son of John Woodfin Burress and Susan Chinn Withers Burress. Nicknamed Pinky because of his red hair, he graduated from McGuire's University School in Richmond in 1910 and then enrolled in the Virginia Military Institute, where he excelled on the football team and graduated in the class of 1914. He and four other members of that class became general officers. Following graduation Burress served as commandant of cadets and football coach at John Marshall High School in Richmond until 1916. Responding to the growing possibility of American involvement in World War I, he applied for a commission in the United States Army. On 30 November 1916 Burress was commissioned a second lieutenant, promoted to first lieutenant that same day, and assigned to the 23d Infantry Regiment, 2d Division.

Promoted temporarily to captain on 25 August 1917, a promotion that became permanent on 12 October of that year, Burress served in France with the 23d Infantry and saw action in the Battles of Château-Thierry, Saint-Mihiel, and Aisne-Marne before returning to the United States in 1919. He received La Solidaridad decoration from Panama and the Chevalieri di Coronna d'Italia. Burress remained in the service but found advancement slow in the small, peacetime army. He was an instructor at the infantry school at Fort Benning, Georgia, when he married Virginia Collier Chappell, of Columbus, Georgia, on 15 November 1922. They had one daughter.

Soon after his marriage Burress returned to Virginia for a two-year assignment as assistant professor of military science and tactics at VMI. He took the army's command courses for infantry officers in 1925 and 1929 and in the latter year on 7 July was promoted to major. Burress graduated from the Command and General Staff School in 1931 and from the Army War College in 1935. He returned once again to VMI in the latter year as commandant of cadets. Reflecting his own lifelong involvement in sports and outdoor activities, he placed a high emphasis on organized physical conditioning and participation in sports by all of the cadets.

Burress was promoted to lieutenant colonel on 18 March 1939 and ordered to duty the next year as a member of the general staff at the Department of War in Washington. In autumn 1941, after being promoted to colonel, he returned to the infantry school at Fort Benning as assistant commandant. On 13 March 1942, three months after the United States entered World War II, Burress was promoted to brigadier general and assigned to Puerto Rico. Five months later, on 9 August, he was promoted to major general and sent to Fort Jackson, South Carolina, where he assumed command of the new 100th Infantry Division when it was activated on 15 November 1942. After two years of preparation, Burress took the 100th Division to Europe and led it through France and Germany, where it distinguished itself during the Vosges Mountains campaign, the liberation of Bitche, France, and the capture of Heilbronn and Stuttgart, Germany. He commanded the division from its formation in 1942 until September 1945, and his ability to inspire loyalty and devotion, already well known at VMI, contributed to his success as a general officer.

Following a brief tour as acting commander of the Twenty-fifth Corps after the war ended, Burress was appointed commanding general of the United States Constabulary in occupied Germany and inspector general of the Eastern Theater of Operations. In this capacity, he handled the investigation of the highly publicized case of officers at a United States Army facility in Lichfield, England, who were charged with brutality against American servicemen jailed there. For his wartime service Burress received the Silver Star for Gallantry in Action, two Bronze Stars, the Distinguished Service Medal, the Legion of Merit, the Legion of Honor, and France's Croix de Guerre.

Burress returned to the United States in 1948 as commander of the Infantry Center at Fort Benning, Georgia. After brief tours in Europe commanding the Sixth and Seventh Corps in 1951 and 1952, respectively, he was promoted to lieutenant general and on 1 January 1953 was given command of the First Army in New York. Burress was honored with a parade through New York City in November 1954 before retiring from active duty on 2 December of that year. Throughout the era of Cold War nuclear proliferation, the general, who always referred to himself as a doughboy, remained a strong advocate of large army ground forces. Returning to Virginia, Burress served as chief executive officer of the Virginia 350th Anniversary Commission and used his executive experience and planning ability to oversee the complex programs of the commemoration. After 1957 he lived in quiet retirement in Salem. His wife died on 10 November 1974. Withers Alexander Burress died in a nursing home in Arlington County on 13 June 1977 and was buried two days later in Arlington National Cemetery.

"Lieutenant General Withers Alexander Burress: A Doughboy's Doughboy," *100th Infantry Division Association News* 21 (Feb. 1978): 1 (por.), 4; personal record and Withers A. Burress Papers, including scrapbooks, VMI; *Record of Service in the World War of V.M.I. Alumni and Their Alma Mater* (1920), 23, 72, 203–204, 385; *Richmond News Leader*, 25 June 1945 (por.), 11 Feb. 1955; *New York Times*, 27 Apr. 1946, 20 Nov. 1954; *Lexington Rockbridge County News*, 24 Jan. 1952; *VMI Alumni Review* 29 (winter 1952/1953): 6; ibid. 54 (winter 1978): 20; family history information confirmed by daughter, Cynthia Kent Burress Dolvin; obituaries in *Richmond Times-Dispatch* and *Washington Post*, both 14 June 1977, and *VMI Alumni Review* 53 (summer 1977): 55.

KEITH ERIC GIBSON

BURROUGHS, Charles Franklin (31 July 1871–24 February 1960), business executive, was born in Sparta, Edgecomb County, North Carolina, the son of Thomas L. Burroughs, a millwright, and Louisa Tyler Burroughs. His father and four of his siblings died when he was young, some of them from tuberculosis. With his mother Burroughs moved to Tarboro, where he attended school and went to work when he was ten years old as an errand boy for Royster and Strudwick, a general store. After his mother's death Burroughs boarded with Frank S. Royster, the store's owner.

Royster and Strudwick became the F. S. Royster Guano Company in 1885, and in 1891 Royster sent Burroughs to Norfolk to open a branch office and to act as the firm's buyer. The company grew rapidly, and at age twenty-four Burroughs became one of its officers. Royster moved the headquarters to Norfolk and in August 1900 incorporated the F. S. Royster Guano Company under Virginia law, with Burroughs as an executive vice president and secretary. Burroughs assumed more responsibility for daily operations as Royster became less involved with the business after 1906. On 27 April 1909 Burroughs married Mabel Chamberlaine. They had one son and one daughter.

In 1912 the company moved its headquarters to the new Royster Building in Norfolk. Before World War I Burroughs traveled to France and Germany to purchase potash, one of the basic materials for manufacturing fertilizer. The company imported nitrate of soda from seabird guano deposits in Chile. With the development of potash production in New Mexico, the availability after World War I of synthetic nitrogen from plants in nearby Hopewell and in Wilmington, North Carolina, and acquisition of phosphate mines in Florida, the company was able to obtain all of its raw materials within the United States. Anticipating these changes in the industry, Burroughs took advantage of the shift from foreign to domestic markets, and by 1924 the F. S. Royster Company had become a sprawling operation of seventeen plants located in eight states. Burroughs became president of the company after Royster's death in 1928. The corporation continued to grow and became one of the Tidewater region's largest civilian employers. In 1958 Burroughs retired as president and became chairman of the board. By the next year the F. S. Royster Company was operating eigh-

teen plants in twelve states and employing more than 1,400 people in Indiana, New York, Ohio, Wisconsin, and every coastal state south of Maryland and east of Louisiana.

Burroughs was a director of the Pamlico Chemical Company and of the Consumers Cotton Oil Company, businesses in which the Royster Company held an interest. He also bred guernseys at his Bayville Farms dairy. Burroughs served for forty years on the board of the Norfolk Academy and played an important part in the growth of Norfolk General Hospital, to which he donated a chapel in memory of his wife, who had died on 26 November 1954. A self-educated man, he developed a love of reading and a taste for history and mathematics. Charles Franklin Burroughs died at his home in Norfolk on 24 February 1960 and was buried in Cedar Grove Cemetery in that city.

Tyler, *Men of Mark*, 2d ser., 413–414 (por. facing 413); business and personal information furnished by son, Charles Franklin Burroughs Jr.; Norfolk City Marriage Register; SCC Charter Book, 41:300, 42:398; business statistics from *Moody's Industrial Manual*, 1924, 1959, 1960; obituaries and editorial tributes in *Norfolk Ledger-Dispatch* and *Norfolk Virginian-Pilot,* both 25 Feb. 1960.

DONALD W. GUNTER

BURROWS, John Lansing (14 February 1814–2 January 1893), Baptist minister, was born in Albany, New York, the son of Samuel Burrows and Elizabeth Lansing Burrows. He was educated in Germantown, Pennsylvania, and at Union College in Schenectady, New York. Burrows also studied theology at Andover Theological Seminary (later Andover Newton Theological School) in Massachusetts. He was ordained by the Poughkeepsie Baptist Church in New York in 1835, the same year that he married Adeline Benthuysen. They had two sons and one daughter.

J. Lansing Burrows served as co-pastor of a Baptist church in New York City for one year and then moved to Kentucky, where he taught school in Elizabethtown and Shelbyville, founded several Baptist churches, and helped organize the Baptist General Association of Kentucky. In 1840 he was called to the Fifth Baptist Church in Philadelphia, and four years later he led in organizing the Broad Street Baptist Church in the same city. Burrows edited the *American Baptist Register, for 1852*, a 500-page directory of churches and ministers that the American Baptist Publication Society issued in 1853.

In 1854 the First Baptist Church of Richmond called Burrows to its pulpit. Even though some members of the church opposed the installation of a minister from the North, he became a southerner by choice and endeared himself to the city. For the next twenty years Burrows was a civic leader in Richmond. During the Civil War he regularly preached to Confederate soldiers, both as pastor of one of the largest churches in the capital of the Confederacy and as a favorite clergyman in the army camps, where he often preached as many as four times a day. Burrows ministered in the local hospitals and as an active member of the Richmond Ambulance Corps often visited the field to comfort the wounded and remove them from the battlefield. At least one of his sermons was published in tract form as *The Christian Scholar and Soldier* (1864) and widely distributed in the army. At the end of the war Burrows consoled his congregation by reminding them that the loss of the war was of less consequence than the loss of God's favor.

Burrows served as president of the Baptist General Association of Virginia for four terms, in 1867, 1868, 1882, and 1883; as a vice president of the Southern Baptist Convention in 1867, 1871, and 1874; and as president of the Foreign Mission Board of the Southern Baptist Convention in 1866 and from 1868 to 1873. He published several of his sermons as pamphlets, and he composed a history of the First Baptist Church for inclusion in *The First Century of the First Baptist Church of Richmond, Virginia, 1780–1880* (1880). Burrows was a gifted orator in great demand for public-speaking engagements, and he influenced many young men to enter the ministry. A friend of education, he was a professor of evidence of Christianity at the Richmond Female Institute, and he sat on the board of Richmond College (later the University of Richmond) from 1855 to 1875 and again from 1882 until his death. Burrows took part in reopening Richmond College after the Civil War, and he organized and directed the memorial campaign that raised $150,000 for the college in 1872 and 1873.

In 1874, following the death of his wife on 22 August of that year, Burrows moved to Broadway Baptist Church in Louisville, Kentucky, and then in 1882 to the Freemason Street Baptist Church in Norfolk. At the latter church he conducted several extended revivals. In 1887 Burrows published two volumes of sermons and lectures, bound together as one, *What Baptists Believe and Other Discourses* and *The Curse and the Cross and Other Sermons*. He resigned from his Norfolk church on 2 January 1891 because of failing health. In his honor the Freemason Street Church named one of its mission churches the Burrows Memorial Baptist Church. In his last years he lived in Augusta, Georgia, with his son, also a Baptist minister, and served as pastor of a rural church about thirty miles away. John Lansing Burrows died at the home of one of his congregants in Stellaville, Jefferson County, Georgia, on 2 January 1893 and was buried in Hollywood Cemetery in Richmond.

George Braxton Taylor, *Virginia Baptist Ministers: Fourth Series* (1913), 170–186; Woodford B. Hackley, *Faces on the Wall: Brief Sketches of the Men and Women whose Portraits and Busts were on the Campus of the University of Richmond in 1955* (1972), 13–14 (por. facing 62); George W. McDaniel, *The First Baptist Church, Richmond, Va.* (1916), 14–15; Blanche Sydnor White, *First Baptist Church, Richmond, 1780–1955* (1955), 223–224; William Latane Lumpkin, *The History of the Freemason Street Baptist Church, 1848–1970* (1973), 91–97; volume of obituaries and articles relating to death in son Lansing Burrows's papers, Southern Baptist Historical Library and Archives, Nashville, Tenn.; obituaries and editorial tributes in *Norfolk Landmark* and *Richmond Dispatch*, both 3 Jan. 1893, and *Religious Herald*, 12 Jan. 1893 (por.); memorials in Southern Baptist Convention *Proceedings* (1893): frontispiece, vi, 42, and [First Baptist Church, Richmond], *Dr. John Lansing Burrows. Died in Stellaville, Ga., . . . Age, Seventy-Nine* (1893).

FRED ANDERSON

BURRUSS, Julian Ashby (16 August 1876– 4 January 1947), president of the State Normal and Industrial School for Women at Harrisonburg and of Virginia Agricultural and Mechanical College and Polytechnic Institute, was born in Richmond, the son of Woodson Cheadle Burruss, a contractor, and Cora McDowell Burruss. After attending public schools in Richmond, he entered Virginia Agricultural and Mechanical College and Polytechnic Institute, from which he graduated with a B.S. in civil engineering in 1898. After further study at Richmond College, Burruss taught at Reinhart Normal College in Waleska, Cherokee County, Georgia, and at Speers-Langford Military Academy and the Searcy Female Institute, both in Searcy, White County, Arkansas.

Burruss became principal of the Leigh School in Richmond in 1901. As director of manual arts in the Richmond public schools from 1904 to 1908, he introduced the first vocational education system in the city. Studying during the summer, Burruss enrolled in concurrent graduate courses and in 1906 received both an M.A. in anthropology from Columbia University and an A.M. from Teachers College at the same university. On 18 June 1907 he married Rachel Cleveland Ebbert in Covington, Kentucky. They had one son and one daughter.

In 1908 Burruss became the first president of the State Normal and Industrial School for Women at Harrisonburg (later James Madison University). During his tenure the student enrollment grew from 209 to 306 and the faculty from 15 to 26, and he doubled the number of buildings to six. Burruss helped the school become a pioneer in the field of industrial education, especially in home economics. It was one of the first colleges in the nation to emphasize rural community development and education programs, and it was unique in managing a one-room practice school several miles from its campus. Burruss inaugurated the four-quarter school year in Virginia, and he also offered the first college-level correspondence courses, which allowed teachers to continue their education and promoted the efficient use of state educational resources. He gained a reputation as a good financial manager and assisted Governor Westmoreland Davis in devising a new state budget system.

Burruss continued to pursue his own education during the summers, and in 1921 he completed his doctorate in education at the University of Chicago. His dissertation, published as *A Study of the Business Administration of Colleges Based on an Examination of the Practices of Land-Grant Colleges in the Making and Using of Budgets* (1921), was pertinent to his new job. In 1919 Burruss had become

president of Virginia Agricultural and Mechanical College and Polytechnic Institute, which became Virginia Polytechnic Institute in 1944 while he was still president. He stabilized the school's finances, hired a business manager, and kept the college within its budget for most of his administration, which spanned the Great Depression of the 1930s. At the same time Burruss fostered tremendous growth. When he became president the college's physical plant was valued at $1,051,500, the buildings were in disrepair, and 244 faculty members served a student body of approximately 700. When he retired in 1945 the property was valued at $8,500,000, the faculty numbered 760, and the student enrollment had increased to 3,300, making Virginia Tech the largest institution of higher education in Virginia. Much of the growth occurred during the 1930s, when Burruss successfully negotiated two large grants to the college from the Public Works Administration for landscaping and for construction of much-needed dormitories, classrooms, a dining hall, a student activities building, water facilities, roads, and walkways. Julian A. Burruss Hall, built during the years 1934–1936 and named for him in 1944, includes a 3,000-seat auditorium that was once one of the largest in the South.

Burruss was a strong proponent of useful education that prepared students for service to the state that was providing them educational opportunities. Soon after arriving at the college he reorganized the curriculum. He modernized and strengthened the agricultural and engineering components in particular and added a premedical specialty and courses in coal-mining engineering and physical education. Burruss established the Engineering Experiment Station in 1921, the same year that the college began admitting women in all departments. By the end of his career Virginia Polytechnic Institute had a national reputation for excellence in several fields of engineering and agriculture.

Burruss's service to the commonwealth of Virginia included a term as president of the Virginia State Teachers Association in 1912–1913 and stints on the Virginia Board of Agriculture and Immigration and the board of the Virginia Truck Experiment Station. Burruss served as a trustee of Mary Baldwin College and was chancellor of Radford College in 1944 and 1945. From 1938 to 1939 he was president of the Association of Land Grant Colleges and Universities. Burruss was seriously considered for the presidencies of the Medical College of Virginia in 1923 and Oklahoma Agricultural and Mechanical College (later Oklahoma State University) in 1928. Besides membership in a number of educational associations, he was active in other fields. He was a member from 1924 to 1925 of the governor's board on simplification and economy in state and local government, and from 1928 through 1930, the last year as chair, he served on a state commission that studied the condition of Virginia's farmers. Burruss also sat on state commissions studying crop pests, geology, medical education, and rural electrification, and he belonged to the Appalachian Forest Research Council. In 1937 *Progressive Farmer* magazine named him the man of the year in Virginia agriculture. Burruss served as president of the Harrisonburg Chamber of Commerce and headed the Virginia State Chamber of Commerce's committee on industrial development. In 1929 and 1930 he was district governor of Rotary International. In Blacksburg Burruss was an elder in the Presbyterian Church, an active Mason, and a member of numerous college societies. Hampden-Sydney College honored him with an LL.D. in 1937.

On 10 January 1945 Burruss fractured a vertebra in an automobile accident. He never fully recovered, and the board of visitors named him president emeritus on 15 May of that year. Julian Ashby Burruss died in Blacksburg on 4 January 1947 and was buried in Riverview Cemetery in Richmond.

NCAB, 43:24–26 (giving erroneous 1874 birth date); Julian Ashby Burruss Papers, VPI; *Virginia Journal of Education* 1 (July 1908): 19; D. L. Kinnear, *The First 100 Years: A History of the Virginia Polytechnic Institute and State University* (1972), 253–335 (por. following 306); feature article in *Richmond Times-Dispatch,* 25 June 1944; Burruss's published addresses include *A Unified System of Education for Virginia from the Standpoint of the Colleges* (1932), "Education and Virginia's Forward Movement," *Bulletin of Virginia Polytechnic Institute* 20, no. 3x (1927): supplement, and *Some Qualitative Effects of the Present Economic Situation on the Colleges* (1932); pors. in President's Room, James Madison University Library, and in Board Room, President's Suite, Burruss Hall, VPI; obituaries in *Richmond*

News Leader, 4 Jan. 1947 (with editorial tribute 6 Jan. 1947), *New York Times,* 5 Jan. 1947, *Richmond Times-Dispatch,* 5 Jan. 1947 (with editorial tribute 6 Jan. 1947), *Harrisonburg Daily News-Record,* 6 Jan. 1947, and *Techgram,* 15 Jan. 1947 (with pors. and birth date).

THOMAS C. HUNT

BURTON, Clarence Godber (14 December 1886–18 January 1982), member of the House of Representatives, was born in Providence, Rhode Island, the son of Joseph Godber Burton, an English immigrant, and Annie Stevens Severn Burton. At the turn of the century the family moved to Lynchburg, where Burton's father founded the Lynchburg Hosiery Company (later the Lynchburg Hosiery Mills, Inc.). After graduation from Lynchburg High School, Burton attended Piedmont Business College. In 1907 he became treasurer of the Lynchburg Hosiery Mills and in 1921 succeeded his father as president of the company. Burton's other business interests included raising cattle and banking. From 1924 to 1980 he held key positions as director and president of the Commercial Trust and Savings Bank in Lynchburg and of the American Federal Savings and Loan Association.

Burton served on the Lynchburg school board from 1938 to 1941 and became its vice chairman. For twenty years he also served on the boards of Randolph-Macon College in Ashland and Randolph-Macon Woman's College in Lynchburg and as chairman of the executive committee of the latter. A lifelong Democrat who did not identify himself with any particular faction within the party, Burton viewed public office as a civic responsibility. During World War II he chaired the local Selective Service Board and sat on the appeals board. In 1942 Burton was elected to the Lynchburg city council, and he served from 1942 to 1946 as vice mayor and from 1946 to 1948 as mayor of the city.

Burton resigned as mayor in 1948 to run for the House of Representatives from the eight-county Sixth District, which also included the cities of Clifton Forge, Lynchburg, Radford, and Roanoke. He easily won simultaneous election to the 80th Congress to fill the seat vacant since James Lindsay Almond's resignation in April and to a full term in the 81st Congress. Burton took his seat on 31 December 1948 in the closing days of the 80th Congress. He was reelected in 1950. During his tenure Burton served on the Committees on Banking and Currency and on Veterans' Affairs and also on a select committee to study the problems of small businesses. He believed his most important act as a congressman was successfully opposing amendments to weaken the Defense Production Act of 1952, which allocated global materials in short supply since World War II.

In 1952 Republican Richard Harding Poff, a twenty-nine-year-old attorney from Radford, defeated Burton in his second bid for reelection. The campaign was noticeably void of any real issues. Although the Republican Party had had no real presence in Lynchburg, a group of citizens interested in establishing a two-party system saw an opportunity to use the immense popularity of the Republican presidential candidate Dwight David Eisenhower. With Poff's agreement to challenge Burton, they formed a Lynchburg GOP committee and united behind the long-shot candidacy of Poff. Burton carried Lynchburg, but he lost the race in Botetourt and Roanoke Counties and the city of Roanoke. Eisenhower's popularity definitely boosted Poff's candidacy, and labor leaders commented afterward that there was no real difference between Burton and Poff and that many working-class voters did not bother to go to the polls.

Burton then retired from politics, but he continued to serve the community in a variety of roles. He held leadership positions at various times with the Memorial Hospital, the Lynchburg Chamber of Commerce, the Miller Female Orphan Asylum, the Boy Scout Area Council, the Rotary and Elks Clubs, the Appalachian Trail Club (of which he was a founder), and the Memorial United Methodist Church, and he served on the Board of Zoning Appeals from 1957 to 1977. Burton owned a farm at Forest and kept a herd of a hundred polled Hereford cattle.

Clarence Godber Burton never married. He died at Virginia Baptist Hospital in Lynchburg on 18 January 1982 at the age of ninety-five and was buried in Spring Hill Cemetery in that city.

Birth date in most printed sources and Social Security application, Social Security Administration, Office of Earnings Operations, Baltimore, Md.; variant birth date of 31 Dec.

1886 in feature article in *Lynchburg News*, 26 Nov. 1959; information provided by nephew Clarence Burton Gerhardt; *Lynchburg News*, 3 Nov. 1948, 2–6 Nov. 1952; *Congressional Record*, 82d Cong., 2d sess., 7629–7631, 7633–7634, 7717–7718; obituaries in *Lynchburg Daily Advance* (por.) and *Richmond News Leader,* both 19 Jan. 1982, and *Richmond Times-Dispatch*, 20 Jan. 1982; editorial tribute in *Lynchburg News*, 25 Jan. 1982.

PAUL R. WAIBEL

BURTON, James Henry (17 August 1823–18 October 1894), armorer, was born at Shannondale Springs in Jefferson County. His parents were of English birth, but their names are not recorded, and little is known about his family and upbringing. Burton attended an academy in West Chester, Pennsylvania, and at the age of sixteen found work in the machine shops of Baltimore, Maryland. After an apprenticeship of four years he returned to Jefferson County to work as a machinist in the rifle works at the United States armory at Harpers Ferry. During the 1840s Burton participated in the introduction of mass production of interchangeable parts and proved his talent at adapting and devising new machinery. He was appointed foreman of machinists in 1845 and four years later became acting master armorer. Burton regularly visited manufacturers and armories in New England to study advanced industrial processes and obtain equipment. In 1849 he modified the pointed, hollow-base rifle bullet invented by Claude-Étienne Minié for the French army by adding lubricated grooves around the base to prevent fouling and improve accuracy. The United States Army adopted it in 1855. The famed Civil War "Minie ball" was thus Burton's bullet.

In 1854 Burton moved to Chicopee, Massachusetts, to work for a private arms manufacturer. About that same time the British government decided to adopt mass production of interchangeable parts for its armaments industry and sent representatives to Massachusetts to purchase equipment and recruit skilled workers. Barely a year after leaving Virginia, Burton became chief engineer of the Royal Small Arms Factory at Enfield, near London, where he supervised fabrication of machinery to make Enfield rifles and experimented with the manufacture of Sharps carbines.

In May 1844 Burton married Cornelia Frances Mauzy, a native of Harpers Ferry whose father was a surveyor and employee of the armory. They had two sons and one daughter. Cornelia Burton died in England about 1858, and on 4 June 1859 Burton married Eugenia Harper Mauzy, the younger sister of his first wife. They had five sons and five daughters. His declining health forced Burton to resign from the Royal Small Arms Factory in 1860. The British government paid him a substantial bonus in appreciation of his efforts and also paid the expenses when the family returned to America that October.

By then the sectional conflict had worsened, and the commonwealth of Virginia had reactivated its Richmond armory and contracted with the Tredegar ironworks to supply machinery for making guns. The company hired Burton soon after his return to the United States. He directed the production effort and visited Northern armories and manufacturers to obtain information and equipment. On 18 April 1861, the day after the state convention voted for secession, Virginia troops occupied the armory at Harpers Ferry and shipped the machinery to Richmond. Burton, as a lieutenant colonel of ordnance for Virginia, supervised the shipment and installation of the machinery. He soon had the Richmond armory manufacturing muskets and an armory in Fayetteville, North Carolina, producing rifles.

On 2 September 1861 Burton became superintendent of armories of the Confederacy, under Josiah Gorgas, chief of ordnance. Private gun manufacturers also sought expert assistance from the respected Burton. Unfortunately, some of his proposed partnerships with manufacturers verged on outright conflicts of interest. Gorgas firmly warned him against any such financial arrangements well before a Confederate congressman complained of them in a speech on 19 April 1862. Burton immediately sent Gorgas his resignation and angrily declared that his only objective had been providing the Confederacy with weapons swiftly and efficiently. Gorgas refused to accept the resignation, and Burton returned to his post.

In May 1862 Burton traveled to Georgia to establish a large armory at Macon, but a shortage of skilled laborers retarded production. The following summer he returned to England to purchase machinery, but little of it reached the Confederacy before the war's end. Burton struggled to maintain production at the Macon armory as the war came to Georgia. On 9 June 1864 Gorgas appointed him general inspector of Confederate armories, and as communication grew more difficult Gorgas gave him complete authority over the Confederate armories in Georgia and Florida, effective 21 February 1865. The war ended for Burton on 20 April 1865, when Union cavalry occupied Macon.

Later that year Burton and his family moved back to England. In the spring of 1868 they returned to a farm in Loudoun County and remained there until 1871, when he once again moved to England to direct an English firm's contract to construct a rifle factory in Russia. He also supervised an armory with an arms contract from the German government, but the strain of overseeing both projects sapped his health. Burton and his large family settled on a farm in Frederick County. In 1890 he sold that property and moved to Winchester. James Henry Burton died in Winchester on 18 October 1894 and was buried there in Mount Hebron Cemetery.

J. E. Norris, *History of the Lower Shenandoah Valley* (1890), 612–614; birth date in French Biographies; William B. Edwards, "One-Man Armory: Colonel J. H. Burton," *Virginia Cavalcade* 12 (autumn 1962): 28–33; Richard Mauzy, *Genealogical Record of the Descendants of Henry Mauzy* (1911), 40–41; Quarles, *Worthy Lives,* 50–51 (por.); James H. Burton Papers, Yale University and Duke; James H. Burton Collection (including Burton's notes and pencil sketches), Harpers Ferry National Historical Park, Harpers Ferry, W.Va.; Jefferson Co. Marriage Register, 1859 (WPA typescript); Compiled Service Records; Frank E. Vandiver, *Ploughshares Into Swords: Josiah Gorgas and Confederate Ordnance* (1952); William A. Albaugh, *The Confederate Brass-Framed Colt and Whitney* (1955), 26–48; Merritt Roe Smith, *Harpers Ferry Armory and the New Technology: The Challenge of Change* (1977); Matthew W. Norman, *Colonel Burton's Spiller and Burr Revolver: An Untimely Venture in Confederate Small-Arms Manufacturing* (1996); obituary in *Baltimore Sun,* 19 Oct. 1894, reprinted in *Winchester Times,* 24 Oct. 1894.

JOHN T. KNEEBONE

BURWELL, Carter (25 October 1716–by 26 October 1756), planter and member of the House of Burgesses, was the son of Elizabeth

Carter Burwell and her first husband, Nathaniel Burwell (1680–1721), and was born at his father's Fairfield plantation on Carter's Creek in Gloucester County. His paternal grandfather was Lewis Burwell (d. 1710), a wealthy Gloucester County planter, and his maternal grandfather was Robert "King" Carter (d. 1732), one of the wealthiest men in North America, who served as president of the governor's Council. Burwell's elder brother Lewis Burwell (d. 1756) and one of his younger brothers, Robert Burwell, also served on the Council. After the death of Burwell's father, King Carter served as his guardian. In 1724 his mother married George Nicholas, a Williamsburg physician.

About the time of his mother's remarriage Burwell entered the grammar school of the College of William and Mary. When he reached his majority he came into a substantial inheritance from his father, and in 1734, under the terms of King Carter's will, Burwell inherited much more land, including an interest in a vast tract in the lower Shenandoah Valley. From his grandfather he also inherited 1,400 acres near the James River on the border of James City and York Counties with the stipulation that the plantation there be called Carter's Grove. In December 1737 Burwell was named a member of the quorum in the new commission of the peace for James City County, and by 1752 he was the presiding justice. On 5 January 1738 he married Lucy Ludwell Grymes, whose father was a wealthy Middlesex County planter and a member of the Council. They had six or seven daughters and three sons, the best known of whom was Nathaniel Burwell (1750–1814), who represented James City County in the Convention of 1788.

Burwell was elected to the House of Burgesses from James City County in 1742 and reelected twice. He served until 1755, by which time he chaired the influential Committee of Privileges and Elections and was a ranking member of the Committee of Propositions and Grievances. A young man of intelligence and talent with powerful family connections, he served on committees for financing the frontier wars and overseeing the construction of a new capitol. A political ally of John Robinson, Speaker of the House of Burgesses and treasurer of Virginia,

Burwell reportedly assisted Robinson in managing the flow of business by prodding a member with his cane to prompt him to speak as desired.

Burwell was twice proposed for membership on the governor's Council. In July 1752 Lieutenant Governor Robert Dinwiddie recommended Burwell, among several others, for the seat vacated by the death of William Dawson, the bishop of London's commissary in Virginia, but Dawson's brother and successor, Thomas Dawson, was appointed instead. Councillor John Blair (ca. 1687–1771) recommended Burwell for another vacancy in 1754, but this time Dinwiddie objected, acknowledging that Burwell was "very well Qualified for a Seat at the Board" but observing that Burwell's brother was then the president of the Council and two of his brothers-in-law were also members, making "too many of one Family."

Five years after Burwell assumed ownership of Carter's Grove plantation he initiated a building program and employed brick mason David Minetree, carpenter John Wheatley, and artisan Richard Baylis to direct the finishing of the interior. With their assistance, and by adapting designs in his copy of William Salmon's *Palladio Londinensis,* Burwell conceived and between 1751 and 1755 erected a plantation house that was a masterpiece of early Georgian architecture in Virginia. The two-and-one-half-story brick mansion had a hipped roof and was flanked by dependencies standing free from the house at either side and parallel to the main axis, each a story and a half high with end chimneys. Elegant in proportion and beautiful in detail, Carter's Grove has subsequently been enlarged and much altered, but it remains one of the gems of colonial Virginia's architecture.

By that time Burwell owned more than 3,000 acres in James City County and more than ninety slaves. Archaeological excavations and plantation records relating to his slaves have revealed much about how his workers and their families lived during and after his time. Not yet forty years old when he completed Carter's Grove, Carter Burwell died less than two years later. He wrote his will on 6 May 1756, added a codicil on 14 May, and died on an unrecorded date between then and 26 October 1756, when the will was proved in the General Court. Burwell was buried probably in the graveyard at Carter's Grove.

George Harrison Burwell III, *Sketch of Carter Burwell (1716–1756)* [1961]; birth recorded in Robert W. Robins, comp., *The Register of Abingdon Parish, Gloucester County, Virginia, 1677–1780* (1981), 28; *Williamsburg Virginia Gazette*, 6 Jan. 1738; Mary A. Stephenson, *Carter's Grove Plantation: A History* (1964), esp. 1–54, 255, 259–303; Jack P. Greene, ed., *The Diary of Colonel Landon Carter of Sabine Hall, 1752–1778* (1965; repr. 1987), 1:85; Robert Dinwiddie to Board of Trade, 28 July 1752, PRO CO 5/1327, fol. 221, and 29 Jan. 1754, CO 5/1328, fols. 41–42 (quotations); John Blair to bishop of London, 25 Jan. 1754, Fulham Palace Papers, Lambeth Palace Library, Eng., 13:118–119; Lorena S. Walsh, *From Calabar to Carter's Grove: The History of a Virginia Slave Community* (1997), esp. 48–49, 67, 109–110, 119–123, 176, 188–189, 205; plantation ledgers and other records in Burwell Papers, CW; copy of will in Burwell Family Papers, UVA.

Daphne Gentry

BURWELL, Lewis (bap. 5 March 1622–ca. 19 November 1652), merchant and founder of the Burwell family in Virginia, was born in Bedfordshire, England, the son of Edward Burwell and Dorothy Bedell Burwell, and was baptized in Ampthill Parish. His family connections undoubtedly explain his immigration to Virginia. His uncles Gabriel Bedell and John Bedell, who were members of the Virginia Company of London, arrived in Jamestown in 1608 and were named in the second charter of the colony in 1609 and on other documents through 1624. One of his sisters married a London merchant who acquired a plantation on Queen's Creek in York County. Following the death of Burwell's father in 1626, his mother married Roger Wingate, who in 1633 participated in one of the first attempts to plant a colony in what became North Carolina and who served on the governor's Council in Virginia from 1640 to 1642.

Burwell may have accompanied his stepfather to America in 1633, but if so he probably returned to England the following year. Burwell had settled in Virginia by January 1641. The records of Accomack County between 1641 and 1647 and of York County after 1645 show him acting with and on behalf of his elder brother William Burwell and other local merchants. Lewis Burwell acquired his first land in 1648, when he and a friend received 2,300 acres on the south bank of the lower part of the York River. Later in 1648 he claimed the headrights inherited from his stepfather and patented 2,350 acres on the north bank of the York River. In that same year Burwell's mother conveyed to him all the rents due at Wingate's death in 1642, and thereafter his wealth grew rapidly. On consecutive days in 1650 he received 1,600 acres in Northumberland County and two adjoining tracts of 500 acres each on the south bank of the Potomac River. Two years later Burwell patented another 200 acres.

Sometime after August 1650 Burwell married Lucy Higginson, the first of a long series of marriages by which the Burwell family substantially increased its wealth and social status. Their only child, Lewis Burwell (d. 1710), built on his father's legacy, partly through connections and property acquired by virtue of Lucy Higginson Burwell's second marriage in 1653 to William Bernard, a member of the Council from 1641 until his death in 1665, and her third to Philip Ludwell, who was appointed to the Council in 1675, the year of her death.

A major in the militia and often identified as a gentleman, Burwell evidently never held political office, but his family ties and the prominence of many of his near neighbors guaranteed that he was well known and respected by persons able to advance his fortunes. Marital alliances and the seemingly insatiable desire for land are common themes in the rise of the great families that dominated Virginia during most of the colonial period, and few families more clearly illustrate these themes than the Burwells.

About the time of his marriage Burwell settled on his land on Carter's Creek in Gloucester County. By then he was suffering from a debilitating illness that is not identified in the records. Lewis Burwell died probably on 19 November 1652, although his gravestone when it was still legible reportedly indicated that he died in the thirty-third year of his life on 19 November 1658. Several extant documents demonstrate that he died before November 1653, and his widow had married William Bernard by August 1653, suggesting that the gravestone inscription was in error or had been incorrectly transcribed. Burwell was buried in the family cemetery, but his body was later moved to the yard of Abingdon Church in Gloucester County.

John L. Blair, "The Rise of the Burwells," *VMHB* 72 (1964): 304–312; F. G. Emmison, ed., *Bedfordshire Parish Registers* (1931–1948), 17:A3; Susie M. Ames, ed., *County Court Records of Accomack-Northampton, Virginia, 1640–1645* (1973), 53–54 (first record in Virginia, 11 Jan. 1641); *Cavaliers and Pioneers*, 1:171, 184, 199, 208–209, 266; one letter printed in *VMHB* 9 (1902): 331; gravestone inscription printed in Meade, *Old Churches*, 1:353, and *WMQ*, 1st ser., 2 (1894): 220.

JOHN L. BLAIR

BURWELL, Lewis (1651 or 1652–19 December 1710), planter, was born probably in Gloucester County, the only child of Lewis Burwell (1622–1652) and Lucy Higginson Burwell. Less than a year after his father's death, his mother married William Bernard, a member of the governor's Council, with whom she had three children before he died on 31 March 1665. By November 1667 she had married Philip Ludwell, who became a councillor eight years later and with whom she had two children. Burwell thus grew up as part of a politically prominent, wealthy, and extended family. About 1674 he married Abigail Smith, the niece and heir of Nathaniel Bacon (1620–1692), who was also a councillor. They had four sons and six daughters before her death on 12 November 1692. Sometime between 4 March 1694 and 21 November 1695 Burwell married Martha Lear Cole, daughter of John Lear, who had served on the Council, and widow of William Cole, yet another councillor. They probably had two sons and three daughters.

Burwell made good use of the connections he gained through the profitable marriages of his mother and greatly enlarged the fortune he had inherited from his father. Already related to the powerful Ludwell family, he saw his sons and daughters marry into the Armistead, Bassett, Berkeley, Carter, and Harrison families. By the 1690s the marriage alliances were no longer one-sided. In six of the seven counties in which he paid taxes in 1704, Burwell was one of the largest landowners, and in Charles City County he owned 8,000 acres, more than any other person. He paid taxes on 26,650 acres that year and was one of the wealthiest men in Virginia. His son Nathaniel Burwell (1680–1721) lived until his death at Fairfield, the striking brick mansion that Burwell had built in the 1690s on Carter's Creek in Gloucester County; another son, Lewis Burwell (d. 1743), lived at Kingsmill, part of the former Bacon estate in James City County; and his daughter Lucy Burwell was the object of a renowned and turbulent courtship by Francis Nicholson, but she spurned the governor and married Edmund Berkeley (d. ca. 1719), of Barn Elms in Middlesex County.

Burwell was a popular member of Tidewater Virginia society, and his name appears regularly in the diary of William Byrd (1674–1744). Burwell became a militia major, a governor, or trustee, of the College of William and Mary, and a trustee of the city of Williamsburg. His name is not included on any extant list of justices of the peace, but a man of his stature would normally have served on the county court, and the loss of most of the Gloucester County records makes it impossible to rule this service out. In 1698 Burwell served a single term in the House of Burgesses, where he sat on the Committee for Propositions and Grievances. Membership on the governor's Council was the highest office to which a Virginian could then realistically aspire, and it usually marked a man or his family as having reached the pinnacle of Virginia society. On 5 September 1700 the Privy Council appointed Burwell to the Council, but on 13 October 1701 he wrote to the Board of Trade and citing his poor health, but perhaps also believing that his strained relationship with Nicholson would make membership on the Council unpleasant, asked to be excused from service. On 14 May 1702 the Privy Council accepted the Board of Trade's recommendation that Burwell's appointment as councillor be withdrawn, and he consequently never served.

Burwell was the central figure in the rise of a prominent Virginia family. By concentrating on acquiring land and pursuing family connections, he became one of the wealthiest men of his time and maximized his descendants' ability to succeed. Among the many evidences of his prosperity was his donation of a lavish set of communion silver to Abingdon Parish. Lewis Burwell died at his plantation on King's Creek in York County on 19 December 1710. He was buried at Fairfield in Gloucester County, but his remains were later moved to Abingdon Church.

John L. Blair, "The Rise of the Burwells," *VMHB* 72 (1964): 312–329; age given as forty-one in 16 Sept. 1693 deposition, PRO C 22/1003, fol. 1, cited in *National Genealogical Society Quarterly* 70 (1982): 41; Everard Kidder Meade, "The Children of Major Lewis Burwell II, of Gloucester County in the Ancient Colony of Virginia," *Proceedings of the Clarke County Historical Association* 4 (1944): 5–28; Thomas Tileston Waterman and John A. Barrows, *Domestic Colonial Architecture of Tidewater Virginia* (1932), 30–35; Francis Nicholson Papers, 1680–1721, CW; PRO CO 391/13, fol. 204, CO 391/15, fol. 200, and Lewis Burwell to Board of Trade, 13 Oct. 1701, CO 5/1312, pt. 1, fols. 105–106; Louis B. Wright and Marion Tinling, eds., *The Secret Diary of William Byrd of Westover, 1709–1712* (1941), esp. 275 (reference to funeral on 23 Dec. 1710); will in York Co. Orders, Wills, Etc., 14: pt. 1, 60–64; death date from gravestone inscription, printed in *WMQ*, 1st ser., 2 (1894): 221.

CHRISTOPHER F. LEE

BURWELL, Lewis (d. 19 November 1743), planter, was born probably in York County, the son of Lewis Burwell (d. 1710) and his second wife, Martha Lear Cole Burwell. The date of his birth is not recorded, but in June 1718 his half brother Nathaniel Burwell (1680–1721) complained that Lewis Burwell could scarcely write, spell, or do his sums correctly and was likely to spend his life as a "Blockhead." This characterization may suggest that he was then still a pupil at the College of William and Mary and therefore was born probably closer to the date of his mother's death in August 1704 than to the date of his parents' marriage in 1694 or 1695.

On another unrecorded date, probably about 1720, Burwell married Elizabeth Armistead, the sister-in-law of his half brother James Burwell. They lived at one of the large properties he acquired on the north bank of the James River south of Williamsburg and had at least two sons. In December 1725 Burwell became a member of the vestry of Bruton Parish, and on 15 August 1728 the governor appointed him to the vacant position of naval officer, a lucrative post from which he drew large fees as overseer of the collection of royal customs and enforcer of the trade and navigation acts. The site of his office quickly became known as Burwell's Ferry. He was listed as a justice in a new commission of the peace for James City County on 15 December 1737, but he may already have been a member of the county court for some time previously. Burwell represented James City County in the House

of Burgesses from 1742 until his death and served on the Committee of Privileges and Elections.

By 1736 Burwell owned more than 2,000 acres in James City and York Counties, 1,800 acres in Isle of Wight County, and an additional 4,800 acres in King William County that he had inherited from his father. He then erected a large new mansion at his Kingsmill plantation, near both Burwell's Ferry and the site where his nephew Carter Burwell built Carter's Grove a few years later. Kingsmill was an impressive demonstration of the Georgian building boom that swept up the Virginia rivers after the construction of the governor's palace in Williamsburg, and it was overshadowed by only a few of the larger James River plantation mansions such as Westover. Thereafter often known as Lewis Burwell of Kingsmill, to distinguish him from several close relatives of the same name, Burwell was a conspicuous and consequential public man.

Burwell's elder son and namesake succeeded him as naval officer but eventually moved out of Kingsmill and with his brother Armistead Burwell and their sons established themselves as prominent gentlemen in Southside Virginia, leaving the Tidewater Burwells in possession of most of the choice Charles City, Gloucester, James City, and York County properties and public offices. Burwell's namesake grandson sold Kingsmill during the 1780s, and during the 1840s the elegant mansion burned, events that Burwell certainly never anticipated in the 1730s when laying out "great sums of money, in building a mansion-house, and other out-houses, and in making gardens, and other considerable improvements . . . intending the same for the seat of the eldest son of the family" and succeeding generations of Burwells at Kingsmill. Lewis Burwell died, probably at Kingsmill, on 19 November 1743, and was most likely buried in the family cemetery there.

Alan Simpson, "The Kingsmill Dynasty—A Tale of Three Mansions," *Colonial Williamsburg* 14 (spring 1992): 10–24; Nathaniel Burwell to brother, 13 June 1718, in *WMQ*, 1st ser., 7 (1898): 43–44 (first quotation); Hening, *Statutes*, 4:534–537 (second quotation); *Executive Journals of Council*, 4:184, 413; Mary R. M. Goodwin, "'Kingsmill' Plantation: James City County, Virginia" (1958 typescript report;

1989 microfiche ed.), CW; Ann Camille Wells, "Kingsmill Plantation: A Cultural Analysis" (master's thesis, UVA School of Architecture, 1976); William M. Kelso, *Kingsmill Plantations, 1619–1800: Archaeology of Country Life in Colonial Virginia* (1984), esp. 41–45; death date in William Gooch to earl of Albemarle, 21 Nov. 1743, Newcastle Papers, Home Correspondence, 16, fol. 267, British Library, Add. 32701.

ALAN SIMPSON

BURWELL, Lewis (1711 or 1712–6 May 1756), member of the Council, was born at Fairfield, the residence on Carter's Creek in Gloucester County of his parents, Elizabeth Carter Burwell and her first husband, Nathaniel Burwell (1680–1721). His grandfathers were Lewis Burwell (d. 1710), a wealthy Gloucester County planter, and Robert "King" Carter (d. 1732), one of the wealthiest men in North America, who served as president of the governor's Council. Burwell's younger brother, Carter Burwell, who built Carter's Grove in James City County, was twice nominated for the Council but not appointed, and his youngest brother, Robert Burwell, sat on the Council at the time of the American Revolution. In 1724 his mother remarried, to George Nicholas, a Williamsburg physician. According to the directions of his father's will, Burwell's guardian, King Carter, sent him to England to be educated. He attended Eton from 1722 to 1729, when at the age of seventeen he matriculated at Gonville and Caius College of Cambridge University. Burwell remained there for four years. Like many young men of his time, he did not take a degree, but he may have begun to study law in London at the Inner Temple in February 1733 a few months before he returned to Virginia after receiving news of the death of King Carter.

Burwell inherited a large amount of property from both parents' sides of the family. The success of a series of lawsuits to settle inheritance rights to property in England and Virginia made him one of the wealthiest young men in the colony. Burwell continued to study law for a time after he returned to Virginia but evidently never practiced. During the third week of October 1736 he married Mary Willis. They had two or three sons and three daughters before she died in May 1746. His eldest son, Lewis Burwell (d. 1779), served in the Convention of 1776.

Lieutenant Governor William Gooch noticed that Burwell returned to Virginia with a reserved and haughty manner that did not favorably impress his fellow colonists. Nevertheless, in 1742 Burwell was elected to the House of Burgesses from Gloucester County and named to the Committees of Privileges and Elections and of Propositions and Grievances. After serving in the short session that met from 6 May to 19 June, he joined the top ranks of Virginia leadership. On 10 February 1743 the king appointed Burwell to the governor's Council. He took his seat on 4 August 1743 and remained a councillor until his death thirteen years later.

At the death of Thomas Lee on 14 November 1750, Burwell became the senior member of the Council, and because the governor and lieutenant governor were both out of Virginia at the time, he served as president, in effect acting governor of Virginia, until the arrival of Lieutenant Governor Robert Dinwiddie on 21 November 1751. No General Assembly met during Burwell's administration, but he continued Gooch's efforts to maintain peace with the Indians in the Ohio Valley, and he selected Joshua Fry and Peter Jefferson to prepare a new map of Virginia. Thus partly responsible for the famous Fry-Jefferson map, Burwell recognized its importance and remarked of Fry that "considering that we are yet a Country of Woods, it is surprising how he could draw so beautiful a Map of it."

Often referred to in Virginia history as President Lewis Burwell, to distinguish him from several near-contemporaries of the same name, he was closely related to several other members of the Council. A sister married William Nelson (1711–1772), and his brother Carter Burwell married a sister of Philip Grymes. In the spring of 1751 Burwell's ill health led him to visit one of the medicinal springs in western Virginia, and on several occasions the Council met at his Gloucester County residence, presumably because of his inability to travel to Williamsburg. After Dinwiddie took office Burwell never again attended the Council. The lieutenant governor wanted to replace him with a member who could participate, but the Burwells were so well connected among the powerful families of Virginia that he took no action. Dinwiddie identified the cause of Burwell's incapacity as "a distemper in the Mind," which may have resulted from a cancer or tumor. A nineteenth-century writer asserted that Burwell had injured his head in a fall from his horse while in England and that the lingering effects of the wound caused his poor health and death. Lewis Burwell died at Fairfield in Gloucester County on 6 May 1756 and was buried probably in the family cemetery there. His remains were later moved along with those of other family members to the yard of Abingdon Church.

John Venn and J. A. Venn, *Alumni Cantabrigienses* (1922–1954), pt. 1, 1:269, gives age as seventeen on 18 June 1729; William Hamilton Bryson, ed., "A Letter of Lewis Burwell to James Burrough, July 8, 1734," *VMHB* 81 (1973): 405–414; *Williamsburg Virginia Gazette*, 29 Oct. 1736, 27 June 1751; Hening, *Statutes*, 8:663–664; PRO CO 5/1325, fols. 97–98; *Executive Journals of Council*, 5:129, 345–371; letters as president in PRO CO 5/1327; Burwell to Commissioners for Trade and Plantations, 21 Aug. 1751, PRO CO 5/1327, fols. 163–165A (first quotation); Robert Dinwiddie to Board of Trade, 20 Mar. 1756, PRO CO 5/1328, fols. 198–199; Robert A. Brock, ed., *The Official Records of Robert Dinwiddie, Lieutenant-Governor of the Colony of Virginia, 1751–1758* (1883–1884), 2:377 (second quotation); Benjamin Blake Minor, "History of Virginia" (MS, ca. mid-1840s), in Benjamin Blake Minor Papers, LVA; death notice in *Annapolis Maryland Gazette*, 20 May 1756.

RANDALL SHROCK

BURWELL, Lewis (d. by 19 March 1779), member of the Convention of 1776, was born probably late in the 1730s at Fairfield on Carter's Creek in Gloucester County, the son of Lewis Burwell (d. 1756) and Mary Willis Burwell. His father served as president of the Council and was acting governor of Virginia in 1750 and 1751. Little is known about Burwell's childhood or education, but contrary to what has been written about him, he did not attend Eton, Oxford, or Cambridge or gain admission to the Inns of Court, at each of which his father and some of his other relatives of the same name were educated. Following his father's death Burwell inherited about 7,000 acres in Gloucester County and other large holdings elsewhere, including approximately 5,000 acres on Bull Run in Prince William County. He inherited and resided at his father's Fairfield estate, one of the largest and oldest plantation houses in a region of the Tidewater famed even then for its spacious dwellings.

By about 1760 Burwell had married his near neighbor Judith Page, of Rosewell, like him a descendant of Robert "King" Carter (d. 1732) and in turn a niece and sister of other councillors. They had two or three sons and two daughters before her death in September 1777. Burwell appears to have been hit hard by the recession early in the 1770s and tried to sell a large tract of land to pay the very "considerable fortunes" that his father's will had promised to his several sisters. He also had many large claims on his landed wealth, some probably inherited, some perhaps self-acquired. Burwell spent heavily on blooded racehorses, and although he won some handsome purses, he doubtless lost some, too. Whether for that or other reasons, his financial condition appears to have been precarious, as was his physical health.

Burwell was a justice of the peace in Gloucester County beginning in 1765, and in 1767 he was sheriff. From 1769 until 1776 he represented the county in the House of Burgesses. Burwell sat on the Committees for Courts of Justice, of Privileges and Elections, and of Religion, but he never moved into the ranks of the leadership. He took the side of the colonial protestors during the disputes leading up to the American Revolution. Burwell was eligible to serve in all five of the Virginia conventions that met from August 1774 to July 1776 but was absent from the fourth convention and from parts of the third and fifth, probably because of poor health. At the Convention of 1776 he was a member of the Committee of Privileges and Elections. On 3 July 1776 Burwell drew pay for about thirty-two of the fifty-two days of active session. No vote tallies were taken at the convention, but because each major decision passed unanimously, if he was well enough to attend on the day of each pertinent roll call he voted for independence on 15 May, for the Virginia Declaration of Rights on 12 June, and for adoption of the first written constitution of Virginia on 29 June 1776.

Burwell also represented Gloucester County in the House of Delegates from 1776 to 1778. He served in a low-ranking position on the Committee of Privileges and Elections. Lewis Burwell's death was reported without date and without comment in Dixon and Nicolson's *Williamsburg Virginia Gazette* of 19 March 1779. He was buried probably in the family cemetery at Fairfield. Within weeks Burwell's fine stable of horses and his valuable household furniture went on the auction block. His death brought to an end a full century of Burwell family residence and political distinction at Carter's Creek in Gloucester County.

Family history established in Hening, *Statutes*, 8:663–665 (quotation); Gloucester Co. Tax Accounts, 1770–1771, LVA; *Williamsburg Virginia Gazette* (Purdie and Dixon), 16 May 1766, 27 Oct. 1768; ibid. (Purdie), 12 Sept. 1777; *Revolutionary Virginia*, 7:22, 78, 691; death notice in *Williamsburg Virginia Gazette* (Dixon and Nicolson), 19 Mar. 1779; elegy in *WMQ*, 1st ser., 1 (1907): 162–163; estate sales in *Williamsburg Virginia Gazette* (Dixon and Nicolson), 9 Apr., 8 May 1779.

BRENT TARTER

BURWELL, Lucy (21 November 1683–16 December 1716), principal in a cause célèbre, was the daughter of Lewis Burwell (d. 1710) and Abigail Smith Burwell and was born probably at Fairfield plantation on Carter's Creek in Gloucester County. When she was about seventeen years old Governor Francis Nicholson began courting her with love letters and visits. He also directed written appeals to Burwell's parents, soliciting their assistance in the courtship. Nicholson's nomination of Lewis Burwell to the governor's Council during the summer of 1700, an honor that he subsequently refused, may not have been coincidental. Lucy Burwell did not return the forty-five-year-old governor's affections. She continued to entertain other men, including Edmund Berkeley (d. ca. 1719), a well-educated man some twelve years her senior. As Nicholson's courtship foundered he became desperate and resorted to threats and temper tantrums. Burwell ultimately married Berkeley on 1 December 1703.

The loss of Burwell provoked the governor to violence. His subsequent taunts and threats directed at the powerful Burwells and their many allies galvanized the Virginia elite's resistance to him. Already disliked by many of the colony's leading men for his heavy-handed attempts to impose unpopular policies, Nicholson lost more

allies by his intemperate reaction to his failed courtship. Six men, including four who were in some way related to Burwell, signed a petition against Nicholson in 1703. After complaints of Nicholson's inappropriate behavior reached London, Queen Anne removed him from his post.

In rejecting the governor Burwell was probably not just acquiescing in her father's wishes. He had publicly declared that his daughter was completely free to choose a husband. Even Nicholson did not believe that she acted at her father's behest, but he suspected that members of the Burwell family had turned her against him with tales of immoral and violent conduct. Burwell need not have based her decision on gossip, however. Having witnessed Nicholson's embarrassing displays of passion and read his occasionally menacing love poems, she may have come genuinely to dislike him.

Like other elite women of her generation, Burwell may simply have been an independent spirit. Several of her contemporaries, including Sarah Harrison Blair, Lucy Parke Byrd, and Frances Parke Custis, responded to patriarchal threats and entreaties with intransigence. Burwell's decision to reject the courtship of Nicholson is best read as a choice of future happiness over pure political expedience by a young woman who knew her own mind and was not easily intimidated. Undoubtedly her decision was made easier by the knowledge that marriage into the Berkeley family also offered political advantages to the Burwells. At a time when leading Virginians were searching for a dignified regional identity and attempting to check the power of the governor, Burwell's refusal of Nicholson did much both to legitimize the Virginia elite's grievances against him and to provide compelling evidence of his despotic and dishonorable tendencies. In exercising her prerogative to choose her own husband, surely the most public and free act of her short life, Lucy Burwell became, in the annals of Virginia folklore, a symbol of regional resistance to the abuse of power.

Burwell's temperament was not perpetually combative, however, if her tombstone epitaph at Barn Elms in Middlesex County is to be believed. Her spouse there asserted of their married life that "she never in all the time she lived with her

Husband gave him so much as once cause to be displeased with Her." Lucy Burwell Berkeley bore at least two sons and three daughters during her thirteen-year marriage, a fact that may account in part for Edmund Berkeley's satisfaction with his wife and may have contributed to her death at the age of thirty-three on 16 December 1716.

Birth date in Robert W. Robins, comp., *The Register of Abingdon Parish, Gloucester County, Virginia, 1677–1780* (1981), 28; marriage date in Berkeley family Bible record, Berkeley Family Papers, 1653–1930, UVA (LVA photocopy); variant marriage date of 1 Dec. 1704 can be inferred from epitaph; relevant documents in Francis Nicholson Papers, CW, in Berkeley Family Papers, UVA, and in PRO CO 5/1314, fols. 20–25; some of Nicholson's courtship letters and poems, transcribed in Papers of Society for the Propagation of the Gospel in Foreign Parts, LC, are printed in Polly Cary Legg, "The Governor's 'Extacy of Trouble,'" *WMQ*, 2d ser., 22 (1942): 389–398; Fairfax Downey, "The Governor Goes A-Wooing: The Swashbuckling Courtship of Nicholson of Virginia, 1699–1705," *VMHB* 55 (1947): 6–19; Kathleen M. Brown, *Good Wives, Nasty Wenches, and Anxious Patriarchs: Gender, Race, and Power in Colonial Virginia* (1996), 254–257; death date in epitaph, printed in *WMQ*, 1st ser., 12 (1904): 244 (quotation).

KATHLEEN M. BROWN

BURWELL, Nathaniel (15 April 1750–29 March 1814), member of the Convention of 1788, was born on an Easter Sunday at Carter's Grove plantation in James City County, the son of Carter Burwell and Lucy Ludwell Grymes Burwell. He attended the College of William and Mary, beginning in the grammar school, and continued to study past his twenty-second birthday. In July 1772 he received the college's Botetourt Medal for scholarship. His father died when Burwell was six, and when he came of age in 1771 he inherited control of a large landed estate in Tidewater Virginia and in the lower Shenandoah Valley, including his father's Carter's Grove plantation and mansion in James City County. On 28 November 1772 Burwell married his cousin Susanna Grymes, of Middlesex County. They had seven sons and one daughter before her death on 24 July 1788.

During Burwell's management of Carter's Grove the plantation prospered, and he also moved some of his slaves to his Frederick County property and improved production there during the 1770s and 1780s. As the proprietor of a major plantation and a member of a leading

family he succeeded to the offices appropriate to his station. Burwell was appointed to the James City County Court on 6 November 1772, was a colonel in the militia by 1774, and served on the James City County Committee that same year. On 27 November 1776 he became county lieutenant, the commander of the county's militia. Burwell represented James City County in the House of Delegates in 1778 and 1779 and served on the Committee of Propositions and Grievances during both years and on the Committee of Religion in 1779. He was elected again in 1782 and served on the Committee of Propositions and Grievances during the short session in May but missed the poorly attended October session. Burwell was also one of the directors of the Public Hospital in Williamsburg.

In 1788 Burwell was one of two men elected to represent James City County in a convention called to consider the proposed constitution of the United States. He did not take an active part in the debates, but his opinions were well known. Burwell voted against insisting on amendments prior to ratification and against reducing the taxing power of Congress, and on 25 June 1788 he voted to ratify the Constitution.

Burwell's wife died scarcely a month after the convention adjourned, and on 24 January 1789 he married Lucy Page Baylor, widow of George Baylor (1752–1784). They had five sons and three daughters. Burwell transferred his seat from James City County to Frederick County not long after his second marriage. By 1790 he owned approximately 8,000 acres of land in the lower Shenandoah Valley. Burwell lived in the portion of Frederick County that in 1836, after his death, became Clarke County. During the 1790s he constructed Carter Hall, one of the largest and most elegant stone mansions in that part of Virginia. Burwell named it in honor of his great-grandfather, Robert "King" Carter (d. 1732), from whom the family had inherited the land. Burwell established a ferry on the Shenandoah River, erected two gristmills, two distilleries, a cooper's shop, an iron forge, a sawmill, and a tannery, and built a school for his children and other local students. Burwell also had a passion for breeding fine horses.

Nathaniel Burwell died at Carter Hall on 29 March 1814 and was buried nearby in the Old Chapel cemetery.

Mary A. Stephenson, *Carter's Grove Plantation: A History* (1964), 56 (por.), 57–75, 217–223, 255–258, 313–318, reproduces family Bible records giving dates of birth (some accounts incorrectly adjust his birth date under Gregorian calendar to 26 Apr. 1750), marriages, and death; Stuart E. Brown Jr., *Burwell Kith and Kin of the Immigrant, Lewis Burwell (1621–1653) and Burwell Virginia Tidewater Plantation Mansion*s (1994); Brown and Ann Barton Brown, *Carter Hall* (1975), esp. 1–10; Lorena S. Walsh, *From Calabar to Carter's Grove: The History of a Virginia Slave Community* (1997), 121–133, 190–191, 205–207, 215–219; Carter's Grove plantation ledgers and other records in Burwell Papers, CW; Burwell Family Papers, VHS; Kaminski, *Ratification,* 8:515, 516, 9:896, 10:1539, 1540, 1557, 1565; Frederick Co. Superior Court Will Book, 2:404–408.

STUART E. BROWN JR.

BURWELL, Robert (3 June 1720–30 January 1777), member of the Council, was the son of Elizabeth Carter Burwell and her first husband, Nathaniel Burwell (1680–1721), and was born probably at Fairfield, his father's plantation on Carter's Creek in Abingdon Parish, Gloucester County. His grandfathers were Lewis Burwell (d. 1710), a wealthy Gloucester County planter, and Robert "King" Carter (d. 1732), one of the wealthiest men in North America, who served as president of the governor's Council. His elder brothers included Lewis Burwell (d. 1756), who also served as president of the Council, and Carter Burwell, who built Carter's Grove in James City County.

Very little is known about Burwell's early life. His father died shortly after Burwell's birth, and in 1724 his mother married a second time, to George Nicholas, a Williamsburg physician. Burwell inherited large estates in Frederick, Isle of Wight, and Prince William Counties and perhaps elsewhere, as well as at least one tract in North Carolina. For most of his adult life he lived in Isle of Wight County, which he represented in the House of Burgesses from 1752 to 1758. Burwell was a vestryman of Newport Parish, one of the first trustees of the town of Smithfield in 1752, and in 1763 one of the incorporators of the Dismal Swamp Company. About 1742 he married Sarah Nelson, of Yorktown, half sister of William Nelson (1711–1772) and Thomas Nelson (1716–1782), both of whom became presidents of the Council. William Nelson, in turn, married one of Burwell's sisters, which made Robert Burwell an uncle of Thomas Nelson (1738–1789), a signer of the Declaration of Independence and future governor of Virginia. Burwell and his wife had one son and one daughter.

In April 1762, following the death of Philip Grymes, a member of the Council and a relative by marriage of Carter Burwell, family or business associates in London quietly and quickly arranged for Robert Burwell's appointment to the Council. When the news reached Williamsburg at the end of July it provoked shock and disbelief because, as Lieutenant Governor Francis Fauquier put it, of some rumored defect in Burwell's "mental Qualifications, and an unwarrantable Impetuosity of Temper." Burwell duly took the oath and was admitted to the Council on 30 July 1762, but at that same meeting his kinsman Thomas Nelson suggested that the Council adopt an address to the king requesting "that he would be graciously pleas'd to appoint some other more able and discreet Person in the Room of Mr. Burwell." The other councillors postponed the motion, and after Burwell had served on the Council for a few months Fauquier admitted that the doubts about his fitness to serve had subsided. Burwell sat on the Council throughout the remainder of the colonial period.

Burwell had financial problems. Early in the 1770s he attempted to sell some of his land. He eventually had to bequeath a plantation to his son-in-law because he could not raise the £1,000 cash dowry he had promised his daughter at the time of her marriage to John Page (1743–1808), of Rosewell, who was a member of the Council at the end of the colonial period, its first president under the Constitution of 1776, and still later governor of Virginia. Early in March 1770 Burwell's wife died, plunging him into depression. Both of his children were by then grown and living away from home, and he had nothing to occupy his time except financial worries. Burwell's loneliness came to an end on the last day of December 1774, when he married Mary Blair Braxton, widow of George Braxton (d. 1761) and a sister-in-law of Carter Braxton, who was another signer of the Declaration of Independence and who later served on the Council of State.

Nothing is definitely known about Burwell's attitude toward the imperial crises that resulted in independence in 1776. Whether because of some lingering uncertainties about his intelligence or temperament, some unrecorded Loyalist leanings, or premonitions of failing health, nobody seriously considered him for any responsible position when the new government of the commonwealth of Virginia was established in July 1776. Robert Burwell lived quietly with his second wife at her Newington estate in King and Queen County until his death there on 30 January 1777. The place of his burial is not recorded.

Birth and baptismal dates in Robert W. Robins, comp., *The Register of Abingdon Parish, Gloucester County, Virginia, 1677–1780* (1981), 29; some old accounts mistakenly give a middle name of Carter; Hening, *Statutes*, 8:448–450; Emory G. Evans, "The Nelsons: A Biographical Study of a Virginia Family in the Eighteenth Century" (Ph.D. diss., UVA, 1957), 23, 30; PRO CO 5/1368, fol. 196; John C. Van Horne and George Reese, eds., *The Letter Book of James Abercromby, Colonial Agent, 1751–1773* (1991), 410–412; Reese, ed., *The Official Papers of Francis Fauquier, Lieutenant Governor of Virginia, 1758–1768* (1980–1983), 2:721, 781–783 (first quotation), 929, 956–958 (second quotation); *Executive Journals of Council*, 6:228–229; *Williamsburg Virginia Gazette* (Rind), 8 Mar. 1770; ibid. (Pinkney), 5 Jan. 1775; Jack P. Greene, ed., *The Diary of Colonel Landon Carter of Sabine Hall, 1752–1778* (1965; repr. 1987), 2:720; abstract of lost will in *WMQ*, 1st ser., 7 (1899): 311–313; an 1803 report concerning his debts (PRO T 79/73, fols. 168–169) gives summary of Burwell's financial condition at the time of his death and information about his descendants and their financial difficulties; second marriage and death date in Frederick Horner, *The History of the Blair, Banister, and Braxton Families before and after the Revolution* (1898), 89 (citing family records kept by stepdaughter); death notice in *Williamsburg Virginia Gazette* (Purdie), 14 Feb. 1777.

BRENT TARTER

BURWELL, William Armistead (15 March 1780–16 February 1821), member of the House of Representatives, was born in Mecklenburg County, the son of Thacker Burwell, who died later in 1780, and Mary Armistead Burwell. After attending the College of William and Mary in 1798, he settled in Franklin County, where he used his inheritance to begin acquiring property. By 1820 Burwell owned 5,578 acres of land, about seventy-five slaves, and a library of more than eight hundred volumes. Altogether, his personal property at the time of his death was worth about $33,000.

A moody man who was frequently ill, Burwell visited Thomas Jefferson in Washington in March 1804 while on a recuperative holiday and in May accepted the president's offer to join his household as private secretary. Off and on from the spring of 1804 until the autumn of 1806 he acted in that capacity. Burwell came to consider Jefferson a father figure. He chiefly looked after minor personal matters and took care of visiting dignitaries, but he also assisted the president in preparing two messages to Congress. Burwell was frequently absent from Washington because from 1804 to 1806 he also represented Franklin County in the House of Delegates. There he helped coordinate Jefferson's followers in the assembly when the president's policies came under attack from John Randolph of Roanoke. During the 1804–1805 session Burwell served on the Committees for Courts of Justice and of Privileges and Elections, and during the 1805–1806 session he sat on the Committees for Courts of Justice and of Finance.

In August 1806 Burwell announced his candidacy for the House of Representatives for the district comprising Bedford, Franklin, Henry, and Patrick Counties to fill the vacancy caused by the resignation of Christopher Henderson Clark. Burwell easily won election, entered Congress on 1 December 1806, and was reelected for the remainder of his life. He began his congressional career as an outspoken advocate of Jefferson's policies, and in 1811 he was appointed to the powerful Committee of Ways and Means. Burwell was never a leading member of the House, however, and his influence waned after Jefferson's retirement and slipped further after the War of 1812. He was often critical of the administration of James Monroe. The genial Henry Clay worked well with Burwell and described him as "a most excellent and intelligent person," but John Quincy Adams, a misanthropic colleague with different political instincts, wrote that Burwell "floated down the stream of time with the current, and always had the satisfaction of being in his own eyes a pure and incorruptible patriot. Virginia teems with this brood more than any other State in the Union, and they are far from being the worst men among us. Such men occasionally render service to the nation by preventing harm;

but they are quite as apt to prevent good, and they never do any."

On 3 January 1809 Burwell married Letitia McCreery, niece and heir of Representative William McCreery, of Baltimore, Maryland. Their one surviving child, William McCreery Burwell, represented Bedford County in the General Assembly on several occasions between the 1830s and the mid-1860s. He later lived in New Orleans and there edited *DeBow's Review*. William Armistead Burwell died in Washington on 16 February 1821 and was buried beside the grave of his wife, who had died in December 1816, in a family cemetery near Reisterstown in Carroll County, Maryland. At least a portion of his remains were moved to Congressional Cemetery in Washington, D.C., in December 1839, but later, in December 1850, remains presumed to be those of Burwell and his wife were removed from the family cemetery in Carroll County and re-interred in Green Mount Cemetery in Baltimore.

French Biographies; family records in William McCreery Burwell Papers, UVA; correspondence in William Armistead Burwell Papers (including draft memoirs published as Gerard W. Gawalt, ed., " 'Strict Truth': The Narrative of William Armistead Burwell," *VMHB* 101 [1993]: 103–132), and Thomas Jefferson Papers, both LC, in Burwell Family Papers and Francis Walker Gilmer Papers, UVA, and in several collections at VHS; four letters dated 1807–1815 in Cunningham, *Circular Letters of Congressmen*, 1:511–516, 577–585, 644–652, 939–948; Baltimore Co., Md., Marriage Licenses (1803–1815), 118, Maryland State Archives, Annapolis; Henry Clay to Francis Walker Gilmer, 4 Aug. 1821, in *Clay Papers*, 3:104–105 (first quotation); Charles Francis Adams, ed., *Memoirs of John Quincy Adams* (1874–1877), 5:281–282 (second quotation); *National Intelligencer and Washington Advertiser*, 9 Jan. 1809; Land Tax Returns, Franklin Co., 1820, RG 48, LVA; Ellen G. Miles, *Saint-Mémin and the Neoclassical Profile Portrait in America* (1994), 259 (por.); will and estate inventory in Franklin Co. Will Book, 2:374–376, 402–416; obituary in *Washington Daily National Intelligencer*, 17 Feb. 1821, copied with a few alterations in *Alexandria Gazette* and *Richmond Commercial Compiler*, both 19 Feb. 1821, and *Richmond Enquirer*, 20 Feb. 1821; account of funeral in *Richmond Enquirer*, 22 Feb. 1821.

BRENT TARTER

BUTLER, Sarah Poage Caldwell (21 August 1892–2 December 1983), librarian and civic leader, was born in Wytheville, the daughter of Manley Morrison Caldwell, a lawyer, and Willie Brown Walker Caldwell, a civic leader and later a Republican Party activist. Her parents moved to Roanoke, which had better schools, and her mother became a leader in the Woman's Civic Betterment Club, which lobbied successfully for public health and for improved schools, parks, and playgrounds. The club's objective of a public library remained unrealized, and the future librarian later credited the thwarted project with instilling in her the desire to enter that field.

After graduating from Roanoke City High School in May 1911, Sarah Caldwell entered Mary Baldwin Seminary (later Mary Baldwin College), the alma mater of her mother and grandmother, as a member of the sophomore class, which she served as secretary. She chose coursework to prepare herself to enter the Pratt Institute Library School, in Brooklyn, New York, the following year. Continuing her speedy educational progress, Caldwell received a certificate of graduation from Pratt on 16 June 1913. In September of that year she became one of the eleven members of the Training Class for Library Work with Children at the Cleveland Public Library. The students worked at the library but spent two mornings each week attending lectures and recitations. In 1916 Caldwell received her certificate of completion.

Caldwell returned to New York as a children's librarian at the Hudson Park Branch of the New York Public Library, in Greenwich Village. On 5 December 1917 she married William Wilson Samuel Butler, a Roanoke physician. He enlisted in the navy three months later in answer to a call for more physicians and was ordered to Brooklyn. Until he was reassigned to Roanoke as a recruiting officer in the spring of 1919, Sarah Butler worked as a substitute librarian in New York. The younger of their two sons, Manley Caldwell Butler, served in the House of Representatives from 1972 to 1983.

Shortly after her return to Roanoke, Butler began discussing the benefits that a public library could bring to the city. About fifty representatives of local civic organizations met in January 1920 to form the Roanoke Library Association, and they elected Butler the first chair. In February the association presented plans for renovating the vacant mansion in Elmwood Park as a library, and next month the city council agreed to improve the building and maintain it, provided that the citizens of Roanoke subscribed to a book fund sufficient to support the library.

Butler presided over a meeting of community leaders in April to plan the citywide fundraising campaign. A local banker chaired the campaign, but in spite of endorsements from the clergy and generous publicity from the newspapers, the campaign fell short of its goal and raised only about $21,000. That sum was enough to go forward, however, and on 21 May 1921 the Roanoke Public Library formally opened. The mayor presented the keys to Butler, who accepted them on behalf of the new library's board, of which she was the first president. Within two months the library had 2,599 registered users, of whom more than 1,000 were children. In July 1921 the library board signed a lease on a building for a branch library for Roanoke's black citizens, who had also raised money for the library during the 1920 campaign. Butler presided at its opening on 13 December 1921.

In the autumn of 1922 the Butlers moved for a year to Baltimore, where William Butler studied at the Johns Hopkins University Hospital, and Sarah Butler worked at the Enoch Pratt Free Library. Back in Roanoke she resumed working for the library board and joined other members in unsuccessful efforts to expand the library's overcrowded quarters. Butler remained on the board until December 1930. In April 1925 she became a charter member of the Roanoke Valley Garden Club, which in June 1929 became a member club of the Garden Club of Virginia. One of the club's projects was maintaining the gardens and grounds at Elmwood Park, the site of the library, which earned the Garden Club of Virginia's Massie Distinguished Achievement Medal in 1930. Butler's husband shared her interest in horticulture, and in that year they moved to a new suburban house with two acres of terraced gardens.

Butler was a director at large of the Garden Club of Virginia from 1941 to 1944, first vice president from 1946 to 1948, chair of the finance committee from 1948 to 1950, and president from 1950 to 1952. During her term as president the club completed one of its largest projects, restoration of the gardens off the West Lawn at the University of Virginia. Butler served again as a director at large in 1952 and 1953 and chaired the nominations committee from 1958 to 1960.

Butler became a leader of women's work at Saint John's Episcopal Church and from 1940 to 1942 was first vice president and in 1944 president of the woman's auxiliary of the Diocese of Southwestern Virginia. Wartime restrictions on travel limited the organization's activities, but Butler was no figurehead. In her annual report in 1945 she analyzed structural weaknesses of the auxiliary and expressed regret that it had not realized its potential.

On 1 March 1949 Roanoke voters approved a bond issue for construction of a new public library, which opened early in 1952. Twenty-six years later, when the city proposed to move the library from Elmwood Park to a vacant federal office building, Butler wrote a forceful letter to the *Roanoke Times and World-News* explaining that renovation of the vacant building would cost far more than expanding the existing library, which, she explained, could be accomplished without further encroachment into the park. Her letter (and "superior credentials" on the subject) caused the newspaper to call for reconsideration of the proposed move. The Roanoke City Central Library remained in Elmwood Park.

Sarah Poage Caldwell Butler died in Roanoke on 2 December 1983 and was buried in the city's Evergreen Burial Park. The library board commissioned a bronze sculpture of a child reading a book as a memorial to her, and on 13 November 1988 her two sons spoke at its unveiling at the library in Elmwood Park. On 2 January 2000 the *Roanoke Times* published a special issue on the twentieth century, including feature stories about ten selected city leaders. Sarah Butler, founder of the city's library system, was one of them.

BVS Birth Register, Wythe Co.; BVS Marriage Register, Roanoke Co.; information, including undated typescript autobiography, provided by son M. Caldwell Butler; Barry Floyd Jones, "A History of the Roanoke Public Library, Roanoke, Virginia, 1921–1946" (master's thesis, UNC, 1985); Carolyn Hale Bruce, *Roanoke: A Pictorial History* (1976), 125 (por.); Mrs. James Bland [Christine Hale] Martin, ed., *Follow the Green Arrow: The History of the Garden Club of Virginia, 1920–1970* (1970), 29, 253, 258; *Roanoke World-News*, 6 Dec. 1917, 5, 7 Apr. 1920, 12 Apr. 1971;

Roanoke Times, 20 Mar. 1920, 21, 22 May 1921, 6 Dec. 1930, 12 Oct. 1969, 30 May 1996, 2 Jan. 2000; *Roanoke Times and World-News* (A.M. ed.), 19, 22 (quotation) Aug. 1978, 18 Apr. 1982, 11 Nov. 1988; *Roanoke Times and World-News* (P.M. ed.), 10 Nov. 1988; obituary in *Roanoke Times and World-News* (A.M. ed.), 3 Dec. 1983 (por.).

JOHN T. KNEEBONE

BUTT, Israel LaFayette (3 May 1848–22 January 1916), African Methodist Episcopal Church minister, was born in Norfolk County, the son of John Wesley Butt and Adaline Grimes Butt. His mother died when he was seven or eight years old. Slavery and military service shaped Butt's early years. With his father and a young girl, he escaped slavery in August 1862 and reached a Union army camp in Norfolk County. Brief schooling in Norfolk and a job hauling cordwood preceded Butt's enlistment on 6 January 1864 in Company A of the 38th Regiment, United States Colored Infantry. His unit fought at the Battle of New Market Heights on 28–30 September 1864 and participated in the occupation of Richmond on 3 April 1865 before being reassigned to Texas the following month. Still a private when his regiment was disbanded, Butt mustered out on 25 January 1867 at Indianola, Calhoun County, Texas, and returned to Norfolk, where he began farming a small plot owned by his father. He also worked on the farms of two white men. On 5 December 1867 Butt married Rose Zillah Simmons. They evidently had no children but adopted a daughter during the 1890s.

Butt industriously pursued the education that he had largely been denied as a slave. He learned to read while in the army. The local men under whom he studied included Dempsey Ferebee, who conducted a night school in Norfolk, and Thomas Bayne, a dentist and member of the Convention of 1867–1868. In May 1869 Butt was elected a constable of Tanners Creek Township and three years later a justice of the peace, an office he held for six years, but a religious life rather than a political career most appealed to him.

Staunch Methodism characterized two generations of Butt's family. His maternal grandfather had become a preacher in the African Methodist Episcopal Church. Butt experienced a religious conversion in Texas in May 1866, and he joined Norfolk's Saint John's African Methodist Episcopal Church in August 1867. He decided to become a minister in 1874 and received a license to preach locally in March 1876. Butt attended Richmond Theological Institute (later Virginia Union University) from 1879 to 1881, was fully ordained in the latter year, and in 1887 graduated with a degree in theology from Hampton Normal and Agricultural Institute (later Hampton University).

Butt was first assigned to a mission he established in Norfolk. He spent one year there, three years preaching on the Chesterfield Circuit, and two on the Henry Circuit before spending four years at Hampton. About 1888 Butt became presiding elder of the Danville District for a year and a half. He monitored the development of the various churches, organized new congregations, and made pastoral recommendations to the several bishops who presided in the Virginia Annual Conference. Butt also served briefly on the Staunton Circuit and for about ten and a half years on the Eastern Shore of Virginia before returning to the Tidewater for five years as presiding elder of the Portsmouth District and five years more as presiding elder of the Norfolk District. While he supervised the Portsmouth District he started a mission at Pinner's Point, and he was serving in Norfolk when the John M. Brown Memorial Church was founded in that city in 1904.

Butt was a delegate to the 1900 and 1904 general conferences of the church held in Columbus, Ohio, and Chicago, Illinois, respectively. At the latter meeting he served on the Committee on the Report of the Secretary of Education. He also sat on boards dealing with missionary activities and with the Allen Christian Endeavour League. While based in the Martinsville area, he had taught school and served as a school principal in 1882 and 1883. Butt was a trustee of the Norfolk District School, of Dickerson Memorial College (the church's college in Portsmouth), and of the Girls Training School in Roanoke. He also served on the boards of Kittrell College in North Carolina and Wilberforce University in Ohio. The latter institution awarded him an honorary D.D. in 1903. Butt continued his education throughout his life and in 1905 studied theology through a correspondence course at Payne University in Selma, Alabama. In addition, he researched and wrote *History of African Methodism in Virginia, or Four Decades in the Old Dominion* (1908), which Hampton Institute published.

A widower, Butt married Marie Church in Northampton County on 29 May 1912. Israel LaFayette Butt suffered from asthma, diabetes, and heart disease late in life and died on 22 January 1916 in Franktown, Northampton County. He was buried in Norfolk County.

W. R. Gullins, *The Heroes of the Virginia Annual Conference of the A.M.E. Church* (1899), 31–32; autobiographical statement in *History of African Methodism in Virginia*, 17–24 (frontispiece por.); *Who's Who of the Colored Race* (1915), 55; Compiled Military Service Records, Records of the Adjutant General's Office, RG 94, NARA (gives variant birthplace of Currituck Co., N.C.); BVS Marriage Register, Norfolk Co., 1867 (wife's name given as Rosetta Ives), Northampton Co., 1912; *Journal of the Twenty-First Quadrennial Session of the General Conference of the African Methodist Episcopal Church* (1900); *Proceedings of the Twenty-Second Quadrennial Conference of the African Methodist Episcopal Church* (1904); BVS Death Certificate, Northampton Co.; death notice in *Virginian-Pilot and the Norfolk Landmark*, 26 Jan. 1916.

DENNIS C. DICKERSON

BUTT, Martha Haines (22 November 1833–9 February 1871), writer, was born in Norfolk, the daughter of Francis Butt and Mary Ann Morriss Butt, a milliner. About 1847 she entered Patapsco Female Institute in Ellicott's Mills, Howard County, Maryland, and in 1850 she received an A.M., indicating that she had probably mastered college-level courses. In April 1850 Butt's essay on the "Influence of Music" appeared in the *Patapsco Young Ladies' Magazine*.

Butt made her mark early as a writer. Her most ambitious work was published in Philadelphia just a few years after she left school. Entitled *Antifanaticism: A Tale of the South* (1853), the book was one of five novels that southern women wrote in response to Harriet Beecher Stowe's *Uncle Tom's Cabin* (1852). Although Butt's novel did not achieve the critical or popular success of other rebuttals of *Uncle Tom's Cabin*, it did contain key elements of the southern literary nationalism that was beginning to emerge in the 1850s. In the preface Butt described herself as "a warm-hearted Virginian" determined to defend southern society against Stowe's charge that the cruelty of slavery had undermined the region's morality. Through the story of life on a fictional cotton plantation, Butt portrayed slavery as a benevolent, Christianizing institution. She repeatedly emphasized that slaves were better off than servants in the North and that they did not want freedom. Butt promoted sectional reconciliation by attempting to persuade her readers that if northerners traveled to the South they would come to agree with southern slave owners and adopt proslavery attitudes. The enthralled northern visitors to her fictional plantation became supporters of slavery, and the planter's children married northerners.

Despite the significance of *Antifanaticism* as a political statement, the heart of Butt's literary career was not her one novel but her plentiful poems, stories, and essays. During the 1850s she contributed short pieces to national and regional periodicals, including *Frank Leslie's Illustrated Newspaper* and *Godey's Magazine and Lady's Book*. Butt also wrote two poems for William S. Forrest's promotional compendium, *Historical and Descriptive Sketches of Norfolk and Vicinity* (1853). At the time women's contributions to periodicals were seldom signed, making it impossible to identify all of her publications, but some of her articles appeared under her name or initials. In 1855 Butt became a contributing editor of two short-lived periodicals published by women, the *Kaleidoscope*, a weekly established by Rebecca Brodnax Hicks in Petersburg, and the *Ladies' Repository*, a monthly published in Richmond by a woman known only by the pseudonym Lillie Linden. When controversy arose about the *Ladies' Repository*, apparently concerning its financial practices, Butt publicly severed all connection with the journal.

In 1860 Butt published her second book, a collection of short works entitled *The Leisure Moments of Miss Martha Haines Butt, A.M.* Through moral tales, poems, and personal musings she championed such values as Christian benevolence, companionate marriage, and thrift. Butt pointedly criticized society's preoccupation with fashion, gossip, status, and wealth, but she steered clear of the subject of slavery. In *Leisure Moments* her identity as a Virginian was clearly evident in her meditation on Norfolk's yellow fever epidemic of 1855 and in her paeans to the works of Virginia sculptors William Randolph Barbee and Alexander Galt. By the time this work was published Butt had moved to New York and gained a national reputation not only as an engaging writer of prescriptive verse and prose but also as a beautiful, graceful woman who always dressed with great style.

On 6 July 1865 at Christ Church in Norfolk Butt married Nathan Ives Bennett, of Bridgeport, Connecticut, who was then working as a clerk in the quartermaster department in Norfolk. They lived later in Hartford, Connecticut, and in New York City. Shortly after her marriage she published her final book, *Pastimes with My Little Friends* (1866), a collection of stories for children.

In 1870 Butt became active in two new fields. Although long a forceful advocate of intellectual pursuits for women, in both the *Kaleidoscope* and *Leisure Moments* she had criticized women's rights activists and defended women's traditional role exerting influence primarily through the home. Adopting a new perspective, Butt became a vice president of the Virginia State Woman Suffrage Association at its founding in May 1870. That autumn she announced her intention to attend lectures at the Woman's Medical College of the New York Infirmary, Elizabeth Blackwell's pioneering medical school for women that emphasized preventive medicine, clinical work, and service to the poor.

Developing pneumonia not long thereafter, Martha Haines Butt Bennett died on 9 February 1871 at the Grand Central Hotel in New York City. She was buried in Norfolk.

Biography in *Frank Leslie's Illustrated Newspaper*, 14 Jan. 1860, 110, 112 (por.); variant birth date of 1834, often repeated in bibliographical authorities, in Samuel Austin Allibone, *Critical Dictionary of English Literature, and British and American Authors* (1858–1871), 1:316; Norfolk City Marriage Register, giving age on 6 July 1865 as twenty-six; William S. Forrest, *Historical and Descriptive Sketches of Norfolk and Vicinity* (1853), 357–361; Butt, *Antifanaticism: A Tale of the South* (1853), vii (quotation); brief reviews of *Antifanaticism* in *Godey's Magazine and Lady's Book* 47 (1853): 180, and *Southern Quarterly Review* 24 (1853): 543; *Norfolk Southern Argus*, 4 June 1855; *Richmond Daily Dispatch*, 3 July 1855; *Pastimes with My Little Friends* reviewed in *New York Times*, 19 Sept. 1866; Rebecca Mary Mitchell, "Extending Their Usefulness: Women in Mid-Nineteenth-Century Richmond" (master's thesis, W&M, 1978), 45; Elizabeth R. Varon, *We Mean to Be Counted: White Women and Politics in Antebellum Virginia* (1998), 108, 111–112, 114, 116, 120, 142, 172, 174–175; Sandra Gioia Treadway, "A Most Brilliant Woman: Anna Whitehead Bodeker and the First Woman Suffrage Association in Virginia," *Virginia Cavalcade* 43 (1994): 171; *Richmond Daily Enquirer*, 4 Oct. 1870; obituaries in *New York Times*, 10 Feb. 1871, and *Norfolk Journal*, 11 Feb. 1871 (includes birth date).

ANTOINETTE G. VAN ZELM

BUTTON, Charles William (7 July 1822–29 December 1894), journalist, was born in Harpers Ferry, the son of Charles Button, a blacksmith, and Jane Read Button. He obtained only a limited formal education and was most likely expected to take up a mechanic's trade. Such a fate must have seemed inevitable when Button shouldered the responsibility of looking after his mother and youngest siblings after his father died in 1843.

Nonetheless, Button's religious faith, voracious reading, and political enthusiasm inspired him to write for the newspapers, revealing a remarkable talent for journalism. By 1851, when he began pasting clippings of his published effusions onto the pages of his father's old account book, he was writing political articles for the *Charlestown Virginia Free Press* and contributing regularly to the *Methodist Protestant*, of Baltimore, Maryland. His parents were founders of the local Methodist church, and Button became a member in childhood. Through the church he met and by 1853 had married Mary Elizabeth Zollickoffer, the daughter of a Methodist clergyman and a native of Carroll County, Maryland. They had five sons and four daughters.

Button was an active Methodist layman, often attended the state's annual conference, and between the 1850s and 1870s regularly attended national church conferences as well, but a ministerial career did not suit him. His devotion to the Whig Party was also strong, and he served the party well enough to be appointed postmaster at Harpers Ferry in May 1849, an office he resigned in May 1853 to run for the House of Delegates. Button was elected and served a single one-year term representing Jefferson County, all the while reporting on politics to the local newspapers. As a member of the minority party he was appointed to the relatively insignificant Committee to Examine the Penitentiary.

Soon after his younger brother Joseph Button purchased an interest in the *Bedford Sentinel*, a Whig newspaper, Button moved to Liberty (later the city of Bedford) to join him. On 24 April 1857 Joseph Button announced the sale of his interest in the paper, and on the same day Charles W. Button announced his purchase of the *Lynchburg Virginian*, one of the oldest Whig newspapers in the state. He promised to continue the paper's advocacy of Whig principles, a pledge that proved difficult to keep as the sectional conflict worsened. The paper's masthead slogan, "The Rights of the States, and the Union of the States," concisely expressed the political ground on which Button stood, and in the 1860 presidential election the paper endorsed the Constitutional Union Party as preferable to the Democrats and the Republicans.

The *Lynchburg Virginian* was very much a family affair. Button's three brothers worked there, and as of 1860 two brothers and four unrelated printers shared Button's home with his wife, his three children, his mother, and his sister. Journalism was both highly partisan and personal, and rivalries sometimes provoked heated and enduring animosities. On the afternoon of 23 June 1860, after angry editorials had passed between the *Lynchburg Virginian* and the *Lynchburg Republican*, as the Button brothers walked home they encountered editorial writers from the other paper. An argument began, during which Joseph Button was shot and mortally wounded. The event deeply affected Charles Button, and five days later in an editorial he promised to be "more forbearing" toward others in the future.

Button published the *Lynchburg Virginian* through the Civil War, although the paper had shrunk by 1864 to a single sheet without a masthead. The issue of 31 March 1865 printed a public appeal inviting Button to become a candidate for the Confederate House of Representatives following the resignation of William Cabell Rives. Button agreed to serve if elected, and four other candidates also announced their availability. The election probably did not take place as scheduled on 10 April 1865, one week after the fall of Richmond and one day after the surrender of the Confederate army at Appomattox Court House. Nevertheless, some accounts state that Button won election to the Confederate Congress. If so, the victory was an empty one.

By the beginning of June 1865, publication and delivery of the newspaper to city and rural subscribers had resumed, and the paper had grown to four pages. Button looked forward to amnesty and reconciliation, but in his paper of 15 June 1865 he pronounced the idea of enfranchising African Americans "preposterous." After Congress passed Reconstruction acts to provide such rights to blacks, Button abandoned any hope for cooperation with Republicans. In the autumn of 1865 he unsuccessfully ran for the Senate of Virginia from the district comprising Appomattox, Campbell, and Charlotte Counties, and thereafter he confined himself to supporting other candidates. By 1867 what mattered most to him was electing conservative white men. Thus, although the *Lynchburg Virginian* retained its prewar masthead slogan, Button made it an outspoken advocate of the Virginia Democratic Party against the Republicans and, in the 1880s, the Readjusters. On 2 November 1875 he enjoyed the pleasure of purchasing his former rival, the *Lynchburg Republican*, and absorbing it into his own paper.

After the Democrats finally elected a president in 1884, Button was rewarded with a patronage appointment as postmaster of Lynchburg. In July 1885 he assumed his new duties and left the newspaper under the direction of his sons Charles Fletcher Button and Joseph Button (1865–1943). Senator William Mahone, leader of the Readjusters, opposed Button's appointment and blocked its confirmation. Unable to overcome Mahone's opposition, Button returned to the newspaper after only eighteen months in office.

Button sold the *Lynchburg Virginian* a few months later, on 14 March 1887. He remained in

Lynchburg for several years, looking after his properties and participating in Methodist affairs. Early in 1894 he moved to the Appomattox County farm of his son Joseph Button, who later served as clerk of the Senate of Virginia and the state's first commissioner of insurance. Charles William Button died there of pneumonia on 29 December 1894 and was buried in Lynchburg's Spring Hill Cemetery.

Birth date in French Biographies and *Lynchburg News*, 30 Dec. 1894; Bruce, Tyler, and Morgan, *History of Virginia*, 4:116 (with variant birth date of 25 July 1822); Charles Button Account Book, 1835–1839, and Button letters in several collections, VHS; National Society Daughters of the American Revolution, comp., *Tombstone Inscriptions and Burial Lots* (1981), 248 (father's death); Edward J. Drinkhouse, *History of Methodist Reform* (1899), 2:664–665 (variant birth date of 17 July 1822); Lester J. Cappon, *Virginia Newspapers, 1821–1935: A Bibliography with Historical Introduction and Notes* (1936), 123; *Lynchburg Virginian,* 28 June 1860 (first quotation), 15 June 1865 (second quotation); Presidential Pardons; Record of Appointment of Postmasters, Virginia, Lynchburg, RG 28, NARA; obituaries in *Lynchburg News*, 30, 31 Dec. 1894, and *Charlestown (W.Va.) Free Press*, 9 Jan. 1895.

JOHN T. KNEEBONE

BUTTON, Joseph (31 October 1865–10 November 1943), clerk of the Senate of Virginia and first commissioner of insurance, was born in Lynchburg, the son of Charles William Button, owner of the *Lynchburg Virginian*, and Mary Elizabeth Zollickoffer Button. He was educated in the local public schools. By 1885 Button and an elder brother were helping to operate the family newspaper, and they acted as editors and publishers between 1885 and 1887 while their father was postmaster of Lynchburg. After the family sold the paper later in 1887, Button moved to Florence, Alabama, where he worked in real estate and insurance for two years. He retained a strong interest in Virginia politics, acquired through his father, and reportedly rushed back to Virginia in 1889 in order to vote against William Mahone, then a candidate for governor but who as United States senator had blocked Charles W. Button's confirmation as postmaster of Lynchburg.

Button moved back to Virginia and became a member of Appomattox County's Democratic Party committee during the 1892 presidential campaign. A new state party leadership was then taking form, and the closest political associate of its leader, Thomas Staples Martin, was Henry DeLaWarr "Hal" Flood, of Appomattox County, then a state senator. Flood undoubtedly helped Button gain appointment in 1893 as a clerk in the state treasurer's office in Richmond, and later that year Button unsuccessfully sought election as clerk of the Senate of Virginia.

In 1894 Button returned to Appomattox as an agent for two large fire and life insurance companies, but politics remained a priority. His agency was located in the office of the commonwealth's attorney, Henry D. Flood. By the end of May, Button had become secretary of the Democratic Party committee for the Tenth Congressional District, and shortly afterward he was elected chairman of the county committee. The governor that year placed Flood on a commission to resolve issues still surrounding Virginia's and West Virginia's obligations for public debts incurred before the Civil War, and Flood arranged for Button's appointment as clerk of that commission. On 4 December 1895 Flood nominated Button for clerk of the Senate, and this time the party caucus elected him. Button served until 1906. Flood was elected to the House of Representatives in 1900, and Button became his trusted lieutenant in Virginia by handling political errands and keeping him informed about state politics. Button, the quintessential political insider, was a member of the state Democratic committee from 1894 to 1916 and secretary from 1896 to 1906.

Only two months before Button's election as clerk of the Senate, he and Samuel Lewis Ferguson (chairman and secretary of the county party committee, respectively) became proprietors of the weekly *Appomattox and Buckingham Times*. Button's editorials and hard work on the campaign trail helped the Democrats carry the state in the 1896 presidential race, despite a national Republican victory and the misgivings of many Virginia Democratic leaders about the national party's endorsement of inflationary free-silver monetary policies. Politics mattered more than weekly journalism, and Button and his partner gave up the paper a year after they acquired it.

Button served as secretary of the Virginia Convention of 1901–1902. This state constitutional convention created the State Corporation Commission to regulate railroads and other industries, including insurance. In 1906 the General Assembly passed a bill establishing the Bureau of Insurance and on 10 March elected Button the bureau's first commissioner. The SCC's commissioners refused to accept his election and argued that the constitution gave them the power to appoint their own officers. Button applied to the Virginia Supreme Court of Appeals, which on 1 August 1906 ruled in his favor.

Button's primary obligation as commissioner was safeguarding the fiscal health of insurance companies operating in Virginia. He proved effective as an administrator, gradually reduced his political activities, and eventually resigned from his party committees in 1916. Button published the annual *Virginia Insurance Report*, a comprehensive review of the financial condition of all of the insurance companies and fraternal benefit societies operating in Virginia. He became a leader in the National Association of Insurance Commissioners and served as its president in 1910 and as secretary-treasurer from 1917 to 1929. When the state government was reorganized in 1928, the divisions of insurance and banking were combined under the SCC, and on 1 March 1928 Button became head of the combined division. He resigned on 15 October 1929 to accept the presidency of the Union Life Insurance Company of Virginia. Button also served on the board of the Virginia Military Institute from 1910 to 1918 and from 1922 until his death.

On 1 December 1917 in Bronxville, New York, Button married Annie Donald Shotwell, a widowed native of Chesterfield County. The Buttons lived much of the year in Richmond but maintained a country house in Appomattox County. They had no children. Button served as an adviser on insurance matters to the Federal Home Owners' Loan Corporation in the mid-1930s. He remained an insurance executive until shortly before his death. Joseph Button died of heart failure in Richmond on 10 November 1943. A detail of VMI cadets served as pall-bearers at his funeral in Richmond and at his burial at Spring Hill Cemetery in Lynchburg.

Biographies in Allyn B. Tunis, *Press Reference Book of Prominent Virginians* (1916), 21, Bruce, Tyler, and Morton, *History of Virginia*, 4:116, and Manarin, *Senate Officers*, 314–316 (por.); caricature in *Richmond Times-Dispatch*, 6 Mar. 1906; *Button v. State Corporation Commission* (1906), *Virginia Reports,* 105:634–642; Frank A. Magruder, *Recent Administration in Virginia* (1912), 159–161; marriage announced in *Richmond News Leader*, 3 Dec. 1917; BVS Death Certificate, Richmond City; obituaries in *Richmond News Leader*, 10 Nov. 1943, *New York Times* and *Richmond Times-Dispatch*, both 11 Nov. 1943, and *VMI Alumni Review* 20 (winter 1944): 4; editorial tributes in *Richmond News Leader*, 11 Nov. 1943, and *Richmond Times-Dispatch*, 12 Nov. 1943.

JOHN T. KNEEBONE

BUTTON, Robert Young (2 November 1899–1 September 1977), attorney general of Virginia, was born in Culpeper County, the son of John Young Button, a traveling hardware salesman and farmer, and Margaret Agnes Duncan Button. After graduating in 1917 from Culpeper High School, where he excelled in debating, Button enrolled at the University of Virginia. There he spent five active years and joined the prestigious Raven Society and the Order of the Coif before receiving an LL.B. Button returned to Culpeper to practice law. On 20 August 1931 he married Kathleen Mary Antoinette Cheape, a nurse. They had one son and one daughter.

Following a career path familiar to many other young lawyers, Button took an active role in community affairs, joined a variety of organizations, invested in local businesses, and eventually got involved in politics, beginning with the 1933 election campaign. He sat on the Virginia Parole Board from 1942 to 1945 and on the State Board of Education from 1945 to 1960. Button was a trustee of the Jamestown Corporation during the 1950s and served on the Potomac River Commission in 1958. He was a member of the Virginia Advisory Legislative Council and as chair issued reports on such issues as Virginia's involuntary sterilization laws and the retention, storage, and disposal of state records.

In 1945 Button was elected to the Senate of Virginia from the district comprising Culpeper,

Fauquier, and Loudoun Counties. He was one of a considerable number of small-town attorneys who long accounted for much of the enduring success of the Democratic Party organization that looked to Senator Harry Flood Byrd (1887–1966) for leadership. Button found the Byrd organization's conservative philosophy congenial and devoted his talents to its advancement. He received increasingly important legislative assignments, including appointments to the Committees on Finance, on General Laws, and on Privileges and Elections, and in 1956 he chaired the Committee on Welfare. During his fifteen years in the Senate, Button backed the organization's programs on matters ranging from fiscal conservatism to Massive Resistance. He served on the Commission on Public Education of 1954 (popularly known as the Gray Commission) and the Commission on Public Education of 1959 (popularly known as the Perrow Commission), both created to craft Virginia's response to the United States Supreme Court's ruling that public school segregation was unconstitutional.

In 1961 a group of party leaders persuaded a reluctant Button to run for attorney general on the ticket with Albertis Sydney Harrison for governor and Button's close friend Mills Edwin Godwin Jr. for lieutenant governor. Button and Godwin were both praised and condemned for their prominent support of Massive Resistance, while the more moderate Harrison escaped some of the bitterest criticism of the attempt to thwart court-ordered desegregation of the public schools. All three candidates received comfortable majorities on election day, and four years later Button was easily reelected.

Button's published annual reports document in detail his work and responsibilities during eight years as attorney general. His office defended Virginia's racial segregation laws, legislative reapportionment, voter registration procedures, and the poll tax. Following previous practice, private attorneys were sometimes engaged to handle the difficult litigation of complicated cases. Assistant attorneys general argued two of the most publicized cases that reached the United States Supreme Court during Button's tenure, *Griffin et al.* v. *County School Board of Prince Edward County et al.* (1964) and *Loving et ux.* v. *Virginia* (1967). In both instances the Supreme Court negated the arguments of Button's assistant. In the first case the Court struck down the school board's abolition of the county schools and diversion of tax money to support private segregated academies, and in the second the justices invalidated Virginia's law against interracial marriages.

Button knew that Virginia had little chance of winning some of those cases. Like other leading members of the Byrd organization, he believed that he had to fight what they regarded as the liberal activism of the Supreme Court, whose decisions he condemned as unconstitutional usurpations of the powers of the legislature and of the states. Button often criticized the federal judiciary and charged that the Supreme Court was so concerned with the rights of individuals that it forgot that society also had rights. He blamed its decisions for increased crime and pornography.

Although some people regarded Button as dignified, distant, and blunt, others who knew him better or worked with him closely remembered his kindness, humor, integrity, and dedication. He did not seek a third term in 1969, and in 1970 he resumed his law practice in Culpeper. Button had suffered a heart attack in 1967. He recovered sufficiently to return to work, but his heart remained weak for the remainder of his life. Robert Young Button died on 1 September 1977 after suffering a heart attack in Culpeper and was buried in Culpeper Masonic Cemetery.

Jerry Gass, "Attorney General of Virginia: Robert Y. Button," *Virginia Record* 84 (Jan. 1962): 25, 134–135; Pat Perkins, "Attorney General of Virginia: Robert Young Button," *Virginia Record* 88 (Jan. 1966): 21–22, 111 (pors.); feature article in *Richmond Times-Dispatch*, 11 Jan. 1970; BVS Marriage Register, Charlottesville; some Button letters in George Lawrence Hunter Papers and Thomas Frank Walker Papers, VHS, and in Mills Edwin Godwin Jr. Papers, W&M; *Richmond Times-Dispatch*, 5 Feb., 6 July 1961; *Griffin et al.* v. *County School Board of Prince Edward County et al.* (1964), and *Loving et ux.* v. *Virginia* (1967), *United States Reports*, 377:218–235, 388:1–14; Button, *The Constitutionality of the Voting Rights Act of 1965: A Response to the Attorney General of the United States* (1965); obituaries in *Culpeper Star-Exponent* (pors.), *Richmond Times-Dispatch*, and *Washington Post*, all 2 Sept. 1977.

J. L. BUGG

BUTTS, Evelyn Thomas (22 May 1924–11 March 1993), civil rights activist and Democratic Party leader, was born in Norfolk, the daughter of George Washington Thomas, a laborer, and Lottie Cornick Thomas. Her mother died when Thomas was about ten years old, and she lived for several years with an aunt who instilled in her an interest in politics. She dropped out of school in the tenth grade and on 7 September 1941 married Charles Herbert Butts. They had three daughters. Charles Butts served in the army during World War II and later worked for the Norfolk Naval Air Station. After a wartime injury disabled him, the family was forced to take in other disabled veterans as boarders to supplement the money she earned as a seamstress, and it also had to rely from time to time on public assistance.

Butts began taking part in local civil rights activities during the 1950s and emerged as a strong advocate for vigorous measures against official racial segregation. As president of the Oakwood Civic League she helped persuade Norfolk to erect Rosemont Middle School so that children from the neighborhood would not have to ride the bus to a segregated school across town. In 1961 Butts ran for president of the Norfolk chapter of the National Association for the Advancement of Colored People in opposition to the longtime president, whom she accused of being insufficiently militant. She withdrew from the contest at the last moment after it became clear that she would not be elected. As in all her later political ventures, her fixed opinions and blunt words aroused strong feelings among her supporters and her opponents.

Butts was one of numerous black voters in Norfolk who participated in politics despite the official barriers to African American voting, one of which was the poll tax. At the end of November 1963 she had the Norfolk attorney Joseph A. Jordan file suit in federal court against Governor Albertis Sydney Harrison and several Norfolk officials, charging that the provisions in the Virginia Constitution of 1902 and related state laws requiring payment of a poll tax as a prerequisite for voter registration violated the United States Constitution. Butts's suit asserted that the poll tax placed an undue financial bur-den on the suffrage and that inasmuch as a larger proportion of African Americans than whites could not afford to pay the poll tax, the measure was an engine of racial discrimination and therefore violated the equal protection clause of the Fourteenth Amendment. The suit contained other arguments against the poll tax, but that issue was the central one and the one that survived early legal challenges. With the assistance of civil rights lawyers from the District of Columbia and Michigan, Butts pursued her case *in forma pauperis* all the way to the United States Supreme Court.

Butts's suit was the first but not the only one filed against the Virginia poll tax. Republicans challenged the poll tax on a number of other grounds, and in March 1964 Annie E. Harper and three other African American residents of Fairfax County, with legal assistance furnished in part by the American Civil Liberties Union, filed suit against the Virginia State Board of Elections, similarly charging that the poll tax was unconstitutional. The presiding judge of the United States Court of Appeals for the Fourth Circuit referred Butts's and Harper's cases to the adjudication of a three-judge panel, which dismissed Butts's suit in May 1964 for failure to prosecute the case with due diligence. The next week Butts filed an almost identical suit in the United States District Court, but because of this initial setback and because Butts's lawyers had to overcome objections that the office of Virginia's attorney general lodged against her suit, her case reached the judges later than Harper's. The combined cases were therefore heard under the style *Harper* v. *Virginia State Board of Elections*. The judges heard arguments in Alexandria on 21 October 1964 and on 12 November, adhering to precedents that the United States Supreme Court had established in the 1930s, upheld the constitutionality of the poll tax.

Harper's attorneys almost immediately appealed to the United States Supreme Court. Butts's lawyers, by contrast, lacked the financial resources of the ACLU and did not file their appeal until later, so the style of the combined action remained unchanged. Before the cases were argued, the attorney general of the United

States filed a separate suit against Virginia charging that the poll tax was illegal under the new Voting Rights Act of 1965. Harper's and Butts's cases were argued together on 24 and 25 January 1966. The solicitor general of the United States, Thurgood Marshall, filed a brief *amicus curiae* and also presented oral arguments against the poll tax. On 24 March 1966 the Supreme Court ruled that the poll tax was unconstitutional, as Butts had originally charged. That decision ended more than sixty years of the use of the poll tax to make it difficult for African Americans and poor people to vote.

Butts conducted voter registration campaigns in Norfolk, first in her own Oakwood neighborhood and then citywide, and she helped to found the Concerned Citizens for Political Education, the most influential African American political organization in Norfolk during the 1970s. Through registration drives, political education, endorsements, and working at the polls, the Concerned Citizens in 1968 helped elect Joseph Jordan to Norfolk's city council, its first African American member in the twentieth century, and the following year the citizens' group helped elect William P. Robinson, the first African American ever to represent Norfolk in the House of Delegates. Butts was so influential in local politics that by the end of the 1970s the press regularly referred to her as one of the most powerful black politicians in Norfolk. She ran three times for the city council in her own right but lost in the at-large elections by a narrow margin in 1980, by a larger margin in 1982, and again by a narrow margin in 1984.

During the 1980s the Concerned Citizens lost much of its influence to the biracial Rainbow Coalition, and the largely moribund group ousted Butts from its chairmanship in June 1990. She remained active in Democratic Party politics until late in the 1980s and attended both state and national conventions. Butts served on the board of the Norfolk Redevelopment and Housing Authority for twelve years beginning in 1975, and in 1982 the governor appointed her to the State Board of Housing and Community Development. In 1989 the Norfolk and Portsmouth Bar Association presented her with

its annual Liberty Bell Award for community service, and she also received a lifetime achievement award from the Hampton Roads Black Media Professionals. In November 1995 the city council renamed Elm Street in her honor. Evelyn Thomas Butts died at her Norfolk home on 11 March 1993 and was buried in Forest Lawn Cemetery in that city.

Feature articles in *Norfolk Virginian-Pilot,* 8 Apr. 1967, 7 Nov. 1979, 10 June 1990, and *Norfolk Ledger-Star,* 13 Aug. 1979; family history confirmed by sister Rosanna Thomas Copeland; *Norfolk Virginian-Pilot and Ledger-Star,* 11 Nov. 1979; political campaigns and other community service reported in *Norfolk Journal and Guide, Norfolk Ledger-Star,* and *Norfolk Virginian-Pilot,* 1961–1990; *Harper v. Virginia State Board of Elections* and *Butts v. Harrison* (1964), *Federal Supplement,* 240:270–271; *Harper v. Virginia Board of Elections* (1966), *United States Reports,* 383:663–686; Thomas C. Parramore, Peter C. Stewart, and Tommy L. Bogger, *Norfolk: The First Four Centuries* (1994), 388 (por.), 389, 432; obituaries and editorial tributes in *Norfolk Virginian-Pilot,* 12, 15 Mar. 1993, *Richmond Times-Dispatch,* 13, 15 Mar. 1993, *Norfolk Ledger-Star,* 17 Mar. 1993, and *Norfolk Journal and Guide,* 17–23 Mar. 1993 (por.).

BRENT TARTER

BUXTON, Joseph Thomas (12 December 1875–5 November 1940), physician, was born in Jackson, North Carolina, the son of Samuel N. Buxton and Elizabeth Peele Buxton. He was educated in private schools in Jackson, at Wake Forest College, at the University of North Carolina during the 1893–1894 academic year, and at the University of Pennsylvania's medical school, from which he received an M.D. in 1897. Buxton interned briefly at two hospitals in Philadelphia and then took graduate courses, specializing in surgery, in England, Scotland, and France.

Early in 1899 Buxton moved to Newport News, where one of his uncles and a brother lived, and began his practice. In New York City on 11 June 1899 he married Helen von Lehn, a New Jersey nurse. They had three sons and two daughters. Buxton was chief surgeon when the Newport News General Hospital opened about 1903, but the hospital soon closed after a fire destroyed its second floor and several patients died from complications after their rescue from the burning building. In 1906 he founded Elizabeth Buxton Hospital, which he named for his mother. With borrowed money Buxton erected a small building and added to it during the ensuing decades. By the time of his death he had turned it into the largest hospital in the area. Its 180 beds made it one of the largest family-owned hospitals in Virginia. In 1907 Buxton started a school of nursing at the hospital, thus giving the Peninsula its first combined hospital and nursing school.

Buxton's spacious home, called Rockhaven, appeared to bespeak a large income derived from his medical practice and ownership of the hospital, but in fact he acquired it in 1917 in a peculiar transaction. He struck up a friendship with one of the patients in Elizabeth Buxton Hospital who blamed his illness on his house's location; he and Buxton then traded residences. Buxton had the better part of the bargain, because Rockhaven was much larger than his former house and also much nearer his hospital. Family tradition records that Buxton's stepgrandson, the novelist William Styron, used Rockhaven as a model for the protagonist's home in *Lie Down in Darkness* (1951).

On 19 October 1918 Buxton entered the army medical corps as a captain. He was stationed first at the embarkation hospital in Newport News, and then at Camp Jackson, South Carolina, and at General Hospital No. 12 in Biltmore, North Carolina, before being discharged from service at the Mayo Clinic in Rochester, Minnesota, on 10 February 1919. Buxton was active in such professional and fraternal organizations as the Knights of Pythias, the Nu Sigma Nu and Phi Delta Theta fraternities, and the Medical Society of Virginia, which he served as vice president. He served in the American Medical Association's House of Delegates in 1920, 1922, and 1924 and was a fellow of the American College of Surgeons.

Buxton was one of the leading physicians and surgeons on the Peninsula until a stroke in 1937 forced him to retire, although he retained his post at the hospital as surgeon in charge. His son Dr. Russell von Lehn Buxton took over direction of the hospital and ran it until 1952, when he sold it to the Bernardine Sisters of the Third Order of Saint Francis, which renamed it Mary Immaculate Hospital. During the 1940s Buxton's daughter Elizabeth Buxton Styron was in charge of the nursing school. On 5 November 1940 Joseph Thomas Buxton became ill while walking to the polling place to vote in the presidential election and died of coronary thrombosis shortly after returning home. He was buried in Peninsula Memorial Park.

Tyler, *Encyclopedia*, 5:956–957 (por. facing 955; marriage date of 11 June 1899, confirmed by Census, Warwick Co., 1900); Alexander Crosby Brown, ed., *Newport News' 325 Years* (1946), 222, 227 (por.); Military Service Records (gives incorrect marriage date of 11 June 1900); *Newport News Daily Press*, 3 Nov. 1985, 27 Mar. 1988; obituaries in *Newport News Times-Herald*, 5 Nov. 1940 (editorial tribute 6 Nov. 1940), *Newport News Daily Press*, 6 Nov. 1940, and *Journal of the American Medical Association* 115 (1940): 2296; memorial in *Virginia Medical Monthly* 67 (1940): 775.

BRENT TARTER

BYARS, William (28 November 1776–14 February 1866), member of the Convention of 1829–1830, was born in Louisa County, the son of John Byars, a prosperous farmer, and Elizabeth Thomason Byars. Sometime after the 1781 death of his father Byars moved to Washington County with his mother and siblings. After he reached adulthood he began acquiring property along the Middle Fork of the Holston River. In 1805 and 1807 Byars purchased two parcels of land consisting of 839 acres on Little Holston Creek, which was soon called Byars' Mill Creek, where he amassed one of Washington County's largest estates. The 1807 purchase included a two-story, six-room log house that had served as a tavern for travelers on the so-called Great Wagon Road between the lower Shenandoah Valley and the backcountry settlements in western Virginia and North Carolina. On 26 February 1807 Byars married Elizabeth Beattie. They had four sons and four daughters.

Byars regularly added to his landholdings, some of which he cultivated and some of which he acquired for resale. By 1830 he may have been the largest-scale farmer in Washington County, and in a region with few large slaveholdings his ownership of fifty-eight slaves ranked among the county's highest. Byars produced corn, oats, rye, and wheat, as well as beef, pork, and wool. He owned two distilleries, a gristmill capable of producing 2,500 bushels of meal and 12,000 pounds of flour annually, a water-powered carding machine for wool, and a sawmill that could process 30,000 board feet of lumber a year. About 1819 Byars began construction of a new residence, Brook Hall, that reflected his affluence and status. A Federal structure of twenty-four rooms, the house featured lavish woodwork carved by two English craftsmen during seven years of construction.

Byars became a militia officer as early as May 1800 and reached the rank of colonel before he resigned in 1834. In 1807 he was elected to the first of four consecutive one-year terms representing Washington County in the House of Delegates. During his first and third terms he served on the Committee of Propositions and Grievances, during his second term he was a member of the Committee to Inquire into the Land Office, and during his fourth term he sat on the Committee of Claims. Byars supported internal improvement projects and the protection of the interests of creditors and landowners.

In 1829 Byars was one of four men elected to represent the district consisting of the counties of Lee, Russell, Scott, Tazewell, and Washington in a convention called to revise the state constitution. He served on the Committee on the Bill of Rights. Insofar as the published records show, Byars was not active in the floor debates, but he voted regularly with western delegates for more democratic election procedures and for a larger representation of western counties in the General Assembly. Probably because the constitution included too few of the proposed reforms, he voted against submitting it to the electorate, who ratified it.

In 1833 Byars lost a campaign against John Hall Fulton, an ardent supporter of Andrew Jackson, to represent an eight-county district in the House of Representatives. Byars then retired from elective politics. He continued to be active in local affairs by supporting a number of efforts to encourage agriculture as well as internal improvement projects such as railroad and turnpike construction. A Presbyterian, Byars during the 1830s contributed $600, more than anyone

else, to the founding and construction of the first buildings of Emory and Henry College, a Methodist institution. He served on its board from 1836 until 1862. The college library building, the fine arts center, and a medal for excellence in scientific scholarship are all named in his honor.

Byars's great wealth figured in several legends. One is that he owned 500 slaves. Another is that he kept a locked iron box full of gold and silver under his bed. A third is that at the outbreak of the Civil War Byars loaded a large treasure of gold, silver, and other valuables onto a wagon, drove off into the mountains, and returned several days later with the emptied wagon. The hoard was allegedly never seen again. William Byars died at Brook Hall on 14 February 1866 and was buried in Glade Spring Presbyterian Church Cemetery at Old Glade in Washington County.

Byars Family Genealogical File, Washington Co. Historical Society, Abingdon; J. Cloyd Byars, "Fort Kilmackronen," *Washington County Historical Society Bulletin* 10 (1943): 9–13; Jerry Simpson, "Ghosts Keep Watch in Brook Hall," *Abingdon Washington County News,* 13 May 1965; Marty Hiatt and Craig Roberts Scott, comps., *Washington County, Virginia, Marriages: Ministers' Returns, 1776–1855* (1994), 28; Militia Commission Papers, RG 3, LVA; Calder Loth, ed., *The Virginia Landmarks Register,* 4th ed. (1999), 538; *Richmond Enquirer,* 23 June 1829, 7 May 1833; *Journal of 1829–1830 Convention,* 296–297; Bruce, *Rhetoric of Conservatism,* 37; Catlin, *Convention of 1829–30* (por.); *Semi-Centennial Catalogue and Historical Register of Emory and Henry College, Washington County, Va., 1837–87* (1887), 46–47 (por.); George J. Stevenson, *Increase in Excellence: A History of Emory and Henry College* (1963), 35–36, 38–39, 43, 48, 50, 80; Washington Co. Will Book, 16:406–411.

GEORGE J. STEVENSON

BYRD, David Wellington (1 November 1868– 6 July 1945), physician, was born in Ashland, Ohio, the son of North Carolina natives James F. Byrd and Mary Anna Henderson Byrd. He attended public schools in Ashland and in 1886 entered Baldwin College (later Baldwin-Wallace College) in Berea, Ohio. Baldwin was a coeducational institution that had admitted a few African American students before Byrd. He went there on the recommendation of Joseph E. Stubbs, superintendent of the Ashland public schools before assuming the presidency of the college in 1886. Byrd helped defray his college expenses by tutoring pupils in Latin. He graduated with an A.B. in 1888 and later received an M.A.

Byrd taught for two years in the Ashland public schools and then moved to Rust University (later Rust College) in Holly Springs, Mississippi, where he taught Greek and Latin for four years. In 1892 he became professor of Greek at Central Tennessee College (Walden University from 1901) in Nashville, an institution for blacks founded by the Freedmen's Aid Society of the Methodist Episcopal Church. Several years later he became dean of Central Tennessee's literary department. During Byrd's tenure the college was in poor fiscal health and uncertain about its mission and future. Its president also doubted the value to students of the ancient languages. The school's one viable section was its Meharry Medical Department, which survived the demise of Walden University and became Meharry Medical College. Byrd entered Meharry's freshman medical class in 1897 and obtained an M.D. in 1900, completing the standard four-year course in three years. Two years later he won Meharry's certification as a Ph.C., or pharmaceutical chemist. Byrd served on the medical faculty as instructor in medical chemistry from 1900 to 1904.

From 1904 until his death Byrd practiced medicine in Norfolk. He was active in both the National Medical Association, which he helped found, and the Old Dominion Medical Society—the black counterparts, respectively, of the American Medical Association and the Medical Society of Virginia. A longtime chairman of the executive committee of the Old Dominion Medical Society, Byrd served as president of the National Medical Association for the 1917–1918 term. Like other African Americans in Virginia and elsewhere, he was excluded from membership in white professional organizations. At a 1940 conference of the Old Dominion Medical Society, Byrd led a campaign to reject an offer by the all-white Medical Society of Virginia to extend restricted privileges to black physicians. After studying the question of interracial cooperation the Medical Society of Virginia had concluded to leave the status quo intact while urging white doctors to "extend to the colored doctors of their respective communities every favor that is reasonable." Byrd's successful opposition to the proposal helped keep pressure on the white group to admit black professionals to full membership in the society.

One of Byrd's major clinical concerns was the prevention and treatment of venereal disease. His interest in the subject, initially sparked by the death of a young male patient from syphilis, soon broadened into a public health mission. In 1916 Byrd headed a lively discussion on "Obscure Syphilis" at a meeting of the Old Dominion Medical Society. He published papers on the subject in 1917 and 1922 in the *Journal of the National Medical Association*. Early in the 1930s Byrd established and became director of the Norfolk Public Clinic, reportedly the nation's first treatment center devoted to venereal disease. In 1936 the National Medical Association became the first national organization to endorse the syphilis control program of the United States Public Health Service, and it appointed Byrd to head its Commission on the Eradication of Syphilis. Byrd spoke in January 1937 at the first National Conference on Venereal Disease Control and impressed the surgeon general of the United States with his passionate commitment to solving this devastating health problem. Byrd also testified before a United States Senate subcommittee in behalf of a $3 million appropriation for venereal disease prevention.

Byrd and his colleagues in the National Medical Association perceived syphilis as a major national health concern that crossed class and race lines and opposed the stereotyping of the disease as predominantly a "Negro problem." In 1939, for example, they prevailed on the editor of a medical text to retract a statement that gonorrhea in children "is most commonly received from toilet seats soiled by infected members of the household, such as colored maids." Although Byrd worked closely with the Public Health Service, he may have been unaware of the Tuskegee Syphilis Experiment, which from 1932 to 1972 deliberately withheld treatment from a test group of black men known to be suffering from syphilis. Judging by his principled stands on other matters, Byrd would almost certainly have been outraged.

Byrd served on the staff of Norfolk Community Hospital and belonged to Omega Psi Phi fraternity, the Hiawatha Social Club, the National Association for the Advancement of Colored People, and the Hunton branch of the Young Men's Christian Association. A trustee of Saint John's African Methodist Episcopal Church in Norfolk, he represented the church as an elder at the Virginia Annual Conference. At Durham in 1942 Byrd attended the initial meeting of the Southern Conference on Race Relations. He was among the local leaders who helped found the Norfolk Division of Virginia State College (later Norfolk State University).

On 15 August 1899 Byrd married Wilhelmina Mitchell, who became a pioneer in the Young Women's Christian Association movement in Norfolk and served a term as president of the Women's Auxiliary of the National Medical Association. They had two daughters. David Wellington Byrd died of a coronary occlusion at his home in Norfolk on 6 July 1945 and was buried in Calvary Cemetery in Norfolk.

Who's Who in Colored America 1 (1927): 33; ibid. 2 (1928/1929): 64–65 (por.); ibid. 3 (1930/1932): 77; ibid. 5 (1938/1940): 93, 98; ibid. 6 (1941/1944): 93, 97; Vivian Ovelton Sammons, *Blacks in Science and Medicine* (1990), 44; *Baldwin-Wallace College Bulletin* 10 (Dec. 1924); *Journal of the National Medical Association* 8 (1916): 172, 190–191; *Norfolk Journal and Guide*, 23 Nov. 1940 (por.); Thomas Parran, *Shadow on the Land: Syphilis* (1937), 178–181; Albert L. Hinton, "Fighting Syphilis," *Crisis* 45 (1938): 138–139, 146; Byrd's major papers are in *Journal of the National Medical Association*, including "Some Considerations in a Study of Vascular Tension," 6 (1914): 226–227, "Maternity and Infant Mortality," 9 (1917): 177–180, "Syphilis of the Respiratory Tract and Lungs," 14 (1922): 84–86, "Therapeutic Notes," 29 (1937): 172, "An Appeal to the Women of America to Help Stamp Out Congenital Syphilis," 31 (1939): 127–128, "Report of N.M.A. Commission on Eradication and Prevention of Syphilis," 31 (1939): 270–271, and "Norfolk Public Clinics," 34 (1942): 39–40; venereal disease work and opposition to 1940 Medical Society of Virginia proposal documented in Julius Rosenwald Fund Archives, box 152, folder 7, box 214, folder 11, and box 215, folders 1–2 (second quotation), 4, Fisk University, Nashville, Tenn.; *Virginia Medical Monthly* 67 (1940): 177–178, 571–572 (first quotation on 571); obituaries and memorials in *Richmond Times-Dispatch*, 7 July 1945, *Norfolk Journal and Guide*, 14 July 1945, *Journal of the American Medical Association* 129 (1945): 527, *Journal of the National Medical Association* 37 (1945): 206, and *Baldwin-Wallace Alumnus* (Nov. 1945): 14.

KENNETH R. MANNING

BYRD, Harry Flood (10 June 1887–20 October 1966), governor of Virginia and member of the United States Senate, was born in Martinsburg, West Virginia, the eldest son of Richard Evelyn Byrd (1860–1925) and Eleanor Bolling Flood Byrd, of Winchester. His brothers were Richard Evelyn Byrd (1888–1957), who gained fame as a polar aviator and explorer, and Thomas Bolling Byrd (1890–1968), a lawyer who became Harry Byrd's partner in the apple business. Byrd inherited a strong political lineage. His grandfather Joel Flood served in the General Assembly, and his uncle Henry DeLaWarr "Hal" Flood sat in the House of Representatives for twenty years. Eleanor Byrd's grandfather Charles James Faulkner (1806–1884) was a member of the Convention of 1850–1851, a congressman, and minister to France, and his namesake son (1847–1929) represented West Virginia in the United States Senate. Harry Byrd's father, a descendant of the three William Byrds of colonial Virginia, became a noted attorney, served as Speaker of the House of Delegates, and was influential in the dominant wing of the Virginia Democratic Party.

The trio of Tom, Dick, and Harry Byrd led the "western gang" on the west side of Winchester, where they grew up. Harry Byrd soon tired of formal education and at age fifteen took over the failing family newspaper. Possessing an indefatigable energy and valuing hard work and thrift, he made the *Winchester Evening Star* a profitable business. Byrd bought a second newspaper and started a third, leased some apple orchards, and from 1908 to 1918 was president of the Valley Turnpike Company, which operated the toll road between Winchester and Staunton. With the profits from these ventures he purchased orchards and apple cold-storage facilities and built them into a multimillion-dollar business that brought him financial security and a national reputation as an orchardist.

Before World War I Byrd started a family and began a political career. On 7 October 1913 he married Anne Douglas Beverley, of Winchester. They had three sons and one daughter. Tutored by his father in the intricacies of Virginia politics, Byrd served an appointed term on Winchester's city council starting in 1909 but lost an electoral bid for the same post the next year. In 1916 he began ten years of service in the Senate of Virginia, representing Frederick and Shenandoah Counties, Winchester, and (from 1924) Clarke County. More a behind-the-scenes manipulator than a legislative orator or draftsman, Byrd served on committees dealing with highways and finance, interests that typified his political career thereafter. During World War I he also served as state fuel administrator.

The death of Hal Flood in December 1921 propelled Byrd into a leadership position in the state Democratic Party. Elected state party chairman the next year, he reduced the party debt, mended political fences around the state, and led a battle against the highway bond issue in 1923 that solidified his control of the party organization. Outflanking Governor Elbert Lee Trinkle, his principal rival for party leadership, Byrd advocated a pay-as-you-go plan for building roads, financed by gasoline taxes rather than bonds. He prepared for the campaign in the same diligent and organized fashion he used in all of his political races. The result was an overwhelming victory for him and his antibond forces that confirmed pay-as-you-go as the fiscal policy of Virginia for the next forty years.

Defeating G. Walter Mapp in the party primary and Republican S. Harris Hoge in the general election, Byrd was elected governor of Virginia in 1925 and was sworn into office on 1 February 1926. Despite his reputation as an organization stalwart, Byrd brought a level of activism, competence, imagination, and leadership to the office not witnessed in generations. Relying on his experience in politics and business, he sought to transform the government of Virginia into a lean and efficient provider of services by reorganizing offices and departments and restructuring state finances. Byrd commissioned a survey of the state government by the New York Bureau of Municipal Research, appointed a citizens' committee headed by his friend and mentor William Thomas Reed, and

asked a constitutional commission to recommend changes in the basic law.

The major reorganization that resulted reduced the number of elected state officers from ten to three, abolished many state agencies, and consolidated the others into twelve departments. Along with a new system of accounting, these changes modernized the state government into something like a corporation with a fully empowered business executive at its head. Byrd sponsored a tax program that allocated real estate and personal property taxes to localities and left most other taxes for the state to collect. He also sought to increase the gasoline tax for highway construction and reduce the taxes on capital used in industry and on bonds and notes, hoping thereby to attract more industry and investment to Virginia.

Thanks primarily to Byrd's political skills, his proposals all won easy approval from the General Assembly and the electorate. His friends on Reed's committee tailored the proposals of the Bureau of Municipal Research to suit the governor, and the constitutional commission endorsed all of his suggested amendments. The 1926 and 1928 regular sessions of the assembly and a special session in 1927 rubber-stamped his handiwork and speedily passed the amendments on to a public referendum in June 1928. Leaving nothing to chance, Byrd campaigned vigorously for the proposed reforms, all of which the voters approved, albeit with less ardor than the politicians had demonstrated.

Although political considerations ruled out any serious changes in the notorious fee system by which county officers were compensated and in the structure of county government—both areas where Byrd rejected suggestions by the Bureau of Municipal Research—the governor established a solid record for progressive government. Sustained by the prosperity of the 1920s, his Program of Progress attracted new industries and residents, increased tourism, and left a state surplus exceeding $4 million when his term ended. He supported the creation of Shenandoah National Park and encouraged the restoration of colonial Williamsburg with money supplied by John D. Rockefeller Jr. Byrd was the commonwealth's number one booster and traveled across the state, often by airplane or blimp, to promote roads, tourism, and airport development. He also supported increased appropriations for education, although with less enthusiasm than he gave to highway construction. By blustering when industries increased gasoline prices and telephone rates, Byrd won acclaim as a populist fighting for the ordinary citizen, a reputation strengthened by his advocacy of a strong antilynching bill passed by the legislature in 1928. His governorship reflected the southern business progressivism of the 1920s that emphasized economy and efficiency rather than upgraded services, but even that was no small achievement.

In 1930 Byrd retired to his orchards and Rosemont, his large new house outside Berryville. He was still an energetic young man with a long political career ahead of him. Stockily built, with thinning, sandy hair above the high forehead typical of his family and a cherubic face that belied his maturity but confirmed his youthful vigor, Byrd enjoyed hiking and hunting in the Blue Ridge Mountains and directing work in his orchards. The apple business consumed most of his time, but he kept up his interest in politics. Relying on Richmond friends, especially Reed and Everett Randolph "Ebbie" Combs, Byrd maintained his influence on public affairs in the state. He advised his successor, John Garland Pollard, on necessary fiscal steps to combat the Great Depression, including support for the 1932 Byrd road law that turned county roads over to the state.

Encouraged by Virginians and conservative Democrats elsewhere who were intent on preventing Franklin Delano Roosevelt from becoming president, Byrd undertook an unsuccessful favorite-son presidential campaign in 1932. That was as close as he ever came to the presidency, but he ran a modest protest campaign against Roosevelt in 1944 and received fifteen electoral votes in 1960 from disaffected southern members of the electoral college who chose not to support their parties' nominees.

In March 1933 the governor appointed Byrd to the United States Senate to succeed Claude Augustus Swanson when the latter became secretary of the navy. Reelected by overwhelming margins six times, Byrd became a national spokesman for reduced federal spending, balanced budgets, and states' rights. During more than thirty years in Washington, Byrd adhered to a nineteenth-century Jeffersonian philosophy that favored a laissez-faire political and economic order in which government was unobtrusive and debt-free, state and local interests were protected from federal action, and the individual was at liberty to develop his own potential—a viewpoint that put him at odds with much of rapidly changing American society.

After briefly supporting Roosevelt's efforts to tackle the Great Depression, Byrd became a vociferous critic of the New Deal. He joined a conservative coalition of congressmen fighting government spending and regulation. Byrd's Senate record thereafter was remarkably consistent and negative. He compiled a strong antilabor record by voting against the Wagner National Labor Relations Act giving federal protection to the unionization of workers and for the Smith-Connally War Labor Disputes and Taft-Hartley Acts that restricted union power and activity. Byrd opposed most of the social reforms introduced during his career, and no significant legislation bears his name.

In foreign affairs Byrd was not an isolationist, but his penny-pinching led him to vote against most postwar foreign aid legislation, including the Marshall Plan. Advocating a strong national defense, he strongly criticized delays in Roosevelt's rearmament program before World War II, but once America entered the war Byrd became preoccupied with the growth of the federal government. He insisted on the creation of the Joint Committee on Reduction of Nonessential Federal Expenditures, and under his chairmanship for twenty-four years its reports ridiculed bloated bureaucracy.

By the 1950s Byrd had assumed the role of an elder statesman. He chaired the important Senate Committee on Finance starting in 1955 and won respect for his courage, integrity, and courtliness. Byrd had achieved national prominence as the spokesman for an outdated but still coveted way of life. He became the idol of the conservative business community, and his numerous magazine articles widely disseminated his political ideas. But his positions, particularly on civil rights, alienated him from the increasingly liberal national Democratic Party, and after 1944 he never again endorsed his party's presidential nominee but preferred instead to maintain what he called a "golden silence."

All the while Byrd controlled political events in Virginia. He helped to select its governors, advised them on legislation, and kept the state committed to a pay-as-you-go policy and honest but parsimonious government. As depression and war changed the nature of the commonwealth, however, Byrd found it increasingly difficult to retain his grip. Antiorganization Democrats and "Young Turks," dissidents within the machine, joined with Republicans in criticizing his failure to confront contemporary issues. None was more important than civil rights. Faced with the United States Supreme Court's desegregation decision of 1954, Byrd pushed the state down the road of Massive Resistance and school closings—an embarrassing chapter with which to close a long career of dedicated public service. The eventual defeat of Virginia's Massive Resistance program in the General Assembly as well as in the courts foreshadowed the end of the old politics in Virginia and the capacity of leaders of his generation to direct the course of state politics.

Byrd spent his final years unsuccessfully combating the tax policies, civil rights legislation, and social programs of Presidents John F. Kennedy and Lyndon B. Johnson. His invalid wife died on 25 August 1964, and on 11 November 1965, undoubtedly feeling the effects of a brain tumor, he retired from the United States Senate. His eldest son, Harry Flood Byrd Jr. (b. 1914), succeeded him. Harry Flood Byrd died on 20 October 1966 at his beloved home, Rosemont. He was buried in Mount Hebron Cemetery in Winchester. In 1976 a statue of Byrd was erected at private expense in Capitol Square in Richmond.

Ronald L. Heinemann, *Harry Byrd of Virginia* (1996), with frontispiece por. and pors. opp. 105, 324, contains bibliography of leading primary and secondary sources; place of birth in BVS Birth Register, Frederick Co.; Harry Flood Byrd (1887–1966) Papers, UVA; Harry Flood Byrd Gubernatorial Papers, RG 3, LVA; interviews with Harry F. Byrd Jr. (17 June 1987), Richard E. Byrd (6 June 1989), Bradshaw Beverley Byrd (7 June 1989), and Joseph Massie and Teresa Massie (7 June 1989); marriage reported in *Winchester Evening Star*, 8 Oct. 1913; leading interpretations of major events in Byrd's career include J. Harvie Wilkinson III, *Harry Byrd and the Changing Face of Virginia Politics, 1945–1966* (1968), Robert T. Hawkes, "The Career of Harry Flood Byrd, Sr., to 1933" (Ph.D. diss., UVA, 1975), James W. Ely Jr., *The Crisis of Conservative Virginia: The Byrd Organization and the Politics of Massive Resistance* (1976), James R. Sweeney, "Harry Byrd: Vanished Policies and Enduring Principles," *Virginia Quarterly Review* 52 (1976): 596–612, and Heinemann, *Depression and New Deal in Virginia: The Enduring Dominion* (1983); Hummel and Smith, *Portraits and Statuary*, 16 (por.); obituaries, tributes, and accounts of funeral in *Richmond News Leader*, 20, 21 Oct. 1966, *Winchester Evening News*, 20–22, 24 Oct. 1966, *New York Times*, 21, 24 Oct. 1966, *Richmond Times-Dispatch*, 21, 23, 24 Oct. 1966, and *Washington Post*, 21 Oct. 1966.

RONALD L. HEINEMANN

BYRD, Mary Willing (10 September 1740–March 1814), planter, was born probably in Philadelphia, the home of her parents, Ann Shippen Willing and Charles Willing, a wealthy and respected merchant who twice served that city as mayor. Benjamin Franklin, one of her godfathers, took an interest in her education and sent her histories and parliamentary speeches from Europe. On 29 January 1761 Willing married William Byrd (1728–1777). A recent widower with four sons and one daughter, he was in winter quarters in Philadelphia while commanding a Virginia regiment during the French and Indian War. The couple initially lived in Philadelphia but in 1762 moved to Westover, the Byrd estate in Charles City County. They had four sons and six daughters.

Hopelessly in debt and suspected of Loyalism, William Byrd committed suicide on 1 or 2 January 1777, bequeathing his wife a life interest in most of his property. As sole executrix Mary Willing Byrd faced the enormous task of settling the estate and satisfying her husband's creditors as well as preserving an inheritance for her children. By seeking payment from her husband's debtors and selling off his western lands, residences in Williamsburg and Richmond, slaves, silver, and the incomparable 3,500-volume library of William Byrd (1674–1744), she succeeded in keeping possession of Westover.

That achieved, Byrd watched as the Revolutionary War literally moved into her home. Despite strong family ties to many men serving the British cause, she attempted to tread a fine line of neutrality and thereby preserve her property for her children. In the first week of January 1781 a British force commanded by Benedict Arnold, whose wife was Byrd's first cousin, landed at Westover. The officers confined her to the upper stories of the house, and the army trampled her wheat, knocked down her fences, butchered her milk cows, and used her plant nursery as a stable. Byrd nevertheless received Arnold tactfully and at one point offered one of her younger sons to the distrustful British as hostage for her good behavior.

Shortly after this visitation Byrd applied to the local American commander for a flag of truce to arrange for the return of forty-nine slaves, three horses, and two ferryboats that the British had seized. The general granted the request even though the governor's Council had banned the use of flags for such private purposes. A lieutenant of HMS *Swift*, who happened to be a brother-in-law of Byrd's sister, tried to act under the flag but was detained by George Lee Turberville, an American major. After discovering a letter from Byrd and a cache of brandy, china, broadcloth, and other goods destined for Westover in the British vessel, Turberville and a company of light infantry raided Westover on 21 February, stormed into Byrd's bedroom while she was still asleep, and seized her papers.

Byrd defended herself and her property vigorously. She protested directly to General Friedrich Wilhelm von Steuben that "This surely can not be stiled liberty. It was Liberty that Savages would have blushed at." To Governor Thomas Jefferson she defended herself eloquently against those who doubted her loyalty: "I wish well to all mankind, to America in particular. What am I but an American? All my friends and connexions are in America; my whole property is here—could I wish ill to everything I have an interest in?"

Turberville was arrested and charged with violating a flag of truce, but his court-martial never took place. Byrd was charged in turn with trading with the invading enemy. Her trial,

scheduled to begin on 15 March before a special commission of oyer and terminer in the General Court, was first postponed until 23 March and ultimately never held. Rumors circulated that the witnesses had been discouraged from attending. Disgusted with her treatment by both sides, and perhaps fearful for her family after an arsonist attempted to burn her plantation house, Byrd put Westover up for sale and announced that she would leave Virginia. She stayed, however, and in August 1781 asked Governor Thomas Nelson for yet another flag of truce to aid her continuing efforts to recover her slaves. On the eve of the final British withdrawal from the United States in 1783, Byrd appealed to the British commander to honor the promises of restitution made by a succession of British generals.

Byrd's vigilance and protectiveness in behalf of her family were both remarkable and successful. Placed in a position that she never would have faced if she had not been a wealthy widow, she preserved much of her property and the legacy of one of the great families of colonial Virginia. When Byrd prepared her will in December 1813, she was still in possession of Westover and was able to provide for all of her children and grandchildren. Not until after her death was Westover sold out of the Byrd family.

Contemporary accounts characterized Byrd as a pious, educated, "amiable & excellent Lady." One historian of the family judged that she was twice the man her husband had been. Mary Willing Byrd died during March 1814, but the exact date of her death is not recorded. She directed in her will that she be buried next to her husband, who had asked to be interred in the cemetery of old Westover Church.

MS biography written ca. 1850 by unidentified granddaughter, Robert A. Brock Collection, Huntington (month of death and third quotation); Mildred H. Arthur, "The Widow of Westover and Women's Rights," *Colonial Williamsburg* 12 (summer 1990): 28–34 (por.); birth and marriage dates in Byrd family Bible notes, New York Public Library; Byrd correspondence and related documentation in CW, LVA, and Steuben Papers, New-York Historical Society, printed in *Jefferson Papers*, 3:111, 112–113, 4:668–670, 680–682, 690–692, 5:31–32, 121, 671–705 (first and second quotations on 5:690, 4:691); other Byrd letters at VHS; *Byrd Correspondence*, 2:609–614; Alden Hatch, *The Byrds of Virginia* (1969), 216–224; Hummel and Smith, *Portraits and Statu-*

ary, 16 (por.); will, proved 21 Apr. 1814, in Charles City Co. Will Book, 2:270–273, printed in *VMHB* 6 (1899): 346–358.

SARA B. BEARSS

BYRD, Richard Evelyn (29 December 1801– 1 January 1872), member of the Convention of 1850–1851, was born at the Cottage, his father's 1,000-acre estate in the eastern portion of Frederick County that became Clarke County in 1836. He was the son of Thomas Taylor Byrd and Mary Anne Armistead Byrd, and he was a grandson of William Byrd (1728–1777) and his first wife, Elizabeth Hill Carter Byrd. His father had been a captain in the British army before and during the American Revolution and afterward, in 1785, was the first member of the family to move to northwestern Virginia.

Richard Evelyn Byrd lived all of his adult life in Winchester, where he practiced law. Tall, dignified, and somewhat austere, he was a skillful courtroom advocate. On 6 April 1826 he married a cousin, Anne Harrison, daughter of a prominent King George County planter. By the time she died on 16 October 1841 they had had three sons and one daughter. Between November 1843 and November 1850 Byrd married a widow, Margaret Funsten Bennett. His second marriage produced no children.

A lifelong Democrat, Byrd flourished in the turbulent political climate of the 1840s and 1850s. He represented Winchester and Frederick County in the House of Delegates in the session of 1839–1840 and for three consecutive terms beginning in 1841. During all four terms he sat on the Committee for Courts of Justice, and he also served one session each on committees concerned with roads and internal improvements, the auditor's accounts, banks, and claims. Byrd strongly supported the interests of the Shenandoah Valley and led an unsuccessful fight for free public education, a major issue of contention between western Virginia and a state government dominated by eastern interests. In 1850 he was one of four delegates elected to represent the district consisting of Frederick, Hampshire, and Morgan Counties in a state constitutional convention that met from 14 October 1850 to 1 August 1851. Byrd served on the Committee on the Judiciary. He spoke on 10 March 1851 in favor of apportioning legislative seats on the basis of the adult white population, a proposal of the western reformers, but he missed the key votes on the basis of apportionment. He voted in favor of the constitution as finally approved on 31 July 1851.

In 1851 Byrd and Henry Bedinger, a former congressman from Shepherdstown, were both nominated for the House of Representatives at separate Democratic Party conventions held in the district. In the heated political atmosphere that followed the debates on and the adoption of the Compromise of 1850, Bedinger was perceived by some as a secessionist. Byrd, who owned slaves but was not as radical as Bedinger, withdrew from the race in order to avoid splitting the Democratic vote. Many of Byrd's supporters either sat out the election or voted for the Whig candidate, Charles James Faulkner (1806– 1884), of Berkeley County, who won the bitter contest in what was to be the last Whig victory in a Virginia congressional election.

Byrd's position on slavery and the value of the Union reflected an ambivalence shared by many of his neighbors during the 1850s. He continued to add to his slaveholdings and by 1860 owned twenty-six bondsmen, making him one of the largest owners of slaves in Frederick County. Byrd persisted in his opposition to secession and believed that Southern industries should be encouraged, even to the point of boycotting Northern products, as a means of influencing Northern opinion on the slavery issue. Early in 1861, as Virginia debated whether to follow the cotton states out of the Union, Byrd came to accept the idea of a peaceful separation. In January, he told a public meeting in Winchester that there had been ample provocation for the South's action, and secession would, in fact, prevent a civil war and lead to a reconstructing of the Union.

A colonel in the 51st Regiment of the Virginia militia when the Civil War began, Byrd, who was then sixty years old, took no active role in the war, although in November 1861 he may have served briefly as provost marshal in Winchester. Byrd suffered a paralytic stroke in 1863. When he applied on 30 January 1866 for a presidential pardon, which he was required to do because of the value of his property, he was unable to speak, walk, or even sign his own name. He was granted the pardon on 5 July 1866. Richard Evelyn Byrd died at his home in Winchester on 1 January 1872 and was buried in Old Chapel Cemetery in Clarke County, one mile from where he was born.

Birth and death dates from gravestone inscription as abstracted in Stuart E. Brown Jr., Lorraine F. Myers, and Eileen M. Chappel, *Annals of Clarke County, Virginia* (1983), 2:70; Thomas K. Cartmell, *Shenandoah Valley Pioneers and Their Descendants: A History of Frederick County, Virginia* (1909), 449; Alden Hatch, *The Byrds of Virginia* (1969), 225–230; Quarles, *Worthy Lives,* 53; Richard E. Byrd Papers, VHS; *Charles Town Virginia Free Press,* 28 Oct. 1841, 21 Aug.–16 Oct. 1851; Robert P. Sutton, *Revolution to Secession: Constitution Making in the Old Dominion* (1989), 220; 10 Mar. 1851 speech reported in *Supplement, 1850–1851 Convention Debates,* no. 21; *Winchester Virginian,* 28 May 1851, 30 Jan. 1861; *Martinsburg Gazette,* 5 Aug., 2 Sept. 1851; Presidential Pardons; obituaries in *Winchester Times,* 3 Jan. 1872, *Charles Town Virginia Free Press,* 6 Jan. 1872, and *Berryville Clarke Courier,* 11 Jan. 1872.

MICHAEL J. GORMAN

BYRD, Richard Evelyn (13 August 1860–23 October 1925), Speaker of the House of Delegates, was born in Austin, Texas, the son of William Byrd (d. 1898) and Jennie Rivers Byrd. He was named for his grandfather, Richard Evelyn Byrd (1801–1872), a Winchester attorney and member of the Convention of 1850–1851. William Byrd served as adjutant general of Texas during the first part of the Civil War and then joined the Confederate army and was taken prisoner. After the war the family moved back to Virginia and settled in Winchester. Richard Evelyn Byrd grew up there and went to school at Shenandoah Valley Academy. Following his education at the University of Virginia and subsequent receipt in 1882 of a degree from the University of Maryland School of Law in Baltimore, he returned to Winchester. Byrd was admitted to the bar in 1884 and later the same year won election as commonwealth's attorney of Frederick County, a post he held for twenty years.

On 15 September 1886 in Martinsburg, West Virginia, Byrd married Eleanor Bolling Flood, of Appomattox, whose political lineage influenced his future. Her grandfather Charles James Faulkner (1806–1884) had been minister to France and a Virginia congressman; her uncle, the younger Charles James Faulkner (1847–1929), had been a United States senator from West Virginia; and her brother, Henry DeLaWarr "Hal" Flood, served in the House of Representatives from 1901 to 1921. Their three children, Harry Flood Byrd (1887–1966), Richard Evelyn Byrd (1888–1957), and Thomas Bolling Byrd—Tom, Dick, and Harry, in reverse order—became respectively a businessman and politician, an aviator and polar explorer, and a lawyer and orchardist.

Byrd enjoyed a legendary reputation as a lawyer. His love of books and a photographic memory supported legal arguments that he delivered with persuasive oratory, clarity of reasoning, fluent diction, and humor and wit. A stockily built man of average height, Byrd had the high family forehead, a determined chin, and penetrating eyes; only the spectacles disguised an aggressive, short-tempered character that made him a fearless and pugnacious competitor in the courtroom. When not meeting the demands of public office he invested in local businesses and practiced law in partnership with the future congressman Thomas Walter Harrison. They took cases from rich and poor alike regardless of their ability to pay. In Winchester Byrd was known as Mr. Dick and regarded as a friend of the underdog and of children, to whom he frequently dispensed candy on the streets.

Hal Flood drew Byrd into the inner circle of the Virginia Democratic Party, which was dominated early in the twentieth century by the political machine of Senator Thomas Staples Martin, to whom Flood was a key adviser. Byrd served on the Democratic State Central Committee and in 1905, probably at the urging of Flood, won a seat representing Winchester and Frederick County in the House of Delegates. In the ensuing January–March 1906 legislative session he sat on the Committee on Finance and chaired the Committee for Courts of Justice. Shockingly for one with so little seniority, Byrd was elected Speaker of the House two years later and held that position for six years, a tribute to his popularity in the assembly and to his standing with the leaders of the Martin machine, who did not often reward newcomers or inept leaders and whose skillful use of the powerful Speaker's office helped the Martin machine to influence crucial legislation and House procedures.

Byrd initiated two statutes bearing his name that furthered the interests of the machine. Although he was himself very far from being a teetotaler, in 1908 he sponsored a bill to restrict the liquor traffic in areas lacking police protection. Its passage revealed a tacit alliance between Martin and James Cannon, the Methodist minister who was Virginia's leader in the fight for Prohibition. Byrd's bill prevented a potentially divisive political struggle. Byrd and Martin supported statewide Prohibition when it was approved in 1914. In 1912 Byrd introduced a bill that made state regulation of party primaries mandatory. He also served on the State Education Commission from 1908 to 1912 and the Special Tax Commission from 1910 to 1912.

Byrd's abilities and fairness as a legislative leader won him the admiration of his peers and the gratitude of the organization leadership, but party regularity did not come at the expense of political independence. When his longtime friend from college days, Woodrow Wilson, announced his presidential candidacy in 1912, Byrd quickly rallied to his side in spite of Martin's opposition to Wilson and the prominence of several antimachine leaders in the Wilson campaign. At the state Democratic convention Byrd engineered a compromise that prevented the Virginia delegation to the national convention from uniting behind any one candidate. The Wilson forces were in a minority in the seriously divided Virginia delegation. Byrd successfully maneuvered to prevent the unit rule from being enforced until it became clear that Wilson would win the nomination in any event.

Byrd's early support naturally made him a key consultant to the new president on patronage appointments in Virginia, and his continued allegiance to the machine likely ensured that Martin's faction was amply rewarded in spite of its initial opposition to Wilson. The president appointed Byrd the United States attorney for the Western District of Virginia. He held that office from 1914 to 1920, after which he served as a special assistant to the United States attorney general for several months at the end of Wilson's second term.

Byrd maintained his private law practice during Wilson's presidency and resided primarily in Richmond. He also served on the state's Commission on Economy and Efficiency from 1916 to 1918 and chaired the State Industrial Council of Safety during World War I. A lifelong Episcopalian and a member of the Commonwealth and Westmoreland Clubs, Byrd was also a key adviser and confidante of his son Harry Flood Byrd (1887–1966), who rapidly rose to political prominence at the beginning of the 1920s. He participated strenuously in his son's 1925 gubernatorial campaign by giving speeches and cajoling old friends in the party machine. Worn out from a successful primary effort, Richard Evelyn Byrd died in Richmond on 23 October 1925 after almost a month of hospitalization, only days before the general election that propelled his son into the governor's mansion. He was buried in Mount Hebron Cemetery in Winchester.

Alden Hatch, *The Byrds of Virginia* (1969), 231, 234–237, 419, 421; Tyler, *Men of Mark*, 1:26–29 (por.); Jamerson, *Speakers and Clerks, 1776–1996*, 118–119, which repeats an incorrect death date; Harry Flood Byrd (1887–1966) Papers, UVA; *Winchester Times*, 22 Sept. 1886; interviews with Harry F. Byrd Jr. (17 June 1987) and Joseph Massie and Teresa Massie (7 June 1989); Allen W. Moger, *Virginia: Bourbonism to Byrd, 1870–1925* (1968), 230, 277, 291, 301–302; Hummel and Smith, *Portraits and Statuary*, 17 (por.); obituaries and accounts of funeral in *Richmond Times-Dispatch*, 24–27 Oct. 1925, and *Winchester Evening Star*, 24, 26 Oct. 1925; memorial in *Virginia State Bar Association Proceedings* (1925): 158–162.

RONALD L. HEINEMANN

BYRD, Richard Evelyn (25 October 1888– 11 March 1957), aviator and recipient of the Medal of Honor, was born in Winchester, the son of Richard Evelyn Byrd (1860–1925) and Eleanor Bolling Flood Byrd. His elder brother, Harry Flood Byrd (1887–1966), served as governor of Virginia and as United States senator, and his younger brother, Thomas Bolling Byrd, was an attorney and orchardist. Dick Byrd, as he was usually known, received his early education at Shenandoah Valley Academy. He manifested his love of travel and adventure at the age of twelve or thirteen when he traveled alone to visit a family friend in the Philippines. Byrd continued his education at the Virginia Military Institute (1904–1906), the University of Virginia (1907–1908), and the United States Naval Academy (1908–1912). He was a fine athlete but not an outstanding student.

On 20 January 1915 the handsome, slender young naval officer married Marie Donaldson Ames, a wealthy Boston heiress he had met during her frequent childhood visits to Virginia. They lived in Boston and had one son and three daughters. Byrd retired from the navy in 1916 with the rank of ensign after he was declared physically unsuitable for promotion because of a fragile foot that he had broken several times. Although on the navy's permanently retired list, he returned to active duty for World War I and was promoted to lieutenant junior grade retroactive to his previous service. All of his subsequent promotions required acts of Congress. Byrd received flight training and won his wings on 17 April 1918. He never saw action, but he commanded air stations in Nova Scotia, helped the navy plan the first transatlantic flight, and developed a bubble sextant to aid in aerial navigation at sea. After the war Byrd played a key role in expanding the navy's aeronautical program, for which Congress promoted him to lieutenant commander.

With further naval advancement unlikely, Byrd again left the service to become an independent aviation pioneer. He hoped to find wealthy patrons, make spectacular flights, and then earn fame and fortune by writing, lecturing, and selling the rights to his adventure stories. John D. Rockefeller Jr. and Edsel Ford were the major backers of his Arctic and early Antarctic ventures. In his first exploit, with navy as well as private support, Byrd joined Arctic veteran Donald B. MacMillan in an attempt to explore Greenland by airplane in 1925. Because of bad weather and bickering with MacMillan, Byrd accomplished little. A poor pilot who seldom operated his own airplanes, Byrd flew north from the rim of the Arctic Ocean with pilot Floyd Bennett on 9 May 1926. When they returned Byrd announced that they had been the first to reach the North Pole by air. Congress rewarded him with the Medal of Honor and a

promotion to commander. Byrd then planned to make the first nonstop flight from the United States to Europe. Charles Lindbergh beat him to it, but Byrd and three companions flew the first transatlantic airmail from New York to France on 29 June 1927.

In 1928 Byrd mounted the first Antarctic aviation expedition, with the objective of flying over the South Pole. With two ships, three airplanes, forty-two men, and eighty-four sled dogs, he established a coastal base he called Little America. Byrd flew to the South Pole on 28–29 November 1929 as part of a four-man crew. The expedition discovered Marie Byrd Land, comparable in size to Alaska and named for the commander's wife, and two mountain ranges. It also conducted important scientific research and proved the efficacy of long-distance radio communications. Congress promoted Byrd to rear admiral, and on 21 June 1930 the commonwealth of Virginia awarded him a partially gilded sterling silver presentation sword.

In January 1934 Byrd returned to Little America with a larger expedition. The one-year project featured a larger scientific program and included eight motorized vehicles. While Byrd manned a solitary meteorological outpost 123 miles from Little America, he became so ill from carbon monoxide poisoning that a tractor party had to make an epic winter journey to rescue him. He never fully recovered from this ordeal.

Byrd started to form a third private Antarctic expedition but merged his enterprise with the new United States Antarctic Service. He led the expedition through its year in the Antarctic, from January 1940 to January 1941. During World War II Byrd served in several staff roles, his principal mission being to survey potential air bases in the Pacific, for which he was awarded the Legion of Merit and a Gold Star. After the war he headed two more navy expeditions, Operation Highjump in 1946 and Operation Deep Freeze in 1955, which established a permanent Antarctic base. Byrd was in the Antarctic only briefly during the postwar expeditions. Disdained by the regular navy because of his political promotions, Byrd had little independent authority in the government's expeditions and was little more than a figurehead in the later operations.

Byrd became one of the most famous explorers of his generation. He publicized his adventures with many articles and four books: *Skyward* (1928), *Little America: Aerial Exploration in the Antarctic, The Flight to the South Pole* (1930), *Discovery: The Story of the Second Byrd Antarctic Expedition* (1935), and *Alone* (1938). His lecture tours were, however, never as profitable as he had anticipated. An Episcopalian, Byrd in the 1930s began a longtime commitment to Moral Re-Armament, a movement that promoted religious values and a conservative political agenda. He supported isolationism until just before World War II and founded the Iron Curtain Refugee Campaign of the International Rescue Committee after the war ended.

Byrd was a complex man. His assertion that he flew to the North Pole is in grave doubt on the basis of the limitations of his airplane, reported confessions to friends by both Byrd and Bennett, and the ambiguities in his own diary. Archival research into his first Antarctic expedition has shown that Byrd lied about his personal roles in discoveries and about his aerial navigational achievements, that he battled an alcohol problem, that he fought almost overwhelming fear during his dangerous flights, and that he was suspicious to the point of paranoia. On the other hand, he always put the well-being of his men before his own, risked death several times to save others, and remained unswervingly loyal to those similarly devoted to him. Byrd established the United States presence in Antarctica, contributed significantly to science and geography, advanced the infant technologies of aviation and radio, and pioneered modern techniques for polar operations.

In declining health after his postwar expeditions, Byrd received the Medal of Freedom a few weeks before his death. Richard Evelyn Byrd died of heart failure at his home in Boston on 11 March 1957 and was buried in Arlington National Cemetery.

Alden Hatch, *The Byrds of Virginia* (1969), 241–397 (pors. opp. 248); Richard Evelyn Byrd Papers, Byrd Polar Research Center, Ohio State University, Columbus; other correspondence in Center for Polar and Scientific Archives at NARA and Harry Flood Byrd (1887–1966) Papers, UVA; *Richmond Times-Dispatch*, 21 Jan. 1915; Raimund E. Goerler, ed., *To The Pole: The Diary and Notebook of Richard E. Byrd, 1925–1927* (1998); leading studies include Charles John Vincent Murphy, *Struggle: The Life and Exploits of Commander Richard E. Byrd* (1928), Edwin P. Hoyt, *The Last Explorer: The Adventures of Admiral Byrd* (1968), Richard Montague, *Oceans, Poles and Airmen: The First Flights over Wide Waters and Desolate Ice* (1971), Paul A. Carter, *Little America: Town at the End of the World* (1979), Finn Ronne, *Antarctica, My Destiny: A Personal History by the Last of the Great Polar Explorers* (1979), Lisle A. Rose, *Assault on Eternity: Richard E. Byrd and the Exploration of Antarctica, 1946–47* (1980), Eugene Rodgers, *Beyond the Barrier: The Story of Byrd's First Expedition to Antarctica* (1990), and John H. Bryant and Harold N. Cones, *Dangerous Crossings: The First Modern Polar Expedition, 1925* (2000); obituaries with pors. in *Boston Daily Globe, New York Times,* and *Winchester Evening Star*, all 12 Mar. 1957.

EUGENE RODGERS

BYRD, William (ca. 1652–4 December 1704), merchant, planter, and member of the Council, was born in London, the son of John Byrd, a goldsmith, and Grace Stegge Byrd. His grandfather Thomas Stegge grew wealthy and politically powerful in Virginia during the 1630s and 1640s, and Stegge's namesake son built on what his father had begun. Sometime late in the 1660s Byrd joined his uncle Thomas Stegge in Virginia, and in the spring of 1670 he inherited the bulk of this younger Stegge's estate.

Known in Virginia history as William Byrd I (although he did not so style himself) to distinguish him from his son and grandson of the same name, Byrd became a member of the Henrico County Court and a captain in the militia while still in his twenties. His vision extended principally westward from his residence at the falls of the James River. Byrd became an active Indian trader and explorer. As early as 1671 he was scouting the Piedmont. Both commercial expectations and curiosity about the wilderness may have motivated him, but Byrd took to the woods as if they were his natural habitat. His expeditions took him away from a family he started in 1672 or 1673, when he married Mary Horsmanden Filmer, the daughter of Warham Horsmanden, a Royalist émigré and former member of the governor's Council, and the widow of Samuel Filmer, who in turn was a younger son of Robert Filmer, author of the famed monarchist tract *Patriarcha*

(1680). Their three daughters and two sons included William Byrd (1674–1744), also known as William Byrd II, Byrd's eldest child, namesake, and heir.

Byrd had ties to Nathaniel Bacon (1647–1676) as a neighbor, fellow militia officer, and drinking companion. The two were licensed by Governor Sir William Berkeley in autumn 1675 to trade in furs with western Indians. By March 1676 their operations had been terminated when fighting between the Native Americans and the colonists caused the General Assembly to prohibit regular commercial dealings with the Indians. Susquehannocks killed two of Byrd's men in April, and Bacon experienced a similar loss. Byrd's location at the falls was both vulnerable and strategic enough that the assembly ordered it garrisoned to protect the colony against further incursions, although he was not given the command of the post. After a night of carousing Byrd and two comrades persuaded Bacon to visit an encampment of armed planters who were poised to fight the Indians even without a commission from Berkeley. By assuming command of this expedition Bacon became the leader of what became a rebellion. Byrd's underlying motives may have included disenchantment with a governor who had passed him over, disappointment that he had not been named to the governor's Council, or a desire with Bacon to make up for their suppressed business by seizing a cache of beaver skins that belonged to the Occaneechi, but Byrd also genuinely believed that only an aggressive crusade against the Indians would bring security to the settlers.

Although unhappy with Berkeley and convinced that the colony's safety would best be served by an offensive campaign against the hostile Indian tribes, Byrd proved unwilling to sacrifice his family's welfare by remaining stubbornly loyal to a course of action that would have undoubtedly brought about his personal downfall. He has been criticized for switching sides when the cause that he originally promoted began to ebb. The record, while scant, is compatible with a less judgmental explanation of Byrd's actions. He may well have begun to regret the bold course on which he had helped launch Bacon as soon as he sobered up from their night of fateful camaraderie. Byrd man-

aged to keep himself in the shadows throughout the heated months that followed Bacon's unauthorized expedition against the Occaneechi and Susquehannock Indians in May 1676, and that June Byrd sent his family to safety in England. To what extent Byrd distanced himself from the rebels will probably never be known for certain. He may have abandoned the rebellion only after Bacon died in October, although Byrd later indicated that he had refused to take part after the end of September when Bacon plundered the house of one of the governor's supporters. Although some witnesses contradicted Byrd on this point, he somehow regained Berkeley's favor and by January 1677 was helping the governor round up the last of the rebels.

Byrd showed some skill retreating from the insurrection he had helped to precipitate, but he displayed even greater dexterity at maneuvering in the troubled political waters afterward. He was too shrewd to allow himself to become closely identified with so controversial a figure as Berkeley, especially after the governor and his intimates collided with the royal commissioners sent to Virginia to investigate the causes of the rebellion. Within a month of the commission's arrival Byrd curried favor with its members by informing on two men who had made scandalous remarks about them. The men were fined, and Byrd was poised for advancement.

A new order in provincial politics began with the passing of Bacon and Berkeley from the scene. The Crown responded to the rebellion by diminishing the role of the burgesses, bolstering the authority of the governor, and paying closer attention to Virginia. In this new climate Byrd realized that he had to be more aware and involved in politics at both Jamestown and Whitehall. He won a seat in the House of Burgesses in 1677, representing Henrico County in that year's second session, and soon parlayed his new prominence at the capital into an enhanced position at home. In April or May 1679 he received command over the defense forces at the falls of the James River. By 1680 he was Colonel Byrd, a recognition of his expertise in both commercial and military relations with the Indians. An ally and adviser of Governor Thomas Culpeper, baron Culpeper of Thoresway, Byrd may have helped push through the General Assembly a law giving the governor a permanent salary. The new statute freed the governor from a measure of assembly influence.

On 11 January 1683 Byrd was sworn in as a member of the governor's Council, where he used his knowledge of the frontier and of Native American affairs to help shape policy and appoint agents to deal with the Indians. He had already proved himself to be a swift, ruthless avenger when he retaliated for the murder of a single colonist by killing seven native prisoners from a village whose inhabitants he merely suspected of being guilty. Despite his record, Byrd's reputation did not always shield the men he employed in the Indian trade, for several caravans that he sent out were attacked with resulting losses of lives, goods, and horses. Nevertheless, he persevered and deserves to be remembered as one of the half dozen most important Indian traders of the seventeenth century who exchanged English clothing, farm implements, cookware, and beads for native furs and skins.

Byrd could have easily perceived himself either as an English landed gentleman living in America or as a successful colonial merchant. He fully realized the dreams of immigrants with London mercantile backgrounds who found Virginia, despite its absence of urban centers, to be replete with commercial opportunities. Byrd underwrote the importation of servants and slaves, both to labor in his own fields and for resale to other planters. Over a period of three decades he gained title to almost 30,000 acres of land through purchase, escheat, and patent. More than half of the acreage was amassed through the headright system, with a third of that coming from the importation of African laborers. On the bulk of his land Byrd produced tobacco for shipment on consignment to London merchants. Landing areas along the James River at his plantations in Henrico and later in Charles City County enabled Byrd to operate warehouses and stores that served lesser planters in the interior and added to his own stream of income. In the absence of towns, landing areas functioned as small trading centers usually on or adjacent to a riverside plantation.

Politics provided another avenue to revenue enhancement. Uncompensated public service vied with gainful public employment as valid objectives in the seventeenth century. Service as a burgess, councillor, or militia officer was regarded as a public duty, and incumbents were reimbursed only for expenses. On the other hand the position of auditor-general, which Byrd's uncle had held until his death, was lucrative enough to justify a transatlantic voyage that Byrd made in 1687 primarily to secure the appointment, which gave him responsibility for collecting and accounting for all quitrents and other revenue and fees belonging to the king. Byrd received the combined posts of auditor- and receiver-general on 20 June 1688 and retained them until his death, even though Governor Francis Nicholson and his Council supporters attempted to separate the two offices during the 1690s. Intimations of malfeasance accompanied the separation attempt, but Byrd was probably at least reasonably diligent and honest in his profitable stewardship of the king's revenues. As senior member of the Council, he served as president, or acting governor, from September until 24 October 1700, from April to June 1703, and in August and September 1704. Byrd was also an original trustee of the College of William and Mary.

Building on the wealth of the Stegges, Byrd founded one of the great families of colonial Virginia, but his family life was not typical for a seventeenth-century planter. He wed only once, and the marriage endured until his wife's death in 1699. Mary Byrd appears to have had no offspring from her first marriage, so the Byrd children grew up without the stepbrothers and stepsisters or half siblings common in the complex households characteristic of the region. They did not, however, escape the high incidence of childhood mortality that was prevalent in Virginia. One son died in early childhood, and their daughter Ursula Byrd, who married the historian Robert Beverley (d. 1722), died before her seventeenth birthday, probably as a consequence of childbirth. Long separations characterized the relationship between Byrd and his children. His first son spent more of his early life in England than in Virginia, and one of his daughters married in England and lived thereafter in London.

William Byrd resided at his Westover property in Charles City County during his final years and died there on 4 December 1704. He was buried in the cemetery at old Westover Church.

Death date and age at death of fifty-two on gravestone; Pierre Marambaud, "William Byrd I: A Young Virginia Planter in the 1670s," *VMHB* 81 (1973): 131–150 (por. on 130), and "Colonel William Byrd I: A Fortune Founded on Smoke," *VMHB* 82 (1974): 430–457; John Spencer Bassett, ed., *The Writings of "Colonel William Byrd of Westover in Virginia Esqr."* (1901; repr. 1970), ix–xl; *Byrd Correspondence*, 1:8–191, 2:825–827; presence in Virginia first documented in will of uncle Thomas Stegge, in Prerogative Court of Canterbury, Duke 69; William Byrd Title Book, VHS; contrasting interpretations appear in Martin H. Quitt, "Immigrant Origins of the Virginia Gentry: A Study of Cultural Transmission and Innovation," *WMQ*, 3d ser., 45 (1988): 629–655, and David Hackett Fischer, *Albion's Seed: Four British Folkways in America* (1989), 218; will printed in *VMHB* 48 (1940): 331–334.

MARTIN H. QUITT

BYRD, William (28 March 1674–26 August 1744), member of the Council, writer, and surveyor, was born probably near the falls of the James River in Henrico County, the eldest child of Mary Horsmanden Filmer Byrd and her second husband, William Byrd (ca. 1652–1704). He is usually referred to as William Byrd II (a style that he did not employ) to distinguish him from his father and his only surviving son.

Byrd spent the formative years of his childhood in England. When he was two years old he and his mother temporarily left Virginia to reside with her relatives in Purleigh, Essex County, England. Although Byrd probably returned to Virginia two years later, by the age of seven he was definitely in England in the care of the same relatives, who sent him for nine years to the Felsted School, a prestigious academy in the same shire. He learned Greek and Latin and there probably also acquired his ability to read French, Italian, and Hebrew. After leaving school Byrd worked for tobacco trading companies for two years in London and Rotterdam to learn about commerce and at the same time acquire the social graces of a gentleman. He entered the Middle Temple in 1692 and studied law there for three years while reading widely, attending the theater frequently, and sporting with "naughty jades." Byrd was called to the bar in 1695 and elected to the Royal Society on 29 April 1696, thanks to the patronage of his father's friend Sir Robert Southwell.

These were heady achievements for a young colonial, and one can imagine Byrd's anticipation in the summer of 1696 as he planned his first trip to Virginia in fifteen years. He may well have made the journey with the expectation of staying. The powerful influence of his father and his own superior education helped Byrd win election to the House of Burgesses for the autumn 1696 session, representing Henrico County, but he withdrew from the assembly in October and returned to England to practice law. Although the elder Byrd was undoubtedly disappointed, he accepted his son's decision and drew on his London contacts to assist him. Extended separations had nurtured or reinforced a strong sense of autonomy in Byrd and a commensurate willingness on the part of his father to accommodate it.

In October 1697 the young barrister was admitted to Lincoln's Inn, and two months later he undertook the defense of Governor Sir Edmund Andros, whom Commissary James Blair had charged with impeding the development of the new College of William and Mary. In a hearing over which the bishop of London presided at Lambeth Palace, Byrd was no match for the formidable commissary, who eventually succeeded in having Andros replaced with Francis Nicholson. In October 1698 Byrd obtained appointment as the London agent of the governor's Council, in which position he successfully opposed Nicholson's effort to separate the combined offices of auditor- and receiver-general held by Byrd's father. The breach widened in 1702 after Byrd presented a petition from the General Assembly to the Crown in opposition to Nicholson. The Crown rejected the petition, and Byrd lost his post and failed in a subsequent bid for the influential and lucrative post of secretary of the colony. Although he had learned valuable lessons about court politics, his four years as colonial agent had left him with little to show for either himself or his native country.

At his thirtieth birthday Byrd was unmarried, lacked an official post, and faced uncertain immediate prospects in England. His surviving letters suggest that he was preoccupied with his aristocratic friends and his own mastery of polite manners and wordsmanship. Byrd had learned a great deal about England. A fourteen-week tour in 1701 as the chaperon of Sir John Percival, the eighteen-year-old nephew of Sir Robert Southwell, introduced him to a wide range of clergymen, merchants, borough officials, and country gentlemen. Byrd visited many market towns and indulged his curiosity about the commercial life of these places, as well as their architecture, libraries, and art collections. He took an interest in his father's business and political affairs, but he stretched beyond the older man's world by encircling himself with social types and activities that his father had usually kept on the periphery of his own life.

Early in 1705 Byrd learned of his father's death and returned to Virginia, where he had spent only about five of his thirty-one years, and only a few months during the past quarter century. As principal heir to his father's great estate, Byrd was one of the wealthiest men in the colony, and on 4 May 1706 he married Lucy Parke, the younger legitimate daughter of Daniel Parke, a wealthy man of the world and newly appointed governor of the Leeward Islands, who promised but did not deliver a £1,000 dowry. Parke bequeathed the Byrds the promised marriage portion at his death in 1710, and Byrd then agreed to take over the lands left to his wife's sister in exchange for assuming the debts of the Parke estate. The obligations were much greater than he knew and left him burdened into his old age.

Passion rather than prudence had directed his marital choice, but at that age Byrd seemed incapable of the kind of intimacy that characterizes successful affectionate marriages. Byrd's references to his wife in his diary suggest that she was less of a companion with whom he was emotionally engaged than a subordinate (and sometime insubordinate) figure whom he expected to dominate in the household and in bed. He manifested the same lack of deep attachment in his relationship with their two sons and two daughters. Both sons died in infancy, but neither their lives nor their deaths weighed heavily on Byrd's mind. He was a distant father and husband, psychologically and physically, and often left his family for extended periods on business, political, or social trips. Just as Byrd's father and mother had been willing to send him across the ocean for most of his childhood and early adulthood, he was unwilling or unable to bring his own children and spouse close to himself emotionally even when they resided on the same plantation.

If the prolonged separation from his parents reverberated in the emotional distance Byrd put between himself and his own children, it did not estrange him from his patrimony. He took up his father's estate, but he could not take it for granted that he would be appointed to the offices that his father had held and that he coveted. He secured the post of receiver general, which was separated from the auditorship after his father's death, and in December 1705 he applied for a seat on the governor's Council. Lineage counted, but no colonial post was hereditary. Byrd had to draw on the influence of his and his father's English connections. Nearly four years after initiating the process, he took his seat on the Council on 12 September 1709. He served continuously until his death thirty-five years later.

Nine months after Byrd joined the Council, Lieutenant Governor Alexander Spotswood began his administration. Although Byrd had sought the governorship for himself and was disappointed to be told that he lacked the required military background, he evidently intended to cooperate with Spotswood. They shared a vision of economic and geographic expansion and later discussed a mutual interest in establishing ironworks in Virginia. They moved completely off common ground, however, when the lieutenant governor, over Byrd's opposition, reorganized the collection of quitrents in order to enlarge the royal revenue. Byrd regarded the receiver's office as his own property and Spotswood's actions as a personal affront. Shortly afterward, in March or April 1715 Byrd sailed for England, primarily to take care of some private affairs but with undercutting and removing Spotswood from office undoubtedly high on his transatlantic agenda.

Byrd stayed in London for five years. In November 1716, shortly after his wife joined him in London, she died of smallpox. Symptomatic of his feelings, Byrd began wooing a prospective replacement within two months. He was unsuccessful with several romances until six weeks after his fiftieth birthday, when on 9 May 1724 he married Maria Taylor, the twenty-five-year-old heiress of a Kensington gentleman. Surviving evidence about Byrd's emotional involvement with his second wife and their one son and three daughters is less abundant and less illuminating than about his first.

In England Byrd sold the receiver generalship to a Virginian for £500. The post's profitability had declined, and he found it difficult to manage through a deputy while he remained in England. In 1717 Byrd took credit for the royal veto of two major laws that Spotswood had persuaded the General Assembly to pass, the Tobacco Inspection Act of 1713 and the Indian Trade Act of 1714. The first regulated the quality and distribution of tobacco exports, and the second established a monopoly over commerce with the natives. Both measures were designed to solve longstanding public policy problems, and Byrd's motives very likely flowed more from his personal resentments than from genuine reservations about the merits of the legislation. He eventually proposed himself to serve as the assembly's London agent, and the burgesses first voted to appoint him in May 1718 and then overrode Spotswood's objection by appropriating Byrd's salary that November. The lieutenant governor was not without influence, though, and maneuvered to have Byrd deposed from the Council. The Virginian saved himself only by promising to return to the colony and evidently agreeing to seek a reconciliation with Spotswood.

Byrd returned to Virginia in February 1720, and in April the two men made peace after airing their differences. Byrd viewed himself as representing the people of the colony in both his struggle and his rapprochement with Spotswood. The two men had each given up something and gained something, and neither had succeeded in removing the other. After the accommodation Byrd set sail for England again in the summer of 1721 as paid agent of the burgesses. Some contemporaries believed that he assisted with the removal of Spotswood from office the following year, but Byrd took no credit for Spotswood's dismissal, which resulted largely from the loss of political power by the lieutenant governor's English sponsors.

Byrd remained in England for four and a half years, through most of the administration of Spotswood's successor, Hugh Drysdale. Byrd returned to Virginia the final time in 1726 and resumed attendance at the Council on 28 April. After Drysdale's death in July, Byrd unsuccessfully urged his own patrons in England to nominate him as the next lieutenant governor. Despite the blow this failure dealt to his ambition, he was impressed by Drysdale's successor, William Gooch, with whom he was friendly from the beginning. Gooch appointed Byrd to the joint commission of Virginians and North Carolinians that surveyed the boundary between the two colonies in 1728. Byrd eventually led the Virginia contingent. The lieutenant governor's landmark achievement was passage of the Tobacco Inspection Act of 1730, essentially a reenactment of Spotswood's statute of 1713 that Byrd had had a hand in killing. This time the legislation benefited Byrd directly, for he was one of those whose land was chosen for the construction of a warehouse. The paucity of references to Gooch in Byrd's writings of the 1730s and 1740s and his general preoccupation at this time with private matters rather than public business reflect in part the lieutenant governor's skill at managing the Council.

Byrd showed a continuing interest in land development, public and private. In the autumn of 1733 he conceived the plan to establish what became the cities of Petersburg and Richmond at the falls of the Appomattox and James Rivers, the latter on his own property. Gooch appointed him in September 1736 to a commission to lay out the bounds of the Northern Neck Proprietary. None of the commissioners accompanied the surveyors to their final destination at the headwaters of the Potomac and Rappahannock Rivers, but Byrd wrote the report that was sent to England with the survey in August 1737 and that was ultimately set aside after his death in favor of a finding more in line with the report of a competing commission that Lord Fairfax appointed.

By 1743 Byrd was the senior councillor, but he never had the satisfaction of serving as Council president, or acting governor, as his father had done. Even without that capstone to his career, Byrd was one of the most skillful politicians of his generation and may have had a greater familiarity with the corridors of power in London than any other American. Royal governors could not afford to antagonize him because he had imperial connections and know-how and a proven willingness to go overseas to draw on them. His influence with his fellow Virginia gentry derived from his unique experience and knowledge.

Despite his political influence, Byrd's lasting fame rests more on his personal lifestyle and private writings than it does on his official activities. He was a highly cultivated colonial gentleman who read widely and assembled one of the greatest colonial libraries, consisting of more than 3,500 volumes on history, biography, travel, drama, divinity, architecture, music, philosophy, agriculture, gardening, law, art, science, medicine, and etiquette. The books were written in English, Greek, Latin, French, Italian, Dutch, and Hebrew. Byrd himself wrote in different genres: diaries, letters, poetry, essays, caricatures, histories, and speeches. He experimented with different tones and styles, from the satirical and comically ironic to the serious and imploringly persuasive. Byrd's friends and correspondents in England included some of the most distinguished statesmen, writers, and naturalists. His wide reading was reflected in the cultivated tone of his writings, and the liveliness of his mind found expression in the keen insights and sharp humor of his personal correspondence. Byrd kept a secret diary that was not decoded and published until the twentieth century, but it, together with his other writings, made him the most-written-about Virginian between Captain John Smith and George Washington.

Byrd wrote mostly for his own enjoyment and the amusement or edification of his friends, but he occasionally also wrote for the public. His *Discourse Concerning the Plague, with Some Preservatives against It*, published in London in 1721, touted tobacco as a preventer of infection. Byrd's writings on natural history and "A Journey to the Land of Eden," his account of his 1733 visit to his frontier landholdings, may have been intended to promote immigration to Virginia. For several years he worked on *The History of the Dividing Line betwixt Virginia and North Carolina, Run in the Year of Our Lord 1728* with an eye toward publication. Byrd's most ambitious literary effort, it was based on rough notes that he had kept on the expedition. He intended the artfully crafted narrative for a broad audience, but in a second version, entitled *The Secret History of the Line*, he assigned pseudonyms to members of his party so that he could describe them more frankly. Neither was published in his lifetime, but Byrd's *History of the Dividing Line* has become a classic of early American literature. It may have been a portion or precursor of a larger history of Virginia that does not survive.

During the last decade and a half of his life Byrd devoted himself to rebuilding and improving what has become one of the most important symbols of gentry culture, his plantation at Westover in Charles City County. His father had begun by laying out the best-documented late-seventeenth-century plantation garden, and while Byrd was still in England he befriended the leading botanists of the day, studied natural history, and may have procured English plants for his father. During earlier Virginia residences Byrd enlarged and improved the garden, and after his final return to Virginia he developed a strong attachment to the landscape of his native country. Moreover, his determination to remain in Virginia permanently led him to replace the wooden structure he inherited with a brick mansion, completed by December 1735, that is considered one of the finest American examples of Georgian architecture still standing. There Byrd housed his library and his large collection of portraits, completed his major prose works, and spent much of his time supervising his plantation. At one point he thought that he might have to sell Westover in order to meet his debts, but he was able to discharge them fully before his death.

William Byrd died at Westover on 26 August 1744 and was buried in the garden there.

Birth and death dates on gravestone; Pierre Marambaud, *William Byrd of Westover, 1674–1744* (1971), por. opp. 146; *Byrd Correspondence*, 1:203–442, 2:443–600 (quotation on 474), 827–828; Louis B. Wright and Marion Tinling, eds., *The Secret Diary of William Byrd of Westover, 1709–1712* (1941), and *The London Diary (1717–1721) and Other Writings* (1958); Maude H. Woodfin and Tinling, eds., *Another Secret Diary of William Byrd of Westover, 1739–1741, With Letters and Literary Exercises, 1696–1726* (1942); Wright, ed., *The Prose Works of William Byrd of Westover: Narratives of a Colonial Virginian* (1966); Kevin Berland, Jan Kirsten Gilliam, and Kenneth A. Lockridge, eds., *The Commonplace Book of William Byrd II of Westover* (2001); Northern Neck boundary commission report in Thomas H. Wynne, ed., *History of the Dividing Line and Other Tracts, from the Papers of William Byrd* (1866), 2:83–139; David Meschutt, "William Byrd and His Portrait Collection," *Journal of Early Southern Decorative Arts* 14 (May 1988): 18–46; Kevin J. Hayes, *The Library of William Byrd of Westover* (1997); Margaret Beck Pritchard and Virginia Lascara Sites, *William Byrd II and His Lost History: Engravings of the Americas* (1993); leading interpretations include Wright, *The First Gentlemen of Virginia: Intellectual Qualities of the Early Colonial Ruling Class* (1940), 312–347, Marambaud, "William Byrd of Westover: Cavalier, Diarist, and Chronicler," *VMHB* 78 (1970): 144–183, Michael Zuckerman, "William Byrd's Family," *Perspectives in American History* 12 (1979): 255–311, Kenneth A. Lockridge, *The Diary, and Life, of William Byrd II of Virginia, 1674–1744* (1987), and Paula A. Treckel, "'The Empire of My Heart': The Marriage of William Byrd II and Lucy Parke Byrd," *VMHB* 105 (1997): 125–156.

Martin H. Quitt

BYRD, William (6 September 1728–1 or 2 January 1777), member of the Council, was born and raised at Westover in Charles City County, the only son of William Byrd (1674–1744) and his second wife, Maria Taylor Byrd. His indulgent parents raised him in a style that few upper-class Virginians could match. With a 3,500-volume library and numerous servants at Westover, among the most beautiful of Virginia's eighteenth-century mansions, Byrd had his every wish granted. His father appears to have been attentive to Byrd. He played billiards and cards and bowled with his son and even ran with him at least once, on 21 February 1740, when the elder Byrd was nearly sixty-six.

Known in many Virginia histories as William Byrd III, although it is a style he did not himself use, Byrd was educated with his sisters and some children from neighboring planter families at a school on the Westover estate. His father provided him with books as well as laboratory equipment such as telescopes, a barometer, a thermometer, and a vacuum pump. The elder Byrd had spent most of his first three decades in England, but he did not send his own son abroad to be educated. A mother who could not bear to part with him and fear of smallpox kept the young man in Virginia until after his father's death in 1744. About two years later he went to London to study law at the Middle Temple. Contemporary comments on Byrd's English sojourn highlight his pursuit of pleasure rather than knowledge. He evidently succumbed to many of the dissipations popular with young men of rank and fortune in London, including gambling, a weakness that plagued him throughout his life.

Byrd had returned to Virginia by 14 April 1748, when he married Elizabeth Hill Carter, a member of another of Virginia's great colonial families. They had four sons and one daughter. In the early years of their marriage the young couple probably lived at Belvidere, a mansion overlooking the falls of the James River that he either built or refurbished. Byrd's mother remained at Westover, where she died in 1771.

The young man assumed enormous responsibilities. Not yet twenty-one when he married, Byrd soon gained full control of an estate that included more than 179,000 acres, hundreds of slaves, and numerous mills, fisheries, vessels, warehouses, and a store. Even though he employed business and farm managers, the estate required complicated coordination. Byrd also assumed all of the other roles an upper-class Virginian was expected to fill. In early adulthood he was a justice of the peace in both Halifax and Charles City Counties, where he owned land, and he also served as county lieutenant in Halifax County. In 1752 Byrd was elected to the House of Burgesses from Lunenburg County and served until 1754, when he was appointed to the governor's Council, a post he held until its last meeting in May 1775. Because of his father's experience Byrd was considered knowledgeable on Native American affairs, and in 1756 he and Peter Randolph represented the colony in negotiations with the Catawba and Cherokee Indians in South Carolina. In all of these posts he appears to have served actively and responsibly.

But Byrd could not live within his income, and as early as 1755 he was in dire financial straits. He conveyed his estate in 1756 to seven trustees, who by 1767 had reportedly sold land and slaves worth £40,000, a huge sum that still did not pay off his debts. The total of the debt cannot be accurately calculated, but in 1768 Byrd resorted to a lottery, the prizes for which were to come from the bulk of his estate at the falls of the James River, valued at £56,796. He vainly hoped to raise £50,000 from the sale of tickets in Virginia and England. Byrd sold additional lands, mortgaged slaves and all of the Westover silver, and finally sold for £15,500 the English estate that he had inherited from his mother. Even these efforts did not cover his debts, some of which burdened the Byrd estate well into the nineteenth century.

Byrd's ability to incur such a vast debt before his thirtieth birthday is difficult to explain. Gambling was certainly a major factor. He reportedly lost £10,000 to the duke of Cumberland in one evening in London. A French visitor to Williamsburg describing the popularity of gaming at a tavern in 1765 remarked that Byrd was "never happy but when he has the box and Dices in hand" and added that Byrd had "reduced himself to that Degree by gameing, that few or nobody will Credit him for Ever so small a sum of money." Even after putting his estate in the hands of trustees Byrd continued to spend freely, perhaps because his income, though reduced, remained substantial. Thanks to his status and polish as the head of a distinguished family, a member of the Council, and a handsome gentleman with elegant manners, his friends found him difficult to deal with firmly until it was too late. They generally conceded that he wanted to pay his debts and had a sense of honor and justice, but as Lieutenant Governor Francis Fauquier observed, "his Failing is want of Circumspection and Steadiness."

Debt was not Byrd's only problem. By the mid-1750s his marriage was failing, and in the summer of 1756 a report circulated that he had repudiated his wife. After turning his estate over to the trustees and sending his three eldest children to England in the care of an uncle and aunt, Byrd volunteered for service under John Campbell, earl of Loudoun, then commander of British forces

in North America during the war with France. Byrd did not see his wife again. After writing him affectionate letters that begged him to return, Elizabeth Byrd died on 25 July 1760, a probable suicide.

With one brief exception Byrd was in military service from 1756 until 1761. He served in Nova Scotia, the Carolinas, Virginia, and Pennsylvania. Byrd used his early experience with Indians to recruit them for service against the French. In 1758 he became colonel of the 2d Virginia Regiment, and the following year he succeeded George Washington as commander of the 1st Virginia Regiment. After an abortive campaign against the Cherokee, Byrd resigned his command in September 1761. During his years of military service he never saw battle but served ably, experienced great hardship, and managed to spend large amounts of his own money. Even in the field Byrd supported a costly table that would have done honor to a general. When he was in Pittsburgh in 1759, for example, his mother hired a wagon and sent him eleven dozen bottles of wine and a great deal of coffee, tea, French brandy, English soap, sweetmeats, fine chocolate, and sugar.

While in winter quarters in Philadelphia in 1760 Byrd met Mary Willing, a daughter of Charles Willing, a prominent local merchant and former mayor of the city. They were married on 29 January 1761. At first the Byrds lived in a house he built in Philadelphia, but they had moved to Westover by the autumn of 1762 and spent the remainder of their married life there. They had four sons and six daughters. Byrd resumed his seat on the Council, took an active role in the management of his business affairs, and worked to pay off his debts and provide for his children. In addition to producing large amounts of tobacco, he offered 11,000 bushels of wheat for sale in 1770 alone, and he also operated a lead mine in southwestern Virginia, an iron forge near Richmond, and other profitable ventures. Byrd proved difficult to deal with in business matters. He once refused to pay George Washington rent on a property in Williamsburg and swore at the latter's agent. When John Beale, the manager of Byrd's iron forge, resigned and tried to collect the money owed him, Byrd rudely refused to pay, and Beale found himself unable to sue Byrd because no attorney would take a case against so prominent a member of the Council.

Byrd's later life was not easy. Almost every year someone commented on his desperate circumstances. When an audit disclosed in 1766 that John Robinson (1705–1766), the Speaker of the House of Burgesses and treasurer of Virginia, had illegally lent more than £100,000 of paper money to prominent friends and acquaintances, the colony's leaders learned that Byrd had received the largest amount—£14,921. And things only got worse. He was unable to retire his debts; the lottery was largely a failure; two of his sons ran amok at the College of William and Mary, destroyed property, and threatened the institution's president; and the death of his mother in 1771 left him owing £5,000 to his children by his first wife.

Byrd continued to enjoy a very expensive lifestyle and does not seem to have denied himself or his family in any way. He dispensed lavish hospitality, raced blooded horses, and purchased expensive British army and navy commissions for three of his sons, one of whom he sent off with a riding chair, horses, and a servant. Byrd purchased a house in Williamsburg, hired tutors, and in 1773 bought a new chariot. His life was luxurious but not idle. He apparently worked hard, continued trying to increase his income, and sold some of his eastern land in order to acquire property farther west. He also remained active in public affairs and unsuccessfully sought appointment as secretary of the colony.

On 6 July 1774 a thoroughly unhappy Byrd made his will, disposing of an estate that "thro' my own folly and inattention to accounts the carelessness of some intrusted with the management thereof and the vilany of others, is still greatly incumbered with Debts which imbitters every moment of my Life." The political difficulties between Virginia and the mother country also disturbed him. He had little sympathy with "the frantick patriotism" of many Virginia leaders and urged a moderate approach and continued loyalty to the Crown. On 30 July 1775 he wrote to his old commander, Sir Jeffery Amherst, offering his services to the king and

stating that he still hoped to convince his countrymen of the error of their ways.

In November 1775, however, the royal governor of Virginia offered freedom to slaves who ran away and joined the fight against the Virginia revolutionaries. That proved too much for many moderates, including Byrd, who in December unsuccessfully sought the post of colonel of the 3d Virginia Regiment. On 25 February 1776 Landon Carter heard that Byrd was "going to the Congress to solicit an appointment to be Majr. Genl." If he went to Philadelphia, nothing came of his efforts. On 1 or 2 January 1777 William Byrd, an embittered forty-eight-year-old man, took his own life at Westover. His will directed that he be buried in the cemetery of old Westover Church.

William H. Gaines Jr., "That Wayward Spendthrift: William Byrd the Third, Prodigal Son," *Virginia Cavalcade* 1 (winter 1951): 44–47 (por.); *Byrd Correspondence*, esp. 2:615–821 (fifth quotation on 814), 828–830 (epitaph with 1 Jan. 1777 death date on 614); Marion Tinling, ed., "Some Unpublished Correspondence of William Byrd III," *VMHB* 88 (1980): 277–300; Byrd family Bible notes, New York Public Library; Jane Carson, *Colonial Virginians at Play* (1965), 51, 114, 116, 124, 258; "Autobiography of David Meade," *WMQ*, 1st ser., 13 (1904): 90–94 (with cause of death); PRO T 79/9; "Journal of a French Traveller in the Colonies, 1765," *AHR* 26 (1921): 742 (first and second quotations); George H. Reese, ed., *The Official Papers of Francis Fauquier, Lieutenant Governor of Virginia, 1758–1768* (1980–1983), third quotation on 2:513; Jack P. Greene, ed., *The Diary of Colonel Landon Carter, 1752–1778* (1965), sixth quotation on 2:989; will (fourth quotation), account of estate sale, and 2 Jan. 1777 death date in *Byrd* v. *Byrd* (1838), U.S. Circuit Court, Virginia District, Ended Cases (restored, box 26), LVA; will printed in *VMHB* 9 (1901): 85–88; undated death notice in *Williamsburg Virginia Gazette* (Dixon and Hunter), 3 Jan. 1777; death noted "Yesterday morning, after a short illness," in supplement to *Williamsburg Virginia Gazette* (Purdie), 3 Jan. 1777.

EMORY G. EVANS

BYRNE, Benjamin Wilson (16 May 1820–12 September 1903), member of the Convention of 1861, was born near Burnsville, in that part of Lewis County that became Braxton County in 1836. He was the son of John B. Byrne, a farmer, and Anne Haymond Byrne, whose grandfather served as a colonel in Dunmore's War. Byrne's early education was limited to attending a subscription school during the winter months, but he received enough instruction to prepare him, at age twenty, for enrollment in Rector College near Pruntytown, in Taylor County. After two years of study he left college to enter a private law school in Staunton operated by its founder Lucas Powell Thompson, a judge on the General Court. On 18 September 1849 Byrne married Mary Louisa Holt, daughter of a Methodist minister. They had four daughters, and of their two sons, William E. R. Byrne was a notable West Virginia lawyer, and George Byrne became editor of the *Charleston Gazette*. Mary Holt Byrne's brother Homer A. Holt joined Byrne's law practice in 1853 and much later in his career was appointed to the West Virginia Supreme Court of Appeals.

In 1848, the same year that he completed law school, Byrne was elected from the district of Braxton, Gilmer, and Lewis Counties to a term in the House of Delegates, where he served on the Committee to Examine the Register's Office. Almost a decade later, in December 1857, he returned to the House of Delegates representing the district of Braxton and Nicholas Counties and serving on the Committee of Propositions and Grievances. In addition to politics and law, Byrne was alert to promising business opportunities. In December 1857 he joined fellow lawyer Johnson Newlon Camden in purchasing several tracts of land in Braxton County. By 1858 the two men had acquired more than 20,000 acres in that county alone. The partners soon became interested in oil speculation. In December 1860 the firm of Camden, Byrne, and Company, which also included Gideon Draper Camden, a member of the Convention of 1850–1851, began drilling in Wirt County. Late in January 1861 Byrne was among the jubilant bystanders when oil erupted in a black geyser high above the derrick, guaranteeing profits for the owners and igniting a blaze of speculation that spread to both sides of the upper Ohio Valley.

Shortly after the oil strike, Byrne was elected on 4 February 1861 to represent the counties of Braxton, Clay, Nicholas, and Webster at a state convention, scheduled to open in Richmond on 13 February, to consider Virginia's response to the secession crisis. Byrne, a moderate Unionist, made no major speeches but voted against disunion on 4 April and again on 17 April, when

the convention approved the measure. When the statewide referendum was held on 23 May, however, Byrne's constituents voted to secede and join the Confederacy. On 14 June he reversed his position and added his signature to the Ordinance of Secession.

While Virginia prepared for war, Byrne and Johnson Camden continued to expand their business interests. On 15 March 1861 the General Assembly enacted a statute incorporating the Burning Springs and Oil Line Railroad Company, with Camden and Byrne listed among those authorized to accept stock subscriptions. By July, however, the war was inhibiting their business operations. During the conflict Byrne served as a niter officer and later as an enrolling officer at Staunton.

After the war Byrne settled in Clay County, West Virginia. His return was probably assisted by Johnson Camden, who led efforts to enfranchise those persons who had been disenfranchised for their roles in the Southern rebellion. Camden, who was destined to have an enormous influence on the economic development of the state, was most likely also instrumental in his former partner's return to the oil business, and Byrne resumed petroleum speculation at several sites in West Virginia.

Byrne also resumed his political career and represented Clay and Nicholas Counties in the West Virginia Constitutional Convention of 1872. During the proceedings he chaired the Committee on County Organization and assisted in drafting the constitutional provisions for a public school system. From 4 March 1873 to 3 March 1877 Byrne was state superintendent of free schools, and in 1882 he ran successfully as a Democratic candidate for a Kanawha County seat in the West Virginia Senate. During the 1883 session he chaired the Committee on Free Schools, and during the 1885 session he became chairman of the Committee on Finance. A popular speaker on the campaign trail, Byrne was remembered by one colleague as a walking encyclopedia.

After his political career ended, Byrne pursued other interests. In 1891 he sat on the executive board of the West Virginia Historical and Antiquarian Society, and the following year the governor appointed him to oversee the transfer of land records from Virginia. He was also a regent for the West Virginia Colored Institute (later West Virginia State College), established in March 1891. Benjamin Wilson Byrne died on 12 September 1903 in Charleston, West Virginia, and was buried at nearby Spring Hill Cemetery.

Encyclopaedia of Contemporary Biography of West Virginia (1894), 116–118; W. S. Laidley, *History of Charleston and Kanawha County, West Virginia, and Representative Citizens* (1911), 895–896; William Alexander MacCorkle, *The Recollections of Fifty Years of West Virginia* (1928), 146; Festus P. Summers, *Johnson Newlon Camden: A Study in Individualism* (1937), 58, 67, 73, 85–87, 90, 92, 104–105; *Weston Herald*, 11 Feb. 1861; Reese and Gaines, *Proceedings of 1861 Convention,* 3:163, 4:144; obituary in *Charleston Daily Mail*, 14 Sept. 1903.

RANDALL S. GOODEN

C

CABANISS, Sarah "Sadie" Heath (9 October 1865–11 July 1921), nurse, was born in Petersburg, the daughter of Charles J. Cabaniss, a retired lawyer, and Virginia Elizabeth Heath Cabaniss. Sadie Cabaniss, as she was called, grew up at Bothwell, the family residence in Dinwiddie County. After studying French, German, and Latin at home, she entered Mount Pisgah Academy in King William County at age twelve. Cabaniss wanted to go on to Vassar College after she graduated from the academy at the age of sixteen, but her parents, holding traditional views about the education of young women, sent her instead to Saint Timothy's School in Stevenson, Maryland. She taught as a governess near Tappahannock for one year and then returned to Mount Pisgah as an instructor for the next three years. Cabaniss never married, but about 1886 she informally adopted a nine-year-old child, Emily Baskerville, whom she raised and educated for the next ten years.

Despite the objections of her parents Cabaniss entered the nursing program at the Johns Hopkins University and graduated in 1893. She was the night superintendent at Johns Hopkins Hospital for one year, and then in 1894 she moved to Richmond to work at Old Dominion Hospital. Six months later the hospital's doctors chose Cabaniss to reorganize the hospital and begin a training school for nurses. The Old Dominion Hospital School for Nurses opened under her supervision in April 1895, and the first class of nine students graduated two years later. Cabaniss was offended that Virginians had to rely on northern nursing schools to obtain enough nurses to meet the needs of hospitals and private nursing calls, and she urged state residents to do better. She was particularly concerned about medical care for the poor and encouraged her nursing students to undertake volunteer work at the homes of patients. Cabaniss sent her students to staff Old Dominion Hospital and Sheltering Arms Hospital in Richmond and also to work in rest homes,

orphanages, the city's free dispensary, and the hospital at the R. E. Lee Camp Confederate Soldiers' Home. The school opened a dispensary for white women and children during its first year of operation. Cabaniss also proposed a system of visiting nursing for patients who were unable to afford private duty nurses but unwilling to accept charitable care.

A formidable personality who insisted on rigid discipline and required her students to be models of neatness, order, and sobriety, Cabaniss also had the gift of inspiring pupils to follow her lead. The members of Old Dominion's class of 1900 devoted themselves to care for the poor. They acquired a house in Richmond, and each committed one day and several evenings a week to charity nursing among both white and black patients of all religious denominations. The visiting nurses also established boys' and girls' clubs for children and nursing and cooking classes for women on the model of the Henry Street Settlement in New York City and the visiting nursing program in Norfolk. The Virginia legislature incorporated the Nurses' Settlement on 14 February 1901. Cabaniss resigned from Old Dominion Hospital on 8 April of that year and in the autumn joined the Nurses' Settlement. She served as its director for eight years.

The city of Richmond provided $150 to the Nurses' Settlement during its first year of operation, but the members had to rent out rooms and kitchen space to raise money for their expenses. In December 1901 the Woman's Club of Richmond invited the settlement to explain its mission at a meeting, and as a consequence Lila Meade Valentine and several other members established the Instructive Visiting Nurse Association (IVNA) in February 1902 to support and expand the activities of the settlement. Cabaniss encouraged her colleagues to begin visiting nurse programs in Danville, Leesburg, and Newport News. In 1904 she helped organize the first tuberculosis dispensaries in Virginia, with separate clinics established for white and black patients in Richmond after the city's board of health assumed responsibility in 1906. In 1909 the IVNA won permission from the city of Richmond to place the first official nurse in a public school.

In 1901 Cabaniss became the first president of the Virginia State Association of Nurses (after 1905 the Graduate Nurses Association of Virginia and still later the Virginia Nurses' Association). She served in this post until she became honorary president in 1905. The association worked for passage of a law that in 1903 made Virginia one of the first four states to regulate nursing. Cabaniss chaired the State Board of Examiners of Graduate Nurses for its first nine years. Although she supported allowing African American women to become registered nurses, she agreed with the Graduate Nurses Association's decision in 1907 to restrict membership to whites.

Cabaniss was second vice president of the Nurses' Associated Alumnae of the United States in 1907 when it held its annual meeting in Richmond. Two years later personal health problems led her to resign from both the Nurses' Settlement and the IVNA and to exchange positions with a rural public health nurse in Hanover County in the hope that leaving the city would improve her health. Cabaniss returned to Saint Timothy's in Maryland as a school nurse, but while there in the spring of 1911 she suffered an emotional collapse and was hospitalized in a sanatorium for two and a half years.

In the winter of 1915 Cabaniss moved to Saint Augustine, Florida, where the King's Daughters employed her as a visiting nurse. She began the Neil Neighborhood House Auxiliary, taught domestic science and child care, and organized a kindergarten. In 1916 Cabaniss left Florida to organize public health nurses in North Carolina, and in 1918 she was appointed public health nurse for Port Wentworth, Georgia, a new industrial city that grew up near Savannah during World War I.

After the war Cabaniss returned to Virginia and worked as a school nurse at Foxcroft School in Loudoun County. In 1920 she became a public health nurse in Westmoreland County, where Emily Baskerville Chinn and her family lived.

When her health failed again the following winter, Cabaniss moved into Chinn's home. Her condition deteriorated, and her brother and sister took her into their home in Petersburg for a few weeks before moving her to Westbrook Sanatorium in Richmond. Sarah "Sadie" Heath Cabaniss died there of an acute kidney inflammation on 11 July 1921 and was buried in Blandford Cemetery in Petersburg.

In 1926 the graduate nurses of Virginia endowed a chair in Cabaniss's honor at the University of Virginia, and two years later the university's Department of Education established the Cabaniss Memorial School of Nursing Education. Until 1954 the school offered graduate courses in nursing education. The Medical College of Virginia dedicated Cabaniss Hall in 1928. In May 2001 Cabaniss was among the inaugural class inducted into the Virginia Nursing Hall of Fame.

Anne F. Parsons, "Sadie Heath Cabaniss, Virginia's Pioneer Nurse," *Bits of News From Headquarters: Graduate Nurses' Association of Virginia* 8 (Mar. 1940): 35–41 (gives 1863 birth date); Nannie J. Minor, "Sadie Heath Cabaniss: A Pioneer Nurse in Virginia," Medical College of Virginia *Bulletin* 25 (Jan. 1928): 17–20, reprinted in Virginia Iota State Organization of the Delta Kappa Gamma Society, *Adventures in Teaching: Pioneer Women Educators and Influential Teachers* (1963), 156–160; BVS Birth Register, Dinwiddie Co. (variant birthplace and birth date of 9 Nov. 1865); James Rives Childs, *Reliques of the Rives (Ryves)* (1929), 640, and BVS Death Certificate, Henrico Co., give birth date of 9 Oct. 1865; Cabaniss documents in Instructive Visiting Nurse Association Papers and Virginia Nurses' Association Archives, MCV; Charles R. Robins, "Beginnings in Nursing Education under Sadie Heath Cabaniss at the Old Dominion Hospital," Medical College of Virginia *Bulletin* 25 (Feb. 1929): 3–7 (frontispiece por.); Grace Erickson, "Southern Initiative in Public Health Nursing: The Founding of the Nurses' Settlement and Instructive Visiting Nurse Association of Richmond, Virginia, 1900–1910," *Journal of Nursing History* 3 (1987): 17–29; Hummel and Smith, *Portraits and Statuary*, 18 (por.); obituary in *Petersburg Evening Progress*, 12 July 1921; death notice in *Richmond Times-Dispatch*, 12 July 1921; editorial tribute in *Richmond News Leader*, 19 July 1921; memorials in *American Journal of Nursing* 21 (1921): 843, and *Johns Hopkins Nurses Alumnae Magazine* (Feb. 1927): 2, 4–8.

MARY CARROLL JOHANSEN

CABELL, Benjamin William Sheridan (10 May 1793–19 April 1862), member of the Convention of 1829–1830, was born in Buckingham County, the son of Joseph Cabell (1762–1831) and Pocahontas Rebecca Bolling Cabell. A member of the class of 1807 at Hampden-Sydney College, he later studied law but never practiced. In 1811 Cabell moved with his parents' family to Kentucky but soon returned to Virginia with an aunt and uncle, and by 1814 he was living in Campbell County. On 16 December 1816 he married Sarah Epes Doswell, of Nottoway County. They had seven sons, three daughters, and one other child who died in infancy.

In 1817 Cabell moved to Pittsylvania County and quickly emerged as one of its leading citizens. Three years later he acquired Bridgewater plantation just outside Danville. He and William F. Lewis constructed a large mill for flour, corn, and oil that operated until a flood destroyed it in 1850. Cabell was a promoter of the Danville Manufacturing Company, formed in 1828. He founded the *Danville Reporter*, the town's first newspaper, in 1831 and published it until 1840. Cabell supported the construction of the Danville Canal and represented the town at a railroad convention in Richmond in 1836. He served in 1833 on Danville's first common council. By 1860 the value of Cabell's land and approximately forty slaves was about $25,000.

Cabell represented Pittsylvania County in the House of Delegates for three consecutive terms from 1823 to 1826, for the 1829–1830 session, and for a fifth term in 1838. During these sessions he served on the Committees for Courts of Justice, on Executive Expenditures, on Finance, and on Militia Laws. From 1830 to 1833 he served in the Senate of Virginia from the district comprising Henry, Patrick, and Pittsylvania Counties. Cabell received one vote for Speaker of the Senate in 1831 and eight votes in 1832. He served on the Committees on Internal Improvements and on Privileges and Elections and on a joint committee to examine the Bank of Virginia and the Farmers' Bank of Virginia.

In May 1829 Cabell was one of four delegates elected to represent Franklin, Henry, Patrick, and Pittsylvania Counties in a state constitutional convention. Like many other western Piedmont delegates, Cabell believed that his region was underrepresented in the General Assembly and therefore joined with delegates from the Valley and the western counties in advocating an extension of the suffrage and reapportionment based on the state's white population. Both as a member of the Committee on the Executive Department and on the convention floor Cabell consistently pushed these changes and voted with reformers more than 80 percent of the time. During the convention he occasionally spoke in support of these efforts and offered one resolution on judicial reform. When the final, basically conservative document was presented to the convention for passage, however, Cabell broke with western reformers and voted with eastern delegates to approve the new constitution, which the electorate subsequently adopted.

Cabell was also active in the militia. During the War of 1812 he had been commissioned an ensign and served on the staffs of Brigadier General Joel Leftwich and Major General John Pegram. He was promoted to colonel in 1817. In 1830 the assembly elected Cabell a brigadier general and in 1843 promoted him to major general. He held this commission until the militia act of 1858 voided all general officers' commissions. When the Civil War began Cabell worked tirelessly to obtain commissions for his sons and vainly hoped for the restoration of his own commission as general. The citizens of Pittsylvania County honored him by calling the local volunteer company the Cabell Guards. One of his sons, William Lewis Cabell, became a Confederate brigadier general, and another, George Craighead Cabell, became a lieutenant colonel and later served for twelve years in the House of Representatives. Cabell's health rapidly declined after he learned of the death of his youngest son at Chimborazo Hospital in Richmond in March 1862. Benjamin William Sheridan Cabell died at his home in Pittsylvania County on 19 April 1862. He was buried in Old Grove Street Cemetery in Danville.

Brown, *Cabells*, 252, 511–521 (with birth and death dates); Mary Mackenzie Mack, *History of the Old Grove Cemetery, Danville, Virginia* (1939), 29–30; George W. Dame, *Historical Sketch of the Roman Eagle Lodge, . . . Danville, Va., 1820–1895* (1895), 112–113, giving year of birth as 1792 and death date of 19 Mar. 1862; some 1861 Cabell letters in Governor's Office, Letters Received, RG 3, LVA, and of various dates in several collections, VHS; L. Beatrice W. Hairston, *A Brief History of Danville, Virginia, 1728–1954* (1955), 5–129; Alfred J. Morrison, *College of Hampden*

Sidney: Dictionary of Biography, 1776–1825 [1921], 143–144; *Journal of 1829–1830 Convention*, 296; *Proceedings and Debates of 1829–1830 Convention*, esp. 762–763, 816, 859, 874–875, 882–883; Bruce, *Rhetoric of Conservatism*, 37; Catlin, *Convention of 1829–30* (por.); Militia Commission Papers, RG 3, LVA; Census and Slave Schedule, Pittsylvania Co., 1860.

TRENTON E. HIZER

CABELL, Frederick Mortimer (15 December 1802–2 March 1873), member of the Convention of 1861, was born at Struman, the Nelson County plantation of his father, Frederick Cabell. His mother, Alice Winston Cabell, died when he was eleven years old. His paternal grandfather John Cabell served in the Convention of 1776. Cabell attended Washington College (later Washington and Lee University) during the 1824–1825 session. On 14 March 1846 he married Clara Hawes Coleman, of Nelson County. They had five sons and three daughters.

Cabell represented Nelson County in the House of Delegates as a member of the Whig Party from 1842 through 1846. He served on the Committee of Schools and Colleges from 1842 to 1844, the Committee to Examine the Executive Expenditures in the 1845–1846 session, and the Committee on Agriculture and Manufactures from 1844 through 1846 and chaired the last committee for the 1844–1845 session. In 1851 Cabell narrowly won election to the Senate of Virginia by defeating Democrat James Powell, a two-term delegate from Amherst County. Representing the district composed of Amherst, Buckingham, and Nelson Counties, Cabell served in the Senate from 1852 to 1853 and sat on the Committee on Agriculture and Commerce and the Joint Committee to Examine the Second Auditor's Office.

A successful planter, Cabell by 1860 owned about $49,000 in real estate and $53,000 in personal property, including sixty slaves. On 4 February 1861 he defeated John Howard McCue by a vote of 699 to 229 to represent the county in the state convention called to deal with the secession crisis. Cabell's participation in the convention was uneven. According to pay records he attended the entire session, but on thirty-one days, including the initial vote on secession on 4 April, he failed to vote. Cabell did not introduce any resolutions or make any speeches, except to present instructions from his Nelson County con-

stituents. Passed at a public meeting on 25 March 1861, they demonstrated a marked change in the attitudes of the people who had elected him. At the meeting McCue called for secession, and those in attendance unanimously adopted a resolution stating that Virginia, "having done all that she can or ought to do, consistently with her honor, to preserve the Union," should immediately secede. As instructed, on 17 April 1861 Cabell voted to secede from the Union, and he signed the Ordinance of Secession.

Cabell attended the less momentous June and November meetings of the convention but held no other public office and took no other part in the Civil War. During the conflict he lost about half of his real estate and almost all of his personal property, much of which had included slaves. Still, he retained taxable real estate worth more than $20,000 and therefore had to apply for a presidential pardon, which he received on 25 October 1865. Frederick Mortimer Cabell died at Struman in Nelson County on 2 March 1873 and was probably buried there.

Birth and death dates in Brown, *Cabells*, 264, 266, 588; *Catalogue of the Officers and Alumni of Washington and Lee University, Lexington, Virginia, 1749–1888* (1888), 77; Nelson Co. Marriage Register; *Daily Richmond Enquirer*, 9 Apr. 1846 (giving variant marriage date of 24 Mar. 1846); Census, Nelson Co., 1860, 1870; Personal Property Tax Returns, Nelson Co., 1859–1861, RG 48, LVA; *Lynchburg Virginian*, 15 Dec. 1851; *Lynchburg Daily Virginian*, 7 Feb. 1861; Reese and Gaines, *Proceedings of 1861 Convention*, 2:503 (quotation), 3:163, 4:144; Presidential Pardons; obituaries in *Richmond Daily Whig*, 5 Mar. 1873, *Lynchburg Daily Virginian*, 6 Mar. 1873, and *Richmond Daily Enquirer*, 7 Mar. 1873.

JOHN G. DEAL

CABELL, George Craighead (25 January 1836–23 June 1906), member of the House of Representatives, was born in Danville, the son of Sarah Epes Doswell Cabell and Benjamin William Sheridan Cabell, who became a general in the militia and served in the Convention of 1829–1830. He was educated at the Danville Academy and studied law during the 1856–1857 academic year at the University of Virginia. Cabell returned to Danville and on 20 July 1857 was licensed to practice law in Pittsylvania County. From 1858 to 1861 he was commonwealth's attorney for the city and editor of the *Danville Republican*, which became the

Danville Democratic Appeal. On 25 October 1859 Cabell married Mary Harrison Baird, of Brunswick County. Three of their five sons and two of their three daughters lived to adulthood.

On 25 May 1861 Cabell was commissioned a major of the 18th Regiment Virginia Volunteers. He saw action at the First Battle of Manassas (Bull Run) and at Seven Pines. In a letter written from Danville in June 1862, Cabell petitioned the Confederate secretary of war for the command of a proposed military post at Danville, but nothing came of the request. At Hagerstown, Maryland, on 14 September 1862 he led the 18th Virginia to the summit of South Mountain amid intense Union fire. This action blocked the advance of the United States Army until nightfall, but heavy losses forced the regiment to retreat. Cabell was shot in the face and seriously wounded on 16 May 1864 at Drewry's Bluff. He was promoted to lieutenant colonel on 21 July, but by then he had returned to Danville, his military career finished. Cabell's elder brother William Lewis Cabell became a brigadier general in the Confederate army.

Cabell resumed his law practice and became involved in politics. In November 1874 he was elected as a Democrat to the first of six consecutive terms in the United States House of Representatives from the Fifth Congressional District, which consisted of Danville and the counties of Carroll, Floyd, Franklin, Grayson, Halifax, Henry, Patrick, and Pittsylvania. In 1880 he narrowly defeated John T. Stovall, a Readjuster whose unsuccessful challenge of the outcome charged that Cabell's campaign had used fraud and intimidation to reduce the African American vote on which Readjusters relied. Cabell was a sponsor in 1883 of a campaign tract called the Danville Circular that denounced the Readjusters and African Americans who had won election to Danville's city council. Three days before elections for the General Assembly took place that year, violence erupted on the streets of Danville. Several men were killed, and Cabell intervened to prevent a group of white men from murdering a black Readjuster. Cabell and the Democrats exploited this so-called Danville Riot to discredit the Readjusters, and the Democratic Party regained control of the General Assembly.

Cabell did not often speak at length in Congress, but he was a determined opponent of Republican tariff policies and taxes on southern industries, specifically tobacco and whiskey. In a long and impassioned speech delivered in Congress on 29 May 1876 he excoriated the Republicans for taxing southern products while letting northern manufacturers escape paying their share. Cabell served on the Committee on War Claims during his first two terms. He joined the Committee on Railways and Canals during his second term and became its chair in 1879 during his third term. Cabell sat on the Committee on Invalid Pensions during his fourth term, and during his fifth he was a member of both the Committee on Pacific Railroads and the housekeeping Committee on Ventilation and Acoustics. During his final term he remained on the Committee on Pacific Railroads and gained a seat on the influential Committee on Appropriations. Cabell lost his bid for reelection to a seventh term to Republican John Robert Brown in 1886.

Cabell's wife died on 30 October 1891. On 2 November 1892 he married Ellen Virginia Ashton, of Portsmouth, who died in 1904. They had no children. George Craighead Cabell died on 23 June 1906 in Union Protestant Infirmary in Baltimore, where he had gone for gallstone surgery. He was buried in Green Hill Cemetery in Danville.

Brown, *Cabells*, 513, 519–520; BVS Marriage Register, Brunswick Co., 1859, and Portsmouth, 1892; George C. Cabell Papers, LVA; Duval Porter, ed., *Men, Places and Things* (1891), 298–299; James I. Robertson, *18th Virginia Infantry* (1984), 16, 27, 44; Compiled Service Records; *Congressional Record*, 44th Cong., 1st sess., 3371–3375, reprinted as *Finance and Taxation: Speech of Hon. George C. Cabell, of Virginia, Delivered in the U.S. House of Representatives, May 29, 1876* (1876); *Papers and Testimony in the Contested-Election Case of J. T. Stovall vs. George C. Cabell, from the Fifth Congressional District of Virginia, January 21, 1882*, 47th Cong., 1st sess., 1882, House Misc. Doc. 29, serial 2046; *Report from the Committee on Elections*, 47th Cong., 1st sess., 1882, House Report 1696, serial 2070; Jane Dailey, *Before Jim Crow: The Politics of Race in Postemancipation Virginia* (2000), 119–125, 221; obituaries in *Danville Register*, 24 June 1906, and *Confederate Veteran* 14 (1906): 372–373 (por.).

BRUCE M. JONES

CABELL, Henry Coalter (14 February 1820–31 January 1889), Confederate artillery officer, was born in Richmond, the son of William H. Cabell, then a judge of the Virginia Court of Appeals and former governor of Virginia, and his second wife, Agnes Sarah Bell Gamble Cabell. He graduated from the University of Virginia in 1839 and from its law school in 1842. Cabell then returned to Richmond to practice law in partnership with Sidney Smith Baxter, an attorney general of Virginia, and later with Johnson H. Sands. On 1 May 1850, in Abbeville, South Carolina, Cabell married Jane C. Alston, daughter of a wealthy planter. They had five sons and one daughter.

Cabell rented, although he never purchased, an elegant 1847 Richmond residence that came to be called the Henry Coalter Cabell House, a reflection of his local prominence. He took an active part in Richmond society and from 1856 until his death served on the executive committee of the Virginia Historical Society. Among the many local organizations in which he participated was the militia. He was commissioned a major of the 1st Regiment Virginia Volunteers on 1 December 1857 and on 21 December 1859 became captain in the 4th Regiment Virginia Artillery, also known as the Fayette Artillery. On 25 April 1861 Cabell's artillery battery entered state service and saw its initial action at Gloucester Point in May. On 12 September 1861 he was promoted to lieutenant colonel in command of the new 1st Regiment Virginia Artillery. In the spring of 1862 Cabell served as chief of artillery under John Bankhead Magruder and took part in the siege of Yorktown. Promoted to colonel on 4 July 1862, Cabell was transferred later that month to command of a battalion as chief of artillery in Lafayette McLaws's division. In September 1862 Cabell saw action at the Battle of Sharpsburg (Antietam), and at the Battle of Fredericksburg later that year he commanded the artillery that repulsed Union assaults on the northern end of the battlefield.

Cabell's battalion fought in the Battle of Chancellorsville in 1863 and participated in the attack on the Peach Orchard and in support of Pickett's Charge at Gettysburg in July. In the autumn of 1863 he was attached to the army's reserve artillery in Virginia. The following year Cabell commanded a First Corps artillery battalion in the Battles of the Wilderness, Spotsylvania Court House, North Anna, and Cold Harbor. On several occasions during the siege of Petersburg he acted as chief of artillery for the First Corps. On 30 March 1865 several general officers, including Richard Stoddert Ewell and Edward Porter Alexander, recommended that Cabell be promoted to brigadier general, but there was then no vacancy for him to fill, and he never received the promotion. Alexander later described Cabell as "not only a superb soldier, but a delightful gentleman also." During an engagement with Union cavalry west of Petersburg on 8 April 1865 Cabell and several other artillery officers escaped toward Lynchburg. He therefore did not take part in the surrender at Appomattox Court House. Cabell returned to Richmond, took the oath of allegiance on 26 July 1865, and received a presidential pardon on 1 August.

Cabell promptly resumed his law practice in partnership with his brother-in-law William Daniel, formerly a judge of the Virginia Supreme Court of Appeals. Cabell was active in the business community and served on the boards of the Chesapeake and Ohio Railway Company, the James River and Kanawha Company, and the Virginia Central Railroad. He had owned a substantial amount of property when the Civil War began, but at his death a newspaper obituary writer politely described him as "long embarrassed." On 11 January 1884 his wife died after her clothing caught fire in their home. Henry Coalter Cabell subsequently moved into rooms at the Saint Claire Hotel in Richmond, where he died in his sleep on 31 January 1889. He was buried in Hollywood Cemetery in that city.

Brown, *Cabells*, 280–281, 639–644 (por. facing 640); French Biographies; *Richmond Enquirer*, 17 May 1850; Mary Wingfield Scott, *Old Richmond Neighborhoods* (1950), 188–189; Cabell Family Papers, including signed presidential pardon and Cabell's recollections of Gettysburg (1887), VHS; Compiled Service Records; numerous references in *OR*, ser. 1, vols. 11, 19, 21, 25, 27, 36, 42, 46, 51; Robert H. Moore II, *The Richmond Fayette, Hampden, Thomas, and Blount's Lynchburg Artillery* (1991), esp. 3–8, 147; Gary W. Gallagher, ed., *Fighting for the Confederacy: The Personal Recollections of General Edward Porter Alexander* (1989), 226 (first quotation); Presidential Pardons; *Richmond Daily Dispatch*, 12, 13 Jan. 1884; oil por. in Confederate uniform, VHS; obituaries in *Richmond State*, 31 Jan., 1 Feb. 1889, and *Richmond Daily Times* and *Richmond Dispatch* (second quotation), both 1 Feb. 1889.

GRAHAM T. DOZIER

CABELL, Henry Landon (3 November 1858– 20 June 1936), broker, was born in Richmond, the son of Robert Gamble Cabell (1809–1889), a prosperous physician, and Margaret Sophia Caskie Cabell. The writer James Branch Cabell was his nephew. Cabell attended Thomas H. Norwood's private school in Richmond and by 1881 had become a clerk in the tobacco manufacturing business of Lawrence Lottier. Five years later Cabell entered the insurance business with William O. Skelton as a partner in Skelton and Cabell. During the 1890s his business interests broadened when he formed a partnership with John J. Wilson. The firm of Cabell and Wilson offered a variety of services, acting as real estate agents, brokers, and auctioneers in addition to arranging loans for its clients. In 1892 Cabell was also the cashier at the People's Building Loan and Trust Company, a position he held for more than a decade. Having successfully established himself in the Richmond business community, he married Adah Wymond on 27 April 1897 at the home of her parents in Louisville, Kentucky. They had three sons.

H. Landon Cabell prospered in real estate and banking. In 1902 he was a vice president and secretary of the Richmond Trust and Safe Deposit Company, secretary of the Richmond and Manchester Land Company, secretary and treasurer of the Powhatan Land and Improvement Company, and a vice president of the Metropolitan Bank of Virginia. By 1905 Cabell had also become the manager of the People's Building Loan and Trust Company. He became a director of First National Bank in Richmond in January 1911 and remained on its board for more than fifteen years. Cabell was president of the city's Chamber of Commerce from 1902 to 1904.

Early in 1904 Cabell allied himself with Carter Wheelwright Branch, a son of Thomas Branch, who since 1880 had been directing C. W. Branch and Company, his own Richmond brokerage business. Branch obtained a two-year loan of seats on the New York Cotton Exchange and the Chicago Board of Trade. By April the two

partners, along with Howard S. Gray, of New York, had opened the brokerage firm of Branch, Cabell, and Company. In 1905 Cabell purchased a seat on the New York Stock Exchange for $82,000, thus enabling the company to buy and sell securities on the exchange floor.

Cabell closely managed the affairs of Branch Cabell and took sole charge of the firm after Branch's death in 1911. He brought in his eldest son, William Wymond Cabell, and Basil Magruder Jones as partners in 1920 and had added two more partners by the end of the decade. Cabell guided the company through the early years of the Great Depression and remained the senior partner until his death. At that time William Wymond Cabell succeeded his father as head of the company and, building on its solid foundation and excellent reputation, oversaw the expansion of Branch Cabell after World War II. It grew into a strong regional brokerage house with branch offices in Harrisonburg, Lynchburg, and Waynesboro. Branch Cabell absorbed the Richmond investment firm of Branch and Company in 1975 and remained one of the largest and most successful independent brokerage firms in the state until a Boston company, Tucker Anthony Sutro, purchased it in September 2000.

Cabell was also prominent in various Richmond civic and social activities. He was a founding member of Richmond's Red Cross chapter, served on its advisory board, and was elected a vice chairman in March 1917. In 1920 he was elected president of the Virginia Society of the Cincinnati and served as a trustee for almost thirty years. After a long period of poor health, Henry Landon Cabell died of a heart attack at his home in Richmond on 20 June 1936. He was buried in Hollywood Cemetery in that city.

Brown, *Cabells*, 625; early business connections documented in Richmond city directories, 1881–1906, Andrew Morrison, ed., *Richmond, Virginia, and the New South* [ca. 1889], 65, 71, Morrison, ed., *City on the James: Richmond, Virginia* (1893), 70, 90, and George W. Engelhardt, ed., *Richmond, Virginia: The City on the James* (1902/1903), 27, 49–50; *Richmond Times*, 28 Apr. 1897; 1904 partnership and stock exchange loan agreements in Branch and Company Records, VHS; *Inside Branch Cabell and Company* [ca. 1979]; *Richmond Times-Dispatch,* 10 Apr. 1904, 15

Sept. 2000; *Richmond News Leader*, 25 Jan. 1975; BVS Death Certificate, Richmond City; obituaries and editorial tributes in *Richmond News Leader*, 20 (por.), 25 June 1936, and *Richmond Times-Dispatch*, 21 June 1936 (por.); obituary in *New York Times*, 21 June 1936.

MARIANNE E. JULIENNE

CABELL, James Branch (14 April 1879–5 May 1958), writer, was born in Richmond, the son of Robert Gamble Cabell (1847–1922), a physician who was then assistant superintendent of the Central Lunatic Asylum in Petersburg, and Anne Harris Branch Cabell, the beautiful and headstrong daughter of James Read Branch and granddaughter of Thomas Branch, both prominent investment bankers. For a conservative southern gentleman, Cabell led a life curiously marked by scandal. He matriculated in 1894 at the College of William and Mary, and during a distinguished undergraduate career he was engaged by the college while an upperclassman to teach undergraduates French and Greek. His reputation, however, was nearly destroyed by a false rumor that he had participated in a homosexual orgy involving the college librarian and a few other members of Cabell's fraternity. This weirdly hysterical piece of campus gossip led to his temporary withdrawal from the college and his abandonment of his courtship of Gabriella Moncure, a young woman whose beguiling unattainability later haunted his novels as Dorothy in *Jurgen* (1919) and Melior in *The High Place* (1923).

After graduating in June 1898, Cabell worked briefly as a reporter in New York City. On his return to Richmond he again found himself the subject of a malicious rumor, that he had murdered a cousin with whom his mother was allegedly having an affair. Although the victim's family conducted an investigation that revealed the identities of the real killers, the truth about the murder, which for various reasons would have sullied the family's name, was allowed to remain obscure, and Cabell spent the rest of his life dogged by innuendos and shady allegations.

A shy, somewhat cool young man with literary ambitions, Cabell found refuge in genealogy. Aided by Branch money, he spent much of his young adulthood researching the family pedigree, an employment that allowed him to travel in France and the British Isles and eventually enabled him to improve his mother's social standing in Virginia. Cabell published the first results of his research in *Branchiana: Being a Partial Account of the Branch Family in Virginia* (1907). On 8 November 1913 he married Rebecca Priscilla Bradley Shepherd, a widow with five children. They had one son.

In the meantime Cabell's short stories were being published in such fashionable periodicals as the *Smart Set* and *Harper's Monthly Magazine*. His first novel, *The Eagle's Shadow,* a drawing-room comedy reminiscent of the plays of William Congreve, appeared in 1904. In the next few years Cabell published several books with different presses, including *The Cords of Vanity* (1909), *Chivalry* (1909), *The Soul of Melicent* (1913; reissued as *Domnei* in 1920), and *The Rivet in Grandfather's Neck* (1915). These early works tended to be comedies of manners, but he was also drawn to the popular medievalism of the day best represented by *A Connecticut Yankee in King Arthur's Court* and *When Knighthood Was in Flower.* Howard Pyle illustrated some of Cabell's works, but his novels sold poorly, and successive publishers dropped him.

Guy Holt, Cabell's friend and editor at the publishing house Robert M. McBride and Company, which published *The Rivet in Grandfather's Neck*, enthusiastically supported Cabell's maturing efforts. *The Cream of the Jest* (1917), one of Cabell's best and most important works, was the first to draw serious critical attention. Burton Rascoe, of the *Chicago Tribune*, and H. L. Mencken praised the work and became Cabell's ardent champions. In 1919 Cabell published *Beyond Life,* a kind of formalist credo in which he first launched his lifelong attack on literary realism. His ideas apparently struck the right note at a time when American writers were striving to replace the genteel tradition with a new literary sophistication and daring. Cabell found himself at the center of a literary circle bearing his name and including such prominent writers as the young F. Scott Fitzgerald, Joseph Hergesheimer, Carl Van Vechten, and Elinor Wylie.

Cabell gained his greatest notoriety in 1919 with the publication of *Jurgen,* a novel that evolved out of a story originally published in the *Smart Set*. In a coy, suggestive narrative, the eponymous hero of *Jurgen* sails through a series of sexual liaisons with a female vampire, a fertility goddess, and Arthurian maidens before ultimately reaffirming to himself the sanity of domestic, wedded harmony. Many people missed the moral of the story, however, and the director of the New York Society for the Suppression of Vice charged that the novel was obscene and quickly had the printing plates seized and the book banned. Overnight, *Jurgen* became a cause célèbre, lifting Cabell from obscurity to fame as one of America's most-discussed novelists. After the obscenity trial resulted in acquittal in October 1922, *Jurgen* became a bestseller and its author became a cult idol for a generation desperate to transcend American provincialism and attain a new Continental knowingness in matters of literature and sex.

Cabell's next novels, such as *The High Place* (1923), *The Silver Stallion* (1926), and *Something about Eve* (1927), enjoyed critical and commercial success. Incorporating these titles and revised versions of some earlier works into an eighteen-volume set entitled *Biography of the Life of Manuel* (1927–1930), he created an entire fictional world called Poictesme, with its own local legends, First Families, customs, and peculiarities, a world very much like Cabell's Virginia. The *Biography* is replete with genealogical and cartographical guides to its invented history and terrain. It traces the descendants of Manuel, a medieval swineherd who becomes the ruler of Poictesme, from humble French beginnings through the court intrigues of the seventeenth-century ancien régime, continuing into the English Enlightenment, and concluding in twentieth-century Virginia. The multi-volume design of the *Biography* created a formal unity crucial to Cabell's sense of literary aesthetics and provided an important, though inadequately acknowledged, influence on southern fiction that can be seen in such cumulations as Ellen Glasgow's Virginia Edition and William Faulkner's Yoknapatawpha novels. To distinguish the *Biography* from his later works, Cabell published under the truncated name Branch Cabell from 1932 through 1946. In *Let Me Lie: Being in the*

Main an Ethnological Account of the Remarkable Commonwealth of Virginia and the Making of Its History (1947), he reverted to his full name.

Cabell's aestheticism eventually worked against him. The intellectual climate turned decidedly toward left-wing radicalism during the 1930s, and he was subjected to brutal criticism. The irony is that far from being a snob, Cabell had always pursued popular success, and he frequently expressed disdain for such avant-garde novelists as Faulkner and James Joyce. His own critical taste ran to odd choices, such as Marjorie Kinnan Rawlings and Booth Tarkington. Cabell enjoyed the acclaim that *Jurgen* brought and reveled in his celebrity and fame. The body of his work, if carefully considered, reveals a writer who was deeply committed to literature as a positive social force. Still, his readers seem to have been influenced by the harsh judgment of his critics and eventually viewed his cool aestheticism with disfavor.

Cabell and his wife were both active in Virginia's patriotic societies, and she was among the first women to work for the preservation of the state's historic records. He was a genealogist for the Sons of the American Revolution and a member of the First Families of Virginia, the Society of the Cincinnati, and the fraternities Phi Beta Kappa and Kappa Alpha. During the 1920s Cabell served as historian for the Society of Colonial Wars in the State of Virginia and as an editor for the Virginia War History Commission, which published records and accounts of Virginians' participation in World War I. Such credentials did little to boost his fame in the 1930s. As his distant, patrician image began to work against him, Cabell's popularity dwindled, as did the sales of his books. Yet he continued to write with no apparent bitterness. Although never recovering his former success, he added some impressive works to his canon, particularly *The Nightmare Has Triplets* (1934–1937), a trilogy with Joycean echoes, and *The First Gentleman of America* (1942), a novel set in Spanish Florida. From 1932 through 1935 Cabell served as an editor of the *American Spectator*, a short-lived literary newspaper whose other contributing editors included Sherwood Anderson,

Theodore Dreiser, Eugene O'Neill, and Louis Untermeyer.

After 1935 Cabell resided in relative obscurity in Richmond and spent vacations in Saint Augustine, Florida. His wife died on 29 March 1949, and on 15 June 1950 in a civil ceremony (followed by a church ceremony two days later) Cabell married Margaret Waller Freeman, who had been an editor of the *Reviewer*, the acclaimed Richmond journal, in the 1920s when Cabell, Hergesheimer, and Mencken were all associated with it. Cabell's reputation languished until the eminent critic Edmund Wilson published "The James Branch Cabell Case Reopened" in the 21 April 1956 issue of the *New Yorker*. Wilson regarded Cabell as an important representative of the southern literary tradition and pleaded for a serious reappraisal of his accomplishments. A sounding call for a Cabell revival, Wilson's essay did not win over critics or readers. Joe Lee Davis published a critical retrospective of Cabell's career in 1962, and thereafter several journals and newsletters devoted to him, such as *Kalki,* thrived briefly but then perished. Two editions of Cabell's letters were published after his death, and on the centennial of his birth a volume of favorable critical essays edited by M. Thomas Inge and Edgar E. MacDonald appeared, but they led to little renewed interest in his writings.

Cabell's fame, always close to moribund, has never quite died. Some of his novels enjoy a cult status in the science fiction and fantasy field, and in the latter decades of the twentieth century some critics attempted to reassess him in the light of post-Modernism by exploring his work as a precursor to the fantastic satire of the 1960s and 1970s. Yet Cabell's aristocratic lineage and his undeserved reputation for aloofness and elitism took their critical toll. He has been remembered most often in association with Mencken, his primary champion, and Glasgow, his friend and fellow Richmonder, or as he had predicted and as the headline of his *New York Times* obituary identified him, simply as the author of *Jurgen*.

Cabell's personal book collection is preserved in the library named for him at Virginia Commonwealth University in Richmond. He lived his last years in seclusion following a heart

attack and a minor stroke. James Branch Cabell died of a cerebral hemorrhage at his home in Richmond on 5 May 1958 and was buried in the graveyard of Emmanuel Episcopal Church in Henrico County. In 1959 the remains of Cabell and his first wife were reinterred in Hollywood Cemetery in Richmond.

Joe Lee Davis, *James Branch Cabell* (1962); Edgar E. MacDonald, *James Branch Cabell and Richmond-in-Virginia* (1993), pors.; autobiographical material in Cabell, *Some of Us: An Essay in Epitaphs* (1930), *Let Me Lie: Being in the Main an Ethnological Account of the Remarkable Commonwealth of Virginia and the Making of Its History* (1947), and *As I Remember It: Some Epilogues in Recollection* (1955); James Branch Cabell Papers, UVA and VCU; BVS Birth Register, Richmond City; Padraic Colum and Margaret Freeman Cabell, eds., *Between Friends: Letters of James Branch Cabell and Others* (1962); Edward Wagenknecht, ed., *The Letters of James Branch Cabell* (1975); James N. Hall, *James Branch Cabell: A Complete Bibliography* (1974); M. Thomas Inge and Edgar E. MacDonald, eds., *James Branch Cabell: Centennial Essays* (1983); Stephen R. Wetta, "Artful Contamination: Genre and the Novel in the Works of James Branch Cabell, 1919–1927" (Ph.D. diss., New York University, 1998); *Richmond Times-Dispatch*, 8 Nov. 1913, 17 June 1950; Hall, *Portraits*, 42–43 (por.); obituaries in *New York Times*, *Richmond News Leader*, and *Richmond Times-Dispatch*, all 6 May 1958.

STEPHEN R. WETTA

CABELL, James Lawrence (26 August 1813–13 August 1889), medical educator and public health advocate, was born probably on the Nelson County farm of his parents, George Cabell and Susanna Wyatt Cabell. Shortly after his mother's death in 1817, the family moved to Richmond, where his father practiced medicine without relinquishing his land and slaves in Nelson County. Following his father's death in 1827, Cabell became the ward of his uncle William H. Cabell, then a judge of the Virginia Court of Appeals. Two years later another uncle, Joseph Carrington Cabell, of Warminster in Nelson County, became his guardian. The change in Cabell's guardianship coincided with his matriculation at the University of Virginia in September 1829.

After receiving an M.A. on 18 July 1833, Cabell entered the medical school of the University of Maryland in Baltimore. He earned his medical degree on 10 September 1834 and completed his formal education with service as a medical resident for a year and a half at the

Baltimore Alms House. In December 1836 Cabell traveled to France in hopes of continuing his medical education in Paris. Although satisfied with his life and work there, he did not stay long in Europe. On 14 May 1837 Cabell applied for the vacant position of professor of medicine at the University of Virginia. He was appointed professor of anatomy and surgery and in December 1837 began more than half a century on the faculty. On 5 February 1839 Cabell married Margaret Nicholson Gibbons in Charlottesville. They had no children but raised the orphaned daughter of one of his brothers.

Cabell rapidly overcame any concerns members of the university community may have entertained about his youth. He demonstrated a facile knowledge and skill in medicine. Shouldering his share of responsibility, he served as chairman of the faculty in 1846 and 1847. At that time the university had no president, and the chairman of the faculty was the university's chief administrative official. A decade later Cabell wrote and published a substantial book entitled *The Testimony of Modern Science to the Unity of Mankind: Being a Summary of the Conclusions Announced by the Highest Authorities in the Several Departments of Physiology, Zoology, and Comparative Philology in Favor of the Specific Unity and Common Origin of All the Varieties of Man* (1859). At a time when some southern writers supported the view that human races they regarded as inferior to northern Europeans may have had a separate creation, Cabell argued that the best evidence from a variety of scientific studies supported the biblical teaching that all people descended from one creation.

Cabell continued to teach at the University of Virginia during the Civil War, but he also served as the surgeon in charge of Confederate military hospitals in Charlottesville and Danville. In 1867 he spearheaded a campaign against a proposed merger of the University of Virginia's medical school with the Medical College of Virginia, in Richmond. Cabell attended the November 1870 founding session of the Medical Society of Virginia. He served on its Committee of Publications, chaired its Committee on Hygiene and Public Health, and was president of the society for the 1876–

1877 term. Cabell's 1877 presidential address called for state legislation to improve public health, regulate the practice of medicine, and bar unqualified practitioners. By 1870 he had become resident physician at the Hot Springs in Bath County, and in 1872 the medicinal springs' expanded promotional pamphlet was issued as *An Account of the Hot Springs, Bath County, Va., and an Analysis of the Waters, with a Treatise by Prof. J. L. Cabell, M.D., of the University of Virginia, Resident Physician, on the Value of the Thermal Baths*. In 1873 Cabell received an honorary doctorate of law from Hampden-Sydney College.

Cabell was the first president of the Virginia State Board of Health after its creation in 1872, but in his presidential address to the Medical Society of Virginia in 1877 he sharply criticized the General Assembly for inadequately funding the board. In 1879 he became president of the American Public Health Association. That same year the president of the United States appointed Cabell to the new National Board of Health, and its members elected him president. His tenure was troubled. Uncertainties about the board's authority and disagreements among board members made organizing and directing its activities difficult. Cabell wanted to participate fully in the board's work, but personal financial problems, exacerbated by the failure in 1875 of a bank in which he was a major stockholder, required him to continue teaching and prevented him from moving to Washington, D.C., to devote full time to the board. Despite these difficulties Cabell served as president of the short-lived board until 1884, when he retired from public medical service. Three years earlier his groundbreaking work in public health was recognized internationally by the Société Royale de Médecine Publique in Brussels, Belgium.

By late in the 1880s Cabell's health was deteriorating. In July 1889 he stepped down as professor of anatomy and gave up teaching, although he nominally retained his chairs of physiology and surgery. James Lawrence Cabell died at his adopted daughter's summer residence in Albemarle County on 13 August 1889 and was buried in the University of Virginia Cemetery in Charlottesville.

Biographies in Medical Society of Virginia, *Transactions* (1889): 292–296, and Bruce, *University of Virginia*, 2:175–180; birth and death dates on gravestone; Brown, *Cabells*, 283, 651–653 (por.); Albemarle Co. Marriage Register; James Lawrence Cabell Correspondence and University of Virginia, Department of Medicine, Papers, 1867, both UVA; Records of the National Board of Health, RG 90, NARA; some Cabell letters in John Shaw Billings Papers, New York Public Library, and in Cabell Family Letters, LVA; Compiled Service Records; published annual reports, Virginia State Board of Health, 1872–1874; Wyndham B. Blanton, *Medicine in Virginia in the Nineteenth Century* (1933); Wyndham D. Miles, "History of the National Board of Health, 1879–1893" (1970 typescript), Wyndham D. Miles Papers, U.S. National Library of Medicine, Bethesda, Md.; Cabell's other publications include *Lecture Introductory to the Course on Anatomy and Surgery, in the University of Virginia, for the Session of 1837–1838* (1838), *Syllabus of the Lectures on Physiology and Histology Including the Outlines of Comparative Anatomy, Delivered at the University of Virginia* (1853), "On the Ventilation of School Houses" and "School-Room Diseases Arising from Avoidable Causes," *Educational Journal of Virginia* 4 (1873): 253–261, 338–346, "Address in State Medicine and Public Hygiene," American Medical Association, *Transactions* (1876): 551–583, and presidential address in Medical Society of Virginia, *Transactions* (1877): 141–162; John Terrill Lovell Autograph Album, 1851–1855, VHS (por.); Albemarle Co. Will Book, 29:626–629; death notice and editorial tribute in *Washington Post*, 14, 15 Aug. 1889; obituaries in *New York Times* and *Richmond Dispatch*, both 14 Aug. 1889, *Charlottesville Chronicle*, 16 Aug. 1889, and *Virginia Medical Monthly* 16 (1889): 492–494; tributes in *Addresses Commemorative of James L. Cabell, Delivered at the University of Virginia, July 1st, 1890* (1890).

JAMES A. JACOBS

CABELL, John (d. by 12 June 1815), member of the Convention of 1776, was the son of William Cabell (1700–1774), a prominent physician, and his first wife, Elizabeth Burks Cabell. He must have been conceived either before his father's departure for England in 1735 or after his return in 1741. Little is known about Cabell's early years or his studies, although his parents probably ensured that he was well educated, as were all their other children. His brothers included Joseph Cabell, who served in the General Assembly, and William Cabell (1730–1798), who served in the Conventions of 1776 and 1788. On 20 May 1762 Cabell married Paulina Jordon. They had seven sons and three daughters, but three sons died before reaching adulthood. Cabell's wife died on 31 July 1781, and on 19 July 1787 he married Elizabeth Brierton Jones. They had no children. When Cabell drew up his will shortly before his death, he also provided for his two sons and one daughter by Frances Johnson.

Cabell acquired large tracts of land in Buckingham County, and at his death he possessed more than 3,000 acres on which he raised tobacco and livestock, including horses and cattle. In October 1764 the General Assembly established a public ferry across the Fluvanna River (now the James River) connecting his estates. Cabell had become a captain in the Buckingham County militia by September 1763, and by 1767 he had been appointed a justice of the peace for the county. When Virginia's counties formed committees in 1775 to enforce the economic measures adopted by the Continental Congress to pressure the British into repealing unpopular tax measures and then to organize for the defense of the colony, he was elected chairman of the Buckingham County Committee. The Virginia Committee of Safety appointed Cabell county lieutenant, or commander of the Buckingham County militia, on 26 September 1775.

In April 1776 he was elected to the last of the Revolutionary Conventions and attended its sessions in Williamsburg from 6 May through 5 July. There Cabell served on the Committee of Propositions and Grievances. He and fellow Buckingham County delegate Charles Patteson received instructions from their constituents directing them to call for a complete break with England and to work for a constitution guaranteeing full representation and free elections. Even before these instructions reached Williamsburg, Cabell had voted on 15 May 1776 to instruct the Virginia delegates to Congress to introduce a resolution declaring the colonies independent. He was probably also present on 12 and 29 June 1776 when the convention unanimously adopted the Virginia Declaration of Rights and the first constitution of Virginia.

Cabell represented Buckingham County in the House of Delegates in 1776 and again served on the Committee of Propositions and Grievances. He was reelected to one-year terms in 1777, 1780, and 1783, although he did not always attend. In the last session he served on the Committee of Privileges and Elections. After the Revolutionary War Cabell continued to manage his plantations and serve as a justice of the peace. In November 1788 the assembly appointed him a trustee for the town of Greensville in Buckingham County. John Cabell dated his will on 22 April 1815 and died sometime between then and 12 June 1815, when the will was proved in the Buckingham County Court.

Brown, *Cabells*, 154–158; French Biographies give birth date as ca. 1735 or 1736 and death in May 1815; Hening, *Statutes*, 8:44, 12:661; *Revolutionary Virginia*, 4:80, 84, 6:347, 353, 7:60, 109–112; Land and Personal Property Tax Returns, 1782–1815, Amherst and Buckingham Cos., RG 48, LVA; record of will in Edythe Rucker Whitley, *Genealogical Records of Buckingham County, Virginia* (1984), 77.

MARIANNE E. JULIENNE

CABELL, Joseph (19 September 1732– 1 March 1798), member of the General Assembly, was born in Goochland County, the son of William Cabell (1700–1774) and his first wife, Elizabeth Burks Cabell. He received his early education from a local tutor, and his father, a prominent physician, later trained him in medicine and surgery. Among his brothers were John Cabell and William Cabell (1730–1798), both of whom served in the Convention of 1776. Early in the 1740s the family moved west to an estate in what became the southern part of Albemarle County in 1744.

Cabell first entered public life in September 1751 when he was appointed a deputy sheriff for Albemarle County, a post he held until 1755. By 1760 he had become a justice of the peace. In 1761 Amherst and Buckingham Counties were formed from the southern portion of Albemarle County where Cabell's property centered, leaving his landholdings spread among the three counties. His primary estate was in Buckingham County. There Cabell was named a justice of the peace in May 1765, and he represented the county in the House of Burgesses from 1761 to 1771. He was appointed to the Committees for Courts of Justice and of Propositions and Grievances, but he did not attend every session. In November 1766 the General Assembly granted Cabell the right to establish a ferry from his land in Buckingham County across the Fluvanna River (now the James River), which remained in operation until 1788.

When the governor dissolved the House of Burgesses in May 1769 Cabell joined many of his fellow members at the Raleigh Tavern to approve a nonimportation agreement in response to the perceived injustices committed by Parliament against the colonies. The next year he signed a second agreement to strengthen the colony's boycott of British goods. Virginia also attempted to develop its own resources so as not to be dependent on Great Britain for necessary supplies. In 1771 Cabell and several other prominent planters formed the Albemarle Furnace Company, an iron-manufacturing venture that did not succeed.

Cabell moved to his estate in Amherst County about 1771 and became active in that county's affairs. He represented the county in the House of Burgesses for the 1772–1774 and 1775–1776 terms and served on the Committees of Propositions and Grievances, Public Claims, and Religion. In 1775 Cabell was a member of the Amherst County Committee. He also attended the first four Revolutionary Conventions between August 1774 and January 1776. They named Virginia's delegates to the Continental Congress, authorized the arming of the militia, and created the Virginia Committee of Safety. Cabell either was defeated or chose not to be a candidate in the April 1776 election for members of the last of the series of conventions. He represented Amherst County in the House of Delegates in 1776 and 1778 and on 6 July of the latter year became the county lieutenant, the commanding officer of the county militia.

In April 1779 Cabell sold his property in Amherst and returned to Buckingham County. He was again elected to the House of Delegates for the 1780–1781 session, and then from 1781 to 1786 he represented the district composed of Albemarle, Amherst, Buckingham, and Fluvanna Counties in the Senate of Virginia. Cabell was elected to the House of Delegates again in 1787 and sat on the Committee on Propositions and Grievances. He did not neglect his extensive landholdings and contributed some of the hemp, livestock, and tobacco he produced to the support of the Revolution. By the time of his death Cabell had acquired more than 17,000 acres and owned more than fifty slaves. As one of the wealthiest men in his part of Virginia he did not need to practice medicine as a career, but he reportedly gained renown as a surgeon.

On 18 October 1752 Cabell married Mary Hopkins, of Goochland County. They had two sons and four daughters. Joseph Cabell died at his home in Buckingham County on 1 March 1798 and was buried in the family cemetery there.

Brown, *Cabells*, 141–153, quoting gravestone inscription with birth and death dates; Goochland Co. Marriage Bonds; *Revolutionary Virginia*, 1:76, 82, 2:356; Land and Personal Property Tax Returns, Albemarle, Amherst, Buckingham, and Fluvanna Cos., 1782–1799, RG 48, LVA; Wills from the Treasurer's Office, 1787–1867, Acc. 28458, LVA.

MARIANNE E. JULIENNE

CABELL, Joseph Carrington (28 December 1778–5 February 1856), member of the Senate of Virginia and president of the James River and Kanawha Company, was born at Liberty Hall plantation in Amherst County, the son of Nicholas Cabell and Hannah Carrington Cabell. He attended Hampden-Sydney College during the 1795–1796 term and the College of William and Mary from 1796 to 1798. At first an indifferent student, Cabell returned to Amherst County and read law with his brother William H. Cabell, later governor of Virginia and judge of the Virginia Court of Appeals. In 1800 Cabell went back to William and Mary for another year to attend law lectures by St. George Tucker and then moved to Richmond to study law. He may have engaged in serious study on his own, because his mentors Thomas Jefferson and Tucker drew up long reading lists for him.

A variety of illnesses that troubled Cabell throughout his life soon forced him to abandon his studies. Convincing his relatives that a foreign sojourn would broaden his education and restore his health, he traveled throughout Europe from 1803 to 1806 and socialized with well-connected Americans in England, France, the Low Countries, and Italy. Cabell's traveling companion for part of the time was Washington Irving.

Cabell returned to Virginia in 1806 and on 1 January 1807 married Tucker's stepdaughter Mary Walker Carter in Williamsburg. Later in 1807 Cabell served as a member of the federal grand jury that indicted Aaron Burr for treason.

His Jeffersonian Republican sentiments were reflected in his vote to indict the former vice president, but he later acknowledged that the case against Burr was weak.

Cabell apparently never practiced law. Instead, his third stay in Williamsburg whetted his appetite for politics, the favorite pastime of Virginia gentlemen. Although he acquired Corotoman, a large estate in Lancaster County, as part of his wife's inheritance, he moved in 1808 to Edgewood, a plantation he had purchased in Amherst County. Almost immediately Cabell was elected to the House of Delegates from Amherst for the 1808–1809 session. Late in 1807 Nelson County was created out of the part of Amherst County where Cabell resided, and the formation of the new county government, combined with his family connections, offered him a chance to move quickly up the political ladder. Cabell became a justice of the peace in 1808 and the following year was elected to the House of Delegates from Nelson County and served on the Committee of Privileges and Elections. In 1810 he was elected to the Senate of Virginia from the district initially composed of the counties of Albemarle, Amherst, Buckingham, Fluvanna, and Nelson. Cabell served in the Senate until 1829 and chaired the Committee of Privileges and Elections in 1814.

In the first years of his legislative service Cabell, reflecting an aristocratic mind-set that was at war with his republican political beliefs, developed a distaste for public life and politicians. Objecting to the ambition and flexible principles he perceived in his colleagues, he remained largely inactive during his early years in the assembly. Cabell's poor health also limited his enthusiasm and encouraged him to hire a substitute during the opening months of the War of 1812, although he briefly served in person when the British invaded the Chesapeake in 1814.

Cabell's political lethargy came to an end after the war when he became one of the most active and influential members of the Senate. He leaped into the struggle to charter and fund Central College, later the University of Virginia. Thomas Jefferson tapped Cabell in 1815 to lead the legislative fight to establish the university. Inspired by the former president's vision of republican education, Cabell adopted the cause as his own and persevered through years of bitter battles over the site for the institution and its appetite for public funds. Cabell led the effort in 1818 and 1819 to commit Virginia to making the college at Charlottesville the state's principal university instead of expanding either the College of William and Mary or Washington College (later Washington and Lee University) in Lexington. After securing approval of the charter, he pushed through a bill to permit the university's board of visitors to borrow money, and in 1825 he blocked a proposed move of William and Mary to Richmond that was perceived as a threat to the new university.

Cabell remained associated with the university long after its opening in 1825. He served on its first board of visitors, and his influence in Richmond was crucial in diverting money to the university from a variety of sources. After his retirement from active politics Cabell served as rector of the University of Virginia from 1834 to 1836. He returned to that post after embarrassing student riots in 1845 and remained on the job until shortly before his death in 1856. Cabell's interest in education also led him to propose during the 1820s that a college preparatory school be established in Nelson County, and he drew plans for the buildings. The school was never opened, but Cabell's drawings probably served as the basis for the buildings erected during the 1830s for Randolph-Macon College's first campus, at Boydton in Mecklenburg County.

Cabell's long years of fighting for the university took a toll on both his health and his personal finances, and he retired from the Senate in 1829. Yet his zeal for the economic development of Virginia soon led him back into politics to fight for the James River and Kanawha Canal. Begun in the 1780s, the canal had been envisioned as a continuous water transport route between Richmond and the Ohio River, but by the 1820s financial problems and conservative management had resulted in limited construction, consisting only of a short route around the falls of the James River at Richmond. The success of New York's Erie Canal inspired Cabell and others to revive the old plan. Aroused by

his service as a representative of Nelson County at a statewide convention on internal improvements held at Charlottesville in 1828, he returned to the House of Delegates in 1831 to lobby for the westward extension of the canal. As a leading member of the Committee of Roads and Internal Navigation, Cabell drafted a new act of incorporation and secured legislative approval in the spring of 1832. In subsequent years he convinced the assembly to fund the project and to authorize Virginia's banks to purchase its stock. He served in the General Assembly through the 1834–1835 session.

In May 1835 Cabell was elected the first president of the reorganized James River and Kanawha Company. Construction had reached Lynchburg by 1840, but the continuing depression of the ensuing decade slowed the canal's extension and forced the company to borrow heavily. Cabell also inadvertently hurt the project through an unyielding insistence on a continuous canal route to the Ohio River rather than accept a compromise that involved building a railroad through part of the western mountains. Financial scandals also embarrassed the company, and in 1842 a flood severely damaged portions of the canal. A legislative investigation cleared Cabell of charges of mismanagement following those episodes. The troubles scarred him, however, and he resigned the presidency in 1846. The canal transported a large volume of traffic until after the Civil War, but construction stopped at Buchanan in 1854, and the company's stockholders never realized a profit from their investment.

Cabell's later years were marked by a steady withdrawal from public life. He apparently adhered to the old principles of Jeffersonian Republicanism more as a result of Virginia patriotism and his friendship with Jefferson than from dedication to the emerging principles of popular democracy. Cabell's conservatism left him increasingly out of step with his neighbors. During the 1820s and 1830s he opposed Virginia's emerging Democratic Party, and unlike many other inhabitants of the Piedmont and points west he supported continued apportionment of the assembly on a basis that gave the eastern counties with their large populations of slaves a larger representation than their adult white population entitled them to. Many of Cabell's neighbors, on the other hand, supported western reformers who advocated apportionment of seats based solely on the number of white men. His position on legislative apportionment and his support for federal tariffs led to his defeat for reelection to the House of Delegates in 1835. In the summer of 1850 Cabell ran for a seat in the state constitutional convention that assembled later that year, but his continued support for the old basis of representation was hopelessly out of touch with the convictions of his neighbors, and he was easily defeated. His loyalty to an anachronistic brand of gentry politics limited his general popularity. Regarded highly enough to be asked to run for Congress and, reportedly, to have been asked to serve in the cabinet, Cabell was so conservative and suffered from such poor health that he probably could never have realized any loftier ambitions he might have possessed. His political career was played entirely on the Virginia stage, where he was nevertheless one of the most influential and respected men of the antebellum period.

Cabell and his wife had no children, but he served as a mentor and father figure to many younger members of the numerous Cabell family, particularly his nephew Nathaniel Francis Cabell, who became a writer and historian. Joseph Carrington Cabell died at Edgewood plantation in Nelson County on 5 February 1856 and was buried in the family cemetery in the garden.

Gravestone and biographies in [Nathaniel Francis Cabell], *Early History of the University of Virginia, as Contained in the Letters of Thomas Jefferson and Joseph C. Cabell* (1856), xxvii–xxxvi, and family history series signed "Shockoe Grit," *Daily Richmond Whig*, 14, 20, 22 Oct. 1868, all give birth date of 28 Dec. 1778, but Brown, *Cabells*, 186, 286–290, and French Biographies both give variant birth date of 26 Dec. 1778; Carol Minor Tanner, "Joseph C. Cabell, 1778–1856" (Ph.D. diss., UVA, 1948); Cabell Family Papers, UVA; letters in various collections at LC, LVA, UVA, and VHS; Bruce, *University of Virginia*, esp. 1:145–157; H. Trevor Colbourn, "The Reading of Joseph Carrington Cabell: 'A List of Books on Various Subjects Recommended to a Young Man . . . ,'" *Studies in Bibliography* 13 (1960): 179–188; Douglas R. Egerton, "To the Tombs of the Capulets: Charles Fenton Mercer and Public Education in Virginia, 1816–1817," *VMHB* 93 (1985): 155–174 (por. on 173); Thomas W. Dolan, "Origins of the First Campus of Randolph-Macon College: An Architectural Note," *VMHB* 93 (1985): 427–434; Wayland Fuller Dunaway, *History of the James River and Kanawha Company* (1922); Langhorne Gibson, *Cabell's Canal: The Story of the James River and Kanawha* (2000); *Daily Richmond Whig*, 4–6 Mar. 1829; *To the Voters of Nelson, Amherst and Albemarle . . .* (broadside including Cabell letter, [13 July 1850], UVA); Hummel and Smith, *Portraits and Statuary*, 18 (por.); obituary in *Richmond Daily Whig*, 9 Feb. 1856; memorial in *Daily Richmond Enquirer*, 12 Feb. 1856.

LYNN A. NELSON

CABELL, Mary Virginia Ellet (24 January 1839–4 July 1930), a founding officer of the National Society Daughters of the American Revolution, was born at Point of Honor in her mother's hometown of Lynchburg, the daughter of Charles Ellet and Elvira Augusta Daniel Ellet. Her father was a noted civil engineer and moved frequently during her childhood. Ellet lived in such varied places as Cuba, Niagara Falls, Philadelphia, and several cities in Virginia, including Wheeling, where her father erected the then-longest suspension bridge in the world, across the Ohio River. The family resided in Europe in 1855. Educated by her father, Ellet became proficient in French and German and developed an interest in history. She spent the momentous winter of 1860–1861 in Richmond, where John Brown Baldwin and Alexander Hugh Holmes Stuart escorted her to sessions of the state secession convention.

Ellet's father died in 1862 of wounds suffered while commanding a fleet of United States steam rams on the Mississippi River during the Civil War, and her mother and younger brother both died not long thereafter, leaving her to care for her two younger siblings at their residence in Philadelphia. In that city on 9 July 1867 she married her cousin William Daniel Cabell, of Nelson County, a widower with two daughters. They had three sons and three daughters. William Cabell had lost much of his wealth during the Civil War and in 1865 had opened the Norwood School (Norwood High School after 1873 and Norwood High School and College after 1876) on his Nelson County property. Many of its graduates matriculated at the University of Virginia, where he had been educated. He was a leader for many years of the university's alumni association.

William Cabell ceased being principal of Norwood in 1879. In 1881, after they sold the school, the Cabells moved to Washington, D.C., and opened the Norwood Institute, an exclusive school for girls, of which they were joint directors. Cabell and her husband became well known for their educational work, and while they lived in Washington they were prominent members of society. On 11 October 1890 she was one of eighteen women who attended the organizing meeting of the National Society Daughters of the American Revolution. Cabell presided at the meeting and was elected one of the vice presidents general. Caroline Scott Harrison, wife of the president of the United States, accepted election as president general on the condition that she not shoulder any functional responsibility. Cabell was then named vice president presiding. She directed the organization and presided over its meetings, many of which were held at the Cabells' large and elegant residence, as was an elaborate reception to publicize the new organization in 1891.

Following Harrison's death Cabell became acting president general and was nominated for president general in February 1893, but she withdrew in favor of Letitia Greene Stevenson, wife of the vice president of the United States, who accepted the office on terms similar to Harrison's. Cabell was named president presiding, recognition of her role as principal director of the society since its founding. While she was in charge the DAR enrolled thousands of members in approximately 150 chapters in thirty-five states and the District of Columbia; founded a journal, the *American Monthly Magazine* (later *Daughters of the American Revolution Magazine*); and made plans to erect a national headquarters building in Washington. Cabell was one of the society's delegates at the World's Congress of Representative Women in Chicago in May 1893 and delivered an address entitled "The Ethical Influence of Woman in Education." It exalted the maternal role of women and emphasized their special social responsibility to educate their children properly. Cabell remained president presiding of the DAR until she resigned on 5 October 1893.

In 1897 the Cabells retired from management of the Norwood Institute and moved back to Norwood in Nelson County. She attended national meetings of the DAR from time to time through World War I but did not join a state chapter. The DAR named Cabell honorary vice president general in 1898, and in 1901, in recognition of her services during the founding decade, the society created for her the office of honorary president presiding. After her husband died on 18 February 1904 while visiting his daughter in Berryville, she lived in Chicago with two of her daughters. Mary Virginia Ellet Cabell died in Michigan City, Indiana, on 4 July 1930 and was buried in Green Hill Cemetery in Berryville.

Ellen Hardin Walworth, "Mrs. William D. Cabell," *American Monthly Magazine* 1 (1892): 114–120 (frontispiece por.); Willard and Livermore, *Woman of the Century*, 144–145; Brown, *Cabells*, 427–428; feature article in *Lynchburg News*, 10 Oct. 1965; Cabell correspondence and documents in Papers of William Daniel Cabell and the Cabell and Ellet Families (including Cabell's diaries, journals, and commonplace books, 1853–1925, and DAR speeches), UVA, in Mary Virginia Ellet Cabell Papers, National Society Daughters of the American Revolution Archives, DAR Library, Washington, D.C., and in Cabell Family Letters, LVA; Ann Arnold Hunter, *A Century of Service: The Story of the DAR* (1991), 8–10, 45–52; Cabell, "The Ethical Influence of Woman in Education," *American Monthly Magazine* 2 (1893): 615–620; obituaries in *New York Times* and *Winchester Evening Star*, both 7 July 1930; memorials in *Daughters of the American Revolution Magazine* 64 (1930): 479–480, and *Virginia State Conference of the National Society of the Daughters of the American Revolution* (1930): 79.

GLENN R. GRAY

CABELL, Nathaniel Francis (23 July 1807– 1 September 1891), writer, the son of Nicholas Cabell and Margaret Read Cabell, was born at Warminster in that part of Amherst County that at the end of December 1807 became Nelson County. After his father died in 1809, his devoutly Presbyterian mother raised him, while his uncle Joseph Carrington Cabell, who became a prominent member of the General Assembly, advised him on his reading and education. Cabell received an A.B. from Hampden-Sydney College in 1825 and a B.L. from Harvard College in 1827. For the next four years he practiced law in Prince Edward County. On 14 September 1831 at Bremo in Fluvanna County he married Anne

Blaws Cocke. They had two sons and four daughters. Soon after his marriage Cabell returned to Nelson County, where he inherited Liberty Hall, a Cabell family plantation, and became one of the region's most prominent planters.

Through various friends and relatives Cabell became acquainted with the doctrines of the Church of the New Jerusalem (commonly referred to as the New Church, or simply as Swedenborgianism). Based on the writings of the eighteenth-century Swedish scientist and theologian Emanuel Swedenborg, the New Church attracted many Americans discouraged by the harshness of Calvinist theology and the antirationalism of American evangelicalism. Swedenborg's writings promised insight into deep symbolic meanings of Scripture, emphasized reason and free will, and described a God of love and forgiveness. Cabell, who had begun to grow disillusioned with Calvinism and sectarian conflict during his days at Hampden-Sydney, left the Presbyterian Church in 1837 and was baptized into the New Church in 1842.

Cabell became a prominent spokesman and theologian for the New Church. His pamphlets defending and explaining the church's doctrines include *An Article on the New Christian Church for Rupp's "History of all Religious Denominations in the United States"* (1844), *A Letter on a Trinal Order for the Ministry of the New Church* (1848), *Reply to Rev. Dr. Pond's "Swedenborgianism Reviewed," with a Preliminary Letter,* by R. K. Crallé (1848), and *The Triads of Scripture* (1866), the first part of a series that he did not complete. Cabell wrote essays for the *New Jerusalem Magazine*, the *New Jerusalem Messenger*, and the *New-Churchman*. His extended study of Saint Paul's theology entitled "Horae Paulinae" appeared in serial form in the *New Jerusalem Messenger* in 1873 and 1874.

Cabell's interests ranged widely. He lectured on agriculture, published articles on that subject in the *Farmer's Register*, and at the urging of the Virginia State Agricultural Society collected sources for a history of Virginia agriculture that he hoped to write. Cabell completed only a small portion of the narrative, which appeared in five parts in *De Bow's Review* in 1858 and was later issued in pamphlet form as

Early History of Agriculture in Virginia (n.d.). He lectured on literature and wrote *The Progress of Literature during the Preceding Century when Viewed from a Religious Standpoint* (1868). Cabell also interested himself in history. He edited a volume entitled *Early History of the University of Virginia as Contained in the Letters of Thomas Jefferson and Joseph C. Cabell* (1856), and between December 1857 and May 1860 he serialized in the *Southern Literary Messenger* a collection of historical letters from the papers of Richard Henry Lee that had recently been deposited in the University of Virginia's library. Cabell also compiled extensive notes and memoirs concerning the Cabell and Carrington families, which served as the basis for *The Cabells and Their Kin* (1895), the monumental work of his relative Alexander Brown.

Cabell took no part in the Civil War, but because at the end of the conflict he possessed real estate worth more than $20,000, he had to apply for, and in October 1865 received, a presidential pardon. In 1867, five years after his wife died on 20 February 1862, Cabell married Mary M. Keller, of Baltimore. They had no children. In his later years he lived with family members in the town of Bedford. Nathaniel Francis Cabell died there on 1 September 1891 and was buried in the family cemetery at Liberty Hall in Nelson County.

Willard H. Hinkley, *Nathaniel Francis Cabell, 1807–1891* [ca. 1891]; family history series signed "Shockoe Grit," *Daily Richmond Whig,* 2, 11 Nov. 1868; Brown, *Cabells,* 657–660 (por.), giving birth, marriage, and death dates; variant first marriage date of 13 Sept. 1831 in *Norfolk American Beacon and Virginia and North-Carolina Gazette,* 22 Sept. 1831; letters in several Cabell family collections, UVA, and in Nathaniel Francis Cabell Papers and Edmund Ruffin Papers, VHS; Nathaniel Francis Cabell Collection of Papers Relating to Virginia's Agricultural History, 1771–1879, Acc. 2, LVA; Cabell, "Some Fragments of an Intended Report on the Post Revolutionary History of Agriculture in Virginia," ed. E. G. Swem, *WMQ,* 1st ser., 26 (1918): 145–168; Presidential Pardons.

LYNN A. NELSON

CABELL, Royal Eubank (12 March 1878–8 September 1950), attorney and Republican Party leader, was born at Inglewood in Nelson County, the son of Patrick Henry Cabell and Elizabeth Willis Eubank Cabell. His father, a grandson of Congressman Samuel Jordan Cabell, was a public school educator and Confederate veteran. Cabell attended the local public schools and received a B.A. from Roanoke College in 1897 and an A.M. from Princeton University a year later. Cabell entered the University of Virginia to study law but transferred to Richmond College (later the University of Richmond), from which he received a law degree in 1902. He began his law practice in Richmond that same year with his brother Patrick Henry Carey Cabell under the firm name Cabell and Cabell. On 12 November 1908 he married Lillian Hoge Lorraine in Richmond. They had three sons and one daughter.

Cabell became active in Republican Party politics soon after establishing his law practice. He was a Republican candidate for presidential elector in 1904, and President Theodore Roosevelt named him postmaster of the city of Richmond. Confirmed by the Senate, Cabell served from 7 February 1906 until 1 September 1909, when President William Howard Taft appointed him commissioner of internal revenue. In the years before the federal income tax, the commissioner's principal responsibility was administration of the federal laws concerning alcoholic beverages, the manufacture of which was subject to an excise. Cabell attracted national attention early in 1913 when a congressional committee made public his report to the secretary of the treasury about collection of taxes on whiskey at the Old Nick Distillery Company, in North Carolina. A federal judge had blocked enforcement of three of Cabell's orders directing that the alcohol be seized and sold for the payment of taxes. In his report Cabell enumerated the illegal actions the company was believed to have employed to avoid paying the taxes and severely criticized the judge for protecting the company. The judge then ordered Cabell to submit to examination by a commissioner, but acting on instructions from the secretary of the treasury, Cabell declined to answer any questions. Cabell supported Taft against Roosevelt at the divisive 1912 Republican National Convention and resigned as commissioner of internal revenue at the end of Taft's administration in March 1913.

Cabell remained in the public eye. During the campaign against statewide Prohibition in Virginia, he delivered a speech in Richmond on 14 May 1914 that was later widely reprinted and circulated. Cabell began by expressing his belief that Prohibition laws could neither stop nor diminish production or consumption of alcohol. He asserted that Prohibition was impossible to enforce and cited statistics demonstrating that it increased crime and social problems and placed distribution of "the vilest kinds of liquor and liquor substitutes" in the hands of "the baser and lower portions of the population." Statewide Prohibition, unlike local-option laws of the kind then in effect in Virginia, would also undermine local government, Cabell warned. His efforts were largely unsuccessful. A statewide Prohibition referendum passed in Virginia on 22 September 1914 by a margin of more than three to two. It permitted each householder to obtain for private consumption one quart of liquor, three gallons of beer, or one gallon of wine per month from outside the state. Virginia remained officially dry until 1933, when national Prohibition was repealed and the state adopted new laws to regulate the sale and consumption of alcohol.

After the 1910s Cabell's name appeared less often in the public spotlight until June 1936, when he addressed a Richmond meeting of the bankers' section of the National Association of Credit Men. Highly critical of Democratic president Franklin Delano Roosevelt, Cabell used his quick humor, spiced with Prohibition-era metaphors, to charge that the New Deal had taken the country on a "jolly boondoggling drunk, but the bottle is empty and the nation economically must sober up."

Cabell practiced law with Cabell and Cabell and its successor firms from 1913 until his death. His client list included several major national manufacturing, processing, and financial companies. Cabell's success enabled him to amass an estate valued at $337,500. His work in the field of tax law was recognized nationally in 1943 when Northwestern University awarded him an honorary doctorate of laws. In 1947 Cabell drafted a new tax code for the city of Richmond. A leader of the Virginia State Bar Association eulogized him at the annual meeting in 1951 as "without doubt the ablest tax lawyer in this section of the country," but he was not so well known to the public as he might have been had he specialized in a different field of the law.

Cabell's namesake son also became an attorney, won the 1956 Republican Party nomination for the House of Representatives from the district that included the city of Richmond, and later served as chairman of the State Library Board. Royal Eubank Cabell died of a heart attack at his home in Richmond on 8 September 1950 and was buried in Hollywood Cemetery in that city.

NCAB, 40:292; BVS Birth Register, Nelson Co.; BVS Marriage Register, Richmond City; Records of Appointment of Postmasters, Virginia, Henrico Co., RG 28, NARA; *New York Times*, 17, 19 Jan. 1913, 12 June 1936 (third quotation); Cabell, *The Issues Involved in Statewide Prohibition* (1914), first and second quotations on 7 (printed in condensed form in *Richmond Times-Dispatch*, 15 May 1914); Cabell, "Facts About Kansas 'On the Water Wagon,'" *Leslie's Illustrated Weekly Newspaper,* 12 Nov. 1914, 466, 481 (reprinted in *The Two Banner Prohibition States: Being a Careful Review of Conditions in Maine and Kansas under Prohibition Legislation* [1914], 21–32, por. on 21); *Richmond Times-Dispatch*, 15 Sept. 1950; obituaries in *Richmond News Leader*, 8 Sept. 1950, and *New York Times* and *Richmond Times-Dispatch*, both 9 Sept. 1950; editorial tribute in *Richmond News Leader*, 9 Sept. 1950; memorial in *Virginia State Bar Association Proceedings* (1951): 135–137 (fourth quotation).

GEORGE HARRISON GILLIAM

CABELL, Samuel Jordan (15 December 1756–4 August 1818), member of the Convention of 1788 and member of the House of Representatives, was born in the portion of Albemarle County that in 1761 became Amherst County, the son of Margaret Jordan Cabell and William Cabell (1730–1798), a member of the Conventions of 1776 and 1788. He was educated at a school conducted by Peter Fontaine and from 1772 to 1775 attended the College of William and Mary. In February 1776 Cabell's father, then serving as a member of the Virginia Committee of Safety, helped him secure appointment as captain of a company of Amherst County riflemen recruited for service in the 6th Virginia Regiment.

Cabell took part in the Battle of Trenton on 26 December 1776 and served under Daniel Morgan in 1777. An able officer, he was promoted to major on 20 December 1777 and lieu-

tenant colonel on 15 December 1778. Through promotions, transfers, and renumbering of regiments Cabell served as major of the 14th Virginia Regiment from 20 December 1777 to 14 September 1778 and of the 10th Virginia Regiment from then until 15 December 1778 and as lieutenant colonel of the 8th Virginia Regiment from 15 December 1778 to 12 May 1779, of the 5th Virginia Regiment from then until 4 July 1779, and of the 4th Virginia Regiment from then until 12 February 1781. During March and April 1780 he marched the 4th Regiment to Charleston, South Carolina, where he was captured on 12 May and held as a prisoner of war. During his imprisonment Cabell was transferred to the 7th Virginia Regiment on 12 February 1781. Paroled in August of that year, he then returned to Amherst County and was granted a brevet promotion to colonel at the end of his service in 1783.

On 15 November 1781 Cabell married Sarah Syme, of Hanover County, whose father was a half brother of Patrick Henry. They had five sons and four daughters and after 1785 lived at Soldier's Joy, the large mansion Cabell erected in the northern part of Amherst County. He became county lieutenant in 1784 and the following year was elected to the first of eight consecutive one-year terms in the House of Delegates. Cabell served on the Committee on Claims in 1785, 1787, and 1788, on the Committee for Courts of Justice in 1792, on the Committee of Privileges and Elections in 1789, 1791, and 1792, and on the Committee of Propositions and Grievances in 1785, 1787, 1788, 1791, and 1792. He probably allied himself politically with Henry. In 1788 when Cabell and his father were elected with little opposition to represent Amherst County in the state convention called to consider ratification of the United States Constitution, they voted with Henry to require amendment of the document before ratification, and after that motion failed they voted with Henry against ratification.

In the spring of 1795 Cabell defeated Congressman Francis Walker in the election for the House of Representatives in the Fourteenth District, consisting of Albemarle, Amherst, Fluvanna, and Goochland Counties. Cabell won reelection three times in succession. His distrust of a strong national government, which had contributed to his opposition to the Constitution, drew him into Thomas Jefferson's political camp. The boldness that had served Cabell well in the army led him into an almost unique political difficulty in 1797. In January of that year, in one of his occasional public letters to his constituents, he severely criticized President George Washington. Cabell suggested that Washington's policies were biased toward Great Britain and could provoke war with France, America's former ally and the world's only other republic. He concluded that Washington's policies were dangerous to republican government in the United States. The intensity of Cabell's language elicited an even more intense response from Federalists, among them James Iredell, an associate justice of the United States Supreme Court, who denounced the government's critics from the bench in open court in Richmond on 22 May 1797. Then, in what may have been a preconcerted move, the federal grand jury returned a "Presentment" against Cabell's letter as a "real evil" that was "ruinous to the peace, happiness and independence of these United States." The judge's attacks and the grand jury's official condemnation of Cabell's circular letter prompted one of his constituents, Vice President Thomas Jefferson, to demand that the federal courts be stripped of the means of interfering with legitimate political and legislative actions, and the episode contributed directly to Jefferson's better-known attempts to limit the scope of federal authority during the crisis over the Alien and Sedition Acts of 1798.

Cabell reportedly spent two nights on a cot in the chamber of the House of Representatives in February 1801 while working to elect Jefferson president, but when Cabell ran for a fifth term in 1803, Jefferson's son-in-law Thomas Mann Randolph unexpectedly opposed him. After Randolph defeated Cabell by 13 votes out of more than 1,800 cast, Cabell announced that he would contest the outcome, but he never presented any evidence of irregularity at the polls. Cabell continued to manage his plantation, which lay in the part of Amherst County that in December 1807 became the county of Nelson.

He owned more than 5,000 acres of land, worth more than $8,000, in the new county, and he was one of its first justices of the peace. An active original member of the Society of the Cincinnati in Virginia, he was well known for his hospitality at his large and elegant mansion until his wife's death on 15 May 1814. Samuel Jordan Cabell died at Soldier's Joy in Nelson County on 4 August 1818 and was buried in the family cemetery there.

Brown, *Cabells*, 191–206, gives birth, marriage, and death dates and details of military career from family records; a few letters in various collections at VHS; Francis B. Heitman, *Historical Register of Officers of the Continental Army*, rev. ed. (1914), 138–139; E. M. Sanchez-Saavedra, *A Guide to Virginia Military Organizations in the American Revolution, 1774–1787* (1978), 42, 46, 49, 53, 57, 63, 70, 89; Kaminski, *Ratification*, 8:90–91, 108, 234, 9:569–570, 10:1538, 1540, 1557, 1565; *Madison: Congressional Series*, 15:467–468, 486–487; Cunningham, *Circular Letters of Congressmen*, 1:39–43, 67–71, 115–120, 177–182; Maeva Marcus et al., eds., *The Documentary History of the Supreme Court of the United States, 1789–1800* (1985–), 3:149–150, 181 (quotations), 183–194, 197–219; Daniel P. Jordan, *Political Leadership in Jefferson's Virginia* (1983), 70, 89, 147, 155–156; William H. Gaines Jr., *Thomas Mann Randolph, Jefferson's Son-in-Law* (1966), 50–52; Land Tax Returns, Amherst Co., 1807, Nelson Co., 1809, RG 48, LVA; Virginius Dabney, *Bicentennial History and Roster of the Society of the Cincinnati in the State of Virginia, 1783–1983* (1983), 123; obituaries in *Richmond Enquirer*, 8 Sept. 1818, and *Washington Daily National Intelligencer*, 12 Sept. 1818.

BRENT TARTER

CABELL, William (9 March 1700–12 April 1774), physician, surveyor, and founder of the Cabell family in Virginia, was born in Warminster, England, the son of Nicholas Cabbell and Rachel Hooper Cabbell. As late as the 1750s he often spelled his surname with two *b*s, as did some of his contemporaries, but the spelling "Cabell" became standard in Virginia long before his death. As the eldest surviving son of a respectable family, Cabell received an excellent education, and he probably studied at the Royal College of Medicine and Surgery in London. He may also have served as a surgeon in the Royal Navy or temporarily ministered to sailors aboard ship. According to an unverified family tradition, when the man-of-war to which he was attached stopped in Virginia, Cabell took the opportunity to explore the colony as far west as the falls of the James River. He returned to

England, resigned from the navy, and in September 1723 sailed from Bristol aboard the *Nevis Merchant.*

On 28 December 1723 Cabell witnessed a deed in Henrico County. About 1726 he married Elizabeth Burks. They had five sons and one daughter and lived in the Licking Hole Creek area of western Henrico County that became part of Goochland County in 1728. During a public life of nearly fifty years Cabell served as county coroner, churchwarden, justice of the peace, and sheriff. Either he or his namesake son represented Albemarle County in the House of Burgesses from 1756 to 1758 and sat during that time on the Committee for Courts of Justice. Cabell's son William Cabell (1730–1798) was a member of the Conventions of 1776 and 1788, his son John Cabell also served in the Convention of 1776, and his son Joseph Cabell was a longtime member of the General Assembly.

More important than Cabell's service in public office was his long association with John Mayo and Joshua Fry in the capacity of assistant surveyor. Cabell played a prominent role in the settlement of the Piedmont in the vicinity of the James River. Between 1730 and 1734 he made several entries for land in Mayo's survey books, but he did not follow through and obtain titles to the property at that time. In September 1735 Cabell sailed for England to settle family affairs resulting from the death of his father in August 1730 and the deaths of other relatives in 1733 and 1734. His mother died in October 1737, and several other relatives died shortly thereafter, requiring him to remain in England until September or October 1741. During his absence Cabell's wife used a power of attorney to manage his properties. At his return he owned 7,952 acres of land, including a 1,200-acre tract obtained on grants his wife received on his behalf during his absence.

Cabell resumed surveying after his return to Virginia and added to his already extensive estate. As a surveyor he was able to identify and claim fertile land on reasonable terms. Cabell moved farther west to the confluence of Swan Creek and the James River in the portion of Goochland County that became Albemarle County in 1744 and Amherst County in 1761.

There he built a house that he called Swan Creek and that was later called Liberty Hall. Cabell also erected a mill, a storehouse, and a warehouse at a town that he named Warminster for his home in England. This new community was a thriving commercial center for more than half a century. In 1753 Cabell relinquished his position as surveyor to his namesake son. By that time he owned more than 26,000 acres of land. Cabell sold some of it but retained the best for himself or his children, for whom he provided generously before his death. The property that he acquired enabled his children and their descendants to marry into other prominent Virginia families, enjoy prestige and prosperity, and play responsible roles in the economic and political life of Virginia.

Cabell practiced medicine until about 1770. He imported some of his medicines, concocted others from native plants, and sold them at his apothecary shop. Cabell's surviving journals indicate that he treated his patients with blisters, boluses, cordials, drops, emetics, pills, plasters, powders, purges, and sweats. Like other physicians of the time he visited his patients, but he also established a private hospital near Swan Creek. Patients paid for their board and necessities at the hospital but paid for medical treatment only if Cabell cured them. Unlike other contemporary physicians, for an additional payment he guaranteed his cures, but if a patient died, his artisans made coffins and handled burial arrangements. They also crafted wooden limbs when necessary.

Cabell was described as tall and spare, lithe and active, with great powers of endurance. Until a gun he was holding misfired and disfigured his face, he was considered handsome. Cabell's large library contained the latest medical books. He kept a small stable of horses and sometimes engaged in gentlemanly wagers. Cabell's wife died on 21 September 1756. On 27 September 1762 he married Margaret Meredith, widow of Samuel Meredith, of Hanover County. They had no children before her death on 26 February 1768. Following two years of failing health, William Cabell died at his Amherst County home on 12 April 1774 and was buried in the family cemetery there.

Register of Births and Baptisms of Dissenter Children, Warminster Saint Denys, Wiltshire Record Office, Trowbridge, Eng., recording birth of sons named William Cabbell to Nicholas Cabbell on both 24 Aug. 1698 and 9 Mar. 1700; the elder son likely died and the name was then reused for the next boy; gravestone originally gave birth date as 9 Mar. 1687 and age at death as eighty-seven but was corrected by 1955 to read 9 Mar. 1699 and age at death as seventy-five years; family history signed "Shockoe Grit," *Daily Richmond Whig*, 28 Oct. 1868, and Nathaniel Francis Cabell, compiled notes on the Cabell and Carrington families, VHS, both with gravestone inscription giving death date and incorrect 9 Mar. 1687 birth date; Brown, *Cabells*, 34–78; Anna Marie Mitchell, "Dr. William Cabell, The Pioneer and Founder" (master's thesis, UVA, 1939); Randolph Wall Cabell, *20th Century Cabells and Their Kin* (1993), 22–39 (frontispiece por.); Cabell Family Papers, UVA and VHS; Peter Wilson Coldham, ed., *Complete Book of Emigrants* (1987–), 3:312 (date of emigration); Henrico Co. Miscellaneous Court Records, 2:603 (first record in Virginia); 27 Aug. 1735 power of attorney in Goochland Co. Deed Book, 3:234; Wyndham B. Blanton, *Medicine in Virginia in the Eighteenth Century* (1931); Amherst Co. Will Book, 1:262.

DAPHNE GENTRY

CABELL, William (13 March 1730–23 March 1798), member of the Convention of 1776 and member of the Convention of 1788, was born near Licking Hole Creek in Goochland County, the son of William Cabell (1700–1774), a prominent physician and surveyor, and his first wife, Elizabeth Burks Cabell. His brothers included John Cabell, who served in the Convention of 1776, and Joseph Cabell, a longtime member of the General Assembly. William Cabell's formal education is undocumented, but he was most likely schooled at home and perhaps then at the College of William and Mary. Before he attained his majority he began assisting his father with his surveying duties.

Cabell was frequently referred to in contemporary records as William Cabell Jr. Family histories and other secondary accounts often call him Colonel William Cabell to distinguish him from his father, who in those sources has often been styled Dr. William Cabell. The younger Cabell lived in the southern portion of Albemarle County that in 1761 became Amherst County. Surviving records do not make it clear whether it was Cabell or his father who was elected to the House of Burgesses from Albemarle County in 1756 and served during that time on the Committee for Courts of Justice, but Cabell was either reelected or elected for the first time in 1758. In April 1763 his father deeded him 1,785 acres of land, to which he added by grant and purchase until at one time his property may have exceeded 25,000 acres. Even at the time of his death Cabell owned more than 13,000 acres of land in addition to the plantation where he lived. He held the public offices expected of a wealthy gentleman: vestryman of Saint Anne's Parish, coroner, justice of the peace, sheriff, and officer in the county militia. Cabell became a colonel in the Albemarle County militia on 11 October 1760 and the following year was the first county lieutenant, or commander of the militia, of Amherst County. He was also a county surveyor and a member of the county court.

Early in 1756 Cabell married Margaret Jordan. Their three daughters and four sons included Samuel Jordan Cabell, who served in the House of Representatives. William Cabell represented Amherst County in the House of Burgesses from 1761 until the American Revolution. The absence of his name from the journals for several of the early sessions suggests that he was unable to attend, arrived too late to be appointed to a major committee, or perhaps initially failed to play a significant part in the legislative process. By the end of the 1760s, however, Cabell often served on the influential Committees of Privileges and Elections and of Propositions and Grievances, and during the final session of the House of Burgesses in June 1775 he also sat on the Committee for Religion.

Cabell supported the protests against Parliament that agitated the colony and the assembly during the decade before independence. In 1769, after the governor had dissolved the assembly for adopting vigorous protest resolutions and Cabell and other burgesses had signed an agreement to cooperate in their efforts to persuade Parliament to repeal acts they found odious, Cabell noted in his diary that he had been unanimously reelected to the House of Burgesses. Five years later, after the governor dismissed the assembly for protesting the Coercive, or Intolerable, Acts, Cabell proudly recorded in his diary that he was again reelected without opposition. He attended all five of the Revolutionary Conventions that met between

August 1774 and July 1776. On 17 August 1775 Cabell was elected to the eleven-member Virginia Committee of Safety, which in effect governed Virginia until the next July. He was one of only two committee members not from the Tidewater or a port city. During the convention that met from May to July 1776 and ordered the Virginia delegates in the Second Continental Congress to move a declaration of independence, Cabell served on the Committee of Propositions and Grievances and the committee that introduced the drafts of the Virginia Declaration of Rights and the first constitution of Virginia. Although he missed several days during the sessions of that convention, he was probably present to vote for both documents.

In September 1776 Cabell was one of two men elected to the new Senate of Virginia from the district of Albemarle, Amherst, and Buckingham Counties. He was assigned to the Committee of Privileges and Elections, which he chaired during the May 1779 session. Cabell served in the Senate until his term expired in March 1781. On 12 June of that year he and two other men were elected to the Council of State, but he declined the appointment two days later and preferred instead to hold the seat in the House of Delegates to which he had been elected that spring. There Cabell was ranking member of the Committee of Privileges and Elections during the May 1781 session. He sat on the Committee on Trade in the October 1781 session, the Committee of Propositions and Grievances in both of the 1782 sessions, and the Committee of Privileges and Elections in May 1783. In the October 1781 session, the May and October 1782 sessions, and the May 1783 session Cabell chaired the Committee for Religion. At that time Thomas Jefferson's bill to establish religious freedom threatened the disestablishment of the Church of England. Because the bill had been debated in the House while Cabell was serving in the Senate and did not pass until after he retired from the House, his opinion of Jefferson's proposal is unclear, but, like his brothers, he probably favored adoption of what became the Virginia Statute for Religious Freedom.

Cabell returned to the House of Delegates for two consecutive one-year terms beginning in 1787. In the October session of that year he was ranking member of the Committee for Religion and served on the Committees on Claims, of Privileges and Elections, and of Propositions and Grievances. During the short session of June 1788 Cabell was ranking member of the Committee of Privileges and Elections. During the next full session in October 1788, he chaired the Committee of Propositions and Grievances and once again sat on the Committees of Privileges and Elections and for Religion.

On 3 March 1788 Cabell and his son Samuel Jordan Cabell were elected without serious opposition to represent Amherst County in the convention called to consider ratification of the proposed constitution of the United States. At the time both men were widely reported to be opposed to the Constitution as drafted. At the convention Cabell was appointed to the Committee of Privileges and Elections. He did not take part in the debates, so far as the records show, and he voted with other antifederalists in favor of prior amendments, in favor of reducing the power of Congress to impose taxes, and against ratification.

Cabell joined other opponents of the Constitution in trying to block the election of James Madison to the House of Representatives in 1789, but at the same time he was chosen a presidential elector from his district and fulfilled his promise to his constituents by voting for George Washington as the country's first president. Cabell was an original trustee when Hampden-Sydney College was chartered in 1783. He owned a part interest in an ironworks in Albemarle County, and from 20 October 1785 until at least 1791 he was a director of the James River Company, which planned to clear obstructed passages of the river and open it to commercial navigation. William Cabell died on 23 March 1798, most likely at Union Hill, his Amherst County home, and was buried in the family cemetery there.

Hugh Blair Grigsby, *The Virginia Convention of 1776* (1855), 113–119; Brown, *Cabells*, 78, 81–141, including birth and death dates and extracts from diaries; Randolph B. Campbell and L. Moody Simms Jr., "Revolutionary Virginian: The Life and Times of Colonel William Cabell," *Virginia Phoenix* 7 (1974): 53–61; William Cabell Papers, LVA;

Cabell Family Papers, UVA and VHS; *Revolutionary Virginia*; Kaminski, *Ratification*, 8:67, 90–91, 108, 234, 9:569–570, 909, 10:1538, 1540, 1557, 1562, 1565; Thomas E. Buckley, S.J., *Church and State in Revolutionary Virginia, 1776–1787* (1977), 51–52; Amherst Co. Will Book, 3:466–470.

DAPHNE GENTRY

CABELL, William H. (16 December 1772–12 January 1853), governor of Virginia and judge of the Virginia Court of Appeals, was born at Boston Hill in Cumberland County, the son of Nicholas Cabell and Hannah Carrington Cabell. Reared in a wealthy and politically prominent family, he was closely related to many men of importance in Virginia, and his brother Joseph Carrington Cabell became the first president of the James River and Kanawha Company. Cabell reportedly added the initial *H* to his name to distinguish himself from several other William Cabells. His acquaintance Hugh Blair Grigsby referred to him in 1860 as William Henry Cabell, but there is no other evidence for a middle name.

Cabell received a classical education from private tutors, attended Hampden-Sydney College from 1785 through 1789, and graduated from the College of William and Mary in July 1793 with the first bachelor of law degree awarded by that college. He read law for a time in Richmond and received his license to practice on 13 June 1794. Cabell moved to Amherst County and on 9 April 1795 married Elizabeth Cabell, a cousin. They had two sons and one daughter before her death from consumption, or tuberculosis, on 5 November 1801. Cabell spent the next several months in Charleston, South Carolina, before returning to Amherst County. On 11 March 1805 he married Agnes Sarah Bell Gamble, daughter of Robert Gamble, one of the wealthiest men in Richmond. They had three daughters and five sons, among them Henry Coalter Cabell, who became a director of the James River and Kanawha Company and of the Chesapeake and Ohio Railroad Company and won fame as a Confederate artillery officer.

Cabell was elected to the House of Delegates from Amherst County in 1796, 1798, and four times in succession from 1802 through 1805. He served five one-year terms and the first few days of a sixth. A Jeffersonian Republican, he voted in December 1798 for the Virginia Resolutions that condemned the Alien and Sedition Acts, but in general his tenure in the assembly was unremarkable. Cabell served on the Committee of Propositions and Grievances during the 1798–1799 legislature and on the Committee for Courts of Justice in the 1798–1799, 1804–1805, and 1805–1806 sessions. He never held a major committee chairmanship. In 1800 and 1804 Cabell was a presidential elector for Thomas Jefferson.

On 6 December 1805, soon after the start of Cabell's sixth legislative term, the General Assembly elected him governor of Virginia. He defeated Alexander McRae, an outspoken Republican, by a vote of 99 to 90. Cabell was only thirty-two years old when he took office on 11 December 1805 and may have been elected because he was acceptable to Jefferson's supporters, to dissident Republicans led by John Randolph of Roanoke, and to some Federalists. The assembly reelected Cabell in 1806 and 1807. He served the legal maximum of three consecutive one-year terms and relinquished office on 12 December 1808.

Cabell's years as governor were largely taken up with routine duties related to collecting taxes, administering the state penitentiary, dealing with Revolutionary War land bounties, constructing turnpikes, and appointing numerous state and local officials. By far his most time-consuming responsibility was the regulation of the state militia. Cabell approved the formation of new militia companies, answered requests for supplies, contracted for arms, and commissioned militia officers. The most dramatic event of his administration occurred on 22 June 1807, when the British warship *Leopard*, ostensibly searching for British deserters, attacked the American frigate *Chesapeake* off the Virginia coast. Regarding the British action as both illegal and savage, Cabell ordered militia units, arms, and supplies sent to the Norfolk vicinity. By mid-July the crisis had ended, without further violence, after the British ships sailed from Hampton Roads.

Cabell displayed a thoughtful and judicious approach in making decisions as governor. He repeatedly advised correspondents which actions were beyond the purview of his office or reported that he had taken action only with the advice of the Council of State. Even during the *Chesapeake* affair, although Cabell was quick to mobilize the state's resources, he recognized the superior jurisdiction of the federal government and acted defensively and prudently. So attentive was Cabell to the law that in August 1808 he admonished the Brunswick County jailer for confining a prisoner to a cell with inadequate air circulation that might imperil the prisoner's health. Cabell recommended that the jailer take the prisoner out of his cell occasionally in order to keep him alive until the date of his scheduled execution.

Early in 1809, a few weeks after Cabell's final term as governor concluded, the General Assembly divided Kanawha County and named the new jurisdiction Cabell County. His deliberate and thorough approach to decision-making both prepared and recommended him for the next stage of his professional life. On 14 December 1808 the assembly elected Cabell a judge of the General Court. For more than two years he conducted civil trials and heard appeals in criminal cases in the counties of Charles City, Elizabeth City, Gloucester, James City, King William, Mathews, Middlesex, New Kent, Warwick, and York. In March 1811 the governor appointed Cabell to a vacancy on the Virginia Court of Appeals, which became the Supreme Court of Appeals under the new state constitution of 1830, and in 1831 the assembly reelected him. As the senior member he became president of the court on 18 January 1842, but his deteriorating physical condition caused him to miss several sessions in 1850 and 1851. The Constitution of 1851 required the judges to be elected by popular vote, and because of his poor health Cabell was not a candidate in the May 1852 election. His forty-one years of service made him, along with his near-contemporary Francis Taliaferro Brooke, among the longest-serving judges in the history of the court.

Beginning with his first reported opinion in *Cooke* v. *Piles* in April 1811, Cabell embarked on a steady and solid judicial career that reflected the same deliberate and analytical characteristics he had displayed as governor. He filed few separate opinions. More often than not Cabell's views corresponded with those of the majority, and he tended to write succinct explanations of the facts and the law as he understood them. Judicial scholars have noted that although he provided concise, convincing decisions and asserted his opinion when the need arose, he usually followed stronger-willed justices such as Spencer Roane and Henry St. George Tucker. Cabell also possessed the rare ability to keep an open mind and sometimes even reversed a previous decision.

The most important case Cabell heard occurred early in his judicial career. The issues in *Hunter* v. *Martin* (1814) revolved around the right to appeal decisions made in the Virginia Court of Appeals to the United States Supreme Court. Cabell and his colleagues unanimously ruled that the United States Constitution and the federal Judiciary Act of 1789 did not authorize the federal courts to hear appeals from rulings of the highest state courts. Recalling his 1798 vote for the Virginia Resolutions, Cabell wrote that the power of the United States Supreme Court to hear appellate cases infringed on the jurisdiction of the state courts. Ultimately the Supreme Court reversed the decision of the Virginia Court of Appeals.

William H. Cabell died at his Richmond home on 12 January 1853. His funeral took place at Saint Paul's Episcopal Church, which he had joined in 1851, and he was buried in Shockoe Cemetery in Richmond. The Supreme Court of Appeals published a long resolution honoring Cabell's gentleness of character, patience, and impartiality and concluded that it was as "natural to love as to honor him."

Biographies in Brown, *Cabells*, 271–281 (por. facing 272), Robert A. Brock, *Virginia and Virginians* (1888), 1:98–103, and Henry C. Riely, "William H. Cabell," *Virginia State Bar Association Proceedings* (1930): 581–612; middle name Henry in Hugh Blair Grigsby, *Discourse on the Life and Character of the Hon. Littleton Waller Tazewell* (1860), 13, accepted in French Biographies; autobiographical "Memo. of certain periods in the life of W. H. Cabell" and other records in Cabell Family Papers, VHS; William H. Cabell Executive Papers, RG 3, LVA; *Richmond Enquirer*, 10 Dec. 1805; Edwin M. Gaines, "Governor Cabell and the Republican Schism in Virginia, 1805–08," *Essays in History* 2 (1955): 40–52; Gaines, "The *Chesapeake* Affair: Virginians Mobilize to Defend National Honor," *VMHB* 64 (1956):

131–142; Supreme Court of Appeals Papers, RG 100, LVA; *Cooke* v. *Piles* (1811) (2 Munford), *Virginia Reports*, 16:151–154; *Hunter* v. *Martin* (1814) (4 Munford), *Virginia Reports*, 18:1–59; Hummel and Smith, *Portraits and Statuary*, 19 (pors.); obituaries and tributes in *Richmond Dispatch*, 14, 17 Jan. 1853, *Richmond Enquirer*, 14 Jan. 1853 (with incorrect death date of 13 Jan. 1853), and *Richmond Whig and Public Advertiser*, 14, 21 Jan. 1853 (quotation).

JOHN G. DEAL

CABELL, William Lewis (1 January 1827–22 February 1911), Confederate army officer, was born in Danville, the son of Sarah Epes Doswell Cabell and Benjamin William Sheridan Cabell, who became a general in the militia and served in the Convention of 1829–1830. His brother George Craighead Cabell represented Virginia's Fifth District in Congress for twelve years after the Civil War. Cabell was educated at a local school and received instruction at home from his father. In July 1846 he entered the United States Military Academy. After graduating thirty-third in a class of forty-four in 1850, Cabell reported to the 7th Infantry Regiment as a brevet second lieutenant. In April 1851 he began a decade of service at forts in the West, where he was a quartermaster and achieved the rank of captain in 1858. On 22 July 1856 Cabell married Harriet A. Rector near Fort Smith, Arkansas. Of their seven children, four sons and a daughter lived to adulthood.

In April 1861 Cabell resigned from the army and offered his services to the governor of Arkansas, but he almost immediately departed for Montgomery, Alabama, to join the Confederate States Army. Commissioned a major, he was assigned to Richmond as chief quartermaster and commissary officer for Virginia. Cabell joined the staff of General Pierre G. T. Beauregard at Manassas as chief quartermaster and later served under General Joseph Eggleston Johnston. In the autumn of 1861 he helped Beauregard and Johnston design a Confederate battle flag that could be readily distinguished from the United States flag.

Cabell was transferred to the Trans-Mississippi District as chief quartermaster under Major General Earl Van Dorn in January 1862. That spring Cabell briefly commanded troops along the White River in central Arkansas, and Van Dorn recommended Cabell's promotion to brigadier general, which became effective on 20 January 1863. Cabell demonstrated his logistical skill when he supervised the speedy transfer of Van Dorn's army to the east side of the Mississippi River in March 1862 after the Confederate defeat at Pea Ridge (Elkhorn Tavern), the engagement that ensured that Missouri remained in the Union.

In his next assignment, as commander of the 1st Brigade, 2d Division, Army of the West, Cabell saw considerable action and earned the nickname Old Tige, or tiger. In October 1862 his brigade distinguished itself under heavy fire at the Battle of Corinth, where he was wounded in the foot. In action during the retreat to Holly Springs, Mississippi, Cabell's horse fell on him, badly injuring his leg. While recuperating he served first as inspection officer and then as chief quartermaster for the Trans-Mississippi Department.

Early in 1863 Cabell returned to the field as commander of the District of Northwest Arkansas and led his troops against Union forces in Arkansas and the Indian Territory. He reorganized his troops in 1864 to defend against the Union army in the Red River campaign in Arkansas. On 18 April of that year Cabell led his cavalry brigade in a signal victory against the Union expeditionary force of Major General Frederick Steele at Poison Spring, Arkansas, a rout that culminated in the massacre of troops of the 1st Regiment Kansas Colored Infantry. That autumn the brigade took part in the ill-fated raid into Missouri and Kansas under the command of Major General Sterling Price, who afterward commended Cabell for the brigade's assault against heavily defended Fort Davidson at Pilot Knob, Missouri. On 25 October 1864 Cabell and fellow brigadier general John Sappington Marmaduke were captured at the Battle of Mine Creek on the Little Osage River in Kansas. Confined first on Johnson's Island in Lake Erie and then at Fort Warren on George's Island in Boston Harbor, Cabell took the loyalty oath on 24 July 1865 and was released a month later.

Cabell returned to his wife's home state of Arkansas and became a lawyer. In 1872 he moved his family to Dallas, Texas, in search of greater economic opportunity. Cabell's various political and professional posts during the next four decades included service as mayor of Dallas from January 1874 to April 1876, April 1877 to April 1879, and April 1883 to April 1885; vice president of the Texas Trunk Railroad Company from about 1879 to 1883; United States marshal for the Northern District of Texas from 1885 to 1889; and delegate to the Democratic National Conventions in 1884 and 1892. In 1893 and 1894 he was a supervisor of the Louisiana Lottery Company and continued until 1907 to fill that position for the company's successor in Central America, the Honduran national lottery.

Cabell was commander of the Trans-Mississippi Department of the United Confederate Veterans from 1890 until 1910, when he was named honorary commander in chief for life. An enthusiastic supporter of the UCV, he tirelessly advocated pensions for veterans, establishment of and support for Confederate rest homes, and public memorials. Cabell chaired the UCV committee on the Jefferson Davis monument that was erected in Richmond in 1907 and served on the committee that promoted the construction of the Confederate Memorial Institute, popularly known as Battle Abbey, also in Richmond. His daughter, Katie Cabell Currie, shared his enthusiasm for the Lost Cause and served a two-year term as president general of the United Daughters of the Confederacy from 1897 to 1899.

William Lewis Cabell died in Dallas of bronchitis on 22 February 1911 and was buried in Greenwood Cemetery in that city.

Brown, *Cabells*, 515–518; Paul Harvey Jr., *Old Tige: General William L. Cabell, CSA* (1970), pors. following 38; "Gen. W. L. Cabell," *Confederate Veteran* 2 (1894): 67–68; MS memoirs, Dallas County Historical Society, Dallas, Tex.; Compiled Service Records; numerous references in *OR*; "The Confederate States' Flag," *SHSP* 31 (1903): 68–69; Cabell, *Report of the Part Cabell's Brigade Took in What is Called "Price's Raid into Missouri and Kansas in the Fall of 1864"* [1900]; Presidential Pardons; obituaries in *Dallas Morning News* and *Richmond Times-Dispatch*, both 23 Feb. 1911, and *Confederate Veteran* 19 (1911): 179–180.

ANTOINETTE G. VAN ZELM

CALCOTT, Mary Alexander Whitworth (10 May 1871–21 July 1960), civic leader, was born in Norfolk, the daughter of John Stansfield Whitworth, a railroad machinist and engineer, and Emily Brickhouse Smith Whitworth. She was educated at home by tutors and later attended a private school in the Berkeley section of the city. Her father forbade her to pursue her ambition of attending college and becoming a teacher. On 21 November 1889 she married Alexander Oag Calcott, a Scottish sailor who had become a naturalized citizen in 1884 and was then a steamboat pilot in Norfolk. By 1910 he had become an assistant inspector at the city's United States Customs House.

For two decades after her marriage Calcott devoted herself to the duties of motherhood. Her first child, a son, was born ten months after her wedding, and she had four more sons and one daughter. By 1912 Calcott was finally able to fulfill her ambition for public service and joined the Berkeley Home and School League, an organization that worked to improve the city's school system by lobbying for playgrounds, lunchrooms, and increased teacher salaries. As a leader in the Berkeley unit, she was instrumental in organizing the city's leagues into a united federation. Her evident determination, acuity, and intellect made Calcott an effective first president of the Norfolk City Federation of Home and School Leagues in 1922. She was elected to a second term in 1926.

In 1927 Calcott became only the second woman to serve on the Norfolk school board. She held office for twenty-five years, and in 1946 the members elected her vice chair. Calcott advocated improvement of the city's educational resources and worked for better school lunches, new school buildings, and plentiful supplies for students and teachers. The task facing her and the board was daunting. When its first public high school opened in 1894, Norfolk had been the nation's only city that had more than 5,000 inhabitants but lacked a high school, and two years later the city still had the lowest percentage of public school enrollment in the state. During Calcott's tenure on the school board, attendance improved, and the board hired additional teachers and maintained open-air classrooms designed to offer fresh air, nutritious diet, and rest periods for students susceptible to tuberculosis. Perhaps because she had been denied the opportunity to teach, Calcott believed that teachers played a pivotal role in improving education. She argued for salary increases and more rigorous training for teachers, and it was probably no coincidence that her daughter became a college English professor.

Calcott believed that all children, regardless of race or economic status, deserved an education. She sat on the advisory board and executive committee for the Norfolk branch of Virginia Union University (later Norfolk State University) and chaired the Tidewater Area Negro Girl Scout movement. A Confederate veteran's daughter and member of the United Daughters of the Confederacy, Calcott nevertheless joined the local Women's Council for Interracial Cooperation, which pressed for improvement of the city's slums. The council, along with the Norfolk Education Association, to which she also belonged, boldly called for the reopening of the city's schools in 1958 after the governor had closed them rather than allow them to be desegregated.

Calcott's interest in the welfare of children extended to child health programs. While on the school board she supported open-air classrooms financed by the Norfolk Anti-Tuberculosis League and the Federation of Home and School Leagues. Calcott was active in both organizations, and as president of the former from 1933 to 1951 she took a leading role in providing free X-ray testing to promote early detection and treatment of the disease.

Calcott received many honors. The governor appointed her to the board of visitors of the University of Virginia in 1944, a local civic group named her Norfolk's First Citizen in 1945, and the Golden Rule Foundation named her the Virginia State Mother in 1948. Shortly before her retirement from the school board in 1952 the board named an elementary school in the Ocean View section of the city in her honor, perhaps the first city school to be named for a living person. Mary Alexander Whitworth Calcott died in Norfolk on 21 July 1960 and was buried in Riverside Memorial Park in that city.

Birth date in autobiographical data Calcott supplied to Sue Ruffin Tyler, Tyler Family Papers Group D, W&M; Norfolk Co. Marriage Register; Calcott to Colgate W. Darden Jr., 20 June 1944, Colgate Whitehead Darden Jr. Executive Papers, RG 3, LVA; *Tidewater Trail* 2 (May 1928): 7; ibid. 4 (Feb. 1933): 10; ibid. 18 (Jan. 1946): 5–6; *Virginia Journal of Education* 38 (1945): 282; *Commonwealth* 13 (Mar. 1946): 15–16; *Norfolk Ledger-Dispatch*, 13 Dec. 1945, 25 Jan. 1946, 9 Mar. 1951, 11, 16 July 1952; *Richmond News Leader*, 1 Apr. 1948; *Norfolk Virginian-Pilot*, 27 Aug., 12 Sept. 1951, 2 May, 15 July 1952, 20 Sept. 1953 (por.); *Virginia and the Virginia County* 5 (Oct. 1951): 12, 48; *Norfolk Ledger-Dispatch and Portsmouth Star*, 5 Mar. 1956, 11 May 1957; Henry S. Rorer, *History of Norfolk Public Schools, 1681–1968* (1968), 147–151, 181–182, 205, 249–251, 271; obituary in *Norfolk Virginian-Pilot*, 22 July 1960.

JENNIFER DAVIS McDAID

CALDWELL, Alexander (ca. 1774–ca. 1 April 1839), United States District Court judge, was born probably in New Jersey, the son of James Caldwell and Elizabeth Alexander Caldwell, who had emigrated from Ireland. Early in the 1770s they acquired 800 acres adjacent to Bogg's Run (later Caldwell's Run), near the site of the future city of Wheeling in the region of northwestern Virginia that in 1776 became Ohio County. His father was one of the first justices of the peace for the new county, and his brother James Caldwell served in the House of Representatives from Ohio from 1813 to 1817. A nephew, Alfred Caldwell, became a prominent member of the Senate of Virginia and a leader of the Republican Party. Alexander Caldwell grew up on the family farm and attended an academy in Canonsburg, Pennsylvania. On 2 February 1803 in Lancaster, Pennsylvania, he married Eliza Jane Halsted. They had two sons and seven daughters.

Caldwell initially practiced law with Phillip Doddridge, who represented the northwestern Virginia district in the House of Representatives from 1829 to 1832. By 1801 Caldwell had moved to Wheeling and became a prominent citizen there. He won election in 1816 to represent Ohio County in the House of Delegates for a one-year term and served on the Committee of Propositions and Grievances. In 1818 and 1819 Caldwell served as president of the board of the Lancasterian Academy, the first major educational institution in Wheeling, and he gave an address of welcome when the marquis de Lafayette stopped in the town in 1825 on his tour of the United States.

Caldwell's political views are not well known, but he was no admirer of Andrew

Jackson and probably supported Henry Clay in the presidential election of 1824. Not long thereafter the judge of the United States District Court for the Western District of Virginia died, and a number of Caldwell's colleagues, including members of the Ohio County bar, recommended him for the vacancy. Henry Clay, then the secretary of state, received the recommendations. President John Quincy Adams preferred other candidates, but after two of them declined he appointed Caldwell on 28 October 1825, and the Senate confirmed him on 3 January 1826.

Caldwell closed his private law practice and served as a federal judge until his death thirteen years later, although his role as a magistrate did not keep him from continuing to express his preference for Clay and dislike for Jackson. Caldwell's large district included most of Virginia west of the Blue Ridge, and he held court in Clarksburg, Lewisburg, Staunton, and Wytheville. His court was the venue for the trial of civil, criminal, and commercial disputes that arose under federal law, but except at Clarksburg the docket was seldom crowded, and he tried relatively few cases.

Alexander Caldwell died of consumption, or tuberculosis, in or near Wheeling, probably on 1 April 1839.

"James Caldwell of Washington County, Pennsylvania, and Ohio County, (West) Virginia" (undated typescript, copy in DVB Files), gives undocumented birth date of 1 Nov. 1774; standard reference works on federal judges give variant birth dates in 1774; Hannah D. Pittman, ed., *Americans of Gentle Birth and Their Ancestors: A Genealogical Encyclopedia* (1903–1907), 1:47, uniquely gives middle name Hillyard without citing any authority; Gibson L. Cranmer et al., *History of the Upper Ohio Valley, With Family History and Biographical Sketches* (1890), 1:238–239, 550; Cranmer, *History of Wheeling City and Ohio County, West Virginia, and Representative Citizens* (1902), 220–222, 245; *Lancaster (Pa.) Intelligencer and Weekly Advertiser*, 8 Feb. 1803; 1825 address in Edgar Ewing Brandon, ed., *A Pilgrimage of Liberty: A Contemporary Account of the Triumphal Tour of General Lafayette* (1944), 354–357; a few letters in Illinois State Historical Society, Springfield, and VHS; judicial appointment and a few letters in *Clay Papers*, 4:214–215, 235, 240, 773, 780, 835, 5:179, 801, 7:86; Ohio Co. Will Book, 2:32–33; death notices in *American Beacon and Norfolk and Portsmouth Daily Advertiser* and *Washington Daily National Intelligencer*, both 12 Apr. 1839, report death "on Monday evening last" (8 Apr. 1839), and death notice in *Richmond Enquirer,* 16 Apr. 1839, reports death on 8 Apr. 1839, but death notice in *Richmond Whig*

and Public Advertiser, 9 Apr. 1839, and Ohio Co. bar association memorial in *Wheeling Tri-Weekly Times and Advertiser*, 4 Apr. 1839, indicate earlier date, most likely Monday, 1 Apr. 1839.

THOMAS E. WHITE

CALDWELL, Alfred (4 June 1817–3 May 1868), member of the Senate of Virginia and Republican Party leader, was born in Saint Clairsville, Ohio, the son of James Caldwell, a member of the House of Representatives from 1813 to 1817, and Anne Booker Caldwell. His uncle Alexander Caldwell, of Wheeling, served as United States District Court judge from 1825 until 1839. Caldwell received an A.B. from Washington College (later Washington and Jefferson College) in Washington, Pennsylvania, in 1836 and a B.L. from Harvard University in 1838. He settled in Wheeling to practice law and on 16 August 1839 married Martha Baird. They had three sons, five daughters, and one other child who died in infancy. On 16 August 1860, approximately a year after his wife died, Caldwell married Alice Wheat, of Wheeling. They had two sons and three daughters. Caldwell's namesake son by his first wife served as attorney general of West Virginia from 1885 to 1893.

Caldwell was elected mayor of Wheeling in January 1850, reelected in 1851, and won the office again in 1856 and 1857. In 1856 he defended the right of Virginia's small Republican Party to meet in Wheeling and denounced the violence that resulted from the controversial assembly. Like many other public men from western Virginia, Caldwell, who had been a Whig, believed that eastern politicians slighted the interests of the western counties. His developing antislavery positions estranged him even more from the easterners. Caldwell moved from the Whig Party's support for white workers and free labor into opposition to slavery and eventually into the Republican Party. In 1857 he was elected to a four-year term in the Senate of Virginia from the district composed of Brooke, Hancock, and Ohio Counties. He was appointed to the Committee for Courts of Justice and the minor Committee to Examine the Clerk's Office, and two years later he served on the same two committees as well as the important Committee on Finance and Claims. The unreservedly outspoken Caldwell endorsed and voted for bills to ameliorate the condition of slaves, circulated copies of Hinton R. Helper's antislavery book, *The Impending Crisis of the South: How to Meet It* (1857), and denounced slavery and slave-holders. Richmond newspapers branded him a dangerous abolitionist, and slave owners threatened him with physical violence.

In 1860 Caldwell chaired the small Virginia delegation to the Republican National Convention in Chicago, where he supported Abraham Lincoln for president. Caldwell was attending his last session of the Senate of Virginia in Richmond when the secession convention began its deliberations in February 1861. That spring he joined western delegates in initiating the meetings that led to the creation of West Virginia. Caldwell did not participate in the formation of the new state, however, because on 12 August 1861 Lincoln appointed him United States consul in the kingdom of Hawaii. Caldwell was stationed at Honolulu from 1 November 1861 to 7 January 1867, when, at the insistence of the United States minister to Hawaii, the secretary of state suspended him for collusion in a scheme to enrich himself and his son-in-law by overcharging the government for services rendered. When he was suspended the consul's accounts were also in arrears almost $4,000. Alfred Caldwell returned to Wheeling, where he died on 3 May 1868 and was buried in the local Mount Wood Cemetery.

Encyclopaedia of Contemporary Biography of West Virginia (1894), 139–140, gives dates of birth and first marriage; Thomas Condit Miller and Hu Maxwell, *West Virginia and Its People* (1913), 2:12–18; *Wheeling Daily Intelligencer*, 17 Aug. 1860; W. G. Bean, "John Letcher and the Slavery Issue in Virginia's Gubernatorial Contest of 1858–1859," *JSH* 20 (1954): 37; Henry T. Shanks, *The Secession Movement in Virginia, 1847–1861* (1934), 212, 271; official correspondence, including documentation of charges against Caldwell and his unsuccessful refutations, in Dispatches from United States Consuls in Honolulu, 1861–1868, and Dispatches from United States Ministers to Hawaii, 1864–1867, both in General Records, Department of State, RG 59, NARA; corruption described in Frederick Anderson, Michael B. Frank, and Kenneth M. Sanderson, eds., *Mark Twain's Notebooks and Journals* (1975–1979), 1:185–186; obituaries in *Wheeling Daily Intelligencer* and *Wheeling Daily Register*, both 4 May 1868.

CONNIE PARK RICE

CALDWELL, Nancy Melvina "Vinnie" (4 August 1868–11 February 1956), member of the House of Delegates, was born in the town of Middlebrook in Augusta County, the daughter of John Barger Caldwell, a farmer, and Fannie Givens Caldwell, both natives of Craig County. When she was two years old her parents moved the family to Carroll County, onto land that later became part of the town of Galax. Caldwell attended the local public school and at her mother's urging took and passed an examination to become a teacher. Sometime in the 1880s she began teaching in the public schools in Carroll and Grayson Counties and attended a summer normal institute to obtain her teaching certificate. Caldwell also studied art briefly at Centenary College in Cleveland, Tennessee.

Miss Vinnie, as she came to be known, taught at a series of a dozen schools until late in the 1890s. Frustrated by her low salary and the difficulties of teaching in an impoverished rural school system, she learned to sew and worked for a time as a seamstress in Richmond. Caldwell then moved to Lynchburg, where she took a business course at a school and then taught there for two years. Later she found employment as a stenographer. About 1903 Caldwell became a traveling sales representative. Crisscrossing the South by train and canvassing small towns door-to-door, she spent several years demonstrating first medicine and then a dustless broom. For several years she lived in Florida. By 1920 she had returned to Galax, where she helped to run the Bluemont Hotel, which her family then owned. Caldwell joined the Galax Music Club and the local chapter of the Business and Professional Women's Club. She also involved herself in welfare work in behalf of children and was instrumental in obtaining state assistance for a number of orphaned and physically handicapped youth and their families.

Caldwell probably became involved in local politics after women gained the right to vote in 1920. In 1927, under circumstances that are no longer clear, the Democratic Party in Carroll County nominated her for the county's seat in the House of Delegates. Although southwestern Virginia was a stronghold of the Republican Party and Republicans captured every other major office in the county that year, Caldwell defeated her opponent, Republican Humes L. Franklin, by a vote of 1,990 to 1,895. She joined Sallie Cook Booker, of Henry County, Sarah Lee Fain, of Norfolk, and Helen Ruth Henderson, of Buchanan County, as the only women in the General Assembly when it convened in January 1928. All four were current or former schoolteachers. Caldwell served on the Committees on Asylums and Prisons, on Manufactures and Mechanic Arts, and on Schools and Colleges.

Caldwell did not seek reelection in 1929 but maintained a keen interest in current events for the rest of her life. She devoted herself to welfare work in the Galax area and remained active in the community into her eighties. Her health began to decline early in the 1950s, and she became a semi-invalid confined to a wheelchair. Nancy Melvina "Vinnie" Caldwell died at her home in Galax on 11 February 1956 and was buried in the Caldwell-Givens family cemetery there.

Biography in Galax Historical Committee, *The Bicentennial Celebration of Galax, Virginia, June 13–19, 1976* [1976], 52–54; birth date (possibly from data provided by Caldwell) in E. Griffith Dodson, *The General Assembly of the Commonwealth of Virginia, 1919–1939* (1939), 225 (por. facing 54); Election Records, no. 230, RG 13, LVA; *Roanoke Times*, 9, 10 Nov. 1927; *Richmond Times-Dispatch*, 10, 11 Nov. 1927, 12 Jan. 1928 (por.); gravestone transcribed in Suzanne Burow, ed., *Cemetery Records of Carroll County, Virginia* (1990), 342; obituary in *Galax Gazette*, 13 Feb. 1956.

SANDRA GIOIA TREADWAY

CALDWELL, Willie Brown Walker (29 November 1860–21 March 1946), civic leader and Republican Party leader, was born in Newbern, Pulaski County, the daughter of James Alexander Walker and Sarah Ann Poage Walker. Her father was an attorney, a brigadier general in the Confederate army, the lieutenant governor of Virginia from 1878 to 1882, and a Republican member of the House of Representatives from 1895 to 1899. Willie Walker's unflinching adulation of her father shaped her life more than any other force. From an early age she was fascinated by politics and civic affairs and drawn to educational and intellectual pursuits.

During most of Walker's childhood and adolescence her mother was in ill health and often confined to bed. Walker's aunt Mary W. Woods, who lived with the family from 1865 until her death in 1874, acted as her surrogate mother. Educated at home and in a small public school in Newbern that her father helped organize after the Civil War, Walker entered the Augusta Female Seminary (later Mary Baldwin College) in 1876 and excelled as a student. After six months, however, she was forced to leave because of failing health. Walker continued her education at home and also assumed the demands of household management. Equally important, she became her father's constant companion, legal assistant, and political confidant.

In 1879 the family moved to Wytheville. There, on 13 June 1888, Walker married Manley Morrison Caldwell, a local attorney. They had one son and two daughters and lived in her father's house until after both of her parents had died. In 1906 the Caldwells moved to Roanoke, where she immediately began organizing local women in civic reform causes. Caldwell was a founder on 7 December 1906 of the Woman's Civic Betterment Club. Roanoke's rapidly increasing population had outgrown its housing, recreation, sanitation, and other civic resources, and early in 1907 the club commissioned a sanitation study of the city and also a remodeling plan by the landscape architect John Nolen, of Massachusetts. Nolen's plan was never implemented, but the club instituted many other improvement projects, including cleanup campaigns, construction of public playgrounds, and stricter food and milk inspections. Through market boycotts it encouraged farmers to store and package their foods properly. Caldwell believed that the civic club movement was the ideal vehicle to mobilize women "for the uplift of the world" in the years before woman suffrage and overt political participation. She served as the Roanoke club's first vice president and was president from 1908 to 1912.

Caldwell soon widened her sphere of influence. She attended the first meeting of the Virginia Federation of Women's Clubs in 1908 and from 1912 to 1915 was president of the federation. During her presidency the federation's membership doubled, and Caldwell initiated civic programs, publicity committees, and library development projects. She also became involved in national affairs, and even though she had not initially supported the woman suffrage movement, at a Republican Party conference in Washington, D.C., she accepted the task of organizing the newly enfranchised women of Virginia in preparation for the 1920 presidential election. Caldwell attended the Republican National Conventions in 1920 and 1924. In the latter year the party for the first time elected women to the national committee, and she became the first Republican national committeewoman from Virginia, for two four-year terms. The 1925 Republican State Convention nominated Caldwell for state superintendent of public instruction, the last time that office was an elective one, but the entire Republican ticket lost by large margins to the Democrats in the general election.

During the 1928 presidential campaign Caldwell was at the center of a brief national controversy, one of many episodes in which the Catholicism of the Democratic Party candidate, Alfred E. Smith, became an issue. An official Republican Party letter bearing Caldwell's stamped signature and containing anti-Catholic language was published in the *Washington Post* on 29 September. She acknowledged dictating and sending the letter but denied responsibility for the specific inflammatory phrases. Instead, Caldwell suggested that her secretary might have added her own words to the letter. The Republican candidate, Herbert Hoover, quickly and publicly repudiated the remarks contained in the letter.

In 1933 Caldwell began teaching a class at the National Business College in Roanoke. Her intended audience was businesspeople, whom she instructed in communication and interpersonal skills. The popularity of the course led to a radio show, and Caldwell also traveled around the state lecturing on the subject to clubs and organizations. She retired from teaching about 1940 after suffering a serious fall.

Caldwell was a founding member of what became the Thursday Morning Music Club, a regent of the National Society Daughters of the American Revolution, an honorary member of the Magic City Garden Club, and a member of the Roanoke Study Club. She wrote throughout her life and published several short stories and two novels, *The Tie That Binds: A Story of the North and the South* (1895) and *Donald McElroy, Scotch Irishman* (1918). Caldwell also composed a book-length biography of her father, which her grandson Manley Caldwell Butler, a member of the House of Representatives from 1972 to 1983, published as *Stonewall Jim: A Biography of General James A. Walker, C.S.A.* (1990).

Caldwell's example inspired her daughter Sarah Poage Caldwell Butler to lead a successful campaign for the establishment of a public library in Roanoke, one of the improvement projects that she had been unable to complete herself. Willie Brown Walker Caldwell died at her home in Roanoke on 21 March 1946 and was buried in the city's Evergreen Burial Park.

Biographies in John William Leonard, ed., *Woman's Who's Who of America, 1914–1915* (1915), 155, Durward Howes, Mary L. Braun, and Rose Garvey, eds., *American Women: The Standard Biographical Dictionary of Notable Women* (1939), 3:140, and Etta Belle Walker Northington, *A History of the Virginia Federation of Women's Clubs, 1907–1957* [1958], 47–50; Pulaski Co. Birth Register; BVS Marriage Register, Wythe Co.; information provided by grandson Manley Caldwell Butler; typed biographical memorandum, ca. 1927, in Butler's possession, 2001 (photocopy in DVB Files); two 1940 typescripts, based in part on interviews with Caldwell, in WPA Biographies; *Roanoke Times*, 17 May 1908 (quotation), 12 Mar. 1939; obituaries and editorial tributes in *Roanoke World-News*, 21 (por.), 23 Mar. 1946, *Roanoke Times*, 22, 23 (por.) Mar. 1946, and *Virginia Club Woman* 18 (Apr. 1946): 24.

STACY G. MOORE

CALFEE, Ernest William (23 November 1886–27 October 1942), mayor of Pulaski, was born in Pulaski, the son of Gustavus A. Calfee, a merchant, and Camille Baughan Calfee. He attended the local public schools and graduated in 1904 from Pulaski's high school. About 1905 Calfee went to work in a real estate and insurance business operated by his uncle Leander S. Calfee, who was a member of the Pulaski Board of Trade, an early version of the town's Chamber of Commerce. After his uncle's death in 1910, Calfee managed the business until January 1915, by which time he was involved in

Pulaski's political and business affairs. He was elected to the town council in June 1912 and won reelection two years later. Although he was one of the youngest council members, in January 1915 the council chose Calfee to fill the vacancy created by the death of the incumbent mayor. The demands of the office coincided perfectly with his interests and abilities. An able and resourceful administrator, Calfee was returned to office each election until his death twenty-seven years later.

Several months after winning his first full term as mayor in June 1916, Calfee became a vice president of the League of Virginia Municipalities at its annual conference held in Clifton Forge. This early exercise in governmental cooperation had a more practical application in the autumn of 1918 when Pulaski was hard hit by a deadly worldwide outbreak of influenza. As the epidemic spread through the town Calfee acted quickly to close schools, churches, and businesses, set up an emergency hospital and a community kitchen, and organize a citizens' committee with headquarters in his office to coordinate the efforts of doctors and relief workers. His calls for help from other localities brought emergency assistance and medical support from Richmond, Roanoke, and as far away as Washington, D.C., and New York City. Ninety-two townspeople died before the epidemic abated, but the toll would have been higher had it not been for Calfee's leadership and the community's tireless efforts.

Calfee presided over a prospering town. Pulaski's population nearly doubled between 1900 and 1920. Commercial development initially kept pace, but in 1920 two of the town's larger industries closed, crippling the local economy. When Calfee and other businessmen learned that leaders in nearby counties were planning a new furniture factory, he spearheaded an appeal to local firms to help purchase town lots on which to construct it. They raised more than $17,000 and acquired more than twelve acres of land, which they conveyed to the manufacturers. In 1923 the Coleman-Vaughan Furniture Company (after 1927 the Coleman Furniture Corporation) was chartered, spurring the growth of other industries in the town.

Pulaski was moving from dependence on the zinc and iron industries that had created the town toward a more diversified economy. Calfee's leadership in successfully bringing new businesses to the town extended that trend. By 1929 Pulaski County boasted thirty-two manufacturing firms, twenty-seven of them concentrated in the county seat. Few other southwestern Virginia communities could match Pulaski's steady economic growth.

During the Great Depression of the 1930s Calfee gave unselfishly of his time in aiding the unemployed. With county officials he applied to the Reconstruction Finance Corporation for a grant of $160,000 and received $54,000 to furnish work for the unemployed during the winter of 1932–1933. Calfee lobbied for federal funds and state approval for highway construction to employ local workers during the depression. He even urged owners of vacant town lots to allow needy citizens to cultivate them as garden plots. After the passage of the National Industrial Recovery Act in 1933, Calfee chaired the local NRA committee and worked closely with other officials on the recovery program. In September 1933 nearly 10,000 people gathered in Pulaski for a "Recovery Parade." Despite the event's optimistic spirit, the county still had considerable unemployment. Calfee, who as committee chairman was scheduled to lead the parade, chose instead to march with the unemployed men in the last contingent.

During his tenure as mayor, Calfee strengthened Pulaski's economic base by acquiring federal funds to build streets, bridges, water and sewer lines, and parks. Until 1930 he maintained a financial interest in his insurance business. By July 1927 Calfee was a director of the Pulaski National Bank, and he sat on the boards of several local corporations, including the Virginia Maid Hosiery Mills, the Paul Knitting Mills, and the Southwest Publishing Company. In 1935 he took over direction of the ailing Coleman Furniture Corporation, in which many local residents had invested and were employed. As president and treasurer, Calfee labored up until the time of his death to keep the business afloat.

Calfee chaired the county fuel committee during World War I and served on the local defense council, and during the early months of World War II he directed local civil defense work. He was well known in Masonic circles and active in other fraternal organizations as well. A Democrat, Calfee was a delegate to several of the party's district conventions. One of his last public acts came in August 1939 as president of the Pulaski County Centennial Commission. Calfee oversaw preparations for the six-day celebration of the county's founding. The events took place at the town athletic field that he was instrumental in having built in 1935. In his honor it is called Calfee Park.

Calfee never married but took a paternal interest in the mountain community where he was born. A shy man who lived a public life but preferred to work behind the scenes, he could be found most evenings at his office in the municipal building settling minor disputes, deliberating with officials, or otherwise conducting the town's affairs. Ernest William Calfee died in a Pulaski hospital on 27 October 1942, two weeks after suffering two heart attacks. His body lay in state at the First Presbyterian Church and was buried in Oakwood Cemetery in Pulaski. In tribute to Calfee all the businesses in Pulaski closed for two hours during the funeral service, and all flags flew at half staff.

Biographies in Glass and Glass, *Virginia Democracy*, 3:736–737 (giving 6 Nov. 1889 birth date), and *Pulaski Southwest Times*, 14 June 1998; birth probably recorded mistakenly on 1 Dec. 1886 under name Ernest Linwood Calfee in BVS Birth Register, Pulaski Co.; information provided by R. Lloyd Mathews; Conway Howard Smith, *The Land That Is Pulaski County* (1981), 423–431, 447, 450–452; *Pulaski Southwest Times and News-Review*, 29 Sept. 1916, 9 June 1920, 13 Aug. 1939; Malita Warden Murphy and James L. Douthat, *Gates to Glory: Cemeteries of Pulaski County, Virginia* (1983), 7; obituaries and editorial tributes in *Pulaski Southwest Times* (por. and birth date of 23 Nov. 1886) and *Roanoke World-News,* both 27 Oct. 1942, and *Roanoke Times,* 28 Oct. 1942.

DONALD W. GUNTER

CALISCH, Edith Elliott Lindeman (21 March 1898–22 December 1984), journalist and lyricist, was born in Pittsburgh, Pennsylvania, the daughter of Sidney Oaks Lindeman and Mae McIntyre Elliott Lindeman. Her father's work as a salesman kept the family moving frequently when she was young, but in 1908 they settled in her father's hometown of Dayton, Ohio. The Lindemans were Jewish and the Elliotts were Christian, but Mae Lindeman converted after her marriage and in June 1911 Edith Lindeman was confirmed at the Dayton synagogue. In March 1913 a flood destroyed Sidney Lindeman's business, and the family moved to Richmond, where he had business contacts. Edith Lindeman attended Virginia Randolph Ellett's school (later Saint Catherine's School) for a year and then matriculated at John Marshall High School. In 1916 she entered the Collegiate School for Girls, where a teacher recognized her writing ability and encouraged her to attend Barnard College in New York City. In 1917 Lindeman enrolled in Barnard to take prejournalism courses but left in 1919 after four semesters.

In Richmond on 3 May 1920 Lindeman married A. Woolner Calisch, whom she had known since high school. They had one son and two daughters. In 1924 they moved with her parents to Greensboro, North Carolina, where her father managed and her husband was a vice president of a business distributing products for the Delco Light Company and the Frigidaire Corporation. Calisch wrote advertising booklets for both companies. The business was hit hard by the Great Depression, and in 1931 the family returned to Richmond.

At the request of her father-in-law Edward Nathan Calisch, an eminent rabbi, she wrote two books, *Bible Tales for the Very Young* (1930) and *Bible Tales for Young People* (1934), for use in Sabbath schools. Calisch also published a one-act play entitled *The Jews Who Stood by Washington* (1932), a collection of Jewish legends for young people entitled *Fairy Tales from Grandfather's Big Book* (1938), and *Three Score and Twenty: A Brief Biography of Edward Nathan Calisch* (1945). In 1933 she became the *Richmond Times-Dispatch*'s part-time motion picture reviewer and during the next thirty years reviewed more than 6,000 films. Calisch became an editor for the children's page in 1934 and editor of the entertainment pages the following year. She also established herself as a respected drama critic. Deeply interested in theater, she promoted local efforts as well as those of the Barter Theater, in Abingdon. In 1956 Calisch suggested that the Barksdale Theatre, in Hanover County, offer dinner along with the evening performance. This practice provided needed additional revenue for the new theater, and in adopting her suggestion Barksdale may have become the first dinner theater in the country.

Early in the 1950s Calisch became a songwriter. She wrote lyrics under her maiden name of Edith Lindeman, and Carl Stutz, then an announcer at WRVA radio station, composed the music. They wrote more than a dozen songs together. An early effort, "Cling to Me," did not attract much attention, but the next attempt was a big success, although several publishers initially rejected it. Kitty Kallen's recording of "Little Things Mean a Lot" on the Decca label climbed to the top of the music charts, was the number one song in the country for nine weeks in 1954, and was voted the year's most popular song in polls taken by the music industry. Other stars who recorded the song included the McGuire Sisters, the country singer Margo Smith, and the rhythm-and-blues artists Billy Ward and His Dominoes. Calisch and Stutz's "Blackberry Winter," written in 1952, was recorded by Mary Higdon "Sunshine Sue" Workman, of WRVA's popular show, *Old Dominion Barn Dance*, but it was most successful as the "B" side of Mitch Miller's 1955 top-selling recording of "The Yellow Rose of Texas." Perry Como recorded their song "I Know" in May 1959, and it reached number forty-seven on the music charts. British singer Tom Jones reprised the tune nearly a decade later. In 1953 Calisch and Stutz composed a western ballad, "Red Headed Stranger." Originally intended for Como, the song achieved its greatest success in 1975 when the country music singer Willie Nelson used it as the title track and thematic basis of the best-selling album that established him as a top recording artist.

In 1959 Calisch's friends at the Barksdale Theatre held a surprise party for her. Guests from the entertainment world included representatives from Metro-Goldwyn-Mayer and the composer Johnny Mercer. In 1964 Calisch retired, although she still occasionally contributed articles to the newspaper. She remained active in Congregation Beth Ahabah through-

out her adult life. In 1977 the Songwriters Hall of Fame recognized her work at a ceremony in New York, and in 1984 the Barksdale Theatre dedicated to her a history of its first thirty-one years. Edith Elliott Lindeman Calisch died on 22 December 1984 at a Henrico County nursing home and was buried in Hebrew Cemetery in Richmond. A *Richmond Times-Dispatch* obituary singled out for special commendation her "tremendous contribution to the cultural life of this community" and the "strong coverage she provided for the area's regional theaters in their formative years."

John Simons, ed., *Who's Who in American Jewry* (1939), 3:154; Durward Howes, Mary L. Braun, and Rose Garvey, eds., *American Women* (1939), 3:141; transcript of autobiographical oral recollections, 14 July 1975, for Congregation Beth Ahabah Museum and Archives, Richmond (copy in DVB Files); *Generations: Journal of Congregation Beth Ahabah Museum and Archives Trust* 3 (Oct. 1990): 1–6 (pors.); BVS Marriage Register, Richmond City; information provided by daughters Frances Calisch Rothenberg and Virginia Calisch Fairman; Muriel McAuley, Nancy Kilgore, and David Kilgore, *Going On . . . Barksdale Theatre: The First Thirty-One Years* (1984), 3, 12, 18, 47; William Bien, " 'Little Things . . .' Mean a Lot to Two Tunesmiths," *Virginia and the Virginia Record* 76 (July 1954): 16–17; feature articles in *Richmond News Leader,* 6 Jan. 1962, 24 Mar. 1987, and *Richmond Times-Dispatch,* 3 May 1971, 24 Mar. 1987; obituaries in *Richmond News Leader* and *Richmond Times-Dispatch* (quotations), both 24 Dec. 1984, and *Washington Post,* 26 Dec. 1984.

DONALD W. GUNTER

CALISCH, Edward Nathan (23 June 1865–7 January 1946), rabbi, was born in Toledo, Ohio, the son of Hartog (Henry) Salomon Calisch, a language instructor, and Rebecca van Noorden Calisch, both of whom immigrated to the United States from the Netherlands in 1856. Calisch spent his boyhood in Chicago, where the great fire of 1871 wiped out the family's possessions. A few years later his father died. At age ten Calisch went to work as a cash boy in a department store, but the meager wages that he and his elder brother earned could not support the family. In 1876 his impoverished mother placed him in a Jewish orphanage in Cleveland. There Calisch excelled in his studies, especially in oratory. In 1879 he attracted the notice of Isaac Mayer Wise, an early advocate of Reform Judaism and the founder of Hebrew Union College in Cincinnati, America's first rabbinical seminary. Wise decided that Calisch should become a rabbi and be trained at the seminary.

For four years Calisch attended Hughes High School in the mornings and the preparatory department of Hebrew Union College in the afternoons. After graduating from high school he undertook a similar regimen for another four years. He began his day with secular courses at the University of Cincinnati and concluded it with rabbinical studies at Hebrew Union College. Calisch graduated with two degrees in 1887 and a reputation as one of the best pulpit orators in the seminary.

In 1886 Calisch had served as a student rabbi for the high holidays at Congregation Anshai Emeth in Peoria, Illinois, and he so impressed the congregants that they offered him the pulpit following his graduation. He spent four happy years in Peoria. Calisch enjoyed guiding his own congregation. In Peoria on 22 January 1890 he married Gisela Woolner, a native of Vienna, Austria. One of their four sons died in infancy and their only daughter died in an automobile accident in 1911. His daughter-in-law Edith Elliott Lindeman Calisch became a successful journalist and lyricist and wrote Calisch's biography.

In January 1891 the rabbi of Congregation Beth Ahabah in Richmond died. A congregation member at whose wedding Calisch had recently officiated persuaded Beth Ahabah to invite Calisch to Richmond for an interview. Offered the position, he accepted and in September 1891 at the age of twenty-six took over the pulpit of the sixth-oldest Jewish congregation in the United States.

Calisch was a firm yet beloved leader of Beth Ahabah, remembered fondly years after his death by congregation members he had married or taught in the religious school. A tall, handsome man with great powers of eloquence, he steered Beth Ahabah away from its earlier Orthodox leanings and toward full participation in Reform Judaism. Men and women sat together in the sanctuary, congregants no longer covered their heads during services, confirmation rather than bar mitzvah became the rite of passage into adulthood, and the most important

service of the week became Friday evening rather than Saturday morning. A man of seemingly endless energy, Calisch prepared a revised *Book of Prayer for Jewish Worship* (1893), which Beth Ahabah used for two decades until the adoption of the *Union Prayer Book*, and he wrote *A Child's Bible: Being the Incidents and Narratives of Sacred Scriptures, Simply Told* (1894) for use by the religious school.

Beth Ahabah became one of the premier Reform congregations in the United States. Under Calisch's longtime leadership it embraced the tenets of the 1885 Pittsburgh Platform, which articulated a vision of modern Judaism free from the rituals and practices of either ancient Palestine or medieval Europe. Reform aspired to be a modern faith, concerned with the society around it. In a nation relatively free of anti-Semitism, Jews could be indistinguishable from their Christian neighbors except in matters of faith. The vision proved attractive to prosperous, assimilating Jews of the late nineteenth and early twentieth centuries, especially in the South. Beth Ahabah clung to the classic tenets of the Pittsburgh Platform long after the Reform movement began to revive older elements of faith and ritual and rethink what modern Judaism meant.

Calisch's participation in the civic affairs of Richmond and beyond was also important to his congregation. For decades Christian ministers had been active in public affairs, delivering addresses and prayers on public occasions and giving sermons in neighboring congregations. The Reform ethos called for rabbis to engage in these activities as well, as another proof that except for their religious beliefs Jews were as patriotic, as civically engaged, and as public-spirited as their Christian neighbors. Calisch was part of that generation of Reform rabbis described by some scholars as emissaries to the Christians. In 1892 he was one of the first rabbis to deliver an opening prayer at the United States House of Representatives, and during the next fifty years he gave hundreds of speeches in Virginia, throughout the country, and even overseas. At Mount Vernon in 1899 Calisch gave the address and benediction at a nationwide Masonic celebration of the centennial of George

Washington's death, the only person on the program who was neither a high-ranking Freemason nor a government official. On 13 June 1901 he gave the prayer at the second day's session of Virginia's constitutional convention, a clear recognition of his high standing among the state's political leaders. In 1913 Calisch returned to Mount Vernon to speak and afterward went to the White House for lunch with President William Howard Taft, who requested that he pronounce the traditional motzei prayer before eating. In 1930 and 1937 he spoke at the Tomb of the Unknown Soldier in Arlington National Cemetery. Throughout his tenure in Richmond, Calisch was a popular speaker at civic groups such as the Rotary (to which he belonged), and he also took an active public part in the local chapter of the Red Cross and many other community organizations. In May 1915 he addressed a rally of the Equal Suffrage League of Virginia on the steps of the State Capitol.

Calisch was widely recognized as a leader in establishing good interfaith relationships in Richmond and in gaining for Jews a greater acceptance by the Christian community. When Grace Baptist Church burned in 1896, he immediately offered the use of Beth Ahabah for Sunday services until it could be rebuilt. The church gladly accepted, an action that would have seemed impossible earlier in the century. When fire struck Grove Avenue Baptist Church four years later, Calisch made a similar offer. He pioneered in establishing joint Thanksgiving services by Beth Ahabah and First Baptist Church, and he cooperated closely with several of Virginia's leading Baptist ministers in their campaign to preserve strict separation of church and state by opposing mandatory Bible readings in public schools.

Calisch also made his mark as a scholar. In 1901 he enrolled in the graduate school at the University of Virginia. He received an M.A. in 1903 and a Ph.D. in 1908 with a dissertation published as *The Jew in English Literature, as Author and as Subject* (1909). Even though he maintained his full-time duties at Beth Ahabah, Calisch found time to join the Washington Literary Society and the university debating team and won election to the prestigious Raven Soci-

ety and the university chapter of Phi Beta Kappa. His extensive list of publications thereafter included essays on public affairs and lighter subjects and two textbooks for Jewish education, *Methods of Teaching Biblical History, Junior Grade* (1914) and *Methods of Teaching Jewish History, Senior Grade* (1914). A member of the liturgy committee of the Reform movement, Calisch helped revise the *Union Prayer Book* and wrote a number of the new prayers. He also wrote an eighty-page *History of Congregation "Beth Ahaba," Richmond, Virginia, From Its Organization to Its Sixtieth Anniversary, 1841–1901* (ca. 1901; reprinted 1926).

The congregation grew in wealth and membership during Calisch's tenure. When he arrived in 1891 it numbered a scant 100 families and held services in an old building on Eleventh Street. In 1904 Beth Ahabah completed construction of a synagogue on West Franklin Street, and membership grew to more than 450 families by 1930. Being rabbi of a premier congregation enhanced Calisch's prestige, but his activities, especially in the broader Jewish community, reflected well on the temple in turn. He served two terms (1921–1923) as president of the Central Conference of American Rabbis, the national body of Reform rabbis, and he was a member of B'nai B'rith, the national Jewish fraternal organization.

As a mark of its appreciation, Beth Ahabah in 1925 gave Calisch a one-year sabbatical with full pay and funds to allow him to travel around the world. His reputation as an orator won him many invitations to speak, and he addressed the Jewish community in Shanghai and Rotary Clubs in Tokyo. In Delhi Calisch lunched with the viceroy of India. He returned greatly refreshed and embarked on another two decades of service to Beth Ahabah.

These years did not prove peaceful, either in the world or in Jewish communal affairs. The rise of Nazism in Germany aroused Calisch's fears, and during the 1930s he spoke out strongly against German treatment of Jews. Despite the threat to European Jewry, he firmly opposed the growing Zionist movement, which called for the reestablishment of a Jewish homeland in Palestine. Although the times had changed greatly, Calisch adhered until the end of his life to the 1885 Pittsburgh Platform, which proclaimed Jews a religious community and not a distinct nation that should have its own state. To him, Jewish nationalism undermined Jews' credibility as loyal Americans. Calisch was a founder of the American Council for Judaism, a group created in 1943 to fight Zionism. He brought many members of Beth Ahabah into the council, and for many years, well after the establishment of the state of Israel, Beth Ahabah had the reputation of being an anti-Zionist congregation.

Despite this growing controversy within American Jewry and within the Reform movement, Calisch remained beloved by his congregation and widely respected in the city and beyond. He received an honorary doctorate of Hebrew law from Hebrew Union College in 1925, and in 1940 the University of Richmond awarded him an honorary doctorate of law. In his later years Calisch received honors and awards from many groups in recognition of his contributions to the community. In December 1939 the *Richmond Times-Dispatch* placed him on its Virginia Honor Roll and described him as one of the most brilliant and beloved churchmen in the country.

Calisch's wife died on 14 February 1927 following several years of paralysis and invalidism. In Brookline, Massachusetts, on 17 July 1927 he married Essie B. Straus Labenberg, a Richmond widow. In 1945 Calisch reached his eightieth year, and although no one in the congregation suggested that he retire, he asked for and in June received rabbi emeritus status. He did not long enjoy his retirement, however. While vacationing in July he suffered a cerebral embolism, and thereafter his health steadily deteriorated. Edward Nathan Calisch died in his room at the Hotel Jefferson in Richmond on 7 January 1946 and was buried two days later in the city's Hebrew Cemetery. His widow died seven weeks later.

Biographies in Tyler, *Men of Mark*, 2d ser., 49–51, John Simons, ed., *Who's Who in American Jewry* (1939), 3:154, *The Light Burns On, 1841, 1891, 1941: Centennial Anniversary Congregation Beth Ahabah, Golden Jubilee, Dr. Edward N. Calisch* (1941), 1–5, Edith Lindeman Calisch, *Three Score and Twenty: A Brief Biography of Edward Nathan Calisch* (1945), frontispiece por., and Claire M. Rosenbaum, "Rabbi Edward N. Calisch: A Man of His Time and Ours," and Frances C. Rothenberg and Nikki C. Fairman, comps., "Remembrances of Rabbi Edward N. Calisch," *Generations: Journal of Congregation Beth Ahabah Museum and Archives Trust* 4 (Oct. 1991): 1–4, 4–5; feature articles in *Commonwealth* 12 (June 1945): 16, and *Richmond Times-Dispatch*, 31 Dec. 1939, 10 June 1945; Edward Nathan Calisch Papers, Congregation Beth Ahabah Museum and Archives, Richmond; second marriage in *Richmond News Leader*, 16 July 1927; Herbert T. Ezekiel and Gaston Lichtenstein, *The History of the Jews of Richmond from 1769 to 1917* (1917); Myron Berman, *Richmond's Jewry, 1769–1976: Shabbat in Shockoe* (1979); Melvin I. Urofsky, *Commonwealth and Community: The Jewish Experience in Virginia* (1997), 111–112, 129, 144, 163; obituaries in *New York Times*, 8 Jan. 1946, *Richmond News Leader* and *Richmond Times-Dispatch*, both 8–9 Jan. 1946; editorial tributes in *Richmond News Leader*, 8 Jan. 1946, and *Richmond Times-Dispatch*, 9 Jan. 1946.

MELVIN I. UROFSKY

CALL, Daniel (5 May 1765–20 May 1840), attorney and law reporter, was born probably at Pittsfield in Prince George County and was most likely the son of William Call, who served as county lieutenant during the American Revolution. His mother's name and the details of his early life and education are not known. Call studied law under George Wythe during the 1780s and by October 1787 had married Wythe's niece Elizabeth Taliaferro. She died shortly after the birth in 1793 of their only child, a daughter.

Call launched his legal career in Petersburg in the autumn of 1786 by commencing his practice in the courts of that town and of the surrounding counties. Five years later, on 9 June 1791, he qualified to practice before the Virginia Court of Appeals and began to turn his attention to the more sophisticated appellate practice in Richmond, where the superior courts of the commonwealth and also the federal district and circuit courts met, but he maintained an active practice—and apparently a residence—in Petersburg until near the end of the decade.

Call took out a marriage bond on 12 May 1797 and on that day or soon thereafter married Lucy Nelson Ambler, one of the four daughters of Jaquelin Ambler, the treasurer of Virginia, and a sister-in-law of Richmond's most prominent attorney and statesman, John Marshall. They had one daughter. Following his marriage

Call moved to Richmond and soon joined Marshall in the top ranks of the city's legal profession, which was then the finest bar in the state. He enlarged his circle of acquaintances further as a member of the famous Barbecue Club. Call lived for several years in a small house located between John Marshall's residence and the State Capitol, but after his practice increased he moved into a larger house only a few yards from Marshall's home. In 1796 Marshall had recommended that George Washington appoint Call United States attorney for the district of Virginia, a post that eluded Call only because the president had already promised it to another Virginian. When Bushrod Washington relinquished his law practice to become an associate justice of the United States Supreme Court in 1798, he turned his practice over to Call, and Marshall did the same when he was appointed chief justice in 1801.

Call specialized in land law and equity cases. His practice dealt with valuable real property and the settlement of family estates, among the most lucrative fields for a skilled attorney. Call began to dominate the practice in the state's highest courts by arguing more cases than almost any other leading attorney. Surviving evidence, both documentary and anecdotal, suggests that he could be brusque and officious toward his clients, but he was much sought after and won renown as a knowledgeable, skilled, and tenacious advocate.

Unlike many of his colleagues, Call eschewed politics and did not run for public office. He usually voiced his opinions only to a small coterie of associates, but his political leanings were generally known. A staunch Federalist early in his career, he later supported Henry Clay and thoroughly disliked Andrew Jackson. Call invested some of his earnings in land in Richmond and in Henrico County, and he also bought land in the midwestern states, but his purchases were not so extensive that he could be described as a land speculator. For a number of years he served both as general counsel and as a director of the Mutual Assurance Society, against Fire on Buildings, of the State of Virginia.

Call is best known for his work publishing the case law of the commonwealth. Until 1820

Virginia courts had no official law reporters and few published records of the decisions of its highest tribunal. Call personally undertook the arduous task of gathering case notes, copies of opinions, and other documents from his own files and from judges and fellow attorneys (most notably from his longtime friend St. George Tucker and from Marshall) in order to produce a usable set of precedents for the bench and bar. Call's first three volumes, bearing the title *Reports of Cases Argued and Adjudged in the Court of Appeals of Virginia* and covering the period from April 1797 through May 1803, were issued in 1801, 1802, and 1805. Much later, in 1833, he published three more volumes primarily treating cases decided in the first Court of Appeals between 1779 and 1789, additional decisions in the new Court of Appeals between 1789 and 1803, some previously unreported rulings of the same court decided between 1803 and 1818, and four decisions of the United States Circuit Court made between 1793 and 1825. Call's Reports, as they were then known, comprise volumes five through ten of the official *Virginia Reports* series of the decisions of the Supreme Court of Virginia and its predecessors.

When Call published the last in his series of reports he dedicated the volumes to the judges of the Court of Appeals and in the preface bid his colleagues at the bar a fond professional farewell. He had virtually closed his appellate practice several years earlier, although he continued to represent some former clients in simple legal transactions until the end of his life. Daniel Call died at his home in Richmond on 20 May 1840 and was buried next to the grave of his longtime friend John Marshall in Shockoe Cemetery in that city.

French Biographies give birth date of 5 May but variant birth year of 1755; Shockoe Cemetery interment record (LVA microfilm) gives age at death as seventy-five, suggesting birth in 1765, a year more consistent with Call's entering law practice in 1786; Arthur G. Smith, "Daniel Call," in *The Virginia Law Reporters before 1880,* ed. W. Hamilton Bryson (1977), 16–18; E. Lee Shepard, "Sketches of the Old Richmond Bar: Daniel Call," *Richmond Quarterly* 11 (winter 1988): 1–8; Daniel Call Papers, VM/RHC, and Call letters in collections at Huntington, UVA, VHS, W&M, and Yale University, and in *Washington: Retirement Series,* 3:311, and *Clay Papers,* 3:789–790; *Virginia Gazette and Petersburg Intelligencer,* 14 Sept.

1786; Henrico Co. Marriage Bonds, 1797; a report that Daniel Call was elected to Congress in 1792 (*Calendar of Virginia State Papers*, 5:450) was based on incomplete returns from a district in which Call did not live and probably referred to another man of the same name; Mary Wingfield Scott, *Houses of Old Richmond* (1941), 27, 39–41; obituary in *Richmond Enquirer*, 22 May 1840; memorials in *Richmond Enquirer*, 22 May 1840, and *Richmond Whig and Public Advertiser*, 26 May 1840.

E. LEE SHEPARD

CALL, Norman (29 March 1880–25 May 1959), president of the Richmond, Fredericksburg, and Potomac Railroad Company, was born in Richmond, the son of Manfred Call, an agricultural-implement manufacturer, and Sarah Elizabeth Watt Call. He attended Richmond's public schools and took classes at the Virginia Mechanics' Institute in that city before becoming a stenographer and clerk for the Richmond Locomotive and Machine Works at the age of eighteen. Call won rapid promotion to director of the purchasing department.

On 1 November 1901 Call left to become secretary to the president of the Richmond, Fredericksburg, and Potomac Railroad Company. There he also advanced rapidly, and on 15 September 1910 he was appointed secretary of the railroad and assistant treasurer. Call was promoted to assistant to the president on 19 April 1917 and served as the corporation's principal officer during World War I, when the federal government controlled the country's railroads. On 26 February 1920, on recommendation from the railroad's president, William H. White, the board of directors elected Call to the new position of vice president with an annual salary of $7,000. White died on 5 August 1920, and the board of directors divided over the choice of his successor. The candidates were Call and the railroad's general counsel, Eppa Hunton (1855–1932). Call informed the board that the office of vice president had been established because White had intended for him to be his successor. Some board members, however, believed that Call did not possess the stature and influence that they considered necessary in consequence of the state government's being a large stockholder in the railroad. Hunton won the election on 16 September 1920 and served as president until his death on 5 March 1932.

On 11 March 1932, although Call was not the first choice of all the board members, they unanimously elected him president of the Richmond, Fredericksburg, and Potomac Railroad Company with a salary of $12,000 a year. Call became president at an inopportune time. The Great Depression had caused the railroad's net income to drop from $2,200,000 in 1928 to $292,000 in 1933. Under Call's sound management, however, the railroad continued to earn profits, albeit at a reduced rate, through the 1930s, and it paid a dividend every year from 1932 to 1939. World War II and the resulting military buildup brought sharply increased business and profits to the strategically located RF&P, which contributed greatly to the war effort in transporting both freight and passengers. The war was the high point of passenger traffic on the railroad. During the remainder of the 1940s and the 1950s the RF&P experienced decreased profits in both its passenger and freight divisions as a result of competition from airlines, automobiles, coastal shipping, and the trucking industries.

Call retired as president on 1 January 1955, leaving a legacy of good fiscal management and railroad improvement. During his presidency the RF&P paid off its bonded indebtedness of more than $7 million, called in and retired $4 million of 6 percent nonvoting stock, increased investments in transportation property by more than $22 million, and converted its locomotives from steam to diesel. Call was fond of remarking that the RF&P "may not be as long as some railroads, but it's just as wide."

Call also served as president of the Richmond Terminal Railway Company, the RF&P Transportation Company, and the Richmond Land Corporation. He was vice president of Richmond-Greyhound Lines, Inc., and of the Union Terminal Corporation of Richmond, and he sat on the boards of directors of the First and Merchants National Bank of Richmond, the Fruit Growers Express Company, the Home Owners Corporation, and Mount Vernon. Call was also active in the community and served as an officer in the annual community chest drives, as president of the Richmond Rotary Club in 1921 and 1922, and as president of the Richmond

Safety Council. He was a director of the Richmond Civic Musical Association. As a young man Call was a soloist at Saint Paul's Episcopal Church and in retirement enjoyed an impressive collection of symphonic and opera recordings. In 1930 he was instrumental in attracting the touring Metropolitan Opera Company to Richmond. Call also belonged to the American Railway Engineering Association, the American Society of Mechanical Engineers, the Benevolent and Protective Order of Elks, the Freemasons, Ginter Park Presbyterian Church, the Sons of the American Revolution, and the chambers of commerce of Richmond and Fredericksburg.

On 30 September 1903 Call married Eileen M. Hearon, of Abingdon. They had two sons and two daughters. She died on 25 September 1941, and on 6 April 1942 he married Anne Murray, of Ardmore, Pennsylvania. They had no children. Norman Call continued to reside in Richmond during his retirement and died of cancer in the city on 25 May 1959. He was buried in Hollywood Cemetery in Richmond.

Biographies in *NCAB*, 44:484–485, Bruce, Tyler, and Morton, *History of Virginia*, 4:125–126, Glass and Glass, *Virginia Democracy*, 3:57–59, Tyler, *Men of Mark*, 2d ser., 101–103 (por. facing 101), and *Commonwealth* 22 (Oct. 1955): 34; feature story in *Richmond News Leader*, 17 Dec. 1954; BVS Birth Register, Richmond City; first marriage in Russell Co. Marriage Register; second marriage in *Richmond Times-Dispatch*, 7 Apr. 1942; Minute Books of the Richmond, Fredericksburg, and Potomac Railroad Company, LVA; Richmond, Fredericksburg, and Potomac Railroad Company Records, VHS; 1920 appointment of Hunton in Westmoreland Davis Executive Papers, box 22, RG 3, LVA; C. Coleman McGehee, "I've Been Working on the Railroad: The Saga of the Richmond, Fredericksburg and Potomac Railroad Company" (master's thesis, University of Richmond, 1992), 22–29; Knights of the Golden Trail Records, 1921–1961, VHS (por.); obituaries in *New York Times*, *Richmond News Leader* (quotation), and *Richmond Times-Dispatch*, all 26 May 1959; editorial tribute in *Richmond Times-Dispatch*, 28 May 1959.

GERALD P. GAIDMORE II

CALLAHAN, Charles Hilliard (22 August 1858–31 July 1944), Masonic leader, was born in Aquia Mills, Stafford County, the son of Allen Tupper Callahan and Sarah Mildred Ennis Callahan. The family had moved to Prince William County by 1870 and then to Fairfax County about 1875. Callahan attended public schools before working as a laborer on his father's farm and clerking in a general store. In 1889 he moved to Alexandria, where he worked as a carpenter for several years. On 22 October 1890 Callahan married Mary Elizabeth Appich. They had one son and four daughters. Callahan became deputy commissioner of revenue for Alexandria in 1895. Three years later he became commissioner of revenue of the city and until his death was reelected without significant opposition. His son succeeded him in office in 1944.

Callahan joined the Freemasons in 1904 and five years later became Worshipful Master for the first of two successive terms in the Alexandria-Washington Lodge, the lodge over which George Washington had presided while serving as president of the United States. Callahan urged that Masons in America work together to build a memorial to Washington that would include a permanent space to display the artifacts of his life that the Alexandria-Washington Lodge had preserved, including a portrait by William Williams. Under Callahan's leadership representatives of grand lodges from several states met in Alexandria on 22 February 1910 and adopted his resolutions for establishing the George Washington Masonic National Memorial Association. Callahan drew up the organization's constitution and served on the board of directors and the executive committee. For the site the association selected Shooter's Hill in Alexandria, part of a tract that George Washington had once owned and the location Thomas Jefferson and James Madison had once proposed for the United States Capitol. As part of the campaign to raise funds and to mark the subsequent completion of the project, Callahan wrote *Washington: The Man and the Mason* (1913) and *The Memorial to Washington: An Historic Souvenir* (1932).

After more than a decade of fund-raising, Callahan took part in the memorial's groundbreaking on 5 June 1922. With President Calvin Coolidge and Chief Justice William Howard Taft he laid the memorial's cornerstone on 1 November 1923, using the same trowel Washington had used in 1793 to lay the first stone of the United States Capitol. Nine more years of fund-raising and construction preceded the dedication on 12 May 1932. Callahan was master of ceremonies at the dedication of the George Washington Masonic National Memorial, with President Herbert Hoover in attendance. The design of the $5 million memorial, a granite tower 337 feet, 6 inches high, standing atop seven landscaped terraces, was inspired by Greek and Roman towers erected to mark harbors and symbolized Washington's guiding spirit.

Callahan served as Grand Master of Masons in Virginia from 1924 to 1926. On 22 February 1944 the Masons of Virginia unveiled a bust of Callahan at the memorial, and the road in front was named Callahan Drive in his honor. In addition to his interest in the memorial Callahan also supported preservation of local historic sites. In 1930 he published a small pamphlet, *Gadsby's Tavern*, as part of a fund-raising effort to restore that property. Charles Hilliard Callahan died in an Alexandria hospital on 31 July 1944. City offices closed and flags flew at half staff while the Grand Lodge of Masons in Virginia conducted his burial service at Bethel Cemetery in Alexandria.

Biographies in Tyler, *Encyclopedia*, 5:681–682, and Philip Alexander Bruce, *Virginia: Rebirth of the Old Dominion* (1929), 5:129–131; birth may be listed in Stafford Co. Birth Register as H. C. Callahan on 15 May 1858; *Washington Post*, 23 Oct. 1890; *Virginia Masonic Herald and Virginia Masonic Journal* 27 (June 1932): 16–17 (por.); Richard A. Rutyna and Peter C. Stewart, *The History of Freemasonry in Virginia* (1998), 380–381; Elmer R. Arn, *The George Washington Masonic National Memorial Association* (1939); *Alexandria Gazette*, 1 Nov. 1923, 12 May 1932; *New York Times*, 2 Nov. 1923, 13 May 1932; *Proceedings of the Most Worshipful Grand Lodge of Ancient, Free and Accepted Masons of the Commonwealth of Virginia* (1924): 19–25, 63–65, 74–78; ibid. (1926): 14, 44–45; ibid. (1933): 3–44; obituaries in *Alexandria Gazette*, 1, 2 Aug. 1944, and *Washington Post*, 2 Aug. 1944; editorial tribute in *Alexandria Gazette*, 1 Aug. 1944; memorials in *Proceedings of the Most Worshipful Grand Lodge of Ancient, Free and Accepted Masons of the Commonwealth of Virginia* (1945): 21–22, [126–127].

MARY CARROLL JOHANSEN

CALLAWAY, James (25 December 1735– 1 November 1809), iron manufacturer, was born in Orange County, the son of William Callaway and his first wife, Elizabeth Tilley Callaway. Some accounts may confuse episodes in his life with facts pertaining to his uncle of the same name. Richard Callaway, another uncle, played

an important role in the settlement of Kentucky. By 1746 Callaway's family had moved to the section of Lunenburg County that in 1753 became Bedford County. His father owned extensive property there, provided the land for the new courthouse (later the town of New London), was one of the first justices of the peace and a colonel of the militia during the French and Indian War, and represented Bedford County in the House of Burgesses from 1755 to 1758 and from 1761 to 1765.

James Callaway secured a marriage bond on 24 November 1756 and on that date or soon thereafter married Sarah Tate. They had five sons and seven daughters. Sarah Tate Callaway died sometime after the birth of her last child in 1773. Callaway won election in July 1765 to succeed his father in the House of Burgesses that assembled in 1766, but he either did not seek reelection in 1768 or was defeated. In 1770 he opened a store in Bedford County in partnership with Alexander Trent and Peterfield Trent, of Rocky Ridge in Chesterfield County. Callaway shipped tobacco to the Trents, who sold it to English merchants, from whom they acquired dry goods and other merchandise that Callaway in turn sold to the planters. He enjoyed a near monopoly in his region of Virginia when the American Revolution interrupted commerce.

Callaway served on the Bedford County Committee of Safety in 1775, and by early in 1776 he had become one of the supervisors of the public lead mines in southern Fincastle County (in what later became Wythe County). He directed the mines until Charles Lynch succeeded him on 5 December 1777. Callaway may have then collaborated with David Ross in operating the Oxford Iron Works in Bedford County.

On 22 September 1777 Callaway received a marriage bond and on that date or soon afterward married Elizabeth Early. They had ten children, of whom six sons and one daughter survived to adulthood. In June 1779 Callaway and his new father-in-law, Jeremiah Early, purchased a bloomery forge in nearby Henry County. They almost immediately built a blast furnace, which still stands in Rocky Mount, and a new forge, which does not. Enhanced demand for iron during the Revolutionary War accelerated the growth of the new company, named the Washington Iron Works. By July 1779 its products were advertised as far away as South Carolina. Jeremiah Early died in 1779, and within two years Callaway owned two-thirds of the company. Thomas Jefferson estimated in his *Notes on the State of Virginia* (written in 1781–1782) that 25 percent of the bar iron and 14 percent of the pig iron produced in Virginia came from the Washington Iron Works.

Callaway became county lieutenant, or commander of the Bedford County militia, on 28 December 1778. During the Revolution he occasionally took part in measures to defend the southwestern part of the state. In several incidents in 1780 Callaway and other militia officers, including Lynch, broke up a suspected Loyalist conspiracy at the lead mine. They or others operating with their permission intimidated, jailed, or whipped suspected Loyalists, or forced them to join the American army. The incidents were most likely the origin of the term *lynch law*, which initially referred to organized extralegal punishment of suspects. In 1782 the General Assembly passed a bill that retroactively legalized the acts of Callaway, Lynch, and two other men.

After the war Callaway built a business office, a gristmill, a sawmill, a store, a tavern, and new quarters for the slaves who labored at his ironworks and the related blacksmith's shop, stables, and storage sheds. By 1809 the company had acquired 18,908 acres of land in order to supply the insatiable demand of the furnace for charcoal. When the county of Franklin was formed from Bedford and Henry Counties, the first court met on 2 January 1786 at one of Callaway's four houses at the ironworks. From a small beginning as a bloomery forge, the Washington Iron Works grew into a significant frontier industry and remained the principal manufacturer in Franklin County until a flood destroyed the furnace on 22 August 1851. Callaway also purchased Carron Iron Works, a nearby competitor, about 1801 or 1802, thus securing his domination of the local iron industry.

Callaway was a justice of the peace in Bedford County from at least 3 April 1767 until 26 November 1780, when he became sheriff of the county until Campbell County was organized in 1782. From 7 February 1782 until at least December 1787 he was a justice of the peace for Campbell County, and he was county lieutenant from February 1782 until at least 1 December 1786. Callaway moved back to Bedford County in 1789 and was presiding judge of the county court from that year until 14 May 1804, when he became sheriff, a post he held until 5 July 1806. In December 1795 he became a founding trustee of the New London Academy for boys.

Callaway's second wife died sometime after the birth of her last child in 1796. By 15 October 1800 Callaway had married the twice-widowed Mary Langhorne Calland Turpin. They had no children. James Callaway died on 1 November 1809 and was buried in the Callaway-Steptoe family cemetery near his home, not far from New London in Bedford County. His estate included approximately 114,000 acres in five counties, including the courthouse town in Franklin County, and a personal estate valued in the inventory at £17,694.

Birth date in nineteenth-century Callaway-Early-Anderson Bible records, Misc. Bible Records Collection, no. 2, LVA; undocumented variant birth dates of 21 Dec. 1736 in Mary Denham Ackerly and Lula Eastman Jeter Parker, *"Our Kin": The Genealogies of Some of the Early Families Who Made History in the Founding and Development of Bedford County, Virginia* (1930; repr. 1976), 296, of 25 Dec. 1736 (with erroneous death date of 11 Jan. 1809) in *Ancestors of the Patrick Henry Chapter, NSDAR Members, 1981, Martinsville, Virginia* (1981), and of 31 Dec. 1736 in *Campbell County, Virginia, Family Cemeteries* (1998), 5:18; Bedford Co. Marriage Bonds, 1756, 1777; date of third marriage estimated from Cumberland Co. Deed Book, 8:408; business records in *Callaway* v. *Dobson's Administrators* (1811), U.S. Circuit Court, Fifth Circuit, Virginia District, Ended Cases (unrestored, oversize file 2), Box 221, LVA; John S. Salmon, *The Washington Iron Works of Franklin County, Virginia, 1773–1850* (1986), 19–42; John S. Salmon and Emily J. Salmon, *Franklin County, Virginia, 1786–1986: A Bicentennial History* (1993), esp. 106–112; Hening, *Statutes*, 11:134–135; Thomas Jefferson, *Notes on the State of Virginia*, ed. William Peden (1954), 27–28; Census, Franklin Co., Industry Schedule, 1820; will and estate inventory in Bedford Co. Will Book, 3:214–217, 228–233; obituary in *Richmond Virginia Argus*, 14 Nov. 1809, reprinted from *Lynchburg Press*.

JOHN S. SALMON
EMILY J. SALMON

CALLAWAY, Richard (ca. 1717–ca. 8 March 1780), a founder of Boonesborough, Kentucky, was born in the northwestern portion of Essex County that in 1728 became Caroline County. His father was Joseph Callaway, son of an immigrant of the same name, but the name of his mother is unknown. About 1738, a few years after the deaths of their parents, Richard Callaway and several of his brothers ventured westward. They were among the first white men to farm in the vicinity of Big Otter Creek in the section of Lunenburg County that in 1753 became Bedford County. Callaway's brother William Callaway is regarded as one of the founders of the new county, and his nephew James Callaway became an important iron manufacturer during the American Revolution.

Richard Callaway became surveyor of Lunenburg County in April 1751. To obtain the position one needed a license from the College of William and Mary, a circumstance that may account for an undocumented tradition that he attended the college. Callaway also served as a constable in Lunenburg County and began acquiring land, perhaps as much as 9,000 acres in all. When Bedford County was created out of Lunenburg County he became a justice of the peace, and he served as a trustee of and perhaps surveyed the site for the county seat, later the town of New London. In July 1745 Callaway married Frances Walton, whose brother later became the surveyor of Bedford County, a connection that may have helped in his acquisition of property. Callaway had at least four sons and six or seven daughters before his wife died, probably early in the 1760s. By September 1768 he had married a widow, Elizabeth Jones Hoy. They had several more children, perhaps as many as two sons and two daughters. The Callaway brothers were active militia officers during the French and Indian War, and according to family tradition Richard Callaway and two of his brothers commanded three of Virginia's frontier forts.

Callaway sold or otherwise lost most of his land and property by the end of 1774. Financial difficulties, his family's venturesome tradition, or connections in North Carolina, where Richard Henderson's expedition to establish a new colony in Kentucky was assembling, impelled Callaway in March 1775 to join the march west. Led by Daniel Boone, Callaway and others marked the Wilderness Road to the new settlement of Boonesborough. Callaway helped lay off town lots, lived in a cabin there, conducted a large party, including his family, to the settlement, and then raised crops and livestock nearby. Claiming 3,000 acres of land, he was a justice of the peace, served in the short-lived Transylvania assembly, and was author of its judiciary statute.

Henderson's colonial experiment collapsed at the beginning of the American Revolution, and Virginia created Kentucky County in December 1776. Callaway was a justice of the peace for the new county and in June 1777 was appointed a colonel in the militia. By the end of the decade he claimed as much as 6,000 acres of Kentucky land. Callaway was elected to the House of Delegates in 1777 and again in 1779. During his first term he served on the Committee of Public Claims, and during his second he presented petitions to authorize a ferry across the Kentucky River and to create the town of Boonesborough. Callaway and Boone were appointed trustees of the new town, although apparently neither served.

In the summer of 1776 daughters of Boone and Callaway wandered away from the safety of the Boonesborough stockade and fell into the hands of the Indians. Callaway and Boone each led search parties; Boone's group recovered the girls. Callaway's relationship with Boone eventually became strained, perhaps as a consequence of Boone's early celebrity but perhaps, too, as a product of inevitable conflicts resulting from their holding similar offices and shouldering similar responsibilities without a clear priority of rank. When the town came under siege in 1778, Callaway resisted with ferocity and ingenuity and perhaps helped to construct a makeshift cannon. Boone's conduct produced allegations that he had been in collusion with the British and the Indians, and Callaway had him court-martialed. When Boone was acquitted and promoted, Callaway became bitter.

About 8 March 1780 while building a town ferryboat, Richard Callaway and at least one companion were killed by Indians near Boonesborough. His body was buried in an unmarked grave near the fort. Kentucky's Calloway County, using a variant spelling, was named in his honor in 1822.

The complicated and incomplete record is confused by conflicting texts (Callaway Family File, Kentucky Historical Society, Frankfort; Callaway family Bible records, LVA) derived in turn from a family Bible that might have been Richard Callaway's or his namesake son's (Joseph A. Callaway, "Colonel Richard Callaway's Family Bible," *Callaway Journal* 6 [1981]: 28–29); biography by nephew Elijah Callaway (1845), Draper MSS, 5DD20–44; the most judicious and best-documented assessments are Mrs. A. E. Hart, "The Callaway Family of Virginia and Some Kentucky Descendants" (1929 typescript), LC, and Sherrill Williams, "Colonel Richard Callaway of Virginia and Kentucky," *Callaway Journal* 6 (1981): 75–89, which plausibly suggests 1717 birth year; less reliable biographies are Charles W. Bryan Jr., "Richard Callaway, Kentucky Pioneer," *Filson Club History Quarterly* 9 (1935): 35–50, and R. Alexander Bate, "Colonel Richard Callaway, 1722–1780," ibid. 29 (1955): 3–20, 166–178; many original records and references in Kentucky Series, Draper MSS; other documents printed in George W. Ranck, *Boonesborough: Its Founding, Pioneer Struggles, Indian Experiences, Transylvania Days, and Revolutionary Annals* (1901); death described as of Mar. 1780 in John David Shane, ed., "The Henderson Company Ledger," *Filson Club History Quarterly* 21 (1947): 27, 33; family Bible gives erroneous death date of 8 Mar. 1778; undocumented death date of 8 Mar. 1780 in Lyman C. Draper, *The Life of Daniel Boone*, ed. Ted Franklin Belue (1998), 558.

JAMES RUSSELL HARRIS

CALLENDER, James Thomson (1757 or 1758–17 July 1803), journalist, was born in Scotland, but the place and date of his birth and the names of his parents are not known. He may have been the son of a tobacco merchant, and he was probably orphaned at an early age. Callender obtained a basic classical education and a strong dose of Calvinism. In 1782 he became a clerk in a public office in Edinburgh, where he learned firsthand about corruption and misuse of influence. Callender became a registered messenger at arms in 1787. He entered Edinburgh's literary circle through the publication of several anonymous pamphlets and poems, including *Deformities of Dr. Samuel Johnson* (1782), a pamphlet critical of the famed author and disparager of Scotland. The work showed Callender to be both a well-read man and a slashing writer.

An intense Scottish nationalist, Callender published a series of pamphlets that brought him into conflict with the authorities. His *Political Progress of Great Britain (Part 1)* (1792) led to an interrogation late in December 1792, and early in January a warrant was issued for his arrest. After he failed to attend the court proceedings, Callender was declared an outlaw and went into hiding in Dublin, where he associated with leaders of the Society of United Irishmen. In spring 1793, leaving his wife (whose name is unknown) and three children in Scotland, he immigrated to the United States and arrived in May 1793.

Through his Irish connections, Callender obtained work in Matthew Carey's Philadelphia bookstore and ultimately became the congressional reporter for Andrew Brown's *Philadelphia Gazette*, a position he held until the spring of 1796. In a period of intensifying partisanship, Callender became intimately associated with the emerging Republican Party and earned the enmity of leading Federalists. Between 1794 and 1798 he contributed anonymous news articles and columns critical of the administrations of George Washington and John Adams to the *Philadelphia Aurora*. Besides republishing his earlier works, Callender produced new pamphlets attacking the policies of the American government, especially those regarding trade, as subordinating American interests to those of the British government. Callender and other radical émigrés shared an Anglophobia and an urban economic nationalism. They rejected not only Alexander Hamilton's fiscal program but also the agrarianism of the Virginia planters of their own party. Callender's reputation was further enhanced by William Cobbett's virulent attacks on his work in *Porcupine's Gazette,* one of Philadelphia's Federalist newspapers. During this time Callender's wife and children joined him in Philadelphia, and a fourth child was born before May 1796.

Callender achieved his first great notoriety by reporting on Hamilton's adulterous affair with Maria Reynolds in the *History of the United States for 1796* (1797). Life in Philadelphia eventually became hazardous for the outspoken journalist. In addition to the recurrence of yellow fever, threats to his personal safety, and mounting personal financial problems, Callender's livelihood was threatened by the adoption of the Alien and Sedition Acts, which sought to muzzle political criticism of the government. By the summer of 1798 his wife had died. Coming under increasing attack for his activities and hoping to remove any danger that he might be deported once the Naturalization and Alien Acts of 1798 passed, Callender on 4 June petitioned for American citizenship. The following month he abandoned Philadelphia for the relative safety of Virginia, leaving his children behind.

For several months Callender stayed at the Loudoun County plantation of Senator Stevens Thomson Mason, and then in May 1799 he moved to Richmond. He contributed articles critical of the Adams administration to the leading local Republican newspaper, the *Richmond Examiner*, and published his most famous work, *The Prospect Before Us, Volume 1* (1800), a highly partisan political history of the 1790s with a decidedly southern emphasis and numerous insulting remarks about Adams and his policies. On 24 May 1800 the United States District Court grand jury indicted Callender for sedition, and after a sensational trial presided over by United States Supreme Court associate justice Samuel Chase, Callender was convicted on 3 June 1800, sentenced to jail for nine months, and fined $200. His trial and imprisonment made Callender a political martyr. Republicans raised money for his relief, and the Republican press throughout the country condemned Chase's partisan behavior during the trial and made suppression of the press an issue in that year's presidential election. While incarcerated Callender wrote and published two more volumes of *The Prospect Before Us.*

Released from jail, Callender resumed his activities with renewed enthusiasm, much to the dismay of moderate Republicans. Because Thomas Jefferson had covertly supported his journalistic efforts in Philadelphia and openly encouraged him in Virginia, Callender viewed him as a patron whose obligations were enhanced by his incarceration and sufferings. Not surprisingly, after Jefferson became president in March 1801 Callender expected a par-

don and immediate remission of his fine, and he also insisted on being appointed postmaster of Richmond. Jefferson retroactively pardoned Callender after his release but failed to bestow a government job.

Bitterly disappointed, Callender severed his ties with the *Richmond Examiner* and gravitated to the *Richmond Recorder: or, Lady's and Gentleman's Miscellany*, a newspaper in which he acquired a part interest in February 1802. Much to the surprise and chagrin of his former allies, he repudiated the Republicans and openly criticized the Jefferson administration with the same strong invective he had formerly directed toward the Federalists. Beginning in September 1802 Callender published a series of articles in the *Recorder* accusing Jefferson of maintaining a long relationship with his slave Sally Hemings and fathering her children. Jeffersonians at the time and many subsequent Jefferson biographers discounted Callender's assertions and emphasized his partisan bias, but recent scholarship suggests that even though vengeance certainly prompted Callender to publish his critical articles about Jefferson's personal life, he was probably reporting accurately.

Circulation of the *Recorder* increased briefly, spurred by reports of Callender's public altercation in December 1802 with George Hay, the Republican attorney who had represented him at his sedition trial, but sustained publishing success proved as elusive as ever. Amid threats of violence from Richmond Republicans, Callender quarreled with his coeditor over money and, facing an uncertain economic future, withdrew from the *Richmond Recorder* in April 1803. James Thomson Callender, who often found solace in drink during periods of crisis, drowned in the James River at Richmond on 17 July 1803 and was buried in a local church cemetery later the same day. A coroner's jury returned a verdict of accidental drowning as a result of intoxication.

Michael Durey, *"With the Hammer of Truth": James Thomson Callender and America's Early National Heroes* (1990), including bibliography of Callender's publications; Charles A. Jellison, "That Scoundrel Callender," *VMHB* 67 (1959): 295–306; letters in Andrew Stuart Papers, National Library of Scotland, Edinburgh, in Worthington Chauncey Ford, ed.,

Thomas Jefferson and James Thomson Callender, 1798–1802 (1897), in *Madison: Congressional Series*, 16:366–367 (Callender states he was "in my thirty ninth year" on 28 May 1796), 17:457–458, and in *Madison: Secretary of State Series*, 1:117–120, 144–145; *Trial of James Thompson Callender for Sedition* (1804); Joshua D. Rothman, "James Callender and Social Knowledge of Interracial Sex in Antebellum Virginia," in *Sally Hemings and Thomas Jefferson: History, Memory, and Civic Culture*, ed. Jan Ellen Lewis and Peter S. Onuf (1999), 87–113; obituaries in *Richmond Examiner*, 20, 28 July 1803, both alleging suicide, and *Richmond Recorder*, 20 July 1803.

WHITMAN H. RIDGWAY

CALLIS, William Overton (23 March 1757–30 March 1814), member of the Convention of 1788, was the son of William Callis and Mary Cosby Callis. He was born probably in Westmoreland County, where his family was involved in shipbuilding, but after the death of his father in the spring of 1758 his mother moved the family to her native Louisa County. The particulars of Callis's childhood and education are not known, but he clearly developed broad intellectual interests. At his death he owned about ninety books, including works by William Shakespeare and Henry Fielding, and his obituary remarked on his "most vigorous and well cultivated mind."

As a young man Callis served in the Revolutionary War. He joined the minute service late in 1775 and by 28 June 1776 had been appointed quartermaster sergeant of the 1st Battalion of Minutemen. After receiving a commission in the 4th Regiment Virginia Infantry of the Continental Line on 27 September 1776, Callis was promoted to lieutenant on 12 January 1777. Suffering from respiratory problems as a result of being wounded by a cannonball either at the Battle of Germantown or the Battle of Monmouth, he gave up his Continental army commission on 27 September 1778 and departed for the West Indies early in 1779 in an effort to regain his health. In June 1780 an apparently recovered Callis returned to Virginia and became a captain in a regiment of militia cavalry that December. He eventually rose to major and served as aide de camp to General Thomas Nelson (1738–1789) during the siege of Yorktown. Callis joined the Society of the Cincinnati as an original member in 1791 and became lieutenant colonel of the 40th Regiment Virginia militia on 13 January 1794 in Louisa County.

In March 1788 Callis was one of two delegates elected to represent Louisa County in the Virginia convention called to consider ratification of the proposed constitution of the United States. He arrived in Richmond for the first session on 2 June and was present for the entire convention, but insofar as the records reveal he did not speak during the debates. Callis voted against requiring prior amendments before approving the constitution and for ratification on 25 June. Also in 1788 he represented Louisa County in the House of Delegates and sat on the Committees of Claims and of Propositions and Grievances. Callis allied himself with the Jeffersonian Republicans throughout his General Assembly service. He was reelected delegate eight more times, from 1790 to 1793, in 1795, and from 1797 to 1799. During his later terms Callis sat on the Committees for Courts of Justice, of Privileges and Elections, of Propositions and Grievances, and of Religion, and he chaired the Committee of Claims for three sessions in 1795, 1797–1798, and 1798–1799. He served Louisa County as a justice of the peace on numerous occasions and was sheriff from 1804 to 1806.

Callis married Martha Winston on 23 October 1782. They had one son and two daughters before her death on 29 April 1788. On 4 May 1790 he married Anne Price, of Hanover County, and they had four sons and five daughters. Callis and his family prospered at his Cuckooville plantation, with support from his inheritance and military compensation and the operation of a tavern on the property. In 1814 he owned 434.5 acres in Louisa County and a personal estate valued at $4,527.40, including sixteen slaves. After several years of declining health, William Overton Callis died at his home in Louisa County on 30 March 1814 of "prevailing Epidemic Typhous Influenza." He may have been buried with other members of his second wife's family in the yard of Fork Episcopal Church in Hanover County.

Biography in Ransom B. True, "Louisa County and the Virginia Convention of 1788," *Louisa County Historical Magazine* 3 (June 1971): 17–19; Kenneth McCoy Lancaster, "William Overton Callis of Louisa County," *Louisa County Historical Magazine* 13 (summer 1981): 3–7 (por.); Compiled Service Records of Virginia Soldiers Who Served in the American Army during the Revolutionary War, War Department Collection of Revolutionary War Records, RG 93, NARA; Revolutionary War Pension and Bounty-Land Warrant Application Files, RG 15, NARA (including birth and marriage dates from family register, certified by widow on 20 Aug. 1838); *Madison: Congressional Series*, 16:445, and seven Callis letters in vols. 8, 13–14; Kaminski, *Ratification*, 10:1538–1540, 1557, 1565; Louisa Co. Court Order and Minute Books; Mutual Assurance Society Declarations, nos. 875, 876 (1802), LVA; will and estate inventory in Louisa Co. Will Book, 5:489–491, 577–579; obituary in *Richmond Enquirer*, 8 June 1814 (quotations).

JAMES A. JACOBS

CALROW, Charles James (21 September 1877–27 November 1938), architect and planner, was born in Norfolk as Charles C. Smith, the son of Frank B. Smith and Eva Smith. He was later adopted by James Hatton Calrow, an architect and builder, and Ida V. Ashley Calrow and renamed Charles James Calrow. After completing his formal education in the Norfolk public schools Calrow began an apprenticeship in 1894 in the Norfolk office of the architectural firm of Carpenter and Peebles, where he acquired practical drafting and planning skills presented through classically based Beaux Arts methodology. When James Edwin Ruthven Carpenter later established an independent practice, Calrow joined him and by 1900 had become superintendent of the firm.

As an ensign in the United States Navy during the Spanish-American War, Calrow served in the Caribbean and thereafter was a lieutenant in the naval battalion of the Virginia militia. About 1904 he formed a partnership with Finlay Forbes Ferguson. They practiced together, at times with one or another third partner, until 1917. Notable local commissions that they completed included the Norfolk National Bank (1909) and the Royster Building (1911), as well as numerous large residences in the city. During the 1920s Calrow headed his own firm with a variety of partners. His work continued to reflect his Beaux Arts training, but his design for the Virginia Electric and Power Company Building (1930) employed more modern streamlined detailing. Calrow was active in the American Legion and the American Institute of Architects. He served in 1925 as secretary of the Norfolk Society of Architects.

On 10 January 1907 Calrow married Sue Leary Russell, of Norfolk. They had one son. Despite his naval background Calrow joined the army in May 1917, shortly after America entered World War I. He received a year of training in military engineering in northern Virginia, Washington, D.C., and Alabama before leaving for France on 19 June 1918. A captain, Calrow assisted in the preparation and inspection of battle plans and troop movements. He served in the 104th Army Engineers and later on the general staff of the First Army. Discharged with the rank of major on 26 May 1919, Calrow returned to Norfolk, where his interest in engineering and planning gradually drew him into public service. On 28 August 1924 he was appointed to the city's Planning Commission. Calrow attended the commission's meetings regularly until 1935 and was particularly insightful in matters relating to traffic management. In 1933 he became a district administrator for the federal government's Civil Works Administration and served concurrently on its engineering council.

By a joint resolution passed on 21 February 1934, the General Assembly created the State Planning Board, financed mainly through private grant money and with its members appointed by the governor. Calrow became a consultant to the board and relinquished his Norfolk practice, although he retained a residence in that city. On 1 February 1935 he became consultant-director, and during the next two years he lectured and wrote about government planning. Calrow sought to cultivate a regional planning consciousness based on the interlocking interests of Virginia and its neighboring states. He maintained, however, that regulations based on information provided by planners working in an expert advisory capacity to the policymakers could be prepared by existing local, state, and federal agencies, thus negating the need for additional regional jurisdictions. In August 1935 the president appointed Calrow one of the Virginia representatives on the National Resources Committee.

On 8 March 1938 the General Assembly made the State Planning Board a fully state-funded agency. At the board's meeting on 6 July

1938, it named Calrow director with duties similar to those he had held the previous three years. On 14 October 1938, however, he learned that he had lung cancer. His health deteriorated rapidly, and Charles James Calrow died of pneumonia in Richmond on 27 November 1938. He was buried in Arlington National Cemetery.

Biographies in Daniel Decatur Moore et al., eds., *Men of the South: A Work for the Newspaper Reference Library* (1922), 707 (por.), 750, Bruce, Tyler, and Morton, *History of Virginia*, 4:439, Glass and Glass, *Virginia Democracy*, 2:608–609, Rowland Andrews Egger, Raymond Uhl, and Vincent Shea, eds., *Who's Who in Public Administration Research in Virginia* (1938), 7–8, and Henry F. Withey and Elsie Rathburn Withey, eds., *Biographical Dictionary of American Architects (Deceased)* (1970), 105–106; Norfolk City Birth Register with 22 Sept. 1877 date (possibly date recorded); 21 Sept. 1877 birth date in most published reference sources, Military Service Records, BVS Death Certificate, and several obituaries; Norfolk City Marriage License with adoption noted; family information provided by son, Charles James Calrow Jr.; *F. F. Ferguson and Chas. J. Calrow, Architects, Norfolk, Virginia* (ca. 1910 advertising booklet), Norfolk Public Library; Wells and Dalton, *Virginia Architects*, 64, 140–143; Norfolk City Planning Commission Minutes, 1922–1939, Department of Planning, Norfolk; Virginia State Planning Board, *Report* 1 (1935); Virginia State Planning Board Minutes, RG 54, LVA; some correspondence in James H. Price Executive Papers, Governor's Office, Letters Received and Sent, RG 3, LVA; Calrow's writings include "Battle of Chaffin's Farm: A Study" (1932 report, National Park Service), "Evolution of State Planning," *Commonwealth* 1 (Dec. 1934): 10, 28, "Interstate Cooperation" and "The Planner Faces a New Job," *National Municipal Review* 25 (1936): 445–451, 464, and 613–616, and "Reflections on Regionalism," *State Government* 9 (1936): 193–195; obituaries in *Norfolk Ledger-Dispatch*, *Norfolk Virginian-Pilot*, *Richmond News Leader* (por.), and *Richmond Times-Dispatch*, all 28 Nov. 1938; editorial tributes in *Richmond News Leader*, 28 Nov. 1938, and *Norfolk Ledger-Dispatch*, *Norfolk Virginian-Pilot*, and *Richmond Times-Dispatch*, all 29 Nov. 1938.

JAMES A. JACOBS

CALTHORPE, Christopher (bap. 22 April 1605–by 23 April 1662), member of the House of Burgesses, was the son of Christopher Calthorpe and Maud Thurton Calthorpe, of Norfolk County, England. He was probably born there and on 22 April 1605 was baptized in Cockthorpe Parish in that county. The family of Calthorpe (also spelled Calthrop) was respectable and well connected. His paternal grandfather was a knight, and he may have been distantly related to Nathaniel Bacon (1620–1692), who became a member of the Council while Calthorpe was living in Virginia.

Calthorpe arrived in Virginia aboard the *Furtherance* in 1622. George Sandys, the treasurer of the colony, offered him a room in his house, introduced him to the governor, and advised him how to succeed, but Calthorpe was then only about eighteen years old, and the next spring Sandys wrote of Calthorpe's inauspicious first months in the colony: "At the first he kept Companie too much with the Inferiours, who hung vpon him while his good liquor lasted." Calthorpe then spent unprofitable time with "a man of no good example" before joining Thomas Purefoy's household in 1623 or 1624 in what became Elizabeth City County.

Purefoy, who became a member of the governor's Council a decade later, may have had a stronger influence on Calthorpe than did Sandys. In 1628 Calthorpe purchased 100 acres of land near Purefoy's property. Three years later, after the governor and Council opened for settlement the region that became York County, he acquired 500 acres at "the New Poquoson" adjoining a small watercourse later known as Calthorpe's Creek. In 1636 Calthorpe received patents that secured his title to 1,100 acres in New Poquoson Parish and 100 acres in Warwick County. He named his property Thropland after the family estate in England.

Calthorpe was a captain in the county militia from 1635 to 1648, major by 1652, lieutenant colonel in 1655, and colonel from 1656 to 1661, and he was a justice of the peace from 1652 to 1661. He represented York County in the House of Burgesses in the sessions that met in March and October 1644, Elizabeth City County in the assembly of February 1645, and York County again in the assemblies of November 1645 and March 1646, November 1652, July 1653, and March and October 1660. Although there is no evidence that Calthorpe served as a vestryman, the New Poquoson Parish church was on his property.

Calthorpe's family life is poorly documented. County records mention his wife, Ann Calthorpe, and indicate that they were married by the mid-1640s. They had at least one son and three daughters. Indentured servants also lived in the household or on Calthorpe's property, and he relied on tenants to develop sections of his plantation. He lived a longer life than many early immigrants, and his ownership of land and occupation of public offices indicate that he was more successful and more respected than most of his neighbors. Calthorpe did not, however, move into the top rank of colonial society, nor did his children. In that, he was a more nearly typical colonist. Unlike some other planters living in his vicinity during the 1650s, Calthorpe did not replace indentured servants from England with imported Africans or descendants of Africans, although this initial failure to participate in the new labor economy need not necessarily have worked to his family's economic disadvantage.

In April 1661 the York County Court replaced Calthorpe as a justice of the peace because he had left Virginia, having gone south in search of unsettled land. In a deed executed on 13 January 1662 he identified himself as "Christopher Calthorpe, late of New Poquoson in the county of York in Virginia now of Carolina to the South of Virginia." Christopher Calthorpe died between then and 23 April 1662, when his widow appointed an attorney to present evidence on Calthorpe's nuncupative will to the York County Court. The October 1662 inventory of his estate, which was valued at 30,480 pounds of tobacco and cask, showed that five tenants then lived on his property. Calthorpe's house had at least two well-furnished rooms, his farm had a shed, he owned several draft oxen, and corn and tobacco were growing in his fields. He also owned one or more beehives, on which the appraisers did not set a value.

Adventurers of Purse and Person, 54, 149–153; "The Calthorpes," *WMQ,* 1st ser., 2 (1894): 106–112, 160–168, 275–276; John Anderson Brayton, "A Royal Descent for Christopher Calthorpe of York Co., Va.," *Virginia Genealogist* 40 (1996): 67–70; George Sandys to Samuel Wrote, 28 Mar. 1623, in Kingsbury, *Virginia Company,* 4:67–68 (first and second quotations; first appearance in Virginia); *Cavaliers and Pioneers,* 1:12, 26 (third quotation), 34, 39, 44; public offices and family data in York Co. records, esp. York Co. Deeds, Orders, Wills, Etc., 3:118, 157 (fourth quotation), 161 (widow appoints attorney), 164, 172, 180 (estate inventory).

JULIE RICHTER

CALVERT, Cornelius (13 March 1724– 5 November 1804), mayor of Norfolk, was born in Norfolk, one of eleven sons of Cornelius Calvert and Mary Saunders Calvert. His father was one of the city's first and most prosperous ship captains and leading merchants. The Calvert brothers were mischievous and high-spirited boys, of whom ten went to sea. Like their father, most succeeded and became masters of their own merchant ships, and several returned to live in Norfolk and take part in the city's civic life. On 19 June 1749 Calvert married Elizabeth Thoroughgood, of Princess Anne County. They had one son and two daughters.

After retiring from the sea, Calvert prospered as a leading Norfolk merchant. When the city was burned at the beginning of 1776, his real estate and warehouse inventory there, valued at more than £2,300, made him one of the fifteen largest losers by the fire. Beginning in 1764 Calvert served for many years as a justice of the peace in Norfolk County. In 1766 he was a member of the Norfolk Sons of Liberty that organized to support the General Assembly in its protests against the Stamp Act. Nine years later Calvert served on the Norfolk County Committee that was elected to support the measures that the First Continental Congress and the Virginia Revolutionary Conventions adopted to protest the Coercive Acts. Elected to Norfolk's common council on 8 July 1761, he became an alderman six years later. Calvert served two one-year terms as mayor of the borough, beginning on 24 June 1768 and 24 June 1778.

Days after he began his first term, Calvert became embroiled in the first Norfolk anti-inoculation riot, precipitated by residents who feared that the procedure, new to the area, would spread smallpox, not prevent it. He supported immunization, and after he allowed three of his slaves to be inoculated a second riot took place in May 1769. Rioters, among them his brother Joseph, the borough sergeant, attacked Calvert's house, broke dozens of windows, and demanded an end to the inoculations. Calvert initiated several civil suits against the rioters, in which Thomas Jefferson represented the inoculators. Conversely, criminal charges for conspiring to spread smallpox were brought against Calvert and John Dalgleish, the physician who administered the inoculations. Defended by John Blair (1731–1800) and Edmund Pendleton, the two men were acquitted. Calvert's second term as mayor was no easier as the city government scarcely functioned in the aftermath of the fire that on 1 January 1776 destroyed most of Norfolk and caused many of its residents to abandon the city. He remained an alderman until his death.

Calvert was a wealthy and respectable gentleman, but his combative personality and personal self-righteousness often placed him in conflict with other local leaders. He twice accused fellow vestrymen of Elizabeth River Parish of misapplying funds, and he led a prolonged campaign of accusation against fellow alderman and keeper of the revenue Paul Loyall, whose accounts of funds raised for maintaining the night watch were muddled and in arrears during the Revolutionary War. Of all the members of Norfolk's common hall, only Calvert among the aldermen and his brother John Calvert among the councillors supported a popular movement that in 1787 persuaded the assembly to grant Norfolk a new charter that for the first time conferred on the city's citizens the right to elect the members of the common council. Before that reform the council had filled its own vacancies and also elected councilmen to vacancies on the board of aldermen. Cornelius Calvert publicly denounced the old charter as undemocratic and government under its terms as despotic and unaccountable. During more than two years in which the question of charter revision dominated and divided Norfolk's politics, he was the old regime's most vocal and intemperate critic.

Although he characterized his opponents as haughty aristocrats, Calvert was haughty and aristocratic himself. He did not believe in democracy but in the right of men of property and good family to conduct the affairs of government in a fair and honest manner. Artisans and laborers, in Calvert's opinion, would always be too ignorant to be trusted with the franchise. Ten years after succeeding in democratizing Norfolk's city charter, he praised the Alien and Sedition Acts as "excellent bills," the first "to drive unruly foreigners away, and the other to keep in order the unruly mob."

The mixed messages that Calvert's words and actions conveyed exemplified in some measure the changes through which he lived. One result was a decidedly uncharacteristic newspaper obituary that appeared on the day after his death. At a time when newspapers seldom published more than death notices or high encomiums, the printer of the *Norfolk Gazette and Publick Ledger* thought himself justified in commenting on Calvert's conduct: "When party dissentions agitated the minds of our citizens, his station obliged him to act the part which he approved. Whether this be eulogized by friends, or blamed by those of opposite opinions, is now (to him) immaterial. However venial his failings, or conspicuous his virtues, they are now called to a superior audit."

Cornelius Calvert died in Norfolk on 5 November 1804. The place of his burial is not recorded.

Incorrectly transcribed birth date of 18 Mar. 1724 in Calvert family Bible records, LVA; Charles B. Cross Jr., ed., *Memoirs of Helen Calvert Maxwell Read* (1970), 25, 27–30, reproduces original record showing birth date of 13 Mar. 1724; Princess Anne Co. Marriage Bonds; Brent Tarter, ed., *The Order Book and Related Papers of the Common Hall of the Borough of Norfolk, Virginia, 1736–1798* (1979), esp. 18–26; *Revolutionary Virginia*, 1:46–48, 3:327, 365–366, 5:273–274, 325, 342, 6:528; Frank L. Dewey, *Thomas Jefferson, Lawyer* (1986), 45–56; *Williamsburg Virginia Gazette* (Rind), supplement for 25 Aug. 1768; *Williamsburg Virginia Gazette* (Purdie and Dixon), 9 Jan. 1772; Edward C. Carter II et al., eds., *The Virginia Journals of Benjamin Henry Latrobe, 1795–1798* (1977), 2:441 (por.), 445–447 (first quotation), 536–537; *Report of the Commissioners . . . to Ascertain the Losses Occasioned to Individuals by the Burning of Norfolk and Portsmouth,* Doc. 43, appended to *JHD*, 1835–1836 sess.; will and estate inventory in Norfolk City Will Book, 2:270–271, 296–297; obituary in *Norfolk Gazette and Publick Ledger*, 6 Nov. 1804 (second quotation).

BRENT TARTER

CALVERT, John Strother (30 November 1806–10 May 1870), treasurer of Virginia, was born in the portion of Culpeper County that became Rappahannock County in 1833. His parents were Ralls Calvert and Mary Wade Strother Calvert. His father owned Calvert Mills, a complex consisting of a gristmill, a sawmill, and other manufacturing facilities. Nothing is known of Calvert's childhood and education. He took out a marriage bond on 29 June 1833 and then or soon thereafter married Catherine Ann Salvage in Rockingham County. They lived in New Market in Shenandoah County and had two sons and two daughters before Catherine Calvert died on 1 March 1845.

In June 1842 Calvert became treasurer and clerk of the Valley Turnpike Company, which constructed and operated a toll road between Staunton and Winchester. He was acting superintendent of the turnpike periodically between 1848 and the end of 1850 and owned twenty shares of company stock in 1854. In 1849 Calvert was named a trustee of Shenandale College, a New Market school that never opened, and the following year he was a trustee for the New Market Female Seminary.

Calvert was elected to the House of Delegates from Shenandoah County in 1850 and served on the Committee to Examine the Penitentiary, the Committee on the Western Lunatic Asylum, and a joint committee to examine the bonds of public officers. On the third day of the session he proposed that the Valley Turnpike Company be permitted to suspend the payment of dividends until the company's debts were paid, and the assembly enacted a bill authorizing the suspension. Calvert introduced five other measures that did not pass. Perhaps frustrated during his first legislative experience, he persuaded the House to adopt a rule that "no member shall speak more than ten minutes on the same subject" for the remainder of the session.

Calvert did not run again for the House of Delegates until 1855, when he was elected by a margin of almost 500 votes over the nearest competitor. He served on the Committee of Roads and Internal Navigation and the Joint Committee on Executive Expenditures. Calvert unsuccessfully tried to get the state to relinquish its share in the Valley Turnpike Company to private stockholders. He proposed a total of sixteen measures, six of which became law, including charters for three new Shenandoah County turnpike companies, a new fire-fighting company for Woodstock, and a resolution authorizing the Board of Public Works to purchase any internal improvement company that might be offered for sale.

On 6 February 1856 the assembly by a vote of 143 to 2 elected Calvert state treasurer, to take office on 1 January 1857. As treasurer, Calvert served in a subordinate capacity to the auditor of public accounts (also known as the first auditor), Jonathan McCally Bennett, who was the state's chief financial officer. The treasurer received and disbursed money on warrants from the first and second auditors, the latter being responsible for certain selected funds, including the internal improvements and literary funds. One of Calvert's sons served as his second clerk for most of his tenure and the other also worked in the office briefly.

Throughout the Civil War the auditors and treasurer performed their duties so well that the state ran a budget surplus and thus did not collect property and license taxes from March 1864 through February 1865. On the night of 2–3 April 1865 the Confederates evacuated Richmond, and the state government collapsed. In his escape from the city Calvert carried with him and thus saved from descruction many valuable archival records. He returned them safely to the Capitol in June. On 10 January 1866 the assembly again elected Calvert state treasurer. He took office five days later and served until the commanding general of Military District Number One removed him on 17 April 1868 at the request of Governor Henry Horatio Wells.

Wells charged that Calvert had kept money belonging to the state instead of returning it to the Virginia treasury after the war had ended. The state had borrowed $21,000 early in 1865 and issued bonds of obligation for its repayment. At the time of the April evacuation the first auditor had taken the balance with him for safekeeping, and in August 1865 he turned over the remaining $2,207 to Calvert, who then expended almost half of that sum according to the wartime governor's prior instructions. In December 1865 Calvert informed the House of Delegates' Committee for Courts of Justice, which was investigating the matter, that he could account for the remaining $1,211.30, of which $119.97 was still in his hands.

The committee reported to the House that Calvert and other officers of the Confederate state of Virginia "cannot be regarded by us as having been the agents or representatives of the people of Virginia, for any purpose; and we, as the agents and representatives of those people, cannot claim title to the money in question merely because it was acquired and held by them." The assembly washed its hands of the matter and referred all claimants to the courts to settle their claims as private citizens. Wells disagreed and persuaded the general to remove Calvert from office. The ouster prompted some of the governor's critics to charge that he was attempting to feather his own nest by replacing a former Confederate state treasurer with a man who would acquiesce in Wells's scheme to sell the state's stock in one railroad company to another railroad company and perhaps benefit personally as a result.

After his removal from office Calvert remained in Richmond and served first as general agent and then as president of the Southern Mutual Insurance Company. On 27 April 1870 he was injured in the collapse of the floor of the Supreme Court of Appeals in the Capitol, an incident that killed about sixty people and injured more than two hundred others. His left leg was fractured below the knee, his right hip was broken, and the hipbone perforated his bowel. John Strother Calvert died at the Monumental Hotel in Richmond on 10 May 1870. He was buried in Saint Matthew's (later Reformation Lutheran Church's) Cemetery in New Market.

Birth date from gravestone transcribed in Duane L. Borden, *Tombstone Inscriptions: New Market, Mt. Jackson, and Edinburg Vicinities, Shenandoah County, Virginia* (1984), 35; Ella Foy O'Gorman, comp., *Descendants of Virginia Calverts* (1947), 130, 201–202; Index to Rockingham Co. Marriage Registers; Valley Turnpike Correspondence, Reports, Etc., 1841–1847, Board of Public Works, RG 57, LVA; Minutes of Board of Directors Meetings, Valley Turnpike Company Records, LVA; *JHD*, 1850–1851 sess., 291 (first quotation); John W. Wayland, *A History of Shenandoah County, Virginia* (1927), 529–530, 592; *Richmond Enquirer*, 30 Apr. 1850, 1 June 1855; *Report of the Committee for Courts of Justice Relative to Distribution of Certain Gold*, 20 Dec. 1865, Doc. 11, supplement to *JHD*, 1865–1866 sess., 3–5 (second quotation on 4), 7; *Richmond Daily Enquirer and Examiner*, 20 Apr. 1868; *Petersburg Daily Index*, 28 Apr. 1868, 11 May 1870; obituaries in *Richmond Daily Enquirer* and *Richmond Daily Whig*, both 11 May 1870, and *Rockingham Register*, 19 May 1870; editorial tribute in *Staunton Vindicator*, 13 May 1870.

EMILY J. SALMON

CALWELL, James (ca. 1773–8 April 1851), proprietor of the White Sulphur Springs resort, was born in Maryland, but the exact place and date of his birth are unknown. His parents were probably Samuel Calwell, or Caldwell, and a woman whose maiden surname was Taggart. About 1795 Calwell visited what was then known as Bowyer's Sulphur Spring in Greenbrier County. There he met Mary, or Polly, Bowyer, daughter of Michael Bowyer, the owner and manager of the springs and a small group of nearby cabins, and Calwell married her on 12 December 1797. They lived in Baltimore and had nine sons and three daughters. Calwell's business, shipping grain to Europe and importing such luxury goods as French clothing to the United States, prospered during the next decade and a half.

About 1807 Michael Bowyer died, leaving the main portion of his estate—including the mineral springs and a new tavern—to his eldest son, James Bowyer, who divided the 950 acres of land among his six siblings, including Polly Calwell. James Calwell purchased the furnishings and household equipment from the estate and became actively involved in the resort, which James Bowyer and others continued to manage. Setbacks to Calwell's shipping business during the War of 1812, in which he was wounded defending Fort McHenry near Baltimore, convinced him that his future fortune lay at his wife's family's mineral-water resort. By 1819 he had bought out all but one of his in-laws' shares and assumed sole proprietorship of the resort.

Calwell borrowed $20,000 from Baltimore associates and began a series of improvements to the springs. He moved to White Sulphur Springs and was for a decade the proprietor and principal manager of the increasingly popular resort. Calwell transformed an establishment that consisted of a few crude cabins and tents into the South's premier vacation spot. He erected a pavilion over the main spring and topped it with a carved wooden figure of a female Indian clutching arrows in one hand and a bowl, symbolizing healing, in the other. The statue was later replaced by a representation of Hygeia, the classical goddess of health. Calwell constructed cottages, bathhouses, and other buildings to give an image of an idyllic retreat where people could relax and recuperate surrounded by the stylish trappings of civilization and good company. Beginning in 1838 a resident physician was on hand to advise his guests.

A trip to White Sulphur Springs became *de rigueur* for many wealthy, influential, or fashionable southern families. Political leaders including Henry Clay, Andrew Jackson, Martin Van Buren, and others made well-publicized visits to forge or reinforce alliances with leading southerners. The popularity of the resort increased to such an extent that Calwell had difficulty housing all of the people who arrived each summer. The resort's high style earned him the respect and friendship of many of his elite guests; he and Clay, for example, corresponded for at least twenty-five years. Calwell became well known, too, as a personification of the well-mannered and well-dressed old-style Virginia gentleman.

Calwell may have represented the ideal of the Virginia gentleman, but he lived the reality of a failed businessman. Despite his accomplishments, his resort struggled financially. His initial investors called in their loans, forcing Calwell to turn to his guests for funds. Fortunately, friendship and business mixed well for him, and he borrowed $27,000 from one of his regular guests, South Carolina planter Richard Singleton. Calwell was thereby able to increase the resort's capacity by adding new cabins. He received additional income by renting out privately owned cottages to other guests when the owners were not in residence and by charging his established weekly rate to the owners of these private dwellings when they visited his springs. The short season that began late in June and concluded late in September never provided enough revenue to meet all of Calwell's expenses, however. He retired from active daily management of White Sulphur Springs in the mid-1820s, leaving his son William B. Calwell in charge of the popular but unprofitable institution. Calwell continued as host, however. By 1845 the resort had expanded from its original 950 acres to nearly 7,000.

Mary Bowyer Calwell died on 28 August 1842, and in November of that year Calwell placed the institution in trust to guarantee his debts. White Sulphur Springs was secure in its fame but insecure in its finances when James Calwell died at his residence there on 8 April 1851. He was buried on the property. The writer of his obituary in the county's weekly newspaper declared that he "died without an enemy, and left an inheritance of character richer and brighter & more enduring than all the gold or rubies of earth." That must have provided small solace to his heirs, because Calwell owed more than $400,000 at the time of his death, and a few years later the family was forced to sell its interests in White Sulphur Springs.

Encyclopaedia of Contemporary Biography of West Virginia (1894), 172–173 (gives 1773 birth date in Harford Co., Md., without documentation); death date at age seventy-eight on gravestone; Census, Greenbrier Co., 1850, gives Maryland as place of birth and age of seventy-four on 10 Sept. 1850; Calwell Papers, Greenbrier Archives, White Sulphur Springs, W.Va.; some Calwell letters in Singleton Family Papers, University of South Carolina, Columbia; correspondence with Henry Clay in *Clay Papers*, vols. 5–6, 8, 10; Robert S. Conte, *The History of the Greenbrier: America's Resort* (1989), 7–14, 18–27, 33–37, 43–44 (por. on 8); wife's death in *Richmond Whig and Public Advertiser*, 9 Sept. 1842; obituary in *Lewisburg Chronicle*, 10 Apr. 1851 (quotation), giving age at death as seventy-seven, reprinted in *Richmond Whig and Public Advertiser*, 18 Apr. 1851.

THOMAS A. CHAMBERS

CAMDEN, Gideon Draper (31 August 1805– 22 April 1891), member of the Convention of 1850–1851, was born in Montgomery County, Maryland, the son of Henry Camden, a Methodist minister, and Mary Belt Sprigg Camden. When he was young the family moved to Virginia and lived in the Collins settlement in Lewis County. After moving to Weston in 1822, Camden worked as an assistant to the county clerk and the clerk of the superior court and about 1826 became county clerk himself. In March 1827 he left to study law in Wythe County under Alexander Smyth, a member of the House of Representatives. Camden completed his studies and later that same year was admitted to the bar of Lewis County. On 24 February 1825 he married Sarah Hoffman, a native of Culpeper County. They had three sons and four daughters, one of whom married Caleb Boggess, a member of the Convention of 1861.

Camden entered politics and was elected to represent Lewis County in the House of Delegates for the 1828–1829 session. He served on the Committee of Roads and Internal Navigation. In 1830 Camden was elected to another term but, probably because of financial concerns, resigned before the session began to become clerk of the superior court of Lewis County.

Camden moved to Clarksburg in 1834 and practiced law in partnership with John James Allen, a member of the House of Representatives. The partnership lasted until 1836 when Allen became a judge, beginning his rise to the Virginia Supreme Court of Appeals. In 1843 Camden formed a partnership with Jonathan McCally Bennett, who later became the auditor of public accounts of Virginia. Active in realms other than the law, Camden was a trustee of the Northwestern Virginia Academy, at Clarksburg, in 1841. His political ambitions remained unfulfilled. In 1845 Camden was the Whig candidate for the House of Representatives in the fifteen-county Fourteenth District, but he lost to Democrat Joseph Johnson, later governor of Virginia, by about 300 votes out of nearly 6,000 cast. Camden remained active in the Whig Party and in 1848 was a delegate to the state and national party conventions.

In the summer of 1850 these political connections helped Camden win election as one of four men representing Doddridge, Harrison, Ritchie, Tyler, Wetzel, and Wood Counties in a convention called to revise the state constitution. He served on the Committees on the Legislative Department of the Government and on Western Land Titles, the latter reflecting his interest in land speculation. Camden was active at the convention and spoke, sometimes at great length, in favor of extending white male suffrage, restricting the size and power of the legislature, abolishing the county courts and Council of State, creating a statewide system of public education, and establishing a banking system similar to that in New York. Along with the majority of delegates from the western districts he voted for representation in the General Assembly based on the white population and for adoption of the new constitution.

Camden quickly benefited from reforms adopted at the convention. For several years previous he had unsuccessfully schemed for a legislative appointment to the circuit court bench. Under the new constitution, the voters elected circuit court judges, and in May 1852 Camden easily won election as judge of the Twenty-first Circuit Court, which included the counties of Barbour, Harrison, Marion, Preston, Randolph, Taylor, and Upshur. He was reelected in 1860 for a second eight-year term, which the Civil War prevented him from completing.

Initially opposed to secession, Camden sided with Virginia following the state's withdrawal from the Union in April 1861. The Convention of 1861 elected him a delegate to the Provisional Confederate Congress, then meeting in Montgomery, but he chose not to travel to Alabama and never served. Because of his pro-Southern leanings, Camden was forced to leave Unionist Harrison County by November 1861. He traveled to Richmond and remained there probably until March 1862, when he returned to western Virginia and eventually settled in Rockbridge County. Camden returned to Clarksburg, West Virginia, in the autumn of 1865 and reentered politics in 1872 when he won election as a Democrat to a four-year term in the West Virginia Senate.

Camden's lifelong involvement in a variety of land, oil, coal, timber, and railroad ventures made him very wealthy. His business partners included Benjamin Wilson Byrne, a member of the Convention of 1861. In 1850 Camden possessed $50,000 in real estate and about seven slaves. By 1870, despite his absence from Clarksburg for most of the war, he owned real estate worth about $100,000 and $15,000 in personal assets. Camden's relatives, most of whom were strong Unionists, probably protected his property and wealth from confiscation during the war. At the time of his death he was reputedly the largest landholder in West Virginia.

Camden's wife died in Clarksburg on 8 February 1879. On 3 October 1883 he married Almira Hornor Davis, a widow. They had no children. Probably seeking relief from chronic back and abdominal pain, Gideon Draper Camden visited the medicinal spa at Hot Springs, Arkansas, where he died on 22 April 1891. Six years after Camden's death, his widow became the second wife of George Wesley Atkinson, author and governor of West Virginia from 1897 until 1901.

Birth and marriage dates from family records and Roy Bird Cook, "Line of Gideon Draper Camden" (undated typescript), both in Roy Bird Cook Papers, WVU; Atkinson and Gibbens, *Prominent Men*, 2:945–948; John Edmund Stealey III, "Gideon Draper Camden: A Whig of Western Virginia," *West Virginia History* 26 (1965): 13–30; Glenn F. Massay, "The Lost Years—Gideon Draper Camden and the Confederacy," *West Virginia History* 25 (1964): 190–194 (with incorrect death date); Louis Reed, "Footnote to Judge Gideon Draper Camden," *West Virginia History* 26 (1965): 191–194; Dorothy Davis, *History of Harrison County, West Virginia* (1970), 96 (por.), 611–613; Gideon Draper Camden Papers, VHS and WVU; *Daily Richmond Enquirer*, 12 May 1845; *Richmond Enquirer*, 30 Aug., 3 Sept. 1850; *Journal of 1850–1851 Convention*, 59, 111, 226, 419; *Register of Debates, 1850–1851 Convention*, 306–307; *Supplement, 1850–1851 Convention Debates*, nos. 17, 42; Reese, *Journals and Papers of 1861 Convention*, vol. 1, Journal, 214, 243; land acquisitions from 1840s to early in the 1860s in Virginia Land Office Patents, RG 4, LVA; Harrison Co. Will Book, 7:248–251; obituary in *Parkersburg (W.Va.) Daily State Journal*, 23 Apr. 1891 (with 5 Aug. 1805 birth date and 1824 first marriage date).

C. Stinson Lindenzweig

CAMERON, Alexander (1 November 1832– 3 February 1915), tobacco manufacturer, was born in Grantown, Inverness-shire, Scotland, the son of Alexander Cameron, a farmer and merchant, and Elizabeth Grant Cameron. His father died in 1840, and the following year his mother married James Cruikshanks, a shoemaker. In 1841 the family moved to Petersburg, where Cameron's mother died in January 1848. He attended the local schools, and, following the path of his elder brother, William Cameron, he had entered the tobacco business of David Dunlop by 1850.

Cameron later joined his brother's tobacco-manufacturing company, Cameron and Crawford, which opened in Petersburg about 1858. William Cameron kept his factory operating during the Civil War, while Alexander Cameron reportedly ran the Union blockades between North Carolina and Nassau and deposited his earnings in England, which left the Cameron

brothers with much-needed cash and good credit at the end of the war. Immediately afterward, William Cameron began expanding the family's tobacco business to Australia, where the brothers eventually opened factories in Adelaide, Brisbane, Melbourne, and Sydney. By 1866 Alexander Cameron had moved to Richmond, probably at the urging of his brother, and founded Alexander Cameron and Company to manufacture plug tobacco. Also, in conjunction with their brothers-in-law, the Camerons opened factories in Kentucky and England during the 1860s. They secured a profitable contract to supply tobacco to the British navy.

By 1870 the tobacco-manufacturing companies owned by Alexander Cameron, William Cameron, and their younger brother, George Cameron, were among the largest in Richmond and Petersburg, and by continuing to expand their business throughout the remainder of the century, they made it one of the largest such enterprises operated by Americans at that time. They sold tobacco around much of the world through agents in Australia, China, India, Japan, South Africa, Europe, and North America. Although each company operated independently, they all worked together buying, manufacturing, and selling all forms of tobacco products, including cigarettes, cigars, plug tobacco, and smoking tobacco. In 1886 William Cameron retired, leaving the management of the far-flung business in the hands of Alexander Cameron and George Cameron, who purchased another Richmond firm within two years to create A. and G. Cameron and Sizer, later known as Cameron and Cameron.

By early in the 1890s the Camerons' factories in Richmond and Petersburg alone employed hundreds of workers and could produce as much as four million pounds of tobacco each year. Alexander Cameron and his partners began to face increasing competition from the American Tobacco Company, created in 1890, which continually undercut the prices of independent manufacturers. Cameron attempted to compete but ultimately decided to retire from the business, and by 1904 he had sold the Cameron factories to the new British-American Tobacco Company.

On 1 September 1868 Cameron married Mary Parke Haxall at her family's estate in Orange County. They had six sons, four daughters, and another child who died young. The family enjoyed substantial wealth and occasionally traveled abroad. During one of these visits in 1875 Cameron and his wife were presented to Queen Victoria. Cameron was prominent in Richmond business and society and served as a director of the city's Chamber of Commerce and of the State Bank of Virginia. With several of his sons he was also a founding director of the Cameron-Tennant Machine Works in 1899. Cameron remained close to his Scottish roots, retained his accent, and hosted an annual pheasant supper at which he served birds brought over from Scotland.

In June 1914 Cameron suffered a stroke at his family's summer home in Orange County. He recovered and returned to Richmond, but on 3 February 1915 Alexander Cameron died at his home of pneumonia. He was buried in the family plot at Hollywood Cemetery in Richmond.

NCAB, 7:321–322; Tyler, *Encyclopedia*, 4:258–260 (por.); Philip Alexander Bruce, *Virginia: Rebirth of the Old Dominion* (1929), 3:391–392 (por. facing 391); Cameron and Grant-Cameron family Bible records, LVA; *Petersburg Daily Index*, 7 Sept. 1868; *Petersburg Index and Appeal*, 19 Apr. 1875; Andrew Morrison, ed., *City on the James: Richmond, Virginia* (1893), 126–128; Joseph C. Robert, *The Story of Tobacco in America* (1949), 81, 131; correspondence and documents related to Cameron tobacco companies in British-American Tobacco Company, Ltd., Papers, Duke; BVS Death Certificate, Richmond City; obituaries in *New York Times*, *Petersburg Daily Index-Appeal*, *Richmond News Leader*, and *Richmond Times-Dispatch*, all 4 Feb. 1915; editorial tributes in *Richmond News Leader*, 4 Feb. 1915, and *Richmond Times-Dispatch*, 5 Feb. 1915; memorial in *VMHB* 24 (1916): xxxvii–xlii.

MARIANNE E. JULIENNE

CAMERON, William (11 August 1829–26 October 1902), tobacco manufacturer, was born in Grantown, Inverness-shire, Scotland, the son of Alexander Cameron, a farmer and merchant, and Elizabeth Grant Cameron. His father died in April 1840, and his mother married again in 1841. That same year the family moved to Petersburg, where Cameron's mother died in January 1848. He probably received some education in Scotland and briefly attended school in Petersburg before he began working in the tobacco factory of David Dunlop. Cameron became a United States citizen after taking the oath of allegiance at age twenty-one. In October 1852 he married Martha Louisa Russell. Their one son died in 1859.

Cameron learned his lessons well at Dunlop's factory, and by 1858 he had opened in Petersburg with Robert Crawford a tobacco-manufacturing business styled Cameron and Crawford. On 9 November 1858 Cameron received patent number 22,014 for the first press to use hydraulic power in the manufacture of plug, or chewing, tobacco, one of the few mechanical innovations in the tobacco industry during the antebellum period. Cameron and Crawford continued operating successfully during the Civil War. In 1867 Cameron had to apply for a presidential pardon, even though he had taken no direct part in the war, because he was then worth more than $20,000.

Immediately after the war Cameron began expanding his tobacco business. In May 1865 he left Virginia on an eighteen-month trip to Europe and Australia, where he and his brothers opened factories during the 1870s in Adelaide, Brisbane, Melbourne, and Sydney. A younger brother, Alexander Cameron, went to Richmond and in 1866 established a factory there. The next year William Cameron brought their younger brother George Cameron into a partnership at his factory in Petersburg designated William Cameron and Brother. Cameron also turned to his two brothers-in-law to extend his production, and they opened factories in Kentucky and England during the 1860s. He used his connections to obtain a lucrative contract with the British navy after the Civil War. Each company operated independently, but they worked in concert to sell Cameron tobacco products worldwide. Their companies conducted trade throughout Africa, Asia, Europe, and North America and were also involved in the sale and distribution of leaf tobacco. The Australian companies reportedly supplied 75 percent of the manufactured tobacco for Australia and India. The combined businesses of the Cameron brothers were among the largest operated by Americans during the late-nineteenth century.

Cameron's tobacco companies alone ranked with the largest tobacco manufacturers in Petersburg. They employed hundreds in their factories and in 1880 produced more than $270,000 worth of tobacco.

By June 1886 Cameron had sold his interest to his brothers and retired from his tobacco business, possibly as a result of poor health. In July 1887 he formed a new partnership with William J. Young, the former manager of the Camerons' Australian factories, to create Cameron and Company. This new venture proved unsuccessful, and in September 1892 Cameron and Company was dissolved. In the meantime, in October 1890 Cameron and his brother George Cameron founded Cameron Tobacco Company in Petersburg, which operated for several years.

Cameron entered local politics. While serving on the Petersburg common council as a Democrat from 1888 to 1892, he chaired the Committee on Gas and Light. In October 1892 he resigned from the council and moved to Washington, D.C. While visiting his summer home in Wytheville with his wife, William Cameron died of heart failure on 26 October 1902. He was buried in Blandford Cemetery in Petersburg.

Birth and death dates in Cameron family Bible records, LVA; tombstone inscription gives variant dates of 14 Aug. 1829 and 27 Oct. 1902; Edward A. Wyatt, "Rise of Industry in Ante-Bellum Petersburg," *WMQ*, 2d ser., 17 (1937): 14; *Report of the Commissioner of Patents for the Year 1858*, 2:279, 3:456, 35th Cong., 2d sess. (1859), House Ex. Doc. 105, serials 1010, 1011; Presidential Pardons; Edward Pollock, *Historical and Industrial Guide to Petersburg, Virginia* [ca. 1884], 116–117; Nannie May Tilley, *The Bright-Tobacco Industry, 1860–1929* (1948), 490, 603; Joseph C. Robert, *The Story of Tobacco in America* (1949), 81, 131; Fay Campbell Kaynor, "George Campbell (1834–1917)," 3–4, 7–8 (1988 typescript), Jane Maud Campbell Papers, Schlesinger Library, Radcliffe Institute, Cambridge, Mass.; Census, Industrial Schedule, Dinwiddie Co., 1880; SCC Charter Book, 13:398, 38:140; letters and documents relating to Cameron in Young Family Papers, VHS; *Petersburg Daily Index-Appeal*, 25 May 1888, 13, 27 May, 4 Oct. 1892; obituaries (giving 26 Oct. 1902 death date) in *Petersburg Daily Index-Appeal* and *Richmond Dispatch*, both 28 Oct. 1902.

MARIANNE E. JULIENNE

CAMERON, William Evelyn (29 November 1842–25 January 1927), journalist, governor of

Virginia, and member of the Convention of 1901–1902, was born in Petersburg, the son of Walker Anderson Cameron, a cotton broker, and Elizabeth Page Walker Cameron. His mother was related to the Byrd and Harrison families, and his father to John Cameron, a Scottish clergyman who had served as the rector of Blandford Church in Petersburg.

Growing up in Petersburg, Cameron attended local schools and developed interests in history, music, and poetry. After his parents died he lived with two unmarried aunts in Petersburg before enrolling in 1857 in a military academy in Hillsboro, North Carolina. Two years later Cameron went to live with an uncle in Saint Louis, Missouri. Following a brief, undistinguished sojourn as a student at Washington College in that city, he worked as an assistant purser on a Mississippi River steamboat. Nomination in 1860 for a cadetship at the United States Military Academy at West Point, New York, rekindled Cameron's zeal for academic pursuits, and he received preparatory tutoring in Missouri from John F. Reynolds, a captain in the United States Army.

At the start of the Civil War Cameron broke off his studies. Joining a secessionist militia company stationed on the outskirts of Saint Louis, he was captured but escaped and began an arduous journey back to Virginia. Cameron reported to Confederate authorities in Norfolk and was assigned to a Petersburg militia contingent that became part of the 12th Regiment Virginia Infantry. On 14 June 1861 he was elected a second lieutenant, and on 18 May 1862 he was commissioned a first lieutenant and appointed a regimental adjutant. Wounded at the Second Battle of Manassas (Bull Run) in August 1862, Cameron was transferred to Brigadier General William Mahone's command as brigade inspector and commenced a close association with Mahone, a fellow Petersburg resident, that lasted for more than two decades. Promoted to captain and assistant adjutant-general as of 2 November 1863, Cameron served in the Army of Northern Virginia until the surrender at Appomattox Court House.

In his early twenties when the Confederacy collapsed, Cameron returned to civilian life in

Petersburg. On 1 October 1868 in Saint Paul, Minnesota, he married Louisa Clarinda Egerton, of Petersburg. They had two sons and one daughter. The economic hardships of the postwar era hastened Cameron's entrance into the professional arena. He read law with a Petersburg attorney, but journalism exerted a more powerful attraction. Between 1865 and 1875 Cameron served in editorial capacities at a succession of newspapers: the *Petersburg Daily News*, the *Norfolk Virginian*, the *Petersburg Daily Index* (in which, with Mahone's backing, he purchased a financial interest), the *Richmond Whig* (which Mahone controlled), the *Richmond Enquirer*, and the *Petersburg Evening Star*. Cameron wrote poems and Civil War articles for sale to various publications. He also worked briefly in 1869 as an administrative secretary to Governor Gilbert Carlton Walker.

Cameron vigorously supported the Conservative Party in its struggles against the Radical Republicans and in 1870 was the party's unsuccessful candidate for Petersburg's seat in the state senate. His journalistic sallies against Robert William Hughes, editor of the Republican *Richmond State Journal*, led to a duel in 1869 in which Cameron was wounded. Although vociferously critical of those he called carpetbaggers and scalawags, he accepted such Republican innovations as African American suffrage and a tax-supported public school system. These pragmatic stands were popular with many Petersburg residents, who beginning in 1876 elected Cameron to three consecutive two-year terms as mayor. That year he was also admitted to the practice of law in the local courts, and he wrote for the editorial pages of the short-lived *Petersburg Evening Star* and for the *Richmond Whig*.

Issues involving Virginia's massive public debt took center stage in state politics and split the Conservative Party into bitterly antagonistic factions. Funders demanded full payment of the principal and interest, while Readjusters proposed to reduce the amount of the principal to be repaid and to refinance the debt at lower interest. The split between the factions gave the Republican minority the balance of political power in the state. Cameron initially supported the Fun-

ders and argued that Virginia was honor-bound to repay its creditors regardless of the budgetary hardships the commitment imposed. As the depression-ridden 1870s wore on, however, he began to side with the Readjusters. Difficulties with his personal finances may have encouraged Cameron's change of heart, but his ties with Mahone exerted a more decisive influence. During a failed bid for the Conservative nomination for governor in 1877, Mahone announced support for Readjuster principles, and Cameron signaled his new allegiance by acting as a floor leader of Mahone's delegates at the party convention.

Cameron followed Mahone down a path that led in 1879 to the creation of an independent Readjuster Party and two years later to an alliance with national and state Republicans. In June 1881, a few months after Mahone took office as one of Virginia's United States senators, Cameron secured the gubernatorial nomination of the new Readjuster-Republican coalition. An outpouring of support from whites in western counties and from blacks in the Tidewater and Southside enabled him to defeat his Funder opponent, John Warwick Daniel, by more than 12,000 votes in November. Supporters of the coalition also won majorities in both houses of the General Assembly. Cameron's inauguration on 1 January 1882 marked the onset of a period of intense governmental activism. Within a few weeks he was affixing his signature to legislation that slashed the debt, dramatically boosted expenditures for the public schools, and financed an array of public improvements, including the founding of Virginia Normal and Collegiate Institute (later Virginia State University) and the construction of Central Lunatic Asylum (later Central State Hospital), both located in or near Petersburg, to serve the needs of black Virginians. The Readjusters also repealed the poll tax, abolished the whipping post, imposed harsher penalties on duelists, gave tax relief to farmers and small businessmen, tripled the revenue assessments on railroads, and established a state inspection program for commercially marketed fertilizers. Placing the prestige of his office behind these initiatives, Cameron also moved to curtail violations of Virginia's laws governing the harvesting of shellfish. He personally led militia units in raids that resulted in the arrest of scores of so-called Chesapeake Bay "oyster pirates."

Egalitarian reforms and executive dynamism were hallmarks of Cameron's administration. So too were political turbulence and partisan intrigue. Inspired by Mahone's unabashed manipulation of federal patronage, Cameron took similar advantage of his own state-level powers of appointment and removal and even attempted in several instances to oust hostile officials before their terms expired. Amid rising protests against bossism and machine politics, the governor unsuccessfully pressured a special session of the General Assembly to gerrymander congressional districts and to restructure the circuit court system so that Funder judges could be discharged from their posts. Frustrated by legislative intransigence, Cameron subsequently sparked an even greater furor by replacing Richmond's Funder-dominated school board with new appointees, several of whom were black.

The administration's foes (who began to call themselves Democrats in 1883) effectively exploited these controversial developments. At the outset of that year's legislative races they pragmatically disavowed their allegiance to the state's creditors and instead began to denounce spoilsmanship, Mahone's party leadership, and the alleged willingness of Cameron and his associates to "Africanize" Virginia in pursuit of political gain. These tactics, accentuated by a bloody racial clash in Danville a few days before the 1883 election, paid handsome dividends at the polls. A dramatic upsurge in white voter turnout enabled the Democrats to win large majorities in both houses of the General Assembly.

Shaken by this setback, Cameron faced ever-proliferating adversities during the last two years of his gubernatorial term. Democratic legislators purged many of his allies from administrative posts, investigated his sometimes imprudent handling of public funds, and routinely overrode his vetoes of flagrantly partisan measures such as the Anderson-McCormick election law of 1884. Equally troublesome for

Cameron, his ties with Mahone began to deteriorate. Mahone insisted on absolute control over the battered remnants of the old coalition, which renamed itself the Republican Party of Virginia in 1884. Cameron's term ended on 1 January 1886. Scorned by the Democrats and increasingly powerless within his own party, he had tested the limits of political dissent in post-Reconstruction Virginia.

Only forty-three years old, Cameron still had a long and multifaceted career ahead of him. He established a law practice in Petersburg in 1886, but other professional pursuits attracted his energies as well. A two-year stint in Chicago, first as an agent and then as official historian of the World's Columbian Exposition, resulted in Cameron's most extensive literary effort, an 800-page chronicle entitled *The World's Fair, Being a Pictorial History of the Columbian Exposition* (1893). With the cooling of the antagonisms generated by his gubernatorial term, Virginia's cultural and intellectual establishment welcomed Cameron back into its elite circles. He participated in Lost Cause commemorative activities, published articles in Confederate veterans' journals, and received appointment as commissioner-general of the 1907 Jamestown Ter-Centennial Exposition.

Cameron also reestablished himself as a figure of some importance in Virginia politics, albeit at the cost of betraying the egalitarian principles that he had earlier espoused. His two-year stay in strike-plagued Chicago may have helped push him more firmly into hard-line conservatism. Six years of intraparty clashes with Mahone ended in 1890 when Cameron announced his decision to leave the Republican Party. He lambasted national Republican policies as detrimental to states' rights and to southern economic needs. In 1896, proclaiming his support for a dissident faction of the Democratic Party that refused to support William Jennings Bryan and the free coinage of silver, Cameron took to the campaign trail once again. His debt-repudiation past a distant memory, he denounced Bryan and free silver in speeches from one end of Virginia to the other, but few voters heeded Cameron's appeals in behalf of the gold Democrats.

The progressive impulse at the turn of the century afforded a more favorable venue for Cameron's maverick, independent-minded brand of reactionism. Endorsed by local Democrats, he was elected over token opposition in 1901 as one of the two Petersburg representatives to a state constitutional convention. Although such delegates as one-time foe John W. Daniel, then a United States senator, enjoyed greater prestige and influence, Cameron played a substantial role. He chaired the Committee on the Executive Department and served on the Committee on the Judiciary. Under his leadership the Committee on the Executive Department successfully advocated constitutional provisions strengthening the governor's authority to discharge subordinate officials and permitting him to return bills to the General Assembly with suggested amendments.

In floor debates Cameron defended the Committee on the Judiciary's insistence that judges should continue to be chosen by the legislature, a stance that provoked the ire of western delegates who favored popular election. Unswayed by appeals from the convention's hopelessly outnumbered Republicans, he supported the reinstitution of the poll tax and the adoption of other registration restrictions intended to reduce the number of African American voters. As the proceedings entered their final stage, Cameron introduced the motion for approval of the Constitution of 1902, but he opposed the majority's decision to proclaim the new fundamental law rather than submit it to the electorate for endorsement or rejection. Even this futile gesture reflected something less than a full defense of democratic principles. As Cameron saw it, ratification could best be accomplished through a referendum in which only literate, tax-paying white men would be allowed to participate. He had traversed a broad expanse of ideological terrain since leading the biracial Readjuster-Republican coalition to victory in 1881.

Cameron hoped that his performance at the convention would set the stage for a sustained political comeback, but he withdrew from a 1904 bid for the Fourth District Democratic congressional nomination because of poor health. His old passion for journalism then resurfaced. Joining the staff of the *Norfolk Virginian-Pilot* in April 1906, Cameron soon took charge of its editorial page and remained at the helm of that newspaper, which became the *Virginian-Pilot and the Norfolk Landmark* in 1912, until he retired in September 1919.

Cameron's wife died in January 1908. He divided his final years between stays with his daughter in Tallahassee, Florida, and with one of his sons in Louisa County. William Evelyn Cameron died in Louisa County on 25 January 1927 and was buried not far from the grave of William Mahone in Petersburg's Blandford Cemetery. The Democratic press lamented the passing of a brave soldier, a talented journalist, and a colorful figure from Virginia's past. Devoting scant attention to the reforms of Cameron's gubernatorial term, obituaries instead emphasized his independence of character and his unwillingness to submit to factional dictates, especially as manifested in his bolt from the Republican Party.

Men of Mark, 1:106–111; Walter T. Calhoun and James Tice Moore, "William Evelyn Cameron: Restless Readjuster," in *The Governors of Virginia, 1860–1978,* ed. Edward Younger and James Tice Moore (1982), 94–109 (por. on 94); birth date in Pollard Questionnaires; Compiled Service Records; *Petersburg Index,* 17 Oct. 1868; William E. Cameron Papers, UVA; William E. Cameron Executive Papers, RG 3, LVA; Cameron letters in George William Bagby Papers, Chamberlayne Family Papers, and David Addison Weisiger Papers, all VHS, in Harrison Holt Riddleberger Papers, W&M, in William Mahone Papers, Duke, and in Susie Cameron Whitfield Papers, Florida State University, Tallahassee; James Tice Moore, *Two Paths to the New South: The Virginia Debt Controversy, 1870–1883* (1974); Moore, "Gunfire on the Chesapeake: Governor Cameron and the Oyster Pirates, 1882–1885," *VMHB* 90 (1982): 367–377; Lenoir Chambers and Joseph E. Shank, *Salt Water and Printer's Ink: Norfolk and Its Newspapers, 1865–1965* (1967); *Journal of 1901–1902 Convention,* 35, 49, 487, 504, 535; *Proceedings and Debates of 1901–1902 Convention,* 1:71–78, 1025–1030, 1421–1425; *Convention of 1901–1902 Photographs* (por.); Cameron's writings include "The Life and Character of Robert Edward Lee," *SHSP* 29 (1901): 82–99, "The Southern Cause," *SHSP* 30 (1902): 360–368, and a poem, "In the Twilight," *Petersburg Index-Appeal,* 4 June 1881; obituaries in *Petersburg Progress-Index, Richmond News Leader, Richmond Times-Dispatch,* and *Virginian-Pilot and the Norfolk Landmark,* all 26 Jan. 1927; editorial tributes in *Petersburg Progress-Index,* 26 Jan. 1927, and *Richmond Times-Dispatch* and *Virginian-Pilot and the Norfolk Landmark,* both 27 Jan. 1927.

JAMES TICE MOORE

CAMM, Frank (8 January 1895–15 December 1976), army officer, was born in Lynchburg, the son of Katherine Ambler Jellis Camm and her second husband, John Camm. His father was at various times president and secretary-treasurer of the Camm Brothers Bottling Company, which produced soda water. The family frequently spent summers at Saint Moor, the Ambler family estate near Monroe in Amherst County. After the bottling plant closed, the family moved permanently to Amherst in 1913. That autumn Camm enrolled at the Virginia Agricultural and Mechanical College and Polytechnic Institute (later Virginia Polytechnic Institute and State University), intending to major in civil engineering. The following year he transferred to the University of Virginia, where he served as an editor of the law review and in 1917 received a law degree.

Camm entered the United States Army on 27 November 1917 as a second lieutenant in the 55th Artillery Division. He participated in the Aisne-Marne and Meuse-Argonne campaigns in France as a radio officer and was commended by his regimental commander for maintaining communications under enemy fire. Camm once escaped serious injury or death when a German artillery shell landed within five feet of him but did not explode. While in France he attended the Saumur Field Artillery School and Camp Saint Maur Tractor Artillery School. Camm was promoted to first lieutenant on a temporary basis on 28 July 1918 and permanently as of 7 August 1919.

Although discharged from the army on 30 June 1920, Camm decided to remain in the service. Assigned to the 81st Field Artillery, he was successively stationed at Fort Knox, Kentucky, and Fort Sheridan, Illinois. After attending the field artillery school at Fort Sill, Oklahoma, in 1924, Camm taught military science to the Reserve Officer Training Corps at Harvard University from 1926 to 1930. Camm was promoted to captain on 14 September 1928. From 1930 to 1934 he was stationed at Fort Bragg, North Carolina, and from 1934 to 1936 was adjutant to the 13th Field Artillery Brigade at Schofield Barracks in Hawaii. Camm taught military science for the ROTC at Xavier University, in Cincinnati, from 1936 to 1940 and was pro-

moted to major on 1 November 1937 and to lieutenant colonel on 29 November 1940. Following completion of the command and general staff course in 1941, he commanded the 56th Field Artillery at Fort Jackson, South Carolina, and after finishing the division officers' course the next year he was promoted to colonel on 12 August 1942 and appointed executive officer of the 78th Division artillery stationed at Camp Butner, North Carolina.

Camm was promoted to the temporary rank of brigadier general in command of the 78th Division's artillery on 30 April 1943 while the division was preparing for the invasion of Europe. He arrived in England with the division in the autumn of 1944 and took part in the drive on the Rhine River from Kesternich to Remagen during the Ardennes, Rhineland, and Central European campaigns in winter and spring 1945. For his World War II service, Camm received the Legion of Merit, the Bronze Star with Oak Leaf Clusters, the French Legion d'Honneur, and the French Croix de Guerre. He reverted to his permanent rank of colonel on 31 January 1946 and spent two years in Germany assigned to the 31st Anti-Aircraft Artillery Brigade and as special field representative of the Office of the Foreign Liquidation Commissioner. Assignment to the Pentagon as deputy to the army chief of staff for combat arms followed from 1948 to 1950, and from 1950 to 1951 Camm was assistant chief of career management for the Department of the Army. Promoted to brigadier general on 15 January 1951, he concluded his career as chief of the military assistance advisory group at the United States embassy in Lisbon, Portugal, during the buildup of forces by the North Atlantic Treaty Organization. Camm retired on 31 August 1954.

In Chattanooga, Tennessee, on 3 June 1921 Camm married Felicia Beall Taylor. They had three sons and one daughter. Their son Frank Ambler Camm served with distinction in the 78th Division during and after World War II and retired from the army as a lieutenant general in 1977. After his own retirement Camm divided his time between Washington and Saint Moor and became active in civic affairs. He chaired a committee of the Virginia division of the

American Cancer Society in 1955 and was its vice president in 1960–1961. His wife died on 22 April 1974 from injuries she received when she and a rescuer jumped from the second story of the Camms' burning house. Frank Camm died at the James River Nursing Home in Newport News on 15 December 1976 and was buried in Arlington National Cemetery.

Pecquet du Bellet, *Virginia Families*, 1:133–135; *Lynchburg News*, 9 June 1921; Frank Camm to Arthur Kyle Davis, 29 May 1922, World War I History Commission Records, RG 66, LVA; Arthur Kyle Davis, ed., *Virginians of Distinguished Service of the World War* (1923), 22; army career documented in annual *Official Army Register*s; *Lightning: The History of the 78th Infantry Division* (1947), 19 (por.), 257, 260, 286, 287; Shelby L. Stanton, *Order of Battle, U.S. Army, World War II* (1984), 145–147; *New York Times*, 30 Aug. 1954; *Army Navy Air Force Journal* 92 (4 Sept. 1954): 13; *Washington Post,* 18, 23 Apr. 1974; obituaries in *Lynchburg News*, 21 Dec. 1976, and *Washington Post*, 22 Dec. 1976.

ROGER E. CHRISTMAN

CAMM, John (bap. 25 June 1717–by 15 February 1779), Anglican minister, president of the College of William and Mary, and member of the Council, was born in the coastal town of Hornsea in the East Riding of Yorkshire, England, the son of Thomas Camm and Ann Atkinson Camm. He was educated at a school in the nearby town of Beverley and admitted on 16 June 1738 to Trinity College, Cambridge University, as one of the sizars, poorer students who worked as servants in exchange for a reduction in fees. Camm was elected to a scholarship on 10 April 1741 and received an A.B. early the next year. The bishop of Lincoln ordained him an Anglican priest on 28 March 1742.

Camm soon moved to Virginia and on 1 August 1745 became rector of Newport Parish, in Isle of Wight County. In 1749 he transferred to Yorkhampton Parish in York County, and on 5 May he was appointed one of the two professors of divinity at the College of William and Mary. In 1755 Camm gave up a growing school he was operating at his own house and took up residence at the college in exchange for an augmented salary. He began making his mark as an outspoken and often cantankerous leader of the clergy, the faculty, and supporters of the British empire. Camm first achieved public prominence at a convention of Virginia's Anglican ministers

held from 30 October to 1 November 1754, during which he was appointed to three committees and elected a founding trustee of a fund for the relief of widows and orphans of poor clergymen. He served this charity, first as a trustee and from 1766 as treasurer, until about 1778.

Camm gained additional prominence in 1757 after the governor's Council removed John Brunskill Jr. from Hamilton Parish in Prince William County and forbade him to act as a clergyman in Virginia. Brunskill had been accused of several crimes and moral offenses. The bishop of London failed either to exercise disciplinary authority himself or to grant it to the commissary, his principal representative in the colony, but Camm refused to recognize the right of a lay body to deprive a minister of his office and invited Brunskill to preach in his own pulpit. After failing to persuade Commissary Thomas Dawson to convene the clergy so that they might voice their grievances in a petition to the bishop, Camm and ten other ministers called a meeting for 31 August 1757. The gathering was thinly attended, but the effort so enraged the lieutenant governor that he unsuccessfully urged a grand jury to indict the men who called the meeting.

Camm was the most prominent spokesman for the Virginia clergy during more than a decade of bitter public debate following the General Assembly's adoption in 1755 and 1758 of temporary laws permitting all kinds of obligations payable in tobacco to be discharged at a rate of approximately two pence in current money per pound of tobacco. Poor harvests in those years reduced the supply of tobacco and raised its price. By law parish rectors received an annual salary of 16,000 pounds of tobacco, and they were incensed at what amounted to the denial of windfall profits in years of high prices that would offset declines when tobacco prices were low. Camm tried to persuade the commissary to hold a clerical convocation to craft an official protest, and when the commissary refused, Camm appealed over his head as the first signatory and probable author of a 29 November 1755 protest from eight clergymen to the bishop of London against the first Two Penny Act.

Tobacco prices rose high enough after passage of the second Two Penny Act in October 1758 that the law seriously reduced ministerial income and brought the rage of Camm and his colleagues to a boil. Again thwarted in their bid for an official convocation, they called a meeting on their own authority. Thirty-five ministers, half of the colony's Anglican clergymen, attended, and all but one voted to subsidize a trip by Camm to England to seek to have the act overturned.

Camm had arrived in London by mid-May 1759 and proved adept at maneuvering in the corridors of power. He presented memorials to the Board of Trade and to the king that ignored the economic reasons for the Two Penny Acts and interpreted them instead as intentional attacks on clerical independence and the royal prerogative. Camm persuaded the bishop of London and the archbishop of Canterbury to lobby in his behalf, and on 10 August 1759 the Privy Council disallowed both Two Penny Acts and two other Virginia laws that had altered royally approved statutes setting clerical salaries. He failed, however, in his effort to have the laws explicitly declared invalid from their inception.

Camm returned to Virginia bearing copies of the order disallowing the Two Penny Acts and an additional instruction to Lieutenant Governor Francis Fauquier ordering him to refrain from approving any statute without a clause suspending its operation until the arrival of royal confirmation. Accompanied by two fellow clergymen, Camm presented this implicit rebuke to Fauquier on 27 June 1760. An extraordinary scene ensued. Fauquier had heard rumors that the acts were disallowed, and he regarded the copy of the instructions that Camm presented to him, which were unsealed, worn, and dirty, as the official version. He accused Camm of opening official documents without authorization. Furious at this apparent invasion of privacy, at what he perceived as an undue delay in presenting the papers, and at Camm's having taken the precaution of bringing witnesses to the interview, Fauquier ordered him never to enter his doors again and then made the insult even more pointed by calling in his slaves and ordering them to deny Camm admittance in the future. Camm stoutly denied that he had tampered with the papers, but for the remainder of the lieutenant governor's tenure Fauquier sought to isolate Camm by urging anyone seeking the governor's favor to cut friendly relations with the clergyman, whom he described as "a clever man with a bad head & a worse heart."

Before returning to Virginia Camm initiated what became known as the Parsons' Cause, the test case in the efforts of ministers to recover legal damages for the difference between the actual price of tobacco in 1758 and the cash equivalent mandated by the Two Penny Act. He argued that the disallowance of the act was meaningless unless damages accrued from the passage of the act, rather than from its disallowance, which had been officially announced well after the act had already expired. The General Court finally ruled against Camm by one vote on 10 April 1764. He lost a subsequent appeal to the Privy Council on a technicality in 1767 but was still trying to revive the litigation two years later.

In 1763 Camm published *A Single and Distinct View of the Act, Vulgarly entitled, the Two-Penny Act*, in which he printed his own parish's tithable list and used it to argue that the Two Penny Act was a peculiar way to alleviate economic distress, because it benefited disproportionately the wealthy elite that least needed help. Subsequently attacked in separate pamphlets by Landon Carter and Richard Bland, Camm defended himself from the two men, whom he derisively called "the Colonels." In *A Review of the Rector Detected: or the Colonel Reconnoitered* (1764; described as "Part the First"), he asserted that the Two Penny Act encroached on the king's authority, damaged the church, and undermined justice, property, and commerce. Venturing into poetry and other extended satirical touches in *Critical Remarks On a Letter ascribed to Common Sense . . .* (1765; possibly the second installment promised in 1764), Camm denied Bland's assertion that only the Virginia assembly had the right to legislate on purely internal Virginia affairs and remarked pointedly on the hypocrisy of assertions by slaveholders of the rights of free men. Camm's uncompromising campaign won him only Pyrrhic victories. He successfully undermined the ability of the assembly to alter ministerial salaries, but his efforts strengthened anticlerical feeling and opposition to effective British control over the colony.

Camm played an equally aggressive role in battles between the faculty and visitors of the College of William and Mary. The problems were rooted in the failure of the college charter to delineate the division of authority between the board of visitors, composed largely of influential laymen, and the almost exclusively clerical faculty. With ample grounds for interference supplied by its often weak presidents and the checkered and occasionally scandalous behavior of some faculty members, the visitors persistently sought to exert greater control, and the faculty, who could often agree on little else, bitterly opposed them. One key question was who had the right to discharge faculty members. The issue arose in September 1757 when the visitors dismissed one of the ushers. Camm led a group of professors who insisted that this power resided solely in the faculty. The visitors then dismissed Camm on 14 December 1757 after he refused to back down. He appealed his ouster to the General Court and eventually to the Privy Council, and for several months he and two other fired professors refused to relinquish their rooms at the college. They eventually moved out, but Camm continued to press his case and finally obtained an Order in Council on 16 March 1763 reinstating him with back pay. He resumed his place on the faculty on 18 January 1764.

Camm's restoration with such convincing proofs of his strong connections in London made him effectively untouchable. In 1765 the visitors sought to enforce a rule against multiple officeholding by demanding that Camm give up either his teaching position or his parish. He insisted on treating the hearing as a judicial proceeding, denied its authority, and threatened another appeal to England. The baffled board declined to proceed. Similarly, after Camm married Elizabeth Hansford, of York County, on 8 July 1769, the visitors again backed down when he ignored their reminder that faculty were required to reside at the college. The union of the middle-aged bachelor with a teenager he had baptized as an infant inspired some amused con-

temporary comment and a possibly apocryphal reminiscence that Camm had gone to sue on another's behalf and been invited to speak for himself. The couple had three sons and two daughters.

For several years late in the 1760s Camm filled William and Mary's chairs of moral and natural philosophy as well as his own of divinity. In the spring of 1770 he drafted an eloquent faculty protest against a proposal to admit to advanced study those students who lacked training in Greek and Latin. He insisted that the plan would subvert the college's primary mission of training students for the professions. A year later Camm took the lead in an effort to obtain endorsement of a plan to create a resident Anglican episcopate in America. He maintained that a bishop would provide much-needed internal governance for the clergy and remove the need for prospective ministers to travel overseas for ordination, while posing no threat to religious dissenters or the purse strings of the laity. During the ensuing public debate Camm defended the proposal in three essays in Purdie and Dixon's *Williamsburg Virginia Gazette* in the summer of 1771, but in the face of strident opposition it came to nothing.

Camm nevertheless soon obtained the three top offices to which a Virginia clergyman could aspire. On 20 June 1771 James Horrocks, the commissary of Virginia and president of William and Mary, sailed for England, ostensibly to improve his health but perhaps in hope of returning as the first bishop of Virginia. Despite some initial reservations about accepting the appointment, Camm took over as acting president of the college. After Horrocks died and with a surprising dearth of recorded opposition, given Camm's reputation for pugnacious defense of views increasingly out of favor in Virginia, the visitors elected him president of William and Mary on 27 July 1772. He had also been appointed commissary by 30 June, and on 31 July he was appointed to the governor's Council and took his seat on that body on 26 October 1772.

William and Mary initially thrived under Camm's leadership. The college balanced its budget, kept its faculty at full strength, and resumed its building program. It awarded baccalaureate degrees for the first time on 15 August 1772, and at the same exercise it began recognizing academic excellence by conferring the Botetourt Medal. Phi Beta Kappa was also founded at William and Mary during Camm's administration, although it began as a typical student literary society rather than the academic honor organization into which it eventually evolved.

Unlike fellow Englishmen on the faculty who left the colony as the Revolution approached, Camm stayed at his post but kept an uncharacteristically low profile. Still, no one doubted where his loyalty lay, and by the summer of 1775 Camm was one of only three councillors from whom the royal governor believed he could reasonably hope to receive assistance. Camm made no overtly Loyalist act, however, until 29 November 1776, when at a faculty meeting he opposed a proposal by James Madison (1749–1812) to strike references to the monarch from surveyors' licenses issued under the college's authority. Madison had evidently chosen circuitous wording in the hope that Camm would give his tacit consent, but the president courageously declined this tactful bow to his feelings and opposed the motion as a violation of the royal charter. The visitors could not ignore such a stance and sometime between 10 May and 5 September 1777 removed him for neglect and misconduct.

John Camm apparently remained unmolested as the minister of Yorkhampton Parish until his death early in 1779. On 15 February 1779 the York County Court directed four men to "Appraise in Current money the Slaves & personal Estate of John Camm Clk. decd." Two resulting inventories show that he owned more than twenty slaves and had extensive holdings of fine furniture, silver, china, and other luxury consumer goods.

Lyon G. Tyler, "Descendants of John Camm, President of William and Mary College," *WMQ*, 1st ser., 4 (1895–1896): 61–62, 275–278; Tyler, "Sketch of John Camm," *WMQ*, 1st ser., 19 (1910): 28–30; Homer D. Kemp, "The Reverend John Camm: 'To Raise a Flame and Live in It,'" in *Essays in Early Virginia Literature Honoring Richard Beale Davis*, ed. J. A. Leo Lemay (1977), 165–180; baptism in Hornsea Parish Records, Register PE 30/2, Archives and Records Service, East Riding of Yorkshire Council, Eng.; John Venn and J. A. Venn, *Alumni Cantabrigienses* (1922–1927), 1:285; arrival in Virginia by about Aug. 1744 documented in *WMQ*, 1st ser., 7 (1898): 39; Newport Parish Vestry Book (1724–1772), 118, LVA; only known copy of a Camm sermon printed ca. 1772, lacking title page, Waller Family Papers, CW, reprinted with introduction in Jack P. Greene, "A Mirror of Virtue for a Declining Land: John Camm's Funeral Sermon for William Nelson," in Lemay, *Essays in Early Virginia Literature*, 181–201; Camm letters and petitions in Fulham Palace Papers, Lambeth Palace Library, Eng., in PRO CO 5/1329, in Richard Bland, *Colonel Dismounted: or the Rector Vindicated* (1764), appendix, viii–xxvii, in *WMQ*, 1st ser., 2 (1894): 237–239, and in *Williamsburg Virginia Gazette* (Purdie and Dixon), 7 Apr. 1768 (two letters); William Stevens Perry, ed., *Papers Relating to the History of the Church in Virginia, A.D. 1650–1776* (1870), 386–388, 414–532 (first quotation on 478); George Reese, ed., *The Official Papers of Francis Fauquier, Lieutenant Governor of Virginia, 1758–1768* (1980–1983), 1:144–145, 383–384, 2:552–554, 933, 3:1404–1405; *Williamsburg Virginia Gazette* (Purdie and Dixon), 13 July 1769, 13, 20 June, 11 July, 15, 22 Aug. 1771, 30 July, 20 Aug., 22, 29 Oct. 1772; ibid. (Purdie), 4 Apr. 1777; Journal of President and Masters of the College of William and Mary, Archives, W&M; Richard L. Morton, *Colonial Virginia* (1960), 2:759–819; Susan H. Godson et al., *The College of William and Mary: A History* (1993), 1:90–128; J. E. Morpurgo, *Their Majesties' Royall Colledge: William and Mary in the Seventeenth and Eighteenth Centuries* (1976); Robert Polk Thomson, "The Reform of the College of William and Mary, 1763–1780," *Proceedings of the American Philosophical Society* 115 (1971): 187–213; York Co. Order Book, 4:203 (second quotation); York Co. Wills and Inventories, 22:442–445, 487; posthumous sale of library advertised in *Williamsburg Virginia Gazette* (Dixon and Nicolson), 16 Apr. 1779.

J. JEFFERSON LOONEY

CAMMACK, John Walter (28 April 1875– 11 February 1958), president of Averett College, was born in Orange County, the son of George Walter Cammack and Mary Jane Pidgeon Cammack. His father died of typhoid fever in 1878, and his mother, originally a North Carolina Quaker, raised him and his siblings, taught Sunday school at nearby New Hope Baptist Church, and provided lodging for its pastor. Little is known of Cammack's childhood or early education. He attended Fredericksburg College and graduated from Richmond College (later the University of Richmond) with a B.A. in 1900 and an M.A. in 1901. Cammack was ordained a Baptist minister on 24 March 1901 and then entered the Southern Baptist Theological Seminary in Louisville, Kentucky, from which he received a Th.M. in 1903. He took graduate courses in English literature and moral philosophy at the University of Virginia during the 1903–1904 academic year.

Cammack began his ministerial career at the Baptist church in Onancock in Accomack County and served there from 1904 to 1907. On 14 June 1905 he married Bessie Clay Hagan, a graduate of Richmond Women's College (later Westhampton College of the University of Richmond). They had no children. From 1907 to 1910 Cammack was pastor in Buckhannon, West Virginia. After returning to Richmond in the latter year, he became associate editor of the *Religious Herald*, a Baptist weekly newspaper, and continued in that capacity for about five years. Starting about this time Cammack took an increasingly responsible role in Baptist educational work. He served as secretary of the Baptist Education Commission of Virginia from 1915 to 1924. Cammack belonged to the Southern Baptist Convention Education Commission that was organized in 1915 and led to the creation in 1919 of the convention's Education Board (later renamed the Education Commission), of which he served as corresponding secretary from 1924 to 1927. Cammack was also a financial agent and fund-raiser for Richmond College, which awarded him a D.D. in 1913.

In May 1927 Cammack was named the president of Averett College, a Baptist preparatory school and junior college for women in Danville. He took office almost immediately and energetically, but the Great Depression, which began two years later, made raising funds difficult. During his nine-year tenure he increased the college's small endowment and almost doubled the school's enrollment to more than 400 students, in part because he allowed parents to pay whatever they could rather than requiring the full stated fees for tuition, room, and board. Averett College received full accreditation from the Southern Association of Colleges and Secondary Schools in 1928. The college erected a modern science and music building, an athletic field, and a president's house, and it enlarged the library. Cammack encouraged the expansion of extracurricular activities, including the band, the school newspaper, Baptist student union and missionary groups, and extended field trips for the students.

While he was president Cammack wrote a regular column, "News and Notes from Here and There," for the *Religious Herald*. The column usually consisted of brief notes on the activities of ministers and church groups as reported to him by correspondents throughout Virginia and the South. Occasionally these notes were interspersed with brief musings of the author. Cammack was an outspoken temperance proponent, as was his mentor, Robert Healy Pitt, longtime editor and publisher of the *Religious Herald*. Both Cammack and the Averett College newspaper, *Chanticleer*, rejoiced after Republican Herbert Hoover defeated Democrat Alfred E. Smith, a Catholic and opponent of Prohibition, in the 1928 presidential election. Not hesitating to express his indignation at the repeal of Prohibition in 1933, Cammack vented his outrage at politicians and journalists who supported repeal.

In his column of 5 December 1935 Cammack reported that several students had written him to complain that professors in one or more of Virginia's public colleges were expressing blasphemous or antireligious opinions and coming to class under the influence of alcohol. He also wrote that one college president had made a speech while inebriated and another had hosted a faculty reception from which some professors left drunk. Although the report was embedded in his regular column of innocuous news items, the Associated Press picked up the story, and some Virginia newspaper editors who had opposed Prohibition called on Cammack to divulge the names of the people involved. Pitt, who had been away from his editorial desk because of the illness and death of a son, had not seen Cammack's column before it was published. He immediately issued an apology for breaking a longtime rule by printing unsubstantiated charges that might lead readers to suspect innocent persons of impropriety. Cammack initially declined to identify his informants but insisted that the reports were true and that the episodes were well known within their respective college communities. He further noted that similar episodes had occurred in private colleges, including his own, which he had promptly dealt with. In a calculated move, early in January 1936 Cammack offered to share the details of his information with several editors, but he afterward stated that he had received no replies to the offer.

Although Cammack had taken a leave of absence from Averett College in 1934 and had suffered health problems in 1935 that forced him to relinquish some of his official duties to Vice President Curtis Vance Bishop, Cammack surprised the college's trustees at their meeting on 31 January 1936 by resigning effective 31 March of that year in order to accept a joint call to become pastor of the Baptist church in Fork Union and the chaplain and director of religious education at Fork Union Military Academy. Board members denied that his resignation was related to the recent controversy, nor is there evidence that the faculty, which had agreed to a 20 percent reduction in salary the previous December, was dissatisfied with him. Cammack resided in Fork Union and served in the three capacities until he retired as pastor emeritus in 1943. He then moved to Richmond, where he was active in Virginia Baptist work. A Freemason for more than fifty years, Cammack wrote a *History of Richmond Lodge, No. 10 A.F. and A.M. from 1909 through 1950* (1952).

Cammack's wife died on 25 June 1952. Sometime later he married Olive Martin and moved to Phoenix, Arizona. They had no children. John Walter Cammack returned to Richmond, where he died on 11 February 1958, and was buried in Hollywood Cemetery in that city.

Birth date verified by BVS; BVS Marriage Register, Richmond City, 1905; Jack Irby Hayes, *A History of Averett College* (1984), 83–92 (por. on 86), 97–98; Cammack, *History of Richmond Lodge, No. 10 A.F. and A.M. from 1909 through 1950* (frontispiece por.); *Virginia Baptist Annual* (1927): 64, (1928): 78–79, (1929): 58, (1930): 70, (1931): 77, (1933): 105–106, (1934): 73–74, (1935): 106–107, (1936): 117–118; *Religious Herald*, 5, 19 Dec. 1935, 16 Jan., 26 Mar., 9 Apr. 1936; *Danville Bee*, 9, 12, 16, 17, 19 Dec. 1935, 1, 27 Feb., 13, 20, 21 Mar. 1936; *Richmond Times-Dispatch*, 9, 20 Dec. 1935; por. at Averett College, Danville; obituaries in *Danville Bee, Danville Register, Richmond News Leader,* and *Richmond Times-Dispatch*, all 12 Feb. 1958, *Religious Herald*, 20 Feb. 1958, and *Virginia Baptist Annual* (1958): 105.

GAIL V. TATUM

CAMP, Hugh Douglas (4 April 1903–17 April 1974), lumber and paper manufacturer, was born in the town of Franklin, the son of Caroline Fountain Savage Camp and James Leonidas

Camp (1857–1925), vice president and general manager of the Camp Manufacturing Company. His uncle Paul Douglas Camp was founding president of the company. Educated in local public schools, Camp completed his secondary schooling at Woodberry Forest School, attended Wake Forest College in 1921–1922, and spent the academic years 1922–1923 and 1923–1924 at the University of Virginia. More interested initially in textile manufacture than in his family's multistate lumber empire, Camp took classes at the Philadelphia Textile School (later the Philadelphia College of Textiles and Science) and worked for the Simmons Company, a manufacturer of synthetic and cotton fabrics, in Roanoke Rapids, North Carolina. He became a vice president of the company in 1926 and served as general superintendent of its textile mills in Roanoke, Virginia, and in Paterson, New Jersey. On 20 April 1927 Camp married Ada Norris Coleman, of Selma, Alabama. They had one daughter.

In the mid-1930s the Camp Manufacturing Company, then headed by Camp's elder brother James Leonidas Camp Jr. (1895–1983), began exploring ways to increase profitability by expanding into papermaking, using as raw material the pulpwood and other byproducts of its logging and lumber operations. In November 1936 J. L. Camp Jr., Hugh Camp, and officers of the Albemarle Paper Company, of Richmond, and the Chesapeake Corporation, of West Point, agreed to erect a $3.5 million, 200-ton paper mill adjacent to the Camp Manufacturing Company's lumber mill in Franklin. On 11 January 1937 the three companies chartered the Chesapeake-Camp Corporation with J. L. Camp Jr. as president and Hugh Camp as general manager of paper production and assistant secretary-treasurer. Albemarle Paper withdrew from the arrangement in the spring of 1937. With Camp Manufacturing providing nearly 40 percent of the wood residue required for pulping, the new mill began commercial operation in January 1938. Chesapeake-Camp turned a profit almost immediately on production of approximately 150 tons per day of paperboard and kraft paper for bags and wrapping. In 1940 Camp Manufacturing purchased Chesapeake

Corporation's shares. The two Camp firms consolidated in October 1944 under the name Chesapeake-Camp Corporation and in July 1945 became the Camp Manufacturing Company, Inc.

Much of the firms' success after 1938 resulted from Hugh Camp's managerial skills. Although he joked that when he joined the company he did not know which was the front end of a paper machine, he understood machinery and appreciated technological innovations. By 1948 Camp had introduced a new type of log barker, the first of its kind in the United States, which efficiently provided pulpwood equaling the annual growth of 50,000 acres of pine timberland. He also created a chemical division to exploit the inevitable byproducts of lumber and paper production, and the company profited from the production and sale of turpentine and tall oil, used in detergent, insecticide, linoleum, and paint. Other end products included garbage and grocery bags, hand towels, kraft and crepe paper, polish, soap, waxed paper, window shades, and even ashtrays, gaskets, flooring, and tabletops. Camp Manufacturing was one of the largest integrated forestry industries in Virginia. In 1949 it had an annual capacity of 50 million board feet of lumber, 100,000 tons of sulfate pulp, and 75,000 tons of kraft paper, and the company owned 230,000 acres of timberland in three states.

Camp became executive vice president in 1954. He needed a large infusion of capital to expand and began seeking a merger. In May 1956 the company announced a merger with Union Bag and Paper Corporation, a New York–based company with $123 million in annual sales in 1955, compared to Camp's $27.6 million. Following approval by Camp stockholders on 12 July 1956, the two companies merged as Union Bag–Camp Paper Corporation (after April 1966 Union Camp Corporation), headquartered first in New York City and after 1969 in Wayne, New Jersey. J. L. Camp Jr. stepped down as president of Camp Manufacturing in March 1956 to become chairman of the board, and Hugh Camp succeeded his brother as president. After the formation of Union Bag–Camp Paper, Hugh Camp moved to New York City as the new company's executive

vice president. In 1960 he became chairman of the board.

Under Camp's effective leadership, Union Camp acquired specialized box and bag plants in Georgia, Maryland, Massachusetts, and Pennsylvania. In 1961 the corporation purchased Write Right, a manufacturer of school supplies, and four years later it acquired a manufacturer of corrugated boxes in Barcelona, Spain, the first of a series of container plants that Union Camp built or bought there and in the Canary Islands, Chile, Ireland, and Puerto Rico. When International Paper purchased Union Camp in a $6.6 billion stock transaction in November 1998, the corporation employed 18,300 people and earned $4.5 billion that fiscal year.

Suffering from heart disease, Camp stepped down as chairman of the board in 1972 but remained a director of the corporation until his death. During his residence in Virginia he was a director of First and Merchants National Bank of Richmond and of the Vaughan and Company Bank in Franklin, and while living in New York he served on the board of the First National Bank of New Jersey. Most of the Camps were devout Baptists, but Hugh Camp joined the Episcopal Church, served on his local vestry, and at the time of his death was a member of Saint James Episcopal Church in New York City. He continued the family tradition of philanthropy by serving as a director of the Camp Foundation, established in 1942 to fund education, health care, libraries, and recreational facilities in Franklin and Southampton County. He indulged his love of engines, obtained a private pilot's license, and became a competitive yachtsman. Hugh Douglas Camp died at Roosevelt Hospital in New York City on 17 April 1974 and was buried in Poplar Springs Cemetery in Franklin.

Parke Rouse Jr., *The Timber Tycoons: The Camp Families of Virginia and Florida and Their Empire, 1887–1987* (1988), pors.; Rogers Dey Whichard, ed., *The History of Lower Tidewater Virginia* (1959), 3:405–406; SCC Charter Book, 184:192, 290:500, 425:572; Camp Manufacturing Company, *Sixty Years of Progress* (1948); "Camp: A Continuing Family Industry," *Virginia Forests* 4 (May/June 1949): 6–7, 13; *Moody's Industrial Manual*, 1956; Alonzo Thomas Dill, *Chesapeake, Pioneer Papermaker: A History of the Company and Its Communities* (1968; repr. 1987), 141–146; W. Craig McClelland, *Union Camp Corporation: A Legacy of Lead-

ership (1995), esp. 19–20; obituaries in *New York Times*, *Richmond News Leader*, and *Richmond Times-Dispatch*, all 18 Apr. 1974, *Norfolk Virginian-Pilot*, 19 Apr. 1974, and *Virginia Forests* 29 (spring/summer 1974): 28 (por.).

SARA B. BEARSS

CAMP, James Leonidas (7 June 1895–27 February 1983), lumber and paper manufacturer, was born in the town of Franklin, the son of Caroline Fountain Savage Camp and James Leonidas Camp (1857–1925), vice president and general manager of the Camp Manufacturing Company. He attended the Franklin Military Academy and Franklin High School and in 1914 received an A.B. from Wake Forest College. While singing professionally he completed one year of graduate work in voice at Columbia University. Although Camp had hoped to pursue a music career, the death of his elder brother from tuberculosis in January 1913 led him to reconsider that course and return to Franklin, where he began working at one of the Camp Manufacturing Company's lumber plants. The United States' entrance into World War I interrupted his mastering of the family business. As a midshipman in the United States Navy Air Corps in 1918, J. L. Camp Jr. (as he signed his name as an adult) served as an aviation chief rigger. After his return from military service in the Fifth Naval District, he joined Camp Manufacturing's sales department and in 1921 became vice president in charge of sales, in effect fourth vice president of the company.

Following the death of the company's founding president, Paul Douglas Camp, in February 1924, Camp's father, who had held the controlling interest since 1915, became president of Camp Manufacturing and began to impose greater fiscal regularity on the informally operated family timber concerns. He suffered from diabetes and heart disease, however, and died on 4 December 1925. At the annual organizational meeting on 13 February 1926, Camp succeeded his father as president of Camp Manufacturing, which at that time produced about 124 million board feet of lumber each year, with annual sales approaching $3.5 million.

The company's profits steadily increased until the onset of the Great Depression, when reduced demand for lumber in the construction industry forced deep wage cuts for the 2,000 Camp Manufacturing employees. By 1938 production was reduced to about 50 million board feet of lumber per year. Although its storage facilities were full, the company continued to buy and manufacture lumber throughout the depression in order to provide jobs for local men. Seeking to boost profits and to exploit more fully the family business's large timber resources, Camp expanded the family logging and lumber interests into papermaking. With the Albemarle Paper Company, of Richmond, and the Chesapeake Corporation, of West Point, Camp Manufacturing chartered the Chesapeake-Camp Corporation on 11 January 1937. With Camp as president and his brother Hugh Douglas Camp as general manager of paper production, the new company erected a pulp and paper mill immediately adjoining the Camp lumber mill in Franklin. The new mill began operating early in January 1938, with 255 employees producing paperboard and kraft paper for bags and wrapping. Albemarle Paper had bowed out of the enterprise in the spring of 1937, and, despite the mill's profitability, Chesapeake sold its shares to Camp in 1940. In October 1944 the two Camp firms consolidated, first under the name Chesapeake-Camp Corporation and in July 1945 under the name Camp Manufacturing Company, Inc. By 1949 the company boasted annual capacities of 50 million board feet of lumber, 100,000 tons of sulfate pulp, and 75,000 tons of kraft paper. Its lumber, pulp, paper, and chemical divisions employed 1,050 people with an annual payroll of $3.5 million. Camp Manufacturing owned 230,000 acres of forest reserves in North Carolina, South Carolina, and Virginia. In 1951 it added another manufacturing plant to produce white paper.

In March 1956 Camp became chairman of the board, and Hugh Douglas Camp was elected president. For two years the Camp firm had been negotiating a merger with Union Bag and Paper Corporation, of New York, a company with $123 million in annual sales in 1955, compared to Camp's $27.6 million. The merger, announced in May 1956, was approved by stockholders on 12 July of that year, when the two companies merged to form Union

Bag–Camp Paper Corporation (after April 1966 Union Camp Corporation), headquartered first in New York City and after 1969 in Wayne, New Jersey. Remaining in Franklin, Camp became vice chairman and then chairman of the board of Union Bag–Camp Paper. After he retired as an active executive in 1960, he chaired the executive committee for another nine years.

Camp's expertise and managerial skills won him appointments as director or trustee of the American Forest Products Industries, Inc., the American Paper and Pulp Association, the National Association of Manufacturers, and the National Lumber Manufacturers Association. In April 1943 he helped found Virginia Forests, Inc. (later the Virginia Forestry Association), an organization to share forest management techniques and conservation strategies among timberland owners. Camp's commitment to conservation influenced Union Camp to make a series of important land donations in the 1970s: almost 50,000 acres in the Dismal Swamp to the Nature Conservancy in 1973, the 1,700-acre coastal Turtle Island to the South Carolina Wildlife and Marine Resources Department, and the Tower Hill plantation in Sussex County and a 10-acre surrounding site to the National Trust for Historic Preservation as part of the celebration of the nation's bicentennial in 1976.

A Baptist like most other members of his family and committed to education, Camp was a trustee of the University of Richmond from 1943 to 1969 and sat on its standing committee on scholarships. He became chairman of the board of the Virginia Foundation for Independent Colleges in 1963 and helped raise nearly $1 million during each of his three years in office. Camp also sat on the governing boards of the University of Virginia Graduate School of Business Administration and the Crozer Theological Seminary, in Chester, Pennsylvania. He served as president of the Camp Foundation, started in 1942 to provide funding for educational opportunities, hospitals, libraries, and recreational facilities in the Franklin area, and he established the J. L. Camp Foundation, Inc., in 1946 to support the arts, education, health care, and religious activities in Virginia. Along with other family members, Camp headed the

drive that built the Southampton Memorial Hospital in Franklin. He founded a Young Men's Christian Association in Franklin that bears his name, but a dream of building a forestry museum in his hometown remained unfulfilled.

Camp's professional activities and philanthropy won him recognition and numerous awards. In 1955 the Franklin Business and Professional Women's Club named him Franklin's First Citizen, and three years later he received an honorary D.Sc. from the University of Richmond. In 1961 the Virginia State Chamber of Commerce presented Camp with its Distinguished Service Award. Virginia Forests, Inc., chose him as its Man of the Year in Forestry in 1967.

On 21 May 1918 Camp married Mary Frances Clay, a native of Selma, Alabama, who graduated from Westhampton College in Richmond. They had one son. She died on 26 December 1969, and on 27 March 1971 Camp married Alma Williams Truitt. They had no children. James Leonidas Camp suffered from Parkinson's disease late in life and died at his home, Wyndie Crest, in Franklin on 27 February 1983. He was buried in the local Poplar Springs Cemetery.

Parke Rouse Jr., *The Timber Tycoons: The Camp Families of Virginia and Florida and Their Empire, 1887–1987* (1988), pors.; biographies in *Virginia Forests* 4 (May/June 1949): 5, Rogers Dey Whichard, ed., *The History of Lower Tidewater Virginia* (1959), 3:403–404, and *NCAB* (1960), 1:343–344; "James L. Camp, Jr.: Man of the Year in Forestry," *Virginia Forests* 23 (spring 1968): 7, 36; several Camp letters in Shelton H. Short Papers, VHS; SCC Charter Book, 184:192, 207:555, 215:534, 643, 246:568, 267:314, 290:500, 620, 316:801, 329:567, 336:173, 425:572, 460:143, 480:73, 660:309; "Camp: A Continuing Family Industry," *Virginia Forests* 4 (May/June 1949): 6–7, 13; *Moody's Industrial Manual*, 1956; *Commonwealth* 30 (1963): 12–13; Alonzo Thomas Dill, *Chesapeake, Pioneer Papermaker: A History of the Company and Its Communities* (1968; repr. 1987), 141–146; obituaries in *Norfolk Virginian-Pilot* and *Richmond Times-Dispatch*, both 28 Feb. 1983, and *New York Times*, 1 Mar. 1983.

SARA B. BEARSS

CAMP, Paul Douglas (25 October 1849–5 February 1924), lumber manufacturer, was born near Franklin in Southampton County, the son of George Camp, a slaveholding farmer and wheelwright, and his second wife, Sarah Cutchins Camp. He received an abbreviated education at home and in a local school. During the Civil

War he helped run an elder sister's farm while her husband served in the Confederate army.

In 1870 P. D. Camp became superintendent of logging for the timber operation of his elder brothers, John Stafford Camp and William Nelson Camp. Seeking to expand into manufacturing, P. D. Camp borrowed money in 1876 to purchase a sawmill at Delaware on the Nottoway River in Southampton County. Two years later he bought another mill in Hertford County, North Carolina. Camp's two mills, operating as P. D. Camp and Company, annually processed 1.5 million board feet of lumber for shipment to Baltimore, New York, Philadelphia, and Washington, D.C. In 1880 he admitted his brother James Leonidas Camp (1857–1925) to his business as a partner. The new firm of P. D. and J. L. Camp increased mill capacity to 5 million board feet annually. On 22 January 1880 Camp married Ella Virginia Cobb, also of Franklin. They had eleven children, of whom three sons and five daughters lived to adulthood. In addition, the son of Camp's half sister grew up in his household and later acted as bookkeeper for the family firm.

In 1886 P. D. and J. L. Camp purchased a steam-powered single-circular-saw mill on the Blackwater River near Franklin. Founded in 1855 and then owned by Robert Johnson Neely and William Neely, the mill was the largest in southeastern Virginia. The acquisition allowed the Camps to increase their annual capacity to 12 million board feet of high-grade pine, oak, and cypress lumber. On 21 November 1887 Camp and his brothers incorporated the Camp Manufacturing Company with P. D. Camp as president, J. L. Camp as vice president and general manager, Robert Judson Camp as secretary and treasurer, and Benjamin Franklin Camp, John Stafford Camp, and William Nelson Camp as directors. The Franklin mill, remodeled and modernized in 1891, produced 20 million board feet of lumber the next year. The company purchased the Arringdale plant near Franklin in 1896, a plant at Butterworth in Dinwiddie County in 1902, and large tracts of woodland in Florida, North Carolina, South Carolina, and Virginia, including 40,000 acres in the Dismal Swamp, about a quarter of the total swampland.

To market its wood products the Camp family affiliated in 1903 with a wholesale distributor in New York City. That firm, Wiley, Harker, and Camp Company, allowed the Camps to extend their timber empire still further by acquiring the Angola, Cape Fear, and Carolina Lumber Companies in North Carolina and the Marion County Lumber Company in South Carolina.

Frugal and austere, Camp enjoyed physical labor and had a keen eye for valuable woodland. A contemporary noted that he would buy anything if given five years to pay. His expansive vision and indulgent hand with relatives working in the family's lumber concerns exacerbated the company's difficulties during the nationwide panic of 1907. Facing bankruptcy, Camp and his brothers, according to family tradition, were advised to place their houses in their wives' names to save them from company creditors. P. D. Camp declared, "If I go, I go clean. I wouldn't hold even this pocketknife back," and his brothers immediately concurred. Impressed, a Wilmington banker placed his institution's assets at their disposal. In fact, only by securing loans from five banks, floating a $2.25 million bond, severing its relationship with Wiley, Harker, and Camp, and cutting ties to failing Camp family operations in Florida did the Camp Manufacturing Company manage to weather its financial difficulties. By the time of P. D. Camp's death, however, Camp Manufacturing was the largest lumber company on the East Coast and produced 125 million board feet of lumber annually. The Camp family and its enterprises defined the town of Franklin.

Besides his hands-on direction of the Camp Manufacturing Company, Camp also served as an officer or director of several of his brothers' operations, including the Albion Mining and Manufacturing Company, which produced phosphate, the R. J. and B. F. Camp Lumber Company, and the Franklin Phosphate Company, all in Florida; the Santee Lumber Company, in South Carolina; the Roanoke Railway Company, which began operating in North Carolina in 1910; and the Giles County Lumber Company, in Virginia. In 1897 Camp built The Elms, a comfortable gabled Victorian brick-and-stucco mansion in Franklin, but he also maintained his agricultural roots by operating a sizable dairy farm. A dedicated Baptist, he served on the State Mission Board of the Baptist General Association of Virginia and as the Blackwater Baptist Association's trustee of the Baptist orphanage in Salem. His contributions helped establish the George and Sallie Cutchins Camp Memorial Foundation's chair of Bible in the University of Richmond's Department of Religion. In his will, written on 10 January 1923, Camp left generous sums to the Baptist State Mission Boards of North Carolina, South Carolina, and Virginia and to his local Sycamore Baptist Church to pay for a new building and to underwrite the minister's salary. Many of the bequests had to be delayed, however, because of continuing cash shortages related to business expansion, informal practices that allowed the Camp brothers to borrow freely from their family concern, and a market glut following World War I.

Paul Douglas Camp died of heart disease at Johnston-Willis Hospital in Richmond on 5 February 1924. Nine prominent Baptist ministers conducted his funeral at The Elms, and thirty-three honorary pallbearers accompanied his body to Poplar Springs Cemetery in Franklin. A month later J. L. Camp became president of the company, but he suffered from heart disease and diabetes and died on 4 December 1925. He was in turn succeeded as head of the firm by his namesake son, James Leonidas Camp (1895–1983). Following the creation of Virginia's community college system, two of P. D. Camp's daughters, Ruth Cutchins Camp Campbell McDougall and Willie Antoinette Camp Younts, donated ninety-two acres of their father's farmland as the site for the Paul D. Camp Community College, which opened in Franklin in 1971.

Parke Rouse Jr., *The Timber Tycoons: The Camp Families of Virginia and Florida and Their Empire, 1887–1987* (1988), including several pors., quotation on 112, and will; biographies in *NCAB*, 37:289–290 (gives variant marriage date of 29 Jan. 1880), and Daniel Decatur Moore et al., eds., *Men of the South: A Work for the Newspaper Reference Library* (1922), 708, 750; BVS Marriage Register, Southampton Co.; SCC Charter Book, 6:465–468, 51:123, 62:405, 83:414; "Pine Products of the Atlantic Coast," *American Lumberman* (15 June 1907): 51–67; BVS Death Certificate, Richmond City; death notice in *Richmond Times-Dispatch*, 7 Feb. 1924; obituaries in *Norfolk Ledger-Dispatch*, 6 Feb. 1924, and *Norfolk Virginian-Pilot*, 8 Feb. 1924.

SARA B. BEARSS

CAMPBELL, Albert Henry (23 October 1826–23 February 1899), civil engineer and Confederate army officer, was born in Charleston, the son of Mason Campbell, a newspaper publisher during the 1820s and 1830s, and Mary Stone Chaddock Campbell. He attended Mercer Academy in Charleston until 1844, when he transferred to Brown University in Providence, Rhode Island, from which he received a B.A. in 1847 and an M.A. in 1850. On 20 December 1847 Campbell married Mary Paine Stebbins in Providence. They had three sons and one daughter.

Armed with a letter of recommendation from Brown's president, Francis Wayland, Campbell began a successful career as a civil engineer specializing in railroad surveying and construction. For eighteen months he was an assistant engineer laying out the route of the Orange and Alexandria Railroad. On 15 April 1851 Campbell successfully applied to the Virginia Board of Public Works for appointment to survey the route for a new railroad between Norfolk and Petersburg. He began work on 1 June 1851, but within several months the field party found itself falling behind its anticipated schedule as it struggled through the Dismal Swamp. Despite the delays Campbell finished the survey by December 1851, when he submitted his final report and map to the board.

In 1853 Campbell became the principal assistant railroad engineer of an expedition authorized by Congress to seek a practical and economical route for a railroad from the Mississippi River to the Pacific Ocean along 35° north latitude. Lieutenant Amiel W. Whipple, of the United States Army Corps of Topographical Engineers, commanded the party, which left Fort Smith, Arkansas, on 14 July 1853 and reached the Pacific Ocean at San Pedro, California, on 23 March 1854. Campbell's notable accomplishments on the journey included his discovery and mapping of a suitable pass over the Continental Divide near present-day Gallup, New Mexico. Whipple named the pass in Campbell's honor. Campbell wrote "Grades and Curves

Required," chapter 5 in Whipple's preliminary report, extracts of which were published in volume 3 of *Reports of Explorations and Surveys to Ascertain the Most Practicable and Economical Route for a Railroad from the Mississippi River to the Pacific Ocean* (1855–1860). Three full-page color lithographic views in that volume were based on Campbell's sketches.

Campbell was again in the field in November 1854 as the civil engineer of the exploring party led by Lieutenant John G. Parke in search of a coastal railroad route between Los Angeles and San Francisco. Parke's report, published in volume 7 of the *Reports of Explorations and Surveys*, includes eight color lithographic scenes in California and southern Arizona prepared from sketches that Campbell drew.

In 1857 Campbell became general superintendent of the new Pacific Wagon Road Office in the Department of the Interior. He and the secretary of the interior soon found that from their offices in Washington it was nearly impossible for them to direct the surveying and construction of the four wagon roads that Congress had authorized. Much of the department's efforts to improve overland communication with the Pacific coast in the 1850s consequently became mired in controversy.

On 19 April 1861, two days after the Virginia convention voted to secede from the Union, Campbell resigned and returned to his native state. He worked as a clerk in the Confederate Post Office Department in Richmond until 6 June 1862, when he was commissioned a captain in the Confederate army's Provisional Corps of Engineers. Promoted to major on 19 October 1864, Campbell was chief of the Topographical Department of the Department of Northern Virginia with responsibility for providing maps for the army's commanders. He organized the topographical department, hired new surveyors, obtained surveying and drafting equipment, and formed reconnaissance parties. From surveys that the parties prepared in the field Campbell's department produced detailed pen-and-ink county and regional maps of much of eastern Virginia, the Piedmont, part of the Shenandoah Valley, and eastern North Carolina

as far south as Wilmington. One of his most difficult tasks was to produce multiple copies from the master maps. In 1864 Campbell introduced photography to replace time-consuming hand-copying. The process that he employed to transfer an ink image on tracing paper to a chemically sensitized paper had been patented in Richmond on 5 February 1864. Photography significantly reduced the time required to copy maps, but it was still a slow, inefficient method compared to the United States Army's duplication of maps by lithography.

Much of what is known about the operations of the Topographical Department is recorded in Campbell's 1888 article in *Century Magazine*. He then believed that most of the maps that the department had produced had been lost or destroyed during the April 1865 evacuation of Richmond. Unknown to Campbell and others at the time, however, Major General Jeremy Francis Gilmer, chief of the Confederate War Department's Engineer Bureau, had preserved several hundred maps, and in subsequent years his heirs presented them to several institutions, including the Southern Historical Collection at the University of North Carolina and the Virginia Historical Society.

Paroled at Appomattox Court House on 9 April 1865, Campbell joined his wife and children in Liberty (later the city of Bedford), where they had resided during much of the war. He took the oath of allegiance there on 20 July 1865. In search of work Campbell returned to Rhode Island, where he was employed at one time by the Horsford Acid Chemical Company and later by the *Providence Journal*. In 1869 he moved back to his native Charleston, West Virginia, and resumed his successful career as a civil engineer. From 1869 until his retirement in 1893 Campbell worked for several new and expanding railroad lines in that state, including the Chesapeake and Ohio Railroad Company.

Following his retirement Campbell moved to Ravenswood, West Virginia, where his son was rector of the Episcopal church. Albert Henry Campbell died in Ravenswood on 23 February 1899 and was temporarily interred there. According to his wishes and following the death of his invalid wife, their bodies were buried on 28 October 1903 in the Confederate Officers' Section of Hollywood Cemetery in Richmond.

Biography in *Historical Catalogue of Brown University, 1764–1904* (1905), 209; family and professional information supplied by grandson Charles S. Campbell in Robert H. George Papers, Brown University; Campbell letters in Norfolk and Petersburg Railroad records, Board of Public Works Papers, RG 57, LVA; Campbell maps in collections of LC, MOC, UNC, VHS, and United States Military Academy, West Point, N.Y.; George Leslie Albright, *Official Explorations for Pacific Railroads, 1853–1855* (1921), 110–111, 122, 155; Robert Taft, *Artists and Illustrators of the Old West, 1850–1900* (1953), 27, 28, 264–266; Robert H. George, "Brunonians in Confederate Ranks, 1861–1865," *Books at Brown* 20 (1965): 31–34; Stephenson and McKee, *Virginia in Maps*, 197–199; Compiled Service Records; Campbell, "The Lost War Maps of the Confederates," *Century Magazine* 35 (1888): 479–481; obituaries in *Ravenswood News*, 1 Mar. 1899, and *Charleston Daily Gazette*, 4 Mar. 1899.

RICHARD W. STEPHENSON

CAMPBELL, Alexander (12 September 1788–4 March 1866), Disciples of Christ minister and member of the Convention of 1829–1830, was born in County Antrim, Ireland, the son of Jane Corneigle Campbell and Thomas Campbell, a studious and irenic minister in the Seceder Presbyterian Church. In 1805 Campbell assisted at his father's new classical academy in County Armagh. Two years later Thomas Campbell, distressed by the sectarian strife prevalent within the church and in the area, immigrated to Washington County, Pennsylvania. The rest of the family attempted to follow in 1808, but shipwreck forced them to winter in Glasgow. During the traumatic misadventure at sea, Campbell decided to enter the ministry. He enrolled in Glasgow University and also studied with the famed evangelists and reformers James Alexander Haldane and Robert Haldane, who probably introduced him to the primitivist religious ideas Campbell later adopted.

By the time Campbell and his family joined his father in Pennsylvania in 1809, Thomas Campbell had left the Seceder Presbyterian Church. The break came largely over his unwillingness to enforce closed communion, a practice that would have denied communion to most of the scattered Christians to whom he was ministering in western Pennsylvania. Thomas Campbell and a few followers formed the Christian Association of Washington. In *The Declaration and Address of the Christian Association of Washington, Pennsylvania* (1809), they stated the central tenets that Alexander Campbell spent his life defending: a plea for Christian unity based on a restoration of the faith and practice of the primitive New Testament church, a defense of Christian liberty, and an optimistic hope that a millennial Christian age was nearing. Campbell blended the principles of the *Declaration* with the primitivist ideas he had encountered in Glasgow. In 1811 the Christian Association of Washington reorganized itself as the Brush Run Church, and on 1 January 1812 Campbell was ordained to the ministry. Almost immediately he replaced his father as the primary leader of the nascent independent religious reform movement.

During his first decade in America, Campbell settled on a number of theological conclusions that made irreversible his decision to sever all denominational connections. In 1812 he embraced believers' baptism by immersion and from 1815 until about 1830 was loosely affiliated with the Redstone Baptist Association, where his recruits came to be known as Reforming Baptists. In 1816 Campbell preached a controversial "Sermon on the Law" at a Baptist association meeting, in which he denied the authority of Old Testament law for Christians, thus undercutting basic Calvinistic beliefs. His study of the Greek texts on which many of his innovative views were based led him to publish an original translation of the New Testament, *The Living Oracles* (1826). Many of Campbell's critics judged the translation a presumptuous undertaking for a young western preacher, but it was repeatedly reprinted, and later scholars regarded it as one of the better nineteenth-century efforts to revise the New Testament.

On 12 March 1811 Campbell married Margaret Brown, of Brooke County, and resided at Bethany in that county for the remainder of his life. They had one son and seven daughters before her death on 22 October 1827. On 31 July 1828 Campbell married Selina Huntingdon Bakewell, a confidante of his first wife. An able and forceful woman, she became a respected teacher among the Disciples of Christ and frequently wrote for the movement's periodicals. They had three sons and three daughters. Of Campbell's fourteen children, only four survived him.

Campbell possessed an impressive intellect, and his fame as a preacher spread throughout western Virginia. He delivered hundreds of sermons each year and made annual tours that carried him throughout most of the United States and in 1847 to Great Britain, Ireland, and France. Campbell refused remuneration for preaching, a commitment made possible by the property acquired through his first marriage and by successful business ventures in publishing, farming, and raising sheep. In 1823 he began issuing a monthly magazine, the *Christian Baptist*. Campbell wrote *Psalms, Hymns and Spiritual Songs* (1828), *Delusions: An Analysis of the Book of Mormon* (1832), *The Christian Preacher's Companion* (1836), *The Christian Hymnbook* (1843), *Christian Baptism—With Its Antecedents and Consequences* (1851), *Popular Lectures and Addresses* (1863), a biography of his father, *Memoirs of Elder Thomas Campbell* (1861), and the posthumously published *Familiar Lectures on the Pentateuch* (1867). His published works, including the *Christian Baptist* and its successor, the *Millennial Harbinger*, fill almost sixty volumes. The success of his publishing efforts led the government to establish a post office in Bethany, and for thirty years Campbell served as postmaster. He founded Buffalo Academy in Brooke County in 1819 and ran it for several years, and in 1840 he established Bethany College and served as its president until his death. The college trained many of the first generation of leaders of the Disciples of Christ.

Campbell's growing fame and heterodox views on baptism and other subjects led him into a series of highly publicized public debates attended by large audiences and widely read in published form. In 1820 he debated the Presbyterian John Walker in Mount Pleasant, Ohio, with the exchange published as *Infant Sprinkling Proved to Be a Human Tradition* (1820). In two subsequent debates with Presbyterian clergymen Campbell fleshed out his ideas on the baptism of believers and the divisiveness of creeds. His exchange with William L. McCalla was published as *A Debate on Christian Baptism* (1824). For two weeks in November 1843 before large crowds in Lexington, Kentucky, Campbell debated Nathan L. Rice, chosen by the Synod of Kentucky to stem the defection of Presbyterians to the Disciples. Henry Clay moderated the exchange, which was published in a book of more than 900 pages, *A Debate Between Rev. A. Campbell and Rev. N. L. Rice, on the Action, Subject, Design and Administrator of Christian Baptism* (1844). In 1837, in another much-publicized confrontation, Campbell debated the Catholic archbishop John Baptist Purcell for eight days in Cincinnati on whether the Catholic Church was "catholic, apostolic, or holy." Campbell's positions and resulting publication, *A Debate on the Roman Catholic Religion* (1837), endeared him to the growing anti-Catholic movement in the West.

By then Campbell had become one of the most famous religious leaders in the United States. He attracted and often responded to criticism from other clergymen, including the Virginia Baptist ministers Andrew Broaddus (1770–1848), with whom he engaged in a debate on baptism, and Jeremiah Bell Jeter, who analyzed Campbell's movement at length in *Campbellism Examined* (1855). In 1829 Campbell gained attention in Great Britain when he debated Robert Owen, a famed Welsh atheist, philanthropist, and reformer, with whom he became close friends. They conducted a public eight-day discussion in Cincinnati, published as *A Debate on the Evidences of Christianity* (1829). Afterward Campbell returned to his home, where, heralded as a hero for defending Christianity against the dual scourges of atheism and socialism, he received Owen as a houseguest.

In May 1829 Campbell was elected one of four delegates to represent the district of Brooke, Monongalia, Ohio, Preston, and Tyler Counties in a convention called to revise the Virginia constitution. He was appointed to the Committee on the Judicial Department of Government. Undaunted by the presence of some of the state's most illustrious statesmen and jurists, Campbell won respect as an eloquent spokesman for the reformers from western Virginia. He forcefully advocated extending the suffrage to almost all adult white men, apportioning seats in the House of Delegates on the basis of the white population, establishing a statewide system of public education, and allowing voters to elect judges of the county courts. Conservatives, among them John Randolph of Roanoke, with whom Campbell verbally clashed, controlled the convention, and Campbell, disappointed with the constitution that the convention drafted, voted against it. His constituents agreed, and the Brooke County electorate voted 371 to 0 against ratifying the document, which nonetheless won approval statewide. While attending the convention in Richmond, Campbell preached regularly to large audiences, including some convention delegates, in the city's churches.

From 1823 to 1830 Campbell's *Christian Baptist* was filled with sharp and sometimes witty caricatures of the weaknesses of religious leaders, but he also developed seriously and at length the major doctrinal positions that became the theological foundation of the Disciples of Christ. In a series of thirty articles on "A Restoration of the Ancient Order of Things" and in another of ten articles on the "Ancient Gospel" he laid out his understanding of New Testament church organization and worship, including the weekly observance of the Lord's Supper, and his views on the plan of salvation. Campbell fleshed out his restoration ideas in *Christianity Restored* (1835) and revised them in *The Christian System* (1839).

By 1830 the Reforming Baptists had established scores of independent congregations and numbered about 10,000 members, generally calling themselves Disciples of Christ. Disciples leaders became increasingly aware of other reform movements that shared their primitivist notions concerning New Testament organization and worship. The movement that most closely paralleled the Disciples was the Christian movement led by Barton W. Stone, and in 1832 its approximately 8,000 members joined forces with the Reformers and became known variously as the Christian Church, Churches of Christ, and Disciples of Christ.

Campbell was the uncontested leader of the new movement, which by the time of his death in 1866 had perhaps 200,000 members, making it the fifth-largest Protestant denomination in the nation and the largest religious group of American origin. Symbolizing his transition from iconoclast to denominational leader, he replaced the *Christian Baptist* in 1830 with the *Millennial Harbinger*, which generally presented a more constructive viewpoint. The Disciples of Christ remained a loose collection of independent, autonomous congregations reflecting Campbell's early criticism of religious societies and denominational organizations. Nonetheless, he encouraged the growth of a variety of regional conventions in the 1840s, and in 1849 he was elected president of the first general convention of the Disciples. Campbell was also the first president of the American Christian Missionary Society, which was founded at the same convention.

Campbell imbibed deeply the optimistic assumptions of the early nineteenth century. He believed that the emergence of American democracy and his own efforts to restore New Testament Christianity foreshadowed the beginning of a prophetic period of peace, prosperity, and righteousness. His millennialism was in fact strongly postmillennial and anticipated an inevitable improvement in the human condition as people came to understand the laws of nature and accept the law of God. Campbell believed that the natural and spiritual progress of his generation would culminate in a period of divine peace and prosperity before Jesus returned.

Campbell's millennial views contributed to his support for political and social reform. He was deeply committed to universal public education and extension of the suffrage. Campbell freed the slaves that he had acquired through marriage and supported the moderate antislavery movement. As sectional animosities deepened after the 1830s, he became increasingly disillusioned and gloomy about the future. In *A Tract for the People of Kentucky* (1849), addressed to the Disciples of that state, Campbell recommended a constitutional amendment to end slavery there, but he refused to endorse radical measures. He watched apprehensively as advocates and opponents of abolition threatened political and religious schism.

In Campbell's last years his millennial enthusiasm waned. The Disciples of Christ increasingly divided into bickering camps, some reflecting his early sectarian demands for a restoration of New Testament patterns and others drawing on the appeals for Christian unity that characterized his writings after 1835. Campbell was also saddened by the inexorable descent of the nation into sectional bitterness and division and found himself vilified in the 1850s by radical Disciples in both the North and the South because of his moderate views on slavery. His nephew Archibald W. Campbell, editor of the *Wheeling Daily Intelligencer*, became one of the most important and controversial critics of slavery in western Virginia. The Civil War divided Campbell's church and his family as well as the nation, and Bethany College was nearly destroyed.

Alexander Campbell's mind deteriorated during the Civil War, and he died at his home in Bethany, West Virginia, on 4 March 1866 and was buried in the family cemetery there. His chief legacy is the Disciples of Christ religious movement. At the end of the twentieth century, three major groups of churches—the Christian Church, Church of Christ, and Disciples of Christ—traced their origins to Campbell's reforms.

Robert Richardson, *Memoirs of Alexander Campbell* (1868–1870), frontispiece por. and birth date on 1:19; Alexander Campbell Papers, Bethany College, Bethany, W.Va.; Robert Frederick West, *Alexander Campbell and Natural Religion* (1948); Harold L. Lunger, *The Political Ethics of Alexander Campbell* (1954); Perry E. Gresham, comp., *The Sage of Bethany: A Pioneer in Broadcloth* (1960); David Edwin Harrell Jr., *Quest for a Christian America: The Disciples of Christ and American Society to 1866* (1966); James M. Seale, ed., *Lectures in Honor of the Alexander Campbell Bicentennial, 1788–1988* (1988); Loretta M. Long, *The Life of Selina Campbell: A Fellow Soldier in the Cause of Restoration* (2001); Records of Appointment of Postmasters, Virginia, Brooke Co., RG 28, NARA; William M. Moorhouse, "Alexander Campbell and the Virginia Constitutional Convention of 1829–1830," *Virginia Cavalcade* 24 (1975): 184–191; *Proceedings and Debates of 1829–1830 Convention*, 42–43, 116–124, 383–390, 496–497, 525–530, 750, 786–787, 831, 850–851; *Journal of 1829–1830 Convention*, 297; Bruce, *Rhetoric of Conservatism*, 34, 36–37, 43, 53–56, 78, 84, 102, 125; Catlin, *Convention of 1829–30* (por.); obituary (with 1789 birth year) in *Wheeling Daily Intelligencer*, 6 Mar. 1866; obituary (with 1786 birth year), funeral sermon, and memorials in *Millennial Harbinger* 37 (1866): 122–144, 186–189, 193–208.

DAVID EDWIN HARRELL JR.

CAMPBELL, Archibald W. (4 April 1833–13 February 1899), journalist and Republican Party leader, was born in Jefferson County, Ohio, the son of Archibald W. Campbell and Phoebe Campbell. His father was a physician and a younger brother of Alexander Campbell, the religious reformer and member of the Convention of 1829–1830. Campbell grew up in or near Bethany, in Brooke County, where his uncle had founded Bethany College and his father practiced medicine. He graduated from Bethany College in 1852 and studied law at Hamilton College Law School in New York, where he met William Henry Seward. Within a few years Campbell followed Seward into the new Republican Party and, like him, became an abolitionist.

Campbell returned to Virginia and settled in Wheeling. In the autumn of 1856 he and John F. McDermot purchased the *Wheeling Daily Intelligencer*. On 9 October of that year Campbell became the editor. During the next two years he used the *Intelligencer* to express his antislavery views. It became not only the first Republican daily newspaper in Virginia but also perhaps the best known and most influential Virginia newspaper outside Richmond. Campbell unsuccessfully proposed in 1859 that the second national convention of the Republican Party meet the following year in Wheeling. It met, instead, in Chicago, where he was a delegate supporting Seward for president. Afterward Campbell warmly endorsed the nomination of Abraham Lincoln, who received about 800 votes in Ohio County in the November election.

Campbell believed that the proslavery policies of Virginia's state government were injurious to northwestern Virginia, but he did not initially expect that Lincoln's election would result in Virginia's secession or that the western counties would in turn separate from Virginia. His attitude quickly changed when the Convention of 1861 adopted the Ordinance of Secession. Thereafter Campbell used the *Wheeling Daily Intelligencer* to argue that the interests of western Virginia and of democracy required the establishment of a new state. He was one of the most influential leaders in the statehood movement and strongly supported the abolition of slavery by the first West Virginia constitution.

Campbell remained a loyal Republican during and after the Civil War, but he occasionally differed with national party leaders when he believed that the interests of the party ran contrary to those of West Virginia. He dissented on withholding suffrage from former supporters of the Confederacy, on refusing to make an alliance with the Greenback Party, and on a proposed third presidential term for Ulysses S. Grant in 1880. So strong was Campbell's opposition to party leaders in 1880 that some considered expelling him from the national convention. He forcefully argued his case at the convention, retained his seat, and also received some credit for the eventual nomination for president of his friend James A. Garfield. Although frequently urged to seek public office, Campbell rejected suggestions that he run for the United States Senate or jockey for a position in Garfield's cabinet.

In Wheeling on 10 March 1864 Campbell married Annie W. Crawford. They had one son and one daughter. Sometime after her death he married a second time to a woman named Mary H., surname unknown, with whom he had at least one daughter. During the 1880s he gradually relinquished his role as editor and publisher of the *Intelligencer* in order to pursue other business interests. Archibald W. Campbell died following a stroke at his sister's home in Webster Groves, Missouri, on 13 February 1899. He was buried in Greenwood Cemetery in Wheeling, West Virginia.

Biographies giving birth date in Gibson Lamb Cranmer et al., *History of the Upper Ohio Valley* (1890), 1:241–246, Atkinson and Gibbens, *Prominent Men*, 507–513, and Granville Davisson Hall, *The Rending of Virginia: A History* (1902; repr. 2000), 582–588 (por. on 583); Archibald W. Campbell Papers, WVU; Ohio Co. Marriage Register, 1864; *Wheeling Daily Intelligencer*, 12 Mar. 1864; Myra Gladys Gray, "A. W. Campbell—Party Builder," *West Virginia History* 7 (1946): 221–237; Donovan H. Bond, "How the *Wheeling Intelligencer* Became a Republican Organ," *West Virginia History* 11 (1949): 160–184; William S. Hitchcock, "The Limits of Southern Unionism: Virginia Conservatives and the Gubernatorial Election of 1859," *JSH* 47 (1981): 68; excerpts from Campbell's writings and speeches printed in Elizabeth Cometti and Festus P. Summers, eds., *The Thirty-Fifth State: A Documentary History of West Virginia* (1966), 299–300, 366–368, 452–456, 478–479, and Hall, *Rending of Virginia*, 154, 211–213, 271–272, 384–390; obituaries, editorial tributes, and accounts of funeral in *Wheeling Intelligencer*, 14–17 Feb. 1899, and *Wheeling Register*, 14, 16, 17 Feb. 1899.

Douglas J. MacGregor

CAMPBELL, Arthur (3 November 1743–8 August 1811), member of the Convention of 1776, was born in Augusta County, the son of David Campbell and Mary Hamilton Campbell, both children of Scots-Irish immigrants who settled in western Virginia in the 1720s. The marriages of his six brothers and sisters connected the Campbells to many of the most influential families in the region. In September 1758, while serving in a company of Virginia rangers during the French and Indian War, Campbell was captured by Wyandot Indians and held captive until he escaped near Fort Detroit two years later. He returned to his family, who had presumed that he was dead, received a grant for 2,000 acres of land, and began a career in landownership and speculation. By the time of his death Campbell's landholdings totaled almost 15,000 acres.

About 1769 Campbell moved with his family to the Holston River region. In 1773 he married his cousin Margaret Campbell. They had six sons and six daughters and lived at Royal Oak (later the site of Marion). Campbell became a justice of the peace in the new county of Fincastle in 1773. The following year he was a major in command of county volunteers who guarded the southwestern Virginia frontier during Dunmore's War. Campbell was an original member of the Fincastle County Committee, established on 20 January 1775, and during the ensuing months he kept his eye on frontier defense and on opportunities for land acquisition in Kentucky. He may have been engaged in Richard Henderson's attempt to create a separate western colony of Transylvania. That attempt pitted members of rival land companies against one another, and Campbell became embroiled in controversies resulting from Henderson's venture.

In April 1776 Campbell became a lieutenant colonel in the Fincastle County militia, and he and William Russell won election to represent the county in the fifth and last of the Revolutionary Conventions. Campbell served on the standing Committees of Propositions and Grievances and on Public Claims and on drafting committees for measures to stimulate manufacture of munitions, to enlarge the 9th Virginia

Regiment, and to raise four troops of cavalry to defend the frontiers. He voted for independence on 15 May, for the Virginia Declaration of Rights on 12 June, and for the first constitution of Virginia on 29 June.

Campbell returned to Williamsburg in October 1776 as a member of the House of Delegates and took seats on the Committees of Propositions and Grievances and on Public Claims. He strenuously opposed a bill to divide Fincastle County into two new counties, one to include Kentucky, and perhaps viewed the measure as a threat to Henderson's western landholdings. After passage late in 1776 of an amended bill dividing Fincastle into three new counties (Kentucky in the west, Montgomery in the north, and Washington in the south), Campbell became the first county lieutenant of Washington County and presiding justice of its court. His local political position secure, he helped coordinate operations against Indians and Loyalists in the Virginia backcountry throughout the Revolutionary War. Campbell was elected to one-year terms in the House of Delegates in 1778, 1782, and 1783. He arrived at the 1778 assembly too late to be appointed to a major standing committee, but he served on the Committee of Propositions and Grievances during the 1782 and 1783 sessions and also sat on the Committees for Courts of Justice and of Privileges and Elections in 1782.

By 1785 Campbell owned almost 5,500 acres in Washington County, far more than any of its other residents. Like many other ambitious frontier settlers, he built his public career through a combination of entrepreneurship, local leadership, and connections with political patrons from Virginia's Tidewater elite. A large man of impressive appearance, Campbell read and traveled widely, especially after the Revolution, and was a fluent conversationalist. His nephew David Campbell (1779–1859), later a governor of Virginia, remembered that he was "hasty and excitable and disposed to be overbearing; and was often engaged in violent personal quarrels."

Campbell's relationship with eastern Virginia leaders changed in the 1780s when he developed connections with the separatist movement that was attempting to establish a state of Franklin in western North Carolina. Believing that a new southwestern state would provide people in his area of Virginia with a more responsive legislature and better protection from the Indians, he led the effort to transfer jurisdiction over Washington County from Virginia to Franklin. When Governor Patrick Henry learned of these activities, he dispatched William Russell to suppress the perceived revolt. Henry's action must have been galling to Campbell. Russell had been his sometime colleague and frequent competitor for office in the county for a decade, and Russell had recently become Henry's brother-in-law by marrying the widow of Campbell's own cousin and brother-in-law Brigadier General William Campbell (1745–1781). The two men were even then contesting guardianship of the general's children. At the June 1785 meeting of the Washington County Court, Russell executed Henry's order to strip Campbell of his appointed offices. Henry also pushed through legislation that defined separatist activity as treason.

Campbell's political estrangement from Virginia proved short-lived, and his local standing remained undimmed. He won election to the House of Delegates in 1786 and 1787 and served on the Committee for Courts of Justice during both sessions and on the Committee for Religion in 1787. In the latter year the new governor, Edmund Randolph, reappointed Campbell justice of the peace and county lieutenant. During the winter of 1787–1788 Campbell took a leading role in meetings at the Washington County courthouse at which local political leaders drafted amendments to the proposed constitution of the United States, many of which were intended to weaken the power of the new national government, to abridge the influence of the president and the Senate, and to require that a bill of rights be added.

Campbell nevertheless became an active Federalist during the 1790s. George Washington appointed him an Indian agent in 1793, and the postmaster general gave him responsibility for transporting the mail between Staunton and Abingdon. Campbell resigned all of his public offices by 1799. Ten years later he moved to the

Yellow Creek settlement in Kentucky (later the site of Middlesboro), near some of his children and other family members. Arthur Campbell died there of cancer on 8 August 1811. His will directed that he be buried at Gideon's Tenements near Cumberland Gap.

Lewis Preston Summers, *History of Southwest Virginia, 1746–1786, Washington County, 1777–1870* (1903), esp. 463–464, quoting birth and death dates from now-lost grave marker; Robert L. Kincaid, "Colonel Arthur Campbell: Frontier Leader and Patriot," in Historical Society of Washington County *Publications*, ser. 2, 1 (1965): 2–18; Hartwell L. Quinn, *Arthur Campbell: Pioneer and Patriot of the Old Southwest* (1990); Arthur Campbell Papers, Filson Historical Society, Louisville, Ky.; Campbell letters in David Campbell Papers, Duke, and Draper MSS, esp. ser. DD, QQ (quotation in David Campbell to Lyman C. Draper, 12 Dec. 1840, 10DD6); *Revolutionary Virginia*, vols. 2, 4–7; James William Hagy, "Arthur Campbell and the Origins of Kentucky: A Reassessment," *Filson Club History Quarterly* 55 (1981): 344–374; Peter J. Kastor, "'Equitable Rights and Privileges': The Divided Loyalties in Washington County, Virginia, during the Franklin Separatist Crisis," *VMHB* 105 (1997): 193–226; Kaminski, *Ratification*, 8:283–284, 472–475, 9:769–779; will and estate settlement in Knox Co., Ky., Will Book, A:38–45, 78–82.

PETER J. KASTOR

CAMPBELL, Charles (1 May 1807–11 July 1876), historian, was born in Petersburg, the son of John Wilson Campbell, a printer and bookseller, and Mildred Walker Moore Campbell, a sometime schoolteacher. He was educated at Peter Cooke's school in Petersburg and at the College of New Jersey (later Princeton University), where he joined the American Whig Society and received an A.B. in 1825. Campbell studied at the law school of Henry St. George Tucker in Winchester but because of his feeble health, which left him in a state of physical and mental exhaustion in 1829, did not practice law.

Following his recovery Campbell worked briefly as an engineer during the construction of the Petersburg Railroad and in 1834 moved to Glencoe, Alabama, where he taught for two years at an academy for boys. He married Elvira N. Callaway, of Monroe County, Tennessee, on 13 September 1836, shortly before he moved back to Petersburg. She died on 8 August 1837, soon after the birth of a son. Campbell remarried on 4 September 1850, to Anna Burdsall, of Rahway, New Jersey. They had four children,

of whom two daughters and one son lived to adulthood. On returning to Petersburg Campbell worked for his father, who served as collector of customs in that city. From 1840 to 1843 he owned and edited the *Petersburg American Statesman*, and in 1849 he took part in founding the *Petersburg Southside Democrat*. From 1842 to 1855 Campbell operated a private school in Petersburg, and from the latter year until 1870 he served as principal at the Anderson Seminary, one of the city's better schools for boys. He was mild mannered but a gentleman of the old school who kept a stout switch at his desk for disciplining students. Campbell participated in and preserved the records of the Petersburg Library Association, the Petersburg Lyceum, and the Petersburg Young Men's Literary Society.

Campbell may have used his father's brief *History of Virginia, from Its Discovery Till the Year 1781* (1813) as a textbook when he began teaching in Petersburg. He indulged his own interest in history during visits to historic sites and on rambles through old cemeteries, and he collected manuscripts and other documents that furnished the basis for historical articles that he published in the *Southern Literary Messenger* and the *Virginia Historical Register*. Campbell edited two volumes of *The Bland Papers: Being a Selection from the Manuscripts of Colonel Theodorick Bland, Jr., of Prince George County, Virginia, to Which are Prefixed an Introduction, and a Memoir of Colonel Bland* (1840–1843), one of the first published collections of family papers produced in Virginia. He generously shared the fruits of his research with William Meade during the latter's preparation of *Old Churches, Ministers, and Families of Virginia* (1857), and he corresponded with many of the leading historians of his generation. In 1855 Campbell wrote an introduction to a new edition of Robert Beverley's *History of Virginia in Four Parts*, based on the 1722 revised edition. He also edited *The Orderly Book of That Portion of the American Army Stationed at or near Williamsburg, Va., under the Command of General Andrew Lewis, from March 18th, 1776, to August 28th, 1776* (1860) and in 1868 published both a *Genealogy of the Spotswood Family in Scotland and Virginia* and *Some Materials to*

Serve for a Brief Memoir of John Daly Burk, the Petersburg resident who in 1804 and 1805 had completed three volumes of a history of colonial Virginia. In the 1840s Campbell interviewed Isaac Jefferson, formerly a slave at Monticello, and although he prepared the text of the resulting memoir for publication about 1871, it was not printed until 1951.

Campbell's most important work began as a series of articles on Virginia history serialized in the *Southern Literary Messenger* and published in Richmond as *Introduction to the History of the Colony and Ancient Dominion of Virginia* (1847). In 1860 the Philadelphia publisher J. B. Lippincott issued an enlarged edition with an expanded section on the American Revolution under the title *History of the Colony and Ancient Dominion of Virginia*. As with the short history of Virginia that his father wrote and the longer history that Burk began, Campbell's history covered Virginia from its founding through the end of the Revolutionary War. The first edition of the *History* was favorably considered in the *North American Review* in October 1848, and Campbell used complimentary letters obtained from such well-known authors as Jared Sparks, of Harvard University, to promote the sale of the volume.

Relying on original sources compiled by Samuel Purchas, John Smith, and others and making use of Beverley's *History*, William Stith's 1747 history of Virginia, and William Waller Hening's valuable collection of Virginia laws, Campbell produced the most accurate of the nineteenth-century histories of the colony and a work perfectly suited to the intellectual climate in mid-nineteenth-century Virginia. He devoted fully a quarter of the 750-page second edition to the struggles of the founders during the period of the Virginia Company of London and nearly a third to the American Revolution and its origins. Like Burk, Campbell viewed the political development of the colony as a long preparation for the American Revolution. He characterized Bacon's Rebellion of 1676 as "a miniature prototype of the revolution of 1688 in England, and of 1776 in America." Campbell wrote about the Native Americans with some respect, although he adopted the language of

his sources and condemned the Indians for treachery during the uprisings of 1622 and 1644. In the 1860 edition he concluded with many of his contemporaries that "while their fate cannot fail to excite commiseration, it may reasonably be concluded that the perpetual possession of this country by the aborigines would have been incompatible with the designs of Providence in promoting the welfare of mankind." About slavery Campbell had little to say beyond a short chapter justifying the institution on religious and practical grounds. In ruminating on the introduction of the first African laborers into Virginia, he concluded, "While the cruel slave-trade was prompted by a remorseless cupidity, an inscrutable Providence turned the wickedness of men into the means of bringing about beneficent results. The system of slavery, doubtless, entailed many evils on slave and slave-holder, and, perhaps, the greater on the latter. These evils are the tax paid for the elevation of the negro from his aboriginal condition."

Following the Civil War Campbell contemplated a new edition of his *History* that would have continued the story through the end of that war, but he did not undertake the task because of his poor health. Charles Campbell died on 11 July 1876 at the Western Lunatic Asylum in Staunton and was buried in Blandford Cemetery in Petersburg.

R. A. Brock, "Charles Campbell, the Historian of Virginia," *Potter's American Monthly* 7 (1876): 425–427 (por.); Edward A. Wyatt IV, *Charles Campbell, Virginia's "Old Mortality"* (1935); William Howell Cryer, "Charles Campbell: Early Life and Works (1807–1847)" (master's thesis, W&M, 1947); biographies in *New-England Historical and Genealogical Register* 31 (1877): 127–128, Margaret Campbell Pilcher, *Historical Sketches of the Campbell, Pilcher and Kindred Families* [ca. 1911], 224–228, and Tyler, *Encyclopedia*, 2:225; Charles Campbell Papers, Duke and W&M; several Campbell letters in Hugh Blair Grigsby and Edmund Ruffin Papers, VHS; Lester J. Cappon, ed., "Correspondence between Charles Campbell and Lyman C. Draper, 1846–1872," *WMQ*, 3d ser., 3 (1946): 70–116; Marian Lois Moran, ed., "The Diary of Charles Campbell, October 5, 1861–April 5, 1862" (master's thesis, W&M, 1966); Edward A. Wyatt IV, "Schools and Libraries in Petersburg, Virginia, Prior to 1861," *Tyler's Quarterly* 19 (1937): 65–84; Campbell, *History of the Colony and Ancient Dominion of Virginia* (1860), 146 (quotation on slavery), 167 (on Native Americans), 288 (on Bacon's Rebellion); Rayford W. Logan, ed., *Memoirs of a Monticello Slave, as Dictated to Charles Campbell in the 1840's by Isaac, One of Thomas Jefferson's*

Slaves (1951), esp. 5–7; obituaries in *Petersburg Index-Appeal*, 12 July 1876, and *Richmond Daily Dispatch,* 13 July 1876.

BRENT TARTER

CAMPBELL, Christiana Burdett (ca. 1723–25 March 1792), innkeeper, was the daughter of John Burdett, a Williamsburg innkeeper, and Mary Burdett. Her father died by 18 August 1746 and bequeathed her a share of his estate worth at least £300 sterling, including three slaves. Sometime after 21 September 1747 she married Ebenezer Campbell and presumably moved with him to Blandford, later part of Petersburg, where he was an apothecary. They had two daughters, one possibly born after the death of Ebenezer Campbell, whose estate was advertised for sale on 14 August 1752. In an odd act of remembrance, the younger daughter was named Ebenezer.

Christiana Campbell had returned to Williamsburg by 7 October 1753, when she had a slave baptized at Bruton Parish Church. She showed her continuing interest in converting and educating her slaves by sending some of them to the Bray School, which taught black children in Williamsburg between 1760 and 1774. Probably starting no later than 1755, when she was purchasing large quantities of beef and wheat, Campbell became one of the capital's most prominent tavern keepers, operating at no fewer than three successive locations. She specialized in offering what she described as "genteel Accommodations, and the very best Entertainment" to a clientele of gentlemen that included George Washington, who between 1761 and 1774 often lodged or dined at her establishments during his visits to Williamsburg. Campbell's signed receipts to Washington attest to her literacy at a time when many women lacked this attainment. Thomas Jefferson also dined regularly at her taverns between 1771 and 1777, but his acquaintance was slight enough that he gave her first name as Catherine when indexing his accounts.

By 18 November 1760 Campbell was renting a lot on the south side of Duke of Gloucester Street subsequently occupied by James Anderson, the prominent blacksmith and public armorer. Sometime between 25 June 1767

and 16 May 1771, and probably before October 1768, she became proprietor of what contemporary records called the Coffee House, close to the Capitol on the north side of Duke of Gloucester Street.

In an advertisement dated 3 October 1771 Campbell announced that she had moved just east of the Capitol to what is now Waller Street. There she opened her tavern in a building constructed in the mid-1750s and recently vacated by innkeeper Jane Vobe, who soon resumed her own operations at the King's Arms Tavern. Campbell stated that she would reserve rooms for gentlemen who had lodged with her before. Her one-story tavern, measuring about sixty feet by twenty-four feet with a cellar and a separate kitchen structure, had a public room large enough to serve as a ballroom for the local Masonic lodge. Campbell rented the buildings and the two lots on which they stood from the estate of Nathaniel Walthoe until 5 January 1774, when she finalized her 29 July 1773 purchase of the property at auction for £598 10s. current money. Walthoe himself, formerly her landlord at the Coffee House, had contributed to the purchase with a £200 bequest in appreciation of her integrity and virtue.

Williamsburg suffered an economic decline after Richmond became the new state capital in April 1780. Some tradespeople moved to the new seat of government, but Campbell stayed behind and evidently chose to retire. The only contemporary description of her came from Alexander Macaulay, to whom she denied service on 25 February 1783, stating that she had closed her tavern several years before. The disgruntled traveler portrayed Campbell as "a little old Woman, about four feet high; & equally thick, a little turn up Pug nose, a mouth screw'd up to one side; in short, nothing in any part of her appearance in the least inviting." Macaulay also said that her house had a "cold, poverty struck appearance," but her ownership that year of thirteen slaves and four cattle suggests that she had provided well for herself. Campbell unsuccessfully sought to auction her Williamsburg real estate on 12 March and 8 October 1787, but in the latter sale she had better luck disposing of her household furnishings. She evidently moved thereafter to Fredericksburg, where her younger daughter lived.

Christiana Burdett Campbell died on 25 March 1792 and was buried in the Masonic Cemetery at Fredericksburg with a fulsome epitaph attesting to her kindness and generosity. Her Waller Street tavern burned about 1859, but the opening by the Colonial Williamsburg Foundation of the reconstructed Christiana Campbell's Tavern as a working restaurant on 16 April 1956 has made her name recognizable to generations of hungry tourists.

Mary A. Stephenson and Patricia Gibbs, "Christiana Campbell's Tavern Historical Report" (1952 and 1975 typescript reports; 1990 microfiche ed.), CW; some sources give first name as Christian; father's will in York Co. Wills and Inventories, 20:37–38; estate sales of father and husband advertised in *Williamsburg Virginia Gazette*, 4 Sept. 1746, 14 Aug. 1752; York Co. Judgments and Orders (1746–1752), 34; William Archer Rutherfoord Goodwin, ed., *The Record of Bruton Parish Church*, 2d ed. (1941), 155; John C. Van Horne, ed., *Religious Philanthropy and Colonial Slavery: The American Correspondence of the Associates of Dr. Bray, 1717–1777* (1985), 241, 278; York Co. Deed Book, 6:309–311, 8:385–389; *Williamsburg Virginia Gazette* (Purdie and Dixon), 25 June 1767, 16 May, 3 Oct. 1771 (first quotation), 20 May 1773; two Campbell receipts to Washington at Morgan Library, New York, and a third, at CW, reproduced in Donald Jackson and Dorothy Twohig, eds., *The Diaries of George Washington* (1976–1979), 3:101; Walthoe's will in Prerogative Court of Canterbury, Taverner 240; *WMQ*, 1st ser., 11 (1903): 187–188 (second and third quotations), and 25 (1917): 152; Personal Property Tax Returns, Williamsburg, 1783, RG 48, LVA; Mutual Assurance Society Declarations, no. 485 (1801), LVA; *Richmond Virginia Gazette and Weekly Advertiser*, 22 Feb., 27 Sept. 1787; Mary Campbell Russell to Ebenezer "Ebe" Campbell Day, 13 Nov. 1787, Papers of Scott and Richards Mercantile Firm, UVA; *Williamsburg Virginia Gazette*, 13 Apr. 1956; death date and death in seventieth year on grave marker in Masonic Cemetery, Fredericksburg, quoted in Dora C. Jett, *Minor Sketches of Major Folk and Where They Sleep: The Old Masonic Burying Ground, Fredericksburg, Virginia* (1928), 24–25.

J. JEFFERSON LOONEY

CAMPBELL, Clarence Jackson (31 May 1863–25 February 1926), member of the Convention of 1901–1902, was born in Amherst County, the son of Joel Henry Campbell and Maria Louise Staples Campbell. He grew up on his father's farm, was educated in local private schools, and graduated from the Virginia Military Institute in 1884. Campbell was an instructor at Kenmore High School in Amherst during the mid-1880s and later served as county surveyor. On 22 November 1884 he married Sarah Freeman Parr, of Amherst County. They had three sons and five daughters.

Campbell represented Amherst County in the House of Delegates from 1891 to 1894. During his first two-year term he served on the Committees on Enrolled Bills, on the Library, on Retrenchment and Economy, and on Schools and Colleges. He chaired the Committee on Schools and Colleges during his second term, continued to sit on the Committee on Retrenchment and Economy, and served on the Committee on Printing. Campbell studied law during that time and was admitted to the bar in 1894. Elected to a third term in the House of Delegates in 1897, he served on the Committees for Courts of Justice, on Federal Relations and Resolutions, and on Schools and Colleges. In 1898 the governor appointed Campbell to the vacant position of judge of Amherst County, and on 18 December 1899 the assembly elected him to a full term.

In April 1901 Campbell won the Democratic nomination for a seat in a convention called to revise the constitution of Virginia, and in the election on 23 May he defeated the Republican nominee Samuel C. Allen by a vote of 1,566 to 919. Campbell served on the Committee on Public Institutions and Prisons. He did not attend the convention with any specific proposals in mind, and he participated only occasionally in the floor debates but spoke in behalf of retaining the old county court system and having the state superintendent of public instruction elected by the voters. Campbell opposed and voted against the restrictive suffrage provisions that the convention approved, which were designed to disfranchise as many African American men as possible. He had previously stated his fear that the proposals would also result in the disfranchisement of white men. Campbell spoke and voted against a successful move to proclaim the new constitution in effect without submitting it to the voters in a referendum as the Democratic Party convention of 1901 had promised. Despite Campbell's previous opposition to these provisions, on 6 June he voted with the majority to approve the new constitution.

On 24 June 1902, two days before the convention adjourned, Campbell presided over a session of the Amherst County Court to hear an appeal from Charles H. Crawford, a Baptist minister and agent of the Anti-Saloon League of America who had organized Virginia's branch of the league in 1901 and was directing the state campaign for Prohibition. Earlier in the spring Campbell had ruled that druggists could sell "medicated" alcohol in certain districts. In criticizing the opinion Crawford sarcastically remarked that he wondered "which had been doctored most, the whiskey or the judge." Campbell cited Crawford for contempt of court. On 24 June Crawford's attorney, future governor William Hodges Mann, argued so forcefully that the law did not authorize a citation for contempt under those circumstances that Campbell had no choice but to rule in Crawford's favor. Enraged that Crawford refused to apologize, the judge left the bench, returned to the courthouse with a horsewhip, and severely beat Crawford about the head and shoulders in front of numerous witnesses. Campbell informed the county sheriff of what he had done and then returned to Richmond on the train to resume his seat in the convention.

When the next session of the General Assembly convened, members of the bar in Amherst County and Lynchburg lodged ten complaints of misbehavior against Campbell. The House of Delegates and the Senate of Virginia found Campbell guilty on four counts of inexcusable impropriety: complicity in the illegal sale of alcohol by a druggist, the assault on Crawford, an attempt to influence the judge whom he thought would try the case of assault, and improperly handling a case involving the issuance of business licenses in the county. By a substantial majority both houses adopted a joint resolution that removed Campbell from office as of 12 May 1903.

In 1890 Campbell had purchased and began publishing the weekly *Amherst New Era,* and his son C. Moncure Campbell joined him as editor in 1906. The elder Campbell once again became sole editor in 1922 and continued in that position until he retired two years later. He was active in the Virginia Press Association and

served as its president in 1910. Campbell also resumed the practice of law for several years after he was removed from the bench. He was elected to one more two-year term in the House of Delegates for the 1922–1923 sessions and was appointed to the Committees on House Expenses, on Retrenchment and Economy, on Special, Private, and Local Legislation, and, ironically, for Courts of Justice.

Sometime after the death of Campbell's wife on 20 November 1917 and before January 1920, he married Minnie Coffey. They had one daughter. Clarence Jackson Campbell suffered a stroke in 1924 or 1925 and died on 25 February 1926 in a Lynchburg hospital. He was buried in the Amherst County Public Cemetery, near the town of Amherst.

Tyler, *Encyclopedia*, 5:745; birth date of 31 May 1863 in Pollard Questionnaires and Mary Frances Boxley, *Gravestone Inscriptions in Amherst County, Virginia* (1985), 236; BVS Marriage Register, Amherst Co., 1884; *Amherst New Era*, 9, 16 May 1901; *Richmond Dispatch*, 12 June 1901, 25–28 June 1902 (quotation in 28 June 1902); *Richmond Times*, 12 June 1901; Election Records, no. 47, RG 13, LVA; *Journal of 1901–1902 Convention*, 487, 504, 535; *Proceedings and Debates of 1901–1902 Convention,* 1:256–259, 1005–1007, 1073–1074, 1087–1088, 1492–1503; *Convention of 1901–1902 Photographs* (por.); Walter A. Watson, *Notes on Southside Virginia*, ed. Mrs. Walter A. Watson and Wilmer L. Hall (1925), 214; *Lynchburg Daily News*, 25 June 1902; *JHD,* 1902–1904 sess., 128–129, 195, 436–443, 447–449, 474–475, 492, 512, 600–607, 638–641, 833–834; *JSV,* 1902–1904 sess., 316, 331–335, 347, 360–361, 479, 489–490, 568–574, 614–615, 649, 651, 677; Campbell's defense printed in *Answer of C. J. Campbell,* Doc. 7, appended to *JSV,* 1902–1904 sess.; BVS Death Certificate, Campbell Co. (with variant birth year of 1862); obituaries in *Richmond News Leader*, 25 Feb. 1926 (por.), and *Lynchburg News* and *Richmond Times-Dispatch*, both 26 Feb. 1926.

BRENT TARTER

CAMPBELL, David (7 August 1779–19 March 1859), governor of Virginia, was born in the part of Washington County that in 1832 became Smyth County, the eldest of eight children of John Campbell and Elizabeth McDonald Campbell. His father was the clerk of Washington County for many years and owned excellent farmland at Hall's Bottom near Abingdon. Nurtured by seven years of education under tutors his father subsidized, Campbell aspired to a career in public service and the economic independence that he believed it required. Throughout his life he advised several of his similarly ambitious younger brothers and assisted in furthering their careers. Edward Campbell served in the Convention of 1829–1830; James Campbell became a prominent attorney and member of the Tennessee legislature; and John Campbell (d. by 29 January 1867) served on the Council of State and as United States treasurer.

Campbell began studying law in 1800 under an uncle in eastern Tennessee, but on 15 May of that year he married his cousin Maria (Mary) Hamilton Campbell and soon returned to Abingdon, where he was his father's deputy in the clerk's office. During the 1810s he traveled and became a successful Abingdon merchant and land investor. Campbell used his political connections to obtain a commission on 6 July 1812 as a major in the 12th Infantry Regiment, United States Army. He spent two winters in camp near the Canadian border and was promoted to lieutenant colonel of the 20th Infantry Regiment on 12 March 1813. Failing to receive a desired posting to Norfolk, Campbell resigned from the army on 28 January 1814 and returned home.

Campbell lost his first campaign for public office, a race for the Senate of Virginia in 1816, but four years later he was elected to represent the state senate district consisting of Lee, Russell, Scott, Tazewell, and Washington Counties. During the first three years of his four-year term Campbell served on the Committee of Privileges and Elections. In all four years he sat on the Committee to Inspect the Manufactory of Arms and the joint Committee for Examining the Treasurer's Accounts. In 1822 he was named to a committee to examine the books of the principal chartered banks in Virginia, in the second and third years to the new Committee of Internal Improvement, in his third and fourth years to the new Committee of Claims, and in his final year to the new Committee on General Laws. He did not seek reelection. Early in 1824 Campbell succeeded his father as county clerk and soon thereafter began construction of Montcalm, a large and handsome house near Abingdon. When he and his wife moved in three years later they took with them several slaves and a new

portrait of Campbell by artist John Wesley Jarvis. They had no children, but they guided the education of several nieces and nephews, some of whom resided with them at Montcalm for extended periods.

Campbell considered himself a Jeffersonian. On their way home from his last session in the state senate in 1824, he and his wife spent several days at Monticello. Campbell rejected the strict Calvinism of the Presbyterian Church in which he had been raised. He was, like Jefferson, a freethinker in religious matters and valued moral action over religious doctrine and ritual. Campbell was also a civic reformer. He made repeated efforts to improve private and public education in Washington County, and he supported projects to develop road and river transportation and construct railroads in the region.

Campbell supported William Harris Crawford for president in 1824, Andrew Jackson four years later and again in 1832, and Martin Van Buren in 1836. As a skilled politician, he and other members of the Campbell family formed durable alliances with eastern Virginia's political leaders, culminating first on 31 January 1834 when the General Assembly elected Campbell a major general of militia and then on 20 January 1837 when it elected him governor of Virginia for a three-year term that began on 31 March of that year.

Campbell and his wife entertained lavishly and often at the Executive Mansion. An able and respected administrator, he urged the assembly to stimulate road and railroad construction in the state with an improvement proposal that would have cost more than $5.1 million. Campbell advocated the creation of a statewide, compulsory school system of 8,000 public schools with 4,000 teachers, each conducting three months of classes at two schools that would be open to all white children, which would have replaced the system that since 1818 had provided only meager educational opportunities to the indigent. The assembly did not support most of his proposals, but it adopted his recommendations to establish in Staunton the Virginia Institution for the Education of the Deaf and Dumb and of the Blind (later the Virginia School for the Deaf and the Blind), to incorporate

Abingdon Female Academy, and to eliminate solitary confinement of prisoners in the State Penitentiary.

Campbell's greatest success came in a crisis he had not expected, brought on by the national economic depression that began about the time he entered office. With gold and silver in short supply, many state-chartered banks refused to redeem paper money with specie, which according to state law meant that some could lose their charters. In 1837 Campbell exercised the governor's rarely used power to call a special session of the assembly. At his suggestion it temporarily suspended the penalties, thus saving the banks and their depositors from financial disaster. The depression that lasted throughout Campbell's term limited the assembly's ability to enact his economic and educational proposals.

Unfortunately for his political future, Campbell's leadership in the banking crisis pulled him into the strong crosscurrents of the evolving Second Party System. Taking his cues from such friends and supporters as his brothers James Campbell and John Campbell, his nephew William Bowen Campbell, then a Whig congressman from Tennessee, and Virginia senator William Cabell Rives, Campbell alienated many of his former allies when in 1838 and 1839 he opposed the fiscal and monetary policies of President Martin Van Buren. Having cut himself off from the mainline Democrats, Campbell joined Rives's conservative Democrats and then moved gradually into the Whig Party by the time his term ended. In the process he lost whatever chance he may have had to be elected to the United States Senate.

In the final months of his term Campbell's wife suffered a serious nervous or mental breakdown that exacerbated domestic tensions in the household between her and the niece who was living with them. Moreover, the family's long periods in Richmond gave the slaves who remained at Montcalm new experiences of autonomy. After Campbell returned to Montcalm in 1840, his life became difficult. His concern about the alcoholism of his brother John Campbell, his slaves' increasingly independent behavior, and his wife's worsening mental con-

dition all made his retirement stressful. Campbell served as a justice of the peace, a local school commissioner, a trustee of both Emory and Henry College and Abingdon Female Academy, and a director of the new Abingdon branch of the Exchange Bank of Norfolk. He enjoyed reading and researching his family's history, and he prepared several biographical memoranda about his own life and the lives of some of his colorful and influential relations.

Plagued by tuberculosis and facial skin cancer in the 1850s, Campbell found his major help not in his relatives but in his household slaves. Although by the mid-1850s his physical weakness and his wife's mental condition rendered his slaves almost independent of his authority, most of them, especially David Bird, gave their infirm and lonely owners the help they needed. In consequence, Campbell freed Bird in his will and left generous bequests to him and several other slaves. Campbell remained interested in politics and denounced what he regarded as the recklessly divisive tactics of some northerners and some southerners over slavery. Believing that southern slavery was ultimately doomed by the progress of liberal democracy, he predicted that southern secession would hasten the institution's destruction. David Campbell died at Montcalm on 19 March 1859 and was buried in the cemetery of Sinking Spring Presbyterian Church near Abingdon. His wife died on 6 October 1859 and was buried beside him.

Birth date in autobiographical letter to Lyman C. Draper, 5 July 1852, Draper MSS, 10DD89, and on gravestone; erroneous 2 Aug. 1779 date in Robert A. Brock, *Virginia and Virginians* (1888), 1:178–180, later copied in some other reference works; Norma Taylor Mitchell, "The Political Career of Governor David Campbell of Virginia" (Ph.D. diss., Duke, 1967); Mitchell, "Making the Most of Life's Opportunities: A Slave Woman and Her Family in Abingdon, Virginia," in *Beyond Image and Convention: Explorations in Southern Women's History*, ed. Janet L. Coryell et al. (1998), 74–98; Campbell Family Papers, Duke (marriage date in David Campbell to Mary Campbell, 15 May 1837); David Campbell Executive Papers, RG 3, LVA; numerous letters in several series, esp. 10DD, in Draper MSS, and in William Cabell Rives Papers, LC; Howard Braverman, "The Economic and Political Background of the Conservative Revolt in Virginia," *VMHB* 60 (1952): 266–287; Anthony F. Upton, "The Road to Power in Virginia in the Early Nineteenth Century," *VMHB* 62 (1954): 259–280; Hummel and Smith, *Portraits and Statuary*, 20 (por.); will and estate inventory in Washington Co. Will Book, 14:402–407, 441–444; death described in William B. Campbell to Lyman C. Draper, 24 May 1859, Draper MSS, 10DD97; obituaries in *Daily Richmond Enquirer* and *Richmond Daily Dispatch,* both 24 Mar. 1859.

NORMA TAYLOR MITCHELL

CAMPBELL, Edmund Douglas (12 March 1899–7 December 1995), attorney, was born on the campus of Washington and Lee University in Lexington, where his father was a professor of geology and later dean of the college. He was the son of Henry Donald Campbell and Martha Miller Campbell and the grandson of John Lyle Campbell, who had also taught geology there for many years. Campbell enrolled in the university at age fifteen and graduated in 1918 as valedictorian of his class. After serving in the army for six weeks at the end of World War I, he continued his education and in 1920 received a master's degree in economics from Harvard University. Campbell then returned to Washington and Lee, where he served as an assistant professor of commerce in 1921–1922 and in 1922 graduated first in his class from the law school.

Ed Campbell, as he was known, was admitted to the bar in Washington, D.C., in 1921 and opened a law practice there. On 15 August 1925 he married Esther Anne Butterworth, in Arlington County, where they lived and had one son and one daughter before her death on 2 July 1934. On 16 June 1936 in Winston-Salem, North Carolina, Campbell married Margaret Elizabeth Pfohl, daughter of a Moravian bishop and at that time the dean at Mary Baldwin College in Staunton. They had twin sons in 1941.

Campbell entered politics in 1936 when he won election to the Arlington Public Utilities Commission, of which he became chair. Arlington was then making a transition from a traditional northern Virginia county to a middle-class suburb of Washington, D.C. Thousands of civil servants, drawn by the expansion of federal agencies, moved into Arlington. Their demands for improved services, especially in public education, inevitably clashed with the low-tax, minimal government views of the Democratic Party's controlling faction under the leadership of Harry Flood Byrd (1887–1966). Promising to address the needs of the county's new resi-

dents, Campbell won election to the Arlington County board of supervisors in 1940. He served on the board, including two one-year terms as chair, until 1946. Campbell also took a leading role in forming the nonpartisan civic association Arlingtonians for a Better County. In 1947 the General Assembly granted Arlington the right, unique in Virginia at that time, to elect members of its school board. Elizabeth Campbell, who became her husband's full partner in public life, ran successfully in the first school board election in November of that year. She served from 1948 to 1956 and again from 1960 to 1962.

When the growth of Arlington and its neighboring localities resulted in the creation of a new, tenth congressional district for Virginia, Campbell sought the 1952 Democratic nomination for the seat. After defeating a Byrd organization candidate in the primary, Campbell ran in the general election without the organization's backing and lost by a narrow margin to Republican Joel Thomas Broyhill. Campbell's greatest influence on public policy in Virginia came in the years following the Supreme Court's 1954 ruling in *Brown* v. *Board of Education* that mandatory racial segregation in public education was unconstitutional. Acting in compliance with the Court's 1955 implementation decree, the Arlington school board, chaired by Elizabeth Campbell, prepared a plan for gradual desegregation. In March 1956 members of the General Assembly angrily denounced the plan and passed a bill terminating the right of the county's citizens to elect school board members.

Later that year the assembly adopted a Massive Resistance plan designed to block any desegregation of the public schools. Its centerpiece was a series of laws requiring the governor to close any public school under a federal desegregation order and to cut off all state funds for the school's operation should the locality try to reopen it. The Campbells were among the people in Northern Virginia most active in organizing effective political opposition to Massive Resistance. In April 1958 they helped organize the Arlington Committee to Preserve Public Schools, which rapidly grew to 4,300 members by November of that year. Campbell opposed segregation, but he and his wife agreed that as a tactical measure it was prudent to limit committee membership to whites. The committee framed the question before the public not in emotional terms of segregation versus integration but as a choice between Massive Resistance and preserving the public schools.

Arlington was spared any school closings because a federal judge delayed desegregation there until 1959. Two other federal judges, however, issued desegregation orders for nine schools in the cities of Charlottesville and Norfolk and in Warren County, after which the governor enforced the school-closing statutes. The closing of Norfolk's public white secondary schools idled 10,000 students and led parents to organize the Norfolk Committee for Public Schools, modeled on the Arlington committee. The Norfolk group tried to enlist a local attorney to bring suit in federal court to reopen the schools. Unsuccessful in their efforts, they asked Campbell, who agreed on the condition that Norfolk attorney Archie L. Boswell would assist him. The three-judge federal panel hearing the case set aside the suit filed by attorneys for the African American students in favor of the plaintiffs Campbell and Boswell represented. The Norfolk city council then voted to cut funds for all public African American secondary schools, thus shutting another 7,000 students out of school. Campbell successfully obtained an injunction from federal judge Walter Edward Hoffman to block the board's decision. In addition to the legal action, Campbell sought to expand his Arlington committee strategy by joining with others to form the Virginia Committee for Public Schools. On 19 January 1959 the federal court in *James* v. *Almond*, the case Campbell had argued, ruled that the school-closing laws were unconstitutional, and on the same day the state's highest court found that those laws violated the Virginia constitution. Massive Resistance was thus legally defeated.

In 1962 Campbell brought suit in federal court on behalf of Northern Virginia legislators and voters who contended that their region and the cities in the lower Tidewater area were underrepresented in the reapportionment of the General Assembly adopted that year. He again united legal and political action to effect signif-

icant change that shifted legislative strength from the rural areas that had supported Massive Resistance to the urban areas that had accepted desegregation and favored a more active state government. Following a victory by Campbell in the three-judge district court, Virginia appealed the decision to the United States Supreme Court. The Court joined the Virginia case, *Davis* v. *Mann,* with five other cases and in its 1964 decision in *Reynolds* v. *Sims* agreed with Campbell's argument that the standard of "one person, one vote" applied to apportionment of state legislative seats as well as to congressional districts.

Campbell practiced law for another quarter century with his Washington firm of Douglas, Obear, and Campbell and later Jackson and Campbell. He served for a time on the Board of Governors of the American Bar Association and in 1961 and 1962 was president of the Bar Association of the District of Columbia. Campbell became legal counsel for Mary Baldwin College. He sat on its board from 1942 to 1976 and acted thereafter as an associate trustee and later trustee emeritus until his death. Campbell was always helpful to young attorneys, and his sympathy for them was institutionalized at Washington and Lee University with the Edmund D. Campbell Public Interest Loan Fund to assist graduates of the law school in repaying their educational loans. Campbell's wife was active in many educational and civic organizations in Arlington and the District of Columbia and was a founder and one of the most influential officers of the capital's educational television station, WETA. Both earned many honors during their careers, and in 1989 both received honorary doctorates from Washington and Lee.

In 1994 Campbell published *Musings of a 95 Year Old*, a short book of essays that explained his commitment to social issues within the larger context of his religious and ethical values. Edmund Douglas Campbell died at his home in Arlington on 7 December 1995 and was buried in the Stonewall Jackson Memorial Cemetery in Lexington.

Family information supplied by widow, Elizabeth P. Campbell, and son Benjamin P. Campbell; BVS Marriage Register, Arlington Co., 1925; *Washington Post*, 17 June 1936;

some letters in Archie L. Boswell Papers, Old Dominion University; James H. Hershman Jr., "Massive Resistance Meets Its Match: The Emergence of a Pro–Public School Majority," in *The Moderates' Dilemma: Massive Resistance to School Desegregation in Virginia,* ed. Matthew D. Lassiter and Andrew B. Lewis (1998), 104–133; feature articles in *Washington Post,* 1 Feb. 1984, 13 June 1991, 11 Dec. 1995, and *Washington Times,* 12 Dec. 1995; obituaries in *Washington Post,* 9 Dec. 1995, *New York Times,* 10 Dec. 1995, *Washington Times,* 11 Dec. 1995, *Lexington News-Gazette,* 13 Dec. 1995, and *Washington and Lee University Alumni Magazine* 70 (winter 1996): 47; editorial tributes in *Arlington Journal* and *Washington Times,* both 12 Dec. 1995, *Richmond Free Press,* 14–16 Dec. 1995, and *Washington Post,* 17 Dec. 1995; memorial in *Washington and Lee Law Review* 53 (1996): 1211–1227 (por. on 1210).

JAMES H. HERSHMAN JR.

CAMPBELL, Edmund Schureman (28 October 1884–8 May 1950), architect, was born in Freehold, New Jersey, the son of James Wall Schureman Campbell and Mary Valentine Campbell. He studied architecture at the Massachusetts Institute of Technology and received a B.S. in 1906 and an M.S. the next year. Campbell traveled in Europe from 1911 to 1912 and studied architecture at the École des Beaux-Arts in Paris. He taught in Pittsburgh at the Carnegie Institute of Technology (later Carnegie Mellon University) from 1912 until 1914, when he became the head of the architecture department at the Armour Institute of Technology (later the Illinois Institute of Technology), in Chicago. In 1918 Campbell married Catherine McEnerny. They had three sons.

From 1924 to 1927 Campbell was dean of the Beaux Arts Institute of Design in New York City. In the latter year he moved to Virginia as the fourth head of the division of art and architecture at the University of Virginia's McIntire School of Fine Arts. Under his leadership during the ensuing twenty-three years the school grew from a three-member faculty to a ten-member department and gained a reputation as one of the premier schools for the study of architectural history in the South. Campbell added courses in drawing and design, offered a class in measured drawings, and encouraged students to document historic structures in Virginia. Adapting methods that originated at the École des Beaux-Arts and the Beaux Arts Institute of Design, he continued a curriculum that included projects and competitions. The university's students participated in a competition that the New York institute conducted, in which the best student received a scholarship that permitted him to attend the École des Beaux-Arts and take an architectural tour of Europe.

Campbell was recognized as a leading critic of architecture and became an expert on the architecture of Thomas Jefferson. He was also an accomplished watercolor painter whose works were exhibited nationally and featured in a 1922 exhibition at the American Academy of Fine Arts. Campbell served as the curator of the university's art collection and designed the Thomas H. Bayly Memorial Museum of Art, which opened in 1935. The art and architecture school also remodeled and enlarged its home, Fayerweather Hall, in 1938. Campbell simultaneously was an active architect who left his mark on the University of Virginia and the Charlottesville area. In 1929 he designed the remodeling of Thomas Jefferson's Farmington into a country club, and for the university grounds he participated with other architects in the design of the Monroe Hill dormitories and Monroe Hall (both 1929), Scott Stadium (1931), the Clark Memorial Hall law school building (1932), and the Lady Astor squash courts (1937). At the time of his death Campbell was serving as a consulting architect for the enlargement and remodeling of the university's Alumni Hall.

Campbell was a member of the American Institute of Architects, the Virginia state examining board for architects, the Virginia Art Commission, and the Water Color Society of Virginia. During his service on the architectural advisory board of Colonial Williamsburg, Inc., his desire to produce aesthetically pleasing designs regardless of surviving architectural evidence placed him in conflict with other board members, especially over the restoration of the College of William and Mary's main building. Edmund Schureman Campbell died on 8 May 1950 at the Mayflower Hotel in Washington, D.C., where he was attending a meeting of the American Institute of Architects. In 1970 the University of Virginia opened a new building for the School of Architecture and named it Campbell Hall in his honor.

Wells and Dalton, *Virginia Architects*, 65; Edmund S. Campbell Papers and some architectural drawings in various collections, UVA; Douglas McVarish et al., "The History of Architectural Education at the University of Virginia," *Colonnade: The Newsjournal of the University of Virginia School of Architecture* (summer 1988, winter 1989, and summer–autumn 1989); Virginius Dabney, *Mr. Jefferson's University: A History* (1981), 360, 362, 573, 574; William B. O'Neal, *Pictorial History of the University of Virginia*, 2d ed. (1976), 50, 128, 130, 131, 167, 186; Susan Tyler Hitchcock, *The University of Virginia: A Pictorial History* (1999), 113, 194, 195 (por.); K. Edward Lay, "Charlottesville's Architectural Legacy," *Magazine of Albemarle County History* 46 (1988), 62, 64, 77, 78; Lay, *The Architecture of Jefferson Country: Charlottesville and Albemarle County, Virginia* (2000), 142, 184, 282, 284, 286, 290, 292, 293; Charles B. Hosmer Jr., *Preservation Comes of Age: From Williamsburg to the National Trust, 1926–1949* (1981), 37, 39, 545, 551, 899, 910, 966–970; Edward A. Chappell and Mark R. Wenger, "Fiske Kimball and Colonial Williamsburg," *Colonial Williamsburg Research Review* 6 (1995/1996): 14–17; obituaries in *Charlottesville Daily Progress*, 9 May 1950, *New York Times*, *Richmond Times-Dispatch*, and *Washington Post*, all 10 May 1950, and *University of Virginia Alumni News* 38 (May 1950): 1, 24.

BRYAN CLARK GREEN

CAMPBELL, Edward (1781–25 February 1833), member of the Convention of 1829–1830, was born at Hall's Bottom near Abingdon in Washington County, the son of John Campbell and Elizabeth McDonald Campbell. A member of a close-knit family, he was a younger brother of David Campbell, elected governor of Virginia in 1837, and an elder brother of John Campbell (d. by 29 January 1867), a member of the Council and treasurer of the United States. Assisted and advised by David Campbell, he attended various schools in and around Abingdon before entering Washington Academy in Lexington (later Washington and Lee University). After completing his education, Campbell returned to Abingdon and began the practice of law. On 25 February 1813 he married Rhoda Trigg. Their three daughters and six sons included John Arthur Campbell, a member of the Convention of 1861, and Joseph Trigg Campbell, a member of the Convention of 1867–1868.

Although several of his brothers became active in politics, Campbell generally seemed content to remain in Washington County and advise them. In 1813, however, he ran for the House of Representatives as a Republican but lost to the incumbent Federalist congressman Daniel Sheffey. Campbell was also once considered for a judgeship but was not appointed. Despite these setbacks, his reputation as a lawyer and his family connections helped him become commonwealth's attorney for Lee, Russell, Scott, and Washington Counties.

Aided by a large majority of the votes cast in Washington County, Campbell was one of four delegates elected in the spring of 1829 to represent the district consisting of Lee, Russell, Scott, Tazewell, and Washington Counties in a convention called to revise the constitution of Virginia. During the convention, which met from 5 October 1829 to 15 January 1830, Campbell and his colleagues from the western counties advocated reform of the old constitution to extend the suffrage to all adult white males and to reapportion the General Assembly based on Virginia's white population. As Virginia's population had grown and moved westward, political power under the old apportionment scheme, which allocated two delegates to each county regardless of its population, remained concentrated in the hands of a shrinking minority of the state's population in the Tidewater and Piedmont. Campbell and other supporters of reform contended that the existing apportionment violated republican principles.

A member of the Committee on the Executive Department, Campbell said little in debates, but he was a critical observer of the proceedings. He objected to the choice of the aging James Monroe as president of the convention, believing him to be unfit and incompetent. Campbell conceded that many of the conservatives were able men, but he consistently opposed their proposals, which he believed were all designed to thwart efforts at reform. When the convention passed a revised constitution, which neither extended suffrage nor reapportioned the legislature, Campbell and almost all of the other western reformers voted against it. His constituents in Washington County, however, voted 556 to 175 to ratify the document, which also won approval statewide.

Campbell resumed his duties as commonwealth's attorney, but he was ill during the winter of 1832–1833, and his health took a turn for the worse while attending court business in Scott County in February. Back home at Hall's Bottom, he suffered an attack of inflammatory rheumatism, an ailment from which he had suffered before. The rheumatism attacked his heart, and Edward Campbell died in Washington County on 25 February 1833. He was buried near Abingdon in the cemetery at Sinking Spring Presbyterian Church.

Brief biographies in Lewis Preston Summers, *History of Southwest Virginia, 1746–1786, Washington County, 1777–1870* (1903), 774, and Summers, "The Heart of the Holston Country," Washington County Historical Society of Abingdon, Virginia, *Bulletin* 9 (Apr. 1943): n.p.; birth year and death date in Campbell family Bible records, 1742–1949, Acc. 23395, LVA; Montgomery Co. Marriage Bonds; Campbell Family Papers, Duke (death described in David Campbell to William B. Campbell, 1 Mar. 1833); *Richmond Enquirer*, 23 Apr. 1813, 23 June 1829; *Journal of 1829–1830 Convention*, 297; *Proceedings and Debates of 1829–1830 Convention*, 903; Bruce, *Rhetoric of Conservatism*, 37; Catlin, *Convention of 1829–30* (por.); estate inventory in Washington Co. Will Book, 6:356–358; obituary in *Richmond Enquirer*, 9 Mar. 1833.

TRENTON E. HIZER

CAMPBELL, Elizabeth Henry. See RUSSELL, Elizabeth Henry Campbell.

CAMPBELL, Graham Cox (9 November 1847–2 December 1915),

Presbyterian missionary and educator, was born in Middle Stewiacke, Colchester County, Nova Scotia, the son of Henry M. Campbell and Eleanor C. Rutherford Campbell. Little is recorded about his life until 1869, when he immigrated to the United States. Campbell received a B.A. from the University of Minnesota in 1877 and an M.A. from the same institution in 1880. In the latter year he also graduated from Auburn Theological Seminary in New York and was ordained by the Presbytery of Saint Paul. On 17 August 1880 Campbell married Laura A. Kreis, of Monticello, Minnesota. They had three sons and two daughters.

Campbell and his wife embarked on careers as missionaries soon after their marriage. The Board of Foreign Missions of the Presbyterian Church in the U.S.A. assigned them to the mission at Baraka on the Gabon River in West Africa, which they reached in January 1881.

Campbell had responsibility for the boys' school at the mission, was superintendent of the Sunday school, preached every other Sunday, and in December of that year became treasurer for the mission. A severe illness in 1883 forced him to return to the United States to recuperate. After resuming his work on the Gabon, Campbell was stricken with a near-fatal fever and forced to end his career as a foreign missionary. He returned home, and by May 1887 the mission board had accepted his resignation.

For the next three years Campbell worked in Arkansas as a school superintendent for the Presbyterian Board of Missions for Freedmen. In 1890 the board sent him to Virginia as president of Ingleside Seminary, one of three educational institutions for African American girls that the board sponsored in the South. A tuition-free school in Amelia County, Ingleside had its roots in the earliest attempt by the northern Presbyterian Church to educate southern blacks. In 1864 Samantha Jane Neil had started a school for children and adults under a large oak tree in Amelia Court House. When Campbell arrived the need for a larger school to accommodate the many girls seeking an education at Ingleside was evident. In 1891 the board began construction of a new facility in Burkeville, which had the advantage of being at the junction of the Norfolk and Western Railroad and the Richmond and Danville Railroad. The new Ingleside Seminary opened in October 1892 with ninety students.

Girls from as far away as New Jersey and New York undertook a five-year program of Bible studies, a liberal-arts curriculum including American history, English literature, languages, mathematics, and music, and practical classes in cooking, housekeeping, and sewing. The Presbyterian Church emphasized the evangelical nature of its schools but realized that religious instruction was more valuable when combined with a strong education. On 23 May 1906 a fire destroyed Ingleside, but the missions board built a new and larger brick school, which opened in October 1907. By 1914 Campbell's dedication to offering quality education had won the institution accreditation from the Virginia State Board of Education, which meant that the school's graduates could receive teaching certificates without taking an examination. Ingleside then had a faculty of about fifteen and more than one hundred students.

On the evening of 2 December 1915 Campbell and two students entered an outbuilding to inspect the malfunctioning acetylene gas plant used for lighting the school. One of the students carried a lantern, which ignited the gas and caused an explosion. Graham Cox Campbell and the student carrying the lantern were killed. Campbell's widow served as acting superintendent until the board appointed a successor. Ingleside Seminary continued operating until the 1930s, when the Great Depression forced many northern churches to eliminate their schools in the South.

Edgar Sutton Robinson, ed., *The Ministerial Directory of the Ministers in "The Presbyterian Church in the United States" (Southern), and in "The Presbyterian Church in the United States of America" (Northern)* (1898), 1:199; marriage verified by Office of County Auditor-Treasurer, Wright Co., Minn.; Board of Foreign Missions of the Presbyterian Church in the U.S.A., *Annual Reports* (1881–1887); *Woman's Work for Woman: A Union Magazine* 12 (1882): 121–122, 182–183; Ingleside Seminary *Catalogues*, 1892/1894, 1897/1898, 1913/1916; seminary mentioned often in church and missionary publications, esp. *Assembly Herald, Church at Home and Abroad,* and *Home Mission Monthly*; Census, Nottoway Co., 1900, 1910; BVS Death Certificate, Nottoway Co., giving birth date; obituaries in *Richmond Planet,* 4 Dec. 1915, and *Farmville Herald,* 10 Dec. 1915; memorial in *Assembly Herald* 22 (1916): 410; account of explosion and memorial in Ingleside Seminary, *Catalog* (1913/1916), 37–38, 39–40 (por. on 8).

MARIANNE E. JULIENNE

CAMPBELL, Henry Wood (9 July 1866–31 March 1931), dentist, was born in Amherst County, the son of Thomas Horace Brown Campbell, a farmer and Methodist minister, and Henry Virginia Wood Campbell. Educated in the local public schools and by private tutors, he entered the University of Maryland in Baltimore and on 13 March 1889 graduated with a D.D.S. Campbell then moved to Suffolk and began his professional practice. On 4 June 1895 his father officiated in Suffolk when Campbell married Emmeline Eley. Their two daughters and two sons included Thomas Wood Campbell, who also became a dentist and practiced with him in Suffolk.

H. Wood Campbell was active in the dental profession throughout his career. Soon after beginning his practice he joined the Virginia State Dental Association and was president in 1894 and 1895. In 1896 Campbell was appointed to the State Board of Dental Examiners (later the State Board of Dentistry). He was president of the board from 1901 to 1916. After a brief absence he was a member again from 1919 until his death and served as president from 1921 to 1931. Campbell served one term as president of the National Association of Dental Examiners, in 1905–1906. As an informal mentor to younger members of the profession, he earned the nickname Big Chief.

Committed to establishing and maintaining high standards in the profession, Campbell sat in 1907 on a committee of the Virginia State Dental Association charged with securing the passage of a law to require students to obtain a medical degree before entering dental school. The General Assembly passed such a bill in 1910, but before it was scheduled to take effect in 1914 the assembly replaced it with a law requiring aspiring dentists to obtain a degree from an accredited dental school before being permitted to take the examinations administered by the state board of examiners. As chair of the society's legislative committee in 1915, Campbell presented a proposal to have a dental representative on the State Board of Health, a suggestion that won legislative approval the following year. Prohibition was then in effect in Virginia, and Campbell's legislative committee also lobbied successfully to have the law changed to ensure that dentists were not denied access to ethyl or grain alcohol for use in their practices.

Campbell urged dentists to take a strong interest in scientific research. At the 1914 meeting of the Southern Branch of the National Dental Association he stated, "Preventive medicine is occupying the minds of the medical profession today, and should take a firmer hold of the dental profession. . . . If more of us engaged in scientific research, we would make more rapid strides."

Campbell was president of Suffolk's town council from 1903 to 1907 and was president of the Suffolk city council from 1913 to 1915. During World War I he served on the local draft board's medical advisory panel. Campbell was president of the Suffolk Mutual Building and Loan Association during the 1920s, a director of the American Bank and Trust Company in Suffolk, and a member and sometime president of the Suffolk Chamber of Commerce. He sat on the board of Main Street Methodist Church, was active as a Freemason, and served as president of the Lions Club. Henry Wood Campbell died on 31 March 1931 after suffering a heart attack at his home in Suffolk and was buried in the city's Cedar Hill Cemetery.

Horace Gibson Campbell, "The Campbell Story: A History of Thomas Horace Brown Campbell and His Descendants" (unpaginated 1970 typescript, LVA), with photograph of family Bible record giving birth date; BVS Birth Register, Amherst Co., gives variant 7 July 1866 birth date; biographies in Eugene Fauntleroy Cordell, *University of Maryland, 1807–1907 . . . with Biographical Sketches and Portraits of its Founders, Benefactors, Regents, Faculty and Alumni* (1907), 2:276, and Philip Alexander Bruce, *Virginia: Rebirth of the Old Dominion* (1929), 3:200–201; BVS Marriage Register, Nansemond Co.; Hermie Wait Powell, ed., *100 Years of Dentistry in Virginia* (1969), 31 (por.), 33–35; *Dental Cosmos: A Monthly Record of Dental Science* 56 (1914): 483 (quotation); Campbell, "The Colleges and the State Boards," ibid. 59 (1917): 629–632; obituaries in *Norfolk Ledger-Dispatch* and *Portsmouth Star*, both 1 Apr. 1931; obituary and editorial tribute in *Suffolk News-Herald*, 1, 2 Apr. 1931; memorials in *Bulletin of the Virginia State Dental Association* 8 (1931): 32–33, 34–36, and *Dental Cosmos: A Monthly Record of Dental Science* 73 (1931): 835.

CAROL ROWLEY

CAMPBELL, Jane Maud (13 March 1869–24 April 1947), librarian, was born near Liverpool, England, the daughter of George Campbell and Jane Cameron Campbell. Her parents were natives of Scotland who met in Petersburg, where her mother's brothers, Alexander Cameron and William Cameron, were prominent tobacco manufacturers and merchants. When the Civil War began the family moved to Great Britain, where Jane Maud Campbell was born. Following the death of Campbell's mother on 19 July 1870, her father on 28 August 1873 married Rosalie Higgenbotham, of Richmond. Campbell's father declared bankruptcy in 1879, sold his English properties, and returned to Virginia. Campbell attended school in Rich-

mond for a year before her father sent her and her sister to Scotland to continue their education at the Ladies' College of the University of Edinburgh. Campbell dropped her first name in favor of Maud, which she regarded as more grown-up but which her family and friends turned into Maudie. As a professional librarian, she identified herself as J. Maud Campbell. The sisters returned to the United States about 1887, and Campbell worked with her father as he struggled to make a success in Burkeville, in Charles Town, West Virginia, and in East Orange, New Jersey.

In 1901 Campbell became an assistant in the reference room of the Newark Public Library. The director, Frank P. Hill, and his successor in 1902, John Cotton Dana, a leading advocate of public access to books and information, recognized Campbell's talent and encouraged her to involve the library in the community through traveling libraries and deposit stations. In October 1902 she became library director in Passaic, New Jersey, a small, heavily industrial city with a large immigrant population. Following Dana's example Campbell made the library an information center for immigrants unfamiliar with the language and customs of their new country and equipped the library with books in the languages—eleven of them in addition to English—spoken by the library's patrons. Her work, which she described in public addresses and in the professional literature, helped alert the American Library Association to the need for adding books in foreign languages to public library collections. With help from local informants Campbell contributed select bibliographies of books in Hungarian and Russian to the association's Foreign Book List series.

Campbell also organized an evening school at her library to teach English to adults. The school charged tuition, but she was convinced that adult immigrants should have the same tuition-free public education as their children and persuaded the state's governor of the value of evening schools. On 10 April 1906 he appointed Campbell one of the three members of the New Jersey Immigration Commission. She was the first woman to serve on a

New Jersey state commission. It recommended legislation to establish statewide adult evening schools, and Campbell used her contacts with immigrant organizations to lobby successfully for the bill's passage.

In May 1910 Campbell became director of educational programs for the North American Civic League for Immigrants, in New York City. She experimented with textbooks in foreign languages and with educational motion pictures to teach immigrant workers about their jobs. Campbell made a special effort to develop educational opportunities for immigrant women in settings where they would hear spoken English. On 2 September 1913 the Free Public Library Commission of Massachusetts hired her as its first agent for library work for alien residents. Within two years Campbell established sixty traveling libraries in foreign languages and in English for beginners and traveled the state to encourage public libraries to serve non-English-speakers. Her father lived with her in Brookline from 1914 until his death in December 1917.

Despite Campbell's development of a highly regarded program for library service to immigrants, her salary remained unchanged after eight years. By 1921 she was looking for another position, preferably nearer her relatives in Virginia and West Virginia. The trustees of the Jones Memorial Library, in Lynchburg, sought a director, and in September 1921 Campbell expressed her interest in the job. Mary Frances Watts Jones, who had established and operated the George M. Jones Memorial Library to honor her husband, a wealthy businessman, had died on 14 October 1920, leaving all her property, valued at about $500,000, to the library. The trustees interviewed Campbell on 5 November 1921 and offered her the position of director two days later.

Campbell began work in January 1922. By February she had gotten repairs to the plumbing and wiring under way and was planning a series of public concerts and lectures at the library. In March she began organizing a branch library at Fort Hill, which opened on 8 May 1924, and a year later Campbell arranged for another branch library to be housed at the new Dunbar High School for African Americans. She hired Anne Spencer, a poet later associated with the Harlem Renaissance, who directed the library until the branch closed in 1946. By 1931 the Jones Memorial Library supported three branch libraries and two deposit stations.

Campbell took part in the reorganization of the moribund Virginia Library Association in Richmond on 28–29 November 1922. The members elected her the association's representative to the Southeastern Library Association. Elected VLA's first vice president for 1923–1924, Campbell with the association's support drafted legislation compelling the boards of supervisors of Virginia's counties to establish free public libraries. She convinced her state senator, Alfred Dickinson Barksdale, to introduce the bill in 1924. Barksdale consulted with other legislators and with the state librarian Henry Read McIlwaine and on their advice revised the bill to make it permissive rather than mandatory. The bill passed but had little effect. During its first five years only one new county public library, made possible by a private gift, was established. Campbell was elected president of the Virginia Library Association for 1924–1925 and served again as first vice president in 1933–1934.

The Great Depression had a severe effect on Virginia public libraries and on the private endowment of the Jones Memorial Library. In January 1933 the trustees reduced staff salaries and directed Campbell to cut operating expenses. Salaries did not return to 1932 levels until 1937. After a dip in the mid-1930s, circulation of library materials rose and peaked at 346,890 in 1940 (compared to 32,398 in 1921). When staff members entered government service during World War II, the depleted endowment contained no funds to hire replacements. Late in 1943 the library requested that the school board cover half the salaries of the branch librarians, and two years later Campbell recommended that the branch libraries be closed at the end of the current school year. With services curtailed at the branch libraries and the deposit stations closed to save money, circulation of library materials declined every year after 1940 and fell to 158,511 in 1946.

On 9 December 1946 Campbell submitted her resignation because of ill health. The trustees asked her to continue, working the hours that she chose, until a successor could be found. In January 1947 the trustees agreed to a pension of $75 a month from 1 February, when Campbell formally retired, until 31 December "or until further notice." She never married but enjoyed a close relationship with her younger relatives, among them the architect Thomas Tileston Waterman, who designed her house in Lynchburg, and two great-nieces, who attended Randolph-Macon Woman's College in that city. Jane Maud Campbell died of bladder cancer on 24 April 1947. She was buried in Spring Hill Cemetery in Lynchburg two days later, and the Jones Memorial Library closed in her honor. Campbell had been a pioneering leader in the national expansion of public library services to all members of the community, but her turn to service at a small city library in Virginia caused the wider profession almost to forget her. In Lynchburg, however, as the library's trustees put it, "she was more than a librarian; she personified the institution."

Fay Campbell Reed Kaynor, "'A Most Progressive Woman': Lynchburg's Librarian Jane Maud Campbell (1869–1947)," *Randolph-Macon Woman's College Alumnae Bulletin* 80 (Dec. 1986): 16–19, 50–51 (pors. on 16, 17, 51); Plummer Alston Jones Jr., *Libraries, Immigrants, and the American Experience* (1999), 40–62 (por. on 38); Jane Maud Campbell Papers, Schlesinger Library, Radcliffe Institute, Cambridge, Mass.; George M. Jones Library Association Record Book, 1921–1930, and Minute Book 2 (quotations on 164, 176), Jones Memorial Library, Lynchburg; Virginia Library Association Records, LVA; *Lynchburg News*, 20 July 1923; *Lynchburg Daily Advance*, 8 Jan. 1947; Campbell's publications include "The Small City Library," *Library Journal* 28 (July 1903): 50–52, "Supplying Books in Foreign Languages in Public Libraries," 29 (Feb. 1904): 65–67, "What the Foreigner Has Done for One Library," 38 (Nov. 1913): 610–615, "The Public Library and the Immigrant," *New York Libraries* 1 (1908): 100–105, 132–136, *Selected List of Hungarian Books* (1907), and *Selected List of Russian Books* (1916); obituaries and editorial tributes in *Lynchburg Daily Advance*, 24, 25 Apr. 1947, and *Lynchburg News* and *Richmond Times-Dispatch*, both 25 Apr. 1947.
JOHN T. KNEEBONE

CAMPBELL, John (1705–1782). See **LOUDOUN, John Campbell, fourth earl of.**

CAMPBELL, John (d. 19 October 1799), a founder of Louisville, Kentucky, was born probably in County Tyrone, Ireland, the son of Allan Campbell, later identified as of the town of Strabane in that county. Campbell's father married at least twice, but the name of Campbell's mother is not known. Campbell was born probably during the mid- or late 1730s, and he was probably still young when he arrived in North America to serve as a messenger on the staff of Major General Edward Braddock during the latter's expedition against Fort Duquesne from February to July 1755. Campbell remained in Pennsylvania after the conclusion of that ill-fated campaign and by 1758 was living at Fort Pitt. During the next two decades he worked in Pittsburgh for several firms, most based in Philadelphia and involved in the western trade. He also clerked and performed surveying work for George Croghan, who conducted an extensive trade with the tribes in the Ohio Valley. One or more of Campbell's brothers and a sister eventually joined him in the New World. Campbell seems never to have married.

Campbell provisioned Virginia militia units in the West and in 1774 received a commission from the governor of Virginia as a justice of the peace for the district of West Augusta County. He was elected to the West Augusta County Committee of Correspondence on 16 May 1775 and sided with the Virginians during protracted disputes over whether Fort Pitt and its fertile surroundings were in Virginia or Pennsylvania. Associated in business and land deals with John Connolly, Campbell was not implicated in Connolly's Loyalist plot when it was discovered late in 1775. On 9 November 1776 Campbell became a justice of the peace and on 4 March 1777 county lieutenant, or commander of the militia, of the new Virginia county of Yohogania.

Late in 1777 when Croghan and several other men with whom Campbell had worked were suspected of Loyalism, Campbell was arrested and briefly jailed. During the summer of 1779 he visited the Falls of the Ohio, where in 1774 he and Connolly had begun investing in land on the south bank of the Ohio River. Because of Connolly's Loyalism, Virginia escheated his land for the site of Louisville. In October 1779 Campbell survived an Indian attack but was taken prisoner by the Shawnee, who turned him over to the British. Described as a "determined avowed Rebel," he was held for three years. Embittered that the Virginians had not freed him sooner, Campbell nevertheless remained loyal to the new state and moved to Louisville, where he served as colonel and quartermaster of George Rogers Clark's Illinois Regiment, Virginia State Forces, and from 1783 to 1792 chaired the local commission for apportioning land granted to the regiment's veterans.

Securing new statutes to strengthen his claim to the land at the falls, Campbell acquired a large amount of property in Kentucky, especially in Jefferson County near Louisville. Possibly hoping to open up more land for acquisition and settlement than was permitted under Virginia's policies, he became a leader in the movement to separate Kentucky from Virginia. After it became clear that if Kentucky became a state it would adhere to Virginia's land policies, Campbell switched to the opposition. He was one of nine delegates from Jefferson County to the first Kentucky Convention that met from December 1784 to January 1785. Campbell withdrew in disgust from the second convention in May 1785 over procedural disputes and his faction's waning control of the separation movement. Campbell represented Jefferson County in the House of Delegates from 1786 to 1788 and again in 1790 and 1791. He served on the drafting committee for the so-called Second Enabling Act that was passed in January 1787 and that in effect delayed the establishment of the new state of Kentucky.

Campbell was a member of Kentucky's 1792 constitutional convention but exerted little influence. Later that year he was elected from Jefferson County to the Senate of Kentucky and sat on the Committee of Propositions and Grievances. By then Campbell was a wealthy man. He served on the Transylvania Seminary's board of directors, and in 1794 Campbell County, Kentucky, was named for him. After moving to Fayette County, where his sister lived and he owned land, he was again elected to the Senate of Kentucky in 1796, and in 1798 he became Speaker of the Senate. John Campbell died suddenly at his Senate desk in the capitol in Frankfort on 19 October 1799. He was buried in an unmarked grave on his Fayette County prop-

erty. Lawsuits resulting from the settlement of his large estate dragged on until 1874.

John Campbell to John Smith and Buchannon, 17 July 1755, in *Minutes of the Provincial Council of Pennsylvania, from the Organization to the Termination of the Proprietary Government* (1851–1852), 6:481; letters and other documents in John Campbell Letters, Frontier Wars Papers, and George Rogers Clark Papers, Draper MSS, printed in part in Reuben Gold Thwaites and Louise Phelps Kellogg, eds., *Revolution on the Upper Ohio, 1775–1777* (1908), and *Frontier Defense on the Upper Ohio, 1777–1778* (1912), Kellogg, ed., *Frontier Advance on the Upper Ohio, 1778–1779* (1916), and James Alton James, ed., *George Rogers Clark Papers* (1912–1926), in Governor's Office, Letters Received, RG 3, LVA, printed in part in *Calendar of Virginia State Papers*, vols. 1, 3, and in Haldimand Manuscripts, British Museum, printed in part in Michigan Pioneer and Historical Society, *Historical Collections* (1892), vols. 19, 20 (quotation on 20:78); *Revolutionary Virginia*, vols. 3–7; Hening, *Statutes*, 7:179, 187, 193, 10:293–295, 11:276–277, 321–322, 12:395–396, 13:310–311; Patricia Watlington, *The Partisan Spirit: Kentucky Politics, 1779–1792* (1972); legal documents and estate settlement papers in George Washington Hull Papers, Filson Historical Society, Louisville, Ky.; Samuel W. Thomas, ed., *Views of Louisville Since 1766* (1971), 12 (por. of doubtful authenticity); wills dated 25 July 1786 and 5 Apr. 1791 in Reuben T. Durrett Collection, Miscellaneous Manuscripts, boxes 4, 5, University of Chicago; death notice in *Lexington Kentucky Gazette*, 24 Oct. 1799.

JAMES RUSSELL HARRIS

CAMPBELL, John (1787 or 1788–by 29 January 1867), member of the Council and treasurer of the United States, was born in Washington County, the son of John Campbell and Elizabeth McDonald Campbell. His extended family was prominent in southwestern Virginia and Tennessee and well connected to eastern Virginia's political leaders. Campbell's father was a well-to-do farmer and the clerk of the county court. His brothers included David Campbell, a governor of Virginia, Edward Campbell, a member of the Convention of 1829–1830, and James Campbell, a prominent attorney and member of the Tennessee legislature. David Campbell served as his principal mentor and helped him obtain an education in the Washington County schools, at the College of New Jersey (later Princeton University), and at Washington College in Lexington (later Washington and Lee University). John Campbell then read law in Staunton with Chapman Johnson.

From a young age Campbell showed exceptional promise in politics. A diligent and insightful student of the American constitutional system, he became an excellent writer and public speaker. After beginning the practice of law in Washington County, Campbell was elected to the House of Delegates in 1810 and reelected in 1811. He served on the Committee of Claims during his first term and on the Committee for Courts of Justice during his second. Early in his second term, on 7 January 1812, the assembly elected Campbell to the Council of State. He completed his term in the House of Delegates and took his seat on the Council on 1 June 1812. Residing in Richmond and working with the state's principal political leaders, Campbell soon became well known among them. He used his political connections to help David Campbell obtain a commission in the United States Army in 1812 and by 1816 sat on the Republican Party's central corresponding committee. Campbell had a good attendance record, but his service as a councillor was irksome and unrewarding both financially and intellectually.

Campbell attended his last Council meeting on 7 July 1817 and soon thereafter left Virginia with his brother James Campbell in search of better opportunities. Campbell purchased land in Alabama and in 1819 served as secretary of the Alabama constitutional convention. His initially bright prospects soon turned bleak. Campbell's Virginia friends were not immediately successful in Alabama politics, his brother declined to practice law with him, his speculative ambitions collapsed in the financial panic of 1819, and he failed in his efforts both to win appointment as Alabama's secretary of state and to persuade President James Monroe to appoint him United States attorney for the state.

After practicing law briefly in Tennessee, Campbell returned to Virginia, where David Campbell, then a member of the Senate of Virginia, helped him get reelected to the Council on 13 January 1821. By then Campbell stated that he could not read without green spectacles and described himself as half blind. He resumed his regular attendance at the Council on 13 June 1821 and served through the end of April 1829. Frustrated in the fulfillment of his ambitions, Campbell found that his service on the Council of State had become not a stepping-stone to a more important political position, as it was for some other young men, but a continuing dead end.

Campbell enjoyed an active social life in Richmond, perhaps too much given his growing addiction to alcohol. He never married. In 1828 new opportunities arose for him when Andrew Jackson, a political ally of the Campbell family since the 1790s, was elected president. In April 1829 Jackson instructed Secretary of State Martin Van Buren to offer Campbell the position of treasurer of the United States, a post with an annual salary of $3,000 and important accounting duties but no policy-making responsibilities. David Campbell, who accompanied him to Washington and assisted in the hiring of his clerks, hoped that in this prestigious and responsible new position his brother would moderate or stop his drinking. Campbell continued his abuse of alcohol, however, which was well known within the administration.

Campbell became increasingly critical of Jackson following the president's removal of government funds from the Second Bank of the United States early in the 1830s. In 1836 he flirted with supporting the presidential candidacy of Senator Hugh Lawson White, of Tennessee, rather than Martin Van Buren, whom the Democratic Party nominated and elected president. In August and September 1837 Campbell published a series of anonymous "Letters from Washington" in the *Richmond Enquirer* criticizing Van Buren's policies. After Congress authorized the printing of $10 million in treasury notes that same year, Campbell admitted that his physical strength and eyesight were unequal to the task of signing his name on the notes. Van Buren suggested that Campbell accept a diplomatic appointment in Colombia, but Campbell angrily rejected the idea. In the spring of 1839 the president and secretary of the treasury finally forced Campbell to resign effective 1 July of that year, ostensibly because of failing health, but undoubtedly because of his drinking and political opposition.

Campbell returned to Washington County and for the next fifteen years supported the Whig Party. The change in party affiliation did his political fortunes no good, and his continued reputation for intemperance rendered futile his and David Campbell's efforts to get him a new appointment in Washington after the Whig victory in the presidential election of 1840 or to get him reelected to the Virginia Council.

Campbell resided for the remainder of his life on his father's former farm in Washington County. From time to time he joined David Campbell at political and internal improvement conventions in southwestern Virginia, and he wrote occasional political pieces for newspapers. Campbell also made several visits to Tennessee, perhaps in search of new opportunities. A restless man, he was often seen riding about Washington County, sometimes for days at a time. Campbell began writing a history of the county, but he may not have completed it, and the manuscript has been lost. Excerpts appeared in Henry Howe's *Historical Collections of Virginia* (1845), and later historians relied on it or copied it without attribution, thus placing Campbell's imprint on the written history of his native county.

Campbell wrote his will on 25 April 1865. Perhaps oblivious to changes then taking place in Virginia, he directed that after his death a nephew free his slave, Richard, if the laws of Virginia would allow Richard to remain in the state as a free man. The outcome of the Civil War had, of course, rendered all these stipulations moot. John Campbell died probably in Washington County sometime late in 1866 or early in 1867, and certainly before 29 January 1867, when his will was proved in the Washington County Court. If he was buried in the family section of the cemetery at Sinking Spring Presbyterian Church near Abingdon, no stone now marks his grave.

Biography in Lewis Preston Summers, *History of Southwest Virginia, 1746–1786, Washington County, 1777–1870* (1903), 792–793 (with 1791 year of birth and por.); Campbell Family Papers, Duke (age given as fifteen in annotation on John Campbell to David Campbell, 25 June 1802); Norma Taylor Mitchell, "The Political Career of Governor David Campbell of Virginia" (Ph.D. diss., Duke, 1967), esp. chaps. 1–2 and pp. 126, 140–141, 213–215, 221–224, 247; Anthony F. Upton, "The Road to Power in Virginia in the Early Nineteenth Century," *VMHB* 62 (1954): 259–280; Campbell letters in William Cabell Rives Papers and Martin Van Buren Papers (including John Campbell to Martin Van Buren, 21 Apr. 1829, accepting treasurer appointment), both LC; *Journal of the Convention of the Alabama Territory Begun July 5, 1819* (1819; repr. 1909); Campbell, "On the Financial and Other Measures of the Administration," 25 Mar. 1840, in Slemp and Preston, *Addresses*, 134–146; Campbell's "historical sketch of Washington county," in Henry Howe, *Historical Collections of Virginia* (1845), 500–506; Washington Co. Minute Book, 17:60–61 (recording will on 29 Jan. 1867); will (with recording date of 28 Feb. 1867) in Washington Co. Will Book, 17:105–106.

NORMA TAYLOR MITCHELL

CAMPBELL, John Arthur (3 October 1823–17 June 1886), member of the Convention of 1861, was born at Hall's Bottom in Washington County, the residence of his parents, Edward Campbell, a member of the Convention of 1829–1830, and Rhoda Trigg Campbell. His uncle David Campbell was governor of Virginia from 1837 to 1840, and his uncle John Campbell (d. by 29 January 1867) was a member of the Council of State and treasurer of the United States. One of his brothers, Joseph Trigg Campbell, was a member of the Convention of 1867–1868.

Campbell was educated at the Abingdon Academy and spent the years 1839 to 1841 at Emory and Henry College. He graduated from the Virginia Military Institute in 1844 as a first captain, fourth in his class, ranking first in both conduct and tactics, and delivered the salutatorian address. After reading law with his brother-in-law Connally Findlay Trigg, he was admitted to the bar in Washington County on 24 August 1846. Campbell moved to Nashville, Tennessee, the following year but remained only briefly before returning to Abingdon, where he began a law practice that lasted off and on for forty-three years. On 19 April 1849 he married Mary Branch, of Washington County. They had no children.

Beginning in the summer of 1849 Campbell helped promote the development of the Virginia and Tennessee Railroad Company, which reached Abingdon in the autumn of 1856, and eventually purchased stock in the company. In 1850 he was elected secretary of the new agricultural society in Washington County. Campbell also served as an officer in the Abingdon division of the Sons of Temperance. In 1851 he ran as a Whig for a seat in the House of Delegates but lost by little more than 100 votes. Supporting a moderate tariff and the democratic reforms embodied in the Virginia Constitution of 1851, Campbell attracted attention as far away as the capital, where the *Richmond Whig and Public Advertiser* touted him as the Whig Party's newest star in Washington County. The following year Campbell attended the state and national Whig Party conventions, but other than serving on the Abingdon town council in 1860 he did not hold public office. He owned eight slaves in 1860.

On 4 February 1861 Campbell was one of two Unionist candidates elected by a large margin to represent Washington County in a state convention called to consider secession. One of the advocates of secession whom he defeated was John Buchanan Floyd, a former governor and secretary of war. Before Campbell departed for Richmond he helped quell a hostile confrontation in Abingdon between advocates and opponents of secession. Campbell served on the convention's Committee on Privileges and Elections and on a special committee chaired by Waitman Thomas Willey to draft an amendment to Virginia's constitution to guarantee equal and uniform taxation throughout the commonwealth, but the convention ignored the proposal. On 4 April 1861 Campbell voted with the majority against secession and later approved a proposal to delay secession long enough to gain the support of the other border states. On 17 April he voted with the majority to adopt the Ordinance of Secession. Campbell returned to Richmond later in the year to attend the third session of the convention in November and December 1861 and then was a member of the Committee of Military Affairs.

In May 1861 while the convention was still in session Campbell began drilling volunteers and recruiting a unit that became the 48th Regiment Virginia Infantry. In spite of objections from Floyd and others based on Campbell's Unionism, the governor appointed Campbell colonel of the regiment. He received his commission on 27 June 1861 and except when attending the convention in November and December commanded the regiment for the remainder of the year. It took part in the war in western Virginia in the summer, served in a supporting role during the Cheat Mountain campaign in the autumn, and was transferred in December 1861 to the command of Thomas J. "Stonewall" Jackson for the expedition to Romney in January 1862. Campbell joined ten other brigade and regimental commanders in petitioning Brigadier General William Wing Loring to remove his army from Romney. Loring bypassed the chain of command to evacuate Romney, and the resulting controversy led to Jackson's temporary resignation.

Campbell and the 48th fought with Jackson in the Shenandoah Valley during the spring. Reelected colonel on 21 April 1862, Campbell was commended for his command of the 2d Brigade at McDowell on 8 May 1862. At Winchester on 25 May he was wounded severely in the right arm while accompanying Jackson on a reconnaissance. Campbell spent several months recuperating and possibly trying to secure a promotion to brigadier general. He resigned his commission on 14 October 1862 after Jackson, perhaps remembering Campbell's earlier support of Loring, chose Lieutenant Colonel John Robert Jones over him to command the 2d Brigade. His resignation was accepted two days later. Although reportedly well liked by his men, Campbell was noted as a hesitant and uncertain leader.

Returning to Abingdon, Campbell helped organize home guard companies and was elected first lieutenant of a unit on 22 June 1863. He lived at Acklin (or Ackland), the home of James C. Greenway, a relative by marriage. In 1864 Confederate cavalry leader John Hunt Morgan used Acklin as his headquarters, and after Morgan was killed early in September of that year his body was placed in the parlor, where hundreds of people paid their last respects.

On 16 October 1862 Campbell won election as judge of the Seventeenth Judicial Circuit, comprising the counties of Lee, Russell, Scott, Smyth, Tazewell, and Washington. In February 1866 Governor Francis Harrison Pierpont nominated and the General Assembly confirmed Campbell as judge of the new Sixteenth Judicial Circuit, which included the counties of the old Seventeenth Circuit plus Bland, Buchanan, and Wise Counties. In May 1867

Campbell presided over a murder case that ended with the first legal execution in Tazewell County. He served until March 1869, when he was removed from office under the authority of a congressional resolution prohibiting former Confederate military officers from holding civil positions in the provisional governments of Virginia and Texas.

Campbell resumed the practice of law. He also enjoyed a longtime association with Emory and Henry College, beginning with service on the school's examining committee from 1855 to 1857. He was a member of the board of visitors in 1865 and 1866 and of the board of trustees from 1866 until his death, including seventeen years as board president and ex-officio president of the joint board (1868–1886). In 1880 Campbell helped reorganize the school faculty. He also was a member and sometime president of the board of trustees for Martha Washington College in Abingdon, a college for women founded by the Holston Conference of the Methodist Episcopal Church. Campbell was on the committee appointed to purchase property for the school, served as president of the first board of trustees when the school opened in 1860, and was credited with proposing the college name. He also sat on the board of Abingdon Male Academy.

After an illness of several months, which included paralysis and the loss of the use of his right arm, John Arthur Campbell died at his home in Abingdon on 17 June 1886. He was buried in the local cemetery at Sinking Spring Presbyterian Church.

Lewis Preston Summers, *History of Southwest Virginia, 1746–1786, Washington County, 1777–1870* (1903), 512–513, 771 (por.); birth, marriage, and death dates in Branch family Bible records, Acc. 23394, LVA; Campbell alumnus file, VMI; *Abingdon Virginian*, 17 Feb., 14 Apr. 1849, 13 Dec. 1851, 3 Jan. 1852, 1 Apr. 1854, 10, 24, 31 Oct. 1862, 26 June, 18 Sept. 1863, 1 Apr. 1864, 2 Mar. 1866; *Abingdon Democrat*, 29 Nov. 1851, 1 May 1852, 8 Feb. 1861; *Richmond Whig and Public Advertiser*, 2 Jan. 1852; Reese and Gaines, *Proceedings of 1861 Convention*, 3:163, 263–264, 4:119–121, 144, 567; May 1861 correspondence file, John Letcher Executive Papers, RG 3, LVA; John D. Chapla, *48th Virginia Infantry* (1989), esp. 97 (por.), 112; Compiled Service Records; *OR,* 1st ser., 2:955–956, 12: pt. 1, 478–480, 767, 769; Campbell to secretary of war, 14 Oct. 1862, Confederate States War Department Records, RG 109, NARA; Washington Co. Will Book, 22:257–259; obituary in *Abingdon Weekly Virginian*, 24 June 1886; memorials in *Abingdon Weekly Virginian*, 1 July 1886, and *Abingdon Southwest Examiner*, 3 July 1886.

DALE F. HARTER

CAMPBELL, John Lyle (7 December 1818– 2 February 1886), geologist and educator, was born at Timber Ridge in Rockbridge County, the son of Robert Smith Campbell and Mary Isabella Paxton Campbell. His father was a farmer, commissary at the Virginia Military Institute, and commissioner of revenue of Rockbridge County. One of his grandfathers helped found Liberty Hall Academy, which became Washington College and later Washington and Lee University. Campbell attended Washington College and received a B.A. in 1843 and an M.A. three years later.

Campbell began teaching at an academy for boys in Staunton shortly after receiving his first degree. Two years later he helped to found the Henry Clay Society, a Staunton debating club, in which he once took the negative side in a public debate on whether slavery was compatible with republican government. On 8 July 1846 in Staunton, Campbell married Harriet Peters Bailey, daughter of Rufus William Bailey, founder of Augusta Female Seminary (later Mary Baldwin College). They had five sons and five daughters. Campbell taught briefly at a boys' school in Richmond, Kentucky, before returning to Virginia in the autumn of 1851 as Robinson Professor of Physical Science at Washington College. He taught chemistry, geology, and mineralogy there until his death thirty-five years later and was one of four faculty members who remained at the college and kept it alive during the Civil War.

Campbell's first major publication was *A Manual of Scientific and Practical Agriculture, for the School and the Farm* (1859), a volume of more than 400 pages. He was active in the Rockbridge Agricultural and Mechanical Society and during 1863 contributed a regular column on agricultural and gardening topics to the *Lexington Gazette*. In December 1864 Campbell became part owner, publisher, and for a time editor of the newspaper. Although he gave up both positions at the beginning of January 1866 at the insistence of the college's trustees, he nevertheless continued to print scientific observations on weather and other topics in the paper. On 1 December 1877 Campbell published in the *Richmond Daily Dispatch* a learned analysis of reports of a bright meteor that flashed across the Virginia sky during the afternoon of 20 November.

Probably at the request of his friend William Henry Ruffner, the first superintendent of public instruction in Virginia, and with the acquiescence of the college's president, Robert Edward Lee, Campbell in 1870 accepted the position of superintendent of the new public school system in Rockbridge County. He held the post for twelve years without relinquishing his professorship at the college. Campbell created a system of free public education for all pupils regardless of race or economic standing. Emphasizing reading as the basis for a good education, he grouped students according to their abilities and regularly evaluated the schools throughout the county, including the controversial Colored Sabbath School that Thomas J. Jackson had founded in connection with the Lexington Presbyterian Church in 1856. Campbell was an elder in the church at that time and held the office until his death.

Following the Civil War Campbell became one of Virginia's best-known and most influential geologists. On his own or in cooperation with other men, among them his son and fellow geologist Henry Donald Campbell, he prepared more than fifty analyses, maps, and reports. Campbell's geological investigations were often associated with construction of railroads in Virginia and elsewhere. Many of them dealt with the geological history and mineral resources of western Virginia. The largest of Campbell's reports on Virginia topics published during the 1870s and 1880s was the 119-page *Geology and Mineral Resources of the James River Valley, Virginia, U.S.A.* (1882). As with the work of other geologists such as Charles Rufus Boyd and the better-known Jedediah Hotchkiss, Campbell added substantially to the scientific record of the region and made practical contributions to the economic exploitation of its resources.

Campbell's eminence made him the natural person to review in 1885 the important posthumous book of his friend and sometime colleague William Barton Rogers, *A Reprint of Annual Reports and Other Papers, on the Geology of the Virginias,* which consisted of the collected pre–Civil War scientific papers of that pioneering Virginia geologist. Campbell's review, written in cooperation with his son Henry Donald Campbell and published in two installments in the *American Journal of Science*, emphasized the importance of Rogers's work and bluntly criticized the General Assembly of Virginia for not following the advice of the Board of Public Works in the 1840s that it publish the reports at that time, when they could have had a beneficial effect. Recognizing that they contained information that still had economic value late in the nineteenth century, Campbell also remarked that Rogers "was laying an important part of the foundation of our grand system of American Geology, the superstructure of which has been in process of erection for half a century and more, and is not yet completed." The practical usefulness and scientific significance that Campbell praised in Rogers's reports also characterized his own work, which was associated with economic development but also employed the latest scientific insights as part of an emerging worldwide literature on geology and geologic history.

Hampden-Sydney College awarded Campbell an honorary LL.D. in 1881. His influence at Washington College (Washington and Lee University after 1871) did not end even with his death. His son John Lyle Campbell (1854–1913) was secretary of the faculty and treasurer of the university from 1877 until 1913, and his son and collaborator Henry Donald Campbell succeeded him as Robinson Professor in 1887 and taught until 1934. For more than eighty years after Campbell joined the faculty, he or one or more of his sons was a man of importance at Washington and Lee.

In 1884 Campbell fell and seriously injured his left arm, which had to be amputated at the elbow. John Lyle Campbell never fully recovered and died at his home in Lexington on 2 February 1886. He was buried in that city in the cemetery at the Lexington Presbyterian Church (later Stonewall Jackson Memorial Cemetery).

Birth date on gravestone; Gerald M. Petty, ed., *Notes on Some Descendants of Duncan Campbell, of Ireland* (1966), I-444; biography and bibliography of geological publications on Virginia topics in Joseph K. Roberts, *Annotated Geological Bibliography of Virginia* (1942), 11, 35–39, 141–148; John Lyle Campbell Papers, Southern Historical Collection, UNC; John Lyle Campbell Papers, MS Memoranda of Proceedings as County Superintendent of Schools for Rockbridge Co., Withrow Scrapbooks, and por., all W&L; *Staunton Spectator, and General Advertiser*, 16 July 1846; Ollinger Crenshaw, *General Lee's College: The Rise and Growth of Washington and Lee University* (1969), 88–89, 133–135, 140, 231, 241; Rockbridge Retired Teachers Association, *A Brief History of Public Education in Rockbridge County, Lexington, Buena Vista, 1748–1980* (1980), 27–33, 50–51; *American Journal of Science*, 3d ser., 30 (1885): 357–374 (quotation on 359), and 31 (1886): 193–202; obituaries in *Lexington Gazette*, 4 Feb. 1886, *Lexington Rockbridge County News*, 5 Feb. 1886, and *Harrisonburg Rockingham Register*, 11 Feb. 1886; account of funeral and editorial tribute in *Lexington Gazette*, 11, 18 Feb. 1886.

MARGARET R. RHETT

CAMPBELL, Joseph Trigg (28 November 1827–16 April 1876), member of the Convention of 1867–1868, was born in Washington County, the son of Edward Campbell, who served in the Convention of 1829–1830, and Rhoda Trigg Campbell. His brother John Arthur Campbell represented Washington County in the Convention of 1861, and his uncles included David Campbell, governor of Virginia, and John Campbell (d. by 29 January 1867), who twice sat on the Council of State and served as treasurer of the United States. He grew up at Hall's Bottom in Washington County, in the large brick house his father had built near the log cabin in which his grandfather had lived when he first settled in the region in the 1770s. Campbell was educated at the Abingdon Male Academy and from 1846 to 1848 studied law at the University of Virginia.

Admitted to the bar in 1849, Campbell practiced law in Abingdon during the 1850s. On 8 October 1856 he married Mary Campbell Preston, who also lived in Abingdon. They had two sons and two daughters. Shortly after Virginia seceded from the Union, Campbell became a first lieutenant on 22 April 1861 and six weeks later was made adjutant of the 37th Regiment Virginia Infantry. After an attack of what was called "camp fever" produced an atrophy of the muscles in his left shoulder, he resigned on 22 March 1862, returned home, and served from 1863 to 1865 as commonwealth's attorney of Washington County.

In October 1867 Campbell was elected one of two delegates to represent the counties of Smyth and Washington in a convention called to write a new constitution for Virginia. On behalf of the conservative members he opened the convention by nominating Norval Wilson, a Methodist minister and delegate from Frederick County, to be president of the convention, but as anticipated the radicals and reformers elected John C. Underwood instead. Brigadier General John McAllister Schofield described both Campbell and Wilson as unreconstructed Confederates. Campbell sat on the Committee on the Judiciary, excepting County and Corporation Courts. Possibly in poor health during and following the convention, he sometimes did not attend its sessions and seldom spoke during the portion of the convention for which the debates were recorded. Campbell missed a number of the most important votes but when in attendance voted regularly against the reformers. On 17 April 1868 he voted against the constitution that the convention wrote, which was ratified in 1869.

A speech Campbell made on the subject of Freemasonry and education at the laying of the cornerstone for a new building at the Abingdon Male Academy has been printed as representative of his oratory. He wrote his will in July 1871 during a stay at Warm Springs and appointed his wife and two brothers to act as his executors. Joseph Trigg Campbell died in Washington County on 16 April 1876 and was buried in the cemetery at Sinking Spring Presbyterian Church near Abingdon.

Birth and death dates from gravestone as documented in Catherine S. McConnell, *High on a Windy Hill* (1968), 79; Lewis Preston Summers, *History of Southwest Virginia, 1746–1786, Washington County, 1777–1870* (1903), 513, 775 (por.); BVS Marriage Register, Washington Co.; Compiled Service Records; Thomas M. Rankin, *37th Virginia Infantry* (1987), 102; Election Records, no. 427, RG 13, LVA; Hume, "Membership of Convention of 1867–1868," 481; Lowe, "Virginia's Reconstruction Convention," 357; *Debates and Proceedings of 1867–1868 Convention*, 7, 405; *Journal of 1867–1868 Convention*, 389; Slemp and Preston, *Addresses*, 225–233; Washington Co. Will Book, 19:98–99.

MARY B. KEGLEY
BRENT TARTER

CAMPBELL, Preston White (24 January 1874–2 or 3 July 1954), member of the Convention of 1901–1902 and judge of the Virginia Supreme Court of Appeals, was born in Abingdon, the son of Ellen Sheffey White Campbell and Edward McDonald Campbell, a surgeon who served on the staff of Major General James Ewell Brown Stuart during the Civil War. The Campbell, Sheffey, and White families had long and distinguished histories in the law, and the Campbells had been prominent in Washington County since before the American Revolution. Campbell was named for an uncle, John Preston White, who became chief justice of the Texas Court of Appeals. Campbell's father died in 1878, leaving his mother to bring up her eight children.

Campbell was educated at Abingdon Male Academy, where he pitched for the baseball team and played on one of the first rugby teams in southwestern Virginia. He read law in the local office of Francis B. Hutton and was admitted to the bar in 1896. Campbell attended the University of Virginia from 1896 to 1897 but did not graduate. He won a medal for debate and once introduced William Jennings Bryan, who spoke to a large crowd in Charlottesville. Campbell practiced law in Abingdon from 1897 to 1911. On 9 April 1914 he married Louise Elwood Howard, in Lynchburg. They had three sons. Campbell's eldest son and namesake, a member of the United States Army Air Corps during World War II, was killed in 1944 during a bombing mission over Germany.

In May 1901 Campbell was one of two delegates elected to represent the district comprising Washington County and the city of Bristol in a convention called to revise the constitution of Virginia. He was the fifth member of the Campbell family to represent Washington County or its predecessor, Fincastle County, in a state convention since 1776. The youngest delegate at the convention, Campbell served on the Committee on the Bill of Rights. He announced at the beginning of the convention that he would support a provision to depoliticize county school superintendents. Campbell seldom spoke during the convention, but when he did it was on an issue of importance to him or his constituents. He objected to the wording of a clause that would have prevented Bristol from having its own separate courts, and he supported an unsuccessful motion that would have guaranteed a minimum appropriation for the University of Virginia. Campbell also spoke in favor of permitting communities to adopt Prohibition by local option. He voted with the majority on the three most important votes that the convention took: in favor of restrictive suffrage provisions that the convention adopted on 4 April 1902, to proclaim the constitution in effect without submitting it to a ratification referendum, and to adopt the new constitution.

A member in good standing of the dominant faction of the Democratic Party throughout his adult life, Campbell served from 1911 to 1914 as commonwealth's attorney for Washington County. On 25 March 1914 he was appointed to the vacant judgeship of the Twenty-third Circuit, comprising the counties of Scott, Smyth, and Washington, and was subsequently elected to a full term. On 23 January 1924 the Democrats in the General Assembly met to nominate a judge for a vacant seat on the Virginia Supreme Court of Appeals. After seven ballots on which no candidate received a majority, the members united and nominated Campbell by acclamation. The assembly formally elected him without opposition six days later. Campbell qualified for his seat on the bench on 31 January 1924 and began his term the following day. After the death of Chief Justice Robert R. Prentis on 25 November 1931, Campbell as the senior member in continuous service automatically became chief justice. He served as chief justice of the court until he retired on 1 October 1946.

Campbell wrote 528 opinions during his twenty-two years on the Supreme Court of Appeals. Perhaps the most memorable was his vigorous solo dissent in the 1945 case *Staples* v. *Gilmer*. In 1944 the General Assembly had submitted to the voters a proposal for calling a convention to draft an amendment to the state constitution to exempt members of the armed forces from certain voter registration and poll tax requirements. The assembly's proposal restricted the convention to the consideration of that topic only. When a case that reached the Supreme Court of Appeals asked whether the assembly could place limits on a convention, the court upheld the power of the assembly, but Campbell dissented and stated forcefully that the assembly lacked constitutional authority to limit the work of a constituent convention. To support his opinion he quoted extensively from the debates in the Convention of 1901–1902 that he had attended. "It is because of my conscientious conviction that the act in question is subversive of my every concept of democratic principles," Campbell wrote, "that I feel constrained to dissent."

Hampden-Sydney College awarded Campbell an honorary LL.D. in 1939. For many years he was an elder and trustee of Sinking Spring Presbyterian Church in Abingdon. He was also a founder and member of the board of directors of the Historical Society of Washington County. Preston White Campbell died during the night of 2–3 July 1954 in a hospital in Johnson City, Tennessee, and was buried in Knollkreg Memorial Park in Abingdon.

Birth date in Pollard Questionnaires; biographies in *Richmond Times*, 12 June 1901, Tyler, *Men of Mark*, 3:60–62 (giving variant birth date of 4 Jan. 1874), and *Richmond Times-Dispatch*, Sunday magazine section, 9 Feb. 1936; BVS Marriage Register, Lynchburg; Election Records, no. 47, RG 13, LVA; *Proceedings and Debates of 1901–1902 Convention*, 1:230–231, 1476–1477, 2:1718–1719, 2605; *Journal of 1901–1902 Convention*, 487, 504, 535; *Convention of 1901–1902 Photographs* (por.); *Richmond Times-Dispatch*, 24 Jan. 1924; *Richmond News Leader*, 26 Nov. 1931; *Staples* v. *Gilmer* (1945), *Virginia Reports*, 183:613–642 (Campbell's dissent on 632–637, quotation on 633); Hummel and Smith, *Portraits and Statuary*, 21 (por.); death date of 2 July on tombstone inscription printed in Historical Society of Washington County, comp., *High on a Windy Hill, Volume 2: Cemeteries of Washington County, Virginia*, corrected ed. (2000), 167; obituaries giving death date of 3 July in *Bristol Virginia-Tennessean* and *Richmond News Leader*, both 3 July 1954, and *Bristol Herald Courier* and *Richmond Times-Dispatch*, both 4 July 1954; editorial tribute in *Richmond Times-Dispatch*, 6 July 1954; memorial in *Virginia State Bar Association Proceedings* (1954): 121–123 (giving death date of 2 July).

HARRY L. CARRICO

CAMPBELL, Richard (d. 8 September 1781), Continental army officer, was residing in the southern part of Frederick County in 1772 when it became Dunmore County (later Shenandoah County). The date and place of his birth and the names of his parents are unknown. Beginning in the mid-1760s his name appears from time to time in the Frederick County records as a witness to deeds, and in July 1768 he and his wife, Rebecca Campbell, whose maiden name is unrecorded, sold 150 acres of land, situated probably near the site of the town of Woodstock, where they lived and had five sons. In May 1772 Campbell received a license to operate an ordinary at his house. The following month he became a deputy sheriff, with duties such as housing prisoners and maintaining the county jail. Campbell was reappointed on 22 November 1774, and in November of the following year he was instructed to take a census in a district of the county. The incomplete census of Dunmore County is the only known surviving census of a Virginia county from the period.

Events soon overshadowed the daily routine of earning a living and Campbell's duties as a minor county official. In January 1775 the Dunmore County Committee held its first meeting at his tavern. One year later, on about 23 January 1776, the committee chose Campbell and Jonathan Clark to command the two companies of riflemen being recruited in the county for service in the 8th Virginia Regiment, also known as the German Regiment, under the command of Campbell's neighbor John Peter Gabriel Muhlenberg. Clark commanded the company of German-speaking soldiers and Campbell the English-speaking company. Commissioned a captain on 19 February 1776, Campbell marched during the summer to Charleston, South Carolina, but his unit saw no action. General Charles Lee promoted Campbell to major of the regiment, his commission to date from 10 August 1777.

By then Campbell had marched to Pennsylvania, where he probably participated in the Battle of Brandywine on 11 September 1777. On 29 September he was transferred to the 13th Virginia Regiment, and in May 1778 he was ordered to York, Pennsylvania. For the next two and a half years and under a succession of commanders Campbell participated in the defense of western Pennsylvania. Receiving a brevet promotion to lieutenant colonel to rank from 20 February 1778, he was stationed for most of the time at Fort Pitt, but during inconclusive forays by his commanders into the western territory he occasionally commanded small outposts in the upper Ohio Valley. On 14 September 1778 Campbell's regiment was reorganized as the 9th Virginia Regiment under the command of John Gibson.

Frustrated that his severely depleted regiment could do little as a result of expiration of enlistments, and believing that his skills could be put to better use elsewhere, Campbell wrote directly to George Washington on 16 March 1780 requesting a transfer. He explained, "When I Stept forth in the Armey it was my determination to Render my Cuntry Ever Service, In my Power & wish to be allways where i Could take an Active Part, & as there has Been Officers Ordered from Differant Reigts: To Command Troops to the Southward I Should be Glad to meet with the Same Indulgence." On 12 February 1781 Campbell finally received the coveted orders transferring him to the 4th Virginia Regiment and sending him to Virginia. Later that month he led 400 men to North Carolina, where he reported to General Nathanael Greene's headquarters on or about 10 March.

Campbell participated in the last four major engagements of the war in the Carolinas. At Guilford Courthouse in North Carolina on 15 March 1781 his regiment helped inflict heavy losses on the British. At Hobkirk's Hill, near Camden, South Carolina, Campbell was wounded on 25 April as he rallied his men. On 18 June 1781 he and Henry "Light-Horse Harry" Lee (1756–1818) led coordinated attacks on Fort Holmes and on the Star Redoubt near the South Carolina village of Ninety-Six. Campbell's regiment suffered heavy casualties in a gallant, unsuccessful assault on the redoubt. On 8 September 1781 at Eutaw Springs, South Carolina, one of the war's hardest-fought actions, Greene's army was defeated but inflicted such heavy losses on the British army that it withdrew to Charleston, leaving the Carolinas virtually liberated. Richard Campbell was mortally wounded leading a charge that broke a British counterattack. Many years later Lee's son added a footnote to his father's account of Campbell's death. He reported that Campbell lived long enough to learn that the enemy troops were retreating and that his final words, in imitation of

those of General James Wolfe at Quebec in 1759, were "I die contented." Campbell was probably buried near the battlefield. One of his sons was present on the occasion, and a few days later Greene wrote to the governor of Virginia praising Campbell as "a brave, active, and intrepid Soldier."

John W. Wayland, *A History of Shenandoah County, Virginia* (1927), 106, 107, 110, 111; BW; LOMC; census in W. Twyman Williams Collection of Dunmore and Shenandoah Counties Revolutionary War Papers, 1775–1814, LVA, printed in Gaius Marcus Brumbaugh, *Revolutionary War Records: Volume I, Virginia* (1936), 591–593; *Revolutionary Virginia*, esp. 2:228–229, 6:19; Francis B. Heitman, *Historical Register of Officers of the Continental Army during the War of the Revolution*, rev. ed. (1914), 142; E. M. Sanchez-Saavedra, comp., *A Guide to Virginia Military Organizations in the American Revolution, 1774–1787* (1978), 41–43, 55, 56, 60, 68–69; Campbell to George Washington, 16 Mar. 1780, George Washington Papers, LC (first quotation); numerous references and letters in Louise Phelps Kellogg, ed., *Frontier Advance on the Upper Ohio, 1778–1779* (1916), Kellogg, ed., *Frontier Retreat on the Upper Ohio, 1779–1781* (1917), and Richard K. Showman et al., eds., *The Papers of General Nathanael Greene* (1976–   ), vols. 7–9 (third quotation on 9:351); Henry Lee (1756–1818), *Memoirs of the War in the Southern Department of the United States*, 2d ed., ed. Henry Lee (1787–1837) (1827), 162–183, 222, 337–338 (second quotation); Shenandoah Co. Will Book, A:419–420.

Donald W. Gunter

CAMPBELL, Stuart Bland (14 April 1888–17 November 1973), attorney and member of the House of Delegates, was born in Wytheville, the son of Archibald Alexander Campbell, a schoolmaster-turned-lawyer, and Susie Lee Stuart Campbell, a half sister of Henry Carter Stuart, governor of Virginia from 1914 to 1918. At age fourteen Campbell entered Hampden-Sydney College, of which his father was a trustee, and after serving as president of his class graduated in 1906. He taught school in Wytheville before entering the law school of the University of Virginia, from which he graduated in 1910. Campbell returned to Wytheville and began the practice of law in partnership with his father.

In the autumn of 1911 Campbell won election as a Democrat to a four-year term as commonwealth's attorney of Wythe County. From April to December 1912 he was the chief prosecutor in the trials of Floyd Allen and his kinsmen for their parts in a notorious shootout at the

Carroll County courthouse on 14 March 1912. Wythe County juries found Allen guilty of murder in the first degree but settled on lesser sentences for the others. A Washington County jury subsequently convicted Claude Swanson Allen of first-degree murder, and both men were executed. One of the men killed in the shootout was Circuit Court judge Thornton Lemmon Massie. Campbell's father was appointed Massie's successor, thus dissolving the law partnership. Instead of seeking reelection in 1915, Stuart B. Campbell resumed his private law practice handling both civil and criminal cases throughout southwestern Virginia.

On 30 September 1915 Campbell married Mary Rebecca Miles in Smyth County. They had one daughter and one son, Stuart B. Campbell Jr., who practiced law with his father after 1941 and who became a prominent Presbyterian layman. Campbell joined the United States Naval Reserve during World War I. He achieved the noncommissioned rank of chief yeoman but was still in officer training school at Princeton University when the war ended, after which he returned to Wytheville.

On 16 June 1921 Campbell was appointed to the Board of Examiners of Applicants for Admission to the Bar (later the Virginia Board of Bar Examiners), which operated under the authority of the Virginia Supreme Court of Appeals. Campbell served without interruption until he retired in 1969, a total of forty-eight years, and was president for half that time, from 9 May 1944. He estimated in 1958 that every board member devoted six weeks each year to drafting the examination questions, assessing the papers produced by prospective lawyers, and conferring afterward with representatives from the state's law schools to ensure that the board's questions and grading reflected current legal teaching. In 1938 Campbell helped to organize the Virginia State Bar, an administrative agency of the Supreme Court of Appeals, and became a charter member of its executive committee.

A member of the Virginia State Bar Association since 1912, Campbell was elected to its executive committee in 1930 and served as president in 1935–1936. His presidential address, "Suggested Changes in Practice and Procedure,"

proposed methods to improve the convenience and speed of legal proceedings in Virginia. At the association's 1936 meeting Campbell was elected the Virginia representative to the new House of Delegates of the American Bar Association. He served continuously until 1958. Campbell was also elected a fellow of the American Bar Foundation and received that organization's Fifty Year Award in 1961. The Virginia State Bar Association honored him in 1965 as a life member.

In 1941 Campbell was elected to the first of three two-year terms in the House of Delegates representing Wythe County. Aware that the county had more Republicans than Democrats, he sought to avoid partisanship and tried to evaluate legislation impartially. Because the political organization of Harry Flood Byrd (1887–1966) controlled state government, Campbell won a reputation as one of the assembly's few independent members. He served on the Committees for Courts of Justice, Federal Relations and Resolutions, and Retrenchment and Economy during all three terms, on the Committee on Finance during his first two terms, and on the Committee on Mining and Mineral Resources during his second and third terms. In 1942 and 1943 Campbell also chaired a House commission to study the healing arts in Virginia, and in 1944 he was a member of a House commission on improving the administration of justice.

On 14 May 1945, during a special session of the assembly, Campbell became chair of the Suffrage Commission charged with studying the state's voter registration laws. A coalition of forces including African Americans supported by the National Association for the Advancement of Colored People, the Virginia Voters' League, white anti-Byrd liberals, and some leading journalists pushed for changes in the Virginia laws that restricted the size and composition of the electorate, with particular focus on the poll tax. Leaders of the Byrd organization, who benefited from the existing laws, realized the growing strength of the opposition and went along with formation of a study commission. Campbell held public hearings throughout the state, and late in 1945 the commission recommended that the poll tax be abolished and replaced by an annual registration, a literacy test, and such other requirements as the assembly might prescribe.

The changes that Campbell's commission proposed required amendment of the state constitution. The proposals had to be approved in two consecutive sessions of the General Assembly and then submitted to the voters for ratification, a process that took four years. By the time the so-called Campbell amendments went before the voters in 1949, a groundswell of opposition had developed. Supporters of an expanded electorate considered the literacy test and the possibility of further restrictive requirements by the Byrd-controlled General Assembly to be as bad as the poll tax, while the Byrd organization was at best lukewarm about the amendments and may have desired their defeat. Campbell defended the amendments but to no avail. On 8 November 1949 the state's voters rejected them so overwhelmingly that they failed to receive a majority in any city or county.

Campbell retired from the assembly in 1947 because of the demands of his law practice and other business responsibilities. He had succeeded his father as president of the First National Bank of Wytheville (later the First National Farmers Bank) and remained an officer for more than thirty years, until the bank's merger early in the 1960s with the Roanoke-based First National Exchange Bank of Virginia. An avid hunter and fisherman, Campbell was also a Freemason, active in the local Presbyterian church and Rotary Club, and a charter member of the Wythe County Historical Society. Stuart Bland Campbell died in a hospital in Wytheville on 17 November 1973 and was buried in the city's East End Cemetery.

E. Randolph Trice, *The Elks Parade: A Centennial History and Catalogue of Members of Upsilon Chapter of Kappa Sigma* (1983), 24–25; J. C. Schwarz, ed., *Who's Who in Law* (1937), 147; E. Griffith Dodson, *The General Assembly of the Commonwealth of Virginia, 1940–1960* (1961), 510; 1973 interview with Campbell, Oral History Project of Wytheville Community College; Mary B. Kegley, *Wythe County, Virginia: A Bicentennial History* (1989), 250; BVS Marriage Register, Smyth County; *Commonwealth* 2 (Sept. 1935): 19; Campbell, "Suggested Changes in Practice and Procedure" and report on bar examiners, *Virginia State Bar Association Proceedings* (1936): 263–276 (frontispiece por.), and (1958): 26–37; *Richmond News Leader*, 1 Apr. 1947; Andrew Buni, *The Negro in Virginia Politics,* *1902–1965* (1967), 138–140; William Bryan Crawley Jr., *Bill Tuck: A Political Life in Harry Byrd's Virginia* (1978), 193–197; Ronald L. Heinemann, *Harry Byrd of Virginia* (1996), 272–273; obituaries in *Richmond Times-Dispatch,* 18 Nov. 1973, and *Wytheville Southwest Virginia Enterprise*, 20 Nov. 1973 (por. and editorial tribute); memorials in *Wytheville Southwest Virginia Enterprise*, 18 July 1974, and *Virginia State Bar Association Proceedings* (1975): 232–234.

JOHN T. KNEEBONE

CAMPBELL, William (bap. 1 September 1745–22 August 1781), Revolutionary War militia officer, was born in Augusta County, the son of Charles Campbell, a farmer, and Margaret Buchanan Campbell. He was baptized at Tinkling Spring Presbyterian Church on 1 September 1745. Campbell received the best education available in the vicinity, being privately tutored and attending Augusta Academy, a forerunner of Washington and Lee University. A tall, strong, imposing man with sandy red hair and blue eyes, he had a fiery temper but was noted for his courtesy. Confident in himself, Campbell inspired confidence in others and was ideally suited to lead Virginia frontiersmen.

When his father died in 1767, Campbell inherited a large estate that included many acres in southwestern Virginia. Moving there in 1768 and relocating his mother and sisters there four years later, he established a plantation, Aspenvale, about twenty miles from present-day Abingdon in what became Smyth County in 1832. Campbell was already a prominent local gentleman when the government of the newly created Fincastle County was organized in 1773, and he became one of its justices of the peace in April of that year. He was a captain in the county militia in 1774 during Dunmore's War, but he did not take part in any fighting. On 20 January 1775 Campbell was elected to the Fincastle County Committee, which adopted an address to the Virginia members of the First Continental Congress pledging support for congressional efforts to redress colonial grievances. By September of that year he had recruited a company of Fincastle County riflemen that was taken into the 1st Virginia Regiment under the command of Patrick Henry. Campbell received a captain's commission dating from 15 December 1775. While serving in Williamsburg he became a close friend of Henry and on 2 April 1776 married Henry's sister, Elizabeth Henry, in Hanover County. They had one son and one daughter.

On 9 October 1776 Campbell resigned his commission and returned to Aspenvale. When Washington County was created he was one of its first justices of the peace. Campbell was also a trustee for the county seat, and he helped survey and sell lots in a new town, later named Abingdon. In 1777 he was one of the Virginia commissioners to draw a boundary line between Virginia and the Cherokee nation. Campbell was appointed lieutenant colonel of the 10th Regiment of Virginia militia that same year and was promoted to colonel three years later. As a local militia commander he fought to maintain peace on the Virginia frontier, ruthlessly suppressing British Loyalists and paying little attention to their civil liberties. Without mercy Campbell destroyed or confiscated Loyalist property and may have executed as many as twelve men without trial. On one occasion he summarily hanged a counterfeiter who was discovered with incriminating documents. In 1779 Campbell participated in a series of militia actions against a band of Loyalists who threatened the strategically important lead mines in Montgomery County. The General Assembly passed an act late that year to immunize Campbell and his second in command from any prosecution or lawsuits resulting from their suppression of the insurrections, inasmuch as "the necessary measures taken for that purpose may not be strictly warranted by law, although justifiable from the immediate urgency and imminence of the danger."

The voters of Washington County elected Campbell to the House of Delegates in the spring of 1780. He was appointed to the Committee of Propositions and Grievances but served only a short time. On 15 June 1780 the governor named Campbell commander of an expedition against the Cherokees and ordered him into what is now eastern Tennessee. He did not go, however, because he was diverted again to defend the lead mines from renewed Loyalist attack, a danger that men under his command ended in August 1780.

Campbell learned in the autumn of 1780 that a Loyalist militia force of more than 1,000 men was threatening the backcountry of western North Carolina. Late in September he led Washington County militia to a rendezvous of frontiersmen at Sycamore Shoals on the upper Watauga River. On 2 October the other militia officers appointed him commander of the little army of about 900 men in its attack on the Loyalist position on Kings Mountain. Campbell's forces surrounded the mountain position on 7 October and surprised the Loyalists, who were under the command of British major Patrick Ferguson, by charging directly up the steep slope. Using trees as cover, Campbell's men fired on their exposed enemies and gained the top of the ridge. After Ferguson was killed, the Loyalists surrendered, and Campbell's triumph was complete. The Battle of Kings Mountain was one of the most dramatic and important American victories in the southern theater during the war. It devastated earl Cornwallis's left and delayed the British advance into North Carolina long enough to allow General Nathanael Greene to reorganize the American forces. Congress officially congratulated Campbell for the victory on 13 November 1780, and four days later the Senate of Virginia approved a House of Delegates resolution to reward him with a sword and a horse.

Early in 1781 Campbell and his militiamen joined Greene's army to oppose Cornwallis's renewed advance into North Carolina. At Wetzell's Mill on 6 March Campbell was involved in a skirmish with British cavalry. Nine days later at the Battle of Guilford Courthouse he fought under the immediate command of Henry "Light-Horse Harry" Lee (1756–1818) on the left of Greene's line. His forces mauled by the enemy, Campbell bitterly charged that Lee had left him unsupported during the battle, but Greene praised Campbell for his bravery. Elected again to the assembly in the spring of 1781 and named to the Committee of Privileges and Elections, Campbell did not serve because on 14 June 1781 the legislature appointed him a brigadier general of militia. He duly marched to join the marquis de Lafayette's army in eastern Virginia. After campaigning in July and early in August Campbell was struck down by fever and chest pains. Retiring to Rocky Mills, the Hanover County residence of his wife's half brother, William Campbell died there on 22 August 1781, apparently of a heart attack, and was buried in Hanover County. In August 1832 his body was moved to the family graveyard at Aspenvale in Smyth County. The assembly named a new county for him in November 1781. Campbell's widow married William Russell, a member of the Convention of 1776, and became a linchpin in a personal and political power struggle between Russell and William Campbell's cousin and brother-in-law Arthur Campbell, also a member of the Convention of 1776.

David G. Malgee, "A Frontier Biography: William Campbell of King's Mountain" (master's thesis, University of Richmond, 1983); Agnes Graham Sanders Riley, *Brigadier General William Campbell, 1745–1781* (1985); baptism recorded in Howard McKnight Wilson, *The Tinkling Spring, Headwater of Freedom: A Study of the Church and Her People, 1732–1952* (1954), 471; marriage and death dates in Thomas L. Preston, *A Sketch of Mrs. Elizabeth Russell, Wife of General William Campbell, and Sister of Patrick Henry* (1888), 7; Lyman C. Draper, *King's Mountain and Its Heroes: History of the Battle of King's Mountain, October 7th, 1780, and the Events Which Led to It* (1881), esp. 378–402; E. T. Crowson, "Colonel William Campbell and the Battle of Kings Mountain," *Virginia Cavalcade* 30 (1980): 22–29; Emory G. Evans, "Trouble in the Back-country: Disaffection in Southwest Virginia during the American Revolution," in *An Uncivil War: The Southern Backcountry during the American Revolution*, ed. Ronald Hoffman et al. (1985), 179–212; Hening, *Statutes*, 10:195 (quotation); Campbell letters in Campbell-Preston-Floyd Papers, LC, and Preston Family Papers, VHS; numerous papers and references in Draper MSS, in *Revolutionary Virginia*, vols. 2, 4–7, in Stanley J. Idzerda et al., eds., *Lafayette in the Age of the American Revolution* (1977–1983), esp. 4:359, in *Jefferson Papers*, vols. 3–5, and in Richard K. Showman et al., eds., *The Papers of General Nathanael Greene* (1976–), vols. 6–7; Worthington C. Ford et al., eds., *Journals of the Continental Congress, 1774–1789* (1904–1937), 18:1048–1049; *JHD*, Oct. 1780 sess., 18, 26; *Richmond Virginia Gazette*, 18 Nov. 1780; Washington Co. Will Book, 1:20–22; reinterment in Elizabeth Lemmon Sayers, *Smyth County, Virginia* (1983), 1:178, 180.

PAUL DAVID NELSON

CAMPBELL, William (1778 or 1779–23 January 1845), member of the Convention of 1829–1830, was born in Bedford County, the son of Thomas Campbell and Mary Church Campbell. Little is known about his personal life, in part because several other men of the same name lived in the county, and references to them have produced confusion in local and family history literature. He was not, as some old accounts state, a grandson of Patrick Henry, nor was he the local tavern keeper of that name or the son of that man. Inheriting some property from his father and gaining at least some education, Campbell became a planter. He owned forty slaves in 1830 and thirty-six in 1840. Campbell married and had children, but their names do not appear in the county's records, and his wife and children all died before he did. He believed that he was the father of the two sons of Ruth Nelson Bennett, and in his will he provided for them modestly.

Starting in January 1798 with a commission as ensign, Campbell served in the Virginia militia for thirty-three years. He was a lieutenant when he commanded his company at Fort Norfolk during the War of 1812 and held the rank of colonel when he resigned on 23 February 1831. Campbell represented Bedford County in the House of Delegates for five consecutive one-year terms from 1816 to 1821. He served on the Committee of Propositions and Grievances in every session except 1817–1818, when he sat on the Committee of Claims. Campbell was a member of the Committee to Examine the Register's Office from 1817 to 1820 and the Committee on the Armory from 1820 to 1821.

In May 1829 Campbell was one of four men elected to represent the counties of Bedford, Buckingham, and Campbell in a convention called to revise the constitution of Virginia. Along with most of the other delegates from the western Piedmont, he believed that his region was underrepresented in the General Assembly and supported proposals by western delegates to reapportion the assembly based on the white population of the state and to extend the suffrage to all adult white males. Campbell was one of several reformers who served on the prestigious select committee that determined how the business of the convention was to be conducted. He also served on the Committee to Consider the Legislative Department of the Government, to which the important questions of apportionment and suffrage were referred. The committee voted 13 to 11 to recommend that apportionment of the House of Delegates be based on the state's white population but by a tie vote rejected a proposal to apportion the Senate of Virginia in the same way. Campbell supported the reform proposal on both votes.

Throughout the convention Campbell nearly always voted with the reformers. Unable to win all that they wished, however, he and many other Piedmont delegates accepted a compromise that increased representation for their counties. Assured of more representation in the General Assembly, Campbell voted with the majority in favor of the revised constitution, which neither reapportioned the assembly according to the white population nor extended the suffrage. Bedford County voters agreed with Campbell and with a tally of 609 to 36 voted to ratify the constitution, which was also approved statewide.

In 1830 Campbell won election to the Senate of Virginia from the new district consisting of Bedford and Franklin Counties. He was repeatedly reelected and served until his death. Campbell sat on the Committee of Privileges and Elections and also on the committees appointed to examine the armory and the treasurer's accounts. In 1843 his colleagues elected him speaker pro tempore. While attending the Senate two years later he fell ill. William Campbell wrote a will on 17 January and died in his rooms at the Columbian Hotel in Richmond on 23 January 1845. Both houses of the assembly adjourned in his honor the next day, and on 25 January the governor, members of the assembly, and other state and local officials attended his elaborate funeral procession from the hotel to the city's Shockoe Cemetery, where he was buried.

Age at death given as sixty-six in Shockoe Cemetery interment record; Margaret Campbell Pilcher, *Historical Sketches of the Campbell, Pilcher, and Kindred Families* (1911), 245–246; Census, Bedford Co., 1830, 1840; militia service and a few letters in Militia Commission Papers, Executive Department, Governor's Office, RG 3, LVA; Stuart Lee Butler, *A Guide to Virginia Militia Units in the War of 1812* (1988), 51, 236, 237; *Richmond Enquirer*, 2, 5 June 1829; *Proceedings and Debates of 1829–1830 Convention*, 882, 903; Bruce, *Rhetoric of Conservatism*, 37; Catlin, *Convention of 1829–30* (por.); Bedford County Will Book, 12:210–211; death notice and account of funeral in *Richmond Enquirer*, 25 Jan. 1845; obituary and memorial in *Lynchburg Virginian*, 30 Jan. 1845.

TRENTON E. HIZER

CAMPFIELD, William Sanford (20 May 1880–25 January 1948), secretary of the Virginia State Horticultural Society, was born in New Milford, Winnebago County, Illinois, the son of William Bradford Campfield, a farmer, and Jane Thompson Campfield. He attended the University of Illinois in Urbana but before graduating left to read law. Youthful wanderlust soon overcame his commitment to the law, and Campfield spent eight years in the western states. Attracted by the apple orchards in southern Washington, he lived for several years in that state, where through on-the-job experience, supplemented by formal coursework at Oregon Agricultural College (later Oregon State University in Corvallis), he earned a reputation as an expert apple box-packer.

In 1914 Campfield traveled to Virginia to conduct box-packing schools. He remained in the state and worked for five years as county agricultural agent for Augusta and Rockingham Counties. Campfield lived first in Harrisonburg and later in Staunton. In 1921 he became the Virginia representative of American Fruit Growers, a fruit-marketing association. On 1 April 1926 Campfield assumed the position of part-time secretary to the Virginia State Horticultural Society, the organization of the state's commercial fruit growers. Within a few years he transformed the small, debt-ridden society into a fully funded and well-organized business association. Campfield became secretary-treasurer in March 1931 and full-time secretary of the society in 1934. With the bills paid and membership expanding, he enlarged the society's publication, *Virginia Fruit*, which he edited, from a four-page quarterly leaflet into a twenty-page monthly journal that provided growers with valuable information on improving yields and limiting crop damage. During Campfield's twenty-two years of leadership, the society doubled its membership and won recognition as one of the outstanding horticultural societies in the country.

Campfield led campaigns to obtain passage of state laws to control cedar rust, a disease of red cedar trees that threatened to destroy apple orchards. Reflecting his lifelong concern for proper apple packing, he urged growers to adopt better packaging methods. Campfield also persuaded the General Assembly in 1927 to enact a law governing the grading and marketing of fruit, which improved sales of Virginia's apples. Appreciating the importance of good roads to the well-being of his industry, he worked to secure better highways in Virginia, and he also fought for freight rate reductions. Campfield organized advertising programs to highlight the advantages of eating apples. He used his legal training to prepare briefs and lobby Congress to pass bills that prohibited the export of apples that did not meet the standard United States grades for fruit. Realizing that those marketing Virginia's apples shared concerns with growers elsewhere, Campfield pursued closer cooperation with other state societies and helped to organize the Eastern Apple Growers Council, a federation of nineteen horticultural societies that focused on promoting the welfare of the apple-growing industry. His promotion of apple production, improved marketing, and better transportation in Virginia made him well known and respected among business and political leaders in the state, the most important being Harry Flood Byrd (1887–1966), one of the state's largest producers of apples, whose rise to political leadership was based in part on a campaign to improve Virginia's highways.

Campfield married Amelia Sophronia Brakke, a native of Saint Charles, Minnesota, about 1907. They had three sons and one daughter. Single-minded in his work to protect the interests of fruit growers, Campfield maintained that his only hobby was apples. Suffering from ill health, he asked to be temporarily relieved of several of his professional duties effective 1 March 1948. Before the request could take effect, William Sanford Campfield suffered a stroke and died in Staunton on 25 January 1948. He was buried in the city's Thornrose Cemetery. Byrd served as an honorary pallbearer and said of Campfield, "Rarely do you find a secretary who had more efficiency and greater enthusiasm in performing duties."

Biography in *Virginia Fruit* 36 (Feb. 1948): 3–8 (quotation and por.); *Commonwealth* 5 (Feb. 1938): 33; birth date and parents' names confirmed by BVS; family information provided by daughter-in-law Jeanne C. Campfield; Campfield's annual reports as secretary in Virginia State Horticultural Society, *Proceedings* (1926–1947); obituary in *Staunton Evening Leader*, 26 Jan. 1948; memorial in Virginia State Horticultural Society, *Proceedings* (1948): 19.

RONALD L. HEINEMANN

CANADA, David (fl. 1867–1869), member of the Convention of 1867–1868, was born a slave, probably in Halifax County. Almost nothing is known about his life before he was elected one of the county's two convention delegates. Brigadier General John McAllister Schofield, then the military commander of Virginia, wrote that Canada was a stonemason who had been "emancipated by the war." References to Canada and other people in the county who shared his surname appear variously as Canada, Cannady, and even Kennedy. At least two other men in the county, one white and one black, were named David Canada, but his relationship to them, if any, is unknown. He was married to Martha Canada, maiden name unknown, and they had at least one son, named U. S. Grant Canada. A physical description and a caricature of Canada that appeared in the hostile newspaper *Richmond Southern Opinion* suggest that when he served in the convention he was a relatively young man of imposing stature and dark skin.

Conditions in Halifax County after the Civil War resembled those in other rural southern counties. Former slaves sought landownership as the means to secure their freedom, and former masters sought to secure farm laborers at low cost. Freedmen's Bureau agents in the county described numerous disputes over labor contracts, payments, and work discipline. As a stonemason, Canada may have had more advantages in the new free labor market than an agricultural worker would have. Tax lists show that he owned a cow in 1867 and acquired a horse and a second cow the following year. These tax lists identify him as a resident of Republican Grove in the northwestern part of the county, but derisive newspaper references to Canada as the delegate from "Low-Cuss Level" suggest a possible connection with Locust Level, near the midpoint of the county's western boundary with Pittsylvania County.

Under the Reconstruction Act of March 1867, elections were to take place in October of that year for delegates to a convention called to draft a new constitution for Virginia. African American men were permitted for the first time to vote in that election and run for seats in the convention. Three white candidates, identified variously as former Whigs and Conservatives, entered the race. Black men and a few white Radicals gathered at Halifax Court House in September to select candidates. One white man and four black men declared themselves candidates. Several men made speeches, but the meeting broke up without narrowing the field.

Canada was almost certainly one of the candidates and speakers that day. Information about the campaign in Halifax is scant, and no official report of the vote for delegates exists. Black voters were not intimidated in their new role. When the local agent of the Freedmen's Bureau endorsed the white conservative candidates, blacks responded by successfully petitioning for his removal. They also turned out in large numbers on election day, 22 October. More than 2,700 African Americans voted, while fewer than 1,000 whites cast ballots. According to partial returns reported in the newspapers, Canada was the only black candidate to receive votes in every precinct, an indication that he enjoyed countywide support and a good reputation. He probably received no more than a few votes from whites.

Canada was present when the convention assembled in Richmond on 3 December 1867. He was appointed to the Committee on the Basis of Representation and Apportionment but did not play a significant role in the convention's rancorous debates. Referring to him as a sphinx, the *Richmond Southern Opinion* observed that Canada "never speaks, though his nod is Radical." On nearly every important issue he voted with the Radicals, although he voted with the majority in opposition to a requirement for racial integration of the public schools. On 17 January 1868 Canada offered a resolution to appoint a state geologist to help develop the mineral resources of the state and a resolution that Virginia should adopt North Carolina's more efficient and economical tax system. Three days later he introduced a resolution to appoint a state chemist and create an experimental farm to teach scientific agriculture. Because Canada probably could not write (he signed for his convention wages with his mark), someone else most likely prepared the innovative resolutions, all of which died in committee.

The convention adjourned on 17 April 1868, fully expecting that a referendum on the new constitution would soon follow. Even though on 24 April Schofield postponed the vote indefinitely, the campaign over ratification continued. Declaring that whites would never accept domination by blacks, Conservatives in Halifax County, where blacks made up a majority of the population, organized to defeat what they derided as "Dave Cannady's Konsterstewshun." Canada returned to Richmond at the beginning of May to pick up copies of "his Constertutions," as a white journalist wrote it, before speaking in favor of ratification at meetings in Halifax County.

Local law enforcement officers and the military commissioner grew fearful that the political conflict might spark violence. African American speakers at Halifax Court House were silenced on 27 July 1868, and the commonwealth's attorney lectured them and their audience on propriety and the use of courteous language. Canada may have heard the lecture from his cell in the local jail. The previous week, while he was speaking at Meadsville, a disturbance between whites and blacks occurred. Afterward, Canada reported, a party of whites threatened his life, and he appealed to the military commissioner at Halifax Court House for protection. The commissioner found everything quiet in Meadsville, then ordered him to report to Halifax Court House, where on 25 July 1868 he placed Canada under arrest. He was permitted to post bail and leave jail about two weeks later. At the next county court, on 28 September, the grand jury found insufficient grounds to indict Canada.

A year passed before Congress authorized an election to ratify the constitution, which was scheduled for 6 July 1869, at which time the voters were also to elect a new governor and members of the assembly. During the campaign a moderate wing of the Republican Party split from the Radicals and organized as the True Republicans. Conservative Party strategists recognized the opportunity for an alliance, and the Conservative nominees of 1868 for statewide office retired in favor of the True Republican ticket. Conservatives in Halifax County employed a similar tactic by selecting African Americans as two of their three nominees for the House of Delegates. David Canada ran for the House of Delegates, too. The True Republican ticket carried the county by fewer than sixty votes, and the Conservatives also won all three of the county's seats in the House of Delegates. One of the African American victors, Alexander Owen, was a former slave of William L. Owen, a white planter and merchant who had served in the convention with Canada, and reportedly voted in the legislature as his erstwhile master ordered.

What happened to Canada after he lost the election in 1869 is unknown. He probably left Halifax County before the census was taken in 1870. For a few years, however, David Canada took a prominent part in dramatic political events and provided leadership for the freedpeople of Halifax County.

Lowe, "Virginia's Reconstruction Convention," 348 (first quotation); son's birth recorded on undated MS page ca. 1868–1872 inserted in BVS Birth Register, Halifax Co., 1866; BVS Death Certificate, Mecklenburg Co., 17 Aug. 1919, for a Ulysses Grant Cannady (b. ca. 1872), lists father's birthplace as Halifax Co.; monthly reports, Halifax Co., Mar. 1866–Dec. 1868, Freedmen's Bureau Records; Personal Property Tax Returns, Halifax Co., 1866–1870, RG 48, LVA; *Richmond Daily Dispatch*, 13, 26 Sept., 23, 24 Oct. 1867, 7, 12 July 1869; *Richmond Southern Opinion*, 21 Dec. 1867 (third quotation), 28 Mar. 1868 (caricature); *Daily Richmond Whig*, 2 Apr., 2 May (fifth quotation), 20 (fourth quotation), 29 July, 5, 28 Oct. (second quotation) 1868, 16, 18, 26 June 1869; *Petersburg Index*, 3 Aug. 1868; Richard Lowe, *Republicans and Reconstruction in Virginia, 1856–70* (1991), 120–129, 148–155, 165–179; *Journal of 1867–1868 Convention*, 3, 28; *Debates and Proceedings of 1867–1868 Convention*, 486, 495, 520–521; Hume, "Membership of Convention of 1867–1868," 479–481; Halifax Co. Minute Book, 21:296.

JOHN T. KNEEBONE

CANNON, James (13 November 1864–6 September 1944), Methodist bishop and temperance reformer, was born in Salisbury, Maryland, the son of James Cannon, a merchant, and Lydia Robertson Primrose Cannon. His parents were both strong Southern Methodists and among the town's most prominent and affluent citizens. Cannon graduated from the local high school in 1880 and a year later enrolled at Randolph-Macon College, in Ashland. Secular in outlook,

he dreamed of becoming a lawyer and judge, but after a conversion experience at a college revival in 1882 he joined the church and decided to become a Methodist minister. Cannon received a B.A. from Randolph-Macon College in 1884, a B.D. from Princeton Theological Seminary in 1888, and an M.A. from the College of New Jersey (later Princeton University) in 1890.

On 1 August 1888 James Cannon Jr., as he was known throughout his life, married Lura Virginia Bennett, the daughter of William Wallace Bennett, president of Randolph-Macon College. They had two daughters and six sons, one of whom died young. Admitted to the Virginia Conference of the Methodist Episcopal Church South in November 1888, Cannon served pastorates in Charlotte County (1888–1889), Newport News (1889–1891), and Farmville (1891–1894). Extraordinarily energetic and buoyed by the confidence derived from an exceptional education and influential family and church connections, he vigorously challenged the ruling establishment within his conference and denomination. As editor from 1893 to 1903 of the *Southern Methodist Recorder,* which served the Farmville district, and from 1904 to 1918 of the *Baltimore and Richmond Christian Advocate,* the organ of the Virginia Conference, Cannon demonstrated formidable talent as a controversialist. Spokesman for a progressive Southern Methodism, he promoted an aggressive, militant Christianity emphasizing missions, education, and temperance reform.

In private Cannon could be congenial and engaging, but his public persona was harsh and forbidding. Intense and confrontational by nature, he was a ruthless and resourceful political combatant, with a keen mind, an encyclopedic command of detail, and extraordinary self-control. Cannon clashed repeatedly with senior members of his conference. From 1898 to 1902 he came to wider attention during a bitter controversy over the church's method of securing compensation from the federal government for damages to its Nashville publishing house sustained during the Civil War. By 1907 Cannon was the most influential figure in the Virginia Conference, and in that year he became locked in a six-year struggle over control of the

Randolph-Macon system of schools and colleges. He finally prevailed, but his relentless attacks on opponents, especially William Waugh Smith, his former mentor and then president of Randolph-Macon Woman's College, left him with many new enemies and broken friendships.

The militant editor was also a country schoolmaster, admired by countless students and their families across Virginia. Although a successful pastor, Cannon was eager to find a distinctive work of his own, and in 1894 he had become principal of Blackstone Female Institute (later Blackstone College for Girls), in Nottoway County. Under his leadership the school combined Christian education with high school courses, college preparation, and teacher training. Restless and ambitious, Cannon left Blackstone in 1911 to become superintendent of the Southern Assembly, a proposed Methodist center for Christian recreation and education at Lake Junaluska, in the mountains of North Carolina. He supervised its construction, traveled throughout the South to promote it as a new Chautauqua, and opened it, partially completed, on schedule in 1913. The next year Cannon returned to Virginia to resume his post at Blackstone, which added junior college courses in 1915. He resigned a second time from the Blackstone school in 1918 after the Methodist Episcopal Church South's General Conference in Atlanta elected him bishop.

Cannon's elevation resulted largely from his growing prominence in the temperance movement. He was the dominant figure in the Anti-Saloon League of Virginia after 1904, and he mobilized Virginia drys as a powerful new political force. In 1910 Cannon founded a daily dry newspaper, the *Richmond Virginian,* to counter the bitter opposition of most of the state press. It continued to publish until 1920. Cannon led the drys to victory in the statewide Prohibition referendum of 1914 and secured passage of the Mapp Prohibition Act of 1916. Although accused of being an ecclesiastical dictator over Virginia politics, he was undaunted and in 1913 became the chief Washington lobbyist for the Anti-Saloon League of America. Cannon played a major role in the adoption of federal Prohibition legislation, culminating in the Eighteenth Amendment to the Constitution. Early in 1918 he traveled to France and Great Britain as special commissioner of the secretary of war to investigate vice and intemperance among American servicemen on the western front. Later that year Cannon returned to Europe to organize a Paris conference on alcoholism, which led to the formation in 1919 of the World League Against Alcoholism, the international affiliate of the Anti-Saloon League of America.

A Wilsonian internationalist, Cannon became one of the most-traveled Americans of his time. He spent much of the 1920s abroad supervising Southern Methodist missions in the Belgian Congo, Brazil, and Mexico, served as the chief troubleshooter for the World League in Great Britain and on the Continent, and attended international temperance and church conferences across Europe. An active participant in the ecumenical movement, he was also a prominent spokesman for Near East Relief, the American organization that assisted Armenians and other victims of Turkish atrocities in the Middle East. By 1922 Cannon was recognized as an important American voice on international affairs, especially those involving humanitarian or religious causes.

Probably the most progressive figure in Southern Methodism, Cannon challenged the traditionalist establishment led by Bishops Collins Denny, of Richmond, and Warren A. Candler, of Atlanta. In 1925 Cannon was a principal southern supporter of merger during the bitter and unsuccessful struggle to reunite Methodism's northern and southern wings, which had split before the Civil War. His work nevertheless laid the groundwork for unification more than a decade later. An active leader of the Federal Council of Churches and a proponent of social Christianity, Cannon became the chief sponsor and defender in 1927 and 1928 of a controversial pastoral letter that condemned poor living-and-working conditions in the southern textile industry.

Prohibition, however, remained Cannon's primary social concern. He broke with the Democratic Party after it nominated Alfred E. Smith, of New York, for president in 1928.

Smith was an opponent of Prohibition, a product of Tammany Hall politics, and a Catholic. Cannon campaigned vigorously against him and scored a stunning victory. Republican nominee Herbert Hoover carried five southern states, including Virginia, breaking the South's record for Democratic solidarity for the first time since Reconstruction. Cannon was hailed as the foremost champion of dry, Protestant America, but his moment of national triumph was bittersweet and short-lived. Following a long illness his wife died on 27 November 1928, shortly after the presidential election, and in 1929 Cannon's alliance of anti-Smith Democrats and Republicans was defeated in the Virginia gubernatorial election.

In failing health, Cannon was constantly hounded by his enemies, notably Senator Carter Glass, of Virginia, and became embroiled in a series of scandals that generated sensational headlines. At home in the secular world of business and finance, Cannon was exposed in 1929 as a patron of a fraudulent Wall Street investment firm operated by Harry Goldhurst (later the journalist and author Harry Golden). At his church's General Conference of 1930, Cannon's opponents attempted unsuccessfully to defrock him for stock-market gambling. After his marriage in London on 15 July 1930 to Helen Myrtle Hawley McCallum, a widow who had been his secretary and with whom he was rumored to have had an affair while abroad, the church summoned him before a twelve-man investigating committee in February 1931 on various charges of immorality, including adultery. The committee unanimously found Cannon innocent of every charge except stock-market gambling, of which he was cleared by a divided vote. Two United States Senate committees subsequently investigated allegations that he had embezzled campaign money, and he was indicted in October 1931 for violating the federal Corrupt Practices Act during the presidential election of 1928. Following protracted legal maneuvers a federal court finally acquitted Cannon in 1934. The scandals undermined his moral authority, destroyed his political influence, and bitterly divided his church.

With the repeal of Prohibition in 1933, Cannon passed out of the public eye, largely ignored by an embarrassed church and a nation preoccupied with economic rather than moral issues. From 1934 to 1938 he resided in Los Angeles, where he served as bishop of the Southern Methodist conference that included the Pacific coastal states. Cannon retired in 1938 and returned to Richmond, where he wrote his memoirs and cultivated an unlikely friendship with H. L. Mencken, the wet journalist and literary critic. Despite crippling arthritis, the bishop continued to travel extensively and attend church and temperance meetings. James Cannon died in Chicago on 6 September 1944 after suffering a heart attack at a national meeting of the Anti-Saloon League. Following services at Broad Street Methodist Church in Richmond, he was buried in Hollywood Cemetery in that city.

Robert A. Hohner, *Prohibition and Politics: The Life of Bishop James Cannon, Jr.* (1999), contains several pors. and full bibliography of primary and secondary sources; Virginius Dabney, *Dry Messiah: The Life of Bishop Cannon* (1949); memoirs published posthumously as *Bishop Cannon's Own Story: Life As I Have Seen It*, ed. Richard L. Watson Jr. (1955), frontispiece por.; James Cannon Jr. Papers, Duke; Louisa Co. Marriage Register, 1888; second marriage in *New York Times*, 22 July 1930; obituaries in *Richmond News Leader*, 6 Sept. 1944, and *New York Times* and *Richmond Times-Dispatch*, both 7 Sept. 1944; obituary and editorial tribute in *Virginia Methodist Advocate* 6 (14 Sept. 1944): 1, 6, 10; memorial in Methodist Church, Virginia Conference, *Annual* (1944): 140–143 (giving erroneous death date of 16 Sept. 1944).

ROBERT A. HOHNER

Library of Congress Cataloging-in-Publication Data

Dictionary of Virginia biography / editors, John T. Kneebone . . . [et al.].
       p.   cm.
       Includes bibliographical references and index.
       Contents: v. 1. Aaroe–Blanchfield. v. 2. Bland–Cannon.
       ISBN 0-88490-189-0 (v. 1)
       ISBN 0-88490-199-8 (v. 2)
       1. Virginia—Biography—Dictionaries. I. Kneebone, John T.
       F225.D54 1998   98-39746
       920.0755—dc21   CIP

Dictionary of Virginia Biography, Volume 2: *Bland–Cannon* was designed by Sara Daniels Bowersox of the Library of Virginia. Page layout was produced by Frances James of the Virginia Department of General Services, Office of Graphic Communications, using Apple Power Macintosh 7600/120 and QuarkXPress 4.1. Text was composed in Times New Roman and Italic. Printed on acid-free, Glatfelter Writers Offset Natural, 60-lb. text, by Thomson-Shore, Inc., in Dexter, Michigan.